VIRGINIANS & WEST VIRGINIANS 1607-1870

VOLUME 1

Compiled By

Patrick G. Wardell
Lt. Col. U.S. Army Retired

HERITAGE BOOKS
2008

HERITAGE BOOKS
AN IMPRINT OF HERITAGE BOOKS, INC.

Books, CDs, and more—Worldwide

For our listing of thousands of titles see our website at
www.HeritageBooks.com

Published 2008 by
HERITAGE BOOKS, INC.
Publishing Division
100 Railroad Ave. #104
Westminster, Maryland 21157

Copyright © 1986 Patrick G. Wardell

All rights reserved. No part of this book may be reproduced or transmitted in any form or by any means, electronic or mechanical, including photocopying, recording or by any information storage and retrieval system without written permission from the author, except for the inclusion of brief quotations in a review.

International Standard Book Number: 978-1-55613-208-7

FOREWORD

The data in this volume has been abstracted from the three biographical volumes in the six volume History of Virginia, published by the American Historical Society, Inc., of Chicago and New York, in 1924. That work contains a great deal of useful genealogical data which has been largely inaccessible to genealogists because it lacks a proper index, and it has been out of print for so long that it can only be found in a few large libraries today.

The objective of this compendium is to present an abstract of the essential genealogical data on each person mentioned in those three volumes who was a native of Virginia or West Virginia. A typical entry gives, in addition to the name of the principal, his or her data and place of birth followed by the names of his or her father, mother, and spouse(s); children of the principal are not named, unless they were also born in Virginia or West Virginia, in which case they also appear as a principal. Spouses and parents also appear as principals if they were born in Virginia or West Virginia; women are always listed under their maiden name. With this arrangement several generations of a family can frequently be reconstructed in a few minutes starting with any known member of the family.

At the back of this volume there is a surname index to the original volumes from which this data was taken. Researchers wishing to read the full account of a particular family can use this index to order a photocopy of the appropriate page(s) from the original books via the Interlibrary Loan department of their local library.

Question marks have been attached to uncertain data and numerous abbreviations have been used in the interest of brevity.

General Abbreviations

b	born	m	mother
bc	born about	(1)m	first wife of father
Co	County	md	married
d	died	mdc	married about
dc	died about	nr	near
h	husband	w	wife
2h	second husband	2w	second wife

Virginia Counties

Augu	Augusta	Loui	Louisa
Bath	-	Lune	Lunenburg
Bedf	Bedford	Madi	Madison
Blan	Bland	Math	Mathews
Bote	Botetourt	Meck	Mecklenburg
Brun	Brunswick	Midd	Middlesex
Buch	Buchanan	Mont	Montgomery
Buck	Buckingham	Nans	Nansemond
Camp	Campbell	Nels	Nelson
Caro	Caroline	NewK	New Kent
Carr	Carroll	Norf	Norfolk
ChCi	Charles City	Nhtn	Northampton
Char	Charlotte	Nhld	Northumberland
Ches	Chesterfield	Nott	Nottoway
Clar	Clarke	Oran	Orange
Crai	Craig	Page	-
Culp	Culpeper	Patr	Patrick
Cumb	Cumberland	Pitt	Pittsylvania
Dick	Dickenson	Powh	Powhatan
Dinw	Dinwiddie	PrEd	Prince Edward
ElCi	Elizabeth City	PrGe	Prince George
Esse	Essex	PrWi	Prince William
Fauq	Fauquier	PrAn	Princess Anne
Fair	Fairfax	Pula	Pulaski
Floy	Floyd	Rapp	Rappahannock
Fluv	Fluvanna	Rich	Richmond
Fran	Franklin	Roan	Roanoke
Fred	Frederick	Rkbr	Rockbridge
Gile	Giles	Rkhm	Rockingham
Glou	Gloucester	Russ	Russell
Gooc	Goochland	Scot	Scott
Gray	Grayson	Shen	Shenandoah
Greene	-	Smyt	Smyth
Greensville	-	Sout	Southampton
Hali	Halifax	Spot	Spotsylvania
Hano	Hanover	Staf	Stafford
Henrico	-	Surr	Surry
Henry	-	Suss	Sussex
High	Highland	Taze	Tazewell
Isle	Isle of Wight	Warr	Warren
JaCi	James City	Warw	Warwick
KiQu	King and Queen	Wash	Washington
KiGe	King George	West	Westmoreland
KiWi	King William	Wise	-
Lanc	Lancaster	Wyth	Wythe
Lee	-	York	-
Loud	Loudon	Yoho	Yohogania (not now a county)

West Virginia Counties

Barb	Barbour	McDo	McDowell
Berk	Berkeley	Monr	Monroe
Boon	Boone	Morg	Morgan
Brax	Braxton	Nich	Nicholas
Cabe	Cabell	Ohio	-
Calh	Calhoun	Pend	Pendleton
Clay	-	Plea	Pleasants
Dodd	Doddridge	Poca	Pocahontas
Faye	Fayette	Pres	Preston
Gilm	Gilmer	Putn	Putnam
Gran	Grant	Rale	Raleigh
Grbr	Greenbrier	Rand	Randolph
Hamp	Hampshire	Ritc	Ritchie
Hanc	Hancock	Roane	—
Hard	Hardy	Summ	Summers
Harr	Harrison	Tayl	Taylor
Jack	Jackson	Tuck	Tucker
Jeff	Jefferson	Tyle	Tyler
Kana	Kanawha	Upsh	Upshur
Lewi	Lewis	Wayn	Wayne
Linc	Lincoln	Webs	Webster
Loga	Logan	Wetz	Wetzel
Mari	Marion	Wirt	-
Mars	Marshall	Wood	-
Maso	Mason	Wyom	Wyoming

AARON, Charles C, bc1860, Swansonville, Pitt Co, fJohn B, mSarah Oaks
Jacob D, b9/5/1862, Swansonville, Pitt Co, f John B, mSarah Oaks
John B, b1829/30, Pitt Co, d1900, wSarah Oaks
John F, b185-, Swansonville, Pitt Co, fJohn B, mSarah Oaks
John R, b186-, Swansonville, Pitt Co, f John B, mSarah Oaks
Nicholas C, bc1870, Swansonville, Pitt Co, f John B, mSarah Oaks
Thomas R, b18--, pitt Co, fWillis C, wHelen G Pace
ABBOTT, Catherine, b18--, Craig Co, hJohn Painter
Mary, b18--, Brandy Station, Culp Co, 2w of James William Sibert Sr md187-
ABDELL, Jennings W, b18--, Acco Co?, wCassie Underhill
ABELL, Charles R, b185-, Albe Co, fJoshua Rawles, mSusan Ann Duncam
Fannie W, b185-, Albe Co, fJoshua Rawles, mSusan Ann Duncum
John E, b9/19/1857, Albe Co, fJoshua Rawles, mSusan Ann Duncum, wLizzie M Rea, md 11/1893
Joshua Rawles, b1821, Albe Co, wSusan Ann Duncum
Julia, b186-, Albe Co, fJoshua Rawles, mSusan Ann Duncum, hF C Adams
Susie L, b186-, Albe Co, fJoshua Rawles, mSusan Ann Duncum, hA B Gentry
ABERNATHY, Katherine, b18--, Richmond, fAlex, m-- Tinsley, hHenry Hutchinson
ABRAMS, Maria, bc1820, KgWi Co, 1w of William Beverly Bird, md1818
ABY, Emma S, b6/1832, Middletown, Fred Co, fJonas, mBarbara Hulett, hJohn Sigsworth Guyer
Maria, b1848, Clar Co?, d1913, hWilliam Sommerville
ACKER, Amanda, b184-, Rkhm Co, fPeter Jr, mLouisa Ann Barnes,
ACKER (continued)
h-- Cunningham
Charles T, b184-, Rkhm Co, fPeter Jr, mLouisa Ann Barnes
Elizabeth, b181-, Rkhm Co, fPeter Sr, mAnna Maria Driver, hAnthony Acker
Isaac, b183-, Rkhm Co, fPeter Jr, mLouisa Ann Barnes
Jacob B, b183-, Rkhm Co, fPeter Jr, mLouisa Ann Barnes
Jefferson, b183-, Rkhm Co, fPeter Jr, mLouisa Ann Barnes
John, b7/24/1845, Rkhm Co, fPeter Jr, mLouisa Ann Barnes, wMary Jane Funk, md12/28/1875
Louisa, bc1840, Rkhm Co, fPeter Jr, mLouisa Ann Barnes, hAlfred Morris
Mary, b180-, Rkhm Co, fPeter Sr, mAnna Maria Driver, hJohn Swank
Mary, b183-, Rkhm Co, fPeter Jr, mLouisa Ann Barnes, hJoseph Bare
Peter, Jr, b1806, Rkhm Co, fPeter Sr, mAnna Maria Driver, wLouisa Ann Barnes
Peter, III, b184-, Rkhm Co, fPeter Jr, mLouisa Ann Barnes
William, b183-, Rkhm Co, fPeter Jr, mLouisa Ann Barnes
ADAIR, Asa Rogers, b3/20/1846, Bell Point, Gile Co, d1923, fJames, mJane Swart
Ellen, b3/30/1845, Bell Point, Gile Co, fJames, mJane Swart
Hugh T, b10/7/1849, Bell Point, Gile Co, fJames, mJane Swart
James Arthur, b4/9/1857, Bell Point, Gile Co, fJames, mJane Swart
John Alexander, Sr, b6/20/1851, Bell Point, Gile Co, fJames, mJane Swart, 1wVirginia McLaugherty, 2wFannie W Peck
Mary Jane, b3/10/1854, Bell Point, Gile Co, fJames, mJane Swart
Menelius Chapman, b6/30/1862, Bell Point, Gile Co, d1900, fJames, mJane Swart
Robert Wallace, b4/3/1848, Bell Point, Gile Co, fJames, mJane Swart
William, b3/24/1844, Bell

ADAIR (continued)
Point, Gile Co, fJames, mJane Swart
ADAM, Jane Selina, b18--, Alexandria?, hWilliam N McVeigh
ADAMS, ---, bc1790, Loud Co?, wSusan Triplett
--, b1800, Gile Co?, 1h of Margaret Melvina Jordan Harmison
Adella, bc1870, nrBlack Walnut, Hali Co, fJohn R, mMary Stanford
Betsy, b17--, Camp Co, fRobert, hJames Dearing
Catherine, b18--, Shen Co, h--White
Charles, b180-, Fauq Co, fJames, mElizabeth Brandt
Eliza Jane, b4/16/1842, Oran Co, fJohn
Elizabeth, b7/16/1812, Fauq Co, fJames, mElizabeth Brandt, 3w of James H Hathaway, md 185-
F C, bc1850, Albe Co?, wJulia Abell
Gustavus, b180-, Fauq Co, fJames, mElizabeth Brandt
Henry T, b4/21/1848, Fran Co, fSneed T, mCynthia Angle, wJosie White
Henry Ward, Sr, b18--, Camp Co?, wAnna Floyd
Henry Ward, Jr, b1863, Camp Co, fHenry Ward Sr, mAnna Floyd
I H Adams, b18--, Appo Co, wMary Patteson
Isaac, b18--, Camp Co?, wSusan Duval
Jennie, b1860/1, Hali Co, fCharles, hJoel K Tune
John, b18--, Shen Co?, wHannah Zirkle
John Buchanan, b1867, Camp Co, fHenry Ward Sr, mAnna Floyd
John Quincy, b184-, Camp Co?, wMary Saunders
John R, b5/10/1822, Powh Co, fRichard, mAnn B Tucker, 1wAmanda Wade, md1847, 2wMary Stanford, md5/1852
Lelia, bc1870, Gainsboro, Fred Co, fCarson, 2w of Edgar L Hook, md1897/8
Luther C, b1847/8, nrBlack Walnut, Hali Co, fJohn R,

ADAMS (continued)
mAmanda Wade
Margaret, b18--, Pitt Co, hJohn Henry Tabb
Martha Wood, b180-, Fauq Co, fJames, mElizabeth Brandt, hCharles C Smith
Mary Ann, b4/21/1811, Fauq Co, fJames, mElizabeth Brandt, hJames H Hathaway, md11/24/1844
Mary S, b186-, nrBlack Walnut, Hali, fJohn R, mMary Stanford, hZachariah T Pointer
Nicholas Floyd Sr, b1/17/1870, Camp Co, fHenry Ward Sr, mAnna Floyd, wDaisy Thompson, md4/14/1899
Richard, b1792, Hali Co, fWilliam, mMartha A Boyd, wAnn B Tucker
Richard A, b185-, nrBlack Walnut, Hali Co, fJohn R, mMary Stanford
Richard H T, Sr, b11/6/1839, Lynchburg, Camp Co, d1900, fIsaac, mSusan Duval, wSue L Scott
Richard Hill, b1867/8, Lynchburg, Camp Co, d1894, fI H, mMary Patteson, wRosalie Owen Hamner
Rosa, b184-, Camp Co?, fJohn Quincy, mMary Sanders, hJohn William Faulkner, md1843
Sarah "Sallie", b5/13/1810, Fauq Co, d1885, fJames, mElizabeth Brandt, hJohn Jamieson Ashby
Sallie F, b18--, Appo Co, fIsaac, mSusan Duval, 2w of John Wesley Carroll, md7/31/1878
Sallie Chappell, b1849/50, nrBlack Walnut, Hali Co, fJohn, mAmanda Wade, hGeorge C Oliver
Sallie W, b18--, Pitt Co, hW R Rogers
Samuel C, b1854, Pitt Co, fWilliam W, m-- Chandler, wChristiana Wade Dickenson
Samuel Lee, Sr, b10/31/1863, nrBlack Walnut, Hali Co, fJohn R, mMary Standford, wAlice Mitchell, md1/12/1887

ADAMS (continued)
Samuel J, Sr, b1826, (eastern shore), d1903, w-- Johnson
Samuel J, Jr, b1853, Lanc Co, d1896, fSamuel J Sr, m-- Johnson, wFannie Belle Dunaway
Sneed T, b1812, Sago, Fran Co, d1896, wCynthia Angle
Theophilus A, bc1860, nrBlack Walnut, Hali Co, d1918, fJohn R, (2)mMary Stanford
Thomas T, b1860, Camp Co, fHenry Ward, Sr, mAnna Floyd
Thomas Tucker, b186-, nrBlack Walnut, Hali Co, fJohn R, (1)mMary Stanford
Walter E, b186-, nrBlack Walnut, Hali Co, d1918, fJohn R, (1)mMary Stanford
William, b1748, Hali Co, d1812, fJohn F, mSusan Wood, wMartha A Boyd
William H, b186-, nrBlack Walnut, Hali Co, fJohn R, (1)m Mary Stanford
William Henry, b10/4/1870, nr Leesburg, Loud Co, fClinton C, mElizabeth Nichols
William W, b18--, Pitt Co, 1w-- Wilson, 2w-- Chandler
ADAMSON, Ethel, b18--, PrWi Co?, hThomas H Lion
ADDINGTON, Anna, b18--, nrNickelsville, Scot Co, hMartin B Quillen
Charles Cromwell, b10/1777, Culp Co, d1882, fWilliam, m Anne Cromwell, 1wFanny Doty
Dora E, b186-, nrNickelsville, Scot Co, fJoseph M, mKerrenneh Quillan, h-- Porter
Elizabeth, b18--, Scot Co?, hLeroy M Lee
Hugh J, bc 1870, Nickelsville, Scot Co, fWilliam J, mMartha E Porter
John Fleetwood, bc1860, Scot Co?, wKate Addington
John L, bc 1800, Scot Co, f Charles Cromwell, mFanny Doty, wPolly Hilton
Jonathan C, b186-, nrNickelsville, Scot Co, fJoseph M, mKerrenneh Quillan
Joseph M, b2/17/1848, nrNickelsville, Scot Co, fJohn L,

ADDINGTON (continued)
mPolly Hilton, wKerrenneh Quillan
Kate, bc1870, nrNickelsville, Scot Co, fJoseph M, mKerrenneh Quillan, hJohn Fleetwood Addington
William J, b1842, Nickelsville, Scot Co, wMartha E Porter
ADDISON, Alice M, b1862, nrEastville, Nhtn Co, d1880, 1w of James Ambler Jarvis, md1848
Sue, b1849, Nhtn Co, d1921, hJames A Fisher, Sr
AFLICK, James, b18--, Shen Co?, wPolly Baker
AGEE, Nannie, bc1870, Patr Co, hSamuel H Hooker
AGNOR, --, b186-, Collierstown, Rkbr Co, fThomas Bowling, mMartha Elizabeth Sheetman, hF K Carter
Albert S, b186-, Collierstown, Rkbr Co, fThomas Bowling, m Martha Elizabeth Sheetman
Robert Colvin, b5/4/1868, Collierstown, Rkbr Co, fThomas Bowling, mMartha Elizabeth Sheetman
Thomas Bowling, b1834, Collierstown, Rkbr Co, d1920, w Martha Elizabeth Sheetman
W Harvey, b186-, Collierstown, Rkbr Co, fThomas Bowling, m Martha Elizabeth Sheetman
AINSLIE, Peter, b18--, Camp Co?, wCarrie Otney
AKER, Jane, b18--, Wyth Co, h Francis Preston Staley
Matilda Jane, b18--, Wyth co, d187-, 1w of John Mathias Bunts
AKERS, Rennie, b18--, Patr Co, hJohn W Hooker
AKERSON, Alonzo Thomas, bc1855, Pitt Co, d1919, wLizzie Carson
ALBERT, Isaac C, b18--, gile Co, fRiley, wFannie L Vaughn
Jacob, b18--, Simmonsville, Crai Co, wElizabeth Trout
James Franklin, b18--, Lee Co?, wMary Marilda Baker
Nannie Josephine, bc1856, Simmonsville, Crai Co, d1917, fJacob, mElizabeth Trout, h Joseph Cales Given

3

ALBERT (continued)
Nellie, b18--, Portsmouth, Norf Co, hAndrew P Crosby
ALBIN, Ed W, bc1860, Berk Co, fM Harvey, mNora E. Keiff
Emanuel, b1846/7, nrStephens City, Fred Co, d1920, wMargaret Kline
Emma E, b186-, Berk Co?, fM Harvey, mNora E. Keiff, h Charles Addison Lupton, md9/10/1884
Harry D, bc1860, Berk Co?, fM Harvey, mNora E Keiff
M Harvey, b18--, Berk Co?, w Nora E Keiff
Mary "Maime" E, b4/12/1859, Berk Co, fM Harvey, mNora E Keiff, hJohn Edgar Lupton
ALDRIDGE, Jane, b17--, Amhe Co, hJames Sheppard Pendleton
ALESHIRE, Emma C, b18--, Page Co, f--, m-- Brubaker, hDavid F Miller
Martha Jane, b18--, Page Co, hCharles Daniel Price
ALEXANDER, --, bc1860, Rkbr Co, fJohn M, mAnn Eliza Gibson, fFinley W Houston
Amanda, b18--, Carr Co?, hFloyd Quesenberry
Andrew, b17--, Rkbr Co?, wAnn Dandridge Aylett
Annie W, b18--, Fauq Co?, f Thomas H, mMary Elizabeth Wilson, 1hFranklin Ritter, 2hWilliam Joseph Whitlock
Bruce A, bc1860, Rkbr Co, fJohn M, mAnn Eliza Gibson, hW B Douglas
Catherine Foote, b17--, PrWi Co, d186-, fJohn, m-- Foote, hWilliam H Triplett
David, b18--, Augu Co?, fReuben, mSarah Smith, wMargaret Stickley
Elizabeth, b18--, hFrederick Wheelwright
H H, bc1860, Rkbr Co, fJohn M, mAnn Eliza Gibson
Henry Hance, b11/29/1840, Newbern, Pula Co, fJabin Baldwin, mVirginia Hance, wJoanna Allison
Henry M, b18--, Fauq Co?, f Thomas H, mMary Elizabeth Wil-

ALEXANDER (continued)
son
Jabin Baldwin, b18--, Union, Monr Co, WVirginia Hance
Javin Baldwin, b1869/70, nrNewbern, Pula Co, fHenry Hance, mJoanna Allison
Janie Allison, b186-, nrNewbern, Pula Co, fHenry Hance, mJoanna Allison, hOllie Erskin Jordan
Jane Mack, b17--, Nels Co?, hThomas E Fortune
John, b17--, Rkbg Co, fArchibald II, mNancy McClure, w Sarah Gibson
John A, b11/25/1864, Augu Co, fJohn H, mSarah Craun, wJames Ella Selman, md6/28/1889
John Gibson, b5/26/1861, Rkbr Co, fJohn M, mAnn Eliza Gibson, wMary Paxton Patton, md1886
John H, b9/23/1846, Clar Co, fWilliam Carroll, mSusan Catherine Swart, wEmma Hughes
John H, b18--, Augu Co?, fDavid, mMargaret Stickley, wSarah Craun
John W Jr, b1824, Augu Co, fJohn W Sr, wNannie S Sitlington
Laura, b18--, Fauq Co?, fThomas H, mMary Elizabeth Wilson, h-- Klingan
Mary Ann, b12/1806, Rkbr Co?, d1881, fAndrew, mAnn Dandridge Aylett, hFrancis Thomas Anderson
Mary M, b10/7/1849, Middletown, Fred Co, d1917, fJohn H, hJohn William Jackson
Nancy, b17--, hWilliam L Turner
Reuben, b17--, Augu Co?, wSarah Smith
Roberta, b18--, Fauq Co?, f Thomas H, mMary Elizabeth Wilson, hJames T Bromley
Sarah, bc1800, Albe Co?, 1w of Bland Rea
Thomas, b18--, Fauq Co?, fThomas H, mMary Elizabeth Wilson
Thomas H, b18--, Fauq Co, d1875, wMary Elizabeth Wilson
William Carroll, b18--, Clar Co?, 1h of Susan Catherine

4

ALEXANDER (continued)
Swart
ALLAMONG, Virginia, b1853, Hamp Co?, hAlexander Morris
ALLEN, --, b18--, Wyth Co, d1890, hShannon Carr
--, b18--, Powh Co, hMonroe Johns
Alice, b18--, Gile Co?, hWilliam Jefferson Higginbotham
Alphonso S, b18--, fJames, wFrances E Wallace
Anne, b18--, Warr Co?, hSamuel B Gardner
Charles W, b12/14/1861, Rkbr Co, fAlphonso S, mFrances E Wallace, wMay Margaret Camp, md1/1898
David H, b17--, Warr Co, fThomas, mAbigail Miller, wSarah Griffin Taylor
Frank W, b18--, Roan Co, wSarah H McClanahan
George, b1855, "Oral Oaks", Lune Co, fRobert Henderson, mAnn Eliza Bagley, wMollie Burke
Harriet, bc1800, hJoseph Hannah
James, b17--, wJean Steele
John, bc1810, Shen Co?, wFrances Moore
John Jeter, b18--, Amel Co?, wMary Elizabeth Jeter
John J, bc1800, nrBuchanan, Bote Co, fJames, mJean Steele, wMary Jackson
Jones, b17--, Lune Co, fWilliam, mSallie Andrews, wDorothy Gee
Linden, bc1850, Shen Co?, w Frances Margaret Moore
Martha, b1843, 2w of Andrew A McClung
Mary, b18--, Page Co, fIsrael, hJoseph Spangler
Mary, bc1830, Bote Co, fJohn J, mMary Jackson, hWilliam Watts, md10/1850
Robert, b17--, Warr Co, fThomas
Robert Henderson, b3/17/1817, Lune Co, d1902, fJones, mDorothy Gee, wAnn Eliza Bagley, md1836
Sarah Bates, bc1830, Richomnd?, fJames, hAlexander Barclay Guigon, Sr, md8/20/1857

ALLEN (continued)
Sarah Catherine, bc1800, Warr Co?, fRobert, h-- Gardner
Thomas, b17--, Warr Co, fRobert, wAbigail Miller
Thomas G, b18--, Warr Co, fDavid H, mSarah Griffin Taylor, wMary --
Virginia, b18--, Warr Co, f Thomas G, mMary, hFriedrich Musaeus
William, b6/20/1756, Lune Co, wSallie Andrews
ALLERTON, --, b16--, fWilloughby, 1w of Thomas Newton
ALLEY, Ella V, b18--, fWarner T, mMary Roach, hDavis Bottom
Robert E, b18--, Taze Co?, d1839, wVirginia Jones
Warner T, b18--, wMary Roach
ALLISON, Joanna, b2/28/1844, nrDraper, Pula Co, d1909, h Henry Hance Alexander
Mary, b18--, Wash Co, hWilliam Beatie
ALLMUTT, --, b17--, Fair Co?, hFrancis Moore
ALLPORT, Henry Marion, b1/28/1852, Rkhm Co, fJohn IV, mMildred Pendleton Braxton, wNellie Shuman
John III, b17--, Caro Co, fJohn II
John IV, b1800, Caro Co, fJohn III, mMildred Pendleton Braxton
ALMOND, Charles H, Sr, bc1841, Luray, Page Co, d1910, fMann, wElizabeth Rucker
ALPHIN, E P, b186-, Collierstown, Rkbr Co, fThomas, mMary Armstrong
L C, b7/9/1867, Collierstown, Rkbr Co, fThomas, mMary Armstrong, wIda Warren, md1920
Thomas, bc1825, Bote Co, wMary Armstrong
ALSOP, Elizabeth, b17--, Spot Co?, hWilliam Spindle, Jr
Emma Jane, b2/22/1861, "Mt Eoleus", Caro Co, hWilliam F Beazley
ALTAFFER, Joseph, b18--, Rkhm Co?, wElizabeth Carpenter
Margaret, b11/1843, Rkhm Co, dc1884, fJoseph, mElizabeth

ALTAFFER (continued)
 Carpenter, hJohn Hooke Meyerhoeffer
ALTHER, W C, bc 1840, Shen Co, wJane Funkhouser
ALTIZER, Alexander, b18--, Taze Co, fThomas, m-- Beavers, w Nannie Whittaker
 Thomas, b18--, Mont Co, w-- Beavers
ALVERSON, Lucy, b18--, fArmistead, hDarias M Whitlock
AMBLER, Edward, b7/6/1854, Fauq Co, fRichard C, mSusan Marshall, wBessie Lyon, md6/13/1894
 James, b1848, Fauq Co, fRichard C, mSusan Marshall
 Richard C, b18--, wSusan Marshall
AMBURGEY, Aily, b2/12/1832, Russ Co, d1918, hNoah Counts
AMES, Leonard Hall, b1831, Pungoteague, Acco Co, d1911, w Virginia S Joynes
 Leonard O, b8/24/1870, Pungoteague, Acco Co, fLeonard Hall, mVirginia S Joynes, w Lillian S Doughty
 Mary Rebecca, b18--, Acco Co, hJohn Dennis Taylor
 Samuel W, bc1860, Acco Co, wAnnie Mears
 Sarah Jane, bc1800, Acco Co, hJohn B Mears
AMISS, Edward, bc1840, Rapp Co, fElijah
 Edwin J, bc1800, Mont Co?, wSarah Peck
 Elizabeth, b1835, Blackburg, Mont Co, d1907, fEdwin J, mSarah Peck, hWilliam H Palmer, md11/26/1856
 Fannie, bc1840, Rapp Co, fElijah, hBuck Farish
 Frederick Taylor, b11/1/1866, Slate Mills, Rapp Co, fThomas Benjamin, mMary E Miller, w Mary Caroline Weaver, md7/4/1899
 John B, b183-, Rapp Co, fElijah
 Joseph M, bc1840, Rapp Co, d1886, fElijah
 Lila, bc1830, Rapp co, fElijah, h-- Holloway
 Nannie Mary, b186-, Slate

AMISS (continued)
 Mills, Rapp Co, fThomas Benjamin, mMary E Miller, hJ B Martin
 Sarah Elizabeth, b18--, Rapp Co, fElijah, hJames Albert Menefee
 Thomas Benjamin, b7/4/1839, Rapp Co, d1913, fElijah, wMary E Miller
 Thomas Jackson, b1863, Slate Mills, Rapp Co, fThomas Benjamin, mMary E Miller
 William H, b183-, Rapp Co, fElijah
AMMEN, Annie R, bc1870, Fincastle, Bote Co, fM T, mHenrietta --, hSamuel B Smith, md4/8/1888
 M T, b18--, Bote Co?, Henrietta
AMMONETTE, Judith Ann, b18--, Powh Co, hFrederick Rudd
AMOS, Anna, b1864, Cumb Co, h Thomas G Guthrie, md12/17/1884
 Charles, b2/22/1867, Madi Co, fGeorge, wHenrietta Shuck Amos
 George, b18--, Rapp Co, d1906
 Henrietta Shuck, bc1870, Madi Co, fJeff J, mBettie Apperson, hCharles N Amos
 Jeff J, b1842, d1920, wBetttie Apperson
ANDERSON, --, b18--, Cumb Co, hThomas Caldwell
 --, b18--, Rapp Co?, hA B Fishback
 --, bc1840, Camp Co?, wSallie Clark Colvin
 A S, bc1830, Hamp Co?, wFannie Hook
 Agnes Penultima, b1847, Cumb Co, hR B Jones
 Ann, b18--, hThomas F Lewis
 Anna, b11/9/1837, Lynchburg, Camp Co, hJoseph Sutherland II
 Anna, b18--, Lexington, Rkbg Co, fThomas A, hLewis Berkley Cox, Sr
 Anna E, b183-, Buck Co, fJames D, mSarah E Flood, hJesse T Lewis
 Anna Allen, bc1800, hNathan Harris
 Archer, b1838, fJoseph Reid, mSarah Eliza Archer

ANDERSON (continued)
Belle, b18--, Glou Co?, hRichard C Coleman
Betsy, b17--, Loud Co?, hIsaac Gochnauer
Boswell P, b8/13/1847, Albe Co, wSarah D Durkee, md1/2/1879
Caroline, b17--, hHugh Montgomery
Charles E, b18--, wAlice Delaney
Charles Harper, bc1840, wSarah Travers Lewis, md2/15/1872
Charles K, b6/10/1833, Nels Co?, d1898, wMary Barcley Rodes
Edward, b18--, Acco Co, wEstelia Kellam
Elijah Thomas, b1828/9, Heckleys Crossroads, Rapp Co, d1896, wElvira G Payne
Eliza, b18--, fPeyton, mSallie Jones, hThomas B Massie
Eliza, b186-, PrGe Co, fWilliam Watkins Jr, mLaura Elizabeth Marks, hEdward R Sutherland
Elizabeth, b17--, Fauq Co?, fWalter, mSusannah Prow, 2w of Henry Moffett
Elizabeth, b17--, PrEd Co, h John Morton
Elizabeth, b1827, Gray Co, d1906, hJohn Wilkinson
Elizabeth, b1842, Hali Co, hCharles W Tisdale
Ellen G, b184-, "Walnut Hill", Bote Co, fJoseph Reid, mSarah Elizabeth Archer, 1w of William Alexander Anderson, md 1871
Fannie, b1862, Berryville, Clar Co, fMilton, mFrances Mildred Anderson, hJames Silvey
Fannie, bc1870, Acco Co?, fEdward, mEstelia Kellam, hJohn Thomas Benjamin Hyslop, md2/1896
Fannie A, bc 1840, fJoseph Reid, mSarah Eliza Archer, hEdwin L Hobson
Fannie L, bc1860, PrEd Co, d1882, hAlexander Stuart Hall, md1876
Fannie M, bc1840, Buck Co, fJames D, mSarah E Flood, hMayo C Richardson

ANDERSON (continued)
Frances Mildred, b6/3/1833, Clar Co, hMilton Anderson
Francis Thomas, b1808, "Walnut Hill", Bote Co, d1887, fWilliam, mAnna Thomas, wMary Ann Alexander
Gertrude, bc1870, PrGe Co, fWilliam Watkins Jr, mLaura Elizabeth Marks, hWilliam P Richardson
Henrietta, b18--, Camp Co?, fRobert C Sr, mJustina Armistead, hEugene A Richardson
Henry Branson, b18--, Rapp co, fPeyton, m-- Jones, wEsther Eugenia Griffin
Henry W, b186-, PrGe Co, fWilliam Watkins Jr, mLaura Elizabeth Marks
Ida Jane, b10/26/1860, Berryville, Clar Co, fMilton, m Frances Mildred Anderson, h Hugh Thompson Ramey, md2/21/1883
Isaac C, b3/6/1819, Smyt Co, fJohn, mCatherine Killinger, wEliza Jane Dungan
Jackson B, b9/28/1864, nrFlint Hill, Rapp Co, fHenry Branson, mEsther Eugenia Griffin, wIda Virginia Hunt, md12/14/1901
James D, b18--, Cumb Co, wSarah E Flood
James L, b7/27/1847, Buck Co, fJames D, mSarah E Flood, wMirtie S Seal
James Lewis, b1861, Camp Co?, fRobert C Sr, mJustina Armistead
James Madison, b1837, Amel Co, 1wMargaret Oliver Robins, 2w--Jackson
James Powell, b1801, nrAmelia, Amel Co, d1875, wCaroline Scott Branch
John, b1788, Smyt Co, wCatherine Killinger
John, bc1850, Fred Co?, wMinnie McVicar
John F T, bc1850, fJoseph Reid Sr, mSarah Elizabeth Archer
John Fisher, b18--, nrColonial Beach, Nhld Co, wAnn Sanford
John L C, b2/3/1868, Smyt Co, fIsaac C, mEliza Jane Dungan,

ANDERSON (continued)
wRobena Halsey, md9/9/1889
John R, b18--, Camp Co?, fRobert C Sr, mJustina Armistead
John T, b18--, Orleans, Fauq Co, fElijah Thomas, mElvira G Payne
John Thomas, bc1800, "Walnut Hill", Bote co, fWilliam, m Anna Thomas
Joseph Reid, Sr, b2/6/1813, d1892, fWilliam, manna Thomas, 1wSarah Elizabeth Archer, md5/3/1837, 2wMary Pegram
Joseph Reid, Jr, b184-, fJoseph Reid Sr, mSarah Elizabeth Archer
Joseph Walker, b186-, Albe Co, fCharles K, mMary Barcley Rodes
Joseph Walker, b12/12/1838, nrColonial Beach, Nhld Co, d1908, 1wVirginia Watts, 2w Mary Elizabeth George
Julia, b18--, Culp Co?, hWilliam Sydnor Richardson.
Katherine, bc1775, hJohn McNutt
Katherine Virginia, b185-, Camp Co?, fRobert C, Sr, mJustina Armistead
Laura, b186-, PrGe Co, fWilliam Watkins Jr, mLaura Elizabeth Marks, hBurtt S Fenn
Lena, b18--, Hamp Co, hJames LaFollett
Leonard W, b17--, PrEd Co, fRobert C, wMary Morton
Leonard W, b18--, Camp Co?, fRobert C Sr, mJustina Armistead
Llewellyn Lee, b18--, Orleans, Fauq Co, fElijah Thomas, mElvira G Payne
Louisa Caroline, b1842, nrAmelia, Amel Co, fJames Powell, mCaroline Scott Branch, hRichard Henry Marshall
Lucy A, b184-, Buck Co, fJames D, mSarah E Flood, hLewis A Jones
Lucy F, b18--, Camp Co?, fRobert C Sr, mJustina Armistead, hDaniel M McIntosh
Luther Rice, b8/4/1860, nrWolftown, Madi Co, fObadiah, mEmeline Booton, wMalinda E Gil-

ANDERSON (continued)
bert
Mary, b17--, Fauq Co?, fWalter, mSusanna Prow, 1w of Henry Moffett
Mary, b18--, Amel Co, hJosiah M Jordan III
Mary, b184-, fJoseph Reid Sr, mSarah Elizabeth Archer, h Thomas Seddon Bruce
Mary E, b9/2/1869, Albe Co, fCharles K, mMary Barcley Rodes, hEdwin Sherwood Wilson, md11/5/ 1902
Mary Jane, b18--, Shen Co?, hAlfred Hoffman
Mary Milton, b1869, Berryville, Clar Co, fMilton, mFrances Mildred Anderson, hWilliam Duncan
Mary Morton, b185-, Camp Co, fRobert C Sr, mJustina Armistead, hSamuel C Fontaine
Milton, b8/24/1834, Berryville, Clar Co, wFrances Mildred Anderson
Nannie, b185-, Camp Co?, fRobert C Sr, mJustina Armistead, hEmmett L Williams
Noah B C, bc1870, Smyt Co, fIsaac C, mEliza Jane Dungan
Norval, b1857, Clar Co, fMilton, mFrances Mildred Anderson
Olivia, b1823, Albe Co, d1863, hErasmus D Booker
Olivia J, b18--, Meck Co, f Thomas, hSchuyler Bland
Peyton, bc1800, wSallie Jones
Richard D, bc1860, Albe Co, wM Carrie White
Robert, b186-, Smyt Co, fIsaac C, mEliza Jane Dungan
Robert C Sr, b3/16/1823, PrEd, fLeonard W, mMary Morton, wJustina Armistead
Robert C Jr, b18--, Camp Co?, fRobert C Sr, mJustina Armistead
Robert J, b18--, Orleans, Fauq Co, fElijah Thomas, mElvira G Payne
Robert K, b186-, Albe Co, d1920, fCharles K, mMary Barcley Rodes
Rosa H, 183-, Buck co, fJames D, mSarah E Flood, hJoseph W

ANDERSON (continued)
Davis
Sallie, b1867, Berryville, Clar Co, fMilton, mFrances Mildred Anderson, hEd Rhodes
Samuel Armistead, b4/8/1850, Camp Co, fRobert C Sr, mJustina Armistead, wPauline D Daniel, md11/1890
Sarah, b18--, Fred Co?, hJohn B McCormick
Sarah, b18--, Amel Co, fJoseph B, hJeduthon Davis
Sarah F, b18--, Richmond?, hGeorge W Gilliam
Sarah L, b184-, Buck Co, fJames D, mSarah E Flood, hJ J Chalton
Scena, bc1870, Smyt Co, fIsaac C, mEliza Jane Dungan, 1hFrank L. Pierce, 2hSamuel T Copenhaver
Sumner S, b18--, Orleans, Fauq Co, fElijah Thomas, mElvira G Payne
Thomas G, b18--, Orleans, Fauq Co, fElijah Thomas, mElvira G Payne
William Alexander, b5/11/1842, nrFincastle, Bote Co, fFrancis Thomas, mMary Ann Alexander, 1wEllen G Anderson, md1871, 2wMaza Blair, md1875
William Edward, b9/10/1866, PrGe Co, fWilliam Watkins Jr, mLaura Elizabeth Marks, wPearl Horton Venable, md4/30/1901
William Neely, bc1810, "Walnut Hill", Bote Co, fWilliam, m Anna Thomas
William Watkins Sr, b1768, Ches Co, d1858, w--
William Watkins Jr, b9/29/1816, Fancy Farm, Dinw Co, d1900, fWilliam Watkins Sr, wLaura Elizabeth Marks
Willie Ward Sr, b18--, Orleans, Fauq Co, fElijah Thomas, mElvira G Payne, wElvira Louise Luck, md188-
ANDERTON, Marietta, b1865, Acco Co, hJoel T Stant
ANDES, Abram, b18--, Rkhm Co, wSarah Long
B Frank, bc1860, Rkhm Co, wRebecca Catherine Holler

ANDES (continued)
Flora B, bc1860, Rkhm Co, fAbram, mSarah Long, hCharles Benjamin Shrum, md4/4/1888
Rebecca, b18--, Rkhm Co, fHenry, hEmanuel Spitzer
William, bc1860, Rkhm Co, wSusanna Kline
ANDIS, Mary, b18--, Lee Co?, d187-, 1w of John F Skaggs
ANDREW, James Abram, bc1800, Camp Co, wLucy Bell
Lucy Lee, b11/4/1827, Camp Co, fJames Abram, mLucy Bell, h Robert Colvin
ANDREWS, Buford, b6/22/1853, Oran Co, fJohn L, mMary E Twyman, wIrene Scott, md11/15/1893
Charles R, b1/1857, Spotsylvania Court House, Spot Co, fJohn L, mMary E Taylor, 1wMattie McKuney, md11/1/1883, 2wBertha Harris, md12/19/1889
Charles W, bc1800, Clar Co?, wSarah "Sallie" Page
Emma J, b1853, Meck Co D1893, 1w of William T Ozlin
James Barclay, b10/1/1863, "Viewmont", Albe Co, fJohn Summerfield, mOrianna Russell Moon
John L, b10/19/1819, Oran Co, wMary E Twyman
Julian Botts Sr, b10/12/1850, Gooc Co, fDaniel Holmes, mMargaret (Taylor) Whitlock, wEdmonia Osceola Bell
Martha Indie, b1842, Meck Co, d1909, hJames Archer Saunders
Sallie, b17--, Lune Co, hWilliam Allen
William Luther, b2/9/1865, "Viewmont", Albe Co, fJohn Summerfield, mOrianna Russell Moon
ANDRICK, Eugene, bc1850, Rkhm Co?, wRebecca Pence
ANGELL, Anderson, b18--, nrCallaway, Fran Co, fTaylor, m-- Dodd
Bell, bc1870, Boone Mill, Fran Co, fJohn William, hJack Garst
Marshall Jefferson, b18--, nr Callaway, Fran Co, fTaylor, m-- Dodd, wEmma Noel

ANGELL (continued)
Robert Henderson, b1/25/1868, nrCallaway, Fran Co, fMarshall Jefferson, mEmma Noel, wMary J Barlow, md1896
Taylor, b18--, Cumb Co, w-- Dodd
Woodson C, b18--, nr Callaway, Fran Co, fTaylor, m-- Dodd
ANGLE, Benjamin, b12/5/1868, Fran Co, fNathaniel, mSarah Frances Wills, wKate W Angle, md1893
C W, b186-, Fran Co, fNataniel, mSarah Franes Wills
Cynthia, b18--, Fran Co, d1890, hSneed T Adams
James E, b1862/3, Fran Co, fNathaniel, mSarah Frances Wills
Joel W, b186-, Fran Co, fNathaniel, mSarah Frances Wills
John R, b186-, Fran Co, d188-, fNathaniel, mSarah Frances Wills
Kate W, bc1870, Fran Co, fJoel, hBenjamin L Angle, md1893
Nathaniel, b18--, Fran Co, w Sarah Frances Wills
Nathaniel P, b1861, nrFerrum, Fran Co, fNathaniel, mSarah Frances Wills, wMary E Shearer
ANGLIN, Adron, b185-, Patr Co?, wMary K Thomas
Sarah, b17--, Grbr Co, hBennett Ingram Hudkins, md1814
ANSLEY, Harrie C, wHarriet Fuller
APPASON, --, b17--, NewK Co, hGideon Christian
APPERSON, Bettie, b18--, hJeff J Amos
Bettie Octavia, b1869, Culp Co, fRichard, mEmma Partlow, hDavid Oswald, m2/1906
John Samuel, b8/31/1837, nrOrange Court House, Oran Co, fWilliam, wElizabeth Black
Richard, b1828/9, Culp Co?, wEmma Partlow
APPLEWHAITE, Alice Cowles, b18--, Norfolk?, hWilliam Thomas Morris
APPLEWHITE, Thomas Henry, b1/13/1830, Sout Co, d1890, wMary Ann Jarratt

ARBOGAST, Virginia, b1854, High Co, hHarmon Himer Seybert, md6/24/ 1880
ARCHER, --, b186-, Wytheville, Wyth Co, fJames D, mPauline F Bateman, hL A Runyan
--, bc1870, Wytheville, Wyth Co, fJames D, mPauline F Bateman, h A M Brown
Annie Blair, b1836, Ches Co, hJames A Page
E T, bc1866, Wytheville, Wyth Co, fJames D, mPauline F Bateman
Edward C, b18--, Powh Co, wCaroline Wooldridge
James D, b1837, Wyth Co, wPauline Bateman, md1860
John W, b8/1957, Gooc Co, fEdward C, mCaroline Wooldridge, wJennie Lloyd
Sarah Elizabeth, b181-, d1881, fRobert, hJoseph Reid Anderson, md5/3/1837
W F, b186-, Wyth Co, fJames D, mPauline F Bateman
ARGENBRIGHT, Moses W, b1853, Augu Co, wEllen Stogdale
Sallie, b18--, McGaheysville, Rkhm Co, hGeorge Bauserman
ARINGTON, Susan, b18--, Russ Co, hNoah Sykes
ARMBRISTER, James, b18--, Wyth Co?, wNannie Jane Bunts
ARMENTROUT, --, bc1800, Rkhm Co?, wDianna Bertram
Elizabeth, b18--, Rkhm Co?, 2w of James Absalom Young, md187-
Margaret, b18--, Rkhm Co?, h Harvey Liskey
Mary, b18--, Alle Co, 2w of Peter Holmintoller
ARMETROUT, Hugh, bc1860, Rkhm Co, wSarah Will
ARMES, Bessie, bc1860, Char Co, fWillia, hJames R Bell
ARMISTEAD, Anthony, b16--, Eliz Co?, fWilliam, mAnnie --, wHannah Ellison
Anthony, b17--, Eliz Co, fWilliam, wElizabeth Starkey
Edward Winston, b18--, Hali Co, fWilliam Harrison, mSarah Henry, wAnna Hobson Clarke, md1890
Fabian, b12/25/1794, Meck Co,

ARMISTEAD (continued)
 fJohn II, mElizabeth Royster, wVirginia Harrison
 Frances, b16--, Eliz Co?, fWilliam, mAnnie --
 George A, b7/31/1848, PrGe Co, fFabian, mVirginia Harrison, wMary Bland
 James A, b18--, Cumb Co, wJennie Madison
 John I, b17--, Warw Co, fAnthony, mElizabeth Starkey
 John II, b17--, Eliz Co, fJohn I, wElizabeth Royster
 Justina, b1/8/1827, Camp Co, hRobert C Anderson Sr
 Lucy, b17--, York Co?, hThomas Nelson Jr
 Mary Marot, b17--, York Co?, fRobert Booth, hJohn Tyler
 Nancy Miller, b8/24/1829, Buck Co, fJese S, hPhilip Southall Blanton
 Nannie, b18--, fWilliam A, m-- Flippin, hJames D Crump
 Samuel Goode, b17--, wMary Armistead Burwell
 Susan C, b18--, Char Co, fJohn, 1hMonroe R Flippen, 2hThomas Jefferson
 Susannah, bc1800, hWilliam Dandridge
 William, b16--, Eliz Co, fWilliam, mAnnie --
 William, b16--, Eliz Co, fAnthony, mFrances Thompson, w Annie --
 William, b16--, Eliz Co, fAnthony, mHannah Ellison
 William Harrison, b2/8/1820, Petersburg, Dinw Co, d1895, fFabian, mVirginia Harrison, wSarah Henry, md4/23/1844
ARMSTRONG, Catherine, bc1840, Catawba Valley, Roan Co, fEllis, mHarriet Moomaw
 Cora, bc1870, Fair Co, hJohn Sidney Hutton Jr, md1/2/1894
 David M, b3/27/1845, Catawba Valley, Roan Co, fEllis, mHarriet Moomaw, wMary Frances Haley, md1872
 Ellis, b1807, Bote Co, d1884/5, wHarriet Moomaw
 Francis, b183-, Catawba Valley, Roan Co, fEllis, mHarriet Moomaw

ARMSTRONG (continued)
 John, b183-, Catawba Valley, Roan Co, fEllis, mHarriet Moomaw
 Margaret, b184-, Catawba Valley, Roan Co, fEllis, mHarriet Moomaw
 Martha A, b18--, Esse Co, h Thomas M Henley
 Mary, b18--, d1902, hThomas Alphin
 Mary, bc1840, Catawba Valley, Roan Co, fEllis, mHarriet Moomaw
 Samuel Ringgold, b12/10/1846, Woodville, Rapp Co, fWilliam Cleminson, mSarah Catherine Slaughter, wElla Brerington Miller, md11/14/1887
 Susan, b183-, Catawba Valley, Roan Co, fEllis, mHarriet Moomaw
 William Cleminson, b18--, Rapp Co?, fJohn, wSarah Catherine Slaughter
ARNEST, Emily, b18--, West Co, hCharles Yeatman
ARNOLD, Betty, b18--, Bote Co?, hGeorge Rieley
 Cordelia, b1852, Loud Co, hColumbus P Cooper
 Kate, b1845/6, Camp Co, hWalter C Rosser Sr
 Lily Brown, b18--, Camp Co?, fD R, hJohn James Board Sr, md1882
 Susana, b18--, Augu Co, hJoseph B Bowman
ARRINGTON, Daniel, bc1850, Fran Co, wBetty D Dillard
 Sallie Lou, b1868, Motvale, Bedf Co, d1912, hCharles Price Ferrell Jr
 W E, bc1860, Bedf Co?, wLelia M Dooley
ARSELL, Josephine, b18--, Richmond, hIsaac J Mercer
ARTHUR, --, b18--, Camp Co?, hGeorge Claiborne Creasy
 James Lewis, b18--, Bedf Co?, wAmerica Brown
 Kate L, bc1870, Bedf Co, fJames Lewis, mAmerica Brown, hMarcellus Alexander Johnson Sr, md1889

ARTRIP, Mollie, b1850, nrCarterton, Russ Co, d1906, hJohn Taze Howard
ARTZ, Laura, b186-, Shen Co, d1920, fSamuel, 1hSamuel Windle, 2hJohn Rhodes
ASHBROOK, Hiram, b18--, Russ Co?, wMelissa Kiser
Lou May, bc1870, Russ Co, fHiram, mMelissa Kiser, hElbert S Finney, md9/8/1888
ASHBY, Alice, bc1870, Fauq Co, hThomas Richards Leachman
Benjamin, b1745, fJohn
Caroline, b1802, Warr Co, d1870, hAlfred Henry
Carrie, b183-, "Oakwood", Fauq Co, fJohn Jamieson, mSallie Adams, hJohn Odilvie
Henry, b18--, Fauq Co, wMary Delaplane
Henry Stribling, b184-, "Oakwood", Fauq Co, fJohn Jamieson, mSallie Adams
James Jr, b1850, Staf Co, wMary B Moncure
James Samuel, b184-, "Oakwood", Fauq Co, fJohn Jamieson, m Salle Adams
Jennie, bc1850, "Oakwood", Fauq Co, fJohn Jamieson, mSallie Adams, hThurston Woolf
John b1740, Fauq Co, d1815, fRobert, wMary Turner
John, b18--, wEmily Buckner
John Jamieson, b1/12/1802, "Oakwood", Fauq Co, d1864, fSamuel Turner Sr, wSarah "Sallie" Adams
John Turner Sr, b5/15/1841, "Oakwood", Fauq Co, fJohn Jamieson, mSallie Adams, w Louise Herndon, md1/1876
Lucy Strother, bc1850, fJohn, mEmily Buckner, hRobert Randolph Henry
Luther, bc1840, "Oakwood", Fauq Co, fJohn Jamieson, mSallie Adams
Maria S, b18--, Warr Co?, hJames W Conrad
Mary Ann, b10/19/1817, Warr Co, fRobert B, mElizabeth Ash, hCharles Buckner Carroll Rust, md9/12/1839
Mary Ellen, b18--, West Co,

ASHBY (continued)
fThomson, mAnne Stuart Menefee, 1w of Charles Bayne
Mattie C, b183-, "Oakwood", Fauq Co, fJohn Jamieson, m Sallie Adams
Robert B, b4/17/1788, Fauq Co?, fBenjamin, wElizabeth Ash
Samuel Turner, b1780, Fauq Co, fJohn, mMary Turner
Scott, b184-, "Oakwood", Fauq Co, fJohn Jamieson, mSallie Adams
Thomson, bc1790, Fauq Co, fJohn, mMary Turner, wAnne Stuart Menefee
Turner, b8/7/1787, Fauq Co, fJohn, mMary Turner
Turner, b18--, Fauq Co, fTurner
ASHE, William, b1834, Gloucester Point, Glou Co, fWilliam, m-- Stubblefield, wLucy Hayes Hughes
ASHER, John, b186-, York Co?, wVera Marshall
ASHWORTH, Charles, b18--, Rale Co, wJane Lilly
ASTON, Charles H, b18--, KgGe Co, wIda B Welch
ASTON, Carroll, b18--, Camp Co, hJames E Loyd Sr
ATHEY, Mary, b18--, Loud Co, hThomas Coates
ATKINS, Floyd, bc1840, Appo Co?, wSusan J Berkley
Isabella, b18--, Loui Co, h Urias Kendig
James, b18--, Wyth Co?, wMary Rosena Bunts
Mary E, b18--, Albe Co, hRichard H Stratton Sr
ATKINSON, George W, bc1860, Clar Co?, wDaisy Cloud Warden
Homer, b5/27/1848, Petersburg, Dinw Co, fJohn Henry III, m-- Temple, wKittie O Pierce
John, bc1820, wBetty Harrison
John Henry III, b18--, NewK Co, fJohn Henry II, w-- Temple
Will, bc1860, Rkhm Co, wLillie D Hawse
ATWELL, Julia, b18--, hGilbert A Jones
Nancy, b17--, Loud Co?, 1hJames Smith, 2hDavid Gibson
S R, bc1860, wCarrie P Barr

ATWELL (continued)
Sallie A, b18--, West Co, hJames H Parker
ATWOOD, --, bc1850, PrEd Co, fRobert B, mAnna Hill, hM L Harvey
John Randolph Sr, b2/25/1848, PrEd Co, d1912, fRobert B, mAnna Hill, wFlorence Blanton Chernault, md1888
AUSTIN, Martha E, b18--, Buck Co, fArchibald, hIberson Lewis Twyman
Sarah Thomas, bc1800, Hano Co, hWilliam Barrett Sydnor
AVEN, Elizabeth, b1834, Wash Co, hWilliam Wallace McChesney I
AVERY, Aramina, bc1800, Fred Co?, hRobert Barr
AYERS, Rufus, b18--, Scot Co?, wVictoria Morison
AYLET, Pattie, b18--, Nels Co?, hGeorge C Callaway Sr
AYLETT, Ann Dandridge, b17--, Rkbr Co, hAndrew Alexander
Mary Macon, b12/5/1793, Aylett's, KiWi Co, d1815, m-- Henry, hPhilip Fitzhugh
AYLOR, Anna E, b186--, nrPeola Mills, Rapp Co, fStaunton, mMalinda Quaintance, hT Walter Oyler
Aylette W, bc1850, nrPeola Mills, Rapp Co, fStaunton, m Malinda Quaintance
John L, b184-, nrPeola Mills, Rapp Co, fStaunton, mMalinda Quaintance
Joseph W, b184-, nrPeola Mills, Rapp Co, fStaunton, mMalinda Quaintance
Mary E, b18--, Madi Co, hJ C Crigler
Robert Edward Lee, b12/11/1860, nrPeola Mills, Rapp Co, fStaunton, mMalinda Quaintance, wElla K Vaden, md1886
Staunton, b1816, Madi Co, wMalinda Quaintance
William Jackson, b4/1842, nrPeola Mills, Rapp Co, f Staunton, mMalinda Quaintance, wRoberta Jane Bowie
AYRE, Ida B, b18--, Fair Co, fWilliam Ayre, mMartha Ann Reid, hGeorge F Harrison,

AYRE (continued)
md9/1/1880
William, b18--, Fair Co, wMartha Ann Reid
BABCOCK, Blanche W, b186-, nrConcord, Camp Co, fBradley W, mMary Elizabeth Cardell, h-- Sweeney
Bradley C, b186-, nrConcord, Camp Co, fBradley W, mMary Elizabeth Cardwell
Frank E, b186-, nrConcord, Camp Co, fBradley W, mMary Elizabeth Cardwell
Homer Curtis, b5/28/1860, nrConcord, Camp Co, fBradley W, mMary Elizabeth Cardwell, wRosie Blanch Moore
J O, b186-, nrConcord, Camp Co, fBradley W, mMary Elizabeth Cardwell
BABER, Cornelia S, b18--, Albe Co?, 1w of William Wallace Tapscott
BACHELOR, Oliver D, b18--, Camp Co?, wMaude Watts
BAGBY, Alexander Fleet, bc1840, Stevensville, KiQu Co, d1915, fRichard, mDorothy Fleet, wFannie Singleton Walker
George, W, b18--, Richmond?, wLucy Parke Chamberlayne
Martha, bc1870, Richmond?, fGeorge W, mLucy Parke Chamberlayne, hGeorge Gordon Battle, md4/12/ 1898
Richard, b18--, KiQu Co, wDorothy Fleet
Virginia, b18--, KiQu Co?, hJohn Pollard
BAGEANT, Dora, bc1870, Fred Co, fJohn, 1w of Robert Eugene Borden, md2/1906
BAGLEY, Ann Eliza, bc1820, Lune Co, fWilliam, mPhoebe Marshall, hRobert Henderson Allen
Isham Trotter, b1851, Lune Co, d1897, wSusan Epesseay
Nannie E, b18--, Lune Co, fWilliam M, mAnne Gaulding, h George Edward Smith, md11/25/ 1874
William, b18--, Lune Co, w Phoebe Marshall
William M, b18--, Lune Co?, wAnne Gaulding

BAILEY, --, b17--, Fred Co, 2w of Jasper Cather
--, b184-, Whitehall, Albe Co, fWilliam, hHiram Hott
Anne, bc1800, 1h-- Loring, 2hBenjamin L Yates Sr
Charles P, b184-, Whitehall, Albe Co, fWilliam
Fannie L, bc1870, Taze Co, fJesse, mMary Shannon, hJames E Wagner
Flora, b1/21/1840, hClaiborne W Beatie
James, b18--, Surr Co, fJames, wAnna Hobbs
James, bc1840, Smyt Co?, wEtta Sanders
Jesse, b18--, Taze Co?, d1895, wMary Shannon
Jesse R, b1846/7, Whitehall, Albe Co, d1922, fWilliam, w Carrie Parkins
John H, b1828, Lee Co, d1888, wMary Robbins
John P, bc1860, West Co, wMinnie Walker
Mary E, b18--, Nels Co, hT A Gentry
Mildred, b18--, Pitt Co, hJonathan Bennett
Sallie Black, bc1860, Albe Co, hJohn Walker Langford, md3/21/1881
William E, bc1860, Taze Co, fJesse, mMary Shannon
F B, bc1860, Wakefield, Susse Co, fFranklin Lemuel, mBetty
BAIN, Philip David, b12/25/1861, Wakefield, Suss Co, fFranklin Lemuel, mBetty --
BAIRD, Jennie, b18--, Augu Co?, hFrancis Brooke Berkeley
Jennie, b18--, hGeorge Scott McCrae
Sarah, b17--, Meck Co?, hJohn Speed Jr
BAKER, --, bc1840, Clar Co?, wJennie Hardesty
--, b18--, Winchester, Fred Co, hOliver Brown
Abraham, b12/18/1818, nrSt Stephen's Church, Shen Co, fPhilip, mCatherine Stickley
Ananias, b6/23/1827, nrSt Stephen's Church, Shen Co, fPhilip, mCatherine Stickley

BAKER (continued)
Anthony, b18--, nrSt Stephen's Church, Shen Co, fIsaac
Attie, b18--, Clar Co, hThomas Chamblin
Benjamin, b10/19/1824, nrSt Stephen's Church, Shen Co, fPhilip, mCatherine Stickley, wMary Elizabeth Helsley
Benjamin West, b8/16/1846, Glen-dobbin Farm, nrWinchester, Fred Co, fHenry M, mCatherine Grove, wLucy V Hiett, md11/10/1876
Catherine, bc1850, Glendobbin Farm, nrWinchester, Fred Co, fHenry M, mCatherine Grove, 2w of W S White
Catherine, b9/27/1852, nrStephen's Church, Shen Co, fBenjamin, mMary Elizabeth Helsley, hJohn Hinkins
Cornelia, b184-, nrWinchester, Fred Co, d1886, fIsaac Baker, hJames M Cadwallader
Daniel, bc1830, Fred Co?, wLucinda Kline
Drusilla E, b1827, PrEd Co?, hRobert J D Smith, md1846
Edward, b5/16/1863, nrSt Stephen's Church, Shen Co, fBenjamin, mMary Elizabeth Helsley wMartha Rebecca Pifer, md11/5/1888
Elizabeth, b8/11/1815, nrSt Stephen's Church, Shen Co, fPhilip, mCatherine Stickley, hDavid Fetzer
Elizabeth, b18--, Shen Co, fJacob, hJohn Strohsnider
Elizabeth, b183-, Shen Co, fThomas Sr, (2)mAnnie Walters, hAbe Nicholas
Ephraim, b17--, Shen Co, fLewis
Ephraim, bc1860, Shen Co?, wJoanna V Pifer
Flora, b184-, Glendobbin Farm, nrWinchester, Fred Co, fHenry M, mCatherine Grove, hJoseph T Hiett
Florence, b185-, Glendobbin Farm, nrWinchester, Fred Co, fHenry M, mCatherine Grove, hJohn S Miller
George, b185-, Glendobbin Farm, nrWinchester, Fred Co, fHenry

BAKER (continued)
M, mCatherine Grove
H W, b17--, Fred Co?, fHeinrich, mElizabeth Fink, wCatherine Miller
Harriet, b18--, nrSt Stephen's Church, Shen Co, fJacob, hWilliam Swartz
Harriet, b184-, Glendobbin Farm, nrWinchester, Fred Co, fHenry M, mCatherine Grove, hRoland T Bryarly
Henry, b17--, Shen Co, fLewis
Henry M, b1818, Winchester, Fred Co, d1864, fHenry W, mCatherine Miller, wCatherine Grove
Isaac, bc1800, St Stephen's Church, Shen Co, fPhilip Peter
Isaac, b12/8/1816, nrSt Stephen's Church, Shen Co, fPhilip, mCatherine Stickley
Jacob, b17--, St Stephen's Church, Shen Co, fPhilip Peter
Jacob, b183-, Shen Co, fThomas Sr, (2)mAnnie Walters
James, bc1780, Hard Co?, wMagdalene Warden
James R, b18--, Hard Co?, wMary Elizabeth Clagett
John, bc1800, Wash Co, fIsaac, wSusan Hortenstine
John, b18--, Shen Co, fJacob
John A P, b18--, Wash Co, fJohn, mSusan Hortenstine, wSusan Catherine Davis
Jonah, b18--, Warr Co, fHenry
Joseph, b18--, Warr Co, fHenry
Joseph, b18--, Shen Co?, f Thomas Sr, (1)m---
Joseph G, bc1850, Shen Co?, wOlive Viola Copp
Joseph Haskew, b8/13/1869, Wash Co, fJohn A P, mSusan Catherine Davis, wNancy Katherine Taylor, md6/16/1897
Julia, b185-, Glendobbin Farm, nrWinchester, Fred Co, fHenry M, mCatherine Grove, hEdward Jiffkins
Kate, b18--, Warr Co, fHenry, h-- Palmer
Lewis, b17--, St Stephen's Church, Shen Co, fPhilip Peter
Louisa, b18--, Hard Co, fJesse, hHezekiah Clagett

BAKER (continued)
Mary, b18--, Hali Co, hCharles Lacy
Mary Beatrice, b184-, Glendobbin Farm, nrWinchester, Fred Co, fHenry M, mCatherine Grove, hT S Chamberlain
Mary Belle, b9/3/1854, nrSt Stephen's Church, Shen Co, fBenjamin, mMary Elizabeth Helsley, hGeorge H Snarr
Mary Marilda, b18--, Lee Co?, hJames Franklin Albert
Myron, b18--, wLouise Spring
Nellie F, bc1870, fMyron, mLouise Spring, hWilliam F Smyth, md12/1888
Nicholas, b18--, nrSt Stephen's Church, Shen Co, fIsaac
Nicholas W, b4/3/1845, nrWoodstock, Shen Co, fThomas Sr, (2)mAnnie Walters, wVirginia Kibler, md5/1871
Philip, b17--, nrSt Stephen's Church, Shen Co, fPhilip Peter, wCatherine Stickley
Philip, b18--, Shen Co, fJacob
Philip, b18--, Warr Co, fHenry
Philip Peter, b3/30/1833, nrStephen's Church, Shen Co, fPhilip, mCatherine Stickley
Polly, b18--, nrSt Stephen's Church, Shen Co, fIsaac, hJames Aflick
Polly, b183-, Shen Co, fThomas Sr, (2)mAnnie Walters
Rachel A, b18--, nrSt Stephen's Church, Shen Co, fIsaac, 2w of Henry Green Huff, md1877
Sallie, b184-, Shen Co, fThomas Sr, (2)mAnnie Walters, hW H Carpenter
Samuel, b17--, nrSt Stephen's Church, Shen Co, fPhilip Peter
Sarah, b18--, nrSt Stephen's Church, Shen Co, fIsaac
Susan, b1827, Hali Co, hWilliam Aaron Penick
Susan, b18--, Rkhm Co, hElias Pirkey
Thomas Sr, bc1800, Fred Co, dc1850, 2wAnnie Walters
Tina, b18--, nrSt Stephen's Church, Shen Co, fIsaac, h-- Hockman
Tobias, b4/23/1830, nrSt Ste-

BAKER (continued)
   phen's Church, Shen Co, fPhilip, mCatherine Stickley
W H, b18--, Camp Co?, 1h of Eliza Deane
William H, b184--, Glendobbin Farm, nrWinchester, Fred Co, fHenry M, mCatherine Grove
William Hartman, b18--, Fred Co, wMary Rivera Pierce
William Henry, bc1840, Shen Co, fThomas Sr, (2)mAnnie Walters
William Henry, b1855, Winchester, Fred Co, d1916, wEmma Ginn
BALDWIN, Briscoe G, b17--, Augu Co?, wMartha Steele Brown
John, b17--, Bedf Co, fJames, mElizabeth Ferrell, wElizabeth Newberry
John, b1/11/1820, Spring Farm, Augu Co, d1873, fBriscoe G, mMartha Steele Brown, wSusan Madison Peyton, md8/20/1842
Katherine Mackey, b18--, Norfolk, fRobert Frederick, mCaroline M Barton, hBarton Myers Sr
Mary, b18--, Nott Co, 1w of George N Seay
Melinda, b18--, Wise Co?, hVincent Wright
Robert, b1841, Wyth Co, wJanie Loufland
Robert Frederick, b1830, Winchester, Fred Co, d1879, wCaroline M Barton
BALL, Ann, b17--, New Kent, NewK, h-- Miller
Burgess, b7/28/1749, fJeduthum, mElizabeth Burgess, 1wMary Chichester, md7/2/1770, 2w Frances Washington
C W, bc1840, Fred Co?, wRachel E Jackson
Charles A, b186-, nrHonaker, Russ Co, fIsaiah D, wClare Stuart, md1901
Elizabeth Burgess, b3/16/1772, fBurgess, (1)mMary Chichester, hArmistead Long
Frances, b17--, Lanc Co, fJoseph, hRaleigh Downman, md1750
Hannah, b17--, Lanc Co?, hRobert Mitchell, md1746
Hannah, b17--, fRichard, hWil-
BALL (continued)
   liam Montague
Isaiah D, b10/1840, Russ Co, fJohn
James, bc1700, fWilliam II
Jeduthum, b1725, fJames, wElizabeth Burgess
Joseph, b16--, fWilliam
Judith Steptoe, b17--, Fauq Co?, hCharles Coatsworth Ball
Lillian, fJohn, Margaret Shreve, hWilliam M Ellison
Mary, b18--, Windsor Shades, NewK Co, hEdmund Archer Saunders Sr
William II, b16--, fWilliam I
William, b1843, Claredon, Alex Co, d1920, fHoratio, wAmerica A Deeble
BALLARD, Ann, b17--, Albe Co?, hThomas Rea
Elmira, bc1845, Fauq Co?, hJames Pearson
James F, b186-, Camp Co, fWilliam A, (1)m-- Doss
John P, b18--, Albe Co, wJane Francis Powers
Mildred Ann, b18--, Richmond?, hReuben S Powers
Mollie, b186-, nrLynchburg, Camp Co, fWilliam A, (1)m-- Doss, hCharles V Heck
William A, b1832, nrLynchburg, Camp Co, fSamuel G, 1w-- Doss, 2wMartha Martin
William Powers, b11/14/1842, Palmyra, Fluv Co, fJohn P, mJane Frances Powers, 2wMary Elvira Thomason
BALLOU, Kate P, b18--, Danville, Pitt Co, hGeorge W Whaling Sr
BANDY, Isaac T, b1849, Bote Co, fMatthew, mJudith Cauley, w Sarah Jane Hurt
BANE, Jennie, b1856, White Gate, Gile Co, d1884, fWilliam, hJohn D Snidow
Nancy, b9/21/1818, White Gate, Gile Co, d1900, hThomas Jefferson Higginbotham
T Miller, b3/8/1858, Gile Co, wAnnie Hunt
William, b1811, Gile Co, d1898
Wilson, b18--, Roan Co?, 1h of Emeline Owen
Wythe Graham, b1849, White

BANE (continued)
　Gate, Gile Co, fWilliam, wVirginia Hight
BANKHEAD, Ellen, fJames, hPeter Thornton Sr
BANKS, Ruth, b17--, hGeorge W Shelor
BANNER, Kent, b18--, Russ Co?, wJulia Burton
　Mary, b1860, Clinch, Scot Co, hL Lloyd Cox
　Philip S, bc1860, Scot Co, wMelissa J Wolfe
BARBEE, Caroline, b18--, nr Sperryville, Rapp Co, 1w of Thomas Henry Settle
　Charles Andrew Sr, b3/5/1861, PrWi Co, fJames Monroe Sr, (1)mMary Weedon, wMollie V Cornwell, mdOct 1903
　Henry W, bc1860, PrWi Co, f James Monroe Sr, (1)mMary Weedon
　James Monroe Sr, b18--, Fauq Co, d1906, fWilliam, m-- (Chancellor) Wroe, 1wMary Weedon, 2wMartha Ellen Weedon
　James Monroe Jr, b186-, PrWi Co, fJames Monroe Sr, (1)mMary Weedon
　John Barbee, b18--, Fauq Co, fWilliam, m-- (Chancellor) Wroe
　John Chancellor, b186-, PrWi Co, fJames Monroe Sr, (1)mMary Weedon
　John P, b18--, Roan Co, wBessie V Cocke
　Madison Ashby, b186-, PrWi Co, fJames Monroe Sr, (1)mMary Weedon
　Mary Catherine, b18--, Fauq Co, fWilliam, m-- (Chancellor) Wroe, hSamuel H Jones
　Mary Elizabeth, b186-, PrWi Co, fJames Monroe Sr, (1)mMary Weedon, hJ M Ellicott
　Robert, bc1850, Fauq Co?, wSusan Holmes
BARBOUR, James, b1775, d1842
　Jeremiah, b18--, Fran Co?, wMargaret Mattox
　John Fletcher, b11/28/1861, Fran Co, fJeremiah, mMargaret Mattox, wAgnes Laetitia Lavender

BARBOUR (continued)
　Robert S Sr, b1857, Riceville, Hali Co, wBessie K Stovall
BARCLAY, Anna Maria, b18--, Albe Co, fRobert, mSarah Coleman Turner, hEdward H Moon
　Robert, b17--, Albe Co, fThomas, mCharlotte Diggs, wSarah Coleman Turner
　Thomas, b17--, Albe Co?, wCharlotte Diggs
BARE, Joseph, bc1830, Rkhm Co?, wMary Acker
BARGAMIN, Paul, b18--, Richmond?, d1883, wLaura Macomber
BARGELT, Laura E, b7/4/1858, Woodstock, Shen Co, d1897, fWilliam H, mCatherine Fravel, hMilton Hockman Hottel
　Robert Lee, b185-, Woodstock, Shen Co, fWilliam H, mCatherine Fravel, wMary Supinger
　William, b185-, Woodstock, Shen Co, fWilliam H, mCatherine Fravel
BARKDALE, Louisa F, b18--, Hali Co, 2w of John B Crews
BARKER, Elizabeth, b18--, Scot Co?, hJohn F Stair
　Francis Marion, b18--, d1863, wDematrice Ann Noell
　Oscar Bayne, b1861, Bedf Co, fFrancis Marion, mDematrice Ann Noell, wEstelle A Wright
　William Carey, b2/24/1857, Cedar Point, Gooc Co, fFrancis Marion, mDematrice Ann Noell, wHenrietta Hall Jones, md1887
BARKSDALE, Armistead, b184-, nrMeadville, Hali Co, fElisha, mJudith A Barksdale
　Champe T, b12/2/1853, Hali Co, fRandolph V, mFanny Clopton Wimbish
　Clara S, b184-, nrMeadville, Hali Co, fElisha, mJudith A Barksdale
　Elisha, b18--, Hali Co, fNathanial, wJudith A Barksdale
　Elisha, bc1840, Hali Co, wJudith W Barksdale
　James Peter, b184-, nrMeadville, Hali Co, fElisha, mJudith A Barksdale
　Judith A, b1828, Hali Co, d1903, hElisha Barksdale

BARKSDALE (continued)
Judith W, b184-, nrMeadville, Hali Co, d1905, fElisha, mJudith A Braksdale, hElisha Barksdale
Mattie, b18--, Pitt Co, hWilliam I Overbey
Millard M, bc1851, Pitt Co?, wMinnie P Terry
Nathanial B, b184-, Hali Co, fElisha, mJudith A Barksdale
Randolph V, b18--, wFanny Clopton Wimbish
Stanhope F, b184-, nrMeadville, Hali Co, d1903, fElisha, mJudith A Barksdale
William Randolph, b1/6/849, nrMeadville, Hali Co, fElisha, mJudith A Barksdale, 1wHarriet Bailey Craddock, md11/14/1872, 2wVirginia Douglas Watkins, md6/28/1905
BARLEY, --, b18--, Clar Co, hFrank Gordon
Adam, bc1840, Clar Co, wHarriet Gordon
BARLOW, Robert G, b9/8/1842, Williamsburg, JaCo Co, d1917, fRobert Jesse, m-- Graves, 2h of Mary (West) Crandall
Robert Jesse, b1814, NewK Co, d1892, w-- Graves
BARNES, Birdie L, b18--, hRufus K Sanders Sr
Eva, bc1860, Lynchburg, Camp Co, d1909, hJ H Fitzgerald, md12/ 19/1882
Jane Clarkson, b18--, Lune Co, hCharles Betts Hardy
Louisa Ann, bc1810, Rkhm Co?, fTravis, hPeter Acker Jr
Manley Howell, b7/25/1854, JaCi Co, fWilliam Henry, mLucy Saunders, wMaggie A Ferrell, md7/7/1885
Robert L, b18--, Richmond?, wGertrude Hardy
William H, b18--, JaCi Co, wLucy Saunders
BARNETT, Annie, bc1833, Mont Co, fJames, m-- Thomas, hJohn Brown
Charles, bc1830, Mont Co, fJames, m-- Thomas
Giles, bc1830, Mont Co, fJames, m-- Thomas

BARNETT (continued)
James, bc1800, Mont Co, w-- Thomas
James, bc1830, Mont Co, fJames, m-- Thomas
John, b183-, Mont Co, fJames, m--Thomas, wNannie Buford Luck
John Edward, b12/6/1843, Berryville, Clar Co, fNeill, mElizabeth Luke, wLucy Virginia Berlin
Morris L, bc1870, nrMontvale, Bedf Co, fJohn, mNannie Buford Luck
Neill, b18--, Clar Co, wElizabeth Luke
Sarah Helm, b184-, Berryville, Clar Co, fNeill, mElizabeth Luke, hThomas E Gold
BARNEY, Avis, b18--, hDavid N Walker
BARNHART, B E, b186-, Fran Co, wZimania Sink
Betty, b18--, New Hope, Augu Co, fGideon, hNewton C Watts
John H, bc1860, Rkhm Co, wRebecca Wenger
BARNITZ, --, bc1860, Christiansburg, Mont Co, fWilliam Martin, Jr, mElizabeth Craddock, hThomas H Cooper
--, bc1860, Christiansburg, Mont Co, fWilliam Martin, Jr, mElizabeth Craddock, hT R Boom
D G, bc1860, Christiansburg, Mont Co, fWilliam Martin Jr, mElizabeth Craddock
Edward S, b4/18/1859, Christiansburg, Mont Co, fWilliam Martin Jr, mElizabeth Craddock, 1wElla Cockey, 2wBlanche Switzer
Fanny, bc1860, Christiansburg, Mont Co, fWilliam Martin Jr, mElizabeth Craddock, hE D Self
Jenny, bc1860, Christiansburg, Mont Co, fWilliam Martin Jr, mElizabeth Craddock
William F, bc1860, Christiansburg, Mont Co, fWilliam Martin Jr, mElizabeth Craddock
William Martin Jr, b1826, Christiansburg, Mont Co, d1901, fWilliam Martin Sr, wElizabeth Craddock
BARR, Ann, b18--, Fred Co, fRob-

BARR (continued)
ert, mAraminta Avery
Araminta, b18--, Winchester, Fred Co, fHugh, mElizabeth Arnold, hWilliam H Calvert
Carrie F, bc1870, Winchester, Fred Co, fJames W, mElizabeth Dickson Wall, hS R Atwell
Cornelius, b18--, Fred Co, f Robert, mAraminta Avery
Edward M, b18--, Winchester, Fred Co, fRobert Sr, m(1)Mary Catherine Kremer
Elizabeth, b18--, Fred Co, f Robert, mAraminta Avery
Elizabeth C, b18--, Winchester, Fred Co, fCornelius, 1h-- Feaster, 2hJ Luther Mavis, md8/1908
George, bc1830, Fred Co, wEmily Shryock
Hugh, b18--, Fred Co, fRobert, mAraminta Avery, wElizabeth Arnold
James, b18--, Fred Co, fRobert, mAraminta Avery
James W, b18--, Winchester, Fred Co, fRobert, (1)mMary Catherine Kremer, wElizabeth Dickson Hall
John, b18--, Fred Co, fRobert, mAraminta Avery
Julia A, b18--, Winchester, Fred Co, fRobert Sr, (1)mMary Catherine Kremer, hCharles Correll
Louis J, b18--, Winchester, Fred Co, fRobert Sr, (2)mSidney Jackson
Margaret Rebecca, b18--, Winchester, Fred Co, fRobert Sr, (1)mMary Catherine Kremer, hNewton Swartz
Mary Elizabeth, b18--, Winchester, Fred Co, fRobert Sr, (1)mMary Catherine Kremer, hW W Wall
Mollie, bc1869, Hamp Co, fOscar, mLucy Kurel, hA E Dabney
Oscar, b18--, Fred Co, d1910, fHugh, mElizabeth Arnold, 1wLucy Kurel, 2wMary McKinister
Owen, b186-, Winchester, Fred Co, fJames W, mElizabeth Dickson Wall

BARR (continued)
R Frank, b18--, Winchester, Fred Co, fRobert Sr, (2)mSidney Jackson
R Frank II, b6/3/1867, Winchester, Fred Co, fJames W, mElizabeth Dickson Wall
Robert Sr, bc1800, Fred Co, 1wMary Catherine Kremer, 2w Sidney Jackson
Robert, b18--, Fred Co, fRobert, mAraminta Avery
Robert Jr, b18--, Winchester, Fred Co, fRobert Sr, (2)mSidney Jackson
Thomas, bc1870, Hamp Co, fOscar, (1)mLucy Kurel
Virginia, b18--, Winchester, Fred Co, fRobert Sr, (2)mSidney Jackson
Virginia, b186-, Rio, Hamp Co, fOscar, (1)mLucy Kurel, hA Huntsberry
Walter Evans, b9/14/1868, Rio, Hamp Co, fOscar, (1)mLucy Kurel, wSusie C Stine
William Theodore, b6/3/1867, Winchester, Fred Co, fJames W, mElizabeth Dickson Wall, wFlorence E Myers
BARRETT, Anderson, b1773, Albe Co, wRebecca Sutton
George, b18--, Piedmont, Mine Co, fThomas J
Margaret A, b18--, Piedmont, Mine Co, fThomas, m-- Vice, hJ Hunter Williams, md10/27/1886
Margaret Ann Elizabeth, b1/9/1842, Richmond, hWilliam Alpheus Clarke Sr
Nannie, b184-, Albe Co?, hNathaniel W Winston Sr, md11/1865
Thomas J, b18--, Mine Co?, w-- Vice
William Taylor, b3/23/1818, fAnderson, mRebecca Sutton, 1wLucy Jane Wood, 2wElla Edward Wilson
BARRON, Samuel, bc1836, Norfolk, d1891, wAgnes Newton Smith
BARROW, --, bc1840, Rkhm Co, wFannie Blackburn
Lucius, bc1840, Lune Co?, wMary L Smith
Nannie Sue, bc1870, Danville,

BARROW (continued)
Pitt Co, fPeter Thomas, hBenjamin Moore Beckham Sr, md1/9/1891
Nettie, b18--, Fran Co?, 1w of Beverly A Davis Sr
BARRY, Thomas Moran/Moore, b18-- Norfolk, wVirginia Lovett
BARTLETT, Burgess, bc1810, Fauq Co?, wSarah Ann Fishback
BARTON, Barbara, b18--, Fran Co, hHarvey Proffitt
Caroline M, b18--, Fred Co, hRobert Frederick Barton
Charles Marshall, b1833, Fred Co, d186-, wEllen Harvie Marshall
Julianna Grammar, b18--, Winchester, Fred Co, fRichard W, mAlcinda Gibson, hMoses Myers
Mary, b18--, Fauq Co?, hJohn Pulla Smith
Mary Douthat, b8/26/1860, Fauq Co, fCharles Marshall, mEllen Harvie Marshall, hRichard Hewlett Smith, md10/18/1882
Richard W, b17--, Fred Co?, wAlcinda Gibson
BASKERVILLE, George D, d18--, Dinw Co?, wEmma Virginia Ferguson
BASS, Lucy, b17--, 2w of Edward Hatcher
Rosser, bc1860, Lanc Co, wLula Ficklin
BASSETT, Edward M, b18--, Math Co?, wCarrie Virginia Raines
George O, bc1840, Fred Co?, wLydia Gordon
John David Jr, b7/14/1866, Bassett, Henry Co, fJohn H, mNancy J Spencer, wPocahontas Hundley, md1893
John H, bc1834, nrPreston, Henry Co, d1917, wNancy J Spencer
BATEMAN, Pauline F, b1844, Wyth Co, hJames D Archer
BATES, --, bc1850, Shen Co, wLaura Kate Stickley
Eliza, b18--, Nhld Co, hJames S Gilliam
Samuel, bc1840, Hamp Co?, wMary C Cougill
BATHURST, Mary, b17--, fLancelot, hFrancis Meriwether
BATSON, --, b18--, hEnoch Garrett

BATSON (continued)
rett
BATTE, Alexander Watson, b18--, fWilliam, mSarah Parham
Cornelia Alvinia, b18--, Greenville Co, fAlexander Watson, hRobert W Brodnax
BATTILLE, Sarah, b17--, hHenry Fitzhugh II, md1746
BATTLE, Elisha, b1/9/1724, Nans Co, d1799, fWilliam, mSarah Hunter, wElizabeth Sumner, md1742
BAUGH, Edward, b4/4/1852, Powh Co, fWilliam H, mElizabeth Sims, wNannie Rudd, md1879
Mollie, b18--, Loui Co, hElihu Parish
Sallie C, b184-, Powh Co, d186- fWilliam H, mElizabeth Sims
Virginia, b184-, Powh Co, fWilliam H, mElizabeth Sims, h George D Williams
William H, b1813, Pow Co, d1873, fEdward, wElizabeth Sims
Willie, b185-, Powh Co, fWilliam H, mElizabeth Sims, h Luther C Denoon
BAUMGARDNER, J Alexander, b18--, Augu Co?, wSarah McGilvray
BAUSERMAN, --, b18--, Shen Co?, hWilliam H Lichleiter
Ann E, bc1850, Shen Co, fNoah, hMorgan F Schmucker
Erasmus, bc1840, Shen Co, wMary Funkhouser
George, b18--, Page Co, wSallie Argenbright
George R, bc1860, Woodstock, Shen Co, fJoseph, mElizabeth A Wilson
Henry W, bc1860, Woodstock, Shen Co, fJoseph, mElizabeth A Wilson
James R, b186-, Woodstock, Shen Co, fJoseph, mElizabeth A Wilson
Joseph, bc1808, Shen Co, d1876, fHenry, wElizabeth A Wilson
Joseph Morgan, b4/6/1865, Woodstock, Shen Co, fJoseph, mElizabeth A Wilson, wMary E Van Horn, md10/2/1890
BAXLEY, Claude, bc1860, Fauq Co?, wMary Willoughby Newton

BAXLEY (continued)
J Leroy, bc1870, Marshall District, Fauq Co, fClaude, mLena Williams, 1wEmily Hirst, 2wMay (Braxton) Wallace
BAXTER, William F, bc1860, wHenrietta Snapp
BAYLOR, Mary B, b18--, Augu Co, fG M, hJohn S Pirkey
BAYNE, Charles, b11/5/1818, nrBaynesville, West Co, d1885, fRichard, mSusan Pope, 1wMary Ellen Ashby
Howard Randolph, b5/11/1851, Winchester, Fred Co, fCharles, mMary Ellen Ashby, wLizzie S Moore, md4/27/1886
Mathew, b17--, West Co, fMathew Bayne
Richard, b9/13/1789, West Co, d1829, fMathew, wSusan Pope
BAYTOP, Ann Walker Carter, b1819, Glou Co, d1894, hJefferson Stubbs
BEACH, Lillian Lee, b1863, Alexandria, hJ Thomas Cooke
BEADLES, Susan Carr, b18--, hJohn Beverly Dudley I
BEALE, Anna E, b18--, West Co, hJames Walker
Elizabeth Taylor Corbin, b18--, West Co, 1w of William Thomas Davis
George W, b8/21/1842, Hague, West Co, d1921, fRichard Lee Turberville, mLucy Brown, w Mary Anne Bouic, md1879
Josepha Anna, b12/1836, Wheatland, Fred Co, hJoseph McKendree Kennerly
Ollie, bc1870, Nans Co?, hJunius Edgar West
Richard Lee Turberville, b1816, Hague, Wmld Co, fRobert, mAnne Turberville, wLucy Brown
Robert, b17--, Chestnut Hill, Farmers Fork, Rich Co, wAnne Turberville
Samuel, b18--, Spot Co, wSallie Scott
BEALES, Joel E, b3/1843, Loud Co, d1911, fMortimer, 1wMartha Ann Caruthers, 2wJennie Lemon
Mortimer, b1822, Loud Co, dc 1890
BEAMAN, Sallie Louise, b18--,

BEAMAN (continued)
Suffolk, Nans Co, hWilliam John Cohoon
BEAMER, Henderson M, b1/1851, Carr Co, wMary E Cooley
BEAN, Joseph, bc1840, Hayfield, Fred Co, wMargaret Larrick
BEANE, Keturah, b18--, Lanc Co, hWilliam Towles
BEAR, Adam C, b18--, Rkhm Co
John Henry, bc1850, Rkhm Co, fAdam C, wLizzie Stephens
Magdalena, b1751, Page Co?, hPeter Blosser
BEARCRAFT, Sallie, bc1800, Nhtn Co, hJohn Fatherly
BEARD, Archie D, b18--, Amhe Co, wNellie Winn Pendleton
Charles D, b18--, Rkhm Co, wMillie Shaver
Elizabeth, bc1841, Mint Spring, Augu Co, hThomas A Montgomery
R E, bc1850, Nels Co?, wSallie Meeks
BEASLEY, C H, b186--, Amhe Co, fH C, mMary Jennings
Carl M, b18--, wEvelyn Osborne
E C, bc1870, Amhe Co, fH C, mMary Jennings
H C, b18--, Amhe Co?, wMary Jennings
J W, bc1860, Amhe Co?, fH C, mMary Jennings
R P, bc1860, Amhe Co?, fH C, mMary Jennings
BEATIE, Alonzo C, b12/7/1864, Old Town House (now Chilhowie), Smyth Co, fClaiborne W, mFlora Bailey, wElnora Walton, md12/31/1890
Claiborne W, b1/28/1828, Seven Mile Ford, Smyt Co, fRobert, mPauline White, wFlora Bailey
Robert, b1787, nrEmory & Henry College, fWilliam, mMary Allison, wPauline White
William, b18--, Glade Springs, Wash Co, fJohn, mEllen Gilmore, wMary Allison
BEATTY, Bettie, b18--, Fauq Co?, 2w of James Skinner
Fountain, bc1840, Fauq Co?, wAnna Elizabeth Hathaway, md1/4/1865
Lucy, b18--, Fauq Co?, 3w of James Skinner

BEAVEL, Frank, bc1850, Amhe Co?, wAnna McGinnis
BEAVER, Abram, bc1810, Augu Co, wMargaret Myers
BEAVERS, --, b18--, Taze Co, hThomas Altizer
--, bc1860, McDo Co?, wElizabeth Rebecca Waldron
Rebecca, b8/10/1830, Taze Co, d1912, hRice J Waldron
Robert, bc1860, Taze Co, Bettie May Brown
BEAZLEY, Annie, b186-, Ches Co, fR Hunter, mCarrie Virginia Farmer, 1hWilliam Roberts, 2hJohn Headspeth
Edgar T, bc1870, Ches Co, fR Hunter, mCarrie Virginia Farmer
Elizabeth, b18--, Spot Co?, hRichard Wesley Colbert
R Hunter, b1884, Sparta, Caro Co, d1916, wCarrie Virginia Farmer
Robert Chiles Sr, b5/9/1865, Manchester (now S Richmond), Ches Co, fR Hunter, mCarrie Virginia Farmer, 1wFlorence Nichols, md1892, 2wHattie Smith, md2/11/ 1903
Roy P, b186-, Ches Co, fR Hunter, mCarrie Virginia Farmer
William F, b10/10/1851, Sparta, Caro Co, fWilliam O, m-- Foster, wEmma Jane Alsop
BECKHAM, Benjamin Moore, b8/17/ 1868, nrBurkeville, Nott Co, fThomas Moore, mLucy Elizabeth Royall, wNannie Sue Barrow, md6/9/1891
Helen Grey, b186-, nrBurkeville, Nott Co, fThomas Moore, mLucy Elizabeth Royall, hJames W Keith
James Minor, b18--, Culp Co, w-- Flannagan
John Grigsby, b186-, Fauq Co?, wMary Campbell Moore
Minnie, bc1870, Culp Co?, fJames Minor, m-- Flannagan, hGeorge Washington Settle
Paul W, b186-, nrBurkeville, Nott Co, fThomas Moore, mLucy Elizabeth Royall
Samuel R, b186-, nrBurkeville, Nott Co, fThomas Moore, mLucy

BECKHAM (continued)
Elizabeth Royall
BECKLEY, Alfred, b18--, Bote Co, fAlfred, wEmma V ---
Annie Dawson, bc1870, Fincastle, Bote Co, fAlfred, mEmma V ---, hTurner McDowell Sr, md12/28/ 1892
BECKWITH, Henrietta, b18--, Esse Co, hChristopher F Newbill
Sue T, b18--, fT S, 1w of Robert Gilliam Jr, md10/24/1876
BEDINGER, Everett Wade, b1831, Shepherstown, Jeff Co, d1916, wVirginia Lucas
Virginia, b1/23/1842, Charlestown, Jeff Co, hHenry B Michie
BEELER, --, bc1780, Hard Co?, 1h of Sarah Warden
BEERS, Lelia, b18--, Augu Co?, hJoseph B Woodward
BEERY, Frances, bc1800, Rkhm Co?, hDavid Ralston
Frances, b9/9/1848, nrCross Keys, Rkhm Co, hJoseph Showalter
Isaac N, b9/4/1835, Edom, Rkhm Co, fJohn K, mMagdalena Wenger, wSarah Jane Swank
John K, b1801, Edom, Rkhm Co, fJohn, mBarbara Kagy, wMagdalena Wenger
Maggie V, b186-, Edom, Rkhm Co, fIsaac N, mSarah Jane Swank, hJ T Rice
Mary, bc1837, Edom, Rkhm Co, fJohn K, mMagdalena Wenger, hJasper Hawse
Mary Lula, b186-, Edom, Rkhm Co, fIsaac N, mSarah Jane Swank, hIsaac B Wenger
Theresa U, bc1870, Edom, Rkhm Co, fIsaac N, mSarah Jane Swank, hE R Shank
BEGOON, George, b18--, Rkhm Co, wSarah Ann Meyerhoeffer
James, b18--, Rkhm Co, wElizabeth Meyerhoeffer
BEIDLER, Samuel, bc1860, Shen Co, wVernon Smoot
BEIRNE, Richard Foulke Sr, b1856, Lewisburg, Grbr Co, d1891, fPatrick, mElizabeth Foulke, wClara Haxall Grundy
BELCHER, Alice, b18--, Dick Co, fWilliam, mMary Epling, hJames

BELCHER (continued)
Colley Sifers, nc12/29/1886
Annie/Elizabeth, b17--, Bedf Co?, hRichard Bailey
John R, bc1860, Dick Co, wNancy Sifers
Lucy, b18--, Buch Co?, hDaniel R Looney
William L, b18--, Dick Co?, wMary Epling
BELEW, Emma V, b18--, Shen Co, hH H Riddleberger
BELFIELD, Frances, b17--, Rich Co, fThomas Wright, mMary Meriwether, 1hFreeman Walker, 2h Henry Brodnax
Thomas Wright, b17--, Rich Co, wMary Meriwether
BELL, --, bc1820, Clar Co?, 1w of Levi Hiett
--, b18--, Clar Co, fJonah, hThomas Dearmont
--, b18--, Clar Co, fJonah, hPeter Dearmont
--, b18--, Clar Co, fJonah, 1w of Washington Dearmont
Alden, b11/27/1863, Culp Co, fJohn Wesley, mMaria Champe Storrow
Alicia, b18--, Berk Co, hWilliam White
Annie L, b7/17/1869, Gainesville, PrWi Co, fJames W, mSusannah Smith, hWilliam Moore Jordan
Edmonia Osceola, b18--, Augu Co, fWilliam H, hJulian Botts Andrews Sr
Eliza, bc1810, Winchester, Fred Co, fJohn, mElizabeth Sherard, hJoseph Smith
Evelina, b1806, Wyth Co, hIsaac Painter
Harman B, b186-, Winchester, Fred Co, fJohn Newton Sr, (2)mMargaretta Brown
Henderson, b18--, Augu Co, fJames, mBetsey Henderson, wAnne Kinnex
Ida, b18--, Fred Co, adoptive parent, James Bell, hJohn Thwaite, md1887
James, b17--, Augu Co, fJoseph, wBetsey Henderson
James R, b2/7/1870, Henry Co, fWilliam A, mSallie A Martin,

BELL (continued)
wBessie Armes, md1896
James W, b18--, PrWi Co?, wSusanna Smith
John, b2/21/1773, d1837, wElizabeth Sherard
John Newton Sr, b3/23/1810, Winchester, Fred Co, d1890, fJohn, mElizabeth Sherard, 1wRebecca Miller, 2wMargaretta Brown
John Newton Jr, bc1840, Winchester, Fred Co, fJohn Newton Sr, (1)mRebecca Miller
John Wesley, b18--, Culp Co?, wMaria Champe Storrow
John William, b6/13/1838, Loud Co, fJohn W, mSarah Katherine Jones, wMary E Minnich, md5/9/1865
Lucy, bc1800, Camp Co, hJames Abram Andrew
Lydia, b18--, Clar Co?, fJoseph, hCharles R Hardesty
Margaretta Brown, bc1860, Winchester, Fred Co, fJohn Newton Sr, (2)mMargaretta Brown
Maria, bc1810, Winchester, Fred Co, fJohn, mElizabeth Sherard
Mary, b18--, Henry Co, hJohn Waters
Mary Ann, bc1810, Winchester, Fred Co, fJohn, mElizabeth Sherard
Mary Miller, bc1840, Winchester, Fred Co, fJohn Newton Sr, (1)mRebecca Miller
Nancy Selina, bc1810, Winchester, Fred Co, fJohn, mElizabeth Sherard, hWilliam H Streits
Nannie Jane, b18--, Mt Sidney, Augu Co, fJoseph, hJames H Clemer
Richard P Jr, b5/6/1853, Staunton, Augu Co, fHenderson, m Anne Kinney, wEmma Lyle Frazier
Robert Sherard, b181-, Winchester, Fred Co, fJohn, mElizabeth Sherard, wE G Green
Robert Sherard, bc1840, Winchester, Fred Co, d1863, fJohn Newton Sr, (1)mRebecca Miller
Sallie Dixon, bc1810, Winchester, Fred Co, fJohn, mEliza-

BELL (continued)
beth Sherard, hJames D Gilkeson
Samuel A, b184-, Winchester, Fred Co, fJohn Newton Sr, (1)mRebecca Miller
Sarah, b186-, Winchester, Fred Co, fJohn Newton Sr, (2)mMargaretta Brown
Stewart Sr, b9/18/1864, Winchester, Fred Co, fJohn Newton Sr, (2)mMargaretta Brown, w Lanier (Miller) Gray, md12/1/1909
William, b18--, Augu Co, fWilliam J, m-- Shipp, wLavinia Houston
William A, bc1845, Henry Co?, wSallie A Martin
William Atkinson, b184-, Winchester, Fred Co, fJohn Newton Sr, (1)mRebecca Miller
William J D, bc1800, Augu Co, w--Shipp
William J D, b4/3/1868, Augu Co, fWilliam, mLavinia Houston, wClara Cox, md1906
BELO, Mary Louise, b1853, Salem, Roan Co, hWilliam Kenny Early
BELT, Benjamin Lloyd, b186-, Whitmell, Pitt Co, fHumphrey Singleton III, mMolly A Daniel
Humphrey Singleton III, b12/25/1825, Cumb Co, d1888, fHumphrey Singleton Jr, wMolly A Daniel
Humphrey Singleton IV, b3/1/1869, Whitmel, Pitt Co, fHumphrey Singleton III, m Molly A Daniel, wAnnie R Easley, md12/19/1894
Mary Douglas, b186-, Whitmel, Pitt Co, fHumphrey Singleton III, mMolly A Daniel, hHenry A Southall
Townsend W, b18--, Loud Co?, wAnne Thrift
Walter Gilmer, b186-, Whitmel, Pitt Co, fHumphrey Singleton III, mMolly A Daniel
BELVIN, --, b18--, Richmond?, fJohn A, hHenry Newton Price
BENN, Julia A, b18--, hThomas Griffin, md10/7/1865
BENNETT, --, b186-, nrChatham, Pitt Co, fJonathan, mMildred

BENNETT (continued)
Bailey, hS E Ramsey
--, b186-, nrChatham, Pitt Co, fJonathan, mMildred Bailey, hJ G Bennett
Anna, b16--, Ches Co?, hJohn Goode Sr
Ellen, b186-, nrChatham, Pitt Co, fJonathan, mMildred Bailey, h-- Keatts
Jonathan, b18--, Pitt Co, fReuben, wMildred Bailey
J G, bc1860, Pitt Co, w-- Bennett
J T, bc1870, nrChatham, Pitt Co, fJonathan, mMildred Bailey
L H, b186-, Fran Co, wCora E Chitwood
Reuben Alfred, bc1841, Pitt Co, d1915, wElizabeth Katherine Tosh
W H, b186-, nrChatham, Pitt Co, fJonathan, mMildred Bailey
BENSON, Eliza Ann, bc1800, hJoseph Antoine Bilisoly
BERKELEY, Carter, b2/20/1768, Hano Co?, fNelson, mElizabeth Wormeley Carter, 1wCatherine Spots-wood Carter, 2wFrances (Page) Nelson
Carter, b1837, Staunton, Augu Co, d1905, fEdmund, mRandolph Spotswood Brooke, 1wJane Love Gilkeson, md1867, 2wJane Hale
Edmund, b16--, Glou Co, d1718, fEdmund, mMary --, wLucy Burwell
Edmund, b11/26/1704, Midd Co, fEdmund, mLucy Burwell, wMary Nelson
Edmund, b3/17/1801, Hano Co, d1851, fCarter, (1)mCatherine Spotswood Carter, wRandolph Spotswood Brooke
Elizabeth, bc1810, Hano Co, m-- Harrison, hEdward Cunningham
Evelyn Spotswood, bc1870, Augu Co, fFrancis Brooke, mJennie Baird, hCharles Russell Robins Sr, md10/18/1897
Francis Brooke, b18--, Augu Co?, wJennie Baird
Mary, b18--, PrWi Co, hRichard Threlkeld Cox
Matilda Anne, b1840, "The Wheelers", Appo Co, d1920,

BERKELEY (continued)
fGeorge Nelson, mNancy Dickerson, hAlbert Henry Williams Nelson, b5/16/1733, Midd Co, fEdmund, mMary Nelson, wElizabeth Wormeley Carter
BERKLEY, Bettie, b184-, "The Wheelers", Appo Co, fGeorge Nelson, mNancy Dickerson, h Peter Davis
George Nelson, b18--, PrEd Co, fAlexander, wNancy Dickerson
George William, b3/10/1846, "The Wheelers", Appo Co, f George Nelson, mNancy Dickerson, wMary Catherine Dickerson, md12/24/ 1869
James A, b183-, "The Wheelers", Appo Co, fGeorge Nelson, mNancy Didkerson
Mattie F, b184-, "The Wheelers", Appo Co, fGeorge Nelson, mNancy Dickerson, hJames T Dickerson
Mollie, b184-, "The Wheelers", Appo Co, fGeorge Nelson, mNancy Dickerson, hSamuel J Marsh
Susan J, bc1850, "The Wheelers", Appo Co, fGeorge Nelson, mNancy Dickerson, hFloyd Atkins
BERLIN, Lewis, b18--, Clar Co?, wBettie Foster
Lucy Virginia, b5/10/1850, Berryville, Clar Co, hJohn Edward Barnett
Mary C, b1848, Clar Co, fLewis, mBettie Foster, hDoras Huyett Jones
Richard, bc1860, Rkhm Co?, w-- Martz
BERNARD, Frances, b18--, Norf Co?, hWashington Tazewell Capps
John Hipkins, b17--, Warr Co?, wJane Gay Robertson, nd181-
Sarah Ann, b18--, KiGe Co, hJohn A Meredith
BERRY, Damaris Irene, bc1870, Augu Co, fCharles G, hJames Willson McClung, md1894
Ellen, b18--, fGeorge L, mMary Anna Parks, hJohn Madison Burton, md11/1881
Ella G, b18--, Scot Co?, hLewis N Osborne

BERRY (continued)
George L, b18--, wMary Anna Parks
Jospeh, bc1870, Fair Co, fJ Owens, mMary Josephine Gunnell, wAnnette Meade Gibson, md11/16/ 1898
Martin, bc1830, Rkhm Co?, wLizzie Myers
Mary, b18--, Page Co?, hPerry Broyles
BERTRAM, Andrew, b1805, nrKeezletown, Rkhm Co, fJulius, m-- Smith, wElizabeth Burner
Andrew D, b186-, nrKeezletown, Rkhm Co, fPeachy Addison, m Amelia Bowman
Anna, b180-, nrKeezletown, Rkhm Co, fJulius, m-- Smith, h-- Davis
Diannah, bc1800, nrKeezletown, Rkhm Co, fJulius, m-- Smith, h-- Armentrout
George, bc1810, nrKeezletown, Rkhm Co, fJulius, m-- Smith
Hiram Wilbert, b11/8/1868, nrKeezletown, Rkhm Co, fPeachy Addison, mAmelia Bowman, wAlice Lee Gaithere, md12/18/1895
J H, b183-, Shen Co, fAndrew, mElizabeth Burner
John, bc1810, nrKeezletown, Rkhm Co, fJulius, m-- Smith
Lydia, bc1800, nrKeezletown, Rkhm Co, fJulius, m-- Smith, hThomas Davis
Mary, b180-, nrKeezletown, Rkhm Co, fJulius, m-- Smith, h-- Miller
Peachy Addison, bc1831, Rkhm Co, fAndrew, mElizabeth Burner, wAmelia Bowman
Rebecca, bc1830, Rkhm Co, fAndrew, mElizabeth Burner
T A Louisa, bc1830, Rkhm Co, fAndrew, mElizabeth Burner
BESON, Bessie, bc1870, PrWi Co?, hCharles Francis Montgomery Lewis
BEST, Ada Virginia, b18--, fJohn Edward, hJohn Robert Sutphin
Estelle, b7/9/1853, "Belle Ville", Nhld Co, hLloyd B/T Smith
BETTS, Pemelia, bc1800, Meck Co, hHenry Hardy
Sarah Frances, b186-, Henrico

BETTS (continued)
Co, hNorvill Wilson
BEVERLEY, Baynton, bc1850, Scott District, Fauq Co, fRobert, mJane Eliza Carter, hThomas J Chew
Caroline, b18--, Dick Co, h Charles W Gilliam
Eliza, bc1850, Scott District, Fauq Co, fRobert, mJane Eliza Carter, hJ S Mason
Elizabeth, bc1690, Glou Co, hWilliam Randolph
George, bc1850, Wise Co?, wLouisa Roberts
James Bradshaw II, b7/27/1861, Scott District, Fauq Co, fRobert, mJane Eliza Carter, 1wAnnie Maxwell Sloan, md10/30/1889, 2wAmanda Madison Clarke
Jane, b185-, Scott District, Fauq Co, fRobert, mJane Eliza Carter, hJohn T Sloan
John Hill Carter, b9/6/1853, Scott District, Fauq Co, fRobert, mJane Eliza Carter, wRebecca Dulaney, md4/19/1881
Lovely Virginia, b18--, hJohn Twiggs Brown
Robert, b4/10/1856, Scott District, Fauq Co, fRobert, mJane Eliza Carter, wRichardetta Carter
Rebecca, b185-, Scott District, Fauq Co, fRobert, mJane Eliza Carter, hW P Herbert
Sarah, b18--, Esse Co, fJames Bradshaw I, 1w of Edward Cartier Turner
Susanna, bc1700, Glou Co, hJohn Randolph
Virginia, b185-, Scott District, Fauq Co, fRobert, mJane Eliza Carter, hJohn McGill
William, bc1697, Midd Co, fRobert II, mUrsala Byrd
William, b1/12/1852, Scott District, Fauq Co, fRobert, mJane Eliza Carter, wMary Welby Carter, md1875
BEVILLE, Ann Jane, b184-, "Pelion Hill", nrBlackstone, Nott Co, fRenyard P, mEliza Clardy, hDarius A Wilson
Archer C, b185-, "Pelion Hill", nrBlackstone, Nott Co, fRen-

BEVILLE (continued)
yard P, mEliza Clardy
Benjamin P, b185-, "Pelion Hill", nrBlackstone, Nott Co, fRenyard P, mEliza Clardy
Lee L, b185-, "Pelion Hill", nrBlackstone, Nott Co, fRenyard P, mEliza Clardy
Lou Eleanor, b185-, "Pelion Hill", Nott Co, fRenyard P, mEliza Clardy
Mollie S, b185-, "Pelion Hill", nrBlackstone, Nott Co, d1918, fRenyard P, mEliza Clardy
Obedience, b184-, "Pelion Hill", nrBlackstone, Nott Co, fRenyard P, mEliza Clardy, hDavid A Williams
Raps S, b4/4/1856, "Pelion Hill", nrBlackstone, Nott Co, fRenyard P, mEliza Clardy, wSallie F Slaughter, md9/15/1892
BEVINS, George C, b1856, Snowflake, Scot Co, fIsaac, mMargaret Perry, wMartha A Flanary
Isaac, b18--, Scot Co, d1903, wMargaret Perry
Melvina, b1860, Wise Co, hSamuel S Rose
BEYDLER, Mary, b18--, Shen Co, 1w of George Shaver Jr
Rebecca Catherine, b18--, Shen Co, d1916, (2)fSamuel Beydler, mMargaret Fravel, hCalvin Hottle
Samuel, b18--, Shen Co?, 2h of Margaret Fravel
Samuel, b18--, Shen Co, (2)f Samuel, mMargaret Fravel, w-- Smoot
BIBB, Emma, bc1840, Charlottesville, Albe Co, d1910, fWilliam A, hHenry Herbert Harris Sr
Margaret, b18--, Albe Co, d1881, 1w of Henry Morris Gibson, md6/1876
BICKERS, --, bc1850, Nels Co?, wOlivia Fitzpatrick
E Pendleton, bc1850, Powh Co?, wBettie Elam
BICKLEY, Elizabeth, b17--, Hano Co, 1w of Andrew Hart
Nancy, b1828, Castlewood, Russ Co, d1882, hJames H Dickenson

BICKLEY (continued)
Sr
BIDGOOD, Richard M, b1837, Smithfield, Isle Co, wMollie Saunders
BIGGS, --, bc1790, Clar Co?, wAnn McCormick
BILISOLY, Frank Nash, b8/19/1868, Portsmouth, Norf Co, fJoseph Lorenzo, mMary Elizabeth Bourke
Joseph Antoine, b1799, Norfolk, d1881, fAntoine Sylvestre, mMarie Adelaide Accenelli, wEliza Ann Benson
Joseph Lorenzo, b1840, Portsmouth, Norf Co, fJoseph Antoine, mEliza Ann Benson
Leslie A, bc1833, Portsmouth, Norf Co, fJoseph Antoine, mEliza Ann Benson, wRosa Mills
BILLINGSLEY, --, b186-, KiGe Co, d1916, fJoseph A, mElizabeth Johnston, hWilliam N Heflin
Alexander, b186-, KiGe Co, fJoseph A, mElizabeth Johnson
Ella, b186-, KiGe Co, fJoseph A, mElizabeth Johnson
James A, b186-, KiGe Co, fJoseph A, mElizabeth Johnson
Joseph Addison, b18--, Fauq Co, d1893, wWillie R Taylor
Lewis J, b9/1858, KiGe Co, fJoseph A, mElizabeth Johnson
Mary Ann, bc1800, Spot Co, hJohn Lipscomb
Sallie, b186-, KiGe Co, fJoseph A, mElizabeth Johnson, h-- White
William P. b185-, KiGe Co, fJoseph A, mElizabeth Johnson, w-- Rogers
BILLUPS, Octavia, b18--, Math Co, hNelson R Gray Sr
Susanna, b17--, Lune Co?, hJohn Ingram
BINFORD, Estelle, b5/8/1854, Richmond, fJohn James, mPamela Branch Lockett, hCharles Paterson Walford
Fannie Christian, b18--, Appo Co, d1887, 1w of Jonathan Christian Woodson, md1885
John James, b18--, wPamela Branch Lockett
BIRCH, Alice S, b1856, Alexan-

BIRCH (continued)
dria, hAlbert G Thomas
Elizabeth, b18--, Alexandria?, hEdwin K S Deeble
BIRCHETT, Roxana, b18--, Camp Co, hJames Dearing
BIRCKHEAD, Annie, bc1860, Profitt, Albe Co, fEdward F, mCornelia Graves, hCharles P Garth
Edward F, b6/24/1820, Morven Farm, Albe Co, d1907, fThomas, mMildred Ferneyhough, wCornelia Graves
Mollie E, b185-, Profitt, Albe, fEdward F, mCornelia Graves
Nellie R, b185-, Profitt, Albe, fEdward F, mCornelia Graves
Robert G, bc1860, Profitt, Albe, fEdward F, mCornelia Graves
Thea, b185-, Profitt, Albe, fEdward F, mCornelia Graves
Thomas, b1789, Morven Farm, Albe Co, d1834, fEdward F, wMildred Ferneyhough
Thomas G, b6/25/1852, Profitt, Albe Co, d1922, fEdward F, mCornelia Graves, wAnnie L Clowes
BIRD, Bettie G, b184-, Shen Co?, fMark, mSarah C M Hite, hKenner B Stephenson
Charles Austin, b18--, Mill Gap, High Co, wMalinda Bacon
Joanna, b17--, KiQu Co, hPhilemon Bird
Maria Sue, b186-, KiQu Co, fWilliam Beverly, (2)mMartha Catherine Harwood, hWilliam R Spencer
Mark, b18--, Smith Creek, Shen Co, wSarah C M Hite
Martha, b18--, Blan Co?, hJohn L Miller
Martha Fountleroy, b186-, KiQu Co, fWilliam Beverly, (2)mMartha Catherine Harwood, hJohn R Taylor
Mary Ella, b184-, KiQu Co, fWilliam Beverly, (1)mMaria Abrams, hRobert B Purcell
Parmenas, b17--, KiQu Co, f Philemon, mJoanna Bird, wJane Wiley Beverly Corrie Roy
Pilemon, b17--, KiQu Co, wJoan-

BIRD (continued)
na Bird
Preston, b184-, KiQu Co, fWilliam Beverly, (1)mMaria Abrams Sallie Madison, b3/29/1856, Shen Co, fMark, mSarah C M Hite, hWilliam Twyman Williams
Spottswood, b184-, KiQu Co, f William Beverly, (1)mMaria Abrams, wEmma Dudley
William Beverly, b11/2/1818, "Cypress Hall", KiQu Co, fParmenas, mJane Wiley Beverly Corrie Roy, 1wMaria Abrams, 2wMartha Catherine Harwood
William Wallace, b12/23/1866, KiQu Co, fWilliam Beverly, (2)mMartha Catherine Harwood, wSara Preston, md12/15/1896
BIRDSONG, A S, b18--, Suss Co, wGeorgia Hall
Thomas Henry Sr, b8/22/1867, Isle Co, fA S, mGeorgia Hall, wMartha McLemore, md4/17/1895
BISHOP, --, bc1860, Rkhm Co, wVirginia Harnsberger
Carter R I, b18--, wMary Elizabeth Head
Carter R II, b5/22/1849, Petersburg, Dinw Co, fCarter R I, mMary Elizabeth Head, wKate Kirk, md1881
Lucy B, b----, Patr Co, fJoe, hJoseph B Wolfe Sr
Mary, d1796, Fauq Co?, d1870, 2w of Acquilla Glascock
BITZER, George, bc1820, Fauq Co?, wAlcinda Cochran
BLACK, Catherine, b18--, Page Co?, hEmanuel Shaffer
Elizabeth, b18--, Blackburg, Mont Co, fHarvey, mMary Kent, hJohn Samuel Apperson
Harvey, b18--, Blackburg, Mont Co, wMary Kent
William E, b18--, Gile Co?, wJennie Johnston
BLACKARD, Jesse D, bc1852, Meadows of Dan, Patr Co, d1915, wRuth E Turner
BLACKBURN, Eliza, bc1835, Jeff Co, d1897, fR S, mSarah Thomas, hCharles H Smith
John S, b183-, Jeff Co, fR S, mSarah Thomas
BLACKFORD, Benjamin Lewis, BLACKFORD (continued)
b8/5/1835, Fredericksburg, Spot Co, fWilliam Matthews, mMary Berkeley Minor
Charles Minor Sr, b10/17/1833, Fredericksburg, Spot Co, fWilliam Matthews, mMary Berkeley Minor, wSusan Leigh Colston, md2/17/1856
Charles Minor Jr, b9/5/1865, fCharles Minor Sr, mSusan Leigh Colston
Eugene, b4/11/1839, Fredericksburg, Spot Co, fWilliam Matthews, mMary Berkeley Minor
Launcelot Minor, b2/23/1837, Fredericksburg, Spot Co, fWilliam Matthews, mMary Berkeley Minor
Lucy Landon, b11/6/1826, Fredericksburg, Spot Co, fWilliam Matthews, mMary Berkeley Minor, hJohn Paige Davis, md6/10/1847
Mary Isabella, b11/27/1840, Fredericksburg, Spot Co, fWilliam Matthews, mMary Berkeley Minor, hJohn Churchill Cook, md3/16/ 1864
Nannie Colston, b185-, fCharles Minor Sr, mSusan Leigh Colston, hSamuel T Withers
Raleigh Colston, b6/25/1870, fCharles Minor Sr, mSusan Leigh Colston
William Willis, b3/23/1831, Fredericksburg, Spot Co, fWilliam Matthews, mMary Berkeley Minor
BLACKWELL, Ann Elizabeth, bc1800, Lune Co, hRobert Blackwell Jones
Christina, b17--, Lune Co, h Robert Jones
Eleanor H, b18--, Hano Co, hLittleton B Starke
George, bc1800, Wash Co?, w-- Denny
Gertrude, bc1870, Warr Co?, fJohn Davenport, mFannie Grayson?, hCharles Lewis Melton
Hiram Harding, b4/17/1844, Fairfield District, Nhld Co, fWilliam Rout, mHannah N Harding
J Garland, b1/26/1859, Lune Co,

BLACKWELL (continued)
fWilliam Fletcher, mMary Anne Ferguson, wMarion Truly Hatchett
John, bc1800, Fauq Co, fJoseph Jr, mAnn (Eustace) Hull
John Davenport, b18--, Fauq Co, fJohn, wFannie Grayson
Joseph Jr, b1750, Fauq Co, fJoseph Sr, mLucy Steptoe, wAnn (Eustace) Hunt
Judith, b1759, Fauq Co, fJoseph Sr, mLucy Steptoe, hThomas Keith
Mary E, b186-, nrDungannon, Scot Co, d1919, fSamuel D, mMartha J Nash, 1hEmmett B Richmond, 2hCharles E Robertson
Robert Emory, b11/14/1854, Warrenton, Fauq Co, fJohn Davenport, mJulia Ann Butts, w Theela Epia Duncan, md8/28/1877
Samuel D, b1827, Wash Co, d1880, fGeorge, m-- Denny, wMartha J Nash
Sarah Agnes, b2/14/1837, Fauq Co, fWilliam, mAnne Sparke Gordon, hIsham Keith Jr
William, b175-, Fauq Co, fJoseph Sr, mLucy Steptoe
William F C Sr, b4/11/1870, nrDungannon, Scot Co, fSamuel D, mMartha J Nash, wLena M Stair, md1889
William Fletcher, b1824, Lune Co, d1905, wMary Anne Ferguson
BLAIR, John Skinner, b1848, Augu Co, fWilliam Robinson, (2)m-- Wallace, wMinnie Craver
Lucy, b184-, Augu Co, fWilliam Robinson, (2)m-- Wallace, h Lewis McClung
Margaret, b1/8/1839, Richmond, hHenry G Cannon
Margaret, bc1850, Augu Co, f William Robinson, (2)m-- Wallace, hC L Coyner
Robert, b18--, Wyth Co?, wMargaret Terrell
Sarah, b16--, hMiles Cary III
William Robinson, b18--, Augu Co, 2w-- Wallace
BLAKE, --, b18--, Loud Co?, hBenjamin Thompson

BLAKE (continued)
Frances, b18--, Esse Co?, hAustin Brockenbrough
Hannah, b18--, Clar Co?, h George E S Phillips
Jane Louisa, b1826, Tappahannock, Esse Co, d1906, hWat Henry Tyler
BLAND, Archer, b18--, Midd Co?, wPolly Chapman
Anna, b18--, PrGeo Co?, h Charles Gee
Ella, bc1860, Ches Co, fWilliam S, mJosephine Winston, hJosephus A Leslie, md5/12/1879
Frances, b17--, 1hJohn Randolph I, 2hSt George Tucker
James Edward, b9/3/1834, Lombard Grove Farm, KiQu Co, d1900, fRobert, mMary Ann Boyd, wCatherine Gardner Corr
Mary, b17--, Jordens, PrGe Co?, fRichard, mElizabeth Randolph, hHenry Lee II
Mary, b185-, Jordan's Point, PrGe Co, d1909, fTheodorick, mMary Harrison, hGeorge A Armistead
Richard, bc1680, PrGe Co?, wElizabeth Randolph
Robert, b5/3/1800, KiQu Co, wMary Boyd
Schuyler, b18--, Glou Co, f Archer, mPolly Chapman, wOlivia J Anderson
Theodorick, b18--, PrGe Co, wMary Harrison
William S, b18--, Ches Co?, wJosephine Winston
BLANKENBAKER, Polly, b18--, Madi Co, hJohn Wilhoit Miller
BLANKENSHIP, Charles A, bc1850, Ches Co, wJosephine V Walker
BLANKS, --, b18--, Hali Co, hRalph Anderson Dodd
Allen Elizabeth, bc1870, Camp Co?, d1906, hFrancis Edward Turner
James Matthew, b3/13/1818, Charlotte Co, d1884, wJulia Frances Dabbs
William Dabbs, b4/3/1864, Clarksville, Meck Co, d1921, fJames Matthew, mJulia Frances Dabbs, wJulia Watkins, md6/24/1891

BLANTON, A L, bc1860, Spot Co?, 2h of Inez Colbert
Amanda, b186-, Wise Co, d1890, 1w of Isaac N Jones
Charles Armistead, b7/23/1859, Cumb Co, fPhilip Southall, mNancy Miller Armistead, wElizabeth Brown Wallace, md12/27/1888
Charles William Sr, b1841, Cumb Co, wMary Virginia Peters
Charles William Jr, b10/31/1865, Farmville, PrEd Co, fCharles William Sr, mMary Virginia Peters, wMartha King Bugg
David, b17--, fRobert, wFrances Johns
Ella Lee, b1858, Amel Co, h George O Hardy
James, b3/6/1796, Cumb Co, f David, mFrances Johns, wNancy Thornton Walker
Jessie, b5/23/1854, Cumb Co, fPhilip Southall, mNancy Miller Armistead, hWilliam T Johnson
Martha Page, b4/4/1861, Cumb Co, fPhilip Southall, mNancy Miller Armistead
Philip Southall, b6/30/1824, Cumb Co, fJames, mNancy Thornton Walker, wNancy Miller Armistead, md2/5/1852
Prescott, b2/17/1856, Cumb Co, fPhilip Southall, mNancy Miller Armistead
Richard A, b1844, Caro Co, wKate Smett
BLEDSOE, Mathilda, b18--, Fairview, Scot Co, fLovin, h--Moore
BLEMCOE, William, bc1820, Fair Co?, wMary Hutton
BLIND, --, bc1800, Shen Co, hJacob Stickley
BLOOD, George H, b18--, wNannie Morrissett
BLOOMER, Freelin H, b18--, Scot Co?, hLarue Taylor
BLOSSER, Abraham, bc1790, Page Co, fPeter, mMagdalena Bear
Abraham, b3/5/1828, nrHarrisonburg, Rkhm Co, fJonas, mMargaret Burkholder
Anna, b12/19/1840, nrHarrison-

BLOSSER (continued)
burg, Rkhm Co, fJonas, mMargaret Burkholder, hAbraham Culp
Barbara, bc1790, Page Co, f Peter, mMagdalena Bear, hDavid Burkholder
Barbara, b18--, Rkhm Co?, hBenjamin Wenger
David, bc1790, Page Co, fPeter, mMagdalena Bear
David, b7/5/1838, nrHarrisonburg, Rkhm Co, fJonas, mMargaret Burkholder
Elizabeth, b11/12/1845, nrHarrisonburg, Rkhm Co, fJonas, mMargaret Burkholder, hRudulph P Metzler
Frances, b9/28/1825, nrHarrisonburg, Rkhm Co, fJonas, m Margaret Burkholder, hAbraham A Good
Isaac, b6/23/1829, nrHarrisonburg, Rkhm Co, fJonas, mMargaret Burkholder
Jacob, bc1790, Page Co, fPeter, mMagdalena Bear
John, bc1790, Page Co, fPeter, mMagdalena Bear
John, b7/24/1848, nrHarrisonburg, Rkhm Co, fJonas, mMargaret Burkholder
Jonas, b7/10/1791, Page Co, fPeter, mMagdalena Bear, wMargaret Burkholder
Jonas H, b7/16/1851, nrHarrisonburg, Rkhm Co, fJonas, m Margaret Burkholder, 1wAnna Wenger, md12/18/1873, 2wMyrtle Showalter, md5/28/1908
Michael, b12/23/1834, nrHarrisonburg, Rkhm Co, fJonas, m Margaret Burkholder
Peter, bc1790, Page Co, fPeter, mMagdalena Bear
Peter, b12/31/1831, nrHarrisonburg, Rkhm Co, fJonas, mMargaret Burkholder
Shem, b8/28/1843, nrHarrisonburg, Rkhm Co, fJonas, mMargaret Burkholder
BLOXOM, Bettie, b18--, Acco Co, hWilliam E Lewis
William E, b18--, Isle Co, wClara Virginia Lattimer
BLUE, Mary, b18--, hJames Dinges
BOARD, Frank H, b2/10/1832, Bedf

BOARD (continued)
Co, 1h of Buena Vista Brown
John James, b6/13/1859, Hendricks Store (now Moneth), Bedf Co, (1)fFrank H, mBuena Vista Brown
Lilly, bc1860, Hendricks Store (now Moneth), Bedf Co, (1)fFrank H, mBuena Vista Brown, hT C Dennis
Mollie, b186-, hMontez Stephenson
BOATWRIGHT, Herbert Lee Sr, b9/12/1862, Buck Co, fJohn G, mPattie Pendleton Phillips, wMary E Vaughan, md12/12/1889
John G, b18--, Buck Co, d1875, wPattie Pendleton Phillips
BOAZ, Emmett Daniel, b2/10/1855, Howardsville, Nels Co, d1915, fWilliam D, mCornelia Harris, wAda C McCallum, md4/22/1903
William D, b18--, Nels Co?, wCornelia Harris
BOCK, Callie, bc1870, Pula Co, fJohn, mVictoria --, hGeorge Wesley Thomas
BOCOCK, William Henry, b1/4/1865, Halifax Court House, Hali Co, fJohn Holmes I, wBessie Perry Friend
BODELL, George, bc1840, Rkbr Co?, wElla Clinedinst
BOGGS, Beulah, b18--, Alle Co, 1w of Charles Mead Stull
Lewis A, bc1800, Albe Co?, wMary Ann Lewis Scott
Minnie, b18--, nrPound, Wise Co, 2w of Marcus D LaFayette Dotson Sr
BOISSEAU, Annie, b18--, Amel Co?, hRobert E Bridgeforth
Benjamin H, b18--, Dinw Co, wMathilda Gregg
Patrick Henry, b10/17/1850, Dinw Co, fBenjamin H, mMatilda Gregg, wSusie D Wicks, md1881
BOLEN, Columbus Franklin, b185-, nrHillsville, Carr Co, d1903, fWilliam B, mRebecca Morris
David Winton, b8/17/1850, nr Hillsville, Carr Co, fWilliam B, mRebecca Morris, wNannie G Early, md2/21/1877
Elmira, bc1870, Mt Solon, Augu Co, fJames Edward, mSarah

BOLEN (continued)
Hopewell, hB A Carrico
Fielden, b18--, Warr Co, wElmyra Thompson
James Edward, b10/25/1847, Warr Co, d1920, wSarah Hopewell
John W, b185-, nrHillsville, Carr Co, fWilliam B, mRebecca Morris
John W, b12/31/1869, Mt Solon, Augu Co, fJames Edward, mSarah Hopewell, wWilla C Graham, md10/1/1900
Laura M, b184-, Warr Co, fFielden, mElmyra Thompson, hWilliam Aylett Compton, md12/23/1868
Martha Isabella, b185-, nr Hillsville, Carr Co, fWilliam B, mRebecca Morris, hJames L Mitchell
Mary Ellen, b1856, nrHillsville, Carr Co, d1908, fWilliam B, mRebecca Morris
BOLLING, Benjamin, b1746, wSallie Hancock
Elizabeth, b17--, hWilliam Robertson
Jane, bc1690, Cobs, ---- Co, fJohn, hRichard Randolph
Margaret Ann, b18--, hThomas Thweatt Jones
Mary Tabb, b18--, hW F Lee
BOLTON, Mary Elizabeth, bc1859, Rkhm Co, hPeter M Rauhof
BOND, George W, b1798, Scot Co, fWilliam, m-- Davis, wLucy Powers
George W, b18--, Scot Co, f George W, mLucy Powers, wEsther Newberry
George W, b186-, nrCoeburn, Wise Co, fWilliam H, mMary E Newberry
Jefferson D, b186-, nrCoeburn, Wise Co, fWilliam H, mMary E Newberry
Laura, bc1870, nrCoeburn, Wise Co, fWilliam H, mMary E Newberry, hMorgan T Kilgore
Martha Lydia, b1830, Bedf Co, 1hCallahill Wilson, 2hRolley Chapman Overstreet
Mary A, b186-, nrCoeburn, Wise Co, fWilliam H, mMary E Newberry, hOscar F Starnes

BOND (continued)
Oliver B, b186-, nrCoeburn, Wise Co, fWilliam H, mMary E Newberry
Samuel H, b6/10/1867, nrCoeburn, Wise Co, fWilliam H, mMary E Newberry, wElizabeth Richmond, md6/21/1899
Virginia, b186-, nrCoeburn, Wise Co, fWilliam H, mMary E Newberry, hJohn W Kilgore
William, b17--, Amhe Co, w--Davis
William H, b2/14/1835, Scot Co, d1913, fGeorge, mLucy Powers, wMary E Newberry
William H, b8/27/1869, Coeburn, Wise Co, fGeorge W, mEsther Newberry, wElizabeth Wiley, m5/5/1900
William W, bc1870, nrCoeburn, Wise Co, fWilliam H, mMary E Newberry
BONHAM, Lewis A, b186-, Smyt Co, wMinnie Jane Johnston
William B, bc1860, Madi Co?, wMary E Graves
BONNIWELL, Bettie E, bc1870, Acco Co?, hJ Curtis Kelley
BOOKER, Erasmus, b1849, Richmond, d1915, fErasmus D, m Olivia Anderson, wSallie A Eubank
Erasmus D, b1862, d1898, wOlivia Anderson
Ernestine, b1/11/1866, Lynchburg, Camp Co, fJames M, hChristian Sixtus Hutter, md1/21/1885
George Edward Sr, b1824, Buck Co, d1899, fWilliam D, wFanny M Eubank
Mollie Jane, bc1834, PrEd Co, d1917, hNathaniel J Terry
Virginia, b18--, nrCumberland Court House, Cumb Co, d1876, hJ William Smith
BOOM, T R, bc1860, Roan Co?, w--Barnitz
BOON, Fleming, b18--, Fran Co?, wSusan Kinsey
John, b18--, Fran Co, fThomas, wJudia Moore
Louise H, b18--, Fran Co, f Fleming, mSusan Kinsey, hJames Addison Fishburn

BOONE, Walter, bc1860, Norf Co?, wMargaret S Corbitt
BOOTEN, Elizabeth Frances Miranda, b18--, Page Co, hDavid M Dovel
BOOTH, --, bc1810, Crai Co?, wMary A Hannah
Agnes, b1821, Fran Co?, fPeter, hWilliam Thomas Hancock, md1838
Christopher, bc1800, Fran Co, fPeter, wMary L Hancock
Elizabeth, b1/29/1801, Bedf Co?, fPeter, 2w of Benjamin Hancock, md1816
Frances, bc1800, "Belleville", Glou Co, hWarner Taliaferro
John, b17--, Amel Co?, fThomas Peter, b17--, Bedf Co, fJohn
BOOTHE, Clara, bc1800, PrWi Co?, hRobert Weir
Jane, b180--, Buch Co, hMiles E Rowe
Margaret, b1840, Elk Garden, Russ Co, d1878, hJohn C Lockhart
BOOTON, Ambrose, bc1800, Page Co
Elizabeth Walker, b18--, Madi Co, hRobert Davis Twyman
John Kaylor, b8/19/1829, Page Co, d1902, fAmbrose C, wEmily Heiskell Lauck, md1857
BORDEN, Daniel, b182-, nrStrasburg, Shen Co, d1896, fPhilip, mMary Funkhouser
Elizabeth Ann, b182-, nrStrasburg, Shen Co, d1894, fPhilip, mMary Funkhouser, hThomas Matthews
John D, bc1850, Shen Co, 2h of Emma N Schmucker
Joseph, b182-, nrStrasburg, Shen Co, d1876, fPhilip, mMary Funkhouser
Mary C, b18--, Shen Co, hDeWitt A Bowman
Perry, b1822, nrStrasburg, Shen Co, fPhilip, mMary Funkhouser, wEliza Ann Lee
Philip, b1792, Augu Co?, d1868, wMary Funkhouser
Robert Eugene, b1/16/1859, nrStrasburg, Shen Co, fPerry, mEliza Ann Lee, 1wDora B Bageant, md2/1906, 2wCatherine Fitzsimmons, md5/1917

BORTAIN, Jacob, bc1840, Shen Co?, wSaloma S Stirewalt
BORUM, Eugenia, b18--, Math Co, hWilliam Stanley Ransome
BOSCHEN, Henry C, b8/1845, Richmond, fJohn H, mJohanna C Paul, wMargaret Frischkorn
BOSSERMAN, C R, bc1850, Augu Co?, wMary Catherine Garrison
BOSTWICK, Mary, b16--, Gooc Co?, hWilliam Leake
BOSWELL, Annie E, b186-, Jame Co, fWilliam T, mJudith W Hockaday, hE C Chapman
Lucy H, b186-, Jame Co, fWilliam T, mJudith W Hockaday, hJ T Farthing
J Walter, b3/20/1867, Jame Co, fWilliam T, mJudith W Hockaday, wLouise D Hockaday
Jennie P, b18--, Meck Co, h George R Tisdale
Lucy, b1858, Winchester, Fred Co, hIsham Keith Briggs
Robert L, bc1870, Jame Co, fWilliam T, mJudith W Hockaday
Thomas, bc1798, Jame Co, wFrances C Richardson
William T, b1839, Jame Co, fThomas, mFrances C Richardson, wJudith W Hockaday
BOTTOM, Davis, b5/2/1867, Richmond, fSamuel, mHenrietta Judson Gardner, wElla V Alley
Ida Belle, B18--, Richmond, fSamuel, mHenriette Judson Gardner, hMoses E Tuck
Mary, b18--, Ches Co, hJohn Horner, Jr
Samuel, b18--, Henrico Co, w Henrietta Judson Gardner
BOTTS, Anna Ford, bc1870, Staf Co?, fLewis Conner, mVirginia Crigler, hCharles William Browning, md2/20/1889
Lewis Conner, b18--, Staf Co?, wVirginia Crigler
Mary James, b18--, Rapp Co, hClarence J Miller
BOUD, Frances, b18--, Shen Co, hJohn Henry Gardner
BOUDURANT, Angeline, b1832, Buck Co, hWilliam P Hall Sr
James S, b18--, wVirginia Slayton
BOUGHTON, Leah, b186-, Esse Co,

BOUGHTON (continued)
fReuben, mLeah Cauthorne, hWilliam McDonald Lee, md6/28/1888
Reuben, b18--, Esse Co, wLeah Cauthorne
BOULDIN, Alice, b186-, Bedf Co?, fWood, mMartha Daniel, hBoylan Green
Anne, b18--, hElisha E Hundley
Henry Wood, b18--, Char Co, wLela Coles
Joanna Tyler, b1820, Char Co, d1901, fJames Wood, hLouis Bouldin Spencer
Louise, bc1870, Danville, Pitt Co, hCharles Ernest Harper
Nina Daniel, b186-, Bedf Co?, fWood, mMartha Daniel, hBerryman Green
Wood, b1811, Bedf Co?, d1876, wMartha Daniel
BOUTON, George, b18--, Madi Co?, wLucetta Nalle
Mollie, b18--, Madi Co, f George, mLucetta Nalle, hWilliam Jones Cave
BOUTWELL, William Rowe Sr, b18--, Surr Co, d1866, wSarah Crittenden
William Rowe Jr, b11/25/1860, nrJamestown, Surr Co, fWilliam Rowe Sr, mSarah Crittenden, 1wMary E Cocke, 2wRebecca M Elliott
BOWTZ, Mollie Rebecca, b18--, Rkhm Co?, hAndrew Jackson Young, md1887
BOWDEN, Elizabeth, b18--, Acco Co, hRevel Carpenter
BOWE, Amanda Stuart, b1842, Hano Co, 2w of Charles Felix Cross
Hector, b18--, Hano Co, fNathaniel, wMary Ursula Ellis
Nathaniel Woodson, b11/1843, Hano Co, fHector, mMary Ursula Ellis, wEmma Lewis Griffin
Polly, b17--, Hano Co, hOliver Cross
BOWELES, Robert, bc1840, Amhe Co, wMartha Turpin
BOWEN, Fannie E, b1854, nrLuray, Page Co, d1911, (1)fPaul Lee, mAlmyra Josephine Hopper, h William G Conrad, md10/12/1876
Harry C, b18--, Fauq Co?, w

BOWEN (continued)
Georgie C Carmichael
Henry, b17--, Taze Co, fRees, wElen Tate
John, b17--, bVirginia or Wales, d1780, fMoses, wRebecca Reed
John R, b18--, Crai Co?, d1865, 1h of Nancy A Webb
Louisa Smith, b17--, Taze Co, fHenry, mElen Tate, hJohn W Johnston
Paul Lee, b18--, Page Co?, 1h of Almyra Josephine Hopper
Peggy, b17--, Taze Co, fReese, hThomas Gillespie
Reese, b17--, Augu Co, d1780, fJohn
Rees T, b17--, Taze Co?, fHenry, mElen Tate
William, b17--, Augu Co, fJohn, wMary Henry Russell
BOWERS, --, b18--, Pend Co?, hPulser C Smith
--, bc1840, Shen Co, fJacob, h-- Hollar
--, bc1840, Shen Co, fJacob, h-- Jones
Amelia, b183-, Shen Co, fJacob Bower
Caroline, b7/2/1826, Culp Co, d1894, fRobert T, mFannie Leavell, hSamuel Foltz
Catherine, b183-, Shen Co, fJacob Bower
Charles, bc1870, Shen Co, f Isaac, mEllen Painter
George, b183-, Shen Co, fJacob Bower
Isaac, b1829, Shen Co, d1896, fJacob Bower, wEllen Painter
Katherine, bc1800, Shen Co, hPhilip Pence
Luther, bc1870, Shen Co, f Isaac, mEllen Painter
Robert T, bc1800, Culp Co?, wFannie Leavell
William, bc1840, Shen Co, fJacob Bower
BOWIE, E W, bc1860, Roan Co?, wOla May Gish
Roberta Jane, bc1850, Rapp Co, fWilliam K, m-- White, hWilliam Jackson Aylor
William K, b18--, Rapp Co, w-- White

BOWLES, --, b18--, Henry Co?, wEliza Richardson
Aubrey Russel, b9/1870, Fluv Co?, fDrurie Wood Jr, mRegina Elmore
Claude, b18--, Cardwell, Gooc Co, fJames Henry, mSarah Ann Glenn
Drurie Wood Sr, b18--, Fluv Co?, wMary Ann Richardson
Drurie Wood Jr, b12/25/1847, Bowlesville, Fluv Co, fDrurie Wood Sr, mMary Ann Richardson, wRegina Elmore, md1866
Hal, b18--, Cardwell, Gooc Co, fJames Henry, mSarah Ann Glenn
Harriet A, b18--, Cardwell, Gooc Co, fJames Henry, mSarah Ann Glenn, hS H Cottrell
James Cocke, b3/27/1850, Cardwell, Gooc Co, fJames Henry, mSarah Ann Glenn, 1wSarah Adelaide (Swann) Pleasants, 2wAnn Bagby
James Henry, b12/12/1824, Gooc Co, fJohn, mMartha Ann Cocke, 1wSarah Ann Glenn, 2w Sally Dickinson
Jefferson Davis, b18--, Cardwell, Gooc Co, fJames Henry, mSarah Ann Glenn
John, bc1800, Gooc Co, fThomas, wMartha Ann Cocke
Joseph, b18--, Amel Co?, wLucy P Moore
Josephine, b1857, Henrico Co, hIsador Hirschberg
Malcolm S, b8/20/1866, Cardwell, Gooc Co, fJames Henry, mSarah Ann Glenn, wMinnie Alice Everett
Sarah Ann, b18--, Cardwell, Gooc Co, fJames Henry, mSarah Ann Glenn, hO B Taylor
William C, b18--, Cardwell, Gooc Co, fJames Henry, mSarah Ann Glenn
BOWLING, Andrew, b18--, Hard Co?, wFrances Clagett
BOWMAN, --, bc1800, Rkhm Co, hHenry Garber
--, bc1860, Fred Co?, wMary Gardner
--, bc1860, Shen Co, wLydia Ellen Stoner
Addison K, bc1860, nrMt Clin-

BOWMAN (continued)
  ton, Rkhm Cop, fSamuel, mSallie Loftis
Amanda E, b12/3/1853, nrTimberville, Rkhm Co, fDavid, mAnna Good, hWilliam Anderson Pence, md11/1/1877
Amelia, bc1843, Rkhm Co, fDaniel, mMargaret Neff, hPeachy Addison Bertram
Ann, b181-, nrWoodstock, Shen Co, fJacob, m-- Fravel, hDecatur Shipe
Anna M, bc1870, Rkhm Co, fDavid, mAnna Good, hArthur Halterman
Annie, b18--, Rkhm Co, hSylvanus Pence
Berry T, bc1850, Page Co, w-- Shuler
Burder D, b2/27/1860, nrWoodstock, Shen Co, fJacob, mSarah Ann Johnson
Charles Irwin, b186-, nrWoodstock, Shen Co, fDaniel, mMary Elizabeth Hockman
Charles S, bc1864, nrMt Clinton, Rkhm Co, fSamuel, mSallie Loftis, wBettie Deavers
Cornelius P, b9/12/1868, Augu Co, fJacob II, mMary Arehart, wCora Lewis Shuey
Daniel, b18--, wMargaret Neff
Daniel, b10/15/1829, nrWoodstock, Shen Co, d1896, fHenry, mEliza Oglesby, wMary Elizabeth Hockman, md8/14/1855
David, b18--, Rkhm Co?, wAnna Good
DeWitt A, b18--, Shen Co?, wMary C Borden
Dilman J, bc1870, Rkhm Co, fDavid, mAnna Good
Edgar Florence, b12/26/1853, nrWoodstock, Shen Co, fJoseph, mSarah Ann Johnson, hErasmus P Bowman
Elizabeth Frances, b12/30/1864, Rkhm Co, fJoseph, mSarah Flory, hJacob Henry Hall, md1/23/1833
Emeline, b18--, Augu Co, fJacob I, mEliza Clemmer
Emma E, b186-, Augu Co, fJacob II, mMary Arehart, hWilliam A McComb

BOWMAN (continued)
Ephraim, b18--, Shen Co?, wJosephine Dyer
Erasmus P, bc1850, Shen Co?, wEdgar Florence Bowman
Eugene, bc1860, Shen Co, wAnna Laura Stoner
Franklin M, bc1860, Rkhm Co, fDavid, mAnna Good
George, b18--, Augu Co, fJacob I, mEliza Clemmer
George, bc1840, Shen Co?, w Catherine Harpine
George H, bc1847, Warr Co?, wFlorence Ellen King
Gussie V, b186-, Augu Co, fJacob II, mMary Arehart, hGeorge E Hanger
Henry, bc1800, nrWoodstock, Shen Co, wEliza Oglesby
Isaac, b181-, nrWoodstock, Shen Co, fJacob, mMary Fravel
Isaac, bc1825, Shen Co, wBetsy Painter
Isaac, bc1840, Clar Co, wElla Jones
Isaiah, b184-, Ashby District, Shen Co, wAnna E Fravel
Jacob, bc1790, Shen Co?, d1849, wMary Fravel
Jacob II, b18--, fJacob I, mEliza Clemmer
Jacob, b186-, Augu Co, fJacob II, mMary Arehart
James, b18--, Augu Co, fJacob I, mEliza Clemmer
Jane, b18--, Augu Co, fJacob I, mEliza Clemmer
Jennie F, bc1870, Rkhm Co, fDavid, mAnna Good, h-- Wise
Joanna C, bc1860, Rkhm Co, fDavid, mAnna Good, hEzra M Minnick Sr, md4/24/1888
John H, b186-, Augu Co, fJacob II, mMary Arehart, wAnnie Cochran
Joseph, b18--, Rkhm Co, wSarah Flory
Joseph, b11/16/1810, nrWoodstock, Shen Co, d1883, fJacob, mMary Fravel, wSarah Ann Johnson, md10/20/1847
Joseph Hockman, bc1870, nrWoodstock, Shen Co, d1904, fDaniel, mMary Elizabeth Hockman
Josephine D, bc1860, Shen Co,

BOWMAN (continued)
fEphraim, mJosephine Dyer, hGideon Wilkins
Kirby Jacob, b12/14/1867, Bowman, Shen Co, fWhiten, mFannie Rosenberger, wNellie G Bowman, md5/1897
Laura Virginia, bc1850, nrWoodstock, Shen Co, fJoseph, m Sarah Ann Johnson
Lewis, b185-, Hano Co?, wWillie Anna Mann
Luther L, b186-, Augu Co, fJacob II, mMary Arehart
Luther S, b186-, nrMt Clinton, Rkhm Co, fSamuel, mSallie Loftis
Margaret, b18--, Augu Co, fJacob I, mEliza Clemmer
Margaret Elizabeth, b186-, nrWoodstock, Shen Co, fDaniel, mMary Elizabeth Hockman, hSamuel Wisman
Marshall C, b7/21/1848, nrWoodstock, Shen Co, d1904, fJoseph, mSarah Ann Johnson
Mary, b180-, nrWoodstock, Shen Co, fJacob, mMary Fravel
Mary, b18--, Augu Co, fJacob I, mEliza Clemmer
Mary Kate, bc1870, nrWoodstock, Shen Co, fDaniel, mMary Elizabeth Hockman
Paul C, bc1840, Shen Co, wElenora C Stirewalt
Robert, b181-, nrWoodstock, Shen Co, fJacob, mMary Fravel
S L, bc1860, wEdna Myers
Samuel, b181-, nrWoodstock, Shen Co, fJacob, mMary Fravel
Samuel, b18--, Harrisonburg, Rkhm Co, wElizabeth Fitzmeyers
Samuel, b18--, nrMt Clinton, Rkhm Co, d189-, wSallie Loftis
Samuel, b10/12/1832, nrWoodstock, Shen Co, fHenry, mEliza Oglesby, wEllen Hottel
Samuel Godfrey, b4/20/1847, Peach Grove, Rkhm Co, d1917, wRebecca Catherine Filsmoyer, md12/6/1876
Samuel H, bc1840, Shen Co, wEllen Schmucker
Sarah, b184-, Shen Co, fIsaac, mBetsy Painter, hJoseph B Tysinger

BOWMAN (continued)
Sarah Alice, b185-, nrWoodstock, Shen Co, d1919, fJoseph, mSarah Ann Johnson, h William O Coates
Sarah M, bc1851, Hard Co, hJohn J Harper
Solon M, bc1860, Rkhm Co, fDavid, mAnna Good
Susan, b18--, Augu Co, fJacob, mEliza Clemmer
Susanna, b18--, Rkhm Co, hAbram Hinegardner
Whiten, b18--, Bowman, Shen Co, fJacob, mMary Fravel, wFannie Rosenberger
Willa A, b186-, Augu Co, fJacob II, mMary Arehart, hNewton Bosserman
William, b181-, nrWoodstock, Shen Co, fJacob, mMary Fravel, wSarah Rosenberger
William, b184-, Shen Co, f Isaac, mBetsy Painter
William R, b6/1/1870, Bowman, Shen Co, fWhiten, mFannie Rosenberger, wElla Stoner, md6/15/1896
BOWYER, Henry L, b10/8/1853, Fran Co, fHenry Quincy Adams, m-- Webb, wMary Katherine Painter
Henry Quincy Adams, bc1810, Fran Co, w-- Webb
BOXLEY, Bettie, b18--, Loui Co, mSally Ann Lipscomb
Charles, b18--, Loui Co, fJames, mSally Ann Lipscomb
James, b1822, Loui Co, fJoseph I, mWinifred Sandridge, wSally Ann Lipscomb
James, b18--, Loui Co, fJames, mSally Ann LIpscomb
James Garland, b11/4/1842, nrCenterville, Loui Co, fJoseph Clivius, mAnn Ladd, wFenton Bruce Mansfield
Joseph I, bc1800, Loui Co, wWinifred Sandridge
Joseph II, b18--, Loui Co, fJames, mSally Ann Lipscomb
Joseph Clivius, b18--, Loui Co, wAnn Ladd
Lucy, b18--, Loui Co, fJames, mSally Ann Lipscomb
Mary, b18--, Loui Co, fJames,

BOXLEY (continued)
mSally Ann Lipscomb
Sandridge, b18--, Loui Co, fJames, mSally Ann Lipscomb
William W, b7/17/1861, Loui Co, fJames, mSally Ann Lipscomb, 1wFannie Haley, md1883, 2wWillie Saunders, md1902
BOXWELL, Charles, b18--, Fred Co, wMary Jane Cather
BOYD, David, b17--, Nels Co, fAlexander, mAnn Swepson, wElizabeth (Ott) Durell
Henry Curran, b18--, Nels Co, fDavid, mElizabeth (Ott) Durell, wJuliet Ann Massie
John, b1778, fWilliam, mSarah Wilson
Lavinia, b18--, Russ Co?, hTazewell Hill Griffith
Martha, b1751, Hali Co, d1810, hWilliam Adams
Mary Ann, b5/16/1810, KiQu Co, hRobert Bland
Richard, b17--, Meck Co, wPanthea Burwell
Robert Aaron, b18--, Russ Co?, d1913, wAngeline Ball
Sarah, b18--, Russ Co, hNelson Dickenson
Stephen D, bc1840, Fauq Co, wAnnie E Woodward
Stephen Decatur Sr, bc1820, fJohn, mFrances Woodward
Waller Massie Sr, b18--, "Blue Rock", Nels Co, fHenry Curran, mJuliet Anna Massie, wCarrie Yancey
Waller Massie Jr, b5/24/1868, Lynchburg, Camp Co, fWaller Massie Sr, mCarrie Yancey, 2wCaroline Cummings
BOYER, --, b18--, Elk Creek, Gray Co, hJohn Cornett
Andrew Jackson, b183-, Shen Co, fWilliam, mRegina Stickley, wBettie Miley
Annie Regina, b184-, Powell's Fort Valley, Shen Co, fWilliam, mRegina Strickley, hJames Coverstone
Benjamin F, b183-, Powell's Fort Valley, Shen Co, fWilliam, mRegina Strickley, w--Clem
David S, bc1840, Powell's Fort

BOYER (continued)
Valley, Shen Co, fWilliam, mRegina Strickley
Eliza Catherine, b184-, Powell's Fort Valley, Shen Co, fWilliam, mRegina Stickley, hThornton Rittenour
George Alvah, b184-, Powell's Fort Valley, Shen Co, fWilliam, mRegina Stickley
Hugh Franklin, bc1870, Powell's Fort Valley, Shen Co, fJohn D, mRebecca Coverstone
Jacob Erasmus, b184-, Powell's Fort Valley, Shen Co, fWilliam, mRegina Stickley
John D, b1837, Powell's Fort Valley, Shen Co, d1916, fWilliam, mRegina Stickley, wRebecca Coverstone
John Lemuel, bc1870, Powell's Fort Valley, Shen Co, fJohn D, mRebecca Coverstone
William Joseph, b11/15/1868, nrWoodstock, Shen Co, fJohn D, mRebecca Coverstone, wJosephine Stephenson, md9/8/1916
Mary Elizabeth, b184-, Powell's Fort Valley, Shen Co, fWilliam, mRegina Stickley, hJohn L McInturf
Peter, b17--, nrStrasburg, Shen Co
Samuel Edward, bc1850, Powell's Fort Valley, Shen Co, fWilliam, mRegina Stickley
William, b1804, nrStrasburg, Shen Co, d1888, fPeter, wRegina Stickley
William Milton, b183-, Powell's Fort Valley, fWilliam, mRegina Stickley
BOYKIN, Clarence Taylor, b186-, Richmond, fSamuel Henry, m Frances Taylor
Francis Marshall, bc1800, Smithfield, Isle Co, d1866
Francis Marshall, b186-, Richmond, fSamuel Henry, mFrances Taylor
Henry Marshall, b8/30/1860, Richmond, fSamuel Henry, m Frances Taylor, wJuliett Marks, md12/9/1885
Miriam, bc1870, Richmond, fSamuel Henry, mFrances Taylor,

BOYKIN (continued)
  hRobert L Norment
  Samuel Henry, b1833, Smithfield, Isle Co, d1879, fFrancis Marshall, wFrances Taylor, md1859
  William Jacquelin, b186-, Richmond, fSamuel Henry, mFrances Taylor, w-- Harris
BOYS, Maria T, b18--, Augu Co?, hGeorge Moffett Cochran Sr
BRACY, W R, b18--, wJennie Hix
BRADBURY, William L, b18--, Oran Co?, wMary Beverly Shaw
BRADFORD, Lucy A M, bc1820, Oran (now Greene) Co, hWilliam Robinson Stuart
  Robert W, bc1860, Rkhm Co, wLucy Knox Lincoln
BRADLEY, Fannie Bennett, bc1860, Harrisonburg, Rkhm Co, fPhilo, hJohn Gibbons Yancey
  Mary V, b18--, Fran Co, hLevi O Dudley
  Thomas, b18--, Page Co?, wBlanche Judd
  Thomas D, b18--, Pitt Co?, wIsabel
BRADSHAW, Alice Tyler, b18--, hJoseph R Sturgis
  Charles, bc8170, High Co?, w Mattie Keister
  Charles S, b1850, nrBelfast Mills, Russ Co, wMary Douglas Stinson
  Romulus, b1---, Loud Co, wIda Frances Presgrave
BRAGG, Anna E, b18--, Madi Co?, fJames, hJames Madison Wood
  Arthur, bc1820, Fred Co, wMary H Wright
  Ella Louise, b1865, Richmond, fJames E, hRobert E Jones
  Susan Mary, b18--, Rapp Co?, hCharles Lewis Yates
BRAIDWOOD, Maggie, b18--, Acco Co?, hJames A D Savage
BRANCH, Anne, b18--, Richmond?, hRobert Gamble Cadell
  Caroline Scott, b1795, PrEd Co, d1881, fAlbert, hJames Powell Anderson
  Julia N, b18--, Richmond, fDavid Mann, 1h-- Archer, 2hJames M Hogg, md11/2/1878
  Sallie Reade, b18--, hGeorge

BRANCH (continued)
  Brockenbrough McAdams
  Thomas, b17--, fChristopher
  William, b17--, fChristopher
BRANDT, Elizabeth, b9/28/1770, Fauq Co, hJames Adams
BRANHAM, Elizabeth, b1851, Dick Co, hJames T Mullins
BRANSCOME, Herbert, b18--, Carr Co, wNancy ---
  Matilda, b18--, Carr Co, fHerbert, mNancy ---, hJonathan Worrell
  Robert L, bc1860, Carr Co?, wAlice Hylton
BRANSON, Sallie, b17--, Warr Co?, mRebecca Millar, h-- LeHew
BRATTON, J Mitchell, b18--, Bath Co?
BRAXTON, Mary Caperton, bc1870, hHenry Winston Holt, md1894
  Mildred Pendleton, b1802, Fredericksburg, Spot Co, hJohn Allport IV
BRAY, Charles Robert, bc1850, Esse Co?, d1917, wBetty Payne Faulconer
  Winter, bc1850, Esse Co?, d1884, wFannie Ida Faulconer
BREADY, Edith M, bc1870, Herndon, Fair Co, fIsaiah, mKate Walters, hErnest Lee Robey
  Isaiah, b18--, Fair Co?, wKate Walters
BRECKENRIDGE, Elizabeth, b3/31/1794, Bote Co, fJames, hEdward Watts
BRENAMIN, Buena Vista, b186-, Mt Solon, Augu Co, fSamuel I, mElizabeth Neff
  Charles, b186-, Mt Solon, Augu Co, fSamuel I, mElizabeth Neff
  Elizabeth, b185-, Mt Solon, Augu Co, fSamuel I, mElizabeth Neff, h-- Houff
  Ellen, b186-, Mt Solon, Augu Co, fSamuel I, mElizabeth Neff, hCharles Reed
  Jacob Neff, b1/10/1854, Mt Solon, Augu Co, fSamuel I, mElizabeth Neff
  Robert, bc1860, Mt Solon, Augu Co, fSamuel I, mElizabeth Neff
  Samuel I, b1827, nrMt Solon, Augu Co, fAbraham, wElizabeth

BRENAMIN (continued)
Neff Samuel II, b186-, Mt Solon, Augu Co, fSamuel I, mElizabeth Neff
Virginia Neff, bc1860, Mt Solon, Augu Co, fSamuel I, mElizabeth Neff
William W, b185-, Mt Solon, Augu Co, fSamuel I, mElizabeth Neff
BRENNAN, John Jr, b1856, Ceredo, Wayn Co, fJohn Sr, wKate Vale
BRENNER, Annie Elizabeth, b1868, Alexandria, fAnthony, mSarah Campbell, hCharles H Davis
Anthony, b1846, Alexandria, wSarah Campbell
Sarah, b17--, Shen Co, hJohn Pence
BRENT, --, b18--, Lanc Co?, hCharles Nichols Lawson
--, b18--, Amhe Co, 1w of W R Hill
Burr Chinn, b181-, fHugh, mElizabeth Shinn
Elizabeth Marye, b7/31/1792, West Co, fWilliam, mHannah Neale, hEppa Hunton I, md6/23/1811
George W, b18--, fLaFayette, mJulia P Johnson
Hugh, b17--, Old Welbourne, Loud Co, fGeorge, wElizabeth Chinn
Hugh, b18--, fLaFayette, mJulia P Johnson
James Fenton, b181-, fHugh, mElizabeth Chinn
James R, b18--, fLaFayette, mJulia P Johnson
Katie, b18--, Old Welborne, Loud Co, fGeorge
LaFayette, b2/1816, fHugh, mElizabeth Chinn, wJulia P Johnson
Lawrence, b18--, Fauq Co?, wLila Murray
Lawrence D, b12/28/1849, Hopewell Farm, fLaFayette, mJulia P Johnson, wEliza Gordon Murray, md12/11/1889
Lucy, b18--, Alexandria?, hRobert T Thorp
Martin, b18--, Old Welborne, Loud Co, fGeorge

BRENT (continued)
Mary Ann, b181-, fHugh, mElizabeth Chinn, hMeredith Robertson
Randolph S, bc1860, Nhld Co?, wLaura Kendall DeShields
Sallie, b18--, Old Welborne, Loud Co, fGeorge, h-- Powell
Thomas, b18--, Old Welborne, Loud Co, fGeorge
Thomas R, b18--, fLaFayette, mJulia P Johnson
William, b17--, wHannah Neale
Willis, b18--, Old Welborne, Loud Co, fGeorge
BREWER, Adam Hinkle, b1820, Jeff Co, d1905, fJohn, mMary Hinkle, wJane Elizabeth Rhodes
Ann, b182-, Jeff Co, fJohn, mMary Hinkle, h-- Statler
George, b181-, Jeff Co, fJohn, mMary Hinkle
Mary, b182-, Jeff Co, fJohn, mMary Hinkle, h-- Johnson
James Scott, b181-, Jeff Co, fJohn, mMary Hinkle
John, b1780, Jeff Co, wMary Hinkle
John I, b181-, Jeff Co, fJohn, mMary Hinkle
Richard Lewis Sr, b18--, Nans Co, wJudith Ann Robinson
Richard Lewis Jr, b5/27/1864, fRichard Lewis Sr, mJudith Ann Robinson, wLelia J Vellines
Scott William D, b8/26/1859, Rkhm Co, fAdam Hinkle, mJane Elizabeth Rhodes, wFlemma L Swank, md6/19/1890
BREWINGTON, John C, b18--, Lanc Co?, wAnna Lilly
BRICKEY, Ginsey/Gency, b2/20/1840, Fort Blackmore, Scot Co, hHiram Kilgore McConnell Sr
BRIDGEFORTH, George B, b18--, wSallie A Seay
Robert E, b18--, Amel Co?, wAnnie Boisseau
BRIDGES, Thomas, b18--, Norf Co?, wMary Hughes
BRIGGS, Isham Keith Sr, b1851, nrFredericksburg, Staf Co, d1923, fJames Keith, mCharlotte Smith, wLucy Boswell
James Keith, b18--, Staf Co,

BRIGGS (continued)
wCharlotte Smith
BRIGHT, Catherine, b17--, Augu Co, hDavid Lincoln
Oliver, bc1860, Fred Co, wCora Hillyard
BRILL, Jonathan H, bc1830, Hamp Co?, wElizabeth Reid
Lewis, b18--, Fred Co, wMargaret Brill
Margaret, b18--, Fred Co, hLewis Brill
Mary, b18--, nrWinchester, Fred Co, fLewis, mMargaret Brill, hJohn R Robinson
BRINKLEY, James, bc1800, wRebecca Venable
Rebecca, bc1830, fJames, mRebecca Venable, hRobert S LaRue
BRISTOW, Benjamin Sr, b4/15/1741, Midd Co, fEdward, mElizabeth, 1wElizabeth Saunders, 2wSarah ---
Benjamin Jr, b3/19/1772, Midd Co, fBenjamin Sr, (1)mElizabeth Saunders, wAnne Saunders
Bettie, bc1840, nrSaluda, Midd Co, fLarkin Stubblefield, m Catherine Seward, 2w of John W Daniel
Catherine, b183-, nrSaluda, Midd Co, fLarkin Stubblefield, mCatherine Seward
Edward, b6/4/1709, Midd Co, fWilliam, mMargaret Starke, wElizabeth Daniel
Eleven, b17--, Midd Co, fBenjamin Sr, (1)mElizabeth Saunders or (2)mSarah ---
John, b16--, Midd Co?, d1716, fJohn, 1wMichal ---, 2wMary Carter
John P, bc1850, nrSaluda, Midd Co, fLarkin Stubblefield, m Catherine Seward
Joseph A, b183-, nrSaluda, Midd Co, d1903, fLarkin Stubblefield, mCatherine Seward
Larkin Stubblefield, b12/26/1807, Midd Co, d1862, fBenjamin Jr, mAnne Saunders, wCatherine Seward
Louis, b184-, nrSaluda, Midd Co, fLarkin Stubblefield, m Catherine Seward
Myra, bc1830, nrSaluda, Midd

BRISTOW (continued)
Co, fLarkin Stubblefield, m Catherine Seward, hJohn W Daniel
Richard Fuller, bc1840, nrSaluda, Midd Co, fLarkin Stubblefield, mCatherine Seward
Robert S, b11/19/1852, Pleasant View Farm, nrSaluda, Midd Co, fLarkin Stubblefield, mCatherine Seward, 1wLelia W Faulkne, md2/24/1881, 2wNellie Christian, md1896
Weston Sr, b1846, Midd Co, fLewis, mIda Northern
William, b10/1682, Midd Co, d1742, fJohn, (1)mMical ---, wMargaret Starke, md12/7/1704
BRITTAIN, Hervey P, b4/17/1858, Taze Co, fRufus, mSarah Peery, wMary Amanda Gillespie, md6/26/ 1879
Jennie, b185-, Taze Co, fRufus, mSarah Peery, hJohn H Lewis
Joey, b186-, Taze Co, fRufus, mSarah Peery, hDavid G Gillespie
John, bc1860, Taze Co, d1900, fRufus, mSarah Peery
Lewis, b186-, Taze Co, dc1900, fRufus, mSarah Peery
Mary, b18--, Taze Co?, hThomas J Saunders
Robert, b185-, Taze Co, fRufus, mSarah Peery
BRITTLE, Emmet M, bc1870, nrMontreal (now Shipman), Nels Co, fPeyton Oliver, mSallie N Strickland
Peyton Oliver, b1844, Wakefield, Suss Co, wSallie N Strickland
Samuel C, b10/22/1868, Montreal (now Shipman), Nels Co, fPeyton Oliver, mSallie N Strickland, wEllen Fitzhugh Bowen, md6/9/ 1896
BRITTON, --, b18--, Rapp Co?, hJonas Y Menefee
George, bc1840, Clar Co?, wHattie Jones
Rachel, b9/6/1814, Rkhm Co?, hJoseph Funk
BRITTS, Adam F, b18--, Crai Co, wElizabeth Curtis
William L, b3/12/1856, Shawver

BRITTS (continued)
Mill, Taze Co, fAdam F, mElizabeth Curtis, wMaria Nye
BRIZZOLARA, Frank, bRichmond?, wNina ---
BROADDUS, Elizabeth Taliaferro, b1811, Glou Co?, d1849, hBenjamin Thomas Claiborne Robins
BROADWATER, Charles C, b3/28/1862, Nickelsville, Scot Co, wMary LaRue Culbertson
BROCK, Benjamin F, b18--, Bote Co?, wElizabeth Williams
Henry Clay, b2/1845, Richmond, fRobert Kink, mElizabeth Mildred Ragland, wMary Carter Irving
Robert Kink, b18--, Richmond?, fPhilip, wElizabeth Mildred Ragland
BROCKENBROUGH, Austin, b16--, Richmond, fWilliam
Austin, b17--, Richmond, fWilliam
Austin, b18--, Esse Co?, wFrances Blake
Champ, b17--, Richmond, fAustin
Frank, bc1850, Rkbr Co?, wSallie Paxton
Gabriella, b1839, Tappahannock, Esse Co, d1872, fAustin, m Frances Blake, 1w of Joseph William Chinn Jr
Loula, b185-, Richmond, 1w of James Christian Lamb
Lucy Champ, b17--, Richmond, fChamp, hPhilip Wade Thornton, md1815
Sadie, bc1860, Richmond?, 2w of James Christian Lamb
Mary Stevenson, b18--, fWilliam, hWilloughby Newton IV, md1829
William, bc1700, Richmond, f Austin
BROCKMAN, Edward, bc1850, Oran Co, wAlice Cooke
Roberta, b18--, hVernie R Graves
BRODERS, John, b18--, Fair Co?, wVirginia Woodyard
Lilian, b1869, Fair Co?, h Charles C Carlin
BRODNAX, Alexander Watson, b18--, Petersburg, Dinw Co, fRobert Walker Sr, mCornelia Alvinia

BRODNAX (continued)
Batte
Ann, b17--, ChCi Co, fEdward Sr, mElizabeth Hall
Ann Meriwether, b18--, Dinw Co, fMeriwether Bathurst, mAnn Eliza Walker
Anne Walker, bc1870, Petersburg, Dinw Co, fRobert Walker Sr, mCornelia A Batte, hLawrence Ingram, md6/25/1890
Cornelia Batte, b18--, Petersburg, Dinw Co, fRobert Walker Sr, mCornelia Alvina Batte
Daniel Lyon, b18--, Petersburg, Dinw Co, fRobert Walker Sr, mCornelia Alvinia Batte
Edward Sr, b17--, Jamestown, PrEd Co, fWilliam Sr, mRebekah (Champion) Travis, wElizabeth Hall
Edward Jr, b17--, ChCi Co, fEdward Sr, mElizabeth Hall
Elizabeth, b17--, ChCi Co, fEdward Sr, mElizabeth Hall
Elizabeth Power, b17--, Suss Co, fHenry, mAnn Holmes
Elizabeth Rebekah, b17--, Jamestown, PrEd Co, fWilliam Sr, mRebekah (Champion) Travis
Elizabeth Starke Walker, b18--, Dinw Co, fMeriwether Bathurst, mAnn Eliza Walker
Elizabeth Wilkins, b18--, Petersburg, Dinw Co, fRobert Walker Sr, mCornelia Alvinia Batte
Ellen, b18--, Petersburg, Dinw Co, fRobert Walker Sr, mCornelia Alvinia Batte
Freeman, b18--, Dinw Co, fWilliam, mMary Walker
Henry, b17--, ChCi Co, fEdward Sr, mElizabeth Hall, 1wAnn Holmes, 2wFrances (Belfield) Walker
Henry Power, b17--, Susse Co, fHenry, (1)mAnn Holmes
John Belfield, b17--, Dinw Co, fHenry, (2)mFrances (Belfield) Walker
John Wilkins, b3/21/1864, Petersburg, Dinw Co, fRobert Walker Sr, mCornelia Alvinia Batte, wDaisy G (Conway) Reed
Lucy Baskerville, b18--, Pet-

BRODNAX (continued)
ersburg, Dinw Co, fRobert Walker Sr, mCornelia Alvinia Batte
Mary Ann, b17--, Dinw Co, fHenry, (2)mFrances (Belfield) Walker
Meriwether Bathurst, b1799, Dinw Co, fWilliam, mMary Walker, wAnn Eliza Walker
Meriwether Bathurst II, b18--, Petersburg, Dinw Co, fRobert Walker Sr, mCornelia Alvinia Batte
Rebecca, b17--, Dinw Co, fHenry, (2)mFrances (Belfield) Walker
Robert Walker Sr, b1/12/1827, Sout Co, d1886, fMeriwether Bathurst, mAnn Eliza Walker, wCornelia Alvinia Batte, md11/6/1850
Robert Walker Jr, b18--, Petersburg, Dinw Co, fRobert Walker Sr, mCornelia Alvinia Batte
Sallie Parham, b18--, Petersburg, Dinw Co, fRobert Walker Sr, mCorneliz Alvinia Batte
Stephen, b17--, ChCi Co, fEdward Sr, mElizabeth Hall
Susan, b17--, Dinw Co, fHenry, (2)mFrances (Belfield) Walker
William, b3/3/1762, Suss Co, fHenry, (1)mAnn Holmes, wMary Walker
William Jr, b17--, Jamestown, PrEd Co, fWilliam Sr, mRebekah (Champion) Travis
William, 17--, ChCi Co, fEdward Sr, mElizabeth Hall
William, b17--, Dinw Co, fWilliam, mMary Walker
William Holmes, b18--, Petersburg, Dinw Co, fRobert Walker Sr, mCornelia Alvinia Batte
BROKENBROUGH, Frances, b18--, Fredericksburg, Spot Co, 1w of James Robert Foster
BROMLEY, Elizabeth, bc1870, Clar Co, fJohn, mMartha Brown, h--Erb
James T, b18--, Fauq Co?, wRoberta Alexander
John, b18--, Clar Co?, wMartha Brown

BROMLEY (continued)
John H, b186-, Clar Co, fJohn, mMartha Brown
Katie E, bc1870, Clar Co, fJohn, mMartha Brown, 1w of J Luther Maphis, md11/19/1884
Mary (Mollie), b186-, Clar Co, fJohn, mMartha Brown
William S, b186-, Clar Co, fJohn, mMartha Brown
BROOKE, Ann, b18--, Esse Co, hConnor C Mallory
Francis Taliaferro, b17--, Spot Co?, m-- Spotswood
Katie Lee, b1---, fBenjamin F, hBentley Kern
Randolph Spotswood, bc1810, Spot Co, fFrancis Taliaferro, hEdmund Berkeley
Robert, b17--, Spot Co?, m--Spotswood
BROOKS, Alice A, b7/3/1852, Math Co, hDavid R James
Andrew, bc1800, Fran Co, wMary Brown
Ellen, b2/21/1838, Taze Co, fJohn, mNancy Duncan, hSamuel Meadows
John, b18--, Taze Co, wNancy Duncan
John V, bc1840, Hali Co?, wMary A Owen
Mary Ann, bc1810, Fluv Co, hWilliam Alfred Gray
Susie, b5/11/1866, Buck Co, hW T Putney
BROUN, Conway, bc1840, Loud Co?, wAnn R McCormick
W Leroy, bc1830, Hano Co?, w--Fleming
BROWER, --, bc1810, Fair Co?, wAugusta Ford
Eve, bc1800, Augu Co, fDaniel, hDaniel Leedy
BROWN, --, b182-, Augu Co, 1w of Tobias Weller
A M, b18--, Wyth Co?, w--Archer
Albert C, b18--, nrHayfield, Fred Co, fRobert, mBarbara Burridge Cather
Alexander, b186-, Fran Co?, fJohn Spotswood, mMary Patterson
Alexander Gustavus Sr, b2/22/1833, Stephens City,

42

BROWN (continued)
Fred Co, fAlexander Gustavus Scott, mNancy Murphy, wFannie Cooksey
Alexander Gustavus Scott, b1801, Alexandria, fGustavus Alexander, wNancy Murphy
Alexander Stuart, bc1840, wEllen Spiller
Alfred N, b18--, Bote Co, wMary Laughlin
Allen K, bc1850, wNancy J Dudley
America, b18--, Bedf Co, hJames Lewis Arthur, md1889
Andrew S, bc1860, Norfolk?, wMary Minar Segar
Angeline, bc1820, Albe Co, fBasil, hGeorge W Kemper Jr
Annie, b18--, Nhld Co, hJohn E Nelms
Annie, b18--, Winchester, Fred Co, fJoseph, mElizabeth Fout, hRobert G Smith
Annie Eliza, b2/8/1862, Fran Co, d1901, fJohn Spotswood, mMary Patterson, hTarlton Frederick Brown
Annie T, bc1853, Amhe Co, hColin Stokes
Belle B, b18--, fJohn Twiggs, mLovely Virginia Beverly, hLangdon Taylor Christian
Bettie A, b18--, Roan Co, fAlfred N, mMary Laughlin, h Charles D Demit, md10/8/1889
Bettie May, b186-, nrTazewell, Taze Co, fWilliam H, mMary Howard, hRobert P Beavers
Bowling, bc1820, Camp Co?, f Tarlton, mLucy Clark Moorman
Buena Vista, bc1840, Camp Co, 1hFrank H Board, 2hAlexander Arnold
Camilla A, b18--, Spot Co, hJohn L White
Caroline, b18--, Fauq Co?, h Lewis Sisk
Carrie, b18--, Monr Co?, hJames W McNeer
Charles R, b9/29/1864, nrTazewell, Taze Co, fWilliam H, mMary Howard, wSallie Cooper, md12/29/1891
Charles F, bc1850, "Buena Vista", nrHague, West Co, fThom-

BROWN (continued)
as, mSarah Newton
Clara L, b18--, Loud Co, fWilliam H, mMartha Jane Pancoast, hJohn Hatcher
David, bc1800, wChristiana Zuvers
David A, bc1800, Norfolk, wMargaret Forloine
Dora Virginia, b18--, Page Co?, hFielding Wise Kite
Edward H, b186-, Richmond, fJ Thompson Sr, mBettie H Harrison
Eliza, b184-, Fran Co, fFrederick Rives, (1)mJane Prunty
Elizabeth, b18--, Albe Co?, hLouis Campbell
Elizabeth, b18--, Fauq Co?, fJames, hDavid Darius Miller
Elizabeth, bc1850, "Buena Vista", nrHague, West Co, fThomas, mSarah Newton, hWilliam Mayo
Elizabeth, b1850, Winchester, Fred Co, d1913, fOliver, m-- Baker, hLuther Leigh Smith
Elizabeth Cheedle, b1/20/1827, Camp Co?, d1906, fTarlton, mLucy Clark Moorman, 2w of Frederick Rives Brown, md1852
Ella, b186-, nrTazewell, Taze Co, fWilliam H, mMary Howard, hRobert P Buchanan
Emma, b18--, nrHayfield, Fred Co, fRobert, mBarbara Burridge Cather, hJohn Funkhouser
Everett Walker, b2/14/1858, nrMidland, Fauq Co, fWilliam Daniel, mLouisa Johnson, wMary Shannon, md11/9/1887
Fannie, b18--, Maid Co?, h-- Sparks
Fannie May, bc1860, nrMidland, Fauq Co, fWilliam Daniel, mLouisa Johnson, hThomas Wilie
Filmore, bc1860, Fran Co?, fJohn Spotwood, mMary Patterson
Florence, b18--, nrHayfield, Fred Co, fRobert, mBarbara Burridge Cather, hWalker Ritter
Florence, bc1860, nrMidland, Fauq Co, fWilliam Daniel, mLouisa Johnson, hJohn Hicka-

BROWN (continued)
son
Frederick Rives, b7/1/1813, Fran Co, d1896, fJohn, mSallie Rives, 1wJane Prunty, 2wElizabeth Cheedle Brown, md1852
G A, b18--, Henry Co, w-- Matthews
George, bc1860, Fran Co, fJohn Spotswood, mMary Patterson
George F, b1848, "Buena Vista", nrHague, Fred Co, d1909, f Thomas, mSarah Newton, wMary Estell Arnest
Gideon, b17--, Culp Co?, wElizabeth Roberts
Gilbert M, b18--, Rapp Co, fE Lawrence, mElizabeth Jury Yates
Gustavus Alexander, b17--, Alexandria, fWilliam, mCatherine Scott
Hannah Logan, b17--, Fauq Co?, hJames Hunton, md2/6/1786
Hannah M, b18--, Loud Co, fWilliam H, mMartha Jane Pancoast, hAlbert Eugene Fletcher, md2/18/ 1885
Henry Peronneau, b18--, Dinw Co?, wFrances Bland Coalter
Howell Lewis, b1801, Lynchburg, Camp Co, hJane Thompson
Ida, b185-, nrHayfield, Fred Co, fRobert, mBarbara Burridge Cather, hJames T Taylor
J C, b18--, Jeff Co?, fJames M
J Thompson Sr, b5/4/1840, Richmond, fDavid A, mMargaret Forloine, wBettie H Harrison
J Thompson Sr, b1/26/1844, Amhe Co, fHowell Lewis, mJane Thompson, 1wElizabeth Caldwell, md1868, 2wMary Warren
J Thompson Jr, bc1860, Richmond, fJ Thompson Sr, mBettie H Harrison
J Thompson Jr, bc186-, fJ Thompson Sr, (1)mElizabeth Caldwell
Jacob, bc1850, wEmma J Maphis
James Gideon, b1867, Rapp Co, fRobert William, mElizabeth Thornhill, wCora Virginia Reid
James M, b18--, Jeff Co?, fSamuel, mMary Moore
Jefferson A, b18--, Glou Co?,

BROWN (continued)
wHannah Frances Copeland
John, b17--, Rapp Co?, fJohn (bEngland)
John, b17--, Fran Co?, fFrederick, m-- Stegall, wSallie Rives
John, bc1830, Mont Co?, wAnnie Barnett
John M, b18--, Augu Co, wClara Lam
John Robert, b1842, Fran Co, fFrederick Rives, (1)mJane Prunty
John Spotswood, b181-, Fran Co, fJohn, mSallie Rives, wMary Patterson
John Thompson Sr, bc1861, Petersburg, Dinw Co, d1921, f Henry Peronneau, mFrances Bland Coalter, wCarrie Dallas Tucker
John Twiggs, b18--, wLovely Virginia Beverley
John Wesley, b18--, Taze Co, fRobert, mSarah Johnson Sanderson, wNancy Gregory
John William, bc1860, Fran Co, fFrederick Rives, (2)mElizabeth Cheedle Brown
Joseph, b18--, Fred Co?, wElizabeth Fout
Joseph C, bc1860, West Co, wBettie Hall
Joshua, b18--, Loud Co, fWilliam H, mMartha Jane Pancoast
Julia A, b186-, nrTazewell, Taze Co, fWilliam H, mMary Howard, hHaynes Buchanan
Jury Yates, b2/7/1866, Rapp Co, fE Lawrence, mElizabeth Jury Yates, wJulia Adams, md6/2/1897
Kate Agnes, bc1860, Fauq Co, fWilliam Daniel, mLouisa Johnson, hEdward T Hirst
Laura, b185-, nrHayfield, Fred Co, fRobert, mBarbara Burridge Cather, hJoseph A Ritter
Lavonia, b18--, Wash Co, hJoseph Peery
Lucinda, b18--, Culp Co, fWilliam, mSarah Ficklin, hHoratio Gates Moffett Sr
Lucy, b181-, Fran Co, fJohn, mSallie Rives, hGeorge Dicken-

BROWN (continued)
son
Lucy, b18--, Montross, West Co, hRichard Lee Turberville Beale
Lucy Clarke, b5/6/1855, Fran Co, fFrederick Rives, (2)mElizabeth Cheedle Brown, hHenry Clay Lester
Maggie, bc1870, Richmond, fJ Thompson Jr, mBettie H Harrison, hPowhatan F Conway
Maggie Gordon, bc1860, Fauq Co, fWilliam Daniel, mLouisa Johnson, hRobert Guard
Margaret, b1815, Richmond, d1869, 2w of George H Hinton
Margaretta, b18--, Fred Co?, d1907, fJ J Harman, 2w of John Newton Bell
Martha, b18--, Clar Co?, hJohn Bromley
Martha, b1843, Gibson Station, Lee Co, hCharles F Couk
Martha, b6/1866, Richmond, hEdmund Archer Saunders Jr
Martha Steele, bc1800, Augu Co?, fJohn, hBriscoe G Baldwin
Mary, bc1810, Fran Co, fJohn, mSallie Rives, hAndrew Brooks
Mary, b18--, Fred Co, hJohn Griffin
Mary, bc1860, Fran Co, fJohn Spotswood, mMary Patterson
Mary, bc1860, Richmond, fJ Thompson Jr, mBettie H Harrison, hJames Turner Hamlin
Mary Anne, b182-, Camp Co?, fTarlton, mLucy Clark Moorman
Mary E, b1847, nrLincoln, Loud Co, hJohn T Connor Jr
Mary Ellen, b18--, Fred Co, hRichard Brown
Mary Jane, b18--, Taze Co, fJohn Wesley, mNancy Gregory, hJohn Randolph Walker, md12/1/1875
Micajah, bc1830, Camp Co?, f Tarlton, mLucy Clark Moorman
Minnie, bc1860, nrHayfield, Fred Co, fRobert, mBarbara Burridge Cather, hMason Cornelius
Mollie Rose, bc1860, Fauq Co, fWilliam Daniel, mLouisa Johnson, hDelafield Clift
Nancy, b181-, Fran Co, fJohn,

BROWN (continued)
mSallie Rives, hArmistead Gorman
Nannie, b185-, Fran Co, fFrederick Rives, (1)mJane Prunty
Nannie, b186-, Fran Co, fJohn Spotswood, mMary Patterson
Nannie Bell, bc1860, nrTazewell, Taze Co, fWilliam H, mMary Howard, hGeorge W Moss
Nathan, b18--, Loud Co, fWilliam H, mHarriet Lake
Nellie Swann, bc1870, Kanawha Co, fJ C, hHenry W McLaughlin Sr, md8/31/1897
Norburn, b185-, Fran Co?, fJohn Spotswood, mMary Patterson
Oliver, b185-, Fred Co, w-- Baker
Phoebe, bc1810, Fran Co, fJohn, mSallie Rives, h-- Pearson
Polly, b17--, Suss Co, hNicholas Jarratt
Reese, bc1850, Caro Co?, wLucy Jacqueline Gravatt
Reuben, b181-, Fran Co, fJohn, mSallie Rives
Richard, b18--, Fred Co?, wMary Ellen Brown
Richard, bc1830, Camp Co, f Tarlton, mLucy Clark Moorman
Richard, bc1860, West Co?, d1922, wMartha S Hall
Robert, b17--, Cumb Co, fWilliam
Robert, b18--, Cumb Co, fRobert Clement, mJulia Ann Turner, wSarah Johnson Sanderson
Robert, b18--, Fred Co?, fDavid, mChristiana Zuvers, wBarbara Burridge Cather
Robert, bc1850, "Buena Vista", nrHague, West Co, fThomas, mSarah Newton
Robert Clement, b17--, Cumb Co, fRobert, wJulia Ann Turner
Robert William, b18--, Rapp Co, fJohn, wElizabeth Thornhill
Rosa, bc1870, Richlands, Taze Co, fPatton J, hJohn A McHenry, md12/24/1892
Roswell B, b18--, Lanc Co?, wIda Kate Dowing
Sallie, b18--, Hano Co?, hWilliam H Campbell
Sallie, b18--, Loud Co, fWil-

BROWN (continued)
liam H, mMartha Jane Pancoast, hThomas Piggott
Sallie, b181-, Fran Co, fJohn, mSallie Rives, hGreen Jefferson
Sallie F, bc1840, Richmond?, fAlexander Gustavus, mFannie Cooksey, 2w of H Seldon Taylor, md1881
Sallie Fannie, b186-, Fran Co, fJohn Spotswood, mMary Patterson
Samuel, b17--, Jeff Co?, wMary Moore
Sarah, b18--, Culp Co, fWilliam, mSarah Ficklin, hJohn Moffett
Sylvia, b18--, Rkhm Co?, hJohn Cover
Susan, b18--, Loud Co, fWilliam H, mMartha Jane Pancoast, h Fayette G Welsh
Tarlton, b17--, Camp Co?, fTarlton, m-- Napier, wLucy Clark Moorman
Tarlton, bc1820, Camp Co?, f Tarlton, mLucy Clark Moorman
Tarlton Frederick, b9/16/1861, Fran Co, d1895, fFrederick Rives, (2)mElizabeth Cheedle Brown, wAnnie Eliza Brown
Taylor, b185-, Fran Co?, fJohn Spotswood, mMary Patterson
Thomas, b18--, West Co, wSarah Newton
Thomas, bc1850, "Buena Vista", nrHague, West Co, fThomas, mSarah Newton
Thomas P, bc1850, Culp Co?, wSarah Ficklin Moffett
Virgil, b185-, Fran Co?, fJohn Spotswood, mMary Patterson
Virgil A, b1849, Albe Co, wAdelaide Rodes Chapman, md1876
Virginia, b18--, nrHayfield, Fred Co, fRobert, mBarbara Burridge Cather, hJames Howard
Virginia A, b183-, fHenry J, mSusan Ann Hobson, 1w of Christopher Valentine Winfree, md11/14/1860
W Scott, b18--, nrHayfield, Fred Co, fRobert, mBarbara Burridge Cather
Wallace F, b11/24/1867, Rich-

BROWN (continued)
mond, fJ Thompson Sr, mBettie H Harrison, wMartha Stuck, md1888
Wiley, bc1860, Fran Co, fJohn Spotswood, mMary Patterson
William, b17--, Cumb Co, fSamuel
William, bc1800, Culp Co?, f Gideon, mElizabeth Roberts, wSarah Ficklin
William, b181-, Fran Co, fJohn, mSallie Rives
William, b18--, nrGraham, Taze Co, fLow, wJean Kendrick
William Daniel, b1820, Doswell, Hano Co, fDaniel, wLouisa Johnson
William H, b18--, Loud Co?, wMartha Jane Pancoast
William H, b1834, Taze Co, d1913, fWilliam, mJean Kendrick, wMary Howard
William S, b18--, KiGe Co, fSlaughter
BROWNE, --, bc1800, KiQu Co?, 1w of Thomas Beverly Evans
Anna, b6/28/1761, Esse Co, fJames, mMary Spearman
Anne, b10/7/1856, Cumb Co?, fEdward Smith, mJane Margaret Winfree
Cornelia Walton, b4/6/1846, Cumb Co?, fEdward Smith, mJane Margaret Winfree
Daniel, b5/12/1776, Esse Co, fJames, mMary Spearman, wNancy Hobson Walton, md11/24/1808
Daniel Hobson, b9/2/1828, Cumb Co, fDaniel, mNancy Hobson Walton, 1wSally Ann Hatcher, md10/16/ 1851, 2wMildred Minerva Wilkinson, md6/30/1858, 3wCharlotte Virginia Hatcher, md2/18/1874
Dorothy, b12/24/1721, Esse Co, fBuckingham, mElizabeth Mestich
Edward Smith, b4/7/1818, Cumb Co, fDaniel, mNancy Hobson Walton, wJane Margaret Winfree, md5/1845
Elizabeth, b12/26/1712, Esse Co, fBuckingham, mElizabeth Mestich
Elizabeth, b1/6/1757, Esse Co,

BROWNE (continued)
fJames, mMary Spearman
Elizabeth Agnes, b11/13/1822, Cumb Co, fDaniel, mNancy Hobson Walton, hWilliam Thomas Hobson, md12/19/1839
Henry J, b10/12/1811, Cumb Co, fDaniel, mNancy Hobson Walton, wSusan Ann Hobson, md10/24/1833
James, b9/23/1726, Esse Co, fBuckingham, mElizabeth Mestich, wMary Spearman
John, b3/16/1764, fJames, mMary Spearman
Martha, b6/16/1759, fJames, mMary Spearman
Martha Ann, b9/13/1825, Cumb Co, fDaniel, mNancy Hobson Walton, hZachariah Grayson Moorman, md11/24/1846
Mary Christina, b11/21/1819, Cumb Co, fDaniel, mNancy Hobson Walton, hHarrison Jones, md3/10/ 1842
Mary Virginia, b1/9/1849, Cumb Co?, fEdward Smith, mJane Margaret Winfree
Rhoda, b6/18/1769, Esse Co, fJames, mMary Spearman
Robert Walton, b8/28/1813, Cumb Co, fDaniel, mNancy Hobson Walton, wElizabeth Allen Hobson, md4/10/1838
Sallie, b17--, KiQu Co?, hWilliam Fleet
Samuel, b12/11/1710, Esse Co, fBuckingham, mElizabeth Mestich
Thomas, b2/14/1715/6, Esse Co, fBuckingham, mElizabeth Mestich
Thomas, b12/4/1765, Esse Co, fJames, mMary Spearman
Thomas Compton, b12/27/1815, Cumb Co, fDaniel, mNancy Hobson Walton, wMartha James Goodman
William, b10/14/1755, Esse Co, fJames, mMary Spearman
BROWNING, Ada, b18--, Culp Co, hRichard Edmond Luttrell
Ada, b186-, Rapp Co, fJames Harrison, (2)mMariah Louise Corbin
Charles William, b8/27/1863,

BROWNING (continued)
Rapp Co, fJames Harrison, (2)mMariah Louise Corbin, w Anna Ford Botts, md2/20/1889
Ella, bc1860, Rapp Co, fJames Harrison, (2)mMariah Louise Corbin
Ernest, b186-, Rapp Co, fJames Harrison, (2)mMariah Louise Corbin
Eusebia, b18--, Rapp Co?, fJohn Dabney, hBenjamin Franklin Miller
Fannie, b186-, Rapp Co, fJames Harrison, (2)mMariah Louise Corbin
George Washington, b18--, wNannie Verina Dickenson
Gustavus Judson Sr, b5/16/1830, Rapp Co, d1885, wSallie Thomas
Isaiah, b185-, Rapp Co, fJames Harrison, (2)mMariah Louise Corbin
James Harrison, bc1820, Rapp Co, dc1885, fWilliam, 1w-- Duncan, 2wMariah Louise Corbin
John Armistead Sr, b18--, Rapp Co, fWillis, wMary Lewis Willis
John Armistead Jr, b5/24/1865, Washington, Rapp Co, fJohn Armistead Sr, mMary Lewis Willis, wElizabeth Frances Boyd, md10/16/1915
John Strother, b18--, wElizabeth Beale Roberts
Lafayette, b1824, Rapp Co, fJohn I, wSusan Ellen Stallard
Lizzie, bc1860, Rapp Co, fJames Harrison, (2)mMariah Louise Corbin
Lucy, bc1870, Rapp Co, fJames Harrison, (2)mMariah Louise Corbin
Mason, b186-, Rapp Co, fJames Harrison, (2)mMariah Louise Corbin
Presley, b185-, Rapp Co, fJames Harrison, (2)mMariah Louise Corbin
Samuel Russell, b3/8/1853, Rapp Co, fLaFayette, mSusan Ellen Stallard, wLaura L Lillard, md1/2/1879
Sue Duncan, b184-, Rapp Co, fJames Harrison, (1)m-- Duncan

BROWNING (continued)
Thomas Edward, bc1846, Rapp Co, d1916, fJames Harrison, (1)m-- Duncan, wRoberta Chappelear
BROWNLEY, Sarah, b18--, Math Co, hRobert J Gayle
BROYLES, Alice, b1849, Luray, Page Co, fPerry, mMary Berry, hJames A Hammer
Henry F, b184-, Page Co?, fPerry, mMary Berry
Perry, b18--, Page Co?, wMary Berry
BRUBAKER, Andrew, bc1830, Shen Co, w-- Shirley
Elizabeth, b18--, Page Co, d1881, fJacob, hBerryman B Price, md1866
Sallie, bc1870, Luray, Page Co, fJohn, hCharles E Miller
Thomas, bc1840, Page Co?, w-- Koontz
BRUCE, Anne Seddon, b185-, "Staunton Hill", Char Co, d1888, fCharles, mSarah Seddon, 1w of Thomas Nelson Page
Charles, b18--, Hali Co?, d1896, fJames, mElvira Cabell, wSarah Seddon
Ella S, b18--, PrEd Co, d1873, 1w of Drury A Woodson, md9/30/1866
Emma W, b18--, PrEd Co, 2w of Drury A Woodson, md2/1/1877
Henry, b184-, Albe Co, fHarry, mEmma --
Horace, b184-, Albe Co, fHarry, mEmma --
James, b17--, dc1830, 2h of Elvira Cabell
Jennie, b185-, Albe Co, fHarry, mEmma --, hHomer Shiflett
John, bc1850, Albe Co, fHarry, mEmma --
Philip Alexander, b3/7/1856, "Staunton Hill", Char Co, fCharles, mSarah Seddon, wBetty T Taylor, md10/29/1896
Richard A, b1848, Albe Co, fHarry, mEmma --, wFrances Elizabeth Dovel
Thomas Seddon, bc1840, wMary Anderson
Wallace, b184-, Albe Co, fHarry, mEmma --
BRUFFEY, George Pinkney, bc1850,

BRUFFEY (continued)
Rkhm Co?, wIda E Lupton
BRUGH, Benjamin Franklin, b18--, Rkbr Co, wEsterline McClure
Ollin Ulaah, b1/7/1858, Fincastle, Bote Co, fBenjamin Franklen, mEsterline McClure, wAnn Farrow
BRUMBACK, --, bc1840, Page Co, fSamuel, m-- Grove, hRichard Deal
E T, b183-, Page Co, fJohn
Eliza Ann, b183-, Page Co, fJohn
Elizabeth, b186-, nrSpringfield, Page Co, fWilliam Henry, mMary S Huffman
Frances Amanda, b183-, Page Co, fJohn
H F, b183-, Page Co, fJohn
Isaac Milton, bc1847, nrOpequon, Fred Co, wEuphrasia Ellen Funkhouser
Isaac Newton, b183-, Page Co, fSamuel, m-- Grove
J B, b11/20/1839, Page Co, fJohn, mVirginia C Grayson
Jacob, b18--, Page Co, d1853, wNancy Grove
James K, bc1840, Page Co, fSamuel, m-- Grove
John, b1795, Page Co?, dc1876
John, bc1860, Shen Co?, wEmma Shirley
Joseph B, b1842, Fred Co, d1892, w-- Copp
Joseph S, bc1870, nrSpringfield, Page Co, fWilliam Henry, mMary S Huffman
Josephus M, b183-, Page Co, fSamuel, m-- Grove
Martha W, bc1840, fJohn, hJohn Stone
Mary Elizabeth, b183-, Page Co, fJohn
R T, b183-, Page Co, fJohn
Samuel, b18--, Page Co, w-- Grove
T H, b183-, Page Co, fJohn
William Henry, bc1833, Page Co, d1905, fSamuel, m-- Grove, wMary S Huffman
BRUNER, John C, bc1860, Wash Co?, wBuena White
BRUNK, Christian, b1849, Harrisonburg, Rkhm Co, fJohn, mAnn

BRUNK (continued)
 Weaver, wElizabeth Ralston
 John, b18--, Rkhm Co, wAnn Weaver
BRUNNER, --, bc1800, Hamp Co, hJohn Reid
BRYAN, Georgia, b3/11/1837, Eagle Point, Glou Co, hAndrew Glassell Grinnan
 Hannah, bc1800, Rkhm Co, hSamuel Moffett
 John, b17--, w-- Lillard
 John W, b180, Rkhm Co, fHenry, mSarah Shirley, wJulia Frances Southard
 William S, b10/26/1868, fJohn W, mJulia Frances Southard, wLaura Minnie Proctor, md6/8/1913
BRYANT, A G, b184-, Hat Creek, Nels Co, fNelson Sr, mSarah Wright
 Elizabeth, b18--, Bote Co, h Henry T Davis
 Emma, bc1860, Gray Co, fLewis H, mDrusilla Phipps, 1w of James Davis Perkins, md6/1881
 Lewis H, b18--, Gray Co, wDrusilla Phipps
 Luvenia Jackson, b18--, Fluv Co, hWilliam Hudson
 Nelson Sr, b1808, Nels Co, wSarah Wright
 Nelson Jr, b7/9/1838, Hat Creek, Nels Co, fNelson Sr, mSarah Wright, 1wM E Y Hall, md1889, 2wAddie Brent Carter, md8/10/1893
 Ollie, b18--, Scot Co?, 2w of Isaac Williams, md188-
BRYARLY, Roland T, b184-, Fred Co?, wHarriet Baker
BRYCE, Charlotte, b17--, Gooc Co, d1870, hAlexander Spotswood Payne, md1804
BUCHANAN, Ann, b18--, Augu Co, hAddison McCutcheon
 Benjamin Franklin, b10/4/1859, Rich Valley, Smyt Co, fPatrick Campbell Jr, mVirginia Copenhaver, wEleanor F Sheffey, md3/2/1887
 Felix G, bc1850, Smyt Co, w Florence D Sanders
 Haynes, bc1860, Taze Co?, wJulia A Brown

BUCHANAN (continued)
 Horace Graham, bc1860, Wash Co?, fJohn Lee, mFrances Elizabeth Wiley
 James D, bc1870, Rich Valley, Smyt Co, fPatrick Campbell Jr, mVirginia Copenhaver
 Jane, b17--, Wash Co?, fJohn, hJohn Floyd
 John, b17--, Augu Co?, fJames, wMartha Buchanan
 John Lee, b6/19/1831, Ellendale, Smyt Co, fPatrick Campbell Sr, (2)mMargaret Graham, wFrances Elizabeth Wiley
 Martha, b17--, nrStaunton, Augu Co, hJohn Buchanan
 Patrick Campbell Sr, b1799, Rich Valley, Smyt Co, fJohn, mMartha Buchanan, 1wElizabeth Haytor, 2wMargaret Graham
 Patrick Campbell Jr, b12/12/1818, Rich Valley, Smyt Co, d1877, fPatrick Campbell Sr, (1)mElizabeth Haytor, w Virginia Copenhaver
 Robert P, bc1860, Taze Co?, wElla Brown
 Sallie, b17--, Bedf Co?, hJames Sutherland
 Simon P, bc180, Dick Co?, wMartha Keel
 William H, b1869, Rich Valley, Smyt Co, d1920, fPatrick Campbell Jr, mVirginia Copenhaver
BUCHER, Annie, b184-, Stephens City, Fred Co, fJacob Augustus, mElizabeth Lemley, hJohn W Manuel
 David, b181-, nrStephens City, Fred Co, fJohn, m-- Snyder
 Drusilla, bc1820, nrStephens City, Fred Co, fJohn, m-- Snyder
 Ida K, b185-, Stephens City, Fred Co, fJacob Augustus, mElizabeth Lemley, hJohn Lemley
 Jacob Augustus, b1814, nrStephens City, Fred Co, d1891, fJohn, m-- Snyder, wElizabeth Lemley
 John William, b181-, nrStephens City, Fred Co, fJohn, m-- Snyder
 Leah, b181-, nrStephens City, Fred Co, fJohn, m-- Snyder,

BUCHER (continued)
hLewis Smith
Maria, b181-, nrStephens City, Fred Co, fJohn, m-- Snyder
William Melancthon, b12/10/1846, Stephens City, Fred Co, fJacob Augustus, mElizabeth Lemley, wLaura A Hockman
BUCK, Amelia Lee, b1858, Buckton, Warr Co, fJohn G, hFrederick Wilmer Richardson
James F, b18--, Wyth Co?, wLouisa V Holbrook
BUCKLES, Mary Pierce, b1851, Shady Valley, --- Co?, hWilliam J Wasson
BUCKNER, Emily, b18--, hJohn Ashby
Mary S, b18--, "The Neck", Caro Co, fWilliam S B, mMildred Hawes, hWilliam Willis Thornton
BUFORD, Abraham, b17--, Bedf Co?, wNancy Itzen
Agatha, bc1700, Spot Co?, h George Twyman II, md1724
Catherine, bc1800, hHenry H Burwell
Nancy, bc1800, Bedf Co?, fAbraham, mNancy Itzen, hGeorge P Luck
BUHRMAN, Adam, b184-, nrFincastle, Bote Co, fAbraham, m-- Tyler
Asbury, b184-, nrFincastle, Bote Co, fAbraham, m-- Tyler
Joseph Benson, b9/16/1848, nrFincastle, Bote Co, fAbraham, m-- Tyler, wSarah E Lemon, md1880
William H, b184-, nrFincastle, Bote Co, fAbraham, m-- Tyler
BULL, George F, b9/25/1858, nrTimberville, Rkhm Co, fWilliam, mLeanna Cook, wSallie Will
Mary, bc1860, nrTimberville, Rkhm Co, fWilliam, mLeanna Cook, hAaron Showalter
William, b18--, nrTimberville, Rkhm Co, d1863, wLeanna Cook
BULLINGTON, Susan, bc1840, Pitt Co, hElisha B Harvey
BULLOCH, Marie Louise, bc1870, Spot Co, fBenjamin F, hW Con-

BULLOCH (continued)
way Saunders, md11/1891
BULLY, Virginia Satchell, b18--, Hampton, ElCi Co, hVirginius Minson Massenburg
BUMGARDER, Ira, bc1840, Page Co?, w-- Long
BUMGARDNER, Lewis, b18--, Augu Co, fJacob, wHetty Ann Halstead
Virginia, b18--, Augu Co, h Archibald Alexander Sproul
BUNDICK, James E, bc1860, Acco Co?, wMary E Mears
BUNNELL, Hardenia, b1826, Spot Co, d1902, hJames Hall
BUNTING, Kenneth J, b18--, Acco Co?, wAnnie Jones
BUNTS, John Mathas, b1/6/1829, nrWytheville, Wyth Co, d1899, 1wMatilda June Aker, 2wLucinda Elizabeth Carnall, md1873
Mary Rosena, b18--, Wyth Co, fJohn Mathas, (1)mMatilda Jane Aker, hJames Atkins
Nannie Jane, b18--, Wyth Co, fJohn Mathas, (1)mMatilda Jane Aker, hJames Armbrister
BURACKER, Lena, b18--, Page Co?, hJames C Weaver
Mary Alice, b18--, Page Co, fSamuel A, hJohn Beatty Seibert
BURCH, Alice, b18--, Roan Co?, fJames, mElizabeth Gannaway, hOrran Davis Oakey, md10/1887
James, b18--, Roan Co?, wElizabeth Gannaway
BURCHER, Sarah, b17--, NewK Co?, hJohn Whitehead
BURFOOT, W D, bc1850, Richmond, 1h of Eliza Caskie
BURFORD, Emma, b18--, Amhe Co?, hHiram McGinnis
BURGES, Albridgeton Samuel Hardy, bc1810, Sout Co?
Richard Urquhart Sr, b1841, Sout Co, fAlbridgeton Samuel Hardy, wFannie Norfleet Urquhart
BURGESS, --, b18--, Rapp Co?, 2w of James Shumate
Horace Peyton, b18--, Fauq Co, fPeyton, mFrances Newhouse, 1w Elizabeth (Moffett) Cockrill, 2wEmma Silcott

BURGESS (continued)
Horace Turner, b2/22/1863, nrThe Plains, Fauq Co, fHorace Peyton, (1)mElizabeth (Moffett) Cockrill, 1wBettie Smith, md11/21/1889, 2wMary Glascock, md1/14/1915
Josphine L, b1856, nrWarrenton, Fauq Co, fHorace Peyton, (1)m Elizabeth (Moffett) Cockrill, hJohn A Woolf, md1/7/1881
Lydia, b18--, Fauq Co, fPeyton, mFrances Newhouse, hJohn McDonald
Martha, b18--, Fauq Co, fPeyton, mFrances Newhouse
Mattie, b185-, Fauq Co, fHorace Peyton, (1)mElizabeth (Moffett) Cockrill, hWilliam Miller
Melissa, b185-, Fauq Co, fHorace Peyton, (1)mElizabeth (Moffett) Cockrill, hFred H Duncan
Oscar F, b18--, Fauq Co, fPeyton, mFrances Newhouse
Peyton, b18--, Fauq Co, wFrances Newhouse
Winter P, b186-, Fauq Co, fHorace Peyton, (1)mElizabeth (Moffett) Cockrill
BURK, Annie L, b186-, New Market, Shen Co, fHarrison, hSamuel Godfrey Good, md11/1886
Emma S, b186-, New Market, Shen Co, fHarrison
Fannie, bc1860, New Market, Shen Co, fHarrison, hJ W Roberts
George W, b185-, New Market, Shen Co, fHarrison
John P, b186-, New Market, Shen Co, fHarrison
BURKE, Andrew, bc1840, Fair Co, wMargaret Ford
George Washington, b18--, Culp Co?, wNancy Mildred Short, md10/3/1876
John, bc1800, Petersburg, Dinw Co, fLucian, wCaroline Garrettson
Margaret, b18--, Shen Co, h-- Robinson
Mary, b17--, Gile Co?, fThomas, hChristian Snidow
Mollie, b1860, Amel Co, d1888,

BURKE (continued)
hGeorge Thomas Allen
Richard Floyd, b17--, Nott Co?, wElizabeth Greenhill Leigh
Richard Floyd, b12/29/1851, "Pleasant Hill", nrBlackstone, Nott Co, fRichard Henry Leigh, mSarah Irby, wLucy Alice Sears, md5/27/1874
Richard Henry Leigh, b182-, Nott Co, fSamuel Dudley, wSarah Irby
Samuel Dabney, b17--, Nott Co?, fRichard Floyd, mElizabeth Greenhill Leigh
BURKETT, William, bc1840, Shen Co?, wKate Zirkle
BURKHOLDER, Barbara, b17--, Shen Co, hChristian Myers
David, b17--, Page Co?, wBarbara Blosser
Frank, bc1860, Rkhm Co, wEmma Hall
John, b18--, wLucy Huff
Margaret, b9/26/1804, Rkhm Co?, fPeter, hJonas Blosser
BURKS, Eliza, b18--, Pitt Co, hAlbert G Taylor
Sarah, b181-, Bedf Co, d1876, hWilliam L Paxton Jr
BURNER, --, b18--, hAbraham Golladay
Elizabeth, bc1810, Rkhm Co?, hAndrew Bertram
Jennie, b18--, Page Co?, hAlfred Koontz
Joseph, b18--, Shen Co, wRebecca Wisman
Sarah, b18--, fIsrael, hJohn W Santmier
BURNETT, Austin, b1830, Patr Co, d1908, w-- Slaughter
Mahala Agnes, b1848, Patr Co, fAustin, m-- Slaughter, hJames M Hylton
BURNHAM, Robert Franklin, b1848, Albe Co, fLyman, wMary E Clarkson
BURNLEY, Bettie B, b1848, Charlottesville, Albe Co, fDrury W, mCornelia Winston Clark, hThomas Lemen Williamson, md6/7/1876
Drury W, b18--, Albe Co?, wCornelia Winston Clark
BURNS, Jane, b18--, Blan Co,

BURNS (continued)
hLorenzo Dow Dunbar
William, b185-, Fair Co?, wLula Harrison
BURRELL, Nancy, b18--, Salem, Roan Co, hFrederick Johnston
BURROUGHS, Mary Virginia, bc1847, Bedf Co, d1919, fJoseph Nick, hThomas Morgan Jr, mdc1868
Samuel N, bc1860, Bedf Co?, wEmma B Hancock
William, bc1860, Fair Co?, wAlice Shreve
BURRUSS, Robert, bc1840, Oran Co?, wAnn Graves
Woodson Cheadle, b18--, Richmond, wCora Emmett McDowell
BURTNER, Gertrude, bc1870, Keezletown, Rkhm Co, fSolomon, mHarriet Dudley, hJohn N Garber, md12/21/1892
Solomon, b18--, Rkhm Co?, wHarriet Dudley
William, bc1850, Hamp Co?, w Virginia Reid
BURTON, Alexander, b17--, wElizabeth Leftwichy, md4/14/1796
Cornelia, b18--, Camp Co?, fJohn H, mMargaret Macon, hEdward Dunscomb Christian
Jesse Alexander, b18--, Bedf Co?, wDamaris Cobbs
John H, bc1800, Camp Co?, wMargaret Macon
John Madison, b6/7/1848, Bedf Co, fJesse Alexander, mDamaris Cobbs, wEllen Berry, md11/1881
Julia, b18--, Russ Co?, hKent Banner
BURWELL, Agnes Atkinson, b9/28/1850, "Carter Hill", Clar Co, d1921, fGeorge H, hRobert Powell Page Jr, md12/18/1873
Armistead, b17--, Meck Co, f Lewis, (1)m Anne Spotswood, wLucy Crawley
Armistead, b1809, Fran Co, d1882, fJohn Spotswood, mEliza Wood, wMary Elizabeth Hix
Armistead, b4/21/1840, "Woburn", Meck Co, fJohn Armistead, mLucy Penn Guy
Anne Spotswood, b17--, Meck Co, fLewis, (1)mAnne Spotswood, hJohn Stark Ravenscroft

BURWELL (continued)
Blair, b17--, Meck Co, fLewis, (1)mAnne Spotswood, 1wElizabeth Hatcher, 2wDelia Harris
Blair Randolph, b9/15/1850, Taylor's Store, Fran Co, fArmistead, mMary Elizabeth Hix, 1wMary Louise Bodley, 2wHelen Springfellow, md1901
Charles Sturdivant, b3/12/1842, "Woburn", Meck Co, fJohn Armistead, mLucy Penn Guy
Christiana, b17--, Meck Co, fLewis, (1)mAnne Spotswood, hWilliam Hamblin
Edward Bouldin, b2/25/1857, "Woburn", Meck Co, fJohn Armistead, mLucy Penn Guy, wRosa B Sneed
Elizabeth, b167-, fLewis, hBenjamin Harrison
Elizabeth, b17--, fNathaniel, hWilliam Nelson, md2/1738
Elizabeth, b3/6/1844, "Woburn", Meck Co, fJohn Armistead, m Lucy Penn Guy, hC H Pearson
Elizabeth Blair, b17--, Meck Co, fLewis, (1)mAnne Spotswood, hEdward Tabb
Frances, b17--, Glou Co, hJohn Page
Harriet, b17--, Meck Co, fLewis, (1)mAnne Spotswood
Henry H, bc1800, Meck Co, fLewis, (2)mElizabeth Harrison, wCatherine Buford
Jane Blair, bc1800, Meck Co, fLewis, (2)mElizabeth Harrison, hWilliam Eaton
John Armistead, b18--, "Woburn", Meck Co, fArmistead, mLucy Crawley, wLucy Penn Guy
John Eaton, b5/13/1838, "Woburn", Meck Co, d186-, fJohn Armistead, mLucy Penn Guy
John Spotswood, b17--, Meck Co, fLewis, (1)mAnne Spotswood, wEliza Wood
Lewis, b16--, Glou Co?, 1wAbigail Smith
Lewis, b9/26/1745, Meck Co?, 1wAnne Spotswood, 2wElizabeth Harrison
Lewis II, b17--, Meck Co, fLewis, (1)mAnne Spotswood, wSallie Green

BURWELL (continued)
Lucy, b16--, Midd Co?, fLewis, (1)m Abigail Smith, hEdmund Berkeley
Lucy, b18--, "Woburn", Meck Co, fArmistead, mLucy Crawley, h--Sturdivant
Lucy Frances, b10/1/1849, "Woburn", Meck Co, fJohn Armistead, mLucy Penn Guy, hAlexander Overby
Martha Christian, bc1800, Meck Co, fLewis, (2)mElizabeth Harrison, hGrandison Field
Mary Armistead, b17--, Meck Co, fLewis, (1)mAnne Spotswood, hSamuel Goode Armistead
Matilda, b17--, Meck Co, fLewis, (1)mAnne Spotswood
Matilda, b18--, "Woburn", Meck Co, fArmistead, mLucy Crawley, hLewis Burwell
Nancy Taylor, b18--, "Woburn", Meck Co, fArmistead, mLucy Crawley
Nathaniel, b18--, Clar Co, w Dorothy Willing Page
Page, b8/1845, Millwood, Clar Co, fGeorge H, hThomas Hugh Burwell Randolph
Panthea, b17--, Meck Co, fLewis, (1)mAnne Spotswood, hRichard Boyd
Peyton Randolph, bc1800, Meck Co, fLewis, (2)mElizabeth Harrison, wJane Ludwell
Polly, b18--, "Woburn", Meck Co, fArmistead, mLucy Crawley
Sallie Christian, b5/4/1852, "Woburn", Meck Co, fJohn Armistead, mLucy Penn Guy, hTucker T Hamlin
Spotswood, b17--, Meck Co, f Lewis, (1)mAnne Spotswood, wMary Green Marshall
Thomas Guy, b1/5/1835, "Woburn", Meck Co, fJohn Armistead, mLucy Penn Guy
Virginia, b17--, Meck Co, fLewis, (1)mAnne Spotswood
BUSH, Albert, bc1840, Fred Co?, wRachel Campbell
BUSHONG, Mary Elizabeth, b18--, Augu Co, fIsaac A, hMuscoe L Hawkins
BUSTER, Ann, b9/29/1776, hJohn M

BUSTER (continued)
Wingfield
Mary Ann, b18--, Kana Co?, hJoseph D Stratton
Nancy, b1822, Ft Blackmore, Scot Co, d1890, hRobert K Cox
BUTCHER, Edward W, b1852, Petersburg, Dinw Co, wNannie Gilliam
BUTLER, --, bc1800, Caro Co, 2w of Warner Lewis
Alice J, b18--, Hano Co, hJames B Puller
Jane, b17--, Fair Co?, d185-, hCharles Fleming Ford Sr
Virginia, b1838, Richmond, hJames Clark Watson Sr
BUTTON, Caroline Virginia, b18--, Lynchburg, Camp Co, d1898, fCharles W, mMary Elizabeth Zollickoffer, hThomas Edward Coulborn
Charles Fletcher, b18--, Harpers Ferry, Jeff Co, fCharles W, mMary Elizabeth Zollickoffer
Charles W, b7/25/1822, Harpers Ferry, Jeff Co, fCharles, mJane Read, wMary Elizabeth Zollickoffer
Eugene A, b18--, Camp Co, f Charles W, mMary Elizabeth Zollickoffer
Joseph, b10/31/1865, Lynchburg, Camp Co, fCharles, mMary Elizabeth Zollickoffer, wAnnie (Donald) Shotwell
Mary Elizabeth, b18--, Lynchburg, Camp Co, fCharles W, mMary Elizabeth Zollickoffer, hEdwin A Warfield
BYARS, Araminta, b1863, Glade Springs, Wash Co, hJefferson Davis McChesney
Sarah, b18--, Smyt Co, hThomas T Hull
BYERLE, Ella, bc1860, Rkhm Co, fJacob, mMargaret Roller
Fannie M, bc1860, Rkhm Co, fJacob, mMargaret Roller, hJames Robert Lupton, md2/12/1879
Jacob, b18--, Rkhm Co, wMargaret Roller
Jennie, bc1860, Rkhm Co, fJacob, mMargaret Roller

BYERLE (continued)
Lucy, bc1860, Rkhm Co, fJacob, mMargaret Roller
Martha, bc1860, Rkhm Co, fJacob, mMargaret Roller
Peter D, bc1860, Rkhm Co, fJacob, mMargaret Roller
BYERS, Sam Jr, b4/17/1836, nr Burketown, Augu Co, d1915, fSam Sr, mNancy Patterson, 1wCatherine Cline, 2wMartha Sheets
BYRD, A James, bc1860, Acco Co?, wCora Mears
Adam McClintic, b5/6/1869, Williamsville, High Co, fJohn Thomas, mSarah Rebecca McClintic
Andrew Hamilton, b10/19/1790, Bath Co, d1862, fJohn II, m-- Hamilton, wElizabeth Capito
Annie Sue, b186-, Williamsville, High Co, fJohn Thomas, mSarah Rebecca McClintic, hHugh Francisco
Charles Andres, bc1860, Williamsville, High Co, fJohn Thomas, mSarah Rebecca McClintic
Clifton Ellis, b186-, Williamsville, High Co, fJohn Thomas, mSarah Rebecca McClintic
Cornelia, bc1860, Williamsville, High Co, fJohn Thomas, mSarah Rebecca McClintic, h Carroll Garnett
Elizabeth, b17--, Camp Co?, fFrancis Otway, hAlexander Tompkins
Elizabeth, b18--, Mill Gap, High Co, 1w of John Clifton Matheny Sr, md12/22/1864
Elkanah, bc1848, Henry Co, d1910, fLewis D, wFrances Wagington
Francis Otway, b17--, Camp Co?, fWilliam III, mElizabeth Carter
Hale Houston, bc1870, Williamsville, High Co, fJohn Thomas, mSarah Rebecca McClintic
James F, b185-, High Co?, 1h of Minnie Byrd
Jane, b17--, hJohn Page
John Thomas, b5/22/1828, nrWarm Springs, Bath Co, d1912, fAn-

BYRD (continued)
drew Hamilton, mElizabeth Capito, wSarah Rebecca McClintic
Maria Horsemander, b17--, "Westover", Clar Co?, hWilliam E, hJohn Page, md1784
Marshall, b184-, Henry Co, f Lewis D
Matilda, bc1810, Gray Co, hJames Livesay
Minnie, b186-, Williamsville, High Co, fJohn Thomas, mSarah Rebecca McClintic, 1hJames F Byrd, 2hDan L Harry
Samuel, bc1840, Henry Co, fLewis D
Serena, b1835, Bloxom, Acco Co, hWilliam Somers
Thomas, b184-, Henry Co, fLewis D
William III, b17--, Camp Co?, wEliabeth Carter
BYRN, --, bc1730, Clar Co?, wJean McCormick
BYRNE, Nannie, bc1870, Warr Co, fJohn S, 1w of Henry Hawkins Downing
BYRNES, Victoria, b10/1863, Blan Co, hJohn S Cecil
BYRNSIDES, --, b18--, Monr Co?, hBenjamin Alexander Stuart Walker, Sr
BYWATERS, --, bc1800, Fauq Co?, hJames Richard Luttrell
Elizabeth, b18--, Culp Co?, hJames Richard Nelson
Oscar, bc1850, Clar Co?, wAnnie Glaize
CABELL, Annie B, Nels Co, 2w of Ammi Moore Jr, md187-
Annie Woolstan, bc1840, Fred Co?, hHenry Lee Cabell
Elvira, b17--, "Union Hill", 1h-- Henry, 2hJames Bruce
Emma, b18--, Char Co, hPaul S Carrington
George W, bc1800, Nels Co, fSamuel Jordan
Henry Lee, bc1829, Fred Co?, wAnnie Woolstan Cabell
Joseph, b17--, fWilliam, wMary Hopkins, md1752
Louisa, bc1800, "Union Hill", Nels Co, fWilliam H, hHenry Carrington
M Callie, bc1870, Inglewood,

CABELL (continued)
Nels Co, fPatrick Henry, mBettie Eubank
Mayo, bc1800, Nels Co?, wMargaret B Daniel
Patrick Henry, b18--, Inglewood, Nels Co, fGeorge W, wBettie Eubank
Patrick Henry Carey, b186-, Inglewood, Nels Co, fPatrick Henry, mBetty Eubank
Robert G, b18--, Richmond?, wMargaret Caskie
Robert Gamble, b18--, Richmond, wAnne Branch
Sallie, b1830, Camp Co, d1902, 2w of Asa D Dickinson
Samuel Jordan, b1756, Amhe Co?, d1818, fWilliam Jr
Samuel Jordan, b8/22/1867, Stephens City, Fred Co, fHenry Lee, mAnnie Woolstan, wVirginia LeHew, md11/12/1907
William Jr, b1730, Albe Co, fWilliam Sr
William D, b1/13/1834, Union Hill, Nels Co, fMayo, mMargaret B Daniel, wMary V Ellet
CADWALLADER, Anabel, bc1840, nrStephens City, Fred Co, fEzra, hJohn Gregory
Bettie, b184-, nrStephens City, Fred Co, fEzra
Ella, b184-, nrStephens City, Fred Co, fEzra
Fannie, bc1840, nrStephens City, Fred Co fEzra
George, bc1840, nrStephens City, Fred Co, fEzra
James M Sr, b184-, nrStephens City, Fred Co, d1917, fEzra, wCornelia Baker
John, bc1840, nrStephens City, Fred Co, fEzra
Scott, bc1840, nrStephens City, Fred Co, fEzra
CAGE, Carrie, b18--, Hali Co, fFielding, hNewton Isaac Watlhall
CALDWELL, Archibald, b17--, Crai Co, fJames, w-- Trout
Caroline, b18--, Crai Co, fJohn, hWilliam Ellis
Celestine, b18--, Augu Co, h David Dillar Coyner
Charles Russell, b9/1/1869,

CALDWELL (continued)
nrLewisburg, Grbr Co, fD C B
D C B, b18--, Fred Co?, fJoseph Franklin, mAnn Tyler Mitchell
Jennie, b18--, Glebe Farm, nrCumberland Court House, Cumb Co, fThomas, m-- Anderson, hWilliam C Corson
John B, b1836, Crai Co, d1912, wFannie Givens
Joseph Franklin, b17--, Bruceton, Fred Co, wAnn Tyler Mitchell
Susanna, b185-, Crai Co, m-- Smith, hJohn A Ferrel
Thomas, b18--, Cumb Co, w-- Anderson
CALE, Elizabeth, b17--, Hamp Co?, hGeorge Nichols Spaid
CALHOUN, Mary, b18--, Page Co, hS M Kendrick
CALLAHAM, Hillary Mosley, b1840, nrMt Zion, Camp Co, fElisha, wMildred Robinson Maddox
Robert Walsa, b11/17/1867, nrMt Zion, Camp Co, fHillary Mosley, mMildred Robinson Maddox, wMattie Iola Flynn, mdc1889
CALLAWAY, Elizabeth Maxwell, b18--, Fran Co, hThomas Yeatman Mosby
George C Sr, b6/1/1853, Nels Co, fPaul C, wPattie Aylet
Henry Tate, b18--, Fran Co, wTabitha Guerrant
James, b18--, Fran Co, fWilliam, m-- Langhorne, w-- Greer
Matilda, b17--, fWilliam, hJames Leftwich, md11/22/1797
Susan E, b18--, Callaway, Fran Co, fHenry, mTabitha Guerrant, hThomas
Thomas, b18--, nrRockymount, Fran Co, fJames, m-- Greer, wSusan E Callaway
CALLOWAY, Granville, b1814, nr Peterstown, Monr Co, d1898, wMary Hobbs
Margaret, b1844, Athens, Merc Co, fGranville, mMary Hobbs, hWilliam H Robertson
CALLIS, Amelia Frances, b1824, Brun Co, d1894, hSamuel Wilkins Ozlin
Georgeanna, b10/18/1836, Norfolk, fWilliam, m-- Simmons,

CALLIS (continued)
2w of Albert Lawrence West
CALLISON, James H, b11/11/1822, nrMiddlebrook, Augu Co, d1889, fWilliam Jackson, m-- ( ) Harris, wIsabelle Patrick McCutcheon
James S, b1/2/1865, nrMiddlebrook, Augu Co, fJames H, mIsabelle Patrick McCutcheon, wCarrie McClure, md6/29/1891
John, b182-, nrMiddlebrook, Augu Co, fWilliam Jackson, m-- ( ) Harris
Mary Dell, b186-, nrMiddlebrook, Augu Co, fJames H, mIsabbelle Patrick McCutcheon, hM D Waller
William Jackson, b17--, Poca Co, w-- ( ) Harris
CALVERT, G R, bc1840, Rkbr Co, wAnnie Clinedinst
Matthew James Preston Hughes, b18--, Rapp Co?, 1h of Anne B Mosby
William H, bc1833, Fred Co, d1901, wAraminta Barr
CAMDEN, Annie Thompson, b18--, fJohnson M, mAnn Thompson, hBaldwin Day Spilman, md6/1/1886
Belle, b1870, Bryant, Nels Co, d1892, hGeorge T Mawyer
Horsel⸺ Barnes, b18--, Nels Co, wWillie Thomas
John S, b186-, Amhe Co, fRobert M, Louise W Thompson
Robert Lee, b5/11/1861, Amhe Co, fRobert M, mLouise W Thompson
Robert M, b1830, Nels Co, d186-, 1h of Louise W Thompson
CAMM, Elizabeth, b18--, hDavid Patteson
CAMP, Benjamin Franklin, Franklin, Sout Co, fGeorge Jr, mSallie Cutchins
Elizabeth Barron, b18--, fGeorge Washington, mElizabeth Barron Armistead, hTench Francis Tilghman Jr
James Leonidas, b12/30/1857, Franklin, Sout Co, fGeorge Jr, mSallie Cutchins, wCarrie Savage, md10/22/1884
John Stafford, b18--, Franklin,

CAMP (continued)
Sout Co, fGeorge Jr, mSallie Cutchins
John W, b1814, Glou Co, fWilliam S, mFrances V Heywood, wHarriet E Cooper
Mary Eliza, b18--, Franklin, Sout Co, fGeorge Jr, mSallie Cutchins, hJohn A Williams
Paul Douglas, b10/25/1849, Franklin, Sout Co, fGeorge Jr, mSallie Cutchins, wElla Virginia Cobb, md1/29/1880
Robert Judson, b11/9/1854, Franklin, Sout Co, d1915, fGeorge Jr, mSallie Cutchins, wCora Antoinette Vaughan, md6/24/1880
Sarah Virginia, b18--, Franklin, Sout Co, fGeorge Jr, mSallie Cutchins, hNathaniel Norfleet
William Carter, b2/6/1856, Richmond, fJohn W, mHarriet E Cooper, 1wSallie S Young, md10/1882, 2wAnnie Bell, md8/25/1921
William Nelson, b9/17/1847, Franklin, Sout Co, fGeorge Jr, mSallie Cutchins, wTexanna Gay
William S, b17--, Glou Co, wFrances V Heywood
CAMPBELL, Abner, bc1850, nrMiddletown, Fred Co, fRobert
Alexander, b18--, Amhe Co, w Judith Snead
Alexander, b185-, KiWi Co?, wLucy R Garrett
Alexander Spotswood, b18--, Fauq Co, m-- Spotswood, wAnne Horner
Alice Marian, b1869, Hano Co, hWirt Hamilton Cross
Annie, b185-, nrMiddletown, Fred Co, fRobert
Charles Richard, b6/2/1854, nrMiddletown, Fred Co, d1916, fRobert, wEmma S Cooley
Douglas, b17--, Berk Co, fJames, wSarah Wallace Lyle
Edward, bc1790, Wash Co, wRhoda Trigg
Hannah, bc1800, Rkbr Co?, hWilliam Blair Donald
Harry, b18--, Fauq Co, fAlexander Spotswood, mAnne Horner,

CAMPBELL (continued)
w-- Muller
Henry Wood, b7/9/1866, Amhe Co, fThomas H, mHenry Virginia Wood, wEmmie Eley, md6/4/1895
Hugh Lyle, b18--, Berk Co, fDouglas, mSarah Wallace Lyle, wMary Eliza Van Meter
Ira R, bc1850, Russ Co?, wAlly Lockhart
James Alexander, b5/31/1841, Bedf Co, d1895, fAlexander, mJudith Snead, wMary Alice Cox, md2/18/1867
James R, b184-, nrMiddletown, Fred Co, fRobert
Jane, bc1800, Taze Co?, f Charles, hThomas Tate
Josephine Horner, b18--, "Spotswood", Fauq Co, fAlexander Spotswood, mAnne Horner, hAlbert Winmill
Leroy, b18--, mMary Cooke, w Nancy Petty
Louis, b18--, Albe Co, fWiley, wElizabeth Brown
Martha, b18--, Wash Co, hJacob Barnett Kent
Mary, b18--, Abingdon, Wash Co, fEdward, mRhoda Trigg, hConnally Findlay Trigg
Mary, b185-, nrMiddletown, Fred Co, fRobert, hRobert Lindamood
Mary Anne, bc1800, West Co?, hRobert Mayo
Mary Jane, b18--, fAndrew, mAnn Hawkins, hNathaniel Hardin Roberts
Mary L, bc1850, High Co?, fA H, mIsabel Lewis, hLucius Holmes Stephenson
Millie, b18--, Fauq Co?, fAlexander Spotswood, mAnne Horner, hInman Evans
Minnie E, bc1870, Lynchburg, Camp Co, fJames Alexander, mMary Alice Cox, hN D Eller
Nancy, b10/10/1849, nrRoanoke, Meck Co, fLeroy, mNancy Petty, hWilliam Littleberry Williamson
Nannie Rebecca, b11/1842, "Stony Mead", Fred Co, fRobert Madison, mRebecca Lockhart, 2w of William Wood Glass
Olivia Henderson, b18--, Gooc

CAMPBELL (continued)
Co, 3w of William H Hening Sr
Rachel, b184-, nrMiddletown, Fred Co, fRobert, hAlbert Bush
Robert C, b18--, Fauq Co, fAlexander Spotswood, mAnne Horner, w-- Mosby
Robert Madison, b18--, Fred Co?, wRebecca Lockhart
Rosebud, bc1870, Amhe Co, f Thomas H, mHenry Virginia Wood
Sallie, b18--, Wash Co?, hJoseph L C Smith
Thomas H, b1843, Albe Co, fLouis, mElizabeth Brown, w Henry Virginia Wood
Virginia, b186-, Amhe Co, f Thomas H, mHenry Virginia Wood, hGeorge Washington Smith
W P, b186-, Bath Co?, wEmma Trotter McClintic
Walter D, b186-, Lynchburg, Camp Co, fJames Alexander, mMary Alice Cox, wAnne Rockenbach
William, bc1800, Taze Co?, fCharles
William Creighton, b12/6/1850, Gerandstown, Berk Co, fHugh Lyle, mMary Eliza Van Meter, wAnna Gale Child
William H, b18--, Hano Co?, wSallie Brown
CANDLER, John T, b18--, Bedf Co?, wMartha Kiser
CANNADAY, Harriet, b18--, Roan Co?, hFloyd W Edwards
Rhoda Jane, b6/19/1859, Willowton, --- Co, hMastin Clay McCorkle
CANNON, Augusta, b18--, Manassas, PrWi Co, fFrank, mCatherine Woodyard, hJacob Hornbaker
Edward Y, bc1823, Richmond, fHenry Cannon, mElizabeth S Lines
Elizabeth L, bc1870, Richmond, fHenry G, mMargaret Blair, hSamuel M Price
Frederick M, b183-, Richmond, fHenry, mElizabeth S Lines
Henry G, b11/17/1830, Richmond, fHenry, mElizabeth S Lines, wMargaret Blair
Sarah, b18--, Fluv Co, 2w of Henry A Parrish

CANNON (continued)
Thomas B, bc1870, Richmond, fHenry G, mMargaret Blair
CANTER, Daniel, b185-, Fred Co, fIsaac W Jr, mSusan McCauley
Elizabeth, b184-, Fred Co, f Isaac W Jr, mSusan McCauley, h-- Wise
Ettie, b5/10/1857, Fred Co, fIsaac W JR, mSusan McCauley, hGeorge Butler Wright
Isaac W Jr, b1813, nrKernstown, Fred Co, d1897, fIsaac W Sr, wSusan McCauley
Isaac W III, bc1850, Fred Co, fIsaac W Jr, mSusan McCauley
James, b184-, Fred Co, fIsaac W Jr, mSusan McCauley
John, b184-, Fred Co, fIsaac W Jr, mSusan McCauley
Margaret, b185-, Fred Co, f Isaac W Jr, mSusan McCauley
Martha, b185-, Fred Co, fIsaac W Jr, mSusan McCauley, h-- Steele
Susan J, b185-, Fred Co, fIsaac W Jr, mSusan McCauley, h-- Wagner
CANTRELL, Melinda, b18--, Dick Co?, hGeorge Dyer
CAPITO/CAPITEAU, Elizabeth "Betsy", b1/11/1797, Franklin, Pend Co, d1888, hAndrew Hamilton Byrd
CAPPER, E Bruce, b2/25/1862, nrCapon Springs, Hamp Co, f Meridith, mMalinda Spaid
Irene, b185-, nrCapon Springs, Hamp Co, fMeredith, mMalinda Spaid
Jane, b181-, nrCapon Springs, Hamp Co, fMichael, mRebecca La Follette, hWilliam Sollars
John, b18--, nrCapper Springs (now Rockenon Springs), Hamp Co, fMicheal, mRebecca LaFollette
John, b185-, nrCapon Springs, Hamp Co, fMeredith, mMalinda Spaid
Ira S, b185-, nrCapon Springs, Hamp Co, fMeredith, mMalinda Spaid
Letitia, b185-, nrCapon Springs, Hamp Co, fMeredith, mMalinda Spaid

CAPPER (continued)
Lydia, b181-, nrCapper Springs (now Rockenon Springs), Hamp Co, fMichael, mRebecca LaFollette, hNicholas Lee
Mary "Pop", b181-, nrCapper Springs (now Rockenon Springs), Hamp Co, fMichael, mRebecca LaFollette, hJames Garvin
Meredith, b1820, nrCapper Springs (now Rockenon Springs), Hamp Co, d1906, f Micheal, mRebecca LaFollette, wMalinda Spaid
Michael, b17--, Hamp Co, wRebecca LaFollette
Michael John, b2/25/1862, nr Capon Springs, Hamp Co, fMeredith, mMalinda Spaid, wMattie G Bromley, md11/23/1899
Sarah, bc1860, nrCapon Springs, Hamp Co, fMeredith, mMalinda Spaid
Walter, b185-, nrCapon Springs, Hamp Co, fMeredith, mMalinda Spaid
CAPPS, Leonard O, b18--, Norfolk?, wMary F James
Washington Lee, b1/31/1864, Portsmouth, Norf Co, fWashington Tazewell, mFrances Bernard, wEdna Ward, md1911
Washington Tazewell, b18--, Norf Co?, wFrances Bernard
CARBAUGH, Anna M, b18--, Stephens City, Fred Co, fAdam, mMary Groniger, hWilliam F Powers
CARDEN, Robert, bc1850, Hano Co?, wOra Nuckols
CARDER, Charles R, b18--, Rapp Co?, fWilliam, wAnna Rosson
James Madison, bc1814, Bedf Co?, d1890
Macon Page, bc1857, Bedf Co, d1919, fJames Madison, wClara Fifer
CARDOSA, M, bc1830, PrEd Co?, wKatherine Cabell Watkins
CARDWELL, Mary Elizabeth, b18--, nrConcord, Camp Co, d1876, fJohn, hBradley W Babcock
CARICO, Jane, b1852, Gray Co, 2w of Absolom McCarty Jr
Matilda, b1849, Gray Co, d1887,

CARICO (continued)
1w of Absolom McCarty Jr
CARLETON, --, b17--, KiQu Co?, hWilliam Corr
CARLTON, Walter R, bc1860, Nhld Co, wGrace Douglas DeShields
CARLIN, Charles C, b4/4/1866, Alexandria, fWilliam, mElizabeth Eskridge, wLilian Broders
CARMICHAEL, Georgie C, b18--, hHarry C Bowen
CARNE, Amanda Rosalie, bc1860, Alexandria, fWilliam F, mEmma Virginia Markell
William Francis, b10/4/1866, Alexandria, fWilliam F, mEmma Virginia Markell, 1wAnnie Elizabeth Appich, 2wCornelia Stoutenberg
CARNEGY, Anne, bc1800, nrWhitePost, Clar Co, fWilliam, mElizabeth --hThomas Kennerly
William, b17--, nrWhite Post, Clar Co, wElizabeth --
CARNER, John W, b7-28-1846, Bedf Co, wAnnie E Jones
CARNOHAN, Sallie J, b18--, Spot Co?, d1911, hJoseph Patrick Henry Crismond, md1866
CARPENTER, Alfred, b18--, Albe Co?, wFrances White
Elizabeth, b18--, Rkhm Co?, hJoseph Altaffer
Emily Anne, b18--, Madi Co?, fUriel, hFielding Jefferson Smith
Frank, b18--, Bedf Co?, wMary Moore
J C, b184-, Grbr Co, fSamuel
J C, bc1850, Loui Co?, wSallie L Herring
Joseph H Sr, b8/28/1867, Falling Springs, Grbr Co, fSamuel Stuben, mMary Ann Griffin, wEvelyn Harlow, md1897
Mary, b186-, Ashland, Hano Co, fWilliam J, mIndiana H Wingfield, hJames Garrett White, md11/30/1887
Nancy, b12/31/1837, Acco Co, fRevel, mElizabeth Bowden, hJohn W Johnson
R F, b186-, Falling Spring, Grbr Co, fSamuel Stuben, mMary Ann Griffith
Revel, b18--, Acco Co, wEliza-

CARPENTER (continued)
beth Bowden
Samuel, bc1810, Crai Co?, w-- Hannah
Samuel, b18--, Bote Co?, fWilliam
Samuel C, bc1870, Falling Spring, Grbr Co, fSamuel Stubem, mMary Ann Griffith
Samuel Stuben, b1842, Grbr Co, fSamuel, wMary Ann Griffith
Sophia Jane, b18--, Madi Co, hJohn Henry Lillard
Stephen Alfred, b4/23/1851, Albe Co, d1912, fAlfred, mFrances White, wMargaret A Teel, md1/22/1885
Thomas, b18--, Madi Co?, fUriel W H, bc1840, Shen Co, wSallie Baker
William J, b18--, Hano Co?, wIndiana Wingfield
CARPER, John, bc1840, Clar Co?, wSallie Levi
Virginia, bc1860, hJames Reid Wills, md1/21/1880
CARR, Aaron B, b18--, Wash Co?, wMary A --
Ann Winston, b18--, Henry Co?, hGeorge Waller
Clay, b1/13/1868, Warr Co, fJohn Thomas, wSue Bryan Wharton, md4/13/1898
Edward B, b1855, Merc Co, f Shannon, m-- Allen, wEva Mae Elliston
Fannie, b186-, Warr Co, fJohn Thomas, hJ W Eddy
Irene, b186-, Warr Co, fJohn Thomas, hThomas B Levi
James Thomas, b18--, Loud Co?, w-- Hansbrough
Jane B, b17--, hWilson Cary
Jane Cary, b180-, fDabney, h Peyton Harrison
Jesse, bc1870, Warr Co, fJohn Thomas
John Thomas, b18--, Leesburg, Loud Co, d1894, fJames Thomas, m-- Hansbrough
Louisa, b1836, Upperville, Fauq Co, d1896, hEdward Poinsett Tayloe
Lucy, bc1860, Warr Co, fJohn Thomas, hHenry D Levi
Lizzie, b186-, Warr Co, fJohn

CARR (continued)
Thomas, hJacob O Levi
Nannie M, b1848, Pitt Co, d1910, hRobert T Waller
Nannie, bc1870, Warr Co, fJohn Thomas, hR C Levi
Peter H, b1/29/1843, nrLeesburg, Loud Co, wRoberta E Elgin
Sara, b11/19/1719, Caro Co, fThomas, mMary Dabney, hJohn Minor, md11/14/1732
Sarah Elizabeth, b18--, PrAn Co, hJohn B Diggs
Shannon, b18--, Merc Co, d1889, h-- Allen
Thomas, b16--, wMary Dabney
CARRELL, Mary, bc1700, Lanc Co?, hThomas Hunton I
CARRICO, --, b18--, Buck Co?, wElizabeth Heatwole
B A, bc1870, Augu Co?, wElmira Bolen
CARRINGTON, A Berkeley, b1/27/1862, Char Co, fAlexander B, mFrances "Fannie" Venable, wMary Taylor, md1901
A Randolph Sr, b7/1865, Char Co, fHenry Alexander, mCharlotte E Cullen, 1wElla N Gordon, 2wElizabeth Cook
Alexander B, bc1836, Char Co, fPaul S, mEmma Cabell, wFrances Venable
Charles Venable, b7/29/1866, Char Co, fAlexander B, mFrances Venable, wAvis Walker, md6/6/1844
Emma, b1/22/1843, Char Co, f Henry, mLouisa Cabell, hJohn William Riely
Florence A, bc1860, Char Co, fHenry Alexander, mCharlotte E Cullen, hSydney G Stevens
George, b17--, Char Co, fPaul, (1)mMargaret Read, w-- Tucker
Henry, b1792, Char Co, fPaul, (2)mPriscilla Sims, wLouisa Cabell
Henry Alexander, bc1840, Char Co, d1884, fHenry, mLouisa Cabell, wCharlotte E Cullen
Henry, bc1860, Char Co, fHenry Alexander, mCharlotte E Cullen
John Bonaparte, b17--, Char Co, fGeorge, m-- Tucker, wJudith

CARRINGTON (continued)
Wimbish
John Cullen, bc1860, Char Co, d1918, fHenry Alexander, m Charlotte E Cullen
Lottie, bc1860, Char Co, fHenry Alexander, mCharlotte E Cullen, hWilliam Cunningham
Louise, b185-, Char Co, fHenry Alexander, mCharlotte E Cullen, hWilliam Leigh
Louise Cabell, bc1846, Char Co, d1909, fPaul, hAndrew Reid Venable
Mary Anne, b18--, Amel Co, 1w of Thomas Penn Fitzpatrick Sr
Matthew, b186-, Char Co, fHenry Alexander, mCharlotte E Cullen
Otelia M, b185-, Char Co, fHenry Alexander, mCharlotte E Cullen, hJohn S Cunningham
Paul, b3/16/1733, Cumb Co, fGeorge, m-- Mayo, 2wPriscilla Sims, 1wMargaret Read
Paul S, bc1800, Char Co?, wEmma Cabell
Sallie Tucker, b18--, Meck Co, 2w of Thomas Leigh
Tazewell Morton, b2/21/1857, Richmond, fWilliam Tucker, mBettie L Morton, wJulia M Watkins, md1/21/1886
William Cabell, bc1860, Char Co, d1918, fHenry Alexander, mCharlotte E Cullen
William Tucker, b1831, Hali Co, fJohn Bonaparte, mJudith Wimbish, wBettie Morton
CARROLL, --, bc1860, Shen Co, wSarah Elizabeth Stoner
Aandres C, b18--, Loui Co?, fJohn, m-- Perkins, wMartha C Payne
C T, bc1860, Clar Co?, wEmma May Smallwood
E L, bc1860, PrWi Co?, wNannie Neville Leachman
Jacob S, bc1800, wIsabel Layman
James Payne Sr, b3/31/1869, Charlottesville, Albe Co, fAndrew C, mMartha C Payne, wNorah Clarke, md11/1895
John Wesley, b3/3/1832, Staunton, Augu Co, d1898, fJacob S, mIsabel Layman, 1wSarah Elizabeth Compton, md1850, 2wMary B

CARROLL (continued)
Carroll, md1881
John W, bc1860, Charlottesville, Albe Co, fAndrew C, mMartha C Payne
Mary, b1/1/1809, White Oak Grove, Floy Co, d1909, hJoseph Roop
Mary B, b18--, Lynchburg, Camp Co, fJohn Wesley, (1)mSarah Elizabeth Compton, hJohn E Gannaway, md1881
CARSON, Birdie, bc1870, Grant, Gray Co, hRobert E Lee Greear, md3/20/1891
Lizzie, b18--, Pitt Co?, fMatthew Joseph, hAlonzo Thomas Adkerson
Martha, b17--, Fred Co?, hJared Williams
Mollie J, bc1860, Gray Co, fRobert, mMary Edwards, hJames Ambrose Livesay, md11/1/1888
Robert, b18--, Gray Co, wMary Edwards
CARTER, --, b18--, Lanc Co, hDavid H James
Adelina, b18--, Lanc Co?, hW L Gungon Mitchell
Alexander, b18--, Fauq Co, fJ Edward, mFanny Scott
Ann, bc1700, fRobert, hBenjamin Harrison
Anna, b18--, Danville, Pitt Co, hWilliam T Walton
Anne Hill, b17--, PrWi Co, fCharles, mAnne Buller Moore, 2w of Henry "Lighthorse Harry" Lee, md1793
C D, b1852, Nels Co, fThomas S, mElizabeth H Moore, wLucy W Dufner, md8/26/1879
Caroline, bc1800, fCharles, m-- Byrd, hElisha Hall
Catherine Spotswood, b17--, ChCi Co, fCharles, mAnne Buller Moore, 1w of Carter Berkeley
Charles, b17--, f"King" Carter, w-- Byrd
Charles, b17--, wAnne Buller Moore
Charles D, b18--, Smyt Co?, wMary Fulton
Charles M, b7/9/1853, Rye Cove, Scot Co, d1899, fSamuel, mEl-

CARTER (continued)
len Horton, 1wMary Ewing Wood, 2wAlice E Cox
Charles W, bc1800, Albe Co?, wMary Cocke
Christian, b18--, Fauq Co, fJ Edward, mFannie Scott
Cora Lee, b11/1870, Wicomico Church, Nhld Co, hBernard E Keane
Cowan W, b11/13/1849, Rye Cove, Scot Co, d1912, fSamuel, wEmily Gilen Waters
Edward, b8/19/1843, nrSalem (now Marshall), Fauq Co, f Richard Henry, wJeanie Turner, md9/1867
Elisha V, b1827, Nels Co, d1896, wMary J Patterson
Eliza, b18--, Fauq Co, fJ Edward, mFannie Scott
Eliza M, b1853, Buck Co, h Charles W Hardiman
Elizabeth, b17--, Camp Co?, hWilliam Byrd III
Elizabeth, b182-, Clar Co, 2w of Levi Hiett
Elizabeth Hill, b18--, Richmond?, hJohn Wickham
Elizabeth Wormeley, b17--, Richmond, fLandon, hNelson Berkeley
Emma, b18--, Floy Co, hHenry Quesenberry
F K, bc1860, Rkbr Co?, w-- Agnor
Fannie, bc1830, Fauq Co, fRichard Henry, mMary Welby DeButts, hR Taylor Scott
French Pendleton, b18--, Rapp Co, fJohn Ferguson, wJudith Terry Miller
George W, b1839, Nels Co, f Thomas S, mElizabeth H Moore
Hill, bc1800, 1h of -- Skipwith
Isaac V, bc1850, Russ Co?, wMary E Meade
J Alexander, b5/5/1848, Scott District, Fauq Co, fRichard Henry, mMary Welby DeButts, wMary S Henley
J DeButts, bc1850, Fauq Co, fRichard Henry, mMary Welby DeButts
J Edward, b17--, Fauq Co, wFannie Scott

CARTER (continued)
James Gibbon, b12/19/853, Richmond, fWilliam Gibbon, mEliza Archer Talley, wDora L Rockner, md1887
Jane Eliza, bc1830, Fauq Co, fJohn Hill, mBaynton Turner, hRobert Beverley
John Armistead, bc1809, fLandon, (2)mMary Armistead, w Richardella DeButts
John Ferguson, b18--, Rapp Co?, fJohn Alexander
John Hill, bc1810, wBaynton Turner
Josiah, b18--, Fauq Co, fJ Edward, mFannie Scott
John L, b18--, Fauq Co, wVirginia Rawlings
Judith, b17--, f"King" Carter
Landon, b16--, Rich Co, fRobert "King", (2)mElizabeth Landon, wElizabeth Wormeley
Landonia, b18--, Fauq Co, fJ Edward, mFannie Scott, hRobert Lawler
Laura J, b18--, Carr Co, fWalter C, mLucy Ann Jennings, hRobert G Wilkinson, md9/14/1880
Louisiana Franklin, b18--, Pitt Co, hThomas David Neal
Lucy A, b10/1838, PrEd Co, d1912, hWilliam K Priddy
Lucy Landon, b17--, Caro Co, hJohn Minor
Margaret, b18--, Russ Co?, d1898, hJohn T Lampkin
Margaret Bruce, bc1870, Smyt Co, fCharles D, mMary Fulton, hHenry Carter Stuart, md2/26/1896
Martha Champ, b4/6/1830, Charlottesville, Albe Co, d1902, fCharles W, mMary Cocke, hMoses Green Peyton
Mary, bc1700, Midd Co?, hJohn Bristow
Mary Lucy, b1831, Point of Forks, Cumb Co, fWilliam, mElizabeth Mayo, hAndrew Jackson Ford Sr
Mary Nicholas, bc1840, Nels Co, d1922, hD H Lee Martz
Mary Taylor, b5/1831, Smithfield, Russ Co, 1w of William

CARTER (continued)
Alexander Stuart
Mary Welby, b185-, Fauq Co, fRichard Henry, mMary Welby DeButts, hWilliam Beverley
Merry, b17--, wFannie Leftwich
Nancy, bc1800, Scot Co, 1w of Emanuel Hutchinson
Nannie, b1850, Clifton, Caro Co, hSamuel C Redd
Nannie, b185-, Fauq Co, fRichard Henry, mMary Welby DeButts, hEdward C Turner
R Welby, b3/11/1837, nrRectortown, Fauq Co, fJohn Armistead, mRichardella DeButts, wSophia Carter, md7/3/1867
Rebecca Welby, b186-, Fauq Co, fEdward, mJeanie Turner
Richard H, b185-, Fauq Co, fRichard Henry, mMary Welby DeButts
Richard Henry, b18--, nrUpperville, Fauq Co, fJ Edward, mFannie Scott, wMary Welby DeButts
Richardetta, b185-, Fauq Co, fRichard Henry, mMary Welby DeButts, hRobert Beverley
Robert N, bc1840, Amhe Co?, wMelvina Turpin
Rosa, b1846, Rye Cove, Scot Co, hGeorge R Dove
S L, b18--, Nels Co, wEugenia L Shields
S S, b1840, Nels Co, fThomas S, mElizabeth H Moore
Sadie, bc1870, Fauq Co, fEdward, mJeanie Turner, hIrwin Fleming
Samuel, b18--, Rye Cove, Scot Co, wEllen Horton
Selina, b184-, Fauq Co, fRichard Henry, mMary Welby DeButts, hJohn H Washington
Shirley, b18--, Rapp Co?, wLucy Meade Hite
Sophia, b3/11/1841, Upperville, Fauq Co, fRichard Henry, hR Welby Carter, md7/3/1867
Thomas S, b1791, Bedf Co, wElizabeth H Moore
Virginia, b18--, Fauq Co, fJ Edward, mFannie Scott
Walter C, b18--, Carr Co?, wLucy Ann Jennings

CARTER (continued)
Willa E, b18--, Nels Co, fThomas S, mElizabeth H Moore, hDavid Bondurant
William, bc1800, wElizabeth Mayo
William Fitzhugh, b18--, Fauq Co, fJ Edward, mFannie Scott
William G, b1866, Independent Hill, PrWi Co, fHenry Everett, mAnn Golden, wMargaret Jane Espey
William Gibbon, b18--, Richmond?, fJames, mMary Gibbon, wEliza Archer Talley
William P, bc1840, Clar Co?, wLucy Randolph Page
CARTWRIGHT, David C, b8/29/1865, Baileysville, Wyom Co, fThomas, mMinerva Morgan, wMary L Taylor
George W, b186-, Baileysville, Wyom Co, fThomas, mMinerva Morgan
Thomas, b18--, Cabe Co, fMoses, mClara Murphy, wMinerva Morgan
Thomas E, b186-, Baileysville, Wyom Co, fThomas, mMinerva Morgan
CARUTHERS, Martha Ann, b18--, Loud Co, 1w of Joel E Beales
CARVER, Joseph S, b1861, Augu Co, wBarbara A Hollar
Margaret, b18--, KiGe Co, h Thacker Rogers
Mary, b18--, Richmond?, hRussell Winch
Mary, b18--, Rkhm Co, hRobert Phillips
CARY, Alexander, b18--, Rapp Co, wEliza Ricketts
Alice, b185-, Glou Co, fEdward B S, mEliza Smith
Archibald, b1721, d1787, wMary Randolph
Charles Edward, b4/4/1847, Glou Co, fEdward B S, mEliza Smith, wVirginia Willis
Edward B S, b18--, Glou Co, wEliza Smith
Elizabeth, b17--, Ches Co, h Benjamin Watkins
Lessie, b184-, Glou Co, fEdward B S, mEliza Smith, 1hFrench Strother, 2hJ Hairston Seawell
Lucius Falkland, b12/14/1815,

CARY (continued)
Oak Hill, Fluv Co, fMiles IV, wLucy Ann Henley
Lucy S, b184-, Glou Co, fEdward B S, mEliza Smith
Mary, b17--, Cumb Co?, 1w of Carter Page
Miles II, bc1655, Warw Co, fMiles, mAnn Taylor, wMary Wilson
Miles III, b16--, fMiles II, mMary Wilson, wSarah Blair
Miles IV, b17--, fWilson, mJane B Carr
Samuel B, bc1850, Glou Co, fEdward B S, mEliza Smith
Virginia, b184-, Glou Co, fEdward B S, mEliza Smith, h-- Horner
Wilson, b17--, fMiles III, m Sarah Blair, wJane B Carr
CASEY, Alice J, bc1870, Lynchburg, Camp Co, fJames, mMary Quinn
Charles M, b9/8/1866, Lynchburg, Camp Co, fJames, mMary Quinn, wMargaret Mallan, md1892
James F, b186-, Lynchburg, Camp Co, fJames, mMary Quinn
Mary A, b186-, Lynchburg, Camp Co, fJames, mMary Quinn, hF J Doherty
P H, b186-, Lynchburg, Camp Co, fJames, mMary Quinn
Rosa E, bc1870, Lynchburg, Camp Co, fJames, mMary Quinn, hWilliam McGrath
CASKIE, Eliza, b18--, Richmond, fJames, mEliza Pinchum, h-- London
Eliza, b185-, Richmond, fJohn Samuel, mFannie Johnson, 1hW D Burke, 2hGeorge Evans
Ellen, b18--, Richmond, fJames, mEliza Pinchum, hRobert Hutchinson
George Evans, b3/20/1858, Richmond, d1919, fJohn Samuel, mFannie Johnson, wRimbrough Ligon, md187-
Harriet Augusta, b18--, Richmond, fJames, mEliza Pinchum, hJohn Scott, md1850
James, b184-, Richmond, fJohn Samuel, mFannie Johnson

CASKIE (continued)
John, bc1850, Richmond, fJohn Samuel, mFannie Johnson
John Samuel, b18--, Richmond, fJames, mEliza Pinchum
Margaret, b18--, Richmond, fJames, mEliza Pinchum, hRobert G Cabell
Nannie, b18--, Richmond, fJames, mEliza Pinchum
Norma Randolph, bc1870, Roan Co?, fJames A, 1w of Aylett B Coleman Sr, md1895
William, b185-, Richmond, fJohn Samuel, mFannie Johnson
CASON, Ann E, b1817, Spot Co, hJames B Rawlings
Elizabeth, b18--, PrAn Co, hJohn West
CASSELL, Elizabeth, bc1800, Wyth Co, 3w of David Whitman
CATHER, Adeline, b181-, Fred Co, fJames, mAnne Howard, hJohn Purcell
Amanda, bc1820, Fred Co, fJames, mAnne Howard
Annie, b184-, Fred Co, fClark, mMargaret Lupton
Barbara Burridge, b18--, Fred Co, fJames, hRobert Brown
Charles F, b18--, Fred Co, fWilliam, mCaroline Smith
Christina, b18--, Fred Co, f Washington, m-- Robinson, h Henry de Haven
Clark, b1816, Fred Co, d1861, fJames, mAnne Howard, wMargaret Lupton
Clark, b185-, Fred Co, fClark, mMargaret Lupton
David, bc1800, Fred Co, fJasper, (2)m-- Bailey
Elizabeth, bc1850, Fred Co, fClark, mMargaret Lupton
Frances, b18--, Fred Co, fJohn, hJonah Lupton Cather
J Howard, b181-, Fred Co, fJames, mAnne Howard, wMillicent Lupton
Howard, b185-, Fred Co, fClark, mMargaret Lupton
J Howard Gore, b18--, Fred Co, fSydney, mMahlon Gore
James, bc1785, Fred Co, fJasper, mBarbara Lawrence, wAnne Howard

CATHER (continued)
James, bc1850, Fred Co, wIda S Lupton
James, b185-, Fred Co, fClark, mMargaret Lupton
Jane, bc1800, Fred Co, fJasper, (2)m-- Bailey
John, bc1780, Fred Co, fJasper, (1)mBarbara Lawrence
John, b181-, Fred Co, fJames, mAnne Howard, wJane Russell
John, b18--, Fred Co, fWashington, m-- Robinson
Jonah Lupton, b7/3/1852, Fred Co, d1915, fClark, mMargaret Lupton, wFrances E Cather
Joshua, b18--, Fred Co, fSydney, mMahlon Gore
Margaret, b178-, Fred Co, fJasper, (1)mBarbara Lawrence
Mary, b177-, Fred Co, fJasper, (1)mBarbara Lawrence
Mary Jane, b18--, Fred Co, fWashington, m-- Robinson, hCharles Boxwell
May, bc1800, Fred Co, fJasper, (2)m-- Bailey
Perry, b181-, Fred Co, fJames, mAnne Howard
Perry Gore, b18--, Fred Co, fSydney, mMahlon Gore
Robert, bc1800, Fred Co, fJasper, (2)m-- Bailey
Robert N, b18--, Fred Co, f Washington, m-- Robinson, wRhoda E Rodgers
Sarah, b185-, Fred Co, fClark, mMargaret Lupton
Silas, b18--, Fred Co, fWashington, m-- Robinson
Sydney, bc1820, Fred Co, fJames, mAnne Howard, wMahlon Gore
Thomas, b177-, Fred Co, fJasper, (1)mBarbara Lawrence
Thomas, b18--, Fred Co, fWashington, m-- Robinson
Washington, b18--, Fred Co, w-- Robinson
William, bc1800, Fred Co, fJasper, (2)m-- Bailey
William, b181-, Fred Co, fJames, mAnne Howard, wCaroline Smith
William, b185-, Fred Co, fClark, mMargaret Lupton

CATLETT, Mary Armistead, b18--, Glou Co, hMaryus Jones, md12/10/ 1873
Maria Breckinridge, b18--, f Nathaniel Pendleton, mElizabeth Breckinridge, hArmistead Churchill Gordon
CATLIN, Ella Virginia, b18--, Churchill, Rich Co, hJohn Lincoln Sydnor, md1864
CATON, Ella, b18--, nrShepherdstown, Jeff Co, d1899, fGeorge W, mMargaret --, hJames Flanagan
George W, b18--, Jeff Co?, wMargaret --
CATRON, Rody J, b2/12/1853, nrCrockett, Wyth Co, d1921, hTandy F Dix
CAULEY, Judith, b18--, Bedf Co, hMatthew Bandy
CAUTHORN, Annie Elizabeth, b1845, Esse Co, hWilliam J Newbill
CAUTHORNE, India Elizabeth, b12/17/ 1837, Esse Co, hAlfred A Rudd
Leah, b18--, Esse Co?, hReuben Boughton
CAVANAUGH, Winifred, b16--, Rapp Co, fPhilemon, hLewis Davis Yancey, md1710
CAVE, Belfield, b17--, Madi Co, wCrimora Jones
William Jones, b18--, Madi Co, d1895, fBelfield, mCrimora Jones, wMollie Bouton
CAWOOD, Nannie B, b18--, Lee Co?, hCampbell Slemp
CECIL, Fannie, b18--, Pula Co?, hWilliam H Keister
John S, b9/19/1856, Dublin, Pula Co, fJohn H, mMary Ellen Trinkle, wVictoria Byrnes
Margaret, b1858, Pula Co, h Wyndham R Gilmer
William B, bc1860, Carr Co?, 2h of Elva Early
CHAFFIN, Deborah, b18--, h Charles Graham Kizer
Emily, b18--, Wyth Co, hWilliam Crockett
CHALKLEY, Achilles, b17--, Ches Co
Anna C, b18--, Ches Co, fWilliam Benjamin, mMary Washing-

CHALKLEY (continued)
ton Nunnally
Benjamin Otis, b18--, Ches Co, fWilliam Benjamin, mMary Washington Nunnally
Eva A, b18--, Ches Co, fWilliam Benjamin, mMary Washington Nunnally, h-- Stanton
Gideon P, b18--, Ches Co, wElizabeth Perdue
Mary Lillian, b18--, Ches Co, fWilliam Benjamin, mMary Washington Nunnally, h-- Gregory
Roger H, b18--, Ches Co, fWilliam Benjamin, mMary Washington Nunnally
Spencer, b17--, Ches Co, fAchilles, wRebecca Farmer
William Benjamin, b4/10/1833, nrDrewrys Bluff, Ches Co, fSpencer, mRebecca Farmer, wMary Washington Nunnally
CHALTON, J J, bc1840, Buck Co?, wSarah L Anderson
CHAMBERLAIN, Grace, b18--, Warrentown, Fauq Co, fJames L, mEllen Holmes, hAlexander Scott Hamilton, md10/1892
T S, bc1840, Fred Co?, wMary Beatrice Baker
William, bc1850, Fran Co?, w Matilda Hughes Dillard
William, bc1850, Albe Co?, w Mary Peyton
CHAMBERLAYNE, Lucy Parke, b18--, Richmond?, hGeorge W Bagby
CHAMBERS, Edward, bc1800, Meck Co?, wLucy Tucker
Virginia, b5/4/1832, Boydton, Meck Co, fEdward, mLucy Tucker, hAlexander Thompson Laird
CHAMBLIN, Lizzie, b18--, Fauq Co?, hDaniel H Green Sr
Thomas, bc1844, Clar Co?, wAttie Baker
CHANCELLOR, --, bc1800, PrWi Co?, 1h-- Wroe, 2hWilliam Barbee
--, b18--, Fauq Co?, wJulia Herndon
Leona, b18--, fMelzi S, mLucy Frazier, 1w of James R Rawlings, md10/1877
Melzi S, b18--, wLucy Frazier
CHANDLER, --, b18--, Pitt Co?, hWilliam W Adams

CHANDLER (continued)
Edward Massie, bc1853, Rkhm Co, d1883, fSamuel W, mSusan Huffman, wSusan Fannie Tutwiler
Elizabeth, bc1850, Rkhm Co, fSamuel W, mSusan Huffman, hDaniel Sandy
Esta, b185-, Rkhm Co, fSamuel, mSusan Huffman
Harry, bc1860, Rkhm Co?, wMaggie Wagner
Joseph Alsop, bc1828, Caro Co, d1902, wEmeline Josephine White
Julian Alvin Carroll, b186-, Guinea, Caro Co, fJoseph Alsop, mEmeline Josephine White, wLenon Burton Duke, md7/10/1897
Maggie, b185-, Rkhm Co, fSamuel W, mSusan Huffman, hEdward Ruebush
Sarah Ann, b184-, Rkhm Co, fSamuel, mSusan Huffman, hJohn Earman
Sue, b1844, hHenry Harrison Moore
CHAPIN, Charles, bc1850, Fair Co?, wCarrie Stuart Harrison
William Taylor Sr, b18--, Lexington, Rkbr Co, d1878, wMartha Kerfoot
CHAPMAN, Ann Pendleton, bc1800, PrWi Co?, fThomas, hJohn Leachman
Annie, bc1840, Ripplemead, Gile Co, fDavid Johnston Sr, mSarah Pepper, hJames W English
Araminta, bc1800, Gile Co?, hGuy D French
Catherine, b1836, Middletown, Fred Co, hWilliam Pannett Jr
Cornelia Jane, b184-, Ripplemead, Gile Co, fDavid Johnston Sr, mSarah Pepper, hSamuel E Lybrook
David Johnston Sr, b1793, Ripplemead, Gile Co, d1856, f Isaac, mElian Johnston, wSarah Pepper
David Johnston Jr, b9/16/1850, Ripplemead, Gile Co, fDavid Johnston Sr, mSarah Pepper
E C, b18--, NewK Co?, wAnnie E Boswell
Isaac, b17--, Ripplemead, Gile

CHAPMAN (continued)
Co, fJohn, wElian Johnston
James Rayburn Pepper, bc1840, Ripplemead, Gile Co, fDavid Johnston Sr, mSarah Pepper
Kizziah, b17--, fIsaac, hThomas Fowler
Malinda, b184-, Ripplemead, Gile Co, fDavid Johnston Sr, mSarah Pepper, hSamuel S Dinwiddie
Polly, b18--, Glou Co?, hArcher Bland
Rachel, b17--, Gile Co, hJohn Snidow
William, bc1840, Ripplemead, Gile Co, d1867, fDavid Johnston Sr, mSarah Pepper
CHAPPELEAR, Adaline, b1836, nrHume, Fauq Co, fBenjamin, m-- Fletcher, hWilliam J Williams
Benjamin, bc1800, Fauq Co?, w-- Fletcher
Roberta, b18--, nrDelaplane, Fauq Co, d1919, fBenjamin, m-- Fletcher, hThomas Edward Browning
CHAPPELL, A M, b18--, wMary Seay
Elizabeth, b3/23/1750, Amel Co, fJames, mSusannah Hudson, h Henry Cox, md7/31/1775
James, b17--, Amel Co?, wSusannah Hudson
John Robert I, b1844, Suss Co, d1899, wNannie Stewart
John Robert Sr, bc1870, Suss Co, fJohn Robert I, mNannie Stewart, wEmma Roy Mitchell
CHARLTON, Elizabeth, b18--, Camp Co?, hRobert L Woolwine
Evaline Matilda, b1/7/1820, Mont Co, fWilliam H, m-- Carter, hAndrew Jackson Lucas
Nancy, b18--, Mont Co?, h Charles D Lucas
CHARTERS, Estelle, b18--, Spot Co, hThomas Scott
CHASE, Charles C, bc1870, Dick Co, fJohn P, mNancy L Dunbar
Emory B, bc1870, Dick Co, fJohn P, mNancy L Dunbar
Minnie B, b186-, Dick Co, fJohn P, mNancy L Dunbar, hGranville M Jones
Roland E, b8/14/1867, Dick Co,

CHASE (continued)
d1891, fJohn P, mNancy L Dunbar, wMary L Chase
CHEATE, J A, bc1860, Albe Co, wMalvina T Minor
CHEATHAM, Ann, b17--, hEdward Hatcher
Lucy, b17--, Ches Co?, hValentine Winfree, md1/3/1783
Pauline, b11/7/1850, Lune Co, hWilliam A Wilson
CHEATWOOD, Fanny C, bc1870, Camp Co?, fLeighton, mMary P Hurt, hThomas Ashby Watts Sr
Leighton, b18--, Camp Co?, w Mary P Hurt
CHERNAULT, Florence Blanton, b18--, Richmond, fJames Lewis, mSue L Donnavant, hJohn Randolph Atwood, md1888
James Lewis, b18--, Richmond?, wSue L Donnavant
CHERRY, John William, b12/24/1854, Norf Co, fJohn, mJulia Ann --, wMary A Pebworth, md2/23/1876
Cherry, b18--, Norfolk, d186-, wJulia Ann --
CHESHIRE, George W, b18--, Norfolk?, wLetitia
CHEVOLIN, Elise, b18--, Richmond, hJacob M Pirkey
CHEW, Thomas J, b18--, Fauq Co?, wBaynton Beverly
CHICHESTER, Daniel McCarty, b8/20/1834, Fair Co, d1896, fWilliam Henry, mJane Peyton, wAgnes Robinson Moncure
Mary, b1753, 1w of Burgess Ball, md7/2/1770
Mary E, b186-, Fair Co, fDaniel McCarty, mAgnes Robinson Moncure, hJohn Latane Lewis
Richard Henry Lee, b4/18/1870, Fair Co, fDaniel McCarty, mAgnes Robinson Moncure, wVirginia Belle Wallace, md6/6/1895
William Henry, bc1800, Fair Co, wJane Peyton
CHILD, Anna Gale, b18--, Jeff Co?, fJohn A, hWilliam Creighton Campbell
CHILDRESS, Elizabeth, b18--, Char Co, hWilliam H Wilborn
CHILDREY, Kate Cowles, b4/4/1860, Henrico Co, hGeorge

CHILDREY (continued)
Kinsey Roper
CHILDS, Mildred, b18--, Fauq Co?, hJames Strother
Sarah Elizabeth, b1/31/1822, Fauq Co, d1903, fWilliam A, mNancy Lewis, hWilliam H Lake
William H, bc1800, Fauq Co?, wNancy Lewis
CHILES, Charles Marshall, b18--, Kernstown, Fred Co, fJohn B, mSarah Wise
Cornelius, b182-, nrWhitehall, Berk Co, fMason
Elizabeth, bc1700, York Co?, hHenry Tyler II
John B, b11/1824, nrWhitehall, Berk Co, d1905, fMason, wSarah Wise
Mahlon, b182-, nrWhitehall, Berk Co, fMason
Mahlon, b18--, Kernstown, Fred Co, fJohn B, mSarah Wise
Mason, b17--, Berk Co, d184-, fBenjamin
R E, b18--, Kernstown, Fred Co, fJohn B, mSarah Wise
Samuel E, b18--, Kernstown, Fred Co, fJohn B, mSarah Wise, wSallie Osburn, md4/4/1895
CHILTON, Alice, b1858, Norwood, Lanc Co, hRobert Opie Norris Sr
C B, b18--, Culp Co?, wHarriet Hamilton
Estelle R, bc1870, Lanc Co, fRalph H, mSue Edmonds, hThomas Joseph Downing
Ralph H, b18--, Lanc Co?, wSue Edmonds
CHINN, Austin Brockenbrough, b186-, Tappahannock, Esse Co, fJoseph William, (1)mGabriella Brockenbrough
Catherine, b17--, hReuben Murray
Elizabeth, b18--, fHugh, mElizabeth Ashe, hHugh Brent
Joseph William Sr, bc1800, Oakley, Lanc Co, wMarianna Smith
Joseph William Jr, b2/13/1836, "Sion House", Rich Co, d1908, fJoseph William Sr, mMarianna Smith, 1wGabriella Brockenbrough, 2wJosephine I Lane
Joseph William III, b2/15/1866,

CHINN (continued)
Tappahannock, Esse Co, fJoseph William Jr, (1)mGarbiella Brockenbrough, wSarah Fairfax Douglas, md12/14/1899
Lucy Leland, b18--, Epping Forest, Lanc Co, hJames Bailey Jett
CHISMAN, Samuel Read, b18--, ElCi Co?, w-- Whiting
CHITWOOD, Amanda, bc1850, Carr Co, fEdmund, mMaria Ogle, hC A Watson
Cora E, bc1870, Rocky Mount, Fran Co, fHenry Clay, mGillie Ann Divers, hL H Bennett
Edmund, b18--, Fran Co, d1881, wMaria Ogle
Henry Clay, b1844-, nrRocky Mount, Fran Co, d1915, fRandolph, mCecelia Dillon, wGillie Ann Divers
Joel, b17--, Fran Co, wSally Short
Randolph, b1800, Fran Co, d1894/5, fJoel, mSally, wCecelia Dillon
Randolph, b1851, Carr Co, d1913, fEdwin, mMaria Ogle, wEllen Smith
S M, b186-, Rocky Mount, Fran Co, fHenry Clay, mGillie Ann Divers
William T, b12/28/1869, Rocky Mount, Fran Co, fHenry Clay, mGillie Ann Divers, wMary White, md1898
CHOWNING, Hattie Lee, b18--, Midd Co, fJames, mEliza Smith, hRichard Beverly Segar, md11/26/1885
James, b18--, Midd Co?, wEliza Smith
Mary H, b18--, nrLancaster Court House, Lanc Co, d1872, 1w of Herbert Pollard Hall
CHRISMAN, John, bc1860, Clar Co, wBlanche Sprint
William, bc1830, Shen Co?, w Margaret Neeb
CHRIST, Hampton R, bc1850, Amhe Co?, wElizabeth E Parrish
CHRISTIAN, Ann Elizabeth, bc1820, ChCi Co, fJames, h Lycurgus Lamb
Annie Willis, b18--, NewK Co,

CHRISTIAN (continued)
fWilliam Edmond, mAnne E Taylor, hWilliam B Langley
Bartholomew D, b18--, NewK Co, fJohn D, m-- Dandridge
Edward Dudley, b185-, Lynchburg, Camp Co, fEdward Dunscomb, mCornelia Burton
Edward Dunscomb, b1823, Lynchburg, Camp Co, fHenry Asbury, mLucy Wood Dunscomb, wCornelia Burton
Eliza J, b1844, ChCi Co, hWilliam Archer Royall
Elizabeth, b17--, NewK Co, h Samuel Waddill
Elizabeth Augusta, b1826, fSamuel, hRobert Henry Glass
Elizabeth D, b185-, Lynchburg, Camp Co, fEdward Dunscomb, mCornelia Burton
Edmonia, b18--, Lewi Co, hGeorge Dawson
Frank Patteson Sr, b11/18/1858, Lynchburg, Camp Co, fEdward Dunscomb, mCornelia Burton, wMary Lucretia Dearing, md1/28/1890
Frank W, bc1850, Richmond?, wBessie Palmer
Gideon, b17--, NewK Co, w-- Appason
Grace Cowan, b185-, Lynchburg, Camp Co, fEdward Dunscomb, mCornelia Burton
Henry, b17--, Camp Co?, fWilliam
Henry Asbury, bc1800, Camp Co, fHenry, mMartha Patteson, w Lucy Wood Dunscomb
James, bc1700, ChCi Co?, fThomas
James, b17--, ChCi Co?, fJoseph
John D, bc1800, NewK Co, w-- Dandridge
John E, b18--, Pitt Co?, wElizabeth Watson
John H, b185-, Lynchburg, Camp Co, fEdward Dunscomb, mCornelia Burton
Langdon Taylor, b5/26/1853, NewK Co, fWilliam Edmund, m Anne E Taylor, wBelle B Brown, md10/5/1881
Laura K, b18--, NewK Co, fWilliam Edmund, mAnne E Taylor,

CHRISTIAN (continued)
  hJohn G Livesay
  Mary Elizabeth, b18--, Appo Co, hJohn William Woodson, md185-Nellie, b18--, Midd Co?, fWilliam S, mHelen Steptoe, 2w of Robert S Bristow, md1896
  Octavia Dandridge, b18--, NewK Co, fBartholomew D, hJohn N Harris
  Samuel, bc1800, Camp Co, fHenry
  Sarah Stovall, bc1800, Nels Co, hWilliam Dillard, md1824
  Susan Beverly, b18--, ChCi Co, hJoseph Walter Harwood Sr
  Thomas, b16--, ChCi Co, fThomas
  Thomas, b18--, wEllen Delaney
  William, b17--, ChCi Co?, fJames
  William Asbury, b186-, Lynchburg, Camp Co, fEdward Dunscomb, mCornelia Burton
  William Edmund, b18--, NewK Co, fGideon, m-- Appason, wAnne E Taylor
  William S, b18--, Midd Co?, wHelen Steptoe
  William Thomas, b18--, NewK Co, fWilliam Edmund, mAnne E Taylor
CHUMBLEY, Asa Harper, b8/1808, Mont Co, d1903, wEliza Hudson
  Joseph H, b1844, Pula Co, d1917, fAsa Harper, mEliza Hudson, wEllen Hannah Shell
CHURCHMAN, John S, b18--, Augu Co, wFrances Crawford
  John W, b9/12/1857, Staunton, Augu Co, fJohn S, mFrances Crawford, wAnnie Goodwin Johnston
CLAGETT, Frances, b18--, Hard Co, fHezekiah, mLouisa Baker, hAndrew Bolling
  Hezekiah Norton, b18--, Hard Co, fHezekiah, mLouisa Baker
  James Henry, b18--, Hard Co, fHezekiah, mLouisa Baker
  John Baker, b18--, Hard Co, fHezekiah, mLouisa Baker
  Mary Elizabeth, b18--, Hard Co, fHezekiah, mLouisa Baker, hJames R Baker
  Naylor Inskeep, b18--, Hard Co, fHezekiah, mLouisa Baker
  Susan, b18--, Hard Co, fHeze-

CLAGETT (continued)
  kiah, mLouisa Baker, hJacob Warden, md1/28/1860
  William B, b18--, Hard Co, fHezekiah, mLouisa Baker
CLAIBORNE, Mary Abia, bc1800, h-- Morris
  Octavia, b18--, KiWi Co, hJohn Skyron Lewis
CLARDY, Eliza, b18--, Nott Co, d1869, fBenjamin, hRenyard B Beville
CLARK, Abram Irvin, b1817, Hat Creek, Camp Co, d1906, fPaulett, mMary Tacker Irvin, wZuleika Lemmon Withers, md1854
  Alexander Storton, b18--, PrEd Co, fThomas, m-- Madison, w Fannie Wooton
  Bettie A, b3/24/1846, Hali Co?, hMonroe Worth Dickerson
  Cornelia Winston, b18--, Albe Co, hDrury W Burnley
  Edward L, b12/9/1870, Patr Co, fJoseph M, mElla Virginia Jefferson, wAnna Massey, md1896
  Elizabeth, b18--, Pitt Co?, fJohn A, hJohn E Hughes Sr
  Elizabeth, b1/15/1838, Lee Co, hWilliam Witt
  Frank, b18--, nrAbingdon, Wash Co, wCatherine White
  George H, bc1848, Fred Co, wSarah Wingeter
  Harriet, b18--, Glade Springs, Wash Co, hCharles F Lincoln
  Harrison, bc1830, Patr Co, fJacob, mJane Stovall
  Hughes, bc1830, Patr Co, fJacob, mJane Stovall
  J Paulett, b4/2/1870, Hat Creek, Camp Co, fOrthodox Creed, mElizabeth (Payne) Nowlin, wFannie Yuolle, md6/1903
  J W, bc1850, Ches Co, wWillie H Walker
  Jacob, b18--, Henr Co, wJane Stovall
  James Thomas, b6/20/1854, Falkland Farm, PrEd Co, fAlexander Storton, mFannie Wootton, w Sallie Hester Foster
  John, b17--, Loui Co, fFrancis, wAnn Paulett
  Joseph L, b186-, Patr Co, fJoseph M, mElla Virginia Jeffer-

CLARK (continued)
son
Joseph M, b4/8/1833, Patr Co, d1892, fJacob, mJane Stovall, wElla Virginia Jefferson
Julia Ann, b18--, Fred Co?, hJames Lewis
Katherine, b18--, Portsmouth, Norf Co, hWilliam Tipton
Lucy, b17--, Camp Co, hThomas Moorman
Lyman Emery, b18--, wAlice Lear
Martha, b18--, NewK Co, hWilliam Timberlake
Martha Jane Elizabeth, b18--, nrMeadowview, Wash Co, fFrank, mCatherine White, hWilliam R DeFriece
Mary, b18--, nrNorth River, Augu Co, hAdam Stover
Mary E L, b18--, Shen Co?, hAlex Osburn
Montraville C, bc1860, Russ Co?, wAlta J Finney
Orthodox Creed, b10/2/1814, Hat Creek, Camp Co, fPaulett, m Mary Tacker Irvin, wElizabeth (Payne) Nowlin
Paulett, b17--, Camp Co, fJohn, mAnn Paulett, wMary Tacker Irvin
Sallie, b18--, Fluv Co, d1888, hJames Clayton Reed
Sophia Ruby, b18--, Fauq Co, hA J Clark
Thomas, bc1800, w-- Madison
Thomas, bc1830, Patr Co, fJacob, mJane Stovall
William Hughes, b186-, Patr Co, fJoseph M, mElla Virginia Jefferson
CLARKE, Amanda Madison, bc1870, The Plains, Fauq Co, fEdwin B, mJudith Taliaferro, hJames Bradshaw Beverley
Anne Hobson, b18--, Hali Co, fEppa, mMary Robinson, hEdward Winston Armistead, md1890
Carrie Lee, b3/4/1866, Richmond, fWilliam Alpheus Sr, mMargaret Anne Elizabeth Barrett
Catherine, bc1800, hJoseph Lee
Dandridge W, b1796, NewK Co, wMartha R Pumphrey
Edwin B, b18--, Fauq Co?, wJu-

CLARKE (continued)
dith Taliaferro
Elizabeth, b17--, Powh Co, h William Hopkins
Eppa, b18--, Hali Co?, wMary Robinson
John H, b18--, Clar Co?, wMollie Levi
John L, b18--, Camp Co?, d1897, wSara D Luck
Judith, b16--, Midd Co?, hAbraham Trigg
L A, bc1860, PrWi Co?, wLucy Margaret Lynn
Minnie D, b18--, Nels Co?, hWilliam D Meeks, md9/1886
Morton E, bc1860, Midd Co, wIda Waverly Lawson
Norah, bc1870, Albe Co, fThomas J, hJames Payne Carroll Sr, md11/1895
William Alpheus Sr, b1831, NewK Co, fDandridge W, mMartha R Pumphrey, wMargaret Anne Elizabeth Barrett
William D, b1857, PrWi Co, wStella Lynn
CLARKSON, J Crawford, b4/6/1866, nrStuarts Draft, Augu Co, fJohn J N, mMartha J McComb, wLelia May Harvey, md1889
John J N, b18--, Roseland, Nels Co, wMartha J McComb
Mary E, b18--, Albe Co, hRobert Franklin Burnham
CLARKSTON, Henry H, bc1840, Lee Co?, wMary Ann Witt
James, bc1830, Lee Co?, wRebecca Witt
CLAUD, Jesse Cornelius, b18--, Sout Co, d1911, wMadeline Lesles
CLAY, --, b17--, Smyt Co, hJohn Sifers
--, b18--, Camp Co, 1w of John Waller
CLAYBROOK, Edwin, bc1830, West Co?, wJudith White Newton
CLAYTON, David, b18--, Fred Co?, wJane Peebles
Mary Frances, b1852, Fred Co, fDavid, mJane Peebles, hGeorge W Kurtz, md5/1871
CLEATON, Thomas, b18--, Meck Co, fThomas, w-- Thacker
Thomas Hicks, b18--, Grvl Co,

CLEATON (continued)
 fThomas, m-- Thacker, wMary W Dameron
CLEEK, Adam G, b18--, Bath Co?, wMary Miller
 Adam G, bc1830, Jackson River Valley, fJohn Cleek II, mSallie Kime
 David G, bc1830, Jackson River Valley, fJohn Cleek II, mSallie Kime
 George W Sr, b6/3/1835, Jackson River Valley, fJohn Cleek II, mSallie Kime, wMalcena Lightner, md11/26/1867
 John I, b1777, Rkbr Co, fJacob, mChristinia Croddy, wJane Gwin
 John II, b5/12/1803, Jackson River Valley, fJohn I, mJane Gwin, wSallie Kime
 John III, bc1830, Jackson River Valley, fJohn II, mSallie Kime
 Lillah B, b186-, Bath Co, fAdam G, mMary Miller, hFloyd Lee LaRue, md11/13/1884
CLEGG, Elizabeth Catherine, b1850, KiQu Co, fThomas, hMiles E Didlake
CLEM, --, bc1840, Powell's Fort Valley, Shen Co, fElias, hBenjamin Boyer
 Daniel, bc1840, Powell's Fort Valley, Shen Co, fElias
 Elias, bc1795, Shen Co, d188-
 Hiram, bc1840, Powell's Fort Valley, Shen Co, fElias
 Jacob B Sr, b5/1844, Powell's Fort Valley, Shen Co, fElias, wSallie J Kibler
 John A, b7/16/1846, Edith, Shen Co, fJoshua, mSallie Ross, wJane Shuff
 Lewis, bc1840, Powell's Fort Valley, Shen Co, fElias
 Regina, bc1840, Powell's Fort Valley, Shen Co, fElias, hSamuel Holmes
CLEMENT, B M, b186-, Pitt Co, fH C Sr, mHarriet Morrison
 H C Sr, b18--, Pitt Co?, wHarriet Morrison
 H C Jr, b186-, Pitt Co, fH C Sr, mHarriet Morrison
 Mary Royal, bc1870, Pitt Co, fH C Sr, mHarriet Morrison
 S A, bc1870, Pitt Co, fH C Sr,

CLEMENT (continued)
 mHarriet Morrison
 S P, bc1870, Pitt Co, fH C Sr, mHarriet Morrison
CLEMENTS, Lucy, b18--, KiWi Co?, hOtis Palmer
CLEMER, Francis, b18--, Augu Co, wJennie Nelson Harris
 Grace Engle, b186-, Fairfield, Rkbr Co, fJames H, mNannie Jane Bell, hJ E Hess
 James H, bc1841, Rkbr Co, d1903, fFrancis, mJennie Nelson Harris, wNannie Jane Bell
 William Bell, b186-, Fairfield, Rkbr Co, fJames H, mNannie Jane Bell, wMary Rebecca Davis, md1903
CLEMMER, Jay Franklin Sr, b10/17/1852, "Silver Brook Farm", Augu Co, fDavid, wMary Preston Hogshead, md1883
 Mariah Louise, b18--, Rkbr Co, d1900, hWilliam S Humphries
 Sarah J, b10/20/1845, nrMiddlebrook, Augu Co, fWilliam K, hRobert D Firebaugh
CLENDENEN, Milton Lee, b1834, Princeton, Merc Co, d1915, wJosephine Adams
CLENDENING, Ruth H, b18--, nr Hillsboro, Loud Co, hHugh S Thompson
CLENSHAW, Emily, b18--, Richmond?, hGeorge W Nolley
CLEVELAND, Anna, b18--, Jeff Co?, hFrank Stipes
CLEVENGER, Sarah, b18--, Clar Co?, hWilliam Hardesty
CLEVINGER, John W, b1850, Buch Co, fLevi, mPricey Mateney, wMelvina Deal
 Levi, b1820, Buch Co, d1915, fJohn W, mMollie Stiltner, wPricey Mateney
CLICK, Joseph, bc1820, wAnnie Driver
CLINE, --, bc1830, Shen Co?, wAnnie Newman
 Amanda Frances, b186-, Wardensville, Hard Co, fLevi, mElizabeth A Landacre, hA Randolph Ginn
 Anna, b18--, Rkhm Co?, hEmanuel Hoover
 Asa, b18--, Hamp Co?, wRebecca

CLINE (continued)
Spaid
Benjamin, bc1850, Rkhm Co, w Annie R Driver
Catherine, b18--, Shen Co?, d1882, fSamuel, 1w of Sam Byers Jr
Catherine, b18--, Rkhm Co?, hJewitt Messick
David, bc1850, Rkhm Co, wMary E Driver
David Cowan Sr, b4/28/1867, Wardensville, Hard Co, fLevi, mElizabeth A Landacre, 1wAmanda Funkhouser, 2wAnnie Gertrude Keys, md8/14/1907
Eliza, b182-, nrMaurertown, Shen Co, fJohn
Jennie, b186-, Hamp Co, fAsa, mRebecca Spaid, hThomas Jackson Orndorff
John, bc1830, nrMaurertown, Shen Co, fJohn
Joseph, bc1820, Rkhm Co, wMary Flory
Levi, b1824, nrMaurertown, Shen Co, d1889, fJohn, wElizabeth A Landacre
Mary, b18--, Rkhm Co?, hJohn Wampler
Polly, b182-, nrMaurertown, Shen Co, fJohn
William, b182-, nrMaurertown, Shen Co, fJohn
CLINEDINST, --, bc1850, Shen Co, wAnna Newland
Alice, b184-, Rkbr Co, fJacob, mAnna Karg, hGeorge Crim
Andrew, b181-, Augu Co, fMichael, m-- Rumbough
Annie, b184-, Rkbr Co, fJacob, mAnnie Karg, hG R Calvert
Charles Edward, b5/21/1856, New Market, Shen Co, fJacob, mAnnie Karg, wCarrie E Keyser, md11/14/1882
Eliza, b1838, Pt Defiance, Rkbr Co, fJacob, mAnnie Karg, hJ W Crim
Ella, b184-, Rkbr Co, fJacob, mAnnie Karg, hGeorge Bodell
George, b184-, Rkbr Co, fJacob, mAnnie Karg
Jacob, b3/1/1815, Augu Co, f Michael, m-- Rumbough, wAnnie Karg

CLINEDINST (continued)
Jacob R, bc1840, Rkbr Co, fJacob, mAnnie Karg
James, bc1820, Augu Co, fMichael, m-- Rumbough
John, b181-, Augu Co, fMichael, m-- Rumbough
John W, b8/10/1837, Brownsburg, Rkbr Co, fJacob, mAnnie Karg
Mary, bc1820, Augu Co, fMichael, m-- Rumbough, hWilliam Morrison
Mary, b184-, Rkbr Co, fJacob, mAnnie Karg, hWilliam H Wright
Rebecca, bc1820, Augu Co, f Michael, m-- Rumbough, hDavid Horshour
Thomas McDowell, bc1850, Rkbr Co, fJacob, mAnna Karg
William, b18--, Augu Co, fMichael, m-- Rumbough
CLINTON, Mary, b18--, Smyt Co?, hJohn Parrish
CLOPTON, Anne Gunn, bc1800, Henrico Co, fDavid, hRobert Mosby Pulliam
CLOWER, Julia, b18--, Rkhm Co?, hJohn R Saum
CLOWES, Annie L, b2/27/1863, Lexington, Rkbr Co, hThomas G Birckhead
CLOWSER, Sarah Catherine, bc1850, Hayfield, Fred Co, fJosiah, hJohn Lucius Summers, bc1877
CLOYD, Mary, b18--, fDavid Sr, mMargaret Campbell, hJames M McGavock
COALTER, Frances Bland, b18--, Dinw Co?, hHenry Peronneau Brown
COATES, Thomas, b18--, Loud Co, d1885, wMary Athey
COBB, Amonette, b18--, Buck Co?, hWilliam W Forbes
Benjamin E, b1859, Sout Co, fJeremiah, wMaggie Westray
Ella Virginia, b18--, fJohn Madison, mEdith March, hPaul Douglas Camp, md1/29/1880
Jeremiah, b18--, Sout Co
COBBS, Damaris, b18--, Bedf Co?, hJesse Alexander Burton
Emma Williams, b10/25/1822, "Glen Alpin", Bedf Co, d1875, fWilliam, hEdward Sixtus Hut-

COBBS (continued)
ter, md10/7/1840
William Walton, bc1834, Pitt Co, fJohn James, wLouise Flournoy
COCHRAN, Alcinda, bc1820, Landmark, Fauq Co, fJohn, mEllen Reid, hGeorge Bitzer
Elizabeth Jane, b18--, "Landmark Farm", Fauq Co, fJohn Thomas Sr, mElizabeth Lodge, hHugh Tiffany
George L, b18--, Fauq Co, wSallie George Moffett Sr, bc1800, Augu Co?, wMaria T Boys
George Moffett Jr, b2/26/1832, "Elk Meadows", nrStribling, Augu Co, d1900, fGeorge Moffett Sr, mMaria T Boys, wMargaret Lynn Peyton, md10/4/1866
Hulda, bc1820, Landmark, Fauq Co, fJohn, mEllen Reid, hAlfred Hampton
James, b182-, Landmark, Fauq Co, fJohn, mEllen Reid
James Robert, b18--, "Landmark Farm", Fauq Co, fJohn Thomas Sr, mElizabeth Lodge
Jane, b181-, Landmark, Fauq Co, fJohn, mEllen Reid, hJames Priest
Jane St Clair, b18--, Augu Co?, hHenry Harrison
John Thomas Sr, bc1826, Landmark, Fauq Co, d1905, fJohn, mEllen Reid, wElizabeth Lodge
John Thomas Jr, b18--, "Landmark Farms", Fauq Co, fJohn Thomas Sr, mElizabeth Lodge
Joseph Walter, b18--, "Landmark Farms", Fauq Co, fJohn Thomas Sr, mElizabeth Lodge
Laura Virginia, b18--, "Landmark Farms", Fauq Co, fJohn Thomas Sr, mElizabeth Lodge, hRobert Elgin
Martha, b18--, Fran Co, hIsaac Via
Mary Ann, b18--, Fauq Co?, fGeorge L, mSallie --, hRobert Thomas Glascock
Mary Henrietta, b18--, "Landmark Farms", Fauq Co, fJohn Thomas Sr, mElizabeth Lodge, hDwight Nevit

COCHRAN (continued)
Nathan, b182-, Landmark, Fauq Co, fJohn, mEllen Reid
Rebecca Ellen, b18--, "Landmark Farm", Fauq Co, fJohn Thomas Sr, mElizabeth Lodge, hJames H Skinner, md11/16/1876
Robert, b181-, Landmark, Fauq Co, fJohn, mEllen Reid
S Lodge, bc1850, Fauq Co?, wAddie Whitacre
Samuel, b18--, "Landmark Farm", Fauq Co, fJohn Thomas Sr, mElizabeth Lodge
Stephen, b181-, Landmark, Fauq Co, fJohn, mEllen Reid
Susan, b186-, Staunton, Augu Co, fGeorge Moffett Jr, mMargaret Lynn Peyton, hAlbert A Daub
COCK, Ann Eliza, b186-, Hampton, ElCi Co, hJohn Cutler Robinson
COCKE, A R, b185-, Camp Co, fAlonzo, mFanny Rice
Alonzo, b18--, Camp Co, d186-, 2h of Fanny J Rice, md185-
Bessie V, b18--, Roan Co, f Charles Lewis, mSusan Virginia Pleasants, hJohn P Barbee
Charles H, b18--, Roan Co, d1898, fCharles Lewis, mSusan Virginia Pleasants, wElla Kirven
Charles Lewis, b2/21/1820, "Edgehill", KiWi Co, d1901, fJames, mElizabeth Fox, wSusan Virginia Pleasants, md12/31/1840
Charlotte M, b18--, Albe Co, fCharles, hWilliam Gordon, md11/27/1884
Elizabeth Pleasants, b17--, Henrico Co, fJames Jr
Henry Harrison, b1794, Montpelier, Surr Co
James, b1666, Henrico Co, d1721, fThomas, mMargaret () Jones, wElizabeth Pleasants
James Sr, b1692, Henrico Co, d1765, fJames, mElizabeth Pleasants
James Jr, b17--, Henrico Co, d1772, fJames Sr, wSusanna Lewis
James, b1783, KiWi Co, fWilliam, mSara New, wElizabeth

COCKE(continued)
Fox
Jane, b17--, Henrico Co, fJames Jr, mSusanna Lewis
John, b17--, Henrico Co, fJames Jr, mSusanna Lewis
Joseph J, b18--, Henrico Co, fCharles Lewis, mSusan Virginia Pleasants
Leila Virginia, b18--, Henrico Co, fCharles Lewis, mSusan Virginia Pleasants, hJoseph A Turner
Lucian Howard Sr, b18--, Hollins College, Roan Co, f Charles Lewis, mSusan Virginia, 1wLelia Smith, 2wSarah (Johnson) Hagan
Mary, bc1800, Albe Co?, fJames Powell, hCharles W Carter
Mary, b18--, Henrico Co?, f Charles Lewis, mSusan Virginia Pleasants, hC W Hayward
Mary E, b18--, Petersburg, Dinw Co, d1917, 1w of William Rowe Boutwell Jr
Mary Monroe, b4/13/1857, fHenry Harrison, hWalter Buck Richards, md6/20/1889
Mary Susan, b5/10/1852, Scottsville, Albe Co, hThomas S Heath
Matty L, b18--, Roan Co, f Charles Lewis, mSusan Virginia Pleasants
Rosa, b18--, Henrico Co?, f Charles Lewis, mSusan Virginia Pleasants, hW R L Smith
Rosalie, bc1860, Camp Co, fAlonzo, mFanny Rice
Sally, b17--, hThomas Massie
Sara Lewis, b17--, Henrico Co, fJames Jr, mSusanna Lewis
Sarah Lewis, b18--, Henrico Co, d1899, fCharles Lewis, mSusan Virginia Pleasants
Susanna, b17--, Henrico Co, fJames Jr, mSusanna Lewis
Thomas, b1638, Henrico Co, d1696, fRichard Sr
William, b17--, Henrico Co, fJames Jr, mSusanna Lewis, wSarah New, md1779
COCKRELL, Lilian, b8/6/1861, Reeville, Nhld Co, fLittleton, mAgnes B Harcum, hGeorge N

COCKRELL (continued)
Reed, md5/6/1886
Littleton, b18--, Nhld Co, wAgnes B Harcum
COE, Joseph, bc1830, Hamp Co?, wMargaret Cougill
COFER, --, b18--, Montvale, Bedf Co, hCharles Price Ferrell, SR
Abner B, b1842, Surr Co, f Isaac, m-- Jones, wSusan Ann Womble
Isaac, b18--, Surr Co, 2w-- Jones
Thomas A, b18--, Surr Co, f Isaac, m-- Jones
COFFELT, Elizabeth Ann, b18--, Shen Co?, fGeorge, hJohn M Maphis
Fannie Bell, b186-, Shen Co, fGeorge, hEdwin Hollingsworth
COFFER, Ella, bc1860, Fair Co?, d1909, 1w of Milton D Hall, md6/1881
COFFEY, Mary Steele, b18--, Richmond?, hCoason W Parrish
COFFMAN, Adelaide, b18--, Shen Co?, 1w of Jacob Strayer
Albert, bc1850, Rkhm Co?, wSallie Garber
Alice M, b18--, Fred Co?, 2w of George W Hillyard, md188-
Catherine, b18--, hAbsolom Dellinger, md9/4/1838
Catherine, bc1830, nrMt Olive, Shen Co, fGeorge, hHenry Hottel
Elizabeth, b18--, Rkhm Co?, hJohn Hopkins
George, b186-, Clar Co?, wNannie Smallwood
Sarah Jane, b1844, nrWoodstock, Shen Co, hSamuel A Wine
Susannah, b18--, Shen Co, hJacob Good
Tirzah A, b18--, Shen Co, fWilliam, mSarah A ---, hJerome Paul Stirewalt, md10/6/1878
William, b18--, Shen Co, wSarah
COGBILL, --, b18--, Ches Co, 1w of William N Perdue
Marcus A, bc1820, Chesterfield Court House, Ches Co
Nathan H, bc1820, Chesterfield Court House, Ches Co
Philip Valentine, b1/24/1861, Chesterfield Court House, Ches

COGBILL (continued)
Co, fWilliam Tilghman, mLucy Winfree, wJulia Amelia Truehart
Virginia Alice, b18--, Ches Co, fAugustus E, hLeonidas Wells
William Tilghman, b1821, Chesterfield Court House, Ches Co, d186-, wLucy Winfree
COGGIN, John, b1840, Sout Co, d1915, wParthenia Spivey
COHOON, William John, b18--, Suffolk, Nans Co, wSallie Louise Beaman
COINER, Adaline, b182-, nrStaunton, Augu Co, fMichael, hSamuel Pelter
Bettie L, bc1860, Augu Co, fDavid, mSusan B Whitmore
Bertie, bc1860, Augu Co, fDavid, mSusan B Whitmore, hT E Rhodes
David, b5/1825, nrStaunton, Augu Co, d1897, fMichael Coyner, wSusan B Whitmore, md1850
Franklin, bc1820, nrStaunton, Augu Co, fMichael
Harvey, b181-, nrStaunton, Augu Co, fMichael
Ida P, b185-, Augu Co, fDavid, mSusan B Whitmore, hGeorge M Grove
John, b182-, nrStaunton, Augu Co, fMichael
Lemuel, b185-, Augu Co, fDavid, mSusan B Whitmore
Millard A, b185-, Augu Co, fDavid, mSusan B Whitmore
J Wade, b186-, Augu Co, fDavid, mSusan B Whitmore
Samuel, b182-, nrStaunton, Augu Co, fMichael Coyner
Susan, bc1820, nrStaunton, Augu Co, fMichael, h-- Brenneman
William, bc1820, nrStaunton, Augu Co, fMichael Coyner
William H, bc1870, Augu Co, fDavid, mSusan B Whitmore
COKE, Mary, b18--, KiQu Co, hJohn Motley
COLAW, Anderson N, b1846, Crabbottom, High Co, fCornelius, mMary Elizabeth Newman
Cornelius, b1819, Crabbottom, High Co, fJacob, mMary Sutton, wMary Elizabeth Newman, md1845

COLAW (continued)
Georgianna, b1847, Crabbottom, High Co, fCornelius, mMary Elizabeth Newman, hM C Mauzy
John Marvin, b3/16/1860, Crabbottom, High Co, fCornelius, mMary Elizabeth Newman, 1wJosie M Judy, md10/21/1886, 2w Elizabeth J Gibson, md9/4/1895
Louise M, b186-, Crabbottom, High Co, fCornelius, mMary Elizabeth Newman, hW E Snyder
COLBERT, Chastine Wesley, b186-, Spot Co, fRichard Wesley, mElizabeth Beazley
Inez, bc1870, Spot Co, fRichard Wesley, mElizabeth Beazley, 1h Rosso Massey, 2hA L Blanton
James B, b9/8/1865, Spot Co, fRichard Wesley, mElizabeth Beazley, 1wBelle Ellis, 2wVirginia E Gressitt, md1901
Lucian Richard, bc1870, Spot Co, fRichard Wesley, mElizabeth Beazley
Richard Wesley, b18--, Spot Co?, wElizabeth Beazley
Samantha, b18--, Salem, Harr Co, d1922, fStrother, mSallie Morgan, hCharles O Embrey, md10/ 1869
Strother, b18--, Harr Co?, w Sallie Morgan
COLE, Delia, b18--, PrWi Co?, hJohn A Ratcliff Sr
Elton, b18--, Upper Zion, Caro Co, 2w of George Winfree
COLEMAN, --, b18--, 2w of George Keith Taylor
--, bc1860, Fauq Co, wSusie Green
Abigail Jean, b6/4/1846, Buch Co, d1903, hLewis Grayson Stacy
Aylett B, b9/27/1870, "Elk Hill", Nels Co, fHawes Nicholas, mNannie Elizabeth Watson, 1wNorma Randolph Caskie, md1895, 2wElizabeth Dabney
Charles Woolfolk Sr, b18--, Caro Co, wMary Graham Gardner
Charles Woolfolk Jr, bc1870, Caro Co, fCharles Woolfolk Sr, mMary Graham Gardner, wVirginia Griffin, md1891
Ethelbert Algernon, b18--, f

COLEMAN (continued)
Henry Embrey, mAnne Gordon, wMartha Frances Ragsdale
Hawes N, b183-, Nels Co, fJohn J, mKatherine "Kitty" Hawes, wNannie Elizabeth Watson
Haweise, b17--, Spot Co?, fJohn
Henry Embrey, b17--, fJohn, mSarah Embrey, wAnne Gordon
Henry Frank, b18--, wJane Patrick
John, b17--, Glou Co, wSarah Embrey
John J, bc1800, Nels Co?, w Katherine "Kitty" Hawes
Lewis Minor, bc1840, Hano Co, d186-
Martha J, b18--, Glou Co, hBenjamin Carr Newcomb
Mary A, b1845, Roan Co, 2w of Thomas E Kizer
Mary A, b185-, Appo Co, hAlfred E Torrence
Mary Kate, b1832, Nels Co, fJohn J, mKatherine "Kitty" Hawes, hCharles D Everett
Maury J, b186-, "Elk Hill", Nels Co, fHawes Nicholas, m Nannie Elizabeth Watson
Nannie, b18--, hRichard P Craddock
Nathaniel Ragsdale, b7/19/1843, Hali Co, fEthelbert Algernon, (2)mMaria Francis Ragsdale, wAnne Nelson Page
Rebecca, b18--, 1w of George Keith Taylor
Richard C, b18--, Glou Co?, wBelle Anderson
Robert, bc1840, Hano Co, mMary O Samuel, b17--, Spot Co?, fJohn
Samuel W, b18--, wMary Owen
Samuella Haweise, b1856, Spot Co, fSpencer, 3w of Thomas Penn Fitzpatrick, md1880
Spencer, b17--, Spot Co?, fJohn
Spencer, bc1800, Spot Co?, fSpencer
Susan Withers, b18--, Caro Co, hLuther Wright
COLES, Lela, b18--, Nhld Co, hHenry Wood Bouldin
Mary, b17--, Fluv Co, fWilliam, hJohn Payne
COLLEY, Bart B, b18--, Dick Co,

COLLEY (continued)
wNannie E Neel
James, bc1800, Sand Lick, Dick Co, fRichard, mCrissey Counts, wLouemma Ferrell
James M, b18--, Dick Co, 2h of Eliza Jane Counts
Josephine, b18--, Sand Lick, Russ Co, fJames Colley, mLouemma Ferrell, hJonathan Linder Sifers
Louise, b18--, Greene Co, h George Anderson Lawrence
Mildred, b18--, Russ Co?, hJames Lockhart
Richard, b17--, Saltville, Smyt Co, wCrissey Counts
Sallie, b18--, Sand Lick, Dick Co, hPreston Mullins
COLLIE, Elizabeth Ann, b18--, Pitt Co, fCarter, hGeorge W Giles
COLLIER, Charles, b186-, Mc Gaheysville, Rkhm Co, fHudson, mFrances Elliott
Elizabeth, b18--, Oran Co, hB F Payne
Frances, b17--, York Co, h Charles Hutcheson
Hudson, b18--, Greene Co?, wFrances Elliot
John, b2/14/1847, Carr Co, f Lorenzo Dow, mSarah L Cox, wLaura E Hylton, md1877
John, b186-, McGaheysville, Rkhm Co, fHudson, mFrances Elliott
John H, b18--, Lee Co?, wSusan Virginia Slemp
Laura Frances, bc1870, Rkhm Co, fHudson, mFrances Elliott, hJohn Holmes Moore, md1893
Lorenzo Dow, b18--, Carr Co, wSarah L Cox
Mary, b18--, Albe Co?, hThomas H Totty
Mollie, bc1870, McGaheysville, Rkhm Co, fHudson, mFrances Elliott, hJohn Kisling
COLLINS, Elmyra Virginia, b18--, Gile Co, hWilliam Jackson Garten
James Ball, b1819, Nels Co, fSamuel, wElizabeth Shields
Lewis Preston Sr, b1862, Greenville, Augu Co, fJames Ball,

COLLINS (continued)
mElizabeth Shields, wElla Bolling Moorman
Lizzie B, b18--, Portsmouth, Morf Co, fWilliam, hJohn Thompson Hill
COLONNA, --, bc1820, Acco Co?, 1h of Mary Kate Powell
Charles Jones, bc1849, Acco Co?, d1920, wMargaret Okeson Dunston
COLQUOHOUN, Barbara, b18--, Wash Co?, hLilburn Henderson Trigg
COLSTON, Anne Fisher, b1827, Charlottesville, Albe Co, d1883, 2w of John Barbee Minor
Charles, b1690, fWilliam, wSusanna Traverse
Elizabeth Marshall, b17--, Berk Co, fRaleigh, mElizabeth Marshall, hRobert Alfred Williams
Raleigh, b17--, fTraverse, (2)m Susanna Opie, wElizabeth Marshall
Susan Leigh, bc1840, fThomas Marshall, mEliza Jacqueline Fisher, hCharles Minor Blackford, md2/17/1856
Thomas Marshall, b17--, Berk Co, fRaleigh, mElizabeth Marshall, wEliza Jacqueline Fisher
Traverse, b1712, fCharles Colston, mSusanna Traverse, 2wSusannah Opie
Wesley, bc1850, Shen Co?, wSarah E Funkhouser
COLVIN, Edward B, b184-, Camp Co, fRobert, mLucy Lee Andrew
Frank H, b184-, Camp Co, fRobert, mLucy Lee Andrew
Harry, b180-, Culp Co, fMason, mCatherine Stringfellow
Howard, bc1810, Culp Co, fMason, mCatherine Stringfellow
Howard H, b184-, Camp Co, fRobert, mLucy Lee Andrew
James M, b180-, Culp Co, fMason, mCatherine Stringfellow
John, b180-, Culp Co, fMason, mCatherine Stringfellow
Lucy, b181-, Culp Co, fMason, mCatherine Stringfellow, h-- Thornton
Martha, b181-, Culp Co, fMason, mCatherine Stringfellow

COLVIN (continued)
Nathaniel, b180-, Culp Co, fMason, mCatherine Stringfellow
Robert, b10/31/1811, Culp Co, fMason, mCatherine Stringfellow, wLucy Lee Andrew
Robert Mason, b5/13/1845, Camp Co, fRobert, mLucy Lee Andrew, wLelia Susan Reynolds
Sallie Clark, bc1850, Camp Co, fRobert, mLucy Lee Andrew, h-- Anderson
Susie Virginia, b18--, Culp Co?, fWilliam, hTandy William Guinn
William O, b184-, Camp Co, fRobert, mLucy Lee Andrew
COMBS, David Carroll, b1850, Carr Co, fJoseph, wRachel Payne
John M, b1818, d1881
John William, b1842, nrHonaker, Russ Co, d1880, fJohn M, wLadora Jane Kiser
Lawrence R, b18--, Lanc Co?, wMinnie Jacobs
Mary, b17--, Loud Co?, hHugh Rogers
COMPTON, Conaway, b18--, Culp Co, wKate Wright
Kate, b18--, Rkbr Co, 1w of David Dunlop III, md1/18/1866
Sarah Elizabeth, b18--, Lynchburg, Camp Co, d1877, fWilliam, 1w of John Wesley Carroll, md1850
William Aylett, b3/17/1845, Page Co, fZachariah James, mEliza McKay, wLaura M Bolen, md12/23/1868
Zachariah James, b18--, Page Co?, wEliza McKay
COMSTOCK, --, b18--, Rkhm Co?, wMartha Riddel
CONE, William, bc1830, Shen Co, wBarbara Shirley
CONLEY, Morton, b18--, Amhe Co, wGertrude Massey
CONN, Sarah P, b11/28/1812, Fair Co, hJonathan Huddleson
CONNALLY, George Franklin, b18--, Hali Co, wMildred Lewis
Henry, bc1840, Hali Co, d1919, fGeorge Franklin, mMildred Lewis
James F, b11/10/1844, Hali Co,

CONNALLY (continued)
fGeorge Franklin, mMildred Lewis, wAlice W Franklin, md1895
Martha Ann, bc1840, Hali Co, fGeorge Franklin, mMildred Lewis, 2w of David Elliott
Mary, bc1840, Hali Co, fGeorge Franklin, mMildred Lewis, hJohn Lipscomb
Robert, b184-, Hali Co, d1907, fGeorge Franklin, mMildred Lewis
Sarah, bc1840, Hali Co, fGeorge Franklin, mMildred Lewis, 1w of David Elliott
Walter, bc1840, Hali Co, f George Franklin, mMildred Lewis
William H, b184-, Hali Co, d1910, fGeorge Franklin, mMildred Lewis
CONNELLEE, James, b18--, Rich Co?, wWillie A --
CONNER, Benjamin C, bc1840, w Bettie Tyler
Susan A, bc1870, Loud Co, 1w of William T Robey Sr, md1891
CONNOR, James Arthur, b186-, Philomont, Loud Co, fJohn T Jr, mMary E Brown
John T Sr, b18--, Loud Co?, d186-, wSusan A Lyne
John T Jr, b1844, Loud Co, fJohn T Sr, mSusan A Lyne, wMary E Brown
Susan Alice, bc1870, Philomont, Loud Co, fJohn T Jr, mMary E Brown, hWilliam T Robey
CONRAD, Catherine, b177-, Fred Co, fFrederick Sr, mMarie Clara Ley
Catherine E, b183-, Winchester, Fred Co, fRobert Young Sr, mElizabeth Powell
Charles Frederick, b184-, Winchester, Fred Co, fRobert Young Sr, mElizabeth Powell, wLouisa Grant
Charles, b185-, Warr Co, fJames W, mMaria S Ashby
Cuthbert, b184-, Winchester, Fred Co, fRobert Young Sr, mElizabeth Powell, wSarah Harris
Daniel, b10/6/1771, Fred Co,

CONRAD (continued)
dc1806, fFrederick, mMarie Clara Ley, wRebecca Holmes
Daniel, b183-, Winchester, Fred Co, fRobert Young Sr, mElizabeth Powell, wSusan Davis
David H, b180-, Fred Co, fDaniel, mRebecca Holmes
Edward, b177-, Fred Co, fFrederick Sr, mMarie Clara Ley
Elizabeth, b177-, Fred Co, fFrederick Sr, mMarie Clara Ley
Elizabeth, bc1870, fHolmes, (2)mGeorgie Bryan Forman, hW D Smith
Francis Edward, b184-, Winchester, Fred Co, fRobert Young Sr, mElizabeth Powell, wMary Harrison
Frederick Jr, b177-, Fred Co, fFrederick Sr, mMarie Clara Ley
James W, b1812, Warr Co, wMaria S Ashby
Holmes, b1/31/1840, Winchester, Fred Co, fRobert Young Sr, mElizabeth Powell, 1wMary Magruder, 2wGeorgie Bryan Forman, md1/2/ 1868
John, b1777-, Fred Co, fFrederick Sr, mMarie Clara Ley
Maud, b18--, Richmond?, hWilliam J Perry Jr
Powell, b183-, Winchester, Fred Co, fRobert Young Sr, mElizabeth Powell
Robert Young Sr, b12/27/1805, Fred Co, d1875, fDaniel, mRebecca Holmes, wElizabeth Powell
Robert Young Jr, b183-, Winchester, Fred Co, dc1860, f Robert Young Sr, mElizabeth Powell
Sarah, b184-, Winchester, Fred Co, fRobert Young Sr, mElizabeth Powell, hA M Fauntleroy
William G, b8/3/1848, Warr Co, fJames W, mMaria S Ashby, wFannie E Bowen, md10/122/1876
CANSALVO, Charles Wright, b10/5/ 1810, Norfolk, d1849, fWilliam II, mSarah Wright, wEliza Ann Riggins
Eugene Herbert, b3/27/1848,

CANSALVO (continued)
Norfolk, d1893, fCharles Wright, mEliza Ann Riggins, wMary Josephine Sykes
William II, b1769, PrAn Co, d1814, fWilliam, mElizabeth Pallette, wSarah Wright, md 1791
CONWAY, Elizabeth, b18--, hHenry Fitzhugh IV
Louisa Roberta, b18--, 2w of Francis C Fitzhugh
Mary, b18--, Staf Co, hRichard C L Moncure
Nellie, b18--, Oran Co?, hWilliam Byrd Willis
Powhatan F, bc1860, Richmond?, wMaggie Brown
COOK, Fannie P, b1870, Pitt Co, d1910, hThomas Alfred Yeatts
Henry H, b1855, Blan Co, fZachariah, mSarah Crabtree, wMartha L Fox
J Churchill, bc1840, wMary Isabella Blackford
James, bc1860, Fauq Co?, wRebecca Parr
John A, b18--, Buch Co, wNancy Virginia Stinson
John Esten, bc1840, Clar Co?, wMary Francis Page
Leanna, bc1838, Cherry Grove, Rkhm Co, d1914, fWilliam, h William Bull
Zachariah, b18--, Taze Co, w Sarah Crabtree
COOKE, Alice, b185-, Oran Co, fJames Madison, mAnne Elizabeth Hawkins, hEdward Brockman
Giles, b18--, Front Royal, Warr Co, wElizabeth Lane
Henry L, b1850, Front Royal, Warr Co, d1918, fGiles, mElizabeth Lane, wAlice W Slemmer
J Frank, b1834, Alexandria
J T, b185-, Oran Co, fJames Madison, mAnne Elizabeth Hawkins
J Thomas, b1860, Alexandria, 1wLillian Lee Beach
James Edward, b8/26/1856, Oran Co, fJames Madison, mAnne Elizabeth Hawkins, wMedora Payne
James Madison, b182-, Culp Co, fJohn R, wAnne Elizabeth Hawkins

COOKE (continued)
Lechmere Rittenhouse, bc1857, Portsmouth, Norf Co
Mary St Clair, b18--, Richmond?, hJames Gordon, md11/26/1856
Susanna, b16--, hHenry Fitzhugh I
COOKSEY, Fannie, b1833-, Fair Co, hAlexander Gustavus Brown Sr
Hartwell P, b18--, Lune Co, wEvelyn Royall
Mary Frances, bc1860, Lune Co, fHartwell P, mEvelyn Royall, hJohn Leroy Yates, md4/7/1881
COOLEY, Emma S, bc1870, Fred Co?, hCharles Richard Campbell
Frank, bc1860, Page Co?, w-- Hottel
Mary E, b1862, Carr Co, d1917, hHenderson M Beamer
Peter F, b18--, Shen Co?, w Sarah Schmucker
S W, bc1850, Fred Co?, wMaria Louise Wright
COONTZ, Mary Elizabeth, bc1816, Winchester, Fred Co, d1904, fPeter, hMichael B Copenhaver
COOPER, --, bc1820, Loud Co, hJohn Cooper
Amanda, b184-, Loud Co, fJohn, m-- Cooper
Arabella, b184-, nrCedarville, Warr Co, 1w of James William Sibert Sr
Columbus P, b1848, Loud Co, fJohn, m-- Cooper, wCordelia Arnold
Edward, bc1870, Merc Co, fJohn, mMaria Padberry
Harriet E, bc1830, hJohn W Camp
Ignatius, b18--, Rkhm Co, wSallie J Keller
Jennie, b18--, Alexandria?, hNicholas Dawson
John, b1814, Loud Co, w-- Cooper
John, b18--, wMaria Padberry
Sallie, bc1870, Merc Co, fJohn, mMaria Padberry, hCharles R Brown, md12/29/1891
Thomas H, bc1860, Roan Co, w-- Barnitz
COOTES, Eugene Baylor, bc1860, Shen Co?, wFreddie Louise

79

COOTES (continued) Moore
COPELAND, Deborah, b17--, Loud Co, hSamuel Purcell
Hannah Frances, b18--, Glou Co, hJefferson A Brown
COPENHAVER, Charles Faulkner, b7/6/1859, Millwood, Clar Co, fMichael B, mMary Elizabeth Coontz, wMary Eva Hodgson, md11/20/1907
George, b180-, Winchester, Fred Co, fMichael
George W, bc1850, Millwood, Clar Co, fMichael B, mMary Elizabeth Coontz
James C, bc1870, nrMarion, Smyt Co, fWilliam H, mNancy Caroline Dungan
Jane, b185-, Millwood, Clar Co, fMichael B, mMary Elizabeth Coontz, hLewis Long
John Worth, bc1850, Millwood, Clar Co, fMichael B, mMary Elizabeth Coontz
Josephine, bc1850, Millwood, Clar Co, fMichael B, mMary Elizabeth Coontz
Julia, b185-, Millwood, Clar Co, fMichael B, mMary Elizabeth Coontz
Margaret, b180-, Winchester, Fred Co, fMichael, hDavid Barrett
Mary Susan, bc1850, Millwood, Clarke Co, fMichael B, mMary Elizabeth Coontz
Meek Hampton, bc1870, nrMarion, Smyt Co, fWilliam H, mNancy Caroline Dungan
Melissa, b186-, nrMarion, Smyt Co, fWilliam H, mNancy Caroline Dungan, hWiley Senter
Michael B, b1807, Winchester, Fred Co, d1864, fMichael, w Mary Elizabeth Coontz
Robert J, b186-, nrMarion, Smyt Co, fWilliam H, mNancy Caroline Dungan
Sallie, bc1830, Wyth Co, 1w of John G Kegley
Samuel, bc1800, Smyt Co, wEliza Tilson
Samuel T, bc1860, Smyt Co, wScena Anderson
Susie, bc1870, nrMarion, Smyt

COPENHAVER (continued) Co, fWilliam H, mNancy Caroline Dungan, hRobert Gollehon
Virginia, b5/21/1830, Seven Mile Ford, Smyt Co, d1871, hPatrick Campbell Buchanan Jr
Virginia, b186-, nrMarion, Smyt Co, fWilliam H, mNancy Caroline Dungan, hA W Edwards
William H, b1829, Smyt Co, fSamuel, mEliza Tilson, wNancy Caroline Dungan
COPP, --, b11/11/1851, nrWoodstock, Shen Co, fJacob, Rebecca Huffman, hJoseph B Brumback
Ada Arlena, b186-, nrStrasburg, Shen Co, fJohn Eli, mJoanna Arlena Glaize, hLeopold Frenkel
Barbara Joanna, bc1860, nrStrasburg, Shen Co, fJohn Eli, mJoanna Arlena Glaize, hWilliam A Hockman
Frances, b183-, nrMaurertown, Shen Co, fJohn, mBarbara Shaver, hJonas Wakeman
George, b17--, Shen Co, fAndrew
George Andrew, b11/1/1858, nrStrasburg, Shen Co, fJohn Eli, mJoanna Arlena Glaize, wEmma Ester Maphis, md11/30/1882
George W, b183-, nrMaurertown, Shen Co, fJohn, mBarbara Shaver
Jacob, b18--, Shen Co?, wRebecca Huffman
John, bc1800, nrMaurertown, Shen Co, fGeorge, wBarbara Shaver
John Eli, b7/1/1835, nrMaurertown, Shen Co, d1917, fJohn, mBarbara Shaver, wJoanna Arlena Glaize, md1/17/1856
Mary Frances, b185-, nrStrasburg, Shen Co, fJohn Eli, mJoanna Arlena Glaize, hWilliam H Spiggle
Olive Viola, b186-, nrStrasburg, Shen Co, fJohn Eli, mJoanna Arlena Glaize, hJoseph G Baker
Sarah, bc1830, nrMaurertown, Shen Co, fJohn, mBarbara Shaver, hNoah Hockman
Zedekiah Hetzel, b186-, nr

COPP (continued)
Strasburg, Shen Co, fJohn Eli, mJoanna Arlena Glaize
COPPRIDGE, Joel, b184-, nrChatham, Pitt Co, fMalberry, mParthenia Watson
William David, b9/4/1859, nr Chatham, Pitt Co, fMalberry, mParthenia Watson, wMollie E Ferguson, md12/11/1884
CORBIN, --, bc1800, Culp Co, fJames Parke, 1hFarley Fontleroy
Elizabeth, b18--, Culp Co?, hWilliam Major
Laetitia, b16--, hRichard Lee II
Mariah Louise, b18--, Rapp Co, m-- Fletcher, hJames Harrison Browning
Virginia Ann, b1848, Laneville Plantation, Warw Co, d1888, hJohn R Parker
CORBITT, Charles L, b10/21/1862, Boykins, Sout Co, fJames Madison, mMartha Ann Whitney, wJosephine Weston, md11/21/1899
James Howard, b4/29/1869, Boykins, Sout Co, fJames Madison, mMartha Ann Whitney, wRoberta Clifford Ansley, md1902
James Madison, b2/9/1829, Sout Co, d1901, wMartha Ann Whitney, md4/30/1861
Margaret S, b186-, Boykins, Sout Co, d1897, fJames Madison, mMartha Ann Whitney, h Walter Boone
Martha S, b186-, Boykins, Sout Co, fJames Madison, mMartha Ann Whitney, hJames N Peed
CORDER, Elijah Sr, b18--, Burkes Garden, Taze Co, w-- Osborne
Elijah Jr, b1851, Scot Co, fElijah Sr, m-- Osborne, wMargaret Ramey
CORKER, Martha Jane, b2/17/1862, Henrico Co, hRobert Julius Smith
CORLEY, Malvina, b18--, Bath Co, fThomas, hJudson Chennoweth Goddin
CORNELIUS, Mason, b18--, Hedgesville, Berk Co, wMinnie Brown
CORNETT, John, b18--, nrElk Creek, Gray Co, w-- Boyer

CORNETT
Kenley C, b1843, Elk Creek, Gray Co, d1919, fJohn, wMary Wright
CORNS, John B, b1801, Patr Co, wElizabeth Cutler
Mary E, b1855, Cornsville, Scot Co, fJohn B, mElizabeth Cutler, hRobert Burns Quillin
CORNWELL, Montraville, b18--, PrWi Co?, 2wAnne Elizabeth Posey
Samuel E, b18--, Alexandria, wMary Virginia Vernon
William C, bc1860, Fred Co, wEmma Gardner
CORR, --, b18--, KiQu Co, hJohn Didlake
Catherine Gardner, b10/17/1838, Corr's Landing, nrWest Point, KiWi Co, hJames Edward Bland
Harry L, b185-, nrWhite Marsh, Glou Co, fLevi Pace, (2)mAnn Watlington
Levi Pace, b12/1818, KiQu Co, d1897, fWilliam, m-- Carleton, 1wMartha Ann Stubblefield, 2wAnn Watlington
Mary Frances, b185-, nrWhite Marsh, Glou Co, fLevi Pace, (2)mAnn Watlington, hArcher H Robins
Ptolemy W, b185-, nrWhite Marsh, Glou Co, fLevi Pace, (2)mAnn Watlington
Thomas R, b185-, nrWhite Marsh, Glou Co, fLevi Pace, (2)mAnn Watlington
William, b17--, w-- Carleton
William Ellis Sr, b4/22/1849, nrWhite Marsh, Glou Co, fLevi Pace, (1)mMartha Ann Stubblefield, 1wSantie M Jones, md1884, 2wMary Dudley Jones
CORRELL, Charles, b18--, Fred Co?, wJulia A Barr
CORSON, Lelia K, b186-, Glebe Farm, nrCumberland Court House, Cumb Co, d1904, fWilliam C, mJennie Caldwell, 1w of Philip J Flippen
William C, b18--, Camp Co, wJennie Caldwell
William M, b7/20/1869, Glebe Farm, nrCumberland Court House, Cumb Co, fWilliam C,

CORSON (continued)
mJennie Caldwell
CORVIN, John P, b18--, Wyth Co?, d1922, wMarkham R Kegley
COSBY, Cornelia C, b18--, hJefferson Davis Van Benthuysen
David, bc1700, Caro Co?, wMary Garland Overton
Elizabeth, b17--, Caro Co?, fDavid, mMary Garland Overton, hJohn Minor
Ira L, b2/28/1858, nrRichmond, fPhilip L, mCharlotte Adkinson, wLina E Duncan
Jane E, b18--, Pitt Co?, hE H Miller
Philip L, b18--, nrRichmond, wCharlotte Adkinson
COSTINE, Elizabeth, b18--, nrNeenah, West Co, hJoseph Warren Hutt Sr
COTTRELL, Nora A, b18--, Richmond, fRichard, hWilliam Davidson Diuguid, md11/8/1880
Samuel H, b18--, Gooc Co, fJohn W, wJulia Crump
COTTY, Margaret, b1786-, Fred Co?, hHenry Larrick
COUCH, Elizabeth, b18--, Russ Co, hWilliam W McCoy
Emma, b1837, Petersburg, Dinw Co, d1897, hJohn Brooks Davis
James H, bc1860, PrEd Co?, wSallie Love Terry
Rebecca, b17--, Gooc Co, fSamuel, hAnthony Robinson Sr
William, bc1860, PrEd Co?, wGeorgia Anna Terry
William, b1/24/1869, Appo Co, fJames M, mBetty E Durphey, wClaudine Bradshaw, md5/12/1887
COUGILL, Clarence E, b6/25/1868, nrStephens City, Fred Co, fJohn W, mCatherine Long, w Rosa B, md5/30/1892
James, b183-, Hamp Co, fJohn T, mCatherine McKee
John T, b18--, Hamp Co, wCatherine McKee
John W, b7/1845, Hamp Co, d1914, fJohn T, mCatherine McKee, wCatherine Long, md9/1867
Joseph, bc1840, Hamp Co, fJohn T, mCatherine McKee

COUGILL (continued)
Margaret, b183-, Hamp Co, fJohn T, mCatherine McKee, hJoseph Coe
Mary C, b184-, Hamp Co, fJohn T, mCatherine McKee, hSamuel Bates
Mary R, bc1870, nrStephens City, Fred Co, fJohn W, mCatherine Long
COUK, Benjamin F, b186-, Jonesville, Lee Co, fCharles F, mMartha Brown
Charles Edgar, b5/30/1869, Jonesville, Lee Co, fCharles F, mMartha Brown, wAlice Reed, md7/11/1900
Charles F, b1838, Jonesville, Lee Co, fCharles, mSusan Beck, wMartha Brown
J Morgan, bc1860, Jonesville, Lee Co, fCharles F, mMartha Brown
William R, b187-, Jonesville, Lee Co, fCharles F, mMartha Brown
COUNTS, --, b17--, hJacob Rasnick
Crissey, b17--, Russ Co, hRichard Colley
Eliza Jane, b18--, Dick Co, d1918, 1hJoshua D Pressley, 2hJames M Colley
Eliza Jane, b3/12/1863, nrAily, Dick Co, fNoah, mAily Amburgey, hWilliam B Sutherland
John, b17--, d1802, wMagdalene
John, b17--, Shen Co, d1843, fJohn, mMagdalene --, wMargaret "Peggy" Kelley
Joshua, b8/27/1801, Russ Co, fJohn, mMargaret "Peggy" Kelley, 1wMartha Kiser
Noah, b4/21/1831, Cleveland, Russ Co, d1898, fJoshua, (1)mMartha Kiser, wAily Amburgey
Richard L, bc1860, Russ Co?, wEdith S Meade
Sylvia, b10/5/1826, Cleveland, Russ Co, d1916, fJoshua, (1)mMartha Kiser, hWilliam Sutherland
COUSEL, John, bc1850, Camp Co?, wSallie A Harvey
COUSINS, Susan, b18--, Pitt Co?,

COUSINS (continued)
  hKerr Farley
COVER, Alice Grace, bc1870, Elkton, Rkhm Co, fJohn, mSylvia Brown, hReuben B Stipes
  John, b18--, Rkhm Co?, wSylvia Brown
COVERSTONE, James, bc1840, Shen Co, fJohn, wAnnie Regina Boyer
  Mary, b18--, Powell's Fort Valley, Shen Co, hJacob Neeb
  Rebecca, b184-, Powell's Fort Valley, Shen Co, d1921, fJohn, hJohn D Boyer
COVINGTON, Mary L, b18--, Ches Co, d1876, 1w of William Mc Kendree Evans, md1868
COWAN, Mary, b17--, 2w of Robert Graham
  Nancy, b17--, hJohnson Howard
  Nancy Ann, b1834, Holston Valley, Scot Co, 3w of William M Gray
COWDERY, Fannie, b18--, hJohn Purviance Leigh
COWHERD, Winifred, b17--, Culp Co?, fJames, hWilliam Twyman I
COWLES, Martha "Pattie" Burton, b1845, Petersburg, Dinw Co, d1885, fHenry B, hEdwin Murray Mann Sr, md1865
  Mary Drew, b186-, JaCi Co?, fPeter T, mLaura Hubbard, h Robert Lee Spencer
  Peter I, b18--, JaCi Co?, w Laura Hubbard
COWLING, Mary, b18--, Richmond, hWilliam C Perrow
COX, Cora, b3/19/1868, nrAlhambra, Nels Co, fThaddeus C, mBettie Massie, hJohn H Massie, md9/1893
  David L, b17--, Ft Blackmore, Scot Co, fWilliam B
  Edwin P, b5/2/1870, Blan Co, fHenry Winston, mMartha H Wooldridge, wSallie Bland Clarke, md4/10/1898
  Elizabeth, b18--, West Co?, 1w of Edward Colville Griffith
  Henry, bc1700, Ches Co, wJudith
  Henry Sr, b5/3/1737, Henrico Co, fHenry, mJudith --, wElizabeth Chappell, md7/31/1775
  Henry Jr, b3/23/1778, Ches Co, d1856, fHenry Sr, mElizabeth

COX (continued)
  Chappell, wMary Traylor, md11/21/1805
  Henry Winston, b12/9/1835, Clover Hill, Ches Co, fJames H, mMartha Reid Law, wMartha H Wooldridge, md11/8/1859
  James H, b2/16/1810, Clover Hill, Ches Co, d1877, fHenry Jr, mMary Traylor, wMartha Reid Law
  James P, b1842, Clover Hill, Ches Co, d1879, fJames H, mMartha Reid Law
  Jane, b17--, hFrances Hopkins
  John Hopkins, b1851, Clover Hill, Ches Co, d1893, fJames H, mMartha Reid Law
  Joseph Edwin, b183-, Clover Hill, Ches Co, d1861, fJames H, mMartha Reid Law
  Joseph M, b12/8/1854, Ft Blackmore, Scot Co, fRobert K, mNancy Buster, wVictoria McClelland
  Kate Virginia, bc1840, Clover Hill, Ches Co, fJames H, mMartha Reid Law, hThomas M Logan
  L Lloyd, b1858, Ft Blackmore, Scot Co, fRobert, mNancy Buster, wMary Banner
  Lewis Berkeley Sr, b1849, Loud Co, fRichard Threlkeld, mMary Berkeley, wElinor Jackson Junkin
  Louella, b18--, Gray Co?, hJames M Kyle
  Lucy, b18--, Russ Co, hJames D Wright
  Mary A, b1852, nrFt Blackmore, Scot Co, hGeorge A Johnson
  Mary Alice, b18--, Bedf Co?, fThomas McFarland, hJames Alexander Campbell, md2/18/1867
  Melville B, b1841, nrIndependence, Gray Co, fSamuel, m-- Thomas, wMartha E Fulton
  Minerva Archer, b5/30/1814, Ches Co, fHenry Jr, mMary Traylor, hDaniel Spencer Wooldridge, md1835
  Richard Threlkeld, b18--, Loud Co, fJohn, wMary Berkeley
  Robert K, b1822, Ft Blackmore, Scot Co, d1887, fDavid L, wNancy Buster

COX (continued)
Sarah L, b18--, Carr Co, hLorenzo Dow Collier
Sue T, b18--, Suss Co, hHenry T West
Thaddeus C, b18--, Nels Co?, wBettie Massie
William B, b17--, Ft Blackmore, Scot Co, fDaniel
William E, b18--, Lanc Co, wAddie Locke
William Law, b1845, Clover Hill, Ches Co, d1899, fJames H, mMartha Reid Law
Winifred, b18--, fVincent, m Anne Payne, 1w of Matthew Rust
COYNER, Artemus Dillar, b4/28/1847, Augu Co, d1919, fDavid Dillar, mCelestine Caldwell, wElizabeth Fauber
C L, bc1840, Augu Co?, wMargaret Blair
David Dillar, b1816, Waynesboro, Augu Co, d1894, fGeorge Michael, m-- Dillar, wCelestine Caldwell
CRABBE, Walter Randolph, b18--, West Co?, wElizabeth Zimmerman
CRABILL, Mary, bc1800, Shen Co, 1h-- Kagey, 2hGeorge Shaver Jr
CRABTREE, Eliza, b12/25/1855, Russ Co, d1888, hJohn C Gilbert
Sarah, b18--, Blan Co, hZachariah Cook
CRADDALL, Margaret Ann, b18--, Mont Co, hDavis Stephens
CRADDOCK, Charles J, b18--, Hali Co?, d1866, wFannie Y Easley
Elizabeth, b1831, Meck Co, d1893, fEdward, hWilliam Martin Barnitz Jr
Harriet Bailey, b185-, Hali Co, fCharles J, mFannie Y Easley, 1w of William R Barksdale, md11/14/ 1872
John Wimbish Sr, b8/14/1858, Halifax Court House, Hali Co, fCharles J, mFanny Y Easley, 1wMary Peachy Gilmer, md12/6/ 1886, 2wEliza (Deane) Baker
Richard P, b18--, wNannie Coleman
CRAIG, --, bc1800, wMartha Triplett
--, b185-, Arli Co?, wMary

CRAIG (continued)
Duncan
Casper, bc1840, Shen Co?, wMalinda Triplett
Clementine, b18--, Mont Co, hEdward Hammett
George Samuel, b9/14/1850, Craigstown, Augu Co, fJames, wAnnie C Doyle
J J, bc1850, Nels Co, wSallie McGinnis
James, b18--, Craigsville, Augu Co, fSamuel C, mElizabeth Bratton
Mary, b17--, wRobert Graham
Mary, b1803, Wyth Co, hJohn Gray
Mildred S, b1858, Albe Co, hJames W Wood
Robert, b18--, Craigsville, Augu Co, fSamuel C, mElizabeth Bratton, 1wSusan Bell, 2wEmma Hamilton
Susan Frances, b18--, Augu Co, hBenjamin Overton Ferguson
CRAIGEN, Laura, b1837, Greenspring, Hamp Co, hJames Bonifant
CRAIGHEAD, Sallie, b18--, Fran Co, d1879, fThomas L, mLucinda ---, 2w of John Hill Matthews
Thomas L, b18--, Fran Co, wLucinda CRALLE, Calista Rosser, b9/4/1808, fLindsay, mAnn Rosser, hArmistead Long Jr
Joseph B, b11/11/1846, Heathsville, Nhld Co, wClara Annie Eubank
Lelia, b1840, Kenbridge, Lune Co, d1878, hRobert M Dickinson
Lindsay, b17--, wAnn Rosser
Sallie, b1799, Powh Co, fRichard Kenner, hColin Stokes
CRANDALL, --, b18--, JaCi Co, 1h of Mary West
CRANFORD, Mary, b18--, 1hJohn Seay, 2hJohn Lowhorne
CRANK, Ida Blanche, bc1870, Loui Co, fJohn R, mSusan M Perkins, hDaniel Webster Perkins, md5/ 1895
John R, b18--, Loui Co, wSusan M Perkins
Martha, b18--, hA J Parish
CRAUN, Sarah, b18--, Rkhm Co, hJohn H Alexander

CRAWFORD, Bettie, bc1800, Augu Co, hWilliam Ingles
Charles A, b7/16/1852, Richmond, fJacob Valentine, mLouisa A Johnson, wNellie L Wightman
Ellie M, b18--, hJohn Frank Elliott, md1/19/1879
Frances, b18--, Staunton, Augu Co, hJohn S Churchman
Maggie, b18--, Russ Co, hLeonidas Webb
Mary Elizabeth, b2/28/1853, Walker's Creek, Blan Co, d1923, fWilliam, hRalph A Stafford
Mary Jane, b18--, Richmond, hDaniel Toomey
CRAWLEY, Charles Wesley, b11/21/1825, Char Co, d1890, fWilliam, mSarah Davis, wMargaret Julia Tinsley
Hannah Fennell, bc1870, nrFarmville, PrEd Co, fCharles Wesley, mMargaret Julia Tinsley
James Wilber, bc1870, nrFarmville, PrEd Co, fCharles Wesley, mMargaret Julia Tinsley
Kenner Tinsley, b186-, nrFarmville, PrEd Co, fCharles Wesley, mMargaret Julia Tinsley
Nannie, b18--, Hali Co, 1w of Richard A Singleton
Sarah E, b1855, Prospect, PrEd Co, hWilliam Montgomery Duvall
William, bc1800, Char Co, d1853, wSarah Davis
CREAMER, Harriett, b18--, Jeff Co?, hThomas Fritts
CREASY, George Claiborne, b18--, Bedf Co, w-- Arthur
Gustavus Adolphus, b18--, Camp Co, fGeorge Claiborne, m-- Arthur, wSallie Claiborne Tucker
Thomas Claiborne, b18--, Bedf Co, fGeorge Claiborne, m-- Arthur, wEliza Lavalette Elliott
CREIGH, Jane Lynn, b18--, Albe Co?, 2w of Egbert Read Watson, md4/29/1856
Sabina Lewis Stuart, b18--, Albe Co, hJohn Rodes Woods
CREIGHTON, William Jr, b17--, Berk Co, fWilliam Sr

CRENSHAW, Charles A, b186-, Fauq Co, fLarkin Hardy, mAnnie Glascock, wLeila Lambert
Dibrell, b182-, Nott Co, fWilliam
Dibrell Duncan, b5/15/1869, Rockburn, Fauq Co, fLarkin Hardy, mAnnie Glascock, wFannie G Quinn
Edmond Massey, bc1870, Rockburn, Fauq Co, fLarkin Hardy, mAnnie Glascock, wDonata Poindexter
Emma Samantha, b18--, Bedf Co, fSamuel H, mPriscilla Jones, 2w of Elijah G McClannahan
Fannie, bc1800, hStephen Clifton Hurt
Frances Edmonia, b1831, Hano Co, hWilliam W Newman, md1867
Gertrude, b186-, Fauq Co, fLarkin Hardey, mAnnie Glascock
Larkin Hardey, b1832, Blackstone, Nott Co, d1902, fWilliam, wAnnie Glascock
Samuel H, b17--, Bedf Co, wPriscilla Jones
William, b182-, Nott Co, fWilliam
CRESSEY, Jeanette, bc1870, Albe Co, hThomas L Rhodes
CREWS, Ada B, b12/1863, Ches Co, hJames Thomas Lacy Sr
B S, bc1860, Hali Co, fJohn B, (2)mLouisa F Barkdale
James D, b9/12/1862, Hali Co, fJohn B, (2)mLouisa F Barkdale, 1wElla Pettus Grasty, md1888, 2wSallie F Holt
John B, b18--, Hali Co, 1w Margaret Sydnor, 2wLouisa F Barkdale
Virginia, b18--, Pitt Co, hEdmond Fitzgerald
CRIDLIN, John N, b2/19/1836, West Co, d1916, 1wSarah E Snyder, 2wMartha Wood
CRIGLER, Belle, bc1870, Madi Co, fJ C, mMary E Aylor, 1w of Jackson Lee Fray, md1901
J C, b18--, Madi Co, wMary E Aylor
Virginia, b18--, Staf Co?, fRobert, hLewis Conner Botts
CRIM, George, bc1840, Rkbr Co, wAlice Clinedinst

CRIM (continued)
J W, bc1830, Rkbr Co, wEliza Clinedinst
CRISMAN, Jacob, bc1840, Fred Co?, wNancy Catherine Larrick
Sarah, b5/18/1757, Hard Co, hWilliam Warden
CRISMOND, Arthur H, bc1870, Spot Co, fJoseph Patrick Henry, mSallie J Carnohan, wEllen B Burke
John B, b1791, Glou Co, wVirginia McDaniel
Joseph Patrick Henry, b5/6/1846, Caro Co, fJohn B, mVirginia McDaniel, wSallie J Carnohan, md1866
CRISS, Mary, b18--, hHugh Holmes Lee
CRIST, Andrew J, b1836, nrTimberville, Rkhm Co, fJohn, m-- May, wChristina Kline
Jacob H, b186-, nrBroadway, Rkhm Co, fAndrew J, mChristina Kline
John, bc1800, Rkhm Co?, w-- May
Mollie C, b186-, nrBroadway, Rkhm Co, fAndrew J, mChristina Kline, h-- Miller
Noah R, b2/27/1867, nrBroadway, Rkhm Co, fAndrew J, mChristina Kline, wEtta S Kiser, md4/27/1898
Samuel K, bc1860, nrBroadway, Rkhm Co, fAndrew J, mChristina Kline
Sara F, b186-, nrBroadway, Rkhm Co, fAndrew J, mChristina Kline
CRITTENDEN, Richard M, b9/29/1825, Esse Co, fWilliam G, mMary Thomas, wLucy A James
Sarah, b18--, Surr Co?, hWilliam Rowe Boutwell Sr
W J, b11/26/1859, Fauq Co, fRichard M, mLucy A James, 2wMrs Claiborne Rice Mason
William G, bc1800, Esse Co, wMary Thomas
CROCKETT, Elizabeth, b18--, Wayn Co?, hJohn Tabor
Jane, b17--, Pula Co?, d1844, hJohn S Draper Jr
Joseph, b17--, Wyth Co?, wJane Devine
Joseph, b17--, Wyth Co?,

CROCKETT (continued)
fJoseph, mJane Devine, wCatherine Montgomery
Mary, b5/23/1778, fJames, mMary Drake, hJames McGavock, md 4/24/1797
Robert, b18--, Wyth Co, wVirginia Crockett
Sallie, b18--, Wyth Co, hJohn C Raper
Susan, bc1810, Wytheville, Wyth Co, fJoseph, mCatherine Montgomery, hWilliam Hickman Spiller Sr
Virginia, b18--, hRobert Crockett
William, b18--, Wyth Co, wEmily Chaffin
William Chaffin, b4/1853, Wyth Co, d1921, fWilliam, mEmily Chaffin, wWillie Crump
CROMER, Eveline, bc1825, nrElkton, Rkhm Co, fJoseph, mMary Harnsberger, hRudolf Myers
Joseph, bc1800, Rkhm Co?, wMary Harnsberger
CROOKS, Margaret P, b18--, fRobert Nelson, hSydney Smith
CROPP, --, b18--, fC B, hWilliam White
James, bc1860, wJennie B Ramey
CROSBY, Andrew P, b18--, Norfolk, wNellie Albert
CROSS, --, bc1800, Russ Co, hIsaiah Fuller
Charles Felix, b1818, Hano Co, fOliver, mPolly Bowe, 2wAmanda Stuart Bowe
Oliver, b17--, Hano Co, wPolly Bowe
Wirt Hamilton, b1859, Hano Co, fCharles Felix, mAmanda Stuart Bowe, wAlice Marian Campbell
CROUCH, --, bc1860, Wise Co?, wEliza A Greear
Charles N, b18--, Wayn Co?, wAlice Wilson
Elizabeth S, b18--, hHowson Wallace
CROUSE, Mary, b18--, Augu Co, hBenjamin F Moomaw
CROW, Catherine Eugeinia, bc1839, Clar Co, d1907, fThomas, hJohn Brazier Glover
Martha A, b18--, Appo, hJohn E Johnson

CROWDER, Charles Womack Sr, b1857, Cumb Co, d1911, fJohn Edmund, wLucy Anne Jeter
Florence, bc1870, Camp Co, fWilliam R, m Victoria Moore, hOscar S Engledove, md1/1/1890
John Edmund, b18--, Cumb Co, fWilson
William R, b18--, Camp Co?, wVictoria Moore
CROWTHER, Virginia, b18--, Nhld Co?, hThomas J Marsh
CROXTON, Louisa, b18--, Buck Co?, hJohn G Morris
CRUM, ---, bc1850, Augu Co?, wMattie Orebaugh
CRUMBAKER, Elizabeth, b1773, Loud Co, d1825, hPhilip Heater
CRUMP, Anna Bigger, b18--, fRobert H, mSarah Dobson, hThomas J Bowles
Elizabeth, b18--, NewK Co, d1896, fStanope, mMary Wright, 1w of Robert Andrew Folkes, md12/15/1869
James D, b8/23/1848, Richmond, fRobert H, mSarah Dobson, wNannie Armistead, md11/4/1875
Julia, b18--, Richmond?, fRobert H, mSarah Dobson, hSamuel H Cottrell
Mary, b18--, Richmond, fRobert H, mSarah Dobson, hWilliam D West
Robert H, b1822, NewK Co, fFielding, wSarah Dobson
Robert Shields, b18--, Richmond, fRobert H, mSarah Dobson
Willie, b4/1858, Crumps Bottom, Summ Co, d1916, hWilliam Chaffin Crockett
CRUMPACKER, Owen, b18--, Bedf Co, wAilie Ann Heim
Sarinda, b18--, Franklin Co, fOwen, mAilie Ann Heim, hStephen P Guerrant Sr
CRUMPTON, Lucy Jane, b18--, Danville, Pitt Co, fJames, hWilliam H Loyd, md10/15/1856
CRUSER, Handford Thornton Sr, b9/17/1858, wJosie Ironmonger
CRUTCHFIELD, Josephine, b1838, Richmond, hThomas White Sydnor
CRUTE, J N, b18--, Buck Co?, w-- Gannaway
J Wyatt, bc1850, Melrose Farm,

CRUTE (continued)
Buck Co, fJohn Venable, (1)m Martha Pettis Smith
John, bc1800, PrEd Co, fJohn, w-- Ligon
John Venable, b6/24/1825, PrEd Co, fJohn, m-- Ligon, 1wMartha Pettis Smith, 2wBettie Powers, 3w---
Joseph Marshall, b9/26/1855, Melrose Farm, Buck Co, fJohn Venable, (1)mMartha Pettis Smith, wHattie Paulett
Martha K, b185-, Melrose Farm, Buck Co, fJohn Venable, (1)m Martha Pettis Smith, hWilliam E Garnett
CULBERTSON, Mary Larue, b6/6/1862, Nickelsville, Scot Co, hCharles C Broadwater
Polly, b18--, Scot Co?, hSamuel D Stallard
CULLEN, Charlotte E, b18--, Char Co?, d1888, hHenry Alexander Carrington
CUMMING, Hugh S, b1869
CUMMINGS, Frank P, b18--, Mont Co?, wGeorgie Pepper
CUNNINGHAM, --, bc1840, Rkhm Co?, wAmanda Acker
Ariana Peyton, b8/9/1835, Oakland, PrEd Co, fEdward, mElizabeth Berkeley, hWilliam Washington Wight
J J, b18--, Amhe Co?, wMary Jordan
Mary, b1857, Holston, Wash Co, hWesley Long
Nannie Maria, b11/30/1849, nrPamplin, PrEd Co, fNewton, hWillis Hopkins Ligon
William, bc1860, Char Co?, hLottie Carrington
CURLING, Laura, bc1870, Norf Co?, hMartin W Hall
CURRELL, Elizabeth, b18--, PrWi Co, hLuther Lynn
Judith, b18--, Lanc Co, hAnthony M Sanders
CURTIS, --, bc1800, Culp Co, hDaniel Hall
Elizabeth, b18--, hAdam F Britts
Frank, b18--, Fauq Co?, wMary Payne
Humphrey Howard, bc1830, Mul-

CURTIS (continued)
berry Island (now Fort Eustis), Warw Co, d1881, wMariah Elizabeth Whitaker
J M, bc1830, Rich Neck, Warw Co
CUSHING, Carrie, b18--, Staf Co, hE Taylor Rollins
Henrietta, b18--, Augu Co, dc1860, 1w of Samuel M Yost
CUSTER, --, bc1800, Fred Co?, h-- Hillyard
Virginia "Kate", b1834, Taze Co, d1884, 1w of Robert B Witten
CUTCHINS, Sol, b1855, Isle Co, wRoberta Oppenhimer
CUTLER, ELizabeth, b18--, hJohn B Corns
DABBS, Frances, bc1800, Hali Co?, hJosiah Dabbs
Josiah, bc1800, Hali Co?, wFrances Dabbs
Julia Frances, b11/21/1829, Hali Co, d1909, fJosiah, mFrances Elizabeth Dabbs, hJames Matthew Blanks
DABNEY, A E, b186-, Fred Co?, wMollie Barr
Ann, b17--, Hano Co, hAlexander Stuart II
Catherine, b18--, hThomas Walker
Chiswell Sr, b7/25/1844, nr Marysville, Camp Co, fJohn B, mElizabeth Towles, wLucy Fontaine, md1873
Elizabeth, b18--, Lynchburg, Camp Co, dc1885, fChiswell, hJohn Scaisbrook Langhorne
Gordon, b185-, "Dunlora", Albe Co, fWilliam S
John B, b18--, Camp Co?, wElizabeth Towles
Lucy, b18--, Camp Co?, hVan Rensselaer Otey
Marion Gordon, b3/20/1858, "Dunlora", Albe Co, d1911, fWilliam S, mSusan Gordon, hJohn B Moon
Mary, bc1700, Caro Co?, hThomas Carr
R A, bc1850, Richmond?, wVirginia H Taylor
Walter D, b185-, "Dunlora", Albe Co, d1899, fWilliam S, mSusan Gordon

DABNEY (continued)
William C, bc185 , "Dunlora", Albe Co, d1894, fWilliam S, mSusan Gordon, wJane Belle Minor
William S, b18--, Albe Co?, wSusan Gordon
William Taylor, b6/12/1868, fRobert A E, mVirginia M ---, wMary R French, md11/5/1885
DADE, Margaret, b18--, Culp Co?, hEdward Smith
DAGGETT, Clifton, bc1860, Fair Co?, wEmma Shreve
DAINGERFIELD, Ellenor N, b186-, Rose Hill, Esse Co, fHenry Willis, mCourtney T Upshur
George Withe, b10/15/1870, Rose Hill, Esse Co, fHenry Willis, mCourtney T Upshur, wLucy B Mallory, md1/31/1907
Henry, b186-, Rose Hill, Esse Co, fHenry Willia, mCourtney T Upshur
Henry Willis, b1824, Greenfield, Esse Co, d1907, fJohn, wCourtney T Upshur
John, bc1860, Rose Hill, Esse Co, fHenry Willis, mCourtney T Upshur
Lou B, b186-, Rose Hill, Esse Co, fHenry Willis, mCourtney T Upshur
William, b186-, Rose Hill, Esse Co, fHenry Willis, mCourtney T Upshur
DALTON, Adaline, b18--, Floyd Co, hElijah Dalton
Lelia Harriett, b1867, Nott Co, hJohn Thomas Green Jr
Mary, b17--, Patr Co?, hArchelaus Hughes
DAME, Ellen Page, b12/5/1849, Danville, Pitt Co, fGeorge Washington, mMary Maria Page, hRobert Brydon
DAMERON, Mary W, b18--, Brun Co, fWilliam, mMary Mangum, hThomas Hicks Cleaton
William, b18--, Brun Co?, wMary Mangum
DANCE, Edward, b17--, Ches Co, wMartha Pride
John, bc1800, Ches Co?, wElizabeth Owen Winfree, md1/1824
Martha, b17--, Ches Co, fEd-

DANCE (continued)
 ward, mMartha Pride, hWilliam Parrin Law
 Willis J, b18--, Char Co?, wBirtea Williamson
DANDRIDGE, Bartholomew, b17--, NewK Co, w-- Clayton
 Cyane (Sianna) Armistead, b1800, NewK Co, fWilliam, mSusanna Armistead, hJohn Williams
 Martha, b17--, Gooc Co?, fNathaniel West, mDorothea Spotswood, hAlexander Spotswood Payne
 Nathaniel West, b17--, Gooc Co?, wDorothea Spotswood
 William, b17--, NewK Co?, fBartholomew, m-- Clayton, wSusannah Armistead
DANIEL, Elizabeth, b9/5/1716, Midd Co?, hEdward Bristow
 Elvira, b18--, Camp Co, hChristopher Columbus Harvey
 Joel W, b18--, wMartha S Dupuy
 John W, bc1830, Midd Co, 1wMyra Bristow, 2wBettie Bristow
 John Warwick, b18--, Camp Co?, fWilliam Jr
 Margaret B, b18--, Camp Co, fWilliam Sr, hMayo Cabell
 Martha, b18--, Camp Co, fWilliam Sr, hWood Bouldin
 Mary Long, b18--, fJoseph J, hGeorge Loyall Gordon
 Molly A, b6/10/1835, Pitt Co, hHumphrey Singleton Belt III
 Nicie Haws, b10/11/1831, Loui Co?, fPeter M, hWilliam Quarles Thomson
 Sarah Ann Warwick, b18--, Camp Co?, d1918, fWilliam Jr, hDon Peters Halsey Sr, md3/7/1866
 William Jr, b18--, Camp Co, fWilliam Sr
DANIELS, Warner, b18--, Gray Co?, wNannie Phipps
DANNER, Hugh, bc1830, Shen Co?, wEmma Newman
DARDEN, Dempsey, bc1840, Holy Neck, Nans Co, fWilliam, mNancy Langston
 Mary Elizabeth, b11/16/1839, Holy Neck, Nans Co, fWilliam, mNancy Langston, hLuther Rawls, md5/30/ 1867

DARDEN (continued)
 William, b18--, Nans Co?, wNancy Langston
DARNELL, Harry Mauze Darnell, b9/13/1857, Fran Co, fRichard, mSusan ---, wMary Louisa Hairston, md7/5/1881
 Richard, b18--, Fran Co, wSusan
DARST, Alice, bc1870, Pula Co?, d1889, fJohn B, mMary E Yost, 1w of Edward W Early
 John B, b18--, Pula Co?, wMary E Yost
DAUB, Albert A, bc1860, wSusan Cochran
DAVENPORT, Catherine, bc1800, Culp Co?, hJames G Ficklen
 Martha Blackwell, b4/7/1813, Gooc Co, hJames Hoye Jr
 Mary, b1857, Sharps, Rich Co, hThomas N Oldham
DAVIDSON, --, b18--, Rkbr Co?, hWilliam Youell
 Albert, b18--, Rkbr Co, d1865, fJames Dorman
 Andrew Baker, b17--, Rkbr Co?, m-- Baker, wSusan Dorman
 B M, bc1850, Nels Co?, wEva P Harris
 Charles A, b18--, Rkbr Co, d1879, fJames Dorman
 Clara, b18--, Rkbr Co, fJames Dorman, hAndrew D Estill
 Frederick, b18--, Rkbr Co, d186-, fJames Dorman
 Greenlee, b18--, Rkbr Co, d186- fJames Dorman
 James Dorman, b11/7/1808, nr Lexington, Rkbr Co, d1882, fAndrew Baker, mSusan Dorman
 Louisa Maria, bc1800, Fred Co?, hIsaac Hite
 Mary, b18--, Rkbr Co, d1894, fJames Dorman
 Mary Lee, b8/15/1866, Wise Co, fWilliam R, mJemima Pendleton, hWade Hampton Roberts Sr, md2/17/1886
 Matilda, bc1835, Taze (now Blan) Co, hJames R Witten
 Paulina, b8/1825, Appo Co, d1885, fSamuel, hGeorge A Diuguid
 Rebecca, b1842, Merc Co, d1922, hJeremiah C Rush
 Robert J, b18--, wAnna McBryde

DAVIDSON (continued)
William, bc1860, Wyth Co?, wElizabeth Poole
William W, b18--, Rkbr Co, d1869, fJames Dorman
DAVIES, Ada B, bc1870, "Linden", nrEdgehill, KiGe Co, fFrederick Staunton, mEmma Rogers
Arthur B Sr, b1826, fFrancis A
Arthur B Jr, b7/1/1866, Amhe Co, fArthur B Sr, mHarriet Pierce
Frederick, bc1800, "Linden", nr Edgehill, KiGe Co, w-- Downman
Frederick Staunton, b1831, "Linden", nrEdgehill, KiGe Co, d1904, fFrederick, m-- Downman, wEmma L Rogers
George W, bc1870, "Linden", nrEdgehill, KiGe Co, fFrederick Staunton, mEmma L Rogers
Julia, b18--, Culp Co, 1w of William H Hening Sr
DAVIS, --, b17--, Scot Co?, hWilliam Bond
--, bc1800, Rkhm Co?, wAnna Bertram
--, bc1800, Rkbr Co?, hMathias Lam
Alice, b18--, Petersburg, Dinw Co, fWilliam Thomas Sr, (1)m Elizabeth Tayloe Corbin Beale, hOlive Branch Morgan
Americus, b18--, Alexandria, fWilliam
Ann D, b18--, Augu Co?, hS L Mayo
Archibald, b18--, Isle Co, fJohn
Arthur Kyle Sr, b7/16/1867, Petersburg, Dinw Co, fWilliam Thomas, (2)mCarolina Virginia Robinson, wLucy Pryor McIlwaine
Aurelia, b18--, Alexandria, fWilliam
Beverly A Sr, b9/27/1868, Fran Co, fDavid H, mNancy G ---, 1wNettie Barrow, 2w-- Bradley
C Boyd, bc1860, Wyth Co, fWilliam, mFrances Elizabeth Earheart
Carolina Robinson, b186-, Petersburg, Dinw Co, d188-, fWilliams Thomas, (2)mCarolina Virginia Robinson

DAVIS (continued)
Charles H, b1866, Alexandria, wAnnie Elizabeth Brenner
Clara, bc1870, Norfolk, fM L T, hWilliam T Hughes, md6/17/1896 D C, bc1850, Rkhm Co, wAnnie Wyant
David H, bc1832, Henry Co, d186-, wNancy ---
Dora, b186-, Bristow, PrWi Co, fThomas K, mMartha Purcell
E Marco, b186-, Wyth Co, d1923, fWilliam, mFrances Elizabeth Earheart
Elizabeth, b17--, Albe Co, fIsaac, hRichard Durrett III
Elizabeth, b18--, nrAshland, Hano Co, hWilliam D Haden
Elizabeth, b18--, Gray Co, d1897, hJames A Gilbert
Elizabeth, b18--, Bote Co?, hWilliam A Gilliam
Emma, b184-, Petersburg, Dinw Co, fWilliams Thomas, (1)mElizabeth Tayloe Corbin Beale, hT L H Young
Fletcher, 18--, Alexandria, fWilliam
Friend William, b184-, Amhe Co, d1906, fWilliam Minor, m-- Eubank
George, b18--, Fauq Co, wEva Murray
George Beauregard, b7/21/1861, Vernon Mills, Fauq Co, fGeorge W, mSallie Ann Lucy Smith, wMedora Z Stephenson, md12/1907
George W, b18--, Alexandria, fWilliam, wLucy Smith
Harriet, bc1800, Fair Co, hJohn Kinchelow
Henry, b18--, Fluv Co?, wNettie Thomas
Henry, b186-, Vernon Mills, Fauq Co, fGeorge W, mSallie Ann Lucy Smith
Henry E, b186-, Wyth Co, d1922, fWilliam, mFrances Elizabeth Earheart
Henry T, b18--, nrRichmond, wElizabeth Bryant
Herbert, bc1860, Bristow, PrWi Co, fThomas K, mMartha Purcell
Ida O, bc1870, Wyth Co, fWilliam, mFrances Elizabeth Ear-

DAVIS (continued)
heart, hJack J Fagg
Isaac III, b6/9/1754, Albe Co?, wElizabeth Kirtley
James T, b185-, Bristow, PrWi Co, fThomas K, mMartha Purcell
Jefferson Davis, b18--, Nels Co, wIda Kendrick
Jennie M, b184-, Amhe Co, fWilliam Minor, m-- Eubank
John, b17--, Louis Co, fWilliam, mMary Gosney, wAnn Jennings
John Brooks, b1825, Glou Co, d1906, wEmma Couch
John Dannie, bc1831, PrEd Co, d1920, wMary Frances Smith, md1872
John Gibson, b186-, KiWi Co, fJohn Brooks, mEmma Couch
John Morgan, b186-, Vernon Mills, Fauq Co, fGeorge W, mSallie Ann Lucy Smith
John Staige Sr, b18--, Albe Co?, fJohn Andrew Gardner
John Staige Jr, b1866, Charlottesville, Albe Co, fJohn Staige Sr
Joseph Claiborne, bc1847, Petersburg, Dinw Co, fWilliam Thomas, (1)mElizabeth Tayloe Corbin Beale
Joseph W, bc1830, Buck Co?, wRosa H Anderson
L Morgan, b18--, Alexandria, fWilliam
Lavinia, b186-, KiWi Co, fJohn Brooks, mEmma Couch, hEugene Roane
Margaret Hewman, b184--, Amhe Co, fWilliam Minor, m-- Eubank, hCharles P Hendricks
Martha Macon, b118--, Midd Co, 1w of John Barbee Minor
Mary, b18--, Taze Co, fThomas, mMary Laird, hJulius C Williams
Mary, b1767, Spring Creek, Wirt Co, hWilliam McCain Gray
Mary, b18--, Alexandria, hThomas Rudd
Mary Anne, bc1830, Wise Co, d1914, hJasper Marion Wolfe
Mary E, b1859, Wyth Co, hThomas J Warren
Mary Rebecca, bc1870, Bote Co,

DAVIS (continued)
fHenry T, mElizabeth Bryant, hWilliam Bell Clemer, md1903
Mary J, b186-, Wyth Co, fWilliam, mFrances Elizabeth Earheart, hJames B Painter
Mattie, b18--, Petersburg, Dinw Co, fWilliams Thomas, (1)mElizabeth Tayloe Corbin Beale, hWilliam Arthur Shepard
Minnie, b185-, Bristow, PrWi Co, fThomas K, mMartha Purcell, hE P Gaines
Mittie, b18--, Brun Co, hEdward M Harris
Mollie G, b184-, Amhe Co, d1911, fWilliam Minor, m-- Eubank
Octavia, bc1850, Taze Co, d1900, hWilliam Cyrus Williams
Peter, bc1830, Appo Co?, wBettie Berkley
Richard Beale, b18--, Petersburg, Dinw Co, dc1900, fWilliams Thomas Sr, (1)mElizabeth Tayloe Corbin Beale
Robert E, bc1843, ChCi Co, fArchibald, wMary E Lacey
Robert Hutchinson, b12/19/1858, Bristow, PrWi Co, fThomas K, mMartha Purcell, wAnnie Laurie Harrison, md10/1881
Samuel, b1837, Mont Co, d1909, wAmanda Painter
Sannie Robinson, b186-, Petersburg, Dinw Co, fWilliams Thomas Sr, (2)mCarolina Virginia Robinson, hClarence Preston Ehrman
Sarah, b17--, Madi Co, hAnthony Twyman
Sarah, bc1800, Char Co, d1853, hWilliam Crawley
Susan Catherine, b18--, Smyt Co, hJohn A P Baker
Susan, b18--, Fred Co?, hDaniel Conrad
Thomas, bc1800, Rkhm Co, wLydia Bertram
Thomas, b18--, Taze Co, wMary Laird
Thomas K, b18--, Fair Co, w-- Simpson
Thomas N Sr, b1842, Amhe Co, fWilliam Minor, m-- Eubank, w E Blanch Thompson, md2/11/1874

DAVIS (continued)
William, b17--, Loui Co, wMary Gosney
William, b18--, Wyth Co, fEli, wFrances Elizabeth Earheart
William, b185-, Bristow, PrWi Co, fThomas K, mMartha Purcell
William Anderson, b10/5/1850, Cumb Co, fJeduthon, mSarah Anderson, wSallie Wyatt Guy
William Arthur, bc1860, Vernon Mills, Fauq Co, fGeorge W, mSallie Ann Lucy Smith
William Blackstone, bc1860, Fred Co?, wHarriett Wood Glass
William Couch, b186-, KiWi Co, fJohn Brooks, mEmma Couch
William Hoomes, b18--, Petersburg, Dinw Co, fWilliams Thomas Sr, (1)mElizabeth Tayloe Corbin Beale
William Minor, b18--, Camp Co?, fJohn, mAnn Jennings, w--Eubank
Williams Thomas Sr, b1816, Glou Co, d1888, fWilliam Edwards, 1wElizabeth Tayloe Corbin Beale, 2wCarolina Virginia Robinson
Williams Thomas Jr, b186-, Petersburg, Dinw Co, fWilliams Thomas Sr, (2)mCarolina Virginia Robinson
Willis Golder, b1/26/1857, Vernon Mills, Fauq Co, fGeorge W, mSallie Ann Lucy Smith, wEdwina Haddox, md12/18/1884
DAWSON, George, b18--, Lewi Co?, wEdmonia Christian
Nannie, b18--, Morg Co?, hC P Dyche
Nicholas, b18--, Alexandria, wJennie Cooper
DAY, Annie, bc1800, Gray Co, hLewis Roberts
David, b186-, Wyth Co?, wIna Nunley
Eliza, b1832, fBaldwin, mLucretia Guthrie, hEdward M Spilman
DEAL, Melvina, b1855, Buch Co, fJames Harvey, hJohn W Clevinger
Richard, bc1830, Page Co, w--Brumback
DEANE, Eliza, b18--, Camp Co, fFrank, 1hW H Baker, 2h John

DEANE (continued)
William Craddock
DEANS, Joseph, bc1755, Norf Co, fWilliam, 1wSarah Graham, 2wMargaret Higginbotham
Joseph Franklin, b5/20/1839, Norf Co, fWilliam II, mElizabeth Wise, wBettie Lightfoot Poindexter
William II, bc1800, Nort Co, fJoseph, (2)mSarah Graham, wElizabeth Wise
DEARING, James, b17--, Camp Co?, d1811, fEdward, wBetsy Adams
James, b4/25/1840, Camp Co, d1865, fJames Griffin, mMary Anna Lynch, wRoxanna Birchett
James Griffin, b1800, Camp Co, d1843, fJames, mBetsy Adams, wMary Anna Lynch, md1834
Mary Lucretia, b18--, Camp Co, fJames, mRozana Birchett, hFrank Patteson Christian Sr
DEARMONT, Peter, b18--, Clar Co, fMichael, mLucy Ferguson, w--Bell
Sallie, b18--, Clar Co, fMichael, mLucy Ferguson, h--McMurray
Thomas, b18--, Clar Co, fMichael, mLucy Ferguson, w--Bell
Washington, b18--, Clar Co, fMichael, mLucy Ferguson, 1w--Bell, 2wJane () Poague
DEASY, Jeremiah M, bc1850, wMary Elizabeth Ryan
DEATHERAGE, Thomas A, bc1860, wHattie Anderson
DEATLEY, Elizabeth, b17--, Rich Co?, fChristopher, hFamous Ficklin
DEATON, Alice V, b185-, Alle Co, fJohn T, mGranville D Haynes, hRobert Jones
Charles, bc1850, Alle Co, fJohn T, mGranville D Haynes
George T, b8/19/1859, Alle Co, fJohn T, mGranville D Haynes
James Alfred, b8/19/1859, Alle Co, fJohn T, mGranville D Haynes, wLillian Manning, md2/12/1891
John T, b1825, nrSalem, Roan Co, d1877, fLevi, wGranville D Haynes

DEATON (continued)
 Joseph L, b185-, Alle Co, fJohn T, mGranville D Haynes
 Levi, b1790, Roan Co, d1871
 Mary N, bc1870, Wyth Co?, fJohn, hWilliam Thomas Poole, md9/7/1889
 Naomi, b185-, Alle Co, fJohn T, mGranville D Haynes, hWilliam T Poole
 William T, b185-, Alle Co, fJohn T, mGranville D Haynes
DEAVERS, Bettie, bc1870, Rkhm Co, fThornton, hCharles S Bowman
DeBUSK, Ellen, b1/15/1838, Lee Co, hJohn B F Witt
DeBUTTS, Daniel Dulany, b184-, "Mt Welby", nrLinden, Fauq Co, fRichard Earle, mSarah Hall, wFrances Sydnor
 Dulany Forrest, b4/15/1861, "Mt Welby", nrLinden, Fauq Co, fRichard Earle, mSarah Hall, wEmma Ashby, md1/9/1895
 Edward Herbert, b186-, "Mt Welby", nrLinden, Fauq Co, fRichard Earle, mSarah Earle, wJulia de Butts
 Gertrude, b184-, "Mt Welby", nrLinden, Fauq Co, fRichard Earle, mSarah Hall, hGeorge Trumbo
 Ida, b185-, "Mt Welby", nrLinden, Fauq Co, fRichard Earle, mSarah Hall, hWilliam H Hall
 John Henry, b179-, nrAlexandria, fSamuel, mMary Welby, wSophia Forrest, md1818
 Julia, bc1870, Fauq Co?, hEdward Herbert deButts
 Louisa, b184-, "Mt Welby", nrLinden, Fauq Co, fRichard Earle, mSarah Hall
 Mary Ann, b179-, nrAlexandria, fSamuel, mMary Welby, hJohn Peyton Dulany
 Mary Welby, b18--, fRichard Welby, hRichard Henry Carter
 Mary Welby, b12/18/1852, "Mt Welby", nrLinden, Fauq Co, fRichard Earle, mSarah Hall, hWilliam Bias Gatewood
 Richard, b179-, nrAlexandria, fSamuel, mMary Welby
 Richard Earle, b1823, nrAlexan-

DeBUTTS (continued)
dria, fJohn Henry, mSophia Forrest, wSarah Hall, md1844
 Richardella, b18--, Fauq Co, fWelby, mLouisa Dulany, hJohn Armistead Carter
 Rosa Earle, bc1860, "Mt Welby", nrLinden, Fauq Co, fRichard Earle, mSarah Hall
 Sarah, b185-, "Mt Welby", nr Linden, Fauq Co, fRichard Earle, mSarah Hall, hGeorge A Roszel
DeCORMIS, James B, b1819, Norfolk, d1884, fJoseph L, wMargaret Williams
DEEBLE, America A, b1847, nrChain Bridge, Arli Co, fEdwin K S, mElizabeth Birch, hWilliam Ball
 Edwin K S, b18--, Alexandria, wElizabeth Birch
DeFRIECE, Riceley, b18--, Gray Co?, wBashy Bartlett
 William R, b4/15/1852, Gray Co, fRiceley, mBashy Bartlett, wMartha Jane Elizabeth Clark
DeHAVEN, Henry, b18--, Fred Co?, wChristina Cather
DeJARNETTE, Caroline Hampton, bc1870, Pine Forest, Spot Co, fElliott Hawse Jr, mEvelyn May Magruder, hWilliam L Keyser, md1891
 Caroline Harris, b18--, hSamuel G Staples
 Daniel, b18--, Spot Co?, fElliott Hawse Sr
 Elizabeth, bc1800, Spot Co, hWilliam Hart
 Elliott Hawse Sr, b18--, fElliott, m-- Hampton
 Elliott Hawes Jr, b18--, Spot Co?, fElliott Hawes Sr, wEvelyn May Magruder
DELANEY, Alice, b18--, Hano Co, fJohn, mSallie Ford, hCharles E Anderson
 Belle, b18--, Hano Co, fJohn, mSallie Ford, hWilliam Ransburg
 Bettey, b18--, Hano Co, fJohn, mSallie Ford, hGeorge Tyler
 Ellen, b18--, Hano Co, fJohn, mSallie Ford, hThomas Christian

DELANEY (continued)
Fannie, b18--, Hano Co, fJohn, mSallie Ford, hWilton Farmer
Howard Monroe, b18--, Richmond, fSamuel Martin, mMary E (Farmer) Jones
James M, b18--, Hano Co, fJohn, mSallie Ford, wMary Jenkins
John, b18--, Hano Co, fJohn, mSallie Ford
Julia Ann, b18--, Hano Co, fJohn, mSallie Ford, hBeverley Morrissett
Samuel Martin, b1842, Hano Co, fJohn, mSallie Ford, 2h of Mary E Farmer
Walter Franklin, b7/24/1868, Richmond, fSamuel Martin, mMary E (Farmer) Jones, wOceola Carson Fussell
DELAPLANE, Mary, b18--, Fauq Co, fWashington E, mMartha Gougar, hHenry Ashby
Washington E, bc1812, Buckland, PrWi Co, fJacob, wMartha Gougar
DELK, Sallie Whitman, bc1870, Appo Co?, hJoel Walker Flood
DELLINGER, Absolom, b8/24/1817, nrMt Jackson, Shen Co, fMartin, mDorothy --, wCatherine Coffman/Kauffman, md9/4/1838
George W, b184-, Clar Co?, fAbsolom, mCatherine Coffman/Kauffman, wAnnie C Wisman, md12/30/1869
Madaline, b18--, Rkhm Co, hWilliam Will
Miranda, b18--, Shen Co, hJoshua Helsley
DELP, Chapman, b18--, Gray Co?, wBettie Phipps
George L, b18--, Gray Co?, wCharlotte Hale
DeMAIN, W H, b18--, PrWi Co?, wMollie Montgomery Lewis
DEMING, Portia, b18--, Norfolk?, hCharles Henry Langley
DENBY, Andrew Jackson, b18--, Norfolk?, wVirginia Philips
DENIT, --, bc1860, Salem, Roan Co, fJohn, mNancy Parish, hG L Sears
--, bc1860, Salem, Roan Co, fJohn, mNancy Parish, hE M Fitzgerald

DENIT (continued)
--, bc1860, Salem, Roan Co, fJohn, mNancy Parish, hA H Magee
--, bc1860, Salem, Roan Co, fJohn, mNancy Parish, hJ T Forsythe
--, bc1860, Salem, Roan Co, fJohn, mNancy Parish, hJ G Hitckok
Charles D, b6/24/1862, Salem, Roan Co, fJohn, mNancy Parish, wBettie A Brown, md10/8/1889
H W, bc1854, Salem, Roan Co, d1913, fJohn, mNancy Parish
John, b1820, Shen Co, d1901, wNancy Parish
J H, bc1860, Salem, Roan Co, fJohn, mNancy Parish
DeNITE, Sarah, b18--, Albe Co?, hThomas Driscoll
DENNIS, Edwin, b18--, fJacob, 2wMargaret Melvina (Jordan) Adams
Ella B, b18--, Acco Co?, fRufus G, 2w of G Fred Floyd Sr, md8/1898
T C, b18--, Bedf Co?, wLilly Board
Willie Lee, b6/7/1869, nrPearisburg, Gile Co, fEdwin, (2)mMargaret Melvina Jordan, wMary A Fletcher
DENNY, --, bc1800, Wash Co?, hGeorge Blackwell
DENOON, Luther C, bc1850, Powh Co?, wWillie Baugh
DENTON, Albina, b18--, Bote Co, hGeorge Layman
DeSHIELDS, Ella Lomax, b185-, Heathsville, Nhld Co, fHenry Clay, mSarah Wheelwright, hWilliam C Snow
Grace Douglas, b186-, Richmond?, fHenry Clay, mSarah Wheelwright, hWalter R Carlton
Henry Clay, b1832, Heathsville, Nhld Co, d1884, fJoseph, (3)mThebadeaux Crudeson, wSarah Wheelwright
Laura Kendall, b186-, Heathsville, Nhld Co, fHenry Clay, mSarah Wheelwright, hRandolph S Brent
Louise Thebadeaux, b186-, Heathsville, Nhld Co, fHenry

DeSHIELDS (continued)
Clay, mSarah Wheelwright
DESKINS, John W, bc1860, Russ Co?, wAda Ratliff
DETTOR, Ann, bc1838, Albe Co, fJoseph, mPeggy Schultz, hFrederick Hughson
Joseph, bc1800, Albe Co, fJohn, wPeggy Schultz
DEVANY, Walter Leslie Sr, b18--, Suss Co?, wAnne Wells
DEVER, Sarah, b18--, Bath Co?, hWilliam H Moore
DEVIER, D Clint, bc1870, Rkhm Co, fAllen, wIda Bell
DEVINE, Jane, b17--, Wyth Co?, hJoseph Crockett
DEVOR, Prudence, b18--, Blan Co, hIsaac Kegley
DEW, Alice Catherine, b1841, KiQu Co, 2w of Andrew Browne Evans
  Benjamin Franklin, b18--, KiQu Co, fThomas, wMary Susan Garnett
  Elizabeth, b185-, Sunny Bank Farm, nrNorth Garden, Albe Co, fThomas Roderick, mElizabeth Hart
  James Harvie, b10/18/1843, Newton, KiQu Co, d1914, fBenjamin Franklin, mMary Susan Garnett, wBessie Martin, md1885
  John G, b184-, Newton, KiQu Co, fBenjamin Franklin, mMary Susan Garnett
  John Mason, b186-, KiQu Co?, wLillian Shepherd Segar
  Mary Emma, bc1840, KiQu Co, 1w of Andrew Browne Evans
  Thomas, b18--, KiQu Co, fThomas
DeWITT, Lafayette, bc1838, Bedf Co, wSarah E --
DEYERLE, Benjamin, b18--, Roan Co?, wSusan Shaeffer
  Berryman, b185-, Roan Co, fBenjamin, mSusan Shaeffer
  Bettie, bc1850, Roan Co, fBenjamin, mSusan Shaeffer
  Charles, bc1840, Roan Co, fBenjamin, mSusan Shaeffer
  George, b184-, Roan Co, fBenjamin, mSusan Shaeffer
  Henry S, b1848, Roan Co, fBenjamin, mSusan Shaeffer, wSallie Price

DEYERLE (continued)
  Julia, bc1850, Roan Co, fBenjamin, mSusan Shaeffer
  Susan, bc1850, Roan Co, fBenjamin, mSusan Shaeffer
DICK, --, bc1860, KiGe Co?, wFlorence Rogers
DICKENSON, Christiana Wade, b1854, Pitt Co, fDavid D, mJane Evans, hSamuel C Adams
  David D, b18--, Pitt Co, wJane Evans
  Elizabeth, b185-, nrCastlewood, Russ Co, fJames H, Sr, mNancy Bickley, hCharles C Fisher
  Georgia A, bc1870, Russ Co, fNelson, mSarah Boyd, hJohn L Litz
  James, b17--, Castlewood, Russ Co, wMary Gray
  James H, Sr, b1821, Castlewood, Russ Co, d1894, fJames, mMary Gray, wNancy Bickley
  James H, Jr, b185-, nrCastlewood, Russ Co, fJames M, Sr, mNancy Bickley
  Mary, b18--, Russ Co, hJohn Richmond
  Mary V, b185-, nrCastlewood, Russ Co, fJames H, Sr, mNancy Bickley, hSamuel B Shomaker
  Robert Walter, b6/7/1857, nr Castlewood, Russ Co, fJames H, Sr, mNancy Bickley, wRose D Earnest, md1/29/1884
  Nannie Verina, b18--, hGeorge Washington Browning
  Nelson, b18--, Russ Co?, wSarah Boyd
  William T, bc1850, nrCastlewood, Russ Co, d1914, fJames H, Sr, mNancy Bickley
DICKERSON, Benjamin, bc1840, Char Co, fBenjamin G, mOna Sowell
  Benjamin F, b9/12/1862, Greene Co, fJohn C, mMary Ann Wetsel, wSusie Tyler Hoopes, md4/7/1897
  Benjamin G, b18--, Char Co, wOna Sowell
  Burdine, bc1839, Floy Co, d1922, wNancy Sowers
  Caroline, b1832, nrCastlewood, Russ Co, d1916, hJoseph B Gilmer

DICKERSON (continued)
Henry H, b18--, Russ Co?, wCornelia Quarls
James T, bc1840, Char Co, fBenjamin G, mOna Sowell, wMattie F Berkley
John C, b18--, Greene Co, wMary Ann Wetsel
John W, bc1840, Char Co, Benjamin G, mOna Sowell
Leonidas C, Sr, b4/19/1869, Floy Co, fBurdine, mNancy Sowers, wCarrie Leigh Moore, md10/15/1902
Leverge, b18--, Camp Co?, fWilliam J, hAlsen Franklin Thomas
Mary Catherine, b184-, Char Co, fBenjamin G, mOna Sowell, hGeorge William Berkley
Monroe Worth, b7/15/1850, Hali Co, d1921, fNathan, m-- Moses, wBettie A Clark
Nancy, b18--, Appo Co, hGeorge Nelson Berkley
Nathan, b18--, Hali Co?, w-- Moses
DICKEY, Laura M, bc1870, Gray Co, fJohn M, hCharles Clark Lincoln, md11/23/1893
DICKIE, James, b2/3/1854, Castle Hall Farm, Nels Co, d1914, fWilliam Lewis, mElizabeth Ann Lightfoot Grasty, wEmily Louise Grasty
William Lewis, b18--, KiQu Co, wElizabeth Ann Lightfoot Grasty
DICKINSON, Asa D, b1824, Nott Co, d1885, 1w-- Michaux, 2w Sallie Cabell
Alexander B, b9/11/1869, Worsham, PrEd Co, fRobert M, mLelia Cralle
Arthur G, bc1850, Spot Co, fHugh Mercer, mSusan Mansfield
Bartie, bc1870, Spot Co, fRobert H, mMary F Hicks, hJames Harris
Emma, b185-, Spot Co, fHugh Mercer, mSusan Mansfield, hVavisaw Powell
F P, b7/10/1858, Spot Co, fHugh Mercer, mSusan Mansfield, wMyrtle Pulliam, md12/20/1893
Florence, bc1850, Spot Co, fHugh Mercer, mSusan Mansfield, hQuintus Richards
George, bc1800, Fran Co, wLucy Brown
Hugh Mercer, b18--, Spot Co, wSusan Mansfield
Hugh Quarles, b5/28/1855, Spot Co, fHugh Mercer, mSusan Mansfield, wMary Haws Thomson, md7/15/1902
M H, b12/16/1868, Spot Co, Robert H, mMary F Hicks, 1w Lillie Robinson, 2wLulu R Jones, md1906
Martha, b18--, Bath Co?, hJames R Ervin
Martha, b18--, Nott Co?, hJohn Harding
Mary Micheaux, b186-, Worsham PrEd Co, fRobert M, mLelia Cralle, hDon Peters Halsey, Jr, md1894
Robert H, b10/21/1839, Spot Co, wMary F Hicks
Robert M, b12/2/1840, PrEd Co, d1898, fAsa D, m-- Michaux, wLelia Cralle
Sally, b1700, Bedf Co?, 2w of Thomas Johnson
Smelt Winston, b1852, Loui Co, m-- Winston, wSarah Belle Look
William, b18--, PrWi Co?, wElizabeth Leachman
William C, bc1850, Spot Co, fHugh Mercer, mSusan Mansfield
DIDLAKE, John, b18--, KiQu Co, w-- Corr
Miles E, b1850, KiQu Co, fJohn, m-- Corr, wElizabeth Catherine Clegg
Winfield, bc1850, KiQu Co, w-- Bray
DIGGES, --, b17--, fDudley, hJohn Stratton
Daniel D M, b18--, Roan Co, wMartha Price
Ida Martha, b18--, Roan Co?, d1920, fDaniel D M, mMartha Price, hThomas W Miller, md 1882
DIGGS, --, b18--, hSterling T Oliver
Alexander, b7/1833, Laban, Math Co, d1922, wElizabeth Hudgins
Carrie W, b1869, Math Co, d1921, hSands Smith, Jr

DIGGS (continued)
Charlotte, b17--, Albe Co?, hThomas Barclay
Drew, b18--, Math Co, d186-, wMartha Hudgins
John B, b18--, Math Co, d187-, wSarah Elizabeth Carr
John L, b1845, Math Co, wMary Eliza Weston
Viola, b18--, Math Co, fDrew, mMartha Hudgins, hThomas Diggs Hudgins, Jr, md1/6/1881
William L, b11/1/1862, Peary, Math Co, fAlexander J, mElizabeth Hudgins, wAlice Hudgins, md1892
DILL, John, b18--, Andrew, wEliza Peck
DILLARD, A Hughes, Sr, bc1813, Henry Co, d1901, fJohn, wMartha A Dillard
A Hughes, Jr, bc1850, Martinsville, Henr Co, fA Hughes, Sr, mMartha A Dillard
Alice, b18--, Scottsville, Albe Co, fGeorge W, mLucy J Dillard
Annie Lacy, bc1870, Nels Co, fWillis Howard, mMariah Woodward Tyree, hHugh Roy Millar, md1/20/1892
Benjamin L, b9/4/1857, Scottsville, Albe Co, fGeorge W, mLucy J Dillard, 1wMaude Baptist, md9/1893, 2w-- Horsley, md1918
Betty D, bc1850, Martinsville, Henry Co, fA Hughes, Sr, mMartha A Dillard, hDaniel Arrington
Charles, bc1850, nrBroadway, Rkhm Co, fJesse, Sr, mAnnie Emswiller
Elizabeth, b18--, Nels Co?, d1892, fJames Spotswood, hJohn James Dillard, md5/13/1847
Erasmus, bc1850, nrBroadway, Rkhm Co, fJesse, Sr, mAnnie Emswiller
Fannie, b18--, nrBroadway, Rkhm Co, fJesse, Sr, mAnnie Emswiller
Frank, b184-, nrBroadway, Rkhm Co, d186-, fJesse, Sr, mAnnie Emswiller
George, bc1850, nrBroadway, Rkhm Co, fJesse, Sr, mAnnie

DILLARD (continued)
Emswiller, wSallie Springle
George, b18--, Scottsville, Albe Co, fGeorge W, mLucy J Dillard
George, b18--, Bowling Green, Caro Co, wLucy J Dillard
James, b1729, Nels Co, d1794, fJames Stephen, Jr, mLucy Wise, wMary Ann Hunt, m1748
James, b1755, Nels Co?, fJames, mMary Ann Hunt, wJane Starke, m1782
James Daniel, b18--, Scottsville, Albe Co, fGeorge W, mLucy J Dillard
James Spotswood, b1850, Nels Co, d1898, fJohn J, mElizabeth Dillard, w Ella Woodroof
James Stephen, Jr, b1698, Nels Co?, fJames Stephen, Sr, mLouisa Page, wLucy Wise, md1724
James VanMeter, b184-, nrBroadway, Rkhm Co, fJesse, Sr, mAnnie Emswiller, 1wLucinda Eaton, 2wBettie Williams
Jennie, b185-, nrBroadway, Rkhm Co, fJesse, Sr, mAnnie Emswiller
Jesse Sr, b18--, wAnnie Emswiller
Jesse, Jr, bc1850, nrBroadway, Rkhm Co, fJesse, Sr, mAnnie Emswiller
John James, b10/4/1824, Nels Co?, d1892, fWilliam, mSarah Stovall Christian, wElizabeth Dillard, md5/13/1847
John L, bc1850, Martinsville, Henry Co, fA Hughes, Sr, mMartha A Dillard
John W, b8/12/1852, Pendleton, Nels Co, fJohn James, mElizabeth Dillard, wEmma Tell White, md1880
Julia B, b18--, Scottsville, Albe Co, fGeorge W, mLucy J Dillard, hBalbour Gillespie
Kate, bc1850, nrBroadway, Rkhm Co, fJesse, Sr, mAnnie Emswiller Lucy J, b18--, Spot Co, hGeoorge W Dillard
Mary E, b18--, Scottsville, Albe Co, fGeorge W, mLucy J Dillard, hJames P Holidy

DILLARD (continued)
Matilda Hughes, bc1850, Martinsville, Henry Co, fA Hughes, Sr, mMartha A Dillard, hWilliam Chamberlain
Mattie, b185-, nrBroadway, Rkhm Co, fJesse, Sr, mAnnie Emswiller, hWill Lambert
Nora L, b18--, Scottsville, Albe Co, fGeoge W, mLucy J Dillard
Pattie, bc1850, Martinsville, Henry Co, fA Hughes, Sr, mMartha A Dillard, hWilliam Penn
Peter H, b10/15/1850, Martinsville, Henry Co, fA Hughes, Sr, mMartha A Dillard, wLydia Nash, md11/6/1872
William, b1797, Nels Co?, d1880, fJames, mJane Starke, wSarah Stovall Christian, md1824
William B, b18--, Scottsville, Albe Co, fGeorge W, mLucy J Dillard
Willis Howard, b18--, Nels Co, fJackson, wMariah Woodward Tyree
DILLON, Agnes, b18--, Albe Co?, fMichael, mMargaret Cluskey, hWilliam Lewis Randolph
Cecelia, b18--, Fran Co?, fSamuel, hRandolph Chitwood
Edward, Sr, b1834, PrEd Co, d1897, wFrances Ann Polk
DILLWORTH James, bc1840, Rkhm Co?, wAddie Blackburn
DINGES, Anne R, b1834, nrMiddletown, Fred Co, d1907, fDavid, mKittie Miller, hW Strother Kline
David, bc1800, Fred Co, wCatherine "Kittie" Miller
Elizabeth, b1824, Woodstock, Shen Co, d189-, fDavid, mCatherine Miller, hIsaac Rhodes
Fannie, b183-, nrMiddltown, Fred Co, fDavid, hBenjamin Stickley
Jackson, b18--, Shen Co, wMary Frances Grandstaff
James, b18--, wMary Blue
Mary Elizabeth, b1837, fJames, mMary Blue, hJacob N Shryock

DINGES (continued)
Virginia, b18--, Woodstock, Shen Co, fDavid, mCatherine Miller, hWade Muse
DINGLEDINE, E Z, b18--, Shen Co, fJohn Balser, mLydia Zirkle
William Johnson, b18--, Shen Co, fJohn Balser, mLydia Zirkle, wElla J Black
DINGUS, John, bc1860, Wise Co?, wMartha S Greear
DINKLE, Elizabeth, 18--, Rkhm Co, hJohn Thuma
DINWIDDLE, Samuel S, bc1840, Gile Co?, wMalinda Chapman
DIRTING, Mary, b1833, nrEdinburg, Shen Co, d1910, hJohn T Hutcheson
DIUGUID, David b181-, Lynchburg, Camp Co, d1864, fSampson, (1)mMartha Patterson
George A, Sr, b11/5/1820, Lynchburg, Camp Co, fSampson, (1)mMartha Pattison, wPaulina Davidson
George A, Jr, b185-, Lynchburg, Camp Co, fGeorge A, Sr, mPaulina Davidson
Harriett, b182-, Lynchburg, Camp Co, fSampson, (1)mMartha Pattison, hWilliam Diuguid
James E, bc1850, Lynchburg, Camp Co, fGeorge A, Sr, mPaulina Davidson
Jesse T, b185-, Lynchburg, Camp Co, fGeorge, Sr, mPaulina Davidson
Sampson, b1794, Bck Co, d1856, 1wMartha Pattison, 2wMargaret () Early
William, b181-, Lynchburg, Camp Co, wHarriett Diuguid
William Davidson, b9/10/1851, Lynchburg, Camp Co, fGeorge A, Sr, mPaulina Davidson, wNora A Cottrell, md11/8/1880
DIVERS, Ananias, bc1800, Fran Co, wPolly Holland
John H, b18--, Fran Co, wMary
Gillie Ann, bc1843, Redwood, Fran Co, d1910, fOliver Perry, mUrsula Dudley, hHenry Clay Chitwood
Oliver Perry, b18--, Fran Co, fAnanias, mPolly Holland, wUrsula Dudley

DIX, Margaret, b1862, Acco Co, hEdward T Parks
Tandy F, b12/14/1842, Wyth Co, d1907, fTandy, wRody J Catron
DIXON, Elizabeth, b17--, hJoseph Timberlake
John A, bc1860, Gray Co, 2h of Victoria Greear
Marlon M, b186-, Augu Co, fMat, m-- ( ) Fry
Mat, b18--, Augu Co, 2h of -- () Fry
Mervin, b186-, bAugu Co, fMat, m-- ( ) Fry
DOBBINS, Mary Ann, b1838, Hampton, ElCi Co, hJoseph B Herbert
DODD, --, b18--, Cumb Co?, hTaylor Angell
Ralph Anderson, b18--, nrChatham, Pitt Co, w-- Blanks
William S, b1840, Chatham, Pitt Co, fRalph Anderson, m-- Blanks, wFannie Taylor Owen
DODGE, Henry William, Jr, b12/4/1850, Upperville, Fauquier Co, fHenry William, Sr, mAbigail Brown, wIrene Stacey
Margaret, b18--, Fauq Co, hWilliam Kerfoot
DODSON, Bettie, b18--, Pitt Co?, d191-, hPatrick Henry Terry, m11/1875
Beverly S, b1/1861, Pitt Co, fPaul, mMartha Dodson, wMary A Ingram
Charles, bc1820, PrWi Co?, wCatherine Mars Lewis
Martha, b18--, Pitt Co, hPaul Dodson
Mary Dasie, bc1870, Norfolk?, fRichard S, mMaria Pfeltz, hAbram Looney McClellam, md1/1/1895
Paul, b18--, Pitt Co, wMartha Dodson
Paul H, bc1860, Lune Co, wAddie Moore Yates
Richard S, b18--, Norfolk?, wMaria Pfeltz
DOE, Mary Virginia, b1843, Danville, Pitt Co, hJohn Thomas Keen
DOGAN, J F, bc1850, PrWi Co?, wEdith May Leachman
DOHERTY, F J, bc1860, Camp Co?,

DOHERTY (continued) wMary A Casey
Mollie E, b1800, Richmond, fJohn E, mNora --, hJohn H Hinchman
DONAGHE, Mary Elizabeth, b18--, Fauq Co?, hAndrew J Silling
DONALD, William A, b10/23/1823, Donaldsburg, Rkbr Co, fWilliam Blair, mHannah Campbell, wMargaret J Humphreys
William Blair, bc1800, Donaldsburg, Rkbr Co, wHannah Campbell
Samuel Moore, b3/12/1861, Vesuvius, Rkbr Co, fWilliam A, mMargaret J Humphreys, 1wMary Brown Watson, md1884, 2wMary E Hanger, md1901
DONALDSON, Harriett, b18--, Loud Co, hWilliam McDonough
DONAVAN, G W, b18--, Rkhm Co?, d1905, wElizabeth Weller
Nettie V, b4/1868, nrSinger Glen, Rkhm Co, fG W, mElizabeth Weller, hS Henton Swank, md3/21/1890
DONIPHAN, Sarah C, bc1860, Camp Co?, 2w of Christopher Valentine Winfree
DONNAN, Alexander, b18--, Petersburg, Dinw Co, fDavid, mMary Stewart
Ann Melville, b18--, Richmond, fWilliam S, Sr, mMary A Donnan, hFletcher M Conner
Bettie Lee, b4/20/1856, Richmond, fGeorge Wallace, mLouisa Pettyjohn, h William T Shields
David, b18--, Richmond, fWilliam S, Sr, mMary A Donnan
Elizabeth Stewart, b1844, Richmond, fWilliam S, Sr, mMary A Donnan, hAlbert A Wilson
Etta, b18--, Petersburg, Dinw Co, fAlexander, hWilliam Hodges Mann
George Wallace, b1828, Richmond, fAlexander, mMarie Stewart, wLouisa Pettyjohn
John, b2/9/1857, Richmond, fWilliam S, Sr, mMary A Donnan, wLizzie Glenn Hunt
William S, Jr, b18--, Richmond, fWilliam S, Sr, mMary A Donnan
DONNAVANT, Sue L, b18--, Rich-

DONNAVANT (continued) mond?, hJames Lewis Chernault
DONOHOE, Stephen George, b18--, Loud Co?, wMary A LeGrand
Stephen Roszel, b2/1/1851, Loud Co, d1921, fStephen George, mMary A LeGrand, 1wHeloise Eubank, 2wSusan Lindsay Moore
DOOLEY, --,, bc1870, Dooley Farm, nrBedford, Bedf Co, fJames A, mSaluda E Veter, hH G Ramsey
Addison N, b186-, Dooley Farm, nrBedford, Bedf Co, fJames A, mSaluda A Veter
Albert H, b186-, Dooley Farm, nrBedford, Bedf Co, fJames A, mSaluda A Veter
Fred J, b186-, Dooley Farm, nrBedford, Bedf Co, fJames A, mSaluda A Veter
James A, bc1834, Bedf Co, d1917, wSaluda A Veter
Lelia M, b186-, Dooley Farm, nrBedford, Bedf Co, fJames A, mSaluda A Veter, hW E Arrington
Lula, b186-, Dooley Farm, nrBedford, Bedf Co, fJames A, mSaluda A Veter, hCharles R Walker
W I, bc1860, Bedf Co?, w-- McMenaway
Waverley H, b186-, Dooley Farm, nrBedford, Bedf Co, fJames A, mSaluda A Veter
William, bc1860, Roan Co?, w-- Scott
William R, b2/15/1867, Dooley Farm, nrBedford, Bedf Co, fJames A, mSaluda A Veter, 1wLaura J Ferguson, md1894, 2wFlorence J Sampson, md1915
DOOM, --, bc1800, Augu Co?, hJohn Patterson
--, bc1860, Rkhm Co? wSarah C Good
DOORS, Flora E, b2/14/1840, hJames Sudduth
DOOSING, John W, b1/1/1846, nr Catawba, Roan Co, d1917, fWilliam, wElla Thomas
William, b1800, Roan Co, d1863, fJacob
DORMAN, Susan, b17--, Rkbr Co?, hAndrew Baker Davidson

DORRELL, James R, bc1840, Fauq Co?, wSallie E Woodward
DORTCH, Mollie J, b1857, Meck Co, 2w of William T Ozlin
DOTSON, Celestie B, bc1870, Pound, Wise Co, fMarcus D LaFayette, Sr, (1)mLetha Hilton, hEmmett A Swindall
Daniel, b18--, Wise Co, wNancy Robinson
Emily, b8/6/1847, Wise Co, hJames H Long
Marcus D, Sr, b2/24/1850, Pound, Wise Co, fDaniel, mNancy Robinson, 1wLetha Hilton, 2wMinnie E Boggs, 3wRosa Mullins
Nancy C, bc1870, Pound, Wise Co, fMarcus D LaFayette, Sr, (1)mLetha Hilton, hCalvin A Swindall
Sophronia, b18--, Wise Co?, hElbert Fulton
William W G, b5/30/1868, Pound, Wise Co, fMarcus D LaFayette, Sr, (1)mLetha Hilton, 1wNannie Hillman, md10/1888, 2wElizabeth (Wright) Lewis, md8/1911
DOUGHERTY, Lula L, bc1870, Scot Co, fNathan B, mEllen Perry, 2w of Robert M Addington, md3/27/1867
Nathan B, b18--, Scot Co, wEllen Perry
DOUGHTY, Lillian S, b1869, Pungoteague, Acco Co, hLeonard O Ames
DOUGLAS, Catherine, b18--, Arnolds Valley, ---- Co?, fJohn W, hJohn W Eads
Louisa, b18--, fJohn W, hMilton Hatcher
Mary S, b18--, Rich Co?, fWilliam G, mMary Hayden, hMeredith Columbus Lewis, md4/20/1881
Thaddeus, b18--, Nhld Co, wAlice -
W B, bc1850, Rkbr Co?, wBruce A Alexander
William G, b18--, Rich Co?, wMary Hayden
William Walter, b18--, Rich Co?, wBettie Landon
DOUTHAT, Sarah, b18--, Bedf Co?, h-- Luck

DOVE, Herschel, b10/9/1869, Rye Cove, Scot Co, fGeorge R, mRose Carter, hWorth Graham J A, bc1860, Bote Co?, wLula Huff
Maude, bc1870, Rye Cove, Scot Co, fGeorge R, mRosa Carter, hCharles H Leonard
Minnie L, b186-, Rye Cove, Scot Co, fGeorge R, mRose Carter,. hCharles J White
DOVEL, --, bc1840, Rkhm Co?, wMattie Thuma
Daniel, b18--, Rkhm Co?, wMary Long
David M, b18--, Page Co, wElizabeth Frances Miranda Booten
Frances Elizabeth, b1851, Rkhm Co, fDaniel, mMary Long, hRichard A Bruce
Mittie Gertrude, b18--, Page Co, fDavid M, mElizabeth Thomas Miller, md12/9/1886
Tabitha, b17--, Rkhm Co?, hJohn Shuler
DOVELL, Early Beauregard, b18--, Madi Co?, fD T
DOWDELL, Beulah Wood, bc1870, Loud Co, fFlavius, m-- Leslie, 1w of Worthington Waters Holton
Flavius, b18--, Loud Co?, w -- Leslie
DOWDY, Sarah, b1851, Patr Co, hSilas G Stump
DOWELL, Charles, bc1820, Albe Co, wNancy Hall
George, bc1860, Rkhm Co, wVirginia Hall
Ann, b18--, Fauq Co?, hAndrew Woolf
Catherine E, bc1820, fJohn, mAgnes Welch, hHenry M Woolf
John, b17--, wAgnes Welch
Julia, bc1820, fJohn, mAgnes Welch
Landy, b1840, nrDumfries, PrWi Co, fWilliam F "Landy", mSarah Turner
Maggie, bc1840, nrDumfries, PrWi Co, fWilliam F "Landy", mSarah Turner, 1w of Robert Waters
Mary C, b184-, nrDumfries, PrWi Co, fWilliam F "Landy", mSarah Turner, hGeorge Matthews Rat-

DOWELL (continued)
cliffe, md11/2/1865
Melinda, bc1850, nrDumfries, PrWi Co, fWilliam F "Landy", mSara Turner, hRobert Merchant
Murray, bc1840, nrDumfries, PrWi Co, fWilliam F "Landy", mSarah Turner
Peter, b184-, nrDumfries, PrWi Co, fWilliam F "Landy", mSarah Turner
Sarah, b184-, nrDumfries, PrWi Co, fWilliam F "Landy", mSarah Turner, 2w of Robert Waters
William F "Landy", b18--, PrWi Co, d186-, wSarah Turner
Willie A, b18--, nrDumfries, PrWi Co, fWilliam F "Landy", mSarah Turner
DOWNEY, E A, bc1850, wMabel C Irvin
Emma Susan, b12/14/1861, nr Edinburg, Shen Co, fJackson, hWilliam Harvey Santmiers
DOWNING, Hannah Virginia, bc1870, "Edgely", Lanc Co, fSamuel, Sr, (2)mAnnie D Rice, hW M Pinkard
Henry Hawkins, b4/20/1853, Fauq Co, fJohn H, mFannie Scott, 1wNannie Byrne, 2wCaroline E Long
Ida Kate, b18--, Lanc Co, fSamuel, Sr, (1)mCatherine Payne, hRoswell B Brown
James A, b18--, Shen Co?, wMary Jane Harman
John Beverley, b18--, Lanc Co, d1875, fSamuel, Sr, (1)mCatherine Payne
John H, b18--, Fauq Co?, wFannie Scott
Lillian Armstrong, bc1870, "Edgely", Lanc Co, fSamuel, Sr, (2)mAnnie D Rice, hRobert S Jett
Maria, b18--, Lanc Co, fSamuel, Sr, ()mCatherine Payne, hGiles F Eubank
Mary Evelyn, b8/14/1869, nr Stephens City, Shen Co, fJames A, mMary Jane Harman, hPeter B Stickley, md10/14/1896
Robert J, b18--, Lanc Co, d1893, fSamuel, Sr, (1)mCatherine Payne

DOWNING (continued)
Samuel, b17--, "Levelfields", Nhld Co, wMary Edwards
Samuel, Sr, b5/8/1808, "Levelfields", Nhld Co, d1891, fSamuel, Mary Edwards, 1wCatherine Payne, 2wAnnie D Rice
Samuel, Jr, b18--, Lanc Co, d1885, fSamuel, Sr, (1)mCatherine Payne
Sarah Belle, b18--, "Chatham", Bridgetown, Nhtn Co, d1919, 2w of James Ambler Jarvis
Thomas Joseph, b5/25/1868, "Edgely", Lanc Co, fSamuel, Sr, (2)mAnnie D Rice, wEstelle R Chilton, md11/26/1890

DOWNMAN, --, bc1800, Richmond, hFrederick Davies
Harriet, b18--, Fauq Co?, fR B Lee Fleming
Lavina, bc1820, hGeorge Hamilton II
Margaret, bc1760, Lanc Co, fRaleigh, mFrances Ball, hWilliam Ball Mitchell
Raleigh, b17--, Lanc Co?, wFrances Ball, md1750
William, b16--, Richmond?, wMillion Travers

DOYLE, --, bc1820, Jeff Co?, wSophia Jones
Annie C, b1/16/1850, Malden, Kana Co, fSamuel, mElecta --
James Theodore, bc1830, Dinw Co?, d1892, wMary Virginia Rives

DRAKE, David W, b18--, Augu Co?, wKate M Slaughter
Emily S, b1869, Staunton, Augu Co, fDavid W, mKate M Slaughter, hHenry C Kelsey, md11/23/1891

DRAPER, Elsa S, bc1870, Henry Co?, hPeter A Prillaman
John S, Jr, b1750, Drapers Meadows, Pula Co, dc1844, fJohn S, Sr, mBetsy Robertson, wJane Crockett
John Samuel, Sr, b1/1829, Wytheville, Wyth Co, d1904, fJoseph, mJane Sayers, wJanie Hairston
Joseph, b1800, Drapers Valley, Pula Co, dc1835, fJohn S, Jr, mJane Crockett, wJane Sayers

DREWRY, Emmet A, b18--, nr Drewryville, Sout Co, fJames Humphrey, b17--, fSamuel, m-- Simmons, w-- Simmons
James, b18--, nrDrewryville, Sout Co, fHumphrey, m-- Simmons, 2wMartha Thomas
James David, b18--, nrDrewryville, Sout Co, fJames,
John W, b18--, nrDrewryville, Sout Co, fJames, (2)mMartha Thomas 1wMartha Frances
Samuel, b18--, nrDrewryville, Sout Co, fHumphrey, m-- Simmons
Samuel Blount, b4/3/1852, nr Drewryville, Sout Co, fJames, (2)mMartha Thomas, wVirginia Branch
Vernon T, b18--, nrDrewryville, Sout Co, fJames, (2)mMartha Thomas
Virginia Martin, b18--, hDavid L Pulliam
William Humphrey, b1832, fJohn W, mMartha Frances, wCaroline Williams Barnes
William Sidney, b7/14/1869, Petersburg, Dinw Co, fWilliam Humphrey, mCaroline Williams Barnes, wVirginia D Watkins, md1910

DRIGG, Evelyn, b18--, Petersburg, Dinw Co, fWesley, mAugustina --, hJames M Mullen
Wesley, b18--, wAugustina --

DRINARD, Sallie, b1862, Richmond, fSimon, hJohn H Stout

DRISCOLL, Orin M, b1849, Albe Co, fThomas, mSarah DeNite, wMattie Jane Flanagan
Thomas, b18--, Albe Co, wSarah DeNite

DRISH, Robert, b183-, Clar Co?, wArrissa Smallwood

DRIVER, Anna Maria, b12/3/1764, Rkhm Co, fLouis, mBarbara --, hPeter Acker, Sr
Anna, b18--, Rkhm Co, d1912, hFrederick Wampler
Annie, b182-, nrTimberville, Rkhm Co, fSamuel, Sr, hJoseph Click
Annie R, b185-, Rkhm Co, fJohn W, mCatherine Myers, hBenjamin Cline

DRIVER (continued)
Cornelius, b2/9/1850, Rkhm Co, fJohn W, mCatherine Myers, wRebecca M Hoover, md11/20/1873
John W, b1827, nrTimberville, Rkhm Co, d1893, fSamuel, Sr, wCatherine Myers
Mary E, b185-, Rkhm Co, fJohn W, mCatherine Myrs, hDavid Cline
Mattie C, b185-, Rkhm Co, fJohn W, mCatherine Myers, hNewton Wine
Samuel Jr, bc1830, nrTimberville, Rkhm Co, fSamuel Dreiber/Driver, Sr
Samuel H, b183-, Rkhm Co?, wAnnie Myers
DRUMMOND, Hugh P P, b18--, Norfolk?, d1917
DRYFUSS, David, bc1850, Camp Co?, wDelia Guggenheimer
DuBOIS, Rebecca, b17--, Warr Co, mCatherine --, h-- Miller
DUDLEY, --, b18--, Rkhm Co, hJohn Tutwiler
Belle, b18--, KiWi Co, fJohn Beverley, mSusan Carr Beadles hJohn C Walford
Beverley Roy, b1866, KiWi Co, fJohn Beverley, mSusan Carr Beadles, wHettie James Barlow
Cynthia, b185-, nrDublin, Pula Co, fHugh, mMary J Shufflebarger, hJames C Fink
David W, b185-, nrDublin, Pula Co, fHugh, mMary J Shufflebarger
Emma, b18--, KiQu Co, hSpotswood Bird
Fannie R, b185-, nrDublin, Pula Co, fHugh, mMary J Shufflebarger, hJames G McGuire
Fannie Taylor, b18--, Rapp Co, hJohn W Wood
Harriet, b18--, Rkhm Co?, hSolomon Burtner
James F, b4/9/1860, nrFalls Mills, Taze Co, fHugh, mMary J Shufflebarger, wEvelina Tabor, md11/19/1884
Jessie Mary, bc1860, Culp Co, fWilliam T, mAchsah Miller, hWilliam Walter Moffett, md2/22/1883

DUDLEY (continued)
John Beverley, b18--, wSusan Carr Beadles
Levi O, bc1836, Fran Co, wMary V Bradley
Linda H, b18--, KiWi Co, fJohn Beverley, mSusan Carr Beadles, hAnderson B Cosby
Margaret, b186-, Pula Co, fHugh, mMary J Shufflebarger, hGranger Thompson
Nancy J, b185-, nrDublin, Pula Co, fHugh, mMary J Shufflebarger, hAllen K Brown
Oliver W, Sr, b7/15/1856, Fran Co, fSilas J, mAnn Park Smith, wLucy Estes, md1894
R H, bc1850, Augu Co?, wMantie Myers
Robert, b185-, Esse Co?, wLucy Bird Hoskins
Silas J, b18--, Fran Co, wAnn Park Smith
Sue, b18--, KiWi Co, fJohn Beverley, mSusan Carr Beadles
Ursula, b18--, Fran Co, hOliver Perry Divers
William E, b185-, Pula Co, fHugh, mMary J Shufflebarger
William T, b18--, Rapp Co?, wAchsah Miller
DUFF, Elizabeth, b1840, on Wallen's Creek, Lee Co, d1901, hWilliam Henderson Nickels
DUFFEL, Elizabeth Leonard, b18-- Fredricksburg, Spot Co, fJames, mRebecca Leonard, hThomas Jefferson Watson, Jr
DUKE, Elizabeth Barcley, b18--, Albe Co?, hRobert Rodes
Mary Willoughby, bc1850, Albe Co?, fRichard Thomas Walker, Sr, mElizabeth Scott Eskridge, hClaude M Lee
Richard, b17--, Albe Co?, wMaria Walker
Richard Thomas Walker, Sr, b6/6/1822, nrCharlottesville, Albe Co, fRichard, mMaria Walker, wElizabeth Scott Eskridge
Richard Thomas Walker, Jr, b8/27/1853, nrCharlottesville, Albe Co, fRichard Thomas Walker, Sr, mElizabeth Scott Eskridge, wEdith R Slaughter, md10/1/1884

DUKE (continued)
William Richard, b7/1/1848, Lewisburg, Grbr Co, fRichard Thomas Walker, Sr, mElizabeth Scott Eskridge
DUKES, Perry C, bc1850, Arli Co?, wMalinda Virginia Turner
DULANY, H Rosier, bc1860, Oakley, nrUpperville, Fauq Co, fHenry Grafton, mIda Powell
Henry Grafton, b18--, Fauq Co?, wIda Powell
John Peyton, bc1790, wMary Ann Welby
Marietta, bc1860, Oakley, nrUpperville, Fauq Co, fHenry Grafton, mIda Powell, hHarry S Belt
Rebecca, b11/1859, Oakley, nr Upperville, Fauq Co, fHenry Grafton, mIda Powell, hJohn Hill Carter Beverley, md4/19/1881
Richard, b18--, fJohn Peyton, mMary Ann Welby
DULLE, R B, bc1860, Augu Co?, wIrene Garrison
DUNAWAY, Fannie Belle, b1862, Lanc Co, hSamuel J Adams, Jr
DUNBAR, Ann, b10/22/1852, Blan Co, fLorenzo Dow, mJane Burns, hIsaac Edward French
Lorenzo Dow, b18--, Blan Co, wJane Burns
Nancy L, b1842, Gile Co, d1923, hJohn P Chase
DUNCAN, Celia, b17--, Albe Co, fGeorge, mAnne --, 1hShadrach Ogles, 2hLewis Hancock, md12/29/1778
Edward, bc1870, Alexandria, fJohn, mMartha Norton
Elizabeth, b1845, Rye Cove, Scot Co, 1w of James Buchanan Richmond
Franklin, b18--, fEldridge
Fred H, b18--, wMelissa Burgess
Harriet, b186-, Alexandria, fJohn, mMartha Norton, hJohn Simmons
Hattie V, bc1850, Arli Co, fJames
James A, b18--, d1877
James H, b18--, fEldridge
John B, bc1850, Arli Co, fJames
John Hoplins, b18--, Scot Co?,

DUNCAN (continued)
d1900, wEva Taylor
Mary, bc1850, Arli Co, fJames, h-- Craig
Mildred Roberts, b18--, Rapp Co, fEldridge, hSilas Browning Lillard
Nancy, b18--, Gile Co, hJohn Brooks
R R, b18--, fEldridge
Sarah, b18--, PrAn Co?, hGeorge L Fentress
Theela Epia, b185-, fJames A, hRobert Emory Blackwell, md8/28/1877
William, bc1860, Berryville, Clar Co, fMilton, mFrances Mildred Anderson, wMary Milton Anderson
William, b1857, Arli Co, d1910, fJames, wAmelia Haag
William, b186-, Alexandria, fJohn Duncan, mMartha Norton
DUNCUM, Susan Ann, b18--, Albe Co, hJoshua Rawles Abell
DUNGAN, Eliza Jane, b1843, Smyt Co, hIsaac C Anderson
Nancy Caroline, b1842, Seven Mile Ford, Smyt Co, hWilliam H Copenhaven
DUNKLEE, Helen, b18--, fCharles H, mMary Parrish, hRobert W Lacey
Virginia, b18--, fCharles H, mMary Parrish, hCharles A Johnston, md5/5/1881
DUNLAP, Henry, b18--, Pula Co?, wMinnie Humphreys
John Morris, Sr, b2/25/1866, Halltown, Jeff Co, fWilliam Henry, mKatherine Bland, wMary Ida Stouffer, md1887
Mary Kinneford, b1837, Hamp Co?, d1897, fWilliam, hMahlon Garvin
William Henry, b18--, Halltown, Jeff Co, d1890, wKatherine Bland
DUNLOP, David III, b11/6/1841, nrPetersburg, Dinw Co, d1902, fDavid II, mAnna Mercer Minger, 1wKate Compton, md1/18/1866, 2wMary Carling Johnston, md2/4/1896
David, IV, b186-, Petersburg, Dinw Co, d1916, fDavid III,

104

DUNLOP (continued)
(1)mKate Compton
Eliza C, b186-, Petersburg, Dinw Co, hJohn E Johnson
DUNN, Fannie E, b1853, Petersburg, Dinw Co, hJoseph Budd
Thomas E, bc1840, Smyt Co?, wCaledonia Sanders
DUNNINGTON, Walter Gray, Sr, bc1850, Farmville, PrEd Co, d1922, fJames William, wIndia Knight
DUNTON, Margaret Nelson, b6/2/1869, Nassawadox, Nhtn Co, hGeorge J Fatherly
DUNSTON, Margaret Okeson, b18--, Norfolk?, d1892, hCharles Jones Colonna
DUPUY, Edward Lawrence, b2/1/1859, Falkland Farm, PrEd Co, fJoseph, (2)mSarah Walker, wEmily D Watkins, md1/3/1889
Elvia E, b184-, Falkland Frm, PrEd Co, fJoseph, (2)mSarah Walker, hAlbert G Jeffress
Henry Watkins, b186-, Falkland Farm, PrEd Co, d188-, fJoseph (2)mSarah Walker
James Asa, b185-, Falkland Farm, PrEd Co, d1917, fJoseph, (2)m Sarah Walker
Jane N, b184-, Falkland Farm, PrEd Co, fJoseph, (2)mSarah Walker
John, b17--, Nott Co, wMary Purnell
Joseph, b1804, Nott Co, d1869, fJohn, mMary Purnell, 1w-- Edmonds, 2wSarah Walker
Joseph, b184-, Falkland Farm, PrEd Co, fJoseph, (2)mSarah Walker
Martha S, b18--, hJoel W Daniel
Mary, b18--, PrEd Co?, hRichard H Watkins
Mollie Towns, b184-, Falkland Farm, PrEd Co, fJoseph, (2)m Sarah Walker
Pocahontas, b1846, Bethlehem Church, PrEd Co, d1899, hLewis B Johnston
Sarah Louisa, bc1850, Falkland Farm, PrEd Co, fJoseph, (2)m Sarah Walker, hGeorge W Reed
William Purnell, bc1845, Falkland Farm, PrEd Co, d1904,

DUPUY (continued)
fJoseph, (2)mSarah Walker
DURHAM, Mary, b18--, KiQu Co?, hWilliam Kerr
DURRETT, Elizabeth, b17--, Albe Co?, hJacob Watts
Elizabeth, bc1770, fRichard III, mElizabeth Davis, hJames Watts
Richard III, b1735, fRichard Watts, mAbigail Terrell, wElizabeth Davis
Winston, bc1770, fRichard III, mElizabeth Davis, wBetsey Watts
DUVAL, Josephine, b18--, Spot Co?, hSylvanus Jackson Quinn
Susan, b18--, Camp Co?, fWilliam, hIsaac Adams
DUVALL, William Montgomery, b1846, Spot Co, d1913, wSarah E Crawley
DWYER, James H, b18--, Rkhm Co?, wAda Sprinkle
DYCHE, C P, b18--, Morg Co?, wNannie Dawson
DYE, Cary, bc1860, Fair Co?, wMary Shreve
Winfield, bc1860, Fair Co?, wLucy Harrison
DYER, Gerge, b18--, Dick Co?, wMelinda Cantrell
Josephine, b18--, Pend Co, hEphraim Bowman
Louise, b2/5/1848, Stratton, Dick Co, hJasper Sutherland, mdc1868
Martha, bc1800, Henry Co, hLewis Gravely
EADS, Catherine Elizabeth, nrFalling Springs Church, Rkbr Co, fJohn W, mCatherine Douglas, hSamuel Steele Miller
John W, b1800, Gooc Co, wCatherine Douglas
EAGLE, Jemimah, b1847, High Co, hHenry Harrison Jones
Samuel C, b18--, High Co?, wMartha Carico
EAKIN, James R, bc1860, wMary T Frazier
EAKISS, Myrtle, b1869, nrMcCoy, Mont Co, hGeorge a McCoy
EARHART, Sarah, b2/22/1817, Shen Co, d1896, hWilliam Filsmoyer
EARHEART, Frances Elizabeth,

EARHEART (continued)
b18--, Wyth Co, hWilliam Davis
Margaret, b10/25/1831, Wyth Co, d1911, hDavid Huddle
EARLY, Alice, b185-, nrHillsville, Carr Co, fJames W, (1)m-- Kenney
Annie, b186-, nrHillsville, Carr Co, fJames W, (2)mRhoda Wygal, hRobert H Glendy
Annie Lee, bc1870, Gile Co, fJames K, hHarvey B McDonald, md2/1892
Antoinette, b18--, Madison, Madi Co, fWilliam M, hWilliam Keith Skinker
Edward W, Sr, b2/21/1864, Hillsville, Carr Co, fJames W, (2)mRhoda Wygal, 1wAlice Darst, md6/16/1889, 2wIndia Howard, md9/18/1893
Elizabeth, bc1833, Rkhm Co?, d1909, fHenry, mSallie Showalter, hAbram Garber
Elva, b186-, nrHillsville, Carr Co, fJames W, (2)mRhoda Wygal, 1hJohn Root, 2hWilliam B Cecil
Henry, bc1800, Rkhm Co?, wSallie Showalter
Jacob, bc1830, Rkhm Co?, fHenry, mSallie Showalter
James N, b185-, nrHillsville, Carr Co, fJames W, (1)m-- Kenney
James W, b1817, Wyth Co, d1897, fJohn, 1w-- Kenney, 2wRhoda Wygal
John, b17--, fJoshua, mMary Leftwich
John, b182-, Rkhm Co?, fHenry, mSallie Showalter
John, b184-, nrHillsville, Carr Co, fJames W, (1)m-- Kenney
Jonas, b18--, Shen Co?, wLeah Hoover
Jonah, bc1850, Shen Co, fJonas, mLeah Hoover, wMary Kagey
Joshua, b17--, wMary Leftwich
Jubal A, b11/3/1816, Fran Co
Laura H, b185-, nrHillsville, Carr Co, fJames W, (1)m-- Kenney
Margaret, b18--, Wash Co?, hRush Jackson
Martha Douglas, b18--, Camp Co, hElbridge George Haden,

EARLY (continued)
md2/29/1876
Motaline, b183-, Rkhm Co, fHenry, mSallie Showalter
Nannie G, b18--, Carr Co, fPeter, mJane Worrell, hDavid Winton Bolen, md2/21/1877
Peter, b18--, Carr Co?, wJane Worrell
Peter S, bc1850, nrHillsville, Carr Co, fJames W, (1)m-- Kenney
Rebecca, b18--, Shen Co?, fJonas, mLeah Hoover, hJacob B Garber
Rhoda, b184-, nrHillsville, Carr Co, fJames W, (1)m-- Kenney, hJ Alison Smith
Samuel, b183-, Rkhm Co, fHenry, mSallie Showalter
Sarah, b18--, Albe Co?, hGarrett W Martin
Sarah, b184-, nrHillsville, Carr Co, fJames W, (1)m-- Kenney, hJames McMurran
Susan Margaret, b18--, Richmond?, hThomas E Powers
Susanna, b183-, Rkhm Co?, fHenry, mSallie Showalter, hDaniel Hale
William Kenney, b1847, nrHillsville, Carr Co, fJames W, (1)m-- Kenney, wMary Louise Belo
EARMAN, John, bc1840, Rkhm Co?, wSarah Ann Chandler
EARNEST, James Austin, b3/9/1853, Hano Co, fGeorge, wMary Elizabeth Talley
Rosa, b18--, Russ Co, hRobert Walter Dickenson
EASLEY, Annie R, bc1870, South Boston, Hali Co, fHenry, mNannie P Owen, hHumphrey Singleton Belt IV, md12/19/1894
Fannie Y, b18--, Hali Co?, hCharles J Craddock
George W, b1847, Level Green, Crai Co, fJohn W, (1)mEmily Thompson, wMinnie Chapman McComas
Harriet, b18--, Hali Co, d1902, hWilliam Owen
Henry, b18--, Hali Co?, wNannie P Owen
James Stone, b1804, Pitt Co,

EASLEY (continued)
d1879, fRobert, wElizabeth Holt
John W, b18--, Hali Co, fWilliam, mAgnes White, 1wEmily Thompson, 2wMinerva Pack
Mary Agnes, b3/20/1849, Gile Co, d1922, hJames W Williams
Nancy, bc1800, Hali Co, hJohn Owen
R Holt, b10/31/1857, Halifax, Hali Co, fJames Stone, mElizabeth Holt, wLouisa E Gilmer
Thomas, b184-, Hali Co, wHallie Owen
William, b17--, Hali Co, wAgnes White
EAST, David E, b11/16/1847, nrBrownsburg, Rkbr Co, fWilliam E, mAmanda Strong, wMargaret McCutcheon, md6/8/1882
William E, b182-, Rkbr Co, d1855, fDavid C, wAmanda Strong
EASTHAM, Ada Virginia, b3/12/1854, Rapp Co, d1895, hJames William Miller, mdc1882
Lee B, bc1860, Rapp Co, wMary B Tavenner
EATON, Clara O, bc1860, PrAn Co, fMoses J, 2w of Abel Erastus Kellam
Lucinda, bc1852, Rkhm Co, d1885, fSamuel, hJames Van Meter Dillard
EBERS, Perry F, b18--, Rkhm Co?, wJane A Spitzer
EBERT, Charles M, b10/9/1858, Fred Co, fWilliam H, mAnna Ridgeway, wGaybrella (Wageley) Tharp, md3/19/1919
John E, b1/11/1853, Fred Co, fWilliam H, mAnna Ridgeway
Martin P, b185-, Fred Co, fWilliam H, mAnna Ridgeway
EBERSOLE, --, bc1860, Fred Co?, wGertrude White
EBY, Laura, b18--, Jeff Co, hJ H March
ECHOLS, Mattison, b18--, Crai Co?, wJosephine Reynolds
EDDINS, Hiram, b18--, Greene Co, w-- Moyers
Margaret, b18--, Greene Co, fHiram, m-- Moyers, hThomas A Miller

EDDY, J W, bc1860, Jeff Co?, wFannie Carr
Theodore, bc1850, Fred Co?, wMary Virginia Williams
William N, bc1820, Fred Co?, wMary Williams
EDINGTON, James, bc1800, Roan Co?, wLouisa Stratton
Sarah Jane, bc1829, Roan Co, d1896, fJames, mLouisa Stratton, 2w of William Woods
EDMONDS, --, b18--, Char Co?, 1w of Joseph Dupuy
Anne Wharton, b1814, Acco Co, hGeorge Bowdoin Mapp
Elias E, b18--, wSarah Battaile Fitzhugh
Elizabeth, b18--, fElias E, mSarah Battaile Fitzhugh, hJohn Henry Parrott, Sr
Fannie, b18--, Char Co?, hCharles A Hundley
Helen Matilda, b18--, Fauq Co, hJames Ferguson
Henry Jeter, Sr, b1833, Lanc Co, fRalph, (3)mMary Eustace, 1wEmma Flippo, 2wSallie A Stott
Henry Jeter, Jr, b8/14/1866, Lanc Co, fHenry Jeter, Sr, (1)mEmma Flippo, wSarah Frances Cox, md6/15/1898
Laura, b186-, Lanc Co, fHenry Jeter, Sr, (1)mEmma Flippo, 1hWilliam A Eubank, 2hRobert M Sherman
Ralph, bc1800, Lanc Co, 3wMary Eustace
Sue, b18--, Lanc Co?, hRalph H Chilton
EDMONDSON, --, b18--, Wash Co, 1w of James Keys
Annah Mabel, bc1870, Warr Co, fSanford, mMary Huff, hClarence Moreland Edmondson, md 4/9/1903
John Wesley, b1829, Wash Co, d1910, fWilliam, mMatilda Wedding, wMartha Jane Hawthorne
Lydia Belle, b186-, Wash Co, fWilliam, mMatilda Wedding, hDavid C Snodgrass
Matilda Jane, bc1870, Wash Co, fWilliam, mMatilda Wedding, hPreston E Wolfe
Sanford, b18--, Warren Co,

EDMUNDSON (continued)
wMary Huff
William, b1800, Liberty Hall, Wash Co, d1875, wMatilda Wedding
William James, b5/7/1867, nrMeadowview, Wash Co, fJohn Wesley, mMartha Jane Hawthorne, wPolly Preston, md6/30/1899
EDMUNDS, --, bc1800, Lanc Co, 3w of Addison H Hall
Elizabeth Hodges, b18--, Char Co, fJoseph Nicholas, 2w of Edward R Monroe
EDMUNDSON, Ellen M, b1843, Salem, Roan Co, d1919, fHenry A, hAllen Taylor Eskridge, Sr
Henry A, b1815, Mont Co, d1890
EDWARDS, A W, b18--, Smyt Co?, wVirginia Copenhaver
Eunice Victoria, b1853, Hicksville, Blan Co, hJohn P Hicks, Sr
Floyd W, b18--, Roan Co?, wHarriet Cannaday
Harriet, b18--, KiWi Co, hLarkin Garrett
James W, b1/1/1860, Cap, Carr Co, fMartin, mMelinda Melton, wJulia Ann Winesett
Louisa, b18--, KiGe Co, d1848, 1w of Thacker Rogers
Luther Rice,. b18--, nrFranklin, Sout Co, fJordan
Martin, b1821, Carr Co, d1861, wMelinda Melton
Mary, b17--, Fleets Point, Nhld Co, hSamuel Downing
Mary, b18--, Gray Co, hRobert Carson
Mary Catherine, b1862, nrEdwardsville, Nhld Co, 3w of Aquila Hatton
Ruth Alma, b11/23/1867, Richmond, hWilliam H Spencer, md7/25/1888
EFFINGER, Emma V, b6/28/1850, Rkhm Co, d1913, fGeorge W, hEdwin Robert Shue, Sr
J Fred, b18--, Rkhm Co?, wFannie S Smith
Laura W, b18--, nrLexington, Rkbr Co, d1893, hHope W Massie
Maria G, b18--, Nels Co?, hWilliam Massie

EGE, Samuel, b17--, Richmond, fJacob, wElizabeth Walker
Samuel H, b17--, Richmond, fSamuel, mElizabeth Walker
Sarah Lambert, b17--, Richmond, fSamuel, mElizabeth Walker, hJohn Enders
EGGLESTON, Beverley P, b7/12/1850, Charlotte Court House, Char Co, fJohn William, mLucy Nash Morton, wFannie P Ligon
David Quinn, b185-, Charlotte Court House, Char Co, fJohn William, mLucy Nash Morton
John William, b18--, Nott Co, d1896, wLucy Nash Morton
Joseph Dupuy, b11/13/1867, Marble Hill, PrEd Co, fJoseph Dupuy, mAnne Carrington Booker
EHRMAN, Clarence Preston, bc1860, Dinw Co?, wSannie Robinson Davis
ELAM, Albert Perry, b1815, Powh Co, fBeverly, wMary Elizabeth Foese
Bettie, b185-, Powh Co, fAlbert Perry, mMary Elizabeth Foese, hE Pendleton Bickers
Henningham, b18--, hWilliam H Wilson
James Beverly, b12/29/1847, Powh Co, fAlbert Perry, mMary Elizabeth Foese, wBetty Taylor, md1874
John Thomas, bc1850, Powh Co, fAlbert Perry, mMary Elizabeth Foese
Mary Susan, b18--, Char Co?, hSamuel Moore II, md4/27/1853
Virginia Caroline, b184-, Powh Co, fAlbert Perry, mMary Elizabeth Foese, hJohn E Owens
ELDER, Nancy, b18--, Camp Co, hCharles Scott
ELDRIDGE, --, b18--, Buck Co, fRolfe, Jr, hRobert Kincaid Irving
Lucy, b18--, Buck Co, fRolfe, hJ H Fitzgerald
Rolfe Eldridge, Jr, b17--, Buck Co, fRolfe, Sr
ELGIN, Rebecca Jane, b18--, Loud Co, d1866, 1h-- Nixon, 2h Robert Whitacre
Robert, b18--, Fauq Co?, wLaura Virginia Cochran

ELGIN (continued)
 Roberta E, b10/1847, nrLeesburg, Loud Co, hPeter H Carr
ELKIN, --, b17--, Henry Co, hRobert Pedigo
ELLER, N D, b186-, Camp Co?, wMinnie E Campbell
 Virginia Alice, b1866, Floy Co, hGeorge W Shelor
ELLET, Cornelia Daniel, b18--, Wheeling, Ohio Co, d1874, fCharles, hAmmi Moore, Jr, md1873
 Mary V, b18--, hWilliam D Gabell
 John Archer, b1824, Nott Co?, d1899, wJane Maxey
ELLETT, John R, b185-, Ellet's Mill, Nott Co, fJohn Archer, mJane Maxey
 Martha S, b18--, Ches Co, hEdward A Maxey
 Octavia A, b11/20/1844, Powh Co, d1921, m-- Speers, hJoseph E Maxey
 William W, b1855, Ellett's Mill, Nott Co, fJohn Archer, mJane Maxey, wMary Elizabeth Enroughty
ELLICOTT, J M, bc1860, PrEd Co?, wMary Elizabeth Barbee
ELLINGER, Harvey, bc1850, Rkhm Co?, wAnnie Riddel
 Samuel H, bc1850, Rkhm Co, wJennie Riddel
 William Henry, bc1860, Cumb Co?, fRobert Smith, mMatilda McShaw
ELLINGTON, Annie, bPrEd Co, hJames E McCoy
ELLIOTT, --, b18--, Henrico Co?, 1h-- Jennings, 2hJames Dutoy Vaughan
 David, bc1840, Hali Co?, 1w Sarah Connally, 2wMartha Ann Connally
 Eliza Lavalette, b18--, Camp Co, hThomas Clairborne Creasy
 Frances, b18--, Rkhm Co?, hHudson Collier
 John Frank, b7/21/1849, Mortonsville, ---- Co, fParrott, m-- Catterton, wEllie M Crawford, m1/19/1879
 John L, bc1850, PrWi Co?, wNessie L Leachman

ELLIOTT (continued)
 Susan G, b1828, Locustville, Acco Co, d1860, fWilliam, 1w of Fred Floyd, Sr
ELLIS, Belle, bc1870, 1w of James B Colbert
 Floyd McComas, b11/30/1860, Monr Co, fWilliam, mCaroline Caldwell, 1wLetha McComas, 2w Clara Fargo
 Jacob, b17--, wAnn Rutledge
 Richard Shelton, Sr, b18--, Nels Co?, wAnne Francis Perkin
 Richard Shelton, Jr, b10/11/1853, Afton Farm, Nels Co, d1914, fRichard Shelton, Sr, mAnne Frances Perkin, wRebecca McClue
 William, b18--, fJacob, mAnn Rutledge, wCaroline Caldwell
ELLISON, Amanda E, bc1860, Falls Church, Fair Co, fWilliam H, mElizabeth Fish
 Edwin H, bc1860, Falls Church, Fair Co, fWilliam H, mElizabeth Fish
 Hannah, b16--, ElCi Co?, hAnthony Armistead
 John F, bc1860, Falls Church, Fair Co, fWilliam H, mElizabeth Fish
 William M, b10/3/1859, Falls Church, Fair Co, fWilliam H, mElizabeth Fish, wLillian Ball, md11/23/1883
ELLISTON, Eva Mae, b1860, Monr Co, hEdward B Carr
ELIZEY, Lewis, b18--, wRosanna McIllhany
 Rose Mortimer, b18--, fLewis, mRosanna McIllhany, hFrancis McCormick
ELMORE, Regina, b7/31/1847, Fluv Co, d1906, fCharles, hDrurie Wood Bowles, md1866
ELSEA, Mary E, b4/1866, Clar Co, fAlbert, hWilliam Walton Smallwood, Sr, md12/2/1882
ELSWICK, --, bc1850, Blan Co?, wDorothy Alice Walker
ELY, Emmie, bc1870, hHenry Wood Campbell, md6/4/1895
 A Mack, bc1870, nrJonesville, Lee Co, fThomas S, mMalinda Willis
 Alexander M, bc1800, Lee Co,

ELY (continued)
fRobert, w-- McMillen
Andrew M, bc1830, nrJonesville, Lee Co, fAlexander M, m-- Mc Millen
Mollie Sue, b186-, nrJonesville, Lee Co, fThomas S, mMalinda Willis, hSamuel B Poteet
Polly, b1828, Lee Co, d1887, hWilliam Smith
Robert, b17--, Lee Co, fThomas Smith
Robert, b18--, Lee Co, wSusan Gibbs
Thomas S, b3/2/1832, nrJonesville, Lee Co, fAlexander M, m-- McMillen, wMalinda Willis
EMBREY, Charles O, b1845, Culp Co, wSamantha E Colbert, md10/1869
Henry, Jr, b17--, fHenry, Sr
Sarah, b17--, Staf Co, hJohn Coleman
EMMONS, --, b17--, Culp Co, hJoseph Field
EMSWILLER, Annie, b18--, Rkhm Co?, hJesse Dillard, Sr
ENDERS, Elizabeth Walker, b18--, Richmond, fJohn, mSarah Lambert Ege, hWilliam Palmer
John, b17--, Richmond, wSarah Lambert Ege
Mary, b18--, Richmond, hPoitiaux Robinson
ENGLEDOVE, Alfred S, b1815, Big Lick (now Roanoke), Roan Co, d1890, wMary Ann Lydick
Oscar S, b10/25/1866, Lynchburg, Camp Co, fAlfred S, mMary Ann Lydick, wFlorence Crowder, md1/1/1890
ENGLEMAN, Peter M, bc1858, Augu Co, wEmma Virginia Trout
ENGLISH, Cave, b18--, Alexandria?, wMary Wigginson
Ida P, b18--, Alexandria?, fCave, mMary Wigginson, hGeorge Ficklin Major, md9/3/1879
James W, bc1840, Gile Co?, wAnnie Chapman
John A, b18--, Shen Co?, w-- Johnson
Josephine, b184-, Augu Co?, fJohn A, m-- Johnson, hGeorge

ENGLISH (continued)
Hupp Eyster
Mary Anne, b18--, Fran Co?, hPeter Lewis Hancock
ENROUGHTY, Mary Elizabeth, b1854, Burkeville, Nott Co, d1906, hWilliam W Ellett
EOFF, Louisa Garnett, bc1869, Rkbr Co, d1912, m-- Williamson, hEdward Lacy Graham, Jr
EPES, Fannie Washington, b12/15/1851, Nott Co, hJohn S Epes
Francis W, bc1870, Nott Co, fJohn S, mFannie Washington Epes
James Fletcher, b184-, Nott Co, fThomas Freeman, mJacqueline Segar Hardaway
John S, b10/15/1847, Nott Co, fThomas Freeman, mJacqueline Segar Hardaway, wFannie Washington Epes
Mary Helen, b1822, Nott Co, d1870, hWilliam Jordan Harris
Theodorick Pryor, b1854, Nott Co, d1911, fThomas Freeman, mJacqueline Hardaway, wJoanna Tyler Spencer
Thomas Freeman, b1814, nrBlackstone, Nott Co, wJacqueline Segar Hardaway
EPPARD, Nancy, b18--, Rkhm Co?, d1890, hZachariah Taylor, Jr
EPPES, John W, bc1800, 1w-- Jefferson, 2wMartha B Jones
Sarah A, b18--, Buck Co?, fJohn W, (2)mMartha B Jones, hE W Hubard
ERVIN, James R, b18--, Bath Co?, wMartha Dickinson
Margaret A, b18--, Bath Co, fJames R, mMartha Dickinson, hWilliam Miller McAllister
ERWIN, Elizabeth, b18--, hThomas Whitehead
ESKRIDGE, Alexander P, b1803, Bote Co, wJulia Taylor
Allen Taylor, b1845, Fincastle, Bote Co, d1914, fAlexander P, mJulia Taylor, wEllen M Edmunson
Elizabeth Scott, b18--, Rkhm Co?, hRichard Thomas Walker Duke, Sr
Sarah, b1707, West Co, fGeorge, hWilloughby Newton I

ESTES, Lucy, b18--, Danville, Pitt Co, fJ Howard, hOliver W Dudley, Sr, md1894
Lucy Guinn, b1834, Nels Co, hEgbert Granville Vaughn
Maggie E, b1864, Lawrenceville, Brun Co, hJohn William Ponton
Mary, b18--, hJeremiah M Meadows
ETCHISON, Mary Elizabeth, bc1854, Jeff Co, hMoses Wood
ETTER, Charles M, bc1870, nr Rural Retreat, Wyth Co, fJohn Jacob, mSarah Ellen Neff
Ephraim, b18--, Wyth Co, w-- Wampler
James Stuart, b2/28/1868, nr Rural Retreat, Wyth Co, fJohn Jacob, mSarah Ellen Neff, wCora Philippi, md12/18/1891
John Jacob, b1841, Wyth Co, d1881, fEphraim, m-- Wampler, wSarah Ellen Neff
EUBANK, --, bc1823, Amhe Co, d1864, fThomas N, hWilliam Minor Davis
Bettie, b18--, Nels Co?, hPatrick Henry Cabell
Clara Anna, b1858, Lanc Co, hJoseph B Cralle
Edward Fendall, bc1830, KiWi Co, fJames, mJane Rebecca Ragland
Fannie Alice, b1854, Prospect Farm, nrLocklies, Midd Co, hThomas J Stiff
Fanny M, b1848, Albe Co, hGeorge Edward Booker, Sr
Giles F, b18--, Lanc Co?, wMaria Downing
James, b18--, Glou Co?, fRichard, wJane Rebecca Ragland
James Clayton, b1834, KiQu Co
James Nelson, bc1840, KiWi Co, d1919, fJames, mJane Rebecca Ragland
Mary E, b1836, Prospect Farm, Midd Co, d1871, hJohn E Segar
Patrick Henry, bc1850, KiWi Co, fJames, mJane Rebecca Ragland
Richard, b17--, Gloucester Point, Glou Co, fJohn
Sallie A, b1850, Lanc Co, d1921, hErasmus C Booker
William A, bc1860, Lanc Co?, 2h of Laura Edmonds

EUBANK (continued)
William Shelton, b184-, KiWi Co, d1905, fJames, mJane Rebecca Ragland, wRose Lee James
EUSTACE, Mary, bc1800, Lanc Co, 3w of Ralph Edmonds
EUTSLER, George W, bc1854, Augu Co?, d1911
Marcellus D, bc1848, Augu Co?, d1915, wSusan Antoinette Ramsay
EVANS, --. bc1850, Fred Co?, wAmelia Shryock
Andrew Browne, b9/1830, KiQi Co, d1912, fThomas Beverly, (1)m-- Browne, 1wMary Emma Dew, 2wAlice Catherine Dew
C H, bc1870, Nels Co?, fJohn T, mLouise W Thompson
D S, bc1850, Camp Co?, wWillie Robertson
Eleano, b1820, Richmond, fWilliam, hJames M Taylor, Sr
Eleanor, b186-, Petersburg, Dinw Co, fWilliam McKendree, (1)mMary L Covington, hCharles L Shackelford
Ellen, b1840, Nhtn Co, hJoshua S Warren
George, bc1850, Richmond?, 2h of Eliza Caskie
Inman, b18--, wMillie Campbell
Jane, b18--, Roan Co, hDavid D Dickenson
John T, bc1830, Nels Co, 2h of Louise W Thompson
Mary Emma, bc1870, "Edgewood Farm", KiQu Co, Andrew Browne, Sr, (2)mAlice Catherine Dew
Nannie Lee, b186-, "Edgewood Farm", Midd Co, fAndrew Browne, Sr, (1)mMary Emma Dew, 2w of John Randolph Segar
S V, b186-, Nels Co, fJohn T, (2)mLouse W Thompson
Thomas Beverly, bc1800, KiQu Co, 1w-- Browne, 2w-- Healy, 3w-- Woodward
William Arthur, bc1870, Petersburg, Dinw Co, fWilliam McKendree, (1)mMary L Covington, wCora Belle Mahone
William McKendree, b2/1/1847, Richmond, fWilliam, (3)mMargaret Patrick, 1wMary L Cov-

EVANS (continued)
  ington, m1868, 2wMattie F Taylor, md1877, 3wLelia Louise Pizzini, md1880
EVERETT, Alice Harrison, bc1860, Albe Co, fCharles D, mMary Kate Coleman, h-- Fry
  Aylett L, b186-, Albe Co, fCharles D, mMary Kate Coleman
  Charles D, b1812, Albe Co, d1876, wMary Kate Coleman
  Ellen E, b12/20/1861, Nels Co?, hWalter C Miller
  Hester Hawes, bc1860, Albe Co, fCharles D, mMary Kate Coleman
  John C, b9/21/1862, Albe Co, fCharles D, mMary Kate Coleman, wNellie G Martin, md8/26/1885
  Joseph Walker, b186-, Albe Co, fCharles D, mMary Kate Coleman
  Louise Everett, bc1860, Albe Co, fCharles D, mMary Kate Coleman, hC L Scott
  Mary K, bc1860, Albe Co, fCharles D, mMary Kate Coleman
EWELL, Jesse Baynes, bc1847, PrAn Co, d1918, fSolomon, wAngeline Fentress
  Sallie E, b1867, Acco Co, hRobert J Mason
EWING, --, b18--, Fred Co, wElizabeth Gardner
  William Henry, b18--, wMargaret Anna Vaughan
EYSTER, George Hupp, b3/4/1840, nrStrasburg, Shen Co, fWilliam D, mMary Hupp, wJosephine English, md1859
FABER, Beatrice, b18--, hJohn Shelton Patton
FADELY, Hattie, bc1850, Loud Co?, hAlfred Glascock
  Henry J, b18--, Loud Co?, wMary Estelle Johnson
FAGG, Jack J, bc1860, Wyth Co?, wIda O Davis
FAIR, J W, bc1860, Patr Co?, wMary R Via
FAIREY, John C, bc1850, Aril Co?, 2h of Janie Caroline Turner
FAIRFAX, Martha, b18--, fJohn Walter, hThomas Bolling Robertson, Sr
FAISON, James Oscar, Sr, b8/3/

FAISON (continued)
  1870, Surr Co, fJohn Robert, mBettie Lane, wAnnie Bland Gee, md1902
  John Robert, b18--, wBettie Lane
FALLS, Calvin, bc1860, Roan Co?, w-- Scott
FANSLER, --, bc1860, Shen Co, wSallie Irwin
  George, bc1840, Shen Co, wMary Hottel
FANT, --, b17--, Culp Co?, hFielding Ficklen
  Charles C, b185-, Culp Co?, wMary V Hathaway, md12/22/1894
FARGO, Clara, bc1870, mMatilda Mott, 2w of Floyd Estill Ellis
FARINHOLT, --, b1805, NewK Co, (father of Luther Farinholt)
  Luther, b1846, NewK Co, wJennie Slater
FARISH, Buck, bc1830, Caro Co?, wFannie Amiss
  F P, b18--, fA J, mMartha Crank, 1wEmma S Farish, 2wKate Sinclair
  Sallie, b18--, nrCharlottesville, Albe Co, fA J, mMartha Crank, hGeorge Loflund
  T M, b18--, nrCharlottesville, Albe Co, fA J, mMartha Crank, 1wJulia Randolph, 2wNannie Mann
  William G, b6/29/1846, nrCharlottesville, Albe Co, fA J, mMartha Crank, wMaggie V Hunter
FARLAND, Margaret Fenwick, b186-, Esse Co, hJohn Lesslie Hall
FARLEY, Sallie P, b1/21/1863, Danville, Pitt Co, fKerr, mSusan Cousins, hBenjamin Shimer Motley
FARMER, Carrie Virginia, b1843, Caro Co, d1917, hR Hunter Beazley
  Mary E, b1838, Caro Co, 1h-- Jones, 2hSamuel Martin Delaney
  Rebecca, b17--, Ches Co, hSpencer Chalkley
  Wilton, b18--, wFannie Delaney
FARRAR, Ann Goode, b18--, Meck Co, fSamuel II, mLucy Hudson, hJoseph Collier Hutcheson
  George, b17--, nrRichmond,

FARRAR (continued)
d1772, fWilliam II, wJudith Jefferson
J Clough, b18--, wJosephine Hooker
John, b17--, Meck Co, fGeorge, mJudith Jefferson
Mary Elizabeth, b8/7/1845, Worsham, PrEd Co, d1920, hWilliam Henry Verser
Samuel II, b17--, Meck Co, fSamuel I, wLucy Hudson
T L, bc1860, Albe Co?, wJane Shackelford
William II, b16--, fWilliam I
FARRIER, Alpha Jacob, b18--, Crai Co, wHarriet Pence
Martin P, Sr, b1869, Crai Co, fAlpha Jacob, mHarriet Pence, wMamie Foote
FARROW, Ann, b1859, Daleville, Bote Co, fEnos S, hOllin Ulaah Brugh
FARTHING, J T, b18--, NewK Co?, wLucy H Boswell
Mary, bc1800, Pitt Co?, hShimer Watson
FATHERLY, George, b6/1860, Franktown, Nhtn Co, fWilliam J, mMary S Thomas, wMargaret Nelson Dunton
John, bc1800, Nhtn Co, fJohn, wSallie Bearcraft
William J, b18--, Eastville, Nhtn Co, fJohn, mSallie Bearcraft, wMary S Thomas
FATIC, --, b18--, Rkhm Co?, 2w of Benjamin Myers
FAUBER, Elizabeth, b8/1847, Waynesboro, Augu Co, hArtemus Dillar Coyner
Mary Ann, b18--, Augu Co, hWellington H Watts
FAUGREE, Mary, b18--, Monr Co, hJesse Taylor
FAULCONER, Benjamin O, b18--, Oran Co?, wMary Massie
Bettie Payne, b185-, nrMillers Tavern, Esse Co, fJohn Waller, Sr, mElizabeth Susan Waring, hCharles Robert Bray
Fannie Ida, b185-, nrMillers Tavern, Esse Co, d1884, fJohn Waller, Sr, mElizabeth Susan Waring, hWinter Bray
James William, b18--, Oran Co,

FAULCONER (continued)
fBenjamin O, mMary Massie, wLillie Ellis, md1/1874
John Waller, Sr, b1820, KiQu Co, fThomas, 1h of Elizabeth Susan Waring
John Waller, Jr, b6/9/1856, nrMillers Tavern, Esse Co, fJohn Waller, Sr, mElizabeth Susan Waring, wCarrie Colgin Jones, md12/5/1888
FAULKNER, Charles James, Sr, b7/1849, Hali Co, fLeander, mSarah Green, wLucy Harrison
Ella W, b18--, Appo Co?, 2w of Joel Walker Flood
Gabriel, b18--, Richmond?, wCelestia Mosely
Isaac Hamilton, b18--, Fred Co?, wJulia Nolton
James, bc1850, wLucy R Larrick
John William, b1843, Winchester, Fred Co, d1893, fIsaac Hamilton, mJulia Nolton, wRosa Adams
Leander, b18--, Hali Co?, wSarah Green
Lelia W, b18--, Richmond, d1894, fGabriel, mCelestia Mosely, 1w of Robert S Bristow, md2/24/1881
Mary Elizabeth, b8/10/1850, Halifax, Hali Co, hThomas Watkins Leigh, Sr
William Sanders, b186-, Lynchburg, Camp Co, fJohn William, mRose Adams
FAUNTLEROY, A M, bc1840, Fred Co?, wSarah Conrad
Janet, b18--, Loud Co?, hPowell Harrison
John, bc1810, wLavinia Turner
FECTIG, Ida, b18--, Loud Co, hSamuel S Lutz
FEILD, Maria Louisa, b18--, Suss Co, hEdwin E Parham
FEILDER, Jane, b17--, PrWi Co?, hAlexander Keys
FELLOWS, Harry A, b18--, Fauq Co?, wAlice Murray
FELTHAUS, bc1860, wElizabeth Alice Ryan
FENN, Burt, bc1860, PrGe Co?, wLaura Anderson
FENTON, Rachel, b5/5/1795, Fred Co, hAbel Jackson

FENTRESS, Angeline, b18--, PrAn Co, d1903, hJesse Baynes Ewell
George L, b18--, PrAn Co?, wSarah Duncan
Joseph Henry, b18--, PrAn Co, wMargaret Anne Laud
FERGUSON, Benjamin Overton, b18--, Augu Co, wSusan Frances Craig
Elizabeth, b18--, Bote Co, hJames McDowell
Elizabeth Byron, bc1860, Craigsville, Augu Co, fBenjamin Overton, mSusan Frances Craig, hJohn Mills Goodloe
Emma Virginia, b18--, Dinw Co, hGeorge D Baskerville
George L, b10/18/1839, wMartha Victoria Lewis
J A, b18--, Bedf Co, wMary ----
James, b18--, Fauq Co?, wHelen Matilda Edmonds
Laura J, b18--, Bedf Co?, d1905, fJ A, mMary, 1w of William R Dooley, md1894
Lucy, b18--, Clar Co?, hMichael Dearmont
Marshall, bc1860, Clar Co?, wJulia Sprint
Mary Anne, b1829, Dinw Co, d1908, hWilliam Fletcher Blackwell
Mollie E, b18--, Pitt Co, hWilliam David Coppridge, md12/11/1884
Samuel Lewis, b10/18/1869, nr Appomattox Court House, Appo Co, fGeorge LaFayette, mMartha Victoria Lewis, wAdelia Celestia Mann, md2/12/1896
Sydnor Gilbert, b11/12/1845, nrParis, Fauq Co, d1904, fJames, mHelen Matilda Edmonds, wKatherine Hanson Finnell, md12/1873
FERREL, Alpha J, b18--, Crai Co, fJackson, m-- Smith
E Madison, b18--, Crai Co, fJackson, m-- Smith
Jackson, bc1800, Crai Co?, w-- Smith
John A, b18--, Crai Co, d1902, fJackson, m-- Smith, wSusan Caldwell
Lloyd P, b5/28/1854, Crai Co, fJohn A, mSusan Caldwell,

FERREL (continued)
1wMary A Ruble, 2wLillian Givens
William S, b18--, Crai Co, fJackson, m-- Smith
FERRELL, Byrd Lanier, bc1800, Hali Co?, wAnna Dennis Reeves
Charles Price, Sr, b18--, Montvale, Bedf Co, w-- Cofer
Charles Price, Jr, b5/6/1852, Montvale, Bedf Co, fCharles Price, Sr, m-- Cofer, wSallie Lou Arrington
Lena, bc1870, Danville, Pitt Co, fPeter William, mLucy Carter Neal, hTurner Ashby Weller
Louemma, bc1800, New Garden, Russ Co, hJames Colley
Peter William, b5/31/1832, "Cherry Hill", Hali Co, fByrd Lanier, mAnna Dennis Reeves, wLucy Carter Neal, md1862
FERRIS, Alice, b1857, Fair Co?, hDaniel Thompson
Elizabeth, b16--, hRobert Woodson
FETZER, David, bc1800, Shen Co?, wElizabeth Baker
FEWELL, Ira, b186-, Clar Co?, wMargaret Smallwood
Thomas T, b18--, PrWi Co?, wSarah Ann Leachman
FICKLEN, Benjamin, b17--, KiGe Co, fWilliam, mSarah ----
Benjamin, b17--, KiGe Co?, fBenjamin, mSusannah Foushee
Catharine, bc1860, Pitt Co?, fJohn Fielding, mSarah Jane Slaughter, hHumphrey Robinson
Fielding, b17--, Culp Co?, fBenjamin, w-- Fant
Harry Campbell, b186-, Danville, Pitt Co, fJohn Fielding, mSarah Jane Slaughter, wMary Louise Nelson Tucker, md9/16/1916
James, bc1860, Pitt Co?, fJohn Fielding, mSarah Jane Slaughter
James G, bc1800, Culp Co, fFielding, m-- Fant, wCatherine Davenport
John Davenport, bc1860, Pitt Co?, fJohn Fielding, mSarah Jane Slaughter, wMary V Lyon
John Fielding, b7/1/1824, Culp

FICKLEN (continued)
Co?, d1872, fJames G, mCatherine Davenport, wSarah Anne Slaughter
Warren S, bc1860, Pitt Co, fJohn Fielding, mSarah Jane, wLucy B Langhorne
FICKLIN, Christopher DeAtley, b1798, Rich Co, d1850, fFamous, mElizabeth DeAtley, 1wLouisa Franklin, 2wMary Wright
Famous, b17--, Staf Co, fBenjamin, mSusannah Foushee, wElizabeth DeAtley
Lula, bc1870, Litwalton, Lanc Co, fThomas Dorsey, Sr, mAnn Lyell, hRosser Bass
Mary Virginia, b18--, Culp Co?, fGeorge, hLangdon C Major
Richard Lyell, b186--, Litwalton, Lanc Co, d1916, fThomas Dorsey, Sr, mAnn Lyell
Sarah, bc1800, Culp Co, fFielding, m-- Fant, hWilliam Brown
Thomas Dorsey, Sr, b1835, Rich Co, d1888, fChristopher DeAtley, (2)mMary Wright, wAnn Lyell
Virginia, b18--, Rich Co, hWilliam Oldham
FIELD, Catheirne, b1812, Culp Co, fJoseph, m-- Emmons, hJames Mastin
Elizabeth, b18--, hJohn Yancey
Grandison, bc1800, wMartha Christian Burwell
Harriett, b18--, Suss Co, 1w of James D Howle
Joseph, b1781, Culp Co, w-- Emmons
FIELDS, Rebecca, b1803, Russ Co?, d1903, hAdam Wilson
FIFER, Clara, b19/19/1859, Rkhm Co, fEllis, mLavigna Ray, hMacon Page Carder
Ellis, b18--, Rkhm Co?, wLavigna Ray
FILSMOYER, Elizabeth, b184-, Ashby District, Shen Co, fWilliam, mSarah Earhart, hMichael Pence
Homer, b184-, Ashby District, Shen Co, fWilliam, mSarah Earhart
Jacob, b184-, Ashby District,

FILSMOYER (continued)
Shen Co, d186-, fWilliam, mSarah Earhart
Rebecca Catherine, b1/1/1847, Ashby District, Shen Co, fWilliam, mSarah Earhart, hSamuel Godfrey Bowman, md12/6/1876
William, b1/1814, Ashby District, Shen Co, d1895, wSarah Earhart
FINCH, Eva, b17--, hJames Watson
FINDLAY, Elizabeth, b17--, Mont Co?, hJoseph Trigg
Margaret, b17--, Mont Co?, 1w of Abram Trigg
Rachel, b17--, Mont Co?, hWilliam Trigg, md1/14/1806
FINK, James C, bc1850, Taze Co, wCynthia Dudley
FINKBINE, Ida F, b18--, Fred Co, hFrederick Adam Shryock
FINLEY, Lavinia Elizabeth, b18-- Augu Co, hMatthew Pilson
FINNELL, Hanson, b18--, Warr Co?, mKatherine Hanson, wMary
Katherine Hanson, bc1850, Warr Co, fHanson, mMary --, hSydnor Gilbert Ferguson, md12/1873
FINNEY, Alta J, b186-, Swords Creek, Russ Co, fLilburn, mMelissa E Wilson, hMontraville C Clark
Benjamin, b17--, Ches Co?, 1h of Hannah Watkins
Elbert S, b6/12/1858, Swords Creek, Russ Co, fLilburn, mMelissa E, wLou May Ashbrook, md9/8/1888
George, b17--, w-- Wilson
Helen, b1830, Buchanan (now Pattonsburg), Bote Co, 2w of Peter Butler Johnston
Ida F, b186-, Swords Creek, Russ Co, fLilburn, mMelissa E Wilson, hThomas P Robinson
Lilburn, b10/4/1827, Lebanon District, Russ Co, fReuben, mElizabeth Johnson, wMelissa E Wilson
Lou May, bc1870, Swords Creek, Russ Co, fLilburn, mMelissa E Wilson, hJohn L Horton
Mary Alice, bc1860, Swords Creek, Russ Co, fLilburn, mMelissa E Wilson, hJ Tobert Snodgrass

FINNEY (continued)
Otis T, b186-, Swords Creek, Russ Co, fLilburn, mMelissa E Wilson
Reuben, b1802, nrLebanon, Russ Co, fGeorge, m-- Wilson, wElizabeth Johnson
Tiney, bc1870, Swords Creek, Russ Co, fLilburn, mMelissa E Wilson, hWilliam P Mundy
FIREBAUGH, --, bc1860, Rkhm Co?, wAnnie Harnsberger
Robert D, b1842, "Willow Grove", nrRockbridge Baths, Rkbr Co, d1913, wSarah J Clemmer
FISH, --, bc1800, Warr Co?, wAidelaide Triplett
Elizabeth, b18--, Alexandria, hWilliam H Ellison
FISHBACK, Alice, b184-, Rapp Co, fAb, m-- Anderson, hBenjamin Putnam
Daniel, b181-, Fauq. Co, fNelson, mAnn Welch
George, bc1810, Fauq Co?, wMartha Jane Fishback
John Nelson, Sr, b9/17/1823, Fauq Co, fNelson, mAnn Welch, wAnn Elizabeth Jackson
John R, bc1846, Rapp Cop, d1897, fAb, m-- Anderson, wMary Jane Sisk
Josiah T, b11/1819, Fauq Co, fNelson, mAnn Welch
Martha Jane, bc1820, Fauq Co, fNelson, mAnn Welch, hGeorge Fishback
Mary, bc1840, Rapp Co, fAb, m-- Anderson, h-- Jones
Nelson, bc1778, Fauq Co, wAnn Welch, md11/24/1814
Sarah Ann, b181-, Fauq Co, fNelson, mAnn Welch, hBurgess Bartlett
William A, b184-, Rapp Co, fAb, m-- Anderson
FISHBURN, James Addison, b18--, Fran Co?, fSamuel
John Robert, bc1830, Sydnorsville, Fran Co, fJacob, mAnn Waggoner
Junius Blair, b9/27/1865, Fran Co, fJames Addison, mLouise H Boon, wGrace Theresa Parker, md1893

FISHBURN (continued)
Reuben Harvey, b2/27/1835, Sydnorsville, Fran Co, fJacob, mAnn Waggoner, wEmma Virginia Phillips, md4/27/1873
Tipton T, bc1830, Sydnorsville, Fran Co, fJacob, mAnn Waggoner
FISHBURNE, Anne Blaine, b18--, Albe Co, fDaniel, (2)mMargaret Lynn Guthrie
Clement D, b5/26/1832, Albe Co, fDaniel, (1)mAnn B Rodes, 1w Sarah Harrison Waddell, md 1857, 2wElizabeth Wood, md1867
Daniel, bc1800, Augu Co, 1wAnne Blackwell Rodes, 2wMargaret Lynn Guthrie
Elliott Guthrie, b1842, Albe Co, fDaniel, (2)mMargaret Lynn Guthrie, wElla Van Lear
James Abbott, b1850, Albe Co, fDaniel, (2)mMargaret Lynn Guthrie
Junius M, b18--, Albe Co, fDaniel, (1)mAnn B Rodes, wJulia Miller Junkin
Mary Catherine, b18--, Albe Co, fDaniel, (1)mAnn B Rodes, hCharles P Estill
Richard Baker, b18--, Albe Co, fDaniel, (2)mMargaret Lynn Guthrie
William N, b18--, Albe Co, fDaniel, (2)mMargaret Lynn Guthrie
FISHER, --, b18--, Fauq Co?, wPatsy Payne
Anna, bc1850, Fisher's Hill, Shen Co, fIsaac, Jr, mSusan Pitman, hHugh Stickley
Belie, bc1850, Fisher's Hill, Shen Co, fIsaac, Jr, mSusan Pitman
Billie, bc1850, Fisher's Hill, Shen Co, fIsaac, Jr, mSusan Pitman
Charles, b1859, Fisher's Hill, Shen Co, fIsaac, Jr, mSusan Pitman, wMary Elizabeth Pifer
Charles C, bc1850, Russ Co?, wElizabeth Dickenson
Clara, bc1850, Fisher's Hill, Shen Co, fIsaac, Jr, mSusan Pitman, hJacob Haney
David, b184-, Fisher's Hill, Shen Co, fIsaac, Jr, mSusan

FISHER (continued)
Pitman
Eliza Jacqueline, bc1800, hThomas Marshall Colston
Elizabeth, b17--, hJohn Nash
Frank, b184-, Fisher's Hill, Shen Co, fIsaac, Jr, mSusan Pitman
George, b17--, Shen Co?, d1814, wBarbara --
Isaac, Jr, b18--, Fisher's Hill, Shen Co, fIsaac, Sr, wSusan Pitman
James A, Sr, b1835, Acco Co, d1892, fJohn, wSue Addison
Jesse, bc1840, Rkbr Co?, wBettie Paxton
John, b184-, Fisher's Hill, Shen Co, fIsaac, Jr, mSusan Pitman
John A, bc1870, Locustville, Acco Co, fJames A, Sr, mSue Addison
Joseph, bc1850, Fisher's Hill, Shen Co, fIsaac, Jr, mSusan Pitman
Mat, bc1850, Fisher's Hill, Shen Co, fIsaac, Jr, mSusan Pitman
Noah, b184-, Fisher's Hill, Shen Co, fIsaac, Jr, mSusan Pitman
Samuel, b184-, Fisher's Hill, Shen Co, fIsaac, Jr, mSusan Pitman
Sarah, b5/15/1796, Shen Co?, d1868, fGeorge, mBarbara --, hAbraham Funkhouser
FITCHETT, --, b18--, Nhtn Co, hThomas Henry Nottingham
Irene, bc1870, Math Co, fWilliam M, mLucy E Soles, hJames Warren Dorsey Haynes, Sr, md12/28/1891
Sabra Polk, b18--, nrCapeville, Nhtn Co, d1896, hTully A T Joynes, Sr
William M, b18--, Math Co?, wLucy E Soles
FITTS, Robert Sydnor, b3/22/1857, Pitt Co, fTandy W, mJulia Tinsley, wSallie B Dulin, md12/16/1884
Tandy W, b18--, Pitt Co, wJulia Tinsley
FITZGERALD, Alfred B, b18--,

FITZGERALD (continued)
Pitt Co, fThomas, wTheodosia Lipscomb
E M, b18--, Roan Co, w-- Denit
Edmond, b18--, Pitt Co?, wVirginia Crews
Elizabeth T, b185-, Buck Co, fJ H, Sr, mLucy Eldredge
F E, bc1850, Buck Co?, fJ H, Sr, mLucy Eldredge
Fannie, b185-, Buck Co?, fJ H, Sr, mLucy Eldredge
George, bc1800, Nott Co, fFrancis, 3wSallie Tazewell
J H, Sr, b18--, Nott Co, wLucy Eldredge
J H, Jr, b1/18/1855, Buck Co, fJ H, Sr, mLucy Eldredge, wEva Barnes, md12/19/1882
John, bc1850, Nott Co?, wCaroline Matilda Harris
Littleton, Sr, b1847, Nott Co, fGeorge, (3)mSallie Tazewell, wAlice Flournoy
Thomas B, b8/23/1840, Hali Co, fAlfred B, mTheodosia Lipscomb, wMartha J, md1868
FITZHUGH, Ann, b17--, Amhe Co?, hRobert Rose
Frances Temple, bc1800, Caro Co, d1873, fWilliam, (1)m--, hIsaac Kurtz
Francis C, b8/12/1838, Barboursville, Oan Co, fJames Madison, mMary Stuart, 1wMargaret Glassell Conway, 2w Louise Roberta Conway
Francis Wilbur, b18--, fFrancis C, (2)mLouise Roberta Conway
George, bc1690, "Bedford", KiGe Co, fWilliam, mSarah/Mary Tucker
Glassell, b18--, fFrancis C, (1)mMargaret Glassell Conway
Henry, b1/15/1686or7, "Bedford", KiGe Co, fWilliam, mSarah/Mary Tucker, wSusanna Cooke
Henry, b8/10/1723, "Bedford", KiGe Co, fHenry, mSusanna Cooke, wSarah Battille, md1746
Henry, b17--, fHenry, mSarah Battaille, wElizabeth Stith
Henry, b18--, fHenry, mElizabeth Stith, wElizabeth Conway
James Stuart, b18--, fFrancis

FITZHUGH (continued)
C, (1)mMargaret Glassell Conway
John, bc1690, "Bedford", KiGe Co, fWilliam, mSarah/Mary Tucker
John, b17--, KiGe Co, wLucy Redd
Lafayette Henry, b18--, "Shooters Hill", Midd Co, d1905, fPhilip, mMary Macon Aylett, wAnnie Elizabeth Bullitt
Louise Conway, b18--, fFrancis C, (1)mMargaret Glassell Conway
Mary Macon Aylett, b18--, Nhtn Co, fPhilip Aylett, mGeorgiana Tankard, hWilliam Bullitt Fitzhugh, md12/22/1881
Mildred Covell, b18--, fFrancis C, (1)mMargaret Glassell Conway, hThomas R Hill
Nellie Catlett, b18--, fFrancis C, (2)mLouise Roberta Conway, hJohn P Sneed
Philip, b17--, Midd Co, fJohn, mLucy Redd, wMary Macon Aylett
Philip, b18--, "Shooters Hill", Midd Co, fPhilip, mMary Macon Aylett, wGeorgiana Tankard
Sarah Battaile, b18--, fHenry, mElizabeth Stith, hElias E Edmonds
Thomas, b168-, "Bedford", KiGe Co, fWilliam, mSarah/Mary Tucker
William, bc1680, "Bedford", KiGe Co, fWilliam, mSarah/Mary Tucker
FITZMEYERS, Elizabeth, b18--, Shen Co, hSamuel Bowman
FITZPATRICK, Alexander, bc1800, Nels Co, wBethelinda Penn
Frances, bc1800, Pitt Co?, hSamuel T Miller
Olivia, b185-, Arrington, Nels Co, fThomas Penn, (1)mMary Anne Carrington, h-- Bickers
Thomas Penn, Sr, b1826, Nels Co, d1897, fAlexander, mBethelinda Penn, 1wMary Anne Carrington, 3wSamuella Haweise Coleman, md1880
Thomas Penn, Jr, b185-, Arrington, Nels Co, fThomas Penn, Sr, (1)mMary Anne Carrington

FITZPATRICK (continued)
Walter Carrington, b6/1851, Arrington, Nels Co, fThomas Penn, Sr, (1)mMary Anne Carrington, wEmma Maud Wheeler
FITZWILSON, Sarah, bc1800, Richmond, 2w of Jesse Hopkins Turner
FIX, Philip, bc1800, Augu Co?, wCatherine Fulwiler
Rebecca, bc1836, Augu Co?, d1900, fPhilip, mCatherine Fulwiler, hJacob S Garrison
FLAHERTY, Elizabeth, b18--, High Co?, 2w of John Clifton Matheny, Sr
FLANAGAN, bc1850, Jeff Co, fJames, mFannie Griggs, hCharles A Harper
Fannie, b185-, Jeff C, fJames, mFannie Griggs
James, b1847, Jeff Co, d1916, fJames, mFannie Griggs, wElla Caton
John G, b185-, Jeff Co, fJames, mFannie Griggs
Laura V, b185-, Jeff Co, fJames, mFannie Griggs, hGeorge W Moore
Madison, b18--, Cumb Co, wCatherine Elizabeth Montague
Mary, bc1840, Jeff Co, fJames, mFannie Griggs, hJohn J Lichleiter
Mattie Jane, b1856, Flanagan Mills, Cumb Co, fMadison, mCatherine Elizabeth Montague, hOrin M Driscoll
FLANNAGAN, --, b18--, Culp Co?, hJames M Beckham
Hugh, b186-, Charlottesville, Albe Co, fRichard Knight, mSibelia Josephine Pitman
James, Sr, b17--, Albe Co, fAmbrose
James, Jr, b18--, Fluv Co, fJames, Sr, wMary Johnson
Lawrence Edward, b186-, Charlottesville, Albe Co, fRichard Knight, mSibelia Josephine Pitman
Maud, b186-, Charlottesville, Albe Co, fRichard Knight, mSibelia Josephine Pitman
Richard Knight, b1832, Fluv Co, fJames, Jr, mMary Johnson,

FLANNAGAN (continued)
wSibelia Josephine Pitman
Roy Knight, b11/23/1870, Charlottesville, Albe Co, wLucy Catesby Jones, md10/1896
William Waddell, b18--, Fluv Co, d1864, wElizabeth Henson
FLANARY, Calvin, b18--, d1891
Elbert Sevier, b5/18/1855, nr Dryden, Lee Co, fElkanah, mNancy Young, wEmily Russell Pennington
Elkanah, b1809, wNancy Young
Martha A, b3/4/1866, Wood, Scot Co, fWilliam, mFlorence Gray, hGeorge c Bevins
Mary, b18--, Scot Co?, hWhitfield Starnes
William, b1838, nrWood, Scot Co, d1915, fCalvin, wFlorence Gay
FLANNERY, Thomas, b18--, Lee Co?, wMary Pennington
FLEET, Dorothy, b18--, KiQu Co, fWilliam III, mSallie Browne, hRichard Bagby
James E, b18--, KiQu Co?, wRuby P Garnett
Sallie Ann, b5/17/1840, Math Co, d1914, 2w of Thomas Y Lawson, Sr
Sarah, bc1800, KiGe Co?, hAugustine Parrott
Susan Pierce, b183-, Math Co, d186--, 1w of Thomas Y Lawson, Sr
William III, b17--, KiQu Co?, wSallie Browne
FLEETWOOD, Purnell, b8/17/1847, Suss Co, fWilliam, mMary Cannon
FLEISHER, Ratie, b8/1870, Meadowdale, High Co, fJames A, hJacob W Hevener, md6/8/1892
FLEMING, --, bc1840, Chantilly, Hano Co, fGeorge, Sr, mMary O () Coleman, h-- Schooler
--, bc1840, Chantilly, Hano Co, fGeorge, Sr, mMary O () Coleman, hW Leroy Brown
--, bc1840, Chantilly, Hano Co, fGeorge, Sr, mMary O () Coleman, hM E Morris
B S, b183-, Fauq Co?, wEugenia M Payne
Elizabeth A, b18--, Rapp Co?,

FLEMING (continued)
fThomas, mElizabeth Roscoe, hThompson H Richards, md8/12/1826
Elizabeth Julia, b1721, Amel Co, hThomas Spencer, md1741
Eudora, b1857, Spot Co, d1908, hSamuel E Kendig
George, Sr, bc1800, fGeorge, wMary O ( ) Coleman
George, Jr, b184-, fGeorge, Sr, mMary O ( ) Coleman
Hannah, b17--, Rapp Co?, hThomas Fleming, md9/26/1795
Malcolm, b184-, Chantilly, Hano Co, fGeorge, Sr, mMary O ( ) Coleman
R B Lee, b18--, Fauq Co, wHarriet Downman
Thomas, bc1800, Rapp Co, fThomas, mHannah Fleming, wElizabeth Roscoe
Vivian Minor, b4/18/1844, Chantilly, Hano Co, fGeorge, mMary O () Coleman, wEmily White
William T, b184-, Chanitlly, Hano Co, fGeorge, Sr, mMary O ( ) Coleman
FLEMMING, Ann, b17--, Fluv Co, hJosias Payne
FLETCHER, --, b17--, Fauq Co?, hBenjamin Chappelear
A E, b18--, Augu Co?, wVirginia Paul
Albert, Sr, b18--, Fauq Co, wSarah Withers
Albert Eugene, b9/20/1850, nr Upperville, Fauq Co, fWilliam, mHarriet Lake, wHannah M Brown, md2/18/1885
Alpheus, b18--, Fauq Co, fWilliam, mHarriet Lake
Benjamin, b18--, Fauq Co, fWilliam, mHarriet Lake
Edward, b181-, Rapp Co?, wMargaret Miller
Eliza, b18--, Fauq Co, fWilliam, mHarriet Lake
Elizabeth, b18--, fJohn, mMary Baker
Elizabeth A, b18--, Fauq Co, fJohn, mTacy Gibson, hJoshua Fletcher, Sr
Emily, b18--, Fauq Co, fJohn, mTacy Gibson, 2w of Thomas Glascock

FLETCHER (continued)
Gibson, b18--, fJohn, mMary Baker
I P, bc1870, Harrisonburg, Rkhm Co, fA K, mVirginia Paul
Ida, b18--, Augu Co?, 2w of John Newton Opis, md1878
Isaac, b18--, Fauq Co, fWilliam, mHarriet Lake
Jane, b18--, Russ Co, hWalter A Howard
John E, b18--, Fauq Co, fWilliam, mHarriet Lake
John T, b18--, fWilliam, mLouise Funston
Joshua, Fr, b9/5/1849, nrUpperville, Fauq Co, fJoshua, Sr, mElizabeth A Fletcher, 1w Marion Pritchard Carter, 2w Lula Foster
Kate L, b184-, Fauq Co, fWilliam, mHarriet Lake
Marion F, b18--, Fauq Co, fWilliam, mHarriet Lake
Mary A, bc1870, Buch Co?, fWilliam, mMartha Fuller, hWillie Lee Dennis, md6/12/1890
Mary Lucinda, b1848, Russ Co, hGeorge B White
Mary Moore, bc1870, Harrisonburg, Rkhm Co, fA K, mVirginia Paul, hJ Silor Garrison, md9/4/1900
Mollie C, b184-, Fauq Co, fWilliam, mHarriet Lake
Robert, b18--, Fauq Co, fWilliam, Harriet Lake
Robert, b1/1/1839, nrUpperville, Fauq Co, d1901, fJoshua, Jr, mElizabeth A Fletcher, wTacy Glascock
Robert, bc1860, Fauq Co?, wMary Kincheloe
Thaddeus Norris, Sr, b18--, Culp Co, wGeorgia Owen Latham
W M, b18--, Fred Co?, wEmily G Smith
William, bc1804, nrUpperville, Fauq Co, fRobert E, wHarriet Lake
William, b18--, Buch Co?, wMartha Fuller
William, b184-, Fauq Co?, wMollie Skinner
William H, b184-, Fauq Co, fWilliam, mHarriet Lake

FLIPPEN, Ida, b18--, Cumb Co, hAndrew J Gray, Sr
John James, b8/16/1845, Farmville, PrEd Co, fMonroe R, mSusan C Armistead, wLucy E Haskins, md1868
Monroe R, b18--, Cumb Co, 1h of Susan C Armistead
Philip, b18--, Cumb Co?, 1w Lelia K Corson, 2wRosalie Hill Corson
FLIPPO, Emma, b1840, Lanc Co, d1876, 1w of Henry Jeter Edmonds, Sr
Samuel Wood, bc1842, Caro Co?, wMattie Patrick
FLOOD, Elinor Bolling, b18--, Appo Co, fJoel Walker, (2)m Ella W Faulkner, hRichard Evelyn Byrd, Sr, md9/15/1886
Henry, b17--, Buck Co, fJohn
Henry, b18--, Appo Co?, fJoel W
Henry Delaware, b9/2/1865, Appo Co, d1921, fJoel Walker, (2)mElla W Faulkner, wAnna V Portner, md4/18/1914
Joel W, bc1800, Appo Co, fHenry
Joel Walker, b18--, Appo Co, fHenry, 1wSallie Whitman Delk, 2wElla Faulkner
Sarah E, b18--, Buck Co, hJames D Anderson
FLORA, George B, b4/20/1848, Fran Co, wAnna L Peters
FLORY, --, b18--, Rkhm Co?, hDavid Holler
Abram, b183-, Mill Creek, Rkhm Co, fSamuel, mElizabeth Young, wBarbara Snell
Anne Rebecca, b5/8/1864, Timberville, Rkhm Co, fDaniel, mSusan Wampler, hJohn Henry Hoover, md11/5/1885
Bettie, b183-, Mill Creek, Rkhm Co, fSamuel, mElizabeth Young, hJoseph Salyards
Catherine, bc1828, Mill Creek, Rkhm Co, fSamuel, mElizabeth Young, hSamuel Good
Daniel, b1832, Mill Creek, Rkhm Co, d1901, fSamuel, mElizabeth Young, wSusan Wampler
Hannah, bc1830, Mill Creek, Rkhm Co, fSamuel, mElizabeth Young, hWilliam Haugh
Isaac, bc1870, nrTimberville,

FLORY (continued)
  Rkhm Co, fDaniel, mSusan Wampler
  John, bc1820, Rkhm Co?, wFrances Garber
  John Samuel, b3/29/1866, nrTimberville, Rkhm Co, fDaniel, mSusan Wampler, wWinnie Mikesell, md8/18/1908
  Joseph F, b186-, nrTimberville, Rkhm Co, fDaniel, mSusan Wampler
  Mary, b182-, Mill Creek, Rkhm Co, fSamuel, mElizabeth Young, hJoseph Cline
  Mary Catherine, b186-, nrTimberville, Rkhm Co, fDaniel, mSusan Wampler, hJulius A Miller
  Nancy, b182-, Mill Creek, Rkhm Co, fSamuel, mElizabeth Young, hWilliam Rodeffer
  Noah, b183-, Mill Creek, Rkhm Co, fSamuel, mElizabeth Young, wSophie Showalter
  Samuel, b12/5/1801, nrPleasant Valley, Rkhm Co, d1869, wElizabeth Young
  Sarah, b18--, Rkhm Co, hJoseph Bowman
FLOURNOY, Alice, bc1860, PrEd Co, hLittleton Fitzgerald, Sr
  Louise, bc1845, hWilliam Watson Cobbs
FLOYD, Anna, b18--, Camp Co, hHenry Ward Adams
  Benjamin Rush, b18--, Wash Co, fJohn, mLetitia Preston
  Carey S, b186-, Locustville, Acco Co, fFred, (2)mIndiana F Jones
  Fred, b6/8/1827, Bradford's Neck, Acco Co, d1875, 1wSusan G Elliott, 2wIndiana F Jones
  G Fred, Sr, b2/8/1859, Locustville, Acco Co, fFred, (1)m Susan G Elliott, 1wMary E Swanger, md6/6/1888, 2wElla B Dennis, md8/1898
  John, b17--, wJane Buchanan
  John, b17--, Wash Co?, fJohn, mJane Buchanan, wLetitia Preston
  John, bc1870, Camp Co?, wAnne West Adams
  John B, b18--, Wash Co, fJohn,

FLOURNOY (continued)
  mLetitia Preston
  Nellie, b18--, Camp Co?, hPeter Johnson Otey
  Nicketti, b18--, Wash Co, fJohn, mLetitia Preson, hJohn W Johnston
  Richard S, b186-, Locustville, Acco Co, fFred, (2)mIndiana F Jones
  William E, b185-, Locustville, Acco Co, fFred, (1)mSusan G Elliott
  William P, b18--, Wash Co, fJohn, mLetitia Preston
FLYNN, James, b18--, Fauq Co, wRachel Hunter
  Mattie Iola, bc1870, Gladys, Camp Co, fC Washington
FOESE, Mary Elizabeth, bc1820, Powh Co, hAlbert Perry Elam
FOGG, Henry, b18--, Mari Co?, wSarah Haun
FOGLE, S P, bc1850, Shen Co?, wMary Susan Good
FOLEY, Benjamin Franklin, b1844, Loud Co, d1915, fWilliam, wSarah J Rust
  Maggie, b184-, Loud Co, fWilliam
  Moses, b184-, Loud Co, fWilliam
  Oswald, b184-, Loud Co, d186-, fWilliam
  William, b184-, Loud Co, fWilliam
FOLKES, Joseph, b1793, ChCi Co, fElijah, 2wHannah Irby
  Robert Andrew, b12/7/1845, ChCi Co, fJoseph, (2)mHannah Irby, 1wElizabeth Crump, md12/15/1869, 2wMary Edna Montague, md9/24/1901
FOLTZ, A M, bc1860, Rkhm Co?, w-- Bowman
  Charles S, bc1860, nrCulpeper, Culp Co, fSamuel, mCaroline Bowers
  David, bc1850, Page Co?, w-- Shuler
  Edward L, b186-, nrCulpeper, Culp Co, fSamuel, mCaroline Bowers
  George T, b4/18/1867, nrCulpeper, Culp Co, fSamuel, mCaroline Bowers, wMary M Broders, md1/1899

FOLTZ (continued)
James B, bc1850, Shen Co, wVictoria Sine
James Perry, b18--, Page Co, fJoel, wLaura Alice Snyder
Joel, bc1805, Page Co?, d1894
John C, bc1850, nrCulpeper, Culp Co, fSamuel, mCaroline Bowers
Joseph, b185-, nrCulpeper, Culp Co, fSamuel, mCaroline Bowers
Mary, b185-, nrCulpeper, Culp Co, fSamuel, mCaroline Bowers, hWilliam Vaughan
Philip, b186-, nrCulpeper, Culp Co, fSamuel, mCaroline Bowers
Robert M, bc1850, nrCulpeper, Culp Co, fSamuel, mCaroline Bowers
Samuel, b11/22/1818, nrNewport, Page Co, fReuben, mElizabeth Kite, wCaroline Bowers
Sarah, b18--, Page Co?, hGeorge Thomas Shuler
FONTAINE, Elizabeth Ballard, bc1820, Pitt Co, hWilliam Witcher Keen I
Lucy, b18--, Pitt Co, d1917, hChiswell Dabney, Sr, md1873
FONTLEROY, Farley, b17--, Culp Co?, 1h of -- Corbin
FOOTE, --, b17--, PrWi Co?, hJohn Alexander
FORBES, Nannie Edwards, bc1860, Buck Co?, fWilliam W, mAmonette Cobb, hAsa Dickinson Watkins, md9/25/1856
William W, b18--, Buck Co?, wAmonette Cobb
FORD, Adaline, bc1820, Fairfax Court House, Fair Co, fCharles Fleming, Sr, mJane Butler
Amanda, bc1820, Fairfax Court House, Fair Co, fCharles Fleming, Sr, mJane Butler
Andrew Jackson, Sr, PrEd Co, fWilliam C, mMargaret Rice, wMary Lucy Carter
Andrew Jackson, Jr, Richmond, fAndrew Jackson, Sr, mMary Lucy Carter
Annie, b184-, Fair Co, fFrederick Mortimer, (1)mSarah Lane
Augusta, b181-, nrFairfax Court House, Fair Co, fCharles Fleming, Sr, mJane Butler, h--

FORD (continued)
Brower
Belle K, b184-, Fair Co, fFrederick Mortimer, Sr, (1)mSarah Lane, hCharles F Miles
Bolling Wellford, b18--, Richmond, fAndrew Jackson, Sr, mMary Lucy Carter
Campbell F, bc1870, Cumb Co, hM E Massie
Charles Fleming, Sr, b17--, Fair Co?, mElizabeth Keith, wJane Butler
Charles Fleming, Jr, b181-, nrFairfax Court House, Fair Co, fCharles Fleming, Sr, mJane Butler
Charles Fleming III, bc1860, Fair Co, fFrederick Mortimer, Sr, (2)mMargaret Tyler
Edward Rodolph, b181-, nrFairfax Court House, Fair Co, fCharles Fleming, Sr, mJane Butler
Elizabeth Keith, bc1810, nr Fairfax Court House, Fair Co, fCharles Fleming, Sr, mJane Butler, h-- Sweatman
Elizabeth Keith, b186-, Fair Co? fFrederick Mortimer, Sr, (2)mMargret Tyler, hA L Jameison
Evelina, bc1810, nrFairfax Court House, Fair Co, fCharles Fleming, Sr, mJane Butler, h-- Samuels
Florence B, b18--, Richmond, fAndrew Jackson, Sr, mMary Lucy Carter, hCharles E Quincy
Frances, b18--, hJohn J Wicks
Frederick Mortimer, Sr, bc1811, nrFairfax Court House, Fair Co, d1897, fCharles Fleming, Sr, mJane Butler, 1wSarah Lane, 2wMargaret Tyler
Frederick Mortimer, Jr, b185-, Fair Co, fFrederick Mortimer, Sr, (1)mSarah Lane
George Tyler, b185-, Fair Co, fFrederick Mortimer, Sr, (2)mMargaret Tyler
John M, b184-, Fair Co, fFrederick Mortimer, Sr, (1)mSarah Lane
Jonathan, b18--, Richmond, fRoyal, wAnnie J Hudgins

FORD (continued)
Kate, b7/7/1833, Henrico Co, hRobert James Throckmorton
Margaret, bc1850, Fair Co, fFrederick Mortimer, Sr, (1)m Sarah Lane, hAndrew Burke
Mary Lee, b18--, Richmond, fAndrew Jackson, Sr, mMary Lucy Carter, hCarroll C Bitting, Jr
Mary Randolph, b181-, nrFairfax Court House, Fair Co, fCharles Fleming, Sr, mJane Butler, h-- Simpson
Mary Taylor, bc1860, Fair Co, fFrederick Mortimer, Sr, (2)m Margaret Tyler, hE R Sweatman
Sallie, b18--, Hano Co, hJohn Delaney
Sallie, bc1841, Fair Co, fFrederick Mortimer, Sr, (1)mSarah Lane
Vernon Hebb, b186-, Luray, Page Co, fFrederick Mortimer, Sr, (2)mMargaret Tyler
Walter, b184-, Fair Co, d1865, fFrederick Mortimer, Sr, (1)m Sarah Lane
William C, b1783, PrEd Co, wMargaret Rice
William Crank, b11/8/1866, Luray, Page Co, fFrederick Mortimer, Sr, (2)mMargaret Tyler, wElizabeth Miller Heller, md1/10/1900
William E, bc1820, nrFairfax Court House, Fair Co, fCharles Fleming, Sr, mJane Butler
FOREMAN, Maacah, b3/2/1797, fAlexander, hJames Green Martin
FORLOINE, Margaret, b1823, Ches Co, hDavid A Brown
FORREST, Sophia, bc1800, hJohn Henry deButts, md1844
FORSYTHE, J T, b18--, Roan Co, w-- Denit
FORTUNE, Connie F, b2/3/1856, nrLovingston, Nels Co, fGeorge W, Sr, mNancy H Stewart
Cora, bc1860, nrLovingston, Nels Co, fGeorge W, Sr, mNancy H Stewart, hW H Loving
George W, Sr, b3/25/1812, Nels Co, d1898, fThomas E, mJane Mark Alexander, wNancy H Stewart

FORTUNE (continued)
George W, Jr, bc1860, nrLovingston, Nels Co, fGeorge W, Sr, mNancy H Stewart, wAdsonia Harvey
Margaret, b185-, nrLovington, Nels Co, fGeorge W, Sr, mNancy H Stewart, hRobert E Gleason
Mary W, b185-, nrLovingston, Nels Co, fGeorge W, Sr, mNancy H Stewart, hW C Stevens
Nannie J, bc1860, nrLovingston, Nels Co, fGeorge W, Sr, mNancy H Stewart
Susan B, bc1860, nrLovingston, Nels Co, fGeorge W, Sr, mNancy H Stewart
Thomas E, b17--, Nels Co, wJane Mack Alexander
FOSTER, --, b1801, Oran Co, d1879, hWilliam O Beazley
Anna, b184-, Fauq Co, fJames William, mLucelia Hunton
Benjamin, bc1860, Buck Co?, wAngeline Guthrie
Bettie, b18--, Clar Co, hLewis Berlin
Cornelia, b4/10/1856, Fauq Co, fThomas R, hRobert Eden Peyton, Jr
Isaac, b4/10/1778, PrWi Co, wPriscilla Hunton
Jacob G, b18--, Page Co?, wVirginia Sours
James Robert, b10/14/1850, Fauq Co, fJames William, mLucelia Hunton, 1wFrances Brokenbrough, 2wMary DeButts Carter, md1/30/1894
James William, bc810, fIsaac, mPriscilla Hunton, wLucelia Hunton
James Hunton, bc1810, fIsaac, mPriscilla Hunton
John Hunton, b185-, Fauq Co, fJames William mLucelia Hunton
Joseph L, b18--, Appo Co?, wBessie Royster
Lula, b18--, Marshall, Fauq Co, fJames, 1w of Joshua Fletcher, Jr
Maria, b18--, Hali Co, hJohn Osborne
Mary, bc1800, Math Co, hJesse Hudgins
Mary Elizabeth, bc1810, fIsaac,

FOSTER (continued)
mPriscilla Hunton
Mary Fitzhugh, b184-, Fauq Co,
fJames William, mLucelia Hunton, hJohn Morton Ramey
Matilda, b17--, hThomas Wigglesworth
Ora, bc1870, Buck Co?, fN B,
hJames H Lewis
Sallie Hester, b6/1862, PrEd
Co, hJames Thomas Clark
Thomas Redmond, bc1810, fIsaac,
mPriscilla Hunton
FOUSHEE, Susannah, b17--, Staf
Co?, hBenjamin Ficklin II
FOUT, Elizabeth, b18--, Fred
Co?, hJoseph Brown
FOUTS, Elizabeth, bc1842, Bedf
Co?, d1918, hJames Wesley
Scott
FOWLER, Amanda, b18--, nrSeven
Pines, Hano Co, hJames Clark
Smith
Everett, bc1840, Clar Co?,
wLucy Smallwood
Mary A, b18--, Monroe (now Summers) Co, fThomas, mKizziah
Chapman, hJames David Johnston
FOWLES, Ella, b18--, Lune Co?,
hEdward W Gary
FOWLKES, --, b18--, Lune Co,
hLouis N Gee
L J, b18--, Henry Co, fWilliam,
mLeonora J ---
William, b18--, Henry Co, 1h of
Leonora J ---
William D, b18--, Henry Co,
d1922, fWilliam, mLeonora J --
FOX, --, b18--, Fauq Co?, wAgnes
Heflin
A P, b18--, Walkerton, KiQu Co,
wSophia Hart
Charles L, b18--. Wyth Co?,
wMary Graham
Elizabeth, bc1800, KiWi Co,
fThomas, mLeah Lipscomb,
hJames Cocke
Elizabeth Lewis, b186-, Wyth
Co, fCharles L, mMary Graham,
hJohn Thompson Graham, md6/6/
1889
James, b186-, fA P, mSophia
Hart
James, b1838, Richmond, fRichard, wMary Louise Redwood
Josephine, b9/10/1858, Hano Co,

FOX (continued)
hAime Maurice Bazile
Martha L, b1863, Burkes Garden,
Taze Co, hHenry H Cook
Philadelphia Claibourne, b17--,
fThomas, hJohn Wigglesworth
Thomas, b17--, KiWi Co?, wLeah
Lipscomb
FRANCE, Harrison Carter, b1818,
Parr Co, wKatherine Penn
John Gordon, b1858, Henry Co,
fHarrison Carter, mKatherine
Penn, wDaisie Wayne
Susan Barbara France, b18--,
Henry Co, fHarrison Carter,
mKatherine Penn, hJohn Harrell
Schoolfield, Sr
FRANCES, Martha, b18--, 1w of
John W Drewry
FRANCIS, Charles W, bc1870, Floy
Co, fWilliam H, mEliza Shelor
Cora, b18--, Old Point Comfort,
ElCi Co, fRobert, hWilliam
Walker Scott, Sr, md11/25/1887
Emma, b1856, Christiansburg,
Mont co, fJohn R, hLilburn R
Litton
Flora McIvor, bc1870, Floy Co,
fWilliam H, mEliza A Shelor,
hIsaac Eldridge Huff
John T, bc1850, Powh Co?, wMildred Lee
Miles, b18--, 1wJane Hall
William H, b1839, Mont Co,
d1879, fMiles, mJane Hall,
wEliza A Shelor
FRANKLIN, Alice W, b18--, Appo
Co?, fJ R, hJames F Connally,
md1895
James, bc1850, Loud Co?, wCatherine Green
Louisa, bc1800, Rich Co, 1w of
Christopher DeAtley Ficklin
Martha, bc1870, Camp Co, fJacob
H, 2w of Elijah E Menefee,
md2/3/1908
FRASIER, Katherine, b18--, Upperville, Loud Co, fThomas,
mCatherine Hall, hPembroke
Somerset Gochnauer
Thomas, b18--, Loud Co?, wCatherine Hall
FRAVEL, Anna E, b18--, fSamuel,
hIsaiah Bowman
Ann, b9/25/1818, Shen Co,
d1873, hIsaac Hottel

FRAVEL (continued)
Catheirne, b18--, Woodstock, Shen Co, hWilliam H Bargelt
Charles F, b1860, Woodstock, Shen Co, fJohn H, mJane Bruce, wIda B Hottle
John H, b1822, Woodstock, Shen Co, wJane Bruce
Margaret, b7/22/1812, Shen Co?, 1hJoseph Hockman, 2hSamuel Beydler
Mary, bc1790, Shen Co, hJacob Bowman
Rebecca, bc1840, Shen Co, d1894, fJonathan, 2w of Abraham Rhodes
FRAY, Ephraim, bc1800, Madi Co?, fJohn, w-- Dutton
Ephraim Dutton, b18--, Madi Co, wSusan Marion Wayland
Jackson Lee, b8/25/1862, Madi Co, fJoseph Michael, mElizabeth Anne Keyser, 1wBelle Crigler, md1901, 2wRoberta Browning, md5/1905
John Dutton, bc1860, Madi Co, fJoseph Michael, mElizabeth Ann Keyser, wFlorence Hilton Jackson
Joseph Michael, bc1840, Madi Co, fEphraim, mSusan Marion Wayland, wElizabeth Anne Keyser
William Henry, b3/31/1844, Madi Co, fEphraim Dutton, mSusan Marion Wayland, wEmma Roberts Miller, md2/15/1872
FRAZIER, Emma Lyle, b18--, Augu Co, hRichard P Bell, Sr
George Andrew, bc1800, Gile Co, w-- Dillon
John, b18--, Scot Co, d1861, Lucy Pennington
J Tyler, b11/22/1840, Gile Co, fGeorge Andrew, m-- Dillon, wMaria Virginia Taylor
Lucy, b18--, hMelzi S Chancellor
Mary T, b186-, Taze Co, fJ Tyler, mMaria Virginia Taylor, hJames R Eakin
Rebecca, b18--, Scot Co, hThomas Greear
Sallie S, bc1870, Taze Co, fJ Tyler, mMaria Virginia Taylor, hJoseph B Kirk

FRAZIER (continued)
William, b184-, Scot Co, d1894, fJohn, mLucy Pennington, wEmily Taylor
FRED, Eliza, b18--, Fauq Co?, 2w of Luke Edward Woodward, Sr
Mary Catherine, b1/24/1832, Loud Co?, fThomas, mRachel Palmer, 2w of Hugh Thomas Swart, md5/19/1858
Thomas, b18--, Loud Co?, wRachel Palmer
FREE, Bettie, bc1860, nrDumfries, PrWi Co, fWilliam R, mLaura V Merchant, hH J Jonas
Clara, b186-, nrDumfries, PrWi Co, fWilliam R, mLaura V Merchant
Gertrude, b186-, nrDumfries, PrWi Co, fWilliam R, mLaura V Merchant, hBolling Thomas
Lamartine, b186-, nrDumfries, PrWi Co, fWilliam R, mLaura V Merchant
William Raymond, b5/27/1861, nrDumfreis, PrWi Co, fWilliam R, mLaura V Merchant, wAlice Black Adamson
FREEMAN, Amanda, b18--, Bedf Co, hDavid Poindexter
Jane, b6/26/1857, Wise Co, fJoseph, mSarah Powers, hPeter F Hutchinson
Joseph, b1832, Wise Co, wSarah Powers
Leigh R, bc1840, Shen Co?, wAda Virginia Miller
Margaret Adams, b10/1825, Richmond, fSamuel, hCharles W Purcell, Jr
FRENCH, David, b17--, West Co?, fMatthew, mSarah "Sallie" Payne
Guy C, bc1800, Gile Co, fDavid, wAraminta Chapman
Hugh, b18--, gile Co, wRachel Frye
Isaac Edward, b4/13/1849, Gile Co, fHugh, mRachel Frye, wAnn Dunbar
Mary R, b18--, hWilliam Taylor Dabney
Matthew, b17--, West Co?, wSarah "Sallie" Payne
Minerva Ann, b18--, Gile Co?, hThomas Jefferson McComas

FRENCH (continued)
Sarah, b1832, Pearisburg, Gile Co, fGuy D, mAraminta Chapman, hWilliam W McComas
FRENKEL, Leopold, bc1850, Fred Co?, wAda Arlena Copp
FRIEND, Alice, b18--, Ches Co, hRichard N Thweatt
Bessie Perry, bc1870, White Hill, nrPetersburg, Dinw Co, hWilliam Henry Bocock
C N, b18--, wHattie Perdue
Charles, b18--, PrGe Co?, fNathaniel, mElizabeth ---, wMary Minge
John Gilliam, b10/15/1849, PrGe Co?, fCharles, mMary Minge, 1wElla Mills, 2wJennie B Green
Nathaniel, b18--, PrGe Co?, wElizabeth ---
FRIES, Elizabeth, b18--, Fred Co?, fMichael, 2w of Solomon Glaize, mdc1840
Florence, b9/15/1867, Fred Co, fJesse, mMary Jane Fries, hMartin Summers Glaize, md11/20/1895
Jacob, b18--, Fred Co?, wJane - Jane Elizabeth, bc1840, Fred Co?, fMartin Fries, hJohn W Glaize
Jesse, b18--, Fred Co, wMary Jane Fries
Mary Jane, b18--, Fred Co, fJacob, mJane ---, hJesse Fries
FRILEY, Edith, bc1800, Castlewood, Russ Co, hHenry M Meade
FRISCHKORN, Margaret, b1850, Richmond, hHenry C Boschen
FRITTS, Charles William, b8/12/1863, Jeff Co, d1921, fThomas, mHarriet Creamer, wValley V Dellinger, md12/16/1903
Thomas, b18--, Jeff Co?, wHarriett Creamer
FRITZ, Catheirne, b18--, Oran Co?, d1904, hJames R Graves
FROST, Ann, b17--, Clar Co?, 2w of Francis McCormick
Thomas L, b18--, Fauq Co?, wElizabeth McG Murray
FRY, --, bc1850, Albe Co?, wAlice Harrison Everett
--, b18--, Shen Co?, hMilton Grandstaff

FRY (continued)
James A, b185-, Augu Co, fHarvey
James A, b18--, Rkhm Co, wAnna Wine
Joseph E, bc1850, Fred Co?, wLillie Funkhouser
Newton W, b185-, Augu Co, fHarvey
Richard Watson, b18--, Richmond, fWilliam Henry, mJane Watson, wEleanor Mitchell
William F, b1861, Augu Co, d1920, fHarvey, wNannie Landis
William Henry, b18--, Richmond?, wJane Watson
FRYE, Rachel, b18--, Gile Co, hHugh French
FUDGE, Andrew, b18--, nrCovington, Alle Co, fConrad, m-- Warwick
Andrew, b186-, nrCovington, Alle Co, fRobert Andrew, mAnnie E Gilmer
Charles Archer, Sr, b4/22/1870, nrCovington, Alle Co, fRobert Andrew, mAnnie E Gilmer, wEdith Haynes, md1904
Harriet L, bc1841, Taze Co, d1922, hAchilles James Tynes
Martha Elizabeth, b18--, nr Covington, Alle Co, fAndrew, hWilliam A Gilliam
Mary Ann, b1821, Covington, Alle Co, hHenry B Harman
Robert Andrew, b1848, nrCovington, Alle Co, fAndrew, wAnnie E Gilmer
FUGATE, James C, b1854, Rye Cove, Scot Co, fRufus Boyd, mSarah Young, wMargaret Thomas
Rufus Boyd, b18--, Rye Cove, fZachariah, m-- Seymour, wSarah Young
Zachariah, b17--, Russ Co, w-- Seymour
FULK, Frank, bc1860, Rkhm Co?, 2h of Emma Jeanetta Swank
FULLER, Amy J, b2/7/1861, Coeburn, Wise Co, fNoah A, hAugustus McFarland Vicars
Harriet, b18--, Taze Co?, hCharles H Reynolds
Isiah, b1795, Lebanon, Russ Co, fAbram, m-- Baldwin, w-- Cross
Martha, b18--, Buch Co?, hWil-

FULLER (continued)
liam Fletcher
Mary, b18--, Richmond?, hEnoch Winch
Remley A, b10/5/1851, Lebanon, Russ Co, Isaiah, m-- Cross, wMartha Hartsock
FULTON, Elbert, b18--, Wise Co?, wSophronia Dotson
Elizabeth, b18--, Leesburg, Loud Co, fWilliam, mMary Shumate, hRobert Lynn
Lee, b18--, Loud Co, fWilliam, mMary Shumate
Martha E, b18--, Gray Co, hMelville B Cox
Mary, b18--, Smyt Co?, hCharles D Carter
Minitree Jones, b4/10/1867, Gray Co, fSamuel Monroe, mMary Catherine Reid, wElizabeth Owen Bowman
Rebecca, b1857, Wash Co, hNathan Dillard
William, b18--, Loud Co, wMary Shumate
William II, b18--, Loud Co, fWilliam, mMary Shumate
FULWIDER, Catherine, b18--, Augu Co?, hPhilip Fix
FUNK, Benjamin, b182-, Alle Co, fJoseph, (2)mRachel Britton
Clarence, bc1870, nrStrasburg, Shen Co, fObed S, mRegina Stover
Davis, b181-, Singer Glen, Rkhm Co, fJoseph, Sr, (2)mRachel Britton
Granville I, b186-, nrStrasburg, Shen Co, fObed S, mRegina Stover
H A, b186-, nrStrasburg, Shen Co, fJoseph, (1)mMartha Funkhouser
Hannah, b182-, Singer Glen, Rkhm Co, fJoseph, Sr, (2)m Rachel Britton, h-- Baer
Jesse H, b186-, nrStrasburg, Shen Co, fObed S, mRegina Stover
John, bc1830, Rkhm Co, wMary E Swank
John, bc1830, Shen Co, wSarah Shaver
Joseph, Jr, b181-, Singer Glen, Rkhm Co, fJoseph, Sr, (2)m

FUNK (continued)
Rachel Britton
Joseph, b185-, Singer Glen, Rkhm Co, fTimothy, mSusan Ruebush
Joseph, b11/1/1830, nrStrasburg, Shen Co, d1899, 1wMartha Funkhouser, 2wMary Margaret Stickley
Joseph, bc1840, Shen Co?, wMary Frances Swank
John, b182-, Singer Glen, Rkhm Co, fJoseph, Sr, (2)mRachel Britton
Mary b7/4/1815, Singer Glen, Rkhm Co, fJoseph, Sr, (2)m Rachel Britton, hJohn Kieffer
Mary Jane, b9/13/1851, Singer Glen, Rkhm Co, fTimothy, mSusan Ruebush, hJohn Acker, md12/28/1875
Mollie, b18--, Shen Co?, fGeorge, 2w of Harrison Lindamood
Obed S, b18--, nrStrasburg, Shen Co, wRegina Stover
Rose, bc1870, nrStrasburg, Shen Co, fObed S, mRegina Stover, hAbram Stickley
Ruth, bc1870, nrStrasburg, Shen Co, fObed S, mRegina Stover
Sallie, b11/17/1867, nrStrasburg, Shen Co, fObed S, mRegina Stover, hPhilip Samuel Rhodes
Samuel, bc1820, Singer Glen, Rkhm Co, fJoseph, Sr, (2)m Rachel Britton
Solomon, bc1830, Singer Glen, Rkhm Co, fJoseph, Sr, (2)m Rachel Britton
Timothy, b182-, Singer Glen, Rkhm Co, fJoseph, Sr, (2)m Rachel Britton, wSusanna Ruebush
W C, b185-, Singer Glen, Rkhm Co, fTimothy, mSusan Ruebush
FUNKHOUSER, Abraham, b8/15/1789, Shen Co?, d1863, fJacob, mDorothy Huddle, wSarah Fisher
Abram Paul, b12/10/1853, Rkhm Co, fSamuel, mElizabeth Paul, wMinnie S King, md6/3/1880
Amanda, bc1870, nrWardensville, Hard Co, d1902, fNoah, mLucy Webster, 1w of David Cowan

FUNKHAUSER (continued)
Cline
Andrew, b18--, Shen Co, fGeorge, 1wMary Zering, 2wElizabeth Rinker
Andrew Alberta, b185-, nrMt Jackson, Shen Co, fAndrew, (2)mElizabeth Rinker
Bird, bc1850, nrWoodstock, Shen Co, fPhilip A, Sr, mElizabeth Hottel, hDavid Neff
Carrie, bc1860, nrStephens City, Fred Co, fJoseph E, (2)m-- Beeler, hAlexander Whetsel
Casper, bc1840, nrMt Jackson, Shen Co, d1914, fAndrew, (2)m Elizabeth Rinker, wSarah Elizabeth Snapp
Catherine, b182-, Page Co?, d1902, hFerdinand Schmucker
Charles Andrew, b9/20/1867, Mt Jackson, Shen Co, fCasper, mSarah Elizabeth Snapp, 1wMaud Irene Snapp, md6/26/1895, 2w Edith Virginia Suter, md1/2/1919
Charles Edward, b3/3/1853, nrStephens City, Fred Co, fJoseph E, (1)m-- Harman, 1w Bertie Huffman, 2wAmelia Gardiner
Daniel C, b18--, Fred Co?, wSarah Catherine Hershberger
Edgar Bright, b186-, Mt Jackson, Shen Co, fCasper, mSarah Elizabeth Snapp
Ella Vernon, b186-, Mt Jackson, Shen Co, fCasper, mSarah Elizabeth Snapp, hJ H Ruebush
Euphrasia, b185-, nrStephens City, Fred Co, fJoseph E, (1)m-- Harman, hIsaac Milton Brumback
George, b178-, Shen Co, fJacob, mDorothy Huddle
George A, b184-, nrMt Jackson, Shen Co, fAndrew, (2)mElizabeth Rinker
Harriet, b18--, nrMt Jackson, Shen Co, fAndrew (1)mMary Zering, h-- Kerr
Iva, b186-, nrStephens City, Fred Co, fJoseph E (3)mEliza Johnson, hFrank Bowman
Jacob, b1750, Shen Co, d1801,

FUNKHAUSER (continued)
fJohn, mMary --, wDorothy Huddle
Jacob Otterbein, bc1870, Mt Jackson, Shen Co, fCasper, mSarah Elizabeth Snapp
Jane, b184-, nrWoodstock, Shen Co, fPhilip A, Sr, mElizabeth Hottel, hW C Alther
Jennie A, b185-, nrMt Jackson, Shen Co, fAndrew, (2)mElizabeth Rinker, hRobert R Rinker
John, b18--, Fred Co?, wEmma Brown
John B, bc1850, Shen Co?, wCaroline Sine
Joseph E, b18--, Fred Co, 1w-- Harman, 2w-- Beeler, 3wEliza Johnson
Lewis, J, b5/18/1842, nrWoodstock, Shen Co, fPhilip A, Sr, mElizabeth Hottel, wMary Catherine Wisman
Lillie, b185-, nrStephens City, Fred Co, fJoseph E, (2)m-- Beeler, hJoseph E Fry
Maggie, b184-, nrWoodstock, Shen Co, fPhilip A, Sr, mElizabeth Hottel
Martha, b18--, Shen Co?, fMartin, hJoseph Funk
Mary, bc1800, Shen Co, fDaniel, d1886, hPhilip Borden
Mary, b184-, nrWoodstock, Shen Co, fPhilip A, Sr, mElizabeth Hottel, hErasmus Bauserman
Monroe, bc1840, nrMt Jackson, Shen Co, fAndrew, (2)mElizabeth Rinker
Newton E, b185-, nrStephens City, Fred Co, fJoseph E (2)m -- Beeler
Noah, b18--, Hard Co?, wLucy Webster
Philip A, Sr, bc1813, Shen Co, wElizabeth Hottel
Philip A, Jr, b184-, nrWoodstock, Shen Co, fPhilip A, Sr, mElizabeth Hottel, wSallie Zering
Rebecca, b3/30/1825, Funkhouser Hollow, Shen Co, hIsaac Pifer
Samuel, b9/25/1823, Rkhm Co?, d1864, fAbraham, mSarah Fisher, wElizabeth Paul
Sarah E, bc1850, nrMt Jackson,

FUNKHAUSER (continued)
Shen Co, fAndrew, (2)mElizabeth Rinker, hWesley Colton Scott, b186-, nrStehens City, Fred Co, fJoseph E, (2)m-- Beeler
Turner Lee, b186-, Mt Jackson, Shen Co, fCasper, mSarah Elizabeth Snapp
William M, b186-, Mt Jackson, Shen Co, fCasper, mSarah Elizabeth Snapp
FUNSTON, Louise, b18--, fOliver H, hJohn T Fletcher
FUQUA, Mary, bc1800, fJoseph, mCelia --, 2w of William Leftwich, Jr, md8/22/1826
Nannie, b18--, Gooc Co?, hJohn M Vaughan
FURR, Harrison, b18--, Augu Co?, wElizabeth Johnson
Mary E, b18--, Augu Co?, d1875, fHarrison, mElizabeth Johnson, hJames Andrew Riddle, Jr, md185-
FUSSELL, Oceola Carson, b18--, Henrico Co, fThomas F, mMary Elizabeth Irby, hWalter Franklin Delaney
Thomas, b18--, Henrico Co, wMary Elizabeth Irby
GAINES, E P, b18--, PrWi Co?, wMinnie Davis
Martha E, b18--, Loud Co?, hFrank E Robey
R E, b186-, Richmond?, wJanet M Harris
William, bc1820, Shen Co?, wSarah E Moore
GALE, Sarah Elizabeth, bEstillville (now Gate City), Scot Co, hJohn Jefferson Wolford
GAMBLE, Jesse, J, b18--, McDo Co?, wMary Prather
Mary, b18--, McDo Co, d1897, fJesse J, mMary Prather, 1w of John W Waldron, md2/1/1877
GAN, --, bc1860, Bote Co?, wElvora Leslie
GANDER, D H, bc1850, Page Co?, wEmma Shaffer
GANNAWAY, --, b18--, "Edgewood", Buck Co, fWilliam E, mKatherine Grigg, hJ N Crute
Catherine, bc1870, Lynchburg, Camp Co, hClarence W Taylor

GANNAWAY (continued)
Elizabeth, b18--, Roan Co, hJames Burch
John E, Sr, b18--, "Edgewood", Buck Co, fWilliam E, mKatherine Grigg, wMary B Carroll, md1881
Richard, b18--, "Edgewood", Buck Co, fWilliam E, mKatherine Grigg
William E, b1825, Buck Co, fJohn, wKatherine Grigg
GANNON, John M, bc1840, Lanc Co?, wElizabeth Rowe
GANT, Lovell, bc1850, Clar Co?, wCatherine Hiett
GARBER, --, bc1800, Rkhm Co, hSamuel Kline
Abram, b1834, Dayton Community, Rkhm Co, fHenry, m-- Bowman, wElizabeth Early
Albert Jefferson, b1839, Augu Co?
Benjamin Franklin, b9/11/1861, Dayton, Rkhm Co, fAbram, mElizabeth Early, wAnnie Zeminia Kiser
C D, bc1850, Augu Co?, Mollie Pirkey
Catherine, b184-, Rkhm Co, fMartin, mElizabeth Wine, hWilliam Anderson Will
David, b182-, Rkhm Co, w-- Miller
Edward T, b2/9/1869, Cook Creek, Rkhm Co, fJoel, mAnnie Harshbarger, wRebecca Burnshire, md9/19/1895
Elizabeth, b18--, Rkhm Co, hDaniel Neff
Fannie, b186-, nrBridgewater, Rkhm Co, fJoel, mAnna Harshbarger, hWill Hale
Frances, b182-, Dayton, Rkhm Co, fHenry, m-- Bowman, hJohn Flory
Jacob, b1844, Shen Co, fSamuel, mHannah Myers, wRebecca Early
Jennie, b186-, Dayton, Rkhm Co, fAbram, mElizabeth Early, hJohn Gillis
Joel, b1829, Dayton Community, Rkhm Co, fHenry, m-- Bowman, wAnna Harshbarger
John Newton, b11/22/1862, nrBridgewater, Rkhm Co, fJoel,

GARBER (continued)
  mAnna Harshbarger, wGertrude Burtner, md12/21/1892
  Joseph, b186-, Dayton, Rkhm Co, fAbram, mElizabeth Early
  Lizzie, bc1860, nrBridgewater, Rkhm co, fJoel, mAnna Harshbarger, hWilliam Pence
  Margaret, b18--, hThomas Jefferson Michie
  Margaret Susan Singleton, b1839, Staunton, Augu Co, fAlbert Jefferson
  Martin, b18--, Rkhm Co, wElizabeth Wine
  Maud, b18--, Norfolk?, fReuben, hHarry K Wolcott, md189-
  Noah E, bc1870, nrBridgewater, Rkhm Co, fJoel, mAnna Harshbarger
  Rebecca, b3/17/1854, Augu Co, fDavid, m-- Miller, hJoseph M Kagey, md4/2/1874
  Sallie, bc1847, Rkhm Co?, d1912, fMartin, mElizabeth Wine, hBenjamin Allen Myers
  Sallie, b185-, Dayton, Rkhm Co, fAbram, mElzabeth Early, hAlbert Coffman
  Sallie, b186-, nrBridgewater, Rkhm Co, fJoel, mAnna Harshbarger, hJoel Miller
  Samuel, b18--, Shen Co, wHannah Myers
  Sarah, b182-, Dayton Community, Rkhm Co, fHenry, m-- Bowman, hGeorge Shaver
  Solomon, b183-, Dayton Community, Rkhm Co, fHenry, m-- Bowman
  Solomon, b186-, Dayton, Rkhm Co, fAbram, mElizabeth Early
  Susan, b18--, Rkhm Co?, hDaniel Kiser
GARDNER, Adolphus C, b7/22/1860, nrGardner, Russ Co, fZadock N, mMary Jane Honaker, wClementine Lipford
  Denny, bc1870, Hillsville, Carr Co, fWilliam Rush, mCassie Mattin
  Elizabeth, b18--, Fred Co, fJohn, (2)m---, h-- Ewing
  Emma, bc1870, Opequon District, Fred Co, fJohn Henry, mFrances Boud, hWilliam C Cornwell

GARDNER (continued)
  George W, bc1840, Mont Co?, wRuth A McDonald
  George, bc1860, Rkhm Co, wMaggie Moore
  Henrietta Judson, b1844, Richmond, fThomas H, mSarah Turner, hSamuel Bottom
  James L, b18--, Fred Co, fJohn, (2)m---
  James Lewis, b1/27/1864, Opequon District, Fred Co, fJohn Henry, mFrances Boud, wSeverine M Hammock, md3/1886
  John Henry, b18--, Fred Co, fJohn, (2)m---, wFrances Boud
  Joseph E, b11/15/1869, Hillsville, Carr Co, fWilliam Rush, mCassie Martin, wAlberta B Hurst
  Lena B, bc1860, nrGardner, Russ Co, fZadock N, mMary Jane Honaker, hJames H Hurst
  Mary, b186-, Opequon District, Fred Co, fJohn Henry, mFrances Boud, h-- Bowman
  Mary Graham, b18--, Smyt Co, hCharles Woolfolk Coleman, Sr
  Mathew, bc1800, nrHillsville, Carr Co, fJames
  Minnie, bc1870, Opequon District, Fred Co, fJohn Henry, mFrances Boud, h--Rowsey
  Nancy, b180-, Fred Co, dc1875, fJohn, (1)m---, h-- Newcombe
  Rebecca B, bc1860, Warr Co?, fSamuel B, mAnne Allen, hNelson Samuel Waller
  Samuel B, b18--, Warr Co?, mSarah Catherine Allen, wAnne Allen
  Rosa, b186-, Opequon District, Fred Co, fJohn Henry, mFrances Boud, hJ W Headley
  Sarah, b18--, Fred Co, fJohn, (2)m---, hSamuel White
  Thomas H, b1803, Henrico Co, wSarah Turner
  Victoria, bc1853, nrHayfield, Fred Co, fWilliam P, hJames T McIlwee
  Washington, bc1800, nrHillsville, Carr Co, fJames
  William B, b18--, Pitt Co, wBettie D Versen
  William Rush, b1848, Hills-

GARDNER (continued)
ville, Carr Co, d1887, fMathew, wCassie Martin
Zadock N, b3/14/1825, Christiansburg, Mont Co, fJohn II, wMary Jane Honaker
GARGES, Mary Elizabeth, b18--, Bedf Co, m-- Laughlin, hWilliam H Hardy
GARLAND, Ann, b17--, Amhe Co, hRuben Pendleton
Anna E, b18--, hJoseph Sutherland
Martha Henry, b18--, Amhe Co, fSamuel M, 2w of Thomas Whitehead
Nannie Rose, b18--, Lynchburg, Camp Co, hGilbert Simrall Meem, Sr
Samuel, b12/16/1830, Lynchburg, Camp Co, d1862, wEliza Meem
GARLICK, Elizabeth, b18--, hJohn Taliaferro Jones
GARNER, John Henceford, b1792, West Co, wAnn E Littrell
John Wyatt, b8/27/1847, Staf Co, fJohn Henceford, mAnn E Littrell, wFrances Marian Alexander Jones
Sarah, b18--, Tappahannock, Esse Co, hWilliam Rowe
GARNETT, Carroll, bc1860, High Co?, wCornelia Byrd
Elizabeth, b17--, Madi Co, hWilliam Twyman II
James M, b18--, Culp Co, wCornelia Wingfield
Maria Mercer, b1806, Esse Co, hJohn Peyton McGuire, Sr, md10/4/1827
Mary Allen, b18--, KiQu Co?, hWilliam D Gresham
Mary Susan, b18--, KiQu Co, fReuben M, hBenjamin Franklin Dew
Ruby P, b18--, KiQu Co?, hJames R Fleet
Sarah Elizabeth, bc1836, Esse Co, fMuscoe, hJohn Trible Thomas Hundley, Sr
Theodore Stenford, Jr, b184-, Richmond, d1915, fTheodore Stenford, Sr
William E, bc1850, Buck Co?, wMartha K Crute
GARRETT, --, bc1800, KiQu Co,

GARRETT (continued)
hBird Hoskins
Benjamin Camm, b12/22/1861, "Longwood", KiWi Co, fCamm S, mCaroline Elizabeth Harris, wAda G McEnery
Camm S, b2/9/1821, "Willow Green", KiWi Co, fLarkin, m-- Wiley, wCaroline Elizabeth Harris
Cincinnatus, b11/11/1850, nr King William Court House, KiWi Co, fLardin, mHarriet Edwards, wMary Emma Neale
Edwin E, b10/21/1870, Mt Gilead, Loud Co, fWilliam E, mFreelove B Shreve, wAgnes Hall Dibrell
Elizabeth A, bc1852, Albe Co, d1922, fJohn Bolling, mNannie Harrison, hSamuel H Purcell
Enoch, b18--, Loud Co, w-- Batson
Esther, b18--, Loud Co, fWilliam E, mFreelove B Shreve, hGilbert Bush
Hannah E, b1--, Loud Co, fWilliam E, mFreelove B Shreve, hHarry B Chamblin
James Alfred, b18--, Loud Co, fWilliam E, mFreelove B Shreve
John Bolling, b18--, Albe Co?, fAlexander, mEvelina Kennon Bolling, wNannie Harrison
John D, b18--, Loud Co, fWilliam E, mFreelove B Shreve
John W, b185-, "Longwood", KiWi Co, fCamm S, mCaroline Elizabeth Harris
Larkin, b17--, KiQu Co, w-- Wiley
Larkin, bc1820, nrKing William Court House, KiWi Co, fLarkin, m-- Wiley, wHarriet Edwards
Lucy R, b185-, "Longwood", KiWi Co, fCamm S, mCaroline Elizabeth Harris, hAlexander Campbell
Paul W, b18--, Loud Co, fWilliam E, mFreelove B Shreve
Sallie R, b186-, "Longwood", KiWi Co, fCamm S, mCaroline Elizabeth Harris, hWilliam H Hall
Thomas H, bc1860, "Longwood", KiWi Co, fCamm S, mCaroline

GARRETT (continued)
Elizabeth Harris
W Frank, b18--, Loud Co, fWilliam E, mFreelove B Shreve
William E, b4/1839, nrPhilomont, Loud Co, fEnoch, m--Batson, wFreelove B Shreve
GARRISON, Aurelius J, b186-, Augu Co, fJacob S, mRebecca Fix
Charles C, b186-, Augu Co, fJacob S, mRebecca Fix
Emily, b18--, hJohn Mullins
Irene, bc1870, Augu Co, fJacob S, mRebecca Fix, hR B Dulle
J Silor, b9/6/1867, nrMiddlebrook, Augu Co, fJacob S, mRebecca Fix, wMary Moore Fletcher, md9/4/1900
Jacob S, b1832, Augu Co, fJoel, mNancy Goodnight, wRebecca Fix, md1858
James W, b185-, Augu Co, fJacob S, mRebecca Fix
Jefferson, b182-, Augu Co, fJoel, mNancy Goodnight
Joel, bc1792, nrRichmond, d1837, wNancy Goodnight
Joseph H, b186-, Augu Co, fJacob S, mRebecca Fix
Louisa, b18--, Warr Co?, fWilliam B, mNancy Littleton, hWilliam Adolphus Simpson
Manley Littleton, b18--, Warr Co?, fWilliam, mNancy Littleton, wCatherine Burgess Jacobs
Martha, b18--, Rkhm Co, hJesse Wyant
Mary, bc1830, Augu Co, fJoel, mNancy Goodnight, hWilliam Rosen
Mary Catherine, bc1860, Augu Co, fJacob S, mRebecca Fix, hC R Bosserman
William, b182-, Augu Co, fJoel, mNancy Goodnight
William B, b18--, Warr Co?, wNancy Littleton
GARST, F J, b185-, Fran Co, fGeorge, (2)mMary Frances Lockett
Frank, b18--, Roan Co, fGeorge, (1)mLucy Linkenauger
George, b18--, Raon Co, fJacob, 1wLucy Linkenauger, 2wMary Frances Lockett

GARST (continued)
J B, b185-, Roan Co?, fGeorge, (2)mMary Frances Lockett
Jack, b12/31/1861, nrRocky Mount, Fran Co, fGeorge, (2)m Mary Frances Lockett, wBell Angell, md4/27/1898
Robert, b18--, Roan Co, fGeorge, (1)mLucy Linkenauger
Taylor, b18--, Roan Co, fGeorge, (1)mLucy Linkenauger
William, b186-, Fran Co, fGeorge, (2)mMary Frances Lockett
GARTEN, William Jackson, b18--, Gile Co?, fJames, wElmyra Virginia Collins
GARTH, Charles P, bc1850, Albe Co?, fJames, wElmyra Virginia Collins
J Woods, Sr, b18--, Albe Co, fWilliam, wMary Edmonds
William, b17--, Albe Co, fThomas
GARVIN, Elias, b183-, nrCapon Springs, Hamp Co, fSamuel, (1)mMalinda Johnson
James, bc1810, Hamp Co?, wMary Capper
James, b18--, nrCapon Springs, Hamp Co, fSamuel, (2)---
John, bc1830, bc1830, Hamp Co, wJane Hook
John W, b183-, nrCapon Springs, Hamp Co, fSamuel, (1)mMalinda Johnson
Mahlon, b12/11/1838, nrCapon Springs, Hamp Co, d1921, fSamuel, (1)mMalinda Johnson, wMary Kinneford Dunlap
Mahlon Calvin, b11/14/1869, nrCapon Springs, Hamp Co, fMahlon, mMary Kinneford Dunlap, wLucy Virginia Smith, md3/19/1907
Mary C, b18--, Hamp Co, fDavid, hArchibald M Hook
Minnie Co, bc1870, nrCapon Springs, Hamp Co, fMahlon, mMary Kinneford Dunlap, hWilliam J Muse
N Beale, b186-, nrCapon Springs, Hamp Co, fMahlon, mMary Kinneford Dunlap
Robert, b18--, nrCapon Springs, Hamp Co, fSamuel, (2)m---

GARVIN (continued)
Richard, b18--, nrCapon Springs, Hamp Co, fSamuel, (2)m---
Samuel, b18--, 1wMalinda Johnson
W Carson, b186-, nrCapon Springs, Hamp Co, fMahlon, mMary Kinneford Dunlap
GARY, Edward W, b18--, Lune Co?, d1922, Ella Fowles
T J, Sr, b1867, Lune Co, wMary Harris Vaughan
GATCH, Martin Wesley, b1847, Norfolk, hClifton Lee, Sr
GATES, Iola M F, b1868, Ches Co, hJohn M Kidd
GATEWOOD, Adaline, b1792, fWilliam, hJordan Bedford Luck
Andrew Cameron Lewis, bc1840, "Mountain Grove", Bath Co, fSamuel Vance, mEugenia S Massie
Lucy Ann, b18--, Caro Co, fJames, hWilliam Augustus Moncure
Sallie Goodwin, b1847, Jamaica, Midd Co, d1882, fWilliam K, m-- Street, hJohn Randolph Segar
William Bias, b7/1846, "Mountain Grove", Bath Co, d1890, fSamuel Vance, mEugenia S Massie, wMary Welby DeButts
William K, b18--, Ben Lomond, Esse Co, w-- Street
GAULDING, Anne, b18--, Lune Co, hWilliam M Bagley
Martha H, b18--, PrEd Co, d1906, hRobert W Priddy
GAWAN, Anna, b18--, West Co, hThomas Moss
GAY, --, bc1800, 2w of Jacob LaRue
Marcellus, bc1850, Page Co?, wElizabeth Miller
Texanna, b18--, fW H, hWilliam Nelson Camp
GAYLE, Robert Finley, Sr, b1/22/1858, Portsmouth, Isle Co, fRobet J, mSarah Brownley, wMay Jeannette Young
Robert J, b18--, Math Co, wSarah Brownley
GEE, Charles, b18--, PrGe Co?, wAnna Bland

GEE (continued)
Dorothy, b17--, Lune Co, fWilliam, hJones Allen
Louis A, b1862, fLouis N, m-- Fowlkes, wMary May
Louis N, b18--, Lune Co, w-- Fowlkes
William, bc1710, Brun Co?, wTibitha Ingram
GENTRY, A B, bc1850, Albe Co, wSusie L Abell
T A, b18--, Buck Co, wMary E Bailey
GEORGE, --, b18--, Lanc Co, 1w of William M Sanders
Mary, b18--, Taze Co?, hJesse M McCall
Mary Elizabeth, b11/6/1852, nrMerry's Point, Lanc Co, 2w of Joseph Walter Anderson
GERMOND, Annie M, b18--, Alexandria, d1897, fJacob, hPatrick F Gorman, Sr
GHOLSON, Anne Jane, b18--, Richmond?, hFrancis Thomas Glasgow
GIBBON, Mary, b18--, Richmond, fJames, hJames Carter
GIBBONS, --, b18--, Grbr Co?, hWilliam Henry Surber
GIBBS, Susan, b18--, Lee Co?, hRobert Ely
GIBSON, --, b18--, Russ Co, hJackson Long
Adeline Douglas, b18--, Richmond?, hRobert B Green
Alcinda, b17--, Fred Co?, hRichard W Barton
Ann Eliza, b18--, d1885, hJohn M Alexander
Annette Meade, bc1870, Loud Co, fGeorge W, mRosanna (Osborne) Purcell, hJoseph Berry, md11/16/1898
David, b17--, Loud Co?, 2h of Nancy Atwell
Elizabeth, b18--, Fran Co, hRobert Sigmon
Elizabeth, b18--, Mont Co?, hJ William Shelburne
Elizabeth J, b8/21/1865, Monterey, High Co, fWilliam D, hJohn Marvin Colaw, md9/4/1895
Fannie, b18--, Fauq Co, hThaddeus Herndon
George W, b1826, Fauq Co, d1896, fJoseph, 2h of Rosanna

GIBSON (continued)
(Osborne) Purcell
Hugh K, b18--, Mont Co?, wSusan A Shelburne
John, b17--, Alexandria?, wRuth
John, b18--, Hano Co?, wBettie Fleet Sydnor
Laura, bc1848, Loud Co, fNelson, hJohn Thomas Maxwell
Mary, b17--, Alexandria?, fJohn, mRuth ---, 2w of Elisha Janney, md3/4/1795
Nancy, b18--, Loui Do?, hJohn Purcell
Sue A, bc1870, Mont Co, fHugh K, mSusan A Shelburne, hWilliam Bullard Kegley, md7/15/1890
GIDEON, Catherine, b18--, Loud Co, fPeter, hMahlon Morris
GIFFIN, John, b18--, Fred Co?, wMary Brown
Lizzie, b1870, Fred Co, d1897, fJohn, mMary Brown, 1w of Edgar L Hook
GILBERT, James A, b1/8/1819, Russ Co, d1903, fJoseph, wElizabeth Davis
John C, b3/8/1858, Russ Co, fJames A, mElizabeth Davis, 1wEliza Crabtree, 2wAmanda J Johnson
Malinda E, b1/27/1860, nrRuckersville, Greene Co, hLuther Rice Anderson
GILES, George W, b18--, Pitt Co, fJames A, wElizabeth Ann Collie
GILKESON, Francis McFarland, b18--, Culp Co?, wFannie Richards Green
James D, bc1810, Fred Co?, wSallie Dixon Bell
Jane Love, b18--, Augu Co, fWilliam, mMarguerite --, 1w of Carter Berkeley, md1867
William, b18--, Augu Co?, wMarguerite --
GILL, William C, b10/15/1843, Ches Co, fWilliam E, wSarah Hayes
GILLAM, Hannah S, b18--, Nott Co?, hJohn E McEnery
GILLESPIE, A P, bc1840, Taze Co?, wNannie Higginbotham
Barbara, b18--, Taze Co,

GILLESPIE (continued)
hGeorge W Gillespie
David C, bc1860, Taze Co, wJoey Brittain
David J, bc1830, Taze Co, wLizzie Sanders
George W, b18--, Taze Co, wBarbara Gillespie
John F, bc1850, Taze Co, wMary Katherine Graham
Margaret, b18--, Taze Co?, hWilliam Williams
Mary Amanda, bc1860, Taze Co, d1911, fGeroge W, mBarbra Gillespie, hHervey P Brittain
Nannie, b1832, Tazewell, Taze Co, hJohn A McCall
Thomas, b17--, Taze Co, wPeggy Bowen
GILLEY, Martha E, b5/26/1852, Pennington Gap, Lee Co, hHenry B Graham
GILLIAM, Annie E, bc1870, Clintwood, Dick Co, fCharles W, mCaroline Beverley, hCharles Andrew Johnson, md8/4/1890
Charles McAlester, bPrGe Co, fRobert, Sr, mCharlotte Isabelle Sanxay
Charles W, bDick Co?, wCaroline Beverley
Charlotte Isabella, b18--, PrGe Co, fRobert, Sr, mCharlotte Isabelle Sanxay
Edna, b1868, PrEd Co, hWilliam Morris
Edward I, b4/25/1850, Mt View Farm, Buck Co, fJohn J, wAda C Steger
Eliza, b18--, PrGe Co, fRobert, Sr, mCharlotte Isabelle Sanxay, hRobert Carter Braxton
Ellen, b18--, PrGe Co, fRobert, Sr, mCharlotte Isabelle Sanxay
Emily G, b18--, PrGe Co, fRobert, Sr, mCharlotte Isabelle Sanxay, hFrancis E Hall
George W, b18--, Richmond?, wSarah F Anderson
James S, b18--, Nhld Co, wEliza Bates
Jane M, b18--, Appo Co, hWilliam Seth Ligon
Janet C, bc1870, Nhld Co, fJames S, mEliza Bates, hJoseph Peirce

GILLIAM (continued)
John, b6/3/1761, PrGe Co, wHannah Sampson
John II, b18--, fRobert, Sr, mCharlotte Isabelle Sanxay
Lucy Skelton, b18--, PrGe Co, fRobert, Sr, mCharlotte Isabelle Sanxay, hGeorge W Tennant
Mary, b18--, hHugh Thomas Nelson, md1871
Mary E, b18--, PrGe Co, fRobert, Sr, mCharlotte Isabelle Sanxay, hWilliam D Porter
Nannie, bc1860, Richmond, fRobert Hobson, hEdward W Butcher
Richard Davenport, b8/14/1855, PrGe Co, fRobert, Sr, mCharlotte Isabelle Sanxay, wIrene Jones
Robert, Sr, b9/17/1796, NewK Co, fJohn, mHannah Sampson, wCharlotte Isabelle Sanxay
Robert Jr, b1/27/1847, PrGe Co, fRoberts, Sr, mCharlotte Isabelle Sanxay, 1wSue T Beckwith, md10/24/1876, 2wMary Love Bragg md4/29/1879
Robert Hobson, b1838, Buck Co
Sophia, b18--, PrGe Co, fRobert, Sr, mCharlotte Isabelle Sanxay, hDavid E Bowden
Virginia H, b18--, Buck Co?, fJohn O, hSamuel Spencer, md1865
William A, bc1837, Bote Co, d1903, fWilliam A, mElizabeth Davis, wMartha Elizabeth Fudge
GILLS, --, b18--, Amel Co, hWilliam Jeter
GILMAN, Fannie Aileen, b18--, hWilton F Sale
GILMER, Annie E, bc1838, Bote Co, d1913, hRobert Andrew Fudge
Axley, b1816, Russ Co, wTemperance Gose
Bettie, b1--, McGaheysville, Rkhm Co, hJames Andrew Riddel, Sr
Charles H, bc1800, Russ Co, d1887, fWilliam, wFrances Gose
Elizabeth, b185-, nrHansonville, Russ Co, fJoseph B,

GILMER (continued)
mCaroline Dickerson
Emma, bc1870, nrHansonville, Russ Co, fJoseph, mCaroline Dickerson, hJohn Hanson
George C, b2/26/1847, Hansonville, Russ Co, fAxley, mTemperance Gose, wNettie Reasor
J Page, bc1860, wCora Ann Lockhart
Jasper H, b186-, nrHansonville, Russ Co, fJoseph B, mCaroline Dickerson
Jay J, bc1870, nrHansonville, Russ Co, d1905, fJoseph, mCaroline Dickerson
Joseph B, b1826, Russ Co, d1893, fWilliam, (2)mElizabeth Wright, wCaroline Dickerson
Louisa E, b2/21/1859, Chatham, Pitt Co, hR Holt Easley
Lucy, b18--, Richmond, hEverard Benjamin Meade
Mary Peachy, b18--, Hali Co, 1w of John Wimbish Craddock, Sr, md12/6/1886
Newton H, bc1860, nrHansonville, Russ Co, fJoseph B, mCaroline Dickerson
Robert L, b186-, nrHansonville, Russ Co, fJoseph B, mCaroline Dickerson
Vincent B, b11/4/1852, Lebanon, Russ Co, wEllen Jane Kelley
William, b17--, Russ Co, 2wElizabeth Wright
William C, bc1860, nrHansonville, Russ Co, fJoseph B, mCaroline Dickerson
Wyndam R, b1843, Russ Co, d1916, fCharles H, mFrances Gose, wMargaret Cecil
GINN, A Randolph, bc1860, Hard Co?, wAmanda Frances Cline
Emma, bc1870, Winchester, Fred Co, d1914, mLucy --, hWilliam Henry Baker
Emma Virginia, bc1870, Winchester, Fred Co, fJames, mJane Hardy, h-- Ginn
James, b18--, Fred Co?, wJane Hardy
GIPSON, Bennie, b18--, Appo Co, d1911, 2w of Jonathan Christian Woodson, md1890
GISH, David, b17--, Roan Co,

GISH (continued)
fDavid, wPolly Wright
Ella, bc1860, nrRoanoke, Roan Co, fGeorge Russell, mMary Adeline Thresher
Frank Anthony, bc1870, nrRoanoke, Roan Co, fGeorge Russell, mMary Adeline Thresher
George Russell, b18--, Roan Co, d1917, fDavid, mPolly Wright, wMary Adeline Thresher
George William, b186-, nrRoanoke, Roan Co, fGeorge Russell, mMary Adeline Thresher
James D, b18--, Roan Co?, wMartha Starkey
Lucy, b18--, Roan Co, fJames D, mMartha Starkey, hLee Long, Sr, md9/5/1891
Mary, bc1800, Daleville, Bote Co, fJacob, hGeorge W Layman
Mary C, b1843, nrAmsterdam, Bote Co, hSamuel L Shaver
Mary Eliza, b18--, Roan Co, fDavid, mPolly Wright
Ola May, bc1870, nrRoanoke, Roan Co, fGeorge Russell, mMary Adeline Thresher, hE W Bowie
Thomas Edward, bc1860, nrRoanoke, Roan Co, fGeorge Russell, mMary Adeline Thresher
GITT, Alice, b18--, Pula Co?, hWalter Moore
GIVENS, Fannie, b1835, Crai Co, d1903, hJohn B Caldwell
Floyd, bc1860, Crai Co?, wFlorence Miller
Joseph Cales, b10/12/1852, Simmonsville, Crai Co, d1921, fJames, mElizabeth Ross, wNannie Josephine Albert
James, b18--, Simmonsville, Crai Co, wElizabeth Ross
Lillian, b18--, Crai Co, 2w of Floyd P Ferrell
GLAIZE, Annie, b185-, nrWinchester, Clar Co, fGeorge, mHarriet Rinker, hOscar Bywaters
Belle, b185-, nrWinchester, Clar Co, fGeorge, mHarriet Rinker, hWill Henshaw
Bettie, bc1860, nrWinchester, Clar Co, fGeorge, mHarriet Rinker, hAlbert Williams
David S, bc1840, Gainesboro

GLAIZE (continued)
District, Fred Co, fSolomon, (2)m Elizabeth Fries
Effie M, b1865, nrWinchester, Clar Co, fGeorge, mHarriet Rinker, hWilliam Hiett
George, b179-, Fred Co, fGeorge, mCatherine Hetzel
George, b18--, Fred Co?, wHarriet Rinker
Geroge F, bc1860, Fred Co, wAlice Elizabeth Stine
Henry, b179-, Fred Co, fGeorge, mCatherine Hetzel
Henry, b185-, nrWinchester, Clar Co, fGeorge, mHarriet Rinker
Hunter, b186-, nrWinchester, Clar Co, fGeorge, mHarriet Rinker
Isaac, bc1830, Gainesboro District, Fred Co, fSolomon, (1)m Elizabeth Streit
Joanna, bc1800, Fred Co, fGeorge, mCatherine Hetzel
Joanna Arlena, b12/23/1837, nrStrasburg, Shen Co, d1918, fJohn H, mBarbara Rosenberger, hJohn Eli Copp, md1/17/1856
John, b186-, nrWinchester, Clar Co, fGeoge, mHarriet Rinker
John H, b179-, Fred Co, fGeorge, mCatherine Hetzel, wBarbara Rosenberger
John William, b11/19/1828, Gainesboro District, Fred Co, d1912, fSolomon, (1)mElizabeth Streit, wJane Elizabeth Fries
Julia A, b182-, Gainesboro District, Fred Co, fSolomon, (1)m Elizabeth Streit, hHenry Stine
Luther, b185-, nrWinchester, Clar Co, fGeorge, mHarriet Rinker
Maria C, bc1830, Gainesboro District, Fred Co, fSolomon, (1)m Elizabeth Streit, hIsaac Stine
Martin Summers, b5/28/1869, Stonewall District, Apple Pie Ridge, Fred Co, fJohn W, mJane Elizabeth Fries, wFlorence Fries, md11/20/1895
Rachel, b184-, Gainesboro District, Fred Co, fSolomon, (2)m Elizabeth Fries

GLAIZE (continued)
Sampson, bc1790, Fred Co, fGeorge, mCatherne Hetzel
Solomon, b1/12/1796, Fred Co, d1878, fGeorge, mCatherine Hetzel, 1wElizabeth Streit, 2w Elizabeth Fries
William, b185-, nrWinchester, Clar Co, fGeorge, mHarriet Rinker

GLASCOCK, --, b17--, Fauq Co?, hSylvester Welch
Alfred, b1837, "Rockburn", Fauq Co, d1880, fAquilla, (2)mMary Bishop, wHattie Fadely
Alfred, b18--, Fauq Co, fAlfred, mHattie Fadely
Agnes, b1860, Fauq Co, fJohn Samuel, hHenry Virginius Glascock, md2/5/1880
Annie, b1830, "Rockburn", Fauq Co, d1909, fAquilla, (1)m Susanna Lake, hLarkin Hardy Crenshaw
Aquilla, b1786, "Rockburn", Fauq Co, d1867, fGeorge, mHanna Rector, 1wSusanna Lake, 2wMary Bishop
Elizabeth, bc1750, Fauq Co, fJohn
Fadely, b18--, Fauq Co, fAlfred, mHattie Fadely
Geroge, b1740, Fauq Co, d1826, fJohn, wHannah Rector
George, b182-, "Rockburn", Fauq Co, fAquilla, (1)mSusanna Lake
Henry, bc1850, Fauq Co, wNannie J Glascock
Henry Virginiaius, b2/4/1851, Scot District, Fauq Co, fRobert Thomas, mMary Ann Cockran, wAgnes Glascock, md2/5/1880
Hezekiah, b174-, Fauq Co, fJohn
John, b174-, Fauq Co, fJohn
John, bc1790, "Rockburn", Fauq Co, fGeoge, mHannah Rector
John Samuel, b182-, nrMarshall, Fauq Co, fHenry
Lillie, b18--, Fauq Co, fAlfred, mHattie Fadely
Ludwell, bc1850, Fauq Co, wSallie N Glascock
Margaret, b174-, Fauq Co, fJohn
Mary, b174-, Fauq Co, fJohn
Mary, b182-, "Rockburn", Fauq

GLASCOCK (continued)
Co, fAquilla, (1)mSusanna Lake, hWilliam Smith
May, b18--, Fauq Co, fAlfred, mHattie Fadely, hLauck Grayson
Nannie J, b185-, nrMashall, Fauq Co, fRobert Thomas, mMary Ann Cochran,, hHenry Glascock
Orra, b18--, Fauq Co, fAlfred, mHattie Fadely, hB S Moore
Robert Thomas, b1821, nrMarshall, Fauq Co, fHenry, wMary Ann Cochran
Sallie N, b185-, nrMarshall, Fauq Co, fRobert Thomas, mMary Ann Cochran, hLudwell Glascock
Sarah, b182-, "Rockburn", Fauq Co, fAquilla, (1)mSusanna Lake, hLevi Hough
Shelton, b185-, nrMarshall, Fauq Co, fRobert Thomas, mMary Ann Cockran
Susanna, bc1750, Fauq Co, fJohn
Tacy, b18--, Fauq Co, d1878, fThomas, mEmily Fletcher, hRobert Fletcher
Thomas, b174-, Fauq Co, fJohn
Thomas, b182-, "Rockburn", Fauq Co, fAquilla, (1)mSusanna Lake, 2wEmily Fletcher
Vidie, bc1830, Fau Co, d1898, hConrad Bitzer Kincheloe
Waynefield, b185-, nrMarshall, Fauq Co, fRobert Thomas, mMary Ann Cochran
William, b178-, "Rockburn", Fauq Co, fGeorge, mHannah Rector
William, b182-, "Rockburn", Fauq Co, fAquilla, (1)mSusanna Lake

GLASGOW, Francis Thomas, b18--, Richmond?, wAnne Jane Gholson
Frank Thomas, b11/16/1854, Fincastle, Bote Co, fWilliam Anderson, mElizabeth Spears
Robert, b18--, Rkbr Co, fArthur, mRebekah (McNutt) McCorkle
Samuel McPheeters, b18--, wMary Finley McIlwaine
William Anderson, b1825, Rkbr Co, fRobert, wElizabeth Spears

GLASS, Carter, bc1840, Pitt Co?, wSusan Monroe
Carter, b1/4/1858, Lynchburg,

GLASS (continued)
Camp Co, fRobert Henry, mElizabeth Augusta Christian, wAurelia Caldwell
Harriett Wood, bc1870, "Rose Hill", Fred Co, fWilliam Wood, (2)mNannie Rebecca Campbell, hWillam Blackstone Davis
Katheirne, b186-, "Rose Hill", Fred Co, fWilliam Wood, (2)mNannie Rebecca Campbell, hHarry Raynor Greene
Robert Henry, b1822, Amhe Co, fThomas, mLavinia Cauthorne, 1wElizabeth Augusta Christian, 2wMeta Sandford
Thomas, b17--, Fred Co, d186-, wCatherine Wood
William Wood, b3/14/1835, "Rose Hill", Fred Co, d1911, fThomas, mCatherine Wood, 1wNannie Luckett, 2wNannie Rebecca Campbell
GLASSCOCK, --, b18--, Hali Co, hCharles Womack
GLEASON, Emmett, b182-, Nels Co
Henry Morris, b12/23/1854, Rkbr Co, fJohn J, mMartha Johnson, 1wMargaret Bibb, md6/1876, 2w Lillie Phillips
James Emmett, b185-, Rkbr Co, fJohn J, mMartha Johnson
John J, b11/23/1823, nrGleason's Gap, Nels Co, d1907, wMartha Johnson
John W, bc1860, Rkbr Co, fJohn J, mMartha Johnson
Martha E, b1850, Rkbr Co, fJohn J, mMartha Johnson, hJ C Matthews
Mary F, b185-, Rkbr Co, fJohn J, mMartha Johnson, hJohn Thomasson
Robert E, bc1850, Nels Co?, wMargaret Fortune
William E, bc1850, Rkbr Co, fJohn J, mMartha Johnson
GLENDY, Robert H, bc1860, Carr Co?, wAlice Early
GLENN, Sarah Ann, b8/14/1830, 1w of James Henry Bowles
GLOVER, Catherne, bc1840, Clar Co, fLewis, mElizabeth Kearney
John Brazier, bc1835, Clar Co, d1881, fLewis, mElizabeth Kearney, wCatheirne Eugenia

GLOVER (continued)
Crow
Kirkland, b183-, Clar Co, fLewis, mElizabeth Kearney
Mary Ann, bc1833, Appo Co, hDavid P Robertson
Thomas L, bc1870, nrWhite Post, Clar Co, fJohn Brazier, mCatherine Eugenia Crow
GOAD, Charles, b1/1/1861, Carr Co, fRobert, mJulia A Webb, wHannah Martin
Robert, b18--, Carr Co, d186-, wJulia A Webb
GOCHENAUR, George, bc1850, Shen Co, wAlice Shaver
GOCHENOUR, --, b18--, Augu Co?, hWilliam Parkins
J H, bc1850, Page Co?, wMattie Shaffer
Sarah Catherine, b12/1833, Shen Co, d1914, fHenry, hJoseph Swift Irwin
GOCHNAUER, David, b9/10/1811, Loud Co, fIsaac, mBetsy Anderson
Elizabeth, b180, Loud Co, fIsaac, mBetsy Anderson
Pembroke Somerset, b18--, Loud Co, fDavid, wKatherine Frasier
Preston B, b18--, Loud Co, fDavid
GODDIN, Clarke Roxanna, b18--, hRichard Worsham
Judson Chennoweth, b18--, Rand Co, wMalvina Corley
GODSEY, Andrew E, b9/1867, nr Cumberland Court House, Cumb Co, fJames B, (1)mKate Talley, wMary C Foster
Drew S, b18--, Scot Co?, wSusan Latture
Fannie, b18--, nrNickelsville, Scot Co, hJames Nickels, Jr
James B, b1836, Cumb Co, d1918, 1wMary Price, 2wKate Talley
GOFF, --, b1830, nrParkersburg, Wood Co, wEliza Skinner
Alice Rhodes, b18--, Gordonsville, Oran Co, mEliza Skinner
Edward, b18--, Gordonsville, Oran Co, mEliza Skinner
James William Johnston, b18--, Gordonsville, Oran Co, mEliza Skinner, wLydia Tracie Gale Wolford

GOLD, thomas E, bc1840, Clar Co?, wSarah Helm Barnett
GOLDSMITH, John, bc1830, wMary Skinker
GOLLADAY, Abraham, b18--, Powell's Fort Valley, Shen Co, w-- Burner
David, b1830, Powell's Fort Valley, Shen Co, d1898, fAbraham, m-- Burner, wMary Sheetz
Jacob, b183-, Powell's Fort Valley, Shen Co, fAbraham, m-- Burner
Lucy C, bc1870, St David's Church, Powell's Fort Valley, Shen Co, fDavid, mMary Sheetz, hAmos Habron
Mary Elizabeth, bc1870, St David's Church, Powell's Fort Valley, Shen Co, fDavid, mMary Sheetz, hR L Walters
GOLLEHON, Samuel F, b18--, Smyt Co, wJosie Anderson
Robert, b18--, Smyt Co, wSusie Copenhaver
GOOD, Anna, b18--, Rkhm Co?, hDavid Bowman
Anna, b11/6/1838, Shen Co, d1911, fJacob, mSusannah Myers, hSamuel Shaver
Annie F, b186-, nrNew Market, Shen Co, fSamuel, mSarah Wampler, hTheodore Layman
Bettie, b186-, Good's Mill, Rkhm Co, fSamuel, mCatherine Flory
Casper N, b186-, nrNew Market, Shen Co, fSamuel, mSarah Wampler
D Saylor, b186-, nrNew Market, Shen Co, fSamuel, mSarah Wampler
D William, b186-, nrNew Market, Shen co, fSamuel, mSarah Wampler
Ernest W, bc1870, Ashby District, Rkhm Co, fFrank, mFrances Showalter
F G, bc1860, Hamp Co?, wLena LaFollett
Frank, bc1840, Ashby District, Rkhm Co, d1921, fSamuel, wFrances Showalter
Isaac Timothy, bc1870, nrNew Market, Shen Co, d1900
Jacob, b18--, Shen Co, wSusannah Myers
GOOD (continued)
Jacob Frederick, b185-, nrNew Market, Shen Co, fSamuel, mSarah Wampler
John S, b186-, Ashby District, Rkhm Co, fFrank, mFrances Showalter
Joseph E, b186-, nrNew Market, Shen Co, d1922, fSamuel, mSarah Wampler
Mary, b183-, Shen Co, fJacob, mSusanna Coffman, hSamuel Wampler
Mary Susan, bc1860, nrNew Market, Shen Co, fSamuel, mSarah Wampler, hS P Fogle
Michael, b183-, Shen Co, fJacob, mSusannah Coffman
Michael A, bc1860, Good's Mill, Rkhm Co, fSamuel, mCatherine Flory
P Ben F, b10/3/1866, Ashby District, Rkhm Co, fFrank, mFrances Showalter, wLetitia Bauserman, md10/14/1893
Peter S, bc1860, Good's Mill, Rkhm Co, fSamuel, mCatherine Flory
Rebecca, b185-, nrNew Market, Shen Co, fSamuel, mSarah Wampler, hD P Wine
Samuel, bc1833, Shen Co, d1914, fJacob, mSusanna Coffman, wSarah Wampler
Samuel, bc1814, nrMcGaheysville, Rkhm Co, d1885, wCatherine Flory
Samuel Godfrey, b3/21/1863, nr New Market, Shen Co, fSamuel, mSarah Wampler, wAnnie L Burk, md11/1886
Sarah C, b186-, Good's Mill, Rkhm Co, fSamuel, mCatherine Flory, h-- Doom
Sewell, bc1860, wMinni I McIlwee
Silvious, b183-, Shen Co, fJacob, mSusanna Coffman
Susan, b186-, Good's Mill, Rkhm Co, fSamuel, mCatherine Flory, hEli S Henkel
Thomas D, b186-, Good's Mill, Rkhm Co, fSamuel, mCatherine Flory
GOODE, --, b17--, Powh Co?,

GOODE (continued)
wMartha Jefferson
Agnes Eppes, b17--, Ches Co?,
fThomas, mAgnes Osborne, hJohn
Tucker
Amarilla, b18--, fWilliam,
mElizabeth Camden, hWillis
Tinsley
J F, b186-, Patr Co?, wMartha
Adeline Via
John, Jr, bc1700, fJohn, Sr,
mAnna Bennett
Lucy, b17--, Powh Co, mMartha
Jefferson, hWilliam Marshall
Thomas, b17--, Ches Co, fJohn,
Jr, wAgnes Osborne
W C, bc1860, Camp Co?, wAnnabelle Victor
William J C, b1849, Ches Co,
fRichard, wPattie Johnson
GOODLOE, James, bc1800, Caro Co,
dc1837, wAnna Winn
Tavener Winn, b1/4/1825, Spot
Co, d1907, fJames, mAnn Winn,
wMary Jane Mills
GOODMAN, Martha, b1822, Powh Co,
d1894, hJohn J Guthrie
Martha James, b18--, hThomas
Compton Browne, md12/21/1837
GOODNIGHT, Nancy, bc1800, Augu
Co?, hJoel Garrison
GOODPASTURE, Jane Lockett,
b1849, Smyt Co, d1912,
hCharles R Johnston
GOODRIDGE, John Henry, bc1860,
Montross, West Co, fJohn,
mMary Jane Greer
Mary Ann, bc1860, Montross,
West Co, fJohn, mMary Jane
Greer, hJohn W Harvey
William Edgar, b1864, Montross,
West Co, fJohn, mMary Jane
Greer, wLizzie Young McKenney
GOODWIN, Albert Thweatt, b17--,
Dinw Co?, fPeterson, wAmelia
Meade
David Everard, b18--, Greenville Co, fAlbert Thweatt
Goodwin, mAmelia Meade, wFanny
Hayes Montgomery
Evelyn, b18--, Fauq Co?,
hArthur Hart
Mary, b18--, nrNorth Garden,
Albe Co, hJames J Thomas
T W, b18--, Roan Co?, wMartha L
Terry

GOODWIN (continued)
William H, b8/24/1845, Nels Co,
wMargaret W Plunkett
GOODWYN, Peterson, b1745, Dinw
Co?, wElizabeth Peterson
GOOLRICK, John T, Sr, b1846,
Fredericksburg, Spot Co,
fPeter, wFannie B White
GORDON, Adam, b184-, Clar Co,
fFrank, m-- Barley
Anne, b17--, hHenry Embry
Coleman
Armistead Churchill, b12/20/
1855, "Edgeworth", Albe Co,
fGeorge Loyall, mMary Long
Daniel, wMaria Breckinridge
Catlett, md10/17/1883
Bennett Taylor, b2/6/1855,
"Huntly", Nels Co, fWilliam,
mCharlotte M Cocke, wAnnie P
Parker, md11/27/1884
Charles C, b185-, "Huntly",
Nels Co, fWilliam, mCharlotte
M Cocke
C T, b18--, Norfolk?, wAlice V
Whitehurst
Conway H, bc1860, Richmond,
fJames, mMary St Clair Cooke
Ella N, b186-, Lynchburg, Camp
Co, d1916, fJ N, 1w of A Randolph Carrington, Sr
George, b184-, Clar Co, d1867,
fFrank, m-- Barley
George Loyall, b18--, fWilliam
Fitzhugh, mElizabeth Lindsay,
wMary Long Daniel
Harriet, b184-, Clar Co,
fFrank, m-- Barley, hAdam Barley
Henry Newton, b185-, Richmond,
fJames, mMary St Clair Cooke
James, b3/18/1826, Richmond,
fJohn Newton, Sr, mLouisiana
Coleman, wMary St Clair Cooke,
md11/26/1856
James Lindsay, b18--, "Edgeworth", Albe Co, fGeorge
Loyall, mMary Long Daniel
James Waddell, b1/8/1869, Richmond, fJames, mMary St Clair
Cooke, wMary Gilmer Meade
John Newton, Sr, b2/15/1793,
Gordonsville, Oran Co,
fNathaniel, mMary Gordon,
wLouisiana Coleman
John Newton, Jr, b182-, Rich-

GORDON (continued)
mond, fJohn Newton, Sr, mLouisiana Coleman
John Peter, b1846, Clar Co, d1919, fFrank, m-- Barley, wSallie Krebs
John W, bc1840, Albe Co?, wEllen Agnes Langford
Lucy Conway, b186-, Richmond, fJames, mMary St Clair Cooke, hHenry Martson Smith
Lydia, bc1850, Clar Co, fFrank, m-- Barley, hGeorge O Bassett
Martha Harvie, b18--, Esse Co, hHenry Waring Latane
Mary, b17--, Urbanna, Midd Co, hNathaniel Gordon
Mary, b17--, Lanc Co?, fJames, hJames Waddell, md10/7/1767
Nathaniel, b10/20/1763, Lanc Co, fJames, (2)mMary Harrison, 2wMary Gordon
S S, bc1860, Rkhm Co?, wCatherine Bright Lincoln
Thomas Alexander, b18--, wJane Yeager
Virginia, b183-, fThomas Alexander, mJane Yeager, hWilliam Anderson Harris
William Fitzhugh, b18--, Oran Co, fJames, wElizabeth Daniel
William S, b185-, Richmond, fJames, mMary St Clair Cooke
GORE, Frances Octavia, b18--, Rapp Co, fJohn E, hCharles L Johnson, Sr
Mahlon, b18--, Fred Co?, hSydney Cather
Joshua, bc1848, Warr Co, wSusie Cornwell
GORMAN, Armistead, bc1810, Fran Co, wNancy Brown
GOSE, Frances, b1810, Russ Co, d1901, hCharles H Gilmer
George B, b186-, Wise Co?, wDarthula E Greear
Nancy P, b1837, nrCastlewood, Russ Co, d1884, hWilliam Rives Meade
Sarah, bc1810, Burkes Garden, Taze Co, fPhilip, hPeter G Litz
Temperance, bc1820, Russ Co, hAxley Gilmer
GOSNEY, Mary, b17--, Loui Co, hWilliam Davis

GOSS, Sarah T, b18--, Albe Co?, hW C Shackelford, Sr
GOUGH, Bettie, b1834, Camp Co, hThomas W Hix
GOULDIN, John Milton, Sr, b18--, Sparta, Caro Co, d187-, wSusan Jones Wright, md187-
GOULSBY, Louise, bc1835, Buck Co, hJames M Jordan
GRAHAM, --, b17--, Clar Co?, hLevi McCormick
Archibald, Sr, bc1800, Rkbr Co, fEdward, wMartha Lyle
Archibald, Jr, bc1840, Rkbr Co, fArchibald, Sr, mMartha Lyle
Archibald T, b185-, nrGraham, Taze Co, fWilliam L, mLouisa Bowen Thompson
Amanda Rebecca, bc1860, nr Graham, Taze Co, fWilliam L, mLouisa Bowen Thompson, hCharles P Greever
Bettie Peirce, b1850, Wyth Co, d1921, fDavid P, mMartha Peirce, hJohn Williamson Robinson
Burton, b186-, Drapers Valley, Pula Co, fThompson Sayers, mEllen Grills, hJoseph --
Charles M, b7/11/1861, nrTazewell, Taze Co, fRobert Graig, (2)mCynthia McDonald
David P, b18--, Wyth Co?, wMartha Peirce
Edward Lacy, Sr, bc1830, Rkbr Co, fArchibald, Sr, mMartha Lyle
Edward Lacy, Jr, bc1864, Rkbr Co, d1921, fEdward Lacy, Sr, wLouisa Garnett Eoff
Ellen, b186-, Drapers Valley, Pula Co, fThompson Sayers
Henry B, b7/5/1853, Pennington Gap, Lee Co, fJohn P, mAmerica Pennington, wMartha E Gilley
John A, b183-, Rkbr Co, fArchibald, Sr, mMartha Lyle
John B, b4/30/1861, nrGraham, Taze Co, fWilliam L, mLouisa Bowen Thompson, wPauline Witten
John P, b1831, Pennington Gap, Lee Co, d1891, fHenry, wAmerica Pennington
John Thompson, b5/18/1864, Drapers Valley, Pula Co, fThomp-

GRAHAM (continued)
son Sayers, mEllen Grills, wElizabeth Lewis Fox, md6/6/1889
Joseph, bc1800, Drapers Valley, Pula Co, fRobert, (2)mMary Cowan, wLucy Sayers
Margaret, bc1810, Smyt Co?, 2w of Patrick Campbell Buchanan, Sr
Margaret, bc1832, Rkbr Co, d1902, fArchibald, Sr, mMartha Lyle, hSamuel Couch Robinson
Mary, b18--, Wyth Co?, hCharles L Fox
Mary A H, b18--, Wyth Co, hDavid Denton Hull, Sr
Mary Katherine, b185-, nrGraham, Taze Co, d1920, fWilliam L, mLouisa Bowen Thompson, hJohn F Gillespie
Matilda, bc1793, Culp Co, fJoseph, hGeorge W Kemper, Sr
Ned, bc1870, Rkhm Co, fWilliam
Rebecca, b184-, nrTazewell, Taze Co, fRobert Craig, (1)m Elizabeth Witten, hRobert Tarter
Robert Craig, b1814, Chatham Hill, Smyt Co, d1855, fSamuel, mRachel Montgomery, 1wElizabeth Witten, 2wCynthia McDonald
Roger, bc1870, Rkhm Co, fWilliam
Samuel Cecil, b1/1/1846, nr Tazewell, Taze Co, d1923, fRobert Craig, (1)mElizabeth Witten, 1wAnnie Elizabeth Spotts, 2wMinnie Cox, 3wClaire Guillaume
Samuel M, b185-, nrGraham, Taze Co, fWilliam L, mLouisa Bowen Thompson
Sarah, b17--, Norf Co, hJoseph Deans
Thompson Sayers, b1828, Drapers Valley, Pula Co, fJoseph, mLucy Sayers, wEllen Grills
Virginia, b186-, Drapers Valley, Pula Co, fThompson Sayers, mEllen Grills, hCochran Preston
Willa C, bc1870, Rkhm Co, fWilliam, hJohn W Bolen, md10/1/1900

GRAHAM (continued)
William L, b10/8/1820, Chatham Hill, Smyt Co, d1908, fSamuel, mRachel Montgomery, wLouisa Bowen Thompson
William L, bc1830, Rkbr Co, fArchibald, Sr, mMartha Lyle
William R, b186-, nrGraham, Taze Co, fWilliam L, mLouisa Bowen Thompson
GRANDSTAFF, --, b18--, Shen Co, hJacob Snapp
Ann Elizabeth, b18--, nrWoodstock, Shen Co, fGeorge W, mMary Reeder, hWilliam J Koontz
Armistead, b18--, nrWoodstock, Shen Co, fGeorge W, mMary Reeder, w-- Parker
Artemissa, b18--, Shen Co, fGeorge W, mMary Reeder, hRichard Miller
Ellen, b18--, nrWoodstock, Shen Co, fGeorge W, mMary Reeder, hJohn R Miller
George W, b17--, nr Woodstock, Shen Co, d1867, wMary Reeder
John James, b18--, Shen Co, fGeorge W, mMary Reeder
Marcus P, b18--, nrWoodstock, Shen Co, fGeorge W, mMary Reeder, w-- Miller
Mary Frances, b18--, Shen Co, fGeorge W, mMary Reeder, hJackson Dinges
Milton, b18--, nrWoodstock, Shen Co, fGeorge W, mMary Reeder, w-- Fry
Sarah, b18--, Shen Co?, hJ M Ludwig
GRANGER, Isabella, b1846, Richmond, hAnthony W Wright
GRANT, --, b18--, Shallow Ford, Wash Co, hJohn Wasson
Louisa, b18--, Fred Co?, hCharles Frederick Conrad
GRANTHAM, Frances Kercheval, b18--, Jeff Co, fJoseph, hGeorge Henry Riely
GRASTY, Elizabeth Ann Lightfoot, b18--, Oran Co, hWilliam Lewis Dickie
Ella Pettus, b186-, Pitt Co?, 1w of James D Crews
GRAVATT, Charles Urquart, b185-, Port Royal, Carol Co, d1922,

GRAVATT (continued)
fJohn James, Sr, mMary Eliza Smith, wFlorence Marshall
John, b18--, KiGe Co, wEllen --
John James, Sr, b18--, Caro Co?, wMary Eliza Smith
John James, Jr, b5/14/1854, Port Royal, Caro Co, fJohn James, Sr, mMary Eliza Smith, wIndia Wray Jones
Lucy Jacqueline, b185-, Port Royal, Caro Co, fJohn James, Sr, mMary Eliza Smith, hReese Brown
Mary Ambler, b185-, Port Royal, Caro Co, fJohn James, Sr, mMary Eliza Smith
Pinckney Alexander, b1841, KiGe Co, d1909, fJohn, mEllen --, wAnne Lilbourne Moncure
William Loyall, b12/15/1858, Port Royal, Caro Co, fJohn James, Sr, mMary Eliza Smith
GRAVELY, Chester B, b18--, Roan Co?, wEmma Pedigo
Eliza, b18--, Henry Co?, 1w of Elijah Richardson
Jabez, b18--, Henry Co?, d186-
Joseph, b17--, Henry Co?, wEleanor Cox
Kate, b18--, Henry Co?, hJohn T Hundley
Lewis, bc1800, Henry Co, fJoseph, mEleanor Cox, wMartha Dyer
Martha, b18--, Henry Co, fLewis, mMartha Dyer, 1w of John F Pedigo
Mary, b18--, Henry Co, hHenry D Peters
Rachel, b18, Henry Co, fLewis, mMartha Dyer, 2w of John F Pedigo
GRAVES, --, bc1850, Shen Co?, 1h of Emma N Schmucker
--, bc1800, Suss Co, hWilliamson Howle
--, b18--, NewK Co?, hRobert Jesse Barlow
Alice Overton, b186, Bedf Co, fWilliam Fountain, mMary J Johnson
Ann, bc1840, Oran Co, fLewis, mFannie White, hRobert Burruss
Asa, b1/25/1780, Madi Co, d1840, fThomas, wSarah Kirtley

GRAVES (continued)
Benjamin, bc1830, Oran Co, fLewis, mFannie White
Benjamin S, b186, Madi Co, fFrancis Edward, mMary Peach Hamilton
Clinton, b183, Oran Co, fLewis, mFannie White
Cornelia, b1826, Solitude Farm, Madi Co, d1896, hEdward F Birckhead
Elmira, b18, Suss Co, hJames Alexander Temple
Florence Olivia, bc1870, Bedf Co, fWilliam Fountain, mMary J Johnson
Frances, b2/20/1842, Oran Co, fLewis, mFannie White, hWilliam Notley Greene
Francis Edward, b18, Madi Co, fAsa Graves, mSarah Kirtley, wMary Peach Hamilton
Frank Peyton, bc1860, Bedf Co, fWilliam Fountain, mMary J Johnson
J P, bc1840, Pitt Co?, wMary J Monroe
James R, b1820, Oran Co, d1913, fLewis, mFannie White, wCatherine Fritz
John, bc1700, Spot Co?, fRichard
John, b183, Oran Co, fLewis, mFannie White
John Thomas, b185, Bedf Co, fWilliam Fountain, mMary J Johnson, wIda F Wright, md10/11/1883
Joseph Pleasant, b186, Bedf Co, fWilliam Fountain, mMary J Johnson
Lewis, b17, Oran Co?, fIsaac, m Holliday, wFannie White
Lewis W, b8/22/1862, Oran Co, fJames R, mCatherine Fritz, wLillian Priest, md1888
Lucian A, b186, Madi Co, fFrancis Edward, mMary Peach Hamilton
Martha, b1822, Albe Co, d1896, hLewis J Thomas
Mary E, b186, Madi Co, fFrancis Edward, mMary Peach Hamiton, hWilliam B Bonham
Mary Willie, b185, Bedf Co, fWilliam Fountain, mMary J

GRAVES (continued)
Johnson
Minnie James, b186, Bedf Co, fWilliam Fountain, mMary J Johnson
Nannie Curtis, b186, Bedf Co, fWilliam Fountain, mMary J Johnson
Nannie Leslie, b186, Bedf Co, fWilliam Fountain, mMary J Johnson
Oscar, bc1870, Bedf Co, fWilliam Fountain, mMary J Johnson
Peyton, Jr, bc1800, nrBerger's Store, Pitts Co, d1836, fPeyton, Sr, wNancy B Hurt
Ralph, b16, fJohn
Richard, b16, fRalph
Richard, b18, Loui Co, d186, wSusan Kean
Richie Morris, b1864, Loui Co, fRichard, mSusan Kean, hJohn Peyton McGuire III
S Hamilton, b10/28/1866, Madi Co, fFrancis Edward, mMary Peach Hamilton
Stuart, b186, Bedf Co, fWilliam Fountain, mMary J Johnson
Thomas, b11/17/1733, Spot Co, (now Madi Co), fJohn
Thomas, bc1830, Oran Co, fLewis, mFannie White
Vernie, b18, Spot Co, fBenjamin Franklin, wRoberta Banks Brockman
William Fountain, b9/26/1832, nrBerger's Store, Pitt Co, fPeyton, Jr, mNancy B Hurt, wMary J Johnson, md1856
Winnie, b184, Oran Co, fLewis, mFannie White
GRAY, --, bc1810, Dinw Co, hAlbert Haddon
Alexander McFarland, b17, Russ Co, wHarriett Mason
Andrew J, Sr, b1850, Manchester, Ches Co, fWilliam, mSusan Ann Pleasants, wIda Flippen
Alphonso Alexander, b5/22/1834, Fluv Co, fWilliam Alfred, mMary Ann Brooks, 2wBettie Ann Leftwich, 1wSallie Ferrell Shepherd
Birdie M, bc1870, Math Co, fNelson R, mOctavia Billups, hRichard C Hayne

GRAY (continued)
Calvin B, bc1860, Math Co, fNelson R, mOctavia Billups
Carrie Esther, b186, Math Co, fNelson R, mOctavia Billups, 2w of Hansford P Roane
H P, bc1860, Richmond?, w Mosby
Harvey, b18, Scot Co?, wEmily Stair
Helen Cabell, b18, Richmond, fWilliam, mSusan Ann Pleasants, hOsbourn Wattson, md10/30/1865
James T, b18, Manchester, Ches Co, fWilliam, mSusan Ann Pleasants
John, b1796, Wash Co, fWilliam McCain, mMary Davis, wMary Craig
Lillie, bc1870, Scot Co, fHarvey, mEmily Stair, hHenry Charles Lane Richmond, md1/9/1896
Lucy Anne, b1/2/1839, nrWood, Scot Co, d1923, fAlexander McFarland, mHarriet Mason, hStephen J Nickels
Marionette, b186, Math Co, fNelson R, mOctavia Billups, 1w of Henry H Roane
Mary, bc1770, Gooc Co, hJacob Woodson
Mary, b17, Castlewood, Russ Co, hJames Dickenson
Nelson R, Jr, b186, Math Co, d1922, fNelson R, Sr, mOctavia Billups
Robert E, b186, Math Co, fNelson R, Sr, mOctavia Billups
Robert H, b1860, nrAbingdon, Wash Co, fWilliam M, (3)mNancy Ann Cowan, wMicajah Watkins King
Roswell P, bc1860, Math Co, fNelson R, Sr, mOctavia Billups
William, b17, fJohn, wJane Guerrant
William, b1810, PrEd Co, wSusan Ann Pleasants
William Alfred, b1803, Gooc Co, fWilliam, Jane Guerrant, wMary Ann Brooks
William M, b1824, Max Meadows, Wyth Co, fJohn, mMary Craig, 3wNancy Ann Cowan

GRAY (continued)
William McCain, b1764, nrHall's Bottoms, Wash Co, fJohn, mJean McCain, wMary Davis
Willie Blanche, b186, Fluv Co, fAlphonso Alexander, (1)m Sallie Terrell Shepherd, hFrank Terry Shepherd
Zachary Taylor, b3/17/1867, Math Co, fNelsoan R, Sr, mOctavia Billups, wMatilda Taliaferro Rose, md3/6/1895
Zora, b18, Fred Co?, hMarcus J Snapp
GRAYBILL, --, bc1800, Shen Co, hJohn Swartz
Virginia, b18, Roan Co?, 1w of John C Moomaw, Sr
GRAYSON, Fannie, b18, Fauq Co, 2w of John D Blackwell
Lauck, b18, Fauq Co?, wMay Glascock
Virginia C, b9/16/1839, Page Co, d1921, fBenjamin F, hJ B Brumback
GREANOR, Margaret S, b18, fWilliam, hWilliam F White
GREEAR, Alonzo Napoleon, b186, Grant, Grayson Cao, fEli Washington, mLoudema Young
Darthula E, b186, nrCoeburn, Wise Co, fFrancis B, (2)mPriscilla Stallard, hGeorge B Gose
Eli Washington, b1833, Grant, Gray Co, d1898, fShadrick, mBettie Baker, wLoudema Young
Eliza A, b186, nrCoeburn, Wise Co, fFrancis B, (2)mPriscilla Stallard, h Crouch
Francis B, b6/22/1819, Gray Co, fNoah, 1wSarah Mullens, md 1851, 2wPriscilla Stallard, md 1854
James L, b1861, Scot C, fThomas, mRebecca Frazier, wSarah E Meade
James Noah, b2/27/1859, nrCoeburn, Wise Co, fFrancis B, (2)mPriscilla Stallard, wBessie E Earnest, md6/17/1886
Martha S, b186, nrCoeburn, Wise Co, fFrancis B, (2)mPriscilla Stallard, hJohn Dingus
Mary E, b185, nrCoeburn, Wise Co, fFrancis B, (2)mPriscilla Stallard, hWilson Holbrook

GREEAR (continued)
Nancy S, b7/12/1865, nrCoeburn, Wise Co, fFrancis B, (2)mPriscilla Stallard, hBenjamin Franklin Hillman
Nellie J, bc1870, Grant, Gray Co, fEli Washington, mLoudema Young, hCharles W Ray
Noah, b1792, Gray Ci, d1872
Robert E Lee, b2/3/1869, Grant, Gray Co, fEli Washington, mLoudema Young, wBirdie M Carson, md3/20/1891
Shadrick, bc1800, Fran Co, wBettie Baker
Thomas, b18, Gray Co, d1863, wRebecca Frazier
Victoria, b186, Grant, Gray Co, fEli Washington, mLoudema Young, 1hMitchell M Hash, 2hJohn A Dixon
William Clayborne, b186, Grant, Gray Co, fEli Washington, mLoudema Young
William O, b185, nrCoeburn, Wise Co, fFrancis B, (2)mPriscilla Stallard
GREEN, Berryman, b7/25/1864, Greenwood Farm, Char Co, fWilliam E, mJennie Elliott Boylan, wNina Daniel Bouldin, md7/2/1891
Berryman, Jr, b17, nrRichmond, fBerryman, Sr
Boylan, bc1857, Greenwood Farm, Char Co, fWilliam E, mJennie Elliott Boylan, wAlice H Bouldin
Catherine, bc1850, Alexandria, fJohn E, (2)mMary Woody, hJames Franklin
Clement Read, bc1856, Greenwood Farm, Cahr Co, fWilliam E, mJennie Elliott Boylan
Daniel H, Sr, b18, Fauq Co, wLizzie Chamblin
Daniel H, Jr, bc1870, Rectortown, Fauq Co, fDaniel H, Sr, mLizzie Chamblin
E G, b181, Fred Co?, hRobert Sherard Bell
Edwin H, bc1860, Greenwood Farm, Char Co, fWilliam E, mJennie Elliott Boylan
Fannie Richards, b18, fArchibald M, hFrancis McFarland

GREEN (continued)
Gilkeson
Isaac Carrington, bc1863, Greenwood Farm, fWilliam E, mJennie Elliott Boylan
Jennie B, b185, Greenwood Farm, Char Co, fWilliam E, mJennie Elliott Boylan, 2w of John Gilliam Friend
John E, b1798, d1889, 2wMary Woody
John Thomas, Sr, b1834, Lune Co, d1898, wLula Tucker
John Thomas, Jr, b1859, Lune Co, fJohn Thomas, Sr, mLula Tucker, wLelia Harriett Dalton
Julia Arondel, bc1800, Culp Co, fMoses, hBernard Peyton
Julia Belle, bc1850, Richmond?, 1w of H Seldon Taylor, md2/1868
Kate, bc1870, Rectortown, Fauq Co, fDaniel H, Sr, mLizzie Chamblin, hGraham Pierce
Kate B, b186, Greenwood Farm, Char Co, fWilliam E, mJennie Elliott Boylan, hWilliam N Page
Mary, b184, Alexandria, fJohn E, (2)mMary Woody, hWallace Mc Donough
Miranda, b185, Alexandria, fJohn E, (2)mMary Woody, hWilliam Grimes
Montford K, b186, Greenwood Farm, Char Co, fWilliam E, mJennie Elliott Boylan
Nathaniel, b18, Richmond?, wMary Sledd
Richard F, Sr, b1855, Alexandria, d1923, fJohn E, (2)mMary Woody, wEugenia McDonough
Robert B, b18, Richmond?, wAdeline Douglas Gibson
Rosalie, bc1820, Farm Hill, nrMannboro, Amel Co, hRichard Feild Taylor, Jr
Sallie, b17, Amel Co, fArmistead, hLewis Burwell II
Sarah, b18, Hali Co, hLeander Faulkner
Shepherd Co, b186, Greenwood Farm, Char Co, fWilliam E, mJennie Elliott Boylan
Susie, b186, Rectortown, Fauq Co, fDaniel H, Sr, mLizzie

GREEN (continued)
Chamblin, h Coleman
Thomas Hope, b17, nrRichmond, fBerryman, Sr, w Morton
W T, bc1850, Pitt Co?, wMary S Hughes
William Booker, b1787, PrEd Co, d1870, fThomas Hope, m Morton, wAnne Read
William Booker, b185, Greenwood Farm, Car Co, fWilliam E, mJennie Elliott Boylan
William E, b1829, Greenwood Farm, Char Co, fWilliam Booker, mAnne Read, wJennie Elliott Boylan
GREENE, Alexander, b18, Oran Co?, wKatie Rogers
Harry Raynor, bc1860, Fred Co?, wKatherine Glass
James R, b184, Oran Co?, fAlexander, mKatie Rogers
William Notley, b2/7/1842, Oran Co?, fAlexander, mKatie Rogers, wFrances Graves
GREER, Catherina B, bc1800, 3w of William Leftwich, Jr, md 2/27/ 1839
Mary Jane, b18--, Port Royal, Caro Co, hJohn Goodridge
GREEVER, Charles P, bc1850, Taze Co?, wAmanda Rebecca Greever
GREGG, Albina, b17--, Alexandria?, 1w of Elisha Janney
B G, b18--, Augu Co?, wKatherine Smith
Edgar B, b18--, Loud Co, fWilliam, wMary Nichols
John, b184--, PrWi Co, fJohn W, mOrra Emma Kenyon
John W, b18--, PrWi Co?, wOrra Emma Kenyon
Laura E, bc1847, PrWi Co, d1908, fJohn W, mOrra Emma Kenyon, hMarshall Selecman
Martha Jordan, b18--, Grvl Co, hWilliam M Jones
Mary, b184--, PrWi Co, fJohn W, mOrra Emma Kenyon, hGeorge Storer
Matilda, b18--, Dinw Co, hBenjamin H Boisseau
Myron, b184-, PrWi Co, fJohn W, mOrra Emma Kenyon
GREGORY, Bettie, b18--, Richmond?, hJohn R Hockaday

GREGORY (continued)
Emmet D, b5/11/1861, nrDillwyn, Buck Co
John, bc1830, Fred Co?, wAnabel Cadwallader
Nancy, b18--, Cumb Co, hJohn Wesley Brown
Richard Clairborne, b1776, Dinw Co, m-- Claiborne
Sarah C, b18--, hWilliam Hatcher
Werter Hancock, b8/31/1846, Lune Co, fRichard Claiborne, 1wSallie J Payne, 2wLillie B Thomas
GRESHAM, Albert B, bc1850, KiQu Co?, wEllen B Jones
Elijah, b17--, KiQu Co, fSamuel
Jessie, b4/27/1847, KiQu Co, hHenry Robinson Pollard, Sr
Kate, b1851, Woodlawn Farm, KiQu Co, d1893, hLewis Armistead Tyler
Thomas, b3/27/1867, Ches Co, fWilliam A, mNannie Haskins Meador, wLelia Gluyas, md12/27/1894
Thomas Butt, bc1842, PrAn Co, d1917, fThomas B, wPermelia Lena Smith
William A, b7/1838, Ches Co, fElijah, mMaria Goode, wNannie Haskins Meador
William D, b18--, KiQu Co?, wMary Allen Garnett
GREY, Esther virginia, b1843, Nickelsville, Scot Co, d1918, hRansom R Rollins
GRICE, George W, b5/16/1824, Portsmouth, Norf Co, fJoseph, mAbigail Cox
Joseph, b9/29/1869, Portsmouth, Norf Co, fGeorge W, mHenrietta Harding
GRIFFIN, Elizabeth, bc1790, Roan Co?, dc1870, hGreen McClanahan
Emma Lewis, b1850, Henrico Co, hNathaniel Woodson Bowe
Esther Eugenia, b18--, fEdward Griffin, hHenry Branson Anderson
Samuel, bc1840, Bedf Co?, wAnn Roy Hutter
Thomas, b183-, wJulia A Benn, md10/7/1865
Virginia, bc1870, fThomas,

GRIFFIN (continued)
mJulia A Benn, hCharles Woolfolk Coleman, md1891
GRIFFITH, Edward Colville, b18-- 1wElizabeth Cox, 2wJulia Hungerford
Edward Colville, bc1870, Thompson's Hill, West Co, fFrederick, mFrances Brockenbrough Tyler
Frederick, b1841, Thompson's Hill, West Co, fEdward Colville, (1)mElizabeth Cox, wFrances Brockenbrough Tyler
Frederick, b3/25/1868, West Co, fFrederick, mFrances Brockenbrough Tyler, wCharity Evelyn Yeatman, md9/14/1897
Hubert F, b18--, Page Co, fJohn, wBettie S Sindlinger
Isaac, b17--, fOwen, mJennie Gillespie, w-- Hale
John F, b1/29/1849, Russ Co, fTazewell Hill, mLavinia Boyd, wAlice Whitt
Mahala, b18--, Russ Co, hFullen Robinson
Mary Ann, b1842, Grbr Co, fCaleb, hSamuel Stuben Carpenter
Nannie Goode, b1865, Cumb Co, hJoseph Robert Johnson, Sr
Philip Smith, b186-, Thompson's Hill, West Co, fFrederick, mFrances Brockenbrough Tyler
Tazewell Hill, b18--, Patr Co, fIsaac, m-- Hale, wLavinia Boyd
Thomas, b18--, wLula Winter
William Fairfax, bc1870, Thompson's Hill, West Co, fFrederick, mFrances Brockenbrough Tyler
GRIGG, Evelyn, b18--, Petersburg, Dinw Co, hJames M Mullen
Katherine, bc1833, Buck Co?, hWilliam E Gannaway
GRIGGS, Fannie, b18--, Jeff Co?, hJames Flanagan
GRIGSBY, Elizabeth, bc1780, hWilliam McNutt
GRILLS, Ellen, b1834, nrRadford, Mont Co, d1882, hThompson Sayers Graham
GRIM, --, bc1860, Albe Co?, wBeulah E Totty

GRIMES, William, bc1850, Loud Co?, wMiranda Green
GRIMM, Charles, bc1840, Fred Co?, wHattie Hardy
Susan, b17--, h-- Huff
GRIMSLEY, Daniel A, b18--, Rkbr Co?, fBarnett
Martha Ann, b18--, Rkbr Co, fBarnett, hGeorge Godfrey Wood, mdc1857
GRINNAN, Andrew Glassell, Sr, b8/14/1827, Fredericksburg, Spot Co, wGeorgia Bryan
Andrew Glassell, Jr, b186-, fAndrew Glassell, Sr, mGeorgia Bryan
Bessie C, b186-, Madi Co, fAndrew Glassell, Sr, mGeorgia Bryan
Daniel, bc1860, fAndrew Glassell, Sr, mGeorgia Bryan
Nina S, b186-, Madi Co, fAndrew Glassell, Sr, mGeorgia Bryan
R Bryan, bc1860, Madi Co, fAndrew Glassell, Sr, mGeorgia Bryan
St George T, b4/6/1870, Madi Co, fAndrew Glassell, Sr, mGeorgia Bryan, wSusie F Dabney, md4/18/1906
GRIZZARD, Henry Thomas, b1846, wBettie ---
James William, b1/22/1846, nr Jarratt, Susse Co, fHenry Thomas, (3)mBettie --, 1wAdiline Antoinette Smith, md12/15/1866, 2w Bettie Smith, md3/12/1874, 3wLaura Smith
GROSSCLOSE, Adeline Elizabeth, b18--, Blan Co, d1900, hElias Repass
Jennie, bc1870, Ceres, Blan Co, 1w of Henry Edward Peery
GROVE, --, b18--, Page Co?, hSamuel Brumback
Ann, bc1820, Stephens City, Fred Co, fIsaac, m-- Shipe, h-- McCormick
Annie, b18--, Rkhm Co, hIsaac Winegoard
Benjamin, b182-, Stephens City, Fred Co, d1922, fIsaac, m-- Shipe
Catherine, b18--, Winchester, Fred Co, d1914, fWilliam H, mMary --, hHenry M Baker

GROVE (continued)
Charles E, b185-, Dodd Co?, d1910, fLewis William, mAnn Elizabeth Lewin
C H, b18--, Roan Co, w-- Denit
Charles H, b184-, Luray, Page Co, fEmanuel
Daniel Latimer, bc1850, Dodd Co, fLewis William, mAnn Elizabeth Lewin
Emanuel, bc1812, Page Co, d1890
Francis Asbury, b184-, Dodd Co, fLewis William, mAnn Elizabeth Lewin
George M, bc1850, Augu Co?, wIda P Coiner
Harvey, b182-, Stephens City, Fred Co, d186-, fIsaac, m-- Shipe
Henry, b181-, Stephens City, Fred Co, fIsaac, m-- Shipe
Isaac, bc1800, Fred Co?, w-- Shipe
John W, b12/16/1844, Luray, Page Co, fEmanuel, wLaura Brumback, md4/20/1880
Lewis William, bc1824, Stephens City, Fred Co, d1905, fIsaac, m-- Shipe, wAnn Elizabeth Lewin
Martin Luther, b9/11/1848, Dodd Co, fLewis William, mAnn Elizabeth Lewin, wJulia Mary Allen Miller, md8/12/1872
Nancy, b18--, Page Co, hJacob Brumback
Rebecca, b182-, Stephens City, Fred Co, fIsasc, m-- Shipe, hJoseph Marston
William D, b185-, Dodd Co, d1916, fLewis William, mAnn Elizabeth Lewin
William H, b17--, Fred Co, wMary --
GRUBB, Alexander, b18--, Gray Co?, d1922, wEmma Taylor
Hiram W, b186-, Wyth Co?, wVirginia R Kegley
GRUBBS, John L, b18--, Richmond?, wMollie Wingfield
Mary Ann, b1840, PrEd Co, d1918, 2w of William Schumaker
Nannie Winston, bc1870, Richmond?, fJohn L, mMollie Wingfield, hGeorge Barret Sydnor, md10/27/ 1892

GRUBBS (continued)
William, b18--, Warr Co?, wJanie Trenary
GRUNDY, Clara Haxall, bc1860, fThomas B, mClara Haxall, hRichard F Beirne
Thomas B, b18--, wClara Haxall
GRUNYON, Margaret, b17--, Lanc Co, hRichard Ball Mitchell
GRUVER, --, bc1860, Fred Co?, wMary S White
Benjamin F, b18--, Warr Co?, wMaggie Snyder
GRYMES, Benjamin R, b1830, KiGe Co?, d1913, fGeorge Nicholas, mAnn Eilbeck Mason, wRebecca Johnson, md1860
George Nicholas, b1795, KiGe Co?, wAnn Eilbeck Mason
Lucy, b17--, fCharles, hHenry Lee II
Lucy, b17--, Midd Co, fPhilip, mMary Randolph, hThomas Nelson, md7/29/1762
Philip, b17--, Midd Co?, wMary Randolph
GUARD, Amos, bc1830, Fred Co?, w-- Kline
Susan Alexander, b18--, Rapp Co?, hCharles Fremont Menefee
GUERRANT, Hattie, b183-, Gooc Co, hWilliam Miller II
James F, bc1870, Fran Co, fStephen P, Sr, mSarinda Crumpacker, wMary Saul
Jane, b17--, hWilliam Gray
John, b17--, fJohn
John R, bc1850, Powh Co?, wCatherine Randolph Lee
Peter, bc1800, fJohn
Stephen P, Sr, b18--, Fran Co, fPeter, wSarinda Crumpacker
Tabitha, b18--, Fran Co, hHenry Tate Callaway
GUGGENHEIMER, Charles M, bc1860, Lynchburg, Camp Co, fNathaniel, mCilla Guggenheimer, wMinnie Lee Rosenbaum
Delia, b185-, Lynchburg, Camp Co, fNathaniel, mCilla Guggenheimer, hDavid Dryfuss
Hortense, b185-, Lynchburg, Camp Co, fNathaniel, mCilla Guggenheimer, hReuben Lindheim
Leo, bc1850, Camp Co, wPauline Guggenheimer

GUGGENHEIMER (continued)
Pauline, bc1860, Lynchburg, Camp Co, fNathaniel, mCilla Guggenheimer, hLeo Guggenheimer
Sidney, bc1850, Lynchburg, Camp Co, fNathaniel, mCilla Guggenheimer
GUIGON, Alexander Barclay, Sr, b2/13/1831, Richmond, fAuguste, mEllen Smithey, wSarah Bates Allen, md8/20/1857
Alexander Barclay, Jr, bc1860, Richmond?, fAlexander Barclay, Sr, mSarah Bates Allen
GULLION, Esther, b1795, Sharon Springs Farm, Blan Co, d1880, hReuben Repass
GUINN, Tandy William, b18--, Culp Co?, fWilliam, wSusie Virginia Colvin
GUNNELL, George West, b17--, Fair Co, fHenry, mSarah West, 1wLucien Ratcliffe, 2wEmeline Young
Henry, b17--, Fair Co, fWilliam, w-- Minor
Henry, b17--, Fair Co, fHenry, m-- Minor, wSarah West
Mary Josephine, b18--, Fair Co, fGeorge West, (2)mEmeline Young, hJ Owens Berry
GUTHRIE, Angeline, b186-, Buck Co, fJohn J, mMartha Goodman, hBenjamin Foster
Balfour, b186-, Buck Co, fJohn J, mMartha Goodman
Bulford, bc1860, Buck Co, fJohn J, mMartha Goodman
Emily, b1838, Buck Co, hWilliam Williams
Forrest, Sr, b10/14/1864, Buck Co, fJohn J, mMartha Goodman, wMary Spencer, md1899
John J, b1819, Buck Co, fWilliam, wMartha Goodman
Margaret Lynn, b18--, Augu Co, hDaniel Fishburne
Martha, bc1860, Buck Co, fJohn J, mMartha Goodman, hW B Shepard
Thomas G, b5/26/1852, Mt Pleasant Farm, Buck Co, fJohn J, mMartha Goodman, wAnna Amos, md12/17/1884
GUY, Jackson, b18--, Good Co,

GUY (continued)
fSamuel A, mAmanda Jackson
John Henry, Sr, b1833, Loui Co, fSamuel Atwell, mAnne Harrison Wyatt, wMary Ellen Ranson
Lucy Penn, b18--, fThomas, mLucy Penn Hunt, hJohn Armistead Burwell
Sallie Wyatt, b4/1851, Gooc Co, fSamuel A, mAmanda Jackson, hWilliam Anderson Davis
Samuel Atwell, bc1800, Loui Co, wAnne Harrison Wyatt
Thomas, b17--, wLucy Penn Hunt
GUYER, Augusta B, bc1860, Middletown, Fred Co, fJohn Sigsworth, mEmma S Aby
Charles Belle, bc1860, Middletown, Fred Co, fJohn Sigsworth, mEmma S Aby
Maggie M, b186-, Middletown, Fred Co, fJohn Sigsworth, mEmma S Aby, hSamuel F Rhodes, md9/10/1885
Minnie, b185-, Middletown, Fred Co, fJohn Sigsworth, mEmma S Aby
Samuel B, b186-, Middletown, Fred Co, fJohn Sigsworth, mEmma S Aby
Virginius, b186-, Middletown, Fred Co, fJohn Sigsworth, mEmma s Aby
GWALTNEY, Annie Melville, bc1870, Roanoke, Roan Co, fJames, mSusan V Haley, hWalter Roland Hancock, md2/10/1898
James, b18--, Roan Co?, wSusan V Haley
GWIN, Jane, b17--, fDavid, hJohn Cleek
GWYNN, Nancy, b18--, Bath Co?, fJohn, Sr, 1w of Hugh McLaughlin
HAAG, Amelia, b1862, Arli Co, hWilliam Duncan
HABRON, Amos, bc186-, Shen Co?, wLucy C Golladay
HACKETT, --, b17--, Oran Co, hJohnny Scott
HACKNEY, Thomas, bc1860, Russ Co?, wSarah Ratliff
HADDON, Albert, b1800, Dinw Co, w-- Gray
Thomas Gray, Sr, b1848, Dinw

HADDON (continued)
Co, fAlbert, m-- Gray, wMusa D Hargrave
HADDOX, Clinton, b18--, Rapp Co?, wDollie Smith
Edwina, b1857, Rapp Co, fClinton, mDollie Smith, hW Golder Davis
HADEN, Asa D, bc1800, Fluv Co, wSusan Lane
Blanche, b18--, Fluv Co, d1899, hGeorge Perkins
Elbridge George, b9/17/1853, Fluv Co, fWilliam D, mElizabeth Davis, wMartha Douglas Early, md2/29/1876
George, bc1800, Fluv Co, wSarah Lane
John R, b18--, Fluv Co, fWilliam D, mElizabeth Davis
Nancy, b17--, Fluv Co, fJohn M, hWilliam S Lane
Patsy M, bc1850, Richmond?, hCharles D Purcell
William D, b7/7/1808, Fluv Co, fWilliam, wElizabeth Davis
William E, b18--, Fluv Co, fWilliam D, mElizabeth Davis
HAINES, Alice, bWinchester, Fred Co, fJohathan H, mMary Hagan, h-- Baker
Charles E, b185-, Winchester, Fred Co, fJonathan, mMary Fagan
Daniel F, b185-, Winchester, Fred Co, fJonathan, mMary Fagan
George W, b6/29/1855, Winchester, Fred Co, fJonathan, mMary Fagan, wSusie Tyler Herndon, md7/1880
Gertrude, bc1860, Winchester, Fred Co, fJonathan H, mMary Fagan
John B, b185-, Winchester, Fred Co, fJonathan H, mMary Fagan
Jonathan H, bc1824, Winchester, Fred Co, wMary Fagan
Margaret, b186-, Charlestown, Jeff Co, fJonathan, mMary Fagan
Martha, bc1860, Winchester, Fred Co, fJonathan, mMary Fagan, h-- Collins
Mary S, bc1820, Fred Co, d1894, hJosiah Jackson

HAIRSTON, Janie, b1839, Marrowbone, Henry Co, d1904, hJohn Samuel Draper, Sr
Mary Louisa, bc1860, Martinsville, Henry Co, fRobert H, hHarry Mauze Darnell, md7/5/1881
HALDEMAN, Ella, bc1870, Rkhm Co, hIsaac B Wenger
HALE, --, b17--, Patr Co?, hIsaac Griffith
Americus, b1822, d1902, hMarshall Wade
Charlotte, b18--, Gray Co?, hGeorge L Delp
Daniel, bc1830, Rkhm Co?, wSusanna Early
Herbert W, b3/24/1865, Narrows, Gile Co, fWilliam, wMary Symns
Elizabeth, b1806, Gray Co, d1851, 2w of David Whitman
Samuel, bc1850, Shen Co, fDavid M, mMary Miller, wJennie R Kagey
Will, bc1860, Rkhm Co?, wFannie Garber
HALEY, Fannie, b18--, Loui Co, fLittleberry J, mMary Long, 1w of William W Boxley
John, b18--, Mont Co?, wMary Mahon
Lewis Clay, b10/26/1869, Grey Stone, Henry Co, fRobert, mMary C Martin, wMattie Inman, md1896
Mary Frances, bc1850, Christiansburg, Mont Co, fJohn, mMary Mahon, hDavid M Armstrong, md1872
Robert Clay, b1844, Henry Co, wMary C Martin
Susan V, b18--, Roan Co?, hJames Gwaltney
HALL, --, b18--, Carr Co?, wMaggie Thornton
--, bc1850, Bote Co?, wAnna Leslie
Addison H, b1792, Heathsville, Nhld Co, d1872, 1w-- Edmunds, 2w-- Tyler, 3w-- Noyes
Agnes B, b12/9/1843, Mont Co, d1918, hHarvey Roop
Alexander Stuart, b17--, Augu Co, wJean Paxton
Alexander Stuart, b7/26/1852, Buck Co, fWilliam P, Sr, mAn-

HALL (continued)
geline Bondurant, 1wFannie L Anderson, md1876, 2wMildred M Ellis, md2/18/1908
Annye L, bc1870, Hillsville, Carr Co, mMaggie Thornton, hLawson Worrell, md6/25/1902
B Franklin, b186-, nrHarrisonburg, Rkhm Co, fGeorge Gordon, mElizabeth Thomas
Bessie Evelyn, b18--, Richmond, fWilliam Green, mSarah Ann Hatcher, hE Thomas Hatcher, md1890
Bettie, b186-, nrMontross, West Co, fRobert M, (1)mAnnie Jennings, hJoseph C Brown
Bettie E, bc1860, Oran Co, fJames, mHardenia Bunnell
Catherine, !b18--, Loud Co?, hThomas Frasier
Charles, b18--, West Co?, wJeannette Powers
Charles R, b18--, Nhld Co, wJosephine Prosser
Daniel, b17--, Staf Co, w-- Curtis
Elisha, b17--, wCaroline Carter
Eliza Cathrene, bc1870, nrMontross, West Co, fRobert M, (2)mSarah Jennings
Elizabeth, b17--, PrGe Co, fThomas, hEdward Broadnax I
Emma, b186-, nrHarrisonburg, Rkhm Co, fGeorge Gordon, mElizabeth Thomas, hFrank Burkholder
Frank M, bc1870, Lanc Co, fHerbert Pollard, (1)mMary H Chowning
George Gordon, b2/26/1827, Albe Co, fThomas, wElizabeth Thomas
George W, b186-, nrHarrisonburg, Rkhm Co, fGeorge Gordon, mElizabeth Thomas
Georgia, b18--, Isle Co, hA S Birdsong
Harvey, b18--, Wise Co?, wMary Jane Roberts
Harvey T, Sr, bc1868, nrBlacksburg, Mont Co, fWilliam Gideon, (2)mEmeline (Owen) Bane, wMary Elizabeth Slaughter, md1901
Henrietta, bc1850, Oran Co, fJames, mHardenia Bunnell

HALL (continued)
Herbert Pollard, b2/6/1841, Lanc Co, fAddison H, 1wMary H Chowning, 2wAnnie Pinckard
Howard Wyche, b12/15/1867, fRobert W, mSarah J Ross, wNancy Walker (Wilson) Bruce, md12/12/1916
Jacob, b18--, Richmond?, wEmily G Moore
Jacob Henry, b1/2/1855, nrHarrisonburg, Rkhm Co, fGeorge Gordon, mElizabeth Thomas, wElizabeth Frances Bowman, md 1/23/1883
James, b1821, Culp Co, d1896, fDaniel, m-- Curtis, wHardenia Bunnell
James O, b185-, Oran Co, fJames, mHardenia Bunnell
Jane, b18--, Mont Co, 1w of Miles Francis
John, bc1820, Albe Co, fThomas
John Byrd, bc1800, fElisha, mCaroline Carter, wHarriet Stringfellow
John Hopkins, Sr, b2/20/1852, Norfolk, wMary C Nelms
John Lesslie, b3/2/1856, Richmond, fJacob, mEmily G Moore, wMargaret Fenwick Farland, md 4/30/1889
John Thomas, b185-, nrHarrisonburg, Rkhm Co, fGeorge Gordon, mElizabeth Thomas
Joseph Isaac, b185-, nrHarrisonburg, Rkhm Co, fGeorge Gordon, mElizabeth Thomas
John W, b1865, Loud Co, fJames M, wAnnie E Holliday
Judson B, b185-, Oran Co, fJames, mHardenia Bunnell
Julia Stringfellow, b18--, Fredericksburg, Spot Co, fJohn Byrd, mHarriet Stringfellow, 2w of William Dixon Henry
Lucy, b182-, Albe Co, fThomas, h-- Walton
Lucy M, bc1860, nrHarrisonburg, Rkhm Co, fGeorge Gordon, mElizabeth Thomas
Luther, bc1850, Rich Co?, wAnnie M Omohundro
Luther, b186-, nrHarrisonburg, Rkhm Co, fGeorge Gordon, mElizabeth Thomas

HALL (continued)
M E Y, b18--, d189-, 1w of Nelson Bryant, Jr, md4/1889
Mace, bc1820, Albe Co, fThomas
Martha, bc1831, Rkbr Co, hIsaac Lam
Martha J, b18--, Hali Co?, hThomas B Fitzgerald
Martha S, bc1870, nrMontross, West Co, fRobert M, (2)mSarah Jennings, hRichard Brown
Martin W, b18--, Norf Co?, wLaura Curling
Mary E, b185-, nrHarrisonburg, Rkhm Co, fGeorge Gordon, mElizabeth Thomas, hB F Landes
Milton D, b9/14/1851, Oran Co, fJames, mHardenia Bunnell, 1wElla Coffer, md6/1881, 2w Elizabeth C Carver, md3/9/1911
Nancy, b182-, Albe Co, fThomas, hCharles Dowel
Richard, bc1800, nrMontross, West Co, fIsaac
Robert, b18--, Rich Co?, wCornelia Jones
Robert M, b2/28/1835, nrMontross, West Co, fRichard, 1w Annie Jennings, 2wSarah Jennings
Robert W, b5/13/1840, Brun Co, fClement, wSarah J Ross
Samuel, bc1850, Rkhm Co, wVictoria Wyant
Sarah, b182-, Fauq Co?, hRichard Earle DeButts, md1844
Snowden C, b1837, Staf Co, fThomas Samuel, wLucinda Hedgman
Tarleton H, b18--, wMollie Harding
Timothy A, b185-, Oran Co, James, mHardenia Bunnell
Virginia, b186-, nrHarrisonburg, Rkhm Co, fGeorge Gordon, mElizabeth Thomas, hGeorge Dowel
William Gideon, b1820, Staunton, Augu Co, fCornelius, 2h of Emeline (Owen) Bane
William Green, b18--, wSarah Ann Hatcher
William H, bc1850, Fauq Co, wIda DeButts
William H, b185-, KiWi Co?, wSallie R Garrett

HALL (continued)
William H, b186-, nrMontross, West Co, fRobert M, (2)mSarah Jennings
William P, Sr, b6/10/1822, Augu Co, fAlexander Stuart, mJean Paxton, wAngeline Bondurant
William P, Jr, b185-, Buck Co, fWilliam P, Sr, mAngeline Bondurant
HALLEY, Elizabeth Reid, b18--, Fair Co, hHenry Simpson Halley
Henry Simpson, b18--, Fair Co?, wElizabeth Reid Halley
Margaret T, b183-, Fair Co, fHenry Simpson, mElizabeth Reid Halley, hJohn Sidney Hutton, Sr, md1858
HALLIGAN, James, b186-, Ream Station, Dinw Co, fJames, mAmanda McKinney
Mary, b186-, Ream Station, Dinw Co, fJames, mAmanda McKinney, hB A McGee
Peter B, b4/11/1870, Ream Station, Dinw Co, fJames, mAmanda McKinney, wJulia M Perkins
HALLOWELL, William Henry, b18--, Nott Co?, 2h of Sarah Irby, md10/23/1867
HALSEY, Aurelia, b18--, Lynchburg, Camp Co, 2w of John Gaw Meem, Jr
Don Peters, Sr, bLynchburg, Camp Co, d1883, fSeth, mJulia D B Peters, wSarah Ann Warwick Daniel, md3/7/1866
Don Peters, Jr, b12/29/1870, Lynchburg, Camp Co, fDon Peters, Sr, mSarah Ann Warwick Daniel, wMary Micheaux Dickinson, md1894
Greenberry B, b18--, Gray Co, wDrucie Hash
Robena, b18--, Gray Co, fGreenberry B, mDrucie Hash, hJohn L C Anderson, md9/9/1889
Seth, bc1800, Camp Co?, wJulia D B Peters
Amanda, b18--, Shen Co, d1915, fLevi, hJohn M Stoner, md12/15/1860
HALTERMAN, Arthur, bc1870, Rkhm Co?, wAnna M Bowman
HAMBLETON, Frances, b17--, Fauq Co?, hRichard Luttrell

HAMBLIN, James Turner, bc1860, Richmond?, wMary Brown
William, b17--, Amel Co, wChristiana Burwell
HAMBRICH, --, b18--, Mont Co, hHenry Surface
HAMILTON, Alexander Scott, b1/18/1859, PrWi Co, fGeorge S, mMary Anna Scott, wGrace Chamberlain, md10/1892
Alice, b18--, Fauq Co, fGeorge S, mMary Anna Scott
Charlotte, b180-, Spot Co, fGeorge, mMaria Slaughter, hWilliam Thornton
Elizabeth, bc1770, Bedf Co?, hJames Watts
Elizabeth Ann, b18--, Cloverdale, Rkbr Co, hPreston Bailey Hogshead, md1833
George II, bc1810, Spot Co, fGeorge, mMaria Slaughter, wLavina Downman
George S, b1830, Fauq Co, fHugh, mJanet Scott, wMary Anna Scott
Harriet, b18--, Fauq Co, fGeorge S, mMary Anna, hC B Chilton
Hugh, b12/1803, Spot Co, fGeorge, mMaria Slaughter, wJanet Scott
J Hopkins, b18--, Wise Co?, wSallie Ann Neal
Jane, b181-, Spot Co, fGeorge, mMaria Slaughter, hJohn L Marye
Jennett, b18--, Fauq Co, fGeorge S, mMary Anna Scott, hJohn D Hamilton
John D, b18--, Fred Co?, wJennett Hamilton
Lillie, b18--, Fauq Co, fGeorge S, mMary Anna Scott, hJohn F Scott
Margaret, bc1810, Spot Co, fGeorge, mMaria Slaughter, hGeorge Thornton
Maria, b180-, Spot Co, fGeorge, mMaria Slaughter, hNelson Page
Mary W, b18--, Fauq Co, fGeorge S, mMary Anna Scott
Matilda, b181-, Spot Co, fGeorge, mMaria Slaughter
Robert S, b181-, Spot Co, fGeorge, mMaria Slaughter

HAMILTON (continued)
Sanders, b8/5/1845, Blan Co, fTimothy, m-- Moore, wSallie Ann Mustard
Sarah, b180-, Spot Co, fGeorge, mMaria Slaughter, hRoots Thompson
Timothy, b18--, w-- Moore
W S, b18--, Fauq Co, fGeorge S, mMary Anna Scott
HAMLET, Edna, b18--, Appo Co, hArcher Lester Woody
HAMLIN, Thomas, b18--, wMartha Reamey
Tucker T, b18--, wSallie Christian Burwell
HAMM, George A, b12/19/1847, Oran Co, wFannie Sisson
HAMMACK, Adolphus, b184-, Lune Co?, wGlendona Eltarina Moore
HAMMAN, Jacob, bc1800, Shen Co?, wDorothy Hottel
HAMMER, Henry, Jr, b1828, Rkhm Co, fHenry, Sr, wMargaret Hawkins
James A, b1848, Elkton, Rkhm Co, fHenry, Jr, mMargaret Hawkins, wAlice Broyles
Walker g, b18--, Camp Co?, wCordelia Ann ---
HAMMETT, Edwrd, b18--, Mont Co, wClementine Craig
Sue, b1846, "Norwood", Mont Co, fEdward, mClementine Craig, hJames Hoge Tyler, md11/16/1868
HAMMOCK, Daniel, bc1840, Hayfield, Fred Co, wAmanda Larrick
Jacob, bc1840, Fred Co?, wMary Larrick
Severine M, Fred Co, d1916, fJacob, mMary Larrick, hJames Lewis Gardner, md3/1886
HAMMOND, Arthur Watson, b3/16/1856, Raleigh Courthouse, Rale Co, fJ M, mRebeca Herndon, wSallie E Minnich, md1890
Frank, bc1860, Raleigh Courthouse, Rale Co, fJ M, mRebecca Herndon
George, b182-, Catawba, Bote Co, d186-
J M, bc1825, Catawba, Bote Co, d1905, wRebecca Herndon
John, bc1820, Shen Co?, 1h of Lydia Maphis
S W, bc1860, Raleigh Courthouse, Rale Co, d1916, fJ M, mRebecca Herndon
HAMNER, Mary Willis, b18--, Albe Co?, 2w of William Wallace Tapscott
Rosalie Owen, bc1870, Lynchburg, Camp Co, d1894, fWalker G, hRichard Hill Adams
HAMPTON, Alfred, b181-, Fauq Co, wHulda Cochran
Margaret, b18--, Henrico Co, hJames Throckmorton
HAMRICK, Samuel M, b18--, Shen Co, d1915, 1wEmma Richrd, 2w Emma O'Deal
HANBACK, --, b18--, Fauq Co, wMartha Ann Heflin
HANCE, Virginia, b18--, nrNewbern, Pula co, fHenry, hJabin Baldwin Allison
HANCOCK, Abram Booth, b10/29/1825, Fran Co, fBenjamin, (2)mElizabeth Booth, 1w Martha Elizabeth Walker
Amanda, b9/9/1834, Char Co, fClement, mMartha A Harvey
Ammon, b186-, Bedf Co, fJohn, mMartha Waller
Benjamin, b175-, Albe (now Fluv) Co, fJohn, mElizabeth Maddox
Benjamin, b6/16/1782, Fluv Co, fLewis, mCelia (Duncan) Oglesby, 1wFannie Holland, md1802, 2wElizabeth Booth, md10/30/1817
Benjamin F, b186-, Bedf Co, fJohn, mMartha Waller
Benjamin Peter, b6/19/1842, Fran Co, fWilliam Thomas, mAgnes Booth, wSarah Frances Hutchinson, md3/21/1865
Betty C, b186-, Fran Co, fCristopher Harrison, mVictoria Street
Catherine, bc1870, Fran Co, fChristopher Harrison, mVictoria Street
Charles Robert, bc1860, Fran Co?, fAbram Booth, mMartha Elizabeth Walker, wSally E Stone
Charles S, b186-, Fran Co,

HANCOCK (continued)
fChristopher Harrison, mVictoria Street
Charles Washington, b5/13/1853, Char Co, fClement, mMartha A Harvey, wEmma Cheesman LaGrande, md12/6/1871
Charlotte Virginia, b3/6/1855, Char Co, fClement, mMartha A Harvey
Christopher Harrison, b11/26/1834, Fran Co, d1893, fBenjamin, wVictoria Street, md1/22/1857
Christopher Harrison, bc1860, Fran Co?, fAbram Booth, mMartha Elizabeth Walker
Clement, b7/16/1810, Char Co, d1858, fMartin, wMartha A Harvey, md11/10/1831
Clement, b3/9/1838, Char Co, d186-, fClement, mMartha A Harvey
Douglas, b181-, Char Co, fMartin
Elizabeth Ann, bc1860, Fran Co?, fAbram Booth, mMartha Elizabeth Walker, hTazewell Price
Elizabeth Maddox, bc1760, Albe (now Fluv) Co, fJohn, mElizabeth Maddox, hWilliam James Mayo
Emma B, bc1860, Bedf Co, d1917, fJohn, mMartha Waller, hSamuel N Burroughs
Emma Minerva, b8/19/1850, Char Co, fClement, mMartha A Harvey
Fannie, bc1790, Fluv Co, fLewis, mCelia (Duncan) Oglesby, hPeter Holland
Field Allen, bc1785, Fluv Co, fLewis, mCelia (Duncan) Oglesby, wSusan Smith
Harris, b5/14/1867, nrCharlottesville, Albe Co, fRichard J, mThomasia Harris, wBelle Lyman Clay, md9/30/1907
Harvey, b181-, Char Co, fMartin
James H, b186-, Bedf Co, fJohn, mMartha Waller
Jane Francs, bc1820, Fran Co, fBenjamin, mElizabeth Booth, hFerdinand Price
John, b1735, Gooc Co, fBenjamin, wElizabeth Maddox, md10/16/1755

HANCOCK (continued)
John, b18--, Bedf Co, fJustus, mHarriet Walden, wMartha Waller
John Allen, bc1780, Fluv Co, fLewis, mCelia (Duncan) Oglesby, wSarah Ryan
John B, bc1860, Fran Co, fChristopher Harrison, mVictoria Street
John H, b186-, Bedf Co, fJohn, mMartha Waller
John Silas, b181-, Fran Co, fBenjamin, mElizabeth Booth, wJulia Morgan
John William, b6/17/1870, Hale's Ford, Fran Co, fBenjamin Peter, mSarah Frances Hutchinson, wMary Carr Leffler, md4/30/1898
Judith, b17--, Albe (now Fluv) Co, fJohn, mElizabeth Maddox, hValentine Mayo
Justus, bc1790, Bedf Co, fSamuel, mNancy Moon, wHarriet Walden
Lewis, b1757, fJohn, mElizabeth Maddox, wCelia (Duncan) Oglesby, md12/28/1778
Lucinda, b178-, Fluv Co, fLewis, mCelia (Duncan) Oglesby, hCharles Powell
Major, bc1760, Albe (now Fluv) Co, fJohn, mElizabeth Maddox
Martha, b11/30/1841, Char Co, fClement, mMartha A Harvey, hJames Jones
Martha Swan, b18--, Fluv Co?, hFrank M Parrish
Mary, bc1760, Albe (now Fluv) Co, fJohn, mElizabeth Maddox
Mary Elizabeth, b8/16/1836, Char Co, fClement, mMartha A Harvey
Mary Ella, b3/14/1858, Fran Co?, fAbram Booth, (1)mMartha Elizabeth Walker, hWilliam Leftwich Turner Hopkins, md 12/26/1882
Mary L, b181-, Fran Co, fBenjamin, mFannie Holland, hChristopher Booth
Mocca Pric, b9/30/1840, Char Co, fClement, mMartha A Harvey
Nancy, bc1760, Albe (now Fluv)

HANCOCK (continued)
Co, fJohn, mElizabeth Maddox
Nathan, b180-, Char Co, fMartin
Nathan Martin, b9/1/1832, Char Co, fClement, mMartha A Harvey
Peter Lewis, b181-, Fran Co, fBenjamin, mElizabeth Booth, wMary Anne English
Phoebe, b180-, Fran Co, fBenjamin, mFannie Holland, hRobert Smith
Raleigh Allen, b180-, Fran Ca, fBenjamin, mFannie Holland
Rhoda, bc1760, Albe (now Fluv) Co, fJohn, mElizabeth Maddox
Richard, b3/23/1864, Bedf Co, fJohn, mMartha Waller
Robert J, b186-, Bedf Co, fJohn, mMartha Waller
Sallie, b17--, hBenjamin Bolling
Samuel, b17--, Bedf Co, wNancy Moon, md2/9/1784
Samuel E, bc1860, Bedf Co, fJohn, mMartha Waller
Sarah Ann, b7/8/1845, Char Co, fClement, mMartha A Harvey
Sophia, bc1790, Fluv Co, fLewis, mCelia (Duncan) Oglesby, hWilliam Powell
Susannah, b176-, Albe (now Fluv) Co, fJohn, mElizabeth Maddox
Thomas, b181-, Char Co, fMartin
Thomas Harvey, b7/13/1847, Char Co, fClement, mMartha A Harvey
Walter Scott, b11/19/1869, Fran Co, fAbram Booth, (1)mMartha Elizabeth Walker, wAnn Spencer
William, b175-, Albe (now Fluv) Co, fJohn, mElizabeth Maddox
William A, b185-, Fran Co, fChirstopher Harrison, mVictoria Street
William D, b185-, Bedf Co, fJohn, mMartha Waller
William Thomas, b1814, Fran Co, fBenjamin, mFannie Holland, wAgnes Booth, md1838
HANES, Eugenia, b8/15/1857, Nels Co, hWilliam C White
HANEY, Jacob, bc1850, Shen Co, wClara Fisher
HANGER, David Washington, b3/7/1836, nrWaynesboro, Augu Co, fPeter, 1wSarah Margaret

HANGER (continued)
McCue, 2wSallie Agnes Crawford
Franklin McCue, b7/10/1862, nrFisherville, Augu Co, fDavid Washington, (1)mSarah Margaret McCue, wMartha McDowell
Mary E, bc1870, nrFisherville, Augu Co, fDavid Washington, (1)mSarah Margaret McCue, 2w of Samuel Moore Donald, md1901
Nannie C, bc1870, nrFisherville, Augu Co, fDavid Washington, (1)mSarah Margaret McCue, hA H McCue
Pattie, bc1870, nrFisherville, Augu Co, fDavid Washington, (1)mSarah Margaret McCue
HANKINS, James D, bc1829, Char Co, d1912, wNannie Lovelace
Polly Anna, b1831, Taze Co?, d1915, hJonas R Sparks
HANKLA, Henry, bc1830, Hali Co, 2wEmily Litz
James J, b1865, nrEmory, Wash Co, fHenry, (2)mEmily Litz, wCordelia Wassum
HANKLEY, Ella F, b1865, Marion, Smyt Co, d1913, hWilliam Maxey
HANKS, Creed, b18--, Carr Co?, wMinerva Moore
Flora L, bc1870, Carr Co?, fCreed L, mMinerva Moore, hStephen Ellis Wilkinson, md3/4/1896
HANNAH, --, b181-, Crai Co, fJoseph, mHarriet Allen, hSamuel Carpenter
Andrew, bc1830, Crai Co, fJoseph, mHarriet Allen
Belle C, bc1870, Rkhm Co?, 2w of George Bernard Keezell, md1903
Frank R, b185-, nrOriskany, Bote Co, fJoseph, mCornelia Neal
George, b182-, Crai Co, fJoseph, mHarriet Allen
George William, b185-, nrOriskany, Bote Co, fJoseph, mCornelia Neal
James, b182-, Crai Co, fJoseph, mHarriet Allen
John, bc1820, Crai Co, fJoseph, mHarriet Allen
John L, bc1850, nrOriskany, Bote Co, fJoseph, mCornelia

HANNAH (continued)
Neal
 Joseph, bc1827, Crai Co, d1883, fJoseph, mHarriet Allen, wCornelia Neal
 Joseph E, b11/2/1858, nrOriskany, Bote Co, fJoseph, mCornelia Neal, wAnnie McFarran, md1880
 Kate, b186-, Rkhm Co?, 1w of George Bernard Keezell, md 11/10/1886
 Mary A, b181-, Crai Co, fJoseph, mHarriet Allen, h-- Booth
 Matthew, b182-, Crai Co, fJoseph, mHarriet Allen
 Samuel C, bnrOriskany, Bote Co, fJoseph, mCornelia Neal
HANNAN, Catherine A, b18--, Maso Co?, hJames W Long
HANRAHAN, Virginia Frances, b1841, Portsmouth, Norf Co, d1920, fJames, mSarah Anne Meriken, hRichard Taylor
HANSBROUGH, --, b18--, Loud Co?, hJames Thomas Carr
 James Farish, b18--, Culp Co?, wAnna Ophelia Smith
 Mortimer French, b18--, Fauq Co, wElizabeth Payne
HANSFORD, Mary, b16--, Glou Co?, hThomas Robins
 Mary Buchanan, b18--, Staf Co?, hThomas Robins
HANSON, John, bc1860, Russ Co?, wEmma Gilmer
HARBOR, Judith Virginia, b9/13/1838, Buffalo Ridge, Patr Co, hWalter H Thomas
HARBOUR, Lucinda, b10/7/1826, Patr Co, hAlbert Gallatin Pedigo
 Sarah, b17--, Patr Co, hLewis Pedigo
HARCUM, Agnes B, b18--, Nhld Co?, hLittleton Cockrell
HARDAWAY, Horace, b4/15/1865, "Glenmore", Amel Coa, fJohn Segar, mSallie Gaines Steger
 Jacquelin Segar, b1820, nr Blackstone, Nott Co, fRichard Eggleston, mMary Rutherfoord, hThomas Freeman Epes
 Jennie Gaines, b185-, "Glenmore", Amel Co, fJohn Segar,

HARDAWAY (continued)
mSallie Gaines Steger
 John Segar, bc1820, nrBlackstone, Nott Co, fRichard Eggleston, mMary Rutherfoord, wSallie Gaines Steger, md1850
 John S, b185-, "Glenmore", Amel Co, fJohn Segar, mSallie Gaines Steger
 Kate Harrison, b186-, "Glenmore", Amel Co, fJohn Segar, mSallie Gaines Steger
 Lucy Stanley, b186-, "Glenmore", Amel Co, fJohn Segar, mSallie Gaines Steger
 Mary Rutherfoord, b1859, "Glenmore", Amel Co, d1899, fJohn Segar, mSallie Gaines Steger, hHodijah Meade
 Nannie Winston, b185-, "Glenmore", Amel Co, fJohn Segar, mSallie Gaines Steger
 Richard Eggleston, b17--, Nott Co, fDaniel, wMary Rutherfoord
 Richard Eggleston, b185-, "Glenmore", Amel Co, d1907, fJohn Segar, mSallie Gaines Steger
 Sallie Gaines, b186-, "Glenmore", Amel Co, fJohn Segar, mSallie Gaines Steger
 Thomas Rutherfoord, b186-, "Glenmore", Amel Co, fJohn Segar, mSallie Gaines Steger
 William Old, b186-, "Glenmore", Amel Co, fJohn Segar, mSallie Gaines Steger
HARDESTY, Charles R, b1845, Jeff Co, d1902, fWilliam G, (1)m Sarah Clevenger, wLydia R Bell
 James, bc1820, Jeff Co?, wSarah Jones
 Jennie, b184-, Jeff Co, fWilliam G, (1)mSarah Clevenger, h-- Baker
 Robert N, bc1870, Clar Co, fCharles R, mLydia Bell
 Thomas B, bc1870, Clar Co, fCharles R, mLydia Bell
 William G, b18--, Clar Co?, d1885, 1wSarah Clevenger, 2w-- Bane
HARDIMAN, Charls W, b1848, Buck Co, wEliza M Carter
HARDING, --, b183-, Nhld Co, fCyrus, m-- Martin, hW W

HARDING (continued)
Walker
Clarissa Rebecca, b1835, Nhld Co, d1898, fCyrus, m-- Martin, hSamuel Walker
Cyrus, bc1800, Nhld Co, w-- Martin
John, b18--, Nott Co?, wMartha Dickinson
Mollie, b18--, hTarlton H Hall
Robert Dickinson, b6/3/1863, Burkeville, Nott Co, fJohn, mMartha Dickinson, wJessie Huss, md10/17/1898
HARDY, Charles, Jr, b183-, Winchester, Fred Co, fCharles, Sr
Charles Betts, b1831, Lune Co, d1907, fHenry, mPemelia Betts, wJane Clarkson Barnes
Charles Henry "Harry", b10/18/1870, Winchester, Fred Co, fWilliam, mMary Elizabeth Garges, 1wLaura Wright, wFlorence Eaton
Charles M, b183-, Lune Co?, wSusan L Smith
Dabney, b18--, Lune Co, wMaria Worsham
Edward, b18--, Meck Co?, wPattie Reekes
Edward Carrington, b5/3/1865, Staunton, Augu Co, fRichard W, mMollie Virginia Bowles, wSallie M McCune, md9/18/1894
Emeline, b18--, Dinw Co?, hWilliam P Spain
Eva, b186-, Staunton, Augu Co, fRichard W, mMollie Virginia Bowles, hJohn M Hanger
Fannie, bc1830, Lune Co, fHenry, mPemelia Betts, hJohn H Jones
George O, b9/1855, Lune Co, wElla Lee Blanton
Gertrude, b18--, Richmond?, hRobert L Barnes
Hattie, bc1840, Winchester, Fred Co, fCharles, Sr, hCharles Grimm
Henry, bc1800, Lune co, wPemelia Betts
Henry, bc1830, Shen Co?, wAnnie A Triplett
Jane, bc1840, Winchester, Fred Co, fCharles, Sr, hJames Ginn
John, bc1830, Winchester, Fred

HARDY (continued)
Co, fCharles, Sr
John L, b186-, Staunton, Augu Co, fRichard W, mMollie Virginia Bowles
Lucy, bc1840, Winchester, Fred Co, fCharles, Sr, hHenry Kinzel
Mamie, b186-, Staunton, Augu Co, fRichard W, mMolie Virginia Bowles, hJ M Kelley
Martha, b1827, Camp Co, d1907, hJohn C Shields
Martha, bc1840, Winchester, Fred Co, fCharles, Sr
Mary, bc1840, Winchester, Fred Co, fCharles, Sr, h-- Brown
Mary A, b1805, Lune Co?, d1883, hBenjamin E Smith
Richard, b183-, Winchester, Fred Co, fCharles, Sr
Samuel, bc1830, Winchester, Fred Co, fCharles, Sr
William Baldwin, b186-, Staunton, Augu Co, fRichard W, mMollie Virginia Bowles
William H, b1840, Winchester, Fred Co, fCharles, Sr, mMary Elizabeth Garges
HARGRAVE, Alfred F, b18--, KiQu Co?, wBettie Wolwine
Musa D, b1857, Dinw Co, hThomas Gray Haddon, Sr
HARLESS, --, b18--, Crai Co?, hEnoch Lafon
HARLOW, --, b18--, Grbr Co, (father of Evelyn Harlow)
Benjamin F, b18--, Grbr Co?, wHenrietta C Renick
Evelyn, bc1870, Lewisburg, Grbr Co, hJoseph H Carpenter, Sr, md1897
HARMAN, --, b18--, Stephens City, Fred Co, 1w of Joseph E Funkhouser
Alexander L, b18--, Taze Co, fHenry B, mMary Ann Fudge
Asher W, bc1830, Augu Co, fLewis
Elizabeth, b18--, Taze Co, fHenry B, mMary Ann Fudge, hJ Henry Simmerman
Ellen, b18--, Augu Co, fWilliam Henry, mMargaret Susan Singleton Garber, hEdwin F Surber
Erastus French, b18--, Taze Co,

HARMAN (continued)
fHezekiah A, m-- Brown
Eugenia J, b18--, Taze Co,
fHenry B, mMary Ann Fudge,
hAbram B White
Harriett Katherine, b18--, Taze
Co, fHenry B, mMary Ann Fudge,
hAdulphus G Kiser
Henry B, b9/27/1811, nrTazewell, Taze Co, fHezekiah A,
m-- Brown, wMary Ann Fudge
Henry E, b1/8/1862, Taze Co,
fHenry B, mMary Ann Fudge,
wJennie St Clair, md6/14/1899
Hezekiah A, b17--, Taze Co,
fHenry, w-- Brown
Isabelle, b18--, Taze Co,
fHenry B, mMary Ann Fudge,
hShields S F Harman
John A, b182-, Augu Co, fLewis
Martha J, b18--, Taze Co,
fHenry B, mMary Ann Fudge,
hJohn A Davidson
Mary Jane, b18--, Shen Co?,
hJames A Downing
Michael G, b182-, Augu Co,
fLewis
Rosa, b18--, Taze Co, fHenry B,
mMary Ann Fudge, hGeorge W
Doak
Thomas L, b1830, Augu Co,
fLewis
Willam F, b10/20/1862, Taze Co,
fErastus French, wAmelia
Sayers
William Henry, b2/17/1828, Augu
Co, d1862, fLewis, wMargaret
Susan Singleton Garber
HARMANSON, Margaret, b1860, Acco
Co, d1922, fJames Robins, hEdward Fitchett Nottingham
HARMISON, Bion, b185-, Harr Co,
fCharles, mElizabeth Smith
Blanche, b1/14/1855, Harr Co,
fCharles, mElizabeth Smith,
hCharles Gustavus Hathaway,
md6/1/1881
Charles, b18--, Hamp Co?, wElizabeth Smith
Charles C, b185-, Harr Co,
fCharles, mElizabeth Smith
Frank L, b186-, Harr Co,
fCharles, mElizabeth Smith
George Edward, bc1860, Harr Co,
fCharles, mElizabeth Smith
Lucille, b185-, Harr Co,

HARMISON (continued)
fCharles, mElizabeth Smith,
hAmos B C Whitacre, md6/3/1885
Malcolm, b186-, Harr Co,
fCharles, mElizabeth Smith
Mattie W, b186-, Harr Co,
fCharles, mElizabeth Smith,
h-- Adams
HARMON, Isabel, b18--, Augu Co?,
1w of John Newton Opie, md10/
1866
Martha, b18--, d1894, hJohn W
Horner
HARNSBERGER, Alfred, b186-,
Elkton, Rkhm Co, fCharles B,
mKate Wolf
Amanda J, bc1830, Albe Co?,
fStephen, h-- Miller
Annie, b186-, Elkton, Rkhm Co,
fCharles B, mKate Wolf, h--
Firebaugh
Bessie, b185-, Augu Co, fRobert
S, mRebecca Ann Ingles, hLowry
Lewis
Catherine, bc1830, Albe Co?,
fStephen, hMiletus B Jarman
Charles B, b18--, Rkhm Co?,
wKate Wolf
Charles Edward, bc1870, Elkton,
Rkhm Co, fCharles B, mKate
Wolf
Conrad, b17--, Rkhm Co, fRobert
Edward M, b185-, Augu Co,
fRobert S, mRebecca Ann Ingles
Frances, b4/9/1848, Rkhm Co,
d1920, fHenry B, mElizabeth
Hopkins, hJohn W Blackburn,
md11/19/1872
Henry B, b18--, Rkhm Co?, wElizabeth Hopkins
John Baldwin, bc1860, Augu Co,
fRobert S, mRebecca Ann Ingles
John I, bc1860, Rkhm co?, 1w
Addie Kemper, 2wMatilda Graham
Kemper
Margaret, b17--, Rkhm Co, fConrad, hSamuel Leedy
Mary, bc1800, nrElkton, Rkhm
Co, hJoseph Cromer
Robert S, bc1821, nrPort Republic, Augu Cao, d1883, fStephen, wRebecca Ann Ingles
Stephen, b7/5/1852, Augu Co,
fRobert S, mRebecca Ann
Ingles, wKate Coffman Hopkins,
md5/16/1878

HARNSBERGER (continued)
Virginia, bc1870, Elkton, Rkhm Co, fCharles B, mKate Wolf, h-- Bishop
William Ingles, bc1850, Augu Co, fRobert S, mRebecca Ann Ingles
HARPER, --, bc1860, wHannah Elizabeth Snapp
Charles A, bc1840, Jeff Co?, wAlice Flanagan
Charles Ernest, b1/6/1864, Leesburg, Loud Co, fRobert, mMary Newton, wLouise Bouldin, md1890
Emily D, b1861, Alexandria, d1809, hJames W Morton
John J, bc1847, Hard Co, dc1890, fSamuel, wSarah M Bowman
Joseph, b18--, Hard Co, wPolly
Robert, b18--, Alexandria, wMary Newton
Sallie, b18--, Pitt Co?, 1w of Nathaniel J Terry
Samuel B, b2/15/1869, Hard Co, fJohn J, mSarah M Bowman, wBeulah B Newman, md1891
HARPINE, Abraham, bc1800, nrForestville, Shen Co, fJonathan, wSusanna Zirkle
Abraham II, bc1850, Forestville, Shen Co, fAbraham, mSusanna Zirkle
Catherine, b184-, Forestville, Shen Co, fAbraham, mSusanna Zirkle, hGeorge Bowman
Isaac, bc1800, nrForestville, Shen Co, fJonathan
Jacob, bc1800, nrForestville, Shen Co, fJonathan
Jonathan, b9/15/1842, Forestville, Shen Co, fAbraham, mSusanna Zirkle, wAnna Wine
Mary, bc1850, Forestville, Shen Co, fAbraham, mSusanna Zirkle, hWilliam Kipps
Paul, b184-, Forestville, Shen Co, fAbraham, mSusanna Zirkle
Phillip, bc1800, nrForestville, Shen Co, fJonathan
Rebecca, bc1800, nrForestville, Shen Co, fJonathan, hJohn Whitmire
Selone, b184-, Forestville, Shen Co, fAbraham, mSusanna

HARPINE (continued)
Zirkle
HARRELL, Annie, b18--, Fauq Co?, hAlexander Wallace Phillips
Carson, bc1870, Nans Co, fJohn Weatherly, mMedia Rountree
Cassandra, b18--, Pula Co?, hGeorge Pulliam
Charles O, bc1860, Nans Co, fJohn Weatherly, mMedia Rountree
Clara, b186-, Nans Co, fJohn Weatherly, mMedia Rountree
Edward, bc1870, Nans Co, fJohn Weatherly, mMedia Rountree
George, bc1870, Nans Co, fJohn Weatherly, mMedia Rountree
John B, b186-, Nans Co, fJohn Weatherly, mMedia Rountree
John Weatherly, b18--, Nans Co, fOliver, mMargaret Weatherly, wMedia Rountree
Luther H, b186-, Nans Co, fJohn Weatherly, mMedia Rountree
Nettie, b186-, Nans Co, fJohn Weatherly, mMedia Rountree
Oliver, bc1800, Nans Co, fJohn, wMargaret Weatherly
Robert Lee, b186-, Nans Co, fJohn Weatherly, mMedia Rountree
Sarah Anne, b18--, Henry Co, hWilliam M Schoolfield
S Walter, b18--, Nans Co, fJohn Weatherly, mMedia Rountree, wKate Nowell, md2/1888
William Henry, bc1860, Nans Co, fJohn Weathely, mMedia Rountree
HARRIS, --, b186-, Gooc Co?, hWilliam Jacquelin Boykin
Albert W, b2/22/1814, Nels Co, d1880,, fLee W, 1wMary Woolfolk, 2wEvelyn M (Harris) Scott
Alexander B, b18--, Gooc Co, fDavid Bullock, mLouise Knight
Belle Overton, b18--, fWilliam Anderson, mVirginia Gordon, hRobert A Buckner
Bertha, bc1870, Spot Co, 2w of Charles R Andrews
Caroline, b1870, Lewisburg, Grbr Co, hWilliam H Parrish, Jr
Caroline Elizabeth, b3/17/1824

HARRIS (continued)
nrHanover Junction, Hano Co, d1892, fWilliam Overton, mLucy Butler, hCamm S Garrett
Caroline Matilda, b10/4/1852, nrBlackstone, Nott Co, fWilliam Jordan, mMary Helen Epes, hJohn Fitzgerald
Caroline Overton, bc1870, Albe Co, fWilliam Henry, mHarriet Wash-ington Towles, hJohn Marion Hart, Jr
Catherine, b18--, Loui Co?, hJames D Porter
Cornelia, b18--, Nels Co?, hWilliam D Boaz
David B, b18--, Gooc Co, fDavid Bullock, mLouise Knight
David Bullock, bc1814, d1850, wLouise Knight
Delia, b17--, Powh Co, 2w of Blair Burwell
Edward M, b18--, Brun Co, wMittie Davis
Eva P, b185-, Nels Co, fAlbert W, (2)mEvelyn M (Harris) Scott, hB M Davidson
Eva V, b18--, Gooc Co, fDavid Bullock, mLouise Knight
Evelyn M, b18--, Albe Ca, fHenry Tate, 1hDaniel Scott, 2hAlbert W Harris
Fannie Ross, bc1860, Camp Co, d1898, fW E, 1w of Samuel Hutchings Price
Gertrude, b1853, Lune Co, hJohn B Jones
Gertrude, b1862, Meck Co, fWilliam, hJohn Blackwell Jones
Gertrude, b18--, fWilliam Anderson, mVirginia Gordon, hH Boatwright
Helen Epes, b1863, nrBlackstone, Nott Co, fWilliam Jordan, mMary Helen Epes
Henry, b18--, Loui Co, wSusan Hart
Henry Herbert, Sr, b12/17/1836, Loui Co, d1897, fHenry, mSusan Hart, wEmma Bibb, md11/26/1862
Henry Herbert, Jr, b186-, Loui Co?, fHenry Herbert, Sr, mEmma Bibb
Henry Tate, b1/21/1856, Nels Co, fAlbet W, (2)mEvelyn M (Harris) Scott, wLillie Hill,

HARRIS (continued)
md1884
James, bc1860, Spot Co?, wBartie Dickinson
James Madison, b1797, Powh Co, d1873, wObedience Amanda Harris
James Madison, b10/11/1855, nrBlackstone, Nott Co, d1899, fWilliam Jordan, mMary Helen Epes, wLunette Phillips
Janet M, bc1870, Albe Co?, fHenry Herbert, mEmma Bibb, hR E Gaines
Jennie Nelson, b18--, Rkbr Co, hFrancis Clemer
John N, b1851, NewK Co, wOctavia Dandridge Christian
Julia, b18--, Powh Co, fAlfred Turpin, hDaniel Dee Talley, Sr
Juliana Elizabeth, b18--, Gooc Co, fDavid Bullock, mLouise Knight, hAndrew Kean Leake
Lee W, b1790, Nels Co, d1836, fWilliam Lee
Lucy Wade, b18--, Henry Co?, hJoseph Henry Hundley
M H, bc1850, Camp Co?, wNolie Walthall
Martha Oliver, bc1858, nrBlackstone, Nott Co, fWilliam Jordan, mMary Helen Epes
Margaret W, b92/1858, Batesville, Albe co, fWilliam H, mMary Wayland, hSamuel M Page, md2/20/1884
Mattie Powell, b18--, fWilliam Anderson, mVirginia Gordon
Nathan, bc1800, wAnne Allan Anderson
Obedience Amanda, bc1800, Powh Co, hJames Madison Harris
Otelia V, bc1870, Meck Co, fWilliam W, hRobert Edward Yancey
Peter Epes, b1848, nrBlackstone, Nott Co, d1917, fWilliam Jordan, mMary Helen Epes
Richard, b18--, Gooc Co, fDavid Bullock, mLouise Knight
Richard Herbert, b184-, nr Blackstone, Nott Co, fWilliam Jordan, mMary Helen Epes
Sarah, b18--, Winchester, Fred Co, hCuthbert Conrad
Thomas, bc1860, Carr Co?, wEmma

HARRIS (continued)
Hylton Thomasia, b18--, nrCharlottesville, Albe Coa, hRichard J Hancock
W B, b18--, Taze Co?, wOctavia Williams
William A, b186-, Loui Co, fHenry Herbert, mEmma Bibb
William Anderson, b7/17/1827, Albe Co, fNathan, mAnne Allan Anderson, wVirginia Gordon
William H, b18--, Nels Co, wMary Wayland
William Henry, b18--, Albe Co?, wHarriet Washington Towles
William Jordan, b10/8/1819, Powh Co, fJames Madison, mObedience Amanda Harris, wMary Helen Epes
William Lee, b17--, Nels Co, fLee
William Trent, b18--, Buck Co, d1912, wMary Kerr Morehead, md1885
HARRISON, --, bc169-, Gooc Co, hThomas Randolph
--, bc1860, wLucy V Taliaferro
--, b17--, Ches Co?, fParson, h-- Armistead
--, b18--, nrPennington Gap, Lee Co, hJeremiah Skaggs
Ann, b18--, Cumb Co, hMoses A Spencer
Annie, b18--, Nott Co?, hFayette C Williams
Annie Laurie, bc1860, Clar Co?, fEdward R, mElizabeth Shumate, hRobert Hutchinson Davis
Asberry Shepard, b186-, Germantown, Fair Co, fShepard, mCatherine Townsend
Benjamin, b1645, Surr Co, d1713, fBenjamin, mMary Sidway
Benjamin, b1673, Surr Co, d1730, fBenjamin, wElizabeth Burwell
Benjamin, b1693, Berkeley, ChCi Co, d1745, fBenjamin, mElizabeth Burwell, wAnn Carter
Benjamin, b172-, Cumb Co, fBenjamin, mAnn Carter
Bessie, bc1870, Berk Co, hEdgar Yager Hudson, md6/6/1893
Bessie H, bc1860, Clar Co?, fEdward R, mElizabeth Shumate,

HARRISON (continued)
hS S Simpson
Betty, bc1830, Clifton, Cumb Co, fPeyton, mJane Cary Carr, hJohn Atkinson
Carrie Stuart, b185-, Germantown, Fair Co, fShepard, mCatherine Townsend, hCharles Chapin
Carter Henry, b1726, Cumb Co, fBenjamin, mAnn Carter, wSusanna Randolph
Dabney Carr, Sr, b1829, Clifton, Cumb Co, d1862, fPeyton, mJane Cary Carr, wSallie Pendleton Buchanan
Dabney Carr, Jr, b10/15/1858, Martinsburg, Berk Co, fDabney Carr, Sr, mSallie Pendleton Buchanan, wEllen Robinson Riley, md12/1/ 1899
Dan L, b1850, 2h of Minnie Byrd
Edward Bailey, bc1860, Clar Co?, fEdward R, mElizabeth Shumate
Edward R, bc1835, Warr Co, wElizabeth Shumate
Elizabeth, b17--, 2w of Lewis Burwell
George, b18--, Madi Co?, w-- Fouche
George F, b11/15/1850, Germantown, Fair Co, fShepard, mCatherine Townsend, wIda B Ayre, md9/1/1880
George Hollingsworth, b185-, Rkhm Co, wJosephine Moore
Hannah, b185-, Germantown, Fair Co, fShepard, mCatherine Townsend, hAlbert Wren
Henry, b18--, Augu Co, wJane St Clair Cochran
Henry Tucker, b183-, Clifton, Cumb Co, fPeyton, mJane Cary Carr
James, b185-, Germantown, Fair Co, fShepard, mCatherine Townsend
Jane, b17--, Rkhm Co?, hDaniel Smith
Jane, b18--, nrHyacinth, Nhld Co, hCarson Rowe
Jane Cary, bc1795, "Elk Hill", Cumb Co, fRandolph, hWilliam Fitzhugh Randolph, md9/1/1817
John S, bc1860, KiQu Co?,

HARRISON (continued)
wJosephine Pollard
Juliet, b18--, KiQu Co, hVolney Walker
Lalla B, bc1870, Leesburg, Loud Co, fPowell, mJanet Fauntleroy, 2w of Elijah B White, md1/21/1900
Lucy, bc1800, Lynchburg, Camp Co, fSamuel Jordan, hLorenzo Norvell
Lucy, b1848, "The Wigwam", Amel Co, d1920, fWilliam H, hCharles James Faulkner, Sr
Lucy, b186-, Germantown, Fair Co, fShepard, mCatherine Townsend, hWinfield Dye
Lucy Somerville, b186--, Clar Co, fEdward R, mElizabeth Shumate
Lula, bc1860, Germantown, Fair Co, fShepard, mCatherine Townsend, hWilliam Burns
Mamie C, b18--, Madi Co?, fGeorge, m-- Fouche, hRobert W Sparks
Mary, b17--, Surr Co, fNathaniel, 2w of James Gordon, md11/12/1748
Mary, b18--, Fred Co, hFrancis Edward Conrad
Mary, b18--, PrGe Co, hTheodorick Bland
Mary, bc1830, Clifton, Cumb Co, fPeyton, mJane Cary Carr, hRobert Hunter
Mary Stuart, b18--, fGesner, hFrancis Smith
Nannie, b18--, "Elk Hill", Cumb Co, fRandolph, hJohn Bolling Garrett
Peyton, b1800, Clifton, Cumb Co, d1887, fRandolph, mMary Randolph, wJane Cary Carr
Peyton, b18--, Clifton, Cumb Co, d186-, fPeyton, mJane Cary Carr
Powell, b18--, Loud Co?, wJanet Fauntleroy
Randolph, b1769, Clifton, Cumb Co, fCarter Henry, mSusanna Randolph, wMary Randolph
Randolph, b182-, Clifton, Cumb Co, d186-, fPeyton, mJane Cary Carr
Randolph, b18--, Camp Co,

HARRISON (continued)
wJulia Meem
Randolph, b1/25/1858, Augu Co, fHenry, mJane St Clair Cochran, wJulia Halsey Macon
Robert Lee, b185-, Germantown, Fair Co, fShepard, mCatherine Townsend
Shepard, b1826, Germantown, Fair Co, d1878, fThomas, mHannah Shepard, wCatherine Townsend
Thomas, b1793, Dumfries, PrWi Co, wHannah Shepard
Virginia, b18--, Petersburg, Dinw Co, fWilliam, hFabian Armistead
Virginia, bc1830, Clifton, Cumb Co, fPeyton, mJane Cary Carr, hWilliam Hoge
William Wirt, b182-, Clifton, Cumb Co, fPeyton, mJane Cary Carr
HARSHBARGER, Anna, bc1831, Rkhm Co, fHenry, hJoel Garber
HART, Andrew DeJarnette, Sr, b8/1858, Sunny Bank Farm, nrNorth Garden, Albe Co, fThomas Roderick Dew, mElizabeth Hart, wVirginia Taylor Byrd
Arthur, b18--, Fauq Co, fRobert, mCatheirne R --, wEvelyn Goodwin
Carrie, bc1870, Spot Co, fWilliam Goodwin, mAgnes Sanford, hC N Sutherland
Elizabeth, b18--, Sunny Bank Farm, nrNorth Garden, Albe Co, fWilliam, mElizabeth DeJarnette, hThomas Roderick Dew
Ferdinand, b184-, Fauq Co, fArthur, mEvelyn Goodwin
John, b18--, Fauq Co, fRobert, mCatherine R --
John B, bc1800, Scottsville, Albe Co, fAndrew, mElizabeth Overton Bickley, wJulia Ann Stuart Lyle
John Marion, Sr, b18--, Scottsville, Albe Co, fJohn B, mJulia Ann Stuart Lyle, wFannie Sanford Smith
John Marion, Jr, b1/2/1867, PrEd Co, fJohn Marion, Sr, mFannie Sanford Smith, wCaro-

HART (continued)
line Overton Harris
Robert, b12/18/1785, Fauq Co,
fArthur, wCatherine R --
Robert, b18--, Fauq Co,
fRobert, mCatherine R --
Sophia, b18--, North Garden,
Albe Co, hA P Fox
Susan, b18--, Loui Co, hHenry
Harris
William, bc1800, Sunny Bank
Farm, nrNorth Garden, Albe Co,
fAndrew, (1)mElizabeth Bickley, wElizabeth DeJarnette
William Goodwin, b1846, Fauq
Co, fArthur, mEvelyn Goodwin,
wAgnes Sanford
HARTLEY, Benjamin, b18--, Warr
Co?, wAnnie Threnary
William H, b18--, Wyth Co?,
wMelinda Hill
HARTMAN, John H, b18--, Dinw
Co?, wMilly Pryor Hill
Sarah, b18--, Rkhm Co, d1900,
fDavid, mElizabeth Burkholder,
hAbram Blosser Wenger
HARTSOCK, Lou E, b18--, Scot
Co?, hJohn G Nickels
Martha, b5/1851, Castlewood,
Russ Co, hRemley A Fuller
HARTSOOK, Annie, b1846, Rkbr Co,
hJames Frank Lotts
HARVEY, Adsonia, bc1860, Nels
Co?, hGeorge W Fortune, Jr
Allie H, bc1870, nrPhenix, Char
Co, fHenry W, mSusie R Raine,
hJohn Coleman Priddy,
md9/4/1906
Angie, b1853, Mont Co, hMcClanahan Ingles
Anna Rebecca, b18--, Lexington,
Rkbr Co, d1901, hWilliam Meek
McElwee, md4/1/1851
Betsey, b1812, West Co, d1885,
hWilliam Hutt
C M, b185-, Nels Co, fJohn R,
mVirginia Sanders
Columbus Feton, b10/4/1861,
Marysville, Camp Co, fChristopher Columbus, mElvira G
Daniel
Christopher Columbus, bc1813,
Camp Co, d1886, fJesse, wElvira G Daniel
Edwin Johnson, Sr, b10/5/1864,
Pitt Co, fElisha B, mSusan

HARVEY (continued)
Bullington, wHattie Rangeley,
md1897
Elisha B, b18--, Pitt Co?,
wSusan Bullington
Henry W, b18--, Char Co?,
wSusie R Raine
James T, b12/24/1859, Nels Co,
fJohn R, mVirginia Sanders,
wEugenia Massie, md10/23/1881
John R, b18--, Nels Co, wVirginia Sanders
John W, bc1860, West Co?, wMary
Ann Goodridge
L J, b185-, Nels Co, fJohn R,
mVirginia Sanders
Lelia May, bc1870, Nels Co?, hJ
Crawford Clarkson, md1889
M L, bc1840, Appo Co?, w--
Atwood
Martha A, b10/16/1816, Char Co,
hClem Hancock
Nancy, b17--, Bedf Co?, hThomas
Newell
R L, b185-, Nels Co, fJohn R,
mVirginia Sanders
Sallie A, bc1860, Marysville,
Camp Co, fChristopher Columbus, mElvira G Daniel, hJohn
Cousel
Sarah E, b1835, Nels Co, d1902,
hCharles H Stevens, md1859
W H, bc1860, Marysville, Camp
Co, fChristopher Columbus,
mElvira G Daniel
HARVIE, Courtney Blair, b2/1846,
Dykeland, Amel Co, 1917,
hGeorge Keith Taylor, Sr
James B, b18--, Richmond?,
wMary L Michaux
HARWOOD, Joseph Walter, b18--,
"Weyonoke", ChCi Co, d186-,
wSusan Beverly Christian
Joseph Walter, Jr, b9/5/1860-1,
Ballardsville, ChCi Co,
fJoseph Walter, Sr, mSusan
Beverly Christian, wSallie
Perkins
Martha Catherine, b6/6/1829,
Newington, KiQu Co, 2w of William Beverly Bird
HASH, Allen C, b18--, Gray Co?,
wSarah J Perkins
Drucie, b18--, Gray Co?,
hGreenberry B Halsey
Mitchell M, bc1860, Gray Co?,

HASH (continued)
  1h of Victoria Greear
HASKINS, Abner, b17--, Powh Co, fEdmund
  Jane, b17--, fThomas, mAnn Nash, hThomas Osborne Scott
  John H, b18--, wBettie Seay
  Lucy F, b18--, Meck Co, fC C, hJohn James Flippen, md1868
  Mary Page, bc1800, fAbner, hJohn Meador
  Thomas, b17--, wAnn Nash
HASLETT, Charles, bc1850, Shen Co?, wAlice W Walton
HATCH, John H, Sr, b18--, PrGe Co, d1904, wMartha Temple
  John H, Jr, b1867, PrGe Co, fJohn H, Sr, mMartha Temple, wHettie Neblett
HATCHER, Anna, b18--, hSamuel Rector
  Charlotte Virginia, b18--, 3w of Daniel Hobson Browne, md2/18/1874
  Elizabeth, b17--, 1w of Blair Burwell
  E Thomas, b1/24/1862, Bermuda District, Ches Co, fWilliam E, mMartha A Friend, wBessie Evelyn Hall, md1890
  Edward, b17--, Ches Co, fSamuel, mMary Walthal, 1wAnn Cheatham, 2wLucy Bass
  Eliza Porter, b17--, Gooc Co?, hJosiah Leake, Jr
  John H, b18--, Cumb Co?, wLucy G --
  Margaret, b18--, Ches Co, fWilliam, mSarah C Gregory
  Milton, b18--, wLouisa Douglas
  Richard G, b18--, Ches Co, fWilliam, mSarah C Gregory
  Sally Ann, b18--, 1w of Daniel Hobson Browne, md10/16/1851
  Samuel, b17--, Ches Co, wMary Walthal
  Samuel Clairborne, b5/24/1869, Cumb Co, fJohn H, mLucy G --, wMary L Kern, md1895
  Sarah, b16--, Henrico Co?, fWilliam, h-- Tanner
  Sarah Ann, b18--, fEpps, hWilliam Green Hall
  Sarah E, b5/1839, Rkbr Co, fMilton, mLouisa Douglas, hWilliam M Painter

HATCHER (continued)
  Thomas C, b18--, Ches Co, fWilliam, mSarah C Gregory
  William, bc1800, Ches Co, fEdward, mLucy Bass, wSarah C Gregory
  William E, b7/18/1828, nrRichmond, fWilliam, mSarah C Gregory
HATCHETT, Ann Eliza, b1823, Lune Co, hHenry Stokes, Sr
  Marion Truly, b12/19/1862, Lune Co, hJ Garland Blackwell
  Petronella L, b1817, Lune Co, 2w of George N Seay
HATFIELD, Alexander, b18--, Wyom Co?, wVirginia Lester
HATHAWAY, Anna Elizabeth, b5/1/1846, Fauq Co, fJames H, (2)mMary Ann Adams, hFountain Beatty, md1/4/1865
  Charles Gustavus, b2/6/1850, Fauq Co, fJames H, (2)mMary Ann Adams, wBlanche Harmison
  Fannie Octavia, b9/19/1849, White Stone, Lanc Co, d1920, hElliott W Lawson
  Henry Clay, bc1840, Fauq Co, fJames H, (1)mSarah Franks Weeks
  Henry Lawson, b17--, Fauq Co, w-- Sullivan
  James Adams, b4/5/1848, Fauq Co, fJames H, (2)mMary Ann Adams, wLouise Amelia Underhill, md1/26/1881
  James H, b4/7/1812, Fauq Co, d1892, fHenry Lawson, m-- Sullivan, 1wSarah Frances Weeks, md11/22/1838, 2wMary Ann Adams, 3wElizabeth Adams
  Lucullus, b18--, White Stone, Lanc Co, wMary Eleanor Spriggs
  Mary V, b8/18/1852, Fauq C, fJames H, (2)mMary Ann Adams, hCharles C Fant
  Sarah W, b181-, Fauq Co, fHenry Lawson, m-- Sullivan, hJoseph Smith
HATTON, William H, b9/15/1860, Melfa, Acco Co, fBenjamin C, mEuphemia Martin
HAUCK, Andrew S, bc1860, wGertrude Ann Stine
HAUGH, William, bc1820, Rkhm Co?, wHannah Flory

HAUN, Sarah, b18--, Mari Co?, hHenry Fogg
Sarah, bc1820, Shen Co?, fJacob, 1w of Abraham Rhodes
HAWES, Katherine "Kitty", bc1800, Caro Co, hJohn J Coleman
Mildred, b18--, KiWi Co, fWalker, hWilliam S B Buckner
Richard, b2/6/1797, Caro Co
HAWKINS, Abner W, b18--, Pitt Co?, d186-, wMolly J --
Anne Elizabeth, b18--, Oran Co, fThomas R, hJames Madison Cooke
Charles W, b18--, nrSlate Mills, Rapp Co, fMordecai John Abner, Sr, b6/22/1887, Pitt Co?, fAbner W, mMolly J --, wAnna H --, md11/22/1887
Margaret, b18--, Rkhm Co?, hHenry Hammer, Jr
Muscoe L, b9/9/1837, nrSlate Mills, Rapp Co, fMordecai, wMary Elizabeth Bushong
HAWSE, Enos T, bc1870, Edom, Rkhm Co, fJasper, mMary Beery
Jacob L, b186-, Edom, Rkhm Co, fJasper, mMary Beery
Jasper, b1836, Hard Co, d1906, wMary Beery
John J, b9/28/1866, Edom, Rkhm Co, fJasper, mMary Beery, wDora B Swank, md10/15/1887
Lillie D, bc1870, Edom, Rkhm Co, fJasper, mMary Beery, hWill Atkinson
Maggie L, b186-, Edom, Rkhm Co, fJasper, mMary Beery, hW F Myers
HAWTHORNE, Martha Jane, b1839, Wash Co, d1914, hJohn Wesley Edmondson
Susanna, b18--, Lune Co, hGeorge Inge
HAXALL, Clara, b18--, hThomas B Grundy
HAY, Sarah Henderson, bc1830, Acco Co, hWilliam H Stant
HAYCOCK, Esther Ann, b18--, Warr Co?, hJoshua McKay
HAYDEN, --, bc1780, Hard Co?, wScotia Warden
Mary, b18--, Rich Co?, hWilliam G Douglas
HAYDON, Mary Elizabeth, b1852,

HAYDON (continued)
Irvington, Lanc Co, hJames W Rowe
HAYES, George W, b18--, Smyt Co?, wNiciti Huffard
James Monroe, Sr, b1847, Richmond, fElias Warner, 1wLucy Priddy, 2wAddie Messler
Mary J, bc1870, Smyt Co?, fGeorge W, mNiciti Huffard, hFulton Kegley, md2/17/1898
HAYNE, Richard C, b186-, Math Co?, wBirdie M Gray
HAYNES, Belle M, b18--, Lynchburg, Camp Co, fPowhatan, hWilliam Bruce Mongtomery, Sr
Elizabeth, b17--, Bedf Co, fWilliam, hWilliam Leftwich
Elizabeth, b18--, Fran Co, d1889, hJohn Wesley Johnson, mdc1837
Francis Reed, b9/30/1834, Glou Co, fRichard, m-- Jackson, wElizabeth Catherine Hodges
Granville D, b1819, Alle Co, d1881, hJohn T Deaton
James Warren Dorsey, Sr, b2/15/1868, Cobbs Creek, Math Co, fFrancis Reed, mElizabeth Catherine Hodges, wIrene Fitchett, md12/28/1891
Leah, b186-, Cobbs Creek, Math Co, fFrancis Reed, mElizabeth Catherine Hodges, hCharles C Soles
Richard, b1806, Glou Co, d1879, w-- Jackson
Susie Catherine, b186-, Cobbs Creek, fFrancis Reed, mElizabeth Catherine Hodges, hVivian V Shipley
Theresa Clementine, b186-, Cobbs Creek, fFrancis Reed, mElizabeth Catherine Hodges, hLaFayette M Travers
William, b17--, Alle Co?, fJoseph
William Daniel, b18--, Fran Ca, fJohn O W, wFrances Keen James
HAYNEY, Thaddeus, bc1850, Warr Co?, wElton Rust
HAYNIE, Flora Alice, b1850, Reedville, Nhld Co, hThomas W Jett
Margaret, b18--, Nhld Co, 1w of Fleming P Welch

HAYTOR, Elizabeth, b17--, Taze Co, 1w of Patrick Campbell Buchanan, Sr
HAYWARD, C C, b18--, Roan Co?, wMary Cocke
HEAD, Mary Elizabeth, b18--, hCarter R Bishop
Mary F, b18--, Albe Co?, hRichard F Ward
Melinda, b18--, Scot Co?, hIsaac Peters
Thomas, b18--, Rkhm Co?, wMagdalena Wenger
HEADLEE, Lydia, b18--, hB F Strosnider
HEADLEY, --, b18--, Fred Co, w-- Strickler
Ellen, bc1856, Fred Co?, hCharles W Snapp
Fannie V, b18--, Shen Co, hJohn H Maphis
J W, bc1860, Fred Co?, wRosa Gardner
William A, bc1846, Shen Co, d1879, m-- Strickler, wVirginia C Painter
HEADSPETH, John, b18--, Hali Co?, wAnnie Beazley
HEALY, --, b18--, KiQu Co?, 2w of Thomas Beverly Evans
HEARN, Daniel S, b18--, Russ Co?, wCleo Miles
HEATER, Charles Wunder, b3/17/1853, nrMiddletown, Fred Co, fSolomon, mCaroline H Wunder, wCora A Henkel, md1874
Henry W, b1843, nrMiddletown, Fred Co, d1865, fSolomon, mCaroline H Wunder
John Philip, b3/22/1838, nrMiddletown, Fred Co, d1864, fSolomon, mCaroline H Wunder
Philip, b7/13/1773, Loud Co, d1836, wElizabeth Crumbaker
Solomon, b9/8/1808, Loud Co, d1872, fPhilip, mElizabeth Crumbaker, wCaroline H Wunder
HEATH, Anna, b18--, hDaniel W Lassiter
Harriet, b18--, Gooc Co?, h-- Selden
Thomas S, b9/24/1849, Scottsville, Albe Co, wMary Susan Cocke
HEATWOLE, --, bc1800, Rkhm Co, hDaniel Suter

HEATWOLE (continued)
Elizabeth, b18--, Spring Creek, Rkhm Co, fShem, m-- Shank, h-- Carrico
Gabriel, b18--, Spring Creek, Rkhm Co, fShem, m-- Shank, wEliza Swartz
Henry, b18--, Spring Creek, Rkhm Co, fShem, m-- Shank
Jacob, b18--, Spring Creek, Rkhm Co, fShem, m-- Shank
John Samuel, b8/11/1866, Ashy District, Rkhm Co, fGabriel, mEliza Swartz, 1wSallie Long, 2wMaggie Knott
Martha, b18--, Spring Creek, Rkhm Co, fShem, m-- Shank, h-- Weaver
Martin, b18--, Spring Creek, Rkhm Co, fShem, m-- Shank
Rebecca, b18--, Spring Creek, Rkhm Co, fShem, m-- Shank, hMartin Miller
Shem, bc1800, Rkhm Co, w- Shank
Shem, b18--, Spring Creek, Rkhm Co, fShem, m-- Shank
HECK, Charles V, b18--, Camp Co?, wMollie Ballard
HECKERT, Alice E, b1857, Lewi Co, hPhilip C Urbach
HEDGMAN, Lucinda, b1838, Rose Hill, Staf Co, m-- Mitchell, hSnowden C Hall
HEFLIN, Agnes, bc1840, Fauq Co, fLawson, mAnn Eliza Heflin, h-- Fox
Ann Eliza, b18--, Fauq Co, fWilliam, hLawson Heflin
Jack, bc1840, Fauq Co, fLawson, mAnn Eliza Heflin
James, bc1840, Fauq Co, fLawson, mAnn Eliza Heflin
John, bc1840, Fauq Co, fLawson, mAnn Eliza Heflin
Landonia, bc1840, Fauq Co, fLawson, mAnn Eliza Heflin, h-- Putnam
Lawson, bc1800, Fauq co, wAnn Eliza Heflin
Lawson, b183-, Fauq Co, fLawson, mAnn Eliza Heflin
Louisa, bc1840, Fauq Ca, fLawson, mAnn Eliza Heflin, h-- Kern
Martha Ann, bc1840, Fauq Co, fLawson, mAnn Eliza Heflin,

HEFLIN (continued)
h-- Hanback
Morgan, bc1840, Fauq Co, fLawson, mAnn Eliza Heflin
Robert, b183-, Fauq Co, fLawson, mAnn Eliza Heflin
Susan Elizabeth, b6/7/1837, Fauq Co, fLawson, mAnn Eliza Heflin, hAnton Schwab, md1/20/1858
William N, bc1860, KiGe Co?, w-- Billingsley
HEIM, Ailie Ann, b18--, Bedf Co?, hOwen Crumpacker
HELLER, Adolph, b18--, Shen Co?, wElla Lichleiter
Elizabeth Miller, bc1870, Woodstock, Shen Co, fAdolph, mElla Lichleiter, hWilliam Crank Ford
HELMINTOLLER, Jordan, b1842, Alle Co, dc1915, fPeter, mPolly Johnson, wRebecca Jane Hook
Mariah W, b1840, Alle Co?, fPeter, hCharles Richardson
Matthison, bc1830, Alle Co, fPeter, mPolly Johnson
Peter, b182-, Alle Co, Peter, mPolly Johnson
Peter C, b9/1/1869, Alle Co, fJordan, mRebecca Jane Hook, wGeorgia Snyder, md1899
William, bc1830, Alle Co, fPeter, mPolly Johnson
William b, b186-, Alle Co, fPeter, mRebecca Jane Hook
HELM, Malinda H, bc1833, Floy Co, d1915, hRoley M Simmons, mdc1857
HELMS, Elizabeth, b18--, Floy Co, fJohn, mSally Livesey, hWilliam B Shelor
John, b17--, Fran Co, wSally Livesey
HELSLEY, G P, bc1850, Shen Co?, wJulia Sine
Jacob, b17--, Shen Co?, wMary Heltzel
Joshua, b18--, Shen Co, wMiranda Dellinger
Mary Elizabeth, b18--, Shen Co?, fJacob, mMary Heltzel, hBenjamin Baker
HELTZEL, Mary, bc1800, Shen Co, hJacob Helsley

HENDERSON, --, bc1750, Bedf Co?, wLockey Trigg
Ann, b18--, Cumb Co, fRobert, hWilliam Allen Perkins
Betsy, bc1800, Augu Co?, hJames Bell
Elizabeth, b18--, Oran Co, hJoseph D Reynolds
Florence, b1851, Lynchburg, Camp Co, hWyndam B Robertson
Hiram, bc1840, Smyt Co?, wPolly Sanders
Jane, bc1800, Gile Co?, hAndrew Johnston
Nannie, b184-, Bote Co, d184-, 1w of A P McHenry
Rachel, b18--, Mont Co, fWilliam F, 1w of William D Meeks, md1881
HENDRICK, Louise, b18--, Chesterfield, Buck Co, hDrury W Woodson
HENDRICKS, Rachel, b18--, Russ Co?, hJerry A McFaddin
HENDRY, --, bc1850, Shen Co?, wAnnie W Walton
HENING, Benjamin Cabell, b18--, Powh Co, fWilliam H, Sr, (2)m Pocahontas Megginson
James Garland, bc1870, Carlisle Farm, Jefferson, Powh Co, fWilliam H, (3)mOlivia Henderson Campbell
William H, Sr, b18--, Spring Garden Farm, Powh Co, fWilliam, 1wJulia Davies, 2wPocahontas Megginson, 3wOlivia Henderson Campbell
William Henry, Jr, b186-, Carlisle Farm, Jefferson, Powh Co, fWilliam H, Sr, (3)Olivia Henderson Campbell
HENKEL, Abram Miller, b10/13/1843, Staunton, Augu Co, fSamuel Godfrey, mSusan Koiner, wVirginia Moore
Ambrose, bc1778, Shen Co, fPaul, mElizabeth Negley
Ambrose L, b185-, New Market, Shen Co, d1913, fSocrates, mEleonora Caroline Henkel
Annie L, bc1850, Shen Co, fSamuel Godfrey, mSusan Koiner, h-- Crickenberger
C C, bc1850, Shen Co, fSamuel Godfrey, mSusan Koiner

HENKEL (continued)
Cora A, b6/13/1855, Shen Co, fSamuel Godfrey, mSusan Koiner, hCharles Wunder Heater, md1874
David, bc1796, Shen Co, d1831, fPaul, mElizabeth Negley, wCatherine Hoyle
Eleonora Caroline, b18--, Shen Co, d1890, fAmbrose, hSocrates Henkel
Eli S, bc1860, Rkhm Co?, wSusan Good
Elon Osiander, b5/5/1855, New Market, Shen Co, fSocrates, mEleonora Caroline Henkel, wJulia K Henkel, md11/8/1907
Haller Hippocrates, b4/5/1852, New Market, Shen Co, fSamuel Godfrey, mSusan Koiner, wOlive Turney
Henrietta, b18--, Shen Co, f1886, fElias, hJacob Stirewalt, md1/1833
Ida M, bc1850, Shen Co, fSamuel Godfrey, mSusan Koiner
Julia, bc1838, Shen Co, fSamuel Godfrey, mSusan Koiner, hAbram Schultz Miller
Julia K, bc1870, New Market, Shen Co, fSolon P C, mMaria Miller, hElon Osiander Henkel, md11/8/ 1907
Nancy, b18--, Rkhm Co?, hJohn Wise Sherman
Otto H, bc1860, New Market, Shen Co, fSocrates, mEleonora Caroline Henkel
Rebecca, bc1850, Shen Co, fSamuel Godfrey, mSusan Koiner, h-- Koiner
Samuel Godfrey, b2/12/1807, New Market, Shen Co, fSolomon, mRebecca Miller, wSusan Koiner
Solomon, b11/10/1777, Shen Co, fPaul, mElizabeth Negley, wRebecca Miller
Solon P C, bc1830, Shen Co, wMaria Miller
Sue E, bc1850, Shen Co, fSamuel Godfrey, mSusan Koiner, h-- Moyers
HENLEY, Fannie E, b18--, fJoseph, mBettie Walker, hSamuel P Waddill, md5/16/1882
John Leonard, b7/4/1864, nrTap-

HENLEY (continued)
pahannock, Esse Co, fThomas M, mMartha A Armstrong, 1wNannie F Jeffries, md11/27/1888, 2wary Josephine DeShields, md10/1/1908
Joseph, b18--, wBettie Walker
Leonard, b1807, d1867, wMary Susan Perkins
Lucy Ann, b18--, Williamsburg, JaCi Co, hLucius Falkland Cary
Martha Josephine, b186-, nrTappahannock, Esse Co, fThomas, mMartha A Armstrong
Mary M, b186-, nrTappahannock, Esse Co, fThomas M, mMartha A Armstrong
Mary S, b1848, KiQu Co, fS S, mRobinette Pendleton, hJ Alexander Carter
Norvell Lightfoot, b5/10/1869, JaCi Co, d1923, fRichardson Leonard, mIda Dudley Spencer, wEdmonia Pendleton Turner, md6/16/1897
Richardson Leonard, b1836, Hill Pleasant, JaCi Co, d1897, wIda Dudley Spencer
Robert Y, b186-, nrTappahannock, Esse Co, fThomas M, mMartha A Armstrong
S S, b18--, KiQu Co, wRobinette Pendleton
Sallie S, bc1870, nrTappahannock, Esse Co, fThomas M, mMartha A Armstrong
Thomas A, b186-, nrTappahannock, Esse Co, fThomas M, mMartha A Armstrong
Thomas L, b186-, KiQu Co?, wMay Hoskins
Thomas M, b11/2/1834, Esse Co, fThomas M, mMary Susan Perkins, wMartha A Armstrong
HENRITZE, Samuel B, b18--, Smyt Co, d1899, fWilliam, mMartha --, wEmma Clinton Parrish
William, b18--, Smyt Co?, d186- wMartha --
HENRY, Alfred, b1797, Warr Co, d1855, fNelson, wCaroline Ashby
Betty, bc1840, Howardsville, Warr Co, fAlfred, mCaroline Ashby, hGeorge W Hooper
Edward Winston, b17--, fPatrick

HENRY (continued)
Franklin, bc1840, Howardsville, Warr Co, fAlfred, mCaroline Ashby
George Robert, b2/10/1838, Howardsville, Warr Co, d1907, fAlfred, mCaroline Ashby, wLawson America Huff, md6/18/1867
James, b183-, Howardsville, Warr Co, fAlfred, mCaroline Ashby
Lucy, b17--, hValentine Wood
Martha, b18--, Camp Co?, hRobert Ward
Mary Jane, b183-, Howardsville, Warr Co, fAlfred, mCaroline Ashby, hJohn Myers
Robert Montague, bc1870, Winchester, Fred Co, fGeorge Robert, mLawson America Huff, wStella Marker
Sarah, b18--, Ches Co?, fEdward Winston, hWilliam Harrison Armistead, md4/23/1844
Walter, b186-, Winchester, Fred Co, fGeorge Robert, mLawson America Huff
William, b183-, Howardsville, Warr Co, fAlfred, mCaroline Ashby
HENSHAW, Will, bc1850, Clar Co?, wBelle Glaize
HENSON, Benjamin alben, b18--, nrPoindexter, Loui Co, fBenjamin III, mMary Puryear Wade
Benjamin II, b17--, Henrico Co, fSamuel, m-- ( ) Green
Benjamin III, b1813, nrPoindexter, Loui Co, fClifton, mElizabeth Donivant, wMary Puryear Wade, mdc1838
Bartlett, b17--, Henrico Co, fSamuel, m-- ( ) Green
Bartlett II, b18--, nrPoindexter, Loui Co, fClifton, mElizabeth Donivant
Clifton, b17--, Henrico Co, fSamuel, m-- ( ) Green, wElizabeth Donivant
Cordelia, bc1870, Amhe Co, fPowhatan, (1)m--, hJohn Hotchkiss
David, b18--, nrPoindexter, Loui Co, fClifton, mElizabeth Donivant

HENSON (continued)
Elizabeth, b18--, nrPoindexter, Loui Co, fClifton, mElizabeth Donivant
Elizabeth, b18--, hWilliam Waddell Flannagan
H B, b186-, Amhe co, fPowhatan, (1)m--
James, b18--, nrPoindexter, Loui Co, d186-, fBenjamin III, mMary Puryear Wade
James II, b18--, nrPoindexter, Loui Co, fClifton, mElizabeth Donivant
James William, b10/3/1863, Scottsville, Albe Co, fWilliam Henry, mMarie Antoinette Hoge, wNellie Alexander Parker
Lizzie, b186-, Amhe Co, fPowhatan, (1)m--, hW P Hodge
Lucy, b17--, Henrico Co, fSamuel, m-- ( ) Green
Lucy II, b18--, nrPoindexter, Loui Co, fClifton, mElizabeth Donivant
Martha Elizabeth, b18--, nrPoindexter, Loui Co, fBenjamin III, mMay Puryear Wade
Mary, b17--, Henrico Co, fSamuel, m-- ( ) Green
Mary Louisa, b18--, nrPoindexter, Loui Cao, fBenjamin III, mMary Puryear Wade
Powhatan, b18--, Amhe Co?, 2wMary (Jennings) Beasley
Sallie, b17--, Henrico Co, fSamuel, m-- ( ) Green
Samuel, b1737, Henrico Co, fBenjamin, w-- ( ) Green
Samuel II, b17--, nrPoindexter, Loui Cao, fClifton, mElizabeth Donivant
Samuel Puryear, b18--, nrPoindexter, Loui Co, fBenjamin III, mMary Puryear Wade
William Henry, b8/15/1840, nrPoindexter, Loui Co, fBenjamin III, mMary Puryear Wade, wMarie Antoinette Hoge
HEPLER, C Isaac, b184-, Rkbr Co, wMartha Hickman
HERBERT, Alice, b18--, PrAn Co, hWilliam Whitehurst Old, Sr, md6/23/1870
Joseph B, bc1830, ElCi Co, d186-, wMary Ann Dobbins

HERBERT (continued)
Joseph C, Sr, b1859, Richmond, fJoseph B, mMary Ann Dobbins, wBessie Selden
Thomas, b1/1862, Richmond, fJoseph B, mMary Ann dobbins, wT A Kellam
W P, b18--, Fauq Co, wRebecca Beverley
HERNDON, Alice, b186-, Page Co?, fRichard, mElizabeth Tyler, hCharles H O'Neal
Edward W, bc1860, Camp Co?, wKate Jessie Loyd
John, bc1850, Fauq Co, fThaddeus, mFannie Gibson
John G, bc1860, Wise Co?, wMartha Peirce
George, b185-, Page Co?, fRichard, mElizabeth Tyler
Julia, bc1850, Fauq Co, fThaddeus, mFannie Gibson, h-- Chancellor
Laura, b185-, Fauq Co, fThaddeus, mFannie Gibson, h-- Marshall
Louise, b185-, Fauq Co, fThaddeus, mFannie Gibson, hJohn Turner Ashby, md1/1876
Matilda, b185-, Page Co?, fRichard, mElizabeth Tyler, h-- Stratford
Rebecca, bc1830, nrLynchburg, Camp Co, hJ M Hammond
Sue, b185-, Fauq Co, fThaddeus, mFannie Gibson
Susie Tyler, b4/1860, Luray, Page Co, fRichard, mElizabeth Tyler, hGeorge W Haines, md7/1880
Thaddeus, b18--, Fauq Co, wFannie Gibson
Thler, b186-, Page Co?, fRichard, mElizabeth Tyler
HERRING, C O, b185-, Loui Co, fOscar, mMary E Walton
Frank H, b12/3/1863, Loui Co, fOscar, mMary E Walton, wLouise V Jones, md9/1893
Mary E, bc1860, Loui Co, fOscar, mMary E Walton
Oscar, b18--, wMary E Walton
Sallie L, b185-, Loui Co, fOscar, mMary E Walton, hJ C Carpenter
HERSHBERGER, b18--, Page Co,

HERSHBERGER (continued)
fPendleton, mElizabeth --, hJohn Nathaniel Stirewalt, md11/10/1870
Pendleton, b18--, Page Co?, wElizabeth --
Sarah Catherine, b18--, Fred Co?, fEmanuel, hDaniel C Funkhouser
HERSHBURGER, Mary Susan, b18--, Page Co, hJoseph Huffman
HESS, Bazzle, b7/12/1858, Upsh Co, fNewton, wSarah Wolford
J E, bc1860, Rkbr Co?, wGrace Engle Clemer
HEUSER, Caroline F, bc1870, Wyth Co?, fGuido A, mSarah Jane Sehorn, hJohn Alexander Whitman, md4/12/1889
Guido A, b18--, Wyth Co?, d1904, wSarah Jane Sehorn
Henry Massillon, b2/28/1867, Wytheville, Wyth Co, fGuido A, mSarah Jane Sehorn
HEVENER, Amos, b18--, Hightown, High Co, fJacob, (1)mMary Stone
Elizabeth, b18--, Hightown, High Co, fJacob, (1)mMary Stone, hRas Rhodes
Elizabeth, b186-, Hightown, High Co, fGeorge W, mMary Sommers, hC A Brock
George W, b1831, Hightown, High Co, fJacob, (1)mMary Stone, wMary Sommers
Hannah, 18--, Hightown, High Co, fJacob, (1)mMary Stone
Jacob, b1797, Pend Co, fFrederick, 1wMary Stone, 2wElizabeth Rexrode
Jacob W, b4/24/1863, Hightown, High Co, fGeorge W, mMary Sommers, wRatie M Fleisher, md6/8/1892
Mollie S, b186-, Hightown, High Co, fGeorge W, mMary Sommers, hG D Dudley
Uriah, b18--, Hightown, High Co, fJacob, (1)mMary Stone
William, b3/17/1820, Hightown, High Co, fJacob, (1)mMary Stone, 1wLouvinia Jordan, 2w Barbara Snyder
HEWITT, Anna, b1857, Camp Co?, fR N, hThomas Nelson Langhorne

HEWLETT, Elizabeth, b18--, Manchester, Ches Co, hWilliam Porter Strother
HEYMOND, Catheirne Virginia, bc1870, PrWi Co, hFrank Ashby Lewis, md7/14/1896
HEYWOOD, Frances V, b17--, Glou Co, hWilliam S Camp
HICKMAN, Elizabeth, bc1830, Hamp Co, fJohn T, hEdgar Douglas Newman
Elizabeth, b18--, Shen Co, hBenjamin Pennypacker Newman
Martha, b18--, Bath Co, hC Isaac Hepler
Susan, b18--, Wash Co, hWilliam King Trigg
William T, b2/22/1858, nrParksley, Acco Co, fRichard, wVirginia Lilliston
HICKOK, J G, b18--, Roan Co?, w-- Denit
HICKS, Edgar T, bc1860, Richmond?, wMary Smith
Johh P, Sr, b1850, Hicksville, Blan Co, d1922, fJoseph, wEunice Victoria Edwards
Leon Z, b186-, KiQu Co?, wJuliette Hoskins
Mary F, b12/1/1836, Spot Co, hRobert H Dickinson
HIETT, Catherine, b185-, nrWinchester, Clar Co, fLevi, (2)mElizabeth Carter, hLovell Gant
Edward, b185-, nrWinchester, Clar Co, fLevi, (2)mElizabeth Carter
Elizabeth, bc1840, Clar Co, fLevi, (1)m-- Bell, hArchibald Pittman
Joseph, bc1820, Jeff Co
Joseph, bc1840, Clar Co, fLevi, (1)m-- Bell
Joseph T, bc1840, Fred Co?, wFlora Baker
Levi, bc1820, Jeff Co, 1w-- Bell, 2wElizabeth Carter
Lucy V, b12/25/1850, nrWinchester, Clar Co, fLevi, (2)mElizabeth Carter, hBenjamin West Baker, md11/10/1876
William S, b185-, nrWinchester, Clar Co, fLevi, (2)mElizabeth Carter
HIGGINBOTHAM, --, b18--, Amhe Co, 1w of Peter Butler Johnston
James Bane, b3/6/1846, Taze Co, fThomas Jefferson, mNancy Bane, wSarah Louisa Allen
James G, Sr, b17--, Liberty Hill, Taze Co, fMoses, 2wElizabeth Scott
James G, Jr, b2/1848, Liberty Hill, Taze Co, fJames G, Sr, (2)mElizabeth Scott, wLaura John Stimson
Mary, bc1809, Amhe Co, hBenjamin Jennings Rucker
Nannie, b184-, Taze Co, fThomas Jefferson, mNancy Bane, hA P Gillespie
Thomas Jefferson, b8/1/1817, Liberty Hill, Taze Co, fJames G, Sr, wNancy Bane
William Jefferson, b18--, Gile Co, wAlice Allen
HIGGINBOTHEM, Anna Jane, b18--, Amhe Co, 2w of W R Hill
HIGGINS, Josiah, b17--, wElizabeth Hewlett Pollard
Maria Louisa, b1813, NewK Co, fJosiah, mElizabeth Hewlett Pollard, hJames Robert Moore
HIGGS, Benjamin, bc1800, PrWi Co?, w-- (Lane) Rowles
Julia, b18--, Fair Co, fBenjamin, m-- (Lane) Rwles, hFrancis M Lewis
HIGHT, M K, bc1870, Nels Co, fJohn H, 2w of William Henry Parrish, md6/6/1922
Virginia, b1854, Gile Co, d1899, hWythe Graham Bane
HIGHTMAN, William, bc1860, Jeff Co?, wAnna Stipes
HILL, A G, bc1840, Loui Co?, wBettie V Vest
Anna, b18--, PrEd Co?, hRobert B Atwood
Albert Hudgins, b2/3/1866, Madi Co, fJohn Booton, mVirginia Byrd, wCora Bransford
Ellen T, b18--, KiQu Co, d1910, 3w of John Barbee Minor
Frances, b17--, KiQu Co, hBaylor Walker
James D, b186-, Amhe Co, fW R, (1)m-- Brent
John Thompson, b18--, Ports-

HILL (continued)
mouth, Norf Co, wLizzie B Collins
Josephine T, b1838, NewK Co, hThomas Ball Montague, Jr
Lillie, b18--, Nels Co?, hHenry Tate Harris, md1884
Melinda, b18--, Wyth Co?, hWilliam H Hartley
Milly Pryor, b18--, Dinw Co?, hJohn H Hartman
W R, b18--, Nels Co, d189-, 1w-- Brent, 2wAnne Jane Higginbothem
Williams Collins Hill, b4/15/1868, Portsmouth, fJohn Thompson, mLizzie B Collins
William H, b18--, Norf Co, wCaroline W Tripple
HILLIARD, Emily, b18--, Loud Co?, hJohn Pearson Smart
HILLMAN, Benjamin Franklin, b8/2/1862, Coeburn, Wise Co, fJames Monroe, wNancy S Greear
J Wesley, b18--, Wise Co?, wEllen Victoria Robinson
James Monroe, b1827, Scot Co, fJohn, wElizabeth Stallard
Nannie, b18--, Wise Co, d1907, fJ Wesley, mEllen Victoria Robinson, 1w of William W G Dotson, md10/1888
HILLYARD, --. bc1800, Fred Co, d186-, w-- Custer
Bennett, b183-, nrBerryville, Clar Co, m-- Custer
Caroline, b183-, nrBerryville, Clar Co, m-- Custer, hCharles Newcomb
Cora, b186-, Fred Co, fGeorge W, (1)mJemimah Windle, hOliver Bright
Daniel, b183-, nrBerryville, Clar Co, m-- Custer
George E, b186-, Fred Co, fGeorge W, (1)mJemimah Windle
George W, b3/27/1832, nrBerryville, Clar Co, d1911, m-- Custer, 1wJemimah Windle, 2w Alice M Coffman
Jacob, b183-, nrBerryville, Clar Co, m-- Custer
James, b183-, nrBerryville, Clar Co, m-- Custer
Jemmie, b186-, Fred Co, fGeorge W, (1)mJemimah Windle, hJames

HILLYARD (continued)
B Hudson
Kate, bc1840, nrBerryville, Clar Co, m-- Custer
Mary Virginia, b18--, Fred Co, fGeorge W, (1)mJemima Windle, hJames B Hodgson
Rosser, bc1870, Fred Co, fGeorge W, (1)mJemimah Windle
William Robert, b9/16/1866, Fred Co, fGeorge W, (1)mJemimah Windle, wLucy E Massie, md12/24/1885
HILTON, Polly, b18--, Scot Co, hJohn L Addington
HIMER, Lucinda, b1812, Pend Co, fHarmon, hHenry Seybert
Margaret, b18--, Pend Co, hWilliam A Jones
Mary, b18--, Pend Co, hJ L Shumate
HINCHMAN, John H, b1854, Richmond, wMollie E Doherty
HINEGARDNER, Abram, b18--, Rkhm Co, wSusanna Bowman
HINGARDNER, Samuel, bc1840, Shen Co?, wAnnie E Kagey
HINKINS, John, bc1850, Camp Co?, wCatherine Baker
Peter, b18--, Shen Co?, wLucy McInturff
HINKLE, Corinne, bc1870, Rkbr Co, 2w of William T Robey, Sr
Mary, b17--, Jeff Co?, hJohn Brewer
HINKS, Sarah Ann, b18--, Shen Co, hDavid Miller
HINMAN, Vernetta Ann, b18--, Acco Co?, hThomas A Northam
HINTON, Elizabeth, b17--, Lune Co, hDaniel Taylor
George H, b4/11/1811, Lanc Co, d180, 2wMargaret Brown
James W, b185-, Richmond, fGeorge H, (2)mMargaret Brown
John Braxton, b3/23/1851, Richmond, fGeorge H, (2)mMargaret Brown, wAnna Augusta Croswell
Mary, b184-, Richmond, fGeorge H, (2)mMargaret Brown
William, b185-, Richmond, fGeorge H, (2)mMargaret Brown
HIPKINS, Margaret, b1860, Alexandria, d1902, hRichard Windsor Johnston
HIRONS, E G, bc1860, Bedf Co?,

HIRONS (continued)
w-- Noell
HIRSCHBERG, David, bc1860, Richmond, fJoseph, mCaroline Van Vort
Esther, bc1860, Richmond, fJoseph, mCaroline Van Vort, hMyer Hirschberg
Isador, b1856, Richmond, fJoseph, mCaroline Van Vort, wJosephine Bowles
Myer, bc1860, Richmond?, wEsther Hirschberg
Samuel, bc1860, Richmond, fJoseph, mCaroline Van Vort
HISEY, Catherine, b18--, Shen Co?, d1902, fJohn, hSamuel Saum
Robert Lee, b18--, Page Co?, wEmma Crist
HITE, Clyde M, b186-, Lantz Mills, Shen Ca, fIsaac R, mRhoda F Miley
Cornelius Randolph, Sr, b18--, Rapp Co?, fHugh, wElizabeth Stark
Harvey D, b18--, Lantz Mills, Shen Co, fIsaac R, (1)mLucinda Humpston
Hugh, bc1800, Fred Co, fIsaac, mAnne Tunstall Maury
Hugh, b18--, Rapp Co, d186-, fHugh
Ira T, b186-, Lantz Mills, Shen Co, fIsaac R, (2)mRhoda F Miley
Isaac, b17--, fIsaac, 1wNellie Madison, 2wAnnie Tunstall Maury
Isaac, bc1800, Fred Co, wLouisa Maria Davidson
Isaac R, b1812, Shen Co, f1893, fMichael, 1wLucinda Humpston, 2wRhoda F Miley
Jacquelin, b6/3/1831, Fred Co, fIsaac, mLouisa Maria Davidson, hJohn William Wright
Jennie, b18--, Lant Mills, Shen Co, fIsaac R, (1)mLucinda Humpston
John M, b18--, Lantz Mills, Shen Co, fIsaac R, (1)mLucinda Humpston
Joseph, b18--, Lantz Mills, shen Co, fIsaac R, (1)mLucinda Humpston

HITE (continued)
Lucy Meade, b18--, Rapp Co, fHugh, hShirley Carter
Milton L, b4/12/1858, Lantz Mills, Shen Co, fIsaac R, (2)mRhoda F Miley, wEmma J Sheetz, md7/3/1881
N D, b18--, Shen Co?, w-- Huffman
Sarah C M, b18--, Shen Co?, hMark Bird
William R, bc1860, Lantz Mills, Shen Co, fIsaac R, (2)mRhoda F Miley
HITT, Virginia, b18--, Fauq Co?, hSeth McDonald
HIX, Jennie, b186-, PrEd Co, fThomas W, mBettie Gough, hW R Bracy
Mary A, b186-, PrEd Co, fThomas W, mBettie Gough, hBenjamin Hooper
Mary Elizabeth, b18--, Fran Co, fPatrick, hArmistead Burwell
Thomas B, bc1870, PrEd Co, fThomas W, mBettie Gough
Thomas W, b1832, Appo Co, wBettie Gough
William G, b186-, PrEd Co, fThomas W, mBettie Gough
HIXSON, Elizabeth, b18--, PrWi Co, hJohn R Hornbaker
HOBBS, Anna, b18--, PrGe Co, fP L, hJames Bailey
Mary, b1815, Monr Co?, hGranville Calloway
P L, bc1826, PrGe Co?
HOBSON, --, b18--, "Clover Forest", Gooc Co, fMahlon, hRichard Cunningham Selden
Edwin L, bc1830, wFannie A Anderson
A Mahen, b186-, Howard's Neck, Gooc Co, fJohn David, mMartha Bland Selden
Elizabeth Allen, b18--, hRobert Walton Brown, md4/10/1838
J Cannon, b186-, Howard's Neck, Gooc Co, fJohn David, mMartha Bland Selden
J Selden, bc1860, Howard's Neck, Gooc Co, fJohn David, mMartha Bland Selden
Jennie Kirkpatrick, b18--, Richmond, fGeorge William, mCatherine Hutchinson Kirk-

HOBSON (continued)
patrick, hJohn W Scott
John David, b18--, Richmond, fJohn Cannon, wMartha Bland Selden
Lillie M, b186-, Howard's Neck, Gooc Co, fJohn David, mMartha Bland Selden, hRichard H Wright
Saunders, b5/8/1868, Howard's Neck, Gooc Co, fJohn David, mMartha Bland Selden, wBessie M Martin
Susan Ann, b18--, hHenry J Brown, md10/24/1833
W Plummer, bc1870, Howard's Neck, Gooc Co, fJohn David, mMartha Bland Selden
William Thomas, b18--, wElizabeth Agnes Browne, md12/19/1839
HOCKADAY, John R, b18--, Richmond?, wBettie Gregory
Judith W, bc1840, NewK Co, fWilliam A, mEliza A Ratcliff, hWilliam T Boswell
Louise D, bc1870, Richmond, fJohn R, mBettie Gregory
Willilam A, bc1800, NewK Co, wEliza A Ratcliff
HOCKMAN, --, b18--, Shen Co?, wTina Baker
--, bc1820, Shen Co?, hIsaac Wilkins
Joseph, bc1800, Shen Co?, 1h of Margaret Fravel
Laura A, b1/18/1851, Warr Co, d1919, fSamuel, hWilliam Melancthon Bucher
Mary Elizabeth, b6/10/1835, Shen Co, d1910, fJoseph, mMargaret Fravel, hDaniel Bowman
Milton H, b1832, Shen Co, fJoseph, mMargaret Fravel
Noah, bc1820, Shen Co, wSarah Copp
Philip J, b3/11/1837, Shen Co, d186-, fJoseph, mMargaret Fravel
Whiten, b3/5/1839, Shen Co, d186-, fJoseph, mMargaret Fravel
William, bc1860, Shen Co?, wLou May Saum
William A, bc1850, Shen Co, wBarbara Joanna Copp

HODGE, W P, bc1860, Amhe Co?, wLizzie Henson
HODGES, Elizabeth Catheirne, b8/1840, Cobbs Creek, Math Co, hFrancis Reed Haynes
Louise, b18--, Norf Co, hJohn White
Mary, bc1800, Hano Co, hBenjamin Waller Page
HODGSON, James B, b18--, Fred Co?, wMary Virginia Hillyard
HOFFMAN, Alfred, b18--, Shen Co?, wMary Jane Anderson
Edward Harrison, Sr, b5/22/1850, Strasburg, Shen Co, fAlfred, mMary Jane Anderson, wIndia M Rager, md1898
Isabel, b18--, nrEdinburg, Shen Co, d1911, fAndrew, hJames M Painter
HOGE, Ann Elizabeth, b18--, hJohn Chapman Snidow
Arista, b4/5/1847, Scottsville, Albe Co, fPeter Charles, mSarah Kerr, wCatherine Miller Garber, md10/10/1872
Eliza, bc1820, Pula Co, d184-, fJames, hGeorge Tyler
Elizabeth, b18--, Loud Co, fIsaac, mRachel Neill Scofield
Frederica, b18--, Loud Co, fIsaac, mRachel Neill Scofield, hJohn B Strasburger
Isaac, b2/1814, Loud Co, fJames, mRachel Nichols, wRachel Neill Scofield
Isaac, b18--, Loud Co, fIsaac, mRachel Neill Scofield
James, b17--, Loud Co, wRachel Nichols
James M, b2/15/1839, nrHamilton, Loud Co, fIsaac, mRachel Neill Scofield, wJulia N (Branch) Archer
Josephine, b18--, Loud Co, fIsaac, mRachel Neill Scofield
Lewis, b18--, Loud Co, fIsaac, mRachel Neill Scofield
Margaretta, b18--, Loud Co, fIsaac, mRachel Neill Scofield
Marie Antoinette, b6/28/1837, nrStaunton, Augu Co, fPeter Charles, mSarah Kerr, hWilliam Henry Henson
Peter Charles, b17--, Augu Co, fJame Hogg, m-- Gregory,

HOGE (continued)
wSarah Kerr
Samuel Harris, b18--, Mont Co?, wKatherine Craig Taylor
William, bc1820, wVirginia Harrison
Willie S, b18--, Loud Co, fIsaac, mRachel Neill Scofield
HOGG, James, b17--, Augu Co, fPeter, mElizabeth Taylor, w-- Gregory
HOGGE, Joseph B, bc1850, York Co?, wKetura Hudgins
HOGSHEAD, Elizabeth Lewis, b18-- Augu Co, fPreston Bailey, mElizabeth Ann Hamilton, hF Percival Loth
Emma Bailey, b18--, Augu Co, fPreston Bailey, mElizabeth Ann Hamilton, hCharles P Hanger
Fannie Hamilton, b18--, Augu Co, fPreston Bailey, mElizabeth Ann Hamilton, hJohn Dale Clothier
Harry, b18--, Augu Co, fPreston Bailey, mElizabeth Ann Hamilton, wEmma Peyton Fitz
Mary Preston, b1865, Parnassus, Augu Co, fPreston Bailey, mElizabeth Ann Hamilton, hJay Franklin Clemmer, Sr
Preston Bailey, b9/9/1833, fElijah, mMargaret Kerr, wElizabeth Ann Hamilton, md10/26/1856
Richard, b18--, Augu Co, fPreston Bailey, mElizabeth Ann Hamilton, 1wCora Smiley, 2w Ella Fulton
Thomas, b12/3/1868, Parnassus, Augu Co, fPreston Bailey, mElizabeth Ann Hamilton, wAnnabel Timberlake
HOLBROOK, Louisa, b18--, Wyth Co?, hJames F Buck
Mary Lucy, b1853, Rkhm Co?, hJohn Marshall Stover
Wilson, bc1850, Wise Co?, wMary E Greear
HOLLADAY, Mary Minor, b18--, KiQu Co?, hJacob James Allen Latane
HOLLAND, Charles E, bc1860, Holy Neck, Nans Co, fZachariah Everett, mAnn S Pretlow, wSue

HOLLAND (continued)
Jones
Edward Everett, b2/26/1861, Holy Neck District, Nans Co, fZachariah Everett, mAnn S Pretlow, 1wSarah Otelia Lee, md11/26/1884, 2wEunice Ensor, md9/1920
Fannie, b178-, Bedf Co?, fPete M, 1w of Benjamin Hancock, md1802
Florence R, b186-, Nhtn Co, fNathaniel, mJuliette F Holland, hOtho Fredrick Mears, md11/19/1890
George L, bc1840, Fauq Co?, wJacquelina Payne
Harriett, b18--, Nhtn Co, hPreston E Trower
John Meador, b1778, Bedf Co?, fPeter M
Juliette, b18--, Nhtn Co?, hNathaniel Holland
Nancy, b17--, Bedf Co, hMatthew Wright
Nathaniel, b18--, Nhtn Co?, wJuliette F Holland
Peter, bc1780, Fran Co, fPeter M, wFannie Hancock
Polly, bc1800, Fran Co, hAnanias Divers
Roberta McLaren, b18--, Rapp Co?, hHenry Lloyd Menefee
Zachariah, bc1800, fJob
Zachariah, b18--, Nans Co?, fZachariah, wAnn S Pretlow
HOLLAR, Barbara A, b186-, Augu Co, fGeorge, hJoseph S Carver
Christian, bc1830, Shen Co?, wSusanne Wine
Michael, b18--, Augu Co?, wIda
Samuel, b18--, Shen Co?, wBettie Wisman
Annie, bc1870, nrTimberville, Rkhm Co, fChristian, (1)m--, hSamuel Mohler
Christian, b18--, nrCherry Grove, Rkhm Co, fDavid, m-- Flory, 2wAnnie Wampler
HOLLER, David, b18--, Rkhm Co?, w-- Flory
Rebecca Catherine, bc1870, nrTimberville, Rkhm Co, fChristian, (1)m--, hB Frank Andes
W L, bc1860, Shen Co?, wRosa

HOLLER (continued)
Hutcheson
HOLLIDAY, Annie E, b1864, nrMiddleburg, Loud Co, hJohn W Hall
HOLLINGSWORTH, Edwin, bc1860, Winchester, Fred Co, wFannie Belle Coffelt
HOLLINSWORTH, Lucinda Caroline, b18--, Wyth Co, hJames R Ward
HOLLOMAN, Mary, b18--, hJames Rutter
HOLLOWAY, --, bc1830, Staf Co?, wLila Amiss
HOLMAN, Mary J, bc1860, hCharles M Perrow
Sallie W, b18--, PrEd Co, 1hBenjamin Stephens Hooper, 2hHugh O'Gara
HOLMES, Ann, b17--, Bowling Green, Caro Co, 1w of Henry Brodnax
Annie Eliza, b1/8/1855, Fauq Co, fJohn, mCatherine Ann Strother, hThomas N Russell, md2/4/1873
Jack, b185-, Fauq Co, fJohn, mCatherine Ann Strother
Jennie, bc1850, Fauq Co, fJohn, mCatherine Ann Strother
John, b18--, Fauq Co, wCatherine Ann Strother
Josephine Elizabeth, b1855, Flint Hill, Rapp Co, mMary Tannehill, hJoseph Taylor Thompson
Molly, b18--, PrWi Co, hHenry Fairfax Lynn
Rebecca, b3/21/1779, Stockholm Farm, fred Co, fJoseph, mRebecca Hunter, hDaniel Conrad
Samuel, bc1830, Shen Co?, wRegina Clem
Samuel, b184-, Fauq Co, d186-, fJohn, mCatherine Ann Strother
Susan, bc1850, Fauq Cao, fJohn, mCatherine Ann Strother, hRobert Barbee
Washington, b184-, Fauq Co, fJohn, mCatherine Ann Strother
HOLSINGER, G B, bc1850, Shen Co, wSarah A Kagey
Martha, b18--, Rkhm Co?, hGeorge B Homan
HOLT, Ada Jane, b18--, Char Co, hLeon Leslie Tucker

HOLT (continued)
Edwin Walter, b1843, ElCi Ci, d1877, wSue Cary Howard
Elizabeth, b1825, Halifax, Hali Co, d1894, hJames Stone Easley
Henry Winston, Sr, b9/4/1864, Anchor Plantation, Surry Co, fMicajah Quincy, mVirginia Henry Winston, wMary Caperton Braxton, md1894
James W, bc1860, Page Co?, wMaggie Keyser
Micajah Quincy, b18--, Surr Co?, wVirginia Henry Winston
Richmond W, b186-, Surr Co, fMicajah Quincy, mVirginia Henry Winston
Saxon W, b186-, Surr Co, fMicajah Quincy, mVirginia Henry Winston
HOLTON, Edward T, b7/26/1826, nrThe Plains, Fauq Co, fThomas, m-- West, wMarietta Wade
Julia Ann, b182-, nrThe Plains, Fauq Co, fThomas, m-- West, hHeaton Silcott
HOLTZCLAW, Sallie, b18--, Culp Co?, hJohn W Hudson
HOMAN, Caroline, b18--, Rkhm Co?, hJacob Lincoln
George B, b18--, Rkhm Co?, wMartha Holsinger
HONAKER, Mary Jane, b1837, Honaker, Russ Co, hZadock N Gardner
Viola, b1858, Russ Co?, hWilliam Wilson
HONEYSTOFFLE, Josephine, b18--, nrWinchester, Fred Co, fRufus, mSelma --, hAugustine B Richards
Rufus, b18--, Fred Co?, wSelma
HOOD, --, b18--, Taze Co?, hWilliam Peery
HOOE, Howson, b18--, wMary Dade
Howson, b18--, wHenrietta Daniel
Rice III, b16--, Staf Co?, fRhys, wAnne Howson
Robert Emmett, bc1860, Fair Co?, wIda Elizabeth Hutton
HOOK, Archibald M, bc1839, nrHigh View, Hamp Co, d1903, fRobert, mMary Kelso, wMary C Garvin

HOOK (continued)
- Edgar L, b10/17/1860, Hamp Co, fArchibald M, mMary C Garvin, 1wLizzie Giffin, md/23/1889, 2wLelia Adams
- Fannie, b184-, Highview, Hamp Co, fRobert, mMary KElso, hA S Anderson
- Henson P, b184-, nrHighview, Hamp Co, fRobert, mMary Kelso
- Isaiah P, b184-, nrHighview, Hamp Co, fRobert, mMary Kelso
- Jane, bc1840, nrHighview, Hamp Co, fRobert, mMary Kelso, hJohn Garvin
- John W, b186-, Hamp Co, d1922, fArchibald, mMary C Garvin
- Laura Virginia, b186-, Hamp Co, fArchibald, mMary C Garvin, hJohn W Pease
- Lycurgus C, b184-, nrHighview, Hamp Co, fRobert, mMary Kelso
- Mack B, b7/10/1869, Hook's Mills, Hamp Co, fArchibald, mMary C Garvin, wLuna La-Follett, md11/24/1892
- Marvin, b186-, Hamp Co, fArchibald, mMary C Garvin
- Rebecca Jane, b184-, Alle Co, dc1913, fEli, hJordan Helmintoller
- Robert, b18--, nrHighview, Hamp Co, wMary Kelso
- Robert C, b186-, Hamp Co, fArchibald, mMary C Garvin

HOOKER, J Murray, b18--, Patr Co, fJohn W, mRennie Akers
- John W, b18--, Patr Co?, wRennie Akers
- Samuel H, b18--, Patr Co, fJohn W, mRennie Akers, wNannie Agee

HOOMES, Elizabeth Lee, b17--, Glou Co?, 2w of William Robins, Jr

HOOPER, Benjamin, b18--, PrEd Co?, wMary A Hix
- George W, bc1830, Warr Co?, wBetty Henry

HOOVER, --, bc1800, Rkhm Co?, fJohn, hBenjamin Myers
- Alice V, b3/1851, nrTimberville, Rkhm Co, fBenjamin, mMelvine Sites, hChristian A White
- Benjamin, b18--, nrTimberville, Rkhm Co, fSamuel, wMelvine

HOOVER (continued) Sites
- David, bc1800, Rkhm Co?, fJohn
- Emanuel, b18--, Timberville, Rkhm Co, fSamuel, wAnna Cline
- George H, b185-, nrTimberville, Rkhm Co, fBenjamin, mMelvine Sites, wCornelia Stiegel
- Henry Wise, b12/25/1859, Alle Co, wGeorge Annie --
- Isaac, bc1860, Rkhm Co, 2h of Emma Myers
- John Henry, b12/4/1863, Rkhm Co, fEmanuel, mAnna Cline, wAnne Rebecca Flory, md11/5/1885
- Leah, b18--, Rkhm Co, fSamuel, hJonas Early
- Mary, b184-, nrTimberville, Rkhm Co, fBenjamin, mMelvine Sites, hJohn H Rhodes
- Rebecca M, b185-, Rkhm Co, fEmanuel, mAnna Cline, hCornelius Driver, md11/20/1873
- Samuel, b17--, Rkhm Co?, fJacob
- Samuel Ringo, b1848, nrTimberville, Rkhm Co, d1905, fBenjamin, mMelvine Sites, wMalinda Neff, md1/1872
- William C, b4/17/1870, Timberville, Rkhm Co, fEmanuel, mAnna Cline, wMaggie Josephine Miller, md9/8/1871or2

HOPE, Frank Stanley, b10/21/1855, Portsmouth, Norf Co, fWilliam Meredith, mVirginia Frances Owens, wAnnie M West, md6/20/1883
- Hubert M, b185-, Portsmouth, Norf Co, d1907, fWilliam Meredith, mVirginia Frances Owens
- Ruth Vernon, b185-, Norf Co?, 1w of Abel Erastus Hope, md187-
- William Meredith, b1812, Norf Co?, wVirginia Frances Owens

HOPEWELL, Sallie Machir, b18--, Warr Co, hFrancis Wesley LeHew
- Sarah, b18--, Mt Solon, Augu Co, d1911, hJames Edward Bolen

HOPKINS, Amelia, b17--, fArthur, mElzabeth Pettus
- Anna, b17--, fArthur, mElizabeth Pettus
- Arthur, bc1690, NewK Co, wElizabeth Pettus, md1710-15

HOPKINS (continued)
Arthur, b17--, fArthur, mElizabeth Pettus, w-- Jefferson
Charles, b1736, fJohn
David, b17--, fJohn
Elizabeth, b17--, fArthur, mElizabeth Pettus
Elizabeth, b17--, fJohn
Elizabeth, b18--, Rkhm Co, hHenry B Harnsberger
Elizabeth A, b5/24/1810, Bedf Co, fJohn III, mMary Turner, hI A Quarles, mdc1830
Frances, b17--, fArthur, mElizabeth Pettus
Frances, b1/27/1738, fJohn, hLittleberry Leftwich, md1/13/1778
Francis, bc1737, fJohn, w Jane Cox
Francis, b1/21/1805, Bedf Co, fJohn III, mMary Turner, wEmeline Cook, md10/31/1835
Francis Alexander, b18--, fJohn Calvin, mMaria M Barnes
Harriet Burr, b2/12/1821, Bedf Co, fJohn III, mMary Turner, hRobert G Bell
Isabel, b17--, fArthur, mElizabeth Pettus
James, b17--, fArthur, mElizabeth Pettus
James Turner, b3/6/1803, Bedf Co, fJohn III, mMary Turner, wMary Early, md12/15/1824
Jane, b17--, fArthur, mElizabeth Pettus
Jesse Turner, b12/13/1808, Bedf Co, fJohn III, mMary Turner
John, b17--, fArthur, mElizabeth Pettus
John II, b17--, fJohn
John III, b10/6/1775, Bedf Co, fFrancis, mJane Cox, wMary Turner, md9/2/1800
John Calvin, b8/21/1812, Bedf Co, fJohn III, mMary Turner, 1wMaria M Barnes, md9/22/1839, 2wElizabeth Ann Tabler
John, b18--, Rkhm Co, wElizabeth Coffman
Kate Coffman, b1856, Mt Clinton, Rkhm Co, d1918, fJohn, mElizabeth Coffman, hStephen Harnsberger, md5/16/1878
Lucy, b17--, fArthur, mElizabeth Pettus
Martha, b17--, Bedf Co, fFrancis, mJane Cox, hJohn Walden, md4/6/1786
Mary, b7/14/1739, Bedf Co, fJohn, hJohn Otey
Mary, b17--, fArthur, mElizabeth Pettus, hJoseph Cabell, md1752
Mary Elizabeth, b8/28/1854, Fran Co, fWilliam Leftwich Turner, Sr, mJulia Ann Muse
Mary Jane, b1/31/1819, Bedf Co, fJohn III, mMary Turner, hWilliam Henry Mathews, md2/22/1848
Mildred Turner, b1/9/1862, Fran Co, fWilliam Leftwich Turner, Sr, mJulia Ann Muse
Peter, b17--, fJohn
Price, b17--, Bedf Co, fFrancis, mJane Cox, 1wElizabeth Turner, md1801, 2wFrances G Claytor, md12/13/1812
Sally Leftwich, b11/28/1801, Bedf Co, fJohn III, mMary Turner, hJames G McAllister, md4/17/1820
Samuel, b17--, fArthur, mElizabeth Pettus, wIsabella Taylor
Samuel II, b4/9/1753, fSamuel, mIsabella Taylor, wElizabeth Bugg
Sarah, b17--, fJohn
Virginia, bc1835, "Midway Place", nrHot Springs, Bath Co, d1903, hJoseph w Warren, Sr
William, b17--, fArthur, mElizabeth Pettus, wElizabeth Moon
William, b17--, fJohn
William, b17--, Bedf Co, fFrancis, mJane Cox, wElizabeth Clarke
William Henry, b18--, Bath Co?, wRachel Lewis
William Leftwich Turner, Sr, b12/14/1814, Bedf Co, fJohn III, mMary Turner, wJulia Ann Muse, md12/26/1850
William Leftwich Turner, Jr, b9/30/1860, Fran Co, fWilliam Leftwich Turner, Sr, mJulia Ann Muse, 1wMary Ella Hancock, md12/26/1882 2wMary Ann Rebec-

HOPKINS (continued)
ca Smith, md6/4/1895
William Tipton, b11/22/1863, Portsmouth, Norf Co, fWilliam Tipton, mKatherine Clark, wElizabeth Conn
HOPPER, Almyra Josephine, b18--, Page Co?, 1hPaul Lee Bowen, 2hWillam Kerfoot
HORNBAKER, John R, b18--, PrWi Co?, wElizabeth Hixson
HORNBARGER, John Wade, bc1865, Bland Court House, Blan Co, wMollie Keyser
HORNE, --, b18--, Wash Co, 2w of James Keys
Elizabeth, bc1800, Wyth Co, 1w of David Whitman
Susan, b18--, Richmond?, hEmil O Nolting
HORNER, --, bc1840, Glou Co, wVirginia Cary
Anne, b18--, hAlexander Spotswood Campbell
Belle, b18--, fLevy B, hThomas B Williams
David, b184-, Ches Co, fJohn, Sr
John, Jr, b185-, Ches Co, fJohn, Sr, wMary Bottom
John W, b18--, Berk Co, d1923, m-- Nelson, wMartha Harmon
Levy, b1810, Ches Co
N S, bc1860, Shen Co, wLaura Shirley
HORSHOUR, David, bc1810, Augu Co, wRebecca Clinedinst
HORSLEY, John, b2/21/1845, nr Lovington, Nels Co, wRose E Shelton
John Dunscond, b18--, Rock Cliffe, Nels Co, wFlorence Massie
HORTENSTINE, J W, bc1840, Wash Co
Mary Catherine, b1848, Wash Co, hHenry B Roberts, Jr
Susan, bc1800, Wash Co, hJohn Baker
HORTON, Ellen, b18--, Rye Cove, Scot Co, hSamuel Carter
Flora, b1863, Snowflake, Scot Co, hJohn P Corns
John L, bc1860, Russ Co?, wLou May Finney
William Henry, Sr, b18--, Camp

HORTON (continued)
Co, wMartha Ann Clarkson
William Henry, Jr, b18--, nr Lynchburg, Camp Co, fWilliam Henry, Sr, mMartha Ann Clarkson, wBettie Ann Roberts
William Henry III, b5/11/1862, Nels Co, fWilliam Henry, Jr, mBettie Ann Roberts, wSusie Gray Roberts
HOSKINS, Betsie Lyon, b186-, KiQu Co, fWilliam, mJanet Carter Roy, hAndrew J Montague Bird, bc1800, KiQu Co, w-- Garrett
Blanche, b186-, KiQu Co, fWilliam, mJanet Carter Roy, hJohn Richard Saunders
Charles R, b186-, KiQu Co, fWilliam, mJanet Carter Roy
May, b186-, KiQu Co, fWilliam, mJanet Carter Roy, hThomas L Henley
Juliette, bc1870, KiQu Co, fWilliam, mJanet Carter Roy, hLeon Z Hicks
Lucy Bird, b185-, KiQu Co, fWilliam, mJanet Carter Roy, hRobert Dudley
Willard Dunbar, bc1860, KiQu Co, d1911, fWilliam, mJanet Carter Roy
William, b1/25/1831, Esse (then KiQu) Co, d1895, fBird, m-- Barrett, wJanet Carter Roy
HOTCHKISS, John, bc1860, Amhe Co?, wCordelia Henson
HOTT, Hiram, bc1840, Albe Co, w-- Bailey
HOTTEL, --, bc1850, Shen Co?, wKate Larkins
--, b186-, Page Co?, fJ H, mMary Rader, hFrank Cooley
--, b186-, Page Co?, fJ H, mMary Rader, hRobert Weaver
Amanda, b184-, Shen Co, fIsaac, mAnn Fravel
Ann R, b184-, Shen Co, fIsaac, mAnn Fravel
Catherine, b181-, Shen Co, fDaniel, mMary Jordan, h-- Hockman
Daniel, b17--, Shen Co, fJacob, wMary Jordan
David, bc1810, Shen Co, fDaniel, mMary Jordan

HOTTEL (continued)
Dorothy, bc1810, Shen Co, fDaniel, mMary Jordan, hJacob Hamman
Eli, b181-, Shen Co, fDaniel, mMary Jordan
Elizabeth, bc1820, Shen Co, fDaniel, mMary Jordan, hPhilip A Funkhousr, Sr
Ellen, bc1850, Shen Co, fIsaac, mAnn Fravel, hSamuel Bowman
Emma J, b185-, Shen Co, fIsaac, mAnn Fravel, hWilliam Roller
George H, b5/14/1854, Woodstock, Shen Co, fHenry, mCatherine Coffman, wLaura Lee Painter, md10/31/1878
Henry, b1818, Shen Co, fJoseph, wCatherine Coffman
Irvin, b186-, Page Co?, fJ H, mMary Rader
Isaac, b5/2/1808, Shen Co, f1866, fDaniel, mMary Jordan, wAnn Fravel
J H, b18--, Page Co?, wMary Rader
Jacob, b17--, Shen Co, fGeorge
Jacob, b181-, Shen Co, fDaniel, mMary Jordan
Jared H, b184-, Shen Co, d186-, fIsaac, mAnn Fravel
John, b181-, Shen Co, fDaniel, mMary Jordan
Laura Katherine, b1/17/1864, Page Co?, fJ H, mMary Rader, hWilliam Henry Harrison Shuler, md12/17/1885
Luther, b185-, Woodstock, Shen Ca, fHenry, mCatherine Coffman
Lydia, b181-, Shen Co, fDaniel, mMary Jordan
Lucy Alice, b185-, Shen Co, fIsaac, mAnn Fravel, hCharles Rush
Margaret, b181-, Shen Co, fDaniel, mMary Jordan
Mary, b184-, Shen Co, fIsaac, mAnn Fravel, hGeorge Fansler
Mary, b185-, Woodstock, Shen Co, fHenry, mCatherine Coffman, hLemuel Painter
Milton Hockman, b11/16/1857, Shen Co, fIsaac, mAnn Fravel, wLaura E Bargelt, md12/12/1894
Morgan, bc185-, Woodstock, Shen Co, d186-, fHenry, mCatherine

HOTTEL (continued)
Coffman
Rebecca, bc1820, Hayfield District, Fred Co, d1898, fDavid, hAsa Larrick
Samuel, b181-, Shen Co, fDaniel, mMary Jordan
Silas, bc1840, Shen Co, wVirginia Schmucker
HOTTLE, Calvin, b18--, Shen Co?, wRebecca Catherine Beydler
Ida B, b1862, Woodstock, Shen Co, hCharles F Fravel
HOUFF, --, b18--, Augu Co?, wBettie Brenaman
HOUGH, Levi, bc1820, Fauq Co?, wSarah Glascock
HOUSEMAN, Jacob, bc1810, Augu Co, 2h of Mary Myers
HOUSER, Sarah E, bc1843, Romney, Hamp Co, dc1920, fGeorge, hElias Irvin
HOUSTON, Betty H, b18--, Craigsville, Augu Co, hLewis R Lupton
Catherine Matilda, b18--, Bote Co?, fRutherford Rowland, mMargaret Isabel Steele, hWalter Ashby Plecker, md11/22/1888
Finley W, bc1860, Rkbr Co?, w-- Alexander
Lavinia, b18--, Augu Co, hWilliam Bell
Mary J, b18--, Craigsville, Augu Co, hIsaac Briscoe Lupton
Rutherford Rowland, b18--, Bote Co?, wMargaret Isabel Steele
HOWARD, Albert Tapp, b1863, Floyd, Floy Co, fJoseph Lane, wMinnie E Simmons
Anne Howard, b17--, Fred Co?, hJames Cather
Bettie, b1821, Russ Co, fJohnson, mNancy Cowan, hJohn S Smyth
Evelyn Jane, b1862, Pennington Gap, Lee Co, 2w of John f Skaggs
Frances, b18--, York Co, hJohn R Sheild
Henry, bc1830, Loud Co?, 2h of Emma Tavenner
India, bc1870, Floy Co, d1917, fJoseph, mAnnie Smith, 2w of Edward W Early, Sr, md9/18/

HOWARD Continued)
1893
James, b18--, Fred Co?, wVirginia Brown
John Taze, b10/1846, nrHonaker, Russ Co, fJohn T, mJane Fletcher, wMollie Artrip
John T, b1818, Russ Co, fWalter A, wJane Fletcher
Johnson, b1774, wNancy Cowan
Joseph, b18--, Floy Co?, wAnnie Smith
Kate, b184-, Hano Co, d1909, fEdward C, hRichard Henry Cardwell, md2/9/1865
Lillie D, b18--, Pitt Co, fJoseph, hWilliam T Lawson
Marya, b1837, Russ Co, d1902, hWilliam H Brown
Norman DeVere, bc1830, wAnna Skinker
Sallie, b17--, Char Co?, hSamuel Moore II, md3/9/1805
Sue Cary, b1845, ElCi Co?, d1895, hEdwin Walter Holt
HOWE, Augusta, b18--, Taze Co?, hRobert D Hufford
Mary Elizabeth, b18--, Wyth Co, d1909, hWilliam Wardlaw Minor, md4/5/1863
HOWELL, --, b17--, Gray Co?, hJohn Phipps
HOWERY, Sophia, b18--, Mont Co, hJohn Floyd Meredith
HOWISON, Ann Wood, bc1800, PrWi Co, h-- McIntosh
HOWLE, Annie Parham, b18--, Suss Co, fJames D, (2)mEmma Parham, hGeorge E Booker
James D, b6/9/1824, Suss Co, fWilliamson, m-- Graves, 1w Harriet Field, 2wEmma Parham, 3wMary Frances Moore
Williamson, b1789, Suss Co, w-- Graves
HOWSON, Anne, b16--, fRobert, hRice Hooe III
HOYE, Edward L, bc1850, Gooc Co, fJames, Jr, mMartha Blackwell Davenport
Emma S, b184-, Gooc Co, fJames, Jr, mMartha Blackwell Davenport
Henry H, bc1840, Gooc Co, fJames, Jr, mMartha Blackwell Davenport

HOYLE (continued)
James, Jr, b12/1/1814, Manakin, Gooc Co, fJames, Sr, wMartha Blackwell Davenport
Mildred Ann, b184-, Gooc Co, fJames, Jr, mMartha Blackwell Davenport
Robert James, bc1840, Gooc Co, fJames, Jr, mMartha Blackwell Davenport
Walter S, b12/7/1853, Gooc Co, fJames, Jr, mMartha Blackwell Davenport, 1wEsther Mitchell, md10/9/1895, 2wAnna Owens, md1/25/1905
HUBARD, E B, b186-, Lynchburg, Camp Co, fE W, mJulia Taylor
E W, b1841, Buck Ca, d1915, wJulia Taylor
Edmund Wilcox, Sr, b18--, Buck Co?, wSarah A Eppes
Edmund Wilcox, Jr1, b8/5/1853, Buck Co, fEdmund Wilcox, Sr, mSarah A Eppes, 1wMary May, 2wMargaret Leake
John E, b185-, Buck Co, fEdmund Wilcox, Sr, mSarah A Eppes
Julia T, b186-, Lynchburg, Camp Co, d1904, fE W, mJulia L Taylor
Robert T, bc1870, Lynchburg, Camp Co, fE W, mJulia Taylor
Sue W, b185-, Buck Co, fEdmund Wilcox, Sr, mSarah A Eppes, hJ T Crow
Willie Jones, b7/27/1856, Buck Co, fE W, mSarah A Eppes, wCarrie L Sims
HUBBARD, Benjamin H B, Sr, b8/29/1838, Lanc Co, fJesse, wFannie McClannahan
Burdine, bc1860, Wise Co?, wPolly Anne Roberts
James E, bc1859, ChCi Co, d1916, wEmma S Nimmo
Laura, b18--, JaCi Co?, hPeter T Cowles
HUDDLE, David, b12/18/1824, Wyth Co, d1880, wMargaret Earheart
Dorothy, b17--, Shen Co, d1802, hJacob Funkhouser
James F, b18--, Wyth Co?, wIsabelle Lambert
John Henry, b9/8/1867, Wyth Co, fDavid, mMargaret Earheart, wMary Jones

HUDDLE (continued)
Sallie, b18--, Shen Co?, 1w of Washington Abel Sager, md187-
HUDDLESON, Frank W, b2/26/1867, Woodstock, Shen Co, fJohn, mMary Elizabeth Patterson, wNellie M Moore, md1891
Harry P, b186-, Woodstock, Shen Co, fJohn, mMary Elizabeth Patterson
Sarah M, b186-, Woodstock, Shen Co, fJohn, mMary Elizabeth Patterson
HUDDLESTON, Peter Lee, b8/5/1837, Chambersburg, Bedf Co, fJohn, mSallie Dent
HUDGINS, Alice, bc1870, Laban, Math Co, hWilliam L Diggs, md1892
Annie J, bMath Co?, fRobert, hJonathan Ford
Charles H, bc1840, Math Co, wEugenia Hudgins
Elizabeth, b1831, Laban, Math Co, hAlexander J Diggs
Eugenia, b184-, York Co, fThomas Diggs, Sr, mLucinia Hudgins, hCharles H Hudgins
Henry Clay, b1842, Math Co, d1913, fRobert, wLucrecia S Langhorne
Henry L, b186-, Lynchburg, Camp Co, fHenry Clay, mLucrecia S Langhorne
Humphrey, b184-, York Co, d1863, fThomas Diggs, Sr, mLucinia Hudgins
Jesse, b17--, Math Co, wMary Foster
Jesse F, b185-, York Co, fThomas Diggs, Sr, mLucinia Hudgins
Ketura, b185-, York Cao, fThomas Diggs, Sr, mLucinia Hdgins, hJoseph B Hogge
Lucinia, b1819, Math Co, d1903, fJesse, mMary Foster, hThomas Diggs Hudgins, Sr
Martha, b18--, Math Co, wDrew Diggs
Mary Eliza, b184-, York Co, fThomas Diggs, Sr, mLucinia Hudgins
Mattie A, bc1850, York Co, fThomas Diggs, Sr, mLucinia Hudgins

HUDGINS (continued)
Robert Henry, Jr, b1846, Buck Co, d1915, fRobert Henry, Sr, wLucy Jane Wren
Theophilus, b185-, York Co, d191-, fThomas Diggs, Sr, mLucinia Hudgins
Thomas Diggs, Sr, b1814, Math Co, d1887, fAnthony d, wLucinia Hudgins
Thomas Diggs, Jr, b10/10/1855, York Co, fThomas Diggs, Sr, mLucinia Hudgins, wViola Diggs, md1/6/1881
HUDNALL, Elizabeth Douglas, b18--, Fauq Cao, 1w of Orlando Thompson
HUDSON, --, b182-, Fauq Co, wAnnie Kincheloe
Amanda Jackson, bc1837, Fluv Co?, d1901, fWilliam, mLuvenia Jackson Bryant, 1hWilliam George Lane, Sr, 2hJohn Haden Lane, Jr
Corilla, b3/17/1853, Slate Mills, Rapp Co, hD W Thornhill
Edgar Yager, b3/3/1858, Page Co, fJohn W, mSallie Holtzclaw, wBessie Harrison, md6/6/1893
Eliza, b18--, Augu Co, hAsa Harper Chumbley
Hubert Varner, b124/1853, Page Co, fJames B, mSusan Varner
James B, bc1860, Fred Co?, wJemmie Hillyard
John W, b18--, Culp Co, fJoel, wSallie Holtzclaw
Mary, b17--, Hanover, Hano Co, fCharles, hJohn Wingfield
Susannah, b17--, Amel Co, hJames Chappell
William, b18--, Fluv Co, wLuvenia Jackson Bryant
Wilson Bryant, b183-, Fluv Co?, fWilliam, mLuvenia Jackson Bryant
William L, b6/20/1851, Page Co, fJames B, mSusan Varner, wMartha Y Smoot, md11/1/1877
HUFF, --, b18--, Fauq Co, 2h of Isabella Swart
Annie, b184-, Fred Co, fDaniel, mSarah Walters, 1h-- Cozland, 2h-- Anderson
Charles N, b12/24/1860, nrDale-

HUFF (continued)
ville, Bote Ca, fDavid, mSarah Nininger, wAnna Layman, md1895
Daniel, b1812, Fred Co, mSusan Grimm, wSarah Walters
David, b181-, Fred Co, d186-, mSusan Grimm
David, bc1827, nrEagle Rock, Bote Co, d1876, wSarah Nininger
Henry Green, b1/1/1843, nrMiddletown, Fred Co, fDaniel, mSarah Walters, 1wRebecca Keffer, md11/1867, 2wRachel A Baker, m1877
Isaac, bc1835, Floy Co, wAdeline Kitterman
Isaac Eldridge, b5/26/1866, Floy Co, fIsaac, mAdeline Kitterman, wFlora McIvor Francis
Jennie, b185-, Fred Co, fDaniel, mSarah Walters
John, b181-, Fred Co, mSusan Grimm
John W, b185-, fDaniel, mSarah Walters
Lawson America, bc1850, Fred Co, d1920, fDaniel, mSarah Walters, hGeorge Robert Henry, md1867
Lucy, b185-, Fred Co, fDaniel, mSarah Walters, hJohn Burkholder
Lula, b186-, nrDaleville, Bote Co, fDavid, mSarah Nininger, hJ A Dove
Maria, b184-, Fred Co, fDaniel, mSarah Walters, hMitchell Walters
Martha, b184-, Fred Co, fDaniel, mSarah Walters, hLawrence Moore
Mary, b181-, Fred Co, mSusan Grimm, hCharlson Sloan
Mary, bc1840, Fred Co, fDaniel, mSarah Walters, hSanford Edmonson
Nellie, b186-, nrDaleville, Bote Co, fDavid, mSarah Nininger, hS B Woodson
Solomon, b181-, Fred Co, mSusan Grimm
Susie, b186-, nrDaleville, Bote Co, fDavid, mSarah Nininger, hW H Moomaw
Virginia, b184-, Fred Co,

HUFF (continued)
fDaniel, mSarah Walters
HUFFARD, James W, b1829, Wytheville, Wyth Co, m-- Whitman, wMary Hudson
Niciti, b18--, Smyt Co?, hGeorge W Hayes
Samuel, b7/5/1870,, St Albans, Kana Co, fJames W, mMary Hudson, wAlice E Yost, md6/5/1896
HUFFINES, J C, bc1860, Henry Co?, wNancy G Taylor
HUFFMAN, --, b18--, Shen Co?, hN D Hite
Amanda, b18--, Crai Co?, hJefferson D Sibold
Bertie, b1856,, Page Co, fHenry, hCharles Edward Funkhauser
Joseph, b18--, Page Co?, wMary Susan Hershburger
Maria, bc1833, Augu Co?, d1907, fBenjamin, hLevi Plecker
Marion Luther, b6/2/1860, nr Level Green, Crai Co, d 1923, wMissouri Jane Reynolds, md10/1864
Martin, bc1814, Rkbr Co, d1904
Mary, b12/25/1792, Augu Co?, hJohn Ruebush, Sr
Mary S, bc1850, Page Co?, d1907, fJoseph, mMary Susan Hershburger, hWilliam Henry Brumback
Miriam, bc1800, Madi Co?, hJohn Wesley Wayland, Sr
Oscar E, b12/13/1845, Crai Co, fMartin, wNancy E Lafon
Susan, b18--, Rkhm co?, hSamuel W Chandler
HUFFORD, Robert D, bTaze Co?, wAugusta Howe
HUGGINS, --, bc1860, wBertie Snapp
HUGHES, Archelaus, b17--, Patr Co, wMary Dalton
Augustine Clark, b185-, Pitt Co, fJohn E, Sr, mElzabeth Clark
Charles, bc1860, Nhld Co?, wVirginia E Welch
Emma, bc1860, nrHamilton, Loud Co, fJohn H, hJohn H Alexander
Fannie, bc1860, Pitt Co, fJohn E, Sr, mElizabeth Clark, hJames R Pruden

HUGHES (continued)
George B, b186-, Pitt Co, fJohn E, Sr, mElziabeth Clark
John E, Sr, b18--, PrEd Co, fJohn E B, wElizabeth Clark
John E, Jr, b186-, Pitt Co, fJohn E, Sr, mElizabeth Clark
John P, bc1830, Appo Co?, wVirginia C Nowlin
John Smith, b18--, Rapp Co, wAdeline Spindle
John Spindle, b11/19/1853, Amissville, Rapp Co, fJohn Smith, mAdeline Spindle, wCapitola Luthera Luttrell
Laura Alice, b18--, Char Co, hRobert H Morton
Lizzie, bc1860, Pitt Co?, fJohn E, Sr, mElizabeth Clark, hS N Walker
Lucy Haynes, b1857, Hayes Store, Glou Co, hWilliam H Ashe
Mary, b18--, Norf Co?, hThomas Bridges
Mary Elizabeth, bc1830, Rkhm Co?, fE G F, hAbraham B Lincoln
Mary S, b185-, Pitt Co, fJohn E, Sr, mElizabeth Clark, hW T Green
Nancy, b17--, Patr Co?, fArchelaus, mMary Dalton, hBrett Stovall
Robert Morton, Sr, b9/10/1855, Abingdon, Wash Co, fRobert William, mEliza A Johnston, wMattie L Smith, md1879
Robert William, b6/6/1821, Powhatan, Powh Co, d1901, wEliza M Johnston, md6/4/1850
Rosa, bc1860, Pitt Co, fJohn E, Sr, mElizabeth Clark, hT E Roberts
Thomas Mortimer, b185-, Amissville, Rapp Co, fJohn Smith, mAdeline Spindle
William, bc1820, Rkhm Co, wChristiana Moore
William T, Sr, b12/10/1862, Pitt Co, fJohn E, Sr, mElizabeth Clark, wClara Davis, md6/17/1896
HUGHLETT, Arabella D, b1852, Corinth Church, Nhld Co, 2w of Fleming P Welch

HUGHSON, Frederick, b183-, Louisa Co, fJohn, wAnn Dettor
HULETT, Barbara, bc1800, Fred Co?, hJonas Aby
HULL, David Denton, Sr, b12/26/837, Marion, Smyt Co, fThomas T, mSarah Byars, wMary A H Graham, md7/29/1868
Norton, b1792, Smyt Co, fSamuel II, mBathenia Norton, 1wRemember Ann Thomas, 2wRuth Jones
Pauline A, b1845, nrMarion, Smyt Co, fThomas T, mSarah Byars, hWalter Scott Staley
Thomas T, b2/23/1811, Smyt Co, fNorton, (1)mRemember Ann Thomas, wSarah Byars
HULVEY, Bell Virginia, b18--, Mt Sidney, Augu Co, fWilliam, hMontague Payne
HUMBERT, John, bc1840, Shen Co, wCatherine Wine
HUME, Hannah, b17--, Spot Co?, hHarry Sparks
HUMPHREYS, Margaret J, b18--, Rkbr Co?, hWilliam A Donald
Minnie, b18--, Pula Co?, hHenry Dunlap
HUMPHRIES, --, b18--, Spot Co, wJane Smith
Arthur N, bc1870, Rkbr Co, fWilliam S, mMariah Louise Clemmer
B Clemmer, bc1870, Rkbr Co, fWilliam S, mMariah Louise Clemmer
Carey Aurelius, b8/7/1870, Spot Co, fJohn Robert Powell, mLillian Matilda Kemper, wBena Hill Newhouse, md7/7/1899
John Robert Powell, b18--, Spot Co, mJane Smith, wLillian Matilda Kemper
William Frank, bc1970, Rkbr Co, fWilliam S, mMariah Louise Clemmer, wWillie Berry, m1899
William S, bc1842, Rkbr Co, wMariah Louise Clemmer
HUMPSTON, Lucinda, b18--, Shen Co, 1w of Isaac R Hite
HUMSTON, Benjamin Franklin, b18--, Shen Co, wRebecca Rush
Mamie, b18--, Edinburg, Shen Co, fBenjamin Franklin, mRebecca Rush, hThomas Hatcher Sprint, Sr

HUNDLEY, Andrew, bc1800, nrMontague, Esse Co, wNancy Trible
Augusta, b18--, Bote Co?, fJ W, 1h-- Cobbs, 2hWilliam A Rinehart
Calhoun, bc1860, Dunnsville, Esse Co, fAndrew, mMartha Sizer
Charles A, b18--, Char Co?, wFannie Edmonds
Elijah Dupee, b12/16/1835, nrClover, Hali Co, wElizabeth Glenn Johnston
Elisha E, b1799, wAnne Bouldin
Frances Arthur, b18--, fJosiah, Jr
John T, b18--, Henry Co, fWilliam B, wKate Gravely
John Trible Thomas, Sr, bc1831, Esse Co, d1890, fAndrew, mNancy Trible, wSarah Elizabeth Garnett
John Trible Thomas, Jr, b3/1/1868, Dunnsville, Esse Co, fJohn Trible Thomas, Sr, mSarah Elizabeth Garnett, wSue Fleet Walker, md10/27/1897
Joseph Henry, bc1851, Henry Co?, d1877, wLucy Wade Harris
Josiah, Jr, b17--, fJosiah, Sr
Martha Elizabeth, b1832, nr Charlotte Court House, Char Co, fElisha E, hJames Benjamin Monroe Osborne
Nannie, b18--, Char Co, fCharles A, mFannie Edmonds, hDaniel W Owen, md10/11/1876
Pocahontas, bc1870, Henry Co?, fH B, hJohn David Bassett, Sr
HUNGERFORD, Julia, b18--, West Co?, 2w of Edward Colville Griffith
HUNT, Annie, b11/30/1866, hT Miller Bane
Daniel Robert, b18--, fJohn II, mSallie Tate, wEmma Mebane
Gilbert, bc1800, fJohn
John II, bc1800, fJohn, wSallie Tate
Lucy Penn, b18--, hThomas Guy
Mary Ann, b17--, Nels Co?, hJames Dillard, md1748
HUNTER, --, b18--, Fred Co, wRachel Catherine Stine
Anne Evelina, b17--, fMoses, hHenry St George Tucker

HUNTER (continued)
Caroline Matilda, b18--, Appo Co?, hArthur Alexander LeGrande
Eliza C, b1852, Charles Towne, Jeff Co, hHenry P McNeer
Frederick Campbell Stewart, b18--, KiGe Co, fThomas Lomax, wSusan Rose Turner
Helen, b18--, Hamp Co, hAlfred Moore
Rachel, b18--, Fair Co, hJames Flynn
Rebecca, b17--, Fred Co?, hJoseph Holmes
Robert, bc1820, wMary Harrison
Sarah, bc1700, Nans Co?, hWilliam Battle
Taliferro, b17--, KiGe Co, w-- Lomax
Thomas Lomax, b18--, KiGe Co, fTaliferro, m-- Lomax, 1wMaria T Tennant, 2wJulia S Tayloe
HUNTON, Alexander,, b172-, Lanc Co, fThomas, mMary Carrell
Charles, b178-, Fauq Co, fJames, mHannah Logan Brown
Eppa, b1789, Fauq Co, fJames, mHannah Logan Brown, wElizabeth Marye Brent, md6/23/1811
Eppa II, b9/22/1822, Fauq Co, fEppa, mElizabeth Marye Brent, wLucy Caroline Weir, md6/1848
Eppa, Jr, b4/14/1855, Brentsville, PrWi Co, fEppa II, mLucy Caroline Weir, 1wErva Winston Payne, md11/18/1884, 2wVirginia Semmes Payne, md4/24/1901
James, b7/21/1763, Fauq Co, fWilliam, mJudith Kirk, wHannah Logan Brown, md2/6/1786
John, b172-, Lanc Co, fThomas, mMary Carrell
Lucelia, b18--, hJames William Foster
Priscilla, b17--, hIsaac Foster
Thomas II, b172-, Lanc Co, fThomas, mMary Carrell
William, b172-, Lanc Co, fThomas, mMary Carrell, wJudith Kirk
HUNTSBERRY, A, bc1860, Fred Co?, wVirginia Barr
HUPP, Mary, b181-, Shen Co?, d1854, fMartin, hWilliam D

HUPP (continued)
Eyster
HURFF, Frank, , 18--, Nans Co, wEmily --
HURLEY, Moses, b18--, Buch Co, d1865, fSamuel R
Samuel R, Sr, b1842, Buch Co, fMoses, wMary Jane Lambert
HURN, Helen Rebecca, b18--, Strasburg, Shen Co, hGeorge Madison Spengler
HURT, Emma Margaret, b7/2/1849, Camp Co?, fStephen Clifton, mFannie Crenshaw, hRichard Thomas Watts, md4/22/1875
Isabell E, b16--, Camp Co?, hPhilip Pendleton, m1680
John G, bc1831, Fran Co, wMary E Whitlow
Lou A, b1854, Taze Co, hJohn A McFarlane
Mary P, bc1850, Camp Co?, fStephen Clifton, mFannie Crenshaw, hLeighton Cheatwood
Nancy B, b12/13/1807, Bedf Co, fWilliam, hPeyton Graves, Jr
Sarah Margaret, b18--, Bedf Co, fWilliam, mMary --, 1w of Elijah G McClanahan
Stephen Clifton, bc1800, mMary Elizabeth Preston, wFannie Crenshaw
Sarah Jane, b1849, nrRoanoke, Meck Co, hIsaac T Bandy
HURST, Alpheus, b18--, Fauq Co?, wMildred Payne
Martha Susan, b18--, Math Co, hAlbert Jefferson Wilkins
Mason, b18--, Fauq Co?, wCatherine Payne
HUTCHESON, Adele Frances, b18--, Meck Co, fCharles Sterling, h-- Love
Bettie, b186-, nrEdinburg, Shen Co, fJohn T, mMary Dirting, hEmanuel G Shipe
Charles, b17--, Caro Co, d1807, fJohn, wFrances Collier
Charles Samuel, b186-, Meck Co, fJoseph Collier, mAnne Goode Farrar
Charles Sterling, b181-, Meck Co, fJoseph, mRebecca Neblett
Collier, b17--, Meck Co, fCharles, mFrances Collier
Conway Goode, bc1870, Meck Co,

HUTCHESON (continued)
fJoseph Collier, mAnn Goode Farrar
D Prescott W, bc1860, nrEdinburg, Shen Co, fJohn T, mMary Dirting
Elizabeth Catherine, b186-, nrEdinburg, Shen Co, fJohn T, mMary Dirting, hJoseph Sheetz
Herbert Farrar, b3/20/1869, Meck Co, fJoseph, mAnn Goode Farrar, wMary Hutcheson Young, md10/25/1893
James N, b181-, Meck Co, fJoseph, mRebecca Neblett
James Nathaniel, b186-, Meck Co, fJoseph Collier, mAnn Goode Farrar
John, b17--, Caro Co, fJohn
John, b17--, Meck Co, fCharles, mFrances Collier
John, b185--, nrEdinburg, Shen Co, fJohn T, mMary Dirting
John T, bc1825, Shen Co, dc1870, wMary Dirting
John V, b18--, Meck Co?, d186-, fJoseph C, (2)mMary Valentine
John William, b18--, Meck Co, d186-, fCharles Sterling
Joseph, b17--, Meck Co, fCharles, mFrances Collier, wRebecca Neblett
Joseph C, b18--, Meck Co, fCharles Sterling, 2wMary Valentine
Joseph Clarence, b3/29/1867, nrEdinburg, Shen Co, fJohn T, mMary Dirting, wMinerva E Miller, md12/12/1906
Joseph Colier, b4/11/1816, Meck Co, d1890, fJoseph, mRebecca Neblett, wAnn Goode Farrar
Joseph Emmett, b186-, Meck Co, fJoseph Collier, mAnn Goode Farrar
Lula Rebecca, bc1870, Meck Co, fJoseph Collier, mAnn Goode Farrar, hF A Smaw
Marquis D Lafayette, b185-, nrEdinburg, Shen Co, fJohn T, mMary Dirting
Peter, b17--, Caro Co, fJohn
Richard, b17--, Caro Co, fJohn
Robert S, Sr, b18--, Rkbr Co, fRobert
Robert S, Jr, b5/1845, Rkbr Co,

HUTCHESON (continued)
fRobert S, Sr, wMary Moore Morrison
Rosa, b186-, nrEdinburg, Shen Co, fJohn T, mMary Dirting, hW L Holler
Sterling Neblett, b186-, Meck Co, fJoseph Collier, mAnn Goode Farrar
William O, bc1840, Lune Co?, wRebecca Ann Moore
HUTCHINSON, Emanuel, b 17--, Scot Co, 1wNancy Carter
Emma, b2/22/1859, nrLloyds, Esse Co, hJames T B Lumpkin
Emma D, b18--, Edinburg, Shen Co, hGeorge Thomas Dorsey Collins
Francis, b1825, Scot Co, 1907, fEmanuel, (1)mNancy Carter, wMatilda Howell
George W, b18--, Augu Co, fJohn, w-- Joyce
Henry, b18--, Union, Monr Co, d1909, fGeorge W, m-- Joyce, wKatherine Abernathy
John C, bc1800, Fran Co, wLucy Meredith
Peter F, b5/4/1860, Fran Co, wLucy Meredith
Sarah Frances, b3/19/1838, Glade Hill, Fran Co, fJohn C, mLucy Meredith, hBenjamin Peter Hancock, md3/21/1865
HUTCHISON, Robert, b18--, Richmond?, wEllen Caskie
Sarah, b18--, Fair Co, hThomas Hutton
HUTSELL, Elizabeth, bc1810, Blan (now Wyth) Co, 1898, hAdam Wagner
HUTT, Bradley, bc1870, Montross, West Co, fJoseph Warren, Sr, mElizabeth Costine
Clayburn Butts, b186-, Montross, West Co, fJoseph Warren, Sr, mElizabeth Costine
Constance Virginia, b186-, Montross, West Co, fJoseph Warren, Sr, mElizabeth Costine
Eliza A, b1827, Hickory Farm, nrWarsaw, Rich Co, d1887, fS S, hWilliam H Omohundro
Ernest L, b185-, Rich Co?, wMollie R Omohundro
George Littleton, b186-, Mon-

HUTT (continued)
tross, West Co, fJoseph Warren, Sr, mElizabeth Costine
Hiram M, bc1850, Rich Co?, 1wVirginia Omohundro, 2wLaura C Omohundro
Joseph Warren, Sr, b1834, Montross, West co, d1912, fWilliam, mBetsey Harvey, wElizabeth Costine
Joseph Warren, Jr, b4/11/1861, Montross, West Co, fJoseph Warren, Sr, mElzabeth Costine, wEliza M Hall, md6/28/1900
Mungo Lloyd, bc1860, Montross, West Co, fJoseph Warren, Sr, mElizabeth Costine
William, b1799, West Co, d1847, wBetsey Harvey
William, b186-, Montross, West Co, fJoseph Warren, Sr, mElizabeth Costine
HUTTER, Adaline L, b1844, Camp Co, fGeorge Christian, mHarriet James Risque, hLeroy William Long
Ann Roy, b3/9/1847, "Poplar Forest", Bedf Co, fEdward Sixtus, mEmma William Cobbs, hSamuel Griffin
Charlotte Stannard, b3/19/1857, "Poplar Forest", Bedf Co, fEdward Sixtus, mEmma Williams Cobbs, hJames Risque Hutter
Christian Sixtus, b10/19/1862, "Poplar Forest", Bedf Co, fEdward Sixtus, mEmma Williams Cobbs, wErnestine Booker, md1/21/1885
Edna, b18--, Camp Co, m-- Langhorne, hStephen H Meem
Edward Sixtus, b9/18/1839, Sanduskey, Camp Co, fGeorge Christian, mHarriet James Risque, wNannie Langhorne
Emma Cobbs, b3/16/1855, "Poplar Forest", Bedf Co, fEdward Sixtus, mEmma Williams Cobbs, hJames A Logwood
Ferdinand Charles, b5/16/1831, Camp Co?, fGeorge Christian, mHarriet James Risque
George Edwrd, b3/7/1852, "Poplar Forest", Bedf Co, fEdward Sixtus, mEmma Williams Cobbs
James Risque, b10/18/1841, San-

HUTTER (continued)
duskey, Camp Cao, fGeorge Christian, mHarriet James Risque, wCharlotte Stannard Hutter
William Christian, b3/21/1843, "Poplar Forest", Bedf Co, d1862, fEdward Sixtus, mEmma Williams Cobbs
HUTTON, Ann Louise, b183-, "Huntingdon", Fair Co, fIsaac Gardiner, mRebecca Emeline Smith, hHenry C Nevitt
Arthur Dixon, b18--, Wash Co, wSarah Buchanan Ryburn
Emeline, bc1830, "Huntingdon", Fair Co, fIsaac Gardiner, mRebecca Emeline Smith, hHyat D Reid
Francis Beattie, Sr, b1/28/1858, Glade Spring, Wash Co, fArthur Dixon, mSarah Buchanan Ryburn, 1wJennie Orr Preston, 2wSophia Ruby Clark
Henry Isaac, b3/24/1859, "Huntingdon", Fair Co, fJohn Sidney, Sr, mMargaret T Halley, wMay G (Halley) Broders, md 6/19/1889
Ida Elizabeth, b9/27/1863, "Huntingdon", Fair Co, fJohn Sidney, Sr, mMargaret T Halley, hRobert Emmett Hooe
John Sidney, Sr, b4/1828, "Huntingdon", Fair Co, d1894, fIsaac Gardiner, mRebecca Emeline Smith, wMargaret T Halley, md1858
John Sidney, Jr, b5/5/1860, "Hunt-ingdon", Fair Co, fJohn Sidney, Sr, mMargaret T Halley, wCora Armstrong, md1/2/1894
Mary, b182-, nrAlexandria, fIsaac Gardiner, mRebecca Emeline Smith, hWilliam Blemcoe
Mary Virginia, b186-, "Huntingdon", Fair Co, fJohn Sidney, Sr, mMargaret T Halley, hA Hunter Terrett
Thaddeus S, b183-, "Huntingdon", Fair Co, fIsaac Gardiner, mRebecca Emeline Smith, wBettie Ragan
Thomas, b182-, "Huntingdon", Fair Co, fIsaac Gardiner,

HUTTON (continued)
mRebecca Emeline Smith, wSarah Hutchison
Virginia, b182-, Fair Co, fIsaac Gardiner, mRebecca Emeline Smith, hJohn Terrett
HUYETT, Mary Jane, bc1825, Fred (now Clar) Co, d1866, fAbram, hThomas Jones
Samuel, bc1820, Fred (now Clar) Co, fAbram, wSydney Jones
HYATT, Adanijah G, b7/11/1867, Turkey Cove, Lee Co, fJohn A G, mEliza Ann Slemp, 2h of Elizabeth (Pennington) Orr, md4/11/1902
H Eugene, bc1870, Turkey Cove, Lee Co, fJohn A G, mEliza Ann Slemp
John A G, b4/20/1839, Taze Co, d1922, fUriah G, wEliza Ann Slemp
Lawrence T, b186-, Turkey Cove, Lee Co, fJohn A G, mEliza Ann Slemp
HYLTON, Alice, b186-, nrDugspur. Carr Co, fJames M, mMahala Agnes Burnett, hRobert L Branscome
Laura E, b1861, nrDugspur, Carr Co, d1920, fJames M, mMahala Agnes Burnett, hJohn Collier, md1877
Emma, b186-, nrDugspur, Carr Co, fJames M, mMahala Agnes Burnett, hThomas Harris
James M, b1839, Floy Co, d1921, fBryant, wMahala Agnes Burnett
Lula L, bc1870, nrDugspur, Carr Co, fJames M, mMahala Agnes Burnett, hStephen Wright
HYSLOP, Georgia, b18--, Acco Co?, hThomas Starkey
John Thomas Benjamin, b6/21/1864, Craddock Neck, Acco Co, fJohn W, mMary Kate (Powell) Colonna, wFannie Anderson, md2/1896
John W, b1835, nrCraddockville, Acco Co, d1902, fSmith, 2h of Mary Kate (Powell) Colonna
INGE, Ella Jane, b18--, Lune Co, fGeorge, mSusanna Hawthorne, 2w of Julius Augustus Moore
George, b18--, Lune Co, wSusanna Hawthorne

INGLES, John, b18--, Radford, Mont Co, fWilliam, wAgnes McClanahan
McClanahan, b1848, Radford, Mont Co, d1907, fJohn, mAgnes Mc Clanahan, wAngie Harvey
Rebecca Ann, bc1827, Aug Co?, d1898, fWilliam, mBettie Crawford, hRobert S Harnsberger
William, bc1800, wBettie Crawford
INGRAM, Amelia, bc1830, "Laurel Hill", Lune Co, fSylvanus, mAlice Littlepage Taylor, hWilliam S Rudd, md11/14/1849
Benjamin, bc1710, Brun Co, fJohn, Sr, mHannah --
Charity, b17--, Lune Co, fSamuel, mMargaret --, hBenjamin Jordan
Elizabeth, b171-, Brun Co, fJohn, mHannah --, h-- Vaughan
George, bc1710, Brun Co, fJohn, Sr, mHannah --
James, b17--, Brun Co, fJohn, Sr, mHannah --
Jesse, c1710, Brun Co, fJohn, Sr, mHannah --
John, Sr, b16--, Spot (now Oran) Co, d1763, fTobias, w Hannah --
John, Jr, bc1700, Oran Co, d1760, fJohn, Sr, mHannah --, wElizabeth --
John, b17--, Lune Co, fSamuel, mMargaret --, wSusanna Billups
John H, bc1860, Char Co?, wMattie R Priddy
John Henry, b3/17/1862, Culpeper Court House, Culp Co, d1911, fSylvanus Littlepage, mEliza Smart, wOctavia Page Sublett, md 6/7/1887
Joseph, b171-, Brun Co, fJohn, Sr, mHannah --
Joshua, bc1710. Brun Co, fJohn, Sr, mHannah --
Lawrence, b12/18/1865, "Laurel Hill", Lune Co, fSylvanus Littlepage, mEliza Smart, wAnne Walker Brodnax, md6/25/1890
Martha Roberta, bc1830, "Laurel Hill", Lune Co, fSylvanus, mAlice Littlepage Taylor, hJoseph Henry Snead, md2/11/1851
Mary A, b5/5/1870, Pitt Co,

INGRAM (continued) hBeverly S Dodson
Pines, b17--, Lune Co, fSamuel, mMargaret --, wLucy --
Richard, bc1710, Brun Co, fJohn, Sr, mHannah --
Robert, b17--, Lune Co, d1782, fSamuel, mMargaret --, wElizabeth --
Samuel, b170, Brun Co, d1765, fJohn, Sr, mHannah --, wMargaret --
Samuel, b17--, Lune Co, fRobert, mElizabeth --, wMartha Walker
Sarah, b183-, "Laurel Hill", Lune Co, fSylvanus, mAlice Littlepage Taylor, hAlgernon Sydney Smith, md6/17/1855
Sylvanus, b1776, Lune Co, d1846, fSamuel, mMartha Walker, wAlice Littlepage Taylor
Sylvanus Littlepage, b1832, "Laurel Hill", Lune Co, d1891, fSylvanus, mAlice Littlepage Taylor, wEliza Smart, md5/8/1861
Thomas, b17--, Lune Co, fSamuel, mMargret --
Thomas Locke, b183-, "Laurel Hill", Lune Co, d1896, fSylvanus, mAlice Littlepage Taylor
Tibitha, b171-, Brun Co, fJohn, Sr, mHannah --, hWilliam Gee
William E, b1838, "Laurel Hill", Lune Co, d1873, fSylvanus, mAlice Littlepage Taylor, wElla Jones, md12/12/1866
Mattie, bc1870, Henry Co?, m-- Fuller, hLewis Clay Haley, md1896
INSKEEP, James, b18--, Culp Co, wSophia --
IRBY, Hannah, b1810, ChCi Co, d1845, 2w of Joseph Folkes
Mary Elizabeth, b18--, Henrico Co, hThomas F Fussell
Sarah, b18--, fWilliam Hunt, mSarah Washington Stith, 1hRichard Henry Leigh Bruke, 2hWilliam Henry Hallowell
William Hunt, bc1800, wSarah Washington Smith
IRONMONGER, Elvira Elizabeth, b1846, York Co, d1915, hJohn Henry Marshall

IRVIN, Arthur H, b186-, Hamp Co?, fElias, mSarah E Houser
Elias, bc1833, Columbia Furnace, Shen Co, d1910, wSarah E Houser
Ella Lee, b186-, nrColumbia Furnace, Shen Co, fElias, m Sarah E Houser
George Elkanah, b6/5/1860, Hamp Co, fElias, mSarah E Houser, wRebecca Newland, md10/6/1890
Ira H, b186-, nrColumbia Furnace, Shen Co, fElias, mSarah E Houser
John W, b186-, nrColumbia Furnace, Shen Co, fElias, mSarah E Houser
Mabel C, b186-, Hamp Co, fElias, mSarah E Housr, hE A Downey
Mary Tacker, b17--, fAbram, hPaulett Clark
IRVINE, Abram II, b17--, Rkbr Co, fAbram
Mary C, b18--, Page Co?, hIsaac A Ruffner
Mary Carter, b1845, Buck Co, d1907, fRobert Kincaid, m-- Eldridge, hHenry Clay Brock
IRVING, Mary Kincade, b18--, Amhe Co?, 1w of Thomas Whitehead
Robert Kincaid, b18--, Buck Co?, w-- Eldridge
IRWIN, Clarence P, b186-, Woodstock, Shen Co, fJoseph Swift, mSarah Catherine Gochenour
Hary D, bc1850, Augu Co?, w-- White
Henry H, b9/19/1862, Woodstock, Shen Co, fJoseph Swift, mSarah Catherine Gochenour, wEmma Charlotte Supinger, md6/16/1886
Holmes A, b186-, Woodstock, Shen Co, fJoseph Swift, mSarah Catherine Gochenour
Joseph Swift, b11/30/1817, Woodstock, Shen Co, Joseph, wSarah Catherine Gochenour
Matilda Barryhill, bc1810, Woodstock, Shen Co, d1869, fJoseph, hLeonidas Triplett, Sr, md5/1834
Linden R, bc1860, Woodstock, Shen Co, d1922, fJoseph Swift,

IRWIN (continued)
mSarah Catherine Gochenour
William T, b185-, Woodstock, Shen Co, d1917, fJoseph Swift, mSarah Catherine Gochenour
ISBELL, Lewis D, bc1850, Appo Co?, wMary Elzabeth Woodson
ISELY, --, bc1850, Rkhm Co?, 1h of Ada Ann Swank
ISHAM, Mary, bc1660, fHenry, mCatherine --, hWilliam Randolph
ISLER, Abe, bc1780, Hard Co?, wSarah Warden
ITZEN, Nancy, b17--, Bedf Co?, hAbraham Buford
IVEY, Thaddeus H, b181-, Camp Co?, wMary Cornelia Winfree, md7/1842
Walter G, b18--, wKate Perdue
Willilam Christopher, b4/22/1843, Lynchburg, Camp Co, fThaddeus H, mMary Cornelia Winfree, wEmma Walton Moorman, md12/10/1871
JACK, Charles P, bc1860, Fred Co?, wOctavia L Stine
Mollie, b18--, Hamp Co?, hJohn T Shumaker
JACKSON, --, b18--, Midd Co, hRichard Haynes
--, b186-, Warr Co?, w-- Wharton
--, b18--, Amel Co?, 1w of James Madison Anderson
Abel, b7/23/1786, Fred Co, fJosiah, mRuth Steer, wRachel Fenton
Abigail, b17--, Rapp Co?, hDavid Miller
Abram E, b184-, Free Nation, Fred Co, fJosiah, mMary S Haines
Albert C, b185-, Free Nation, Fred Co, fJosiah, mMary S Haines
Ann Elizabeth, bc1830, Fauq Co?, fGeorge, hJohn Nelson Fishback, Sr
Charles F, bc1850, Free Nation, Fred Co, hJosiah, mMary S Haines
Elliza T, b185-, Free Nation, Fred Co, fJosiah, mMary S Haines, hWalter T McDonald
Fannie, b17--, Mont Co?, hGuy

JACKSON (continued)
Smith Trigg
Florence Hilton, bc1870, Madi Co?, hJohn Dutton Fray
John, b17--, wMary Payne
John William, b12/18/1847, Free Nation, Fred Co, fJosiah, m Mary S Haines, wMary M Alexander
Josiah, b7/31/1816, Fred Co, d1896, fAbel, mRachel Fenton, wMary S Haines
Maria F, bc1850, Free Nation, Fred Co, fJosiah, mMary S Haines, hHerbert C Jacobs
Mary, bc1800, fJohn, mMary Payne, hJohn J Allen
Permelia, bc1800, Char Co, hWilliam B Williamson
Rachel, bc1850, Free Nation, Fred Co, fJosiah, mMary S Haines, hC W Ball
Rush, b18--, Wash Co?, wMargaret Early
Sidney, b18--, Winchester, Fred Co, 2w of Robert Barr
Thomas Henry, bc1861, Bath Co, fAndrew, m-- Williams, wMary Kincaid
JACOB, Annie C, b2/28/1860, Belle Haven, Acco Co, hWilliam F Waters
JACOBS, Edward Burgess, b18--, Warr Co?, wMary Ann Shumate
Herbert C, bc1840, wMaria F Jackson
Minnie, b18--, Lanc Co, hLawrence R Combs
Miriam, b18--, Richmond? hWilliam Jacquelin Taylor
JAMES, --, b18--, Fran Co, d186- (father of Thomas S and Frances Keen James)
Bettie, b18--, PrAn Co, hRobert Woodside Woodhouse, Sr
David H, b1796, Lanc Co, w-- Carter
David R, b1/5/1841, Lanc Co, fDavid H, m-- Carter, wAlice A Brooks
Frances Keen, b18--, Fran Co?, hWilliam Daniel Haynes
Henry Wise, bc1840, Lanc Co, fDavid H, m-- Carter
John, b18--, Pitt Co?, wAngeline Rorer

JAMES (continued)
Lucy A, b1/8/1837, Fauq Co, hRichard M Crittenden
Mary F, b18--, Norf Co, hLeonard O Capps
Robert W, b18--, Wise Co?, wEmma Willard
Rorer A, Sr, b3/1/1859, nrBrosville, Pitt Co, d1921, fJohn, mAngeline Rorer, wAnnie Wilson, md10/12/1892
Rosa Lee, b18--, Norfolk, hWilliam Shelton Eubank, Sr
Susan, bc1803, Bedf Co, d1876, hPeter M Wright
JAMEISON, A L, bc1860, Fair Co?, wElizabeth Keith Ford
JAMESON, Caroline, b18--, Fauq Co?, hSmith S Nottingham
John William, b1/22/1849, Fran Co, fJohn, Jr, mElizabeth Akers, wSarah Elizabeth Webster, md4/4/1878
JAMISON, --, b18--, Fauq Co?, hWillie Miller
Henry, b18--, Fran Co, fJohn
John, b1783, Fran Co
John, b18--, nrBoone's Mill, Fran Co, fJohn, Sr, mCatherine Boone, wElizabeth Akers, md8/2/1844
Samuel William, b4/27/1850, Fran Co, fHenry, mSarah Catherine Showalter, wAlice Peyton Terry
JANNEY, Anna M, b1/11/1854, Hillsboro, Loud Co, fJames C, mRebecca Jane Walker, hHoward W Lippincott
Charles P, Sr, b4/27/1839, Hillsboro, Loud Co, fJames C, mRebecca Jane Walker, wNannie Lee Pollock, md11/23/1868
Elisha, b1761, Alexandria, d1827, 1wAlbina Gregg, md 4/9/1787, 2wMary Gibson, md3/4/1795
James C, b11/20/1804, Alexandria, d1878, fElisha, (2)mMary Gibson, wRebecca Jane Walker
James W, b12/18/1845, Hillsboro, Loud Coa, d1917, fJames C, mRebecca Jane Walker
John, b11/20/1847, Hillsboro, Loud Co, d1921, fJames C, mRebecca Jane Walker

JANNEY (continued)
Mary, b1855, Hillsboro, Loud Co, d1915, fJames C, mRebecca Lane Walker
Nathaniel E, b3/5/1842, Hillsboro, Loud Co, d1916, fJames C, mRebecca Jane Walker
Rebecca T, b4/19/1856, Hillsboro, Loud Co, fJames C, mRebecca Jane Walker, hAlbert B Williams
Robert M, b9/18/1851, Hillsboro, Loud Co, fJames C, mRebecca Jane Walker
Susan W, b11/11/1843, Hillsboro, Loud Co, fJames C, mRebecca Jane Walker
Thomas Gordon, b2/1/1870, Leesburg, Loud Co, fCharles P, Sr, mNannie Lee Pollock
JARMAN, Dabney, bc1800, Albe Co, w-- Maupin
Edgar Littleton, b186-, Albe Co, fWilliam Daniel, mCatherine Goodloe Lindsay
Etta L, bc1850, nrCrozet, Albe Co, fMiletus B, mCatherine Harnsberger, h-- Bethune
Henry Dabney, b186-, Albe Co, fWilliam Daniel, mCatherine Goodloe Lindsay
James Edwin, b186-, Albe Co, fWilliam Daniel, mCatherine Goodloe Lindsay
Joseph Leonard, b11/19/1867, Albe Co, fWilliam Daniel, m Catherine Goodloe Lindsay, wMary Helen Wiley, md12/22/1891
Lulu Jennings, b186-, Albe Co, fWilliam Daniel, mCatherine Goodloe Lindsay, hHenry N Tillman
Miletus B, bc1803, Albe Co, fJames, wCatherine Harnsberger
Miletus Miller, b11/8/1852, nrCrozet, Albe Co, fMiletus B, mCatherine Harnsberger, wLizzie A Taliaferro, md2/20/1884
Robert Melvin, bc1870, Albe Co, fWilliam Daniel, mCatherine Goodloe Lindsay
William Daniel, b5/30/1831, Albe Co, fDabney, m-- Maupin, wCatherine Goodloe Lindsay
JARNAGIN, Milton P, bc1830, wAg-

JARNAGIN (continued)
nes Woodson Watkins
JARRATT, Benjamin Franklin, b18--, Suss Co, fWilliam Nicholas, mElizabeth Wilburn, w Julia Ann Nicholson
Mary Ann, b10/22/1837, Esse Co, d1919, hThomas Henry Applewhite
Nicholas, b17--, wPolly Brown
William Nicholas, b18--, Suss Co, fNicholas, mPolly Brown, wElizabeth Wilburn
JARRETT, Elizabeth, b17--, York Co?, hJohn Tyler
John II, b17--, York Co?, fJohn, wAnne Contesse
JARVIS, James Ambler, b1848, Nhtn Co, d1920, 1wAlice M Addison, 2wSarah Belle Downing
JAVINS, Andrew J, b1870, Monr Co, wAddie Perry
JEFFERSON, --, b17--, hArthur Hopkins
Ella Virginia, bc1837, Pitt Co, hJoseph M Clark
Green, bc1810, Fran Co, wSallie Brown
Judith, b17--, nrRichmond, hGeorge Farrar
Martha, b17--, Powh Co?, h-- Goode
Peter, b17--, wJane Randolph
Thomas, b4/13/1743, fPeter, mJane Randolph, wMartha Wayles Skelton
JEFRESS, Albert G, bc1840, Char Co?, wElvia E Dupuy
Roberta Scott, b18--, Meck Co, d1903, hJohn Wesley Nicholson
Stanley, b18--, wMabel Osborne
JEFFRIES, J M, bc1850, Culp Co?, wPhoebe Ann Motley
Juliett, bc1820, KiQu Co, hJohn Pollard
Mary, bc1831, Fauq Co, d1916, fPresley N, mNancy Utterback, hJohn W Russell
Nannie F, b186-, Tappahannock, Esse Co, f1900, fWilliam G, 1w of John Leonard Henley, md11/27/1888
Presley N, bc1800, Fauq Co, w Nancy Utterback
JENKINS, Joel, b18--, Richmond, d1857, wAnn C Peyton

JENKINS (continued)
Luther Howard, b2/25/1856, Fredericksburg, Spot Co, fJoel H, mAnn C Peyton, wRosa Belle King, md5/20/1879
Mary S, b18--, Hano Co, hJames M Delaney
JENNEY, Elizabeth, b18--, Fran Co, fIsaac, mMartha Radford, hWiley Via
Isaac, b18--, Fran Co, wMartha Radford
JENNINGS, Ann, b17--, Loui Co, hJohn Davis
Annie, bc1840, nrMontross, West Co, 1w of Robert M Hall
Charles L, bc1850, Carr Co?, wEveline Wilkinson
Emily, b4/4/1851, Hillsville, Carr Co, hIsaiah Quesinberry
Henry Kelley, b18--, Shen Co?, wFrances Catherine Harr Long
Lucy Ann, b18--, Carr Co?, hWalter C Carter
Mary, b18--, Amhe Co?, 1hH C Beasley, 2hPowhatan Henson
Mary, b18--, Bedf Co?, hHolcomb White
Sarah, bc1800, Rapp Co?, hCumberland Marshall Johnson
Sarah, b1840, nrMontross, West Co, d1899, 2w of Robert M Hall
Susie Stover, b1862, Strasburg, Shen Co, fHenry Kelley, mFrances Catherine Harr Long, hOrlando Adam Keister
Theodore W, b186-, Strasburg, Shen Co, fHenry Kelley, mFrances Catherine Harr Long
JESSE, Joseph B, b1845, Milford, Caro Co, wAnnie Sarah Thornton
JESSEE, --, b1840, Russ Co, d1905, hAbednego Kiser
Kate, b1837, Caro Co, hThomas H Motley
JETER, John, b18--, Amel Co, fRhodophil
John R, Sr, b4/18/1838, Meck Co, fWilliam, m-- Gills, wRoberta Ellis Walker
Lucy Anne, b1861, Powh Co, fJohn, hCharles Womack Crowder, Sr
Mary Elizabeth, b18--, Amel Co?, hJohn Jeter Allen
Linda K, b12/3/1860, Meck Co,

JETER (continued)
fJohn R, Sr, mRoberta Ellis Walker
T Walker, b18--, Meck Co, fJohn R, Sr, mRoberta Ellis Walker
William, b1802, Meck Co, w-- Gills
William II, b1/12/1864, Meck Co, fJohn R, Sr, mRoberta Ellis Walker
William E, bc1850, Lune Co?, wAnna M Yates
Wortley, b18--, Richmond, fJohn R, Sr, mRoberta Ellis Walker, hRichard E Walker
JETT, Ellen Jane, bc1836, Rapp Co, d1910, fJames, hEdward McCormick
Eva A, bc1870, Reedville, Nhld Co, fThomas W, mFlora Alice Haynie
James Bailey, b18--, Spot Co?, wLucy Leland Chinn
Lulu E, b18--, Fred Co, fJames Bailey, mLucy Leland Chinn, hHarry Orrick Locher, Sr
Thomas Howard, b4/2/1868, Reedville, Nhld Co, fThomas W, mFlora Alice Haynie, wMary Alice Stiff, md9/15/1890
Thomas W, b184-, West Co, d1915, fWilliam, wFlora Alice Haynie
JIFFKINS, Edward, b184-, Fred Co?, wJulia Baker
JOHNS, Edward Lovell, bc1860, Richmond?, 1h of Mary Ellen Scott
Monroe, b18--, Buck Co, w-- Allen
R B, b1849, Buck Co, fMonroe, m-- Allen, wAgnes Penultima Anderson
Ella P, b7/1846, Oran Co, hW H Smith, md12/1867
Frances, bc1800, hDavid Blanton
Mary, b17--, Midd Co?, hWilliam Trigg
JOHNSON, --, b18--, Shen Co?, hJohn A English
--, b18--, Lanc Co?, hSamuel J Adams, Sr
--, bc1820, Jeff Co?, wMary Brewer
Aggie B, b184-, Wytheville, Wyth Co, fJohn L, mElizabeth

JOHNSON (continued)
Neighbours
Agnes E, b18--, Oran Co, hSamuel M Teel
Amanda J, b18--, Buch Co, 2w of John C Gilbert
Ann E, b1833, Alexandria, d1922, hFerdinand Knight
Anna, b1839, Loui Co, hWilliam Henry West
Annie C, b186-, Appo Co, f Charles I, mMartha A Crow, hJames A Mundy, Jr
C E, bc1860, wSusan Moore Wood
Charles I, b10/27/1839, Nels Co, wMartha A Crow
Charles L, Sr, b18--, Rapp Co, fWilliam, wFrances Octavia Gore
Charles W, Sr, b10/20/1840, Elk Garden, Russ Co, d1912, wAnn E Thompson
Cumberland Marshall, b17--, Rapp Co?, wSarah Jennings
Cynthia A, b18--, Acco Co, fJohn W, mNancy Carpenter, hGeorge O Hutchinson
Dorothy, b17--, hPatrick Michie
Eliza, b18--, Warr Co, 3w of Joseph E Funkhouser
Elizabeth, b1811, Honaker, Russ Co, fJohn, hReuben Finney
Elizabeth, b18--, Augu Co?, hHarrison Furr
Elizabeth, b18--, Fauq Co, hJoseph A Billingsley
Emily, b184-, Wytheville, Wyth Co, fJohn L, mElizabeth Neighbours, hIchabod P White
Emma Cooksey, b186-, Rapp Co, fCharles L, mFrances Octavia Gore
Ettie, bc1870, nrPearisburg, Gile Co, fAndrew J, mElizabeth Stewart, hEstell L Stafford
Fannie, b18--, Richmond?, fWilliam R, hGeorge Evans Caskie
Francis, b1797, Bedf Co, fThomas, (2)mSally Dickinson, wNancy Wright
George A, b1847, Duncans Mills, Scot Co, fGeorge W, wMary A Cox
Granderson B, b2/12/1869, Elk Garden, Russ Co, fCharles W, mAnn E Thompson, 1wMollie

JOHNSON (continued)
Webb, md3/21/1891, 2wEvelyn Robinson, md5/18/1901
Helen Edmonia, b18--, Rpp Co?, hGeorge Franklin Reaguer
Herny, b18--, Rapp Co, fWilliam
Hugh L, b185-, Wytheville, Wyth Co, fJohn L, mElizabeth Neighbours
Ida Virginia, b18--, Acco Co, fJohn W, mNancy Carpenter, hJ Lee Phillips
J H, bc1860, Fran Co, fJames, mAmerica E Stone
J M, bc1840, Scot Co, wManie T Morrison
James, b183-, Fran Cao, d186-, 1h of America E Stone
James Wellington, b1850, Gooc Co, wMary E Lewis
John E, b9/27/1867, Appo Co, fCharles I, mMartha A Crow, wEliza C Dunlop, md2/1901
John H, b10/31/1865, Acco Co, fJohn W, mNancy Carpenter, wMargaret Virginia Warrington, md9/19/1905
John H, bc1870, Rapp Cao, f Charles L, mFrances Octavia Gore
John L, b1827, Wyth Co, d1903, fPalser, wElizabeth Neighbours
John Wesley, b18--, Bedf Co, d1868, fMartin Johnson, mSarah Leftwich, wElzabeth Haynes, mdc1837
Joseph Robert, Sr, b18--, Buck Co, d1900, wNannie Goode Griffith
Julia P, b9/11/1815, fAmos, mSarah Nutt, wLafayette Brent
Kate S, bc1850, Wytheville, Wyth Co, fJohn L, mElizabeth Neighbours, hJames Wohlford
Louisa, b18--, Hano Co?, hWilliam Daniel Brown
Louisa A, b1819, KiWi Co, hJacob Valentine Crawford
M Annie, bc1870, Loui Co?, d1906, hWilliam Bledsoe Walton, md1895
Malinda, b18--, Hamp Co?, hSamuel Garvin
Marcellus Alexander, Sr, bc1866, Fran Co, fJohn Wesley, mElizabeth Haynes, wKate L

195

JOHNSON (continued)
Arthur, md1889
Martha, b17--, Ches Co?, hValentine Winfree, Sr
Martin, b18--, Bedf Co, wSarah Leftwich
Mary, b18--, Fluv Co, hJames Flannagan, Jr
Mary Estelle, b18--, Loud Co, hHenry J Fadeley
Mary J, b4/13/1839, Bedf Co, fFrancis, mNancy Wright, hWilliam Fountain Graves, md1856
Mary L, bc1860, Rapp Co, f Charles L, mFrances Octavia Gore
Melissa, b18--, Gile Co?, h Thomas J Stafford
Missouri Ann, b8/1/1848, Lune Co, d1906, hWilliam B Turner
Polly, bc1800, Alle Co?, 1w of Peter Helmintoller
Pattie, b1853, Cumb Co, hWilliam J C Goode
Richard, b18--, Rapp Co, d186-, fWilliam
Robert N, bc1860, Rapp Co, fCharles L, mFrances Octavia Gore
Robert Payne, b11/22/1854, Wytheville, Wyth Co,, fJohn L, mElizabeth Neighbours, wAmanda Virginia Trinkle, md3/22/1877
Robert Temple, b18--, Pitt Co?, wKate Wright
Sabra H, b186-, Rapp Co, f Charles L, mFrances Octavia Gore
Samuel G, b1850, Wytheville, Wyth Co, d1921, fJohn L, mElizabeth Neighbours
Sarah Ann, b11/21/1821, Rapp Co, d1892, fCumberland Marshall, mSarah Jennings, hJoseph Bowman
Silas B, b18--, Rapp Co?, wIda Menefee
Theodosia, b1865, Bedf Co, h David L Wells
Thomas, b17--, Bedf Co, 2wSally Dickinson
Thomas W, bc1860, Fran Co, d1920, fJames, mAmerica E Stone
Virginia Rudasill, b185-, Rapp Co, fCharles L, mFrances Oc-

JOHNSON (continued)
tavia Gore
William, b18--, Rapp Co, fWilliam
William T, b2/17/1856, Amel Co, wJessie Blanton
JOHNSTON, A Nash, b18--, PrEd Co, fAndrew, mAnna Nash
A Nash II, b18--, Bote Co, fPeter Butler, (1)m-- Higginbotham
Ada, b18--, Gile Co, fHarvey G, Sr, (1)mAnnie Snidow
Andrew, b1767, PrEd Co, fPeter, mMartha Butler, wAnna Nash
Andrew, bc1800, wJane Henderson
Andrew, b1770, Culp Co, fDavid, mNannie Abbott
Annie Carrie, b18--, Gile Co, fHarvey G, Sr, (1)mAnnie Snidow, hJohn E Triplett
Charles, b1770, PrEd Co, fPeter, mMartha Butler
Charles A, b6/14/1858, Bedf Co, fPeter Butler, (2)mEllen Finney, wVirginia Dunklee, md5/5/1881
Charles C, bc1800, wEliza Mary Preston
Charles R, b9/9/1843, nrMarion, Smyt Co, d1916, fJohn T, mRachel Snider, wJane Lockett Goodpasture
Edward, b18--, PrEd Co, fAndrew, mAnna Nash
Elian, b17--, Gile Co?, hIsaac Chapman
Eliza M, b7/3/1825, fCharles C, mEliza Mary Preston, hRobert William Hughes, md6/4/1850
Emma J, b18--, Bote Co, fPeter Butler, m-- Higginbotham, hJohn T Martin
Frederick, b1804, d1892, wNancy Burrell
George Ben, b18--, Abingdon, Wash Co, fJohn W, mNicketti Floyd
Harvey Green, Sr, b1824, Pearisburg, Gile Co, d1881, fAndrew, mJane Hendrson, 1wAnnie Snidow, 2wMary (Fowler) Halsey
James Andrew, b18--, Bote Co, fPeter Butler, m-- Higginbotham
James David, b9/29/1828, Pear-

JOHNSTON (continued)
 isburg, Gile C, fAndrew, mJane Henderson
 Jane Bell, b18--, Bedf Co, fPeter Butler, mEllen Finney
 Jennie, b18--, Gile Cao, fHarvey Green, Sr, (1)mAnnie Snidow, hWilliam E Black
 John H, b18--, Bote Co, fPeter Butler, m-- Higginsbotham
 John Nash, bc1800, fAndrew, mAnna Nash, wEliza Ogilvie Bell
 John T, b1815, Rkhm Co, d1888, wRachel Snider
 John W, b17--, fPeter, (1)mMary Wood, wLouisa Smith Bowen
 John W, b18--, fJohn W, mLouisa Smith Bowen, wNicketti Floyd
 John William, b1839, Pattonsburg, Bote Co, fJohn Nash, mEliza Ogilvie Bell, wElizabeth Alexander, md1868
 Lewis B, b1848, Salem, Roan Co, d1907, fFrederick, mNancy Burrell, wPocahontas Dupuy
 Louisa Bowen, b18--, Abingdon, Wash Co, fJohn W, mNicketti Floyd, hDaniel Trigg
 Maggie J, b18--, Bedf Co, fPeter Butler, mEllen Finney, hEugene W Stone
 Mary, b11/21/1870, Buchanan, Bote Co, fJohn William, mElizabeth Alexander
 Mary Carling, bc1870, Ches Co?, 2w of David Dunlop III, md2/4/1896
 Minnie Jane, bc1870, nrMarion, Smyt Co, fCharles R, mRachel Snider, hLewis A Bonham
 Peter II, b1/6/1763, PrEd Co, fPeter, mMartha Butler, 1wMary Wood, 2wAnn Bernard
 Peter Butler, b1802, PrEd Co, fAndrew, mAnna Nash, 1w-- Higginbotham, 2wEllen Finney
 Richard Windsor, b12/24/1851, Arli Co, 1907, fJohn R, wMargaret Hipkins
 Sarah Eliza, b17--, Albe Co?, 1w of Dabney Minor
 William H, b18--, Bote Co, d186-, fPeter Butler, m-- Higginbotham
 William A, b18--, Gile Co,

JOHNSTON (continued)
 fHarvey Green, Sr, (1)mAnnie Snidow
JOLLEY, --, bc1820, Fauq Co?, 1w of Luke Edward Woodward, Sr
JOLLIFFE, Alexander, bc1860, Hamp Co?, wEtta May Reid
JONAS, H J, bc1850, PrWi Co, wBettie Free
JONES, --, bc1830, Rapp Co?, wMary Fishback
 --, b17--, York Co, 1w of Thomas Ball Montague, Sr
 --, b18--, Richmond, 2w of Isaac Cofer
 Ann Lee, b18--, Nhld Co?, fWalter, mAnn Lee, hRobert Eden Payton, Sr
 Annie, b18--, Acco Co?, hKenneth J Bunting
 Annie, b1/14/1843, Rkhm Co, fJohn, hJohn Will
 Annie E, b7/28/1851, Oran Co, hJohn W Garner
 Annie Washington, b186-, Rapp Co, fEdward Thompson, mEliza Edmonia Jones, 1hSamuel T Clopton, 2hWilliam Grimsley Wood
 Austin W, b1798, Brun Co, d1890, wCatherine Prince
 Blanche C, b185-, KiQu Co, fJames Hawkins Claggett, mSallie Smith
 C L, bc1860, Bedf Co?, w-- Noell
 C N, b18--, wMartha Perdue
 Callom B, b1812, Hano Co, fJohn, wMary Wingfield
 Callom B II, b5/15/1842, fCallom B, mMary Wingfield, wSallie Phoebe Newman, md1/29/1855
 Carrie Colgin, b186-, Esse Co, fJohn H, mMaria Russell Nelson, hJohn Waller Faulconer, Jr, md12/5/1888
 Catesby, b18--, Glou Co?, wMary Ann Pollard
 Charles Pinckney, b9/1845, High (then Pend) Co, fJohn M, mPhoebe Jane Dice, wMartha J Wilson
 Claggett Bennett, b4/29/1857, KiQu Co, fJames Hawkins Claggett, mSallie Smith, wJulia Latane, md4/19/1880

JONES (continued)
Cornelia, b18--, Rich Co?, h Robert Hall
Crimora, bRichmond, hBelfield Cave
Daniel Seldon, b7/10/1849, nr Jamestown, JaCi Co, fHenly T, mMary A H Jones, wCarrie Y Powell, md10/10/1873
Dorcas Huyett, b1/10/1850, Jeff Co, fThomas, Sr, mMary Jane Huyett, wMary C Berlin
Edward Thompson, bc1830, Rapp Co, fJohn B, mEliza Miller, wEliza Edmonia Miller
Eli, b18--, Hano Co?, wMary E Chewning
Elizabeth, b18--, Loud Co, f William, mSarah --, hHugh Smith
Elizabeth, b18--, Albe Co?, fJohn, 2w of Bland Rea
Elzabeth, b18--, Hano Co, d1909, hEdward T Mann
Ella, b18--, Lune Co, fPeter Branch, mVirginia Pilkington, hWilliam E Ingram, md12/12/1866
Ella, bc1850, Jeff Co, fThomas, Sr, mMary Jane Huyett
Ellen B, b185-, KiQu Co, fJames Hawkins Claggett, mSallie Smith, hAlbert G Gresham
Elsa, b1850, nrLuttrellsville, Rich Co, d1909, hHenry Carson Rowe
Fielding E, b18--, Bedf Co?, wSarah Spear
Frances Marian Alexander, b12/12/1858, Staf Co, hJohn Wyatt Garner
George M, b183-, Bedf Co?, fFielding E, mSarah Spear
Granville M, bc1860, Dick (then Wise) Co, wMinnie B Chase
Harriet E, b18--, Albe Co, hThomas W Williams
Harriet Meade, b8/10/1864, Dinw Co, fThomas Thweatt, mMargaret Ann Bolling, hWilliam B McIlwaine
Harrison, b181-, Jeff Co, fMatthew, m-- Williamson, wMary Christina Browne, md3/10/1842
Hattie, bc1844, Jeff Co, fThomas, Sr, mMary Jane Huyett,

JONES (continued)
hGeorge Britton
Henley T, b18--, JaCi Co, wMary A H Jones
Henry Harrison, b18--, High Co, wJemimah Eagle
Ida B, b18--, Hano Co, fCallom B, mMary Wingfield, hRufus R Griffith
India Wray, b18--, ElCi Co, hJohn James Gravatt, Jr
Indiana F, b18--, nrOld Point Comfort, ElCi Co, fCarey, 2w of Fred Floyd
Irene, b18--, Surr Co, fWilliam Clayborne, mMary Cauthorn, hRichard Davenport Gilliam
Isaac N, b1861, Lee Co, fJoseph, mSarah Wilson, 1wAmanda Blanton, 2wAnnie Elizabeth Lee
James, b18--, Camp Co?, dc1870, wMartha Hancock
James S, bc1855, KiQu Co, d1894, fJames Hawkins Claggett, mSallie Smith
Jesse, b18--, Buck Co?, wMargaret M Spitzer
Jesse Franklin, b7/21/1870, Washington, Rapp Co, fEdward Thompson, mEliza Edmonia Miller, wWillie Gates Moffitt, md8/10/1910
John, bc1820, Jeff Co, fMatthew, m-- Williamson
John B, b17--, Rapp Co?, wEliza Miller
John B, b1852, Brun Co, fWilliam Robert, mElizabeth Manson, wGertrude Harris
John Blackwell, b1852, Crooked Run, Lune Co, fJohn Robert, mAnn Elizabeth Blackwell Manson, wGertrude Harris
John C, b18--, High Co, fJohn M, mPhoebe Jane Dice
John F, b185-, Russ Co?, wTina V Jones
John H, bc1830, Lune Co?, wFannie Hardy
John H, b18--, Esse Co?, d186-, wMaria Russell Nelson
John J, b1842, Brun Co, d1918, fAustin W, mCatherine Prince, wMargaret Short
John M, b18--, fThomas
John Robert, b10/19/1822,

JONES (continued)
  Crooked Run, Lune Co, d1901, fRobert Blackwell, mAnn Elizabeth Blackwell, wAnn Elizabeth Blackwell Manson
  John Sheldon, b18--, York Co, wJane Eagle
  John Taliaferro, b18--, wElizabeth Garlick
  Josepah, b18--, Lee Co, wSarah Wilson
  Julia E, b18--, Amhe Co, hJohn C Turpin, md1/26/1870
  Leonard, bc1820, Jeff Co, fMatthew, m-- Williamson
  Lewis, b18--, Glou Co, fGabriel, w-- Robinson
  Lewis A, bc1840, Buck Co?, wLucy A Anderson
  Lucy Catesby, b18--, fJohn Taliaferro, mElizabeth Garlick, hRoy Knight Flannagan, md10/1896
  Margaret, b18--, Nans co?, hElisha Rawls
  Margaret, b1854, Crai Co, hJohn F Walker
  Martha J, b18--, Grvl Co, fWilliam M, mMartha Jordan Gregg, hNathaniel J Land
  Mary A H, b18--, JaCi Co, hHenley T Jones
  Mary Dudley, bc1860, Math Co, fWilliam D, 2w of William Ellis Corr, md7/1895
  Mary Elizabeth, b183-, Bedf Co?, fFielding E, mSarah Spear, hJames Winston Watts, md2/22/1854
  Mary F, b18--, Culp Co, hPresley Morehead Rixey
  Maryus, b7/8/1844, Glou Co, d1923, fCatesby, mMary Ann Pollard, wMary Armistead Catlett, md12/10/1873
  Mathew, b184-, Jeff Co, d1922, fThomas, Sr, mMary Jane Huyett
  Mattie Lee, bc1870, Camp Co?, 3w of Francis Edward Turner, Sr, md4/19/1908
  Osborn A, b184-, Jeff Co, f Thomas, Sr, mMary Jane Huyett
  Patsy Saterwhite, b17--, hJohn Shaddock West
  Peter Branch, b18--, Lune Co?, wVirginia Pilkington

JONES (continued)
  Polly, b17--, Pitt Co?, hJoseph Motley
  Priscilla, b17--, Bedf Co?, fGray, Samuel H Crenshaw
  Robert, b17--, Lune Co, 1842, fStephen, wChristina Blackwell
  Robert, bc1850, Taze Co?, wAlice V Deaton
  Robert Blackwell, bc1800, Crooked Run, Lune Co, fRobert, mChristina Blackwell, wAnn Elizabeth Blackwell
  Robert E, b1854, Richmond, f Robert Evans, wElla Louise Bragg
  Robert Evans, b1810, Richmond
  Robert F, bc1860, KiQu Co, fJames Hawkins Claggett, mSallie Smith
  Sallie, bc1800, hPeyton Anderson
  Sallie Dice, b18--, High Co, fJohn M, mPhoebe Jane Dice
  Samuel H, b18--, Fauq Co?, wMary Catherine Barbee
  Santie M, bc1860, Math Co, d1894, fWilliam D, 1w of William Ellis Corr, Sr, md2/1884
  Sarah, bc1820, Jeff Co, fMatthew, m-- Williamson, hJames Hardesty
  Sophia, bc1820, Jeff Co, fMatthew, m-- Williamson, h-- Doyle
  Stephen, b1742, Lune Co, fThomas, Sr
  Sue, b18--, Nans Co, hCharles E Holland
  Sydney, b182-, Jeff Co, fMatthew, m-- Williamson, hSamuel Huyett
  Thomas, b17--, fJoseph, wMary Lee
  Thomas II, bc1820, fThomas, mMary Lee, wAnne Seymour Trowbridge
  Thomas, Jr, b1720, Lune Co, d1785, fThomas, Sr
  Thomas, Sr, bc1827, Jeff Co, fMatthew, m-- Williamson, w Mary Jane Huyett
  Thomas, Jr, bc1840, Jeff Co, fThomas, Sr, mMary Jane Huyett
  Thomas E, b1853, Hano Co, d1908, fEli, mMary E Chewning,

JONES (continued)
wMary A Welch
Thomas G, Sr, b9/22/1843, Midd Co, d1912, fLewis, m-- Robinson, wAlice Perciful
Thomas O, b18--, High Co, fJohn M, mPhoebe Jane Dice
Thomas Thweatt, b1837, Brun Co, wMargaret Ann Bolling
Virginia, b18--, Taze Co?, h Robert E Alley
W A, b18--, Rich Co?, wClaude Douglas Motley
Walter, b17--, Nhld Co?, wAnn Lee
William, b17--, Loud Co?, wSarah --
William, bc1800, Fluv Co?, w Mary Ann Lane
William, b182-, Jeff Co, fMatthew, m-- Williamson
William, bc1840, Shen Co?, w Barbara Will
William Atkinson, b3/21/1849, Warsaw, Rich Co, fThomas II, mAnne Seymour Trowbridge
William M, b18--, Grvl Co, wMartha Jordan Gregg
William Robert, b1804, Brun Co, d1879, wElizabeth Manson
William T, b10/3/1865, Red House, Camp Co, fJames mMartha Hancock, wEstelle Miller, md6/1913
William Z, bc1860, Wyth Co?, wSallie A Kegley
JOPLIN, Bettie, bc1820, Bote Co, 1w of Samuel Noffsinger
JORDAN, Ann, b18--, Page Co, hAndrew Russell Meem
Annie, b18--, Shen Co?, hWilliam Supinger
Annie, b18--, hWilliam M Patton
Benjamin, b17--, Lune Co?, wCharity Ingram
Catherine, b18--, Rapp Co, 2w of Thomas Henry Settle
Charles E, b10/1851, Haymarket, PrWi Co, fJames w, mMary A Sanders, wAlice Moore
Ellen Jane, b18--, hWilliam Watts Parker
Hubert F, b18--, Norfolk, wHarriet --
James M, bc1833, Nels Co, fWilliam Corbin, wLouise Goulsby

JORDAN (continued)
John Pendleton, b184-, Haymarket, PrWi Co, fJames W, mMary A Sanders
John Richard, b184-, Haymarket, PrWi Co, fJames W, mMary A Sanders
Josiah M, b17--, Jordan's Point, PrGe Co, fSamuel III
Josiah M II, b17--, Jordan's Point, PrGe Co, fJosiah M
Josiah III, b18--, Jordan's Point, PrGe Co, fJosiah M II, wMary Christine Anderson
Louvinia, b18--, nrCrabbottom, High Co, fJacob, mMatilda Lance, hWilliam Hevener
Lucretia, b18--, Gile Co, d1890, HJames Huson Woods
Lucy, b18--, Hali Co?, hWilliam Slate
Margaret Melvina, b1831, "Walnut Grove", Gile Co, 1911, 1h-- Adams, 2hEdwin Dennis
Mary, b17--, Shen Co?, hDaniel Hottel
Mary, b186-, nrAllen Creek, Nels Co, James M, mLouise Goulsby, hJ J Cunningham
Mary, bc1870, Camp Co?, d1901, fJohn R, 1w of Elijah E Menefee, md11/26/1889
Mary Jane, b18--, Claremont, PrGe Co, fJosiah M III, mMary Anderson, hWilliam David Temple
Mollie Hoge, b186-, Pula Co, fWilliam T, mLetitia Simmerman, hGary Laughon, Sr, md5/25/1886
Olli Erskin, bc1860, Pula Co?, wJanie Allison Alexander
Samuel II, b16--, Jordan's Point, PrGe Co, fThomas
Samuel III, bc1700, Jordan's Point, PrGe Co, fThomas II
Sarah R, b1845, PrGe Co, hWilliam Joseph Leake, md7/3/1866
Thomas, bc1620, Jordan's Point, PrGe Co, fSamuel, mCicely --
Thomas II, b16--, Jordan's Point, PrGe Co, fSamuel II
Thomas Walden, b18--, Pula Co?, wCatherine Hammond Longley
Thomas Wilkinson, b10/9/1870, nrAllen Creek, Nels Co, fJames

JORDAN (continued)
M, mLouise Goulsby, wBelle W Warren, md1/7/1903
William T, b18--, Pula Co?, wLetitia Simmerman
William Ware, bc1850, Haymarket, PrWi Co, fJames W, mMary A Sanders
Willie Trolinger, bc1870, Pula Co, fWilliam T, mLetitia Simmerman, hHenry Lewis Trolinger, md11/6/1895
JORDON, Mildred Hester, b5/30/1832, Gooc Co, hJacob Woodson Nuckols
JOYCE, --, b18--, Augu Co?, hGeorge W Hutchinson
JOYNER, Houston Clay, bc1840, Amhe Co?, d1909
John Wesley, bc1839, Amhe Co?, d1907, wBell Wren
JOYNES, Alexander Tankard, b184-Onancock, Acco Co, fTully A T, Sr, mSabra Polk Fitchett
George Goodwyn, Sr, b9/6/1856, Onancock, Acco Co, fTully A T, Sr, mSabra Polk Fitchett, 1wSallie W Northam, md11/25/1880, 2wMarguerite E Tyler, md6/26/1923
Tabitha J, b185-, Onancock, Acco Co, fTully A T, Sr, mSabra Polk Fitchett, hSamuel B Hance
Tully A T, Sr, b1815, nrLocustville, Acco Co, d1890, wSabra Polk Fitchett
Tully A T, Jr, b185-, Onancock, Acco co, fTully A T, Sr, mSabra Polk Fitchett
Virginia S, b1839, Pungoteague, Acco Co, d1912, hLeonard Hall Ames
William F, bc1850, Onancock, Acco Co, fTully A T, Sr, mSabra Polk Fitchett
JUDD, Blanche, b18--, Page Co?, hThomas Bradley
JUDY, Josie M, b9/12/1864, fManassah, 1w of John Marvin Colaw, md10/21/1886
JUNKIN, Julia Miller, b18--, hJunius M fishburne
JUSTUS, Mary Jane, b18--, Wyom Co?, hRiley Lester
KACKLEY, Sarah, b18--, hCasper

KACKLEY (continued)
Rinker, Jr
KAGEY, Abram D, b184-, nrNew Market, Shen Co, fDavid M, mMary Miller
Anna, b5/1831, Shen Co, fJacob, mBarbara Neff, hJohn Wesley Wayland, Jr
Annie E, b184-, nrNew Market, Shen Co, fDavid M, mMary Miller, hSamuel Hingardner
Barbara, b17--, Shen Co, fJohn Beery
Barbara, bc1800, Shen Co, 1w of Zachariah Shirley
Catherine E, b18--, Rkhm Co?, hJohn A Roller
Charles Lemuel, b185-, nrNew Market, Shen Co, fDavid, mMary Miller
David M, b1809, nrNew Market, Shen Co, fAbraham, m-- Neff, wMary Miller
Fannie, b185-, nrNew Market, Shen Co, fDavid M, mMary Miller
Isaac B, b184-, nrNew Market, Shen Co, fDavid M, mMary Miller
J S, bc1860, Rkhm Co?, wBettie Isadora Swank
Jacob, bc1800, Shen Co?, wBarbara Neff
Jennie R, b185-, nrNew Market, Shen Co, fDavid M, mMary Miller, hSamuel Hale
Joel, b18--, Shen Co?, wMary C Ruby
John W, b184-, nrNew Market, Shen Co, fDavid M, mMary Miller, wMary Shaver
Joseph M, b2/5/1850, nrNew Market, Shen Co, fDavid M, mMary Miller, wRebecca Garber, md4/2/1874
Mary C, b185-, nrNew Market, Shen Co, fDavid M, mMary Miller, hJonas Early
Sarah A, b185-, nrNew Market, Shen Co, David M, mMary Miller, hG B Holsinger
KANE, Louise Elizabeth, b18--, Scot Co, hHenry Addison Morison
Margaret, b18--, Scot Co?, hSmith H Morison

KARNES, Charles R, b7/4/1867, Low Moor, Alle Co, fBen A, mSarah Griffith
KAVANAUGH, James M, b12/25/1869, Harrisonburg, Rkhm Co, wMary Hickey
KEAN, Fanny Minor, b18--, Alle Co, fAndrew, hSamuel D Leake, md1833
Napoleon B, b18--, Alle Co, fAndrew
Susan, b18--, Loui Co, hRichard Graves
KEANE, Bernard E, bc1860, wCora Lee Carter
KEARNEY, Elziabeth, b18--, hLewis Glover
Mary Catheirne, b18--, Jeff Co?, hWilliam Thomas McQuilkin
KEATTS, --, bc1860, Pitt Co?, wEllen Bennett
KECKLEY, Barbara, bc1800, Shen Co, d1876, hMoses Russell
Mary Jane, b1832, Fred Co, fBenjamin, hJonah Tavenner, md 1865
KEEBLE, Houston, b186-, Bote Co?, wLizzie Shaver
KEEF, Nora E, b18--, Fred Co?, hHarvey M Albin
KEEL, Elizabeth, bc1860, nrClintwood, Dick Co, fWilliam Kellley, mNancy Vanover, h George C Smith
Harmon T, b185-, nrClintwood, Dick Co, fWilliam Kelley, m Nancy Vanover
Henry, b4/16/1855, nrClintwood, Dick Co, fWilliam Kelley, m Nancy Vanover, wNancy Jane McFall, md2/27/1879
Jane, b185-, nrClintwood, Dick Co, d1922, fWilliam Kelley, mNancy Vanover, hFlournoy N Smith
Martha, b184-, nrClintwood, Dick Co, fWilliam Kelley, m Nancy Vanover, hSimon P Buchanan
Mary, bc1850, nrClintwood, Dick Co, d1885, fWilliam Kelley, mNancy Vanover, hElijah Yates
Samuel G, b185-, nrClntwood, Dick Co, d1892, fWilliam Kelley, mNancy Vanover
William J, b185-, nrClintwood,

KEEL (continued) Dick Co, d1917, fWilliam Kelley, mNancy Vanover
KEEN, John Thomas, b1843, Danville, Pitt Co, fWilliam Witcher, mElizabeth Ballard Fontaine, wMary Virginia Doe
Nanni Witcher Keen, b1848, Cottage Hill, Pitt Co, hC D Langhorne
Sallie Ross, b186-, Danville, Pitt Co, fJohn Thomas, mMary Virginia Doe, hGeorge A Watson
William Witcher, b18--, Pitt Co, fJohn, wElizabeth Ballard Fontaine
William Witcher II, b6/23/1870, Danville, Pitt Co, fJohn Thomas, mMary Virginia Doe, wDaisy Wilson, md4/4/1907
KEEZELL, George, b17--, Keezellton, Rkhm Co, d1862, fGeorge Keezell, wAmanda Fitzallen Peale
George Bernard, b7/20/1854, Keezellton, Rkhm Co, fGeorge, mAmanda Fitzallen Peale, 1wKate Hannah, 2wBelle C Hannah
KEFFER, Rebecca, b18--, fJohn, hHenry Green Huff, md11/1867
KEGLEY, Campbell J, b18--, nr Wytheville, Wyth Co, fJohn G, (1)m Sallie Copenhaver
Caroline, b1/24/1850, Wyth Co?, d1919, hAndrew Clay Whitman
Christian, b17--, Wyth Co, fGeorge
Fulton, b7/12/1866, Bland, Blan Co, fMitchell, mMatilda J Johnson, wMary J Hayes, md2/17/1898
George L, b186-, Wyth Co?, wSalome Maude Kegley
George W, b18--, nrWytheville, Wyth Co, fJohn G, (1)mSallie Copenhaver
George W, b18--, nrWytheville, Wyth Co, fJohn G, (1)mSallie Copenhaver
Henry, b18--, nrWytheville, Wyth Co, fJohn G, (1)mSallie Copenhaver
Henry Clinton, b186-, Bland, Blan Co, fMitchell, wMatilda J Johnson

KEGLEY (continued)
Isaac, b1808, nrWytheville, Wyth Co, d1884, fChristian, wPrudence Devor
John G, b1827, Wyth Co, d1902, fMartin, mMary Myers, 1wSallie Copenhaver, 2wMary M Wolford
Markham R, b18--, nrWytheville, Wyth Co, fJohn G, (1)mSallie Copenhaver, hJohn P Corvin
Martin, b9/19/1782, nrWytheville, Wyth Co, d1845, fGeorge, wMary Myers
Mary R, b186-, Bland, Blan Co, fMitchell, mMatilda J Johnson, hWilliam H Tilson
Millard D S, bc1870, nrWytheville, Wyth Co, fJohn G, (2)mMary M Wolford
Mitchell, b18--, Blan Co, f Isaac, mPrudence Devor, wMatilda J Johnson
Nannie A, b186-, nrWytheville, Wyth Co, fJohn G, (2)mMary M Wolford, hJames Harvey Simmerman
Sallie A, b186-, nrWytheville, Wyth Co, fJohn G, (2)mMary M Wolford, hWilliam Z Jones
Virginia R, bc1870, nrWytheville, Wyth Co, fJohn G, (2)mMary M Wolford, hHiram W Grubb
W Scott, b18--, nrWytheville, Wyth Co, John G, (1)mSallie Copenhaver
William Bullard, b5/27/1868, nrWytheville, Wyth Co, fJohn G, (2)mMary M Wolford, wSue A Gibson, md7/15/1890
KEISTER, Adam, Jr, b18--, Strasburg, Shen Cao, Adam, Sr, wCatherine Keister
Ella, b187-, High Co, fWilliam R, mMartha Emma McCoy, hCameron Siron
Emma Catherine, b11/25/1870, Pend Co, fMartin, mElizabeth --, hRobert Franklin Leedy, md3/27/1890
Henry , b186-, High Co, fWilliam R, mMartha Emma McCoy
Martin, b18--, Pend Co?, wElizabeth --
Mattie, b186-, High Co, fWilliam R, mMartha Emma McCoy

KEISTER (continued)
Orlando, bc1864, Strasburg, Shen Co, fAdam, Jr, mCatherine Keister, wSusie Stover Jennings
Signora, bc1870, High Co, fWilliam R, mMartha Emma McCoy, hCharles Bradshaw
Viola, b186-, High Co, fWilliam R, mMartha Emma McCoy, hJoseph Siron
William H, b18--, Pula Co?, wFannie Cecil
William Hampton, b8/18/1865, High Co, fWilliam R, mMartha Emma McCoy, wVirginia Fletcher, md9/4/1900
William R, bc1843, High Co, wMartha Emma McCoy
KEITH, Alexander, b17--, fJames, Sr, mMary Isham Randolph
Ann Gordon, b18--, Fauq Coa, Isham, Jr, mSarah Agnes Blackwell, hEdward M Spilman
Elizabeth, b17--, Fauq Co, fJames, Sr, mMary Isham Randolph, h-- Ford
Harriet, b17--, fThomas, mJudith Blackwell
Isham, bc1735, fJames, Sr, m Mary Isham Randolph, wCharlotte Ashmore
Isham, Sr, b17--, fThomas, m Judith Blackwell, wJuliet Chilton
Isham, Jr, b1833, Fauq Co, fIsham, Sr, mJuliet Chilton, wSarah Agnes Blackwell
Isham III, b18--, Fauq Co, fIsham, Jr, mSarah Agnes Blackwell, wJessie Lee Hall
James, b11/21/1868, Fauq Co, fIsham, Jr, mSarah Agnes Blackwell, wJosephine Noble
James, Sr, b17--, fThomas, m Judith Blackwell, Mary Isham Randolph
James, Jr, b17--, fJames, Sr, mMary Isham Randolph
James W, b186-, Nott Co?, wHelen Grey Beckham
John, b17--, James, Sr, mMary Isham Randolph
John Augustine Chilto, b6/7/1870, Fauq Co, fIsham, Jr, mSarah Agnes Blackwell,

KEITH (continued)
wMary Welby Scott
Judith, b17--, fJames, Sr, m Mary Isham Randolph
Julian Chilton, b18--, Fauq Co, fIsham, Jr, mSarah Agnes Blackwell, 1wMary Lapsley, 2wMargaret Berry
Katherine, b18--, Fauq Co, fIsham, Jr, mSarah Agnes Blackwell
Lucien, b18--, Fauq Co, fIsham, Jr, mSarah Agnes Blackwell, wElizabeth Sharpless
Margaret, b18--, Fauq Co, fIsham, Jr, mSarah Agnes Blackwell, hRobert W Neilson
Marshall, b17--, fThomas, mJudith Blackwell
Mary Isham, b17--, fThomas, mJudith Blackwell
Peter Grant, b17--, fThomas, mJudith Blackwell
Susan, b17--, fThomas, mJudith Blackwell
Tarleton Fleming, b17--, fThomas, mJudith Blackwell
Thomas, bc1755, fJames, Sr, mMary Isham Randolph, wJudith Blackwell, md1774
Thomas R, bc1870, Fair Co?, wEdith M Moore
Virginia Mary, b17--, Fauq Co, fJames, Sr, mMary Isham Randolph, hThomas Marshall, md1754
William Steptoe, b11/17/1855, Fauq Co, fIsham, Jr, mSarah Agnes Blackwell
KELLAM, Abel Erastus, b7/6/1849, Nhtn Co, fSevern F, mMartha --, 1wRuth Vernon Hope, 2wClara O Eaton
David C, b18--, Nhtn Co?, wLucy Nottingham
Estelia, b18--, Acco Co, hEdward Anderson
Jane, b1840, PrAn Co, hIsma W Mears
Severn F, b18--, Acco Co, wMartha --
Sheppard S, b5/12/1834, nrBelle Haven, Acco Co, d1900, fStokeley, wMary Stringer
KELLER, --, b17--, Shen Co, fGeorge, mAnna Hottel, hJacob

KELLER (continued)
Rinker
--, b17--, Shen Co, fGeorge, mAnna Hottel, hHenry Fravel
Anna, b1849, Fred Co, d1923, hJames William Rhodes
George, b17--, Shen Co?, wAnna Hottel
John H, bc1850, Shen Co?, wEmma Walton
Sallie J, b18--, Rkhm Co, hIgnatius Cooper
KELLEY, --, b17--, hTobias Smyth
Ellen Jane, b1/31/1856, Marion, Smyt Co, hVincent B Gilmer
Ernest A, b18--, Richmond, f Samuel A, mMary J Quinn
George, b185-, Hano Co?, wCleverine Ada Mann
J Curtin, bc1870, Acco Co?, wBettie E Bonniwell
Margaret, b17--, Russ Co?, hJohn Counts
Samuel Lee, b6/22/1864, Richmond, fSamuel A, mMary J Quinn
John Jackson, Sr, b1819, Wise Co, d1906
John Jackson, Jr, b2/26/1847, Wise Co, fJohn Jackson, Sr, wElizabeth Jane Lewis
Joseph Luther, b3/4/1867, Smyt Co, fJohn A, mMartha Peck, wMary Eloise Hull
Margaret, b18--, Dick Co, hNoah K Rasnick
Vincent, b18--, Taze Co, fJames P, wMary C May
KELSO, Mary, b18--, Hamp Co?, hRobert Hook
KEMP, --, bc1800, Glou Co?, hRichard Lawson
Tabitha C, b18--, hAlgernon S Vaiden, Sr
Thomas M, b7/19/1836, nrLuray, Page Co, wElizabeth Kibler
KEMPER, Addie, b186-, Port Republic, Rkhm Co, fGeorge W, Jr, (2)mMargaret C Strayer, 1w of John L Harnsberger
Albert S, b1/28/1866, Port Republic, Rkhm Co, fGeorge W, Jr, (2)mMargaret C Strayer, wElizabeth Blackburn, md12/16/1897
B Frank, b181-, Port Republic, Rkhm Co, fGeorge W, Sr, mMa-

KEMPER (continued)
tilda Graham
Caroline, bc1820, Port Republic, Rkhm Co, fGeroge W, Sr, mMatilda Graham, hGeorge D Butler
Charles Joseph, b181-, Port Republic, Rkhm Co, fGeorge W, Sr, mMatilda Graham
Charles L, bc1860, Port Republic, Rkhm Co, fGeorge W, Jr, (2)mMargaret C Strayer
Elizabeth, b181-, Port Republic, Rkhm Co, fGeorge W, Sr, mMatilda Graham, hDavid S Young
George B, b18--, Port Republic, Rkhm Co, d186-, fGeorge W, Jr, (1)mAngeline Brown
George W, Sr, bc1786, Fauq Co, wMatilda Graham
George W, Jr, b12/20/1814, Port Republic, Rkhm Co, fGeorge W, Sr, mMatida Graham, 1wAngeline Brown, 2wMargaret C Strayer
Mary Frances, b18--, Port Republic, Rkhm Co, fGeorge W, Jr, (1)mAngeline Brown, hWilliam H Young
Matilda Graham, b186-, Port Republic, Rkhm Co, fGeorge W, Jr, (2)mMargaret C Strayer, 2w of John I Harnsberger
Walter W, b186-, Port Republic, Rkhm Co, fGeorge W, Jr, (2)m Margaret C Strayer
William M, b18--, Port Republic, Rkhm Co, fGeorge W, Jr, (1)mAngeline Brown
KENDIG, Samuel E, b1856, Spot Co, fUrias, mIsabella Atkins, wEudora Fleming
KENDRICK, Elizabeth, b1854, Luray, Page Co, d1906, fS M, mMary Calhoun, hCharles Everett Carter Peyton, md12/17/1879
Ida, b18--, Buck Co, hJefferson Davis Davis
Jean, b18--, Russ Co, hWilliam Brown
Mattie C, b186-, Buck Co, hWilliam Old Taylor, md1890
S M, b18--, Page Co?, wMary Calhoun
KENDRICKS, Louise, b18--, Camp

KENDRICKS (continued)
Co?, hJohn Watkins
KENNER, Daniel Augustin, b1861, Fauq Co, fGeorge A, (2),mHarriet Rector
George A, b18--, Marshall, Fauq Co, fRodham, Jr, 1wSusan Pendleton, 2wHarriet Rector, md2/22/1859
Harry W, b1864, Fauq Co, fGeorge A, (2)mHarriet Rector
Rodham, Jr, b18--, Fauq Co, fRodham, Sr
Winder, b18--, Fauq Co, fRodham, Sr
KENNERLY, Joseph McKendree, b1826, nrWhite Post, Clar Co, fThomas, mAnne Carnegy, wJosepha Anne Beale
May, bc1870, nrWhite Post, Clar Co, fJoseph McKendree, mJosepha Anne Beale, hJ Hampton Skinker
Susan, bc1800, hChristopher J Terrell
Thomas, bc1800, Rkhm Co, wAnne Carnegy
KENNEY, --, b18--, Carr Co, 1w of James W Early
Madison, b1831, Rkbr Co, d1884, wMary A McGown
KENT, Jacob Barnett, b18--, Mont Co, wMartha Campbell
Margaret, b18--, Mont Co?, hJohn Archer Langhorne
Samuel W, b3/15/1859, Wash Co, fJacob Barnett, mMartha Campbell, wAmanda J (Starritt) Repass
KENYON, Orra Emma, b18--, PrWi Co?, hJohn W Gregg
KERFOOT, Mary Eliza, b18--, Clar Co?, fJohn, hDaniel W Sowers
John B, b18--, Warr Co?, wElizabeth Taylor
Margaret, bc1840, Fred Co?, fJohn B, mElzabeth Taylor, hWilliam Henry Wheelwright
Martha, b18--, Clar Co, hWilliam Taylor Chapin, Sr
William, b18--, Fauq Co?, wMargaret Dodge
KERN, --, bc1800, Shen Co?, hGeorge Shrum
--, b18--, Fauq Co?, wLouisa Heflin

KERN (continued)
Bentley, b1841, Fred Co, fNimrod, mEliza Bentley, wKatie Lee Brooke
Catherine Ann, bc1822, Fred Co, d1889, fAdam, hJames Frederick Shryock
Jacob, bc1800, Shen Co, w-- Stover
John Adam, b1846, Fred Co, fNimrod, mEliza Bentley
Kate, b18--, Fred Co, fNimrod, mEliza Bentley, hWilliam R Harrison
Lucinda, b18--, Shen Co?, hWilliam Larkins
Nimrod, b18--, Fred Co, fAdam, mMargaret --, wEliza Bentley
Susan, bc1840, Shen Co, f1922, fJacob, m-- Stover, hWilliam Stickely
KERR, --, b18--, Shen Co?, wHarriet Funkhouser
Alice, b18--, Nhtn Co?, hHenry L Upshur
Gardner P, bc1850, Rkbr Co?, wMary T McClung
George W, b7/17/1838, nrWare's Church, KiQu Co, fWilliam, mMary Durham, wMary Elizabeth Watlington
Margaret, b18--, Norfolk?, hWilliam Wilson Lamb
Sarah, b17--, fWilliam, mMary Ann Grove, hPeter Charles Hogg
Thomas, b185-, Rkbr Co, wBetty McClung
William, b1808, KiQu Co, d1846, fFrank, wMary Durham
KERRH, Emma E, b8/29/1854, Fredericksburg, Spot Co, hWilliam M Davidson
KESSLER, Adaline, b1835, Bote Co, d1916, fDaniel, hJohn William Layman
KEYS, Alexander, b17--, PrWi Co?, wJane Feilder
E G W, b18--, PrWi Co, fMagruger Jackson, mAnnie McCracken, wElmira H Liming
James, b1820, Wash Co, 1w-- Edmondson, 2w-- Horne
Magruder Jackson, b1814, Occoquan, PrWi Co, fAlexander, mJane Feilder, wAnnie McCracke
KEYSER, Carrie, b10/5/1864, Honeyville, Page Co, fHenry M, mNancy Kite, hCharles Edward Clinedinst, md11/14/1882

KEYSER (continued)
E L, b186-, Honeyville, Page Co, fHenry M, mNancy Kite
Edward Thomas, b18--, Page Co, fNoah, wMary Jane Williams
Elizabeth Anne, b18--, Madi Co?, hJoseph M Fray
Henry M, b18--, Page Co, fJohn, wNancy Kite
Hubert Forest, b4/21/1866, Page Co, fEdward Thomas, mMary Jane Williams, wLula Wood, md12/10/1890
Maggie, bc1870, Honeyville, Page Co, fHenry M, mNancy Hite, hJames W Holt
Mattie K, b18--, Page Co, 2w of Berryman B Price
Mollie, bc1870, Blan Co?, hJohn Wade Hornbarger
Virgie, b186-, Honeyville, Page Co, fHenry M, mNancy Hite, hRobert Lias
William F, b186-, Honeyville, Page Co, fHenry M, mNancy Hite
William L, b9/7/1864, Rapp Co, d1915, fEdward Thomas, mMary Jane Williams, wCaroline Hampton DeJarnett, md1891
KIBLER, Elizabeth, b1842, nrLuray, Page Co, d1896, hThomas M Kemp
George W, b18--, Shen Co?, wSarah Showalter
John, b18--, Shen Co?, wMary Wolverton
Sallie, bc1846, Powell's Fort Valley, Shen Co, hJacob B Clem, Sr
Virginia, b18--, Shen Co, fJohn, mMary Wolverton, hNicholas W Baker, md5/1871
KIDD, --, b17--, Mont Co?, h George Wagner
John M, b3/22/1865, Ches Co, wIola M F Gates
Martha Ellen, bc1830, Buckingham Estate, Midd Co, hOpie Norris
Willam, b18--, Richmond?, wMary Newell
KIDWELL, Julia, b18--, Fair Co, hAllison Thompson

206

KIDWELL (continued)
Mary Ellen, b1849, Upperville, Fauq Co, hWilliam I Robey
KIEFFER, Aldine S, bc1840, Alle Co, fJohn, mMary Funk
John, b18--, Alle Co?, wMary Funk
Lucilla Virginia, b7/23/1843, Alle Co, d1919, fJohn, mMary Funk, hEphraim, md3/28/1861
KILGORE, John W, bc1860, Wise Co?, wVirginia Bond
Morgan T, bc1860, Wise Co?, wLaura Bond
Rebecca, b18--, Scot Co, dc1848, hJoab Watson McConnell
Susanna, b7/30/1830, Scot Co, d1917, hWilliam L Roberts
KILLINGER, Catherine, b1793, Smyt Co, hJohn Anderson
Katherine, b1838, Smyt Co, hJohn Jacob Sherer, Sr
KIMBROUGH, Mary Louisa, b18--, Loui Co?, hFrederick H Sims
KINCAID, Julia, b18--, Grbr Co, hSamuel McCorkle
Mary, b186-, Deerfield, Augu Co, hThomas Henry Jackson
KINCHELOE, Annie, bc1830, nrRectortown, Fauq Co, fHardwick, m-- Hudson
Bertha, bc1860, nrMarkham, Fauq Co, fConrad Bitzer, mVidie Glascock, hMartin Welfley
Blanche, b186-, nrMarkham, Fauq Co, fConrad Bitzer,, mVidie Glascock
Conrad Bitzer, b1832, nrRectortown, Fauq Co, dc1901, fHardwick, wVidie Glascock
Elisha, b182-, nrRectortown, Fauq Co, Hardwick
James M, b185-, nrMarkham, Fauq Co, fConrad Bitzer, mVidie Glascock
John, b1793, nrClifton, Fair Co, fCornelius, mDorcas Wycliffe, wHarriet Davis
Cornelius, b17--, Fair Co, f
Daniel, wDorcas Wycliffe
John William, b182-, nrRectortown, Fauq Co, fHardwick
John William, b7/27/1869, nr Markham, Fauq Co, fConrad Bitzer, mVidie Glascock, wMay Green, md11/1897

KINCHELOE (continued)
Mary, b186-, nrMarkham, Fauq Co, fConrad Bitzer, mVidie Glascock, hRobert Fletcher
Thomas J, b183-, nrRectortown, Fauq Co, fHardwick
William S, b12/1837, Clifton, Fair Co, d1905, fJohn, mHarriet Davis, wAnnie Suddath
KING, Ann, b17--, Mont Co?, hJames Trigg
Camillus, b18--, KiQu Co, fJohn
Delia, bc1870, Rand Co?, d1918, hPrice L Shannon
Elsie, b17--, Mont Co?, hJohn Johns Trigg
Fannie, b1852, nrOmega, Hali Ca, d1888, 2w of Richard A Singleton
Florence Ellen, b18--, Warr Co?, fI N, hGeorge H Bowman
Jeremiah C, b9/3/1846, Henry Co, d1908, fCamillus, wEliza Rangeley, md1870
John, b18--, Richmond?, wSusan E Todd
John, bc1840, Rkhm Co, wEmma Mauzy
John O, b8/11/1852, Albe Co, d1891, fElias W, wMary Ann Marsh
Mary Elizabeth, b1848, Pula Co, d1911, hJames T Trolinger
Robert L, bc1860, wMattie Smith
Rosa Belle, bc1860, Richmond, fJohn, mSusan E Todd, hLuther Howard Jenkins, md5/20/1879
William, b177-, Mont Co?, 1h of Mary Trigg
KINGREE, David, b17--, Shen Co, fJohn
Sallie, bc1800, Shen Co?, fSolomon, hReuben Moore
Solomon, b17--, Shen Co?, fDavid
KINGSBURY, Cora, b18--, West Co, hJoseph W Shackford
KINNEY, Anne, b18--, Augu Co?, hHenderson Bell
Jane Eleanor, b1821, Staunton, Augu Co, fWilliam, hEdwin M Taylor
KINNIER, James W, b18--, Lynchburg, Camp Co, d1915, fWilliam, (2)mVictoria Tanner
Mildred Lelia, b186-, Lynch-

KINNIER (continued)
burg, Camp Co, fWilliam, (1)mMildred Lelia Scruggs
KINSEY, Minnie Rebecca, b18--, nrBoone Mill, Fran Co, fJ H, hMonroe Thomas Sink, md4/14/1896
Susan, b18--, Fran Co, hFleming Boon
KINZEL, Henry, bc1830, Fred Co?, wLucy Hardy
KINZIE, C W, bc1850, Bote Co, wPearl Layman
KIPPS, William, bc1840, Shen Co?, wMary Harpine
KIRBY, Andrew J, b18--, Floy Co?, wElizabeth Liggon
Lelia C, b186-, Floy Co, fAndrew J, mElizabeth Liggon, hBenjamin Schuyler Pedigo, md4/1892
Mary, b17--, York Co, hAnthony Robinson II
KIRK, George W, b18--, Lune Co, wEliza Ann Walker
Joseph B, bc1860, wSallie S Frazier
Judith, bc1730, Lanc Co?, hWilliam Hunton
Kate, b18--, hCarter R Bishop II, md1881
Margaret Agnes, b18--, Lune Co, d1906, fGeorge W, mEliza Ann Walker, hJulius Augustus Moore, md1/12/1882
KIRKNER, Eliza, b18--, Blan Co?, hJacob Trinkle
KIRKPATRICK, Elizabeth, b17--, West Co, hPeter Morison
F Sydnor, b18--, fThomas J
Jennie, b18--, hJames W Scott
John, b1790, Camp Co, d1842, wJane Maria Jellis
Mary, b18--, Lynchburg, Camp Co, fJohn, mJane Maria Jellis, hWilliam Henry Parrish, Sr
KIRTLEY, Sarah, bc1790, Madi Co, hAsa Graves
KISER, Abednego, b1832, Dick Co, w-- Jessee
Daniel, b18--, Rkhm Co?, wSusan Garber
Elihu T, b1870, Dick Co, d1920, fAbednego, m-- Jessee, wLucinda Short
Elizabeth T, bc1860, Dayton,

KISER (continued)
Rkhm Co, fJohn M, mElizabeth Miller, hJoseph Newton Shrum, md10/7/1880
Etta S, bc1870, Rkhm Co, fDaniel, mSusan Garber, hNoah R Crist, md4/27/1898
John M, b18--, Rkhm Co?, wElizabeth Miller
Ladora Jane, b18--, nrCarterton, Bedf Co, fElihu, hJohn William Combs
Martha, b18--, Bedf Co?, hJohn T Candler
Martha, b18--, Russ Co?, d1839, 1w of Joshua Counts
Melissa, b18--, Russ Co, hHiram Ashbrook
KISLING, John, bc1860, Rkhm Co?, wMollie Collier
KITE, Amanda Virginia, b18--, Page Co?, hIsaac Shuler, md 1870
Elizabeth, b1/1/1788, Page Co, d1865, hReuben Foltz
Fielding Wise, b18--, Page Co, wDora Virginia Brown
George L L, bc1825, Page Co?, dc1900
I F, bc1850, Page Co, w-- Shuler
Nancy, b18--, Page Co, fDavid, hHenry M Keyser
Susan Bell, b18--, Page Co, d1914, fGeroge L, hJohn F Long
KITTERMAN, Adeline, bc1839, Floy Co, hIsaac Huff
KIZER, John P, b1795, Luray, Page Co, wHannah A Miller
Thomas E, b1832, Salem, Roan Co, fJohn P, mHannah A Miller, wMinerva C Wiseman
KLINE, --, bc1840, Kline Mill, Fred Co, fJames R, hAmos Guard
Amanda Alice, bc1860, nrYellow Spring, Hamp Co, mRebecca McIvor, hJohn Edward Lincoln
Annie, b18--, Fred Co, fAnthony, h-- Spessard
Anthony, b18--, Fred Co, fAnthony
Christina, bc1840, Rkhm Co, fSamuel, m-- Garber, hAndrew J Crist
Clara, b186-, Fred Co, fW Strother, mAnne R Dinges, hJames I

KLINE (continued)
Wise
Eliza, b18--, Fred Co, fAnthony
F Estes, b3/10/1866, Fred Co, fW Strother, mAnne R Dinges, wNannie Stickley, md1/3/1900
Frances, b183-, Kline Mill, Fred Co, fJames R, hCharles W Powers
Harvey, b186-, Fred Co, fW Strother, mAnne R Dinges
Howard W, bc1870, Fred Co, d1921, fW Strother, mAnne R Dinges
Hugh Boyd, b1/25/1858, Fred Co, fW Strother, mAnne R Dinges, wLillie R Muse, md9/19/1882
James Oscar, b183-, Kline Mill, fFred Co, fJames R
James R, b18--, Fred Co, fAnthony
John, bc1830, Rkhm Co?, wMartha Myers
John Michael, b8/8/1867, nr Broadway, Rkhm Co, fMichael B, mElizabeth Rhodes, wBertie Homan, md11/2/1904
Kate, bc1860, rBroadway, Rkhm Co, fMichael B, mElizabeth Rhodes, hDennis Weimer
Lucinda, b183-, Kline Mill, Fred Co, fJames R, hDaniel Baker
Madison, b186-, nrBroadway, Rkhm Co, fMichael B, mElziabeth Rhodes
Margaret, b18--, Fred Co?, d1896, hEmanuel Albin
Mary, b18--, Rkhm Co?, hChristian Myers
Mary, b183-, Kline Mill, Fred Co, fJames R, hMilton Peery
Mary F, b18--, Fred Co, fAnthony, hJohn Senseny
Michael B, b1826, nrBroadway, Rkhm Co, d1909, wElizabeth Rhodes
Noah, b186-, nrBroadway, Rkhm Co, fMichael B, mElzabeth Rhodes
Octavia, b186-, Fred Co, fW Strother, mAnne R Dinges
Samuel, bc1840, Fred Co?, wAnnie Rhodes
Samuel A, b184-, Kline Mill, Fred Co, fJames R

KLINE (continued)
Samuel R, b186-, nrBroadway, Rkhm Co, fMichael B, mElizabeth Rhodes
Susanna, b186-, nrBroadway, Rkhm Co, fMichael B, mElizabeth Rhodes, hWilliam Andes
W Strother, b4/15/1829, Kline Mill, Fred Co, fJames R, wAnne R Dinges
KLINGAN, --, b18--, wLaura Alexander
KLUGE, Carrie, b18--, hAndrew Y Prarie
KNIGHT, Annie E, bc1870, Alexandria, fFerdinand, mAnn E Johnson, hJohn D Matter
Ferdinand, b1828, Alexandria, d1894, wAnn E Johnson
Herbert C, b186-, Alexandria, fFerdinand, mAnn E Johnson
India, bc1860, PrEd Co, hWalter Gray Dunnington
Joseph Lafayette, b10/16/1866, nrMonitor, Amhe Co, fWilliam Lafayette, mSarah Elizabeth Landrum
Julian D, b186-, Alexandria, fFerdinand, mAnn E Johnson
Robert E, Sr, b6/3/1866, Alexandria, fFerdinand, mAnn E Johnson, wElizabeth E Soper
KNOWLES, Absalom, b12/17/1817, Churchville, Augu Co, fGeroge, mDiana Brooks, wSusan Jane Taylor
A Lee, b12/16/1865, nrChurchville, Augu Co, fAbsalom, mSusan Jane Taylor
KOGER, Martha E, b18--, Patr Co?, hJames R Via
KOINER, --, bc1840, Shen Co?, wRebecca Henkel
Susan, bc1820, Shen Co, hSamuel Godfrey Henkel
KOONTZ, --, bc1848, Page Co, fJames, mJane Snyder, hThomas Brubaker
A C b18--, Augu Co, wLaura Ross
Abram W, b184-, Rkhm Co, fPeter P, mElzabeth Ann Lincoln
Alfred, b18--, Page Co?, wJennie Burner
David E, b184-, Rkhm Co, fPeter P, mElizabeth Ann Lincoln
Eliza, b184-, Rkhm Co, fPeter

KOONTZ (continued)
P, mElizabeth Ann Lincoln
Ella, b18--, Shen Co, fJoseph B McInturff
George Williams, b2/12/1839, Edinburg, Shen Co, fWilliam J, mAnn Elziabeth Grandstaff, wMary T Newman, md12/6/1871
James, b18--, Page Co, fJohn, wJane Snyder, md184-
James William, b184-, Page Co, fJames, mJane Snyder, wElizabeth Catherine Moore
John Edgar, b3./3.1851, Page Co, d1917, fJames, mJane Snyder, wMollie Larkins, md2/2/1882
Julia Ann, b183-, Page Co, hAndrew Jackson Shuler
Mary, b183-, Edinburg, Shen Co, fWilliam J, mAnn Elizabeth Grandstaff, hHenry Tallhelm
Milton, b184-, Edinburg, Shen Co, d1867, fWilliam J, mAnn Elizabeth Grandstaff
Nellie, b184-, Edinburg, Shen Co, fWilliam J, mAnn Elizabeth Grandstaff, hNewton McCann
Peter B, bc1810, Augu Co, wElizabeth Ann Lincoln
Philip, b184-, Rkhm Co, fPeter P, mElizabeth Ann Lincoln
Reuben, b184-, Rkhm Co, fPeter P, mElizabeth Ann Lincoln
Sudie Elizabeth, b18--, Page Co?, fAlfred, mJennie Burner, 1h-- Snyder, 2w of Isaac Shuler
Thomas, bc1850, Page Co, fJames, mJane Snyder
William J, bc1818, Edinburg, Shen Co, 1845, fGeorge, wAnn Elizabeth Grandstaff
Wilson Asbury, b12/6/1850, Rkhm Co, fPeter P, mElizabeth Ann Lincoln, wMary Strole, md11/8/1878
KOWNSELAR, Jane, b18--, Clar Co?, hWilliam Byrd Lee
KREBS, Joshua, b18--, Fred Co, wElizabeth McCormick
Sallie, b185-, nrWinchester, Fred Co, fJoshua, mElizabeth McCormick, hJohn Peter Gordon
KREITE, John E, bc1860, Esse Co?, wEmily Margaret Trible

KREMER, Mary Catherine, b18--, Winchester, Fred Co, 1w of Robert Barr
KRUG, Frederick C, bc1860, Richmond?, wAnnie Sorg
KUREL, Lucy, b18--, Hamp Co?, 1w of Oscar Barr
KURTZ, George W, b3/6/1838, Winchester, Fred Co, fIsaac, mFrances Temple Fitzhugh, w Mary Frances Clayton, md5/1871
Isaac, b7/5/1790, Winchester, Fred Co, d1861, wFrances Temple Fitzhugh
KYGER, --, bc1830, Rkhm Co?, wSallie Miller
KYLE, James H, b18--, Gray Co?, wLouella Cox
Jane, b17--, Bote Co, d1852, hBernard Pitzer
John E, bc1860, Rkbr Co?, wMary Sale
LACY, Alexander S, b3/22/1858, Hali Co, fCharles, mMary Baker, wKate Forrest Baker
Charles, b1820, Hali Co, d1901, fRobert, wMary Baker
James Thomas, Sr, b1/19/1858, Halifax Court House, Hali Co, fMicajah T, wAda B Crews
LACEY, Mary E, b18--, ChCi Co?, hRobert E Davis
LADD, Ann, b18--, Loui Co?, hJoseph Clivius Boxley
LAFFOON, Mary Catherine, b1826, Lune Co, d1900, hThomas Garrett Moore
LAFON, --, b17--, hValentine Winfree III
LA FORCE, Rachel, b18--, Russ Co, hJonas Rasnick
LA FOLLETT, James, b18--, Hamp Co, wLena Anderson
Lena, bc1870, Hamp Co, fJames A mLena Anderson, hF G Good
Rebecca, b17--, Hamp Co?, hMichael Capper
LAFON, Enoch, b18--, Crai Co, w-- Harless
John C, b184-, Crai Co, fEnoch, m-- Harless
Nancy E, b1/23/1851, Crai Co, fEnoch, m-- Harless, hOscar E Huffman
LAIRD, Alexander Thompson, b4/20/1819, nrLexington, Rkbr Co,

LAIRD (continued)
  fJohn, wVirginia Chambers
  Edward Chambers, b10/9/1854, Boydton, Meck Co, fAlexander Thompson, mVirginia Chambers, wCora Holt, md6/9/1880
  Mary, b18--, Taze Co, hThomas David
LAKE, Harriet, b18--, fIsaac, hWilliam Fletcher
  Mary Agnes, b5/8/1851, nrMarshall, Fauq Co, fWilliam H, mSarah Elizabeth Childs, hTheodore Montgomery Triplett, Sr, md12/18/1877
  Susanna, b1790, Fauq Co, d1835, fWilliam, 1w of Aquilla Glascock
  William H, b11/1826, Fauq Co, d1896, wSarah Elizabeth Childs
  William Ludwell, bc1850, nrMarshall, Fauq Co, fWilliam H, mSarah Elizabeth Childs
LAM, Charles Davis, b1/5/1864, Bote Co, fIsaac, mMartha Hall, wAnnie Eliza Moore, md8/7/1895
  Clara, b18--, Augu Co?, hJohn M Brown
  Isaac, bc1829, Rkbr Co, fMathias, m-- Davis, wMartha Hall
LAMB, James Christian, b11/18/1853, ChCi Co, fLycurgus, mAnn Elizabeth Christian, 1wLoula Brockenbrough, 2wSadie Brockenbrough
  John, b184-, ChCi Co, fLycurgus, mAnn Elizabeth Christian
  Lycurgus, bc1814, ChCi Co, wAnn Elizabeth Christian
  Joseph H, b18--, nrElkton, Rkhm Co, wLaura Virginia Maupin
  Margaret, bc1870, Norfolk, fWilliam, mSarah Ann Chaffee, hAlonzo Augustus Bilisoly, md 1902
  William, b9/7/1835, Norfolk, d1905, fWilliam Wilson, mMargaret Kerr, wSarah Ann Chafee, md9/7/1857
  William Wilson, b18--, Norfolk?, wMargaret Kerr
LAMBERT, Isabelle, b18--, Wyth Co?, hJames F Huddle
  John, bc1830, Blan Co, wMary E Walker
  Leila, bc1870, Fauq Co?, h

LAMBERT (continued)
  Charles A Crenshaw
  Lena, b18--, Brun Co, hWaverly T Walker
  Mary Jane, b1844, Wise Co, d1920, hSamuel R Hurley, Sr
  Will, bc1850, Rkhm Co?, wMattie Dillard
LAMBETH, Samuel Summerfield, Sr, b1838, Richmond, fThomas H, wVirginia Jessie Parker
LAMPKIN, John T, b18--, Russ Co?, wMargaret Carter
  Sara Preston, bc1870, Russ Co?, fJohn T, mMargaret Carter, hWilliam Wallace Bird, md12/15/1896
  Susan Lewis, bc1800, hHenderson Lee
LANCASTER, Elma, b186-, Floy Co, fRobert, mOctavia Underwood, hW J Phleger
  John, bc1860, Clar Co?, wKate Sprint
  Robert, bc1831, Floy Co, d1907, wOctavia Underwood
  Robert T, bc1870, Floy Co, fRobert, mOctavia Underwood
LAND, Nathaniel J, b18--, nrBroomfield, Suss Co
LANDACRE, Jesse, bc1800, Hard Co?, wEliza --
  Elizabeth, b18--, Hard Co?, fJesse, mEliza --, hLevi Cline
LANDES, B F, bc1840, Rkhm Co?, wMary E Hall
  William H, b12/12/1858, nrWarm Springs, Bath Co, fJohn, m Catherine A Rose, wHester Virginia Link
LANDIS, Nannie, bc1870, Augu Co, d1899, fErasmus, hWilliam F Fry
LANDON, Bettie, b18--, hWilliam Walter Douglas
LANE, --, bc1800, PrWi Co?, 1h-- Rowles, 2hBenjamin Higgs
  Arthur Hudson, bc1870, Fluv Co, fJohn Haden, Jr, mAmanda Jackson Hudson
  Bettie, b18--, hJohn Robert Faison
  Charles Wesley, bc1870, Fluv Co, fJohn Haden, Jr, mAmanda Jackson Hudson, wMamie Allen
  Elizabeth, b18--, Front Royal,

LANE (continued)
Warr Co, hGiles Cooke
Frances, b17--, Fluv Co?, fLittleberry
George, bc1800, Fluv Co, fWilliam S, mNancy Haden
Henry Lee, b12/12/1867, Fluv Co, fJohn Haden, Jr, mAmanda Jackson Hudson, wLaura S Martin
James F, b186-, Fluv Co, fJohn Haden, Jr, mAmanda Jackson Hudson, wCourtney Hughes
John Edwards, Sr, b2/17/1857, fWilliam George, Sr, mAmanda Jackson Hudson, 1wElla Florence Wisely, 2wRosa Thornton Wright, md1911
John Haden, Sr, bc1800, Fluv Co, fWilliam S, mNancy Haden, 1w-- Timberlake, 2wLucinda B Shepherd
John Haden, Jr, bc1834, Fluv Co, d1919, fJohn Haden, Sr, (2)mLucinda B Shepherd, 2h of Amanda Jackson Hudson
Josephine I, b18--, Esse Co?, 2w of Joseph William Chinn, Jr
Maggie Virginia, bc1860, Fluv Co, fWilliam George, Sr, m Amanda Jackson Hudson, hLewis A Mc Cutchen
Martha, b17--, Fair Co, fJames, hSimon Triplett
Mary Ann, bc1800, Fluv Co, fWilliam S, mNancy Haden, h William Jones
Sarah, bc1800, Fluv Co, fWilliam S, mNancy Haden, hGeorge Haden
Sarah, b181-, Fair Co?, 1w of Frederick Mortimer Ford, Sr
Susan, bc1800, Fluv Co, fWilliam S, mNancy Haden, hAsa D Haden
Unity, b17--, Fluv Co?, fLittleberry, hLansen Rowe
William George, Sr, bc1836, Fluv Co, d1863, fJohn Haden, Sr, 1h of Amanda Jackson Hudson, md1886
William George, Jr, b9/20/1858, Fluv Co, fWilliam George, Sr, mAmanda Jackson Hudson, wZada N Rorer
William S, b17--, Fluv Co?,

LANE (continued)
Littleberry, wNancy Haden
LANG, Anna, bc1860, Bridge Water, Rkhm Co, fSol, mAmanda Fraley, hE B Woodruff
Henry L, b2/16/1863, BridgeWater, Rkhm Co, fSol, mAmanda Fraley, wMargaret Starritt, md1886
LANGFORD, Eliza Agnes, bc1850, Albe Co, fPleasant, Jr, mSusan B Newcomb, hJohn W Gordon
John Walker, b9/25/1850, Albe Co, fPleasant, Jr, mSusan B Newcomb, wSallie Black Bailey, md3/21/1881
Pleasant, Sr, bc1800, Albe Co, fWest
Pleasant, Jr, b18--, Albe Co, fPleasant, Sr, wSusan B Newcomb
LANGHORNE, --, b17--, Warw Co?, hJohn Scaisbrook Langhorne
--, b17--, Fran Co?, 2w of William Callaway
Anne Norvell, b18--, Lynchburg, Camp Co, d1921, fJames M, mEmeline Norvell, hWilliam Nelson Wellford, Sr
Chriswell Dabney, b11/4/1844, Lynchburg, Camp Co, dc1920, fJohn Scaisbrook, mElizabeth Dabney, wNanni Witcher Keen
Elizabeth, b18--, hT M Perkins
Elizabeth Allen, b184-, Mont Co, fJohn Archer, mMargret Kent, hJohn Meem Payne, md12/1863
Elizabeth Dabney, bc1850, Lynchburg, Camp Co, fJohn Scaisbrook, mElizabeth Dabney, hJohn H Lewis
Henry Scaisbrook, b1790, Cumb Co?, fJohn, m-- Langhorne, wFrances Steptoe
James M, b18--, Camp Co?, wEmeline Norvell
John, b16--, Warw Co?, fJohn La Charm of Langhorne, Wales
John, b16--, Warw Co, fJohn
John Archer, b18--, Mont Co?, wMargaret Kent
John Scaisbrook, b1760, Warw Co, d1796, fWilliam, mElizabeth Scaisbrook, w-- Langhorne
John Scaisbrook, bc1823, Cumb

LANGHORNE (continued)
Co, fHenry Scaisbrook, mFrances Steptoe, wElizabeth Dabney
Lucrecia S, bc1850, Norf Co?, d1907, fMaurice, mLucrecia --, hHenry Clay Hudgins
Lucy B, bc1860, Lynchburg, Camp Co, fJohn Scaisbrook, mElizabeth Dabney, hWarren S Ficklen
Mary, b18--, Bote Co, fWilliam, mCatherine Steptoe
Maurice, b1720, Warw Co, d1791, fJohn
Maurice, b1787, Cumb Co?, d1865, fJohn Scaisbrook, m-- Langhorne
Maurice, b18--, Norf Co?, wLucrecia --
Nannie, 184-, Lynchburg, fJohn Scaisbrook, mElizabeth Dabney, hEdward Sixtus Hutter
Thomas Nelson, b1/8/1858, Lynchburg, Camp Co, fJohn Scaisbrook, mElizabeth Dabney, wAnna Hewitt
William, bc1720, Warw Co, fJohn, wElizabeth Scaisbrook
William, b17--, Bote Co?, w Catherine Steptoe
LANGLEY, Charles Henry, b18--, Norf Co?, wPortia Deming
Kate, b2/1/1865, Norfolk, f Charles Henry, mPortia Deming, hCharles Gideon Bosher
LANGSTON, nancy, b18--, Nans Co?, hWilliam Darden
LANHAM, Enoch F, b1859, wMary Elizabeth Pope
Samuel, bc1840, Clar Co?, w Amanda Smallwood
LAREW, R F, bc11850, Rkbr Co?, wElizabeth Poague McClung
LARKINS, Kate, bc1860, Edinburg, Shen Co, fWilliam, mLucinda Kern, h-- Hottel
Mollie, b12/6/1862, Edinburg, Shen Co, fWilliam, mLucinda Kern, hJohn Edgar Koontz, md2/2/1882
William, b18--, Shen Co?, wLucinda Kern
William, bc1860, Edinburg, Shen Co, fWilliam, mLucinda Kern
LARRICK, Amanda, bc1850, Hayfield, Fred Co, fAsa, mRebecca Hottel, hDaniel Hammock

LARRICK (continued)
Asa, b1807, Hayfield District, Fred Co, d1881, fHenry, mMargaret Cotty, wRebecca Hottel
Catherine, b181-, Hayfield District, Fred Co, fHenry, mMargaret Cotty
Cora Lee, b186-, nrMiddletown, Fred Co, fJacob B, Sr, mMary A Scaggs, hPinckney A Scaggs
David, b181-, Hayfield District, Fred Co, fHenry, mMargaret Cotty
David H, b184-, Hayfield, Fred Co, fAsa, mRebecca Hottel
Edgar Olin, b6/16/1857, nrMiddletown, Fred Co, fJacob B, Sr, mMary A Scaggs, wMartha F Haslup
George W, b185-, nrMiddletown, Fred Co, fJacob B, Sr, mMary A Scaggs
Henry, bc1781, Hayfield District, Fred Co, wMargaret Cotty
Herbert S, b186-, nrMiddletown, Fred Co, fJacob B, Sr, mMary A Scaggs
Isaiah E, b185-, Hayfield, Fred Co, fAsa, mRebecca Hottel
Jacob B, Sr, b3/12/1826, nrMiddletown, Fred Co, d1887, wMary A Scaggs
Jacob B, Jr, b186-, nrMiddletown, Fred Co, fJacob B, Sr, mMary A Scaggs
James, b180-, Hayfield District, Fred Co, fHenry, mMargaret Cotty
James, bc1850, Hayfield, Fred Co, fAsa, mRebecca Hottel
James I, b11/30/1859, Middletown, Fred Co, fJacob B, Sr, mMary A Scaggs, wRose Bird, md5/16/1883
John, bc1810, Hayfield District, Fred Co, fHenry, mMargaret Cotty
John Wesley, b2/1/1850, Hayfield, Fred Co, fAsa, mRebecca Hottel, wMargaret A Simpson, md3/10/1880
Lucy R, b185-, nrMiddletown, Fred Co, fJacob B, Sr, mMary A Scaggs, James Faulkner
Margaret, b181-, Hayfield District, Fred Co, fHenry, mMar-

LARRICK (continued) garet Cotty
Margaret, bc1850, Hayfield, Fred Co, fAsa, mRebecca Hottel, hJoseph Bean
Martha, bc1810, Hayfield District, Fred Co, fHenry, mMargaret Cotty
Mary, bc1810, Hayfield District, Fred Co, fHenry, mMargaret Cotty
Mary, b184-, Hayfield, Fred Co, fAsa, mRebecca Hottel, hJacob Hammock
Nancy Catheirne, b184-, Hayfield, Fred Co, fAsa, mRebecca Hottel, hJacob Crisman
Robert A, b186-, nrMiddletown, Fred Co, Jacob B, Sr, mMary A Scaggs
Sallie, b185-, Hayfield, Fred Co, fAsa, mRebecca Hottel, hJohn W Smoke
Sarah E, b185-, nrMiddletown, Fred Co, fJacob B, Sr, mMary A Scaggs, hS M Williams
Susan, b185-, Hayfield, Fred Co, fAsa, mRebecca Hottel, h Joseph Richard
LaRUE, E M, b185-, Bath Co, fRobert S, mRebecca R Brinkley
Emma, b185-, Bath Co, fRobert S, mRebecca R Brinkley, h-- Hall
F T, b185-, Bath Co, fRobert S, mRebecca R, Brinkley
Floyd Lee, b10/24/1859, nrBath Alum (now McClung) Bath Co, fRobert S, mRebecca R Brinkley, wLillah B Cleek, md11/13/1884
Jacob, b17--, Bath Co?, 1wAnna Scott, 2w-- Gay
Mary S, b186-, Bath Co, fRobert S, mRebecca R Brinkley
Robert S, bc1825, Waynesboro, Augu Co, fJacob, (1)mAnna Scott, wRebecca R Brinkley
W S, b186-, Bath Co, fRobert S, mRebecca R Brinkley
LASSITER, Daniel W, b18--, wAnna Heath
LATANE, Ann Susanna, b1799, "Langley Farm", Esse Co, 1w of Warner Lewis
Ann Ursula, b11/5/1826, "Meadow Farm", Esse Co, d1876, hThomas

LATANE (continued) Waring Lewis
Blanche, b18--, fThomas, (2)m Anne Madison Haile
Harry A, b18--, fThomas, (2)m Anne Madison Haile
Henry Waring, b18--, Esse Co, wMartha Harvie Gordon
Jacob James Allen, b1831, KiQu Co?, wMary Minor Holladay
James, b1810, Esse Co, wMarie Rouzzie
John H, bc1860, KiQu Co?, fJacob James Allen, mMary Minor Holladay
Julia, b186-, KiQu Co?, fJacob, James Allen, mMary Minor Holladay, hClaggett Bennett Jones
Lewis, b18--, fThomas, (2)mAnne Madison Haile
Lucy C, b18--, fThomas, (2)m Anne Madison Haile
Mary Susan, b11/1853, Mahockny Farm, Esse Co, f1921, hCharles Jones Sale
Robert Haile, b4/19/1858, KiQu Co, fThomas, (2)mAnne Madison Haile, wClare Wyatt
Susan Elizabeth, b18--, fThomas, (2)mAnne Madison Haile
Thomas, b18--, Esse Co?, fHenry Waring, 2wAnne Madison Haile
William Catesby, b1846, Esse Co, fJames, mMarie Rouzzie, w Susan Wilson
LATHAM, Georgia Owen, b18--, Culp Co?, hThaddeus Norris Fletcher, Sr
LATTIMER, Clara Virginia, b18--, Isle Co, hWilliam E Bloxom
LATTURE, Susan, b18--, Scot Co?, hDrew S Godsey
LAUCK, Emily Heiskell, b3/7/1839, Page Co, fWilliam C, m-- Sours, hJohn Kaylor Booton, md1857
Emily M, bc1830, Page Co, fMorgan A, mMaria Ott, hMoses Walton
Morgan A, bc1800, Page Co, wMaria Ott
William C, b18--, Page Co?, w-- Sours
LAUD, Margaret Anne, b18--, PrAn Co, hJoseph Henry Fentress
LAUGHLIN, Mary, b18--, Lexing-

LAUGHLIN (continued)
ton, Rkbr Co, hAlfred N Brown S O, bc1860, Shen Co?, wMary Magruder
Smith, bc1810, Augu Co?, wDorcas Lincoln
LAUGHON, Alonzo, b185-, nrLeesville, Bedf Co, fJoshua, (1)m Elizabeth White
Beauregard, b186-, nrLeesville, bedf Co, fJoshua, (1)mElizabeth White
Gary, Sr, b5/26/1862, nrLeesville, Bedf Co, fJoshua, (1)mElizabeth White, wMollie Hoge Jordan, md5/25/1886
Isom, b17--, Bedf Co
Joshua, b1818, Bedf Co, d1876, fIsom, 1wElizabeth White, 2w Eliza Quarles
Lavinia E, bc1860, nrLeesville, Bedf Co, fJoshua, (1)mElizabeth White, hJames M White
Oscar, b186-, nrLeesville, Bedf Co, fJoshua, (1)mElizabeth White
Walter, b185-, nrLeesville, Bedf Co, fJoshua, (1)mElizabeth White
LAULA, --, b18--, Rapp Co?, wLucy Menefee
LAVENDER, Agnes Laetitia, b186-, Roan Co?, fTazewell Chilton, mMartha Parcell, hJohn Fletcher Barbour
Tazewell Chilton, b18--, Roan Co?, wMartha Parcell
LAW, Martha Reid, b5/10/1810, Ches Co, d1872, fWilliam Parrin, mMartha Dance, hJames H Cox
LAWLER, Robert, b18--, Fauq Co?, wLandonia Carter
LAWLESS, George W, b18--, Patr Co?, wRosanna Washburn
Robert E, b9/19/1869, Patr Co, George W, mRosanna Washburn, wFlorence D Hall, md6/3/1893
LAWRENCE, --, b18--, Henry Co?, wMary E Richardson
Barbara, b17--, Fred Co?, 1w of Jasper Cather
Gattie, b18--, Nans Co, fJoseph, hLewis H Webb
George Anderson, b18--, Greene Co?, wCharlotte Louise Colley

LAWRENCE (continued)
Joseph, b18--, Nans Co
Mary Elizabeth, b18--, hDaniel James Turner
LAWS, Bolitha J, bc1850, wMamie Menefee
LAWSON, Bertha t, bc1870, Locklies, Midd Co, fThomas Y, Sr, (2)mSallie Ann Fleet
Charles M, b186-, Locklies, Midd Co, fThomas Y, Sr, (2)mSallie Ann Fleet
Charles Nichols, b18--, White Stone, Lance Co, d1864, w-Brent
Elliott W, b12/1/1847, White Stone, Lanc Co, fCharles Nichols, m-- Brent, wFannie Octavia Hathaway
F, b185-, Locklies, Midd Co, fThomas Y, Sr, (1)mSusan Pierce Fleet
Ida Waverly, bc1870, Locklies, Midd Co, fThomas Y, Sr, (2)mSallie Ann Fleet, hMorton E Clarke
Richard, b17--, Glou Co, w-- Kemp
Susan Pierce, b186-, Locklies, Midd Co, fThomas Y, Sr, (2)m Sallie Ann Fleet, hEdward H Whitehurst
Thomas Y, Sr, b5/5/1820, Glou Co, d1893, fRichard, m-- Kemp, 1w Susan Pierce Fleet, 2wSallie Ann Fleet
Thomas Y, Jr, b186-, Locklies, Midd Co, fThomas Y, Sr, (2)mSallie Ann Fleet
William H, b2/14/1862, Locklies, Midd Co, fThomas Y, Sr, (2)mSallie Ann Fleet, wKate B Taliaferro, md10/30/1894
William T, b18--, Patr Co, wLillie D Howard
LAYMAN, Annie, b185-, nrTroutville, Bote Co, fJacob G, mAdaline Kessler, hJ L Riley
Betty E, b186-, Roan Co, fWilliam J, (1)m-- Williams, h-- Smith
Charles T, b186-, nrConner Springs, Bote Co, fLewis G, mLucy Ann Rieley
Dovey, b186-, nrTroutville, Bote Co, d1917, fJacob G,

LAYMAN (continued)
  mAdaline Kessler, hG A Moomaw
  Elizabeth Frances, bc1860, nr Conner Springs, Bote Co, fLewis G, mLucy Ann Rieley
  George H, b18--, Bote Co?, wAlbina Denton
  George W, bc1800, Bote Co, wMary Gish
  George W, b12/18/1868, Roan Co, fWilliam J, (2)mNancy A Webb, wAddie G Reynolds, md7/3/1895
  George William, bc1860, nrConner Springs, Bote Co, Lewis G, mLucy Ann Rieley, wMary Lillie Moomaw, md1890
  Jacob G, b1/15/1835, rTroutville, bote Co, fGeorge W, mMary Gish, wAdaline Kessler
  John William, b5/3/1863, nrTroutville, Bote Co, fJacob G, mAdaline Kessler, wMary Elizabeth Layman, md10/4/1887
  Lewis Edward, bc1870, nrConner Springs, Bote Co, fLewis G, mLucy Ann Rieley
  Lewis G, b1834, nrTroutville, Bote Co, fGeorge W, mMary Gish, wLucy Ann Rieley
  Lucy Berta, bc1870, nrConner Springs, Bote Co, fLewis G, mLucy Ann Rieley
  Marshall, b186-, nrConner Springs, Bote Co, fLewis G, mLucy Ann Rieley
  Mary Elizabeth, b186-, Bote Co, fAbram K, hJohn William Lyman, md10/4/1887
  Nannie, b186-, nrConner Springs, Bote Co, fLewis G, mLucy Ann Rieley
  Pearl, bc1860, nrTroutville, Bote Co, fJacob G, mAdaline Kessler, hC W Kinzie
  Philip, b183-, Bote Co?, fJohn
  Priscilla, bc1870, nrTroutville, Bote Co, fJacob G, mAdaline Kessler, hJohn William Shaver, md1893
  R G, b185-, nrTroutville, Bote Co, fJacob G, mAdaline Kessler
  Theodore, bc1860, Shen Co?, wAnnie F Good
  Virginia Layman, b1860, nrConner Springs, Bote Co, fLewis G, mLucy Ann Rieley

LAYMAN (continued)
  William H, b186-, Roan Co, fWilliam J, (1)m-- Williams
  William J, b6/3/1838, Roan Co, d121, fJohn, 1w-- Williams, 2wNancy A Webb
LAYNE, Louise, b18--, Camp Co, hIsaac Walthall
  Robert L, b18--, Fluv Co
  Robert Jones, fRobert L, wElisha William Winfrey
LEA, David M, Sr, b1826, Richmond, wSarah E Palmer
  David M, Jr, bc1860, Richmond, fDavid M, Sr, mSarah E Palmer
  Helen, bc1870, Richmond, fDavid M, Sr, mSarah E Palmer, hV D Venable
LEACH, --, b18--, hJonas A Leach --, bc1850, Warr Co?, wAddie/ Attie Rust
  Charles, bc1850, Warr Co, 1wIda Leach
LEACHMAN, Catherine, b186-, "Locust Grove", PrWi Co, fJohn Thomas, mElizabeth Ann Lewis
  Charles C, b185-, "Locust Grove", PrWi Co, fJohn Thomas, mElizabeth Ann Lewis
  Edith May, b185-, "Locust Grove", PrWi Co, fJohn Thomas, mElizabeth Ann Leiws, hJ F Dogan
  Elizabeth, b18--, PrWi Co, fJohn, mAnn Pendleton Chapman, hWilliam Dickinson
  John, bc1795, PrWi Co, dc1840, fLeonard, wAnn Pendleton Chapman
  John Pendleton, b12/18/1853, Manassas District, PrWi Co, fJohn Thomas, mElizabeth Ann Lewis, wMary Virginia Strother, md2/6/1884
  John Thomas, b18--, "Locust Grove", PrWi Co, d1914, fJohn, mAnn Pendleton Chapman, wElizabeth Ann Lewis
  Leonard, b17--, PrWi Co?, f Thomas
  Mary Lewis, b185-, "Locust Grove", PrWi Co, fJohn Thomas, mElzabeth Ann Lewis, hCary C Buck
  Nannie Neville, b186-, "Locust Grove", PrWi Co, fJohn Thomas,

LEACHMAN (continued)
mElzabeth Ann Lewis, hE L Carroll
Nessie L, bc1860, "Locust Grove", PrWi Co, fJohn Thomas, mElizabeth Ann Lewis, HJohn LElliott
Robert C, b18--, PrWi Co, fJohn, mAnn Pendleton Chapman
Robert Lee, b186-, "Locust Grove", PrWi Co, fJohn Thomas, mElizabeth Ann Lewis, hL C Lynn
Sarah Ann, b18--, PrWi Co, fJohn, mAnn Pendleton Chapman, hThomas T Fewell
Thomas Richards, b186-, "Locust Grove", PrWi Co, fJohn Thomas, mElizabeth Ann Lewis, wAlice Ashby
William, b18--, PrWi Co, fJohn, mAnn Pendleton Chapman
LEADBEATER, Lucy, b12/11/1837, Alexandria, d1917, fJohn, m Mary P Stabler, hEdgar Speiden, md10/1861
LEAKE, Andrew Kean, b18--, "Rocky Springs", Gooc Co, f Walter D, wJuliana Elizabeth Harris
Elizabeth, b17--, Albe Co, 2w of Andrew Hart
Gay Pendleton, b18--, Charlottesville, Albe Co, fShelton F, 1w of John M White, md1868
J Jordan, b2/13/1870, Ashland, Hano Co, fWilliam Josiah, m Sarah R Jordan, wLisa Foulke Beirne, md12/7/1904
Josiah, Sr, bc1730, Gooc Co, fWalter, mJudith Mask, wAnn Minter
Josiah, Jr, b10/26/1770, Gooc Co, fJosiah, Sr, mAnn Minter, wEliza Porter Hatcher
Samuel D, b12/10/1809, Gooc Co, fJosiah, Jr, mEliza Porter Hatcher, wFanny Minor Kean, md1833
Shelton F, b18--, Albe Co
Walter, bc1704, Gooc Co, fWilliam, mMary Bostwick, wJudith Mask
William Josiah, b9/30/1843, Gooc Co, fSamuel D, mFanny Minor Kean, wSarah R Jordan,

LEAKE (continued)
md7/3/1866
LEAR, Alice, b18--, hLyman Emery Clark
LEATH, --, b18--, Nott Co, hJohn Marshall
Emmett, bc1850, Richmond, wRosa L Taylor
LEAVEL, Fannie, bc1800, Culp Co?, hRobert T Bowers
LeCATO, Margaret, Benson, b6/11/1844, Bradfords Neck, Acco Co, hJohn E Mapp
LEAVENS, Esther, bc1800, Alexandria, hThomas Sanford
LECKEY, Fanny Templeton, b186-, Fancy Hill, Rkbr Co, d1911, fJ Poague, hReuben Grigsby Paxton
W F, b186-, Fancy Hill, Rkbr Co, fJ Poague
LEE, Alexander Y, b1838, Augu Co, d1897, fJoseph, mCatherine Clarke, wFrances McDonald
Annie Elizabeth, b18--, Wise Co, 2w of Isaac N Jones
Catherine Randolph, bc1860, Powh Co, fCharles Carter, mLucy Penn Taylor, hJohn R Guerrant
Charles Carter, b11/8/1798, "Stratford", West Co, d1871, fHenry, (2)mAnne Hill Carter, wLucy Penn Taylor, md5/13/1847
Clifton, Sr, b9/13/1848, Richmond, fLeroy M, mElizabeth Addington, wMartha Wesley Gatch
Edmund Jennings, b1772, fHenry II, mLucy Grymes, mSarah Lee
Eliza Ann, bc1829, Shen Co, d1910, fJohn C, m-- Newell, hPerry Borden
Elizabeth, b18--, Fauq Co?, fCharles, hAbram David Pollock
Elizabeth, b128--, Catawba, Roan Co, hWilliam Henry Nunley
George T, b3/8/1848, Powh Co, fCharles Carter, mLucy Penn Taylor
Gertrude, bc1860, fHugh Holmes, mMary Criss, hJohn Allen Watts, md/12/1880
Hannah, bc1806, Alexandria, fEdmund Jennings, mSarah Lee, hKensey Johns Stewart
Henderson, b1793, wSusan Lewis

LEE (continued)
Lampkin
Henderson, b1866, Lune Co, fHenderson Lewis, mLucy Scott
Henderson Lewis, b1826, Lune Co, fHenderson, mSusan Lewis Lampkin, wLucy Scott
Henry, bc1700, fRichard Lee II, mLaetitia Corbin, wMary Bland
Henry II, b1729, PrWi Co, fHenry, mMary Bland, Lucy Grymes
Henry, b1/29/1756, PrWi Co, fHenry II, mLucy Grymes, 1wMatilda Ludwell, 2wAnne Hill Carter, md1793
Henry, b1849, Powh Co, dc1904, fCharles Carter, mLucy Penn Taylor
Hugh Holmes, b18--, fGeorge H
John C, bc1800, Shen Co, w- Newell
John Penn, b9/11/1867, "Windsor Forest", Powh Co, fCharles Carter, mLucy Penn Taylor, wIsabella Gilman Walker, md12/2/1896
Joseph, b17--, wCatherine Clarke
Leroy M, b18--, Norf Co, wElizabeth Addington
Lettice, bc1755, West Co?, fJohn, mSusanna Smith, hJohn Whiting
Lewis Maury, bc1870, Lune Co, fHenderon Lewis, mLucy Scott
Mildred, bc1850, Powh Co, Charles Carter, mLucy Penn Taylor, hJohn T Francis
Nicholas, bc1810, Hamp Co?, wLydia Capper
Patrck Henry, b18--, Nans Co?, wJoanna Rawles
R R, b18--, Henry Co?, w- Matthews
Richard II, b16--, fRichard, wLaetitia Corbin
Richard, b17--, 1h of Sally Bland Poythress
Ricahrd, b184-, PrWi Co?, wMartha Triplett
Richard Henry, b18--, Clar Co?, fHenry, (1)mMatilda Ludwell
Robert Edward, bc1806, "Stratford", West Co, d1870, fHenry, (2)mAnna Carter
Robert E II, b2/11/1869, Pe-

LEE (continued)
tersburg, Dinw Co, fW H F, mMary Tabb Bolling, wMary Wilkinson (Middleton) Pinckney
Robert R, b1853, Powh Co, f Charles Carter, mLucy Penn Taylor
Sarah, b17--, fRichard Henry, hEdmund Jennings Lee
Sarah Otelia, b1861, Nans Co, d1897, fPatrick Henry, mJoanna Rawles, 1w of Edward Everett Holland, md11/26/1884
Sidney Smth, bc1800, "Stratford", West Co, fHenry, (2)m Anne Hill Carter
Thomas, bc1700, fRichard II, mLaetitia Corbin
W H F, b18--, fRobert E, wMary Tabb Bolling
Warren, bc1860, Albe Co?, wElizabeth B Minor
William Byrd, b18--, Clar Co?, fRichard Henry, wJane Kownselar
William Carter, b1852, Powh Co, d1882, fCharles Carter, mLucy Penn Taylor
LEEDY, Catherine, b18--, nrWoodstock, Shen Co, fJohn Keyser, mElizabeth Ridenour, hWilliam Smith
Charles J, b18--, nrWoodstock, Shen Co, w-- Dean
Daniel, b1795, Rkhm Co, fSamuel, mMargaret Harnesberger, wEve Brower
John, b18--, Harrisonburg, Rkhm Co, fSamuel
John, b1826, Rkhm Co, d1889, fDaniel, mEve Brower, wSarah Ann Mauck
John Keyser, b2/25/1829, Rkhm Co, fJohn, wElizabeth Ridenour
John W, b4/8/1854, nrWoodstock, Shen Co, fJohn Keyser, mElizabeth Ridenour, wDiana Spiggle
Maggie, b18--, nrWoodstock, Shen Co, fJohn Keyser, mElizabeth Ridenour, hPhilip Koontz
Minerva, b18--, nrWoodstock, Shen Co, John Keyser, mElizabeth Ridenour, hFrank Webb
Robert Franklin, b7/28/1863, Leedy's Pump, nrHarrisonburg, Rkhm Co, fJohn, mSarah Ann

LEEDY (continued)
Mauck, wEmma Catherine Keister, md3/27/1890
Samuel, b17--, Rkhm Co, wMargaret Hrnesberger
LeFEVRE, Laura, b11/9/1859, Loud Co, hGeorge W Popkins
LEFTWICH, Augustine, Jr, b11/10/1744, Bedf Co, fAugustine, Sr, 1wMary Turner, 2wMrs Sarah Turner
Bettie Ann, b1/23/1842, nrLiberty (now Bedford City), Bedf Co, 2w of Alphonso Alexander Gray
Elizabeth, b17--, Bedf Co, fWilliam, Sr, mElizabeth Haynes, hAlexander Burton, md4/14/1796
Fannie, b17--, Bedf Co, fAugustine, S, hMerry Carter
Jabez, bc1761, Bedf Co, fAugustine, Sr
James, b17--, Bedf Co, fWilliam, Sr, mElizabeth Haynes, wMatilda Callaway
Jesse, b17--, Bedf Co, fWilliam, Sr, mElizabeth Haynes, wDoshia Trigg, md7/21/1771
Joel, b11/27/1760, Bedf Co, fAugustine, Sr, (1)m--, wNancy Turner
John, b1750, Bedf Co, fAugustine, Sr, (1)m--
John, b17--, Bedf Co, fWilliam, Sr, mElzabeth Haynes, wSusanna Smith, md2/7/1788
Littleberry, b175-, fAugustine, Sr, wFrances Hopkins, md1/13/1778
Mary, b17--, Bedf Co, fAugustine, Sr, (1)m--, hJoshua Early
Mary, b17--, Bedf Co, fWilliam, Sr, mElizabeth Haynes, hWilliam Walton, md2/2/1778
Mildred, b17--, Bedf Co, fWilliam, Sr, mElizabeth Haynes, hFrazier Otey, md11/21/1793
Nancy, b17--, Bedf Co, fAugustine, Sr, (1)m--, hJames Pettross
Pattie L, b18--, Richmond, d1905, hNathaniel J Mason
Rebecca, b17--, Bedf Co, fAugustine, Sr, (1)m--, hJames H L

LEFTWICH (continued)
Moorman Sally, b1/20/1762, Bedf Co, fWilliam, Sr, mElizabeth Haynes, hJames Turner, md8/25/1778
Sarah, b18--, Bedf Co, hMartin Johnson
Thomas L, a bc1800, fWilliam, Jr, mFrances Otey, wMildred Otey Turner, md12/22/1829
Thomas, b1740, Bedf Co, fAugustine, Sr, 1wMary Challis, 2wBethenia Ellis, 3wJane Stratton
Uriah, bc1740, Bedf Co, fAugustine, Sr, wNancy Keith
William, Sr, b10/1737, Bedf Co, fAugustine, Sr, (1)m--, wElizabeth Haynes
William, Jr, b17--, Bedf Co, fWilliam, Sr, mElizabeth Haynes, 1wFrances Otey, md6/17/1788, 2wMary Fuqua, md8/22/1826, 3w Catherina B, Greer, md2/27/1839
LeGRANDE, Arthur Alexander, b18--, Appo Co?, wCaroline Matilda Hunter
Emma Cheesman, b7/2/1852, "Surrender Grounds", Appomattox, Appo Co, fArthur Alexander, mCaroline Matilda Hunter, hCharles Wash-ington Hancock, md12/6/1871
LeHEW, Eda, b17--, Warr Co?, hJacob Van Nort
Eli, b18--, Warr Co, mSallie Branson
Francis Wesley, b18--, Warr Co?, fEli, wSallie Machir Hopewell
LEIGH, Egbert, bc1850, Richmond, wLelia Palmer
Elizabeth Greenhill, b17--, Nott Co?, fTackana Greenhill, hRichard Floyd Burke
John Purviance, b18--, wFannie Cowdery
Southgate, Sr, b186-, fJohn Purviance, mFannie Cowdery, wAlice Creekmore, md1905
Thomas, b18--, Hali Co, fWilliam, 1wSarah Ann Wimbish, 2wSallie Tucker Carrington
Thomas Watkins, b12/13/1846,

LEIGH (continued)
Halifax, Hali Co, fThomas, (2)mSarah Ann Wimbish, wMary Elizabeth Faulkner
William, bc1850, Char Co?, wLouise Carrington
LEMEN, Thomas, b17--, wMary Williamson
LEMLEY, Elizabeth, bc1802, Fred Co?, d1867, hJacob Augustus Bucher
John, bc1850, Fred Co, wIda K Bucher
W F, bc1860, Fred Co, wLillian Shryock
LEMON, Harriet, bc1859, Bote Co?, d1921, fJames M, hBenjamin W Reid
Jennie, b1855, Loud Co, d1922, 2w of Joel E Beales
John B, b18--, Bote Co?, wEliza A Wright
Lula J, b2/1857, Bote Co, fJohn B, mEliza A Wright, hJohn Peter Saul, Sr, md6/1882
Sarah E, b185-, Bote Co?, fJonathan, hJoseph Benson Buhrman, md1880
LEONARD, Emma, b18--, Rich Co, hJames L Motley
LESLES, Madeline, b18--, Sout Co?, hJesse Cornelius Claud
LESLIE, Alonzo C, b185-, nrFincastle, Bote Co, fNathan M, mSusan Wagner
Andrew M, b186-, nrFincastle, Bote Co, fNathan M, mSusan Wagner
Anna, bc1860, nrFincastle, Bote Co, fNathan M, mSusan Wagne, h-- Hall
Charles E, b186-, nrFincastle, Bote Co, fNathan M, mSusan Wagner
Elvora, b186-, nrFincastle, Bote Co, fNathan M, mSusan Wagner, h-- Gan
Howard, b186-, nrFincastle, Bote Co, fNathan M, mSusan Wagner
Josephus, b10/16/1854, nrFincastle, Bote Co, fNathan M, mSusan Wagner, wElla Bland, md5/12/1879
Nannie, b186-, nrFincastle, Bote Co, d1923, fNathan M,

LESLIE (continued)
mSusan Wagner, hDavid H Riley
Nathan M, b1830, Augu Co, d1920, wSusan Wagner
Virginia, b185-, nrFincastle, Bote Co, fNathan M, mSusan Wagner, hWilliam A Ricker
Walter, b185-, nrFincastle, Bote Co, fNathan M, mSusan Wagner
LESNER, John, b18--, Norf Co
John Adam, b6/26/1869, Norfolk, fJohn
LESTER, George W, bc1836, Henry Co, wVictoria Wade
Henry Clay, b2/25/1838, Figsboro, Henry Co, d1913, fWilliam, mFrances Stegall, wLucy Clark Brown, md8/10/1871
Jennie, b18--, Floy Co, hGeorge Shelor
Job E, bc1860, Patr Co?, wMattie M Thomas
Riley, b18--, Wyom Co?, wMary Jane Justus
Virginia, b18--, Wyom Co?, hAlexander Hatfield
William, b17--, Pitt Co, fThomas
William, b18--, Pitt Co, fWilliam, wFrances Stegall
LETCHER, Greenlee Davidson, b7/19/1867, Lexington, Rkbr Co, fJohn
John, b3/29/1813, Lexington, Rkbr Co, fWilliam Houston
LEVI, George W, bc1844, Jeff Co, d1920, fRice W, mGeorgiana Weighley, wSallie Horton
Henry D, b184-, Jeff Co, fRice W, mGeorgiana Weighley, wLucy Carr
Howard C. b185-, Jeff Co, fRice W, mGeorgiana Weighley
Jacob O, b185-, Jeff Co, fRice W, mGeorgiana Weighley, wLizzie Carr
John, b185-, Jeff Co, fRice W, mGeorgiana Weighley
Laney, b185-, Jeff Co, fRice W, mGeorgiana Weighley
Mollie, b184-, Jeff Co, fRice W, mGeorgiana Weighley, hJohn H Clarke
R C, bc1860, Jeff Co, fRice W, mGeorgiana Weighley, wNannie

EVI (continued)
Levi
Rice W, bc1806, Fair Co?, d1866, wGeorgiana Weighley
Sallie, bc1850, Jeff Co, fRice W, mGeorgiana Weigley, hJohn Carper
Thomas B, b184-, Jeff Co, fRice W, mGeorgiana Weighley, wIrene Carr
.EVY, Abraham, b2/28/1831, Richmond, fJacob A, mMartha Ezekiel, wRachael Cornelia Levy
Adah Virginia, b18--, Richmond, fAbraham, mRachael Cornelia Levy, hCharles Strauss
Ernest Coleman, b8/11/1868, Richmond, fAbraham, mRachael Cornelia Levy, wElizabeth Detwiler, md6/19/1912
Martha, b18--, Richmond, fAbraham, mRachael Cornelia Levy, hEdwin Ezekiel
Rachael Cornelia, b3/13/1832, Richmond, hAbraham Levy
.EWIN, Ann Elizabeth, b18--, Warr Co, d1881, hLewis William Grove
LEWIS, --, bc1780, Roan Co?, fAndrew, hElijah McClanahan
--, bc1860, Rkhm Co?, wMary Moore
Agatha, b17--, Augu Co?, fThomas, hJohn Stuart
Andrew, b17--, Augu Co?, d1781, fJohn
Andrew, b17--, fAndrew Lewis
Andrew Jackson, b184-, nrFarnham, Nhld Co, John Ball, (1)mAlice Roeick
Ann, b17--, Spot Co, fZachariah, mAnn Terrell, 1w of James Scott
Ann Montgomery, bc1820, nrManassas, PrWi Co, fFrancis, m Martha Bennett
Ann Susanna, b1848, Mansfield Farm, Esse Co, d1921, fThomas Waring, wAnn Ursula Latane
Benjamin H, b186-, nrManassas, PrWi Co, fFrancis M, mJulia Higgs, wMargaret Pringle
Beverly Crump, Sr, b12/5/1848, Richmond, fWillim, wKate Westwood
Catherine, bc1800, Fauq Co,

LEWIS (continued)
fWilliam, mAnn Montgomery
Catherine, b1863, Mansfield Farm, Esse Co, d1908, fThomas Waring, mAnn Ursula Latane, hWilliam Nathan Morris
Catheirne Mars, bc1820, nrManassas, PrWi Co, fFrancis, m Martha Bennett, hCharles Dodson
Charles, b16--, fjohn, mElizabeth Warner, wMary --
Charles, b17--, Augu Co?, fJohn
Charles, b1---, Glou Co, fJohn, mMildred Warner, wMary Howell
Charles Francis Montgomery, b186-, nrManassas, PrWi Co, fFrancis M, mJulia Higgs, w Bessie Beson
Charles Henry, bc1850, nrFarnham, Nhld Co, fJohn Ball, (1)mAlice Roeick
Eliza, b17--, Bote Co, hMadison Pitzer
Elizabeth Ann, b18--, PrWi Co, fWilliam H, mAnn Montgomery, hJohn Thomas Leachman
Elizabeth Dabney Langhorne, b18--, Camp Co, fJohn H, hDexter Otey
Elizabeth Jane, b5/30/1852, Wise Co, hJohn Jackson Kelly, Jr
Eveline, b1812, nrManassas, PrWi Co, d1895, fFrancis, m Martha Bennett, hHayward Foote Triplett, Sr
Francis, b17--, Fauq Co, fWilliam, mAnn Montgomery, wMartha Bennett
Francis M, b1820, nrManassas, PrWi Co, d1887, fFrancis, m Martha Bennett, wJulia Higgs
Frank Ashby, b7/14/1862, nrManassas, PrWi Co, fFrancis M, mJulia Higgs, wCatherine Virginia Heymond, md7/14/1896
Frank Waring, Sr, b5/28/1857, Litwalton, Lanc Co, fMerriweather, mJulia Ann Saunders, wVirginia Massie, md11/12/1884
George Thomas Ringgold, b1848, Gloucester Point, Glou Co, fJames H, mSarah Ann Snead, wMartha Jane Taylor
Harriet Elizabeth, b185-, Lit-

LEWIS (continued)
walton, Lanc Co, fMerriweather, mJulia Ann Saunders, hR Milton Neale
Helen Stuart, b1858, Brun Co, d1886, fAshton, hNeedham Stuart Turnbull, Sr
Henry, b17--, Fauq Co, fWilliam, mAnn Montgomery
Henry, bc1820, nrManassas, PrWi Co, fFrancis, mMartha Bennett
Henry Waring Latane, b1846, Mansfield Farm, Esse Co, f Thomas Waring, mAnn Ursula Latane
Herbert I, b1/18/1853, KiWi Co, fJohn Skyron, mOctavia Claiborne, wMattie Parks
Howell, b17--, fCharles, wMary Carr
Huldah, b18--, Albe Co?, fD Richmond, hJohn Thomson Scott
Isabel, b18--, Bath Co?, fAugustus, hA H Campbell
J Ed, Sr, bc1870, Toga, Buck Co, d1922, fJesse T, mAnna Anderson, wMay Mahood
James, bc1800, Fauq Co, fWilliam, mAnn Montgomery
James, b18--, Fred Co?, wJulia Ann Clark
James H, b18--, Glou Co, wSarah Ann Snead
James H, b8/1/1869, Toga, Buck Co, fJesse T, mAnna Anderson, wOra Foster
James Meriwether, b11/24/1869, Mansfield Farm, Esse Co, f Thomas Waring, mAnn Ursula Latane, wEllen Harvie Latane, md12/9/1908
Jane, b1---, Albe Co, fRobert, mJane Meriwether, 1hThomas Meriwether, 2hJohn Lewis
Jesse T, bc1830, Buck Co?, wAnna E Anderson
John, b17--, fFielding, wBetty Washington
John, b17--, fJohn, mBetty Washington, wLucy Thornton
John, Jr, b178-, fJohn, Sr, mSarah John, b1---, Gooc Co, fCharles, mMary Howell, 2h of Jane Lewis
John, b1---, Glou Co, fJohn, mMildred Warner

LEWIS (continued)
John, b1---, Glou Co?, wMildred Warner
John Ball, b1821, Nhld Co, d1893, fCharles, 1wAlice Roeick, 2wMary Rice
John H, bc1840, Camp Co?, wElizabeth Dabney Langhorne
John H, bc1850, Taze Co?, d1921, wJennie Brittain
John Latane, b1865, Mansfield Farm, Esse Co, fThomas Waring, mAnn Ursula Latane, wMary E Chichester
John M, b18--, Alle Co, fThomas F, mAnn Anderson, wMargaret Tapp
John Paige, b183-, wLucy Landon Blackford
John Pierce, b185-, nrFarnham, Nhld Co, fJohn Ball, (1)mAlice Roeick
John Skyron, b18--, d1865, wOctavia Clairborne
Joseph, bc1700, Henrico Co, fJohn
Joseph, bc1820, nrManassas, PrWi Co, fFrancis, mMartha Bennett
Joseph, b1858, Mansfield Farm, Esse Co, fThomas Waring, mAnn Ursula Latane
Joseph F, b185-, nrManassas, PrWi Co, fFrancis M, mJulia Higgs, wMary B Moore
Judith, b17--, Albe Co?, hJohn Randolph
Lowry, bc1850, Augu Co?, wBessie Harnsberger
Lucy Cateby, b1854, Mansfield Farm, Esse Co, d1902, fThomas Waring, mAnn Ursula Latane
Margaret, b17--, fNicholas, hDavid Wood
Mars, b185-, nrManassas, PrWi Co, fFrancis M, mJulia Higgs, wHattie Wilcoxen
Martha Victoria, b18--, hGeorge Lafayette Ferguson
Mary E, b1851, hJames Wellington Johnson
Mary Latane, b1851, Mansfield Farm, Esse Co, fThomas Waring, mAnn Ursula Latane, hPhilip Winston Lewis
Melissa, bc1847, Bartonsville,

LEWIS (continued)
Fred Co, d1916, fJames, mJulia Ann Clark, hCharles W McVicar
Melville Luther, bc1850, nrFrnham, Nhld C, fJohn Ball, (1)mAlice Roeick
Meredith Columbus, b8/29/1859, nrFarnham, Nhld Co, fJohn Ball, (1)mAlice Roeick, wMary S Douglas, md4/20/1881
Merriweather, b2/17/1826, Esse Co, d1883, fWarner, (2)m-- Butler, wJulia Ann Saunders
Mildred, b18--, Char Co?, h George Franklin Connally
Mildred Gregory, b3/12/1770, Fredericksburg, Spot Co, fJohn, mLucy Thornton, hWilliam Minor
Mollie Montgomery, b186-, nr Manassas, PrWi Co, fFrancis M, mJulia Higgs, hW H DeMaine
Nancy, bc1800, fWilliam, mAnn Montgomery
Nancy, bc1800, hWilliam H Childs
Nicholas, bc1700, Glou Co, fJohn, mElizabeth Warren
Nicholas, b17--, fNicholas
Philip Winston, bc1850, Esse Co?, wMary Latane Lewis
Rachel, b18--, Bath Co?, hWilliam Henry Hopkins
Robert, b1---, Glou Co, fJohn, mMildred Warner
Sallie Lane, b185-, nrManassas, PrWi Co, fFrancis M, mJulia Higgs
Samuel, b17--, Augu Co?, fJohn
Sarah, b16--, 1w of Robert Woodson
Sarah Ann, b185-, nrFarnham, Nhld Co, fJohn Ball, (1)mAlice Roeick, hJohn Henry Purcell
Sarah Travers, b11/7/1813, Spot Co, hJames McClure Scott
Searles, bc1820, nrManassas, PrWi Co, fFrancis, mMartha Bennett
Susan Allen, b1856, Mansfield Farm, Esse Co, fThomas Waring, mAnn Ursula Latane, hCesla Mason Smoot
Susanna, b17--, Henrico Co, fJoseph, hJames Cocke, Jr
Thomas, b17--, Augu Co?, fJohn

LEWIS (continued)
Thomas, bc1820, nrManassas, PrWi Co, fFrancis, mMartha Bennett
Thomas Deane, b1867, Mansfield Farm, Esse Co, fThomas Waring, mAnn Ursula Latane, wVirginia Alice Lewis
Thomas F, b18--, fHowell, mMary Carter, wAnn Anderson
Thomas Waring, b8/15/1815, Goldberry Farm, Esse Co, d1899, fWarner, (1)mAnn Susanna Latane, wAnn Ursula Latane
Virginia Alice, b186-, nrFarnham, Nhld Co, fJohn Ball, (1)mAlice Roeick, hThomas Deane Lewis
Warner, bc1782, Goldberry Farm, Esse Co, dc1870, 1wAnn Susanna Latane, 2w-- Butler, 3w-- Shepherd
Warner, b1844, Mansfield Farm, Esse Co, d1918, fThomas Waring, mAnn Ursula Latane
William, b17--, Augu Co, fJohn
William, b17--, Fauq Co, fWilliam, mAnn Montgomery
William, bc1820, nrManassas, PrWi Co, fFrancis, mMartha Bennett
William Addison, b184-, nrFarnham, Nhld Co, fJohn Ball, (1)mAlice Roeick
William E, b18--, Acco Co, wBettie Bloxom
William H, b222/1865, nrManassas, PrWi Co, fFrancis M, mJulia Higgs, wAlice Turner, md4/1900
William H, b9/8/1868, Alle Co, fJohn M, mMargaret Tapp, wAnna Strayer
William Latane, b1861, Mansfield Farm, Esse Co, fThomas Waring, mAnn Ursula Latane
Zachariah, b17--, Spot Co?, wAnn Terrell
LIAS, Robert, bc1860, Page Co?, wVirgie Keyser
LICHLEITER, Georgie, b12/12/1858, Shen Co, fWilliam H, m-- Bauserman, hJames Sine
John G, bc1840, Jeff Co, wMary Flanagan

LICHLEITER (continued)
 Ella, b18--, Shen Co?, hAdolph Heller
 William H, b18--, Shen Co, w--Bauserman
LIGGITT, Anna Belle, bc1850, Rckm Co, hThomas G Mauzy
LIGGON, Elizabeth, b18--, Floy Co?, hAndrew J Kirby
LIGHTNER, Elizabeth, b18--, 2w of Hugh McLaughlin
 Malcena, b2/22/1844, Back Creek, Bath Co, fJacob, mNancy Warwick, hGeorge W Cleek, Sr, md11/26/1867
LIGON, --, bc1800, PrEd Co?, hJohn Crute
 Fannie P, b7/1860, Farmville, PrEd Co, d1917, hBeverley P Eggleston
 Mattie O, b18--, Powh Co?, hJames A Tilman
 Rimbrough, b18--, Nels Co, hGeorge Evans Caskie, Sr, md187-
 William Hopkins, b1/19/1851, Appo Co, fWilliam Seth, mJane M Gilliam, wNannie Maria Cunningham
 William Seth, b1814, Powh Co, wJane M Gilliam
LILLARD, --, b17--, hJohn Bryan
 John Henry, bc1839, Madi Co, fHenry, wSophia Jane Carpenter
 Laura L, b18--, Rapp Co, fSilas Browning Lillard, mMildred Roberts Duncan, hSamuel Russell Browning, md1/2/1879
 Lucy Eldridge, b18--, Rapp Co, fSilas Browning, mMildred Roberts Duncan, hJohn James Miller, Sr, md7/7/1886
 Lucy Mildred, b18--, Rapp Co?, fBenjamin, hJames M O'Bannon
 Mary Frances, b18--, Madi Co, fJack, hJoseph Lewis Yowell
 Silas Browning, b18--, Rapp Co?, wMildred Roberts Duncan
LILLISTON, virginia, b1853, nr Accomac Court House, Acco Co, hWilliam T Hickman
LILLY, Anna, b18--, Lanc Co?, hJohn C Brewington
 Jane, b18--, Rale Co?, hCharles V Ashworth
 Margaret, b1848, Harrisonburg,

LILLY (continued)
 Rckm Co, hWesley W McMillen
LINCOLN, Abigail, b181-, Augu Co, fDavid, mCatherine Bright, hJonathan Shaver
 Abraham, b1817, Augu Co, fDavid, mCatherine Bright, wMary Elizabeth Hughes
 Alandson Tilman, b10/23/1858, Broadford, Smyt Co,fCharles F, mHarriet Clark, wLucretia Sexton, md9/11/1889
 Alice M, b185-, Christiansburg, Mont Co, fCharles F, mHarriet Clark, hCharles W White
 Anna E, b186-, Marion, Smyt Co, fCharles F, mHarriet Clark, hWilliam H Fillinger
 B F, b181-, Augu Co, fDavid, mCatherine Bright
 Catherine Bright, bc1860, Rkhm Co, fAbraham, mMary Elizabeth Hughes, hS S Gordon
 Charles Clark, b2/11/1866, Marion, Smyt Co, fCharles F, mHarriet Clark, wLaura M Dickey, md11/23/1893
 David, b17--, Augu Co, wCatherine Bright
 Dorcas, bc1810, Augu Co, fDavid, mCatherine Bright, hSmith Laughlin
 Elizabeth Ann, b181-, Augu Co, fDavid, mCatherine Bright, hPeter B Koontz
 Hattie O, bc1870, Marion, Smyt Co, fCharles F, mHarriet Clark, hJames H Gibboney
 Jacob, b181-, Augu Co, fDavid, mCatherine Bright, wCaroline Homan
 Jetson Jackson, b185-, Rkhm Co, fAbraham, mMary Elizabeth Hughes
 John Edward, b7/22/1856, Rkhm Co, fAbraham, mMary Elizabeth Hughes, wAmanda Alice Kline, md10/22/1878
 Laura M, b186-, Marion, Smyt Co, Charles F, mHarriet Clark, hA F Horne
 Lucy Knox, bc1860, Rkhm Co, fAbraham, mMary Elizabeth Hughes, hRobert W Bradford
 Mattie V, bc1870, Marion, Smyt Co, fCharles F, mHarriet

LINCOLN (continued)
Clark, hJohn H Horne Preston, bc1810, Augu Co, fDavid, mCatherine Bright
Samuel Waldon, bc1860, Rkhm Co, fAbraham, mMary Elizabeth Hughes
Strother, bc1810, Augu Co, f David, mCatherine Bright
Virginia C, b8/2/1850, Lacey Springs, Rkhm Co, fJacob, m Caroline Homan, hJohn W Taylor
Willard Loomis, b10/21/1867, Marion, Smyt Co, fCharles F, mHarriet Clark, wAnnie Navy Smith, md1/24/1900
LINDAMOOD, Arthur Lee, b1/9/1870, Madison District, Shen Co, fHarrison, (1)mElizabeth Rinker, wElla Newland Harrison, bc1848, Ashby District, Shen Co, 1wElizabeth Rinker, 2wMollie Funk
Rebecca E, b1833, Bristol, Wash Co, d1918, hJames H Meade
LINDER, Martha, bc1800, Wash Co, hAmos Sifers
LINDHEIM, Reuben, bc1850, Camp Co?, wHortense Guggenheimer
LINDSAY, Catherine Goodloe, 11/30/ 1831, Albe Co, 1897, fHarry, m-- Maupin, hWilliam Daniel Jarman
Charlotte, b18--, Pitt Co?, fWilliam hJohn Watson
Flora, b18--, Carr Co, 2w of Henry Kyle Lindsay
Harry, b1789, Spot Co, d1874, w-- Maupin
Henry, b17--, Richmond?, fHenry, w-- Smith
Henry, b1811, nrOcala, Carr Co, d1900, fHenry, m-- Smith, w-- Vaughan
Henry Kyle, b8/1859, nrOcala, Carr Co, fHenry, m-- Vaughan, 1w Marilda Orlene Shockley, 2wFlora Lindsay
Mary, b17--, Oran Co?, hJohn Wigglesworth
Susan, bc1800, Fair Co, hAmi Moore
LINDSEY, Edward E, b186-, Clar Co, fJoseph B, mMary E McCormick
Frank S, bc1870, Clar Co, fJo-

LINSEY (continued)
seph B, mMary E McCormick
Joseph B, b18--, Clar Co, d1917, wMary E McCormick
Maggie, b186-, Clar Co, fJoseph B, mMary E McCormick, hA L Glascock
Nannie, b186-, Clar Co, fJoseph B, mMary E McCormick, hT S Lee
LINEWEAVER, Abram, b1858, Rkhm Co, fJohn, wHarriet I Liskey
D C, bc1850, Rkhm Co?, wAmanda Jane Swank
LINKENLAUGER, Lucy, b18--, Roan Co?, 1w of George Garst
LINTZ, William Frederick, Sr, b1840, Richmond, wAnne Wakefield
LION, Thomas H, b18--, PrWi Co?, wEthel Adamson
LIPES, Mary Lewis, bc1846, Bote Co?, d1892, hWilliam A Rinehart
LIPSCOMB, John, bc1800, Spot Co, wMary Ann Billingsley
John, bc1840, Hali Co, wMary Connally
Leah, b17--, KiWi Co?, hThomas Fox
Sally Ann, b1821, Spot Co, fJohn, mMary Ann Billingsley, hJames Boxley
Theodosia, b18--, Hali Co, fClement, hAlfred B Fitzgerald
LISKEY, Harriet I, b1859, Rkhm Co, fHarvey, mMargret Armentrout, hAbram Lineweaver
Harvey, b18--, Rkhm Co?, wMargaret Armentrout
LITTLE, Jane, b18--, Merc Co?, hThomas Llewellyn
John Chapman, b18--, Fauq Co?, wNellie Williams
Mary, b17--, Fred Co?, fWilliam, hWilliam McGuire
LITTLEPAGE, Alice, b17--, KiWi Co?, hDaniel Taylor
LITTLETON, Edgar, Sr, b18--, Loud Co, fThomas, wAntoinette Addison Campbell
Thomas, b18--, nrLeesburg, Loud Co
LITTON, John, b17--, Russ Co?, fSolomon
John W, b1822, Russ Co, fSolomon II, m-- Yonce, wLydia

LITTON (continued)
Whittaker
Lilburn R, b12/2/1852, Elk Garden, Russ Co, fJohn W, mLydia Whittaker, wEmma Francis
Millard Fillmore, b18--, wJemima Scott
Solomon II, bc1800, Russ Co, fJohn, w-- Yonce
LITTRELL, Ann E, bc1800, hJohn Henceford Garner
LITZ, Alma Z, b8/24/1869, Burkes Garden, Taze Co, fJohn T, mElizabeth Thompson, wEtta V Stauber, md12/20/1900
David H, b186-, Burkes Garden, Taze Co, fJohn T, mElizabeth Thompson
Emily, b18--, Wyth Co?, 2w of Henry Hankla
James G, bc1870, Burkes Garden, Taze Co, fJohn T, mElizabeth Thompson
John L, b10/10/1964, Burkes Garden, Taze Co, fJohn T, mElizabeth Thompson, wGeorgia A Dickenson, md3/15/1888
John T, b1832, Burkes Garden, Taze Co, d1901, fPeter G, mSarah Gose, wElizabeth Thompson
Nannie, b186-, Burkes Garden, Taze Co, fJohn T, mElizabeth Thompson, hRagens Sluss
Peter G, b1805, Smyt Co, d1880, wSarah Gose
Peter G, b186-, Burkes Garden, Taze Co, fJohn T, mElizabeth Thompson
Sallie Ann, b186-, Burkes Garden, Taze Co, fJohn T, mElizabeth Thompson, hHarvey McGuire
Samuel T, bc1860, Burkes Garden, Taze Co, fJohn T, mElizabeth Thompson
LIVESAY, Calvin, b1832, Gray Co, fJames, mMatilda Byrd, wHester Pekins
James, b1808, Gray Co, fThomas, wMatilda Byrd
James Ambrose, b12/18/1859, Gray Co, fCalvin, mHester Pekins, wMollie J Carson, md11/1/1888
Thomas, b17--, Gray Co
LIVESEY, Sally, b17--, Fran Co?,

LIVESEY (continued)
fJohn Helms
LLEWELLYN, Lizzie, bc1870, Bluefield, Merc Co, fThomas, mJane Little, hRudolph Schwank
Thomas, b18--, Merc Co?, wJane Little
LLOYD, Charles, b183-, Clar Co?, wMary Smallwood
Fannie, b18--, Clar Co, hFrank Thompson
Jennie, b1860, Ches Co, hJohn W Archer
Joseph W, b1800, wHenrietta Wiley
LOCHER, Charles Hunter, Jr, b10/3/1862, Rkbr Co, fCharles Hunter, Sr, mMary Elizabeth Orrick, wMatilda McClure
Harry Orrick, Sr, b1850, Morg Co, fCharles H, Sr, mMary Elizabeth Orrick, wLulu E Jett
LOCKE, Addie, b18--, Lanc Co?, hWilliam E Cox
Annie, b18--, Jeff Co?, hHierome Opie
Thomas French, bc1842, Jeff Co
LOCKETT, Mary Frances, bc1835, Roan Co, 2w of George Garst
Pamela Branch, b18--, hJohn James Binford
LOCKHART, Ally, bc1860, Russ Co, fJohn C, mMargaret Boothe, hIra R Campbell
Cora Ann, bc1870, Roane Co, fJohn C, mMargaret Boothe, hJ Page Gilmer
James, b18--, Russ Co?, wMildred Colley
James J, b186-, Russ Co?, fJohn C, mMargaret Boothe
John C, b5/13/1838, Russ Co, d1912, fJames, mMildred Colley, wMargret Boothe
John Hiram, b6/18/1868, Roane Co, fJohn C, mMargret Boothe, wMinnie Settle, md12/7/1898
Josiah, b18--, Fred Co?, wMary Odell
Margaret E, b183-, Fred Co, d1891, fJosiah, mMary Odell, hJoshua Smith Lupton
Melvin Lee, b186-, Russ Co, fJohn C, mMargaret Boothe
Rebecca, b18--, Fred Co?, hRobert Madison Campbell

LOCKMILLER, Moses, bc1840, Shen Co, wEmma C Snarr
LODGE, Elizabeth, bc1821, Fauq Co, d1882, fSamuel, mRebecca Russell, hJohn Thomas Cochran, Sr
Samuel, b17--, Fauq Co?, wRebecca Russell
LOFTIS, Sallie, b18--, Rkhm Co?, hSamuel Bowman
LOGAN, thomas M, bc1830, Ches Co?, d1914, wKate Virginia Cox
LOGWOOD, James A, bc1850, Bedf Co?, wEmma Cobbs Hutter
LOMAX, --, b17--, KiGe Co, f Thomas, m-- Taylor, hTaliaferro Hunter
--, b18--, Alexandria?, hDouglas Stuart
Thomas, b17--, Powh Co?, w-- Tayloe
LONDON, --, b18--, Richmond?, wEliza Caskie
LONG, --, b17--, Rkhm Co?, hMichael Shuler
--, bc1850, Page Co, hThomas Spitler
--, bc1850, nrLuray, Page Co, fReuben, hJacob Spitler
--, bc1850, nrLuray, Page Co, fReuben, hIra Bumgardner
Armistead, Sr, b4/26/1762, wElizabeth Burgess Ball
Armistead, Jr, b1/29/1801, f Armistead, Sr, mElizabeth Burgess Ball, wCalista Rosser Cralle
Caroline E, bc1870, Page Co, fMichael, mSusan M Long, 2w of Henry Hawkins Downing
Ernest M, bc1870, KiQu Co?, wElizabeth Pollard
Frances Catherine Harr, b18--, Shen Co?, hHenry Kelley Jennings
Frank, bc1850, nrLuray, Page Co, fReuben
G T, bc1850, Page Co, w-- Shuler
Gideon Lee, b7/31/1865, nrLuray, Page Co, fMichael, mSusan M Long, 1wAmanda V Spangler, md5/15/1889, 2wAnna Malone, md1912
Isaac, Sr, b1790, Page Co, fPhilip, w-- Shuler

LONG (continued)
Isaac, Jr, b181-, Page Co, fIsaac, Sr, m-- Shuler
Jackson, b18--, Russ Co, w- Gibson
James H, b5/19/1844, Russ Co, fJackson, m-- Gibson, wEmily Dotson
James W, b18--, Maso Co?, w Catherine A Hannan
John F, b10/1850, nrLuray, Page Co, fReuben, wSusan Bell Kite, md1875
John William, b18--, Page Co, fPhilip, wSarah Catherine Shirley
Joseph, bc1850, nrLuray, Page Co, fReuben
Julia, bc1840, Rkhm Co, hAlexander Wyant
Leroy William, b1831, Amhe Co, fArmistead, Jr, mCalista Rosser Cralle, wAdalie Laurence Hutter, md1866
Lewis, bc1850, wJane Copenhaver
Mary, b17--, Page Co, fPhilip Lung
Mary, b18--, Rkhm Co?, hDonald Dovel
Mary J, bc1850, nrLuray, Page Co, fReuben, h-- Funkhouser
Michael, b8/31/1818, Page Co, 1887, fIsaac, Sr, m-- Shuler, wSusan M Long
Nicholas, b17--, Page Co, f Philip Lung
Paul, bc1700, Page, fPhilip Lung
Philip, b17--, Page Co, fPaul
Philip, bc1850, nrLuray, Page Co, fReuben
Reuben, b17--, Page Co, fPhilip
Sarah, b18--, Rkhm Co?, hAbram Andes
Susan M, b18--, Page Co, fPhilip, hMichael Long
Wesley, b12/25/1852, Russ Co, wMary Cunningham
William, bc1850, nrLuray, Page Co, fReuben
William M, b18--, Shen Co, wLou Hensley
LONGLEY, Catherine Hammond, b18--, Pula Co?, fEdmund, hThomas Walden Jordan
LOOK, Sarah Belle, b1855, Loui

LOOK (continued)
Co, hSmelt Winston Dickinson
LOONEY, Daniel R, b18--, Buch Co?, wLucy Belcher
LOTTS, James Frank, b1840, Rkbr Co, wAnnie Hartsook
LOUFLAND, Jenie, b18--, Rkhm Co, fL L, mDorcas Lincoln, hRobert Baldwin
LOVE, --, b18--, Meck Co, w Adelle Frances Hutcheson
Alice Neblett, b18--, Meck Co, mAdelle Frances Hutcheson, hJohn Wesley Young
Elizabeth H, b185-, nrHamilton, Loud Co, fFenton M, Sr, mElizabeth Morris, hJohn Pickett
Fenton M, Sr, b1808, nrHamilton, Loud Co, d1896, fJames, wElizabeth Morris
Fenton M, Jr, b6/9/1853, nrHamilton, Loud Co, fFenton M, Sr, mElizabeth Morris, wGertrude T Woolf, md6/1/1881
James Flavius, b184-, nrHamilton, Loud Co, fFenton M, Sr, mElizabeth Morris
Janie A, b184-, nrHamilton, Loud Co, fFenton M, Sr, mElizabeth Morris
Oscar M, bc1850, nrHamilton, Loud Co, fFenton M, Sr, mElizabeth Morris
Susanna C, b184-, nrHamilton, Loud Co, d1868, fFenton M, Sr, mElizabeth Morris
LOVELACE, Hattie B, bc1860, Chatham, Pitt Co, m-- Treadway, hWilliam Young Noell
Nannie, bc1849, Hali Co?, hJames D Hankins
LOVELL, Florida Calhoun, b18--, hJames Alexander Scott, Sr
LOVETT, Virginia, b18--, Norfolk, hThomas Moran Barry
LOVING, Pierce, b18--, Nels Co?, wElizabeth K Payne
Sally, b17--, Nels Co, hWilliam Teas
W H, bc1850, Nels Co?, wCora Fortune
LOWRY, Henry Clay, bc1839, Bedf Co, d1917, fMilton, wElizabeth Quarles
Lucinda A, b1826, Lowry's Crossing, Bedf Co, fWilliam, hAl-

LOWRY (continued)
bert Thornhill
LOYD, Ardelia, bc1860, Lynchburg, Camp Co, fWilliamH, m Lucy Jane Crumpton
James E, Sr, b185-, Lynchburg, Camp Co, fWilliam H, mLucy Jane Crumpton, wCarroll Aston
Jennie, b186-, Lynchburg, Camp Co, fWilliam H, mLucy Jane Crumpton
Kate Jessie, b186-, Lynchburg, Camp Co, fWilliam H, mLucy Jane Crumpton, hEdward W Herndon
Sarah A, bc1870, Lynchburg, Camp Co, fWilliam H, mLucy Jane Crumpton
Spencer C, b17--, Camp Co
William C, b186-, Lynchburg, Camp Co, fWilliam H, mLucy Jane Crumpton
William H, b4/8/1829, Lynchburg, Camp Co, d1894, fSpencer C, wLucy Jane Crumpton, md10/15/1856
LUCAS, Andrew Jackson, b12//1818, nrChristiansburg, Mont Co, fSamuel, wEvaline Matilda Charlton
Charles D, b18--, Mont Co?, wNancy Charlton
Elvina, b18--, Gile Co, hJames H Snidow
James C, b1849, Maybrook, Gile Co, fMiles K, mRachel Atkins, wSallie A Sibold
Miles K, b1823, Maybrook, Gile Co, wRachel Atkins
Olivia Jackson, b9/15/1858, Christiansburg, Mont Co, fAndrew Jackson, mEvaline Matilda Charlton
Virginia, b183-, Charlestown, Jeff Co, d186-, hEverett Wade Bedinger
LUCK, --, b18--, Bedf Co, wSarah Douthat
Angelina, b18--, nrMiddleburg, Loud Co, fJordan Bedford, m Adaline Catewood
Drusilla Ann, b182-, nrMiddleburg, Loud Co, fJordan Bedfrod, mAdaline Gatewood, hJohn M Moran
Elvira Louise, b18--, Roanoke,

LUCK (continued)
  Meck Co, fGeorge S, mLula N -- hWillis Ward Anderson, Sr
  Emily Midred, b18--, nrMiddleburg, Loud Co, fJordan Bedford, mAdaline Gatewood, h Charles W Simpson
  George P, bc1800, Bedf Co?, fJohn, wNancy Buford
  George S, b18--, Meck Co, wLula N --
  John Bedford, b183-, nrMiddleburg, Loud Co, fJordan Bedford, mAdaline Gatewood
  Jordan Bedford, b1791, nr Chilesburg, Spot Co, wAdaline Gatewood
  Nannie, b18--, nrMiddleburg, Loud Co, fJordan Bedford, m Adaline Gatewood, hSamuel L Simpson
  Nannie Buford, bc1840, Bedf Co, fGeorge P, mNancy Buford, hJohn Barnett
  Sara D, b18--, Camp Co?, hJohn L Clarke
  Sue Lewis, bc1870, Bedf Co, m-- Sarah Douthat, hWalter Lee Welborn, md12/20/1896
  WilliamJordan, b4/23/1836, nr Middleburg, Loud Co, fJordan Bedford, mAdaline Gatewood, wRoberta Rector
LUCKETT, John M, b17--, Fauq Co?, wAlsey Newton Murray
  Nannie, b18--, Loud Co, 1w of William Wood Glass
LUDWELL, Jane, bc1800, hPeyton Randolph Burwell
  Matilda, b17--, d179-, 1w of Henry "Lighthorse Harry" Lee
LUDWIG, J M, b18--, Shen Co?, wSarah Grandstaff
LUKE, Elizabeth, b18--, nrBerryville, Clar Co, hNeill Barnett
LUMPKIN, James T B, b10/13/1853, KiQu Co, wEmma Hutchinson
LUPTON, Ann, bc1850, Apple Pie Ridge, Fred Co, fJohn, mLydia Walker, h-- Bond
  Charles Addison, b10/21/1858, Fred Co, fJoshua Smith, mMargaret E Lockhart, wEmma E Albin, md9/10/1884
  Charles E, bc1850, Rkhm Co, d1917, fWilliam Isaac, mMary C

LUPTON (continued)
  Ragan, wMargaret McFarland
  David P, bc1850, Apple Pie Ridge, Fred Co, fJohn, mLydia Walker
  Edward, bc1850, Apple Pie Ridge, Fred Co, fJohn, mLydia Walker
  Hugh Sidwell, b4/20/1845, Apple Pie Ridge, fJohn, mLydia Walker, wMary Speakman
  Ida E, bc1850, Rkhm Co, d1888, fWilliam Isaac, mMary C Ragan, hGeorge Pinkney Bruffey
  Ida S, b185-, Fred Co, Joshua Smith, mMargaret E Lockhart, hJames Cather
  Isaac Brisco, bc1850, Rkhm Co, d1879, fWilliam Isaac, mMary C Ragan, wMary J Houston
  James Robert, b12/17/1854, Rkhm Co, fWilliam Isaac, mMary C Ragan, wFannie M Byerle, md2/12/1879
  John, bc1800, nrWinchester, Fred Co, wMargaret Smith
  John, b18--, Apple Pie Ridge, Fred Co, wLydia Walker
  John Edgar, b12/26/1856, Fred Co, fJoshua Smith, mMargart E Lockhart, mMary E Albin
  John R, b184-, Rkhm Co, fWilliam Isaac, mMary C Ragan, wElizabeth Hurr
  John Robert, bc1830, nrWinchester, Fred Co, fJohn, mMargaret Smith
  Jonah, bc1820, Loud Co?, wMary Elizabeth Tavenner
  Joshua Smith, b1828, nrWinchester, Fred Co, d1891, fJohn, mMargaret Smith, wMargaret E Lockhart
  Lewis R, b184-, Rkhm Co, fWilliam Isaac, mMary C Ragan, wBetty H Houston
  Margaret, b18--, Fred Co?, hClark Cather
  Margaret Bailey, b183-, nrWinchestr, Fred Co, fJohn, mMargaret Smith
  Mary, bc1850, Apple Pie Ridge, Fred Co, fJohn, mLydia Walker, h-- Irish
  Milicent, b18--, Fred Co?, hJ Howard Cather

LUPTON (continued)
Rebecca, bc1850, Apple Pie Ridge, Fred Co, fJohn, mLydia Walker, h-- Broomell
Sarah, b18--, Fred Co, hRichard Simpson
Thomas Gideon, b183-, nrWinchester, Fred Co, fJohn, mMargaret Smith
William, b184-, Rkhm Co, d186-, fWilliam Isaac, mMary C Ragan
William Isaac, b1820, Fred Co, 1861, wMary C Ragan
LUTTRELL, Burrell, bc1837, Culpeper Co, fJames Richard, m-- Bywaters, wMary Nelson
Capitola, b12/18/1860, Culp Co?, fBurrell Edmond, mMary Nelson, hJohn Spindle Hughes
Frank, bc1870, Olive, Culp Co, fBurrell Edmond, mMary Nelson
Hugh Montgomery, b1/18/1868, Olive, Culp C, fBurrell Edmond, mMary Nelson, wAtlanta Singleton, md7/10/1894
James Richard, bc1800, Fauq Co?, fRichard, mFrances Hambleton, w-- Bywaters
Richard, Jr, bc1761, PrWi Co?, wSarah Hambleton
Richard Edmond, b186-, Olive, Culp Co, fBurrell Edmond, m Mary Nelson, wAda Browning
Warren, b187-, Olive, Culp Co, fBurrell Edmond, mMary Nelson
LUTZ, samuel S, b18--, Loud Co?, wIda Fectig
LYBROOK, Samuel E, bc1840, Gile Co?, wCornelia Jane Chapman
LYDICK, Mary Ann, b18-, Camp Co, fWilliam H, hAlfred S Engledove
LYELL, Ann, b1845, Montross, West Co, d1921, hThomas Dorsey Ficklin
Susan, b1852, Montross, West Co, d1920, hL Taylor Rock, Sr
LYLE, Julia Ann Stuart, bc1800, Rkbr Co, fWilliam, hJohn B Hart
Martha, bc1800, Rkbr Co, fWilliam, hArchibald Graham, Sr
Sarah Wallace, bc1800, m-- Creighton, hDouglas Campbell
William b17--, Rkbr Co
LYNCH, Anselm, b17--, Camp Co,

LYNCH (continued)
fCharles
Mary Anna, b18--, Camp Co, fAnselm, hJames Griffin Dearing
LYNE, Susan A, b18--, Loud Co, hJohn T Connor, Sr
LYNN, Absalom T, bc1820, Independent Hill, PrWi Co, fSeymour, mLucy Norman
Benjamin W, b182-, Independent Hill, PrWi Co, fSeymour, mLucy Norman
Frederick Lycurgus, bc1815, Independent Hill, PrWi Co, d1870, fSeymour, mLucy Norman, wJane Elizabeth Selecman
Henry Fairfax, b18--, PrWi Co?, wMolly Holmes
Jennie, bc1820, Independent Hill, PrWi Co, fSeymour, mLucy Norman
L C, bc1860, PrWi Co?, wRoberta Lee Leachman
Lillian, bc1870, PrWi Co?, f Henry Fairfax, mMolly Holmes, hThomas Bolling Robertson, Jr
Lucy Margaret, b186-, Independent Hill, PrWi Co, fFrederick Lycurgus, mJane Elizabeth Selecman, hL A Clarke
Luther, b18--, Loud Co?, wElizabeth Currell
Marshall, b182-, Independent Hill, PrWi Co, fSeymour, mLucy Norman
Robert, b1848, PrWi Co, fLuther, mElizabeth Currell, wElizabeth Fulton
Seymour, b17--, PrWi Co, wLucy Norman
Shirley, b181-, Independent Hill, PrWi Co, fSeymour, mLucy Norman
Stella, b18--, fAlexander, mJane Ashby, hWilliam D Clarke
William Seymour, b10/1/1863, Independent Hill, PrWi Co, fFrederick Lycurgus, mJane Elizabeth Selecman, wLettie L Selecman, md9/1/1886
LYON, Daniel, bc1800, Petersburg, Dinw Co, wAgnes Temple
David S, b1831, Smyt Co, fJacob, mPollie Snodgrass, wNannie Barker

LYON (continued)
Frank, b12/30/1867, Petersburg, Dinw Co, fJohn, mMary Margaret Springs, wGeorgie Hayes Wright, md8/5/1890
Jacob, b1779, Smyt Co, wPollie Snodgrass
John, b9/1827, Petersburg, Dinw Co, fDaniel, mAgnes Temple, wMary Margaret Springs
LYONS, Sally, b1825, Richmond, d1899, fJames, hWilliam Booth Taliaferro, md1856
McADAMS, George Brockenbrough, b18--, wSallie (Reade) Branch
McALLISTER, Joseph Thompson, b2/27/1866, Covington, Alle Co, fAbraham Addams, (1)mJulia Ellen Stratton, 1wRebecca Anderson, md3/18/1893, 2w Marjorie Roosevelt Leary Craft, md4/8/1916
Mary Lydia, bc1870, Covington, Alle Co, fAbraham Addams, (1)mJulia Ellen Stratton
McBRYDE, Anna, b18--, fJohn McLaren, hRobert J Davidson
McCALL, George R, b3/8/1870, nrShraders, Taze Co, fJohn A, mNannie Gillespie, wExie Stevens
Jesse, b18--, nrShraders, Taze Co, fJohn A, mNannie Gillespie
Jesse M, b18--, wMary George
John A, b5/15/1828, nrGlade Springs, Wash Co, wNannie Gillespie
John W, b18--, nrShraders, Taze Co, fJohn A, mNannie Gillespie
Lyde, b18--, nrShraders, Taze Co, fJohn A, mNannie Gillespie
Mollie Octavia, b18--, nr Shraders, Taze Co, fJohn A, mNannie Gillespie, hLuther W Place
Thomas E, b18--, nrShraders, Taze Co, fJohn A, mNannie Gillespie
McCANN, Newton, bc1840, Shen Co?, wNellie Koontz
McCARTHY, Daniel S, b18--, Richmond?, wElla Pendleton
McCARTY, Absolom, Sr, b1809, Scot Co, d1894, w-- Salyers
Absolom, Jr, b1832, Scot Co, d1906, fAbsolom, Sr, m-- Sal-

McCARTY (continued)
yers, 1wMatilda Carico, 2wJane Carico
Fannie, b18--, Loud Co, 2w of Robert Whitacre
Lina, bc1870, nrCoeburn, Wise Co, fAbsolom, Jr, (1)mMatilda Carico, hThomas Minton
W H, bc1860, Fauq Co?, wLula Phillips
McCAULEY, James, b186-, Lee Co?, wMartha Woodward
Susan, b1/25/1815, Kernstown, Fred Co, d1886, fJohn, hIsaac W Carter, Jr
McCAW, Bessie, b18--, Richmond, fJames Brown, hChristopher Tompkins, md11/8/1877
David, bc1800, Richmond?, fJames Drew, wCaroline Matilda Harris, md1827
William Reid, b18--, Richmond, dc1888, fJames Brown, wLavinia Ragland
McCAY, Sarah, b18--, Rapp Co?, hWilson Nicholas Melton
McCHESNEY, Jefferson Davis, b12/17/1861 Wash Co, fWilliam Wallace, mElizabeth Aven, wAraminta Byars
Mary, b17--, Rkbr Co?, hRobert McCormick
William Wallace, b183-, Wash Co, wElizabeth Aven
McCLANAHAN, Agnes, b18--, Roan Co, hJohn Ingles
Blanche, b18--, Roan Co, 2w of Thomas White Sydnor
Elijah, bc1780, Bote Co?, fWilliam, mSarah Neely, w-- Lewis
Elijah, b18--, Roan Co, d1892, fGreen, mElizabeth Griffin, 1wSarah Margaret Hurt, 2w Samantha Crenshaw
Green, b10/3/1782, Bote Co, d1820, fWilliam, mSarah Neely, wElizabeth Griffin
Laura, b18--, nrBig Lick, Roan Co, fElijah G, (1)mSarah Margaret Hurt, hA W Pitzer
Maria Blanche, b18--, nrBig Lick, Roan Co, fElijah, (1)m Sarah Margaret Hurt, hH M White
Nannie, b18--, nrBig Lick, Roan Co, fElijah G, (1)mSarah Mar-

McCHESNEY (continued)
 garet Hurt, hP H Rorer
Robert C, b18--, nrBig Lick, Roan Co, fElijah G, (2)mEmma Samantha Crenshaw
Sarah H, b18--, nrBig Lick, Roan Co, fElijah G, (2)mEmma Samantha Crenshaw, hFrank W Allen
William, b12/25/1740, Staunton, Augu Co, dc1820, fRobert, mSarah Breckenridge, wSarah Neely
William S, b18--, nrBig Lick, Roan Co, fElijah G, (2)mEmma Samantha Crenshaw, wAnnie J (Reilly) Stanard, md4/24/1900
McCLANNAHAN, Fannie, b1852, Nhld Co, d1897, hBenjamin H B Hubbard, Sr
McCLAUGHERTY, Virginia, b1852, nrPearisburg, Gile Co, hJohn Alexander Adair, Sr
McCLELLAN, Victoria, b10/1/1854, Wayland, Scot Co, hJoseph M Cox
McCLINTIC, Adam Alexander, b18-- Bath Co, fMoses, mMartha A Porter
Andrew Bird, b5/12/1842, Bath Co, d1887, fWilliam II, wMary Wise, md7/25/1865
Emma Trotter, bc1870, Bath Co, fAndrew Bird, mMary Wise, hW P Campbell
Fannie Pettus, b18--, Bath Co, fMoses, mMartha A Porter, hWilliam F Shields
John, b186-, Bath Co, fAndrew Bird, mMary Wise
Lizzie Porter, b18--, Bath Co, fMoses, mMartha A Porter
Martha Margaret, b18--, Bath Co, fMoses, mMartha A Porter
Mary Jane, b18--, Bath Co, fMoses, mMartha A Porter
Moses, b17--, Bath Co, fWilliam II, mAlice Mann
Moses, b5/8/1797, Bath Co, fAlexander, mSarah Mann, wMartha A Porter
Moses Hamilton, b11/10/1848, Bath Co, fMoses, mMartha A Porter, wJennie Cameron McDannald
Robert Shields, b18--, Bath Co,

McCLINTIC (continued)
 fMoses, mMartha A Porter
Sarah Rebecca, b12/1/1835, Flowing Springs, Bath Co, d1896, hJohn Thomas Byrd
Sarah Rebecca, b18--, Bath Co, fMoses, mMartha A Porter
Thomas Brown, b18--, Bath Co, fMoses, mMartha A Porter
William, b17--, Bath Co
William II, b1814, Bath Co, d1887, fWilliam
William III, b17--, Bath Co, fWilliam II, mAlice Mann
William Stephen, b18--, Bath Co, fMoses, mMartha A Porter
McCLUER, Napoleon B, bc1838, Rkbr Co, d1904, fWilliam P, wSallie Ann Wilson
William P, b18--, fMoses
McCLUNG, Agnes, bc1830, Clover Creek, High Co, fWilliam, Sr, mRachel Gwin, hWilliam Summers
Andrew A, b1831, nrFairfield, Rkbr Co, fJames, 1wEstelline Montgomery Willson, md1856
Betty, bc1860, "Beech Spring Farm", nrBrownsburg, Rkbr Co, fAndrew A, (1)mEstelline Montgomery Willson, hThomas Kerr
Charles S, b186-, "Beech Spring Farm", nrBrownsburg, Rkbr Co, fAndrew A, (1)mEstelling Montgomery, wAnnie G Wilson
Crawford, bc1830, Clover Creek, High Co, fWilliam, Sr, mRachel Gwin
David G, bc1830, Clover Creek, fWilliam, Sr, mRachel Gwin
Fannie, bc1830, Clover Creek, fWillam, Sr, mRachel Gwin, h-- Sieg
Elizabeth Poague, bc1857, Rkbr Co, fJohn Alexander, mMary Willson, hR F Larew
James Willson, b12/24/1866, "Beech Spring Farm", nrBrownsburg, Rkbr Co, fAndrew A (1)mEstelline Montgomery Willson, wDamaris Irene Berry, md1894
John Alexander, b1826, Rkbr Co, d1910, fBenjamin, wMary Wilson
John H, bc1830, Clover Creek, High Co, fWilliam, Sr, mRachel Gwin

McCLUNG (continued)
John H, bc1851, Rkbr Co, d1922, fJohn Alexander, mMary Willson
Lewis, bc1840, High Co?, wLucy Blair
Louis Martena, b6/1/1846, Clover Creek, High Co, fWilliam, Sr, mRachel Gwin, wSudie Reamer, md11/1873
Margaret, b185-, "Beech Spring Farm", nrBrownsburg, Rkbr Co, d1923, fAndrew A, (1)mEstelline Montgomery Willson
Mary, bc1830, Clover Creek, High Co, fWilliam, Sr, mRachel Gwin, hJohn S McNulty
Mary T, b185-, "Beech Spring Farm", nrBrownsburg, Rkbr Co, fAndrew A, (1)mEstelline Montgomery Willson, hGardner P Kerr
Phebe, b17--, Rkbr Co?, hWilliam Paxton
Phoebe, b186-, "Beech Spring Farm", nrBrownsburg, Rkbr Co, fAndrew A, (1)mEstelline Montgomery Willson, hJ Frank Willson
Robert T, bc1830, Clover Creek, High Co, fWilliam, Sr, mRachel Gwin
Silas Brown, bc1830, Clover Creek, High Co, fWilliam, Sr, mRachel Gwin
Susanna, bc1830, Clove Creek, High Co, fWilliam, Sr, mRachel Gwin
William, Jr, bc1830, Clover Creek, High Co, fWilliam, Sr, mRachel Gwin
William, Sr, b1793, Bath Co, fJohn, Jr, mSarah McCutcheon, wRachel Gwin, m1821
W T, b18--, Bath Co
McCLURE, Carrie, b18--, Augu Co, fJohn P, mMary Wallace, hJames S Callison, md6/29/1891
Esterine, b18--, Rkbr Co, hBenjamin Franklin Brugh
John P, b18--, Augu Co?, wMary Wallace
Mary Stuart, b18--, fAndrew, hJohn Howard McClure
John Howard, b6/30/1854, Augu Co, fJames A, wMary Stuart McClure

McCLURE (continued)
Samuel Finley, b18--, Augu Co, fJames A
Uncus, bc1830, PrEd Co?, wCharlotte Watkins
McCOMAS, Cynthia, b6/1847, Gile Co?, fThomas Jefferson, mMinerva Ann French, hWilliam Hickman Spiller, Jr
Letha, b186-, Huntington, Cabe Co, 1w of Floyd Estill Ellis
Minnie Chapman, b18--, Pearisburg, Gile Co, fWilliam W, mSarah French, hGeorge W Easley
Thomas Jefferson, b18--, Gile Co?, wMinerva Ann French
Willam W, b1827, Cabe Co, d1862, wSarah French
McCOMB, J H, bc1860, Nels Co?, wLucy M Massie
Martha J, b18--, nrStuarts Draft, Augu Co, hJohn J Clarkson
McCONNELL, Anna, b18--, Richmond, hGeorge M Robeson
Henry Madison, bc1870, Mack, Scot Co, fHiram Kilgore, Sr, mGinsey E Brickey
Hiram Kilgore, Sr, b7/25/1838, Nickelsville, Scot Co, fJoab Watson, mRebecca Kilgore, wGinsey E Brickey
Hiram Kilgoe, Jr, bc1870, Mack, Scot Co, fHiram Kilgore, Sr, mGinsey E Bickey
Joab Watson, b18--, dc1881, fGeorge, mSusanna Snavely, wRebecca Kilgore
John Preston, b2/22/1866, Mack, Scot Co, fHiram Kilgore, Sr, mGinsey E Brickey, wClara Louisa Lucas, md5/21/1891
Rebecca Lucy, bc1870, Mack, Scot Co, fHiram Kilgore, Sr, mGinsey E Brickey, hOtto Lubker
Robert Watson, b7/25/1868, Mack, Scot Co, fHiram Kilgore, Sr, mGinsey E Brickey, wAnnie S Tallard, md12/18/1895
McCORKLE, Mastin Clay, b9/3/1853, nrAlderson, Summ Co, fSamuel, mJulia Kincaid, wRhoda Jane Cannaday
Samuel, b18--, Grbr Co, Julia

McCORKLE (continued)
Kincaid
McCORMICK, --, b180-, Clar Co, fWilliam, mElizabeth Rice, hHenry Pogue
--, bc1810, Fred Co?, wAnn Grove
Andrew, b173-, Clar Co?, fJohn
Ann, b17--, Clar Co, fFrancis, (1)m-- Provin
Ann, bc1800, Clar Co, fWilliam, mElizabeth Rice, h-- Biggs
Ann Herndon, b1862, Rapp Co, fEdward, mEllen Jane Jett, hGoodwin Hulings Williams, md3/18/1886
Ann R, bc1840, nrBerryville, Clar Co, fProvince, Sr, mMargaretta Moss, hConway Broun
Charles, b183-, nrBerryville, Clar Co, d186-, fProvince, Sr, mMargaretta Moss
Cyrus, b18--, Berryville, Clar Co, fFrancis, mRose Mortimer Ellzey
Cyrus Halla, b2/15/1809, "Walnut Grove", Rkbr Co, d1884, fRobert, mMary McChesney
Dawson, bc1860, Rapp Co, fEdward, mEllen Jane Jett
Edward, bc1830, "Clermont", nrBerryville, Clar Co, dc1870, wEllen Jane Jett
Elizabeth, b18--, Fred Co, hJoshua Krebe
Elizabeth, b18--, Clar Co, fWilliam, mSarah Neal, hProvince, Jr, md12/6/1871
Elvira Jett, b185-, Rapp Co, fEdward, mEllen Jane Jett, hScollay Moore
Francis, b1734, Clar Co?, fJohn, 1w-- Provin, 2wAnn Frost
Fancis, b18--, Berryville, Clar Co, fThomas, wRose Mortimer Ellzey
Frank, b18--, Berryville, Clar Co, fFrancis, mRose Mortimer Ellzey
George, b173-, Clar Co?, fJohn
Hannah Taylor, b18--, Berryville, Clar Co, fFrancis, mRose Mortimer Ellzey
Harriet, b179-, Clar Co, fWilliam, mElizabeth Rice, hRoss

McCORMICK (continued)
Milton
Hugh H, b184-, nrBerryville, Clar Co, d1870, fProvince, Sr, mMargaretta Moss
Isaac, b17--, Clar Co?, fFrancis, (2)mAnn Frost
James, bc1730, Clar Co?, fJohn
James Jett, b186-, Rapp Co, fEdward, mEllen Jane Jett
Jean, b173-, Clar Co?, fJohn, h-- Byrn
John, b17--, Clar Co, fFrancis, (1)m-- Provin
John, bc1730, Clar Co?, fJohn
John B, b1831, nrWhitehall, Fred Co, fLevi, m-- Graham, wSarah Anderson, md1874
Levi, b17--, Clar Co?, fJohn, w-- Graham
M D, b186-, Rapp Co, fEdward, mEllen Jane Jett
Margaretta, bc1810, Berryville, Clar Co, fFrancis, mRose Mortimer Ellzey, hRoss Milton
Marshall, bc1850, nrBerryville, Clar Co, d1918, fProvince, Sr, mMargaretta Moss
Mary, bc1730, Clar Co?, fJohn, hMagnus Tate
Mary E, b18--, Clar Co, fOttway, hJoseph B Lindsey
Mary Eliza, b10/17/1840, Weeshaw, Clar Co, fFrancis, mRose Mortimer Ellzey, hMarshall MacDonald, md12/17/1867
Nannie Frank, b18--, Berryville, Clar Co, fFrancis, mRose Mortimer Ellzey, hThomas McCormick
Province, b17--, Clar Co, fFrancis, (1)m-- Provin
Province, Sr, b9/9/1797, Clar Co, d1873, fWilliam, mElizabeth Rice, hMargaretta Moss
Province, Jr, b2/18/1847, nr Berryville, Clar Co, fProvince, Sr, mMargaretta Moss, wElizabeth T McCormick, md12/6/1871
Robert, b17--, Rkbr Co?, d1846, wMary McChesney
Rose Ellzey, b18--, Berryville, Clar Co, fFrancis, mRose Mortimer Ellzey, hLorenzo Lewis
Samuel, b17--, Clar Co, fFran-

McCORMICK (continued)
cis, (1)m-- Provin
Samuel, b18--, Berryville, Clar Co, fFrancis, mRose Mortimer Ellzey, wEsther Maria Lewis
Thomas, b17--, Clar Co, fFrancis, (1)m-- Provin
William, b17--, Clar Co, fFrancis, (1)m-- Provin
William, b17--, Clar Co, d1819, fIsaac, wElizabeth Rice, md1/10/1795
William, b17--, Clar Co?, fJohn
William, b18--, Clar Co, wSarah Neal
McCOY, George A, b1859, nrMcCoy, Mont Co, fMoses, wMyrtle Eakiss
Henry, b18--, Pend Co
James E, b184-, Richmond, d1923, m-- Elliott, wAnnie Ellington
John C, b18--, Buch Co?, wPolly
Marion Lafayette, b1843, St Paul, Wise Co, fWilliam W, mElziabeth Couch, wRebecca Rose
Martha Emma, bc1845, Pend Co, fHenry, hWilliam R Keister
Moses, b18--, Mont Co
William W, b18--, wElizabeth Couch
McCRAE, Alan, bc1870, Manchester, Ches Co, fJohn Harris, (3)mEmma Susan Turpin
George Scott, b18--, wJennie Baird
John Harris, b1815, Stony Point, Ches Co, d1905, fAlan, 3wEmma Susan Turpin
McCRARY, John R, b18--, Wash Co?, wFrances Steele
McCUE, Charles, b18--, Nels Co?, wVirginia Pulliam
Margaret H, b18--, hGeorge M Nolley
Massie L, b9/15/1849, nrAfton, Nels Co, d1922, wEmma F Purcell, md11/11/1879
Rebecca, b7/24/1869, nrAfton, Nels Co, fCharles W, mVirginia Pulliam, hRichard Shelton Ellis, Jr, md10/11/1899
Sarah Margart, b18--, fFranklin, 1w of David Washington Hanger

McCUTCHEON, Addison, b18--, Augu Co, wAnn Buchanan
Isabelle Patrick, b18--, Augu Co?, d1897, hJames H Callison
Margaret, b8/4/1847, Augu Co, fAddison, mAnn Buchanan, hDavid E East, md6/8/1882
Sarah, b18--, Augu Co, hJohn McClung, Jr
McDANIEL, Virginia, b18--, Caro Co?, hJohn B Crismond
McDANNALD, Mary W, b1863, Bath Co, fCharles, mEllen --, hChanning C Delaplane
McDONALD, Catherine B, b185-, Bath Co, fCharles, mEllen --, hChanning C Delaplane
Cynthia, b1830, Wyom Co, d1878, 2w of Robert Craig Graham
George S, b17--, Mont Co
George, Jr, b1810, McDonald's Mills, Mont Co, d1886, fGeorge, S, wNancy Sessler
George E, b185-, McDonald's Mills, Mont Co, fGeorge, Jr, mNancy Sessler
Harvey B, b9/26/1856, McDonald's Mills, Mont Co, fGeorge, Jr, mNancy Sessler, wAnnie Lee Early, md2/1892
Mark R, b185-, McDonald's Mills, Mont Co, fGeorge, Jr, mNancy Sessler
Ruth A, bc1850, McDonald's Mills, Mont Co, fGeorge, Jr, mNancy Sessler, hGeorge W Gardiner
Seth, b18--, Fauq Co?, wVirginia Hitt
Susan, b184-, McDonald's Mills, Mont Co, fGeroge, Jr, mNancy Sessler, hJames P Slusser
Walter T, bc1850, Fred Co?, wEliza T Jackson
MacDONALD, Angus William, Sr, b17-- Winchester, Fred Co, fAngus II, mMary McGuire, 1h of Leacy Ann Naylor
Angus II, b12/30.1769, Winchester, Fred Co, fAngus, mAnna Thompson, wMary McGuire, md1/11/1798
Angus William, Jr, b18--, fAngus William, Sr, mLeacy Ann Naylor
Angus, b186-, nrBerryville,

MacDONALD (continued)
Clar Co, fMarshall, mMary Eliza McCormick
Allen, b18--, fAngus William, Sr, mCornelia Peak
Anne Sanford, b18--, fAngus William, Sr, mLeacy Ann Naylor, hJames W Greene
Donald, b18--, fAngus William, Sr, mCornelia Peak
Edward Allen Hitchcock, b18--, fAngus William, Sr, mLeacy Ann Naylor
Ellen, b18--, fAngus William, Sr, mCornelia Peak, James H Lyne
Flora, b18--, fAngus Willim, Sr, mLeacy Ann Taylor, hEustace Williams
Hunter, b18--, fAngus William, Sr, mCornelia Peak
John, b18--, wLydia Burgess
Kenneth, b18--, fAngus William, Sr, mCornelia Peak
Marshall, b10/18/1835, Romney, Hamp Co, fAngus William, Sr, mLeacy Ann Naylor, wMary Eliza McCormick, md12/17/1867
Mary, b18--, fAngus William, Sr, mLeacy Ann Naylor, hThomas Glaiborne Greene
Rose Mortimer Elizey, b186-, nrBerryville, Clar Co, fMarshall, mMary Eliza McCormick
Roy, b18--, fAngus William, Sr, mCornelia Peak
Susan Leacy, b18--, fAngus William, Sr, mLeacy Ann Naylor, hJohn B Stannard
Woodrow, b18--, d186-, fAngus William, Sr, mLeacy Ann Naylor
William, b18--, fAngus William, Sr, mLeacy Ann Naylor
McDONOUGH, Eugenia, b1854, Leesburg, Loud Co, fWilliam, mHarriett Donaldson, hRichard F Green, Sr
Wallace, bc1850, Loud Co, wMary Green
William, b18--, Loud Co?, wHarriett Donaldson
McDOWELL, Cora Emmett, b18--, Richmond?, hWoodson Cheadle Burruss
James, b8/11/1833, Fincastle, Bote Co, d1911, fJames, mElizabeth Ferguson, wAnn Eliza Turner
Margaret Cantey, b18--, hCharles Scott Venable
Turner, Sr, b7/6/1866, Fincastle, Bote Co, James, mAnn Eliza Turner, wAnnie Davison Beckley, md12/28/1892
MACE, --, b17--, Russ Co, hAnthony Witt
McELHANY, John, bc1830, Fauq Co?, wMadge Skinker
McELWEE, Flora, b186-, Lexington, Rkbr Co, fWilliam Meek, Sr, mAnna Rebecca Harvey, h-- Miller
Nannie R, b185-, Lexington, Rkbr Co, fWilliam Meek, Sr, mAnna Rebecca Harvey, h-- Waller
Robert Harvey, b185-, Lexington, Rkbr Co, fWilliam Meek, Sr, mAnna Rebecca Harvey
Trigg, b185-, Lexington, Rkbr Co, fWilliam Meek, Sr, mAnna Rebecca Harvey
Virginia, b186-, Lexington, Rkbr Co, fWilliam Meek, Sr, mAnna Rebecca Harvey, h-- Bartolomew
William Meek, Jr, b1/5/1860, Lexington, Rkbr Co, fWilliam Meek, Sr, mAnna Rebecca Harvey, wFannie Symington, md1910
McENERY, Ada G, bc1870, Nott Co, fJohn E, mHannah S Gillam, hBenjamin Camm Garret, md4/20/1897
John E, b18--, Nott Co?, wHannah S Gillam
McEVOY, Michael Owen, bc1850, wMargaret Ryan
McFADDIN, Abel A, b1860, Hansonville, Russ Co, fJerry A, mRachel Hendricks, wNannie E Martin
Jerry A, b18--, Hansonville, Russ Co, wRachel Hendricks
McFALL, Nancy Jane, b18--, Dick Co, fArthur, hHenry Keel, md 2/27/1879
McFARLAND, James N, b2/24/1842, nrStaunton, Augu Co, fFrancis, mMary Ann Bent, wMary E Wallace

McFARLANE, Ellen, b17--, Augu Co, hThomas Neel
John A, b1839, Russ Co, d1889, wLou A Hurt
McFARRAN, Annie, b18--, Catawba, Bote Co, fMartin, hJoseph E Hannah, md1880
McGAVOCK, Edgar, b9/15/1868, Ft Chiswell, Wyth Co, fJames H, (1)mElizabeth Pointer
Ephraim, b1805, Wyth Co, fJames, mMary Crockett, wAbigail Joult Williamson, md11/17/1840
James, b6/10/1764, fJames M, mMary Cloyd, wMary Crockett, Md4/24/1797
James H, b2/16/1842, Ft Chiswell, Wyth Co, fEphraim, mAbigail Joult Williamson, 1wElizabeth Pointer, 2wEveline Prescott
McGEE, B C, bc1860, Dinw Co?, wMary Halligan
Fannie, b18--, Smyt Co?, hWilliam A Mays
McGHEE, --, b18--, Fran Co, hJack Miles
Hattie S, bc1870, Bedf Co?, 1w of Raswell C Overstreet, md1890
McGILL, John D, bc1810, Midd Co, wAnne Woodward
John, b18--, Fauq Co, wVirginia Beverley
McGILVRAY, Sarah, b18--, Augu Co?, hJ Alexander Baumgardner
McGINNIS, Anna, bc1860, Amhe Co, fHiram, mEmma Burford, hFrank Beavel
Bettis, b186-, Amhe Co, fHiram, mEmma Burford, hJames B Wright
Ella, b185-, Amhe Co, fHiram, mEmma Burford, hJ B Massie
Hiram, b 1815, Amhe Co, fJames, wEmma Burford
John, b186-, amhe Co, fHiram, mEmma Burford
Roberta, b185-, Amhe Co, fHiram, mEmma Burford, hR C Shinnett
Sallie, b185-, Amhe Co, fHiram, mEmma Burford, hJ J Craig
Thomas H, Sr, b10/20/1867, Amhe Co, fHiram, mEmma Burford, wBessie Lea Shipman, md3/30/

McGINNIS (continued)
1897
McGOWN, Mary A, b4/1847, Kerr's Creek, Rkbr Co, d1922, fHarry, mElizabeth Wiltshire, hMadison Kenney
McGRATH, William, bc1860, Camp Co?, wRosa E Casey
McGREGOR, Permelia, b18--, Hali Co?, d1876, hJohn Monroe
McGUFFIN, Adam G, Sr, bc1807, Bath Co, fJames, 1wEliza Orbison, 2wMary Bonner
Adam G, Jr, bc1840, Bath Co, fAdam G, S, (1)mEliza Orbison
Cornelia Jane Lee, bc1860, Bath Co, fAdam G, Sr, (2)mMary Bonner, hCharles Hyde
David, bc1840, Bath Co, fAdam G, Sr, (1)mEliza Orbison
James, bc1850, Bath Co, fAdam G, Sr, (1)mEliza Orbison
John Crawford, b11/18/1858, Warm Springs, Bath Co, fAdam G, Sr, (2)mMary Bonner, 1wMary Agnes Rivercomb, 2wBertie L Wright
McGUIRE, Edward II, b176-, Fred Co, fEdward, wBetsey Holmes
Harvey, bc1860, Taze Co?, wSallie Ann Litz
Hugh Holmes, b11/6/1801, fEdward II, mBetsey Holmes, wAnn Eliza Moss
Hunter Holmes, b2/11/1835, Winchester, Fred Co, fHugh Holmes, mAnn Eliza Moss, wMary Stuart, md12/9/1866
James G, bc1850, Taze Co?, fHugh Dudley, mMay Shufflebarger, wFannie R Dudley
John Peyton, Sr, b9/4/1800, Winchester, Fred Co, fWilliam, mMary Little, wMaria Mercer Garnett, md10/4/1827
John Peyton, Jr, b1836, Henrico Co?, fJohn Peyton, Sr, mMaria Mercer Garnett, wClara Mason, md7/10/1860
John Peyton III, b12/21/1866, Henrico Co, fJohn Peyton, Jr, mClara Mason, wRichie Morris Graves
Mary, b17--, fEdward, mMillicent D'Obee, hAngus McDonald II

McGUIRE (continued)
Stuart, b12/16/1867, Staunton, Augu Co, fHunter Holmes, mMary Stuart, wRuth I Robertson
William, b1765, Fred Co, fEdward, wMary Little
William David, b1810, Winchester, Fred Co, fEdward II, wNancy Boyd Moss
William Edward, b3/1860, Norwood, Clar Co, fWilliam David, mNancy Boyd Moss, wMary Stuart McGuire, md10/9/1894
McHENRY, A P, b1842, nrCatawba, Roan Co, d1914, 1wNannie Henderson, 2wMary Shulters
Charles, b186-, Roan Co, fA P, (1)mNannie Henderson
John A, b9/22/1868, Roan Co, fA P, (1)Nannie Henderson, wRosa Brown, md12/24/1892
MACHIN, --, b17--, Brun Co, hWilliam Palmer
MACHIR, Bettie, b18--, Shen Co?, hJames A Sonner
McILWAINE, Henry Read, b7/12/1864, Farmville, PrEd Co, fJoseph Finley, mSarah Embra Read
James R, b18--, Farmville, PrEd Co, fJoseph Finley, mSarah Embra Read
Jane Braham, b18--, Farmville, PrEd Co, fJoseph Finley, mSarah Embra Read, hHugh A White
Joseph Finley, b1838, Petersburg, Dinw Co, fArchibald Graham, mMartha Dunn, wSarah Embra Read
Lucy Pryor, b18--, Dinw Co?, fRobert B, mLucy Pryor, hArthur Kyle Davis, Sr, md10/12/1890
Mary Finley, b18--, Farmville, PrEd Co, fJoseph Finley, mSarah embra Read, hSamuel McPheeters Glasgow
Nannie Cabell, b18--, Farmville, PrEd Co, fJoseph Finley, mSarah Embra Read, hCarr Moore
Richard, b18--, Farmville, PrEd Co, fJoseph finley, mSarah Embra Read
Robert B, b18--, Dinw Co?,

McILWAINE (continued)
wLucy Pryor
Sarah, b18--, Farmville, PrEd Co, fJoseph Finley, mSarah Embra Read, hHarrington Waddell
McILWEE, Charles A, bc1870, nrHayfield, Fred Co, fJames T, mVictoria Gardner
Isaac, b185-, nrHayfield, Fred Co, fWilliam, mSarah white
James T, bc1850, nrHayfield, Fred Co, fWilliam, mSarah White, wVictoria Gardner
Minni I, bc1870, nrHayfield, Fred Co, fJames T, mVictoria Gardner, hSewell Good
William, b18--, Fred Co?, wSarah White
McINTIRE, george M, Jr, b18--, fGeorge M, Sr, mLouise Ann Davis, wCatherine Ann Clarke
Paul G, b5/28/1860, Charlottesville, Albe Co, fGeorge M, Jr, mCatherine Ann Clarke
McINTOSH, --, b1800, Loud Co, wAnn Wood Howison
Belle, 18--, PrWi Co, mAnn Wood Howison, hBenjamin F Head
James L, b10/8/1837, PrWi Co, mAnn Wood Howison, wMary Elizabeth Wenner
Lodounia, b18--, PrWi Co, mAnn Wood Howison, hRobert Howison
McINTURFF, John L, bc1840, Shen Co, wMary Elizabeth Boyer
Joseph B, b18--, Shen Co, wElla Koontz
Lucy, b18--, Shen Co?, hPeter Hinkins
Monroe, bc1860, Shen Co, wWernie Stickley
McIVOR, Rebecca, b18--, Hard Co?, h-- Kline
McKAY, Eliza, b18--, Warr Co, Zachariah James Compton
Joshua, b18--, Warr Co, d1861, wEsther Ann Haycock
Nannie Antrim, b1847, Warr Co, fJoshua, mEsther Ann Haycock, hJohn Robert Rust
McKEE, Catherine, b18--, Hamp Co?, hJohn T Cougill
James, bc1800, wMargaret Roe
William B, b1832, Wash Co, fJames, mMargaret Roe, wIsa-

McKEE (continued)
bella Tilson
McKINISTER, Mary, b18--, Fred Co?, 2w of Oscar Barr
McKINNEY, Amanda, b18--, Brun Co?, hJames Halligan, mdc1852
Peter Jefferson, b18--, Hali Co, dc1890
Robert Daniel, b9/8/1852, Hali Co, d1923, fPeter Jefferson, wKate Tuck
Samuel B, bc1830, PrEd Co?, wBettie Irving Watkins
McLAUGHERTY, Magdeline, b18--, 1w of George Herveson Walker
Sarah, b18--, Gile Co, 2w of George Walker
McLAUGHLIN, A M, b1844, Grbr Co, fHugh, wMary Price
Cormelia, b1804, hSam Redd
Henry W, Sr, b6/13/1869, Marlinton, Poca Co, fA M, mMary Price, wNellie Swann Brown, md8/31/1897
Hugh, bc1801, Bath Co, d1870, 1wNancy Gwynn, 2wElizabeth Lightner
McLEMORE, Benjamin Franklin, bc1840, Sout Co, d1911, wRosa Ann Westbrook
James Latinus, Sr, b11/18/1866, nrDrewryville, Sout Co, fBenjamin Franklin, mRosa Ann Westbrook, wMary Willis Pretlow, md5/21/1908
Martha, bc1870, nrDrewryville, Sout Co, fBenjamin Franklin, mRosa Ann Westbrook, hThomas Henry Birdsong, Sr, md4/17/1895
McLEOD, Rebecca, b18--, Camp Co?, hHenry Clay Victor
McMANAWAY, --, bc1860, Bedf Co, fC H, mNancy Wright, hW I Dooley
--, bc1860, Bedf Co, fC H, mNancy Wright, hT S Wright
A G, bc1860, Bedf Co, fC H, mNancy Wright
Annie, bc1860, Bedf Co, fC H, mNancy Wright
C G, bc1860, Bedf Co, fC H, mNancy Wright
C H, b18--, Bedf Co?, wNancy Wright
J E, bc1860, Bedf Co, fC H,

McMANAWAY (continued)
mNancy Wright
James M, b12/8/1855, Bedf Co, d1922, fC H, mNancy Wright, wMary R Morgan, md1882
Maggie, bc1860, Bedf Co, fC H, mNancy Wright
McMANUS, Jane, b18--, hEdward M Tearney, Sr
McMATH, Ellen, b4/5/1844, Norfolk, d1922, fJohn P, mEllen Day, hArthur T Mears
John P, b18--, Acco Co, wEllen Day
McMILLEN, b18--, Lee Co, hAlexander M Ely
Richard R, bc1870,, Rkhm Co?, fWesley W, mMargaret Lilly
Wesley, b18--, Pend Co
Wesley W, bc1840, Harrisonburg, Rkhm Co, fWesley, wMargaret Lilly
McMURRAN, James, bc1840, Carr Co, wSarah Early
Robert Lowry, Sr, bc1836, Jeff Co, d1892, wMary Archer Royall
Robert Lowry, Jr, b5/29/1866, Jeff Co?, fRobert Lowry, Sr, mMary Archer Royall, wMargaret Elizabeth Ferebee, md4/30/1901
McNAIR, Mary Elizabeth, b3/9/1841, Augu Co, d1900, fJames, hJohn Hatch Stover
McNEER, Henry P, b1851, Salt Sulphur Springs, Monr Co, d1889, wEliza C Hunter
James W, b1851, Monr Co, d1905, fAndrew, m-- Miller, mCarrie Brown
McNEIL, A S, b18--, Wash Co?, wNannie S --
Sara A, bc1870, Bristol, Wash Co, fA S, mNannie S --, hHomer Edward Jones, md10/4/1893
McNULTY, Frank, b10/23/1827, Poca Co, fJohn, wFrances Margret Wilson
McNUTT, Jane Reed, b18--, PrEd Co?, hHenry E Watkins
John, b17--, fAlexander, wKatherine Anderson
Joseph P, b1847, fRobert Blair, mElizabeth E Peck, wVirginia Adair
Robert Blair, b2/9/1814, Rkbr Co, fWilliam, mElziabeth

McNUTT (continued)
Grigsby, wElizabeth E Peck
Susie, b1864, Rkbr Co, hWilliam A Youell
William, b4/16/1774, Rkbr Co, fJohn, mKatherine Anderson, wElizabeth Grigsby
MACON, Charlotte, b18--, nrKeswck, Albe Co, fGeorge w, mMildred Nelson Meriwether, hFrank Randolph
George, b18--, nrKeswick, Albe Co, fGeorge W, mMildred Nelson Meriwether
George w, b1830, nrNew Kent Court House, NewK Co, fThomas, mVirginia Savage, wMildred Nelson Meriwether
Julia Halsey, b 18--, Shen Co, fJohn G, hRandolph Harrison
Letitia, b1859, Taze Co, hAlexander S Peery
Lyttleton, b18--, nrKeswick, Albe Co, fGeorge W, mMildred Nelson Meriwether
Margaret, bc1800, Camp Co?, hJohn H Burton
Thomas, b18--, fWilliam Hartwell
Thomas, b18--, nrKeswick, Albe Co, fGeorge W, mMildred Nelson Meriwether
William Douglas, b4/17/1869, nr Keswick, Albe Co, fGeorge W, mMildred Nelson Meriwether, 1wMary Johnson, 2wMercy (Hunter) Sherrerd
McQUILKIN, Frank Rush, bc1870, Jeff Co, fWilliam Thomas, mMary Catherine Kearney
Sarah Elizabeth, bc1870, Jeff Co, fWilliam Thomas, mMary Catherine Kearney
Thomas, bc1800, Berk Co, w-- Rush
William Thomas, b18--, Berk Co, fThomas, m-- Rush, wMary Catherine Kearney
McSHAN, Matilda, b18--, hRobert Smith
McVEIGH, Harvey, b12/20/1844, Alexandria, d1923, fWilliam N, mJane Selina Adam, wMary Richardson, md11/28/1872
William N, b18--, Richmond?, wJane Selina Adam

McVICAR, Catherine, b184-, Neffstown, Fred Co, fJohn, mCatherine Thatcher
Charles W, b1845, Neffstown, Fred Co, d1913, fJohn, mCatherine Thatcher, wMelissa Lewis
Henry W, bc1850, Neffstown, Fred Co, fJohn, mCatherine Thatcher
Marion Jenkins, b184-, Neffstown, Fred Co, fJohn, mCatherine Thatcher
Minnie, b185-, Neffstown, Fred Co, fJohn, mCatherine Thatcher, hJohn Anderson
Turner Ashby, b184-, Neffstown, Fred Co, fJohn, mCatherine Thatcher
McWILLIAMS, Gordon, b1/2/1768, Shen Co
Martha, bc1800, Shen Co, d1830, fGordon, 1w of Reuben Moore
MADDOX, Elizabeth, b173-, Gooc Co?, fJohn, mElizabeth --, hJohn Hancock, md10/16/1755
John, b17--, Gooc Co?, d1749, wElizabeth --
Mary, b18--, fJohn C, hDabney O Shackelford
Mildred Robinson, b1850, Camp Co, d1918, hHillary Mosely Callahan
Nelson, bc1810, Nels Co?, wJulia Massie
Sarah, b18--, Staf Co?, fBasil, hThomas Peyton
MADDUX, T Henderon, b18--, Fauq Co, wIda Murray
MADISON, --, bc1800, PrEd Co?, hThomas Clark
Elizabeth, b17--, Bote Co?, hJohn Pitzer
James, b17--, 2h of Dolly (Payne) Todd
Jennie, b18--, Cumb Co?, hJames A Armistead
Lucy, b18--, Oran Co, hJohn Willis
Mary, b17--, hLewis Timberlake
Nellie, b17--, 1w of Isaac Hite
MAGEE, A H, b18--, Roan Co?, w-- Denit
MAGRI, Francis Joseph, bc1870, Lynchburg, Camp Co, fFrancis J, mMary J --
MAGRUDER, Benjamin Henry,

MAGRUDER (continued)
  bc1800, Fluv Co, fJohn Bowie, mSarah B Jones, wMaria Louisa Minor, md12/15/1836
  Evelyn May, b18--, Albe Co?, fBenjamin Henry, hElliott Hawse DeJarnette
  Henry Minor, b2/9/1844, Albe Co, fBenjamin Henry, mMaria Louisa Minor, wSally Gilmer Minor
  Mark W, b5/3/1868, Woodstock, Shen Co, d1921, fPhilip Wilson, mAnnie Ott, wLelia M Riddleberger, md9/1893
  Mary, b18--, Shen Co, 1w of Holmes Conrad
  Mary, bc1870, Woodstock, Shen Co, fPhilip Wilson, mAnnie Ott, hS O Laughlin
  Philip Wilson, b1838, Shen Co, d1907, wAnnie Ott
MAHON, Mary, b18--, Mont Co?, hJohn Haley
MAHONEY, Anna, b17--, Amhe Co?, fDennis, hJohn Whitehead, md2/24/1812
MAHOOD, Fannie, bc1870, Camp Co, hJohn Victor, md1901
  May, bc1870, Buck Co, fC B, hJ Ed Lewis, Sr
MAIDEN, Delilah Frances, b18--, Rkhm Co, d1870, 1w of James Absalom Young
MAJOR, George Ficklin, b2/6/1856, Culp Co, fLangdon C, mMary Virginia Ficklin, wIda P English, md9/3/1879
  John E, b18--, Oak Hill, ChCi Co, d1907, wMaria L Marable
  Landgdon C, b18--, Culp Co, fWilliam, mElizabeth Corbin, wMary Virginia Ficklin
  Richard W, b11/14/1857, Stormont, Midd Co, fWalter Meuse, wElizabeth Blanche Meuse
  Walter Meuse, b1825, Stormont, Midd Co
  William, bc1800, Culp Co?, wElizabeth Corbin
MALLAN, Margaret, bc1870, Lynchburg, Camp Co, fWilliam, hCharles M Casey, md1892
MALLORY, Conner C, b18--, Esse Co?, wAnn Brooke
  Ella L, b18--, Hano Co, hJesse

MALLORY (continued)
  J Porter
MALONE, Mary, b18--, Richmond?, hSamuel S Weatherly
MANESS, Ann, b1857, Fairview, Scot Co, d1895, hThomas Moore
MANGUM, Mar, b18--, Brun Co, hWilliam Dameron
MANN, Alice, b11/5/1762, Bath Co, hWilliam McClintic II, md1782
  Cleverine Ada, bc1860, Broomfield, Hano Co, fEdward T, mElizabeth Jones, hGeorge Kelley
  Edward T, b18--, Ches Co, d1909, fEdward, wElizabeth Jones
  Edwin Murray, Sr, b1845, Williamsburg, JaCi Co, d1885, wMartha Burton Cowles, md1865
  Edwin Murray, Jr, b5/18/1868, Petersburg, Dinw Co, fEdwin Murray, Sr, mMartha Burton Cowles, wSarah Elizabeth Matthews, md12/10/1896
  Eva P, bc1870, Broomfield, Hano Co, fEdward T, mElziabeth Jones
  George C, b7/23/1867, Broomfield, Hano Co, fEdward T, mElizabeth Jones, wVernon Walker, md6/1895
  Henry C, b186-, Petersburg, Dinw co, fEdwin Murray, Sr, mMartha Burton Cowles
  Joel, b18--, Henrico Co
  Lula Lee, b186-, Broomfield, Hano Co, fEdward T, mElizabeth Jones, hJoseph W Willis
  Rosa Alice, b186-, Broomfield, Hano Co, fEdward T, mElizabeth Jones, hJames B Wise
  Thomas Alfred,, b186-, Broomfield, Hano Co, fEdward T, mElizabeth Jones
  William Hodges, b7/30/1843, Williamsburg, JaCi Co, fJohn, mMary Hunter Bowers
  William Hodges, bc1870, Petersburg, Dinw Co, fEdwin Murray, Sr, mMartha Burton Cowles
  Willie Anna, bc1860, Broomfield, Hano Co, d1897, fEdward T, mElizabeth Jones, hLewis Bowman

MANNING, Lillian, b186-, Merc Co?, fJames, mHester A Williams, hJames Alfred Deaton, md2/12/1891
MANSFIELD, Fenton Bruce, b18--, Loui Co, hJames Garland Boxley Susan, b7/15/1822, Loui Co, hHugh Mercer Dickinson
MANSON, Ann Elizabeth Blackwell, b1830, Lune Co, d1913, hJohn Robert Jones
Elizabeth, b1832, Lune Co, d1912, hWilliam Robert Jones
MANUEL, John W, bc1840, Fred Co?, wAnnie Bucher
MAPHIS, Benjamin Franklin, b1855, Saumsville, Shen Co, fJoseph, m-- Rhodes, wClara Virginia Spiker
Charles G, bc1860, Shen Co, fJohn M, mElizabeth Ann Coffelt
David W, b18--, Shen Co
Emma Ester, b11/27/1863, nr Strasburg, Shen Co, fJohn H, mFannie V Headley, hGeorge Andrew Copp, md11/30/1882
Emma J, b185-, Shen Co, fJohn M, mElzabeth Ann Coffelt, hJacob Brown
George, b17--, Shen Co, w-- Miley
J Luther, b10/15/1858, Shen Co, fJohn M, mElizabeth Ann Coffelt, 1wKatie E Bromley, md11/19/1884, 2wElizabeth C (Barr) Feaster
Jennie, b18--, Shen Co, hJohn H Wisman
John H, b18--, Shen Co, wFannie V Headley
John M, b1823, nrWoodstock, Shen Co, fGeorge, m-- Miley, wElizabeth Ann Coffelt
Joseph, b182-, nrEdinburg, Shen Co, fGeorge, m-- Miley, w-- Rhodes
Lillie Belle, b186-, Shen Co, fJohn M, mElizabeth Ann Coffelt
Lydia, b182-, nrWoodstock, Shen Co, fGeorge, m-- Miley, 1hJohn Hammond, 2h-- Gowl
Regina, b18--, Shen Co, hIsaac Painter
Samuel, bc1830, nrWoodstock,

MAPHIS (continued)
Shen Co, fGeorge, m-- Miley
Samuel, bc1850, Shen Co, wSophia A Saum
Samuel Wellington, b186-, Shen Co, fJohn M, mElizabeth Ann Coffelt
MAPP, Bessie, b1870, "Downingsville", Nhtn Co, hAlfred A Mears
Emma S, b18--, Wachapreague, Acco Co, d1914, hBenjamin W Mears
George Bowdoin, b1812, Acco Co, fGeorge T, m-- Harrison, wAnne Wharton Edmonds
John E, b2/1/1845, Wachapreague, Acco Co, fGeroge Bowdoin, mAnne Wharton Ednods, wMargaret Benson LeCato
MARABLE, Maria L, b18--, ChCi Co?, hJohn E Major
MARCH, J H, b18--, Jeff Co?, wLaura A Eby
Mollie A, b185-, Charlestown, Jeff Co, fJ H, mLaura A Eby, hMorgan L Walton, md1/26/1876
MARCHANT, John R, b1832, Glou Co, fThomas, mMary S (Robins) Keeble, wVirginia Blackburn, md1871
Thomas, b1801, wMary S (Robins) Keeble
MARCUSE, Isaac J, b11/16/1867, Richmond
MARKELL, Emma Virginia, b1844, Alexandria, hWilliam F Carne
MARKHAM, Judith, b17--, Ches Co, fJohn, mCatherine Matthews, hArcher Traylor
MARKS, --, bc1830, Fred Co?, wAnn Shryock
Laura Elizabeth, b6/28/1838, PrGe Co, hWilliam Watkins Anderson
MARMADUKE, Lydia Ann, b8/1861, Stratford, West Co, hRichard Henry Stuart
MARR, Harriett, b18--, Albe Co, hMadison Rhodes
MARRS, Elizabeth, b18--, Taze Co, hRaleigh W Pruett
MARSH, Mary Ann, b10/19/1849, Fluv Co, hJohn O King
Samuel J, bc1830, Appo Co?, wMollie Berkley

MARSH (continued)
Thomas J, b18--, Nhld Co?, wVirginia Growther
MARSHALL, --, bc1860, wElsie Snapp
Ada F, b186-, York Co, fJohn Henry, mElvira Elizabeth Ironmonger, hGilbert Taylor
Anna Josephine, b186-, nrAmelia Court House, Amel Co, d188-, fRichard Henry, mLouisa Caroline Anderson
Anna Mariah, bc1860, nrFront Royal, Warr Co, fJames, mLucy Steptoe Marshall
Bessie Lewis, b1843, Markham, Fauq Co, 1888, fEdward Carrington, hWilloughby Newton V
Carrie Branch, b186-, nrAmelia Court House, Amel Co, fRichard Henry, mLouisa Caroline Anderson, hEdward C Way
Charles, bc1760, Fauq Co, fThomas, mVirginia Mary Keith, wLucy Pickett
Charles Coatsworth, bc1800, Fauq Co?, fCharles, mLucy Pickett, wJudith Steptoe Ball
Charles C, bc1850, nrFront Royal, Warr Co, fJames, mLucy Steptoe Marshall
Edward Carrington, b18--, Fauq Co, fJohn
Elizaeth, bc1800, hRaleigh Colston
Ellen Harvie, b18--, hCharles Marshall Barton
George Washington, b1799, Nhtn Co, d1903, wSusan Sparrow
Harriett Alice, bc1870, nrAmelia Court House, Amel Co, fRichard Henry, mLouisa Caroline Anderson
Hester Morris, bc1850, nrFront Royal, Warr Co, fJames, mLucy Steptoe Marshall
James, b3/9/1826, Mt Morris, Fauq Co, 1901, fRobert Morris, mLucy Marshall, wLucy Steptoe Marshall, md1846
James Markham, b3/12/1764, Fauq Co, d1848, fThomas, mVirginia Mary Keith, wHester Morris, md1795
James Markham, bc1850, nrFront Royal, Warr Co, fJames, mLucy

MARSHALL (continued)
Steptoe Marshall
Jaquelin A, bc1850, Fauq Co, wEliza R Turner
John, b175-, Fauq Co, fThomas, mVirginia Mary Keith
John, b1797, nrAmelia Court House, Amel Co, d1856, w-- Leath
John Henry, b9/16/1836, Nhtn Co, fGeorge Washington, mSusan Sparrow, wElvira Elizabeth Ironmonger
John William, b11/19/1869, York Co, fJohn Henry, mElvira Elizabeth Ironmonger, wMarie Adams Kidd, md3/1/1893
Judith Ball, bc1850, nrFront Royal, Warr Co, fJames, mLucy Steptoe Marshall
Lucy, b1796, Fauq Co?, fCharles, mLucy Pickett, hRobert Morris Marshall, md 1819
Lucy, b186-, nrFront Royal, Warr Co, fJames, mLucy Steptoe Marshall, hWilliam Kertley Leathers, md10/11/1889
Mary, b18--, Acco Co, hJ T Merrill
Mary Morris, bc1860, nrFront Royal, fJames, mLucy Steptoe Marshall
Phoebe, bc1800, Meck Co, fWilliam, mLucy Goode, hWilliam Bagley
Presley/Preston, bc1840, Warr Co?, wLou Rust
Richard Anderson, b1/15/1863, nrAmelia Court House, Amel Co, fRichard Henry, mLouisa Caroline Anderson, 1wMattie Rahm Stacy, md9/28/1902, 2wAnnie Robbie, md6/5/1904
Richard Henry, b1843, nrAmelia Court House, Amel Co, 1910, fJohn, m-- Leath, wLouisa Caroline Anderson
Robert Morris, bc1850, nrFront Royal, Warr Co, fJames, mLucy Steptoe Marshall
Susan, b18--, hRichard C Ambler
Susan, b1829, nrJonesville, Lee Co, hAlexander Wynn
Susan Betts, bc1860, nrFront Royal, Warr Co, fJames, mLucy

MARSHALL (continued)
Steptoe Marshall
Thomas, b16--, Dumfries, PrWi Co, fJohn
Thomas, b42/1730, West Co, fJohn, wVirginia Mary Keith, md1754
Vera, bc1870, York Co, fJohn Henry, mElvira Elizabeth Ironmonger, hJohn Asher
William, b17--, fThomas
William, b17--, KiQu Co, fWilliam, wLucy Goode
MARSTON, Joseph, bc1810, Fred Co?, wRebecca Grove
MARTIN, --, bc1800, Nhld Co, fJoseph, hCyrus Harding
Betty Tarpley, b18--, Pitt Co, fChesley, mRebekah Martha White
Cassie, b1848, Carr Co, hWilliam Rush Gardner
Charles, b1830, Hillsville, Carr Co, fJoseph, mElizabeth Webb
Chesley, b4/14/1809, Pitt Co, d1880, fWilliam, mSusan --, wRebekah Martha White
Elizabeth, b18--, Henry Co, hRobert Williams
Euphemia, b1838, Acco Co, hBenjamin Hatton
Garrett W, b18--, Albe Co, wSarah Early
George Alexander, Sr, b9/3/1833, fJames Green, mMaacah Foreman, wGeorgia A Wickens
George Alexander, Jr, b11/26/1862, Richmond, fGeorge Alexander, Sr, mGeorgia A Wickens, wAnnie Louise Peery, md4/1/1891
Hanna, b6/6/1866, Carr Co, hCharles Goad
Harriet R, b18--, Salem, Roan Co, hWilliam J Perry
J B, bc1860, Rapp Co?, wNannie Mary Amiss
James Green, b3/11/1797, nr Great Bridge, Norf Co, fGeorge, mAnn Old, wMaacah Foreman
Jeff Davis, b185-, Philomont, Loud Co, fJohn W, mJane Norris Wyndham
Jennie Mortime, b1865, NewK Co,

MARTIN (continued)
d1909, hWilliam Joseph Parrish, Sr
John Richard, b18--, Pitt Co, fChesley, mRebekah Martha White
John Robertson, b2/9/1854, Appomattox Court House, Appo Co, d1916, fJohn Todd Anderson, mElizabeth Bruce Robertson, wJanie Haskins Scott
John S II, b10/2/1858, fJohn S, mMartha Staples
John T, b18--, wEmma J Johnston
John Todd Anderson, b4/2/1812, Gooc Co, d1859, wElizabeth Bruce Robertson, md2/18/1853
Joseph Merican, b2/20/1853, Philomont, Loud Co, fJohn W, mJane Norris Wyndham, wLizzie Rutter
Lucy, bc1870, Irishburg, Henry Co, fJames Orson, hRobert Pinkney Fagge, md9/21/1890
Marina A, b18--, Norf Co?, fGeorge Alexander, Sr, mGeorgia A Wickens
Martha, b1848, Appo Co, 2w of William A Ballard
Martha Susan, b18--, Pitt Co, fChesley, mRebekah Martha White
Mary Ann, b18--, Pitt Co, fChesley, mRebekah Martha White
Mary C, b1850, Henry Co, hRobert clay
Mary Elizabeth, bc1850, Clar Co?, fJohn W, mJane Norris Wyndham, hJ Seldon Welch
May, b18--, fGeorge Alexander, Sr, mGeorgia A Wickens, hSamuel C Peery
Nannie E, b11/1862, Russ Co, hAbel A McFaddin
Nellie G, b186-, Albe Co, fGarrett W, mSarah Early, hJohn C Everett, md8/26/1885
Nicholas, bc1860, Russ Co, wCora L Meade
Rawley White, b18--, Pitt Co, fChesley, mRebekah Martha White
Rebekah Chesley, b18--, Pitt Co, fChesley, mRebekah Martha White

MARTIN (continued)
Robert A, b18--, Dinw Co?, fWilliam, m-- Macon, wAnne E McIlwaine
Rosabelle, b18--, Camp Co?, hThomas J Moorman
Ruth, bc1800, Jonesville, Lee Co, hJames Miles
Sallie A, bc1848, Henry Co?, hWilliam A Bell
Theresa Fairfax, b18--, fGeorge Alexander, Sr, mGeorgia A Wickens
Thomas, b184-, Patr Co?, wCordelia Pedigo
Thomas A, b184-, Clar Co?, fJohn W, mJane Norris Wyndham
Thomas Staples, b7/29/1847, Scottsville, Albe Co, John S, mMartha Staples
William, b17--, Pitt Co, wSusan
William M, b1866, Petersburg, Dinw Co, fRobert A, mAnne E McIlwaine
William Preston, b2/1861, Hillsville, Carr Co, fCharles, mElizabeth Webb, wLetitia Nester
MARTZ, --, b186-, Rkhm Co, fD H Lee, mMary Nicholas Carter, hRichard Berlin
D H Lee, b3/23/1837, nrLacy Springs, Rkhm Co, d1914, fHiram, wMary Nicholsa Carter, md11/14/1860
Edward Carter, b12/28/1868, Rkhm Co, fD H Lee, mMary Nicholas Carter, wStella Bowcock, md6/27/1904
MARX, Louisa, b17--, Richmond?, hSamuel Myers
MARYE, John L, bc1810, wJane Hamilton
Lucy Mary, b17--, PrWi Co?, hJames Weir
MASK, Judith, b17--, Gooc Co?, hWalter Leake
MASON, --, b16--, PrAn Co?, hSamuel Wilson
Ann Eilbeck, b1798, KiGe Co?, d1862, fGeorge, hGeorge Nicholas Grymes
Clara, b2/16/1840, Chestnut Hill, Fair Co, fMurray, m-- Forsyth, hJohn Peyton McGuire, Jr, md7/10/1860

MASON (continued)
George, b1725, PrWi Co?, d1792
George, b1753, PrWi Co?, fGeorge
Harriet, bc1800, Russ Co, hAlexander McFarland Gray
J S, b18--, Fauq Co, wEliza Beverley
John, b18--, fGeorge, wAnna Maria Murray
Lucy Wiley, b18--, KiGe Co?, hEdward Jacquelin Smith
Julien J, b18--, KiGe Co, fWiley Roy, mSusan Smith, wElizabeth Freeland
Murray, b18--, fJohn, mAnna Maria Murray, w-- Forsyth
Nathaniel J, b18--, Meck Co, d1895, wPattie L Leftwich
Rachel, bc1800, Crai Co?, hJohn M Wood
Robert J, b12/26/1860, Parksley, Acco Co, fSouthy, mSallie Nelson
Southy, b1834, Bloxom, Acco Co
Wiley Roy, b18--, Staf Co, wSusan Smith
MASSENBURG, Anne Eliza, b18--, Sout Co?, fWilliam Albridgton, hThomas Jefferson Pretlow
Virginius Minson, b18--, Hampton ElCi Co, wVirginia Satchell Bully
MASSEY, --, b17--, hHosea Rogers
Rosso, bc1860, Spot Co?, wInez Colbert
MASSIE, Bettie, b18--, Nels Co, fJohn, hThaddeus C Cox
Bland, b11/10/1854, Pharsalia, Nels Co, fWilliam, mMaria C Effinger, wElizabeth Roster Sneed, md11/19/1876
Charles, b186-, Kernstown, Fred Co, fThomas W, mJennie Whissen
Charles W, b18--, Amhe Co, fJoseph H, mSophie Tyree
Cyrus, bc1860, Nels Co, fThomas, mSusan Poindexter
Edmond, bc1776, w-- Wortham
Edmund L, b18--, wLouisa A Swarzman
Edward, bc1850, Warr Co?, wSallie Rust
Emma, b18--, Amhe Co, fJoseph H, mSophie Tyree, hJesse Milner

MASSIE (continued)
Emma, bc1870, Nels Co, fThomas, mSusan Poindexter, hLittleton Miller
Eugenia, bc1861, Nels Co, hJames T Harvey, md10/23/1881
Eugenia S, b2/19/1819, Albe Co, hSamuel Vance Gatewood, md12/2/1835
Florence, b18--, Nels Co?, hJohn Dunscond Horsley
Florence, b18--, Nels Co, hJohn L Tunstall
Gertrude, b18--, Amhe Co, fJoseph H, mSophie Tyree, hMorton Conley
Hope W, b18--, Nels Co, d1892, wLaura W Effinger
J B, bc1850, Amhe Co?, wElla McGinnis
J Page, b18--, Amhe Co, d1920, fJoseph H, mSophie Tyree
James B, b18--, Fred Co?, wVirginia --
John, b181-, nrAlhambra, Nels Co, fEdmond, m-- Wortham
John, b186-, Kernstown, Fred Co, fThomas W, mJennie Whissen
John Henry, b186-, Nels Co, fThomas, mSusan Poindexter, wCora Cox, md9/1893
Joseph A, bc1870, Warr Co, fThomas B, mEliza Anderson
Joseph H, bc1829, Amhe Co, d1915, wSophie Tyree
Julia, b181-, nrAlhambra, Nels Co, fEdmond, m-- Wortham, hNelson Maddox
Juliet Anna, b18--, Nels Co, fThomas, hHenry Curran Boyd
Laura M, bc1870, Nels Co, fHope W, mLaura W Effinger, hJ H McComb
Lucy E, b186-, Kernstown, Fred Co, fThomas W, mJennie Whissen, hWilliam R Hillyard, md12/24/1885
Lucy M, b186-, Nels Co, fHope W, mLaura W Effinger, hHugh H Warde
M E, b9/6/1866, Nels Co, fHope W, mLaura W Effinger, wCambell F Ford
Marie, bc1870, Kernstown, Fred Co, fJames B, mVirginia --, hRobert S Smith

MASSIE (continued)
Mary, b18--, Oran Co?, fJames O, hBenjamin O Faulconer
Mary, b18--, Albe Co, fNathaniel, mSusan Woods, hRobert B Moon
Nathaniel, bc1800, Albe Co, wSusan Woods
Newton, b186-, Nels Co, fThomas, mSusan Poindexter
Polly, b181-, nrAlhambra, Nels Co, fEdmond, m-- Wortham
Robert, bc1870, Kernstown, Fred Co, fThomas W, mJennie Whissen
Susan, b181-, nrAlhambra, Nels Co, fEdmond, m-- Wortham
Susan M, bc1870, Nels Co, fHope W, mLaura W Effinger, hS B Whitehead, Sr
Thomas, b8/22/1747, d1834, fThomas, wSally Cocke
Thomas II, bc1800, fThomas, mSally Cocke
Thomas, b10/1/1818, nrAlhambra, Nels Co, d1912, fEdmond, m-- Wortham, wSusan Poindexter
Thomas, b186-, Nels Co, fThomas, mSusan Poindexter
Thomas B, b18--, Rapp Co?, fThomas II, wEliza Anderson
Thomas W, b18--, Fred Co?, wJennie Whissen
Virginia, b186-, fEdmund L, mLouisa A Swarzman, hFrank Waring Lewis, md11/12/1884
Wade Hampton, b9/30/1869, Warr Co, fThomas B, mEliza Anderson, wLizzie H Fletcher, md 10/14/1896
Walker W, bc1870, Nels Co, fThomas, mSusan Poindexter
Walter, bc1860, Nels Co, fThomas, mSusan Poindexter
Walter Price, b18--, Amhe Co, fJoseph H, mSophie Tyree, wIda Taliaferro
William, bc1800, Nels Co, fThomas, wMaria C Effinger
William, bc1870, Kernstown, Fred Co, fThomas W, mJennie Whissen
MASTIN, James, b1809, Spot Co, fThomas, wCatherine Field
James H, b18--, Spot Co, fJames, mCatherine Field
Joseph T, b5/2/1855, Spot Co,

MASTIN (continued)
fJames, mCatherine Field, wFannie Cowles Nottingham, md 12/10/1879
MATENEY, Price, b18--, Buch Co, d1903, hLevi Clevinger
MATHENY, --, b18--, Alle Co?, 1w of William Schumaker
Abijah, b18--, High Co
Ellen, b18--, Alle Co?, 4w of Charles Meade Stull
John Clifton, Sr, b2/27/1837, Mill Gap, High Co, d1908, fAbijah, 1wElizabeth Byrd, md12/22/1864, 2wElizabeth Flaherty
MATTER, John D, b186-, Alexandria?, wAnnie E Knight
MATTHEWS, --, b186-, Martinsville, Henry Co, fJohn Hill, (2)mSallie Craighead, hR R Lee
--, b186-, Martinsville, Henry Co, fJohn Hill, (2)mSallie Craighead, hG A Brown
--, b186-, Martinsville, Henry Co, fJohn Hill, (2)mSallie Craighead, hT P Parrish
Calvin, b18--, Henry Co?, dc1830, wLucy Mullins
Cyrus A, b18--, Nels Co, wMary Elizabeth Powell
J C, bc1850, Rkbr Co?, wMartha E Gleason
John, bc1840, Rkhm Co?, wOlivia Blackburn
John Hill, b12/7/1837, Horsepasture, Henry Co, fCalvin, mLucy Mullins, 1wAnne Morris, md1857, 2wSallie Craighead, 3wLouisa Shelton, md1881
Thomas, bc1820, Shen Co?, wElizabeth Ann Borden
William H, b18--, Madi Co?, wEliza Taliaferro
William Jefferson, bc1850, Lune Co, wOdelia Moore
William Walter, b11/7/1867, nrAfton, Nels Co, fCyrus A, mMary Elizabeth Powell, wAgnes Grove
MATTOX, Margaret, b18--, Fran Co?, hJeremiah Barbour
MAUCK, Sarah Ann, b1830, Page Co, d1896, fJohn, hJohn Leedy
MAUPIN, --, bc1800, Albe Co, hDabney Maupin

MAUPIN (continued)
--, b1799, Albe Co, d1893, hHarry Lindsay
Laura Virginia, b18--, Rkhm Co?, hJoseph H Lamb
MAURY, Anne Tunstall, b17--, Fred Co?, hIsaac Hite
Mary, b18--, Richmond?, fMatthew, hJames R Werth
Matthew Fontaine, b1806, Spot Co, d1873, fRichard, mDiana Minor
Richard, b17--, Spot Co?, wDiana Minor
MAUZY, --, bc1810, McGaheysville, Rkhm Co, wFrances Rush
Albert G, b18--, Rkhm Co
Emma, b184-, Montevideo District, Rkhm Co, fAlbert G, hJohn King
Fannie, b184-, Montevideo District, Rkhm Co, fAlbert G, hEd S Yancey
Joseph N, b184-, Montevideo District, Rkhm Co, fAlbert G
Thomas G, b1844, Montevideo District, Rkhm Co, d1912, fAlbert G, wAnna Belle Liggitt
MAWYER, George T, b1854, Greenfield, Nels Co, wBelle Camden
MAXEY, Burl, b18--, Fran Co, w-- Richards
Edward A, bc1800, Powh Co, fFields, wMartha S Ellett
Jane, b18--, Nott Co, hJohn Archer Ellett
Joseph E, b3/5/1839, nrPowhatan, Powh Co, fEdward A, mMartha S Ellett, wOctavia A Ellett
William, b9/11/1864, Fran Co, d1923, fBurl, m-- Richards, wElla F Hankley
MAXWELL, Martha H, b1862, Taze Co, hRobert M Sparks
MAY, --, bc1800, Rkhm Co, hJohn Crist
Charles E, b18--, Lune Co, fCharles
Frank, bc1860, Rkhm Co?, wEmma Jeanetta Swank
James M, b18--, Norf Co?, wLucy Monroe
Mary C, b18--, Taze Co, fAndrew Jackson, hVincent Kelly
Mary, b1866, Lune Co, fCharles

MAY (continued)
E, hLouis A Gee
MAYER, Eugene L, b18--, Norf Co
MAYHAN, Rebecca, b1836, nrCallands, Pitt Co, d1908, hWilliam H Ramsey
MAYHEW, Esom, b18--, Berk Co?, w-- Sencendiver
James A, b18--, Clar Co, d1919, fEsom, m-- Sencendiver, wEdith E Fitery
MAYNARD, Mary, b17--, hEdmund Waddill
MAYO, Elizabeth, bc1800, hWilliam Carter
Joseph, b1832, West Co, d1896, fRobert, mMary Anne Campbell, wMary Armstead Tyler
Robert, bc1800, Richmond, wMary Anne Campbell
S L, b18--, Augu Co?, wAnn D Davis
Valentine, b17--, Albe (now Fluv) Co, fJacob, wJudith Hancock
Wat Tyler, b10/1/1870, nrHague, West Co, fJoseph, mMary Armstead Tyler
William, bc1850, West Co, wElizabeth Brown
William James, bc1760, Albe (now Fluv) Co, fJacob, wElizabeth Maddox Hancock
MAYS, William A, b18--, Smyt Co?, wFannie McGee
MEADE, Amelia, b17--, hAlbert Thweatt Godwyn
Charles A, bc1870, Dickensonville, Russ Co, fJames H, mRebecca A Lindamood
Charles G, b186-, nrCastlewood, Russ Co, fWilliam Rives, mNancy P Gose
Cora L, b186-, Dickensonville, Russ Co, fJames H, mRebecca A Lindamood, hNicholas H Martin
Edith S, b186-, Dickensonville, Russ Co, James H, mRebecca A Lindamood, hRichard L Counts
Eliza, b18--, Russ Co?, hJames L Williams
Emmett W, bc1860, Dickensonville, Russ Co, fJames H, mRebecca A Lindamood
Everard Benjamin, b18--, Richmond, wLucy Gilmer

MEADE (continued)
Frank F, b186-, Dickensonville, Russ Co, fJames H, mRebecca A Lindamood
Henry M, bc1800, Richmond, fHenry, wEdith Friley
Hodijah, b1842, wMary Hardaway
James H, b1825, Dickensonville, Russ Co, d1911, fHenry M, mEdith Friley, wRebecca E Lindamood
James O, bc1870, Dickensonville, Russ Co, fJames H, mRebecca A Lindamood
Martha J, b185-, Dickensonville, Russ Co, fJames H, mRebecca A Lindamood, hWilliam G Milton
Mary E, b185-, Dickensonville, Russ Co, fJames H, mRebecca A Lindamood, hIsaac V Carter
Robert C, b9/13/1867, nrCastlewood, Russ Co, fWilliam Rives, mNancy P Gose, wJennie Williams, md1/6/1904
Robert S, b11/10/1866, Dickensonville, Russ Co, fJames H, mRebecca A Lindamood, 1wIndia E Gibson, md12/25/1893, 2w Alice B Exall, md12/31/1919
Sarah E, b1862, Scot Co, hJames L Greear
Tina V, bc1860, Dickensonville, Russ Co, fJames H, mRebecca A Lindamood, hJohn F Jones
Virginia, bc1870, nrCastlewood, Russ Co, fWiliam Rives, mNancy P Gose, hRobert L Smythe
Walter R, bc1870, nrCastlewood, Russ Co, fWilliam Rives, mNancy P Gose
William H, b185-, Dickensonville, Russ Co, d1894, fJames H, mRebecca A Lindamood
William Rives, b1840, nrDickensonville, Russ Co, d1904, fHenry G, mElizabeth Hicks, wNancy P Gose
MEADOR, Nannie Haskins, b18--, fJohn, mMary Page Haskins, hWilliam A Gresham
MEADOWS, Anna, b18--, Merc Co, hRobert M Whited
James Tyler, b12/15/1866, nrStaffordsville, Gile Co, fSamuel, mEllen Brooks, wMin-

MEADOWS (continued)
nie Wood Early, md10/7/1891
Jeremiah M, b18--, fJoel, mMary Estes
Joel, b18--, Greene Co, fJohn
John, b3/10/1800, Greene Co
Joseph, b12/2/1867, Greene Co, fJeremiah M, mMary Estes, wMittie Strole, md10/13/1897
Samuel, b5/5/1825, Monr Co, fJohn, mElziabeth Wyant, wEllen Brooks
MEANS, R, Preston, bc1850, wSarah Palmer
MEARS, Alfred A, b1868,, "Happy Union", nrFrankln, Nhtn Co, fIsma W, mJane Kellam, wBessie Mapp
Annie, b186-, Acco Co, fBenjamin W, mEmma S Mapp, hSamuel W Ames
Arthur T, b9/2/1839, Locustville, Acco Co, fRobert, wEllen McMath
Benjamin W, b1833, Keller, Acco Co, fJohn B, mSarah Jane Ames, wEmma S Mapp
Charles, bc1870, Locustville, Acco Co, fArthur T, mEllem McMath
Charles B, bc1870, Acco Co, fBenjamin W, mEmma S Mapp
Cora, b186-, Acco Co, fBenjamin W, mEmma S Mapp, hA James Byrd
Harry E, b186-, Acco Co, fBenjamin W, mEmma S Mapp
Isma W, b1841, Acco Co, wJane Kellam
John B, bc1800, Acco Co, wSarah Jane Ames
John B, bc1870, Acco Co, fBenjamin W, mEmma S Mapp
Leonard C, b186-, Acco Co, fBenjamin W, mEmma S Mapp
Margaret Anna, b8/28/1856, Acco Co, hWilliam James Somers
Mary E, b186-, Locustville, Acco Co, fArthur T, mEllen McMath, hJames E Bundick
Otho Frederick, Sr, b6/4/1862, Acco Co, fBenjamin W, mEmma S Mapp, wFlorence R Holland, md11/19/1890
MEBANE, Bessie, b4/18/1837, Rich Co, d1913, fAlexander, mEmeline Broaddus Pleasants, hWil-

MEBANE (continued)
liam Broaddus Robins
Emma, bc1840, Rich Co, fAlexander, mEmeline Broaddus Pleasants, hDaniel Robert Hunt
MEDLEY, Harriet, b18--, Madi Co, hDaniel Jenifer Smoot
MEDLICOTT, Elizabeth, b7/6/1845, Glou Co, d1920, hJames New Stubbs
MEEKS, James W C, b18--, nrMassie's Mill, Nels Co, wElowise Wills
Julia, bc1860, nrMassie's Mill, Nels Co, fJames W C, mElowise Wills, hCharles Zolman
Sallie, bc1860, nrMassie's Mill, Nels Co, fJames W C, mElowise Wills, hR E Beard
William D, b9/13/1860, nrMassie's Hill, Nels Co, fJames W C, mElowise Wills, 1wMinnie D Clarke, md9/1886, 2wRachel Henderson, md1881
MEEM, Andrew Russell, bc1830, Lynchburg, Camp Co, fJohn Gaw, Sr, (1)mEliza Campbell Russell, wAnn Jordan
Elise Campbell, b18--, Camp Co, fGilbert Simrall, Sr, mNanne Rose Garland, hDaniel Kelleher
Eliza, bc1830, Lynchburg, Camp Co, fJohn Gaw, Sr, (1)mEliza Campbell Russell, hSamuel Garland
Frances Russell, bc1820, Lynchburg, Camp Co, fJohn Gaw, Sr, (1)mEliza Campbell Russell, hRobert Spotswood Payne
Gilbert, b17--, fPeter, wFrances Simrall
Gilbert Simrall, Sr, bc1830, Lynchburg, Campbell Co, fJohn Gaw, Sr, (1)mElizabeth Campbell Russell, wNannie Rose Garland
Gilbert Simrall, Jr, b18--, Camp Co, fGilbert Simrall, sr, mNannie Rose Garland
Hugh Garland, b18--, Camp Co, fGilbert Simrall, Sr, mNannie Rose Garland
J Lawrence, b18--, Camp Co, fJohn Gaw, Jr, (2)mAurelia Halsey, wPhyllis Deadrick
James Gowan, b18--, Camp Co,

MEEM (continued)
fJohn Gaw Meem, Jr, (1)mNancy Cowan
James Lawrence, b184-, Lynchburg, Camp Co, d186-, fJohn Gaw, Sr, (1)mEliza Campbell Russell
John Gaw, Sr, bc1795, Winchester, Fred Co, dc1873, fGilbert, mFrances Simrall, 1w Eliza Campbell Russell
John Gaw, Jr, b1839, Camp Co, d1908, fJohn Gaw, Sr, (1)m Eliza Campbell Russell, 1w Nannie Cowan, 2wAurelia Halsey
John Gaw III, b18--, Camp Co, fJohn Gaw, Jr, (1)mNancy Cowan
Julia, b18--, Camp Co, fJohn Gaw, Jr, (2)mAurelia Halsey, hRandolph Harrison
Lelia Russell, b18--, fAndrew Russell, mAnn Jordan, hWilliam Daingerfield Peachy
Stephen H, b18--, Camp Co, fJohn Gaw, Jr, (2)mAurelia Halsey, wEdna Hutter
MEGEATH, Martha C, bc1843, Fauq Co?, hWashington L Richards
MEGGINSON, John Thomas, b18--, fWilliam, mAmanda B Babcock, wSarah Emily Smith
Pocahontas, b18--, Nels Co, 2w of William H Hening, Sr
MELSON, Dora, b18--, Accomac Court House, Acco Co, hD Frank White, Sr
MELTON, Charles Lewis, b4/12/1865, Rapp Co, fWilson Nicholas, mSarah McCay, wGertrude Blackwell, md6/24/1896
Melinda, b18--, Carr Co, hMartin Edwards
Wilson Nicholas, b18--, Rapp Co?, wSarah McCay
MENEFEE, Anne Stuart, b17--, Fauq Co?, hThomson Ashby
Bettie, b18--, Rapp Co, fJonas Y, m-- Britton, hJack Pounds
Britton, b18--, Rapp Co, fJonas Y, m-- Britton
Charles Fremont, bc1853, Rapp Co?, wSusan Alexander Guard
Edgar Warren, b186-, nrMt Crawford, Rkhm Co, fSamuel M, mVirginia Tutwiler
Elijah E, Sr, b2/12/1858, Rapp

MENEFEE (continued)
Co, fJames Albert, mSarah Elizabeth Amiss, 1wMary Jordan, md11/26/1889, 2wMartha Franklin, md2/2/1908
Garland, b18--, Rapp Co, fJonas Y, m-- Britton
Hanson J, b1842, Rapp Co, d1920, fJonas Y, m-- Britton
Henry Floyd, b18--, Rapp Co, wRoberta McLaren Holland
Ida, b18--, Rapp Co, hSilas B Johnson
Ida Stribling, b18--, Rapp Co, fJonas Y, m-- Britton, hHoratio Gates Moffett, Jr
James, b18--, Rapp Co, d186-, fJonas Y, m-- Britton
James Albert, b2/24/1806, Rapp Co, d1890, wSarah Elizabeth Amiss
Jane, b18--, Rapp Co, fJonas Y, m-- Britton, hJohn Shank
Jonas Y, bc1800, Rapp Co, w-- Britton
Lucy, b18--, Rapp Co, fJonas Y, m-- Britton, h-- Laula
Mamie, bc1850, Rapp Co, fJames Albert, mSarah Elizabeth Amiss, hBolitha D Laws
Mary L, b86-, nrMt Crawford, Rkhm Co, fSamuel M, mVirginia Tutwiler, hDaniel Stoner
Robet Tilden, bc1870, nrMt Crawford, Rkhm Co, fSamuel M, mVirginia Tutwiler
Samuel M, bc1840, Rapp Co, 1907, fJonas Y, m-- Britton, wVirginia Tutwiler
Thomas, b18--, Rapp Co, fJonas Y, m-- Britton
Thomas J, b186-, nrMt Crawford, Rkhm Co, fSamuel M, mVirginia Tutwiler
William McAtee, b8/6/1866, nrMt Crawford, Rkhm Co, fSamuel M, mVirginia Tutwiler, wAlice Roberta Roller, md3/25/1892
MERCER, Caroline V, b186-, Richmond, fIsaac J, mJosephine Arsell, hWilliam J Young
Charles A, b186-, Richmond, fIsaac J, mJosephine Arsell
Elizabeth Frances, b18--, PrAn Co, hBenjamin S Dey
Isaac J, b18--, Esse Co, fJohn,

MERCER (continued)
wJosephine Arsell
I Morton, bc1870, Richmond,
fIsaac J, mJosephine Arsell
MERCHANT, James Edward, bc1850,
Arli Co?, 1h of Janie Caroline
Turner
Laura V, b7/1833, Dumfries,
PrWi Co, fRobert, hWilliam R
Free
Robert, b184-, PrWi Co?,
wMelinda Dowell
MEREDITH, Charles V, b9/12/1850,
Richmond, fJohn A, mSarah Ann
Bernard, wSophie G Rose
Edward Douglas, b18--, fJohn A,
mSarah Ann Bernard
Eliza Bernard, b18--, fJohn A,
mSarah Ann Bernard, hPreston
Cocke
John A, b18--, NewK Co,
fRobert, mMay Anderson, wSarah
Ann Bernard
John Floyd, b18--, Pula Co,
wSophia Howery
Lelia Bernard, b18--, fJohn A,
mSarah Ann Bernard, hRichard L
Manning
Lucy, b18--, Fran Co, hJohn C
Hutchinson
Lulu Lee, b18--,Pula Co, fJohn
Floyd, mSophia Howery, hJohn
Henry Taylor
Raymond G, b17--, Amhe Co
Sallie, b18--, hRobert T Sydnor
William Bankhead, b18--, Staf
Co, fJaquelin, wMinnie Mullins
William Bernard, b18--, fJohn
A, mSarah Ann Bernard
Wyndham R, b18--, fJohn A,
mSarah Ann Bernard
MERIWETHER, Anne Kinloch, b18--,
hFrederick Winslow Page
Francis, b17--,Esse Co, wMary
Bathurst
Mary, b17--, Esse Co, fFrancis,
mMary Bathurst, hThomas Wright
Belfield
Mildred Nelson, b18--, Albe Co,
hGeorge W Macon
MERRILL, J T, b18--, Acco Co?,
wMary Marshall
MERRITT, John, b18--, Hali Co,
d1919, wLuemma Woolwine
Pearl, b18--, Alle Co?,
hCharles Mead Stull

MERRYMAN, John, bc1846, Appo
Co?, d1890, wMary Spigle
MESSERSMITH, --, bc1800, Wyth
Co?, hGeorge Porter
MESSICK, Jewitt, b18--, Rkhm
Co?, wCatherine Cline
Sarah Ann, b5/7/1835, Rkhm Co,
fJewett, mCatherine Cline,
hSamuel Shrum, md12/1855
METZ, Catherine, b18--, Fred Co,
hJohn S Solenberger
MEUSE, Elizabeth Blanche,
b9/4/1862, Hominy Village,
Midd Co, hRichard W Major
MEYERHOFFER, Elizabeth, b18--,
Rkhm Co, Lewis, mAnn Hooke,
hJames Begoon
Ida, b18--, Rkhm Co, fLewis,
mAnn Hooke
James, b18--, Rkhm Co, fLewis,
mAnn Hooke
John, b18--, Rkhm Co
John Hooke, b18--, Rkhm Co,
fLewis, mAnn Hooke, wMargaret
Altaffer
Lewis, b18--, Rkhm Co, wAnn
Hooke
Lewis B, b18--, Rkhm Co,
fLewis, mAnn Hooke
Lucy, b18--, Rkhm Co, fLewis,
mAnn Hooke, hLewis Riddle
Marshall, b18--, Rkhm Co
Martha Allen,b18--, Rkhm Co,
fLewis, mAnn Hooke, hBrown
Ruebush
Robert, b18--, Rkhm Co, fLewis,
mAnn Hooke
Robert M, bc1860, Augu Co?,
wElizabeth Susan Pirkey
Sarah Ann, b18--, Rkhm Co,
fLewis, mAnn Hooke, hGeorge
Begoon
Thomas, b18--, Rkhm Co, fLewis,
mAnn Hooke
William, b18--, Rkhm Co
MICHAEL, J A, bc1850, Augu Co?,
wIda C Plecker
Lucy, b18--, Augu Co?, hMartin
Shull
Sophia, b18--, d1892, hWilliam
Joseph Whitlock
Sophie, b17--, hAndrew Woolf
W W, bc1850, Augu Co?, hFannie
Plecker
MICHAUX, --, b1810, PrEd Co,
d1850, 1w of Asa D Dickinson

MICHAUX (continued)
Mary, b18--, PrEd Co?, fMiller, hRichard V Watkins
Mary L, b18--, Richmond, hJames B Harvie
Stuart, bc1860, Richmond?, wMartha Garland Whitehead
MICHIE, Armistead R, b18--, fHenry B, mVirginia Bedinger
George R B, b8/28/1870, Staunton, Augu Co, Henry B, mVirginia Bedinger, wHay Watson Perkins
Henry B, b839, Charlestown, Jeff Co, fThomas Jefferson, mMargaret Garber, wVirginia Bedinger
Henry Clay, b1/9/1842, Albe Co, fJames, mFrances Garth, wEunice Dandridge Sykes, md12/10/1867
James, b18--, Albe Co, fJohn Augustus, wFrances Garth
John Augustus, b17--, Albe Co, fWilliam
Patrick, b17--, fRobin/Robert, mAnn Watson, wDorothy Johnson
Robin/Robert, b17--, Albe Co, fJohn, wAnn Watson
Thomas Jefferson, b18--, fPatrick, mDorothy Johnson, wMargaret Garber
Thomas Johnson, b18--, fHenry B, mVirginia Bedinger
William, b17--, Albe Co, fJohn
MICKS, W G, b18--, Norfolk, wCornelia Rathbone
MIDDLETON, Jane, b17--, West Co, fBenjamin, hBenedict Rust, md3/24/1766
MILBY, John H, b8/6/1858, Shacklefords, KiQu Co, fHezekiah H, mLucy Milby
MILES, Ben S, bc1870, Jonesville, Lee Co, fFrancis, mDiana Stanley
Charles C, b186-, Jonesville, Lee Co, fFrancis, mDiana Stanley
Charles F, bc1840, Fair Co?, wBelle K Ford
Cleo, b18--, Russ Co?, hDaniel S Hearon
David T, bc1870, Jonesville, Lee Co, fFrancis, mDiana Stanley

MILES (continued)
Francis, b1839, Jonesville, Lee Co, fJames, mRuth Martin, wDiana Stanley
Henry Morgan, b8/14/1868, Jonesville, Lee Co, fFrancis, mDiana Stanley, wAlpha Hobbs, md9/21/1890
Jack, b18--, Fran Co, w-- Mc Ghee
James, b1793, Jonesville, Lee Co, wRuth Martin
John W, b1/10/1844, Fran Co, fJack, m-- McGhee, wAlice Wade
Mollie, bc1860, Jonesville, Lee Co, fFrancis, mDiana Stanley, hJohn M Parsons
Samuel V S, b186-, Jonesville, Lee Co, fFancis, mDiana Stanley
MILEY, --, b17--, Shen Co, hGeorge Maphis
Bettie, b18--, Shen Co, hAndrew Jackson Boyer
Martin F, b18--, Shen Co?, wCatherine Rhodes
Rhoda F, b7/10/1837, Shen Co, d1887, fMartin F, mCatherine Rhodes, 2w of Isaac R White
MILLAN, J P, bc1860, wMary Ruth Wood
MILLAR, Hugh Roy, bc1860, Warr Co, fMortimer Hamilton, mMary Carson Roy, wAnnie Lacy Dillard, md1/20/1892
Isaac, b17--, Warr Co
Mortimer Hamilton, b18--, Warr Co?, wMary Carson Roy
Rebecca, b17--, Warr Co?, mRebecca DuBois, h-- Branson
Samuel Richardson, b1817, Front Royal, Warr Co, d1861, fIsaac, wSusan Beverly Randolph
Samuel Rolfe, Sr, b5/21/1857, Front Royal, Warr Co, fSamuel Richardson, mSusan Beverly Randolph, wBertha Riedel, md 10/2/1881
MILLER, --, b17--, wAnn Ball
--, bc1860, Rkbr Co?, wFlora McElwee
--, b186-, Greene Co, fThomas A, mMargaret Eddins, hC E Urquhart
--, b18--, Monr Co, hAndrew McNeer

MILLER (continued)
--, bc1800, Rkhm Co? wMary Bertram
--, b1826, d1888, (father of Walter C Miller)
--, b18--, Augu Co, hDavid Garber
--, b18--, Shen Co?, hMarcus P Grandstaff
Abigail, b17--, Warr Co?, hThomas Allen
Abram, b17--, Winchester, Fred Co, fGodfrey Mueller, Sr, mAnna Maria Kurtz, wRebecca Schultz
Abram Schultz, b1830, Winchester, Fred Co, fAbram, mRebecca Schultz, wJulia Henkel
Achsah, b18--, Rapp Co, hWilliam T Dudley
Acsah, bc1820, Rapp Co, fDavid, mAbigail Jackson, hJohn Settle
Ada V, b185-, New Market, Shen Co, fAbram Schultz, mJulia Henkel
Ada Virginia, bc1850, Strasburg, Shen Co, fThomas Jefferson, mKatherine Russell, hLeigh R Freeman
Adam, b17--, Madi Co
Anna, b18--, Spring Creek, Augu Co, fMartin, hAndrew Hess
Anna Josephine, b18--, Rapp Co, fMiddleton, mAnna Louise Hubbs, hPersley Henry O'Bannon, md5/14/1879
Anna Maria, b17--, Winchester, Fred Co, fGodfrey Mueller, Sr, mAnna Maria Kurtz, h-- Wolf
Annie Lee, bc1860, Mont Co, fRobert A, mClara A --, hJames Henry Stuart
B F, bc1860, Rkhm Co?, wNora Myers
Benjamin Franklin, b18--, Rapp Co, wEusebia Browning
C A, bc1860, Bote Co, w-- Rinehart
Carrie B, bc1870, Bedf Co, fWilliam, hEdmund A Overstreet, Sr, md1891
Casper O, b8/7/1857, New Market, Shen Co, fAbram Schultz, mJulia Henkel, wMary C Schumacher, md9/19/1901
Catherine, bc1840, Stonewall

MILLER (continued)
District, Rkhm Co, fDaniel, mMary Saufley, h-- Glick
Catherine, b1847, nrWeyer's Cave, Rkhm Co, fSamuel, m-- Wine, hJohn Wampler
Catherine, bc1800, Fred Co, hDavid Dinges
Charles E, b1866, Elkton, Rkhm Co, fS P H, wSallie Brubaker
Charles M, bc1860, Gooc Co, fWilliam II, mHattie Guerrant
Clarence Alexander, b185-, Strasburg, Shen Co, fThomas Jefferson, mKatherine Russell
Clarence Jackson, b12/22/1869, Washington, Rapp Co, fMiddleton, mAnna L A Hubbs, wSallie Hunt Strother, md11/29/1893
Daniel, b18--, Rkhm Co?, wMary Saufley
David, b17--, Little Washington, Rapp Co, wAbigail Jackson
David, b18--, Shen Co?, wSarah Ann Hinks
David C, bc1860, Fred Co?, wMary Stonewall Jackson Smith
David Darius, b18--, Fauq Co?, fJohn, wElizabeth Brown
David F, b1856, Page Co, fSamuel, wEmma C Aleshire
E H, b18--, Pitt Co, wJane E Cosby
Edgar Patton, b12/12/1861, Lynchburg, Camp Co, fJohn M, mMary E Norvell, wEleanor Selden Lucke, md1903
Eliza, bc1800, fJohn, hJohn B Jones
Eliza Edmonia, bc1840, Rapp Co?, fJohn, hEdward Thompson Jones
Elizabeth, b183-, Winchester, Fred Co, fAbram, mRebecca Schultz, hWilliam S Miller
Elizabeth, bc1840, Stonewall District, Rkhm Co, fDaniel, mMary Saufley, hJohn M Kiser
Elizabeth, b185-, Page Co, fSamuel, hMarcellus Gay
Ella Brerington, b18--, Rapp Co, fBenjamin Franklin, mEusebia Browning, hSamuel Ringgold Armstrong, md11/14/1887
Emma Roberts, b18--, fHenry, hWilliam Henry Fray

MILLER (continued)
Emmett, b186-, Greene Co, fThomas A, mMargaret Eddins
Everett, b186-, Greene Co, fThomas A, mMargaret Eddins
Florence, bc1870, nrSimmonsville, Crai Co, fJohn Jefferson, mMary Wallace, hFloyd Givens
Frank, b183-, Stonewall District, Rkhm Co, fDaniel, mMary Saufley
George, b1840, Stonewall District, Rkhm Co, fDaniel, mMary Saufley wSarah Elizabeth Whitmore
Godfrey, Jr, b17--, Winchester, Fred Co, fGodfrey Mueller, Sr, mAnna Maria Kurtz
Hannah A, bc1800, Roan Co, fJohn P Kizer
H M, bc1860, Albe Co, wMary F Minor
Henry II, b17--, Rapp Co?, fHenry
Henry Co, b1842, Beaver Creek, Rkhm Co, dc1902, wHannah J Snyder
Henry Roberts, bc1850, Culp Co, fJohn Greene, mAnn C --
Ida B, b186-, Ashy District, Rkhm Co, fGeorge, mSarah Elizabeth Whitmore, hJ W Showalter
Ione Cordelia, b185-, Strasburg, Shen Co, fThomas Jefferson, mKatherine Russell, hJames Willis
Isaac, b184-, Stonewall District, Rkhm Co, fDaniel, mMary Saufley
J A, bc1860, Rkhm Co?, wJennie Myers
J G, b181-, Rapp Co, fJohn
J H, b186-, Greene Co, fThomas A, mMargaret Eddins
J W, bc1850, Shen Co?, wSarah Moore
Jackson, b181-, Rapp Co. fJohn
Jacob, bc1830, Shen Co?, wRebecca Wine
Jacob W, b17--, Woodstock, Shen Co, fChristian, w-- McGovern
James, b18--, Greene Co
James Houston, b185-, Strasburg, Shen Co, d1923, fThomas

MILLER (continued)
Jefferson, mKatherine Russell
James N, bc1840, Slate Mills, Rapp Co, fJohn Wilhoit, mPolly Blankenbaker
James Richard, b4/1817, Rapp Co, d1890, fDavid, mAbigail Jackson, wRhoda Miller
James William, b2/13/1848, Rapp Co, fJames Ricahrd, mRhoda Miller, wAda Virginia Eastham
Jane, bc1820, Rapp Co, fDavid, mAbigail Jackson
Jesse, b181-, Rapp Co, fDavid, mAbigail Jackson
Joel, bc1860, Rkhm Co?, wSallie Garber
John, b17--, Winchester, Fred Co, fGodfrey Mueller, Sr, mAnna Maria Kurtz
John, b17--, fHenry II
John, b1800, wSallie Peck
John II, b18--, fJohn
John, b181-, Rapp Co, fDavid, mAbigail Jackson
John Byron, b18--, fJohn II, wRebecca Jane Smith
John Franklin, b5/1/1870, Ashby District, Rkhm Co, fGeorge, mSarah Elizabeth Whitmore, wNellie Harper Lamb, md4/2/1901
John Godfrey, b182-, Winchester, Fred Co, fAbram, mRebecca Schultz
John Greene, b18--, Culp Co?, wAnn C --
John James, Sr, b12/24/1858, Fauq Co, fDavid Darius, mElizabeth Brown, wLucy Eldridge Lillard, md7/7/1886
John Jefferson, b18--, Crai Co, d1895, fJohn, mSallie Peck, wMary Wallace
John L, b18--, Blan Co?, wMartha Bird
John M, b10/5/1827, Cedar Forest, Pitt Co, fSamuel T, mFrances Fitzpatrick, wMary E Norvell
John R, b18--, Shen Co?, d1887, wEllen Grandstaff
John S, bc1850, Fred Co?, wFlorence Baker
John Wilhoit, b4/10/1809, Madi Co, d1905, fAdam, wPolly

MILLER (continued)
Blankenbaker Josephine, b18--, Blan Co, fJohn L, mMartha Bird, hJacob A Miller, md2/1881
Judith Terry, b18--, Rapp Co, fHenry, hFrench Pendleton Carter
Julia Mary Allen, b2/19/1852, Edinburg, Shen Co, d1910, fJohn R, mEllen Grandstaff, hMartin Luther Grove, md8/12/1872
Julius A, bc1860, Rkhm Co?, wMary Catherine Flory
Laura Parran, b18--, Jeff Co?, d1922, hDaniel Dechert
Lewis M, b183-, Winchester, Fred Co, fAbram, mRebecca Schultz
Littleton, bc1860, Nels Co?, wEmma Massie
Lucy, b18--, hJohn Hay Wood
Margaret, bc1820, Rapp Co, fDavid, mAbigail Jackson, hEdward Fletcher
Margaret, bc1840, Stonewall District, Rkhm Co, fDaniel, mMary Saufley, h-- Pence
Maria, bc1830, Winchester, Fred Co, fAbram, mRebecca Schultz, hSolon Henkel
Martha, bc1830, Winchester, Fred Co, fAbram, mRebecca Schultz, hWilliam Zirkle
Martin, b18--, Rkhm Co?, wRebecca Heatwole
Mary, bc1800, Albe Co, 1hRobert Warner Wood
Mary, b18--, hAdam G Cleek
Mary, bc1820, Shen Co, fAbram, hDavid M Kagey
Mary Catherine, b18--, Rapp Co, fWarner, hCharles B Wood
Mary E, bc1836, Slate Mills, Rapp Co, fJohn Wilhoit, mPolly Blankenbaker, hThomas Benjamin Amiss
Mary Margaret, bc1850, Rapp Co, hWashington Rucker
Matthias, b183-, Winchester, Fred Co, fAbram, mRebecca Schultz
Middleton, bc1817, Rapp Co, d1893, fJohn, wAnna L A Hubbs
Mollie A, bc1860, Goochland,

MILLER (continued)
Gooc Co, fWilliam II, mHattie Guerrant, h-- Turney
Moses A, b1928, Rkbr Co, d1887, wCassandra Fidella Sale
Nancy, b18--, Rkhm Co, hJoseph Shickel
Nannie S, b12/29/1854, Mill Brook, nrMiddletown, Shen Co, d1918, fDavid, mSarah Ann Hinks, hWilliam H Smith
Narcissus, bc1800, Goochland, Gooc Co, fWilliam
Oscar D, bc1840, Slate Mills, Rapp Co, fJohn Wilhoit, mPolly Blankenbaker
Peter, b17--, Winchester, Fred Co, fGodfrey Mueller, Sr, mAnna Maria Kurtz
Peter, b185-, Page Co, fSamuel
Peter Guerrant, b8/25/1859, Goochland, Gooc Co, fWilliam, mHattie Guerrant
Philip, b18--, Woodstock, Shen Co, fJacob W, m-- McGovern
Randolph Russell, b184-, Strasburg, Shen Co, d186-, fThomas Jefferson, mKatherine Russell
Rebecca, b17--, Winchester, Fred Co, fGodfrey Mueller, Sr, mAnna Maria Kurtz, hSolomon Henkel
Rebecca, b18--, Fred Co?, d185-1w of John Newton Bell, Sr
Rhoda, b18--, Madison Court House, Madi Co, d1871, fAdam, hJames Richard Miller
Richard, b18--, Shen Co?, wArtemissa Grandstaff
Robert A, b18--, Mont Co?, wClara A --
Sallie, b184-, Stonewall District, Rkhm Co, fDaniel, mMary Saufley, h-- Kyger
Samuel, b18--, Rkhm Co?, w-- Wine
Samuel, b1812, Page Co, fMatthias
Samuel, bc1830, Rkhm Co?, wKate Myers
Samuel Steele, b1822, nrBuffalo Forge, Rkhm Co, wCatherine Elizabeth Eads
Samuel T, b11/22/1789, Richmond, d1870, mAnn Ball, wFrances Fitzpatrick

MILLER (continued)
Thomas A, b18--, Greene Co, fJames, wMargaret Eddins
Thomas Jefferson, b18--, Woodstock, Shen Co, d1894, fJacob W, m-- McGovern, wKatherine Russell
Thomas W, b8/5/1852, Strasburg, Shen Co, d1923, fThomas Jefferson, mKatherine Russell, wIda Martha Digges, md1882
Walter C, b7/2/1855, Nels Co?, wEllen E Everett
Warner, b18--, Rapp Co, fHenry II
Warner, b181-, Rapp Co, fDavid, mAbigail Jackson
Will, bc1860, Fred Co?, wIda Orndorff
William, b17--, Powh Co?, d1846
William, b18--, wMattie Burgess
William II, b1831, Goochland, Gooc, fNarcissus, wHattie Guerrant
William A, bc1825, Cedar Forest, Pitt Co, fSamuel T, mFrances Fitzpatrick
William Eads, b12/28/1859, Buffalo Forge, Rkbr Co, fSamuel Steele, mCatherine Elizabeth Eads, wMinnie Virginia Painter
William S, bc1830, Fred Co?, wElizabeth Miller
William Thomas, b11/20/1863, Greene Co, fThomas, mMargaret Eddins, wMittie Gertrude Dovel
Willie, b18--, Fauq Co, w-- Jamison
MILLNER, J R, bc1860, Camp Co, wLoulie G Victor
MILNER, Jesse, b18--, Amhe Co?, wEmma Massie
MILLS, Ella, b18--, Buck Co, 1w of John Gilliam Friend
MILTON, Ross, bc1790, Clar Co?, wHarriet McCormick
Ross, b18--, Jeff Co, wFrances Duncan
William G, bc1850, Russ Co?, wMartha J Meade
William H, bc1870, Berryville, Clar Co, fWilliam Taylor, mFrances Duncan
William Taylor, b8/17/1836, Jeff Co, fRoss, mMargaretta McCormick, wFrances Duncan

MINGE, Anna Mercer, b18--, Ches Co?, hDavid Dunlop II
Benjamin, b18--, PrGe Co?, wJane --
Mary, b18--, PrGe Co?, fBenjamin, mJane --, hCharles Friend
MINNICH, Charles A, b18--, Bote Co
Mary E, b18--, Rkhm Co?, fJohn, hJohn William Bell
Sallie E, bc1870, Bote Co, fCharles A, hArthur Watson Hammond, md1890
MINNICK, Ezra M, Sr, b3/21/1865, Rkhm Co, wJoanna C Bowman, md4/24/1888
MINOR, --, b17--, Fair Co, hHenry Gunnell
Anne Jacquelin, bc1870, Charlottesville, Albe Co, fJohn Barbee, (2)mAnne Fisher Colston
Charles, b11/4/1810, Loui Co, fLancelott, wLucy Walker Minor
Dabney, b17--, Albe Co, fJames, 1wSarah Eliza Johnston, 2wMartha Jefferson Terrell
Diana, b17--, Spot Co?, hRichard Maury
Elizabeth B, b186-, nrCharlottesville, Albe Co, fWilliam Wardlaw, mMary Elizabeth Howe, hWarren Lee
Garret, b1679, Midd Co, fDoodes, mElizabeth Cocke, wDiane Vivian, md10/17/1706
Jane Bell, b18--, hWilliam C Dabney
John, b6/22/1707, fGarret, mDiane Vivian, wSara Carr, md11/14/1732
John, b11/18/1735, Caro Co, fJohn, mSara Carr, wElizabeth Cosby
John, b1761, Caro Co?, fJohn, mElizabeth Cosby, wLucy Landon Carter
John B, b9/5/1866, Charlottesville, Albe Co, fJohn Barbee, (2)mAnne Fisher Colton, 2h of Mary Ellen Scott, md9/1907
John B, b5/24/1852, Charlottesville, Albe Co, fCharles, mLucy Walker Minor, wVirginia Carr Minor
John Barbee, b6/13/1813, Loui

MINOR (continued)
Co, d1895, fLancelott, mMary Overton Tompkins, 1wMartha Macon Davis, 2wAnne Fisher Colston, 3wEllen T Hill
Lancelott, b1763, Caro Co?, d1848, fJohn, mElizabeth Cosby, wMary Overton Tompkins
Lucian, b1802, Loui Co, fLancelott, mMary Overton Tompkins
Malvina T, b186-, nrCharlottesville, Albe Co, fWilliam Wardlaw, mMary Elizabeth Howe, hJ A Cheate
Maria Louisa, b1817, Loui Co, hBenjamin Henry Magruder, md12/15/1836
Martha Macon, b185-, Charlottesville, Albe Co, d1897, fJohn Barbee, (2)mAnne Fisher Colston, hC Whittle Sams
Mary Berkeley, b12/2/1802, Fredericksburg, Spot Co, fJohn, mLucy Landon Carter, hWilliam Matthews Blackford, md10/12/1825
Mary F, bc1870, nrCharlottesville, Albe Co, fWilliam Laidlaw, mMary Elizabeth Howe, hH M Miller
Mary L, b18--, Bote Co?, d1908, fJohn Barbee, (1)mMartha Macon Davis
Mary Mildred, b11/19/1823, fWarner Washington, mMaria Timberlake, hJohn Pitt Lee Woodward, md10/26/1843
Raleigh Colston, b1/24/1869, Charlottesville, Albe Co, fJohn Barbee, (2)mAnne Fisher Colston, wNatalie Embra Venable, md6/8/1897
Sally Gilmer, b12/9/1839, Charlottesville, Albe Co, hBenjamin Henry Magruder
Susan Colston, bc1860, Charlottesville, Albe Co, fJohn Barbee, (2)mAnne Fisher Colston, hJohn Wilson
Warner Washington, b11/22/1792, Hano Co?, fWilliam, mMildred Gregory Lewis, mMaria Timberlake, md1/28/1819
William, b2/20/1759, Hano Co, fJohn, mElizabeth Cosby, wMildred Gregory Lewis

MINOR (continued)
William H, b186-, nrCharlottesville, Albe Co, fWilliam Wardlaw, mMary Elizabeth Howe
William W, b18--, Gale Hill, Albe Co, fDabney, (1)mSarah Eliza Johnston, wMary Waters Terrell
William Wardlaw, b2/2/1840, Albe Co, fWilliam W, mMary Waters Terrell, wMary Elizabeth Howe, md4/5/1863
MINTER, Ann, b17--, Gooc Co?, hJosiah Leake, Sr
J Willie, b18--, Math Co?, wLillian Ethelyn --
MINTERY, Mary, b17--, Meck Co, 1h-- Taylor, 2hJohn Speed, Sr
MINTON, Thoms, bc1860, Wise Co?, wLina McCarty
Virginia, b1861, nrJonesville, Lee Co, hJonathan Cass Richmond
MISKELL, Mary J, b8/15/1845, Rich Co, hFrank W Mullin
MITCHELL, --, bc1800, Bedf Co, fJames, hSamuel D Rice
Adelina Langville, b186-, Lanc Co, d1916, fW L Gungon, mAdelina Carter, 1w of Francis W Motley, md12/11/1888
Ann Tyler, b17--, Fred Co?, hJoseph Franklin Caldwell
Belva, bc1870, Fran Co, d1899, fThomas B, hJefferson D Sparrow, md1893
Henry Dudley, b17--, Clar Co, fGeorge, wMary Tuley
James, b17--, Bedf Co?, fRobin
James L, bc1850, Carr Co?, wMartha Isabella Bolen
Joseph Downman, Sr, b4/21/1864, "Ridgefield", Lanc Co, fRichard Ball, mCharlotte Belson Thornton, wLouise Estelle Morrison, md12/16/1894
Joseph Tuley, b18--, Augu Co, fhenry Dudley, mMary Tuley, wSarah Campbell
M Esther, bc1870, Gooc Co?, d1899, fTerry
Mary, b17--, Mont Co?, 2w of Abram Trigg
Richard Ball, bc1750, Lanc Co, fRobert, mHannah Ball, wMargaret Gunyon

MITCHELL (continued)
Richard Ball, b18--, Lanc Co, dc1873, fWilliam Ball, mMargaret Downman, wCharlotte Belson Thornton, md1861
Robert, b17--, fWilliam, wHannah Ball, md1746
Tuley Joseph, b1841, Fauq Co, fJoseph Tuley, mSarah Campbell, wBetty Wethered Young, md11/4/1869
W L Gunyon, b18--, Lanc Co?, wAdelina Carter
William Ball, b17--, Lanc Co, fRichard Ball, mMargaret Gunyon, wMargaret Downman
MODESITT, W Stage, bc1846, Page Co
MOFFETT, Anderson, b8/28/1744, Fauq Co, fHenry, (1)mMary Anderson
Daniel, b17--, Fauq Co?, fHenry, (2)mElizabeth Anderson, 1wElizabeth Moore, 2wMary Newman
Daniel Anderson, b185-, Culp Co, fJohn, mSarah Brown
Elizabeth, b18--, Carters Run Valley, fJohn T, 1hRobert Cockrill, 2hHorace Peyton Burgess
George Allen, b5/31/1834, nrNew Market, Shen Co, fSamuel, mHannah Bryan, wMary J Sibert, md11/28/1858
Henry, b1705, 1wMary Anderson, 2wElizabeth Anderson
Horatio Gates, Sr, b18--, Culp Co, fDaniel, (2)mMary Newman, wLucinda Brown
Horatio Gates, Jr, b185-, Rapp Co, d1916, fHoratio Gates, Sr, mLucinda Brown, wIda Stribling Menefee
John, b18--, Culp Co, fDaniel, (2)mMary Newman, wSarah Brown
John Roberts, b185-, Rapp Co, d1892, fJohn, mSarah Brown
Joseph S, b186-, Rkhm Co, fGeorge Allen, mMary J Sibert
Samuel, b17--, Rkhm Co?, fAnderson, wHannah Bryan
Samuel, b18--, Rkhm Co, wHattie Rinker
Sarah Ficklin, b185-, Culp Co, fJohn, mSarah Brown, hThomas P

MOFFETT (continued)
Brown
Thomas Anderson, bc1800, Fauq Co?, fDaniel, (1)mElizabeth Moore
Walter Franklin, b18--, Rapp Co, d1864, fHoratio Gates, Sr, mLucinda Brown
William D, b18--, Rapp Co, fHoratio Gates, Sr, mLucinda Brown
William Franklin, b18--, Rapp Co, fHoratio Gates, Sr, mLucinda Brown
William Walter, b7/19/1854, Culp Co, fJohn, mSarah Brown, wJessie Mary Dudley, md12/22/1883
MOHLER, Samuel, bc1860, Rkhm Co?, wAnnie Holler
MONCURE, Agnes Robinson, b6/6/1844, Staf Co, d1919, fRichard C L, mMary Conway, hDaniel McCarty Chichester
Annie Lilbourne, b1860, "Bowling Green", Caro Co, d1883, hPinckney Alexander Gravatt
Henry, b18--, Richmond, wJulia Warwick
Henry W, b18--, Staf Co, fHenry, mJulia Warwick
Lillie M, b18--, Staf Co, fHenry, mJulia Warwick, hPatterson Bayne
Mary B, b1849, Staf Co, hJames Ashby, Sr
Philip St Leger, b1/27/1867, "Idlewild", nrRuther Glen, Caro Co, fSt Leger Landon, mLucy George Oliver, wGrace Fortesque Terry, md11/17/1915
Richard C L, b18--, Staf Co, wMary Conway
Robert A, b7/1864, Staf Co, fHenry, mJulia Warwick, wAgnes Waller, md12/7/1888
St Leger Landon, b1833, Caro Co, d1898, fWilliam Augustus, mLucy Ann Gatewood, wLucy George Oliver
W Peyton, Sr, b1843, Staf Co, wMary J Hughes
William Augustus, b18--, Staf Co, d1862, wLucy Ann Gatewood
MONROE, Colin A, b18--, Lune Co, wMary J Stokes

258

MONROE (continued)
Edward R, b4/24/1856, Camp Co, fJohn, mPermelia McGregor, 1wIda B Tate, 2wElizabeth Hodges Edmunds
George L, b185-, Camp Co, fJohn, mPermelia McGregor
John, b18--, Hali Co?, d186-, wPermelia McGregor
Lucy, b18--, Norfolk?, hJames M May
Mary J, b184-, Camp Co, fJohn, mPermelia McGregor, hJ P Graves
Mary Kercheval, bc1870, Clar Co, fA M, hEdward Trent Robinson
Susan, bc1850, Camp Co, fJohn, mPermelia McGregor, hCarter Glass
Thomas J, b185-, Camp Co, fJohn, mPermelia McGregor
MONTAGUE, Andrew J, bc1860, KiQu Co?, wBetsie Lyons Hoskins
Catherine Elizabeth, b18--, Flanagan Mills, Cumb Co, hMadison Flanagan
Hill, b12/29/1866, Glou Co, fThomas Ball, mJosephine T Hill, wMary Mead Winston, md6/26/1894
Katherine, b16--, Midd Co?, hGeorge Twyman
Lewis, b18--, Math Co?, wRosa Young
Mary Edna, bc1870, Norfolk, fLewis, mRosa Young, 2w of Robert Andrew Folkes, md9/24/1901
Thomas Ball, Sr, b17--, Glou Co, fWilliam, mHannah Ball, 1w-- Jones, 2w-- Jones
Thomas Ball, Jr, b18--, Glou Co, fThomas Ball, Sr, m-- Jones, wJosephine T Hill
William, b17--, wHannah Ball
MONTGOMERY, Ann, b17--, PrWi Co?, hWilliam Lewis
Catherine, b17--, Wyth Co?, fJohn, hJoseph Crockett
Fanny Hayes, b18--, Rich Co, hDavid Everard Goodwyn
John, b18--, Albe Co
Rachel, b18--, hSamuel Graham
Thomas, b1838, Mint Spring, Augu Co, d1918, fJohn, wEliza-
MONTGOMERY (continued)
beth Beard
MOOMAW, Benjamin F, b18--, Daleville, Bote Co, wMary Crouse G A, bc1860, Bote Co, wDovey Layman
Harriet, b1808, Catawba Valley, Roan Co, d1908, hEllis Armstrong
John C, Sr, b1837, Bonsacks, Roan Co, d1886, fBenjamin F, mMary Crouse, 1wVirginia Graybill, 2wHonoria Elizabeth Bowman
Joseph, b18--, Bote Co?, wPolly Stover
Sallie C, b5/9/1857, Daleville, Bote Co, hBenton D Painter
Martha Ann, b184-, Catawba Valley, Roan Co, fEllis, mHarriet Moomaw
Mary Lillie, b18--, Daleville, Bote Co, fJoseph, mPolly Stover, hGeorge William Layman, md1890
W H, bc1860, Bote Co?, wSusie Huff
MOON, Andrew Floyd, Sr, b10/4/1860, Albe Co, fFleming B, wMary Alice Seay
Breckenridge, b18--, Pitt Co?, wEmma V --
Charlotte, b183-, nrScottsville, Albe Co, fEdward H, mAnna Maria Barclay
Edward H, b18--, Albe Co, wAnna Maria Barclay
Elizabeth, b17--, fJacob, hWilliam Hopkins
Fleming B, b18--, Albe Co
John B, b7/20/1849, Albe Co, d1915, fRobert B, mMary Massie, wMarion Gordon Dabney, md3/20/1878
Martha O, bc1840, Batesville, Albe Co, fSamuel O, hJohn S White
Nancy, b17--, Bedf Co, hSamuel Hancock, md2/9/1784
Orianna Russell, b8/11/1834, nrScottsville, Albe Co, d1883, fEdward H, mAnna Maria Barclay, hJohn Summerfield Andrews, md11/24/1861
Robert B, b18--, Albe Co, wMary Massie

MOORE, --, b18--, Fairview, Scot Co, wMathilda Bledsoe
Addie, b18--, Rapp Co, fGeorge, hJames William Parr, Sr
Alfred, b18--, Hamp Co, wHelen Hunter
Alice, b185-, PrWi Co, fJames H, mHarriet --, hCharles E Jordan
Allen W, b185-, PrEd Co, fSamuel III, mMary Susan Elam
Ami, b17--, Fair Co, fJeremiah, mLydia Renno, wSusan Lindsay
Ammi, Sr, b1809, Jeff Co, d1887, fFrancis, m-- Allmutt, wMary Brewer
Ammi, Jr, b5/30/1846, nrBerryville, Clar Co, fAmmi, Sr, mMary Brewer, 1wCornelia Daniel Ellett, md1873, 2wAnnie B Cabell
Anne Buller, b17--, ChCi Co, hCharles Carter
Annie Eliza, bc1870, Bath Co?, fWilliam H, mSarah Dever, hCharles Davis Lam, md8/7/1895
B S, b18--, Fauq Co?, wOrra Glascock
Bettie, b180-, nrBerryville, Clar Co, fAmmi, Sr, mMary Brewer
Cabell, b185-, PrEd Co, fSamuel II, mMary Susan Elam
Caroline, b18--, Albe Co?, hJohn White
Carr, b18--, wNannie Cabell McIlwaine
Catherine, b181-, nrBerryville, Clar Co, fAmmi, Sr, mMary Brewer
Catherine, b182-, Moores Store, Shen Co, fReuben, mSallie Kingree, hBenjamin D Wierman
Christiana, b182-, nrPleasant Valley, Rkhm Co, fJames Samuel, (2)m--, hWilliam Hughes
Cornelia, b181-, nrBerryville, Clar Co, fAmmi, Sr, mMary Brewer
Dabney, b182-, nrPleasant Valley, Rkhm Co, fJames Samuel
Edith M, b186-, Fairfax, Fair Co, fThomas, mHannah Morris, hThomas R Keith
Edward Mason, b184-, nrKenbridge, Lune Co, fThomas Gar-

MOORE (continued)
rett, mMary Catherine Laffoon
Elizabeth, b17--, Fauq Co?, 1w of Daniel Moffett
Elizabeth, bc1860, PrEd Co, fSamuel III, mMary Susan Elam
Elizabeth Catherine, b185-, Moores Store, Shen Co, fJoseph, mVirginia Moore, hJ W Koontz
Elizabeth H, b1820, Nels Co, hThomas S Carter
Elizabeth Mary, b1/1823, Moores Store, Shen Co, d186, fReuben, mSallie Kingree, hCharles Wunder
Emily G, b18--, Richmond?, hJacob Hall
Erasmus D, b18--, Norfolk?, wMargaret S --
Frances, b181-, Moores Store, Shen Co, fReuben, mSallie Kingree, hJohn Allen
Frances Margaret, b185-, Moores Store, Shen Co, fJoseph, mVirginia Moore, hLinden Allen
Francis, b17--, Fair Co, w-- Allmutt
Freddie Louise, b186-, Moores Store, Shen Co, fJoseph, mVirginia Moore, hEugene Baylor Cootes
George F, bc1850, Lune Co?, wAnna M Yates
George Samuel, b2/22/1866, Pitt Co, fCalvin J, mJane Washington Thompson, wCortelyou Strickland
George W, bc1840, Jeff Co, wLaura V Flanagan
Georgianna, b186-, Moores Store, Shen Co, fJoseph, mVirginia Moore
Glendona Eltarina, b185-, nr Kenbridge, Lune Co, fThomas Garrett, mMary Catherine Laffoon, hAdolphus Hammack
Hannah, bc1830, nrPleasant Valley, fJames Samuel, (2)m--
Helen Stuyvesant, b186-, Fairfax, Fair Co, fThomas, mHannah Morris
Henry, b17--, Char Co, fJohn
Henry, b18--, Fran Co?, wFanny
Henry Harrison, b1839, Meck Co, wSue Chandler

MOORE (continued)
James A, bc1820, nrPleasant Valley, Rkhm Co, fJames Samuel, (1)mElizabeth Messerly
James Robert, b1812, JaCi Co, fJames
Jefferson Davis, b185-, PrEd Co, fSamuel III, mMary Susan Elam
Jennie Morris, b186-, Fairfax, Fair Co, fThomas, mHannah Morris
Jeremiah, b17--, Staf Co, wLydia Renno
John, b182-, Shen Co?, fReuben, Sr, (1)mMartha McWilliams
John Holmes, b1/18/1869, Spring Creek, Rkhm Co, fJohn Horace, mRhoda Ellen Swartz, wLaura Frances Collier, md5/1893
John Horace, b1/1818, nrPleasant Valley, Rkhm Co, fJames Samuel, (1)mElizabeth Messerly, wRhoda Ellen Swartz
Joseph, b17--, Char Co, fJohn
Joseph, b1/4/1818, Moores Store, Shen Co, fReuben, mSallie Kingree, wVirginia Moore
Josephine, b186-, Moores Store, Shen Co, fJoseph, mVirginia Moore, hGeorge Hollingsworth Harrison
Josiah Staunton, b6/18/1843, Richmond, fJames Robert, mMaria L Higgins, wJane Ellen Owens, md3/6/1867
Judia, b18--, Fran Co, fHenry, mFanny --, hJohn Boon
Julia, b18--, nrCliff Mills, Fauq Co, d1920, hAndrew Jackson Parr, Sr
Julius Augustus, b2/6/1852, nr Kenbridge, Lune Co, fThomas Garrett, mMary Catherine Laffoon, wMargaret Agnes Kirk, md1/12/1882
Lawrence, b18--, wMartha Huff
Leisure, b18--, Pitt Co, hJohn Willis Shelton
Lucy P, b18--, hJoseph H Bowles
Maggie, b186-, Spring Creek, Rkhm Co, fJohn Horace, mRhoda Ellen Swartz, hGeorge Gardner
Margaret Lindsay, bc1870, Fairfax, Fair Co, fThomas, mHanna Morris

MOORE (continued)
Martha Virginia, b185-, Moores Store, Shen Co, fJoseph, mVirginia Moore, hMilton Neff
Mary, b17--, Jeff Co?, hSamuel Brown
Mary, b18--, Rapp Co?, hJames E Yates
Mary, b18--, Bedf Co?, hFrank Carpenter
Mary, b186-, Spring Creek, Rkhm Co, fJohn Horace, mRhoda Ellen Swartz, h-- Lewis
Mary B, bc1870, PrWi Co?, hJoseph F Lewis
Mary Campbell, b18--, Fauq Co?, hJohn Grigsby Beckham
Mary Frances, b1830, Suss Co, 3w of James D Howle
Mattie, b187-, Spring Creek, Rkhm Co, fJohn Horace, mRhoda Ellen Swartz, hThomas Patterson
Minerva, b18--, Carr Co?, hCreed L Hanks
Nicholas, b180-, nrBerryville, Clar Co, fAmmi, Sr, mMary Brewer
Odelia, b185-, nrKenbridge, Lune Co, fThomas Garrett, mMary Catherine Laffoon, hWilliam Jefferson Matthews
Phoebe, bc1820, Shen Co?, fReuben, (1)mMartha McWilliams, hJoshua Price
Rebecca Ann, b184-, nrKenbridge, Lune Co, fThomas Garrett, mMary Catherine Laffoon, hWilliam O Hutcheson
Reuben, b17--, Moores Store, Shen Co, fJoseph, wSallie Kingree
Reuben, Sr, b17--, Shen Co, d1859, 1wMartha McWilliams, 2wMillie Hughes
Reuben, Jr, b182-, Shen Co?, fReuben, Sr, (1)mMartha McWilliams
Richard, bc1860, PrEd Co, fSamuel III, mMary Susan Elam
Robert Beverly, b186-, Moores Store, Shen Co, fJoseph, mVirginia Moore
Robert Walton, b2/26/1859, Fairfax, Fair Co, fThomas, mHannah Morris

MOORE (continued)
Rosie Blanche, b186-, Camp Co?, fRobert W, hHomer Curtis Babcock
Samuel, b17--, Char Co, fJohn
Samuel II, b17--, Char Co?, fSamuel, mElizabeth Margaret, wSallie Howard, md3/9/1805
Samuel III, b18--, PrEd Co?, fSamuel II, mSallie Howard, wMary Susan Elam, md4/27/1853
Samuel, b182-, nrPleasant Valley, Rkhm Co, fJames Samuel, (2)m--
Samuel, b186-, Spring Creek, Rkhm Co, fJohn Horace, mRhoda Ellen Swartz, wMinnie Royer
Sarah, b10/6/1853, Char Co, d1917, hWilliam Robert Moore
Sarah, b185-, Moores Store, Shen Co, fJoseph, mVirginia Moore, hJ W Miller
Sarah E, b182, Shen Co?, fReuben, Sr, (1)mMartha McWilliams, hWilliam Gaines
Scollay, bc1850, Rapp Co?, wElvira Jett McCormick
Stanley, b186-, PrEd Co, fSamuel III, mMary Susan Elam
Susan, bc1860, PrEd Co, fSamuel III, mMary Susan Elam
Susan Lindsay, b186-, Fairfax, Fair Co, fThomas, mHannah Morris, 2w of Stephen Roszel Donohoe
Thomas, b7/7/1819, Fair Co, f1899, fAmi, mSusan Lindsay, wHannah Morris
Thomas, b182-, Shen Co, fReuben, Sr, (1)mMartha McWilliams
Thomas, b10/15/1852, Fairview, Scot Co, mMatilda Bledsoe, wAnn Maness
Thomas Earl, b4/20/1859, Moores Store, Shen Co, Joseph, mVirginia Moore
Thomas Garrett, b1823, Lune Co, d1897, fMason, wMary Catherine Laffoon
Victoria, b18--, Camp Co?, hWilliam R Crowder
Virginia, b2/25/1825, Shen Co, d1902, fReuben, Sr, (1)mMartha McWilliams, hJoseph Moore
Virginius Emilus, bc1850, nr Kenbridge, Lune Co, fThomas

MOORE (continued)
Garrett, mMary Catherine Laffoon
Walter, b18--, Pula Co?, wAlice Gitt
William H, b18--, Bath Co?, wSarah Dever
William H, bc1850, Surr Co?, wMary Frances Motley
William Henry, b185-, nrKenbridge, Lune Co, fThomas Garrett, mMary Catherine Laffoon
William O, b18--, Wyth Co?, wPage Waller Taylor
William Robert, b9/3/1854, PrEd Co, fSamuel III, mMary Susan Elam, wSarah Moore
William Thomas, b186-, Spring Creek, Rkhm Co, fJohn Horace, mRhoda Ellen Swartz, 1wMamie Zetty, 2wAda Liskey
MOORMAN, Ella, b18--, nrLynchburg, Camp Co, fThomas, hJohn Henry Parkins
Emma Walton, bc1850, Lynchburg, Camp Co, hWilliam Christopher Ivey, md12/20/1871
Lucy Clark, bc1800, Camp Co, fThomas, mLucy Clark, hTarlton Brown
James H L, b17--, wRebecca Leftwich
Rosabelle, b9/15/1846, Camp Co, fThomas J, mRosabelle Martin, hCharles S Roller, Sr, md10/26/1874
Thomas, b17--, Camp Co?, wLucy Clark
Thomas J, b18--, Camp Co?, wRosabelle Martin
Zachariah Grayson, b18--, wMartha Ann Browne, md11/24/1846
MORGAN, --, b18--, Camp Co?, hGaston Otey
Calvin, b178-, wElizabeth Trigg
Charles Stephen, b6/4/1799, nrMorgantown, Mono Co, fStephen, wAlcinda Gibson Moss
David, b17--, nrMorgantown, Mono Co, fMorgan
Julia, b18--, Fran Co?, hJohn Silas Morgan
Lizzie W, b18--, Floy Co, fWilliam H, hJohn Webb Simmons, Sr, md1887
Olive Branch, b18--, Dinw Co?,

MORGAN (continued)
wAlice Davis
Sallie, b18--, Harr Co?, hStrother Colbert
Stephen, b17--, fDavid Thomas, Jr, bc1844, Bedf Co, d1919, fThomas, Sr, wMary Virginia Burroughs
Thomas Nick, b186-, Bedf Co, fThomas, Jr, mMary Virginia Burroughs
Tolison S, b1857, Guyan, Wyom Co, d1919, fDavid, wSusan Mutters
Virginia, b4/9/1851, Richmond, fCharles Stephen, mAlcinda Gibson Moss, hJohn Enders Robinson
Willie Y, bc1860, Bushfield, West Co, wClara Walker
MORISON, George, b17--, West Co, fPeter, mElizabeth Kirkpatrick, wMary Jane Woods
Henry S K, b6/4/1846, Estilville (now Gate City), Scot Co, d1899, fHenry Addison, mLouisa Elizabeth Kane, wAnnis F Kyle
Katherine, bc1840, Estillville (now Gate City), Scot Co, fHenry Addison, mLouisa Elizabeth Kane, 2w of James B Richmond
Louise Estelle, bc1870, Scot Co, fSmith H, mMargaret Kane, hJoseph Downman Mitchell, Sr, md12/16/1894
Lucretia, bc1840, Estillville (now Gate City), Scot Co, fHenry Addison, mLouisa Elizabeth Kane, hWilliam A Blair
Manie T, c1840, Estillville (now Gate City), Scot Co, fHenry Addison, mLouisa Elizabeth Kane, hJ M Johnson
Smith H, b18--, Scot Co?, wMargaret Kane
Victoria, bc1840, Estillville (now Gate City), Scot Co, fHenry Addison, mLouisa Elizabeth Kane, hRufus A Ayers
MORRIS, --, bc1800, wMary Abia Claiborne
Alexander, b1850, Albe Co, wVirginia Allamong
Alfred, c1840, Rkhm Co?,

MORRIS (continued)
wLouisa Acker
Anne, b18--, Henry Co, fJohn T, mHairston --, 1w of John Hill Matthews, md1857
Elizabeth, b18--, nrPurcellville, Loud Co, fMahlon, mCatherine Gideon, hFenton M Love, Sr
Emma, b18--, fWarren, hL D Warren
James Benjamin, b18--, Buckingham Springs, Buck Co, d1911, fJohn G, mLouisa Croxton, wLucy Sledd Wingfield
John G, b18--, Buckingham Springs, Buck Co, fSamuel, wLouisa Croxton
John T, b18--, Henry Co?, wHairston --
M E, bc1830, Hano Co?, w-- Fleming
Mahlon, b18--, Loud Co, wCatherine Gideon
Marion, bc1840, Lee Co?, wMartha Witt
Martha Ann, b1830, Loui Co, d1870, hDaniel H Perkins
Mary Leigh, b18--, Fluv Co?, mMary Abia Clairborne, hJ Samuel Parrish
Matilda Minor, b18--, Hano Co, hMicajah Woods
William, bc1860, Farmville, PrEd Co, d1893, wEdna Gilliam
William Nathan, bc1860, Esse Co?, wCatherine Lewis
William Thomas, b18--, Math Co, d190-, wAlice Cowles Applewhaite
William Sherwood, b18--, Norfolk, fWilliam Thomas, mAlice Cowles Applewhaite
MORRISON, Frances, b1840, Clifton Forge, Alle Co, d1881, m-- Haynes, 2w of Charles Meade Stull
Harriet, b18--, Pitt Co?, hH C Clement, Sr
John C, bc1840, New Market, Shen Co, wHenrietta Helena Stirewalt
Mary Moore, b1855, Rkbr Co, hRobert S Hutcheson, Jr
Richard Grubbs, b18--, Page Co?, wAlberta Frances Woodward

MORRISON (continued)
William, bc1810, Augu Co, wMary Clinedinst
MORRISS, Garland, b18--, wElla Hillard Sutton
MORRISSETT, Beverley, b18--, wJulia Ann Delaney
Howard, b18--, Ches Co, fLawson, mMary Walker
Lawson, b1838, Ches Co, wMary Walker
Nannie, b18--, Ches Co, fLawson, mMary Walker, hGeorge H Blood
Thomas E, b18--, Ches Co, fLawson, mMary Walker
Warren, b18--, Ches Co, fLawson, mMary Walker
William Jeter, b12/29/1866, Ches Co, fLawson, mMary Walker, wHattie Augusta Nollner
MORTON, --, b17--, nrRichmond?, hThomas Hope Green
Bettie, b1836, Richmond, hWilliam Tucker Carrington
Cabell, bc1860, Char Co?, wAnnie M Williams
Elizabeth, b17--, PrEd Co, fJohn, mElizabeth Anderson, hJacob Woodson
Elizabeth, b18--, Char Co?, hJoshua Warren White
George, b18--, Oran Co, w-- Williams
James W, b1842, Culp Co, d1911, fGeorge, m-- Williams, wEmily D Harper
John, b17--, PrEd Co?, wElizabeth Anderson
Lucy Nash, b18--, Charlotte Court House, Char Co, d1904, hJohn William Eggleston
Mary, b17--, PrEd Co, fHezekiah, hLeonard W Anderson
Robert, b18--, PrEd Co?, d1923, wMildred Henry Watkins
Robert H, b18--, Char Co?, wLaura Alice Hughes
Sallie, b18--, Clarksville, Meck Co, 2w of Henry Wood, Jr, md187-
MOSBY, --, b18--, fJohn S, hRobert C Campbell
--, b186-, Richmond, fJohn A, mElizabeth, hH P Gray
Anne B, b18--, Rapp Co, fThomas

MOSBY (continued)
Yeatman, mElizabeth Maxwell Callaway, 1hMatthew James Preston Hughes Calvert, 2h Robert Taylor Stark, md1/13/1916
Charles L, b9/13/1863, Richmond, fJohn A, mElizabeth Trueheart, wCorinne Nichols, md1894
E J, b186-, Richmond, fJohn A, mElizabeth Trueheart
J A, bc1860, Richmond, d1916, fJohn A, mElizabeth Trueheart
John A, b1822, Richmond, d1899, wElizabeth Trueheart
Robert H, bc1850, Richmond, fJohn A, mElizabeth Trueheart
S B C E, b185-, Richmond, fJohn A, mElizabeth Trueheart
Thomas Yeatman, b18--, Rapp Co?, fWade, wElizabeth Maxwell Callaway
Wade, b17--, Rapp Co?, fWade
William T, bc1854, Richmond, d1894, fJohn A, mElizabeth Trueheart
MOSCHLER, Emma, b18--, Pitt Co, hGeorge Townes Rison, Sr, md1888
MOSELEY, Anne, b18--, Appo Co, hJerry Spears
Arthur, b174-, Bedf Co?, wNancy Trigg
Virginia Pearl, b18--, Sout Co, d1896, hFrank P Pope
MOSELY, Celestia, b18--, Richmond?, hGabriel Faulkner
MOSES, --, b18--, Hali Co?, hNathan Dickerson
MOSS, Alcinda Gibson, b8/28/1811, hCharles Stephen Morgan
Ann Eliza, b17--, Fair Co, fWilliam
F H, bc1860, Nels Co?, w-- Whitehead
George W, bc1850, Taze Co?, wNannie Belle Brown
Henry Clinton, b1854, Tucker Hill, West Co, fThomas, mAnna Gawan, wCharlotte Annie Thrift
Laura, b1870, wJohn Talley
Margaretta, bc1800, Fair Co, d1865, fWilliam, hProvince Mc Cormick, Sr
Nancy Boyd, bc1830, Clar Co?,

MOSS (continued)
  hWilliam David McGuire
  Thomas, b18--, West Co, wAnna Gawan
  William, b17--, Fair Co
  William A, b18--, Buck Co?, wDaisy --
MOTLEY, Anne, bc1850, nrChatham, Pitt Co, fJohn, mJoanna Watson
  Benjamin Shimer, b3/13/1859, nrCallands, Pitt Co, fDavid Samuel, mElizabeth Watson, wSallie P Farley
  Christopher, b184-, nrChatham, Pitt Co, fJohn, mJoanna Watson
  Clarence, b3/8/1843, Woodberry Farm, Rich Co, fJames L, mLouis Tod
  Claude Douglas, b18--, KiQu Co?, fJohn, mMary Coke, hW A Jones
  Daniel, b185-, nrChatham, Pitt Co, fJohn, mJoanna Watson
  David, b1797, nrChatham, Pitt Co, dc1879, wElizabeth Nichols
  David Samuel, b1/3/1831, nr Chatham, Pitt Co, d1862, fDavid, mElizabeth Nichols, wElizabeth Watson, md1850
  Edwin S, b18--, Caro Co, wElvira Thornton
  Elizabeth, b8/2/1861, nrCallands, Pitt Co, fDavid Samuel, mElizabeth Watson, hJohn W Owens
  Emeline, b18--, KiQu Co, fJohn, hWilliam Alexander Saunders
  Francis W, b11/8/1860, Woodberry Farm, Rich Co, fJames L, mLouisa Tod, 1wAdelina Langville Mitchell, md12/11/1888, 2wElma Jones, md6/29/1918
  Hartwell, b184-, nChatham, Pitt Co, fJohn, mJoanna Watson
  James Abel, b9/27/1851, nrCallands, Pitt Co, fDavid Samuel, mElizabeth Watson
  James L, b10/14/1816, KiQu Co, d1893, fJohn, mFrances Watts, wLouisa Tod
  James S, b3/5/1845, Woodberry Farm, Rich Co, d1914, fJames L, mLouisa Tod, wEmma Leonard
  Joanna, b185-, nrChatham, Pitt Co, fJohn, mJoanna Watson
  John, b17--, wFrances Watts

MOTLEY (continued)
  John, b18--, Pitt Co, fJoseph, mPolly Jones, wJoanna Watson
  John, bc1820, KiQu Co, d186-, fJohn, mFrances Watts, wMary Coke
  John, bc1850, nrChatham, Pitt Co, fJohn, mJoanna Watson
  John George, b1/5/1847, Woodberry Farm, Rich Co, d1922, fJames L, mLouisa Tod
  Joseph, b17--, Pitt Co, fDavid, wPolly Jones
  Julien Coke, b18--, KiQu Co, fJohn, mMary Coke
  Levi, b185-, nrChatham, Pitt Co, fJohn, mJoanna Watson
  Mary, bc1850, nrChatham, Pitt Co, fJohn, mJoanna Watson
  Mary Frances, b185-, nrCallands, Pitt Co, fDavid Samuel, mElizabeth Watson, hWilliam H Moore
  Matilda Frances, bc1850, nr Chatham, Pitt Co, d1922, fJohn, mJoanna Watson, hJohn Marion Shelton
  Phoebe Ann, b2/6/1857, nrCallands, Pitt Co, fDavid Samuel, mElizabeth Watson, hJ M Jeffries
  Sarah Elizabeth William, b18--, Pitt Co, hThomas Jefferson Shelton
  Thomas H, b1840, Guinea, Caro Co, fEdwin S, mElvira Thornton, wKate Jessee
  Washington, bc1830, nrChatham, Pitt Co, fDavid, mElizabeth Nichols
MOULTON, Sarah Elizabeth, b5/8/1849, Davis' Mills, Bedf Co, d1914, fBenjamin Hammond, hThomas Key Phelps
MOWERY, Barbara, b18--, Shen Co?, hAdam Sine
MOYERS, --, bc1840, Shen Co, wSue E Henkel
  Emma C, bc1858, Pend Co, hJohn M Stone
  Henry, b18--, Hard Co
  Mary, b1839, Hard Co, fHenry, hHenry Wittig
MULLENS, Sarah, bc1830, nrHolly Creek, Wise Co, 1w of Francis B Greear

MULLIN, Elizabeth M, bc1870, Rich Co, fFrank W, mMary J Miskell, hGeorge R Northam
James T, b1853, Jane, Buch Co, fPreston, mSallie Colley, wElizabeth Branham
Lucy, b18--, Henry Co, fHenry, hCalvin Matthews
Mary Jane, b186-, Fran Co, hElkanah Prillaman
Minnie, b18--, Norfolk?, fJohn, mEmily Garrison, hWilliam Bankhead Meredith
Preston, b1838, Buch Co, d1913, fJames, wSallie Collie
Rosa, b18--, nrPound, Wise Co, 3w of Marcus D Lafayette Dotson, Sr
MUNCY, --, b17--, Taze Co?, hElkanah Wynn
MUNDIE, Mary, b18--, KiWi Co, hDandridge Sale
MUNDY, James A, Jr, bc1860, Buck Co?, fJames A, Sr, wAnnie C Johnson
William P, bc1860, Russ Co?, wTiney Finney
MUNFORD, Thomas Taylor, b3/29/1831, Richmond, fGeorge Wythe
MUNSEY, Elsie, b1826, nrStraffordsville, Gile Co, d1911, hJames Wagner
MURPHY, James C, b183-, Wash Co?, wNannie Byrd Trigg
Nancy, b1812, Cherry Hill, Broo Co, hAlexander Gustavus Scott Brown
Robert, bc1860, Fauq Co?, 2h of Mary Tayloe
MURRAY, Alfred, b6/30/1796, Fauq Co, fReuben, mCatherine Chinn
Alice, b185-, Fauq Co, fJames Enoch, (2)mJane (Welch) O'Bannon
Alice, b186-, Fauq Co, fE Milton, mVirginia Welch, hHarry A Fellows
Alsey Newton, b6/24/1798, Fauq Co, fReuben, mCatherine Chinn, hJohn M Luckett
Anna Maria, b18--, hJohn Mason
Anna Rachel, b7/12/1864, Fauq Co, fE Milton, mVirginia Welch, hDaniel W Swart, md12/1/1886
Enoch Mellon, bc1837, Fauq Co,

MURRAY (continued)
fJames Enoch, (1)m--
E Milton, b1834, Fauq Co, wVirginia Welch
Elizabeth McG, b186-, Fauq Co, fE Milton, mVirginia Welch, hThomas L Frost
Eva, b186-, Fauq Co, fE Milton, mVirginia Welch, hGeorge Davis
Ida, b186-, Fauq Co, fE Milton, mVirginia Welch, hT Henderson Maddux
James Enoch, b11/10/1801, Fauq Co, fReuben, mCatherine Chinn, 2wJane (Welch) O'Bannon
James W, bc1870, Fauq Co, fE Milton, mVirginia Welch
Lila, b186-, Fauq Co, fE Milton, mVirginia Welch, hLawrence Brent
Robert, b8/9/1850, nrThe Plains, Fauq Co, fJames Enoch, (2)mJane (Welch) O'Bannon
Reuben, b1762, wCatherine Chinn
Reuben J, b183-, Fauq Co, fJames Enoch, (1)m--
Theodosia Earnest, bc1870, Bote Co, fJ P, hJames H Scott, md1888
Virginia, b186-, Fauq Co, fE Milton, mVirginia Welch
MURRELL, Jennie, b17--, Albe Co?, hRobert Page
John D, bc1850, Richmond?, wMildred Powell Whitehead
MUSE, Asburina, b1/25/1832, nrBethel, Fred Co, hSamuel Jackson Smith
Henry Lawson, b12/12/1788, fThomas, mElizabeth Tidwell, wElizabeth Swanson, md12/5/1816
Julia Ann, b1/2/1824, Fran Co, fHenry Lawson, mElizabeth Swanson, hWilliam Leftwich Turner Hopkins
Lillie R, b1859,Black Creek District, Fred Co, fWade, mVirginia Dinges, hHugh Boyd Kline
Margaret Jane, b1/26/1884, nr Cave Spring, Roan Co, hStephen Wright
Wade, b18--, Fred Co, wVirginia Dinges
William J, b186-, wMinnie C

MUSE (continued)
Garvin
MUSICK, Gordon, b18--, Russ Co?, wMelissa Stinson
MUSTARD, Sallie Ann, b18--, Blan Co, d1913, hSanders M Hamilton
MUSTOE, Robert L, b186-, Falling Springs Valley, Bath Co, fAnthony, wBessie Moore
MUTTERS, Susan, b1860, Merc Co, hTolison S Morgan
MYERS, A Jackson, b184-, nrTimberville, Rkhm Co, fBenjamin, (2)m-- Fatic
Annie, bc1841, nrTimberville, Rkhm Co, fBenjamin, (2)m-- Fatic, hSamuel H Driver
Barton, Sr, b18--, Norfolk, fMoses, mJulianna Grammar Barton, wKatherine Mackey Baldwin
Benjamin, b180-, Rkhm Co, fSamuel, mBarbara Wine, 1w-- Hoover, 2w-- Fatic
Benjamin Allen, bc1843, nrTimberville, Rkhm Co, fBenjamin, (2)m-- Fatic, wSallie Garber
Betty, bc1830, Rkhm Co, d1907, 2w of Tobias Weller
C W, bc1846, Pitt Co, d1918, wEliza A Owen
Catherine, bc1829, Rkhm Co?, d1889, fBenjamin, (1)m-- Hoover, hJohn W Driver
Catherine, b1850, hGeorge W Pullen
Christian, bc1810, Rkhm Co, fIsaac, wMary Kline
Clara, bc1870, Green Mont, Rkhm Co, fIsaac C, mHannah Ralston, hWill Swank
Edna, bc1870, Rkhm Co, fBenjamin Allen, mSallie Garber, hS L Bowman
Emma, bc1870, Green Mount, Rkhm Co, fIsaac C, mHannah Ralston, 1hCarr Spitzer, 2hIsaac Hoover
Florence E, b186-, Fred Co?, fWilliam H, mMary J Harman
Gasper, Sr, b17--, Rkhm Co, w-- Shoemaker
Gasper, Jr, b182-, Augu Co, fGasper, Sr, m-- Shoemaker
Hannah, b18--, Shen Co, hSamuel Garber
Hannah, b183-, Green Mount, Rkhm Co, fChristian, mMary

MYERS (continued)
Kline, hConrad Rodeffer
Henry, bc1820, Augu Co, fGasper, Sr, m-- Shoemaker
Isaac C, b2/8/1839, Green Mount, Rkhm Co, fChristian, mMary Kline, wHannah E Ralston
Isaac, bc1820, Augu Co?, wRachel Shaver
James, bc1810, Rkhm Co, fIsaac
James O, b186-, Rkhm Co, fBenjamin Allen, mSallie Garber
Jennie, b186-, Green Mount, Rkhm Co, fIsaac C, mHannah Ralston, hJ A Miller
John, b181-, Augu Co, fGasper, Sr, m-- Shoemaker
John, bc1830, Warr Co?, wMary Jane Henry
John H, bc1870, Fred Co?, fWilliam H
John W, b12/21/1868, Green Mount, Rkhm Co, fIsaac C, mHannah Ralston, wLizzie S Wampler, md5/10/1890
Joseph G, b9/1852, Rkhm Co, fRudolf, mEveline Cromer, wMary Graham, md1/13/1880
Julia Ann, bc1820, Augu Co, fGasper, Sr, m-- Shoemaker, h-- Thompson
Kate, b183-, Green Mount, Rkhm Co, fChristian, mMary Kline, hSamuel Miller
Katie, bc1810, Rkhm Co, fIsaac, h-- Wampler
Lizzie, bc1830, Green Mount, Rkhm Co, fChristian, mMary Kline, hMartin Berry
Lucy Ellen, b18--, nrHamilton, Loud Co, hRobert James Nelson Reid
Mantie, b185-, Rkhm Co, fRudolf, mEveline Cromer, hR H Dudley
Margaret, bc1820, Augu Co, fGasper, Sr, m-- Shoemaker, hAbram Beaver
Martha, b183-, Green Mount, Rkhm Co, fChristian, mMary Kline, hJohn Kline
Mary, bc1800, Wyth Co, hMartin Kegley
Mary, bc1820, Augu Co, fGasper, Sr, m-- Shoemaker, 2w of Jacob Houseman

MYERS (continued)
Mary S, b186-, Fred Co?, fWilliam H, mMary J Harman, hJ William Taylor
Michael, bc1830, Green Mount, Rkhm Co, fChristian, mMary Kline
Moses, b4/27/1817, Norfolk, d1881, fSamuel, mLouisa Marx, wJulianna Grammar Barton
Nora, b186-, Green Mount, Rkhm Co, fIsaac C, mHannah Ralston, hB F Miller
Peter, bc1810, Rkhm Co, fIsaac
Polly, bc1810, Rkhm Co, fIsaac
R E Lee, bc1860, Rkhm Co, fRudolf, mEveline Cromer
Raphael, b184-, nrTimberville, Rkhm Co, fBenjamin, (2)m-- Fatic
Rudolf, bc1822, Augu Co, fGasper, Sr, m-- Shoemaker, wEveline Cromer
St A, b185-, Rkhm Co, fRudolf, mEveline Cromer
Samuel, b17--, Shen Co, fChristian, mBarbara Burkholder, wBarbara Wine
Samuel, bc1810, Rkhm Co, fIsaac
Samuel, b181-, Augu Co, fGasper, Sr, m-- Shoemaker
Samuel H, b182-, Rkhm Co, fBenjamin, (1)m-- Hoover
Susanna, b18--, Shen Co, hJacob Good
W F, bc1860, Rkhm Co, wMaggie L Hawse
William, b181-, Augu Co, fGasper, Sr, m-- Shoemaker
William H, b18-, Fred Co?, wMary J Hartman
William H, b185-, Rkhm Co, fRudolf, mEveline Cromer
NALLE, Lucetta, b18--, Madi Co, hGeorge Bouton
Sarah Ellen, b1812, Culp Co, hGarrett Scott
NANCE, Benjamin A, b18--, ChCi Co, fZachariah, wSusan E Stagg
Eaton, b17--, ChCi Co, fJames
Eaton II, b18--, ChCi Co, fZachariah
L M, b10/30/1857, nrRoxbury, ChCi Co, fBenjamin A, mSusan E Stagg, wEdmonia Taylor
Zachariah, bc1800, ChCi Co,

NANCE (continued)
fEaton
NAPIER, --, b17--, Camp Co?, hTarlton Brown
NASH, Ann, b17--, fJohn, hThomas Haskins
Anna, b17--, PrEd Co, fJohn, mElizabeth Fisher, hAndrew Johnston
H M, b18--, Fran Co, fThomas
John, b17--, PrEd Co, wElizabeth Fisher
Lydia, b18--, Fran Co, d1923, fThomas, hPeter H Dillard, md11/6/1872
Martha J, b1835, Russ Co, d1920, hSamuel Blackwell
Thomas, b18--, Fran Co
NAYLOR, Leacy Ann, b18--, fWilliam, mAnne Sanford, 1w of Angus Mac Donald II
NEAL, Armstead, b18--, Amel Co, wEliza Williams
Cornelia, bc1836, Bote Co?, d1820, hJoseph Hannah
Lucy Carter, bc1843, Pitt Co, fThomas David, mLouisiana Franklin Carter, hPeter William Ferrell, md1862
Margaret Ellen, b1843, Roan Co, fArmstead, mEliza Williams, hGeorge Madison Pitzer, Sr
Sallie Ann, b18--, Wise Co, hJ Hopkins Hamilton
Sarah, b18--, Clar Co?, hWilliam McCormick
Thomas David, b18--, Pitt Co, wLouisiana Franklin Carter
NEALE, Emma, b18--, Cedar Lane Farm, KiWi Co, hCincinnatus Garrett
Hannah, b17--, fChristopher, hWilliam Brent
R Milton, bc1850, Lanc Co?, wHarriet Elizabeth Lewis
NEBLETT, Rebecca, b17--, Lune Co, hJoseph Hutcheson
NEEB, Elizabeh, b185-, nrWoodstock, Shen Co, fJacob, mMary Coverstone
John William, b7/13/1855, nr Woodstock, Shen Co, fJacob, mMary Coverstone, wAnna Catherine Saum, md10/25/1886
NEEL, Harriett Williams, b18--, Blan Co, fRobert, mRebecca

NEEL (continued)
Waggoner, hDaniel Alexander Walker
Nannie E, b18--, Dick Co, hBart E Colley
Robert, b17--, Blan Co?, fThomas, mEllen McFarlane, wRebecca Waggoner
Thomas, b17--, Augu Co?, wEllen McFarlane
NEELY, Sarah, b17--, Augu Co?, hWilliam McClanahan
NEFF, --, b17--, Shen Co?, hAbraham Kagey
Barbara, bc1800, Shen Co?, hJacob Kagey
Daniel, b18--, Rkhm Co?, wElizabeth Garber
David, bc1840, Shen Co, wBird Funkhouser
Elizabeth, b1826, Rkhm Co, hSamuel Brenaman
Malinda, b18--, Rkhm Co?, d1922, fDaniel, mElizabeth Garber, hSamuel R Hoover, md1/1872
Margaret, b18--, Rkhm Co, hDaniel Bowman
Milton, bc1850, Shen Co?, wMartha Virginia Moore
Sarah Ellen, b1844, Wyth Co, d1915, hJohn Jacob Etter
Susannah, b18--, Shen Co?, hJacob Wine
NEGLEY, Elizabeth, b17--, Shen Co?, hPaul Henkel
NEIGHBOURS, Elizabeth, b18--, Camp Co, fJames, hJohn L Johnson
James, b17--, Camp Co
NEIKERK, Sallie, b2/1868, Mouth of Wilson, Gray Co, hDavid Pearson Hurley
NELMS, --, b18--, Bedf Co, 1h of Malinda Perkins
John E, b18-, Nhld Co?, wAnnie Brown
Mary C, b11/12/1855, Isle Co, hJohn Hopkins Hall, Sr
NELSON, Charlotte C, bc1870, Fauq Co?, fGeorge Washington, Jr, mMary Nelson Scollay, h-- Holt
Edwin, b18--, Rkhm Co, wElizabeth Weedon
Elizabeth Burwell, b182-, fWil-

NELSON (continued)
liam, mElizabeth Burwell, hJohn Page
Elizabeth W, bc1870, Brentsville, PrWi Co, fEdwin, mElizabeth Weedon, hAustin Ogilvie Weedon, md11/3/1893
Fannie P, b17--, Yorktown, York Co, fThomas, Jr, mLucy Armistead, hJohn Spotsford Wellford, Sr, md1807
Frank, b6/25/1767, Yorktown, York Co, fThomas, mLucy Grymes, wLucy Page
George Washington, Jr, b5/1840, ChCi Co, fGeorge Washington, Sr, wMary Nelson Scollay
Harry Lee, bc1870, Fauq Co?, fGeorge Washington, Jr, mMary Nelson Scollay
Hugh, b9/30/1768, Yorktwn, York Co, fThomas, mLucy Grymes, wEliza Kinloch, md1799
Hugh M, Sr, bc1800, York Co, fFrank, mLucy Page, w-- Holker
Hugh M, Jr, b10/31/1847, "Long Branch", Fred Co, fHugh M, Sr, m-- Holker, wSallie Page Nelson, md4/22/1885
Hugh Thoms, b18--, Albe Co, fRobert William, mVirginia L Nelson, wMary Gilliam, md1871
James E, bc1870, Brentsville, PrWi Co, fEdwin, mElizabeth Weedon
James Richard, bc1800, Culp Co, wElizabeth Bywaters
John H, bc1870, Brentsville, PrWi Co, fEdwin, mElizabeth Weedon
John K, b18--, Rkhm Co
Lucy, b18--, Loui Co, hChiswell Barrett Winston
Lucy, b17--, fThomas, mLucy Grymes, hCarter Page
Maria Russell, b18--, Esse Co?, hJohn H Jones
Mary, b17--, York Co?, hEdmund Berkeley
Mary, b18--, Culp Co, fJames Richard, mElizabeth Bywaters, hBurrell Richard Luttrell
Nannie, b18--, KiWi Co, hOctavus Madison Winston
Patsy B, b1843, Loud Co, hCharles Reed

NELSON (continued)
Paul, bc1870, Brentsville, PrWi Co, fEdwin, mElizabeth Weedon
Philip, b17--, Yorktown, York Co, fThomas, w-- Burwell
Robert William, b1822, Albe Co, fHugh, mLucy Grymes, wVirginia L Nelson
Salle, b1834, Modestown, Acco Co, hSouthy Mason
Sallie Page, bc1800, fFrank, mLucy Grymes, hSamuel Scollay
Sallie Page, bc1867, Fauq Co?, fGeorge Washington, Jr, mMary Nelson Scollay, hHugh M Nelson, Jr
Susan, b17--, fThomas, mLucy Grymes, hFrancis Page
Thomas, b17--, Yorktown, York Co, fThomas, mLucy Grymes, 1h of Frances Page
Thomas, Jr, b17--, York Co?, fThomas, Sr, wFannie P Nelson
Thomas, b12/26/1738, Yorktown, York Co, fWilliam, mElizabeth Burwell, wLucy Grymes, md6/29/1762
Thomas Crease, b186-, Fauq Co?, fGeorge Washington, Jr, mMary Nelson Scollay
Virginia L, b17--, fThomas, hRobert William Nelson
William, b1711, Yorktown, York Co, fThomas, (1)mMargaret Reid, wElizabeth Burwell, md2/1738
NESTER, Letitia, b1868, Willis, Carr Co, hWilliam Preston Martin
NEVIT, Dwight, bFauq Co?, wMary Henrietta Cochran
NEVITT, Ben F, b18--, Fair Co, fHenry C, mAnn Louise Hutton
Henry C, b182-, Fair Co?, wAnn Louise Hutton
NEW, Sara, b17--, Henrico Co, fWilliam, mPatience Russell, hWilliam Cocke, md1779
William, b17--, Henrico Co?, wPatience Russell
NEWBERRY, Elizabeth, b17--, Bedf Co, hJohn Baldwin
Esther, b1845, Coeburn, Wise Co, hGeorge W Bond
Mary E, b12/1832, Blan Co, d192-, hWilliam H Bond

NEWBILL, Charles B, b185-, Esse Co, fWilliam Gresham, mCatherine Seward
Christopher F, b18--, Esse Co, wHenrietta Beckwith
H Logan, bc1850, Esse Co, fWilliam Gresham, mCatherine Seward
Hopie, b18--, Fran Co?, hE H Poindexter
William Gresham, b1822, Esse Co, d1909, wCatherine Seward
William J, b12/1846, Esse Co, fWilliam Gresham, mCatherine Seward, wAnnie Elizabeth Cauthorn
NEWCOMB, Benjamin Carr, b18--, Glou Co, d1900, wMartha J Coleman
Charles, bc1830, Fred Co?, wCaroline Hillyard
John, bc1850, Midd Co?, wMary E Segar
Susan B, b18--, Albe Co, hPleasant Langford, Jr
NEWCOMBE, --, bc1800, Fred Co?, wNancy Gardner
NEWELL, --, b18--, Loud Co?, 1h of Rebecca Jane Elgin
Isabella Eagan, bc1800, Bedf Co?, fThomas, mNancy Harvey, hRichard Davis Watts
Mary, b18--, Richmond?, hWilliam Kidd
Thomas, b17--, Bedf Co?, wNancy Harvey
NEWHOUSE, Frances, b18--, Fauq Co, hPeyton Burgess
Silas Mortimer, b18--, Culp Co?, fSilas Henry, w-- Rixey
NEWLAND, Anna, bc1860, Shen Co, fIsrael, mSusan Rinker, h-- Clinedinst
Ella, b8/24/1866, Shen Co, fIsrael, mSusan Rinker, hHarrison Lindamood
Israel, b18--, Shen Co, wSusan Rinker
Mary, bc1860, Shen Co, fIsrael, mSusan Rinker, h-- Cooper
Rebecca, b12/3/1862, Shen Co, fIsrael, mSusan Rinker, hGeorge Elkanah Irvin, md10/6/1890
Richard, bc1860, Shen Co, fIsrael, mSusan Rinker

NEWMAN, Annie, bc1840, New Market, Shen Co, fWalter, mCaroline Rice, h-- Cline
Benjamin Pennybacker, bc1824, New Market, Shen Co, fWalter, mCharlotte Henrietta Pennybacker, wElizabeth Hickman
Beulah B, bc1870, Augu Co, fJoseph, hSamuel B Harper, md1891
Caroline Mary, b7/23/1862, Liberty Furnace, Shen Co, fBenjamin Pennybacker, mElizabeth Hickman, hMark Bird Wunder, md10/18/1883
Edgar Douglas, b3/26/1854, Woodstock, Shen Co, fBenjamin Pennybacker, mElizabeth Hickman, wMary W Walton
Edmund Walter, bc1870, nrEllerson, Hano Co, fWilliam W, mFrances Edmonia Crenshaw
Edward, b184-, New Market, Shen Co, fWalter, mCaroline Rice
Emma, b184-, New Market, Shen Co, fWalter, mCaroline Rice, hHugh Danner
Isaac, bc1800, Pt Pleasant, Maso Co, fWilliam Walter
John, bc1840, New Market, Shen Co, fWalter, mCaroline Rice
Mary, b17--, Fauq Co?, 2w of Daniel Moffett
Mary Elizabeth, b1824, Crabbottom, High Co, hCornelius Colaw, md1845
Mary T, bc1844, New Market, Shen Co, d1915, fWalter, mCaroline Rice, hGeorge Williams Koontz
Sallie Phoebe, b3/3/1856, Harrisonburg, Rkhm Co, fW N, hCallom B Jones, md1/29/1855
Samuel, bc1849, New Market, Shen Co, d1889, fWalter, mCaroline Rice
Thomas, b1843, York Co, d1902, wMartha Wynne
W T, bc1860, Bedf Co, wLelia B Overstreet
Walter, b18--, nrNew Market, Shen Co, wCaroline Rice
Walter, b185-, Liberty Furnace, Shen Co, fBenjamin Pennybacker, mElizabeth Hickman
William Crenshaw, b3/10/1869,

NEWMAN (continued)
nrEllerson, Hano Co, fWilliam W, mFrances Edmonia Crenshaw, wAnn Coleman Sydnor, md11/5/1905
William W, b1824, Point Pleasant, Maso Co, fIsaac, wFrances Edmonia Crenshaw, md1867
NEWTON, Edward Colston, b4/4/1849, Linden Farm, West Co, d1913, fWilloughby IV, mMary Stevenson Brockenbrough, wLucy Yates
Edward Marshall, b10/19/1870, Markham, Fauq Co, fWilloughby V, mBessie Lewis Marshall, 1w Elizabeth Yates, md11/3/1898, 2wJuliet (Beckham) Yates, md6/27/1918
James Keith Marshall, b186-, Markham, Fauq Co, d1899, fWilloughby V, mBessie Lewis Marshall, wMaie Nelms
John Brockenbrough, Sr, b2/7/1840, Linden, West Co, d1897, fWilloughby IV, mMary Stevenson Brockenbrough, wRoberta Page Williamson
John Brockenbrough, Jr, bc1870, fJohn Brockenbrough, Sr, mRoberta Page Williamson, wLaura Neal, md1890
Judith White, bc1840, Linden, West Co, fWilloughby IV, mMary Stevenson Brockenbrough, hEdwin Claybrook
Mary, b18--, Alexandria, hRobert Harper
Mary Willoughby, b186-, Markham, Fauq Co, fWilloughby V, mBessie Lewis Marshall, hClaude Baxley
May, bc1840, Linden, West Co, fWilloughby IV, mMary Stevenson Brockenbrough, h-- Smith
Rebecca, b186-, Markham, Fauq Co, fWilloughby V, mBessie Lewis Marshall
Robert Murphy, b184-, Linden, West Co, fWilloughby IV, mMary Stevenson Brockenbrough
Sarah, b18--, West Co, hThomas Brown
Thomas, b1678, West Co, fJohn, mRose ( ) Gerrard, 2wElizabeth Starke, md1702, 1w-- Allerton

NEWTON (continued)
William B, b183-, Linden, West Co, d186-, fWilloughby IV, mMary Stevenson Brockenbrough
William Brockenbrough, bc1870, fJohn Brockenbrough, Sr, mRoberta Page Williamson, wMary Shields
Willoughby, bc1702, West Co, fThomas, (1)m-- Allerton, wSarah Eskridge
Willoughby II, b17--, West Co, fWilloughby, mSarah Eskridge, wElizabeth --
Willoughby III, b17--, West Co, fWilloughby II, mElizabeth --, 2h of Sally Bland (Poythress) Lee
Willoughby IV, b1802, West Co, d1875, fWilloughby III, mSally Bland (Poythress) Lee, wMary Stevenson Brockenbrough, md 1829
Willoughby V, b1837, Linden, West Co, fWilloughby IV, mMary Stevenson Brockenbrough, wBessie Lewis Marshall
NICHOLAS, Abe, bc1830, Shen Co?, wElizabeth Baker
Jane Hollis, b17--, Albe Co, hThomas Jeffeson Randolph
William, bc1850, Albe Co?, wMary E Page
NICHOLS, Corinne, bc1870, Richmond?, fJames L, mMary --, hCharles L Mosby, md1894
Edward West, b6/27/1858, Petersburg, Dinw Co, fJames Nathaniel, mAnne Wynn, 1w Edmonia L Waddell, md10/28/1886, 2wEvelyn Junkin Rust, md11/14/1905
Elizabeth, bc1800, Pitt Co, hDavid Motley
Elizabeth, b1848, Loud Co, hClinton C Adams
Florence, bc1870, Camp Co?, d1896, fWilliam E, mSarah Woodall, 1w of Robert Chiles Beazley, Sr, md1892
H W, bc1850, Bedf Co?, wJennie D Wilson
James L, b18--, Rich Co?, wMary
James Nathaniel, b18--, PrGe Co?, wAnne Wynn
Mary S, b1/15/1850, Hali Co,

NICHOLS (continued)
hPeter P Nichols
Peter P, b12/31/1846, nrCrystal Hill, Hali Co, fWilliam, m-- Palmer, wMary S Nichols
Rachel, b17--, Loud Co, fIsaac, hJames Hoge
William, b18--, Hali Co, fJerry, w-- Palmer
William E, b18--, Camp Co?, wSarah Woodall
NICHOLSON, Julia Ann, b18--, Wakefield, Suss Co, hBenjamin Franklin Jarratt
NICKELS, James, Jr, b1807, Nickelsville, Scot Co, d1895, fJames, Sr, wFannie Godsey
John G, b18--, Scot Co, wLou E Hartsock
Joseph T, b1869, nrWood, Scot Co, fStephen J, mLucy Anne Gray
Nannie Jackson, bc1870, Scot Co, d1908, fJohn G, mLou E Hartsock, 1w of Robert M Addington, md10/21/1893
Stephen J, b10/14/1839, nrNickelsville, Scot Co, d1912, fJames, Sr, mFannie Godsey, wLucy Ann Gray
William Barlow, b18--, Scot Co, fWilliam
William Henderson, b3/1/1833, Scot Co, d1916, fWilliam Barlow, wElizabeth Duff
William W, b180-, nrNickelsville, Scot Co, fJames, Sr
NICOL, Sallie Warner, b18--, Madi Co, hHorace Davis Twyman, md8/17/1871
NIMMO, Emma S, b186-, ChCi Co, hJames E Hubbard
NININGER, Sarah, bc1829, Bote Co?, d1880, hDavid Huff
NIXON, -- b18--, Loud Co?, 1h of Rebecca Jane Elgin
NOBLIN, Alexander, b1834, Meck Co, d1897, wElizabeth Virginia Chandler, md1866
NOCK, --, b18--, Acco Co, 1w of Edwin Thomas Powell, Sr
NOEL, Eliza Jones, b18--, Esse Co?, fEdwin F, hJohn Wright
NOELL, --. b186-, Bedf Co, fAlbert L, Sr, mEliza E Turpin, hC L Jones

NOELL (continued)
--, bc1870, Bedf Co, fJ M, mEliza Turpin, hE G Hirons
Albert L, Jr, b8/5/1864, Bedf Co, fAlbert L, Sr, mEliza E Turpin, wCarrie H Smith
Albert L, Sr, bc1830, Bedf Co, d186-, 1h of Eliza E Turpin
Demstrice Ann, b18--, fJohn C, hFrancis Marion Barker
J M, bc1830, Bedf Co, d1910, 2h of Eliza Turpin
James D, b18-, Hali Co?, fJames, wVirginia Penick
William Young, b12/5/1854, Hali Co, fJames D, mVirginia Penick, wHattie B Lovelace, md1878
NOFFSINGER, Charles T, b18--, Bote Co, fSamuel, (1)mBettie Joplin
Ida L, b18--, Bote Co, fSamuel, (1)mBettie Joplin, hGeorge W Saville
Samuel, b1816, Fincastle, Bote Co, d1892, 1wBettie Joplin, 2wHettie M Owen
William, b18--, Bote Co, fSamuel, (1)mBettie Joplin
NOLLEY, Emmett W, b4/29/1845, Clarksville, Meck Co, wJulia McN Tolar
George M, b1860, Richmond, fGeorge W, mEmily Clenshaw, wMargaret H McCue
George W, b18--, Richmond?, wEmily Clenshaw
NOLLINER, Hattie Augusta, b3/6/1861, Petersburg, Dinw Co, hWilliam Jeter Morrissett
NOLTING, Emil O, b18--, Richmond?, wSusan Horne
NOLTON, Julia, b18--, Fred Co?, hIsaac Hamilton Faulkner
NORFLEET, E S, b186-, Nans Co, wRosa M Rawls
NORMAN, Keziah, b17--, hJohn Staples
Lucy, b17--, PrWi Co?, hSeymour Lynn
NORMENT, Robert L, bc1860, Richmond?, wMiriam Boykin
NORRIS, Mary Kelly, b181-, Albe Co, d185-, 1w of Egbert Read Watson, md9/3/1833
Opie, b1821, nrLively, Lanc Co,

NORRIS (continued)
d1863, wMartha Ellen Kidd
Robert Opie, Sr, b12/10/1854, "Lively Oak", nrLively, Lanc Co, fOpie, mMartha Ellen Kidd, wAlice Chilton
NORSWORTHY, Nettie D, bc1870, Norfolk?, hThomas S Southgate
NORTHAM, Sallie W, b18--, Onancock, Acco Co, d1921, fThomas A, mVernetta Ann Hinman, 1w of George Goodwyn Joynes, Sr, md11/25/1880
Thomas A, b18--, Acco Co, wVernetta Ann Hinman
NORTHERN, Ida, b1857, Midd Co, hWeston Bristow, Sr
NORTHRUP, Carrie Belle, b18--, Falls Church, Fair Co, fEli J, mCandace A Barnes, hMerton Elbridge Church
NORVELL, Emeline, b18--, Camp Co, hJames M Langhorne
Lorenzo, bc1800, Camp Co?, wLucy Harrison
Mary E, b183-, Lynchburg, Camp Co, fLorenzo, mLucy Harrison, hJohn M Miller
NOTTINGHAM, Edward Fitchett, b1861, Eastville, Nhtn Co, fThomas Henry, m-- Fitchett, wMargaret Harmanson
Fannie Cowles, b18--, Fauq Co, fSmith S, mCaroline Jameson, hJoseph T Mastin, md12/10/1879
John Evans, b17--, Nhtn Co, wElizabeth Parker Upshur
Lucy, b18--, Nhtn Co, hDavid C Kellam
Smith S, b18--, Fauq Co?, wCaroline Jameson
Thomas Henry, b18--, Nhtn Co, w-- Fitchett
NOWELL, Lucy Wilhemina, bc1800, Camp Co?, fWilliam, hJohn Matthews Otey
NOWLIN, Abraham, b17--, Pitt Co?, fJames II, wMildred Watkins
Bryan Watkins, bc1800, Pitt Co, fAbraham, mMildred Watkins, wMary Spencer
James II, b17--, Pitt Co, fJohn H, mCatherine Ward
John H, bc1840, Appo Co, fBryan Watkins, mMary Spencer wSarah

NOWLIN (continued)
Louisa Woodson Marie E, bc1830,Appo Co, fBryan Watkins, mMary Spencer, hS H Overton
Robert, bc1800, wElizabeth Payne
Virginia C, bc1830, Appo Co, fBryan Watkins, mMary Spencer, hJohn P Hughes
William C, bc1840, Appo Co, fBryan Watkins, mMary Spencer, wVirginia Watkins
NOYES, --, bc1800, Lanc Co?, 2w of Addison H Hall
NUCKOLS, Courtland J, bc1870, Henrico Co, fJacob Woodson, mMildred Hester Jordon
Emma, b186-, Henrico Co, fJacob Woodson, mMildred Hester Jordon, hJohn T St Clair
Hartwell M, b186-, Henrico Co, fJacob Woodson, mMildred Hester Jordon
Hester E, b1833, Gooc Co, hWilliam A Robinson
Israel, b1796, Hano Co, wJane Woodson
Jacob Woodson, b7/30/1836, Hano Co, fIsrael, mJane Woodson, wMildred Hester Jordon
Ora, bc1859, Henrico Co, fJacob Woodson, mMildred Hester Jordon, hRobert Carden
Oscar N, bc1870, Henrico Co, fJacob Woodson, mMildred Hester Jordon
NUCKOLLS, Chestr B, b5/15/1866, Gambetta, Carr Co, fThomas, mJestine Stone, wCarrie Reeves, md1900
Elbert I, bc1870, Gambetta, Carr Co, fThomas, mJestine Stone
Ellis Lee, bc1863, Gambetta, Carr Co, fThomas, mJestine Stone
Henry Clay, b186-, Gambetta, Carr Co, fThomas, mJestine Stone
Hugh, bc1856, Gambetta, Carr Co, fThomas, mJestine Stone
Nathaniel Richards, b185-, Gambetta, Carr Co, fThomas, mJestine Stone
Robert, b17--,Oldtown (now

NUCKOLLS (continued)
Galax), Gray Co, wMargaret Swift
Thomas, b1816, Oldtown (now Galax), Gray Co, d1903, fRobert, mMargaret Swift, wJestine Stone
NUNN, Mollie, b18--, Pula Co, d1895, mVirginia --, hAugustus P Phleger
NUNLEY, Arthur, bc1870, Wyth Co, fWilliam Henry, mElizabeth Lee
Charles W, b5/15/1866, Wyth Co, fWilliam Henry, mElizabeth Lee, wMary Remine
Daniel, bc1870, Wyth Co, fWilliam Henry, mElizabeth Lee
Ina, bc1870, Wyth Co, fWilliam Henry, mElizabeth Lee, hDavid Day
William Henry, b18--, Wash Co, wElizabeth Lee
NUNNALLY, Mary Washington, b3/9/1838, Farmville, PrEd Co, fWashington, mJudith Ann Robertson, hWilliam Benjamin Chalkley
Washington, b18--, wJudith Ann Robertson
NUNNELLY, R H, b18--, wLucy A Perdue
Sarah T, b18--, Ches Co, 2w of William N Perdue
NUTT, Sarah, b18--, fRichard, hAmos Johnson
NYE, Maria, b1858, hWilliam L Britts
OAKEY, Ada A, b184-, Lynchburg, Camp Co, fWilliam, Jr, mAnn G Snead, hDavid Dull
Joel E, b84-, Lynchburg, Camp Co, fWilliam, Jr, mAnn G Snead
John Martin, b2/23/1839, Lynchburg, Camp Co, fWilliam, Jr, mAnn G Snead, 1wEmma L Woolwine, 2wFannie G Barnett
Mary L, b186-, Salem, Roan Co, fWilliam S, mMargaret M Davis
Minnie C, b186-, Salem, Roan Co, fWilliam S, mMargaret M Davis
Nannie S, bc1870, Salem, Roan Co, fWilliam S, mMargaret M Davis
Orran Davis, b0/14/1864, Salem, Roan Co, fWilliam S, mMargaret

OAKEY (continued)
M Davis, wAlice Burch, md10/1887
Robert Woolwine, b10/29/1866, Camp Co?, fJohn Martin, (1)m Emma L Woolwine
Samuel G, b184-, Lynchburg, Camp Co, fWilliam, Jr, mAnn G Snead
Sarah Emma, b184-, Lynchburg, Camp Co, fWilliam, Jr, mAnn G Snead, hE D Mitchell
Uriel H, b184-, Lynchburg, Camp Co, fWilliam, Jr, mAnn G Snead
Virginia C, b184-, Lynchburg, Camp Co, fWilliam, Jr, mAnn G Snead, hCharles J Stephens
Walter H, b186-, Salem, Roan Co, fWilliamS, mMargaret M Davis
William S, b8/24/1836, Lynchburg, Camp Co, d1904, fWilliam, Jr, mAnn G Snead, mMargaret M Davis
OAKS, Sarah, bc1833, Pitt Co, hJohn B Aaron
O'BANNON, James M, b18--, Fauq Co?, fBryant, wLucy Mildred Lillard
Lucy, b18--, Culp Co, hHenry Sparks
Persley Henry, b5/16/1848, Rapp Co, fJames M, mLucy Mildred Lillard, wAnna Josephine Miller, md5/14/1879
OCKER, Mary, b18--, Rkhm Co, fPeter, hJohn Swank
O'CONNOR, John, b18--, Norfolk?, wMary Virginia Taylor
ODELL, Mary, b18--, Fred Co?, hJosiah Lockhart
ODILVIE, John, bc1830, Fauq Co?, wCarrie Ashby
O'GARA, Hugh, b18--, Alle Co?, 2h of Sallie W Holman
OGBURN, Fanny, b18--, hJoseph William Palmer, Sr
OGILVIE, Lucy Ann, b6/6/1821, Jeffersonton, Culp Co, d1901, fJohn, hRobert Weedon
OGLE, Maria, b18--, Fran Co?, hEdmund Chitwood
OGLESBY, Nicholas P, bc1860, Carr Co, d1921, wLavinia Wilkinson
Shadrach, b17--, Fluv Co?, 1h

OGLESBY (continued)
of Celia Duncan
OLDS, James Elisha, Sr, b7/24/1854, nrFentress, Norf Co, fJames McBride, mHulda E --, wAda V Jarvis
Jonathan Whitehead, b18--, PrAn Co?, wAnne Elizabeth Whitehurst
Martha J, b18--, Camp Co, hWilliam H Taylor
Nannie R, b185-, Amhe Co?, 1w of John P Pettyjohn
William Whitehurst, Sr, b11/17/1840, PrAn Co, fJonathan Whitehead, mAnne Elizabeth Whitehurst, wAlice Herbert, md 6/23/1870
OLDHAM, Sallie, b12/25/1853, Rich Co, d1918, hLawson A Weaver
Thomas N, b1846, Ivondale, Rich Co, fWilliam, mVirginia Ficklin, wMary Davenport
William, b18--, Ivondale, Rich Co, wVirginia Ficklin
OLIVER, Eli Edmund, b1819, Fair Co, fJames, mMary Nalley, wAmelia Anne Robey
George C, bc1850, Hali Co, d1914, wSallie Chappell Adams
Harry Diggs, b2/8/1866, Norfolk, fJohn B Diggs, mSarah Elizabeth Carr, wMary F Patton, md11/28/1889
James, b1787, Fair Co, wMary Nalley
Lewis Edmund, b5/27/1847, nr Kenmore, Fair Co, fEli Edmund, mAmelia Anne Robey, wLucretia Alice Tansill
Louisa V, b1857, Fair Co, hJoseph E Clements
Lucy George, b1840, Caro Co, d1922, fPhilip, mElizabeth Keeling Tompkins, hSt Leger Landon Moncure
Philip, b18--, Caro Co?, wElizabeth Keeling Tompkins
Sterling T, b18--, Norfolk?, w-- Diggs
OMOHUNDRO, Annie M, b185-, Hickory Farm, nrWarsaw, Rich Co, fWilliam H, mEliza A Hutt, hLuther Hall
Elizabeth, b3/1844, Edgehill

OMOHUNDRO (continued)
Farm, West Co, hThomas M Omohundro
James E, b186-, Farmers Fork, Rich Co, fThomas M, mElizabeth Omohundro
John Moreland, b186-, Farmers Fork, Rich Co, fThomas M, mElizabeth Omohundro
John Murwin, b5/16/1866, Hickory Farm, nrWarsaw, Rich Co, fWilliam H, mEliza A Hutt, wBessie Carter Walker, md10/31/1889
Laura C, b185-, Hickory Farm, nrWarsaw, Rich Co, fWilliam H, mEliza A Hutt, 2w of Hiram M Hutt
Lou, b185-, Hickory Farm, nr Warsaw, Rich Co, fWilliam H, mEliza A Hutt
Mollie R, bc1860, Hickory Farm, nrWarsaw, Rich Co, fWilliam H, mEliza A Hutt, hErnest L Hutt
Richard Bruce, b11/8/1868, Farmers Fork, Rich Co, fThomas M, mElizabeth Omohundro, wMary Helen Parker
Sallie Blanch, bc1870, Farmers Fork, Rich Co, fThomas M, mElizabeth Omohundro
Thomas, bc1800, nrFarmers Fork, Rich Co
Thomas Edgar, b185-, Hickory Farm, nrWarsaw, Rich Co, fWilliam H, mEliza A Hutt
Thomas Edward, b186-, Farmers Fork, Rich Co, fThomas M, mElizabeth Omohundro
Thomas M, b1831, nrFarmers Fork, Rich Co, fThomas, wElizabeth Omohundro
Virginia, b185-, Hickory Farm, nrWarsaw, Rich Co, fWilliam M, mEliza A Hutt, 1w of Hiram M Hutt
William H, b1827, Farmers Fork, Rich Co, d1886, wEliza A Hutt
William R, bc1860, Hickory Farm, nrWarsaw, Rich Co, fWilliam H, mEliza A Hutt
O'NEAL, Charles H, bc1850, Richmond, wAlice Herndon
O'NEIL, J T, b18--, Richmond, wAnna I Robertson
OPIE, Hiercome Lindsay, b18--,

OPIE (continued)
Jeff Co, wAnnie Locke
John Newton, b3/14/1844, Jeff Co, d1906, fHierome Lindsay, mAnnie Locke, 1wIsabel Harmon, md10/1866, 2wIda Fletcher, md1878
Susanna, bc1720, 2w of Traverse Colston
ORBISON, Eliza, b181-, Rkbr Co, 1w of Adam G McGuffin, Sr
OREBAUGH, --, b2/15/1861, Augu Co, fGeorge A, mBettie A Stoutermyer, hJames Andrew Riddel III, md1885
George A, b18--, Augu Co?, wBettie A Stoutermyer
James, bc1860, Augu Co, fGeorge A, mBettie A Stoutermyer
John H, bc1860, Augu Co, fGeorge A, mBettie A Stoutermyer
Mattie, bc1860, Augu Co, fGeorge A, mBettie A Stoutermyer, h-- Crum
ORNDORFF, Arthur, bc1870, Capon Springs, Hamp Co, fPhilip Setzer, mMary Jane Tevalt
Bruce, bc1870, Capon springs, Hamp Co, fPhilip Setzer, mMary Jane Tevalt
George, b185-, Stonewall District, Fred Co, fPhilip Setzer, mMary Jane Tevalt
Ida, b186-, Capon Springs, Hamp Co, fPhilip Setzer, mMary Jane Tevalt, hWill Miller
Levi, bc1800, Fred Co?, dc1858, wEllen --
Luther E, b186-, Stonewall District, Fred Co, fPhilip Setzer, mMary Jane Tevalt
Minerva, b186-, Stonewall District, Fred Co, fPhilip Setzer, mMary Jane Tevalt, hNimrod Wilson
Nettie C, b186-, Capon Springs, Hamp Co, fPhilip Setzer, mMary Jane Tevalt, hNathan Linaberg
Philip Setzer, b2/16/833, Stonewall District, Fred Co, d1906, fLevi, mEllen --, wMary Jane Tevalt
Robert, b186-, Fred Co?, fPhilip Setzer, mMary Jane Tevalt

ORNDORFF (continued)
Sarah C, b18--, Fred Co?, hJacob Summers
Thomas Jackson, b10/26/1862, Stonewall District, Fred Co, fPhilip Setzer, mMary Jane Tevalt, wJennie Cline
William Martin, bc1860, Stonewall District, Fred Co, fPhilip Setzer, mMary Jane Tevalt
O'ROARK, Emma, b18--, Shen Co?, hJohn W Zirkle
ORR, --, b186-, Lee Co, 1h of Elizabeth Pennington
Robert W, b1843, nrJonesville, Lee Co, wMinerva Wilson
ORRICK, Mary Elizabeth, b1831, Morg Co, fCromwell, hCharles Hess Locher
ORWICK, Sarah, b18--, Shen Co, m-- Warner, hW F Wisman
OSBORNE, -- b18--, Gray Co, 1w of John M Phipps
--, b18--, nrDungannon, Scot Co, hElijah Corder, Sr
OTEY, Ann, bc1870, Lynchburg, Camp Co, fKirkwood, mLucy Minor, hJames A Scott
Carrie, b18--, Camp Co?, fGaston, m-- Morgan, hPeter Ainslie
Dexter, b18--, Camp Co, fWalter Hayes, mSarah Elizabeth Wiatt, wElizabeth Dabney Langhorne Lewis
Frances, b17--, Bedf Co?, fJohn, mMary Hopkins, 1w of William Leftwich, Jr, md6/17/1788
Frazier, b17--, wMildred Leftwich, md11/21/1793
Gaston, b18--, Lynchburg, Camp Co, fJohn Mathews, mLucy Wilhemina Nowell, w-- Morgan
Isaac, b17--, Bedf Co?, fJohn, mMary Hopins, wElizabeth Mathews
James Hervey, b179-, Bedf Co, fIsaac, mElizabeth Mathews
John, b1735, NewK Co?, wMary Hopkins
John Marshall, b18--, Lynchburg, Camp Co, fJohn Mathews, mLucy Wilhelmina Nowell
John Mathews, b10/2/1792, Bedf Co, d1859, fIsaac, mElizabeth

OTEY (continued)
Mathews, wLucy Wilhelmina Nowell
John Mathews, Sr, b2/5/1866, Lynchburg, Camp Co, fKirkwood, mLucy Minor, wMaggie Marshall Murrell, md1898
Kirkwood, Sr, b10/19/1829, Lynchburg, Camp Co, fJohn Mathews, mLucy Wilhelmina Nowell, wLucy Minor
Kirkwood, Jr, bc1870, Lynchburg, Camp Co, fKirkwood, Sr, mLucy Minor
Lucy, b18--, Lynchburg, Camp Co, fJohn Mathews, mLucy Wilhelmina Nowell, hJohn S Walker
Peter Johnson, b12/22/1840, Lynchburg, Camp Co, fJohn Mathews, mLucy Wilhelmina Nowell, wNellie Floyd
Samuel Dexter, b18--, Lynchburg, Camp Co, fJohn Mathews, mLucy Wilhelmina Nowell
Van Rensselaer, b18--, Lynchburg, Camp Co, fJohn Mathews, mLucy Wilhelmina Nowell, wLucy Dabney
Walter Hayes, b18--, Lynchburg, Camp Co, fJohn Mathews, mLucy Wilhelmina Nowell, wSarah Elizabeth Wiatt
OTT, Annie, b18--, Shen Co?, dc1900, hPhilip Wilson Magruder
Elizabeth, b11/27/1783, Dinw Co?, d1833, 1h-- Durell, 2h David Boyd
Maria, bc1800, Page Co, hMorgan A Lauck
OVERBEY, William I, b18--, Pitt Co?, wMattie H Barksdale
OVERBY, Alexander, b18--, wLucy Frances Burwell
OVERSTREET, Alexander B, b186-, Bedf Co, fRolley Chapman, mMartha Lydia Bond
Edmund A, Sr, b1/3/1866, Bedf Co, fRolley Chapman, mMartha Lydia Bond, wCarrie B Miller, md1891
Lelia B, b186-, Bedf Co, fRolley Chapman, mMartha Lydia Bond, hW T Newman
Raswell C. b6/4/1870, Bedf Co, fRolley Chapman, mMartha Lydia

OVERSTREET (continued)
  Bond, 1wHattie S McGhee, md1890, 2wElla B Spradlin
Robert V, b186-, Bedf Co, fRolley Chapman, mMartha Lydia Bond
Rolley Chapman, b1827, Bedf Co, 2h of Martha Lydia Bond
Serena F, bc1860, Bedf Co, fRolley Chapman, mMartha Lydia Bond, hJohn A Preston
OVERTON, --, bc1860, Bote Co?, wElizabeth Robinson
Mary Garland, b17--, Caro Co?, hDavid Cosby
S H, bc1830, Appo Co?, wMarie E Nowlin
OWEN, --, b18--, Meck Co, hWilliam Pool
Archibald A, b185-, Hali Co, fWilliam, mHarriet Easley
Daniel W, b6/24/1852, Black Walnut (now Cluster Springs), Hali Co, fWilliam, mHarriet Easley, wNannie Hundley, md10/11/1876
Eliza A, b18--, Pitt Co, hC W Myers
Emeline, b18--, Roan Co, 1hWilson Bane, 2hWilliam Gideon Hall
Fannie, b185-, Hali Co, fWilliam, mHarriet Easley, hThornton Wilson
Fannie Taylor, b1848, Pitt Co, d1921, hWilliam S Dodd
Hallie, bc1850, Hali Co, fWilliam, mHarriet Easley, hThomas Easley
Helen, b185-, Hali Co, fWilliam, nHarriet Easley, hFred S Whaley
Hettie M, b1823, Bote Co, d1908, 2w of Samuel Noffsinger
John, bc1800, Hali Co, wNancy Easley
John Bailey, b185-, Hali Co, fWilliam, mHarriet Easley
John E, bc1840, Powh Co?, wVirginia Caroline Elam
John J, b8/27/1859, PrEd Co, fThomas J, mLouisa Rudd, wFannie Daniel, md10/1884
Lelia B, b18--, PrEd Co, fThomas J, mLouisa Rudd
Mary, b18--, PrEd Co, fThomas

OVERTON (continued)
  J, mLouisa Rudd, hSamuel W Coleman
Mary A, b184-, Hali Co, fWilliam, mHarriet Easley, hJohn V Brooks
Mattie, b18--, PrEd Co, fThomas J, mLouisa Rudd, hDavid L Sublett
Nannie P, b18--, Hali Co, hHenry Easley
Robert L, b184-, Hali Co, fWilliam, mHarriet Easley
Rufus, bc1860, Hali Co, fWilliam, mHarriet Easley
Thomas, b184-, Hali Co, d186-, fWilliam, mHarriet Easley
Thomas J, b1827, Hali Co, fWilliam
William, b18--, Hali Co, d1883, fJohn, mNancy Easley, wHarriet Easley
OWENS, Jane Ellen, b8/25/1844, Ches Co, fRobert, mCelia Fellows, hJosiah Staunton Moore, md3/6/ 1867
John W, b185-, Pitt Co?, d1886, wElizabeth Motley
Virginia Frances, b18--, Norf Co?, hWilliam Meredith Hope
OWSLEY, Harry Hawkins, b1786, Alexandria
OZLIN, Samuel Wilkins, b1812, Meck Co, d1888, wAmelia Frances Callis
William T, b3/8/1850, Lune Co, fSamuel Wilkins, mAmelia Frances Callis, 1wEmma J Andrews, 2wMollie J Dortch
PACE, Helen G, b1866, Richmond, hThomas R Aaron
M J, bc1860, Roan Co?, w-- Scott
Mary, b18--, Henry Co, fGreenville T, hThomas Jefferson Talbott
PACK, Minerva, b18--, Gile Co, 2w of John W Easley
PADBERRY, Maria, b18--, hJohn Cooper
PAGE, Anne Nelson, b18--, fFrederick Winslow, mAnne Kiloch Meriwether, hNathaniel Ragsdale Coleman
Benjamin Waller, b17--, Hano Co, wMary Hodges

PAGE (continued)
Betsey, b17--, Albe Co, fRobert, mJennie Murrell
Carter, b1758, Cumb Co, 1wMary Cary, 2wLucy Nelson
Dorothy Willing, b18--, "Briars", Chapel District, Clar Co, fRobert Powell, Sr, (1)mMary Francis, hNathaniel Burwell
Eliza Jane, b181-, Albe Co, fSamuel, mEliza Smith
Elizabeth Burwell, bc1840, "Briars", Chapel District, Clar Co, fRobert Powell, Sr, (2)m Susan Grymes Randolph
Frances, b177-, Rosewell, Glou Co, fJohn, mFrances Burwell, 1h Thomas Nelson, 2hCarter Berkeley
Francis, b1774, Rosewell, Glou Co, fJohn, mFrances Burwell, wSusan Nelson
Frank, b18--, fJohn, mElizabeth Burwell Nelson
Frederick Winslow, b18--, wAnne Kinloch Meriwether
George, b17--, Albe Co, fRobert, mJennie Murrell
George, b181-, Albe Co, fSamuel, mEliza Smith
James, b17--, Albe Co, fRobert, mJennie Murrell
James A, b1832, Hano Co, fBnjamin Waller, mMary Hodges, wAnnie Blair Archer
Jennie, b17--, Albe Co, fRobert, mJennie Murrell
John, b4/17/1744, Rosewell, Glou Co, fMann II, 1wFrances Burwell, 2wJane Byrd
John, b17--, Hano Co, fRobert, mSarah Walker, wMaria Horsemander Byrd, md1784
John, b4/26/1821, Hano Co, fFrancis, mSusan Nelson, wElizabeth Burwell Nelson
John W, b185-, Albe Co, fNicholas M, mMary White
Lucy, bc1770, fJohn, mJane Byrd, hFrank Nelson
Lucy Nelson, b18--, Richmond?, hJames Madison Sublett
Lucy Randolph, b184-, "Briars", Chapel District, Clar Co, fRobert Powell, Sr, (2)mSusan

PAGE (continued)
Grymes Randolph, hWilliam P Carter
Mann, b1691, Glou Co, fMatthew, mMary Mann, wJudith Carter
Mann II, b17--, Rosewell, Glou Co, fMann
Maria B, b18--, "Briars", Chapel District, Clar Co, fRobert Powell, Sr, (1)mMary Francis, hMayhew Wainright
Mary, b18--, Nott Co, hE F Slaughter
Mary A, bc1810, Albe Co, fSamuel, mEliza Smith
Mary E, bc1860, Albe Co, fNicholas M, mMary White, hWilliam Nicholas
Mary Frances, b184-, "Briars", Chapel District, Clar Co, fRobert Powell, Sr, (2)mSusan Grymes Randolph, hJohn Esten Cook
Mary Maria, b18--, Cumb Co, fCarter, (2)mLucy Nelson, hGeorge Washington Dame
Mary Mann, b18--, Clar Co, fRobert, hJoseph A Williamson
Matthew, b1659, Glou Co, fJohn, wMary Mann
Matthew, b1762, "Broadneck", Hano Co, d1826, fRobert, wAnn Randolph Meade, md1799
Nancy F, b18--, "Briars", Chapel District, Clar Co, fRobert Powell, Sr, (1)mMary Francis, hJoseph Pleasants Nelson, bc1800, wMaria Hamilton
Nicholas, b17--, Albe Co, fRobert, mJennie Murrell
Nicholas M, b11/2/1810, Albe Co, fSamuel, mEliza Smith, wMary White, md10/9/1849
Robert, b17--, Hano Co?, wSarah Walker
Robert, b17--, wJennie Murrell
Robert, b17--, Albe Co, fRobert, mJennie Murrell
Robert, b5/8/1863, Batesville Community, Albe Co, fNicholas M, mMary White, wAnn Elizabeth Rosser, md1/30/1895
Robert Powell, Sr, bc1790, Hano Co?, fJohn, mMaria Horsemander Byrd, 1wMary Francis, 2wSusan Grymes Burwell

PAGE (continued)
Robert Powell, Jr, b8/26/1846, "Briars", Chapel District, Clar Co, fRobert, Sr, (2)m Susan Grymes Randolph, wAgnes Atkinson Burwell, md12/18/1873
Robert Powell, b18--, Clar Co, wPattie Hardee
Rosewell, b11/21/1858, Hano Co?, fJohn, mElizabeth Burwell Nelson, wSusan Dabney Morris, md1887
Samuel, b17--, Albe Co, fRobert, mJennie Murrell, w Eliza Smith
Samuel Massie, b2/25/1858, Batesville, Albe Co, d1921, fNicholas M, mMary White, wMargaret W Harris, md2/20/1884
Sarah, bc1810, "AnnField", Clar Co, fMatthew, mAnn Randolph Meade, hCharles W Andrews
Thomas Nelson, b4/23/1853, Hano Co?, fJohn, mElizabeth Burwell Nelson, 1wAnne Seddon Bruce, 2wFlorence Lathrop Field, md1893
William, b17--, Albe Co, fRobert, mJennie Murrell
William, b180-, Albe Co, fSamuel, mEliza Smith
William Garrett, bc1860, Albe Co, fNicholas M, mMary White
William N, b185-, Char Co?, wKate B Green
PAGGETT, Carlton A, b18--, Alexandria?, wMary E Talbott
PAINTER, --, b185-, Shen Co, fIsaac, 1w of Jack Smith
Abram, b1798, Pula Co, 1w-- Shepard
Amanda, b1854, nrWolf Glade, Carr Co, hSamuel Daivs
Benton D, b5/6/1856, nrTroutville, Bote Co, fJohn, mCatherine Abbott, wSallie C Moomaw
Betsy, b18--, Shen Co?, hIsaac Bowman
Davis M, b18--, fWilliam M, mSarah E Hatcher
Dorothy v, b7/26/1853, Rkhm Co, hJacob Pence
Ellen, b1837, Shen Co, d1892, fLemuel, hIsaac Bowers
Emeline, b1835, Cripple Creek,

PAINTER (continued)
Wyth Co, d1919, hWilliam Peirce
Hugh M, b186-, Shen Co, fJames M, mIsabel Hoffman
Isaac, b1800, Wyth Co, d1884, fMatthias, wEvelina Bell
Isaac, b18--, Shen Co, wRegina Maphis
James B, bc1860, Wyth Co?, wMary J Davis
James M, bc1834, nrEdinburg, Shen Co, fSamuel A, m-- Spangler, wIsabel Hoffman
James O, bc1870, nrEdinburg, Shen Co, fJames M, mIsabel Hoffman
John, b1807, Mont Co, wCatherine Abbott
Laura Lee, b1/17/1857, Shen Co, d1921, fIsaac, mRegina Maphis, hGeorge H Hottel, md10/31/1878
Lemuel, b18--, Rkhm Co
Lemuel, bc1850, Shen Co, fLemuel, wMary Hottel
Mary Katherine, b1861, Wyth Co, hHenry L Bowyer
Mary Lula, b18--, fWilliam M, mSarah E, hStephen Sanders Simmerman, md10/21/1885
Mathias, b17--, Shen Co
Minnie Virginia, b18--, fWilliam M, mSarah E Hatcher, hWilliam Eads Miller
Nellie, b186-, nrEdinburg, Shen Co, fJames M, mIsabel Hoffman
Samuel A, bc1800, Shen Co, w-- Spangler
Sarah Catherine, b183-, nrEdinburg, Shen Co, fSamuel A, m-- Spangler, hIsaac Sheetz
Thomas L, b7/28/1841, Cripple Creek, Wyth Co, fIsaac, mEvelina Bell, wElla Gillespie
Virginia C, b185-, Shen Co, fIsaac, mRegina Maphis, hWilliam A Headley
Walter T, b18--, fWilliam M, mSarah E Hatcher
William H, b18--, fWilliam M, mSarah E Hatcher
William Isaac, b5/11/1870, Liberty Hill, Taze Co, fThomas L, mElla Gillespie, wDoris Ida Russell, md1/29/1897
William M, b4/1836, Ivanhoe,

PAINTER (continued)
Wyth Co, wSarah E Hatcher
PALLETTE, Elizabeth, b17--, PrAn Co, hWilliam Consalvo
PALMATARY, Fred, b18--, Richmond?, d188-, wMary Elizabeth
PALMER, --, b18--, Hali Co, hWilliam Nichols
--, b18--, Warr Co?, wKate Baker
--, b18--, Fauq Co?, hDavid Stephenson
Bessie, bc1860, Richmond, fWilliam H, mElizabeth Amiss, hFrank W Christian
Charles L, b18--, Meck Co, fJoseph William, mFanny Ogburn
Claudia, b186-, Richmond, fWilliam, mElizabeth Amiss, hW Ormond Young
David Hunter, b18--, Meck Co, fJoseph William, Sr, mFanny Ogburn
Edwin A, b11/15/1865, Mountain View, Mont Co, fWilliam H, mElizabeth Amiss, wAlice Henning, md2/1898
Emma, b183-, Richmond, fWilliam, mElizabeth Walker Enders, hJames Caskie
Fitz Lee, b18--, Meck Co, fJoseph William, Sr, mFanny Ogburn
Joseph William, Sr, b18--, Brun Co, fLuke, wFanny Ogburn
Joseph William, Jr, b18--, Meck Co, fJoseph William, Sr, mFanny Ogburn
Lelia, b185-, Richmond, d1900, fWilliam H, mElizabeth Amiss, hEgbert G Leigh
Luke, b18--, Grvl Co, fWilliam, m-- Machin
Otis, b18--, KiWi Co?, wLucy Clements
Rachel, b18--, Loud Co?, hThomas Fred
Sarah, b1832, Richmond, fWilliam, hDavid M Lea
Sarah, b185-, Richmond, fWilliam H, mElizabeth Amiss, hR Preston Means
William, b17--, Hali Co, w-- Machin
William H, b10/9/1835, Richmond, fWilliam, mElizabeth

PALMER (continued)
Walker Enders, wElizabeth Amiss, md11/17/1856
William H, Jr, b186-, Richmond, fWilliam H, mElizabeth Amiss
PANCOAST, Martha Jane, b18--, Loud Co?, hWilliam H Brown
Rosalie, b186-, Leesburg, Loud Co, 1w of Elijah B White
PANNELL, Elizbeth Letcher, b1801, Pitt Co, hArchibald Stuart
PANNETT, William, Jr, b1829, Fred Co, fWilliam, Sr, mMary Watts, wCatherine Chapman
PANNILL, . D C, b186-, Wyth Co?, wMary M Kegley
PARCELL, Martha, b18--, Roan Co?, hTazewell Chilton Lavender
PARHAM, Edwin E, b1829, Suss Co, fStitch, m-- Massenburg, wMaria Louisa Feild
Edwin Feild, b1/9/1855, Suss Co, fEdwin E, mMaria Louisa Feild, wMary A Lyon
Emma, b18--, Suss Co, 2w of James D Howle
Stitch, bc1800, Suss Co, w-- Massenburg
PARISH, Andrew, b18--, Roan Co?, wMary --
Elihu, b18--, Gooc Co, wMollie Baugh
Julia, b18--, Roan Co?, hJohn Quisenberry
Nancy, b18--, Salem, Roan Co, d1903, fAndrew, mMary --, hJohn Denit
PARKER, Annie M, b1861, Acco Co, hWilliam C West, Sr
Henry, b18--, Hali Co, d1902, 2wMargaret A Smith
Jacob G, b1787, Nhtn Co, wAnn Gertrude Stratton
James H, b18--, West Co?, wSallie A Atwell
Jesse, b18--, Nans Co?, wAnn Elizabeth --
John R, b1837, Suss Co, d1881, wVirginia Ann Corbin
Martha Elizabeth, b18--, hAbram Booth Hancock
Mary Helen, bc1870, West Co, fJames H, mSallie A Atwell, hRichard Bruce Omonhundro,

PARKER (continued)
md5/13/1894
Nellie Alexander, b6/24/1869, Richmond, fWilliam Watts, mEllen Jane Jordan, hJames William Henson, md7/2/1898
Sarah Andrews, b12/31/1822, Nhtn Co, fJacob G, mAnn Gertrude Stratton, hGeorge L Upshur
Strafford M, b18--, wSarah Pearson
Virginia Jessie, b18--, Suffolk, Nans Co, fJesse, mAnn Elizabeth --, hSamuel Summerfield Lambeth, Sr
William Watts, b8--, fStrafford M, mSarah Pearson, wEllen Jane Jordan
PARKINS, Carrie, b18--, Parkins Mills, fWilliam, m-- Gochenour, hJesse R Bailey
John Henry, b18--, Fred Co, fNathan, m-- Sours, wElla Moorman
Nathan, bc1800, nrWinchester, Fred Co, w-- Sours
Samuel H, Sr, bc1860, Augu Co?, wGrace G Warden
Thomas M, b6/8/1866, nrStaunton, Augu Co, fJohn Henry, mElla Moorman, wGertrude Alby, md4/19/1899
William, b18--, Augu Co?, w-- Gochenour
PARKINSON, John W, b18--, wLucinda Roberts
Sallie, b4/1853, Warrenton, Fauq Co, fJohn W, mLucinda Roberts, hDaniel Pollard Wood, md4/17/1877
PARKS, Hannah B, bc1830, Lexington, Rkbr Co, fJoshua, hSchuyler B Smith
Martha, b1848, Gray Co, 1h-- Rutherford, 2hJohn M Phipps
Mary Anna, b18--, hGeorge L Berry
Mattie, b3/31/1860, Norf Co, hHerbert I Lewis
PARR, Alice J, bc1860, Orlean, Fauq Co, fAndrew Jackson, Sr, mJulia Moore
Andrew Jackson, Sr, b6/27/1834, Culp Co, d1921, wJulia Moore
Andrew Jackson, Jr, b186-, Or-

PARR (continued)
lean, Fauq Co, fAndrew Jackson, Sr, mJulia Moore
Anna, b186-, Fauq Co, fJames William, Sr, mAddie Moore, hT F Yates
Asbury, b18--, Culp Co
Dora L, b186-, Orlean, Fauq Co, fAndrew Jackson, Sr, mJulia Moore, hDouglas Wingfield
Effie J, b185-, Orlean, Fauq Co, fAndrew Jackson, Sr, mJulia Moore
George D, b186-, Fauq Co, fJames William, Sr, mAddie Moore
George H, bc1870, Orlean, Fauq Co, fAndrew Jackson, Sr, mJulia Moore
Grace E, b186-, Orlean, Fauq Co, fAndrew Jackson, Sr, mJulia Moore, hJohn E Russell
James M, b2/13/1866, Orlean, Fauq Co, fAndrew Jackson, Sr, mJulia Moore, 1wElizabeth Coffman, md10/17/1894, 2wJennie () Ratcliffe, md10/17/1901, 3wMyrtle J Wilson, md9/10/1912
James William, Sr, bc1837, Culp Co, wAddie Moore
James William, Jr, b6/2/1865, Fauq Co, fJames William, Sr, mAddie Moore, wCecelia Russell
Rebecca, b186-, Orlean, Fauq Co, fAndrew Jackson, Sr, mJulia Moore, hJames Cook
Robert S, bc1860, Fauq Co, fJames William, Sr, mAddie Moore
Sallie, b183-, Culp Co
Sallie Belle, b186-, Orlean, Fauq Co, fAndrew Jackson, Sr, mJulia Moore, hJohn A Walter
PARRISH, Bettie, b1844, Nels Co, d1912, hSamuel Powhatan Parrish
Coason W, b6/5/1803, Richmond?, d1860, wMary Steele Coffey
Elizabeth E, bc1850, Augu Co?, fHenry A Parrish, (2)mSarah Cannon, hHampton R Christ
Emma Clinton, b18--, Smyt Co?, fJohn, mMary Clinton, hSamuel B Henritze
Frank M, b18--, Fluv Co?,

PARRISH (continued)
 wMartha Swan Hancock
Henry A, b18--, Fluv Co, 2wSarah Cannon
J Samuel, b18--, Fluv Co, fFrank M, mMartha Swan Hancock, wMary Leigh Morris
James Scott, Sr, b12/12/1869, fWilliam Henry, Sr, mMary Kirkpatrick, wEdith Winch, md 12/6/1893
James, b1840, Portsmouth, Norf Co, wAlice Virginia Toomer
John, b18--, Smyt Co?, d186-, wMary Clinton
John E, b1846, Gooc Co, wMartha A Rose
John Walker, b184-, Augu Co?, fHenry A, (2)mSarah Cannon
Mary, b18--, hCharles H Dunklee
Mary Lucy, bc1850, Augu Co?, fHenry A, (2)mSarah Cannon, hJohn R Wright
Oscar E, b3/1/1970, Richmond, fJohn E, mMartha A Rose, wMargaret Keer Johnston, md6/21/1893
Samuel Powhatan, b1829, Nels Co, d1905, fWillis Redmond, wBettie Parrish
T P, bc1860, Henry Co?, w-- Matthews
Thomas Kirkpatrick, b18--, fWilliam H, Sr, mMary Kirkpatrick
Virginia, bc1850, Augu Co?, fHenry A, (2)mSarah Cannon, hHoward F Wright
William Henry, Sr, b7/27/1834, fCoason W, mMary Steele Coffey, wMary Kirkpatrick
William Henry, Jr, b1860, Lynchburg, Camp Co, fWilliam Henry, Sr, mMary Kirkpatrick, wCaroline Harris
William Henry, b8/23/1851, Augu Co, fHenry A, (2)mSarah Cannon, 1wLucy A Pondexter, md1880, 2wM K Hight, md6/6/1922
William Joseph, Sr, b9/1/1865, Nels Co, fSamuel Powhatan, mBettie Parrish, wJennie Mortimer Martin
Willis Redmond, bc1800, Nels Co
PARROTT, Augusta Fleet, bc1860,

PARROTT (continued)
 Mt Airy, Fauq Co, fJohn Henry, Sr, mElizabeth Edmonds
Augustine, bc1800, KiGe Co, fJohn, wSarah Fleet
Elizabeth Edmonds, b186-, Mt Airy, Fauq Co, fJohn Henry, Sr, mElizabeth Edmonds
Helen Sydnor, b18--, Mt Airy, Fauq Co, fJohn Henry, Sr, mElizabeth Edmonds
John Henry, Sr, b18--, Math Co, fAugustine, mSarah Fleet, wElizabeth Edmonds
John Henry, Jr, bc1870, Mt Airy, Fauq Co, fJohn Henry, Sr, mElizabeth Edmonds, wJosephine C Cromwell, md1895
Roberta Wallace, b186-, Mt Airy, Fauq Co, fJohn Henry, Sr, mElizabeth Edmonds
Sarah B, bc1860, Mt Airy, Fauq Co, fJohn Henry, Sr, mElizabeth Edmonds
William Temple, bc1870, Mt Airy, Fauq Co, fJohn Henry, Sr, mElizabeth Edmonds
PARSONS, John D, b1836, Acco Co
John M, bc1860, Lee Co?, wMollie Miles
PARTLOW, Emma, bc1830, Culp Co?, hRichard Apperson
PATRICK, Jane, b18--, hHenry Frank Coleman
Mattie, b18--, Caro Co?, fJohn, hSamuel Wood Flippo
Susan H, b18--, Nels Co?, hWilliam Lewis Williams
PATTERSON, Cecelia, bc1832, nr Spring Hill, Augu Co, d1914, fJohn, m-- Doom,, hSamuel F Wagner
Elizabeth, b18--, Buck Co, fTurner, hThomas Smith Wright
Ella Brown, bc1870, nrWytheville, Wyth Co, fJames H, mMary J Umberger, hSelden W Repass
James H, b18--, Wyth Co, d1911, wMary J Umberger
John, bc1800, w-- Doom
Mary, b18--, Fran Co?, hJohn Spotswood Brown
Mary Elizabeth, b9/4/1844, Spring Hill, Augu Co, hJohn Huddleson

PATTERSON (continued)
Mary J, b1841, Nels Co, hElisha V Carter
Nancy, b18--, South River, Augu Co, hSam Byers, Sr
Thomas, b186-, Rkhm Co, wMattie Moore
Turner, bc1800, Buck Co
PATTESON, Agnes, bc1800, Appo Co, hThomas Thornhill
Mary, b18--, Appo Co, hI H Adams
Martha, b17--, Camp Co?, hHenry Christian
Seargent Smith Prentiss, b12/15/1856, Amhe Co, fDavid, mElizabeth Camm
PATTISON, Martha, bc1800, Buck Co?, 1w of Sampson Diuguid
PATTON, Elizabeth, b18--, Newbern, Pula Co, fThomas, mElizabeth Raines, hRobert Edmond Taylor
John Shelton, b1/10/1857, Augu Co, fAlfred Taylor, mVirginia Harris, wBeatrice Faber, md6/10/1881
Mary F, b18--, Norf Co?, hHarry Diggs Oliver
Mary Paxtopn, b186-, Rkbr Co, fJ T, hJohn Gibson Alexander md1886
Thomas, b18--, Pula Co, wElizabeth Raines
William M, b18--, wAnnie Jordan
PAUL, Elizabeth, b18--, Rkhm Co?, fSamuel, mBetsy --, hSamuel Funkhouser
Isaac, b18--, Augu Co
Samuel, b6/25/1804, Rkhm Co, d1857, wBetsy --
Virginia, b18--, Augu Co, fIsaac, hA K Fletcher
PAULETT, Ann, b17--, hJohn Clark
PAXSON, Frances, b18--, Norf Co?, fJoseph, mFrances Wynkoop, hWilliam Ellsworth Hermance, md1892
PAXTON, Bettie, b184-, Rkbr Co, fWilliam L, Jr, mSarah Burks, hJesse Fisher
Charles Hawkins, b185-, Rkbr Co, fWilliam L, Jr, mSarah Burks
Ella, b185-, Rkbr Co, fWilliam L, Jr, mSarah Burks, hIvan

PAXTON (continued)
Pike
Esteline, b18--, Bote Co?, hStarkey Robinson
Jean, bc1800, Augu Co, hAlexander Stuart Hall
John Calvin, b1849, Rkbr Co, fWilliam L, Jr, mSarah Burks, wRebecca Robinson
Joseph L, b184-, Rkbr Co, fWilliam L, Jr, mSarah Burks
Luther, b184-, Rkbr Co, d186-, fWilliam L, Jr, mSarah Burks
Martin L, b184-, nrGlasgow, Rkbr Co, d186-, fWilliam L, Sr, mPhebe McClung
Mary V, b184-, Rkbr Co, fWilliam L, Jr, mSarah Burks
Reuben Grigsby, b2/15/1857, nrGlasgow, Rkbr Co, fWilliam, Jr, mSarah Burks, 1wFanny Templeton Leckey, 2wBelle Gibson, md1918
Sallie, b185-, Rkbr Co, fWilliam L, Jr, mSarah Burks, hFrank Brockenbrough
William L, Sr, b17--, nrGlasgow, Rkbr Co, wPhebe McClung
William L, Jr, b1803, nrGlasgow, Rkbr Co, d1879, fWilliam L, Sr, mPhebe McCling, wSarah Burks
William L III, b184-, Rkbr Co, d186-, fWilliam L, Jr, mSarah Burks
PAYNE, --, b18--, KiGe Co?, 1h of Louise Stiff
Alexander Spotswood, b17--, Gooc Co, d1858, fArcher, mMartha Dandridge, wCharlotte Bryce, md1804
Amos, b18--, Fauq Co, fFrancis, (1)m--, wElizabeth Barton Smith
Amos, b12/8/1852, Pruntytown, Tayl Co, fAmos, mElizabeth Barton Smith, wLaura May Phillips
Archer, b17--, Gooc Co, wMartha Dandridge
B F, b18--, Oran Co, wElizabeth Collier
Betsy, b17--, Fluv Co, fWilliam, mMary Thompson, hGeorge Richardson
Bettie K, b1857, Camp Co,

PAYNE (continued)
hPierce Loving
Catherine, b18--, Lanc Co, 1w of Samuel Downings, Sr
Catherine, b18--, Fauq Co, fFrancis, (1)m--, hMason Hurst
Catherine M, bc1837, Oak Grove, Camp Co, d1905, fPhilip M, hFerdinand A Perrow
Daniel Allen, bc1870, Lynchburg, Camp Co, fJohn Meem, mElizabeth Allen Langhorne, wMary Novell Miller, md12/1900
Doak R, bc1850, McDo?, wJulia Ann Waldron
Dolly, b1772, Fluv Co?, d1855, fJohn, mMary Coles, 1hJohn Todd, 2hJames Madison
Edward A, b183-, nrOrleans, Fauq Co, d186-, fAmos, mElizabeth Barton Smith
Elizabeth, b18--, fJohn S, 1hRobert W Nowlin, 2hOrthodox Creed Clark
Elizabeth, b185-, Pruntytown, Tayl Co, fAmos, mElizabeth Barton Smith, hMortimer French Hansbrough
Elizabeth K, b18--, Nels Co, hPierce Loving
Elvira G, b18--, Orleans, Fauq Co, fThornton, hElijah Thomas Anderson
Emma J, b1846, Fauq Co, fJohn W, hThomas A Russell
Ernestine, b185-, Pruntytown, Tayl Co, fAmos, mElizabeth Barton Smith
Erva Winston, b2/20/1861, Fauq Co, fWilliam Henry Fitzhugh, mMary Elizabeth Payne, 1w of Eppa Hunton, Jr
Eugenia M, bc1841, nrOrleans, Fauq Co, fAmos, mElizabeth Barton Smith, hB S Fleming
Francis, b17--, Fauq Co, fFrancis, 2w-- Hall
George, bc1700, Fluv Co?, wMary Woodson
George, b177-, Fluv Co?, fJohn, mMary Coles
Hugh, b184-, Fauq Co?, fAmos, mElizabeth Barton Smith
Jacquelina, b184-, nrOrleans, Fauq Co, fAmos, mElizabeth Barton Smith, hGeorge L Hol-

PAYNE (continued)
land
James, b18--, Fauq Co, fFrancis, (1)m--
John, b17--, Fluv Co, wMary Coles
John, bc1770, Fluv Co, fJohn, mMary Coles
John, b18--, Fran Co?, wAnnie Richardson
John Barton, b1/26/1855, Pruntytown, Tayl Co, fAmos, mElizabeth Barton Smith
John Meem, b11/1840, Lynchburg, Camp Co, fRobert Spotswood, mFrances Russell, wElizabeth Allen Langhorne, md12/1863
John Richard, bc1848, Loui Co, d1919, wJoanna Whitlock
John Robert, Dandridge, b17--, Gooc Co, fArcher, mMartha Dandridge
John W, b18--, Fauq Co
Josias, b17--, Fluv Co?, fGeorge, mMary Woodson, wAnn Flemming
Lucy, b177-, Fluv Co?, fJohn, mMary Coles, hGeorge S Washington, md1792
Lucy, b18--, Loui Co, hFrederick Wilmer Sims
Lucy, b18--, Loui Co?, hWilliam A Winston
Marshall, b18--, Fauq Co, fFrancis, (1)m--
Martha C, b18--, Loui Co?, hAndrew C Carroll
Mary, bc177-, fJohn, mMary Coles, hJohn Jackson
Mary, b18--, Fauq Co, fFrancis, (1)m--, hFrank Curtis
Mary C, b184-, nrOrleans, Fauq Co, fAmos, mElizabeth Barton Smith, hUpton Payne
Mary Elizabeth, b18--, fWilliam Winter, mMinerva Winston, hWilliam Henry Fitzhugh Payne
Medora, b18--, Oran Co, d1905, fB F, mElizabeth Collier, hJames Edward Cooke
Mildred, b18--, Fauq Co, fFrancis, (1)m--, hAlpheus Hurst
Montague, b1852, Fauq Co, fElijah, wBell Virginia Hulvey
Patsy, b18--, fFrancis, (1)m--, h-- Fisher

PAYNE (continued)
Rachel, b1852, Carr Co, hDavid Carroll Combs
Robert Spotswood, b180-, Gooc Co, fAlexander Spotswood, mCharlotte Brice, wFrances Russell Meem
Sally A, bc1858, Oak Grove, Camp Co, fPhilip M, hFletcher C Perrow
Sallie J, b18--, Pitt Co, 1w of Werter Clairborne Gregory
Sarah, b17--, West Co?, hMatthew French
Susan Catherine, bc1847, Loui Co, d1910, hWilliam Morton Payne
Upton, bc1840, Fauq Co, wMary C Payne
Virginia Semmes, b2/23/1867, Fauq Ca, fWilliam Henry Fitzhugh, mMary Elizabeth Payne, 2w of Eppa Hunton, Jr, md4/24/1901
William, b17--, Fluv Co?, fJosias, mAnn Flemming, wMary Thompson
William Henry Fitzhugh, b18--, wMary Elizabeth Payne
William L, b18--, Madi Co, fJohn J, wMollie Yager
William M, bc1810, Gooc Co, fAlexander Spotswood, mCharlotte Bryce
William Morton, b1/12/1846, Gooc Co, wSusan Catherine Jackson
William Undril, bc1850, Pruntytown, Tayl Co, fAmos, mElizabeth Barton Smith
William Winter, b18--, wMinerva Winston
PEACHY, William Daingerfield, b18--JaCi Co?, wLelia Russell Meem
PEAK, Alonzo, bc1860, nrAltavista, Pitt Co, fWilliam H, mMartha Word
Cornelia, b18--, 2w of Angus William MacDonald, Sr
Henry B, bc1860, nrAltavista, Pitt Co, d1889, fWilliam H, mMartha Word
J Hunter, b18--, West Co?, wStella Thurman
James M, bc1860, nrAltavista,

PEAK (continued)
Pitt Co, fWilliam H, mMartha Word
John A, b185-, nrAltavista, Pitt Co, fWilliam H, mMartha Word
Thomas N, bc1860, nrAltavista, Pitt Co, fWilliam H, mMartha Word
W N, bc1860, nrAltavista, Pitt Co, fWilliam H, mMartha Word
William H, bc1815, Hali Co, d1893, wMartha Word
PEALE, Amanda Fitzallen, b18--, Rkhm Co?, hGeorge Keezell
Walter N, b18--, Augu Co?, wAnnie Smith
PEARCE, Frances W, b1774, Char Co?, d1817, hThomas Cole Spencer, md1796
PEARSON, --, bc1800, Fran Co?, wPhoebe Brown
C H, b18--, wElizabeth Burwell
James, bc1846, Fauq Co, wElmira Ballard
Sarah, b18--, hStafford M Parker
PEASE, John W, b185-, Hamp Co?, wLaura Virginia Cook
PEATROSS, Richard Warner, b183-, Gebe, Caro Co, fRobert Sale, mElizabeth Scott
Richard Warner II, b6/29/1870, Penola, Caro Co, fRobert Oliver, mJulia Archibald Samuel, wMary Sheridan Newman, md4/12/1905
Robert Oliver, bc1835, White Chimneys, Caro Co, d1905, fRobert Sale, mElizabeth Scott, wJulia Archibald Samuel
Robert Sale, bc1800, Caro Co, wElizabeth Scott
PEBWORTH, Mary A, b185-, Norfolk, d1900, hJohn William Cherry, md2/23/1876
PECK, Elizabeth E, hRobert Blair McNutt
Ellen Victoria, b18--, Bote Co, hThomas H Simmerman
Fannie W, b18--, Gile Co, 2w of John Alexander Adair, Sr
John, b17--, Gile Co
Sallie, b1805, Crai Co, hJohn Miller
Sarah, bc1800, Gile Co, fJohn,

PECK (continued)
  hEdwin J Amiss
PEDDICORD, John M, b18--, Roan Co?, wClara Staples
PEDIGO, Abram Lincoln, bc1860, nrThe Hollow, Patr Co, fAlbert Gallatin, mLucinda J Harbour
  Albert Gallatin, b1822, Elamsville, Patr Co, d1911, fLewis, mSarah Harbour, wLucinda J Harbour
  Benjamin Schuyler, b11/18/1855, nrThe Hollow, Patr Co, fAlbert Gallatin, mLucinda J Harbour, wLelia C Kirby, md4/1892
  Cordelia, b185-, nrThe Hollow, Patr Co, fAlbert Gallatin, mLucinda J Harbour, hThomas Martin
  Emma, b18--, Roan Co?, hChester B Gravely
  Emma, b185-, Henry Co, fJohn F, (1)mMartha Gravely
  Henry, bc1800, fRobert, (1)m-- Elkin, w-- Poston
  John Edward, b186-, Henry Co, fJohn F, (2)mRachel Gravely
  John F, b18--, fhenry, m-- Poston, 1wMartha Gravely, 2w Rachel Gravely
  Lewis, b17--, Elamsville, Patr Co, fAbel Peregoy, wSarah Harbour
  Lewis Gravely, b1/23/1858, Henry Co, fJohn F, (1)mMartha Gravely
  Rufus C, bc1860, nrThe Hollow, Patr Co, d1923, fAlbert Gallatin, mLucinda J Harbour
PEEBLES, Jane, b18--, Fred Co?, hDavid Clayton
PEED, James N, bc1860, Norf Co?, wMartha S Corbitt
PEERMAN, James C, b18--, Camp Co?, wMary Jane Elam
  Robert L, b10/12/1870, Rustburg, Camp Co, fJames C, mMary Jane Elam, wBessie Sutherlin, md1912
PEERY, Alexander S, b1855, Taze Co, fWilliam, m-- Hood, wLetitia Macon
  Charles T, bc1860, Taze Co?, wMary Ollie Surface
  Henry Edward, b9/21/1867, Taze Co, 1wJennie Groseclose, 2w

PEERY (continued)
  Kate Buchanan, 3wLillian (Chapell) Hall
  James, b1833, Burkes Garden, Taze Co, fThomas, Jr, wMary L Spotts
  Joseph, b18--, Wash Co, wLavona Brown
  Milton, bc1830, Fred Co?, wMary Kline
  Sarah, b1832, Taze Co, 1904, fHarvey G, hRufus Brittain
  Thomas, Sr, b17--, Augu Co
  Thomas, Jr, bc1800, Burkes Garden, Taze Co, fThomas, Sr
  William, b18--, Taze Co, w-- Hood
PEIRCE, David, bc1870, Fosters Falls, Wyth Co, fWilliam, mEmeline Painter
  Isaac, b186-, Fosters Fall, Wyth Co, fWilliam, mEmeline Painter
  Joseph, b17--, West Co, wAlice Tapscott
  Joseph, b4/15/1864, "Oakley", Lanc Co, fRobert T, Sr, mMary Alice Tapscott, wJanet C Gilliam, md1894
  Martha, b18--, Wuth Co?, hDavid P Graham
  Robert Tunstall, Sr, b1800, West Co, d1874, fJoseph, mAlice Tapscott, wMary Alice Tapscott
  Robert Tunstall, Jr, bc1870, "Oakley", Lanc Co, fRobert Tunstall, Sr, mMary Alice Tapscott
  William, b1812, Wyth Co, d1875, wEmeline Painter
  William, b186-, Fosters Fall, Wyth Co, fWilliam, mEmeline Painter
PEKINS, Hester, b1834, Gray Co, hCalvin Livesay
PENCE, --, bc1830, Rkhm Co, wMargaret Miller
  Adam, b7/24/1834, Shen Co?, fJacob, wSarah Peters
  Casper, b186-, Timberville, Rkhm Co, fSylvanus, mAnnie Bowman
  Conrad, b17--, Shen Co
  Elnora, b185-, Timberville, Rkhm Co, fSylvanus, mAnnie

PENCE (continued)
Bowman
Harriet, b18--, Monr Co, d1916, hAlpha Jacob Farrier
Jacob, b18--, Shen Co?, fPhilip, mAnn Marie Miller, w-- Schaeffer
Jacob, b7/12/1857, Timberville, Rkhm Co, fSylvanus, mAnnie Bowman, wDorothy V Painter
John, b17--, Shen Co, dc1845, fConrad, wSarah Brenner
Jonas, b10/1/1818, Shen Co, d1890, fJohn, mSarah Brenner, wSallie Zirkle
Michael, bc1840, Shen Co, wElizabeth Filsmoyer
Michael, b185-, Shen Co, fJonas, mSallie Zirkle
Milton M, b1846, nrForestville, Shen Co, d1900, fPhilip, mKatherine Bowers, wNannette E Neff
Philip, b1781, nrForestville, Shen Co, d1860, fConrad, wKatherine Bowers
Rebecca, b18--, Shen Co?, hGideon Zirkle
Rebecca, bc1860, Timberville, Rkhm Co, fSylvanus, mAnnie Bowman, hEugene Andrick
Sarah Elizabeth, b185-, Shen Co, fJonas, mSallie Zirkle
Sylvanus, b18--, Rkhm Co, wAnnie Bowman
William, bc1850, Rkhm Co?, wLizzi Garber
William A, bc1850, Shen Co, wMary Hagey Wunder
William Anderson, b7/14/1856, Shen Co, fJonas, mSallie Zirkle, wAmanda Bowman, md11/1/1877
PENDLETON, E Morgan, b18--, wLaura Tucker
Ella, b18--, Richmond?, hDaniel S McCarthy
James Sheppard, b17--, Amhe Co?, fRuben, mAnn Garland, wJane Aldridge
John, bc1690, Camp Co?, fPhilip, mIsabelle Hurt, w-- Tinsley
Nellie Winn, b18--, Amhe Co, fRobert Aldridge, mElizabeth Pierce, hArchie D Beard

PENDLETON (continued)
Robert Aldridge, b18--, Amhe Co, fJames Sheppard, mJane Aldridge, wElizabeth Pierce
Robert Nelson, bc1845, Loui Co, d1905, wFannie Gibson
Robinette, b18--, KiQu Co?, hS S Henley
Ruben, b17--, Camp Co?, fJohn, m-- Tinsley, wAnn Garland
Susan, b18--, 1w of George A Kenner
PENICK, Douglas, b12/19/1866, fGiles A, mNannie Bland, wNannie McKinney
Junius, b185-, Hali Co, fWilliam Aaron, mSusan Baker
Rosa, b185-, Hali Co, fWilliam Aaron, mSusan Baker, hHarper W Shelton
Virginia, b18--, Hali Co?, hJames D Noell
William Aaron, bc1820, PrEd Co, wSusan Baker
William B, b1857, Hali Co, fWilliam Aaron, mSusan Baker, wPattie Roberts
PENN, Abram, b17--, wRuth Stoval
Bethelinda, bc1800, Nels Co?, hAlexander Fitzpatrick
Katherine, b 1819, Patr Co, hHarrison Carter Frances
Lucinda, b9/3/1771, fAbram, mRuth Stoval, hSamuel Penn, md1790
Mary Stoval, bc1800, fGranville, hAbram Stenn Staples
William, bc1850, Henry Co?, wPattie Dillard
PENNINGTON, America, b1833, Pennington Gap, Lee Co, d1907, hJohn P Graham
Ann E, b18--, Lynchburg, Camp Co?, hJohn Bell Tilden Winfree
Elizabeth, bc1870, Lee Co, fWilliam, mLavina Turner, 1h-- Orr, 2hAdanijah G Hyatt
Emily Russell, b9/1/1862, nr Dryden, Lee Co, hElbert Sevier Flanary
Lucy, b18--, Lee Co, hJohn Frazier
Mary, b18--, Lee Co?, hThomas Flannery
William, b18--, Lee Co, wLavina Turner

PEPPER, Georgie, b18--, Mont Co?, wMollie Nunn
Sarah, b18--, Pepper, Mont Co, d1853, hDavid Johnston Chapman, Sr
PERCIFUL, Alice, bChurch View, Midd Co, hThomas G Jones, Sr
PERDUE, Edgar N, b5/24/1855, nrChester, Ches Co, fWilliam N, (2)mSarah T Nunnelly, wPatty Cogbill
Elizabeth, b18--, Ches Co, fWilliam N, (1)m-- Cogbill, hGideon P Chalkley
Everett, b18--, Ches Co, fWilliam N, (1)m-- Cogbill
Fanny, b18--, Ches Co, fWilliam N, (2)mSarah T Nunnelly, hG E Robinson
Hattie, b18--, Ches Ca, fWilliam N, (2)mSarah T Nunnelly, hC N Friend
Kate, b18--, Ches Co, fWilliam N, (2)mSarah T Nunnelly, hWalter G Ivey
Lucy A, b18--, Ches Co, fWilliam N, (1)m-- Cogbill, hR H Nunnelly
Martha, b18--, Ches Co, fWilliam N, (1)m-- Cogbill, hC N Jones
Samuel A, b18--, Ches Co, fWilliam N, (2)mSarah T Nunnelly
Thomas, b18--, Ches Co, fWilliam N, (1)m-- Cogbill
Walter N, b18--, Ches Co, fWilliam N, (2)mSarah T Nunnelly
William N, b18--, 1w-- Cogbill, 2wSarah T Nunnelly
PERKIN, Anne Frances, b18--, hRichard Shelton Ellis, Sr
PERKINS, Callis L, b186-, Loui Co, fDaniel H, mMartha Ann Morris
Daniel, bc1800, Loui Co
Daniel H, b1829, Loui Co, d1912, fDaniel, wMartha Ann Morris
Daniel Webster, b12/11/1866, Loui Co, fDaniel H, mMartha Ann Morris, wIda Blanche Crank, md5/1895
Emma, b186-, Loui Co, fDaniel H, mMartha Ann Morris
George, b12/7/847, Cumb Co?, d1918, fWilliam Allen, mAnn

PERKINS (continued)
Henderson, wEliza Norris Watson
George, b18--, Fluv Co, d1900, wBlanche Haden
Henry D, b186-, Camp Co?, wSarah Ann Brown Whitehead
James David, b2/3/1856, Gray Co, fJohn H, mLucy Young, 1wEmma Bryant, md6/1881, 2w Callie Carson, md12/1915
John C, b186-, Loui Co, fDaniel H, mMartha Ann Morris
John H, b1802, Gray Co, fStephen, mRuth Hitchcock, wLucy Young
Joseph H, b18--, Russ Co?, wCynthia Yates
Leander N, b185-, Gray Co, fJohn H, mLucy Young
Malinda, b18--, Bedf Co?, 1h-- Nelms, 2hThomas J Phelps
Mary Susan, bc1810, Esse Co?, hLeonard Henley
Mollie, b186-, Loui Co, fDaniel H, mMartha Ann Morris
Sallie, b18--, Midd Co, hJoseph Walter Harwood, Jr
Sarah J, bc1850, Gray Co, fJohn H, mLucy Young, hAllen C Hash
Shandy K, b1842, Fluv Co, wMildred Shepherd, md2/9/1871
Susan M, b18--, Loui Co?, hJohn R Crank
T M, b18--, Richmond?, wElizabeth Langhorne
William Allen, b18--, Cumb Co?, wAnn Henderson
William Young, b185-, Gray Co, fJohn H, mLucy Young
PERROW, A D, b18--, Camp Co
Alexander, b184-, Camp Co, fWilliam C, mMary Cowling
Adolphus, b185-, Camp Co, fWilliam C, mMary C Cowling
Bascom M, b185-, Camp Co, fFerdinand A, mCatherine M Payne
Charles, b17--, Nels Co?, w-- Teas
Charles M, b186-, Camp Co, fFerdinand A, mCatherine M Payne, wMary J Holman
Eleanor, b18--, Lovington, Nels Co, fCharles, m-- Teas, hPereguin Wethered Young
Fanny S, bc1870, Camp Co, fA D,

PERROW (continued)
hRobert G Robertson, Sr, md9/18/1896
Ferdinand A, bc1826, Camp Co, d1873, fDaniel, wCatherine M Payne
Fletcher C, bc1844, Camp Co, fWilliam C, mMary Cowling, wSally A Payne
Mitchell, b17--, Buck Co?, f--Perrot/Perreau
Robley M, b3/1/1861, Marysville, Camp Co, fFerdinand A, mCatherine M Payne, wKate H William, md1/20/1892
Stephen, b17-, Buck Co, f--Perrot/Perreau
Stephen II, b184-, Camp Co, fWilliam C, mMary Cowling
William C, bc1808, Camp Co, fStephen, wMary C Cowling
Willis, b184-, Camp Co, fWilliam C, mMary C Cowling
PERRY, D L, bc1850, Augu Co?, wMaggie Riddel
Ellen, b18--, Scot Co, hNathan B Dougherty
Margaret, b18--, Scot Co?, d1907, hIsaac Bevins
PETERS, Anna L, b1/5/1856, Fran Co, hGeorge B Flora
Catherine, b1812, fDavid, mChristina Brubaker, 2w of John R Webster
Catherine, bc1836, Fran Co, d1913, hBenjamin Sink, Sr
George, bc1800, Scot Co, fJacob, w-- Pierson
Henry D, 18--, Henry Co?, wMary Gravely
Herbert Greyson, b9/10/1859, Henry Co, fHenry D, mMary Gravely, wElectra Smith, md 1894
Isaac, b1835, nrGate City, Scot Co, fGeorge, m-- Pierson, wMelinda Head
Julia D B, bc1800, Camp Co, hSeth Halsey
Mary Virginia, b18--, Cumb Co, hCharles William Blanton, Sr
Rhoda J, b18--, Monr Co?, hBenjamin Alexander Stuart Walker, Jr
Sarah, b18--, hAdam Pence
PETTIT, James C, b18--, Nels

PETTIT (continued)
Co?, wMary G Goodwin
Nannie Sue, b18--, Henrico Co, hGeorge Curtis Vanderslice
Virginia E, b1844, d1921, hWilliam G Venable
PETTROSS, James, b17--, wNancy Leftwich
PETTUS, Ann, b17--, Mont Co?, hJames Shelburne
Elizabeth, b16--, fThomas, m--Dabney, hArthur Hopkins, mdc 1715
Thomas, b16--, fThomas
PETTY, --, b186-, Warr Co?, wBelle Wharton
Abner, bc1800, Culp Co, fZacharey, mMary Marshall, wMary Smith
Anne, b18--, Meck Co, hJohn Gibbons Wall
George, b18--, Page Co
Laura, b18--, Rkhm Co?, fGeorge, hJoseph F Taylor, md 1876
Nancy, b18--, nrRoanoke, Meck Co, fAbner, mMary Smith, hLeroy Campbell
PETTYJOHN, George W, b18--, Amhe Co?, wAnn Taylor Reynolds
John P, b2/8/1846, Amhe Co, fGeorge W, mAnn Taylor Reynolds, 1wNannie R Old, 2wBell W Watts
Louisa, b1832, Amhe Co, d1912, hGeorge Wallace Donnan
Walker, b11/2/1870, Camp Co, fJohn P, (1)mNannie R Old, wMary Macon Rains, md1896
PEYTON, Ann C, bc1830, Staf Co, fThomas, mSarah Maddox, hJoel Jenkins
Bernard, bc1800, Culp Co?, wJulia Arondel Green
Bernard, b185-, Charlottesville, Albe Co, d1885, fMoses Green, mMartha Champ Carter
Champ, b185-, Charlottesville, Albe Co, fMoses Green, mMartha Champ Carter
Chandler, b17--, Fauq Co?, wEliza Scott
Charles Everett Carter, b1/5/1855, Charlottesville, Albe Co, fMoses Green, mMartha Champ Carter, wElizabeth Ken-

PEYTON (continued)
drick, md12/17/1879
Henry, b17--, Staf Co, fJohn
Imogene, b186-, Charlottesville, Albe Co, d1922, fMoses Green, mMartha Champ Carter, hWilliam Wertenbaker
Jane, bc1800, Staf Co, hWilliam Henry Chichester
Julia Green, b186-, Charlottesville, Albe Co, fMoses Green, mMartha Champ Carter
Margaret Lynn, b18--, Augu Co, fJohn Howe, hGeorge Moffett Cochran, Jr, md11/4/1866
Mary, bc1860, Charlottesville, Albe Co, d1922, fMoses Green, mMartha Champ Carter, hWilliam Chamberlain
Moses Green, b1/6/1826, "Liberty Hall", Culp Co, d1897, fBernard, mJulia Arondel Green, wMartha Champ Carter
Robert Eden, Sr, b1803, "Gordonsdale", Fauq Co, fChandler, mEliza Scott, wAnn Lee Jones
Robert Eden, Jr, b8/8/1843, "Gordonsdale", Fauq Co, fRobert Eden, Sr, mAnn Lee Jones, wCornelia Foster
Susan Madison, b182-, Augu Co, fJohn Howe, hJohn Brown Baldwin, md9/20/1842
Thomas, bc1800, Staf Co, wSarah Maddox
PFELTZ, Maria, b18--, Norfolk?, hRichard S Dodson
PHELPS, John, b17--, Bedf Co, fJohn
Thomas, b17--, Bedf Co, fJohn
Thomas J, b18--, Fancy Grove, Bedf Co, fThomas, 2h of Malinda (Perkins) Nelms
Thomas Key, b9/21/1847, "Keyton", nrBody Camp, Bedf Co, fThomas J, mMalinda (Perkins) Nelms, wSarah Elizabeth Moulton
PHILLIPS, Abram, b185-, nrMayland, Rkhm Co, fRobert, mMary Carver
Alexander Wallace, b18--, Fauq Co?, wAnnie Harrell
Edward, bc1860, nrMarkham, Fauq Co, fAlexander Wallace, mAnnie Harrell

PHILLIPS (continued)
Emily A, bc1860, nrMayland, Rkhm Co, fRobert, mMary Carver
Emma Virginia, b18--, fJoshua, mSallie Hughes
Ernest, b186-, nrMarkham, Fauq Co, fAlexander Wallace, mAnnie Harell
Fannie, b186-, nrWayland, Rkhm Co, fRobert, mMary Carver
George E S, b18--, Clar Co?, wHannah Blake
Harvey F, b1853, nrMayland, Rkhm Co, fRobert, mMary Carver, wLillie Spitzer
Jennie, b186-, nrPetersburg, PrGe Co, fJohn T, hJohn Whitehead
John H, b185-, nrMayland, Rkhm Co, fRobert, mMary Carver
John T, b18--, PrGe Co
Laura May, b5/22/1861, nrMarkham, Fauq Co, d1920, fAlexander Wallace, mAnnie Harrell, hAmos Payne, md5/22/1879
Lillie, b18--, Albe Co?, d1891, 2w of Henry Morris Gleason, md1882
Lula, b186-, nrMrkham, Fauq Co, fAlexander Wallace, mAnnie Harrell, hW H McCarty
Mary, b17--, York Co, 2w of Anthony Robinson III
Pattie Pendleton, b18--, Albe Co, d1920, hJohn G Boatwright
Robert, b18--, wMary Carver
Turner, b186-, nrMarkham, Fauq C, fAlexander Wallace, mAnnie Harrell
William, bc1860, nrMayland, Rkhm Co, fRobert, mMary Carver
William Jesse, b1845, Acco Co, d1923, wMargaret Ann Savage
PHILIPS, virginia, b18--, Norfolk?, hAndrew Jackson Denby
PHIPPS, Bettie, b18--, Bridle Creek, Gray Co, fJohn M, (1)m-- Osborne, hChapman Delp
Drucilla, b18--, Bridle Creek, Gray Co, fJohn M, (1)m-- Osborne, hHarvey Phipps
Drusilla, b18--, Gray Co?, hLewis H Bryant
Harvey, b18--, Gray Co?, wDrucilla Phipps
John, b17--, Gray Co, fBenja-

PHIPPS (continued)
min, w-- Howell
John M, b1829, Bridle Creek, Gray Co, fJoseph, 1w-- Osborne, 2wMartha (Parks) Rutherford
Joseph K, b18--, Bridle Creek, Gray Co, fJohn M, (1)m-- Osborne
Mollie, b18--, Bridle Creek, fJohn M, (1)m-- Osborne, hHardin Todd
Nannie, b18--, Bridle Creek, Gray Co, (1)m-- Osborne, hWarner Daniels
Preston, b1818, Fox, Gray Co, d1893, fJohn, m-- Howell, wJane Dixton
Preston Columbus, b1849, Gray Co, fPreston, mJane Dixton, wEmeline Osborne
Zachariah, b18--, Bridle Creek, Gray Co, fJohn M, m-- Osborne
PHLEGAR, Archer Allen, b2/22/1846, Christiansburg, Mont Co, d1912, fEli, mAnn C Trigg, wSue Shanks, md6/5/1872
Augustus R, b9/1856, Floy Co, wMollie Nunn
Eli, b1808, Floy Co, d1864, wAnn C Trigg
Jane, b18--, Wash Co?, hGeorge W Summers
PHLEGER, W J, bc1860, Floy Co?, wElma Lancaster
PICKETT, Elizabeth Blackwell, b17--Fauq Co, fMartin, hJohn Scott
John, bc1850, Loud Co?, wElizabeth H Love
Lucy, b17--, Fauq Co?, hCharles Marshall
PIERCE, Amanda, b18--, Arli Co?, hWilliam Plaugher
Annie Pendleton, b1855, Appo Co, hEdwin P Rucker
Elizabeth, b18--, Amhe Co, hRobert Aldridge Pendleton
Graham, bc1860, Fauq Co?, wKate Green
Harriet, b1831, hArthur B Davies, Sr
PIERSON, --, bc1800, Scot Co?, hGeorge Peters
PIFER, Isaac, b11/2/1820, nrStrasburg, Shen Co, wRebecca

PIFER (continued)
Funkhouser
Joanna V, b186-, nrFishers Hill, Shen Co, fIsaac, mRebecca Funkhouser, hEphraim Baker
John H, b186-, nrFishers Hill, Shen Co, fIsaac, mRebecca Funkhouser
Martha Rebecca, b6/28/1868, nrFishers Hill, Shen Co, fIsaac, mRebecca Funkhouser, hEdward Baker, md11/5/1888
Mary Elizabeth, b186-, nrFishers Hill, Shen Co, fIsaac, mRebecca Funkhouser, hCharles Fisher
PIGG, Elizabeth, b17--, Cumb Co?, fJohn, 1w or 2w of Richard Spencer
PILCHER, Mary Bell, b18--, hJohn Henry Worsham
PILKINGTON, Virginia, b18--, Lune Co, hPeter Branch Jones
PILSON, Matthew, b18--, Augu Co?, wLavinia Elizabeth Finley
William Harper, bc1850, Greenville, Augu Co, fMatthew, mLavinia Elizabeth Finley, wLucy Harriet Stout
PINCHUM, Eliza, b18--, Richmond?, hJames Caskie
PINCKARD, Annie, b18--, nrLancaster Court House, Lanc Co, 2w of Herbert Pollard Hall
PINKARD, W M, bc1860, Lanc Co?, wHannah Virginia Downing
PIPER, Bettsey E, b17--, Albe Co?, hGarrett White
PIRKEY, Bell Walker, b186-, nrThe Grottoes, Rkhm Co, fElias, mSusan Baker, mC M Shaver
Elias, bc1828, Rkhm Co?, d1908, wSusan Baker
Elizabeth, b186-, nrThe Grottoes, Rkhm Co, fElias, mSusan Baker, hRobert M Meyerhoeffer
Fannie, bc1870, nrThe Grottoes, Rkhm Co, fElias, mSusan Baker, hGeorge R Root
Jacob M, b5/19/1857, nrThe Grottoes, Rkhm Co, fElias, mSusan Baker, wElise Chevolin
John S, b8/6/1865, nrThe Grottoes, Rkhm Co, fElias, mSusan Baker, wMary B Baylor

PIRKEY (continued)
Mollie, b185-, nrThe Grottoes, Rkhm Co, fElias, mSusan Baker, hC D Garber
PITMAN, Levi, b18--, Shen Co
Sibelia Josephine, b1843, nrMt Jackson, Shen Co, hRichard Knight Flannagan
Susan, b18--, Shen Co, hIsaac Fisher, Jr
PITT, Robert H, b1852, Midd Co, wAnne Clair Robertson
PITTMAN, Archibald, bc1830, Clar Co?, wElizabeth Hiett
PITZER, A W, b18--, Roan Co?, wLaura McClanahan
Armstead Neal, b c1870, nr Salem, Roan Ca, fGeorge Madison, Sr, mMargaret Ellen Neal
Bernard, b17--, Bote Co, d1825, fJohn, mElizabeth Madison, wJane Kyle
Emeline, b18--, Roan Co?, fMadison, hCharles C Tomkins
George Madison, Sr, b18--, nrSalem, Roan Co, d1915, fMadison, mEliza Lewis, wMargaret Ellen Neal
James M, b186-, nrSalem, Roan Co, fGeorge Madison, Sr, mMargaret Ellen Neal
John, b17--, wElizabeth Madison
Madison, b8/24/1789, Bote Co, fBernard, mJane Kyle, wEliza Lewis
PIZZINI, Lelia Louise, b18--, Richmond, 3w of William McKendree Evans, m d1880
PLASTER, Harvey L, b9/1854, Blackford, Russ Co, wMary Elizabeth Ray
Lucy, b18--, Russ Co?, hJerome Bonaparte Whited
PLAUGHER, William, b18--, Arli Co?, wAmanda Pierce
PLEASANTS, Archibald, b17--, wJane Randolph Woodson
Elizabeth, b16--, Henrico Co?, d1751, fJohn, mJane --, hJames Cocke
Emeline Broaddus, b18--, fJohn Woodson, mElizah Coleman, hAlexander Mebane
John Woodson, b17--, fArchibald, mJane Randolph Woodson, wElizah Coleman

PLEASANTS (continued)
Joseph, bc1800, Henrico Co
Joseph, b18--, Clar Co?, wNancy F Page
Susan Ann, b18--, hWilliam Gray
Susanna Virginia, b1/1821, Henrico Co, d1906, fJoseph, hCharles Lewis Cocke, md12/31/1840
PLECKER, Charles Edgar, b186-, Augu Co, fJacob H, mFrances Burton Smoot
Emma Frances, bc1860, Augu Co, fJacob H, mFrances Burton Smoot, hJulius Frederick Ferdinand Cassell
Fannie, b185-, Milnesville, Augu Co, fLevi, mMaria Huffman, hW W Michael
George A, b186-, Milnesville, Augu Co, fLevi, mMaria Huffman
Harriet Elizabeth, b185-, Augu Co, fJacob H, mFrances Burton Smoot, hEdward Franklin Wayman
Horace Medley, bc1860, Augu Co, fJacob H, mFrances Burton Smoot
Ida C, b185-, Milnesville, Augu Co, fLevi, mMaria Huffman, hJ A Michael
Jacob H, b10/13/1829, Augu Co, d1890, fJacob Plecker/Blaecher, mElizabeth Wise/Weisz, wFrancis Burton Smoot, md11/22/1854
John Edmund, b12/19/1852, Milnesville, Augu Co, fLevi, mMaria Huffman
Levi, bc1830, nrMilnesville, Augu Co, wMaria Huffman
Lucy A, bc1860, Milnesville, Augu Co, fLevi, mMaria Huffman
Mary V, b185-, Milnesville, Augu Co, fLevi, mMaria Huffman, hWilliam Wine
May Burton, b186-, Augu Co, fJacob H, mFrances Burton Smoot
Thomas C, b186-, Milnesville, Augu Co, fLevi, mMaria Huffman
Walter Ashby, b4/2/1861, Augu Co, fJacob H, mFrances Burton Smoot, wCatherine Matilda Houston, md11/22/1888
PLUNKETT, Margaret W, b12/1840, Nels Co, hWilliam H Goodwin

POGUE, Henry, bc1790, Clar Co?, w-- McCormick
POINDEXTER, Bettie Lightfoot, b1/15/1851, Ches Co, fEdwin Wilkerson, mFrances Archer Hundley, hJoseph Franklin Deans
David, b18--, Bedf Co, fJack, mDabney --, wAnn --
E H, b18--, Fran Co?, wHopie Newbill
Edwin, b17--, fGeorge Benskin
Edwin Wilkerson, b18--, fEdwin, wFrances Archer Hundley
George II, b16--, fGeorge
George III, b17--, fGeorge II
George Benskin, b17--, fGeorge III
J B, bc1860, Camp Co?, wMattie Walthall
Jack, b17--, Loui Co, wDabney -
John David, b18--, Bedf Co, fDavid, mAnn --, wAmanda Freeman
Lucy A, b18--, 1w of William Henry Parrish, md1880
Mollie Elizabeth, b186-, Fran Co, fE H, mHopie Newbill, hWesley D Wright
Susan, b3/7/1832, Loui Co, d1891, hThomas Massie
POINTER, Zachariah T, bc1860, Hali Co?, d1915, wMary S Adams
POLLARD, Elizabeth, bc1800, Buck Co, hBenjamin Snead
Elizabeth, bc1870, KiQu Co, fHenry Robinson, mJessie Graham, hErnest M Long
Elizabeth H, b17--, fRobert, mAnn Talman, hJosiah Higgins
Henry Robinson, Sr, b11/28/1846, KiQu Co, fJohn, mJuliett Jeffries, wJessie Gresham
Henry Robinson, b12/21/1868, KiQu Co, fHenry Robinson, Sr, mJessie Gresham, wJulia Williams, md3/21/1896
John, b1802, Gooc Co, wJuliett Jeffries
John, b18--, KiQu Co?, wVirginia Bagby
Josephine, bc1870, KiQu Co, fHenry Robinson, Sr, mJessie Gresham, hJohn S Harrison
Lucinda, bc1800, Buck Co, hWilliam Snead

POLLARD (continued)
Mary Ann, b18--, Glou Co, hCatesby Jones
Oranie, bc1800, Buck Co, hGeorge Snead
POLLOCK, Abram David, b18--, Fauq Co?, wElizabeth Lee
Nannie Lee, bc1850, Fauq Co?, d1908, fAbram David, mElizabeth Lee, hCharles P Janney, Sr
PONTON, John William, b1842, PrEd Co, wMaggie E Estes
POOL, Bale, b185-, Meck Co, fWilliam, m-- Owen
Burruss, b1855, Meck Co, fWilliam, m-- Owen, wNannie H Scott, md1875
Selden, b185-, Meck Co, fWilliam, m-- Owen
William, b18--, Meck Co, w-- Owen
POOLE, --, b177-, nrPetersburg, Dinw Co, hHenry Stokes, md1795
Elizabeth, bc1870, Wytheville, Wyth Co, fJoseph, mMatilda Walk, hWilliam Davidson
Joseph, b1837, Wyth Co, wMatilda Walk
Laura, bc1870, Wytheville, Wyth Co, fJoseph, mMatilda Walk, hWill Winesett
William T, bc1850, Alle Co?, wNaomi Deaton
William Thomas, b3/31/1868, Wytheville, Wyth Co, fJoseph, mMatilda Walk, wMary N Deaton, md9/7/1889
POORE, Carrie, bc1870, Richmond, fPeter, mMargaret --, hJoseph E Sorg, md1890
Martha C, b12/24/1817, d1892, hBenjamin Watkins Roper
Peter, b18--, Richmond?, wMargaret --
POPE, Athalia, b18--, Pitt Co?, fThomas, hWilliam Terry
Frank P, bc1829, Sout Co, d1916, wVirginia Pear Moseley
Mary Elizabeth, b1866, hEnoch F Lanham
Susan, b17--, West Co, hRichard Bayne
POPKINS, George W, b2/22/1855, PrWi Co, wLaura LeFevre
PORTER, --, bc1860, Scot Co?,

PORTER (continued)
wDora E Addington
Andrew Johnson, b8/7/1870, Crockett, Wyth Co, fDavid H, mNancy Rosenbaum, wMaude (Cook) Huddle, md12/22/1921
Charles S, bc1860, Crockett, Wyth Co, fDavid H, mNancy Rosenbaum
David H, b1/14/1833, Crockett, Wyth Co, d1915, fGeorge, m-- Messersmith, wNancy Rosenbaum, md185-
George, bc1800, Gray Co, w-- Messersmith
George W, b186-, Crockett, Wyth Co, fDavid H, mNancy Rosenbaum
James D, b18--, Loui Co?, fJames, wCatherine Harris
Jesse J, b18--, Loui Co, fJames D, mCatherine Harris, wElla L Mallory
Martha A, b12/11/1812, Bath Co, hMoses McClintic
Martha E, b1843, nrBrewster, Russ Ca, d1908, hWilliam J Addington
Paulina V, b1851, Scot Co, hForest P Sergent
Philip B, b11/5/1867, Loui Co, fJesse J, mElla L Mallory, wBessie Hanger, md1898
PORTERFIELD, Alexander, b18--, Gile Co
James H, b1846, nrNewport, Gile Co, d1880, fAlexander, wHenrietta V Williams
PORTRUM, J Henry, bc1810, nr Keezletown, Rkhm Co, fJulius Bertram, m-- Smith
Samuel, b181-, nrKeezletown, Rkhm Co, fJulius Bertram, m-- Smith
POSEY, Anne Elizabeth, b18--, PrWi Co?, fJohn, 2w of Montraville Cornwell
POSTON, --, bc1800, Henry Co, hHenry Pedigo
POTEET, Samuel B, b18--, Lee Co?, wMollie Sue Ely
POUNDS, Jack, bRapp Co?, wBettie Menefee
POWELL, --, bc1850, Rkhm Co, wCordelia Wyant
Alexander L, b12/13/1870, Fran Co, fCarles A, mLucy E Rorrer,

POWELL (continued)
wAddie L Conner, md1/10/1900
Carrie Y, b18--, Williamsburg, JaCi Co, fPeter T, hDaniel Seldon Jones, md10/10/1873
Charles, bc1780, Fran Co?, wLucinda Hancock
Charles A, b18--, Pitt Co, d1911
Cuthbert, bc1810, PrWi Co?, wMarietta Turner
Edwin Thomas, b11/14/1853, Lee Mont, Acco Co, d1918, fThomas, 1w-- Nock, 2wEdna Pearl Savage
Elizabeth, b10/10/1809, Middleburg, Loud Co, d1872, hRobert Young Conrad, Sr
Ida, b18--, Fauq Co?, hHenry Grafton Dulany
India, b186-, Stuart, Patr Co, fCharles A, mLucy E Rorrer, hJoshua A Hedgecock, md1885
Laura Holmes, b18--, hJohn Randolph Tucker
Mary Elizabeth, b18--, Nels Co, hCyrus A Matthews
Mary Kate, b1830, Acco Co, 2hJohn W Hyslop, 1h-- Colonna
Nancy Floyd, b17--, KiQu Co?, hRobert Walker
Val, b18--, Spot Co?, wEmma Dickenson
Walter, b186-, Fran Co, fCharles A, mLucy E Rorrer
William, bc1780, Fran Co?, wSophia Hancock
POWERS, Bettie, b18--, Esse Co, 2w of John Venable Crute, md187-
Charles W, b182-, Kline's Mill, Fred Co, fDaniel, wFrances Kline
Daniel, b185-, Kline's Mill, Fred Co, fCharles W, mFrances Kline
Dudley, bc1860, Richmond?, fWilliam H
James, b18--, Richmond
Jane Francis, b18--, KiQu Co, hJohn P Ballard
Jeannette, b18--, West Co, hCharles Hall
Jeremiah, bc1800, Scot Co, w-- Ritchie
Lucy, b1810, Scot Co, d1894, hGeorge Bond

POWERS (continued)
Philip, b18--, Richmond?, wBertha --
Pike, b18--, Richmond
Reuben S, b18--, Richmond, d1864, wMildred Ann Ballard
Robert, b18--, Richmond
Sarah, b1828, Wise Co, fJeremiah, m-- Ritchie, hJoseph Freeman
Thomas E, b2/4/1857, Richmond, fReuben S, mMildred Ann Ballard, wSusan Margaret Early
William F, b3/17/1850, Kline's Mill, Fred Co, fCharles W, mFrances Kline, wAnna M Carbaugh
POYTHRESS, Sally Bland, b17--, West Co, m-- Bland, 1hRichard Lee, 2hWilloughby Newton III
PRARIE, Andrew Y, b18--, wCarrie Kluge
PRATHER, Mary, b18--, McDo Co, hJesse J Gamble
PRATT, G Julian, fWilliam A
PRESLEY, Peter, b16--, Nhld Co?
Winefred, b16--, Nhld Co, fPeter, hAnthony Thornton
PRESSLEY, Ephraim, b18--, w-Colley
Eunice, bc1870, Stratton, Dick Co, hClement V Rasnick
Joshua D, b18--, Dick Co, d1888, fEphraim, m-- Colley, 1h of Eliza Jane Counts
PRESTON, Cochran, bc1860, Pula Co?, wVirginia Graham
Eliza Mary, bc1800, hCharles C Johnston
Jennie Orr, b1/1865, Wash Co, d1910, 1w of Frances Beattie Hutton, Sr
John A, bc1850, Bedf Co, wSerena F Overstreet
Letitia, b17--, fWilliam, mSusanna Smith, hJohn Floyd
Mary, b18--, Wash Co?, hJohn G White
Polly, bc1870, Wash Co, fJohn, hWilliam James Edmondson, md6/30/1899
Mary Elizabeth, b17--, h-- Hurt
Nannie Montgomery, b1842, Wash Co, hJohn C Summers
Robert John, b1841, Wash Co, fJohn, 1wMartha Sheffey, 2w

PRESTON (continued)
Elizabeth S (Stuart) Gravely
PRETLOW, Ann S, b18--, Nans Co?, hZachariah Everett Holland
Thomas Jefferson, b18--, Sout Co?, wAnne Eliza Massenburg
PRETTYMAN, Rebecca, b18--, Wheeling, Ohio Co, hJames W Renforth
PRICE, Berryman, b7/1837, nrElkton, Rkhm Co, d1903, fJacob, mEleanor Rosenberger, 1wElizabeth Brubaker, md1866, 2w Mattie K Keyser
Blanch, b18--, Crai Co?, hIsaac C Wagener
Charles Daniel, bc1848, Loud Co, wMartha Jane Aleshire
Ferdinand, b18--, Fran Co?, wJane Frances Hancock
Florence, b18--, Ballston, -- Co, hRichard B Shreve
Henry Newton, b18--, Richmond?, w-- Belvin
Hutchings B, b18--, PrEd Co, d1851, 1h of Fanny J Rice
Jacob, b18--, nrElkton, Rkhm Co, wEleanor Rosenberger
Jane H, b17--, hJohn Watson
Joshua, bc1810, Shen Co?, wPhoebe Moore
Martha, b18--, Roan Co?, hDaniel D M Digges
Mary, b18--, Cumb Co?, 1w of James B Godsey
Mary, b184-, Poca Co?, hA M McLaughlin
Melvina, b1841, Hano Co, d1913, hOscar Wiley
Robert, b186-, nrNew Market, Shen Co, fBerryman B, (1)mElizabeth Brubaker
Sallie, bc1857, Fran Co, fCyrus, hHenry S Deyerle
Samuel Hutchings, b1/25/1852, Bedf Co, fHutchings B, mFanny J Rice, 1wFannie Rose Harris, md1878, 2wLelia D (Wood) Ruff
Samuel M, bc1860, Richmond?, wElizabeth L Cannon
Tazewell, bc1860, Fran Co?, wElizabeth Ann Hancock
Vernon L, bc1870, nrNew Market, Shen Co, fBerryman B, (1)mElizabeth Brubaker
PRIDDY, Albert Sidney, b12/7/

PRIDDY (continued)
1865, Lune Co, fRobert W, mMartha H Gaulding
John Coleman, b2/3/1868, nr Keysville, Lune Co, fWilliam K, mLucy A Carter, wAlice H Harvey, md9/4/1906
Lucy, b18--, Richmond, 1w of James Monroe Hayes, Jr
Mattie R, b186-, nrKeysville, Lune Co, fWilliam K, mLucy A Carter, hJohn H Ingram
Nannie E, b185-, nrKeysville, Lune Co, fWilliam K, mLucy A Carter, hAlbert G Towler
Robert W, b1827, nrRichmond, Henrico Co, d1901, fRobert, mNancy Dabney Francis, wMartha H Gaulding
William H, b4/1/1861, nrKeysville, Lune Co, d1913, fWilliam K, mLucy A Carter
William K, b1/20/1830, Henrico Co, wLucy A Carter
PRIDE, Martha, b17--, Ches Co, hEdward Dance
PRIDEMORE, Hiram D, b18--, Scot Co?, wSusan Slemp
PRIEST, James, bc1810, Fauq Co?, wJane Cochran
Lillian, bc1870, Oran Co?, d1922, hLewis W Graves
PRILLAMAN, Andrew, b18--, Fran Co
Elkanah, bc1862, Fran Co, fAndrew, wMary Jane Mullis
Peter A, bc1865, Henry Co, d1922, fJames, wElsa S Draper
PRINCE, Catherine, b1797, Suss Co, hAustin W Jones
PRINGLE, Margaret, bc1870, PrWi Co, hBenjamin H Lewis
PRITCHETT, Charles Wesley, Sr, b11/1826, Pitt Co?, d1906, fWilliam E, wLydia A Robertson
Charles Wesley, Jr, b7/1/1864, Pitt Co, fCharles Wesley, Sr, mLydia A Robertson, wS Clay Keesee, md12/12/1888
PROFFIT, Samuel Green, b18--, Fran Co, fJoseph Patterson, mMary Via
PROFFITT, Harvey, bc1800, Fran Co?, wBarbara Barton
Joseph Patterson, b18--, Fran Co, fHarvey, mBarbara Barton,

PROFFITT (continued)
wMary Via
PROSSER, Josephine, b18--, Nhld Co, hCharles R Hall
PROVIN, --, b17--, Clar Co?, 1w of Francis McCormick
PROW, Susannah, bc1700, fCyprin, hWalter Anderson
PRUDEN, A D, bc1860, Isle Co, fJohn Thomas, mSarah Ann Denson
C O, b6/8/1856, Isle Co, d1921, fJohn Thomas, mSarah Ann Denson
James R, bc1860, Pitt Co?, wFannie Hughes
Nathaniel, bc1860, Isle Co, fJohn Thomas, mSarah Ann Denson
PRUETT, Raleigh W, b18--, Taze Co?, wElizabeth Marrs
PRUNTY, Jane, b18--, Fran Co, 1w of Frederick Rives Brown
PUCKETT, John W, bc1860, Dick Co?, wMartha Sifers
William, b18--, Hali Co
PUGH, Arthur, b18--, fLemuel, m-- Twyford
Isadora Charity, bc1861, fLemuel, m-- Twyfod, hCharles Frederick Rinker
Lemuel, b18--, Capon Ridge, Hamp Co, w-- Twyford
PULLEN, Dora, b18--, Bote Co, fSamuel, mMary Deisher, hEdward Flaherty
George W, b1848, Eagle Rock, Bote Co, fSamuel, mMary Deisher, wCatherine Myers
Jacob U, b18--, Bote Co, fSamuel, mMary Deisher
Samuel, b1825, Bote Co, wMary Deisher
PULLER, --, b17--, hWilliam Spindle, Sr
James B, b18--, Hano Co, wAlice J Butler
PULLEY, Mary, bc1700, JaCi Co?, hJames Speed
PULLIAM, Albet Clopton, b1829, Henrico Co, fRobert Mosby, mAnne Gunn Clopton, wElizabeth Loyd
George, b18--, Pula Co, wCassandra Harrell
Mosby, b2/9/1764, Loui Co,

PULLIAM (continued)
wSarah Timberlake
Myrtle, bc1870, Richmond?, hF P Dickinson, md12/20/1893
Robert Mosby, b17--, Henrico Co, fMosby, msarah Timberlake, wAnne Gunn Clopton
Virginia, b18--, Nels Co?, hCharles W McCue
PUMPHREY, Martha R, b18--, NewK Co, hDandridge W Clarke
Sarah, b18--, York Co, hJohn Cary Wade
PURCELL, --, bc1800, Loud Co?, hStacey Tavenner
Annie, b18--, Fred Co, fJohn, mAdeline Cather
Charles D, b5/2/1843, nrLouisa, Loui Co, fJohn, mNancy Gibson, wPatsy M Haden
Charles W, b1/18/1818, Richmond, d1887, fCharles W, Sr, mSarah Ann Broughy, wMargaret Adams Freeman
Clark, b18--, Fred Co, fJohn, mAdeline Cather
Emma F, b10/2/1850, Richmond, fCharles W, Sr, mMargaret Adams Freeman, hMassie L McCue, md11/11/1889
John, bc1810, Fred Co, wAdeline Cather
John Henry, bc1850, Richmond?, wSarah Ann Lewis
Jonah, b17--, Fauq Co?, fSamuel, mDeborah Copeland, wMaria Osborne
Martha, b18--, PrWi Co?, hThomas K Davis
Mary, b18--, Fred Co, fJohn, mAdeline Cather
Perry, b18--, Fred Co, fJohn, mAdeline Cather
Philip T, b185-, Richmond, fCharles W, Jr, mMargaret Adams Freeman
Robert B, bc1840, KiQu Co?, d1898, wMary Ella Bird
Rosanna Osborne, b18--, Loud Co, fJonah, mMaria Osborne, hGeorge W Gibson
Samuel, b17--, Fauq Co?, fThomas, mMary Van Hook, wDeborah Copeland
Samuel H, b12/4/1851, Richmond, fCharles W, Jr, mMargaret

PURCELL (continued)
Adams Freeman, wElizabeth A Garrett, md12/13/1882
Thomas, b17--, PrWi Co, wMary Van Hook
PURNELL, Mary, b17--, Nott Co, hJohn Dupuy
PUTNAM, --, b18--, Fauq Co?, wLandonia F Heflin
Benjamin, b183-, Rapp Co?, wAlice Fishback
PUTNEY, Fannie, b18--, Fluv Co, hJames A Snead
W T, b8/7/1856, Buck Co, wSusie Brooks
QUAINTANCE, Homieselle Victoria, b18--, Rapp Co, hTheodore Lindsay Thurman
Malinda, b1818, Rapp Co, hStaunton Aylor, md1836
QUANTZ, --, bc1850, Fred Co?, wRosa Belle Shryock
QUARLES, Eliza, b18--, Bedf Co?, 2w of Joshua Laughon
Elizabeth, bc1850, Bedf Co, fSamuel, mElizabeth R Steptoe, hHenry Clay Lowry
Julian Minor, b9/25/1848, Caro Co, fPeter, mMary E Waddy, 1wCornelia Stout, md10/1876, 2wCornelia Taylor
N F, b184-, Isle Co, d1862, fPeter, mMary E Waddy
Peter, b18--, Isle Co?, wMary E Waddy
Samuel, b18--, Bedf Co?, wElizabeth R Steptoe
QUARLS, Cornelia, b18--, Russ Co?, hHenry H Dickerson
QUILLAN, Kerrenneh, b1/1846, Quillins Valley, Scot Co, d1910, hJoseph M Addington
QUILLEN, Joseph A, b1843, nrGate City, Scot Co, d1907, fMartin B, mAnna Addington, wFrances S Osborne
Martin B, b18--, nrGate City, Scot Co, wAnna Addington
QUILLIN, James Monroe, b18--, nrGate City, Scot Co, wRena Tate
Robert Burns, b1853, Nickelsville, Scot Co, fJames Monroe, mRena Tate, wMary E Corns
QUINN, Sylvanus Jackson, b18--, Spot Co?, wJosephine Duval

QUESENBERRY, Floyd, b18--, Carr Co, wAmanda Alexander
Henry, b18--, Floy Co?, wEmma Carter
Mamie, b18--, Loui Co, hOscar Littleton Snead
QUESINBERRY, George, b18--, Snake Creek, Carr Co, d1875, fThomas, wJoanna Webb
Isiah, b6/15/1840, Snake Creek, Carr Co, fGeorge, mJoanna Webb, wEmily Jennings
Thomas, b17--, Carr Co
QUISENBERRY, Charles D, b8/1/1862, Oran Co, fDaniel, mSallie Reynolds, wVirginia Coleman, md1902
Daniel, b18--, Oran Co, fVivian, wSallie Reynolds
George, b17--, Oran Co
John, b18--, Roan Co?, wJulia Parish
Vivian, bc1800, Oran Co, fGeorge
RADER, Mary, b18--, Page Co?, wJ H Hottel
RADFORD, Martha, b18--, Fran Co, hIsaac Jenney
RAGAN, Bettie, b18--, Fair Co?, hThaddius S Hutton
Mary C, bc1821, Harrisonburg, Rkhm Co, fDaniel, hWilliam Isaac Lupton
RAGLAND, Elizabeth Mildred, b18--, hRobert Kink Brock
Jane Rebecca, b18--, KiWi Co?, hJames Eubank
Lavinia, b18--, Petersburg, Dinw Co, dc1888, hWilliam Reid McCaw
RAGSDALE, Martha Frances, b18--, 2w of Ethelbert Algernon Coleman
RAHM, Carrie, b18--, Richmond?, hCharles B Stacy
RAILEY, Jenny Price, b18--, hJohn A Sneed
RAINE, Charles A, Jr, b18--, Camp Co?, fCharles A, Sr
Susie R, b18--, Char Co?, hHenry W Harvey
RAINES, Carrie Virginia, b18--, Math Co, hEdward M Bassett
Elizabeth, b18--, Pula Co, hThomas Patton
RALLS, Sophia, b18--, Albe Co,

RALLS (continued)
d1916, hBenjamin L Yates, Sr
RALSTON, Barbara Ann, b182-, Rkhm Co, d1895, fDavid, mFrances Beery, hPeter Swank
Benjamin, b18--, Rkhm Co
Charles Hopkins, b9/21/1860, Mt Clinton, Rkhm Co, wAnnie Bowman Whitmore, md5/22/1890
David, bc1800, Rkhm Co?, wFrances Beery
Elizabeth, b1852, Harrisonburg, Rkhm Co, hChristian H Brunk
Hannah, b9/1834, nrGreen Mount, Rkhm Co, d1919, fDavid, mFrances Beery, hIsaac C Myers
RAMEY, Ashton, b18--, Rapp Co, fThomas A, Sr, (1)m-- Cougill
Charles Franklin, b10/8/1864, Rapp Co, fThomas A, Sr, (2)m Elizabeth Jane Richards, 1w Lucy Lake Skinner
Edward/Edwin, b18--, Rapp Co, fThomas A, Sr, (1)m-- Cougill
Henry/Harry M, b2/4/1863, Rapp Co, fThomas A, Sr, (2)mElizabeth Jane Richards
Hugh Thompson, b2/14/1858, Rapp Co, fThomas A, Sr, (2)mElizabeth Jane Richards, wIda Jane Anderson, md2/21/1883
Jacquelin Sears, b186-, Rapp Co, fThomas A, Sr, (2)mElizabeth Jane Richards
Jennie, b2/2/1866, Rapp Co, fThomas A, Sr, (2)mElizabeth Jane Richards, hJames Cropp
John Martin, b18--, Rapp Co, fThomas A, Sr, (1)m-- Cougill
Lelia/Lillie M, bc1860, Rapp Co, fThomas A, Sr, (2)mElizabeth Jane Richards, hJohn D Varner
Margaret, b1854, nrDungannon, Scot Co, d1921, hElijah Corder, Jr
Robert Lee, b9/19/1869, Rapp Co, fThomas A, Sr, (2)mElizabeth Jane Richards
Thomas A, Sr, b8/5/1817, Clar Co, 1w-- Cougill, 2wElizabeth Jane Richards, md9/5/1854
Thomas A, Jr, b18--, Rapp Co, fThomas A, Sr, (1)m-- Cougill
William, b18--, Rapp Co, d1862, fThomas A, Sr, (1)m-- Cougill

RAMSAY, Susan Antoinette, b18--, nrWaynesboro, Augu Co, hMarcellus D Eutsler
RAMSEY, Catherine, b1843, nr Staunton, Augu Co, hJohn H Taylor
H G, bc1860, Bedf Co?, w-- Dooley
Henry, b18--, Pitt Co, d1885
S E, bc1860, Pitt Co?, w-- Bennett
William H, b1837, nrPullens, Pitt Co, d1917, fHenry, wRebecca Mayhan
RANDOLPH, Annie, b18--, hCalvin Wilson
Beverley, bc1800, Fauq Co, fRobert, wLavinia Heth
Beverley, b6/26/1823, Cumb Co, d1903, fWilliam Fitzhugh, mJane Cary Harrison, wMary Conway Randolph
Dorothea, b17--, fIsham, mJane Rogers, hJohn Woodson
Edward, b169-, Henrico Co, fWilliam mMary Isham, w-- Groves
Elizabeth, b169-, Henrico Co, fWilliam, mMary Isham, hRichard Bland
Elizabeth Carter, b17--, Fauq Co, hThomas Turner
Epes, b17--, fWilliam Eston, m-- Epes
Eston, b185-, Clar Co, fBeverley, mMary Conway Randolph
Henry, bc1690, Henrico Co, fWilliam, mMary Isham
Isham, bc1690, Henrico Co, fWilliam, mMary Isham, wJane Rogers
Jane, b170-, fIsham Randolph, mJane Rogers, hPeter Jefferson
John, bc1690, Henrico Co, fWilliam mMary Isham, wSusanna Beverley
John, b17--, wFrances Bland
John, b17--, Albe Co?, fThomas Mann, mAnn Cary, wJudith Lewis
John II, b17--, fJohn, mFrances Bland
Lucius, b182-, Cumb Co, fWilliam Fitzhugh, mJane Cary Harrison
Margaret Smith, b18--, Albe Co, fThomas Jefferson, mJane Hol-

RANDOLPH (continued)
lins Nicholas, hWilliam Mann Randolph
Mary, b169-, Henrico Co, fWilliam, mMary Isham, h-- Stith
Mary, b17--, JaCi Co?, fJohn, hThomas Nelson
Mary, b177-, Cumb Co?, fThomas Isham, hRandolph Harrison
Mary Conway, bc1830, fPhilip Grymes, hBeverley Randolph
Mary Harrison, b181-, Cumb Co, fWilliam Fitzhugh, mJane Cary Harrison, hGeorge Tabb
Mary Harrison, b185-, Clar Co, fBeverley, mMary Conway Randolph, 1hPercy W Charrington, md6/26/1877, 2hErnest H Astley-Cooper
Mary Isham, b17--, fThomas, hJames Keith, Sr
Mary Magill, b11/12/1833, Fauq Co, fRobert, 2w of Edward Carter Turner
Nancy, b18--, Fauq Co?, fBeverley, mLavinia Heath, hWilliam Henry Kennon
Nathaniel Burwell, bc1850, Clar Co, fBeverley, mMary Conway Randolph
Peyton, b17--, Henrico Co?, fWilliam III, mAnne Carter Harrison, wLucy Harrison
Philip Grymes, bc1800, fArchibald Cary
Philip Grymes, b185-, Clar Co, fBeverley, mMary Conway Randolph
Richard, bc1690, Henrico Co, fWilliam, mMary Isham, wJane Bolling
Robert, b18--, Fauq Co, fRobert
Robert Carter, b11/16/1869, Clar Co, fThomas Hugh Burwell, mPage Burwell
Susan Beverley, b1821, Cumb Co, fThomas Beverley, hSamuel Richardson Millar
Susan Grymes, b18--, Clar Co, fArchibald Cary, 2w of Robert Powel Page, Sr
Susanna, bc1740, Cumb Co?, fIsham, mJane Rogers, hCarter Henry Harrison
Thomas, b168-, Henrico Co, fWilliam, mMary Isham, w--

RANDOLPH (continued)
Harrison Thomas, b17--, albe Co?, fWilliam, wAnn Cary
Thomas, b182-, Cumb Co, fWilliam Fitzhugh, mJane Cary Harrison
Thomas Beverly, bc1793, d1867
Thomas Hugh Burwell, b4/5/1843, Clar Co, fRobert Carter, wPage Burwell
Thomas Isham, b17--, Henrico Co?
Thomas Jefferson, bc1800, Albe Co, fThomas Mann, mMartha Jefferson, wJane Hollins Nicholas
Thomas Jefferson, b7/21/1868, Albe Co, fWilliam Lewis, mAgnes Dillon, 1wLaura Lester, md1895, 2wAnnie Clifton Markli, md1919
Virginius Cary, b182-, Cumb Co, fWilliam Fitzhugh, mJane Cary Harrison
William, b168-, Henrico Co, fWilliam, mMary Isham, wElizabeth Beverley
William III, bc1700, Henrico Co, d1761, fWilliam II, wAnne Carter Harrison
William Eston, b181-, Cumb Co, fWilliam Fitzhugh, mJane Cary Harrison, 1w-- Epes
William Fitzhugh, bc1790, wJane Cary Harrison, md9/11/1817
William Fitzhugh, b185-, Clar Co, fBeverley, mMary Conway Randolph
William Lewis, b18--, Albe Co?, fWilliam Mann, mMargaret Smith Randolph, wAgnes Dillon
William Mann, bc1800, Albe Co?, fJohn, mJudith Lewis, wMargaret Smith Randolph
Winnie, b17--, Fran Co?, hWilliam Short
RANGELEY, Eliza, bc1850, Henry Co, fJohn, mMary Webster, hJeremiah C King, md1870
Hattie, bc1870, Stuart, Patr Co, hEdwin Johnson Harvey, Sr, md1897
RANSBURG, William, wBelle Delaney
RANSON, Mary Ellen, b1849, Jeff Co, hJohn Henry Guy, Sr

RANSONE, William Stanley, b18--, Math Co, wEugenia Borum
RAPER, John C, b18--, Wyth Co?, wSallie Crockett
RASNICK, Clement V, b1867, Selton, Dick Co, fElijah J, mPolly Breeding, wEunice Pressley
Elijah J, b18--, Russ Co, fJonas, mRachel LaForce, wPolly Breeding
Jonas, b18--, Russ Co, fJacob, m-- Counts, wRachel LaForce
Noah K, b18--, Dick Co, wMargaret Kelly
RATCLIFF, Eliza A, b18--, JaCi Co, hWilliam A Hockaday
RATCLIFFE, Anna J, b186-, nrDumfries, PrWi Co, fGeorge Matthews, mMary C Dowell, hH C Speake
George Matthews, b4/9/1845, PrWi Co, fJohn A, Sr, mDelia Cole, wMary C Dowell
George Raymond, b4/12/1870, nr Dumfries, PrWi Co, fGeorge Matthews, mMary C Dowell, wLillian Silling, md9/3/1902
Henry A, b184-, PrWi Co, fJohn A, Sr, mDelia Cole
James E, b184-, PrWi Co, fJohn A, Sr, mDelia Cole
John A, Sr, b18--, Staf (then PrWi) Co, wDelia Cole
John A, Jr, b183-, PrWi Co, fJohn A, Sr, mDelia Cole
Louisiana, bc1800, Fair Co, fRobert, mMildred Wilkinson, hJames Bankhead Taylor Thornton
Lucien, bc1800, Fair Co, 1w of George West Gunnell
Mary J, bc1840, PrWi Co, fJohn A, Sr, mDelia Cole, hJames A Tolson
Richard, b184-, PrWi Co, d186-, fJohn A, Sr, mDelia Cole
Robert, b17--, Fair Co, fRichard, mAnna Bolling, wMildred Wilkinson
William, b184-, PrWi Co, d1922, fJohn A, Sr, mDelia Cole
RATLIFF, Ada, b186-, nrLebanon, Russ Co, fSparell, mNancy Ratliff, hJohn W Deskins
Ben, b10/2/1866, nrLebanon,

RATLIFF (continued)
Russ Co, fSparell, mNancy Ratliff, 1wLydia Ratliff, md10/1/1886, 2wLottie Rowe
George, bc1870, nrLebanon, Russ Co, fSparell, mNancy Ratliff
James, bc1860, nrLebanon, Russ Co, fSparell, mNancy Ratliff
John, b186-, nrLebanon, Russ Co, fSparell, mNancy Ratliff
Lydia, b186-, Buch Co, d1888, fWilliam, mCaroline Ward, 1w of Ben Ratliff, md1886
Nancy, b1827, Buch Co, d1907, hSparell Ratliff
Sarah, b186-, nrLebanon, Russ Co, fSparell, mNancy Ratliff, hThomas Hackney
Sparell, b1826, Buch Co, d1909, fRichard, wNancy Ratliff
William, b18--, Buch Co, wCaroline Ward
RAUHOF, Peter M, b1848, Rkhm Co, wMary Elizabeth Bolton
RAVENSCROFT, John Stark, b17--, wAnne Spotswood Burwell
RAWLES, Joanna, b18--, Nans Co, hPatrick Henry Lee
RAWLINGS, James B, b1809, Oran Co?, wAnn E Cason
James M, bc1830, Albe Co?, wHelen Carter Watson
James R, b5/6/2853, Spot Co, fJames B, mAnne E Cason, 1w Leona Chancellor, md10/1877, 2wLula Williams
James Wesley, b184-, "Rawlingsdale", Fauq Co, fJohn D, mBettie Rector
John D, bc1805, Fauq Co, wBettie Rector
John Henry, b18--, Sout Co?, wMary Jane Williams
John Will, b9/4/1854, "Rawlingsdale", Fauq Co, fJohn D, mBettie Rector, wElvira Kenner, md10/5/1871
Lee, bc1850, "Rawlingsdale", Fauq Co, fJohn D, mBettie Rector
Mit, bc1850, "Rawlingsdale", Fauq Co, fJohn D, mBettie Rector, hJoseph Hampton
Virginia, b184-, "Rawlingsdale", Fauq Co, fJohn D, mBettie Rector, hJohn L Carter

RAWLS, Elisha, b18--, Nans Co?, wMargaret Jones
Gavin, bc1857, Isle Co, 1922
Jesse P, b6/28/1868, Holy Neck, Nans Co, fLuther, mMary Elizabeth Darden
Luther, b6/2/1835, Holy Neck, Nans Co, fElisha, mMargaret Jones, wMary Elizabeth Darden, md5/30/1867
Rosa M, b6/19/1870, Holy Neck, Nans Co, fLuther, mMary Elizabeth Darden, hE S Norfleet
RAY, Charles W, b186-, Gray Co?, wNellie J Greear
Lavigna, b18--, Rkhm Co?, hEllis Pifer
Mary Elizabeth, b3/1863, Blackford, Russ Co, hHarvey L Plaster
REA, Andrew, b17--, Albe Co
Ann, bc1800, Albe Co, fThomas, mAnn Ballard
Bland, bc1800, Albe Co, fThomas, mAnn Ballard, 1wSarah Alexander, 2wElizabeth Jones
Daniel, bc1800, Albe Co, fThomas, mAnn Ballard
James H, b11/11/1839, nrCrozet, Albe Co, d1914, fBland, 1wSallie Black, 2wBetty Black
Jane, bc1800, AlbeCo, fThomas, mAnn Ballard
Jemima, bc1800, Albe Co, fThomas, mAnn Ballard
John, bc1830, nrCrozet, Albe Co, fBland, (1)mSarah Alexander
Joseph, b183-, nrCrozet, Albe Co, fBland, (1)mSarah Alexander
Margaret, bc1800, Albe Co, fThomas, mAnn Ballard
Maria, bc1830, nrCrozet, Albe Co, fBland
Mollie Eliza, bc1830, nrCrozet, Albe Co, fBland, hWilliam Bernard Tilman
Samuel II, bc1800, Albe Co, fThomas, mAnn Ballard
Thomas, b17--, Albe Co?, wAnn Ballard
William T, b183-, nrCrozet, Albe Co, fBland
READ, Anne, b1813, Greenwood Farm, Char Co, fClement, hWil-

READ (continued)
liam Booker Green
Clement, b17--, Greenwood, Char Co, fThomas
Margaret, bc1720, Cumb Co, hPaul Carrington
Sarah Embra, b1842, Farmville, PrEd Co, hJoseph Finley McIlwaine
Thomas, b17--, Ingleside Farm, Char Co
REAGUER, George Franklin, bc1845, Rapp Co, wHelen Edmonia Johnson
REAMER, Sudie, b18--, fDaniel, hLouis Martena McClung
REAMY, Fleming James, bc1870, KiGe Co, fJames S, mAnnis Elizabeth Terrell
James S, b5/12/1838, KiGe Co, wAnnis Elizabeth Terrell, md1/19/1868
REAMEY, Martha, b18--, hThomas Hamlin
REASOR, Nettie, b11/24/1858, Turkey Cove, Lee Co, hGeorge C Gilmer
RECTOR, Bettie, b18--, nrRectortown, Fauq Co, fThomas, hJohn D Rawlings
Edward R, bc1810, Fauq Co?, 1h of Isabella Swart
Hannah, b1750, Fauq Co, d1816, hGeorge Glascock
Harriet, b1834, Rectortown, Fauq Co, fAlfred, 2w of George A Kenner, md2/22/1859
Roberta, b18--, fSamuel, mAnna Hatcher, hWilliam Jordan Luck
Samuel, b18--, wAnna Hatcher
Sarah, b18--, Smyt Co, hWilliam T Senter
REDD, Barbara, bc1850, Caro Co?, fSam, mCormelia McLaughlin
Carey, bc1850, Caro Co?, fSam, mCormelia McLaughlin
Emily, bc1850, Caro Co?, fSam, mCormelia McLaughlin
Eugene, b184-, Caro Co?, fSam, mCormelia McLaughlin
George, b184-, PrEd Co?, wSarah Louise Dupuy
Lucy, b17--, Hano Co, hJohn Fitzhugh
Sam, b1798, Caro Co, wCormelia McLaughlin

REDD (continued)
Samuel C, bc1840, Jericho, Caro Co, fSam, mCormelia McLaughlin, wNannie Carter
REDWOOD, Mary L, b1820, ChCi Co, 1w of Edmund Waddill II
REED, Charles, b18--, Augu Co?, wEllen Brenaman
Hurrah, bc1850, Fauq Co?, 2h of Bessie Woolf
Walter, b1846, Glou Co, d1902
William E, bc1820, Fred Co?, wMargaret Williams
REEKES, Pattie, b18--, Meck Co?, hEdward Hardy
REELY, James T, bc1850, Fred Co, wJessie D Rhodes
REEVES, Anna Dennis, b18--, Lune Co?, fP M, hByrd Lanier Ferrell
Elizabeth, b18--, Wash Co?, hEphraim E Wiley
Nettie V, bc1851, Augu Co, hNewton B Wise
REID, Andrew, b18--, Rkbr Co
Azariah, b183-, Hamp Co, fJohn, m-- Brunner
Benjamin W, bc1842, nrOriskany, Bote Co, d1904, fAndrew, wHarriett Lemon
Cepha S, b186-, Hamp Co, fDorsey, mLouisa Spaid
Charles, b18--, Loud Co, wPatsy B Nelson
Cora Virginia, bc1870, Rapp Co, fJohn Jett, mLucy Penn Rodes, hJames Gideon Brown
Dorsey, b3/1/1832, nrShilo Church & Capon Bridge, Hamp Co, d1907, fJohn, m-- Brunner, wLouisa Spaid, md8/13/1855
Elizabeth, b18--, Acco Co?, hWilliam Robinson Riley
Elizabeth, b183-, Hamp Co, fJohn, m-- Brunner, hJonathan H Brill
Ellen, bc1800, Fauq Co?, hJohn Cochran
Etta May, b186-, Hamp Co, fDorsey, mLouisa Spaid, hAlexander Jolliffe
Evan H, b185-, Hamp Co, d1892, fDorsey, mLouisa Spaid
James, b18--, Rapp Co
John, bc1800, Hamp Co, fJeremiah J, w-- Brunner

REID (continued)
John Jett, bc1848, Rapp Co, fJames, wLucy Penn Rodes
Joseph, b9/13/186, Rapp Co, fMark, mAlice Catlett, wMary Russell Settle, md4/28/1886
Madison Lemuel Pierce, b8/13/1856, Hamp Co, fDorsey, mLouisa Spaid
Margaret, b16--, 1w of Thomas Nelson, md1710
Margaret C, bc1820, Nels Co, hJames L Wills
Martha Ann, b18--, Fair Co?, hWilliam Ayre
Martin, b183-, Hamp Co, fJohn, m-- Brunner
Mary E, bc1860, Hamp Co, fDorsey, mLouisa Spaid, hEugene F Barr
Richard E, b186-, Hamp Co, fDorsey, mLouisa Spaid
Robert James Nelson, b7/7/1869, Lenah, Loud Co, fCharles, mPatsy B Nelson, wLucy Ellen Myers
Virginia, b185-, Hamp Co, fDorsey, mLouisa Spaid, hWilliam Burtner
William, b183-, Hamp Co, fJohn, m-- Brunner
REILLY, Annie J, bc1870, Lexington, Rkbr Co, fD M, mMargaret J --, 1hPhilip B Stanard, 2h William S McClanahan, md4/24/1900
D M, b18--, Rkbr Co?, wMargaret J --
REMINE, Mary, b3/6/1869, Lodi, Wash Co, hCharles W Nunley
REMSBURG, Henry, b17--, Shen Co?, wCatherine Stickley
RENFORTH, James W, b18--, Wheeling, Ohio Co, wRebecca Prettyman
RENICK, Henrietta C, b18--, Grbr Co, hBenjamin F Henlow
RENNO, Lydia, b17--, Staf Co?, hJeremiah Moore
REPASS, Dessie, bc1870, nrCeres, Blan (then Wyth) Co, fElias, mAdeline Elizabeth Grossclose, hSamuel Tibbs
Elias, b11/28/1825, Blan Co, fReuben, mEsther Gullion, wAdeline Elzabeth Grossclose

REPASS (continued)
Guy, b186-, nrCeres, Blan (then Wyth) Co, fElias, mAdeline Elizabeth Grossclose
Hectorine Ibbie, b186-, nrCeres, Blan (then Wyth) Co, fElias, mAdline Elizabeth Grossclose
Lafayette D, b186-, nrCeres, Blan (then Wyth) Co, fElias, mAdeline Elzabeth Grossclose
Raymond Clinton, b10/5/1860, nrCeres, Blan (then Wyth) Co, fElias, mAdeline Elizabeth Grossclose, wJuliet Elizabeth Kitts, md3/8/1891
Reuben, b1797, Wyth Co, d1872, wEsther Gullion
Selden W, bc1860, Wyth Co, wElla Brown Patterson
REYNOLDS, Addie G, bc1870, Crai Co, fJ Hale, hGeorge W Layman, md7/3/1895
Ann Taylor, b18--, nrClifton Forge, Bote Co, hGeorge W Pettyjohn
Charles H, b18--, Taze Co?, wHarriet Fuller
Henry Singleton, b18--, Norf Co?, wMary Watkins
J Hale, b18--, Crai Co
John H, bc1850, Scot Co?, wJaley A Wolfe
Joseph D, b18--, Oran Co?, wElizabeth Henderson
Josephine, b18--, Crai Co?, hMattison Echols
Lelia Susan, b184-, Bedf Co, fTheodore, hRobert Mason Colvin
Lillie Ellis, b18--, Oran Co, fJoseph D, mElizabeth Henderson, hJames William Faulconer, md1/1874
Missouri Jane, b10/1864, Crai Co, hMarion Luther Hoffman
Sallie, b18-, Oran Co, fJoseph D, mElizabeth Henderson, hDaniel Quisenberry
Sarah Eleanor, b18--, hD M Wood
RHEA, Joseph, b18--, Smyt Co?, wEllen Sheffey
RHODES, --, b18--, Saumsville, Shen Co, d1916, hJoseph Maphis
Abraham, b2/14/1794, Shen Co, fMichael, Sr, mAnnie Strickler

RHODES (continued)
Abraham, bc1810, Middletown, Fred Co, fJohn, mMary Senseney
Abraham, b3/3/1817, Shen Co, d1887, fJohn, mEve Saum, 2w Rebecca Fravel, 1wSarah Haun
Abraham S, b185-, Middletown, Fred Co, fIsaac, mElizabeth Dinges
Ann, bc1820, Middletown, Fred Co, fJohn, mMary Senseney, hSamuel Sperry
Anna, b2/9/1790, Shen Co, fMichael, Sr, mAnnie Strickler
Annie, bc1850, Middletown, Fred Co, fIsaac, mElizabeth Dinges, hSamuel Kline
Annie M, b185-, nrToms Brook, Shen Co, fAbraham, (2)mRebecca Fravel
Barbara, b4/24/1796, Shen Co, fMichael, Sr, mAnnie Strickler
Catherine, b18--, Shen Co?, hMartin F Miley
Charles, bc1860, Rhodes Mills, Albe Co, fMadison, mHarriet Marr
Daniel, b2/28/1792, Shen Co, fMichael, Sr, mAnnie Strickler
David, b11/3/1784, Shen Co, fMichael, Sr, mAnnie Strickler
Ed, bc1860, wSallie Anderson
Elizabeth, b18--, Rkhm Co, d1912, hMichael B Kline
Fannie, b184-, Middletown, Fred Co, fIsaac, mElizabeth Dinges, hWilliam Simpson
Isaac, b1818, Middletown, Fred Co, d189-, fJohn, mMary Senseney, wElizabeth Dinges
J B D, b18--, Rkhm Co, wEmma Sipe
Jacob, bc1800, Rkhm Co
Jacob, b181-, Middletown, Fred Co, fJohn, mMary Senseney
James, b181-, Middletown, Fred Co, fJohn, mMary Senseney
James William, b1847, Middletown, Fred Co, fIsaac, mElizabeth Dinges, wAnna Keller
Jane Elizabeth, bc1829, Rkhm Co, d1903, fJacob, hAdam H Brewer
Jeff, b185-, Rhodes Mills, Albe Co, fMadison, mHarriett Marr
Jessie D, b185-, Middletown,

RHODES (continued)
Fred Co, fIsaac, mElizabeth Dinges, hJames T Reely
John, b17--, Fred Co?, wMary Senseney
John, b3/30/1783, Shen Co, fMichael, Sr, mAnnie Strickler, wEve Saum
John, b181-, Middletown, Fred Co, fJohn, mMary Senseney
John, b184-, Middletown, Fred Co, d186-, fIsaac, mElizabeth Dinges
John H, bc1850, nrTom's Brook, Shen Co, d1898, fAbraham, (1)mSarah Haun, wMary Hoover
Madison, b18--, Albe Co, wHarriett Marr
Maggie E, b186-, nrTom's Brook, Shen Co, fAbraham, (2)mRebecca Fravel
Maria, b3/1/1786, Shen Co, fMichael, Sr, mAnnie Strickler
Mary C, bc1860, nrTom's Brook, Shen Co, fAbraham, (2)mRebecca Fravel, hWilliam B Spiggle
Mary Ellen, b184-, Middletown, Fred Co, fIsaac, mElizabeth Dinges, hDavid Stickley
Michael, Sr, b1749, Massanutten, Page Co, d1819, fJohn, mEve Albright, wAnnie Strickler, md1728
Michael, Jr, b8/15/1788, Shen Co, fMichael, Sr, mAnnie Strickler
Michael, b181-, Middletown, Fred Co, fJohn, mMary Senseney
Milton A, b186-, nrTom's Brook, Shen Co, fAbraham, (2)mRebecca Fravel
Neal, b181-, Middletown, Fred Co, fJohn, mMary Senseney
Olin Randolph, b185-, Middletown, fIsaac, mElizabeth Dinges
Philip Samuel, b4/3/1865, nrTom's Brook, Shen Co, fAbraham, (2)mRebecca Fravel, wSallie M Funk, md6/8/1898
Ras, b18--, Rkhm Co?, wElizabeth Hevener
Rebecca, b11/17/1798, Shen Co, fMichael, Sr, mAnnie Strickler
Samuel F, b185-, Middletown, Fred Co, fIsaac, mElizabeth

RHODES (continued)
Dinges, wMaggie M Guyer, md9/10/1885
T E, b185-, Augu Co?, wBertie Coiner
Thomas L, b6/11/1863, Rhodes Mill, Albe Co, fMadison, mHarriett Marr, wJeanette Cressey
Walter, b185-, Rhodes Mill, Albe Co, fMadison, mHarriett Marr
William, bc1850, nrTom's Brook, Shen Co, fAbraham, (1)mSarah Haun
RICE, Annie, b1836, Mt View, Nhld Co, d1918, fHiram G, 2w of Samuel Downing, Sr
Caroline, b18--, New Market, Shen Co, hWalter Newman
Elizabeth, b17--, Clar Co, hWilliam McCormick, md1795
Fanny J, b9/25/1825, Bedf Co, fSamuel D, m-- Mitchell, 1h Hutchings B Price, 2hAlonzo Cocke, md185-
J T, bc1860, Alle Co?, wMaggie V Beery
Margaret, b1785, Farmville, PrEd Co, hWilliam C Ford
Martha Friend, bc1870, Char Co, m-- Smith, hWalter Gregory Williams
Mary, b1841, nrLara, -- Co, d1919, 2w of Joh Ball Lewis
Mollie, bc1860, Richmond?, hPeter Winston, Jr
Samuel D, bc1800, Bedf Co?, w-- Mitchell
RICHARD, Jacob W, bc1820, Fred Co?, wHarriet Williams
Joseph, bc1840, Fred Co, wSusan Larrick
RICHARDS, --, b18--, Fran Co, hBurl Maxey
Augustine B, bc1854, Fred Co, wJosephine Honeystoffle
Elizabeth Jane, bc1830, fThompson H, mElizabeth A Fleming, hThomas A Ramey, Sr, md9/5/1854
Julia, b1863, Abingdon, Wash Co, hLewis J Thomas
Maud C, b1869, Upperville, Fauq Co, fWashington L, mMartha C Megeath, hJohn McCormick
Quintus, b18--, Spot Co?, wFlo-

RICHARDS (continued)
rence Dickenson
Thomas/Thompson H, b5/4/1797, wElizabeth A Fleming, md8/12/1826
Walter Buck, b6/24/1863, nr Riverton, Warr Co, fJames Russell, mElizabeth Mauzey Blakemore, wMary Monroe Cocke, md6/20/1889
Washington L, b18--, Upperville, Fauq Co, wMartha C Megeath
RICHARDSON, Annie, b18--, Fran Co?, hJohn Payne
Charles, b2/1825, nrCovington, Alle Co, fThomas, wMariah Watts Helmintoller
Elijah, bc1823, Henry Co, d1902, fJohn, 1wEliza Gravely, 2wLeonora J (Fowlkes) --
Eliza, b18--, Henry Co?, fElijah, (1)mEliza Gravely, h-- Bowles
Ferdinand Dawson, b1808, Fairfax, Fair Co, fJohn, m-- Dawson, wMary Posey Grigsby
Frances C, bc1800, JaCi Co, hThomas Boswell
Frederick, b1834, Math Co, d1907, fJohn P, wElizabeth Susan White
Frederick Wilmer, b12/16/1853, Fairfax Court House, Fair Co, fFerdinand Dawson, mMary Posey Grigsby, wAmelia Lee Buck, md6/13/1883
George, b17--, Math Co
George, b17--, Fluv Co, wBetsy Payne
John P, b9/3/1801, Math Co, fWilliam
John Wesley, bc1839, Nhtn Co, d1912, wEmma V Wood
Julia, b7/12/1842, fThomas, hAnthony M Snead
Mary, b18--, fWilliam Sydnor, mJulia Anderson, hHarvey McVeigh, md11/28/1872
Mary Ann, b18--, Fluv Co, fGeorge, mBetsy Payne, hDrurie Wood Bowles, Sr
Mary E, b18--, Henry Co?, fElijah, (1)mEliza Gravely, h-- Lawrence
Mary Elizabeth, bc1815, JaCi

RICHARDSON (continued)
  Co, d1877, hWilliam L Spencer
  Mayo C, b183-, Buck Co?, wFannie M Anderson
  Richard Henry, bc1837, JaCi Co, wMarian Claiborne Seymour
  Robert Vulosco, b10/18/1867, nrToana, JaCi Co, fRichard Henry, mMarian Claiborne Seymour, 2wKate B Letherland
  Thomas Shepherd, b11/10/1868, fCharles, mMariah Watts Helmintoller, 1wEdith Pauline Pole, md11/15/1903, 2wFlorence Mabel Corbett, md1/12/1914
  William, b9/14/1776 or 2/4/774, Math Co, fGeorge
  William, b18--, Henry Co?, fElijah, (1)mEliza Gravely
  William P, bc1860, PrGe Co, wGertrude Anderson
  William Sydnor, b18--, Culp Co?, wJulia Anderson
RICHMOND, Henry Charles Lane, b1/21/1868, Jonesville, Lee Co, fJames Buchanan, mElizabeth Duncan, wLillie Gray, md1/9/1896
  Emmett B, bc1860, Scot Co?, 1h of Mary E Blackwell
  James Buchanan, b2/27/1842, Turkey Cove, Lee Co, fJohn, mMary Dickenson, 1wElizabeth Duncan, 2wKate Morrison
  John, b18--, fIsaac, wMary Dickenson
  Jonathan Cass, b18-, Wise Co?, d1922, wVirginia Minton
  Mary, b18--, Wash Co?, hOlin Fisk Wiley
  Mary Amelia, b186-, Jonesville, Lee Co, fJames Buchanan, (1)m Elizabeth Duncan, hJames B Cox
RICKARD, Mary Emma, b18--, Shen Co?, 1w of Samuel M Hamrick
RICKETTS, Elias, b18--, Rapp Co?, wNannie Tannehill
  Eliza, b18--, Rapp Co?, hAlexander Cary
RIDDEL, Anie, b185-, nrMt Solon, Augu Co, fJames Andrew, Jr, mMary E Furr, hHarvey Ellinger
  Edward, b18--, Rkhm Co?, fJames Andrew, Sr, mBettie Gilmer
  Maggie, bc1860, nrMt Solon, Augu Co, fJames Andrew, Jr,

RIDDEL (continued)
  mMary E Furr, hD L Perry
  James Andrew, Sr, b18--, McGaheysville, Rkhm Co, wBettie Gilmer
  James Andrew, Jr, b18--, Rkhm Co?, dc1863, fJames Andrew, Sr, mBettie Gilmer, wMary E Furr, md185-
  Janes Andrew, III, b7/22/1861, nrMt Solon, Augu Co, fJames Andrew, Jr, mMary E Furr, w--Orebaugh, md10/1885
  Jennie, b185-, nrMt Solon, Augu Co, fJames Andrew, Jr, mMary E Furr, hSamuel H Ellinger
  John A, b18--, Rkhm Co?, fJames Andrew, Sr, mBettie Gilmer
  Martha, b18--, Rkhm Co?, fJames Andrew, Sr, mBettie Gilmer, h-- Comstock
  Mary, b18--, Rkhm Co?, fJames Andrew, Sr, mBettie Gilmer, 1h-- Sheets, 2hJohn Sheets
  Matilda, b18--, Rkhm Co?, fJames Andrew, Sr, mBettie Gilmer, 1h-- Wood, 2h-- Wheeler
RIDDELL, Archibald, b18--, Fauq Co, 3h of Susan Swart
RIDDICK, Mary, b18--, Arli Co?, hJames Taylor
RIDDLE, Lewis, b18--, Rkhm Co, wLucy Meyerhoeffer
RIDDLEBERGER, Frank B, b186-, Edinburg, Shen Co, fH H, mEmma V Belew
  H H, b18--, Shen Co?, wEmma V Belew
  Lelia M, b9/23/1867, Edinburg, Shen Co, fH H, mEmma V Belew, hMark W Magruder, md9/1893
  Ralph H, bc1870, Edinburg, Shen Co, fH H, mEmma V Belew
RIDGEWAY, Anna, b6/5/1826, Jeff Co, d1899, fJonas, mLydia --, hCharles M Ebert, md2/19/1852
  Jonas, bc1800, Jeff Co, wLydia
RIELEY, George, b18--, Bote Co, fWilliam, wBetty Arnold
  Lucy Ann, b1838, Blue Ridge Springs, Bote Co, d189-, fGeorge, mBetty Arnold, hLewis G Layman
RIELY, Alexander, b12/25/1766, Berk Co, fJohn, mMargaret

RIELY (continued)
 Brown, wHarriet May Wright Clyma
George Henry, b8/31/1808, Jeff Co, fAlexander, mHarriet May Wright Clyma, wFrances Kercheval Grantham
John William, b2/26/1839, Jeff Co, fGeorge Henry, mFrances Kercheval Grantham, wEmma Carrington
RIFE, W A, b7/22/1848, Augu Co, wEmma Brown Schoppert
RIGGINS, Eliza Ann, b18--, Norfolk?, d1855, hCharles Wright Consalvo
RILEY, David H, bc1860, Bote Co?, d1923, wNannie Leslie
 Fannie, bc1870, Acco Co?, fWilliam Robinson, mElizabeth Reid, hCharles Collins
 J L, bc1850, Bote Co?, wAnnie Layman
 Margaret, b18--, Acco Co?, 3w of Revel J West
 William Robinson, b18--, Acco Co, wElizabth Reid
RINEHART, --, bc1870, nrFincastle, Bote Co, fWilliam A, (1)mMary Lewis Lipes, hC A Miller
 Lula May, bc1870, nrFincastle, Bote Co, fWilliam A, (1)mMary Lewis Lipes, hR C Stokes
 William A, bc1846, nrFincastle, Bote Co, d1922, fJohn, mMartha Sites, 1wMary Lipes, md186-, 2wAugusta (Hundley) Cobbs, md2/5/1907
RINKER, Absolom, bc1800, Shen Co
 Anna Margaret, bc1850, Race Mills, Fred Co, fCasper, Jr, mSarah Kackley, hH N Claggett
 Casper, Sr, bc1800, Gainesboro, Fred Co, 1w-- Pugh
 Casper, Jr, b18--, Fred Co, fCasper, Sr, m-- Pugh, wSarah Kackley
 Charles Frederick, b11/13/1859, Race Mills, Fred Co, fCasper, Jr, mSarah Kackley, 1wIsadora Charity Pugh, md1885, 2wLouisa Dulany Hall, md11/15/1922
 Eliza, b18--, Fred Co, fCasper, Sr, m-- Pugh, h-- Stephenson
 Elizabeth, b18--, Shen Co,

RINKER (continued)
 d1887, 1w of Harrison Lindamood
 Elizabeth, b18--, Shen Co, fAbsalom, 2w of Andrew Funkhouser
 Elizabeth Ann, b5/29/1821, Shen Co, fEphraim, hDaniel Stickley
 Ephraim, bc1800, Shen Co
 Galloway, b18--, Fred Co, fCasper, Sr, (2)m--
 Harriet, b18--, Fred Co?, hGeorge Glaize
 Hattie, b18--, Rkhm Co?, hSamuel Moffett
 Isabel, b18--, Fred Co, fCasper, Sr, (1)m-- Pugh, h-- Hite
 Jacob, b17--, Shen Co, w-- Keller
 Jacob, b18--, Fred Co, fCasper, Sr, (2)m--
 Josiah, b18--, Fred Co, fCasper, Sr, (2)m--
 Lamarian, b18--, Fred Co, fCasper, Sr, (2)m--
 Mary Isabel, bc1850, Race Mills, Fred Co, fCasper, Jr, mSarah Kackley, hH O Pierce
 Robert R, bc1850, Shen Co?, wJennie A Funkhouser
 Susan, b18--, Shen Co, fAbsalom, hIsrael Newland
 William, b18--, Fred Co, fCasper, Sr, (2)m--
 William Franklin, b185-, Race Mills, Fred Co, fCasper, Jr, mSarah Kackley
RIPLEY, Fannie A, b18--, h-- Williamson
 Judith, b17--, Patr Co?, hCharles Thomas
RISON, George Townes, Sr, b2/3/1850, Pitt Co, fWilliam, mSallie Ann Townes, wEmma Moschler, md1888
 William, b18--, amel Co, fJohn, wSallie Ann Townes
RISQUE, Harriet James, b10/6/1807, Fincastle, Bote Co, fJames Beverly, hGeorge Christian Hutter
RITCHIE, --, bc1800, Scot Co, hJeremiah Powers
RITTENOUR, --, bc1810, Rkhm Co, wMary Rush
 Thornton, bc1840, Shen Co,

RITENOUR (continued)
wEliza Catherine Boyer
RITTER, --, b18--, Fred Co, w-- Daily
Frances, b184-, Stonewall District, Fred Co, m-- Daily
Franklin, b18--, Fauq Co?, 1h of Annie W Alexander
Henry, bc1840, Stonewall District, Fred Co, m-- Daily
James, b185-, Stonewall District, Fred Co, m-- Daily
Joseph A, b9/1849, Stonewall District, Fred Co, m-- Daily, wLaura Brown
Martha, bc1840, Stonewall District, Fred Co, m-- Daily, hJack Grimes
Mary, b184-, Stonewall District, Fred Co, m-- Daily, hSamuel Bromley
Oliver T, b18--, Fauq Co?, fFranklin, mAnnie W Alexander
Susan, bc1840, Stonewall District, Fred Co, m-- Daily, hHiram Newcomb
Walker, bc1840, Stonewall District, Fred Co, m-- Daily, wFlorence Brown
RIVERCOMB, George, b18--, High Co
RIVES, Alfred Landon, b18--, Richmond?, fWilliam C
Amelie, b8/23/1863, Richmond, fAlfred Landon, hPrince Pierre Troubetzkoy, md2/18/1896
Joseph, b17--, Fran Co, wMary Spotswood
Mary Virginia, b18--, Dinw Co?, hJames Theodore Doyle
Sallie, b17--, Fran Co?, fJoseph, mMary Spotswood, hJohn Brown
RIXEY, --, b18--, Culp Co?, fCharles William, mFrances Anne Seetle, hSilas Mortimer Newhouse
Charles William, b18--, Culp Co?, wFrances Anne Seetle
John F, bc1850, Culpeper, Culp Co, fPresley Morehead, mMary F Jones
Presley Marion, b7/14/1852, Culpeper, Culp Co, fPresley Morehead, mMary F Jones
Presley Morehead, b18--, Culp

RIXEY (continued)
Co?, wMary F Jones
ROACH, Mary, b18--, hWarner T Alley
ROANE, Eugene, bc1860, KiWi Co?, wLavinia Davis
Harriet Elizabeth, b18--, Glou Co?, hSamuel F Roane
Henry H, b1860, Glou Co, fHenry, mVirginia Anderson, 1wMarinette Gray, 2wCarrie Esther Gray
Matilda Taliaferro, bc1870, Glou Co, fSamuel F, mHarriet Elizabeth Roane, hZachary Taylor Gray, md3/6/1895
Samuel F, b18--, Glou Co?, wHarriet Elizabeth Roane
ROBBINS, Fannie,, b8/4/1862, nr Keokee, Lee Co, 1hWilliam O Smith, 2hElkanah Wynn, Jr
Mary, b1833, Lee Co, hJohn H Bailey
ROBERTS, Arthur, b6/18/1865, East Radford, Mont Co, fGeorge E, mJulia A Cofer
Bettie Ann, b18--, Nels Co, fWilliam Addison, hWilliam Henry Horton, Jr
Cordelia, b186-, Nhtn Co, fAugustus, mMary Eliza Collins, hThaddeus Woodson Jones
Edward, b18--, Meck Co?, wPagie Morgan
Edwin G, b2/10/1864, East Radford, Mont Co, fGeorge E, mJulia A Cofer
Elizabeth, b17--, Culp Co, hWilliam Brown
Elizabeth Beale, b18--, hJohn Strother Browning
Frank E, b2/17/1867, East Radford, Mont Co, fGeorge E, mJulia A Cofer
Harry H, b9/21/1868, East Radford, Mont Co, fGeorge E, mJulia A Cofer
Henry B, Sr, b1810, Wash Co, d1888, wElizabeth Warren
Henry B, Jr, b1846, Wash Co, fHenry B, Sr, mElizabeth Warren, wMary Catherine Hortenstine
J W, bc1850, Shen Co?, wFannie Burk
James A, bc1860, nrWise, Wise

ROBERTS (continued)
Co, fWilliam, mSusanna Kilgore
Lewis, bc1800, Gray Co, wAnnie Day
Louisa, b185-, nrWise, Wise Co, fWilliam L, mSusanna Kilgore, hGeorge Beverley
Lucinda, b18--, hJohn W Parkinson
Mary Jane, b18--, Wise Co?, hHarvey Hall
Nathaniel Hardin, b9/30/1818, Greenfield, Nels Co, wMary Jane Campbell
Nellie D, b18--, Rapp Co?, hB J Wood
Pattie, b1860, Char Co, hWilliam B Penick
Polly Anne, b186-, nrWise, Wise Co, fWilliam L, mSusanna Kilgore, hBurdine Hubbard
Susie Gray, b186-, Monr Co, fNathaniel Hardin, mMary Jane Campbell, hWilliam Henry Horton III
T E, bc1850, Pitt Co?, wRosa Hughes
Wade Hampton, b3/18/1864, nrWise, Wise Co, fWilliam L, mSusanna Kilgore, wMary Lee Davidson
Walter R, b5/28/1860, East Radford, Mont Co, fGeorge E, mJulia A Cofer
William, b186-, Ches Co?, 1h of Annie Beazley
William F, b186-, nrWise, Wise Co, fWilliam L, mSusanna Kilgore
William L, b182-, Lee Co, d1894, fLewis, mAnnie Day, wSusanna Kilgore
ROBERTSON, Alexander F, b2/15/1853, Culp Co, fWilliam A, mSarah Tunstall Farish, wMargaret Briscoe Stuart
Anna I, b18--, Yancey Mills, Albe Co, hCharles H O'Neil
Anne, b17--, fWilliam, hHenry Skipworth
Anne Clair, bc1860, Hano Co, hRobert H Pitt
Archibald, b17--, fWilliam, wElizabeth Bolling
Betsy, b17--, Pula Co?, hJohn S Draper, Sr

ROBERTSON (continued)
Charles E, bc1860, Scot Co?, 2h of Mary E Blackwell
D Mott, b186-, Appo Co, fDavid P, mMary Ann Glover
David P, bc1823, Appo Co, wMary Ann Glover
Elizabeth Bruce, b18--, Appo Co, hJohn Todd Anderson Martin
Frank S, b18--, Wash Co?, wStella Wheeler
Gay, b17--, fWilliam, hJohn Bernard
Granville, bc1870, Athens, Merc Co, fWilliam H, mMargaret Galloway
J H, b185-, Appo Co, fDavid P, mMary Ann Glover
John, b17--, fWilliam, wAnne Trent
John G, b18--, Richmond?, wIsabella W Wilkinson
Joseph F, b18--, West Co, wAlice Sutton
Judith Ann, b18--, hWashington Nunnally
Lindsay, b18--, fThomas Bolling, Sr, mMartha Fairfax
Lydia A, b1831, Pitt Co?, d1893, hCharles Wesley Pritchett, Sr
Mary, b18--, fThomas Bolling, Sr, mMartha Fairfax
Mary B, bc1860, Appo Co, fDavid P, mMary Ann Glover, hJ J Wood
Mercer L, b18--, fThomas Bolling, Sr, mMartha Fairfax
Mittie, bc11860, Appo Co, fDavid P, mMary Ann Glover, hW F Wood
Pocahontas, b18--, Wash Co?, fWyndham, hConnally Findlay Trigg
Powhatan, b18--, fThomas Bolling, Sr, mMartha Fairfax
Robert G, b1/1/1862, Appo Co, fDavid P, mMary Ann Glover, wFanny S Perrow, md9/18/1896
Thomas Bolling, b17--, fWilliam
Thomas Bolling, Sr, b18--, fWilliam, mChristina Williams, wMartha Fairfax
Thomas Bolling, Jr, b18--, fThomas Bolling, Sr, mMartha Fairfax, wLillian Lynn
Walter, b18--, fThomas Bolling,

ROBERTSON (continued)
Sr, mMartha Fairfax
William, b17--, wChristina Williams
William, b17--, Cobbs, Dinw Co, wElizabeth Bolling
William A, b18--, Nott Co?, wIsabella Henry Southall
William H, b1840, nrDublin, Pula Co, d1920, fWilliam, wMargaret Calloway
Willie, bc1860, Appo Co, fDavid P, mMary Ann Glover, hD S Evans
Wyndham, bc1800, Manchester, Ches Co, fWilliam, mElizabeth Bolling, wMary Smith
Wyndham, b1851, Richmond, fWyndham, mMary Smith, wFlorence Henderson
ROBEY, --, b186-, Loud Co, fFrank E, mMartha E Gaines, hW O Whitman
Amelia Anne, b18--, Fair Co, hEli Edmund Oliver
Clarence E, b186-, Loud Co, fFrank E, mMartha E Gaines
E F, bc1860, Loud Co, fFrank E, mMartha E Gaines
Edward L, bc1860, Loud Co, fFrank E, mMartha E Gaines
Ernest Lee, b8/8/1870, Herndon, Fair Co, fWilliam I, mMary Ellen Kidwell, wEdith M Bready, md6/6/1896
Frank E, b18--, Loud Co, wMartha E Gaines
George W, bc1860, Loud Co, fFrank E, mMartha E Gaines
J E, bc1860, Loud Co, fFrank E, mMartha E Gaines
William, b1785, Fair Co
William I, b1832, Fair Co, fWilliam, wMary Ellen Kidwell
William T, Sr, b7/28/1866, Loud Co, fFrank E, mMartha E Gaines, 1wSusan A Conner, md1891, 2w Corinnee Hinkle, md1912, 3wMrs Virginia Wright, md1914
ROBINETTE, Isaac H, b1802, Gray Co, fSamuel III, mAnne Osborne, wMartha Stapleton
Samuel III, b1760, Richmond, d1850, fSamuel II, wAnne Osborne

ROBINETTE (continued)
Samuel R, b7/9/1839, Lee Co, fIsaac H, mMartha Stapleton, wNarcissa Lindsay, md1870
ROBINS, Archer H, bc1850, Glou Co?, wMary Frances Corr
Benjamin Thomas Claiborne, b1808, Glou Co, fWilliam, Jr, (2)mElizabeth Lee Hoomes, wElizabeth Taliaferro Broaddus
Charles Russell, Sr, b12/31/1868, Richmond, fWilliam Broaddus, mBessie Mebane, wEvelyn Spotswood Berkeley, md10/18/1899
Frank Gordon, bc1870, Richmond, fWilliam Broaddus, mBessie Mebane
John, b1͞ ͞ ͞ ͞ Co, fThomas, mMary ҉around
Margaret Olivia, b6/1842, Acco Co, 2w of James Madison Anderson
Mary Giles, b186-, Richmond, fWilliam Broaddus, mBessie Mebane, hHenry P Taylor, Jr
Mary S, b18--, Glou Co, 1h-- Keeble, 2hThomas Marchant
Thomas, b16--, ElCi Co, fJohn, wMary Hansford
William, Sr, b1715, Glou Co, fJohn
William, Jr, b17--, Glou Co, fWilliam, Sr, 2wElizabeth Lee Hoomes
William Broaddus, b3/24/1834, Clay Bank, Glou Co, d1906, fBenjamin Thomas Claiborne, mElizabeth Taliaferro Broaddus, wBessie Mebane
William Randolph, b186-, Richmond, fWilliam Broaddus, mBessie Mebane
ROBINSON, --, b18--, Midd Co, hLewis Jones
--, b18--, Shen Co, wMargaret Burke
--, b18--, Fred Co, hWashington Cather
Andrew Hart, b186-, Bote Co, fStarkey, mEsteline Paxton
Anthony, b5/1/1662, Lanc Co, fJohn, wMary Starkey
Anthony II, b9/9/1711, York Co, fJohn, mFrances Wade, wMary Kirby

ROBINSON (continued)
Anthony III, b6/15/1737, York Co, fAnthony II, mMary Kirby, 2wMary Phillips
Anthony IV, b4/12/1880, York Co, fAnthony III, (2)mMary Phillips, wElizabeth Russell
Anthony, Sr, b17--, York Co?, wRebecca Couch
Anthony, Jr, b17--, York Co?, fAnthony, Sr, mRebecca Couch
David Graham, b186-, Graham's Forge, Wyth Co, fJohn Williamson, mBettie Peirce Graham
Edward Trent, b7/28/1865, Richmond, fSamuel Couch, mMargaret Graham, wMary Kercheval Monroe, md1889
Elizabeth, b17--, Augu Co, fWilliam, hCharles Alexander Stuart
Elizabeth, b186-, Bote Co, fStarkey, mEstelline Paxton, h-- Overton
Elizabeth Taylor, b18--, NewK Co?, fBenjamin, hJohn Daniel Turner
Ellen Victoria, b18--, Wise Co?, hJ Wesley Hillman
Esteline Robinson, b186-, Bote Co, fStarkey, mEsteline Paxton, hA C Walker
Fullen, b18--, Russ Co, wMahala Griffith
G E, b18--, wFanny Perdue
H James Paxton, b185-, Bote Co, fStarkey, mEsteline Paxton
Hannah Ellen, b4/15/1861, Elk Garden, Russ Co, hJames H Thompson
Humphrey, bc1850, Pitt Co?, wCatharine Ficklen
Jack, b184-, Fauq Co?, wFannie Skinner
James L, b2/18/1844, Fred Co, d1915, wSallie G Robinson
John II, b8/25/1685, York Co, fAnthony, mMary Starkey, wFrances Wade
John III, b17--, York Co, fAnthony III, mMary Phillips
John Enders, b7/10/1851, Richmond, fPoitiaux, mMary Enders, wVirginia Morgan
John R, b6/20/1852, Edinburg, Shen Co, d1919, mMargaret

ROBINSON (continued)
Burke, wMary Brill, md1878
John Williamson, b1844, Bdf Co, d1911, wBettie Pierce Graham
Jordan A, bc1860, Bote Co, fStarkey, mEsteline Paxton
Judith Anne, b18--, Ches Co, hRichard Lewis Brewer, Sr
Malcolm Graham, Sr, b9/7/1870, Graham's Forge, Wyth Co, fJohn Williamson, mBettie Peirce Graham, 1wMaggie S Raper, md7/17/1895, 2wMaggie Taylor Crockett, md1/10/1900
Margaret G, b186-, Bote Co, fStarkey, mEsteline Paxton
Mary, b18--, Hali Co?, hEppa Clarke
Mary, b186-, Bote Co, fStarkey, mEsteline Paxton
Nancy, b18--, Russ Co, hDaniel Dotson
Poitiaux, bc1800, fAnthony IV, mElizabeth Russell, wMary Enders
Rebecca, b186-, Bote Co, fStarkey, mEsteline Paxton, hJohn Calvin Paxton, md188-
Sallie G, bc1860, Fred Co, fJosiah, hJames L Robinson
Samuel Couch, bc1822, Gooc Co?, d1872, fAnthony, Jr, wMargaret Graham
Starkey, bc1831, Richmond, wEsteline Paxton
Thomas P, bc1860, Russ Co?, wIda F Finney
William A, b1824, Glou Co, wHester E Nuckols
William , b186-, Bote Co, fStarkey, mEsteline Paxton
Willard Bellamy, b3/.21/1859, Gooc Co, fWilliam A, mHester E Nuckols, wElizabeth Lowry Smith, md6/1887
ROCK, L Taylor, Sr, b1846, Nhld Co, wSusan Lyell
ROCKENBACK, Ann, bc1870, Camp Co?, hWalter D Campbell
ROCKNER, Dora L, bc1860, Richmond?, hJames Gibbon Carter
RODEFFER, Conrad, bc1830, Rkhm Co?, wHannah Myers
William, bc1820, Rkhm Co?, wNancy Flory
RODES, Ann B, b18--, 1w of

RODES (continued)
Daniel Fishburne
Lucy Penn, b18--, Rapp Co?, hJohn Jett Reid
Mary Barcley, b10/3/1840, Millbrook Farm, Albe Co, fRobert, mElizabeth Barcley Duke, hCharles K Anderson
Robert, b18--, Albe Co?, wElizabeth Barcley Duke
Robert Emmett, b3/29/1829, Lynchburg, Camp Co, fDavid, mMartha Yancey
Virginius, bc1830, Lynchburg, Camp Co, fDavid, mMartha Yancey
RODGERS, Rhoda E, b18--, Fred Co, hRobert N Cather
ROE, Margaret, bc1800, hJames McKee
ROEICK, Alice, b12/22/1824, nr Emmetton, Rich Co, d1881, 1w of John Ball Lewis
ROGERS, --, b186-, Waveland, KiGe Co, fThacker, (3)mLouise Stiff, hW P Billingsley
Annie, b18--, Nhld Co, 2w of Aquila A Hatton
C Luther, b1859, Rkhm Co, wAlice Whitesel
Elizabeth, b3/7/1794, Stonehill, Fauq Co, fHugh, mMary Combs, hDaniel W Swart, md1813
Emma L, b8/1839, Waveland, KiGe Co, fThacker, (1)mLouisa Edwards, hFrederick Staunton Davies
Florence, b186-, Waveland, KiGe Co, fThacker, (3)mLouise Stiff, h-- Dick
Hosea, b17--, w-- Massey
Hugh, b17--, fArthur
James E, b184-, Waveland, KiGe Co, fThacker, (1)mLouisa Edwards
John Eaton, Sr, b1836, Loud Co, d1873, wKate Yost
Katie, b18--, Oran Co, hAlexander Greene
Milton, b186-, Fauq Co?, wHester A Whitacre
Minnie, b18--, Nhld Co, 1w of Aquila A Hatton
Mortimer, b2/20/1839, nrMiddleburg, Loud Co, fHamilton, mMary Hawling, wVirginia Tay-

ROGERS (continued)
loe, md1875
Thacker, b1811, KiGe Co, d1877, 1wLouisa Edwards, 2wMargaret Carver, 3wLouise (Stiff) Payne W R, b18--, Pitt Co, wSallie W Adams
William J, b10/25/1845, Waveland, KiGe Co, fThacker, (1)mLouisa Edwards, wEloise Rodier, md12/15/1878
ROLLER, Alice Roberta, b9/1866, Rkhm Co, fGeorge W, mLouise Ann Sherman, hWilliam McAtee Menefee, md3/25/1892
Charles S, Sr, b5/8/1874, Mt Sidney, Augu Co, Jacob, wRosabelle Moorman, md10/26/1874
George W, b18--, Rkhm Co, wLouise Ann Sherman
John A, b18--, Rkhm Co, wCatherine E Kagey
Joseph, bc1860, Shen Co, wElla Shirley
Margaret, b18--, Rkhm Co, hJacob Byerle
William, bc1850, Shen Co?, wEmma J Hottel
ROLLINS, E Taylor, b18--, Staf Co?, wCarrie Cushing
Harrison, b18--, Scot Co
Harry L, b18--, Wise Co?, wBelle O Williamson
Ransom R, b1839, Snowflake, Scot Co, d1915, fHarrison, wEsther Virginia Grey
ROOP, Harvey, b5/4/1848, nr Riner, Mont Co, d1920, fJoseph, mMary Carroll, wAgnes B Hall
Joseph, b1811, nrRiner, Mont Co, d1874, fHenry Rupe, mCatherine Null, wMary Carroll
Redmond I, b7/13/1869, nrRiner, Mont Co, fHarvey, mAgnes B Hall, wElizabeth Shelburne, md 12/11/1901
ROOT, George R, b186-, Augu Co?, wFannie Pirkey
John, bc1860, Carr Co?, 1h of Elva Early
ROPER, Benjamin Watkins, b4/1817, ChCi Co, d1869, wMartha C Poore
George Kinsey, b9/23/1847, Richmond, fBenjamin Watkins,

ROPER (continued)
mMartha C Poore, wKate Cowles Childrey
Mary, bc1850, Richmond, fBenjamin Watkins, mMartha C Poore
RORER, Angeline, b18--, Pitt Co?, hJohn James
P H, b18--, Roan Co?, wNannie McClanahan
Zada N, b18--, Bedf Co, fJ Q, hWilliam George Lane, Jr, md1886
RORRER, Lucy E, bc1841, Bedf Co, hCharles A Powell
ROSCOE, Elizabeth, bc1800, Rapp Co, hThomas Fleming
ROSE, Anne, bc1870, nrMillard, Dick Co, hJames S Sykes
Gustavus A, bc1800, Amhe Co, fHugh
Hugh, b1743, Amhe Co?, fRobert, mAnn Fitzhugh
Martha, b1853, Richmond, hJohn E Parrish
Rebecca, b1844, Leck, Dick Co, d1919, hMarion Lafayette McCoy
Samuel S, b1850, Dick Co, fJohn, mElizabeth Hale, wMelvina Bevins
ROSEN, David H, b18-, Rkbr Co
Flora May, bc1870, Rkbr Co, fDavid H, hJohn T Montgomery, md1893
William, bc1820, Augu Co, wMary Garrison
ROSENBAUM, Bertha V, b18--, Richmond?, hMax Guggenheimer, Jr, md1877
Nancy, b2/4/1839, Crockett, Wyth Co, d1915, hDavid H Porter
ROSENBERGER, Barbara, b18--, Shen Co, hJohn H Glaize
Edmond, bc1800, Shen Co
Eleanor, b18--, Rkhm Co, hJacob Price
Elizabeth, b5/3/1835, New Market, Shen Co, fEdmond, hChristian Shirley
Fannie, b18--, Ashby District, Shen Co, d1920, fJacob, mAnnie Rinker, hWhiten Bowman
Jacob, bc1800, Shen Co, wAnnie Rinker
Sarah, b18--, Shen Co, hWilliam Bowman

ROSS, Amanda, b18--, Patr Co, hJames Wyatt Smith
Elizabeth, b18--, Crai Co?, hJames Givens
Laura, b18--, Augu Co, hA C Koontz
Peter w, b18--, Brun Co, m-- Wyche
Sarah J, b12/10/1842, Brun Co, fPeter W, hRobert W Hall
ROSSER, Ann, b17--, fWilliam, hLindsay Cralle
Ann Elizabeth, b1/29/1869, Pitt Co, hRobert Lee Page, md 1/30/1895
George Thomas, bc1840, Camp Co
Thomas L, b10/15/1836, Camp Co, wElizabeth Barbara Winston
Walter C, Sr, bc1846, Camp Co, wKate Arnold
ROSSON, Anna, b18--, Rapp Co?, fGarland, hCharles R Carder
George W, b18--, Rapp Co?, fGarland
John W, b18--, Rapp Co?, fGarland
ROSZEL, George A, bc1850, Fauq Co, wSarah De Butts
ROUSE, Charles Taylor, b3/3/1849, Smyt Co, fJohn, wMartha E West
John, b1809, Smyt Co, fPaulser
ROWE, Carson, b18--, d1853, wJane Harrison
Elizabeth, bc1850, Irvington, Lanc Co, fWilliam, mSarah Garner, hJohn M Gannon
Frances J, bc1830, Glou Co?, d1906, hPeter William Smith
Henry Carson, b2/7/1853, nrHyacinth, Nhld Co, d1922, fCarson, mJane Harrison, wElsa Jones
James W, b1847, Irvington, Lanc Co, d1885, fWilliam, mSarah Garner, wMary Elizabeth Haydon
Lansen, b17--, Fluv Co?, wUnity Lane
Lottie, bc1870, Buch Co, fMiles E, mJane Boothe, 2w of Ben Ratliff, md11/1900
Miles E, b18--, Buch Co, wJane Boothe
William B, b184-, Irvington, Lanc Co, fWilliam, mSarah Garner

ROWSEY, --, b186-, Fred Co, wMinnie Gardner
ROY, Jane Wiley Beverly Corrie, b17--, KiQu Co?, fBeverly, hParmenas Bird
Janet/Jeannette Carter, b2/14/1836 Ashdale, Esse Co, d1911, hWilliam Hoskins
Mary Carson, b18--, Warr Co?, hMortimer Hamilton Millar
ROYALL, Aubyn, b18--, Danville, Pitt Co, fJoseph, hBoyd F Young
Evelyn, b18--, Lune Co, hHartwell P Cooksey
Joseph, b18--, Powh Co
Lucy Elizabeth, bc1839, Oak Hill, Ches Co, d1918, fS H, hThomas Moore Beckham
Mary Archer, b18--, Jeff Co?, hRobert Lowry McMurran, Sr
William Archer, b1840, Ches Co, fJoseph, wEliza Christian
ROYER, Minnie, bc1870, Rkhm Co?, hSamuel Moore
ROYSTER, Bessie, b18--, Appo Co?, hJoseph L Foster
ROYSTON, John F, bc1860, Clar Co?, wJulia Smallwood
Walter S, bc1860, Clar Co?, wVirginia Smallwood
RUBLE, Mary A, b1856, Crai Co, 1w of Lloyd P Ferrel
RUBY, Mary C, b18--, Shen Co, hJoel Kagey
RUCKER, Benjamin Jennings, bc1809, Amhe Co, wMary Higginbotham
Brack, bc1850, Amhe Co, fBenjamin Jennings, mMary Higginbotham
Daniel, b18--, Lune Co?, wMarianna Rucker
Edwin P, b1853, Amhe Co, fBenjamin Jennings, mMary Higginbotham, wAnnie Pendleton Pierce
Elizabeth, bc1850, Bedf Co, fMonroe, hCharles H Almond, Sr
Ellen, bc1850, Amhe Co, fBenjamin Jennings, mMary Higginbotham, hM E Theiss
James Irrin, bc1870, Amhe Co?, fWashington, mMary Margaret Miller
Marianna, b18--, Lune Co,

RUCKER (continued)
hDaniel Rucker
Paul, bc1850, Amhe Co, fBenjamin Jennings, mMary Higginbotham
Washington, bc1840, Rapp Co?, wMary Margaret Miller
William A, bc1850, Bote Co?, wVirginia Leslie
RUDASILL, Lucy Cornelia, b18--, Rapp Co, fPhilip, hJohn Michael Schwartz
RUDD, Alfred A, b10/13/1835, Ches Co, fRichard, wIndia Elizabeth Cauthorne
Augustus B, b18--, Ches Co, fAlfred A, mIndia Elizabeth Cauthorne
Frederick, b18--, Powh Co?, wJudith Ann Ammonette
Elizabeth, b18--, Ches Co, fAlfred A, mIndia Elizabeth Cauthorne, hH C Sims
Louisa, b1822, PrEd Co, hThomas J Owen
Nannie, bc1860, Powh Co, fFrederick, mJudith Ann Ammonette, hEdward A Baugh, md1879
Richard, bc1800, Ches Co
Thomas, b18--, wMary Davis
William S, b182-, Lune Co, wAmelia Ingram
RUDDER, Lucy, b18--, Lune Co, hJames Turner
RUEBUSH, Brown, b18--, wMartha Ellen Meyerhoeffer
Edward, bc1840, Rkhm Co?, wMaggie Chandler
Ephraim, b9/26/1833, Churchville, Augu Co, fJohn, Sr, mMary Huffman, wLucille Virginia Kieffer, md3/28/1861
George, bc1830, Churchville, Augu Co, fJohn, Sr, mMary Huffman
J H, bc1860, Shen Co?, wElla Vernon Funkhouser
Jacob, bc1830, Churchville, Augu Co, fJohn, Sr, mMary Huffman
James Hott, b10/19/186, Singers Glen, Rkhm Co, fEphraim, mLucille Virginia Kieffer
John, Jr, bc1830, Churchville, Augu Co, fJohn, Sr, mMary

RUEBUSH (continued)
Huffman
Kate, bc1830, Churchville, Augu Co, fJohn, Sr, mMary Huffman
Magdalene, bc1830, Churchville, Augu Co, fJohn, S, mMary Huffman
Peter, bc1830, Churchville, Augu Co, d186-, fJohn, Sr, mMary Huffman
Samuel, bc1830, Churchville, Augu Co, d186-, fJohn, Sr, mMary Huffman
Silas, bc1830, Churchville, Augu Co, John, Sr, mMary Huffman
Susanna, bc1830, Churchville, Augu Co, fJohn, Sr, mMary Huffman, hTimothy Ruebush
RUFF, A W, b18--, High Co?, d189-, 1h of Lelia D Reynolds
RUFFIN, Edmund, b1/5/1794, PrGe Co, d1865
Edmund, b18--, PrGe Co, fEdmund
RUFFNER, Benjamin F, b18--, Page Co?, fIsaac A, mMary C Irvine
Isaac A, b10/4/1808, nrLuray, Page Co, wMary C Irvine
Mary Elizabeth, b10/1842, Page Co?, fIsaac A, mMary C Irvine, hJohn Buckner Trenary, md1868
RUMBOUGH, --, b17--, Shen Co, hMichael Clinedinst
RUNYAN, L A, bc1860, Wyth Co?, w-- Archer
RUSH, Charles R, b11/8/1821, McGaheysville, Rkhm Co, fJohn, m-- Nicholas, wPhoebe Catherine Scott
Charles, bc1850, Shen Co, wLucy Alice Hottel
Elizabeth, bc1820, McGaheysville, Rkhm Co, fJohn, m-- Nicholas
Frances, bc1820, McGaheysville, Rkhm Co, fJohn, m-- Nicholas, h-- Mauzy
Harriet Jane, bc1820, McGaheysville, Rkhm Co, fJohn, m-- Nicholas
Jacob, b17--, McGaheysville, Rkhm Co
Jeremiah C, b1837, Abingdon, Wash Co, d1913, fJeremiah, wRebecca Davidson
John, b17--, McGaheysville,

RUSH (continued)
Rkhm Co, w-- Nicholas
Josephus Branson, b182-, McGaheysville, Rkhm Co, fJohn, m-- Nicholas
Josephus Branson, b5/27/1866, McGaheysville, Rkhm Co, fCharles R, mPhoebe Catherine Scott, wClara E Irwin, md10/7/1896
Mary, bc1820, McGaheysville, Rkhm Co, fJohn, m-- Nicholas, h-- Rittenour
Rebecca, b18--, Shen Co, hBenjamin Franklin Humston
RUSSELL, Andrew, b17--, Wash Co
Eliza Campbell, bc1800, Abingdon, Wash Co, fAndrew, 1w of John Gaw Meem, Sr
Elizabeth, b17--, fWilliam, hAnthony Robinson IV
John Elijah, b5/19/1868, Orlean, Fauq Co, fThomas A, mEmma J Payne, wGrace E Parr, md7/12/1893
John W, bc1822, Fred Co, d1863, wMary Jeffries
Katherine, b1820, Mt Falls, Fred Co, fMoses, mBarbara Keckley, hThomas Jefferson Miller
Margaret Custis, bc1800, Acco Co, hJohn Perry
Mary Henry, b17--, Augu Co?, hWilliam Bowen
Moses, b17--, Mt Falls, Fred Co, fJames, mMary Alexander, wBarbara Keckley
Patience, b17--, Henrico Co, hWilliam New
Rebecca, bc1800, Fauq Co, hSamuel Lodge
Susie, bc1870, Orlean, Fauq Co, fThomas A, mEmma J Payne, hW G Fogg
Thomas A, b18--, Fauq Co, wEmma J Payne
Thomas N, b2/4/1851, Marshall District, Fauq Co, fJohn W, mMary Jeffries, wAnnie Eliza Holmes, md2/4/1873
RUST, --, b18--, Warr Co?, 1w of James Shumate
Addie, bc1850, nrHowesville, Warr Co, fCharles Buckner Carroll, mMary Ann Ashby, 2w of

RUST (continued)
Charles Leach
Ann Susan, b18--, fJohn, mElizabeth Marshall
Anne, b18--, fSamuel, mMartha --, h-- Harrison
Ashby, b184-, nrHowesville, Warr Co, fCharles Buckner Carroll, mMary Ann Ashby
Benedict, b10/25/1743, West Co, fMatthew, (1)mWinifred Cox, 1wJane Middleton, md3/24/1766
Benjamin, b18--, fSamuel, mMartha --
Charles, b184-, nrHowesville, Warr Co, fCharles Buckner Carroll, mMary Ann Ashby
Charles Buckner Carroll, b12/26/1816, Warr Co, fJohn, mElizabeth Marshall, wMary Ann Ashby, md9/12/1839
Comfort M, b18--, fJohn, mElizabeth Marshall, h-- Gardner
Ella, b18--, Rapp Co?, hJames Stark
Elton, b184-, nrHowesville, Warr Co, fCharles Buckner Carroll, mMary Ann Ashby, hThaddeus Haynie
Evelyn Junkin, b18--, Rkbr Co, 2w of Edward West Nichols
Frances, b17--, West Co, fMatthew, (1)mWinifred Cox, h-- Shearman
George, b17--, West Co, fMatthew, (1)mWinifred Cox
George, b17--, West Co, fBenedict, mJane Middleton, w-- Marshall
George, b18--, fSamuel, mMartha
George, b18--, fWilliam, Sr, mAnna Gray
Hannah, b18--, fSamuel, mMartha --, h-- Eskridge
Ida, bc1850, nrHowesville, Warr Co, fCharles Buckner Carroll, mMary Ann Ashby, 1w of Charles Leach
Jeremiah, b18--, fSamuel, mMartha --
John, b2/8/1769, West Co, fBenedict, mJane Middleton, wElizabeth Marshall, md8/13/1797
John, b18--, fWilliam, Sr, mAnna Gray

RUST (continued)
John, b18--, fSamuel, mMartha -
John B, b18--, fJohn, mElizabeth Marshall
John Robert, b6/14/1840, nr Howesville, Warr Co, fCharles Buckner Carroll, mMary Ann Ashby, wNannie Antrim McKay, md12/22/1873
Lou, b184-, nrHowesville, Warr Co, fCharles Buckner Carroll, mMary Ann Ashby, hPreston/Presley Marshall
Martha E, b18--, fJohn, mElizabeth Marshall
Mary, b17--, West Co, fMatthew, (1)mWinifred Cox
Matthew, b17--, West Co, fBenedict, mJane Middleton
Matthew, b17--, fSamuel, mMartha --
Molly, b17--, West Co, fMatthew, (1)mWinifred Cox
Peter, b18--, fSamuel, mMartha --
Rachel, b17--, West Co, fMatthew, (1)mWinifred Cox, h-- Cox
Sallie, b184-, nrHowesville, Warr Co, fCharles Buckner Carroll, mMary Ann Ashby, hEdward Massie
Samuel, b18--, fWilliam, Sr, mAnna Gray, wMartha --
Sarah, b17--, West Co, fMatthew, (1)mWinifred Cox
Sarah J, b184-, Loud Co, hBenjamin Franklin Foley
Sarah Jane, b18--, fJohn, mElizabeth Marshall
Vincent, b17--, West Co, fMatthew, (1)mWinifred Cox
William, b18--, fSamuel, mMartha --
William, Jr, b18--, fWilliam, Sr, mAnna Gray
Winifred, b17--, West Co, fMatthew, (1)mWinifred Cox
RUTHERFOORD, Mary, b17--, Richmond?, fThomas, hRichard Eggleston Hardaway
RUTHERFORD, --, bc1840, Gray Co?, 1h of Martha Parks
Ella, b1852, Richmond, hLewis Wheat
RUTTER, James, b18--, wMary

RUTTER (continued)
Holloman
Lizzie, b10/30/1847, fJames, mMary Holloman, hJoseph Merican Martin, md10/11/1877
RUTZ, Mary Dorothy, b18--, Shen Co?, hSamuel H Snarr
RYAN, Elizabeth Alice, b186-, Henrico Co, fJames, mEllen Mary Finnegan, hRudolph B Felthaus
James Joseph, bc1870, Henrico Co, fJames, mEllen Mary Finnegan
John Matthew, bc1860, Henrico Co, fJames, mEllen Mary Finnegan
Margaret, b185-, Henrico Co, fJames, mEllen Mary Finnegan, hMichael Owen McEvoy
Mary Elizabeth, b185-, Henrico Co, fJames, mEllen Mary Finnegan, hJeremiah M Deasy
Sarah, b17--, Bedf Co?, hJohn Allen Hancock
William Alfred, bc1860, Henrico Co, fJames, mEllen Mary Finnegan
RYBURN, Sarah Buchanan, b18--, Wash Co, hArthur Dixon Hutton
SADLER, Letitia, b18--, Ches Co, 1w of Hiram Lee Walker
SAFFELL, Lucy Anne, b18--, Warr Co, hJames T Venable
SAGER, Barbara, bc1800, Shen Co?, hAbram Smoot
Washington Abel, b18--, Shen Co?, 1wSallie Huddle, 2wReda Smott
ST CLAIR, John T, bc1860, Gooc Co?, wEmma Nuckols
SALE, Cassandra Fidella, b1837, Rkbr Co, d1916, hMoses A Miller
Charles Jones, b1/23/1845, Mahockny Farm, Esse Co, d1898, fDandridge, mMary Mundie, wMary Susan Latane
Dandridge, b18--, nrLloyds, Esse Co, wMary Mundie
John M, b179-, Caro Co?, wLouisa Wade
John T, b186-, Augu Co, fWilliam M, mSarah Esterline Templeton
Mary, b186-, Augu Co, fWilliam

SALE (continued)
M, mSarah Esterline Templeton, hJohn E Kyle
William M, b1838, Augu Co, d1912, fJohn M, mLouisa Wade, wSarah Esterline Templeton
William Wilson, b9/30/1870, Rkbr Co, fWilliam M, mSarah Esterline Templeton, wEdith Dabney Tunis, md1909
Wilton F, b18--, wFannie Aileen Gilman
SALLING, Joseph, b18--, Scot Co?, wDicey Williams
Nancy J, b10/1842, Slant, Scot Co, fJoseph, mDicey Williams, hMilo Taylor
SALYARDS, Joseph, bc1830, Rkhm Co, wBettie Flory
SALYERS, --, b18--, Scot Co, hAbsolom McCarty, Sr
SAMPSON, J W, bc1860, Albe Co, wMinnie R Shackelford
SAMS, C Whittle, bc1850, wMartha Macon Minor
SAMUEL, Julia Archibald, b18--, Caro Co, fArchibald, hRobert Oliver Peatross
SAMUELS, --, bc1810, Fair Co?, wEvelina Ford
Elizabeth, b18--, Shen Co?, 2w of Jacob Strayer
SANDERS, Anthony M, b18--, Math Co, d1867, wJudith Currell
Augustus O, b183-, Saltville, Smyt Co, fJames, mLouisa White
Caledonia, bc1840, Saltville, Smyt Co, fJames, mLouisa White, hThomas E Dunn
Etta, bc1850, Saltville, Smyt Co, fJames, mLouisa White, hJames Bailey
Florence D, b185-, Saltville, Smyt Co, fJames, mLouisa White, hFelix G Buchanan
George W, b4/21/1840, Lanc Co, fAnthony M, mJudith Currell, wLucy A Spriggs
Henry O, b185-, Glou Co?, wMary Henningham Taliaferro
J C, bc1840, Saltville, Smyt Co, fJames, mLouisa White
James, b1797, Wyth Co, d1874, wLouisa White
James Erasmus, bc1870, nrWhite Stone, Lanc Co, fWilliam M,

RUTTER (continued)
Holloman
Lizzie, b10/30/1847, fJames, mMary Holloman, hJoseph Merican Martin, md10/11/1877
RUTZ, Mary Dorothy, b18--, Shen Co?, hSamuel H Snarr
RYAN, Elizabeth Alice, b186-, Henrico Co, fJames, mEllen Mary Finnegan, hRudolph B Felthaus
James Joseph, bc1870, Henrico Co, fJames, mEllen Mary Finnegan
John Matthew, bc1860, Henrico Co, fJames, mEllen Mary Finnegan
Margaret, b185-, Henrico Co, fJames, mEllen Mary Finnegan, hMichael Owen McEvoy
Mary Elizabeth, b185-, Henrico Co, fJames, mEllen Mary Finnegan, hJeremiah M Deasy
Sarah, b17--, Bedf Co?, hJohn Allen Hancock
William Alfred, bc1860, Henrico Co, fJames, mEllen Mary Finnegan
RYBURN, Sarah Buchanan, b18--, Wash Co, hArthur Dixon Hutton
SADLER, Letitia, b18--, Ches Co, 1w of Hiram Lee Walker
SAFFELL, Lucy Anne, b18--, Warr Co, hJames T Venable
SAGER, Barbara, bc1800, Shen Co?, hAbram Smoot
Washington Abel, b18--, Shen Co?, 1wSallie Huddle, 2wReda Smott
ST CLAIR, John T, bc1860, Gooc Co?, wEmma Nuckols
SALE, Cassandra Fidella, b1837, Rkbr Co, d1916, hMoses A Miller
Charles Jones, b1/23/1845, Mahockny Farm, Esse Co, d1898, fDandridge, mMary Mundie, wMary Susan Latane
Dandridge, b18--, nrLloyds, Esse Co, wMary Mundie
John M, b179-, Caro Co?, wLouisa Wade
John T, b186-, Augu Co, fWilliam M, mSarah Esterline Templeton
Mary, b186-, Augu Co, fWilliam

SALE (continued)
M, mSarah Esterline Templeton, hJohn E Kyle
William M, b1838, Augu Co, d1912, fJohn M, mLouisa Wade, wSarah Esterline Templeton
William Wilson, b9/30/1870, Rkbr Co, fWilliam M, mSarah Esterline Templeton, wEdith Dabney Tunis, md1909
Wilton F, b18--, wFannie Aileen Gilman
SALLING, Joseph, b18--, Scot Co?, wDicey Williams
Nancy J, b10/1842, Slant, Scot Co, fJoseph, mDicey Williams, hMilo Taylor
SALYARDS, Joseph, bc1830, Rkhm Co, wBettie Flory
SALYERS, --, b18--, Scot Co, hAbsolom McCarty, Sr
SAMPSON, J W, bc1860, Albe Co, wMinnie R Shackelford
SAMS, C Whittle, bc1850, wMartha Macon Minor
SAMUEL, Julia Archibald, b18--, Caro Co, fArchibald, hRobert Oliver Peatross
SAMUELS, --, bc1810, Fair Co?, wEvelina Ford
Elizabeth, b18--, Shen Co?, 2w of Jacob Strayer
SANDERS, Anthony M, b18--, Math Co, d1867, wJudith Currell
Augustus O, b183-, Saltville, Smyt Co, fJames, mLouisa White
Caledonia, bc1840, Saltville, Smyt Co, fJames, mLouisa White, hThomas E Dunn
Etta, bc1850, Saltville, Smyt Co, fJames, mLouisa White, hJames Bailey
Florence D, b185-, Saltville, Smyt Co, fJames, mLouisa White, hFelix G Buchanan
George W, b4/21/1840, Lanc Co, fAnthony M, mJudith Currell, wLucy A Spriggs
Henry O, b185-, Glou Co?, wMary Henningham Taliaferro
J C, bc1840, Saltville, Smyt Co, fJames, mLouisa White
James, b1797, Wyth Co, d1874, wLouisa White
James Erasmus, bc1870, nrWhite Stone, Lanc Co, fWilliam M,

SANDERS (continued)
(2)mSusan E Williams
John, b18--, nrWhite Stone, Lanc Co, fWilliam M, (1)m-- George
Joseph W, b183-, Saltville, Smyt Co, fJames, mLouisa White
Llewellyn I, b18--, nrWhite Stone, Lanc Co, fWilliam M, (1)m-- George
Lizzie, b183-, Saltville, Smyt Co, fJames, mLouisa White, hDavid JGillespie
Mary A, b18--, PrWi Co?, hJames W Jordan
Polly, b184-, Saltville, Smyt Co, fJames, mLouisa White, hHiram Henderson
Robert A, b185-, Saltville, Smyt Co, fJames, mLouisa White
Rufus K, Sr, b6/25/1863, Saltville, Smyt Co, fJames, mLouisa White, wBirdie L Barnes, md9/4/ 1887
Susie, b185-, Saltville, Smyt Co, fJames, mLouisa White, hThomas T Taylor
Thomas G, bc1860, Saltville, Smyt Co, fJames, mLouisa White
Virginia, b18--, Nels Co, hJohn R Harvey
William, b184-, Saltville, Smyt Co, d186-, fJames, mLouisa White
William M, b1824, Math Co, d1891, 1w-- George, 2wSusan E Williams
SANDERSON, Sarah Johnson, b18--, Cumb Co?, hRobert Brown
SANDRIDGE, Winifred, b18--, Hali Co, hJoseph Boxley
SANDY, Daniel, bc1840, Rkhm Co?, wElizabeth Chandler
SANFORD, --, b18--, Rich Co, (father of Millard F Sanford, b1850)
Agnes, b1/6/1847, Spotsylvania Court House, Spot Co, fWilliam, hWilliam Goodwin Hart
Ann, b18--, nrColonial Beach, Nhld Co, hJohn Fisher Anderson
Catherine Pope, b17--, Rich Co?, hGeorge Wright
Mary, b18--, Alexandria?, fThomas, mEsther Leavens, hJames P Smith

SANFORD (continued)
Millard F, b1850, Montross, West Co, wNellie Nevitt
Thomas, bc1800, Alexandria?, wEsther Leavens
SANGER, Samuel F, b1849, Sangerville, Augu Co, fJohn, mElizabeth Florey, 1wRebecca Thomas, 2wSusan Thomas
SANTMIERS, John W, b18--, Shen Co?, wSarah Burner
William Harvey, b11/20/1856, nr Front Royal, Warr Co, d1918, wEmma Susan Downey
SANXAY, Charlotte Isabel, bc1800, fRichard D, hRobert Gilliam
SARGENT, J B, bc1860, Buck Co?, wFannie Snoddy
SATTERWHITE, -- b17--, Richmond, 1w or 2w of Sylvester Welch
SAUERWINE, William, bc1840, Shen Co?, wCaroline Will
SAUFLEY, Mary, b18--, Rkhm Co?, hDaniel Miller
William, bc1830, Rkhm Co?, wEliza Swank
SAUL, James D, bc1770, Fran Co, d1861
John Peter, Sr, b12/19/1854, Boone's Mill, Fran Co, fWilliam R, wLula J Lemon, md6/1882
Mary, bc1870, Callaway, Fran Co, hJames F Guerrant
William R, b18--, Fran Co, fJames D
SAUM, Anna Catherine, b186-, Saumsville, Shen Co, fSamuel, mCatherine Hisey, hJohn William Neeb, md10/23/1886
Dilman Jefferson, bc1860, Saumsville, Shen Co, fSamuel, mCatherine Hisey
Ella, b18--, Shen Co?, d1878, fAbraham, 1w of Edward B Tapley, md1872
Eve, b17--, Shen Co, hJohn Rhodes
John R, b18--, Rkhm Co?, wJulia Clower
Lou May, bc1866, Saumsville, Shen Co, fSamuel, mCatherine Hisey, hWilliam Hockman
Lucy, b18--, Saumsville, Shen Co, 2w of Edward B Tapley

SAUM (continued)
Mary Frances, b18--, Shen Co, hDavid F Spiker
Samuel, b18--, Saumsville, Shen Co, d1894, wCatherine Hisey
Samuel Eugene, b186-, Saumsville, Shen Co, fSamuel, mCatherine Hisey
Sarah L, bc1860, Saumsville, Shen Co, fSamuel, mCatherine Hisey
Sophia, bc1860, Saumsville, Shen Co, fSamuel, mCatherine Hisey, hSamuel Maphis
William L, b186-, Saumsville, Shen Co, fSamuel, mCatherine Hisey
SAUNDERS, Anne, b17--, Midd Co, hBenjamin Bristow, Jr
Edmund Archr, Sr, b1831, NewK Co, wMary Ball
Edmund Archer, Jr, b8/12/1861, ChCi Co, fEdmund Archer, Sr, mMary Ball, wMartha Brown
Elizabeth, b17--, Midd Co, 1w of Benjamin Bristow, Sr
Eugenia, b18--, KiQu Co, fWilliam Alexander, mEmiline Motley, hRichard H Waring
Gilbert A, bc1870, Whittles Mills, Lune Co, fJames Archer, mMartha Indie Andrews
Henry, bc1860, wAnnie Mary Woolf
Herbert S, b18--, ChCi Co, fEdmund Archer, Sr, mMary Ball
James Archer, b1842, Lune Co, fRobert, mMary Towler, wMartha Indie Andrews
James Sidney, b1/15/1868, Whittles Mills, Lune Co, fJames Archer, mMartha Indie Andrews, wAdella Smith, md12/15/1892
John Richard, b12/19/1869, KiQu Co, fWilliam Alexander, mEmiline Motley, wBlanche Hoskins
Julia Ann, b8/26/1826, Lanc Co, hMerriweather Lewis
Lavinia, bc1820, Caro Co, hReuben Saunders
Letitius Atwater, b1843, Caro Co, fReuben, mLavinia, wJennie E Thompson
Lucy, b18--, JaCi Co, hWilliam Henry Barnes

SAUNDERS (continued)
Mary, b18--, Camp Co?, hJohn Quincy Adams
Mary, b18--, ChCi Co, fEdmund Archer, Sr, mMary Ball, hJames N Williamson, Jr
Mollie, b18--, Buck Co, d1915, hRichard M Bidgood
Reuben, bc1810, Caro Co, wLavinia Saunders
Robert, b1803, Lune Co, d1873, wMary Towler
Robert Thweat, b186-, Whittles Mills, Lune Co, fJames Archer, mMartha Indie Andrews
Thomas J, b18--, wMary Brittain
W Bailey, b18--, ChCi Co, fEdmund Archer, Sr, mMary Ball
W Conway, b5/19/1867, Ashland, Hano Co, fLetitius Atwater, mJennie E Thompson, wMarie Louise Bulloch, md11/1891
William Alexander, b12/26/1829, Caro Co, fReuben, mLavinia Saunders, wEmiline Motley
William C, b18--, KiQu Co, fWilliam Alexander, mEmiline Motley
William Fitzhugh, bc1870, Whittles Mills, Lune Co, fJames Archer, mMartha Indie Andrews
William Spotswood, b18--, KiQu Co, fWilliam Alexander, mEmiline Motley
Willie, b18--, Loui Co, fWilliam, mPamelia Crosby
SAVAGE, James A D, b18--, Acco Co?, wMaggie Braidwood
Margaret Ann, b1848, Acco Co, hWilliam Jesse Phillips
Virginia, b18--, hThomas Macon
SAVILLE, Charles O, b1850, Richmond, fJohn T, wKeith Woodson
George W, b18--, Bote Co, wIda L Noffsinger
John T, b1828
SAYERS, Amelia, b4/5/1866, Sayersville, Taze Co, hWilliam F Harman
Jane, b18--, Wyth Co, d1840, hJoseph Draper
Lucy, bc1800, Drapers Valley, Pula Co hJoseph Graham
SCAGGS, Pinckney A, bc1850, Fred Co?, wCora Lee Larrick

SCAISBROOK, Elizabeth, bc1740, Warw Co?, fHenry, hWilliam Langhorne
SCHERER, John Jacob, bc1800, Wyth Co
John Jacob, Sr, b2/7/1829, Wyth Co, fJohn Jacob, wKatherine Killinger
SCHEUCK, John, bc1830, Shen Co?, wEmily Neeb
SCHLATER, Mabel, bc1870, ElCi Co?, hWilliam C L Taliaferro
SCHMUCKER, Dick L, bc1870, nrToms Brook, Shen Co, fMorgan F, mAnn E Bauserman
Ellen, b184-, nrToms Brook, Shen Co, fFerdinand, mCatherine Funkhouser, hSamuel HBowman
Emma N, b185-, nrToms Brook, Shen Co, fFerdinand, mCatherine Funkhouser, 1h-- Graves, 2hJohn D Borden
Ferdinand, bc1818, Toms Brook, Shen Co, dc1900, wCatherine Funkhouser
George E, b184-, nrToms Brook, Shen Co, fFerdinand, mCatherine Funkhouser
John C, b185-, nrToms Brook, Shen Co, fFerdinand, mCatherine Funkhouser
Martin Luther, bc1850, nrToms Brook, Shen Co, fFerdinand, mCatherine Funkhouser
Morgan F, bc149, nrToms Brook, Shen Co, dc1900, fFerdinand, mCatherine Funkhouser, wAnn E Bauserman
Sarah, b184-, nrToms Brook, Shen Co, fFerdinand, mCatherine Funkhouser, hPeter F Cooley
Virginia, b184-, nrToms Brook, Shen Co, fFerdinand, mCatherine Funkhouser, hSilas Hottel
SCHOOLER, -- bc1830, Hano Co, w-- Fleming
SCHOOLFIELD, John Harrell, Sr, b2/18/1838, Traylorsville, Henry Co, d1920, fWilliam M, mSarah Anne Harrell, wSusan Barbara France, md10/17/1860
William M, b18--, Henry Co?, wSarah Anne Harrell
SCHOPPERT, Emma Brown, b18--,

SCHOPPERT (continued) Augu Co, hW A Rife
SCHULTZ, Peggy, b18--, Albe Co, hJoseph Dettor
Rebecca, bc1800, Fred Co, fJohn, hAbram Miller/Mueller
SCHUMAKER, Charles, b18--, Alle Co, fWilliam, (1)m-- Matheny
David, b17--, Amhe Co?, fWilliam
Gatewood Ledbetter, b5/9/1868, Alle Co, fWilliam, (2)mMary Ann Grubbs, wAlice Maud Mary Butler, md10/5/1896
Jane, b18--, Alle Co, fWilliam, m-- Matheny, hJohn Tucker
William, b18--, Alle Co, fWilliam, m-- Matheny
William, b1/20/1819, Amhe Co, d1890, 1w-- Matheny, 2wMary Ann Grubby
SCHWARTZ, John Michael, b18--, Rapp Co?, fJoseph, wLucy Cornelia Rudasill
SCLATER, Fannie Howard, b18--, Surr Co?, hPeter T Spratley
SCOFIELD, Rachael Neill, b1813, Alexandria, hIsaac Hoge
SCOLLAY, Mary Nelson, bc1850, fSamuel, mSallie Page Nelson, hGeorge Washington Nelson, Jr
Samuel, bc1800, wSallie Page Nelson
SCOTT, --, b186-, nrStewartsville, Bedf Co, fJames Wesley, mElizabeth Fouts, hWilliam Dooley
--, B186-, Bedf Co?, fJames Wesley, mElizabeth Fouts, hM J Pace
--, bc1870, Gishmills (now Vinton), Roan Co, d1889, fJames Wesley, mElizabeth Fouts, hCalvin Falls
Alexander, bc1800, Fauq Co
Anna, bc1800, 1hJacob LaRue
C L, bc1850, Amhe Co?, wLouise Everett
Catherine, b17--, Alexandria, hWilliam Brown
Charles, b18--, Camp Co, wNancy Elder
Charles Francis, b185-, Richmond, fJohn, mHarriet Augusta Caskie
Daniel, b18--, Nels Co?, 1h of

SCOTT (continued)
Evelyn M Harris
David, bc1800, Rkhm Co?, wBarbara Eliza, b17--, Fauq Co?, fJohn, mEliza Gordon, hChandler Peyton
Eliza Caskie, b185-, Richmond, fJohn, mHarriet Augusta Caskie, hRichard C Scott
Elizabeth, b18--, Smyt Co, 2w of James G Higginbotham, Sr
Elizabeth Amanda, b18--, fWm Coleman, m-- Branch, hJohn Archer Scott, Sr
Fannie, bc1800, Fauq Co?, hEdward Carter
Fannie, bc1870, Spot Co, fThomas, mEstelle Charters, hT H Twyman
Fannie, b18--, Fauq Co?, hJohn H Downing
Fanny, b183-, Oran Co, fGarrett, mSarah Ellen Nalle
Garrett, b4/9/1808, Oran Co, fJohn, m-- Terrell, wSarah Ellen Nalle
George T, b183-, Oran Co, fGarrett, mSarah Ellen Nalle
James Alexander, Sr, b1821, Manchester, Ches Co, d1884, fWilliam Irvin, wFlorida Calhoun Lovell
James Caskie, b185-, Richmond, fJohn, mHarriet Augusta Caskie
James H, b7/23/1865, nr Stewartsville (now Crossroads), Bedf Co, fJames Wesley, mElizabeth Fouts, wTheodosia Earnest, md1888
James M, b184-, Oran Co, fGarrett, mSarah Ellen Nalle
James McClure, b8/17/1811, Albe Co, fJames, (2)mMildred Thomson, wSarah Travers Lewis
James W, b18--, wJennie Kirkpatrick
James Wesley, bc1831, Bedf Co?, d1909, wElizabeth Fouts
Janet, b18--, Fredericksburg, Spot Co, fJohn, hHugh Hamilton
Janie Haskins, b6/12/1855, PrEd Co, d1917, hJohn Robertson Martin
Jemima, b18--, hMillard Fillmore Litton
John, b16--, Spot Co, wJane

SCOTT (continued)
Todd
John, b17--, Oran Co, fJohnny, m-- Hackett, w-- Terrell
John, b4/23/1820, "Oakwood", Fauq Co, d1907, fJohn, mElizabeth Blackwell Pickett, wHarriet Augusta Caskie, md1850
John II, Oran Co, fJohn, mJane Terrell
John Archer, Sr, b1800, PrWi Co, fThomas Osborne, mJane Haskins, wElizabeth Amanda Scott
John Archer, Jr, b18--, PrEd Co, fJohn Archer, mElizabeth Amanda Scott, wJennie Walker
John F, b18--, Spot Co?, wLillie Hamilton
John G, b186-, Gish Mills (now Vinton), Roan Co, fJames Wesley, mElizabeth Fouts
John Gordon, bc1860, Richmond, fJohn, mHarriet Augusta Caskie
John Thomson, bc1810, Albe Co, fJames, (2)mMildred Thomson, wHuldah Lewis
John W, b8/22/1855, Oran Co, fWilliam C, mPamelia Graves, wJennie Kirkpatrick, md4/20/1881
Johnny, b17--, Oran Co, fJohn, mJane Todd, w-- Hackett
Joseph Winfield, b18--, Isle Co, d1898, wEmeline Jane Smith
Lily Cabell, b18--, Bedford, Bedf Co, fSamuel B, 3w of Jonathan Christian Woodson
Lucy, b1848, Lune Co, fEdward Chambers, hHenderson Lewis Lee
Martha Ann, b181-, Bedf Co, d1902, hFrancis Nathaniel Watkins
Mary, b17--, PrEd Co, fThomas, hWilliam Watts
Mary Anna, b18--, Fauq Co, fAlexander, hGeorge S Hamilton
Mary Ann Lewis, b180-, Albe Co, fJames, (2)mMildred Thomson, hLewis A Boggs
Mary Ellen, b186-, Richmond, fJohn, mHarriet Augusta Caskie, 1hEdward Lovell Johns, 2hJohn B Minor, md9/1907
Nannie H, b18--, Camp Co, fCharles, mNancy Elder, hBur-

323

SCOTT (continued)
russ Pool, md1875
Nannie S, b1/18/1857, PrEd Co, hLucius d Walton
Nelly Barbour, bc1840, Oran Co, fGarrett, mSarah Ellen Nalle
Philip H, b184-, Oran Co, fGarrett, mSarah Ellen Nalle
Philip H, b187-, Oran Co, fWilliam Wallace, mClaudia Marshall Willis
Phoebe Catheine, bc1832, McGaheysville, Rkhm Co, d1899, fDavid, mBarbara --, hCharles R Rush
R Taylor, b18--, Fauq Co?, wFannie Carter
Richard Co, b18--, Ches Co?, wEliza Caskie Scott
Robert C, bc1860, Camp Co?, wMary Terrell
Robert Eden, b1808, "Oakwood", Fauq Co, d1862, fJohn, mElizabeth Blackwell Pickett
Sallie, b18--, Spot Co?, hSamuel Beale
Samuel, b1818, PrEd Co, fSamuel, wFrances Watson
Sarah, b1859, nrClinchport, Scot Co, d1886, 1w of Isaac Williams
Sarah Travers Lewis, b3/31/1847, Spot Co, fJames McClure, mSarah Travers Lewis, hCharles Harper Anderson, md2/15/1872
Sue L, b18--, Lynchburg, Camp Co, fCharles, hRichard H T Adams, Sr
Thomas Osborne, b17--, PrWi Co, fJames II, mElizabeth Osborne, wJane Haskins
Thomas, b4/1/1843, Spot Co, wEstelle Charters
Thomas, b184-, Oran Co, fGarret, mSarah Ellen Nalle
Waller, b7/4/1859, Oran Co, fJames W, mJennie Kirkpatrick, wKate Childrey
William A, b8/11/1862, Char Co, fSamuel, mFrances Watson, wLucie Buston, md4/24/1894
William C, Oran Co, fJohn II, mAnne Cowheid, wPamelia Graves
William Coleman, b17--, w-- Branch
William Walker, Sr, b2/27/1865,

SCOTT (continued)
York Co, fJoseph Winfield, mEmeline Jane Smith, wCora Francis, md11/25/1887
William Wallace, b4/10/1845, Oran Co, fGarrett, mSarah Ellen White, wClaudia Marshall Willis, md9/29/1869
SCRUGGS,John, b18--, Fauq Co, 2h of Susan Swart
Mildred Lelia, bc1840, Bedf Co, d1866, fReaves, 1w of William Kinnier
Reaves, b18--, Bedf Co
SEAL, Mirtie, b18--, Buck Co?, d1897, hJames L Anderson
SEALS, --, bc1860, Albe Co?, wFlorence S Totty
SEARS, G L, b18--, Roan Co?, w-- Denit
SEATON, James I, b18--, Fauq Co, wCarrie Kenner
SEAWELL, J Hairston, bc1840, Glou Co?, 2h of Lessie Cary
SEAY, Ann, b17--, Cumb Co?, fJames, hBenjamin Wilson
Archer N, b185-, Lune Co, fGeorge N, (2)mPetronella L Hatchett
Austin, bc1800, Amel Co
Bettie, b18--, Nott Co, fGeorge N, (1)mMary Baldwin, hJohn H Haskins
Fannie C, bc1850, fGeorge N, (2)mPetronella L Hatchett
George B, b18--, Nott Co?, fGeorge N, (1)mMary Baldwin
George N, b1839, Amel Co, fAustin, 1wMary Baldwin, 2wPetronella L Hatchett
Haynie Hatchett, b7/28/1860, Lune Co, fGeorge N, (2)mPetronella L Hatchett, wMattie P Davis
John, b185-, Amhe Co?, 1h of Mary Cranford
John M, b185-, Lune Co, fGeorge N, (2)mPetronella L Hatchett
Julia, b5/23/1847, Fork Union, Fluv Co, 2w of William P Snead
Mary, b18--, Nott Co, fGeorge N, (1)mMary Baldwin, hA M Chappell
Mary Alice, b12/25/1860, Fluv Co
Petronella L, bc1850, Lune Co,

SEAY (continued)
fGeorge N, (2)mPetronella L Hatchett
Richard B, b18--, Nott Co?, fGeorge N, (1)mMary Baldwin
Sallie A, b18--, Nott Co, fGeorge N, (1)mMary Baldwin, hGeorge B Bridgeforth
Susan Epes, b1855, Lune Co, fGeorge N, (2)mPetronella L Hatchett, hIsham Trotter Bagley
William Austin, b18--, Nott Co?, fGeorge N, (1)mMary Baldwin
SEDDON, Sarah, b18--, m-- Alexander, hCharles Bruce
SEETLE, Frances Anne, b18--, Culp Co?, hCharles William Rixey
SEGAR, Archer Eubank, b186-, nrJamaica, Midd Co, fJohn E, mMary E Eubank
H Lancelot, b3/21/1869, Midd Co, fJohn Randolph, (1)mSallie Goodwin Gatewood, wAgnes Newton Barron, md1902
James Randolph, bc1860, nr Jamaica, Midd Co, fJohn E, mMary E Eubank
John E, b1826, Midd Co, d1902, fRichard, wMary E Eubank
John Randolph, b1836, Midd Co, d1910, fCyrus, 1wSallie Goodwin Gatewood, 2wNannie Lee Evans
Lillian Shepherd, b187-, Midd Co, fJohn Randolph, (1)mSallie Goodwin Gatewood, hJohn Mason Dew
Mary E, b185-, nrJamaica, Midd Co, fJohn E, mMary E Eubank, hJohn Newcomb
Mary Minar, b186-, Midd Co, fJohn Randolph, (1)mSallie Goodwin Gatewood, hAndrew S Brown
Richard, bc1800, Midd Co
Richard Beverly, b8/13/1861, nrJamaica, Midd Co, fJohn E, mMary E Eubank, wHattie Lee Chowning, md11/26/1885
Thomas Churchill, b186-, nr Jamaica, Midd Co, fJohn E, mMary E Eubank
SEHORN, Sarah Jane, b4/7/1843,

SEHORN (continued)
Rkbr Co, hGuido A Heuser
SEIBERT, John Beatty, b18--, Page Co, hMary Alice Buraker
SELDEN, --, b18--, Gooc Co?, wHarriet Heath
Bessie, b1857, Westover, ChCi Co, hJoseph C Herbert, Sr
Martha Bland, b18--, Westover, ChCi Co, hJohn David Hobson
Richard Cunningham, b184-, "Snowden", Gooc Co, mHarriet Heath, w-- Hobson
SELECMAN, George, bc1800, PrWi Co
Henry, bc1800, PrWi Co
Jane Elizabeth, bc1830, PrWi Co, fWilliam R, mMargaret Selecman, hFrederick Lycurgus Lynn
Lettie M, b10/1/1870, Occoquan, PrWi Co, fMarshall, mLaura E Gregg, hWilliam Seymour Lynn, md9/1/1886
Margaret, bc1800, PrWi Co, fHenry, hWilliam R Selecman
Marshall, bc1840, PrWi Co, d1872, fHenry, wLaura E Gregg
William R, bc1800, PrWi Co, wMargaret Selecman
SELF, E D, bc1860, Mont Co?, wFanny Barnitz
SENSENEY, Mary, b17--, Fred Co?, hJohn Rhodes
Catherine, b182-, Fred Co?, 1w of George Wright
SENSENY, John, Fred Co?, wMary F Kline
SENTER, Bettie, b1851, Smyt Co, hJames K P Slaughter
James H, b11/19/1848, Smyt Co, fWilliam T, mSarah Rector, wHarriet McCrary
Wiley, b18--, Smyt Co?, wMelissa Copenhaver
William T, b18--, Smyt Co, wSarah Rector
SERBER, Jane, b1841, Wash Co, hWilliam Woodward
SERGENT, Forest P, b1848, nrDungannon, Scot Co, wPaulina V Porter
John Franklin, b12/6/1868, nr Dungannon, Scot Co, fForest P, mPaulina V Porter, 1wCallie Pridemore, md4/1/1905, 2wHanna

SERGENT (continued)
B Rollins
Joseph D, bc1866, nrDungannon, Scot Co, d1900, fForest E, mPaulina V Porter
Travis L, bc1870, nrDungannon, Scot Co, fForest P, mPaulina V Porter
SESSLER, Nancy, b1812, nrMcDonald's Mill, Mont Co, d1908, hGeorge McDonald, Jr
SETTLE, George Washington, b18--, Rapp Co, fThomas Henry, (1)m Caroline Barbee or (2)mCatherine Jordan, wMinnie Beckham
John, bc1810, Rapp Co?, wAcsah Miller
Mary Russell, b18--, fThomas Henry, (1)mCaroline Barbee, hJoseph Reid, md4/28/1886
Minnie, bc1870, Russ Co, fRobert, mJulia Taylor, hJohn Hiram Lockhart, md12/7/1898
Robert, b18--, Russ Co?, wJulia Taylor
Thomas Henry, b1813, Flint Hill, Rapp Co, fJoseph, 1w Caroline Barbee, 2wCatherine Jordan
William Barbee, Sr, b1853, Flint Hill, Rapp Co, d1889, fThomas Henry, (1)mCaroline Barbee, wLillian Belle Word
SEWARD, Catherine, b1808, Midd Co, d1883, hLarkin Stubblefield Bristow, md12/28/1828
Catherine, b18--, Esse Co, hWilliam Gresham Newbill
Hatcher S, bc1870, Petersburg, Dinw Co, fSimon, wIda Lee Baldwin, md2/25/1897
Simon, b18--, Surry Court House, Surr Co, d1912
SEXTON, Letitia M, b1/12/1840, Dublin, Pula Co, hElbert S Trinkle
Lucretia, b18--, Smyt Co, fWilliam C, hAlanson Tilman Lincoln
SEYBERT, Andrew, bc1800, High Co, fJacob, mMary Gum
Harmon Himer, b4/2/1850, High Co, fHenry, mLucinda Himer, wVirginia Arbogast, md6/24/1880
Henry, b1805, High Co, fJacob,

SEYBERT (continued)
mMary Gum, wLucinda Himer
Hester, bc1800, High Co, fJacob, mMary Gum
Isaac, bc1800, High Co, fJacob, mMary Gum
Jacob, b1767, fHenry, wMary Gum
Margaret, bc1800, High Co, fJacob, mMary Gum
Mary, bc1800, High Co, fJacob, mMary Gum
SEYMOUR, Marian Claiborne, bc1844, JaCi Co, hRichard Henry Richardson
SHACKELFORD, A C, bc1870, Dovedale, Albe Co, fW C, Sr, mSarah T Goss
Charles D, b18--, Albe Co, fDabney O, mMary Maddox, 1w Elizabeth Blakey, 2wMrs Gertrude Blakey, md1917
Charles L, bc1860, Richmond?, wEleanor Evans
Dabney O, b1822, Albe Co, fDaniel, m-- Carr, wMary Maddox
Grigsby C, b186-, Dovedale, Albe Co, fW C, Sr, mSarah T Goss
Jane, b186-, Dovedale, Albe Co, fW C, Sr, mSarah T Goss, hT L Farrar
John W, b186-, Dovedale, Albe Co, fW C, Sr, mSarah T Goss
Mary A, b186-, Dovedale, Albe Co, fW C, Sr, mSarah T Goss
Minnie R, bc1860, Dovedale, Albe Co, fW C, Sr, mSarah T Goss, hJ W Sampson
O Carr, b18--, Albe Co, fDabney O, mMary Maddox
W C, Sr, b3/24/1835, Stony Point Community, Albe Co, wSarah T Goss
SHACKFORD, Joseph W, b18--, West Co, wCora Kingsbury
Sallie, bc1870, West Co, fJoseph W, mCora Kingsbury, hSamuel B Walker, md5/18/1893
SHADRACH, James M, b1844, Culp Co, d1890, wEmma Terry
SHADWELL, L L, b18--, Shen Co?, wLydia Zirkle
SCHAEFFER, Susan, b18--, Roan Co?, hBenjamin Deyerle
SHAFFER, Emanuel, b18--, dc1865,

SHAFFER (continued)
wCatherine Black
Emma, bc1860, Page Co, fEmanuel, mCatherine, hD H Gander
G W, bc1850, PrWi Co?, wEllen Virginia Swank
John W, b12/28/1858, Page Co, fEmanuel, mCatherine Black, wFannie C Varner
Mattie, bc1860, Page Co, fEmanuel, mCatherine Black, hI H Gochenour
SHANK, --, bc1800, Rkhm Co?, hShem Heatwole
E R, bc1860, Rkhm Co, wTheresa U Beery
John, b18--, Rapp Co?, wJane Menefee
Sarah E, b18--, Rkhm Co, fSamuel, mCatherine Rodes, hDavid H Zigler, md2/14/1885
SHANKS, David C, bc1850, Salem, Roan Co
Sue, b12/28/1850, Salem, Roan Co, hArcher Allen Phlegar, Sr
SHANNON, Mary, b1836, Taze Co, d1917, hJesse Bailey
Price L, b8/22/1869, nrHuttonsville, Rand Co, fMichael, mMary Simpson, 1wDelia King, 2wNora Fitzpatrick
SHAPARD, Clementine P, b18--, Pitt Co, 2w of Patrick Henry Terry, md1913
SHAVER, Albert George, b9/26/1865, Maurertown, Shen Co, fEmanuel B, mLucretia Stone, wCora B Totty, md2/10/1886
Alice, bc1860, nrMaurertown, Shen Co, fSamuel, mAnna Good, hGeorge Gochenour
Barbara, b179-, Maurertown, Shen Co, fGeorge, Sr, mBarbara Stauffferin, hJohn Copp
C M, bc1860, Rkhm Co?, wBell Walker Pirkey
Catherine, b179-, Maurertown, Shen Co, fGeorge, Sr, mBarbara Stauffferin
Cornelius, b183-, Maurertown, Shen Co, fGeorge, Jr, (1)mMary Beydler
Davis Lee, b5/29/1861, nrMaurertown, Shen Co, fSamuel, mAnna Good, wMary L Shaver, md10/28/ 1891

SHAVER (continued)
Elizabeth, bc1800, Maurertown, Shen Co, fGeorge, Sr, mBarbara Stauffferin
Emanuel B, b2/8/1843, Maurertown, Shen Co, fGeorge, Jr, (1)mMary Beydler, wLucretia Stone
Fronica, b179-, Maurertown, Shen Co, fGeorge, Sr, mBarbara Stauffferin
George, Jr, b5/9/1798, Maurertown, Shen Co, d1887, fGeorge, Sr, mBarbara Stauffferin, 1w Mary Beydler, 2wMary (Crabill) Kagey
George, bc1820, Shen Co?, wSarah Garber
George H, b183-, Maurertown, Shen Co, fGeorge, Jr, (1)mMary Beydler
Jonathan, bc1810, Rkhm Co?, wAbigail Lincoln
John William, b10/16/1867, nrArmsterdam, Bote Co, fSamuel L, mMary C Gish, wPriscilla Layman, md1893
Lizzie, bc1870, nrAmsterdam, Bote Co, fSamuel L, mMary C Gish, hHouston Keeble
Magdalene, b179-, Maurertown, Shen Co, fGeorge, Sr, mBarbara Stauffferin
Mary, bc1850, Shen Co?, hJohn W Kagey
Mary C, bc1833, Maurertown, Shen Co, fGeorge, Jr, (1)mMary Beydler
Mary L, b1/2/1869, Shen Co, fEmanuel B, mLucretia Stone, hDavis Lee Shaver, md10/28/1891
Millie, b18--, Rkhm Co?, hCharles D Beard
Rachel, b182-, Maurertown, Shen Co, fGeorge, Jr, (1)mMary Beydler, hIsaac Myers
Samuel A, b3/14/1829, Maurertown, Shen Co, d1911, fGeorge, Jr, (1)mMary Beydler, wAnna Good
Samuel A, b186-, nrAmsterdam, Bote Co, fSamuel L, mMary C Gish
Samuel J, b186-, nrMaurertown, Shen Co, fSamuel, mAnna Good

SHAVER (continued)
Samuel L, b1841, nrHarrisonburg, Rkhm Co, d1911, wMary C Gish
Sarah, b180-, Maurertown, Shen Co, fGeorge, Sr, mBarbara Staufferin
Sarah, bc184-, Maurertown, Shen Co, fGeorge, Jr, (1)mMary Beydler, hJohn Funk
William E, b186-, Maurertown, Shen Co, fEmanuel B, mLucretia Stone
SHAW, Mary Beverly, b18--, Oran Co?, hWilliam L Bradbury
SHEARER, Anna, b18--, Millwood, Clar Co, hJohn W Sprint
Mary E, bc1870, Appo Co?, hNathan P Angle
SHEETMAN, Martha Elizabeth, bc1838, Rkbr Co?, d1906, hThomas Bowling Agnor
SHEETS, --, b18--, Rkhm Co, 1h of Mary Riddel
John, b18--, Rkhm Co?, 2h of Mary Riddel
SHEETZ, Daniel, b18--, Shen Co?, wHarriet Jane Sibert
Emma J, b2/12/1866, Shen Co, fDaniel W, mHarriet Jane Sibert, hMilton H Hite, md2/12/1866
Isaac, bc1830, Shen Co?, wSarah Catherine Painter
Joseph, bc1860, Shen Co?, wElizabeth Catherine Hutcheson
Mary, b18--, nrWoodstock, Shen Co, d1898, fAbram, hDavid Golladay
SHEFFEY, Eleanor F, b186-, Marion, Smyt Co, fJohn Preston, mJosephine Spiller, hBenjamin Franklin Buchanan, md3/2/1887
Ellen, b18--, Smyt Co?, hJoseph Rhea
John Preston, b18--, Smyt Co?, wJosephine Spiller
Martha, b1850, Marion, Smyt Co, 1w of Robert John Preston
SHEILD, Conway Howard, b3/17/1870, Yorktown, York Co, fJohn R, mFrances Howard, wCatherine Stryker
John R, bc1829, Yorktown, York Co, wFrances Howard

SHELBURNE, Cephas, b18--, Mont Co, fSilas, mMary H Stone, wLucy J Wigglewsroth
J William, b18--, Mont Co?, wElizabeth Gibson
James, b17--, Mont Co?, wAnn Pettus
Susan A, b18--, Mont Co?, hHugh K Gibson
Lavinia Catherine, b5/12/1844, Mont Co, fCephas, mLucy J Wigglesworth, hThomas W Spindle, md1870
Silas, bc1800, Mont Co, fJames, mAnn Pettus, wMary H Stone
William James, bc1840, Mont Co, fCephas, mLucy J Wigglesworth
SHELL, Ellen Hannah, b1848, Mont Co, hJoseph H Chumbley
SHELOR, Eliza A, b12/17/1847, Floy Co, fWilliam , mElizabeth Helms, hW H Francis
George, b18--, Floy Co, d186-, wJennie Lester
George W, b17--, Floy Co, wRuth Banks
George W, b1861, Floy Co, d1890, fGeorge, mJennie Lester, wVirginia Alice Eller
William B, b18--, Floy Co, fGeorge W, mRuth Banks, wElizabeth Helms
SHELTON, --, bc1840, Pitt Co?, wAnnie White
Ann Elizabeth, b1842, White Gate, Gile Co, d1920, hGeorge R Surface
Charlotte, bc1840, Pitt Co, fJohn Willis, mLeisure Moore
Edward, b18--, Atlee, Hano Co, w-- Oliver
Ferdinand, b184-, Pitt Co, fJohn Willis, mLeisure Moore
Harper W, bc1850, Hali Co?, wRosa Penick
James, b184-, Pitt Co, fJohn Willis, mLeisure Moore
John Marion, b1844, Pitt Co, d1921, fJohn Willis, mLeisure Moore, wMatilda Frances Motley
John Willis, b18--, Pitt Co, wLeisure Moore
Joseph, b18--, Henry Co
Lucy, bc1849, Henry Co?, d1883, fJoseph, hSamuel C Taylor
Nancy, b183-, Pitt Co, fJohn

SHELTON (continued)
Willis, mLeisure Moore
Peter, b18--, Henry Co, wMagdalen Rose E, b18--, Lovingston, Nels Co, fJohn, hJohn Horsley
Thomas Jefferson, b18--, Pitt Co?, wSarah Elizabeth William Motley
Thomas Wall, b12/8/1870, Ringgold, Pitt Co, fThomas Jefferson, wSarah Elizabeth William Motley
Walter M, b1852, Atlee, Hano Co, fEdward, m-- Oliver, wBertie Winn
William N, b18--, Henry Co, wAnna Robson
Willie, b184-, Pitt Co, fJohn Willis, mLeisure Moore
SHEPARD, Hannah, b1801, Dumfries, PrWi Co, d1861, hThomas Harrison
W B, bc1850, Buck Co?, wMartha Guthrie
SHEPHERD, --, bc1800, 3w of Warner Lewis
Frank Terry, bc1860, Fluv Co, wWillie Blanche Gray
James Leftwich, Sr, b8/17/1864, Fluv Co, wSusie Rives Jackson
Lucinda B, b18--, Fluv Co?, 2w of John Haden Lane, Sr
Mildred, b1843, Fluv Co, hShandy K Perkins, md2/9/1871
Sallie Terrell, bc1840, Fluv Co, 1w of Alphonso Alexander Gray
William, bc1810, Midd Co?, wIsabella Woodward
William Holman, bc1844, Fluv Co, wSarah Elizabeth Vaughan
SHEPPARD, Eliza, bc1800, Richmond?, fNathan, hFrederick Shryock
SHERARD, Elizabeth, b17--, Fred Co?, d1815, fRobert, hJohn Bell
SHERMAN, George F, b18--, Augu Co, w-- Wise
Homer Henkel, b7/27/1870, Rkhm Co, fJohn Wise, mNancy Henkel, 1wLaura Catherine Bowman, md3/24/1896, 2wElla Holmes, md1907
John Wise, b18--, Augu Co, fGeorge F, m-- Wise, wNancy

SHERMAN (continued)
Henkel
Louise Ann, b18--, Augu Co, hGeorge W Roller
Robert M, bc1860, Lanc Co?, 1h of Laura Edmonds
SHICKEL, Joseph, b18--, Rkhm Co, fJacob, wNancy Miller
SHIELDS, Elizabeth, b1821, Augu Co, hJames Ball Collins
James, b17--, Rkbr Co?, d1807
John C, b1820, Rkbr Co, d1904, wMartha Hardy
William T, b10/17/1849, Lynchburg, Camp Co, fJohn C, mMartha Hardy, wBettie Lee Donnan
SHIFLETT, Homer, bc1840, Albe Co?, wJennie Bruce
SHINNETT, R C, bc1850, Amhe Co?, wRoberta McGinnis
SHIPE, --, bc1800, Fred Co, hIsaac Grove
Decatur, bc1810, Shen Co, wAnn Bowman
Emanuel G, bc1860, Shen Co?, wBettie Hutcheson
SHIPLEY, vivian V, bc1860, Math Co?, wSusie Catherine Haynes
SHIPMAN, Bessie Lea, bc1870, Nels Co, hThomas H McGinnis, Sr, md3/30/1897
SHIPP, --, bc1800, Augu Co?, hWilliam H D Bell
SHIRLEY, --, b183-, New Market, Shen Co, fZachariah, (1)mBarbara Kagey, hAndrew Brubaker
Barbara, b183-, New Market, Shen Co, fZachariah, (1)mBarbara Kagey, hWilliam Cone
Bettie, b183-, New Market, Shen Co, d1896, fZachariah, (1)m Barbara Kagey
Christian, b10/31/1835, New Market, Shen Co, d1915, fZachariah, (1)mBarbara Kagey, wElizabeth Rosenberger
Daniel, b186-, New Market, Shen Co, fChristian, mElizabeth Rosenberger
Ella, b186-, New Market, Shen Co, fChristian, mElizabeth Rosenberger, hJoseph Roller
Emma, b186-, New Market, Shen Co, fChristian, mElizabeth Rosenberger, hJohn Brumback
Laura, bc1870, New Market, Shen

SHIRLEY (continued)
Co, fChristian, mElizabeth Rosenberger, hN S Horner
Martin, b183-, New Market, fZachariah, (1)mBarbara Kagey
Samuel P, b183-, New Market, Shen Co, fZachariah, (1)mBarbara Kagey
Sarah Catherine, b18--, hJohn William Long
Thomas, b183-, New Market, Shen Co, fZachariah, (1)mBarbara Kagey
Zachariah, b10/11/1796, New Market, Shen Co, d1875, 1wBarbara Kagey, 2wMrs Jacob Weaver
SHOCKLEY, Marilda Orlene, b18--, Carr Co, d1894, 1w of Henry Kyle Lindsay
SHOMAKER, --, b17--, Rkhm Co?, hGasper Myers, Sr
Samuel B, b184-, Russ Co?, wMary V Dickenson
SHORT, Margaret, b1849, Brun Co, hJohn J Jones
Sally, b17--, Fran Co?, fWilliam, mWinnie Randolph, hJoel Chitwood
William, b17--, Fran Co?, wWinnie Randolph
SHOWALTER, Aaron, bc1850, Rkhm Co, wMary Bull
David, b1804, Pula Co, d1877
Frances, b184-, Rkhm Co, fPeter, hFrank Good
John, b18--, Fran Co
J W, bc1860, Rkhm Co?, wIda B Miller
Joseph, b5/4/1844, nrBroadway, Rkhm Co, wFrances Beery
Josiah Thomas, b1848, Pula Co, d1915, fDavid, wSarah Catherine Vaden
Sallie, b18--, Rkhm Co, hHenry Early
Sarah, b18--, Shen Co?, hGeorge W Kibler
Sarah Catherine, b18--, Fran Co, fJohn, hHenry Jamison
Sophie, bc1840, Rkhm Co, fNoah Flory
SHREVE, Alice, bc1870, Fair Co, fSamuel, mJane Thompson, hWilliam Burroughs
Annie, bc1870, Fair Co, fSamuel, mJane Thompson, 1hWalter

SHREVE (continued)
Crown, 2h-- Hansborough
Emma, bc1870, Fair Co, fSamuel, mJane Thompson, hClifton Daggett
Freelove B, b18--, Loud Co, hWilliam E Garrett
Mary, b186-, Fair Co, fSamuel, mJane Thompson, hCary Dye
Oliver, b186-, Fair Co, fSamuel, mJane Thompson
Richard B, b18--, Ballston, Fair Co, wFlorence Price
Robert, b7/4/1859, Fair Co, fSamuel, mJane Thompson, wAnna Donaldson
Samuel, b1833, Fair Co, d1898, wJane Thompson
Samuel, bc1870, Fair Co, fSamuel, mJane Thompson
SHRUM, Andrew Lee, b186-, Dayton, Rkhm Co, fSamuel, mSarah Ann Messick
Charles Benjamin, b8/6/1864, Dayton, Rkhm Co, fSamuel, mSarah Ann Messick, wFlora B Andes, md4/4/1888
David, b182-, Shen Co, fGeorge, m-- Kern
Frederick, b182-, Shen Co, fGeorge, m-- Kern
George, b17--, w-- Kern
George Edgar, b5/18/1870, Dayton, Rkhm Co, fSamuel, mSarah Ann Messick, wAnnie K Ralston, md4/28/1904
Joseph, b8/27/1824, Shen Co, fGeorge, m-- Kern
Joseph Newton, b7/26/1857, Dayton, Rkhm Co, fSamuel, mSarah Ann Messick, wElizabeth T Kiser, md10/7/1880
Mary "Mollie" Susan, b1860, Dayton, Rkhm Co, fSamuel, mSarah Ann Messick, hReuben Daniel Suter, md10/26/1880
Peachy Messick, b186-, Dayton, Rkhm Co, fSamuel, mSarah Ann Messick
Samuel, b8/27/1824, Shen Co, fGeorge, m-- Kern, wSarah Ann Messick, md12/1855
SHRYOCK, Amelia, b185-, Fred Co, fJames Frederick, mCatherine Ann Kern, h-- Evans
Ann, b182-, Fred Co, fFrede-

SHRYOCK (continued)
rick, mEliza Sheppard, h-- Marks
Annie, b186-, Stephens City, Fred Co, fJacob N, mMary Elizabeth Dinges
Charles E, b181-, Fred Co, fFrederick, mEliza Sheppard
Emily, b182-, Fred Co, fFrederick, mEliza Sheppard, hGeorge Barr
Frederick, bc1800, Fred Co, wEliza Sheppard
Frederick Adam, b4/11/1854, Kernstown, Fred Co, fJames Frederick, mCatherine Ann Kern, wIda F Finkbine
Jacob N, b182-, Fred Co, fFrederick, mEliza Sheppard, wMary Elizabeth Dinges
James Frederick, bc1820, Fred Co, d1864, fFrederick, mEliza Sheppard, wCatherine Ann Kern
John, b182-, Fred Co, fFrederick, mEliza Sheppard
Lillian, bc1870, Stephens City, Fred Co, fJacob N, mMary Elizabeth Dinges, hW F Lemley
Rose Belle, b185-, Fred Co, fJames Frederick, mCatherine Ann Kern, h-- Quantz
Theodore, b185-, Fred Co, fJames Frederick, mCatherine Ann Kern
Thomas, b181-, Fred Co, fFrederick, mEliza Sheppard
Webster H, b186-, Stephens City, Fred Co, fJacob N, mMary Elizabeth Dinges
SHUE, Edwin Robert, b6/3/1847, nrHarrisonburg, Rkhm Co, d1913, fJoseph H, mElizabeth Mary Way, wEmma V Effinger
Edwin Robert, Jr, bc1870, Harrisonburg, Rkhm Co, fEdwin Robert, Sr, mEmma V Effinger
Joseph H, b11/1/1819, Rkhm Co, d1883, wElizabeth Mary Way
Joseph T, b1825, Bote Co, fDaniel, 1w-- Fagg, 2wMary E Merritt
William D, b18--, Blacksburg, Mont Co, fJoseph T, (2)mMary E Merritt
SHUFF, Jane, b18--, fWilliam, hJohn A Clem

SHUFFLEBARGER, Mary J, b1825, Pula Co, d1865, hHugh Dudley
SHULER, --, b185-, Page Co, fJohn, mMary Ann Kite, hBerry T Bowman
--, b185-, Page Co, fJohn, mMary Ann Kite, hDavid Foltz
--, b185-, Page Co, fJohn, mMary Ann Kite, hI F Kite
--, b184-, Page Co, fJohn, mMary Ann Kite, hJohn Strole
--, b18--, Page Co?, hIsaac Long, Sr
--, bc1860, Page Co, fAndrew Jackson, mJulia AnnKoontz, hG T Long
Andrew Jackson, bc1832, Page Co, d1911, wJulia Ann Koontz
Charles, bc1860, Page Co, fAndrew Jackson, mJulia Ann Koontz
David, b185-, Page Co, fAndrew Jackson, mJulia Ann Koontz
Emma J, b185-, Page Co, fAndrew Jackson, mJulia Ann Koontz, h-- Sutphim
George, b17--, Rkhm Co?, fJohn, mTabitha Dovel
George Thomas, b1855, Page Co, fJohn, mMary Ann Kite, wSarah Foltz
I F, b185-, Page Co, fAndrew Jackson, mJulia Ann Koontz
Isaac, b9/26/1848, Page Co, fJohn, mMary Ann Kite, 1wAmanda Virginia Shuler, md1870, 2wSudie Elizabeth (Koontz) Snyder
James Jackson, b185-, Page Co, fJohn, mMary Ann Kite
John, b17--, Rkhm Co?, fMathias, wTabitha Dovel
John, b18--, Page Co?, fGeorge, mMary Ann Kite
John, bc1850, Page Co, fJohn, wMary Ann Kite
John, bc1860, Page Co, fAndrew Jackson, mJulia Ann Koontz
Michael, b17--, Rkhm Co?, fMathias, w-- Long
Michael, b184-, Page Co, d1864, fJohn, mMary Ann Kite
Thomas, b185-, Page Co, fJohn, mMary Ann Kite
William Henry Harrison, b8/30/1854, Page Co, fAndrew Jack-

SHULER (continued)
son, mJulia Ann Koontz, wLaura Katherine Hottel, md12/17/1885
SHULL, Martin, b18--, Augu Co?, wLucy Michael
SHULTERS, Mary, b18--, Wash Co, 2w of A P McHenry
SHUMAKER, John T, b18--, Hamp Co?, wMollie Jack
SHUMAN, Nellie, b12/28/1861, Richmond, hHenry Marion Allport
SHUMATE, Elizabeth, b18--, Warr Co, fJames, m-- Rust or m-- Burgess, hEdward R Harrison
James, b18--, Warr Co?, 1w-- Rust, 2w-- Burgess
Joseph T, b18--, Henry Co, fSamuel, wElizabeth Stone
Mary, b18--, Loud Co?, hWilliam Fulton
Mary Ann, b18--, Warr Co, hEdward Burgess Jacobs
Samuel, b18--, Henry Co
SIBERT, Ernest R, b186-, Clar Co, fJames William, Sr, (1)m Arabella Hooper
Harriet Jane, b18--, Shen Co?, hDaniel W Sheetz
James William, Sr, bc1840, Woodstock, Shen Co, d1919, 1w Arabella Hooper, 2wMary Abbott
James William, Jr, b4/9/1863, Clar Co, fJames William, Sr, (1)m Arabella Cooper, wHenrietta Allsdorf, md10/1900
John, bc1840, Woodstock, Shen Co
Mary J, b18--, Rkhm Co, hGeorge Allen Moffett, md11/28/1858
SIBOLD, Jefferson D, b18--, Crai Co, wAmanda Huffman
Sallie A, b1852, nrNewport, Gile Co, hJames C Lucas
SIDWAY, Mary, bc1620, hBenjamin Harrison
SIFERS, Amos, bc1800, Cove Creek, Smyt Co, fJohn, m-- Clay, wMartha Linder
James Colley, b4/29/1860, nr Haysi, Dick Co, fJonathan Linder, mJosephine Colley, wAlice Belcher, md12/29/1886
Jonathan Linder, b18--, Wash Co, fAmos, mMartha Linder, wJosephine Colley

SIFERS (continued)
Martha, b186-, nrHaysi, Dick Co, fJonathan Linder, mJosephine Colley, hJohn W Puckett
Nancy, b186-, nrHaysi, Dick Co, fJonathan Linder, mJosephine Colley, hJohn R Belcher
Oliver D, b186-, Dick Co, wWinnie W Sifers
William, b186-, nrHaysi, Dick Co, fJonathan Linder, mJosephine Colley
Winnie W, c1870, nrHaysi, Dick Co, fJonathan Linder, mJosephine Colley
SIGMON, James, bc1870, Fran Co, fRobert, mElizabeth Gibson, wNinnie Via
Robert, b18--, Fran Co, wElizabeth Gibson
Robert, bc1870, Fran Co, fRobert, mElizabeth Gibson
SILCOTT, Heaton, bc1820, Fauq Co?, wJulia Ann Holton
SILLING, Andrew J, b18--, Fauq Co?, wMary Elizabeth Donaghe
SILVEY, James, bc1860, wFannie Anderson
SIMMERMAN, James Harvey, bc1860, Wyth Co?, wNannie A Kegley
John P M, b11/18/1821, nrWytheville, Wyth Co, fThomas H, wMary A Simmerman
Letitia, b18--, Pula Co?, hWilliam T Jordan
Mary A, b3/1825, Wyth Co, hJohn P Simmerman
Stephen Sanders, b11/18/1854, nrAustinville, Wyth Co, fJohn P M, mMary A Simmerman, wMary Lula Painter, md10/21/1885
Thomas H, b1828, Wyth Co, d1883, wEllen Victoria Peck
Thomas H, Wyth Co, Christopher, wMary Campbell Sanders
SIMMONS, --, b186-, Floy Co, fRoley M, mMalinda H Helm, hC B Keesee
George W, b186-, Floy Co, fRoley M, mMalinda H Helm
Hamilton W, b186-, Floy Co, d1917, fRoley M, mMalinda H Helm
John Webb, Sr, b1/16/1859, Floy Co, fRoley M, mMalinda H Helm, wLizzie W Morgan, md1887

SIMMONS (continued)
Lula, b9/30/1857, Meck Co, hJohn Hiram Wall
Mattie, b186-, Floy Co, fRoley M, mMalinda H Helm, h-- Martin
Minnie E, b1863, Floy Co, hAlbert Tapp Howard
Roley M, bc1826, Floy Co, d1907, wMalinda H Helm, mdc 1857
Tazewell M, b186-, Floy Co, fRoley M, mMalinda H Helm
Thomas W, b186-, Floy Co, d1898, fRoley M, mMalinda H Helm
W B, b18--, Fincastle, Bote Co
SIMMS, Eliza Mildred, b18--, Albe Co, hEdward Campbell Wingfield
Ella, b18--, Madi Co?, hF P Smith
SIMPSON, --, bc1810, Fair Co?, wMary Randolph Ford
--, b18--, Fair Co, hThomas K Davis
Gustavus Adolphus, bc1830, Warr Co, fSamuel, mMary Carson Williams, wLouisa Garrison
John S, bc1860, Loud Co?, wMary Smoot
Margaret A, b1/21/1859, Loud Co, fRichard, mSarah Lupton, hJohn Wesley Larrick, md3/10/1880
Mary, b18--, Richmond, hMichael Shannon
Richard, b18--, Loud Co, d186-, wSarah Lupton
S S, b18--, PrWi Co?, wBessie H Harrison
William Adolphus, bc1840, Warr Co, fGustavus Adolphus, mLouisa Garrison, wFannie Fravel Rhodes, md6/4/1878
SIMRALL, Frances, b17--, Fred Co?, hGilbert Meem
SIMS, Alice, bc1800, hWilliam Wynn
Carrie L, bc1870, Loui Co, fFrederick H, mMary Louisa Kimbrough, hWillie Jones Hubard
Elizabeth, b18--, Richmond, d1918, hWilliam H Baugh
Frederick H, b18--, Loui Co?, wMary Louisa Kimbrough

SIMS (continued)
Frederick Wilmer, b7/23/1862, Loui Co, fFrederick H, mMary Louisa Kimbrough, wLucy Payne, md9/8/1888
Priscilla, 17--, 2w of Paul Carrington
SINCLAIR, Edward Allen, b18--, Glou Co, wSally Smith
Mary, b18--, Midd Co, hThomas Booth Taliaferro
SINDLINGER, Bettie S, b18--, Page Co?, fJohn W, hHubert F Griffith
SINE, Adam, b18--, nrLiberty Furnace, Shen Co, wBarbara Mowery
Barney, bc1860, Shen Co, fAdam, mBarbara Mowery
Caroline, bc1860, Shen Co, fAdam, mBarbara Mowery, hJohn B Funkhouser
James, b6/17/1855, Shen Co, d1915, fAdam, mBarbara Mowery, wGeorgie Lichleiter
Julia, b185-, Shen Co, fAdam, mBarbara Mowery, hG P Helsley
Katie, b186-, Shen Co, fAdam, mBarbara Mowery
Thomas, b185-, Shen Co, fAdam, mBarbara Mowery
Victoria, bc1860, Shen Co, fAdam, mBarbara Mowery, hJames B Foltz
SINGER, Clara, bc186-, Richmond, fJohn, mPauline --
Ida, bc186-, Richmond, fJohn, mPauline --
John A, b12/22/1861, Richmond, fJohn, mPauline --, wGertrude Lewis, md1885
Julia, bc1860, Richmond, fJohn, mPauline --
SINGLETON, Richard A, b1835, Hali Co?, d1907, 1wFannie King, 2wNannie Crawley
SINK, Benjamin, Sr, bc1829, Fran Co, d1911, fHenry, wCatherine Peters
Benjamin, Jr, b186-, nrBoone Mill, Fran Co, fBenjamin, Sr, mCatherine Peters
Cabell, b186-, nrBoone Mill, Fran Co, fBenjamin, Sr, mCatherine Peters
Emma, bc1860, nrBoone Mill,

SINK (continued)
Fran Co, fBenjamin, Sr, mCatherine Peters
Frank, b186-, nrBoone Mill, Fran Co, fBenjamin, Sr, mCatherine Peters
George W, b186-, nrBoone Mill, Fran Co, fBenjamin, Sr, mCatherine Peters
Gideon, b186-, nrBoone Mill, Fran Co, fBenjamin, Sr, mCatherine Peters
Henry, bc1800, Fran Co
Monroe Thomas, b1/4/1864, nrBoone Mill, Fran Co, fBenjamin, Sr, mCatherine Peters, wMinnie Rebecca Kinsey, md4/14/1896
Owen H, b186-, nrBoone Mill, Fran Co, fBenjamin, Sr, mCatherine Peters
Zimania, b186-, nrBoone Mill, Fran Co, fBenjamin, Sr, mCatherine Peters, hB E Barnhart
SIPE, Emma, b18--, Rkhm Co, fEmanuel, hJ B D Rhodes
SIRON, Cameron, bc1860, High Co, wElla Keister
Joseph, bc1860, High Co, wViola Keister
SISK, Lewis, b18--, Fauq Co?, wCaroline Brown
Mary Jane, b18--, Scott District, Fauq Co, d1904, fLewis, mCaroline Brown, hJohn R Fishback
SISSON, Fannie, b18--, Greene Co, hGeorge A Hamm
SITES, Martha, b18--, Bote Co?, hJohn Rinehart
Melvine, b18--, Rkhm Co?, hBenjamin Hoover
SITLINGTON, Nannie S, b18--, High Co, hJohn W Alexander, Jr
SIZER, Martha, bc1800, Esse Co, 1w or 2w of Andrew Hundley
SKAGGS, Jeremiah, b18--, Turkey Cove, Lee Co, d1862, fJohn, w-- Harrison
John, bc1800, Russ Co
John F, b1853, Turkey Cove, Lee Co, fJeremiah, m-- Harrison, 1wMary Andis, 2wEvelyn Jane Howard
SKEEN, --, b18--, Bout Co,

SKEEN (continued)
(father of Virginia Skeen, md1900)
SKELTON, Maria Ward, b1846, Powh Co, John G, hJohn Langbourne Williams, md10/13/1864
SKIDMORE, Mary Alice, b18--, KiWi Co?, hL E Williams
SKINKER, Anna, b183-, Huntley, Fauq Co, fJames, mElizabeth Chambers, hNorman DeVere Howard
Charles, bc1840, Huntley Co, fJames, mElizabeth Chambers
Elizabeth, b183-, Huntley, Fauq Co, fJames, mElizabeth Chambers, hThomas Smith
J Hampton, bc1860, wMay Kennerly
James, bc1809, Millbank, Fauq Co, fWilliam, wElizabeth Chambers
Madge, bc1830, Huntley, Fauq Co, fJames, mElizabeth Chambers, hJohn McElhany
Mary, bc1830, Huntley, Fauq Co, fJames, mElizabeth Chambers, hJohn Goldsmith
Rose, bc1830, Huntley, Fauq Co, fJames, mElizabeth Chambers, hBeverley Turner
Thomas, bc1810, Millbank, Fauq Co, fWilliam
William, b17--, Millbank, Fauq Co, fSamuel
William Keith, b1838, Huntley, Fauq Co, fJames, mElizabeth Chambers, wAntoinette Early
SKINNER, Annie B, bc1860, nrMiddleburg, Fauq Co, fJames, (2)m Bettie Beattie
Charles, b184-, nrMiddleburg, Fauq Co, fJames, (1)mJane Turner
Edgar, b184-, nrMiddleburg, Fauq Co, fJames, (1)mJane Turner
Eliza, b18--, Oran Co?, h-- Goff
Fannie, b184-, nrMiddleburg, Fauq Co, fJames, (1)mJane Turner, hJack Robinson
James, b18--, Fauq Co, fGabriel, d1876, 1wJane Turner, 2wBettie Beatty, 3wLucy Beatty
James H, b18--, wJoshuanna Ger-

SKINNER (continued)
main
James Henry, b1/15/1848, nrMiddleburg, Fauq Co, fJames, (1)mJane Turner, wRebecca Ellen Cochran
Mollie, b184-, nrMiddleburg, Fauq Co, fJames, (1)mJane Turner, hWilliam Fletcher
William Jefferson, b184-, nr Middleburg, Fauq Co, fJames, (1)mJane Turner
SKIPWORTH, Henry, b17--, wAnne Robertson
SLAGLE, Alfred A, b7/1/1867, Meck Co, fJohn, 1wElla Daniel, md1893
SLATE, William, b18--, Hali Co?, wLucy Jordan
SLATER, Jennie, b1848, Henrico Co, hLuther Farinholt
SLAUGHTER, --, b18--, Patr Co, hAustin Burnett
Albert G, b18--, Augu Co?, fJohn S
Alfred E, b18--, Oran Co, wEugenia Taylor
E F, b18--, Nott Co, wMary Page, md9/15/1892
Edith R, b185-, Camp Co?, hRichard Thomas Walker Duke, Jr, md10/1/1884
John, b17--, Culp Co
John S, b17--, Culp Co, fJohn
Kate M, b18--, Augu Co, fAlbert G, hDavid W Drake
Robert, b17--, Culp Co, fJohn
Sallie F, bc1870, Nott Co?, d1913, fE F, mMary Page, hRaps S Beville, md9/15/1892
Sarah Jane, b18--, Culp Co, hJohn Fielding Ficklen
Sarah Catherine, b18--, Rapp Co?, fWilliam, hWilliam Cleminson Armstrong
William, b17--, Rapp Co?, fMercer
William, b1700, Culp Co, fJohn
SLAYTON, Virginia, b18--, hJames S Bondurant
SLEDD, Mary, b18--, Richmond?, hNathaniel Green
SLEMP, Campbell, b18--, Lee Co?, d1907, wNannie B Cawood
Campbell Bascom, b9/4/1870, fCampbell, mNannie B Cawood

SLEMP (continued)
Eliza Ann, b1841, Turkey Cove, Lee Co, d1920, hJohn A G Hyatt
Susan, b186-, Lee Co, fCampbell, mNannie B Cawood, hHiram D Pridemore
Susan Virginia, b18--, Lee Co?, hJohn H Collier
SLOAN, John T, b18--, Fauq Co?, wJane Beverley
SLUSS, Ragens, bc1860, Taze Co?, wNannie Litz
SLUSSER, James P, bc1840, Mont Co, wSusan McDonald
SMALLWOOD, Amanda, b184-, Clar Co, fBourbon, mEliza Tomblin, hSamuel Lanham
Arrissa, b184-, Clar Co, fBourbon, mEliza Tomblin, hRobert Drish
Bourbon, bc1800, Clar Co, fJames, wEliza Tomblin
Bushrod, b184-, Clar Co, fBourbon, mEliza Tomblin
Emma May, b186-, nrBerryville, Clar Co, fSylvester, mSarah Margaret Thompson, hC T Carroll
George, b184-, Clar Co, fBourbon, mEliza Tomblin
John F, b184-, Clar Co, fBourbon, mEliza Tomblin
Julia, b186-, nrBerryville, Clar Co, fSylvester, mSarah Margaret Thompson, hJohn F Royston
Lucy, b184-, Clar Co, fBourbon, mEliza Tomblin, hEverett Fowler
Margaret, bc1870, nrBerryville, Clar Co, fSylvester, mSarah Margaret Thompson, hIra Fewell
Mary, b184-, Clar Co, fBourbon, mEliza Tomblin, hCharles Lloyd
Nannie, bc1870, nrBerryville, Clar Co, fSylvester, mSarah Margaret Thompson, hGeorge Coffman
Rebecca, b183-, Clar Co, fBourbon, mEliza Tomblin, hJames Tomblin
Sylvester, b1839, Clar Co, d1887, fBourbon, mEliza Tomblin, wSarah Margaret Thompson
Thomas, b18--, Clar Co, fBourbon, mEliza Tomblin

SMALLWOOD (continued)
Virginia, b186-, nrBerryville, Clar Co, fSylvester, mSarah Margaret Thompson, hWalter S Royston
William Walton, b10/16/1863, nrBerryville, Clar Co, fSylvester, mSarah Margaret Thompson, wMary E Elsea, md12/2/1882
SMART, Eliza, b1838, Leesburg, Loud Co, d1883, fJohn Pearson, mEmily Hilliard, hSylvanus Littlepage Ingram, md5/8/1861
John Pearson, b1802, Loud Co?, d1865, wEmily Hilliard
Lafayette, bc1840, Leesburg, Loud Co, fJohn Pearson, mEmily Hilliard
SMETT, Kate, b1854, Caro Co, hRichard A Blanton
SMITH, --, b17--, Richmond?, hHenry Lindsay
--, bc1830, Clar Co?, wMay Newton
--, bc1800, Crai Co, h-- Caldwell
--, bc1800, Crai Co, hJackson Ferrell
--, bc1860, Crai Co?, wBetty E Layman
Abigail, b16--, Glou Co, 1w of Lewis Burwell
Abraham, b17--, Rkhm Co?, fJohn, mMargaret --
Adella, bc1870, Lune Co?, fBenjamin J, mKatherine Walker, hJames Sidney Saunders, md12/15/1892
Adiline Antoinette, b18--, 1w of James William Grizzard
Agnes Newton, bc1850, Nhld Co, fJames, hSamuel Barron
Albert S, b18--, Lune Co
Algernon Sydney, bc1830, Lune Co, wSarah Ingram, md6/17/1855
Alice, b18--, Appo Co, hWilliam C Turpin
Allen, bc1840, nrRomney, Hamp Co, fStephen
Ann, b16--, PrGe Co?, fObediah, hRichard Woodson
Ann, b175-, Bedf Co, fGuy, mAnn Hopkins, hDaniel Trigg
Ann Park, b18--, Pitt Co, fAlbert S, hSilas J Dudley

SMITH (continued)
Anna Mary, b18--, Patr Co, fJames Wyatt, mAmanda Ross, hJohn Lewis Waid
Anna Ophelia, b18--, Culp Co?, fEdward, mMargaret Dade, hJames Farish Hansbrough
Annie, bc1870, Augu Co?, fJohn Green, (1)m-- Taylor, hWalter N Peale
Annie, b18--, Floy Co?, hJoseph Howard
Annie G, b186-, Amherst, Amhe Co, d1893, fJames E, 1w of Francis Edward Turner, Sr
Asbury R, b183-, nrRomney, Hamp Co, fStephen
Benjamin E, Sr, b1801, Lune Co, fJohn, wMary A Hardy
Benjamin E, Jr, bc1840, "Laurel Branches", Lune Co, d1921, fBenjamin E, Sr, mMary A Hardy
Benjamin J, b18--, Lune Co?, wKatherine Walker
Bettie, b18--, Fauq Co, fHenry, 1w of Horace Turner Burgess, md11/21/1889
Byrd, b17--, Cumb Co
Caroline, b18--, Fred Co, hWilliam Cather
Carrie H, bc1870, Fran Co, fH P, hAlbert L Noell, Jr, md1889
Catherine Markham, b17--, Hano Co?, fFrancis, hJames Spiller
Channing B, b186-, Cumb Co, fRobert, mMatilda McShan
Charles C, b180-, Fauq Co?, wMartha Woods Adams
Charles H, bc1833, Berryville, Clar Co, d1904, fTreadwell, wEliza Blackburn
Charlotte, b18--, Staf Co, hJames Keith Briggs
Claudius F, bc1860, wClara Forsyth McGuire
Connie C, bc1870, Cumb Co, fRobert, mMatilda McShan
Daniel, b17--, Rkhm Co?, fJohn, mMargaret --, wJane Harrison
David H, b1/8/1815, nrAdvance Mills, Albe Co, wMary A Parrott
Dollie, b18--, Rapp Co?, hClinton Haddox
Edward, b18--, Culp Co?, wMargaret Dade

SMITH (continued)
Edward Jacquelin, b18--, KiGe Co?, wLucy Wiley mason
Electra, bc1870, Henry Co?, fJames M, hHerbert Greyson Peters, md1894
Eliza, b17--, Albe Co, hSamuel Page
Eliza, b18--, Math Co, hEdward B S Cary
Eliza, b18--,Midd Co, hJames Chowning
Elizabeth, b17--, Roan Co, hJohn Woods
Elizabeth, b18--, Hamp Co?, hCharles Harmison
Elizabeth Barton, b18--, Fauq Co, fJohn Pulla, mMary Barton, hAmos Payne
Elizabeth Lowry, b186-, Esse Co, fWilliam F, mElizabeth Warring, hWillard Bellamy Robinson, md6/1887
Ellen, b1860, Carr Co, hRandolph Chitwood
Emeline Jane, bc1842, Warw Co, hJoseph Winfield Scott
Emily G, bc1870, nrWinchester, Fred Co, fRobert G, mAnnie Brown, hW N Fletcher
Erasmus T, bc1850, nrEdinburg, Shen Co, fJack, (1)m-- Painter
Eula, b18--, nrAdvance Mills, Albe Co, fDavid H, mMary A Parrott, hEd Smith
F P, b18--, Madi Co, wElla Simms
Fannie, b18--, nrAdvance Mills, Albe Co, fDavid H, mMary A Parrott, hJames Fransley
Fannie S, bc1870, Augu Co?, fJohn Green, (1)m-- Taylor, hJ Fred Effinger
Fannie Sanford, b18--, Alexandria?, fJames P, mMary Sanford, hJohn Marion Hart, Sr
Fielding Jefferson, b18--, Madi Co, fFielding, wEmily Jane Carpenter
Flournoy N, bc1850, Dick Co?, wJane Keel
Francis, b177-, Mont Co?, wMary Trigg
Francis, b18--, wMary Stuart Harrison
George C, b18--, Hano Co?,

SMITH (continued)
wMary --
George C, bc1850, Dick Co?, wElizabeth Keel
George Edward, b4/29/1845, "Laurel Branches", Lune Co, fBenjamin E, Sr, mMary A Hardy, wNannie E Bagley, md11/25/1874
George Washington, bc1860, Richmond?, wVirginia Campbell
Grace Allice, b1851, Glou Co, d1881, fPeter William, mFrances J Rowe, hJohn E Smith
Guy, b17--, Bedf Co?, wAnn Hopkins, md11/23/1751
H P, b18--, Fran Co
Henry, b17--, York Co, fLeven
Henry, b17--, Rkhm Co?, fJohn, mMargaret --
Henry Clay, bc1852, Norfolk, d1916, wElla Ward
Henry Marston, b7/19/1859, Richmond, fHiram Moore, mElizabeth Louisa Ames, wLucy Conway Gordon, md11/7/1883
Hugh, b1/28/1793, Loud Co, fJames, mNancy Atwell, wElizabeth Jones
Hugh, bc1800, Alexandria?, wElizabeth Watson
J Alison, bc1840, Carr Co, wRhoda Early
J Mason, b1/10/1869, Oran Co, fW H, mElla P Johns, wHattie B Norfor, md1/17/1894
J Weldon, b186-, nrCumberland Court House, Cumb Co, fJ William, mVirginia Booker
J William, b18--, Cumb Co, d1873, fJohn, wVirginia Booker
Jack, b18--, Shen Co, d186-, 1w-- Painter
Jacob Henry, bc1830, Albe Co?, wMary Kelly Watson
James, b17--, Loud Co?, 1h of Nancy Atwell
James, bc1800, Nhld Co
James, bc1800, Smyt Co?, wNancy Orr
James Absolom Waller, b8/7/1862, "Oldhams", West Co, d1920, fJames R, mAlmeda J Stephens, wElla Josephine Anderson
James D, b6/16/1847, nrAdvance

SMITH (continued)
Mills, fDavid H, mMary A Parrott
James G, b180-, fWillis G, mSallie
James P, b18--, Alexandria?, fHugh, mElizabeth Watson, wMary Sanford
James R, b1835, "Oldhams", West Co, d1895, wAlmeda J Stephens
James T, b183-, nrRomney, Hamp Co, fStephen
James Wyatt, b18--, Fran Co, wAmanda Ross
Jane, b18--, Spot Co, h-- Humphries
John, b17--, Rkhm Co?, fJohn, mMargaret --
John, b17--, Rkhm Co?, fAbraham
John, b17--, Lune Co
John, b18--, Cumb Co, fByrd
John C, b183-, "Laurel Branches", Lune Co, fBenjamin E, Sr, mMary A Hardy
John E, b11/5/1841, Craney Island, Norf Co, wGrace Alice Smith
John Green, b18--, Rkhm Co, fDaniel, mJane Harrison, 1w-- Taylor, 2wSarah McKelden
John, b18--, Fran Co?, d186-, fRobert, mPhoebe Hancock
John N, bc1860, Cumb Co, fRobert, mMatilda McShan
John P, b180-, fWillis G, mSallie John Pulla, bc1800, Fauq Co?, wMary Barton
Jonathan, b18--, Clar Co, fTreadwell, wRebecca Isler
Joseph, b17--, Rkhm Co?, fJohn, mMargaret --
Joseph, bc1810, Fred Co?, wEliza Bell
Joseph B, b180-, fWillis G, mSallie --
Joseph L C, b18--, Wash Co?, wSallie Campbell
Juliet Lyle, b1816, Rkhm Co, d1893, fAbram, hCrawford C Straver
Julia, b18--, Buch Co, hShadrick Stacy
Katherine, bc1870, Augu Co?, fJohn Green, m-- Taylor, hB G Gregg
Lelia, b18--, Charlottesville,

SMITH (continued)
Albe Co, d1899, fFrancis H, mMary Stuart Harrison, 1w of Lucian Howard Cocke, Sr, md1885
Letitia, b186-, Cumb Co, fRobert, mMatilda McShan, hWilliam Henry Ellinger
Lewis, bc1810, Fred Co?, wLeah Bucher
Lloyd B/T, b7/14/1845, Middleburg, Loud Co, fHugh, mElizabeth Jones, wEstelle Betts
Lucius G, bc1870, Augu Co?, fJohn Green, (1)m-- Taylor
Lucy Ann, b18--, Rapp Co?, fCornelius C, hHenry Ashford Smith
Lucy Virginia, b9/1/1864, Fred Co, fSamuel Jackson, mAsburina Muse, hMahlon Calvin Garvin, md3/19/1907
Lula E, b3/1/1870, Rye Cove, Scot Co, hElbert F Wolfe
Margaret A, b18--, Augu Co, d1903, 2w of Henry Parker
Margaret P, bc1810, fWillis G, mSallie --
Marianna, b18--, Morattico Hall, Richmond, hJoseph William Smith
Martha Pettis, b7/2/1828, Buck Co, d1876, 1w of John Venable Crute
Mary, b18--, Abingdon, Wash Co, hWyndham Robertson
Mary, b186-, Cumb Co, fRobert, mMatilda McShan, hEdgar T Hicks
Mary Ann Rebecca, b18--, Fran Co, fSamuel, mMary --, 2w of William Leftwich Turner Hopkins, md6/4/ 1895
Mary Eliza, b18--, Caro Co?, hJohn James Gravatt, Sr
Mary Frances, b1848, PrEd Co, d1884, fJ D, mDrusilla E Baker, hJohn Dannie Davis
Mary Hart, b17--,Caro Co?, hGeorge Tod
Mary L, b184-, "Laurel Branches", Lune Co, fBenjamin E, Sr, mMary A Hardy, hLucius E Barrow
Mary Stonewell Jackson, b186-, Fred Co, d1906, fSamuel Jack-

SMITH (continued)
son, mAsburina Muse, hDavid C Miller
Mattie, bc1870, Cumb Co, fRobert, mMatilda McShan, hRobert L King
Mattie L, b18--, JaCi Co?, fSidney, hRobert Morton Hughes, Sr, md2/19/1879
Nannie E, b184-, "Laurel Branches" Lune Co, fBenjamin E, Sr, mMary A Hardy, hFrank White
Otis M, b184-, nrEdinburg, Shen Co, fJack, (1)m--- Painter
Permelia Lena, b18--, Mt Pleasant, Norf Co, hThomas Butt Gresham
Peter Hamilton, b18--, Culp Co, fPeter, wIda Sparks
Peter William, b1828, Glou Co, d1908, wFrances J Rowe
Polly W, b181-, fWillis G, mSallie
Pulser C, b18--, Pend Co?, w-- Bowers
Rebecca Emeline, bc1800, nr Alexandria, fJohn Frye, hIsaac Gardiner Hutton, md1823
Rebecca Jane, b18--, fCornelius, hJohn Byron Miller
Richard Hewlett, b7/27/1859, Richmond, fSamuel B, mMargaret Strother, wMary Douthat Barton, md10/18/1882
Robert, bc1800, Fran Co, wPhoebe Hancock
Robert, b18--, Cumb Co, wMatilda McShan
Robert Allen, b1791, PrEd Co, wSarah Watkins Spencer, md1818
Robert J D, b1821, PrEd Co, fRobert Allen, mSarah Watkins Spencer, wDrusilla E Baker, md1846
Robert Julius, b2/17/1862, Cumb Co, fRobert, mMatilda McShan, wMartha Jane Corker
Robert S, b10/13/1868, nWinchester, Fred Co, fRobert G, mAnnie Brown, 1wMary Massie, md10/1896, 2wMyrtle R Massie, md1917
Sallie, b10/10/1826, KiQu Co, d1911, hJames Hawkins Claggett Jones

SMITH (continued)
Sally, b18--, York Co, hEdward Allen Sinclair
Sallie Ann Lucy, b6/10/1827, fWillis G, mSallie --, hGeorge W Davis
Sallie B, b184--, "Laurel Branches", Lune Co, fBenjamin E, Sr, mMary A Hardy
Samantha, b183-, nrRomney, Hamp Co, fStephen
Samuel B, b12/25/1856, nrFincastle, Bote Co, fSchuyler W, mHannah B Parks, wAnnie R Ammen, md4/8/1888
Samuel Jackson, b9/7/1828, Fred Co, wAsburina Muse
Sands, Sr, b18--, d186-
Sands, Jr, b1838, Math Co, d1914, fSands, Sr, wCarrie W Diggs
Sarah, b17--, Augu Co?, hReuben Alexander
Sarah J, b1848, Berryville, Clar Co, d1916, fJonathan, mRebecca Isler, hJohn O Crown, md1817
Sarah V, b183-, nrRomney, Hamp Co, d1919, fStephen, hSilas R Snapp
Schuyler B, bc1816, Albe Co, wHannah B Parks
Stephen, bc1802, d1870
Susan, b17--, Bedf Co, fWilliam, hField Allen Hancock
Susan, b18--, hWiley Roy Mason
Susan L, bc1840, "Laurel Branches", Lune Co, fBenjamin E, Sr, mMary A Hardy, hCharles M Hardy
Susanna, b17--, fGuy, mAnn --, hJohn Leftwich, md2/7/1788
Susannah, b18--, PrWi Co?, hJames W Bell
Sydney, b1821, Poquoson District, York Co, d1884, fHenry
Sydney, b6/16/1859, Williamsburg, JaCi Co, fSydney, wMargaret P Crooks
Thomas, bc1830, wElizabeth Skinker
Thomas A, b183-, "Laurel Branches" Lune Co, fBenjamin E, Sr, mMary A Hardy
W D, bc1860, Richmond?, wElizabeth Conrad

SMITH (continued)
W H, b11/1844, Oran Co, wElla P Johns, md12/1867
W R L, b18--, Roan Co?, wRosa Cocke
William, bc1820, Fauq Co?, wMary Glascock
William, b1826, Lee Co, d1889, fJames, mNancy Orr, wPolly Ely
William Armistead, Sr, b1847, nrRoanoke, Roan Co, wLillian Posey
William Edward, b186-, Fred Co, fSamuel Jackson, mAsburina Muse
William F, b18--, Esse Co?, wElizabeth Warring
William H, b1851, nrEdinburg, Shen Co, fJack, (1)m-- Painter, wNannie S Miller
William Henry, Sr, b1843, Charlotte Court House, Char Co, d1921, fThomas, wFannie Mebane
William Jackson, b2/15/1861, Madi Co, fFielding Jefferson, mEmily Anne Carpenter, wFannie C Wood, md2/7/1894
William O, b1/9/1851, nrPennington Gap, Lee Co, d1890, fWilliam, mPolly Ely, 1h of Fannie Robbins
Willie, b18--, nrAdvance Mills, Albe Co, fDavid H, mMary A Parrott, hJohn H Marshall
Willis G, b6/27/1777, wSallie --, md2/10/1806
Willis Golder, bc1810, fWillis G, mSallie --
SMITHEY, Ellen, bc1800, Richmond?, hAuguste Guigon
SMOKE, John W, bc1840, Fred Co?, wSallie Larrick
SMOOT, --, b18--, Shen Co, hSamuel Beydler
A I, b18--, Nels Co?, w-- Whitehead
Annie, b183-, nrWoodstock, Shen Co, fAbram, mBarbara Sager
Annie, bc1860, nrWoodstock, Shen Co, fJames William, mMargaret Stickley, hJosiah Wisman
Cesla Mason, bc1850, Esse Co?, d1910, wSusan Allen Lewis
Daniel Jenifer, b18--, Madi Co?, wHarriet Medley
David F, b183-, nrWoodstock,

SMOOT (continued)
Shen Co, fAbram, mBarbara Sager
Fannie, bc1870, nrWoodstock, Shen Co, fJames William, mMargaret Stickley, hLee Young
Frances Burton, b9/22/1833, Madi Co, d1915, fDaniel Jenifer, mHarriet Medley, hJacob H Plecker, md11/21/1854
George, b183-, nrWoodstock, Shen Co, fAbram, mBarbara Sager
Georgie, b186-, nrWoodstock, Shen Co, fJames William, mMargaret Stickley, hThomas R Stickley
Hampson, b183-, nrWoodstock, Shen Co, fAbram, mBarbara Sager
Henry, b183-, nrWoodstock, Shen Co, fAbram, mBarbara Sager
Henry J, b18--, Page Co?, wMartha C Yager
James Henry, b9/21/1867, nrWoodstock, Shen Co, fJames William, mMargaret Stickley, 1wMary Wisman, 2wNettie H Maphis, md1899
James William, b1831, nrWoodstock, Shen Co, fAbram, mBarbara Sager, wMargaret Stickley
Martha Y, b18--, Page Co?, fHenry J, mMartha C Yager, hWilliam L Hudson, md11/1/1877
Mary, b186-, nrWoodstock, Shen Co, fJames William, mMargaret Stickley, hJohn S Simpson
Thomas R, b186-, Taze Co?, wKatie Litz
Vernon, b186-, nrWoodstock, Shen Co, fJames William, mMargaret Stickley, hSamuel Beidler
SMOTT, Reda, b18--, Shen Co, 2w of Washington Abel Sager, mdc1890
SMYTH, George, b18--, Emory, Wash Co, fJohn S, mBettie Howard
John S, b1819, Wash Co, fTobias, m-- Kelley, wBettie Howard
Mary, b18--, Emory, Wash Co, fJohn S, mBettie Howard, hJames T Neilson

SMYTH (continued)
Robert J, b18--, Emory, Wash Co, fJohn S, mBettie Howard
Tobias, b1778, Wash Co, fJonas S, w-- Kelley
Tobias II, b18--, Emory, Wash Co, fJohn S, mBettie Howard
William F, b8/12/1847, Emory, Wash Co, fJohn S, mBettie Howard, wNellie F Baker, md12/1888
SMYTHE, Robert L, bc1860, Russ Co?, wVirginia A Meade
SNAPP, Betie, bc1870, nrRomney, Hamp Co, fSilas R, mSarah V Smith, h-- Huggins
Charles E, bc1860, nrRomney, Hamp Co, fSilas R, mSarah V Smith
Charles W, bc1855, Fred Co?, wEllen Headley
Elsie, bc1870, nrRomney, Hamp Co, fSilas R, mSarah V Smith, h-- Marshall
Hannah Elizabeth, b186-, nrRomney, Hamp Co, fSilas R, mSarah V Smith, h-- Harper
Henrietta, b186-, nrRomney, Hamp Co, fSilas R, mSarah V Smith, hWilliam F Baxter
Herbert, b186-, nrRomney, Hamp Co, fSilas R, mSarah V Smith
Jacob, b18--, Shen Co, w-- Grandstaff
L R, b186-, nrRomney, Hamp Co, fSilas R, mSarah V Smith
LeRoy Fletcher, b186-, nrRomney, Hamp Co, fSilas R, mSarah V Smith
Marcus J, b18--, Fred Co?, wZora Gray
Marvin L, b186-, nrRomney, Hamp Co, fSilas R, mSarah V Smith
Robert J, b7/17/1865, nrRomney, Hamp Co, fSilas R, mSarah V Smith, wKate Harnsberger, md 12/19/1895
Sarah Elizabeth, b18--, Edinburg, Shen Co, d1915, fJacob, m-- Grandstaff, hCasper Funkhouser
Silas R, bc1830, Hamp Co, d1895, wSarah V Smith
SNARR, Charles O, b185-, Mt Olive, Shen Co, fSamuel H, mMary Dorothy Rutz

SNARR (continued)
Emma C, bc1850, Mt Olive, Shen Co, fSamuel H, hMoses Lockmiller
George H, b1851, Mt Olive, Shen Co, fSamuel H, mMary Dorothy Rutz, wMary Belle Baker
Lemuel Josephus, bc1850, Mt Olive, Shen Co, fSamuel H, mMary Dorothy Rutz
Obed N, b185-, Mt Olive, Shen Co, fSamuel H, mMary Dorothy Rutz
SNAVELY, Sallie, b18--, Smyt Co?, hJohn H Snyder
SNEAD, Ann G, b18--, Camp Co?, hWilliam Okey, Jr
Anthony, b1839, fRichard, wJulia Richardson
Archibald, b17--, Fluv Co
Archibald II, bc1800, Fluv Co, fArchibald
Ben, bc1800, Fluv Co, fArchibald, w-- Pollard
Benjamin, b18--, Fluv Co, fJohn, mSarah Weaver, wElizabeth Pollard
Bettie, bc1830, Fluv Co, fWilliam, mLucinda Pollard, hWillis Curl Thomas
Burwell, bc1800, Fluv Co, fArchibald
Charles, b184-, Fork Union, Fluv Co, fWilliam, mLucinda Pollard
Cornelius P, b18--, Fluv Co, d1912, fBen, wHelen Winn
Elisha, bc1800, Camp Co?, wSusan Thomas
George, b18--, Fluv Co, fJohn, mSarah Weaver, wOranie Pollard
George, bc1800, Fluv Co, fArchibald, wOranie Pollard
James A, b18--, Fork Union, Fluv Co, fCornelius P, mHelen Winn, wFannie Putney
Joseph Henry, b182-, Ches Co?, wMartha Roberta Ingram, md2/11/1851
Judith, b18--, Amhe Co?, hAlexander Campbell
Lula, b18--, Fluv Co, fLuther Rice, mEmma Elliott, hMarion C Thomas
Luther Rice, b18--, Fluv Co, fBenjamin, wEmma Elliott

SNEAD (continued)
Mary Malvina, bc1840, Camp Co?, fElisha, mSusan Thomas, hFayette Williams
Oscar Littleton, bc1859, Loui Co, d1906, wManie Quesenberry
William, b1796, Fluv Co?, fArchibald, wLucinda Pollard
William P, b5/13/1821, Fork Union, Fluv Co, d1902, fWilliam, mLucinda Pollard, 1w--Tapscott, 2wJulia Seay
SNEED, Benjamin, b18--, Albe Co
John A, b18--, Albe Co, wJennie Price Railey
Elizabeth Royster, b18--, Nels Co?, hBland Massie, md11/19/1876
Martha, b18--, Loui Co, hJames M Vest
Rosa B, b18--, fWilliam B, mLouisa Howrad, hEdward Bouldin Burwell
SNELL, Barbara, bc1840, Rkhm Co?, hAbram Flory
SNELLINGS, Adelaide, b18--, Ches Co, 1w of George Winfree
SNIDER, Rachel, bc1820, Smyt Co?, hJohn T Johnston
SNIDOW, Annie, bc1800, Gile Co, 1w of Harvey Green Johnston, Sr
John Chapman, b 18--, wAnn Elizabeth Hoge
John D, b11/17/1847, fJames H, mElvina Lucas, wJennie Bane
James H, b1811, Gile Co, d1886, fJohn, mRachel Chapman, wElvina Lucas
John, b17--, Gile Co, fChristian, mMary Burke, wRachel Chapman
SNODDY, B L, bc1860, Buck Co, wHelen Williams
Fannie, bc1870, Buck Co, fJohn R, mHattie Thornhill, hJ B Sargent
J C, b186-, Buck Co, fJohn R, mHattie Thornhill
J E, c1870, Buck Co, fJohn R, mHattie Thornhill
John R, b2/11/1836, Buck Co, wHattie Thornhill
Maggie, b186-, Buck Co, fJohn R, mHattie Thornhill, hJ M Steger

SNODGRASS, David C, bc1860, Wash Co?, wLydia Belle Edmondson
J Tobert, bc1860, Russ Co?, wMary Alice Finney
Pollie, bc1800, Smyt Co, fJacob Lyon
SNOW, William C, bc1850, Nhld Co?, wElla Lomax DeShields
SNYDER, --, bc1820, Fred Co?, hJohn Bucher
David, b18--, High Co?, wHannah Hevener
Hannah J, b18--, nrOttobine, Rkhm Co, hHenry C Miller
Jane, b18--, Page Co?, fJames, hJames Koontz
John H, b18--, Smyt Co?, wSallie Snavely
Laura Alice, b18--, Page Co?, hJames Perry Foltz
Maggie, b18--, Warr Co, hBenjamin F Gruver
Sarah E, b18--, Salem, Roan Co, d1886, 1w of John N Cridlin
SOLENBERGER, John S, b18--, Fred Co?, wCatherine Metz
SOLES, Charles C, bc1860, Math Co?, wLeah Haynes
Lucy E, b18--, Math Co?, hWilliam M Fitchett
SOLLARS, William, bc1810, Hamp Co?, wJane Capper
SOMERS, William, b1832, Bloxom, Acco Co, wSerena Byrd
William James, b12/15/1853, Bloxom, Acco Co, fWilliam, mSerena Byrd
SOMMERS, Mary, b18--, fSamuel, hGeorge W Hevener
SOMMERVILLE, Charles William, b186- White Post, Clar Co, fWilliam, mMaria Aby
James Aby, b8/12/1869, White Post, Clar Co, fWilliam, mMaria Aby, wJulia Chapin, md1896
Richard C, b186-, White Post, Clar Co, fWilliam, mMaria Aby
William, b1829, Clar Co?, d1876, wMaria Aby
SONNER, James A, b18--, Shen Co, wBettie Machir
SORG, Annie, b186-, Richmond, fPeter, mMollie Rupert, hFrederick C Krug
George, bc1860, Richmond,

SORG (continued)
fPeter, mMollie Rupert
Joseph E, b8/29/1863, Richmond, fPeter, mMollie Rupert, wCarrie Poore, md1890
Kate, b186-, Richmond, d189-, fPeter, mMollie Rupert
Lizzie, b185-, Richmond, fPeter, mMollie Rupert
William A, b 186-, Richmond, fPeter, mMollie Rupert
SOURS, --, b18--, Winchester, Fred Co, hWilliam C Lauck
Virginia, b18--, nrLuray, Page Co, fIsaac, hJacob G Foster
SOUTHALL, Henry A, bc1860, Pitt Co?, wMary Douglas Bent
Isabella Henry, b18--, Nott Co?, hWilliam A Robertson
SOUTHGATE, Thomas M, b18--, Norfolk?, wMary E --
Thomas S, b2/7/1868, Norfolk, fThomas M, mMary E --, wNettie D Norsworthy
SOWARDS, Mack Jesse, b5/1870, Haddonfield, Wise Co, d1903, fJoshua, mRebecca Robinson, wExer Austin
SOWDER, Anthony, bc1800, Floy Co, w-- Snuffer
Valentine, b10/5/1866, Floy Co, fWilliam, mMary Thrash, wSue Edwards, md7/24/1901
William, b1826, Floy Co, d1899, fAnthony, m-- Snuffer, wMary Thrash
SOWELL, Ona, b18--, Char Co, hBenjamin G Dickerson
SOWERS, Annie Eliza, b1/1/1833, nrBerryville, Clar Co, fDaniel W, mMary Eliza Kerfoot, 1w of Hugh Thomas Swart, md12/7/1852
Daniel W, b18--, Clar Co?, wMary Eliza Kerfoot
George H, b18--, Clar Co?, wMattie
Nancy, bc1842, Floy Co?, hBurdine Dickerson
SPAID, Cornelius, b183-, Hamp Co
Frederick,, b17--, Hamp Co
George Nichols, b17--, Hamp Co?, wElizabeth Cale
John, bc1800, Hamp Co?, fGeorge Nichols, mElizabeth Cale
Louisa, bc1836, Hamp Co, hDorsey Reid, md8/13/1855

SPAID (continued)
Malinda, b18--, Hamp Co?, d1900, fJohn, hMeredith Capper
Rebecca, b18--, Hamp Co, hAsa Cline
SPAIN, Myrtis A, bc1870, Dinw Co?, hHerbert Chowning Hall, md9/3/ 1896
William P, b18--, Dinw Co?, wEmeline Hardy
SPANGLER, --, bc1800, Shen Co, hSamuel A Painter
Amanda V, bc1870, Mt Jackson Community, Page Co, fJoseph, mMary Allen, 1w of Gideon Lee Long, md5/15/1889
Joseph, b18--, Page Co?, wMary Allen
SPARKS, George Harrison, Sr, b11/11/1869, Madi Co, fRobert W, mMamie C Harrison, wDaisy L Hoffman, md12/20/1905
Harry, b17--, wHannah Hume
Henry, b18--, Culp Co?, wLucy O'Bannon
Ida, b18--, Culp Co, fHenry, mLucy O'Bannon, hPeter Hamilton Smith
Robert M, b1856, Tazewell, Taze Co, d1915, fJonas R, mPolly Anna Hankins, wMartha H Maxwell
Robert W, b18--, Madi Co?, mFannie Brown, wMamie C Harrison
Thomas, b17--, fJohn
SPARROW, Abner W, bc1829, Pitt Co, wMary Sue Strickland
Edwin F, b186-, nrDanville, Pitt Co, fAbner W, mMary Sue Strickland
Jefferson D, b8/26/1861, nrDanville, Pitt Co, fAbner W, mMary Sue Strickland, wBelva Mitchell, md1893
John B, bc1860, nrDanville, Pitt Co, fAbner W, mMary Sue Strickland
Susan, b18--, Math Co, hGeorge Washington Marshall
SPEAKE, H C, bc1860, PrWi Co?, wAnna J Ratcliffe
SPEAR, Sarah, b18--, Bedf Co, hFielding E Jones
SPEARMAN, Mary, b11/13/1730, Esse Co?, fJob, hJames Browne

SPEARS, Elizabeth, b9/9/1826, Rkhm Co, fCharles, mMargaret Chisman, hWilliam Anderson Glasgow
Jerry, b18--, Appo Co, wAnne Moseley
Lucy Alice, b18--, Appomattox, Appo Co, fJerry, mAnne Moseley, hRichard Floyd Burke, md5/27/ 1874
SPEED, Edward, b18--, Meck Co, fJohn III, mMary Wade, wFrances Young
John, Sr, b17--, Williamsburg, JaCi Co, fJames, mMary Pulley, wMary (Mintery) Taylor
John, Jr, b8/3/1738, fJohn, Sr, mMary (Mintery) Taylor, wSarah Baird
John III, b17--, Meck Co, fJohn, Jr, mSarah Baird, wMary Wade
Joseph H, b9/12/1832, Meck Co
SPEERS, Lina, b18--, nrClinchport, Scot Co, 3w of Isaac Williams
SPEERY, -- bc1780, Hard Co?, wMary Warden
SPEIDEN, Albert, b6/12/1868, Alexandria, fEdgar, mLucy Leadbeater, wEffie Lee Nelson, md10/31/1901
Alice, bc1870, Alexandria, fEdgar, mLucy Leadbeater
Edgar, b186-, Alexandria, fEdgar, mLucy Leadbeater
Lucy, bc1870, Alexandria, fEdgar, mLucy Leadbeater
William L, b186-, Alexandria, d1914, fEdgar, mLucy Leadbeater
SPENCER, Anne Grant, b2/15/1767, Petersburg, Dinw Co, fRichard, mElizabeth Pigg, hDaniel Wooldridge
Elizabeth, bc1850, nrBuckingham Court House, Buck Co, fMoses A, mAnn Harrison
Harriet, b185-, nrBuckingham Court House, Buck Co, fMoses A, mAnn Harrison
Ida Dudley, bc1850, JaCi Co, d1905, hRichardson Leonard Hensley
James, b184-, nrBuckingham Court House, Buck Co, fMoses

SPENCER (continued)
A, mAnn Harrison
Joanna Tyler, b1854, Char Co, fLouis Bouldin, mJoanna Tyler Bouldin, hTheodorick Pryor Epes
John, b12/16/1745, Char Co, d1828, fThomas, mElizabeth Julia Fleming, wSally Watkins
John, b184-, nrBuckingham Court House, Buck Co, fMoses A, mAnn Harrison
Julia, b185-, nrBuckingham Court House, Buck Co, fMoses A, mAnn Harrison, h-- Leake
Louis Bouldin, b1820, Char Co, d1901, wJoanna Tyler Bouldin
Mary, b18--, Appo Co?, hBryan Watkins Nowlin
Mary, bc1870, Dixie Farm, Buck Co, hForrest Guthrie, Sr, md1899
Mary Virginia, b18--, Char Co, hE M Williamson, md1859
Nancy J, bc1839, Patr Co, d1907, hJohn H Bassett
Richard, b17--, Dnw Co?, d1783, 1wElizabeth Pigg, 2wElizabeth
Robert Lee, b6/28/1861, Locust Hill, JaCi Co, fWilliam L, mMary Elizabeth Richardson, wMary Drew Cowles
Samuel, b3/9/1849, nrBuckingham Court House, Buck Co, fMoses A, mAnn Harrison, wVirginia H Gilliam
Sarah Watkins, b1797, Char Co, fThomas Cole, mFrances W Pearce, hRobert Allen Smith, md1818
Thomas, b1721, Char Co?, wElizabeth Julia Fleming, md1741
Thomas Cole, b1774, Char Co, d1860, fJohn, mSally Watkins, wFrances W Pearce, md1796
William H, b6/2/1870, nrBuckingham Court House, Buck Co, fSamuel, mVirginia H Gilliam, wRuth Alma Edwards, md7/25/ 1888
William L, b1805, Spencer-Ordinary, JaCi Co, d1887, wMary Elizabeth Richardson
William R, bc1860, KiQu Co?, wMaria Sue Bird
SPENGLER, George Madison, b18--,

SPENGLER (continued)
  Strasburg, Shen Co, wHelen Rebecca Horn
SPERRY, Samuel, bc1810, Fred Co?, wAnn Rhodes
SPESSARD, John , b1831
  Nathaniel E, b1862, Union, Monr Co, fJohn P, wAlice Houston
SPIGGLE, Diana, b3/12/1852, nr Woodstock, Shen Co, fPeter, mElizabeth Richard, hJohn W Leedy
  Emma, b185-, nrWoodstock, Shen Co, fPeter, mElizabeth Richard, hSilas Copp
  Mary, b185-, nrWoodstock, Shen Co, fPeter, mElizabeth Richard, hWilliam Bydley
  William B, bc1850, Shen Co?, wMary C Rhodes
  William H, b185-, nrWoodstock, Shen Co, fPeter, mElizabeth Rickard, wMary Frances Copp
SPIGLE, Mary, b18--, Appo Co?, d189-, hJohn Merryman
SPIKER, David F, b18--, Shen Co, wMary Frances Saum
  Clara Virginia, b18--, Shen Co, fDavid F, mMary Frances Saum, hBenjamin Franklin Maphis
SPILLER, Ellen, b1838, Wytheville, Wyth Co, 1hAlexander Stuart Brown, 2hWilliam Alexander Stuart
  James, b17--, Lanc Co, wCatherine Markham Smith
  Josephine, b18--, Smyt Co?, hJohn Preston Sheffey
  William Hickman, Sr, b10/1800, Lanc Co, fJames, mCatherine Markham Smith, wSusan Crockett
  William Hickman, Jr, b9/4/1847, Wytheville, Wyth Co, fWilliam Hickman, Sr, mSusan Crockett, wCynthia McComas
  William Hickman III, bc1870, Wyth Co?, fWilliam Hickman, Jr, mCynthia McComas
SPILMAN, Baldwin Day, b18--, Culp Co, fEdward M, mEliza Day, wAnnie Thompson Camden, md6/1/1886
  Edward M, b18--, Culp Co, fConway, mNancy (Fishback) Mason, wEliza Day
  Fayette, b18--, Culp Co, fCon-

SPILMAN (continued)
  way, mNancy (Fishback) Mason
  John Armistead, b18--, Culp Co, fConway, mNancy (Fishback) Mason, wSusan Rogers
  Lucy, b18--, Culp C, fConway, mNancy (Fishback) Mason, h-- Burnley
  Jemima, bc1809, Springfield, Culp Co, fJohn, hPollard Wood
SPINDLE, Adeline, b18--, Rapp Co, hJohn Smith Hughes
  Benjamin, bc1800, Spot Co, fWilliam, Jr, mElizabeth Alsop, wMaria Claibourne Wigglesworth
  Thomas W, b5/21/1835, nrSpotsylvania Court House, Spot Co, fBenjamin, mMaria Claibourne Wigglesworth, wLavinia Catherine Shelburne, md1870
  William, Sr, b17--, fRobert, w-- Puller
  William,Jr, b17--, Spot Co?, fWilliam, Sr, m-- Puller, wElizabeth Alsop
SPITLER, Jacob, bc1840, Page Co?, w-- Long
  Matilda, b18--, Page Co?, hHamilton Varner
  Thomas, bc1840, Page Co?, w-- Long
SPITZER, Carr, bc1860, Rkhm Co, 1h of Emma Myers
  Ellen R, b18--, nrPort Republic, Rkhm Co, fEmanuel, mRebecca Andes
  Emanuel, b1818, Long Meadows, Rkhm Co, d19--, fHenry, wRebecca Andes
  Hannah V, b18--, nrPort Republic, Rkhm Co, fEmanuel, mRebecca Andes
  Jane A, b18--, nrPort Republic, Rkhm Co, fEmanuel, mRebecca Andes, hPerry F Ebers
  Lillie, bc1860, nrMayland, Rkhm Co, fWilliam A, hHrvey F Phillips
  Margaret M, b18--, nrPort Republic, Rkhm Co, fEmanuel, mRebecca Andes, hJesse Jones
  Perry F, b18--, nPort Republic, Rkhm Co, fEmanuel, mRebecca Andes, wMabel B Baldwin
  Sarah J, b18--, nrPort Repub-

SPITZER (continued) lic, Rkhm Co, fEmanuel, mRebecca Andes, hEli Walters
William A, b18--, nrMayland, Rkhm Co
SPIVEY, Parthenia, b7/24/1843, Windsor, Isle Co, hJohn Coggin
SPOTSWOOD, Anne, b17--, fAlexander, 1w of Lewis Burwell
Dorothea, b17--, fAlexander, hNathaniel West Dandridge
Mary, b17--, Fran Co?, hJoseph Rives
SPOTTS, Annie Elizabeth, b18--, Taze Co, 1w of Samuel Cecil Graham
Mary L, b4/5/1847, Cedar Bluff, Taze Co, hJames Peery
SPADLIN, Ella B, bc1870, Bedf Co?, 2w of Raswell C Overstreet, md1903
SPRATLEY, Peter T, b18--, Surr Co?, wFannie Howard Sclater
SPRIGG, James Cresap, Jr, b3/16/1858, nrPetersburg, Dinw Co, fJames Cresap, mLucy Eliason Addison, wGrace Elizabeth Duryea, md12/15/1896
Lucy A, b3/15/1849, Lanc Co, hGeorge W Sanders, Sr
Mary Eleanor, b18--, Lanc Co, hLucullus Hathaway
SPRING, Louise, b18--, hMyron Baker
SPRINGLE, Sallie, bc1860, Buck Co, hGeorge Dillard
SPRINKLE, Ada, b18--, Rkhm Co, fSt Clair, hJames H Dwyer
SPRINT, Blanche, b186-, Millwood, Clar Co, fJohn W, mAnna Shearer, hJohn Chrisman
John W, bc1838, Clar Co, d1917, wAnna Sherer
Jone Trone, b186-, Millwood, Clar Co, fJohn W, mAnna Shearer
Julia, b18--, Millwood, Clar Co, fJohn W, mAnna Shearer, hMarshall Ferguson
Kate, b186-, Millwood, Clar Co, fJohn W, mAnna Shearer, hJohn Lancaster
Thomas Hatcher, Sr, b1859, Millwood, Clar Co, d1911, fJohn W, mAnna Shearer, wMamie Humston

SPROUL, Archibald Alexander, b18--, Augu Co, fJohn, wVirginia Bumgardner
Frances E, bc1824, Augu Co, d1879, fJohn, hWilliam White
William Scott, b18--, Augu Co, fJohn
STABLER, Mary P, b18--, Alexandria?, d1863, hJohn Leadbeater
STACY, Charles B, b18--, Richmond?, wCarrie Rahm
Elias S, b186-, Hurley, Buch Co, d1906, fLewis Grayson, mAbigail Jean Coleman
George P, b18--, Richmond?, wLucy Turner
James R, bc1870, Hurley, Buch Co, fLewis Grayson, mAbigail Jean Coleman
Lewis Grayson, b12/6/1848, Buch Co, d1918, fShadrick, mJulia Smith, wAbigail Jean Coleman
STAFFORD, Estell L, bc1860, Gile Co?, wEttie Johnson
Ettie, bc1870, Gile Co?, fThomas J, mMelissa Johnson, hWilliam H Thompson, md10/1899
Ralph A, b17--, Walker's Creek, Blan Co
Ralph M, b1833, Walker's Creek, Blan Co, dc1923, fRalph A, wMary Elizabeth Crawford
Thomas J, b18--, Gile Co?, wMelissa Johnson
STAIR, Emily, b18--, Scot Co?, hHarvey Gray
John F, b18--, Scot Co?, wElizabeth Barker
Lena M, bc1870, Scot Co, John F, mElizabeth Barker, hWilliam F C Blackwell, Sr, m1/3/1889
STALEY, Francis Preston, b18--, Wyth Co, wJane Aker
Stephen, b17--, Bote Co?, d1815
Walter Scott, b1837, Marion, Smyt Co, fFrancis Preston, mJane Aker, wPauline A Hull
STALLARD, Annie S, bc1870, Scot Co, fSamuel D, mPolly Culbertson, hRobert Watson McConnell, md12/18/1895
Elizabeth, bc1830, Scot Co, hJames Monroe Hillman
Frankie, b1803, Scot Co, d1885, hJacob Wolfe
Priscilla, b1828, Scot Co, 2w

STALLARD (continued)
of Francis B Greear, md1854
Samuel D, b18--, Scot Co?, wPolly Culbertson
Susan Edward, b18--, hLafayette Browning
STANARD, Philip B, b18--, Rkbr Co?, 1h of Annie J Reilly
STANT, Joel T, b1863, Acco Co, fWilliam H, mSarah Henderson Hay, wMarietta Anderton
William H, b1830, Acco Co, wSarah Henderson Hay
STAPLES, Abram Penn, b1793, Stuart, Henry Co, fSamuel, mLucinda Penn, wMary Stoval Penn
Abram Penn II, b8/14/1858, Stuart, Henry Co, fSamuel G, mCaroline Harris DeJarnett, wSallie Clement Hunt
Clara, b18--, Roan Co, hJohn M Peddicord
M P, b3/6/1868, Lune Co
Samuel, b3/23/1762, Buck Co, fJohn, mKeziah Norman, wLucinda Penn, md1790
Samuel G, b11/29/1829, Stuart, Henry Co, fAbram Penn, mMary Stoval Penn, wCarolne Harris DeJarnette
STAPLETON, Martha, b1804, Lee Co, fWilliam, hIsaac H Robinette
STARK, Elizabeth, b18--, Staf Co?, hCornelius Randolph Hite, Sr
James, b18--, Rapp Co?, wElla Rust
James Smith, bc1800, Staf Co, fWilliam
Jane, b17--, Nels Co?, hJames Dillard, md1782
Robert Taylor, b4/9/1869, Rapp Co, fJames, mElla Rust, 2h of Anne B (Mosby) Calvert
William, b18--, Staf Co?, d186- fJames Smith
STARKE, Elizabeth, b1687, West Co, 2w of Thomas Newton, md1702
Littleton B, b18--, Hano Co?, wEleanor H Blackwell
Margaret, b16--, Midd Co?, hWilliam Bristow, md12/7/1682
Mary Rosa, b18--, Nhld Co,

STARKE (continued)
fLittleton B, mEleanor H Blackwell, hCyrus Harding Walker, md1/27/ 1859
STARKEY, Elizabeth, b17--, Warw Co?, hAnthony Armistead
Martha, b18--, Roan Co?, hJames D Gish
Mary, b16--, hAnthony Robinson
Thomas, b18--, Acco Co?, wGeorgia Hyslop
STARNES, Henry T, bc1860, Scot Co?, wCordelia Taylor
James H, bc1860, Scot Co?, wVictoria Taylor
Oscar F, bc1860, Wise Co?, wMary A Bond
Whitfield, b18--, Scot Co?, wMary Flanary
STATLER, --, bc1820, Jeff Co, wAnn Brewer
STAUFFERIN, Barbara, b12/8/1763, Shen Co, hGeorge Shaver, Jr
STEELE, --, bc1850, Fred Co, wMartha J Canter
Frances, b18--, Wash Co?, hJohn R McCrary
Jean, b17--, hJames Allen
Margaret Isabel, b18--, Bote Co?, hRutherford Rowland Houston
STEGALL, --, b18--, Fren Co?, hFrederick Brown
Frances, b18--, Henry Co?, hWilliam Lester
STEGER, Ada C, b 18--, Buck Co, hEdward I Gilliam
J M, c1860, Buck Co?, wMaggie Snoddy
John Harris, b17--, Amel Co?, d1860
Nannie, b18--, hCharles Winston
Sallie Gaines, b18--, "Kennons", Amel Co, dc1872, fJohn Harris, hJohn Segar Hardaway
STEPHENS, Almeda J, b1844, Nhld Co, d1908, hJames R Smith
Betty Montague, bc1870, Cold Springs, Mont Co, fDavis, mMargaret Ann Caddall, hAncil Davidson Witten, md2/1895
Davis, b18--, Mont Co?, wMargaret Ann Craddall
John J, b18--, Spot Co?, wLucy Lizzie, bc1853, d1921, hJohn Henry Bear

STEPHENSON, Adam, b18--, High Co, wCharlotte Wilson
Clorethia, b186-, Fauq Co?, fDavid, m-- Palmer
Irea, b186-, Fauq Co?, fDavid, m-- Palmer, hJames Clothier
John Wilson, b7/24/1850, Monterey, High Co, fAdam, mCharlotte Wilson, wEliza Gatewood Warwick
Josephine, b18--, High Co, fLucius Holmes, mMary C Campbell, hJoseph William Boyer, md9/8/1916
Kenner B, b18--, Shen Co?, wBettie G Bird
Lou L, b1861, Parkersburg, Wood Co, fKenner B, mBettie G Bird, hFrank Stacey Tavenner, md12/1892
Lucius Holme, b2/16/1840, nr Bolar Springs, High Co, d1911, fAdam, mCharlotte Wilson, wMary C Campbell
Maggie, b1863, Marion, Smyt Co, hFrank P Wheeler
Medora Z, b1864, Marshall, Fauq Co, fDavid, m-- Palmer, hGeorge Beauregard Davis
Montez, b186-, Fauq Co?, fDavid, m-- Palmer, wMollie Board
Senora, bc1860, Fauq Co?, fDavid, m-- Palmer, hBenjamin Huffman
STEPTOE, Catherine, b17--, Bote Co?, hWilliam Langhorne
Elizabeth R, b18--, Bedf Co?, hSamuel Quarles
Frances, bc1800, Cumb Co, fJames, hHenry Scalsbrook Langhorne
Helen, b18--, Midd Co, hWilliam S Christian
James, b17--, Cumb Co
Lucy, b17--, hWilliam Blackwell
STEVENS, C Emmet, b7/14/1865, Nels Co, fCharles H, mSarah E Harvey, wEva C Miller, md9/16/1914
Charles H, b1835, Nels Co, d1906, wSarah E Harvey, md1859
Elizabeth, b17--, Fred Co?, hAndreas Whitman
Sydney G, bc1860, Char Co, wFlorence Carrington

STEVENS (continued)
W C, bc1850, Nels Co?, wMary W Fortune
STEWART, Elizabeth, b18--, Gile Co, hAndrew J Thompson
Emma Lee, b1864, Richmond, hJohn H White
Judith, b17--, Scot Co?, fWilliam, hNimrod Taylor, Jr
Kate, b18--, Scot Co?, fJames, hJames A Taylor
Kensey Johns, b1816, fDavid, mSusannah Johns, wHannah Lee
Margaret L, b5/20/1865, nrBig Stone Gap, Wise Co, hBenjamin F Tate
Mary E, b1/31/1847, fKensey Johns, mHannah Lee, hWarner Minor Woodward, md10/28/1869
Nancy H, b11/1812, Nels Co, d1889, hGeorge W Fortune, Sr
Nannie, b1845, Suss Co, hJohn Robert Chappell
William, b17--, Scot Co
STICKLEY, Abraham, b17--, Shen Co, fBenjamin, mAnn Stover
Abraham, b180-, Shen Co, fDavid
Abram, bc1860, Shen Co?, wRose Funk
Amos, bc1800, Shen Co, wMarian Stoner
Annie, b180-, Shen Co, fDavid
Benjamin, b17--, wAnn Stover
Benjamin, b181-, Shen Co, fDavid
Benjamin, b18--, Fred Co?, wFannie Dinges
Catherine, b17--, Shen Co?, d183-, hPhilip Baker
Catherine, b17--, Shen Co, fBenjamin, mAnn Stover, hHenry Remsburg
Daniel, b6/14/1802, Shen Co, d1886, fDavid, wElizabeth Ann Rinker
Daniel L, bc1830, Shen Co, wKatie Stickley
David, b17--, Shen Co, fBenjamin, mAnn Stover
David, b183-, Starsburg, Shen Co, fJacob, m-- Blind
David H, b18--, Fred Co?, wEllen Rhodes
Elijah Carson, bc1870, nrStrasburg, Shen Co, fWilliam, mSusan Kern

STICKLEY (continued)
Elizabeth A, bc1870, nrStrasburg, Shen Co, fWilliam, mSusan Kern
Ezra, b18--, Shen Co, fLevi
Frances, b17--, Shen Co, fBenjamin, mAnn Stover
Frank K, b186-, nrStrasburg, Shen Co, fWilliam, mSusan Kern
Hugh, bc1850, Shen Co, wAnna Fisher
Jacob, bc1800, Strasburg, Shen Co, w-- Blind
James, b181-, Shen Co, fDavid
Katie, b183-, Strasburg, Shen Co, fJacob, m-- Blind, hDaniel L Stickley
Laura Kate, bc1860, Shen Co, fDaniel, mElizabeth Ann Rinker, h-- Bates
Levi, b181-, Shen Co, fDavid
Margaret, b18--, Augu Co?, hDavid Alexander
Margaret, bc1840, Shen Co, fPhilip, hJames William Smoot
Mary Margaret, b18--, Shen Co, fAmos, mMarian Stoner, 2w of Joseph Funk
Mary R, b186-, nrStrasburg, Shen Co, fWilliam, mSusan Kern
Mary Virginia, b185-, Shen Co, d1918, fDaniel, mElizabeth Ann Rinker
Nannie E, bc1870, Fred Co, fBenjamin F, mFannie Dinges, hF Estes Kline, md1/3/1900
Peter B, b183-, Strasburg, Shen Co, d186-, fJacob, m-- Blind
Peter B, b12/13/1863, nrStrasburg, Shen Co, fWilliam, mSusan Kern, wMary Evelyn Downing, md10/14/ 1896
Philip David, b181-, Shen Co, fDavid
Regina, bc1811, Shen Co, d1892, fDavid, hWilliam Boyer
Samuel, b17--, Shen Co, fBenjamin, mAnn Stover
Samuel, bc1810, Shen Co, fDavid
Samuel, b186-, nrStrasburg, Shen Co, fWilliam, mSusan Kern
Thomas R, bc1860, Shen Co, wGeorgie Smoot
Turner Ashby, b11/10/1862, Shen Co, fDaniel, mElizabeth Ann Rinker

STICKLEY (continued)
Vernie, bc1870, nrStrasburg, Shen Co, fWilliam, mSusan Kern, hMonroe McInturff
William, b12/18/1829, Strasburg, Shen Co, d1878, fJacob, m-- Blind, wSusan Kern
William Albert, b186-, nrStrasburg, Shen Co, fWilliam, mSusan Kern
STIEGEL, Cornelia, b18--, Rkhm Co?, hGeorge H Hoover
STIFF, Louise, b18--, KiGe Co?, 1h-- Payne, 2hThacker Rogers
Mary Alice, bc187-, KiGe Co, fJames Hampden, hThomas Howard Jett, md9/15/1890
Thomas J, b1844, nrLocklies, Midd Co, d1911, wFannie Alcie Eubank
William, b18--, Midd Co, d1890, fWilliam N
STILTNER, Mollie, bc1800, Buck Co, hJohn W Clevinger
STIMSON, Laura John, b1860, Floy Co, hJames G Higginbotham, Jr
STINE, Alice Elizabeth, b186-, Fred Co, fHenry, mJulia A Glaize, hGeorge F Glaize
Benjamin Franklin, b186-, Fred Co, fHenry, wJulia A Glaize
Gertrude Ann, b186-, Fred Co, fHenry, mJulia A Glaize, hAndrew S Hauck
Henrietta, bc1860, Fred Co, fHenry, mJulia A Glaize, hWilson Bruyn
Henry, bc1820, Fred Co, wJulia A Glaize
Laura Lee, b186-, Fred Co, fHenry, mJulia A Glaize, hGeorge J Allsdorf
Octavia L, b186-, Fred Co, fHenry, mJulia A Glaize, hCharles P Jack
Rachel Catherine, bc1860, Fred Co, fHenry, mJulia A Glaize, h-- Hunter
Susan C, bc1870, Fred Co, fHenry, mJulia A Glaize, hWalter Evans Barr
STINSON, --, b186--, Warr Co?, wLola Wharton
John, b18--, Russ Co
John Henry, b2/25/1864, Belfast, Russ Co, fSamuel, mAmy

STINSON (continued)
Thompson, wFlorence L Williams, md8/13/1893
Mary Douglas, b1855, nrBelfast Mills, Russ Co, hCharles S Bradshaw
Melissa, b186-, Belfast, Russ Co, fSamuel, mAmy Thompson, hGordon Musick
Nancy Virginia, b18--, Buch Co, hJohn A Cook
Samuel, b18--, Belfast, Russ Co, fJohn, wAmy Thompson
STIPES, Anna, b186-, Harpers Ferry, Jeff Co, fFrank, mAnna Cleveland, hWilliam Hightman
Carrie, bc1870, Harpers Ferry, Jeff Co, fFrank, mAnna Cleveland, hWilliam Middlekauf
Frank, b18--, Harpers Ferry, Jeff Co, wAnna Cleveland
Reuben B, b2/8/1868, Harpers Ferry, Jeff Co, fFrank, mAnna Cleveland, wAlice Grace Cover
STIREWALT, Elenora C, b184-, New Market, Shen Co, fJacob, mHenrietta Henkel, hPaul C Bowman
Henrietta Helena, b184-, New Market, Shen Co, fJacob, mHenrietta Henkel, hJohn C Morrison
Jacob Luther, b184-, New Market, Shen Co, fJacob, mHenrietta Henkel
Jerome Paul, b4/11/1850, New Market, Shen Co, fJacob, mHenrietta Henkel, wTirzah A Coffman, md10/6/1878
John Nathanael, b2/21/1844, New Market, Shen Co, d1907, fJacob, mHenrietta Henkel, wEmily A Hershberger, md11/10/1870
Maria C, b185-, New Market, Shen Co, d1910, fJacob, mHenrietta Henkel
Saloma S, b184-, New Market, Shen Co, fJacob, mHenrietta Henkel, hJacob Bortain
STITH, --, bc1690, wMary Randolph
--, b18--, Brun Co, hRobert D Turnbull
Elizabeth, b17--, hHenry Fitzhugh III
John, b17--, wAnne Washington

STITH (continued)
Sarah Washington, bc1800, fJohn, mAnne Washington, hWilliam Blunt Irby
STOGDALE, Ellen, b1853, Augu Co, hMoses W Argenbright
STOKES, Allen Y, b185-, Lune Co, fHenry, Sr, mAnn Eliza Hatchett
Colin, b8/30/1797, Lune Co, fHenry, m-- Poole, wSallie Cralle
Colin II, b184-, Lune Co, fHenry, Sr, mAnn Eliza Hatchett
Colin, Sr, bc1855, Linwood, PrEd Co, fRichard, wAnnie T Brown
Edward Cralle, bc1850, Lune Co, fHenry, Sr, mAnn Eliza Hatchett
Haynie A, b184-, Lune Co, fHenry, Sr, mAnn Eliza Hatchett
Henry, b17--, Lune Co, w-- Poole, md1795
Henry, Sr, b1820, Lune Co, fColin, mSallie Cralle, wAnn Eliza Hatchett
Henry, Jr, b12/12/1853, Lune Co, fHenry, Sr, mAnn Eliza Hatchett, 1wSarah India Williams, md4/10/1884, 2wLoula (Bennett) Dickinson, md10/6/1920
Mary J, b184-, Lune Co, fHenry, Sr, mAnn Eliza Hatchett, hColin A Monroe
R C, bc1860, Bote Co?, wLula May Rinehart
Sallie Fannie, bc1860, Lune Co, fHenry, Sr, mAnn Eliza Hatchett
William DeMonfort, b185-, Lune Co, fHenry, Sr, mAnn Eliza Hatchett
STONE, America E, bc1841, Fran Co, d1909, 1hJames Johnson, 2hGeorge W Stone
Ernest L, b18--, Mont Co, fJames L, mMattie A Wooten
Eugene W, b1800, Mont Co, fJames L, mMattie A Wooten, wMaggie W Johnston
Eustace B, b18--, Mont Co, fJames L, mMattie A Wooten

STONE (continued)
Frank T, b10/20/1870, Auburn (now Riner), Meck Co, fJames L, mMattie A Wooten
George W, Sr, bc1844, Fran C, d1911, 2h of America E Stone
George W, Jr, b186-, Fran Co, fGeorge W, Sr, mAmerica E Stone
Ila A, b18--, Mont Co, fJames L, mMattie A Wooten, hA Sidney Johnson
James L, b5/4/1834, Whittle's Mill, Meck Co, fWilliam, wMattie A Wooten
Jestine, b1830, Carr Co, d1912, hThomas Nuckolls
John, b183-, Page Co?, wMartha W Brumback
John M, b185-, Pend Co, dc1893, fDaniel C, wEmma C Moyers
Kate E, b18--, Warrenton, Fauq Co, hHamden Murray White, md12/21/1884
Lee, b186-, Fran Co, fGeorge W, Sr, mAmerica E Stone
Lucretia, b5/1844, fFleming, hEmanuel B Shaver
Mary H, b18--, Mont Co?, hSilas Shelburne
Sally E, b18--, Fran Co?, hCharles Robert Hancock
Samuel P, bc1870, Fran Co, fGeorge W, Sr, mAmerica E Stone
William, bc1800, Meck Co
STONER, Anna Laura, bc1870, Shen Co, fJohn M, mAmanda Halsley, hEugene Bowman
D Monroe, b186-, Shen Co, fJohn M, mAmanda Halsey
Daniel, bc1860, Rkhm Co?, wMary L Menefee
John M, b9/27/1839, Shen Co, d1894, wAmanda Halsley, md12/15/1860
Lydia Ellen, b186-, Shen Co, fJohn M, mAmanda Halsley, h-- Bowman
Marian, bc1800, Shen Co, hAmos Stickley
Mary Catherine, b186-, Shen Co, fJohn M, mAmanda Halsey
Samuel Arthur, b186-, Shen Co, fJohn M, mAmanda Halsley
Sarah Elizabeth, b186-, Shen

STONER (continued)
Co, fJohn M, mAmanda Halsley, h-- Carroll
William David, b186-, Shen Co, fJohn M, mAmanda Halsley
STORER, George, bc1840, PrWi Co?, d186-, wMary Gregg
STORROW, Maria Champe, b18--, Culp Co, hJohn Welsey Bell
STOTT, Sallie A, b18--, Lanc Co, 2w of Henry Jeter Edmonds, Sr
STOUT, Carey, bc1860, Culp Co?, wGeorgie Wood
Cornelia, b185-, Augu Co?, d1903, 1w of Julian Minor Quarles, Sr
Lucy Harriet, b185-, Augu Co?, hWilliam Harper Pilson
STOUTERMYER, Bettie A, b18--, Augu Co?, hGeorge A Orebaugh
STOVAL, Ruth, b17--, hAbram Penn
STOVALL, Bessie K, b1867, Meadville, Hali Co, d1923, hRobert S Barbour, Sr
Brett, b17--, Patr Co?, wNancy Hughes
Jane, b18--, Patr Co?, hJacob Clark
STOVER, --, b18--, Shen Co, hJacob Kern
Adam, b17--, Churchville, Augu Co, fSimon, wMary Clark
Ann, b17--, hBenjamin Stickley
John Hatch, b2/27/1842, Churchville, Augu Co, d1907, fAdam, mMary Clark, wMary Elizabeth McNair
John Marshall, b1848, Augu Co, d1877, wMary Lucy Holbrook
Polly, b18--, Bote Co, hJoseph Moomaw
Regina, b18--, Shen Co?, hObed S Funk
STRATFORD, --, bc1850, Richmond?, wMatilda Herndon
STRATTON, Ann Gertrude, bc1800, Nhtn Co, fJohn, m-- Digges, hJacob G Parker
Joseph D, b18--, Kana Co?, wMary Ann Buster
Julia Ellen, b184-, Kana Co, d1906, fJoseph D, mMary Ann Buster, 1w of Abraham Addams McAllister, md5/10/1865
Louisa, bc1800, Roan Co, hJames Edington

STRATTON (continued)
Richard H, Sr, b9/30/1844, Howardsville, Albe Co, wMary E Atkins
Lucy William, b1841, Nels Co?, hAlexander Robert Whitehead
STRAYER, Addie, b18--, Shen Co, fJacob, (1)mAdelaide Coffman
Albert W, b18--, Shen Co, fJacob, (1)mAdelaide Coffman
Clara, b18--, Shen Co, fJacob, (1)mAdelaide Coffman
Crawford C, bc1824, Shen Co, d1897, fJacob, (1)mAdelaide Coffman, wJuliet Lyle Smith
Eliza, b18--, Shen Co, fJacob, (1)mAdelaide Coffman
Ernest S, b1857, Rkhm Co, d1906, fCrawford C, mJuliet Lyle Smith
George G, b18--, Shen Co, fJacob, (2)mElizabeth Samuels
Henry V, b6/1853, Rkhm Co, d1900, fCrawford C, mJuliet Lyle Smith, wElizabeth Hill Carter Wickham, md12/4/1883
Jacob, bc1800, Alexandria, 1wAdelaide Coffman, 2wElizabeth Samuels
Joseph S, b18--, Shen Co, fJacob, (2)mElizabeth Samuels
Margaret, b184-, Shen Co, fJacob, (1)mAdelaide Coffman, 2w of George W Kemper, Jr
McDowella, b185-, Rkhm Co, fCrawford C, mJuliet Lyle Smith
Parker Worth, b18--, Shen Co, fJacob, (2)mElizabeth Samuels
STREET, Victoria, b7/11/1839, d1897, hChristopher Harrison Hancock
STREIT, Elizabeth, bc1800, Albe Co, d1838, fCharles, 1w of Solomon Glaize
STREITS, William H, bc1810, Fred Co?, wNancy Selina Bell
STRICKER, Annie, b17--, Shen Co?, d1829, hMichael Rhodes
STRICKLAND, Cortelyou, b18--, Pitt Co?, fFrancis Marion, mMary Jane Chaney, hGeorge Samuel Moore
Mary Sue, bc1829, Hali Co, f1894, hAbner W Sparrow
Sallie N, b18--, Nels Co,

STRICKLAND (continued)
fZebulon, m-- Wood, hPeyton Oliver Brittle
Zebulon, b18--, w-- Wood
STRICKLER, --, b18--, Fred Co?, fAbraham, w-- Headley
STRINGER, Mary, b1/31/1836, nrBelle Haven, Acco Co, d1912, hSheppard S Kellam
STRINGFELLOW, Catherine, b17--, Culp Co?, hMason Colvin
Harriet, b18--, hJohn Byrd Hall
STROHSNIDER, John, b18--,Shen Co?, wElizabeth Baker
STROLE, Hiram, b18--, Page Co, 1862, wMary C Summers
John, bc1840, Page Co, w-- Shuler
Mary, b18--, Page Co, fHiram, mMary C Summers, hWilson Asbury Koontz, md11/8/1878
STRONG, Amanda, b18--, Rkbr Co, d1892, fElijah, hWilliam E East
STROSNIDER, B F, b18--, wLydia Headlee
STROTHER, Catherine Ann, b18--, Fauq Co, hJohn Holmes
French, bc1840, Glou Co?, 1h of Lessie Cary
George French, b18--, Rapp Co, fJames French, Sr, mSallie Greene Williams
James, b18--, Fauq Co?, wMildred Childs
James French, Sr, b17--, Rapp Co, fFrench, wSallie Greene Williams
James French, Jr, b18--, Rapp Co, fJames French, Sr, mSallie Greene Williams, wMary James Botts
John, b1771, d1805
John, b18--, fWilliam Porter, mElizabeth Hewlett
John R, b18--, Rapp Co, fJames French, Sr, mSallie Greene Williams
Margaret, b2/3/1830, Richmond, fWilliam Porter, mElizabeth Hewlett, hSamuel B Smith, md10/18/ 1855
Mary Virginia, b1861, nrMarkham, Fauq Co, d1915, fJames, mMildred Childs, hJohn Pendleton Leachman, Sr, md2/6/1884

STROTHER (continued)
Philip W, b1800, Rapp Co, fJames French, Sr, mSallie Greene Williams
Robert Q, b18--, fWilliam Porter, mElizabeth Hewlett
Sallie Hunt, bc1870, Rapp Co, fJames French, Jr, mMary James Botts, hClarence J Miller, md11/29/1893
Sydney, b18--, d186-, fWilliam Porter, mElizabeth Hewlett
William A, b18--, fWilliam Porter, mElizabeth Hewlett
William J, 18--, Rapp Co, fJames French, Sr, mSallie Greene Williams
William Johnson, b8/13/1849, Washington, Rapp Co, fJames French, mElizabeth Richardson Roberts
William Porter, b2/14/1798, Richmond, d1874, fJohn
STUART, Alexander II, b1773, Augu Co, fAlexander, wAnn Dabney
Alexander Brown, b1868, Wytheville, Wyth Co, fWillam Alexander, (2)mEllen (Spiller) Brown
Alexander Hugh Holmes, b4/2/1807, Staunton, Augu Co, fArchibald
Archibald, b177-, Augu Co, fAlexander
Archibald, b1796, Camp Co, fAlexander, mAnn Dabney, wElizabeth Letcher Pannell
Augustus Bradford, b18--, Grbr Co, fWilliam Robinson, Sr, mLucy A M Bradford
Charles Alexander, Sr, b17--, Augu Co, fJohn, mAgatha Lewis, wElizabeth Robinson
Charles Alexander, b18--, Grbr Co, fWilliam Robinson, Sr, mLucy A M Bradford
Dale Carter, b185-, Wytheville, Wyth Co, fWilliam Alexander, (1)mMary Taylor Carter
Douglas, b18--, w-- Lomax
Eleanor, bc1770, Augu Co, fAlexander, (1)mMary Patterson, hThomas Walker
Elizabeth Jane, b18--, Grbr Co, fWilliam Robinson, Sr, mLucy A

STUART (continued)
M Bradford
Elizabeth S, b18--, Smyt Co?, 1h-- Gravely, 2hRobert John Preston
Hannah Augusta, b18--, Grbr Co, fWilliam Robinson, Sr, mLucy A M Bradford
Henry Carter, b1/18/1855, Wytheville, Wyth Co, fWilliam Alexander, (1)mMary Taylor Carter, wMargaret Bruce Carter, md2/26/1896
J E B, b18--, Patr Co, fArchibald, mElizabeth Letcher Pannell
James Henry, bc1850, Grbr Co, fWilliam Robinson, Sr, mLucy A M Bradford, wAnnie Lee Miller, md1879
John J. bc1860, Wytheville, Wyth Co, fWilliam Alexander, (1)mMary Taylor Carter
John Joseph, b18--, Grbr Co, fWilliam Robinson, Sr, mLucy A M Bradford
Lucy A M, b18--, Grbr Co, fWilliam Robinson, Sr, mLucy A M Bradford
Margaret Briscoe, b18--, fAlexander H H, mFrances C Baldwin, hAlexander F Robertson
Mary, b18--, Staunton, Augu Co, hHunter Holmes McGuire, md12/9/1866
Mary, b18--, hJames Madison Fitzhugh
Richard Henry, b2/2/1851, KiGe Co, fDouglas, m-- Lomax, wLydia Ann Marmaduke
Susan Spiller, b186-, Wytheville, Wyth Co, fWilliam Alexander, (2)mEllen (Spiller) Brown
Thomas Floyd, b18--, Grbr Co, fWilliam Robinson, Sr, mLucy A M Bradford
William Alexander, b5/2/1826, Patr Co, fArchibald, mElizabeth Letcher Pannell, 1wMary Taylor Carter, 2wEllen (Spiller) Brown
William Robinson, Sr, b1813, Augu Co, fCharles Alexander, mElizabeth Robinson, wLucy A M Bradford

STUART (continued)
William Robinson, Jr, b18--, Grbr Co, fWilliam Robinson, Sr, mLucy A M Bradford
STUBBS, James New, b17--, Glou Co
James New, b10/17/1839, Glou Co, d1919, fJefferson W, mAnn Walker Carter Baytop, wElizabeth Medlicott
Jefferson D, bc1870, Glou Co, fJames New, mElizabeth Medlicott
Jefferson W, b1811, Valley Front Farm, nrGloucester, Glou Co, d1889, fJames New, wAnn Walker Carter Baytop
Joseph M, b186-, Glou Co, fJames New, mElizabeth Medlicott
William Carter, bc1840, Glou Co, fJefferson W, mAnn Walker Carter Baytop
STUBBLEFIELD, Martha Ann, b18--, nrGloucester, Glou Co, d1851, 1w of Levi Pace Corr
STULL, Charles Mead, bc1839, Alle Co, d1910, fJacob C M, 1wBeulah Boggs, 2wFrances Morrison, 3wPearl Merritt, 4w Ellen Matheny
Jacob C M, 18--, Alle Co
John Walter, Sr, b11/23/1870, Richpatch, Alle Co, fCharles Mead, (2)mFrances Morrison, 1wVirginia Thompson, 2wNancy Aiken, md12/27/1906
STUMP, Silas G, b1849, Fran Co, fSilas, wSarah Dowdy
STURGIS, Joseph R, b18--, wAlice Tyler Bradshaw
SUBLETT, Annie Eliza, b1846, Richmond, hWilson Miles Cary
David L, b18--, wMattie Owen
James Madison, b18--, Richmond?, wLucy Nelson Page
Octavia Page, b186-, Manchester (now in Richmond), fJames Madison, mLucy Nelson Page, hJohn Henry Ingram, md6/7/1887
SUDDATH, Annie, b18--, Fair Co, hWilliam S Kincheloe
SUDDUTH, Edloe James, b7/2/1855, Warrenton, Fauq Co, fJames, mFlora E Doors, wLucy M White, md1883

SUDDUTH (continued)
Jerry M, b185-, Warrenton, Fauq Co, fJames, Sr, mFlora E Doors
SULLIVAN, --, b17--, Fauq Co?, hHenry Lawson Hathaway
SUMMERS, Alice, b185-, Hayfield, Fred Co, fJacob, mSarah C Orndorff
Augustus, b184-, Hayfield, Fred Co, fJacob, mSarah E Orndorff
David C, b184-, Hayfield, Fred Co, fJacob, mSarah C Orndorff
Elizabeth, b185-, Hayfield, Fred Co, fJacob, mSarah C Orndorff
George W, b18--, Wash Co?, wJane Phlegar
Jacob, b18--, nrWoodstock, Shen Co, wSarah C Orndorff
John C, b1840, Monr Co, fAndrew Jackson, mMargaret Hawkins, wNannie Montgomery Preston
John Lucius, b6/30/1846, Hayfield, Fred Co, fJacob, mSarah C Orndorff, wSarah Catherine Clowser, md1877
John Preston, b186-, nrAbingdon, Wash Co, fJohn C, mNannie Montgomery Preston
Mary C, b18--, hHiram Strole
Milton, bc1850, Hayfield, Fred Co, fJacob, mSarah C Orndorff
Olivia Wurt, bc1870, nrAbingdon, Wash Co, fJohn C, mNannie Montgomery Preston
William, b185-, Hayfield, Fred Co, fJacob, mSarah C Orndorff
SUMNER, Elizabeth, b17--, hElisha Battle, md1742
SUPINGER, Emma Charlotte, b9/10/1862, Woodstock, Shen Co, fWilliam, mAnnie Jordan, hHenry H Irwin
L J, b186-, Woodstock, Shen Co, fWilliam, mAnnie Jordan
Laura, b186-, Woodstock, Shen Co, fWilliam, mAnnie Jordan
Mary, bc1860, Woodstock, Shen Co, fWilliam, mAnnie Jordan, hRobert Lee Bargelt
Robert, bc1860, Woodstock, Shen Co, fWilliam, mAnnie Jordan
Sallie, bc1860, Woodstock, Shen Co, fWilliam, mAnnie Jordan, h-- Fansler
W J, bc1860, Woodstock, Shen

SUPINGER (continued)
Co, fWilliam, mAnnie Jordan
William, b18--, Shen Co?, wAnnie Jordan
SURBER, Edwin F, b11/4/1849, Grbr Co, fWilliam Henry, m-- Gibbons, wEllen Harman
William Henry, b18--, Grbr Co, d185-, w-- Gibbons
SURFACE, George R, b1845, Blacksburg, Mont Co, d1917, fHenry, m-- Hambrich, wAnn Elizabeth Shelton
Henry, b18--, Mont Co, w-- Hambrich
Mary Ollie, bc1870, Gile Co, fGeorge R, mAnn Elizabeth Shelton, hCharles T Peery
SURGANER, Stephen S, bc1860, Lee Co?, wUrsula Belle Wynne
SUTER, Christian C, bc1870, Rkhm Co, fEmanuel, mElizabeth Swope
David I, bc1870, Rkhm Co, fEmanuel, mElizabeth Swope
Emanuel, b1833, Rkhm Co, d1902, fDaniel, m-- Heatwole, wElizabeth Swope
Emanuel J, b186-, Rkhm Co, fEmanuel, mElizabeth Swope
Eugene C, bc1870, Rkhm Co, fEmanuel, mElizabeth Swope
John R, b186-, Rkhm Co, fEmanuel, mElizabeth Swope
Laura E, b186-, Rkhm Co, fEmanuel, mElizabeth Swope
Lillie H, bc1870, Rkhm Co, fEmanuel, mElizabeth Swope, hAmos Showalter
Perry G, b186-, Rkhm Co, fEmanuel, mElizabeth Swope
Peter S, b186-, Rhm Co, fEmanuel, mElizabeth Swope
Reuben Daniel, b1858, Cooks Creek Community, Rkhm Co, fEmanuel, mElizabeth Swope, wMary Susan Shrum
Virginia, bc1860, Rkhm Co, fEmanuel, mElizabeth Swope, hJacob C Wenger
SUTHERLAND, Alexander, b186-, Dick Co?, wRitter Sutherland
C N, bc1860, Spot Co?, wCarrie Hart
C R, b18--, Albe Co, fJoseph II, mAnna E Anderson
Clara S, b18--, Albe Co,

SUTHERLAND (continued)
fJoseph II, mAnna E Anderson, hT R Morris
Daniel, bc1800, Bedf Co, d1876, fJames, mSallie Buchanan, wPhoebe Fuller
Edward R, bc1860, PrGe Co, wEliza Anderson
Fannie E, b18--, Albe Co, fJoseph II, mAnna E Anderson, hF E Anderson
Jasper, b2/1/1845, Tiny, Dick Co, fWilliam, mSylvia Counts, wLouise Dyer
Joseph II, b7/17/1822, Albe Co, fJoseph, mAnna E Garland, wAnna E Anderson, md2/26/1856
Joseph E, b18--, Albe Co, fJoseph, mAnna E Anderson
M Y, b10/8/1860, North Garden, Albe Co, fJoseph II, mAnna E Anderson, wEthel White, md9/4/1907
Ritter, bc1870, nrTiny, Dick Co, d1898, fWilliam, mSylvia Counts, hAlexander Sutherland
W Floyd, b186-, nrTiny, Dick Co, fWilliam, mSylvia Counts
William, b3/25/1822, nrCarbo, Russ Co, d1909, fDaniel, mPhoebe Fuller, wSylvia Counts
William B, b2/24/1861, nrTiny, Dick Co, fWilliam, mSylvia Counts, wEliza Jane Counts
SUTHERLIN, William T, b18--, Hali Co?, d1893
SUTPHIN, --, bc1850, Pge Co?, wEmma J Shuler
Barnett, b18--, Rapp Co?, fBarnett
John Robert, b18--, Rapp Co, fBarnett, wAda Virginia Best
SUTTON, Alice, b18--, West Co, hJoseph F Robertson
Ella Hillard, b18--, Richmond?, hGarland Morriss
SWAINE, Lucinda, b18--, PrWi Co?, hAlbert Alexander Turner
SWANGER, Mary E, b18--, Locustville, Acco Co, d1894, fEmanuel B, 1w of G Fred Floyd, md6/6/1888
SWANK, --, bc1800, Rkhm Co?, hReuben Swope
Ada Ann, b185-, nrSingers Glen, Rkhm Co, fPeter, mBarbara Ann

SWANK (continued)
Ralston, 1h-- Esely, 2hEdward Teague
Amanda Jane, b185-, nrSingers Glen, Rkhm Co, d1920, fPeter, mBarbara Ann Ralston, hD C Lineweaver
Bettie Isadora, b186-, nr Singers Glen, Rkhm Co, fPeter, mBarbara Ann Ralston, hJ S Kagey
Charles Harvey, bc1860, nr Singers Glen, Rkhm Co, fPeter, mBarbara Ann Ralston
Dora B, b186-, Rkhm Co, fJ Perry, hJohn J Hawse, md10/15/1887
Eliza, bc1830, nrSingers Glen, Rkhm Co, fJohn, mMary Ocker, hWilliam Saufley
Ellen Virginia, b185-, nr Singers Glen, Rkhm Co, fPeter, mBarbara Ann Ralston, hG W Shaffer
Emma Jeanetta, b186-, nrSingers Glen, Rkhm Co, fPeter, mBarbara Ann Ralston, 1hFrank May, 2hFrank Fulk
J Harvey, bc1830, nrSingers Glen, Rkhm Co, fJohn, mMary Ocker
John, b18--, Augu Co, dc1860, fJohn, wMary Ocker
John David, b185-, nrSingers Glen, Rkhm Co, d1883, fPeter, mBarbara Ann Ralston
Mary E, bc1830, nrSingers Glen, Rkhm Co, fJohn, mMary Ocker, hJohn Funk
Mary Frances, bc1850, nrSingers Glen, Rkhm Co, fPeter, mBarbara Ann Ralston, hJoseph H Funk
Peter, bc1826, Rkhm Co, fJohn, mMary Ocker, wBarbara Ann Ralston
S Henton, b10/3/1854, nrSingers Glen, Rkhm Co, fPeter, mBarbara Ann Ralston, wNettie V Donavan, md3/21/1890
Sarah Jane, b11/17/1842, nrSingers Glen, Rkhm Co, fJohn, mMary Ocker, hIsaac N Beery
Will, bc1860, Rkhm Co?, wClara Myers
SWANSON, Claude Augustus, b3/31/

SWANSON (continued)
1862, Swansonville, Pitt Co, fJohn Muse, mCatherine Pritchett
Elizabeth, b6/3/1790, Pitt Co, fWilliam, hHenry Lawson Muse
John Muse, b18--, Pitt Co, wCatherine Pritchett
SWART, Daniel W, b2/29/1856, Elleslie Farm, Clar Co, fHugh Thomas, (1)mAnnie Eliza Sowers, wAnna Rachel Murray, md12/1/1886
Ella R, b186-, Fauq Cao, fHugh Thomas, (2)mMary Catherine Fred
Hugh Thomas, b182-, Box Hill Farm, Fauq Co, fDaniel W, mElizabeth Rogers, 1wAnne Eliza Sowers, md12/7/1852, 2wMary Catherine Fred, md5/9/1858
Isabella, b181-, Fauq Co, fDaniel W, mElizabeth Rogers, 1hEdward Rector, 2h-- Huff
Jane A, b9/30/1813, Fauq Co, d1865, fWilliam R, mElizabeth Rogers, hJames Adair
Mary, b181-, Fauq Co, fDaniel W, mElizabeth Rogers, hJonathan Waters
Sarah, b181-, Fauq Co, fDaniel W, mElizabeth Rogers, hHugh Tiffany
Susan, bc1820, Fauq Co, fDaniel W, mElizabeth Rogers, 1hWilliam Carroll Alexander, 2hJohn Scruggs, 3hArchibald Riddell
Thomas Water, b1/14/1868, Box Hill Farm, Fauq Co, fHugh Thomas, (2)mMary Catherine Fred, wElla Oscar Bennett, md6/14/1895
William Aubrey, 185-, Clar Co, fHugh Thomas, (1)mAnna Eliza Sowers
William R, b17--, Fauq Co?, wElizabeth Rogers
SWARTZ, Eliza, b18--, Shen Co, fJohn, m-- Graybill, hGabriel Heatwole
Jacob, bc1800, Rkhm Co?, w-- Whitehead
John, bc1800, Shen Co?, w-- Graybill
Rhoda Ellen, bc1829, Spring

SWARTZ (continued)
Creek, Rkhm Co, fJacob, m-- Whitehead
Newton, b18--, Fred Co?, wMargaret Rebecca Barr
William, b18--, Shen Co?, wHarriet Baker
SWEATMAN, --, bc1810, Fair Co?, wElizabeth Keith Ford
E R, bc1850, Fair Co?, wMary Taylor Ford
SWEENEY, --, bc1860, Camp Co?, wBlanche W Babcock
SWIFT, Margaret, b17--, Gray Co, hRobert Nuckolls
SWINDALL, Calvin A, bc1860, Wise Co?, wNancy C Dotson
Emmett A, bc1860, Wise Co?, wCelestie B Dotson
SWOPE, Elizabeth, bc1840, Rkhm Co?, fReuben, m-- Swank, hEmanuel Suter
Reuben, bc1800, Rkhm Co, w-- Swank
SYDNOR, Bettie Fleet, bc1840, nrMechanicsville, Hano Co, fWilliam Barrett, mSarah Jane Austin, hJohn Gibson
Bettie Scott, b185-, Nott Co, fThomas White, (2)mBlanche McClanahan
Blanche, b185-, Nott Co, d1923, fThomas White, (2)mBlanche McClanahan
Edward, b186-, Mayfield, Hano Co, fThomas White, mJosephine Crutchfield
Edward Garland, b17--, Hano Co?, wElizabeth White
Edward Garland, b184-, Nott Co, d186-, fThomas White, (1)m-- Chapin
Eugene Beauharnais, b3/15/1869, Beaver Dam, Hano Co, fJohn Lincoln, mElla Virginia Catlin, wSallie Belle Weller
Frances, bc1850, Hali Co, hDaniel Dulany DeButts
George Barret, b10/5/1858, Mayfield, Hano Co, fThomas White, mJosephine Crutchfield, wNannie Winston Grubbs, md10/27/1892
George Boardman, bc1830, nr Mechanicsville, Hano Co, fWilliam Barret, mSarah Jane Aus-

SYDNOR (continued)
tin
Gertrude, b186-, nrMayfield, Hano Co, fThomas White, mJosephine Crutchfield, hAndrew J Nelson
Henry Clinton, bc1840, nrMechanicsville, Hano Co, fWilliam Barret, mSarah Jane Austin
Ida V Lee, bc1870, Beaver Dam, Hano Co, fJohn Lincoln, mElla Virginia Catlin, hI L Lafitte
John Lincoln, bc1830, Hano Co, fWilliam Barret, mSarah Thomas Austin, wElla Virginia Catlin, md1864
Margaret, b18--, Hali Co, 1w of John B Crews
Pearl Garnet, bc1870, Beaver Dam, Hano Co, fJohn Lincoln, mElla Virginia Catlin, hJohn W White
Robert T, b18--, Richmond, wSallie Meredith
Robert Tredway, bc1830, nr Mechanicsville, Hano Co, fWilliam Barret, mSarah Jane Austin
Robert Walton, b184-, Nott Co, fThomas White, (2)mBlanche McClanahan
Ruby Onyx, bc1870, Beaver Dam, Hano Co, fJohn Lincoln, mElla Virginia Catlin, hEdgar Spainhour
Stanley Edward, bc1870, Beaver Dam, Hano Co, fJohn Lincoln, mElla Virginia Catlin
Thomas Garland, b186-, Mayfield, Hano Co, fThomas White, mJosephine Crutchfield
Thomas Lincoln, b4/12/1849, Nott Co, fThomas White, (2)m Blanche McClanahan, wOlivia (Voss) Lindsey, md1902
Thomas White, b18--, Hano Co, fEdward Garland, mElizabeth White, 1w-- Chapin, 2wBlanche McClanahan
Thomas White, bc1820, nrMechanicsville, Hano Co, fWilliam Barret, mSarah Thomas Austin, wJosephine Crutchfield
Walter, bc1830, nrMechanicsville, Hano Co, fWilliam Barret, mSarah Thomas Austin

SYDNOR (continued)
Wilbourne Lee, bc1820, nrMechanicsville, Hano Co, fWilliam Barret, mSarah Thomas Austin
William Austin, bc1870, Beaver Dam, Hano Co, fJohn Lincoln, mElla Virginia Catlin
William Barret, b17--, Hano Co, wSarah Thomas Austin
William Joseph, bc1820, nr Mechanicsville, Hano Co, fWilliam Barret, mSarah Jane Austin
SYKES, George, b18--, Norf Co?, wMarina --
John, b18--, PrAn Co?, wMary --
Mary Josephine, b1850, PrAn Co, d1875, fJohn, mMary --, hEugene Herbert Consalvo
Noah, b18--, Russ Co, wSusan Arington
SYMNS, Mary, b11/8/1870, Forest Hill, -- Co, hHerbert W Hale
TABB, Cynthia Claxton, b7/26/1850, Math Co, d1921, hJohn N Tabb
Edward, b17--, wElizabeth Blair Burwell
George, bc1810, Glou Co, wMary Harrison Randolph
John Henry, b18--, Glou Co, wMargaret Adams
John N, b2/12/1845, Gloucester, Glou Co, d1920, fJohn Henry, mMargaret Adams, wCynthia Claxton Tabb
TABOR, Evelina, b18--, Wayn Co, fJohn, mElizabeth Crockett, hJames F Dudley, md11/19/1884
John, b18--, Wayn Co?, wElizabeth Crockett
TALBOTT, Frank, Sr, b11/10/1870, Danville, Pitt Co, fThomas Jefferson, mMary Pace, 1wGrace Lindsey, md1891, 2wIda Lipscomb, md1898
Mary E, b18--, Alexandria, hCarlton A Paggett
Thomas Jefferson, b18--, Richmond, d1893, wMary Page
TALIAFERRO, Edward Carrington Stanard, b186-, Glou Co, fWilliam Booth, mSally Lyons, wAlice Serpell, md11/10/1908
Eliza, b186-, Madi Co, fFitzhugh, mFrances Twyman, hWil-

TALIAFERRO (continued)
liam H Matthews
Fanny Booth, b186-, Glou Co, fWilliam Booth, mSally Lyons
Fitzhugh, b8/1825, Madi Co?, fBaldwin, wFrances Twyman
Fountain, b18--, Rkhm Co?, wMary Columbia Yancey
George Booth, bc1860, Glou Co, fWilliam Booth, mSally Lyons
Ida, b18--, Amhe Co, fJames M, hWalter Price Massie
James, b18--, Amhe Co
James Lyons, b1/13/1855, Glou Co, fWilliam Booth, mSally N Lyons
Judith, b18--, Fauq Co?, hEdwin B Clarke
Kate B, bc1870, Midd Co, fThomas Booth, mMary Sinclair, hWilliam H Lawson, md10/30/1894
Katie, b4/10/1868, Madi Co, fFitzhugh, mFrances Twyman, hWalter Clifton Aylor
Leah Sedden, b185-, Glou Co, fWilliam Booth, mSally N Lyons
Lizzie A, b186-, nrElkton, Rkhm Co, fFountain, mMary Columbia Yancey, hMiletus Miller Jarman, md2/20/1884
Lucy V, b186-, nrElkton, Rkhm Co, fFountain, mMary Columbia Yancey, h-- Harrison
Mary Henningham, b186-, Glou Co, fWilliam Booth, mSally N Lyons, hHenry O Sanders
Robert E L, b186-, Madi Co, fFitzhugh, mFrances Twyman
Thomas Booth, b182-, "Bellesville", Glou Co, fWarner T, mFrances Booth, wMary Sinclair
Warner T L, b185-, Glou Co, fWilliam, mSally N Lyons, wEmily F Johnson
Warner Throckmorton, b17--, Church Hill, Glou Co, wFrances Booth
William Booth, b12/28/1822, "Bellesville", Glou Co, d1898, fWarner Throckmorton, mFrances Booth, wSally N Lyons, md1856
William C L, b186-, Glou Co, fWilliam Booth, mSally N Lyons, wMabel Schlater
TALLE, William W, bc1850,

TALLE (continued)
  wBettie Welch
TALLEY, Daniel Dee, Sr, b10/17/1842, Clarksville, Meck Co, fNathaniel, wJulia Harris
  Eliza Archer, b18--, Richmond?, hWilliam Gibbon Carter
  John, b1865, wLaura Moss
  Kate, b18--, Cumb Co, 2w of James B Godsey
  Mary Elizabeth, b7/15/1856, Hano Co, hJames Austin Earnest
TALLHELM, Henry, bc1830, Shen Co?, wMary Koontz
TANKARD, Georgiana, b18--, Nhtn Co?, hPhilip Fitzhugh
TANNEHILL, Mary, b18--, Rapp Co?, h-- Holmes
  Nannie, b18--, Rapp Co?, hElias Ricketts
TANNER, Elizabeth, b17--, Henrico Co, fLudowick, m-- Branch, hWilliam Osborne
  Ludowick, bc1700, Henrico Co, mSarah Hatcher
  Victoria, b18--, Lynchburg, Camp Co, d1891, fJohn A, 2w of William Kinnier
TANSILL, Lucretia Alice, b1/19/1846, PrWi Co, hLewis Edmund Oliver
TAPP, Margaret, b18--, hJohn M Lewis
TAPSCOTT, --, b18--, Buck Co, 1w of William P Snead
  Alice, b17--, Edgehill, Lanc Co, hJoseph Pierce
  Benjamin, b18--, Richmond?, wCharlotte Wallace
  J E, bc1860, Buck Co?, wEllen Williams
  Mary Alice, bc1810, Edgehill, Lanc Co, hRobert Tunstall Peirce, Sr
  William Wallace, b8/30/1851, Richmond, fBenjamin, mCharlotte Wallace, 1wCornelia S Baber, 2wMary Willia Hamner
TARTER, Robert, bc1840, Taze Co?, wRebecca Graham
TATE, Benjamin F, b1/16/1861, nrBig Stone Gap, Wise Co, wMargaret L Stewart
  E Carrie, b2/8/1861, Pitt Co, hG H Vaden
  Elen, b17--, Taze Co?, fThomas,

TATE (continued)
  mJane Campbell, hHenry Bowen
  Ida B, b18--, Camp Co?, d1886, 1w of Edward R Monroe
  James, b1741, Rkbr Co, dc1780, wSarah Hall
  John, b1743, Russ Co?, d1828
  Magnus, bc1730, Clar Co?, wMary McCormick
  Rena, b18--, East Stone Gap, Wise Co, hJames Monroe Quillin
  Sallie, b18--, hJohn Hunt II
  Scott, b186-, Wise Co? wKate Meade
  Thomas, bc1800, Taze Co, wJane Campbell
TAVENNER, Albert, b182-, Loud Co, fStacey, m-- Purcell
  Brown, bc1830, Loud Co, 1h of Emma Tavenner
  Emma, b183-, Loud C, fStacey, m-- Purcell, 1hBrown Tavenner, 2hHenry Howard
  Frank Stacey, b4/25/1866, Fred Co, fJonah, mMary Jane Keckley, wLou L Stephenson, md12/1892
  John V, b182-, Loud Co, fStacey, m-- Purcell
  Jonah, b17--, Loud Co?, fGeorge
  Jonah, b2/1832, Loud Co, fStacey, m-- Purcell, wMary Jane Keckley, md1865
  Joseph, b182-, Loud Co, fStacey, m-- Purcell
  Mary B, b186-, Fred Co, fJonah, mMary Jane Keckley, hLee B Eastham
  Mary Elizabeth, b182-, Loud Co, fStacey, m-- Purcell, hJonah Lupton
  Newton, b182-, Loud Co, fStacey, m-- Purcell
  Rebecca, bc1830, Loud Co, fStacey, m-- Purcell
  R D, b186-, Clar Co?, wLizzie M Lindsey
  Stacey, bc1800, Loud Co, fJonah, w-- Purcell
TAYLOE, Benjamin Ogle, bc1870, Fauq Co, fEdward Poinsett, mLouisa Carr
  Edward Carr, b186-, Fauq Co, fEdward Poinsett, mLouisa Carr
  Edward Poinsett, b1830, KiGe Co, d1886, fEdward Thornton,

TAYLOE (continued)
m-- Ogle, wLouisa Carr
Edward Thornton, bc1800, w-- Ogle
George Plater, b1804, Mount Airy, Pitt Co, fJohn, Sr, mMary Ogle, wMary Langhorne
Julia S, b18--, Powh Co, fEdward T, 2w of Thomas Lomax Hunter
Mary, b186-, Fauq Co, fEdward Poinsett, mLouisa Carr, 1h Hiero Taylor, 2hRobert Murphy
Virginia, b18--, Pitt Co?, fGeorge Plater, mMary Langhorne, hMortimer MRogers
William Carr, bc1870, Fauq Co, fEdward Poinsett, mLouisa Carr
TAYLOR, --, b18--, Mont Co?, hSamuel Wallace Thomas
Albert G, b18--, Pitt Co?, wEliza Burks
Alice, b18--, Alderson, Summ Co, fJesse, mMary Faugree, 2hJohn W Waldron, md6/17/1897, 1h-- Baldwin
Alice Littlepage, b18--, "Dove Hill", Lune Co, fDaniel, mElizabeth Hinton, 3w of Sylvanus Ingam
Anne E, b1831, JaCi Co, hWilliam Edmund Christian
Arabelia Sherman, b18--, Staunton, Augu Co, fEdwin M, mJane Eleanor Kinney, hEdward H Fisher
Armistead G, b184-, Amel Co, fRichard Field, Jr, mRosalie Green
Bettie, bc1850, Ches Co, fG Watkins, hJames Beverly Elam, md1874
Betty T, b186-, fJohn Sanders, hPhilip Alexander Bruce
Carrington T, b18--, Staunton, Augu Co, fEdwin M, mJane Eleanor Kinney
Clarence W, b8/17/1870, Hano Co, fJohn R, wCatherine Gannaway
Cordelia, bc1870, Slant, Scot Co, fMilo, mNancy J Salling, hHenry T Starnes
Corlia Letitia, b18--, Pula Co, fRobert Edmond, mElizabeth Patton

TAYLOR (continued)
Cornelia, bc1870, Augu Co?, 2w of Julian Minor Quarles, Sr, md1/1908
Daniel, b17--, KiWi Co?, fDaniel, wAlice Littlepage
Daniel, b17--, "Dove Hill", Lune Co, fWilliam, mMartha Waller, wElizabeth Hinton
Douglas E, b184-, Richmond, fJames M, Sr, mEleanor Evans
Douglas E, b2/22/1870, Richmond, fH Seldon, Sr, mJulia Belle Green
Edmonia, b18--, ChCi Co, fWilliam, hL M Nance
Edward, b18--, Hamp Co
Eleanor, b18--, Staunton, Augu Co, fEdwin M, mJane Eleanor Kinney, hRobert H Fisher
Eliza, b18--, Staunton, Augu Co, fEdwin M, mJane Eleanor Kinney
Elizabeth, b17--, Oran Co?, hBenjamin Walker
Elizabeth, b17--, Augu Co, hPeter Hogg
Elizabeth, bc1800, hHenry Taylor
Elizabeth, b18--, Warr Co?, hJohn B Kerfoot
Emily, b1850, nrRye Cove, Scot Co, d1915, fJames A, hWilliam Frazier
Emma, b18--, Gray Co, hAlexander Grubb
Emma Francina, b18--, Pula Co, fRobert Edmund, mElizabeth Patton
Eugene, bc1860, Camp Co, fWilliam H, mMartha J OLd
Eugenia, b18--, Oran Co?, hAlfred E Slaughter
Eva, b18--, Scot Co?, hJohn Hopkins Duncan
Frances, b1837, Richmond, d1909, fWilliam Jacquelin, mMiriam Jacobs, hSamuel Henry Boykin, md1859
Garland Burnley, b8/9/1855, Aspin Hill, Caro Co, fGeorge Keith, mRebecca Coleman, wLucy Ann Gilmer Magruder
George B, b18--, Nhtn Co?, wFannie Thomas
George Keith, b1833, Taylors-

TAYLOR (continued)
ville, Hano Co, 1wRebecca Coleman, 2w-- Coleman
George Keith, Sr, b4/18/1846, Amel Co, fRichard Field, Jr, mRosalie Green, wCourtney Blair Harvie
George M, b186-, Slant, Scot Co, fMilo, mNancy J Salling
Gilbert, bc1860, York Co?, wAda F Marshall
H Seldon, Sr, b2/21/1849, Richmond, fJames M, Sr, mEleanor Evans, 1wJulia Belle Greene, md2/1868, 2wSallie F Brown, md1881
Henry, b18--, Snowville, Pula Co, fRobert Edmond, mElizabeth Patton, wLulu Lee Meredith
Henry, bc1800, wElizabeth Taylor
Henry P, Jr, bc1860, Richmond?, fHenry P, Sr, wMary Giles Robins
Hiero, bc1860, Fauq Co?, 1h of Mary Tayloe
Hiram H, b183-, nrShenandoah City, Rkhm Co, fZachariah, Jr, mNancy Eppard
Isabella, b17--, hSamuel Hopkins
James, b18--, Arli Co?, wMary Riddick
James A, b1819, Scot Co, d1889, fNimrod, Jr, mJudith Stewart, wKate Stewart
James M, b3/1/1808, NewK Co, wEleanor Evans
James M, Jr, b185-, Richmond, fJames M, Sr, mEleanor Evans
James M, b186-, slant, Scot Co, fMilo, mNancy J Salling
James R, b3/1/1858, Staunton, Augu Co, fEdwin M, mJane Eleanor Kinney, wMariah Marshall Baldwin
James T, b18--, Pula Co, fRobert Edmond, mMatilda Patton
James T, b18--, Fred Co?, wIda Brown
Jesse, b18--, Monr Co?, wMary Faugree
Jessie, bc1870, Mayo, Henry Co, d1907, fSamuel C, mLucy Shelton, hJ H Thacker

TAYLOR (continued)
John F, b4/6/1864, Staunton, Augu Co, fJohn H, mCatherine Ramsey, wIrene Todd, md1893
John H, b1843, nrStaunton, Augu Co, wCatherine Ramsey
John R, bc1860, KiQu Co, fBenjamin T, wMartha Fountleroy Bird
John W, b10/28/1835, nrShenandoah City, Rkhm Co, fZachariah, Jr, mNancy Eppard, wVirginia C Lincoln, md5/21/1868
Joseph F, b12/25/1840, nr Shenandoah City, Rkhm Co, fZachariah, Jr, mNancy Eppard, wLaura Petty, md1876
Joseph Henry, b186-, Slant, Scot Co, fMilo, mNancy J Salling
Joseph Reuben, b1/5/1867, Mayo, Henry Co, fSamuel C, mLucy Shelton, wFlorence Trogdon, md10/12/1910
Julia, b18--, Russ Co?, hRobert Settle
Julia, b18--, Bote Co, fAllen, hAlexander P Eskridge
Jullia Elizabeth, b18--, Pula Co, fRobert Edmond, mElizabeth Patton
Julia L, bc1842, Caro Co, d1918, hE W Hubard
Katherine Craig, b18--, Mont Co, hSamuel Harris Hoge
LaRue, b18--, Scot Co, hFreelin H Bloomer
Lucy Penn, b1828, Stratford, West Co, d1913, hCharles Carter Lee, md5/13/1847
Margaret, b18--, Gooc Co?, 1h-- Whitlock, 2hDaniel Holmes Andrews
Maria Virginia, b3/4/1841, Smyt Co, hJ Tyler Frazier
Martha Jane, b1853, Esse Co, hGeorge Thomas Ringgold Lewis
Mary, b1852, Acco Co, hJohn D Parsons
Mary L, b18--, Pocahontas, Blan Co, fCalvin, mRebecca Reedy, hDavid C Cartwright
Mary M, bc1840, nrShenanhoah City, fZachariah, Jr, mNancy Eppard
Mary N, b186-, Mayo, Henry Co,

TAYLOR (continued)
fSamuel C, mLucy Shelton, hS H Ware
Mary Todd, b17--, Caro Co, fJames, hPeter Thornton, Jr
Mary Virginia, b186-, Portsmouth, Norf Co, fRichard, mVirginia Frances Hanrahan, hJohn O'Connor
Mattie F, b18--, Richmond, d1879, 2w of William McKendree Evans, md1877
Milo, b10/1842, Slant, Scot Co, fJames A, mKate Stewart, wNancy J Sallaing
Nancy G, b186-, Mayo, Henry Co, fSamuel C, mLucy Shelton, hJ C Huffines
Nimrod, Jr, b17--, fNimrod, Sr, wJudith Stewart
Page Waller, b18--, Wyth Co?, hWilliam O Moore
Rebecca Porterfield, b18--, Staunton, Augu Co, fEdwin M, mJane Eleanor Kinney, hJames Foster
Reuben, bc1800, Henry Co?, fGeorge
Richard, b1836, Nans Co, d1903, fWilliamson, wVirginia Frances Hanrahan
Richard Field, Sr, b17--, PrGe Co
Richard Field, Jr, b4/19/1814, Poplar View, Dinw Co, d1899, fRichard Field, Sr, wRosalie Green
Robert Edmond, b18--, Pula Co, fHenry, mElizabeth, wMatilda Patton
Robert Skipwith, b18--, Staunton, Augu Co, fEdwin M, mJane Eleanor Kinney
Rosa L, b185-, Richmond, fJames M, mEleanor Evans, hEmmett Leath
S F, b186-, Mayo, Henry Co, d1922, fSamuel C, mLucy Shelton
Samuel C, bc1837, Henry Co, d1922, fReuben, wLucy Shelton
Sarah Anne, b186-, Portsmouth, Norf Co, fRichard, mVirginia Frances Hanrahan, hGeorge Leonard Whitehurst
Sarah Griffin, b17--, "Clif-

TAYLOR (continued)
ton", Warr Co?, hDavid H Allen
Susan Jane, b18--, Augu Co?, fJohn Henley, hAbsalom Knowles
S T, b18--, Acco Co, wLula --
Thomas T, bc1850, Amyt Co?, wSusie Sanders
Victoria, bc1870, Slant Co, fMilo, mNancy J Salling, hJames H Starnes
Virginia H, b185-, Richmond, fJames M, mEleanor Evans, hR A Dabney
Waller, b17--, "Dove Hill", Lune Co, fWilliam, mMartha Waller
William, b17--, KiWi Co?, fDaniel, mAlice Littlepage, wMartha Waller
William, b17--, "Dove Hill", Lune Co, fDaniel, mElizabeth Hinton
William, b5/10/1853, Smyt Co, wFannie LeGrand Walker
William H, bc1824, Camp Co, wMartha J Old
William H, b18--, ChCi Co
William Jacquelin,, b18--, Richmond?, wMiriam Jacobs
William O, b184-, Richmond, fJames M, Sr, mEleanor Evans
William Old, b8/26/1861, Camp Co, fWilliam H, mMartha J Old, wMattie C Kendrick, md1890
William R, b186-, Portsmouth, Norf Co, fRichard, mVirginia Frances Hanrahan
Williamson, bc1810, Nans Co, d1874
Willie R, bc1861, KiGe Co, d1911, hLewis J Billingsley
Zachariah, Jr, bc1800, Oran Co, d1871, fZachariah, Sr, wNancy Eppard
TAZEWELL, Sallie, b18--, 3w of George Fitzgerald
TEAGUE, Edward, bc1850, Rkhm Co?, 2h of Ada Ann Swank
TEARNEY, Edward M, b1/10/1858, Harpers Ferry, Jeff Co, fEdward M, Sr, mJane McManus
George, bc1860, Harpers Ferry, Jeff Co, fEdward M, Sr, mJane McManus
Joseph F, bc1860, Harpers Ferry, Jeff Co, fEdward M, Sr,

TEARNEY (continued)
mJane McManus
Thomas A, bc1860, Harpers Ferry, Jeff Co, fEdward M, Sr, mJane McManus
TEEL, Margaret A, b11/1/1854, Albe Co, fS M, mAgnes E Johnson, hStephen Alfred Carpenter, md1/22/1885
Samuel M, b18--, Albe Co, wAgnes E Johnson
Stephen S, b6/20/1867, Albe Co, fSamuel M, mAgnes E Johnson, wMary L Howard
TELSON, Isabella, b1837, Smyt Co, hWilliam B McKee
TEMPLE, Agnes, bc1800, Dinw Co?, hDaniel Lyon
James Alexander, b18--, Suss Co, wElmira Graves
Martha, b18--, PrGe Co, hJohn H Hatch, Sr
Rebecca, b18--, Richmond?, hWilson Thomas
William David, b10/9/1845, Jordan's Point, PrGe Co, fJames Alexander, mElmira Graves, wMary Jane Jordan, md1/24/1872
TEMPLETON, Sarah Esterling, bc1835, Fairfield, Rkbr Co, hWilliam M Sale
TENNANT, Maria T, b18--, KiGe Co, hThomas Lomax Hunter
TERRELL, --, b17--, Oran Co, hJohn Scott
Abigail, b10/6/1805, fHenry, (1)mSarah Woodson, 1w of Richard Watts Durrett
Alexander W, bc1830, Penn's Store, Patr Co, fChristopher J, mSusan Kennerly
Alexander W, b7/11/1861, Camp Co, fJohn J, mSue Wade, wLily King, md11/6/1889
Ann, b17--, Spot Co, hZachariah Lewis
Annis Elizabeth, b10/29/1836, Caro Co, d1913, fWilliam, hJames S Reamy, md1/19/1868
Christopher J, bc1800, Camp Co, d1833, wSusan Kennerly
Henry, b16--, 1wSarah Woodson
Jane Elizabeth, b18--, Oran Co?, fUriel, hJohn William Yancey
John J, b7/8/1829, Penn's

TERRELL (continued)
Store, Patr Co, d1922, fChristopher J, mSusan Kennerly, wSue Wade, md3/17/1857
Joseph C, b185-, Camp Co, fJohn J, mSue Wade
Judith, bc1830, Camp Co
Margaret, b18--, Wyth Co?, hRobert Blair
Martha Jefferson, b17--, Albe Co?, 2w of Dabney Minor
Mary, b186-, Camp Co, fJohn J, mSue Wade, hRobert C Scott
Mary Waters, b18--, Loui Co, fRichmond, hWilliam W Minor
Sue, bc1870, Camp Co, fJohn J, mSue Wade
Thomas K, bc1860, Camp Co, fJohn J, mSue Wade
Uriel, b18--, Oran Co
TERRETT, A Hunter, bc1860, Fair Co?, d1922, wMary Virginia Hutton
John, b182-, Fair Co?, d186-, wVirginia Hutton
TERRILL, Henry Towles, b17--, Orange Court House, Oran Co, fEdmund, wFannie Turpin
TERRY, Alice Peyton, b18--, Big Lick, Roan Co, d1921, fPeyton Leftwich, mMary S Trout, hSamuel William Jamison
Annie D, b18--, Big Lick, Roan Co, d1883, fPeyton Leftwich, mMary S Trout
Emma, b10/5/1849, Hano Co, hJames M Shadrach
Georgia Anna, bc1870, PrEd Co, fNathaniel J, (2)mMollie Booker, hWilliam Couch
James, b17--, Pitt Co
John Coles, b184-, Roan Co, wElizabeth Beverley Whittle
Lila M, b18--, Big Lick, Roan Co, fPeyton Leftwich, mMary S Trout
Lucinda, b18--, Big Lick, Roan Co, fPeyton Leftwich, mMary S Trout
Lula, b18--, Meck Co, fStephen W, hJacob D Moss
Martha L, b18--, Big Lick, Roan Co, fPeyton Leftwich, mMary S Trout, hT W Goodwin
Minnie P, bc1860, Pitt Co?, hMillard M Barksdale

TERRY (continued)
Nathaniel, bc1860, Pitt Co, fNathaniel J, (1)mSallie Harper
Nathaniel J, bc1826, Pitt Co, d189-, fBenjamin, 2wMollie Jane Booker, 1wSallie Harper
Patrick Henry, b7/9/1875, Pitt Co, fWilliam, mAthalia Pope, 1wBettie S Dodson, md11/1875, 2wClementine P Shapard, md1913
Peyton Leftwich, b2/2/1835, Camp Co, d1898, fStephen, mLucinda Leftwich, wMary S Trout
Sallie Love, b186-, PrEd Co, fNathaniel J, (2)mMollie Jane Booker, hJames H Couch
William, b18--, Pitt Co, fJames, wAthalia Pope
William P, b186-, PrEd Co, fNathaniel J, (2)mMollie Jane Booker
TEVALT, Isaac, b18--, Fred Co, d1892
Mary Jane, b11/18/1835, Stonewall District, Fred Co, d1923, fIsaac, hPhilip Setzer Orndorff
THACKER, --, b18--, Greensville Co?, hThomas Cleaton
J H, bc1860, Henry Co?, wJessie Taylor
THATCHER, Catherine, b18--, hJohn McVicar
THEISS, M E, b18--, Amhe Co?, wEllen Rucker
THOMAS, --, b18--, Mont Co?, hJames Barnett
--, b18--, Gray Co, hSamuel Cox
Alsen, bc1816, Nels Co, d1900, fEdward, wVirginia C Whitehead
Alsen Franklin, b12/1/1862, nrOakville, Appo Co, fAlsen, mVirginia C Whitehead, wLeverge Dickerson, md6/19/1889
Bolling, bc1850, PrWi Co, wGertrude Free
Charles, b17--, Appo Co, wJudith Ripley
E P M, b181-, Nels Co, fEdward
Elizabeth, b18--, nrHarrisonburg, Rkhm Co, 1w of Samuel F Sanger
Elizabeth, b11/27/1832, Rkhm Co?, fJohn, hGeorge Gordon Hall

THOMAS (continued)
Ella, b4/20/1850, Catawba, Roan Co, d1914, hJohn W Doosing
Fannie, b18--, Nhtn Co?, hGeorge B Taylor
Flora Alice, bc1860, Patr Co, d1923, fWalter H, mJudith Virginia Harbor, hSparrel Tyler Turner
George Wesley, b18--, Mont Co, fSamuel Wallace, m-- Taylor, wCallie Bock
Henry L, b18--, Fair Co, wJane E Thomas
James J, b1843, Nels Co, wMary Goodwin
James W, b186-, Patr Co, fWalter H, mJudith Virginia Turner
Joseph M, b3/3/1860, Char Co, d1912, fLewis J, mMartha Graves, wJulia Richard
Lewis J, b1822, Albe Co, d1896, wMartha Graves
Lillie B, b18--, Salem, Roan Co, 2w of Werter Clairborne Payne
Margaret, b1853, nrClinchport, Scot Co, hJames C Fugate
Marion C, b11/5/1858, Fluv Co, fWillis Curl, mBettie Snead, wLula Snead, md12/5/1888
Mary, bc1800, Midd Co, hWilliam G Crittenden
Mary K, b186-,Patr Co, fWalter H, mJudith Virginia Harbor, hAdron Anglin
Mary L, bc1870, Camp Co?, hErnest Williams
Mary Rebecca, b18--, Isle Co?, hAndrew J Vellines
Mary S, b18--, Cheriton, Nhtn Co, hWilliam H Fatherly
Mattie M, b186-, Patr Co, d1890, fWalter H, mJudith Virginia Turner, hJob E Lester
Minnie, b1863, Richmond, fWilson, mRebecca Temple, hGeorge A Delaplane
Nannie R, b18--, Hali Co, d1883, 1w of John G Lea, md 1873
Nettie, b18--, Fluv Co?, hHenry Davis
Peyton L, b18--, wEliza Weatherall
Remember Ann, b18--, 1w of

THOMAS (continued)
Norton Hull
Richard, bc1800, Patr Co, fCharles, mJudith Ripley, 2w Mattie Turner
Robert E L, b186-, nrOakville, Appo Co, fAlsen, mVirginia C Whitehead
Robert Lee, b11/25/1862, Madison Court House, Culp Co, fPeyton L, mEliza Weatherall
Sallie, b18--, Rapp Co, hGustavus Judson Browning, Sr
Samuel Wallace, b1831, Mont Co, dc1923, w-- Taylor
Susan, b18--, Camp Co, hElisha Snead
Susan, b1850, Harrisonburg, Rkhm Co, 2w of Samuel F Sanger
Walter H, b4/29/1829, Buffalo Ridge, Patr Co, fRichard, mMattie Turner, wJudith Virginia Harbor
Walter S, b186-, nrOakville, Appo Co, fAlsen, mVirginia C Whitehead
William C, bc1870, nrOakville, Appo Co, fAlsen, mVirginia C Whitehead
Willie, b18--, Amhe Co, hHorsely Barnes Camden
Willis Curl, b18--, Fluv Co, wBettie Snead
Wilson, b18--, Richmond?, wRebecca Temple
THOMASON, Mary Elvira, b18--, Henrico Co, 2w of William Powers Ballard
THOMASSON, John, bc1850, Rkbr Co?, wMary F Gleason
THOMPSON, Allison, b18--, Fair Co, wJulia Kidwell
Amy, b18--, fJohn, hSamuel Stinson
Andrew J, b1840, Floy Co, d1909, fHiram, wElizabeth Stewart
Anne E, b12/9/1843, Wash Co, hCharles W Johnson, Sr
Annie, b11/21/1812, Lee Co, d1862, hEdmond Witt, md12/22/1831
Benjamin, b18--, Loud Co?, w-- Blake
Daniel, b8/3/1849, nrVienna, Fair Co, wAlice Ferris

THOMPSON (continued)
E Blanch, b1845, Camp Co?, fHoratio, hThomas N Davis, Sr, md2/11/1874
Elias, b17--, Fauq Co, fJesse, mElizabeth --
Elizabeth, b1840, Burkes Garden, Taze Co, 1898, hJohn T Litz
Elmyra, b18--, Warr Co?, hFielden Bolen
Emily, b1830, Pitt Co, d1859, 1w of John W Easley
Frances, b16--, ElCi Co?, hAnthony Armistead
Frank, b18--, Clar Co?, wFannie Lloyd
Granger, bc1860, Taze Co?, wMargaret Dudley
Hiram, b18--, Floy Co?,
Hugh A, b9/23/1861, Hillsboro, Loud Co, fHugh S, mRuth H Clendening, wHannah E Norris, md9/29/1884
Hugh S, b18--, Hillsboro, Loud Co, fIsrael, wRuth H Clendening
Irving P, b18--, Hillsboro, Loud Co, fHugh S, mRuth H Clendening
J Harry, b18--, Hillsboro, Loud Co, fHugh S, mRuth H Clendening
James H, b9/25/1855, New Garden, Russ Co, wHannah Ellen Robinson
Jane, bc1810, Nels Co, hHowell Lewis Brown
Jane, b18--, Arli Co, hSamuel Shreve
Jennie E, b1846, Caro Co, hLetitius Atwater Saunders
Jeremiah, b184-, nrVienna, Fair Co, fAllison, mJulia Kidwell
Joel, b185-, nrVienna, Fair Co, fAllison, mJulia Kidwell
John Arthur, b18--, Hillsboro, Loud Co, fHugh S, mRuth H Clendening
Joseph Taylor, b1850, Fauq Co, d1888, fOrlando, (1)mElizabeth Douglas Hudnall, wJosephine Elizabeth Holmes
Louisa, bc1850, nrVienna, Fair Co, fAllison, mJulia Kidwell, hWilliam Thompson

THOMPSON (continued)
Louisa Bowen, b1824, nrTazewell Court House, Taze Co, d1888, hWilliam L Graham
Louise W, b1/8/1831, Nels Co, 1hRobert M Camden, 2hJohn T Evans
Maggie, bc1870, nrPearisburg, Gile Co, fAndrew J, mElizabeth Stewart, hJ W Thompson
Mary, b17--, Fluv Co, hWilliam Payne
Mollie S, b186-, nrPearisburg, Gile Co, fAndrew J, mElizabeth Stewart
Orlando, b1821, Fauq Co, d1896, 1wElizabeth Douglas Hudnall, 2wMrs Amanda ( ) O'Bannon, 3wMrs Amanda ( ) Clark
Rachel, b18--, rkbr Co, hW C Whitmore
Roots, bc1800, wSarah Hamilton
Sallie, b18-, Hillsboro, Loud Co, fHugh S, mRuth H Clendening, hRobert W Grubb
Sarah Margaret, b18--, Loud Co?, d1890, fBenjamin, m-- Blake, hSylvester Smallwood
William D, b18--, Hillsboro, Loud Co, fHugh S, mRuth H Clendening
William H, b9/30/1867, nrPearisburg, Gile Co, fAndrew J, mElizabeth Stewart, wEttie Stafford, md10/1899
THOMSON, Mary Haws, b1/5/1864, Loui Co, fWilliam Quarles, mNicie Haws Daniel, hHugh Quarles Dickinson, md7/15/1902
Mildred, b17--, Albe Co, 2w of James Scott
William Quarles, b7/1/1823, Loui Co, wNicie Haws Daniel
THORNHILL, Albert, b1/10/1819, Appo Co, fThomas, mAgnes Patteson, wLucinda A Lowry
Albert B, b7/18/1861, Appo Co, fAlbert, mLucinda A Lowry, wKate Smith, md3/17/1897
Charles W, b18--, Appo Co, fAlbert, mLucinda A Lowry
D W, b12/9/1852, Madi Co, fGeorge, wCorilla Hudson
Elizabeth, b18--, Rapp Co?, fJoseph, hRobert William Brown
Fannie, b18--, Appo Co, fAl-

THORNHILL (continued)
bert, mLucinda Lowry, hEdward C James
Hattie, b8/24/1842, Buck Co, hJohn R Snoddy
Jesse, b17--, (now) Appo Co
Joseph, b18--, Rapp Co?, fThomas
Luther R, b18--, Appo Co, fAlbert, mLucinda A Lowry
Margaret, b18--, Rapp Co?, hJoel Yowell
Mary Agnes, b18--, Appo Co, fAlbert, mLucinda A Lowry, hDavid A Christian
Maude, bc1860, Appo Co, hWilliam McGuffy Woodson
Thomas, b17--, Appo Co, fJesse, wAgnes Patteson
Thomas J, b18--, Appo Co, fAlbert, mLucinda A Lowry
THORNTON, --, bc1800, Culp Co, wLucy Colvin
Annie Sarah, b1844, Hunter's Hill, Caro Co, hJoseph B Jesse
Anthony, b16--, Staf Co, fFrancis, wWinifred Presley
Bickley Buckner, bc1860, PrWi Co, fWilliam Willis, Sr, mMary Susan Buckner
Charlotte Belson, bc1820, Nhld Co?, fPhilip Wade, mLucy Champ Brockenbrough, hRichard Ball Mitchell, md1861
Elvira, b18--, Caro Co, hEdwin S Motley
Francis, b16--, Glou Co?, fWilliam
George, bc1800, wMargaret Hamilton
James Bankhead Taylor, bc1800, fPeter, Jr, mMary Todd Taylor, wLouisiana Ratcliffe
James Bankhead Taylor II, b185-PrWi Co, fWilliam Willis, Sr, mMary Susan Buckner
James H, b18--, Alle Co?, wVictoria --
John Taylor, b17--, Nhld Co, fPresley, wSusan Kenner
Lucy, b17--, hJohn Lewis
Maggie, b18--, Carr Co?, h-- Hall
Mary S, bc1860, PrWi Co, fWilliam Willis, Sr, mMary Susan Buckner

THORNTON (continued)
Mildred Hawes, b1851, PrWi Co, fWilliam Willis, Sr, mMary Susan Buckner, hJames Jenkyn Davies
Nannie Ratcliffe, b185-, PrWi Co, fWilliam Willis, Sr, mMary Susan Buckner, hJohn Boyd Washington
Peter, Sr, b16--, Caro Co?, fAnthony, mWinefred Presley, wEllen Bankhead
Peter, Jr, b1774, Caro Co, fPeter, Sr, mEllen Bankhead, wMary Todd Taylor
Philip Wade, b17--, Nhld Co, fJohn Taylor, mSusan Kenner, wLucy Champ Brockenbrough, md1815
Presley, bc1700, Nhld Co?, fAnthony, mWinifred Presley
Richard Ewell, b1/7/1865, PrWi Co, fWilliam Willis, Sr, mMary Susan Buckner, wSue Plummer, md6/25/ 1891
William, bc1800, wCharlotte Hamilton
William Willis, Sr, b1830, Brentsville, PrWi Co, fJames Bankhead Taylor, mLouisiana Ratcliffe, wMary Susan Buckner
William Willis, Jr, b185-, PrWi Co?, fWilliam Willis, Sr, mMary Susan Buckner
THRASH, Mary, b1829, Floy Co, d1905, hWilliam Sowder
THRESHER, Mary Adaline, b18--, Mill Creek, Bote Co, d1909, fStephen, mMary --, hGeorge Russell Gish
Stephen, b18--, Bote Co?, wMary
THRESLEY, --, bc1800, Midd Co?, 1w of Richard Woodward
THRIFT, Anne, b18--, Loud Co, hTownsend W Belt
Charlotte Annie, b1864, Tucker Hill, West Co, hHenry Clinton Moss
THROCKMORTON, Charles Woodson, b2/1/1861, Richmond, fRobert James, mKate Ford, wMary Ann Wright, md5/12/1886
James, b1804, Henrico Co, fJosiah, mSarah (Williams) Roberts, wMargaret Hampton
Josiah, b17--, Henrico Co

THROCKMORTON (continued)
Robert James, b4/15/1834, Henrico Co, fJames, mMargaret Hampton, wKate Ford
THUMA, Belle, bc1850, Bridgewater, Rkhm Co, fJohn, mElizabeth Dinkle, h-- White
Chapman, bc1850, Bridgewater, Rkhm Co, fJohn, mElizabeth Dinkle
Jack, b1849, Bridgewater, Rkhm Co, fJohn, mElizabeth Dinkle, wBirdie Nichols
John, b18--, Rkhm Co, wElizabeth Dinkle
Marcellus, bc1850, Bridgwater, Rkhm Co, fJohn, mElizabeth Dinkle
Mattie, bc1850, Bridgewater, Rkhm Co, fJohn, mElizabeth Dinkle, h-- Dovel
Robert, b184-, Bridgewater, Rkhm Co, d186-, fJohn, mElizabeth Dinkle
Thomas, b184-, Bridgewater, Rkhm Co, fJohn, mElizabeth Dinkle
THURMAN, Benjamin W, b18--, Albe Co
Charles Ross, b18--, Rapp Co, fTheodore Lindsay, mHomieselle Victoria Quaintance
Francis Lee, b18--, Rapp Co, fTheodore Lindsay, mHomieselle Victoria Quaintance, wLizzie Tate Gill, md1897
J W, b186-, Floy Co?, wAlloway Lancaster
James Oscar, b18--, Rapp Co, fTheodore Lindsay, mHomieselle Victoria Quaintance
Stella, b18--, West Co?, hJ Hunter Peak
Theodore Lindsay, b184-, Albe Co, wHomieselle Victoria Quaintance
Tesora Fendal, b18--, Rapp Co, fTheodore Lindsay, mHomieselle Victoria Quaintance, hArthur Alexander McCorkle
THWEATT, Mary Eppes, b1845, Eppington, Ches Co, fRichard N, mAlice Friend, hGeorge M Wilson
Richard N, b18--, Ches Co, wAlice Friend

TIFFANY, Hugh, bc1810, Fauq Co?, wSarah Swart
Hugh, b18--, Fauq Co?, wElizabeth Jane Cochran
TILDEN, --, bc1800, Camp Co?, hJohn Victor
Cornelia Meyer, b5/25/1798, Fred Co?, fJohn Bell, mJane Chambers, 2w of Christopher Winfree, md11/19/1817
TILGHMAN, Tench Francis, b6/1/1868, Norfolk, fTench Francis, Sr, mElizabeth Barron Camp
TILLEY, Charles, b1776, d1881
Lazarus, b1815, Henry Co, d1909, fCharles
TILLMAN, Henry N, bc1860, Albe Co?, wLulu Jennings Jarman
TILMAN, James A, b18--, Powh Co?, wMattie O Ligon
William Bernard, bc1830, Albe Co, wMollie Eliza Rea
TILSON, eliza, bc1800, Smyt Co, hSamuel Copenhaver
William H, bc1860, Blan Co?, wMary R Kegley
TIMBERLAKE, --, bc1800, Fluv Co?, 1w of John Haden Lane, Sr
Lewis, b1841, nrRichmond, wMary Ellen Humphreys
Joseph, b17--, wElizabeth Dixon
Leonidas Rosser, b12/21/1851, NewK Co, fWilliam, mMartha Clark, wEmma M Cottrell, md1875
Lewis, b17--,fJoseph, mElizabeth Dixon, wMary Madison
Maria, b7/23/1799, fLewis, mMary Madison, hWarner Washington Minor
Sarah, b11/30/1765, Hano Co, hMosby Pulliam
Stephen Davis, b2/20/1747, Fred Co, fStephen Davis, Sr, mFrances A --, wNannie D Bell
William, b18--, ChCi Co, wMartha Clark
TINSLEY, --, b16--, Camp Co?, hJohn Pendleton
Julia, b18--, Pitt Co, hTandy W Fitts
Margaret Julia, b12/1844, Char Co, d1911, hCharles Wesley Crawley
TIPTON, Walter S, b18--, Carr Co?, wPattie Howard

TISDALE, Charles W, bc1840, Meck Co, d187-, fWilliam R, wElizabeth Anderson
George R, b18--, Meck Co, wJennie P Boswell
Thomas M, b6/9/1865, Clarksville, Meck Co, fCharles W, mElizabeth Anderson, wMattie A Drake
William R, bc1800, Lune Co, d1871
TOD, George, b17--, Caro Co, wMary Hart Smith
Louisa, b1/22/1818, Caro Co, d1895, fGeorge, mMary Hart Smith, hFrancis W Motley
TODD, Hardin, b18--, Gray Co?, wMollie Phipps
Jane, b1699, KiQu Co, hJohn Scott
John, bc1770, Fluv Co?, 1h of Dolly Payne
Susan E, b18--, Richmond?, hJohn King
TOLSON, James A, b183-, PrWi Co?, wMary J Ratcliffe
TOMBLIN, Eliza, b18--, Clar Co?, hBourbon Smallwood
James, b183-, Clar Co?, wRebecca Smallwood
TOMKINS, Charles C, b18--, Roan Co, wEmeline Pitzer
TOMPKINS, Alexander, b17--, Camp Co?, wElizabeth Byrd
Anna Munford, b181-, Lynchburg, Camp Co, fAlexander, mElizabeth Byrd, hDaniel Trigg, md 3/14/1838
Christopher Quarles, bc1814, wEllen Wilkins
Christopher, b9/7/1847, Richmond, fChristopher Quarles, mEllen Wilkins, wBessie McCaw, md11/8/ 1877
Elizabeth Keeling, b18--, Caro Co?, hPhilip Oliver
Ellen, b184-, Richmond?, fChristopher Quarles, mEllen Wilkins, hFrank Wise
Henderson F, b18--, PrWi Co?, wElizabeth Bankhead Weir
Mary Overton, b17--, Loui Co?, hLauncelot Minor
William Frazier, bc1850, Richmond, fChristopher Quarles, mEllen Wilkins

TOOMBS, Annie Elizabeth, b1852, Shepard's Church, KiQu Co, d1908, hWilliam H Walker
TOOMER, Alice Virginia, bc1841, hJames Parrish
TOOMEY, Daniel, b18--, Richmond?, wMary Jane Crawford
TORRENCE, Alfred E, b185-, Appo Co, wMary A Coleman
TOSH, Elizabeth Katherine, bc1847, Pitt Co, d1923, hReuben Alfred Bennett
TOTTY, Beulah E, bc1860, Charlottesville, Albe Co, fThomas H, mMary Collier, h-- Grim
Cora B, b186-, Charlottesville, Albe Co, fThomas H, mMary Collier, hAlbert George Shaver, md2/10/1886
Florence S, bc1860, Charlottesville, Albe Co, fThomas H, mMary Collier
H Edward, bc1860, Charlottesville, Albe Co, fThomas H, mMary Collier
James, bc1860, Charlottesville, Albe Co, fThomas H, mMary Collier
Lawrence, bc1860, Charlottesville, Albe Co, fThomas H, mMary Collier
Samuel, b186-, Charlottesville, Albe Co, fThomas H, mMary Collier
Thomas H, b18--, Albe Co?, wMary Collier
William, b186-, Charlottesville, Albe Co, fThomas H, mMary Collier
TOWLER, Albert G, bc1850, Lune Co, wNannie E Priddy
Mary, b1812, Meck Co, d1889, hRobert Saunders
TOWLES, Clarence Spotswood, Sr, b11/22/1870, Lanc Co, fJohn C, mZelia A Towles, wMary Towles, md2/7/1804
Elizabeth, b18--, Camp Co?, hJohn B Dabney
Harriet Washington, b18--, Albe Co?, hWilliam Henry Harris
John C, b11/26/834, Towles Point Farm, Lanc Co, d1921, fWilliam, mKeturah Beane, wZelia A Towles
Nannie Walker, b18--, Spot Co?,

TOWLES (continued)
fThomas T, hHorace L Vaughan
Virginius E, b186-, Lanc Co, fJohn Co, mZelia A Towles
William, b18--, Lanc Co, wKeturah Beane
Zelia A, b4/1/1844, nrWhite Stone, Lanc Co, hJohn C Towles
TOWNES, George, b17--, Amel Co?, wElizabeth Tunstall
Sallie Ann, b18--, Amel Co, fGeorge, mElizabeth Tunstall, hWilliam Rison
TOWNSEND, Alfred, bc1840, wRebecca Tyler
Catherine, b1830, nrFairfax Court House, Fair Co, d1910, hShepard Harrison
TRAMMELL, Mildred, b18--, Fair Co?, hJames A Wells
TRAVERS, Lafayette M, bc1860, Math Co?, wTheresa Clementine Haynes
Million, b16--, Lanc Co?, fWilliam, hWilliam Downman
TRAVERSE, Susanna, bc1690, hCharles Colston
TRAYLOR, Archer, b17--, Ches Co, wJudith Markham
Mary, b17--, Ches Co, fArcher, mJudith Markham, hHenry Cox, Jr, md11/21/1805
TREDWAY, Patty Booker, b3/8/1850, Danville, Pitt Co, fWilliam M, hFletcher Bangs Watson, Sr
William M, b18--, Pitt Co
TRENARY, Annie, b184-, nrNinevah, Warr Co, fJonas A, m-- Leach, hBenjamin Hartley
Frank, b184-, nrNinevah, Warr Co, fJonas A, m-- Leach
Janie, bc1850, nrNinevah, Warr Co, fJonas A, m-- Leach, hWilliam Grubbs
John Buckner, b9/1840, nrNinevah, Warr Co, fJonas A, m-- Leach, wMary Elizabeth Ruffner, md1868
Jonas, b184-, nrNinevah, Warr Co, fJonas A, m-- Leach
Jonas A, b18--, w-- Leach
Marshall, bc1850, nrVinevah, Warr Co, fJonas A, m-- Leach
William Collen, b184-, nrNinevah, Warr Co, fJonas A, m--

TRENARY (continued)
Leach
TRENT, Annie, b17--, hJohn Robertson
TRIBLE, Emily Margaret, b186-, Johnville Farm, Esse Co, fJohn S, mElizabeth Susan Waring, hJohn E Kreite
George Meredith, b186-, Johnville Farm, Esse Co, fJohn S, mElizabeth Susan Waring
John S, b1815, Johnville Farm, Esse Co, d1880, 2h of Elizabeth Susan Waring
Lowry Waring, b186-, Johnville Farm, Esse Co, fJohn S, mElizabeth Susan Waring
Nancy, bc1800, Esse Co?, hAndrew Hundley
Thomas Young, b186-, Johnville Farm, Esse Co, fJohn S, mElizabeth Susan Waring
TRIGG, Abraham, b1684, Midd Co, fDaniel, wJudith Clarke, md1710
Abram, b174-, Bedf Co, fWilliam, mMary Johns
Abram, b1788, Mont Co, d1852, fDaniel, mAnn Smith, 1wMargaret Findlay, 2wMary Mitchell
Ann, b1783, Mont Co, fDaniel, mAnn Smith
Ann C, b18--, Christiansburg, Mont Co, hEli Phlegar
Connally Findlay, b3/8/1810, Abingdon, Wash Co, d1880, fWilliam, mRachel Findlay, wMary Campbell
Connally Findlay, b9/18/1847, Abingdon, Wash Co, d1907, fDaniel, mAnna Munford Tompkins, wPocahontas Robertson
Daniel, bc1650, Midd Co?,
Daniel, b17--, Midd, fAbraham, mJudith Clarke
Daniel, b8/14/1749, Bedf Co, d1819, fWilliam, mMary Johns, wAnn Smith, md1/30/1777
Daniel, b1780, Mont Co, fDaniel, mAnn Smith
Daniel, b9/7/1808, Abingdon, Wash Co, d1853, fWilliam, mRachel Lindsay, wAnna Munford Tompkins, md3/14/1838
Daniel, b3/12/1843, Abingdon, Wash Co, d1909, fDaniel, mAnna

TRIGG (continued)
Munford Tompkins, wLouisa Bowen Johnston
Doshia, b17--, fJohn, hJesse Leftwich, md7/21/1771
Elizabeth, b1790, Mont Co, fDaniel, mAnn Smith, hCalvin Morgan
Guy Smith, b1777, Mont Co, d1808, fDaniel, mAnn Smith, wFannie Jackson
James, b1793, Mont Co, d1819, fDaniel, mAnn Smith, wAnn King
John, b174-, Bedf Co, d1804, fWilliam, mMary Johns
John Johns, b1779, Mont Co, d1817, fDaniel, mAnn Smith, wElsie King
Joseph, b1795, Mont Co, d1831, fDaniel, mAnn Smith, wElizabeth Findlay
Lilburn Henderson, b3/3/1812, Abingdon, Wash Co, d1954, fWilliam, mRachel Findlay, wBarbara Colquohoon
Lockey, b175-, Bedf Co, fWilliam, mMary John, h-- Henderson
Mary, b1781, Mont Co, fDaniel, mAnn Smith, 1hWilliam Kings, 2hFrancis Smith
Nancy, b175-, Bedf Co, fWilliam, mMary Johns, hArthur Moseley
Nannie Byrd, b12/24/1838, Abingdon, Wash Co, fDaniel, mAnna Munford Tompkins, hJames C Greenway
Rhoda, b1795, Mont Co, fDaniel, mAnn Smith, hEdward Campbell
Robert C, b18--, Christiansburg, Mont Co
Sarah, b175-, Bedf Co, fWilliam, mMary Johns
Stephen, b1786, Mont Co, d1814, fDaniel, mAnn Smith
Stephen, b174-, Bedf Co, d1782, fWilliam, mMary Johns
Susanna, b171-, Midd Co, fAbraham, mJudith Clarke
Thomas Preston, b5/23/1851, Abingdon, Wash Co, d1921, fDaniel, mAnna Munford Tompkins, wBettie W White
William, b1716, Midd Co, d1772, fAbraham, mJudith Clarke,

TRIGG (continued)
wMary Johns
William, b174-, Bedf Co, fWilliam, mMary Johns
William, b12/26/1784, Mont Co, d1813, fDaniel, mAnn Smith, wRachel Findlay, md1/14/1806
William King, b1/8/1807, Abingdon, Wash Co, fWilliam, mRachel Findlay, wSusan Hickman
William King, b2/26/1841, Abingdon, Wash Co, d1862, fDaniel, mAnna Munford Tompkins
TRINKLE, Amanda Virginia, b18--, Blan Co?, fJacob, mEliza Kirkner, hRobert Payne Johnson, md3/22/1877
Clarence M, Sr, b10/25/1868, Pula Co, fElbert S, mLetitia M Sexton, wAddie Kent Moore, md6/6/ 1907
Elbert S, b4/22/1834, Dublin, Pula Co, d1883, mSallie Trolinger, wLetitia M Sexton
Jacob, bc1840, Pula Co, mSallie Trolinger, wEliza Kirkner
Stephen, bc1870, Pula Co, fElbert S, mLetitia M Sexton
William, bc1870, Pula Co, d1923, fElbert S, mLetitia M Sexton
TRIPLETT, Aidelaide, bc1810, Front Royal, Warr Co, fWilliam H, mCatherine Foote Alexander, h-- Fish
Alfred V M, b184-, Mt Jackson, Shen Co, d1887, fLeonidas, Sr, mMatilda Barryhill Irwin
Annie A, b183-, Mt Jackson, Shen Co, d1907, fLeonidas, Sr, mMatilda Barryhill Irwin, hHenry Hardy
Arthur W, b184-, PrWi Co, fHayward Foote, Sr, mEveline Lewis
Catherine, b178-, Loud Co, fSimon, mMartha Lane
Elizabeth Foote, bc1810, Front Royal, Warr Co, fWilliam H, mCatherine Foote Alexander
Florence Alexander, b184-, PrWi Co, fHayward Foote, Sr, mEveline Lewis
G S P, b183-, Mt jackson, Shen Co, fLeonidas, Sr, mMatilda

TRIPLETT (continued)
Barryhill Irwin
Hayward Foote, Sr, b1807, Front Royal, Warr Co, d1890, fWilliam H, mCatherine Foote Alexander, wEveline Lewis
Hayward Foote, Jr, bc1840, PrWi Co, fHayward Foote, Sr, mEveline Lewis
James Lane, b178-, Loud Co, fSimon, mMartha Lane
John E, b184-, Mt Jackson, Shen Co, d1913, fLeonidas, Sr, mMatilda Barryhill Irwin, wAnnie Carrie Johnston
Joseph Irwin, b3/14/1845, Shen Co, fLeonidas, Sr, mMatilda Barryhill Irwin
Leonidas, Sr, b9/5/1810, Front Royal, Warr Co, d1890, fWilliam H, mCatherine Foote Alexander, wMatilda Barryhill Irwin, md5/1834
Leonidas, Jr, bc1839, Mt Jackson, Shen Co, fLeonidas, Sr, mMatilda Barryhill Irwin, wLaura (Templeton) Whiton
Leonidas, bc1850, PrWi Co, fHayward Foote, Sr, mEveline Lewis
Lucinda, b178-, Loud Co, fSimon, mMartha Lane
Lucy A, bc1810, Front Royal, Warr Co, fWilliam H, mCatherine Foote Alexander
Malinda, b184-, Mt Jackson, Shen Co, fLeonidas, Sr, mMatilda Barryhill Irwin, hCasper Craig
Martha, bc1810, Front Royal, Warr Co, fWilliam H, mCatherine Foote Alexander, h-- Craig
Martha, b185-, PrWi Co, fHayward Foote, Sr, mEveline Lewis, hRichard Lee
Mary Katherine, bc1840, Shen Co, d1884, fLeonidas, Sr, mMatilda Barryhill Irwin, hJames Trotter
Philip, b179-, Loud Co, fSimon, mMartha Lane
Philip Alexandria, b184-, PrWi Co, fHayward Foote, Sr, mEveline Lewis
Simon, b17--, Loud Co?, d1810,

TRIPLETT (continued)
  wMartha Lane
Simon, bc1790, Loud Co, fSimon, mMartha Lane
Susan, b179-, Loud Co, fSimon, mMartha Lane, h-- Adams
Theodore Montgomery, Sr, b2/14/1848, PrWi Co, fHayward Foote, Sr, mEveline Lewis, wMary Agnes Lake, md12/18/1877
William, b17--, Loud Co
William H, b8/11/1783, Loud Co, d1856, fSimon, mMartha Lane, wCatherine Foote Alexander
William H, bc1840, PrWi Co, fHayward Foote, Sr, mEveline Lewis
William H, b183-, Mt Jackson, Shen Co, fLeonidas, Sr, mMatilda Barryhill Irwin
TROLINGER, Henry Lewis, b7/15/1870, nrDublin, Pula Co, fJames T, mMary Elizabeth King, wWillie Trolingr Jordan, md11/6/1895
James T, b9/8/1842, Dublin, Pula Co, fJohn, mMary Wygal, wMary Elizabeth King
John, b1806, Dublin, Pula Co, d1880, fJohn, wMary Wygal
TRONE, --, b18--, PrWi Co, hAustin B Weedon
TROTTER, James, bc1840, Shen Co?, wMary Katherine Triplett
TROUT, --, b17--, Crai Co, hArchibald Caldwell
Elizabeth, b18-, Simmonsville, Crai Co, hJacob Albert
Emma Virginia, bc1863, Roan Co, hPeter M Engleman
Henry S, b18--, Roan Co, fJohn, mEliza --
John, b18--, Roan Co?, wEliza - Mary S, b18--, Roan Co, fJohn, mEliza --, hPeyton Leftwich Terry
TROWER, Preston e, b18--, Nhtn Co, wHarriett Holland
TRUEHEART, Elizabeth, bc1824, Richmond?, hJohn A Mosby
Julia Amelia, b7/1865, Amel Co, hPhilip Valentine Cogbill
TUCK, Kate, b9/6/1851, Scottsburg, Hali Co, d1913, hRobert Daniel McKinney
Mary S, b9/15/1856, Virgilina,

TUCK (continued)
  Hali Co, hStephen M Wilborn
TUCKER, --, b17--, hGeorge Carrington
--, b18--, hJohn Bonifant
Ann B, b1796, Powh Co, d1842, hRichard Adams
Annie B, b185-, dc1922, fSt George, hLeon Gardiner Tyler, md11/14/1878
Carrie Dallas, b18--, Dinw Co?, fDavid H, hJohn Thompson Brown, Sr
Gertrude, b18--, fJohn Randolph, mLaura Holmes Powell, hJohn L Logan
Henry St George, b12/29/1780, Mattoaca, Che Co, fSt George, (1)mFrances (Bland) Randolph, wAnne Evelina Hunter, md9/23/1806
Henry St George II, b4/5/1853, Winchester, Fred Co, fJohn Randolph, mLaura Holmes Powell, wHenrietta Preston Johnston, md10/25/1877
John, b11/8/1770, Brun Co?, wAgnes Eppes Goode
John, b18--, Alle Co?, wJane Schumaker
John Randolph, b1821, Winchester, Fred Co, fHenry St George, mAnne Evelina Hunter, wLaura Holmes Powell
Laura, b18--, fJohn Randolph, mLaura Holmes Powell, hE Morgan Pendleton
Leon Leslie, b18--,Char Co?, wAda Jane Holt
Lucy, bc1800, Brun Co?, fJohn, mAgnes Eppes Goode, hEdward Chambers
Lula, b1834, Lune Co, d1904, hJohn Thomas Green
Lula, b1834, Lune Co, d1904, wJohn Thomas Green
Mary/Sarah, bc1663, West Co, fJohn, hWilliam Fitzhugh
Mary L, b1847, Vernon Hill, Hali Co, d1921, hPolk Dallas Womack
Pitt Edward, b9/29/1870, Nels Co, fW Dillard, mSusan Wilshire, wMary Cunningham, md1/31/1879
Reuben D, b18--, Warr Co?,

TUCKER (continued)
fClayborne
Sallie Claiborne, b18--, Riceville, Pitt Co, fReuben D, hGustavus Adolphus Creasy
W Dillard, b18--, Amhe Co, wSusan Wilshire
William Younger, b18--, Lee Co?, wNancy Whisman
TULEY, Mary, b17--, Clar Co, hHenry Dudley Mitchell
TUNE, Joel K, bc1828, Hali Co, fJohn, wJennie Adams
TUNSTALL, Corinne, bc1870, Lynchburg, Camp Co, fJohn L, mFlorence Massie
Elizabeth, b17--, Pitt Co, fWilliam, hGeorge Townes
John L, b18--, Lynchburg, Camp Co, wFlorence Massie
Richard Baylor, b7/1/1848, Norfolk, fRobert Baylor
Robert Baylor, b8/3/1818, Norfolk, d1883
W P, b17--, Pitt Co, fWilliam
William M, Sr, b9/21/1869, Lynchburg, Camp Co, fJohn L, mFlorence Massie, 1w-- Peibes, 2wMaria Gleason
TURBERVILLE, Anne, b17--, Hague, West Co, hRobert Beale
TURMAN, Elijah, bc1856, Floy Co, fGeorge, wAdaline Dalton
George, b18--, Floy Co
TURNBULL, Needham Stuart, Sr, b1859, Lawrenceville, Brun Co, d1922, fRobert D, m-- Stith, wHelen Stuart Lewis
Robert D, b1820, Lawrenceville, Brun Co, w-- Stith
TURNER, Albert Alexander, b18--, PrWi Co, d1886, fThomas, wLucinda Jane Swaine
Alice/Alys, bc1870, PrWi Co, hWilliam H Lewis
Ann, b17--, Bedf Co, fJames, mSally Leftwich
Ann Eliza, b9/1840, Finc Co, d1902, fPitticus, hJames Mc Dowell
Baynton, bc1810, PrWi Co, fThomas, mElizabeth Carter Randolph, hJohn Hill Carter
Beverley, bc1830, wRose Skinker
Beverley, b184--, Fauq Co, fEdward Carter, Sr, (1)mSarah

TURNER (continued)
Beverley
Charles, bc1810, PrWi Co, fThomas, mElizabeth Carter Randolph
Daniel James, bc1745, Norfolk?, wMary Elizabeth Lawrence
Daniel Lawrence, b10/25/1869, Portsmouth, Norf Co, fDaniel James, mMary Elizabeth Lawrence, wEve Barcine Denby
Edmonia Pendleton, bc1870, NewK Co, fJohn Daniel, mElizabeth Taylor Robinson, hNorvell Lightfoot Henley, md6/16/1897
Edward C, Jr, b184-, Fauq Co, wNannie Carter
Edward Carter, Sr, b8/1816, PrWi Co, fThomas, mElizabeth Carter Randolph, 1wSarah Beverley, 2wMary Magill Randolph
Edward P, b18--, fThomas, wMary Beverley Turner
Eliza R, bc1850, Fauq Co, fEdward Carter, Sr, (1)mSarah Beverley, hJaquelin A Marshall
Elizabeth, b17--, Bedf Co, fJames, mSally Leftwich, 1w of Price Hopkins, md1801
Fitzhugh, b181-, PrWi Co, fThomas, mElizabeth Carter Randolph
Francis Edward, Sr, b8/28/1861, Alexandria, fAlbert Alexander, mLucinda Jane Swaine, 1wAnnie G Smith, md6/2/1888, 2wAllen Elizabeth Blanks, 3wMattie Lee Jones, md4/19/1908
George M, b18--, Henry Co
Henry, b181-, PrWi Co, fThomas, mElizabeth Carter Randolph
Henry Alexander, b185-, Alexandria, d1889, fAlbert Alexander, mLucinda Jane Swaine
James G, b17--, Bedf Co, fJames, mSally Leftwich
James, b5/7/1759, Bedf Co, fRichard, mNancy John, wSally Leftwich, md8/25/1778
James, b18--, Lune Co, wLucy Rudder
Jane, b18--, Leesburg, Loud Co, fCharles, 1w of James Skinner
Janie Caroline, b185-, Alexandria, fAlbert Alexander, mLucinda Jane Swaine, 1hJames

TURNER (continued)
Edward Merchant, 2hJohn C Fairey
Jeannie, bc1850, fEdward C, Sr, (1)mSarah Beverley, hEdward Carter, md9/1867
Jesse Hoplins, b17--, Bedf Co, fJames, mSally Leftwich, 1wHarriet Burr, 2wSarah Fitzwilson
John Daniel, b18--, NewK Co?, wEliabeth Taylor Robinson
John R, b18--, w-- Armstrong
Joseph A, Sr, b8/6/1839, Grvl Co, wLeila Virginia Cocke
Julia Ann, b17--, Cumb Co, hRobert Clement Brown
Lattie, bc1820, PrWi Co, fThomas, mElizabeth Carter Randolph, hNathan Loughborough
Lavina, b18--, Lee Co?, hWilliam Pennington
Lavinia, b181-, PrWi Co, fThomas, mElizabeth Carter Randolph, hJohn Fauntleroy
Lucy, b18--, Richmond?, hGeorge P Stacy
Lydia Ann, b18--, Loui Co?, d1902, hAndrew Washington Walton
Malinda Virginia, bc1860, Alexandria, fAlbert Alexander, mLucinda Jane Swaine, hPerry C Dukes
Marietta, bc1810, PrWi Co, fThomas, mElizabeth Carter Randolph, hCuthbert Powell
Mary, b17--, Fauq Co, hJohn Ashby
Mary, b1779, Bedf Co, fJames, mSally Leftwich, hJohn Hopkins III, md9/2/1800
Mary Beverley, bc1850, Fauq Co, fEdward Carter, Sr, (1)mSarah Beverley, hEdward P Turner
Mattie, bc1800, Patr Co?, 2w of Richard Thomas
Melancthon, b17--, Bedf Co, fJames, mSally Leftwich
Mildred Otey, bc1800, Bedf Co, fJames, mSally Leftwich, hThomas L Leftwich, md12/22/1829
Nathan Loughborough, bc1850, Fauq Co, fEdward Carter, Sr, (1)m Sarah Beverley

TURNER (continued)
Pitticus, b18--, Nels Co
Randolph, bc1810, PrWi Co, fThomas mElizabeth Carter Randolph
Robert F, b184-, Fauq Co, fEdward Carter, Sr, (1)mSarah Beverley
Ruth E, bc1858, Charleston, Jeff Co, hJesse D Blackard
Sallie Randolph, b186-, Fauq Co, fEdward Carter, Sr, (2)m Mary Magill Randolph, hJohn H Janney
Sarah, b18--, PrWi Co, hWilliam F Dowell
Sarah Coleman, b17--, Albe Co, fJohn, mOrianna Russell, hRobert Barclay
Shirley, b181-, PrWi Co, fThomas, mElizabeth Carter Randolph
Sparrel Tyler, b185-, Patr Co?, wFlora Alice Thomas
Susan Rose, b18--, KiGe Co, fCarolinus, hFrederick Campbell Stewart Hunter
Thomas, b17--, KiG Co, wElizabeth Carter Randolph
Thomas, bc1810, PrWi Co, fThomas, mElizabeth Carter Randolph
Thomas, b184-, Fauq Co, d186-, fEdward Carter, Sr, (1)mSarah Beverley
Virginia, b181-, PrWi Co, fThomas, mElizabeth Carter Randolph
Washington, b1828, Fran Co?, d1890, 1wEve Brubaker, 2w Judith Flory Brumbaugh
William B, b12/5/1845, Lune Co, d1915, fJames, mLucy Rudder, wMissouri Ann Johnson
William L, b17--, Bedf Co, fJames, mSally Leftwich, wNancy Alexander
TURPIN, Eliza, bc1843, Bedf Co, 1hAlbert L Noell, Sr, 2hJ M Noell
Emma Susan, b1829, Manchester, Ches Co, d1906, 3w of John Harris McRae
John C, b4/1842, Amhe Co, fWilliam C, mAlice Smith, wJulia E Jones, md1/26/1870

TURPIN (continued)
Martha, bc1850, Amhe Co, fWilliam C, mAlice Smith, hRobert Bowles
Melvina, bc1850, Amhe Co, fWilliam C, mAlice Smith, hRobert N Carter
William C, b18--, Bedf Co, wAlice Smith
TUTWILER, John, b18--, Rkhm Co?, w-- Dudley
Susan Fannie, b185-, Rkhm Co, fJohn, m-- Dudley, hEdward Massie Chandler
Virginia, bc1843, Rkhm Co?, d1891, fJonathan, hSamuel M Menefee
TWYFORD, --, b18--, hLemuel Pugh
TWYMAN, Anthony, b2/2/1779, Madi Co, fWilliam II, mElizabeth Garnett, 1wSarah Davis
Frances, bc1840, fRobert D, mElizabeth Walker Booton, hFitzhugh Taliaferro
Frances A, b185-, nrWingina, Buck Co, fIverson Lewis, mMartha E Austin
George II, bc1700, Midd Co, fGeorge, mKatherine Montague, wAgatha Buford, md1724
Horace Davis, b7/18/1840, Madi Co, fRobert Davis, mElizabeth Walker Booton, wSallie Warner Nicol, md8/17/1871
Iverson Lewis, b18--, Buck Co?, d1863, wMartha E Austin
John A, b11/27/1856, nrWingina, Buck Co, fIverson Lewis, mMartha E Austin
Mary E, b1822, Oran Co?, hJohn L Andrews
Robert Davis, b1808, Madi Co, fAnthony, mSarah Davis, wElizabeth Walker Booton, md1829
Samuel Rogers, bc1860, nr Wingina, Buck Co, fIverson Lewis, mMartha E Austin
T H, bc1860, Spot Co, wFannie Scott
William, b5/20/1727, Spot Co, fGeorge II, mAgatha Buford, wWinifred Cowherd
William II, b1754, Culp Co, fWilliam, mWinifred Cowherd, wElizabeth Garnett
TYLER, --, bc1810, Lanc Co, 2w

TYLER (continued)
of Addison H Hall
Bettie, b184-, Acco Co, fJohn Dennis, mMary Rebecca Ames, hBenjamin C Conner
Edward Hammett, bc1870, Pula Co, fJames Hoge, mSue Hammett
Frances Brockenbrough, b1/6/1844, Tappahannock, Esse Co, fWat Henry, mJane Louisa Blake, hFrederick Griffith
George, b18--, wBettey Delaney
George, b17--, Caro Co
George, b1817, Caro Co, d1889, wEliza Hoge
George Thomas, Sr, b1843, Acco Co, d1919, fJohn Dennis, mMary Rebecca Ames, 1wAmanda --, 2wMary (Fackler) Sinn, md1874
Henry II, b16--, Williamsburg, JaCi Co, fHenry, wElizabeth Chiles
James Hoge, b8/11/1846, Blenheim, Caro Co, fGeorge, mEliza Hoge, wSue Hammett, md11/16/1868
John, b17--, Williamsburg, JaCi Co, fHenry II, mElizabeth Chiles, wElizabeth Jarrett
John, b2/28/1747, JaCi Co?, fJohn, mElizabeth Jarrett, wMary Marot Armistead
John, b3/29/1790, York Co?, d1862, fJohn, mMary Marot Armistead, 2wJulia Gardiner, md6/26/1844, 1wLetitia Christian, md1813
John Dennis, b18--, Acco Co, fSevern, wMary Rebecca Ames
John S, b184-, Acco Co, fJohn Dennis, mMary Rebecca Ames
Leon Gardiner, bc1850, fJohn, (2)mJulia Gardiner, wAnnie B Tucker, md11/14/1878
Lewis Armistead, b1846, JaCi Co, d1895, wKate Gresham
Margaret, bc1827, Mill Park, PrWi Co, d1871, 2w of Frederick Mortimer Ford, Sr
Mary Armistead, b10/19/1846, Warsaw, Rich Co, fWat Henry, mJane Louisa Blake, hJoseph Mayo
Rebecca, b184-, Acco Co, fJohn Dennis, mMary Rebecca Ames, hAlfred Townsend

TYLER (continued)
Severn, b17--, Acco Co
Wat Henry, b18--, ChCi Co, wJane Louisa Blake
TYNES, Achilles James, b11/29/1833, Shawsville, Mont Co, d1914, wHarriet L Fudge
Buford C, b186-, nrTazewell, Taze Co, fAchilles James, mHarriet L Fudge
Conrad F, bc1870, nrTazewell, Taze Co, fAchilles James, mHarriet L Fudge
Lacey A, bc1870, nrTazewell, Taze Co, fAchilles James, mHarriet L Fudge
TYREE, Mariah Woodward, b18--, Nels Co, fMarkillus Douglas, hWillis Howard Dillard
Sophie, b18--, Amhe Co?, hJoseph H Massie
TYSINGER, Joseph B, b18--, Shen Co?, wSarah Bowman
UMBERGER, Mary J, b9/2/1846, Wyth Co, hJames H Patterson
UNDERHILL, Cassie, b18--, Acco Co, hJennings W Abdell
Louisa Amelia, b18--, Fauq Co, hJames Adam Hathaway, md1/26/1881
UNDERWOOD, Octavia, bc1831, Floy Co, d1914, m-- West, hRobert Lancaster
UPSHUR, Courtney T, b1832, Rose Hill, Esse Co, hHenry Willis Daingerfield
Elizabeth Parker, bc1800, Nhtn Co?, hJohn Evans Nottingham
George L, b1/14/1822, Nhtn Co, fJohn Evans Nottingham, mElizabeth Parker Upshur, wSarah Andrews Parker
Henry L, b185-, Nhtn Co, fGeorge L, mSarah Andrews Parker, wAlice Kerr
John Nottingham, b2/14/1848, Norfolk, fGeorge L, mSarah Andrews Parker, 1wLucy T Whittle, md11/19/1873, 2wElizabeth Spencer Peterkin, md12/11/1879
Sallie Parker, b185-, Nhtn Co, fGeorge L, mSarah Andrews Parker, hThomas C Walston
URBACH, Philip C, Jr, b1843, Weston, Lewi Co, fPhilip C, Sr, wAlice E Heckert
URQUHART, C E, bc1860, Greene Co?, w-- Miller
Fannie Norfleet, b18--, Sout Co, fJames Burwell, hRichard Urquhart Burges, Sr
James Burwell, b18--, Sout Co
UTTERBACK, nancy, bc1800, Fauq Co, hPresley N Jeffries
VADEN, G H, b1851, Hali Co, wE Carrie Tate
Sarah Catherine, b9/23/1843, Ches Co, d1922, hJosiah Thomas Showalter
VAIDEN, Algernon S, Sr, b18--, NewK Co, wTabitha C Kemp
VAIRDEN, --, b17--, Ches Co?, hNelson Winfree
VALENTINE, Mary, b18--, Richmond, 2w of Joseph C Hutcheson
VAN BENTHUYSEN, Jefferson Davis, b18--, wCornelia C Cosby
VANCE, Mary, b3/1/1823, Fred Co, dc1916, hPhilip Benjamin Williams
VANDERSLICE, George Curtis, b18--, Henrico Co?, wNannie Sue Pettit
George Keessee, b11/12/1870, Henrico Co, fGeorge Curtis, mNannie Sue Pettit, wAnnie Ross Phoebus, md1899
VAN HORN, Guy, bc1870, Union, Monr Co
Mary E, b1867, Union, Monr Co, hJoseph M Bauserman, md10/2/1890
Rhuel V, bc1870, Union, Monr Co
Sadie, b186-, Union, Monr Co
VAN LEAR, Ella, b1846, fWilliam, hElliott Guthrie Fishburne
VANMETER, Mary Eliza, b18--, Berk Co?, hHugh Lyle Campbell
VAN NORT, Jacob, b17--, Warr Co, wEda LeHew
Lucinda, b2/19/1808, Front Royal, Warr Co, fJacob, mEda LeHew, hBenjamin Van Nort
Caroline, b1835, Richmond?, hJoseph Hirschberg
VARER, Fannie C, bc1860, Page Co, fHamilton, mMatilda Spitler, hJohn W Shaffer
Hamilton, b18--, Page Co?, wMatilda Spitler
John D, bc1860, wLelia M Ramey
Susan, b18--, Page Co, hJames B

VARER (continued)
Hudson, md3/8/1849
VAUGHAN, --, bc1700, Brun Co?, wElizabeth Ingram
--, b18--, Carr Co, hHenry Lindsay
Cora Antoinette, b18--, Sout Co?, hRobert Judson Camp, md6/24/1880
Fannie Bowling, b18--, hJoseph Henry Vaughan
Garland Estes, b5/9/1870, Danville, Pitt Co, fEgbert Granville, mLucy Guinn Estes, wMarian Jackson, md4/1902
Horace L, b1863, Hano Co, fJoseph Henry, mFannie Bolling, wNannie Towles
James Dutoy, b18--, Henrico Co?, 2h of -- (Elliott) Jennings
John M, b18--, Gooc Co, wNannie Fuqua
Joseph Henry, b18--, wFannie Bowling Vaughan
Margaret Anna, b18--, Lune Co, fH A, hWilliam Henry Ewing
Mary E, b18--, Hali Co, hHerbert Lee Boatwright, Sr, md12/12/1889
William, bc1850, Culp Co?, wMary Foltz
VAUGHN, Egbert Granville, bc1816, Amel Co, fMilton, wLucy Guinn Estes
Fannie L, b18--, Gile Co?, fThomas, hIsaac C Albert
Sarah Elizabeth, bc1850, Amelia Court House, Amel Co, hWilliam Holman Shepherd
VELLINES, Andrew J, b18--, Isle Co?, wMary Rebecca Thomas
Leila J, b18--, Isle Co, fAndrew J, mMary Rebecca Thomas, hRichard Lewis Brewer, Jr
VENABLE, Agnes Woodson, b17--, PrEd Co, hHenry Edward Watkins
Andrew Reid, bc1832, PrEd Co, d1915, wLouise Cabell Carrington
Charles Scott, b128--, wMargaret Cantey McDowell
Clarence Moreland, b4/7/1870, Front Royal, Warr Co, fJames T, mLucy Anne Saffell, wAnnah Mabel Edmondson, md4/9/1903

VENABLE (continued)
Elizabeth, b17--, Cumb Co?, hGoodrich Wilson
Frances, b18--, Farmville, PrEd Co, hAlexander B Carrington
James T, b18--, Warr Co, fJohn, wLucy Ann Saffell
Natalie Embra, bc1870, Charlottesville, Albe Co, fCharles Scott, mMargaret Cantey McDowell, hRaleigh Colston Minor, md6/8/1897
Pearl Horton, bc1870, Farmville, PrEd Co, fWilliam G, mVirginia E Pettit, hWilliam Edward Anderson, md4/30/1901
Rebecca, bc1800, Bath Co, hJames Brinkley
V D, bc1860, Richmond?, wHelen Lea
William G, b7/8/1835, nrFarmville, PrEd Co, d1915, wVirginia E Pettit
William Henry, b9/2/1870, nr Hampden-Sidney, PrEd Co, fAndrew Reid, mLouise Cabell Carrington, wElizabeth Berkley Wight
VERNON, Mary Virginia, b18--, Alexandria?, hSamuel E Cornwell
VERSEN, Bettie D, b18--, Pitt Co, hWilliam B Gardner
VERSER, William Henry, b1/2/1847, nrCrewe, Nott Co, wMary Elizabeth Farrar
VEST, Bettie, bc1850, "Corduroy Farm", Loui Co, fJames M, mMartha Sneed, hA G Hill
Charles B, b10/26/1845, "Corduroy Farm", Loui Co, fJames M, mMartha Sneed
Ida R, bc1850, "Corduroy Farm", Loui Co, fJames M, mMartha Sneed, hJ R Wingfield, md1876
James M, b18--, Loui Co, hMartha Sneed
Louisa M, b1843, "Corduroy Farm", Loui Co, fJames M, mMartha Sneed, hA J Wood
Mary G, b184-, "Corduroy Farm", Loui Co, fJames M, mMartha Sneed
VETER, Saluda A, bc1840, Bedf Co, hJames A Dooley
VIA, George F, bc1870, nrDod-

VIA (continued)
son, Patr Co, fJames R, mMartha E Kroger
Henry W, bc1870, nrDodson, Patr Co, fJames R, mMartha E Kroger
Isaac, b18--, Fran Co, wMartha Cochran
James R, b18--, nrDodson, Patr Co, fFlemmon, wMartha E Kroger
Jesse B, b186-, nrDodson, Patr Co, fJames R, mMartha E Kroger
John Peter, b186-, nrDodson, Patr Co, fJames R, mMartha E Kroger
Martha Adeline, bc1870, nrDodson, Patr Co, fJames R, mMartha E Kroger, hJ F Goode
Mary, b18--, Fran Co, hJoseph Patterson Proffit
Mary R, bc1870, nrDodson, Patr Co, fJames R, mMartha E Kroger, hJ W Fair
Nancy S, bc1870, nrDodson, Patr Co, fJames R, mMartha E Kroger, hA J Wood
Ninnie, bc1870, Fran Co, fWiley, mElizabeth Jenney, hJames Sigmon
Samuel, b18--, Fran Co, d186-, fIsaac, mMartha Cochran
Wiley, b18--, Fran Co, fIsaac, mMartha Cochran, wElizabeth Jenney
William King, b1/10/1868, nr Dodson, Patr Co, d1921, fJames R, mMartha E Kroger, wMary Rose Belle Wood, md2/21/1895
VICARS, Augustus McFarland, b12/26/1852, Cowans Creek, Scot Co, fJoel, wAmy J Fuller
Joel, b18--, Scot Co, fPaul
Paul, b17--, Scot Co, fRobin
VICTOR, Annabelle, b186-, Lynchburg, Camp Co, fHenry Clay, mRebecca McLeod, hW C Goode
Henry Clay, b18--, Lynchburg, Camp Co, fJohn, m-- Tilden, wRebecca McLeod
Henry McLeod, b186-, Lynchburg, Camp Co, fHenry Clay, mRebecca McLeod
John, b17--, Camp Co?, w-- Tilden
John, b2/20/1867, Lynchburg, Camp Co, fHenry Clay, mRebecca McLeod, wFannie Mahood, md1901

VICTOR (continued)
Loulie G, b186-, Lynchburg, Camp Co, fHenry Clay, mRebecca McLeod, hJ R Millner
William Englebert, bc1870, Lynchburg, Camp Co, fHenry Clay, mRebecca McLeod
VIVIAN, Diane, b16--, Midd Co?, hGarret Minor, md10/17/1706
WADDELL, Edmonia L, bc1860, PrGe Co?, d190-, 1w of Edward West Nichols
Harrington, b18--, wSarah McIlwaine
James, b17--, wMary Gordon, md10/7/1767
Sarah Harrison, b18--, d1859, 1w of Clement D Fishburne, md1857
Susanna, b18--, Hano Co, hWilliam West
WADDILL, Charles C, b18--, ChCi Co, fEdmund II, (2)mAnnie L Wight
Edmund, b17--, ChCi Co, fSamuel, mElizabeth Christian, wMary Maynard
Edmund II, b1814, ChCi Co, fEdmund, mMary Maynard, 1wMary L Redwood, 2wAnnie L Wight
Edmund, Jr, b18--, ChCi Co, fEdmund II, (1)mMary L Redwood
Emily Wight, b18--, ChCi Co, fEdmund II, (2)mAnnie L Wight, hW W Bennett
John R, b18--, ChCi Co, fEdmund II, (1)mMary L Redwood
Julia, b18--, ChCi Co, fEdmund II, (2)mAnnie L Wight
Lucy T, b18--, ChCi Co, fEdmund II, (1)mMary L Redwood, hL B Betty
Marguerite, b18--, ChCi Co, fEdmund II, (2)mAnnie L Wight
Mary L, b18--, ChCi Co, fEdmund II, (1)mMary L Redwood, hJames H Christian
Nannie, b18--, ChCi Co, fEdmund II, (1)mMary L Redwood, hJames W Barnes
Nora, b18--, ChCi Co, fEdmund II, (2)mAnnie L Wight, hRobert H Talley
Samuel, b17--, NewK Co, wElizabeth Christian
Samuel P, b12/15/1852, ChCi Co,

WADDILL (continued)
 fEdmund II, (1)mMary L Redwood, wFannie E Henley, md5/16/1882
 William M, b18--, ChCi Co, fEdmund II, (2)mAnnie L Wight
WADDY, Mary E, b18--, Isle Co, hPeter Quarles
WADE, Alice, 1854, Fran Co, d1905, fMarshall E, mAmericus Hale, hJohn W Miles
 Amanda, b18--, Hali Co, d1850, 1w of John R Adams, md1847
 James N, b18--, wDeborah Chaffin
 John Cary, b18-, York Co, wSarah Pumphrey
 Lillie May, b8--, fJames N, mDeborah Chaffin, hCharles Graham Kizer
 Louisa, bc1800, Caro Co?, hJohn M Sale
 Marshall, b1811, Fran Co, d1861, wAmericus Hale
 Mary, b17--, Meck Co, hJohn Speed III
 Sue, b18--, Fran Co, d1919, hJohn J Terrell, md3/17/1857
 Victoria, b18--, Henry Co?, hGeorge W Lester
WAGENER, Isaac C, b18--, Crai Co?, wBlanch Price
WAGGONER, Ann, bc1800, fJohn Melcher, mElizabeth Heiner, hJacob Fishburn
 Christina, b18--, Taze (now Blan) Co, fDaniel, mLucy Ann Day, hThomas Stuart Walker
 Rebecca, b18--, Taze (now Blan) Co, fDaniel, mLucy Ann Day, hRobert Neel
WAGINGTON, Frances, bc1850, Fran Co, fHenry, hElkanah Byrd
WAGNER, ---, bc1850, Fred Co?, wSusan J Canter
 Abigail, b18--, Augu Co, d1883, hJohn Morrison
 Adam, bc1800, Kimberling Valley, Blan (then Gile) Co, fGeorge, m-- Kidd, wElizabeth Hutsell
 David W, b186-, Kimberling Valley, Blan Co, fJames, mElsie Munsey
 George, b17--, Mont Co?, w-- Kidd

WAGNER (continued)
 Jacob A, b3/10/1861, Kimberling Valley, Blan Co, fJames, mElsie Munsey, wJosephine Miller, md12/1881
 James, b1826, Walkers Creek, Blan (then Wyth) Co, d1862, fAdam, mElizabeh Hutsell, wElsie Munsey
 James E, bc1860, wFannie L Bailey
 John F, b12/10/1867, Port Republic, Rkhm Co, fSamuel F, mCecelia Patterson, wBertha V Winegoard, md1/19/1892
 Maggie, bc1870, Port Republic, Rkhm Co, fSamuel F, mCecelia Patterson, hHarry Chandler
 Navo, b186-, Port Republic, Rkhm Co, d1887, fSamuel F, mCecelia Patterson
 Newton L, b186-, Port Republic, Rkhm Co, fSamuel F, mCecelia Patterson
 Samuel F, bc1830, Augu Co, d1880, wCecelia Patterson
 Susan, b1837, nrFincastle, Bote Co, d1884, hNathan M Leslie
WAID, Charles, b18--, Fran Co, fJames, Sr
 George, b18--, Fran Co, fJames, Sr
 James, Jr, b18--, Fran Co, d186-, fJames, Sr
 John Lewis, b18--, Fran Co, fJames, Sr, wAnna Mary Smith
WAKEFIELD, Anne, bc1854, Portsmouth, Norf Co, d1921, hWilliam Frederick Lintz, Sr
WAKEMAN, J O, bc1840, Shen Co?, wLydia Wilkins
 Jonas, bc1830, Shen Co?, d1922, wFrances Copp
WALDEN, Harriet, bc1800, Bedf Co, hJustus Hancock
 John, b17--, wMartha Hopkins, md4/6/1786
WALDON, A A, bc1840, Rkhm Co?, wCatherine Williamson
WALDRON, Alexander R, b185-, nrTazewell, Taze Co, fRice J, mRebecca Beavers
 Elizabeth Rebecca, bc1860, nr Tazewell, Taze Co, fRice J, mRebecca Beaver, h-- Beavers
 John W, b11/14/1852, nrTaze-

WALDRON (continued)
well, Taze Co, fRice J, mRebecca Beavers, 1wMary Gamble, md2/1/1877, 2wMrs Alice (Taylor) Baldwin, md6/17/1897
Julia Ann, b185-, nrTazewell, Taze Co, fRice J, mRebecca Beavers, hDoak R Payne
Moses Hansley, b185-, nrTazewell, Taze Co, fRice J, mRebecca Beavers
Raleigh W, b185-, nrTazewell, Taze Co, fRice J, mRebecca Beavers
Rice J, b1827, Taze Co, d1920, wRebecca Beavers
WALFORD, Charles Paterson, Sr, b12/7/1853, Richmond, fThomas Logan D, wEstelle Binford
Thomas Logan D, b9/25/1829, Henrico Co, fEdward
WALK, Matilda, b1843, Wyth Co, hJoseph Poole
WALKE, John, b17--, Amel Co?, 2h of Hannah Watkins
Martha Hannah, b17--, Amel Co, fJohn, mHannah (Watkins) Finney, hSpence Wooldridge
WALKER, A C, bc1860, Bote Co, wEsteline Robinson
Ajax, b1794, Amhe Co, fRobert, mNancy Floyd Powell, wLucy Meriwether Lewis
Alexander, b175-, Oran Co, fBenjamin, mElizabeth Taylor
Ann Eliza, b18--, Dinw Co, fRobert, hMeriwether Bathurst Brodnax
Annie T, b18--, Crai Co, fGeorge Hervison, (2)mSarah McLaugherty
Avis, b18--, Richmond, fDavid N, mAvis Barney, hCharles Venable Carrington, md6/6/1894
Baylor, b171-, KiQu Co, fJohn, wFrances Hill
Benjamin, b17--, Oran Co?, wElizabeth Taylor
Benjamin, b175-, Oran Co, fBenjamin, mElizabeth Taylor
Benjamin Alexander Stuart, Sr, b180-, nrLurich, Monr Co, fThomas, mEleanor Stuart, w--Byrnsides
Benjamin Alexander Stuart, Jr, b18--, Monr Co?, fBenjamin

WALKER (continued)
Alexander Stuart, Sr, m--Byrnsides, wRhoda J Peters
Benjamin Stuart, b182-, Blan Co, fThomas Stuart, mChristina Waggoner
Bessie Carter, b186-, Bushfield, West Co, fSamuel, mClarissa Rebecca Harding, hJohn M Omohundro, md10/31/1889
Benedict, bc1800, West Co, dc1892, wHannah Wright
Bettie, b18--, hJoseph Henley
Charles Elgan, b185-, Taze (now Blan) Co, fDaniel Alexander, mHarriett Williams Neel
Charles M, b18--, PrEd Co?, d1905, wElla E Warren
Charles R, bc1860, Bedf Co?, wLula Dooley
Clara, bc1870, Bushfield, West Co, fSamuel, mClarissa Rebecca Harding, hWillie Y Morgan
Cyrus Harding, b1/27/1859, "Snowden Park", Nhld Co, fW W, m-- Harding, wMary Rosa Starke, md10/27/1887
Daniel, bc1800, Wyth Co, fDelarious
Daniel Alexander, b4/8/1824, Blan Co, fThomas Stuart, mChristina Waggoner, wHarriett Williams Neel
David M, b8/14/1853, nrChesterfield, Ches Co, fHiram Lee, (1)mLetitia Sadler, wTheodosia Franklin
David N, b18--, wAvis Barney
Dorothy Alice, b185-, Taze (now Blan) Co, fDaniel Alexander, mHarriett Williams Neel, h--Elswick
Eliza Ann, b18--, Lune Co?, hGeorge W Kirk
Elizabeth, b1745, Lune Co, hSamuel Ege
Fannie S, b18--, Crai Co, fGeorge Herveson, (2)mSarah McLaugherty
Fannie Singleton, b1844, Walkerton, KiQu Co, hAlexander Fleet Bagby
Fannie LeGrand, b18--, Smyt Co?, fDaniel, hWilliam Taylor
Freeman, b17--, 1h of Frances Belfield

WALKER (continued)
George Herveson, b18--, Bote Co, d1882, 1wMagdeline McLaugherty, 2wSarah McLaugherty
George T, b18--, Crai Co, fGeorge Herveson, (2)mSarah McLaugherty
Hiram Lee, b18--, nrChesterfield, Ches Co, fLauncelot, 1wLetitia Sadler, 2wElizabeth Wilson
Isabella Gilman, b1865, Lynchburg, Camp Co, fThomas, mCatherine Dabney, hJohn Penn Lee, md12/2/ 1896
James, b176--, Oran Co, fBenjamin, mElizabeth Taylor
James, b18--, West Co?, wAnna E Beale
James Robert McDaniel, b185-, Taze (then Blan) Co, fDaniel Alexander, mHarriett Williams Neel
Jennie, b18--, Buck Co, hJohn Archer Scott, Jr
Jeremiah, b176-, Oran Co, fBenjamin, mElizabeth Taylor
John, b175-, Oran Co, fBenjamin, mElizabeth Taylor
John F, b18--, Bote Co, dc1904, fGeorge Herveson, (1)mMagdeline McLaugherty, wMargaret Jones
John Randolph, b5/12/1850, Taze (now Blan) Co, fDaniel Alexander, mHarriett Williams Neel, wMary Jane Brown, md12/1/1875
John S, b18--, Camp Co? wLucy Otey
Joseph, b176-, Oran Co, fBenjamin, mElizabeth Taylor
Josephine V, b185-, nrChesterfield, Ches Co, fHiram Lee, (1)mLetitia Sadler, hCharles A Blankenship
Katherine, b18--, Lune Co?, hBenjamin J Smith
Laura Ellen, b185-, Taze (then Blan) Co, fDaniel Alexander, mHarriett Williams Neel
Louisa, b18--, Monr Co?, fBenjamin Alexander Stuart, Sr, m-- Byrnsides
Lydia, b18--, Fred Co?, hJohn Lupton
M Lee, b185-, nrChesterfield,

WALKER (continued)
Ches Co, fHiram Lee, (1)m Letitia Sadler
Maria, bc1800, Rkbr Co?, fThomas, hRichard Duke
Martha, b17--, Lune Co, hSamuel Ingram
Martha Elizabeth, b18--, Fran Co, 1w of Abram Booth Walker, md11/3/1847
Mary, b17--, fFreeman, mFrances Belfield, hWilliam Brodnax
Mary, b1845, PrEd Co, hLawson Morrissett
Mary A, b185-, nrChesterfield, Ches Co, fHiram Lee, (1)m Letitia Sadler
Mary E, b183-, Blan Co, fThomas Stuart, mChristina Waggoner, hJohn Lambert
Mattie A, b18--, Crai Co, fGeorge Herveson, (2)mSarah McLaugherty
Minnie, bc1870, Bushfield, West Co, fSamuel, mClarissa Rebecca Harding, hJohn P Bailey
Nancy Thornton, bc1800, hJames Blanton
Rebecca Jane, b6/20/1816, Waterford, Loud Co, hJames C Janney
Robert, b17--, KiQu Co, fBaylor, mFrances Hill, wNancy Floyd Powell
Robert, b176-, Oran Co, fBenjamin, mElizabeth Taylor
Roberta Ellis, b6/24/1839, nrClarkesville, Meck Co, hJohn R Jeter, Jr
S N, bc1850, Pitt Co?, wLizzie Hughes
Samuel, bc1760, Oran Co, fBenjamin, mElizabeth Taylor
Samuel, b1832, "Poplar Plain", West Co, d1897, fBenedict, wClarissa Rebecca Harding
Samuel B, b7/27/1866, Bushfield, West Co, fSamuel, mClarissa Rebecca Harding, wSallie Shackford, md5/18/1893
Sanders, b175-, Oran Co, fBenjamin, mElizabeth Taylor
Sarah, b1815, PrEd Co, d1865, 2w of Joseph Dupuy
Sarah, b17--, Hano Co?, hRobert Page

WALKER (continued)
Thomas, Jr, b17--, fThomas, Sr
Thomas, b1715, KiQu Co, fJohn
Thomas, b12/18/1764, Oran Co, d1853, fBenjamin, mElizabeth Taylor, wEleanor Stuart
Thomas, b18--, wCatherine Dabney
Thomas Fowler, b183-, Blan Co, fThomas Stuart, mChristina Waggoner
Thomas Stuart, b3/1802, nr Lurich, Monr Co, fThomas, mEleanor Stuart, wChristina Waggoner
Vernon, bc1870, West Co, fJames, mAnna E Beale, hGeorge C Mann, md6/1895
Volney, b18--, Haybattle Farm, nrWalkerton, KiQu Co, wJuliet Harrison
W W, b18--, West Co, w-- Harding
Waverly T, b2/3/1855, nrChesterfield, Ches Co, fHiram Lee, (1)mLetitia Sadler, wLena Lambert
William, b175-, Oran Co, fBenjamin, mElizabeth Taylor
William, b18--, Ches Co, fLancelot
William H, b1/9/1846, Haybattle Farm, nrWalkerton, KiQu Co, d1918, fVolney, mJuliet Harrison, wAnnie Elizabeth Toombs
William Pierce, b182-, Blan Co, fThomas Stuart, mChristina Waggoner
Willie H, b185-, nrChesterfield, Ches Co, fHiram Lee, (1)mLetitia Sadler, hJ W Clark
WALL, Elizabeth Dickson, b1838, Winchester, Fred Co, fWilliam T, mElizabeth Van Horn, hJames W Barr
John Gibbons, b18--, Surr Co, wAnne Petty
John Hiram, b9/3/1855, Drakes Branch, Char Co, d1922, fJohn Gibbons, mAnne Petty, wLula Simmons
Joseph Benjamin, bc1870, Meherrin, PrEd Co, wLucy Bidgood
W W, b18--, Fred Co?, wMary Elizabeth Barr
WALLACE, ---, b18--, Fred Co?,

WALLACE (continued)
wSusan J Canter
Charlotte, b18--, Richmond?, fWilliam, hBenjamin Tapscott
Elizabeth Brown, b2/19/1868, Fredericksburg, Spot Co, fHowson, mElizabeth S Crouch, hCharles Armistead Blanton
George Preston, b12/6/1845, Rkbr Co, fSamuel, 2wSusan Bond
Howson, b18--, wElizabeth S Crouch
Mary, b18--, Augu Co?, hJohn P McClure
Mary, b1847, Mont Co, d1883, hJohn Jefferson Miller
Samuel, b1814, Rkbr Co, d1895
Samuel Gordon, b1800, Staf Co?, wMary Buchanan Hansford
Virginia Belle, bc1870, Staf Co, fSamuel Gordon, mMary Buchanon Hansford, hRichard Henry Lee Chichester, md6/6/1895
WALLER, Benjamin, b17--, York Co?, fJohn
John, b18--, nrCody, Hali Co, d1879, 1w-- Clay
Kate, b7/24/1858, Staf Co, hRobert S Barrett, md1876
Martha, b17--, Williamsburg, JaCi Co, fBenjamin, hWilliam Taylor
Martha, b18--, Bedf Co?, hJohn Hancock
Nelson Samuel, b1851, Front Royal, Warr Co, wRebecca B Gardner
Robert T, b9/15/1846, nrCody, Hali Co, fJohn, m-- Clay, wNannie M Carr
WALSTON, Thomas C, bc1850, Nhtn Co?, wSallie Parker Upshur
WALTER, John A, b18--, wSallie Belle Parr
WALTERS, Annie, b18--, Shen Co, d1866, 2w of Thomas Baker, Sr
Eli, b18--, Rkhm Co?, wSarah J Spitzer
Kate, b18--, Fair Co, hIsaiah Bready
Mitchell, b18--, wMaria Huff
R L, c1860, Shen Co?, wMary Elizabeth Golladay
Sarah, b181-, Fred Co, hDaniel Huff

WALTHAL, Mary, b17--, hSamuel Hatcher
WALTHALL, Edgar, b185-, Camp Co, fIsaac, mLouise Layne
Isaac, b18--, Camp Co, wLouise Layne
Mattie, b186-, Camp Co, fIsaac, mLouise Layne, hJ B Poindexter
Newton Isaac, b11/16/1859, Camp Co, d1921, fIsaac, mLouise Layne, wCarrie Cage
Nolie, b185-, Camp Co, fIsaac, mLouise Layne, hM H Harris
R O, b185-, Camp Co, fIsaac, mLouise Layne
Walter E, b185-, Camp Co, fIsaac, mLouise Layne
WALTON, Aggie, b17--, fThomas, Sr, mMartha Cox
Alice W, b185-, Woodstock, Shen Co, fMoses, mEmily M Lauck, hCharles Haslett
Andrew Washington, b18--, Louise Court House, Loui Co, d1899, wLydia Ann Turner
Annie W, b185-, Woodstock, Shen Co, fMoses, mEmily M Lauck, h-- Hendry
Charles Cortlandt, Sr, b1849, Cumb Co, fRichard Payton, mMary J Woodson, wMary Kearney Phillips
David H, b186-, Woodstock, Shen Co, fMoses, mEmily Lauck
Emma, bc1860, Woodstock, Shen Co, fMoses, mEmily Lauck, hJohn H Keller
Fanny, b17--, fThomas, Sr, mMartha Cox
George, b17--, fRobert, mMary Hobson
Josiah, b17--, fRobert, mMary Hobson
Lucius D, b1/26/1847, PrEd Co, wNannie S Scott
Mary E, b18--, hOscar Herring
Morgan L, b10/13/1853, Woodstock, Shen Co, fMoses, mEmily M Lauck, wMollie A March, md1/26/1876
Mary W, b185-, Woodstock, Shen Co, fMoses, mEmily M Lauck, hEdgar D Newman
Moses, b17--, Shen Co
Moses, bc1827, Shen Co, fReuben
Nancy Hobson, b17--, Cumb Co?,

WALTON (continued)
fRobert, mMary Hobson, hDaniel Brown, md11/24/1808
Polly, b17--, fThomas, Sr, mMartha Cox
Reuben, bc1800, nrNew Market, Shen Co, fMoses
Robert, b17--, fThomas, Sr, mMartha Cox, wMary Hobson
Samuel A, b185-, Woodstock, Shen Co, d1920, fMoses, mEmily M Lauck
Thomas, Jr, b17--, fThomas, Sr, mMartha Cox
Thomas III, b17--, fRobert, mMary Hobson
William, b17--, fThomas, Sr, mMartha Cox
William, b17--, wMary Leftwich, md2/2/1778
William Bledsoe, Sr, b11/9/1869, Louisa Court House, Loui Co, fAndrew Washington, mLydia Ann Turner, wM Annie Johnson, md1895
William T, b18--, Danville, Pitt Co, wAnna Carter
WAMPLER, --, bc1810, Rkhm Co?, wKatie Myers
--, b18--, Wyth Co, hEphraim Etter
Annie, b18--, Timberville, Rkhm Co, fMartin, 2w of Christian Hollar
Frederick, b18--, Rkhm Co, d1897, wAnna Driver
John, b18--, Shen Co?, wMary Cline
John, b1835, Broadway, Rkhm Co, wCatherine Miller
John, b186-, Rkhm Co?, fFrederick, mAnna Driver
Joseph, bc1860, Rkhm Co, fFrederick, mAnna Driver
Lizzie S, bc1870, Rkhm Co, fFrederick, mAnna Driver, hJohn W Myers, md5/10/1890
Minnie, bc1870, Rkhm Co, fFrederick, mAnna Driver, h-- Wenger
Samuel, bc1830, Shen Co, wMary Good
Sarah, bc1840, Shen Co, fJohn, hSamuel Good
Saylor, bc1860, Rkhm Co, fFrederick, mAnna Driver

WAMPLER (continued)
Susan, bc1832, Rkhm Co, d1917, fJohn, mMary Cline, hDaniel Flory
WARD, A W, b9/25/1859, Northside, Albe Co, fRichard F, mMary F Head, wElla J W Mayo, md9/7/1881
Caroline, b18--, Buch Co?, hWilliam Ratliff
Catherine, b16--, Pitt Co, fBryan, hJames Nowlan
Charles P, bc1850, Albe Co?, wEliza E Ward
Eliza E, b186--, Northside, Albe Co, fRichard F, mMary F Head, hCharles P Ward
Ella, b18--, Norfolk?, hHenry Clay Smith
J R, b185-, Northside, Albe Co, fRichard F, mMary F Head
James Dearing, b186-, Lynchburg, Camp Co, mMartha Henry
James R, b18--, Wyth Co?, wLucinda Caroline Hollinsworth
L E, b186-, Northside, Albe Co, fRichard F, mMary F Head
Richard F, b18--, Albe Co, fWilliam S, wMary F Head
Robert H, b18--, Camp Co, d1895, mMartha Henry, wSusan Dearing
William H, b185-, Northside, Albe Co, fRichard F, mMary F Head
WARDE, Hugh H, bc1860, Nels Co?, wLucy M Massie
WARDEN, Benjamin, b7/21/1790, Hard Co, fWilliam, mSarah Crisman, wLucinda Van Nort
Benjamin, b183-, Hard Co, fBenjamin, mLucinda Van Nort
Daisy Cloud, b186-, Hard Co, fJacob, mSusan Clagett, hGeorge W Atkinson
Grace G, b186-, Hard Co, fJacob, mSusan Clagett, hSamuel H Parkins
Harry Clagett, b186-, Hard Co, fJacob, mSusan Clagett
Jacob, b178-, Hard Co, fWilliam, mSarah Crisman
Jacob, b8/10/1841, Hard Co, fBenjamin, mLucinda Van Nort, wSusan Clagett, md1/281860
James, bc1750, Hard Co, fWil-

WARDEN (continued)
liam Wallace, mElizabeth Williams
James, b178-, Hard Co, fWilliam, mSarah Crisman
James, bc1840, Hard Co, d186-, fBenjamin, mLucinda Van Nort
Julius, b183-, Hard Co, fBenjamin, mLucinda Van Nort
Magdalene, b178-, Hard Co, fWilliam, mSarah Crisman, hJames Baker
Mary, bc1790, Hard Co, fWilliam, mSarah Crisman, h--Sperry
Nimrod, b178-, Hard Co, fWilliam, mSarah Crisman
Sarah, bc1790, Hard Co, fWilliam, mSarah Crisman, 1h--Beeler, 2hAbe Isler
Scotia, b178-, Hard Co, fWilliam, mSarah Crisman, h--Hayden
William, b1749, Hard Co, fWilliam Wallace, mElizabeth Williams, wSarah Crisman
William Isac, b178-, Hard Co, fWilliam, mSarah Crisman
WARE, S H, bc1860, Henry Co?, wMary N Taylor
WARING, Elizabeth Susan, b1829, nrTappahannock, Esse Co, d1870, fWilliam Lowry, 1hJohn Waller Faulconer, 2hJohn S Trible
Richard H, b18--, wEugenia Saunders
William Lowry, b17--, Esse Co
WARNER, Elizabeth, b16--, hJohn Lewis
Mildred, b1---, Glou Co?, hJohn Lewis
WARREN, Elizabeth, bc1820, Wash Co, hHenry B Roberts, Sr
Ellen, b18--, PrEd Co, hCharles M Walker
Joseph W, Sr, bc1833, Surr Co, d1904, wVirginia Hopkins
Joshua S, b1830, Nhtn Co, wEllen Evans
L D, b18--, wEmma Morris
Littleton Adrian, bc1845, Petersburg, Dinw Co, d1884, fHoward E, wMartha McCabe
Thomas J, b1839, Wash Co, wMary E Davis

WARREN (continued)
William Cabell, b8/26/1870, "Midway Place", nrHot Springs, Bath Co, fJoseph W, Sr, mVirginia Hopkins, wMaud Lewis Hopkins
WARRING, Elizabeth, b18--, Esse Co?, hWilliam F Smith
WARWICK, --, b17--, Warw Co, hConrad Fudge
Corbin, b18--, Richmond?, wSarah --
Julia, b18--, hHenry Moncure
Polly, b17--, Camp Co?, fWilliam, 1w of Christopher Winfree
WASHBURN, Rosanna, b18--, Patr Co?, hGeorge W Lawless
WASHINGTON, Anne, b17--, fLawrence, hJohn Stith
Betty, bc1730, hJohn Lewis
Frances, b17--, fCharles, 2w of Burgess Hall
George S, bc1770, wLucy Payne
John Boyd, bc1850, Caro Co?, wNannie Ratcliffe Thornton
John H, b18--, wSelina Carter
WASSON, John, b1800, Smyt Co, fJohn, w-- Grant
William H, b1846,Smyt Co, d1896, fJohn, m-- Grant, wMary Pierce Buckles
WATERS, Emily Gilen, b18--, Scot Co, hCowan W Carter
Jonathan, bc1810, Fauq Co?, wMary Swart
Robert, bc1840, PrWi Co?, 1w Maggie Dowell, 2wSarah Dowell
Thomas Edmond, b9/25/1869, nrCraig, Roan Co, fJohn, mMary Bell
William, bc1850, 1h of Bessie Woolf
WATKINS, A S, b18--, Oran Co, wMary Watkins
Asa Dickinson, b6/5/1856, nr Farmville, PrEd Co, fFrancis Nathaniel, mMartha Ann Scott, wNannie Edwards Forbes, md9/2/1886
Agnes Woodson, b183-, nrFarmville, PrEd Co, fFrances Nathaniel, mMartha Ann Scott, hMilton P Jarnagin
Benjamin, b17--, Ches Co?, wElizabeth Cary

WATKINS (continued)
Bettie Irving, bc1836, nrFarmville, PrEd Co, d1899, fFrancis Nathaniel, mMartha Ann Scott, hSamuel B McKinney
Charles B, b18--, Meck Co?, wMary Ann Womack
Charles T, bc1860, nrFarmville, PrEd Co, dc1880, fFrancis Nathaniel, mMartha Ann Scott
Charlotte, bc1840, nrFarmville, PrEd Co, fFrancis Nathaniel, mMartha Ann Scott, hUncus McClure
Constant, b17--, Henrico Co?, hObediah Woodson
Emily D, b186-, PrEd Co, fRichard H, mMary Dupuy, hEdward Lawrence Dupuy, md1/3/1889
Francis, b17--, Ches Co, fBenjamin, mElizabeth Cary
Francis, b18--, Chickahominy, Hano Co, fThomas, wAgnes Woodson
Francis Nathaniel, b1812, nr Hampden-Sidney, PrEd Co, fHenry Edward, mAgnes Woodson Venable, wMartha Ann Scott
Frank Sampson, bc1850, nrFarmville, PrEd Co, fFrancis Nathaniel, mMartha Ann Scott
George P, bc1850, Camp Co?, wJinnie Watts
Hannah, b17--, Ches Co, fBenjamin, mElizabeth Cary, 1hBenjamin Finney, 2hJohn Walke
Henry B, b3/13/1859, PrEd Co, fRichard V, mMary Michaux, wBlanch Leveredge, md1886
Henry E, b18--, PrEd Co
Henry E, bc1835, nrFarmville, PrEd Co, dc1900, fFrancis Nathaniel, mMartha Ann Scott, wJane Reed McNutt
Henry Edward, b1783, PrEd Co, f1856, fFrancis, wAgnes Woodson Venable
James A, b18--, ElCi Co?, wMary Whiting
John, b18--, Camp Co?, wLouise Kendricks
Julia, b4/20/1870, Buffalo Springs, Meck Co, fCharles B, mMary Ann Womack, hWilliam Dabbs Blanks, md6/24/1891

WATKINS (continued)
Julia A, b18--, hTazewell Morton Carrington, md1/21/1886
Katherine Cabell, bc1840, nr Farmville, PrEd Co, fFrancis Nathaniel, mMartha Ann Scott, hM Cardosa
Lena Michaux, bc1870, PrEd Co, fRichard V, mMary Michaux
Maggie Leigh, b186-, nrFarmville, PrEd Co, fFrancis Nathaniel, mMartha Ann Scott
Manley, b186-, PrEd Co, fRichard V, mMary Michaux
Mary, b18--, hA S Watkins
Mary, b18--, Norfolk?, hHenry Singleton Reynolds
Micajah, bc1800, Hali Co, hJames King
Mildred, b17--, Pitt Co?, hAbraham Nowlin
Pattie B, b185-, nrFarmville, PrEd Co, fFrancis Nathaniel, mMartha Ann Scott
Rachael, b16--, Malvern Hill, -- Co, 2w of Robert Woodson
Richard H, b18--, PrEd Co?, wMary Dupuy
Richard V, bc1830, PrEd Co, fHenry E, wMary Michaux
Sally, b1748, Cumb Co, dc1786, hJohn Spencer
Samuel Woodson, b185-, nrFarmville, PrEd Co, fFrancis Nathaniel, mMartha Ann Scott
Virginia, bc1840, Appo Co?, hWilliam C Nowlin
Virginia Douglas, b18--, Hali Co?, fRichard V, 2w of William Randolph Barksdale, md6/28/1905
WATLINGTON, Ann, b18--, Robin's Neck, Glou Co, d1897, 2w of Levi Pace Corr
Mary Elizabeth, b4/1/1846, KiQu Co, dc1910, hGeorge W Kerr
WATSON, Ann, b17--, Loui Co, fJames, mBarbary --, hRobert/Robin Michie
Anne, b18--, Pitt Co, hLevi Watson
Annie, bc1870, Buch Co, fJames Clark, Sr, mVirginia Butler, hWilliam Wolf
C A, bc1849, Carr Co, fJohn, mCharlotte Lindsay, wAmanda

WATSON (continued)
Chitwood
Daniel E, bc1800, Albe Co
Egbert Read, b1810, Albe Co, fJohn, mJane H Price, 1wMary Kelly Norris, md9/3/1833, 2wJane Lynn Creigh, md4/29/1856, 3wMrs Elizabeth (White) Kent
Egbert Richard, b184-, Albe Co, fEgbert Read, (1)mMary Kelly Norris
Ella Norris, b184-, Albe Co, fEgbert Read, (1)mMary Kelly Norris, hGeorge Perkins
Elizabeth, b17--, Loui Co, fJames, mBarbary --, h-- Michie
Elizabeth, bc1800, Alexandria, hHugh Smith
Elizabeth, b18--, Chatham, Pitt Co, fThomas Jeffeson, mElizabeth Leonard Duffel, hJohn E Christian
Elizabeth, b10/7/1829, nrChatham, Pitt Co, d1905, fShimer, mMary Farthing, hDavid Samuel Motley, md1850
Emmett St Clair, b1866, Buch Co, fJames Clark, mVirginia Butler, wJulia Butler Winn
Fletcher Bangs, Sr, b11/27/1841, d1917, Chatham, Pitt Co, fThomas Jefferson, Jr, mElizabeth Leonard Duffel, wPatty Booker Tredway, md6/22/1870
Harry Lee, b186-, Buch Co, fJames Clark, Sr, mVirginia Butler
Helen Carter, b184-, Albe Co, fEgbert Read, (1)mMary Kelly Norris, hJames M Rawlings
Hortensia Hay, b183-, Albe Co, fEgbert Read, (1)mMary Kelly Norris
Hubert, b18--, Bedf Co, fJordan, wWillie A White
James, b17--, wEva Finch
James, b17--, Loui Co?, dc1776, wBarbara --
James II, b17--, Loui Co, fJames, mBarbara --
James Clark, b1832, Charlottesville, Albe Co, wVirginia Butler
James Clark, Jr, b186-, Buch

WATSON (continued)
Co, fJames Clark, Sr, mVirginia Butler
Jane, b18--, Richmond?, hWilliam Henry Fry
Joanna, b18--, Pitt Co, fLevi, mAnne, hJohn Motley
John, b17--, fJames, mEva Finch, wJane H Price
John, b18--, Carr Co?, wCharlotte Lindsay
John Davis, b183-, Albe Co, fEgbert Read, (1)mMary Kelly Norris
Jordan, b18--, Bedf Co
Levi, b18--, Pitt Co, wAnne Watson
Mary, b17--, Loui Co, fJames, mBarbara --, hDavid Wood
Mary, b17--, PrEd Co, hObediah Woodson
Mary Kelly, b183-, Albe Co, fEgbert Read, (1)mMary Kelly Norris, hJacob Henry Smith
Mary Brown, b186-, Augu Co?, fJohn M, 1w of Samuel Moore Donald, md1884
Nannie Elizabeth, b18--, Albe Co, fDaniel E, hHawes Nicholas Coleman
Parthenia, b18--, Pitt Co, hMalberry Coppridge
Sally, b17--, Loui Co, fJames, mBarbara --, hHenry Paulette
Shimer, bc1800, Pitt Co, wMary Farthing
Shimer H, bc1830, nrChatham, Pitt Co, d1914, fShimer, mMary Farthing
Sidney, b18--, Albe Co
Thomas Jefferson, Jr, b1806, Chatham, Pitt Co, d1894, fThomas Jefferson, Sr, wElizabeth Leonard Duffel
Wilbur Fisk, b18--, Chatham, Pitt Co, fThomas Jefferson, Jr, mElizabeth Duffel
William B, b186-, Buch Co, fJames Clark, Sr, mVirginia Butler
William Opie, bc1850, Albe Co, fEgbert Read, (1)mMary Kelly Norris
William R, bc1830, nrChatham, Pitt Co, fShimer, mMary Farthing

WATT, Bettie, b1854, Richmond, hManfred Call, Sr
WATTS, Alice, b182-, Flat Creek, Camp Co, fEdward, mElizabeth Breckenbridge
Ann, b181-, Flat Creek, Camp Co, fEdward, mElizabeth Breckenbridge
Bell W, b18--, Amhe Co, 2w of John P Pettyjohn
Betty, bc1770, Culp Co?, fWilliam, hWinston Durrett
Edward, b4/7/1779, PrEd Co, fWilliam, mMary Scott, wElizabeth Breckenbridge
Edward II, b182-, Flat Creek, Camp Co, fEdward, mElizabeth Breckenbridge
Elizabeth, bc1820, Flat Creek, Camp Co, fEdward, mElizabeth Breckenbridge
Emma, b182-, Flat Creek, Camp Co, fEdward, mElizabeth Breckenbridge
Frances, b17--, KiQu Co?, hJohn Motley
Henrietta, bc1830, Flat Creek, Camp Co, fEdward, mElizabeth Breckenbridge
Hubert Bruce, b12/6/1857, Bedf Co, fJames Winston, mMary Elizabeth Jones
Jacob, b1731, Albe Co?, d1821, wElizabeth Durrett
James, b1/21/1767, Culp Co?, d1828, fWilliam, wElizabeth Hamilton
James B, b181-, Flat Creek, Camp Co, fEdward, mElizabeth Breckenbridge
James Winston, b1833, Bedf Co, d1906, fRichard Davis, mIsabella Eagan Newell, wMary Elizabeth Jones, md2/22/1854
Jinnie, b185-, Bedf Co, fJames Winston, mMary Elizabeth HJones, hGeorge P Watkins
John A, bc1740, Portsmouth, Norf Co, fArthur
John Allen, b3/30/1855, Beaver Dam, Bote Co, fWilliam, mMary Allen, wGertrude Lee, md4/12/1880
Letitia, b182-, Flat Creek, Camp Co, fEdward, mElizabeth Breckenbridge

WATTS (continued)
Lucy, bc1770, Culp Co?, fWilliam, h-- Allen
Mary S, b181-, Flat Creek, Camp Co, fEdward, mElizabeth Breckenbridge
Maude, b186-, Bedf Co, fJames Winston, mMary Elizabeth Jones, hOliver D Bachelor
Newton C, b9/7/1852, nrWaynesboro, Augu Co, fWellington H, mMary Ann Fauber, wBetty Barnhart, md1875
Richard Davis, b9/28/1793, Culp Co?, fJames, mElizabeth Hamilton, wIsabella Eagen Newell
Richard Thomas, Sr, b9/5/1838, Bedf Co, d1910, fRichard Davis, mIsabella Eagan Newell, wEmma Margaret Hurt, md4/22/1875
Patsy, bc1770, Culp Co?, h-- White
Thomas Ashby, Sr, b9/9/1866, Bedf Co, fJames Winston, mMary Elizabeth Jones, wFanny C Cheatwood
Virginia, b18--, nrLancaster Court House, Lanc Co, 1w of Joseph Walter Anderson
Washington, b176-, Culp Co?, fWilliam
Washington H, b18--, Albe Co, fDavid, wMary Ann Fauber
William, bc1744, Portsmouth, Norf Co, fArthur, wMary Scott
William, b17--, Albe Co?, fJacob, mElizabeth Durrett
William, b12/20/1817, Flat Creek, Camp Co, fEdward, mElizabeth Breckenbridge, wMary Allen, md10/1850
William, b17--, Culp Co, fThomas
WAY, Edward C, bc1860, wCarrie Branch Marshall
Elizabeth Mary, b8/8/1817, Rkhm Co?, d1869, hJoseph H Shue
WAYLAND, Abram, b18-, Crozet, Albe Co, fJeremiah, wMartha Woodson
Agnes, b186-, nrMt Jackson, Shen Co, fJohn Wesley, Jr, mAnna Kagey, 1hJacob Grabill, 2hRobert Wardell
Charles Lee, b4/25/1861, Augu

WAYLAND (continued)
Co, fAbram, mMartha Woodson, wLizzie Gantt Bourne, md1889
Edward Franklin, bc1850, Augu Co?, wHarriet Elizabeth Plecker
Jacob Wesley, bc1870, nrMt Jackson, Shen Co, fJohn Wesley, Jr, mAnna Kagey
James Worth, b186-, nrMt Jackson, Shen Co, fJohn Wesley, Jr, mAnna Kagey
John Wesley, Sr, bc1800, Madi Co?, wMiriam Huffman
John Wesley, Jr, bc1830, Shen Co, fJohn Wesley, Sr, mMiriam Huffman, wAnna Kagey
Mary, b18--, Albe Co, hWilliam H Harris
Susan Marion, b18--, Madi Co?, hEphraim Dutton Fray
WAYT, John, b18--, Oran Co, 2w Sarah Allen Bell
Newton, b1838, Staunton, Augu Co, fJohn, (2)mSarah Allen Bell, wJulia B Heiskell
WEATHERALL, Eliza, b18--, hPeyton L Thomas
WEATHERLY, Margaret, bc1800, Nans Co, hOliver Harrell
Samuel S, b18--, Richmond?, wMary Malone
WEAVER, --, b18--, Rkhm Co?, wMartha Heatwole
J A, b18--, West Co
Jacob, bc1800, Shen Co
James C, b18--, Page Co?, wLena Buracker
Lawson A, b11/13/1843, West Co, fJ A, wSallie Oldham
Mary Caroline, bc1870, Luray, Page Co, fJames C, mLena Buracker, hFrederick Taylor Amiss, md7/4/1899
Robert, bc1860, Page Co?, w-- Hottel
WEBB, --, b18--, Rkbr Co, hHenry Quincy Adams Bowyer
Elizabeth, b1846, Hillsville, Carr Co, hCharles Martin
Fanny L, b18--, Nans Co, fLewis H, mGattie Lawrence
Joanna, b18--, Snake Creek, Carr Co, hGeorge Quisenberry
Julia A, b18--, Carr Co, d1922, hRobert Goad

WEBB (continued)
Leonidas, b18--, Russ Co?, wMaggie Crawford
Mollie, bc1870, Russ Co?, d1901, fLeonidas, mMaggie Crawford, 1w of Granderson B Johnson, md3/21/ 1891
Nancy A, b11/12/1842, Crai Co?, 1hJohn R Bowen, 2hWilliam J Layman (his 2d wife)
WEBSTER, John R, b11/4/1804, Fran Co, fGeorge, mPeggy Rickard, 2wCatherine Peters
Lucy, b18--, Hard Co?, hNoah Funkhouser
Sarah Elizabeth, b9/14/1849, Fran Co, fJohn R, (2)mCatherine Peters, hJohn William Jameson, md4/4/1878
WEDDING, Matilda, b1808, nrMeadowview, Wash Co, d1839, fAbednego, hWilliam Edmondson
WEEDON, Austin B, b18--, PrWi Co, w-- Trone
Austin Ogilvie, b9/9/1859, Brentsville, PrWi Co, fRobert, mLucy Ann Ogilvie, wElizabeth W Nelson, md11/3/1893
Elizabeth, b18--, Brentsville, PrWi Co, fJohn Catesby, hEdwin Nelson
Ella Virginia, bc1860, fRobert, mLucy Ann Ogilvie
Martha Ellen, b18--, PrWi Co, fAustin B, mTrone, 2w of James Monroe Barbee, Sr
Mary, b18--, PrWi Co, fAustin B, m-- Trone, 1w of James Monroe Barbee, Sr
Mary Elizabeth, bc1860, Brentsville, PWi Co, fRobert, mLucy Ann Ogilvie
Robert, b3/28/1820, PrWi Co, d1906, wLucy Ann Ogilvie
WEEKS, Sarah Frances, b18--, Fauq Co?, 1w of James H Hathaway, md11/22/1838
WEIGHLEY, Georgiana, bc1820, Fair Co, hRice W Levi
WEIMER, Dennia, bc1860, Rkhm Co, wKate Kline
WEIR, Elizabeth Bankhead, b18--, PrWi Co?, fRobert Carter, hHenderson F Tompkins
Lucy Caroline, b2/20/1825, Tappahannock, Esse Co, fRobert,

WEIR (continued)
mClara Boothe, hEppa Hunton II, md6/1848
Robert, bc1800, PrWi Co, fJames, mLucy Mary Marye, wClara Boothe
Robert Carter, b18--, PrWi Co
WELCH, Agnes, b17--, Fauq Co?, hJohn Dowell
Ann, b17--, Fauq Co, fSylvester, m-- Satterwhite, hNelson Fishback
Bettie, b185-, Old Point Comfort, ElCi Co, fThomas, mAnn Pierce, hWilliam W Talle
Fleming P, b1823, Nhld Co, d1878, fJohn, 1wMargret Haynie, 2wArabella D Hughlett
Frank,b185-, Old Point Comfort, ElCi Co, fThomas, mAnn Pierce
Ida B, b18--, Fauq Co, hCharles H Ashton
Jane, bc1811,Fauq Co, fSylvester, m-- Glascock, 1h-- O'Bannon, 2hJames Enoch Murray
J Seldon, b18--, wMary Elizabeth Martin
John, bc1800, Nhld Co
Mary A, b1851, Old Point Comfort, ElCi Co, fThomas, mAnn Pierce, hThomas E Jones
Sylvester, b18--, Fauq Co, w-- Satterwhite, w-- Glascock
T J, b185-, Old Point Comfort, ElCi Co, fThomas, mAnn Pierce
Thomas, b18--, ElCi Co?, wAnn Pierce
Virginia, bc1800, Fauq Co, fSylvester, m-- Satterwhite, hE Milton Murray
Virginia E, bc1870, Nhld Co, fFleming P, (1)mMargaret Haynie, hCharles Hughes
WELFLEY, Martin, b185-, Fauq Co?, wBertha Kincheloe
WELLER, Brown, bc1850, Augu Co, fTobias, (1)m-- Brown
Elizabeth, b18--, Rkhm Co?, hG W Donavan
J N, b186-, Augu Co, fTobias, (2)mBetty Myers
S T, bc1870, Augu Co, fTobias, (2)mBetty Myers
Thomas, bc1860, Augu Co, fTobias, (2)mBetty Myers
Tobias, bc1821, nrMt Sidney,

WELLER (continued)
Augu Co, d1899, 1w-- Brown, 2wBetty Myers
WELLFORD, Armistead Nelson, b18--, Rich Co?, wElizabeth Landon Carter
Emma N, b186-, Lynchburg, Camp Co, fWilliam Nelson, Jr, mAnne Norvell Langhorne
Francis Corbin, b186-, Culp Co, fWilliam Nelson, Jr, mAnne Norvell Langhorne
James L, b186-, Culp Co, fWilliam Nelson, Jr, mAnne Norvell Langhorne
John Francis, b183-, Culp Co, fWilliam Nelson, Sr, m-- (Corbin) Fontleroy
John Spotsford, b17--, Fredericksburg, Spot Co, fRobert, mCatherine Yates, wFannie P Nelson, md1807
Norvell Warren, b186-, Culp Co, fWilliam Nelson, Jr, mAnne Norvell Langhorne
Parke Farley, bc1840, Culp Co, fWilliam Nelson, Sr, m-- (Corbin) Fontleroy
Richard Corbin, b183-, Culp Co, fWilliam Nelson, Sr, m-- (Corbin) Fontleroy
Robert Carter, bc1853, Rich Co, fArmistead Nelson, mElizabeth Landon Carter, wElizabeth Harrison, md1878
William Nelson, Sr, bc1810, Fredericksburg, Spot Co, d1872, fJohn Spotsford, mFannie P Nelson, 2h of -- (Corbin) Fontleroy
William Nelson, Jr, b1836, Culp Co, d1872, fWilliam Nelson, Sr, m-- (Corbin) Fontleroy, wAnne Norvell Langhorne
William Nelson III, b186-, Lynchburg, Camp Co, fWilliam Nelson, Jr, mAnne Norvell Langhorne, wLaura May Simmons, md12/15/1891
WELLS, Anne, b18--, Suss Co?, hWalter Leslie Devany, Sr
David L, b2/14/1862, Bedf Co, wTheodosia Johnson
Ernest H, Sr, b1/4/1869, nr Chesterfield Court House, Ches Co, fLeonidas, mVirginia Alice

WELLS (continued)
Cogbill, wLethia Wingfield Perdue
James A, b18--, Fair Co, wMildred Trammell
Leonidas, b18--, Ches Co, fBaker, wVirginia Alice Cogbill
Lillian, bc1870, Broo Co?, hHarry Hampton Rumble, md1/22/1890
William Baker, b10/3/1864, Patr Co, d1911, wMartha Ann Gentle
WENGER, --, bc1860, Rkhm Co?, wMinnie Wampler
Abraham Blosser, b18--, nrHarrisonburg, Rkhm Co, d1898, fBenjamin Wenger, mBarbara Blosser, wSarah Hartman
Anna, b1/3/1850, nrMilnesville, Augu Co, fDaniel, mSarah --, 1w of Jonas H Blosser
Benjamin, b18--, Rkhm Co, wBarbara Blosser
Daniel, b18--, Augu Co?, wSarah
Isaac B, bc1860, Rkhm Co, wMary Lula Beery
Isaac B, bc1870, nrHarrisonburg, fAbram Blosser, mSarah Hartman, wElla Haldeman
Jacob C, bc1850, Rkhm Co?, wVirginia Suter
Magdalena, b18--, Rkhm Co, hJohn K Beery
Magdalena, b18--, nrHarrisonburg, Rkhm Co, fBenjamin, mBarbara Blosser, hThomas Head
Noah, b18--, nrHarrisonburg, Rkhm Co, fBenamin, mBarbara Blosser
Rebecca, b186-, nrHarrisonburg, Rkhm Co, fAbram Blosser, mSarah Hartman, hJohn H Barnhart
WENNER, Mary Elizabeth, b12/8/1839, nrLovettsville, Loud Co, hJames L McIntosh
WERTENBAKER, William, bc1860, Albe Co, wImogene Peyton
WERTH, James R, b18--, wMary Maury
WEST, Albert Lawrence, b5/10/1825, Laurel Grove, Ches Co, fJohn Shaddock, mPatsy Saterwhite Jones, 1wEmaline Marcella Woodson, 2wGeorgeanna

WEST (continued)
Callis Alexander, bc1845, Loui Co, wCharlotte Bryce Winston
Ann Virginia, b18--, NewK Co, fWilliam, mSusanna Waddell
Annie M, b186-, fJohn, mElizabeth Cason, hFrank Stanley Hope, md6/20/1883
Benjamin, b18--, Richmond, fWilliam Henry, mAnna Johnson
Benjamin F, b18--, NewK Co, fWilliam, mSusanna Waddell
Charles H, b18--, NewK Co, fWilliam, mSusanna Waddell
George W, b18--, NewK Co, fWilliam, mSusanna Waddell
George Callis, b18--, fAlbert Lawrence, (2)mGeorgeanna Callis
H Marion, b18--, Richmond, fWilliam Henry, mAnna Johnson
Henry T, b18--, Suss Co?, wSue T Cox
James E, b18--, NewK Co, fWilliam, mSusanna Waddell
John, b18--, Norf Co, wElizabeth Cason
John B, b18--, NewK Co, fWilliam, mSusanna Waddell
John Shaddock, b17--, wPatsy Saterwhite Jones
John Walter, Sr, b8/12/1864, nrWaverly, Suss Co, fThomas Henry, wAnnie May Capelle
Julia, b18--, Richmond, fWilliam Henry, mAnna Johnson, hJohn E Cox
Junius Edgar, b7/12/1866, Waverly, Suss Co, fHenry T, mSue T Cox, wOllie Beale
Martha E, b1854, Smyt Co, hCharles Taylor Rouse
Martha Tyree, b18--, fAlbert Lawrence, (2)mGeorgeanna Callis
Mary, b9/3/1846, JaCi Co, d1913, 1h-- Crandall, 2hRobert G Barlowe
Revel, bc1800, Acco Co
Revel H, b18--, Acco Co, fRevel, 3wMargaret Riley
Sarah, b17--, Fair Co, fHugh, Jr, hHenry Gunnell
Thomas Henry, b18--, Waverley, Suss Co

WEST (continued)
Thomas J, b18--, NewK Co, fWilliam, mSusanna Waddell
Whitfield, bc1832, Pitt Co?, wFlorilla Wood
William, b18--, KiWi Co, wSusanna Waddell
William C, Sr, b2/28/1859, Acco Co, fRevel H, (3)mMargaret Riley, wAnnie M Parker
William Callis, b18--, fAlbert Lawrence, (2)mGeorgeanna Callis
William Henry, b18--, NewK Co, fWilliam, mSusanna Waddell, wAnna Johnson
WESTBROOK, Rosa Ann, bc1846, Sout Co, d1894, hBenjamin Franklin McLemore
WESTCOTT, Gustave Teagle, b18--, Acco Co, wJulia Wise
WESTON, Mary Eliza, b18--, hJohn L Diggs
WESTWOOD, Kate, nrPortsmouth, Norf Co, hBeverly Crump, Sr
WETHERED, Mary, bc1800, hJohn Young
WETSEL, Mary Ann, bRkhm Co, hJohn C Dickerson
WHALEY, Fred S, bc1850, Hali Co?, wHelen Owen
WHALING, Alexander Lewis, b18--, Roan Co
George W, Sr, b1862, Salem, Roan Co, fAlexander Lewis, wKate P Ballou
H M, bc1860, Salem, Raon Co, fAlexander Lewis
Thornton, bc1860, Salem, Roan Co, fAlexander Lewis
WHARTON, -- b186-, Culp Co, fJames, mMary Elizabeth Wharton, h-- Jackson
Belle, bc1870, Culp Co, fJames, mMary Elizabeth Wharton, h-- Petty
James, b18--, Culp Co?, wMary Elizabeth Wharton
Lola, bc1870, Culp Co, fJames, mMary Elizabeth Wharton, h-- Stinson
Mary Elizabeth, b18--, Culp Co?, hJames Wharton
R Woolwine, b18--, Patr Co
Sallie, bc1870, Patr Co, fR Woolwine, hMalvern Vance Sted-

WHARTON (continued)
man, md9/3/1888
Sue Bryan, b11/10/1866, Culp Co, fJames, mMary Elizabeth Wharton, hClay Carr
WHEAT, Lewis, b1856, Rkhm Co, wElla Rutherford
Lucy, b18--, Bedf Co, fHazel, hWilliam White
WHEELER, --, b18--, Rkhm Co?, 2h of Matilda Riddel
Benjamin E, b5/24/1870, nrCharlottesville, Albe Co, fDavid H, mMary Frances Foster, wLonnie B Wagner, md1899
David H, b18--, nrAfton, Albe Co, fDavid
Emma Maud, b9/30/1857, Amherst Court House, Amhe Co, hWalter Carrington Fitzpatrick
Frank P, b1861, Smyt Co, fWilliam C, wMaggie Stephenson
Stella, b18--, Wash Co?, hFrank S Robertson
William C, b18--, Smyt Co
WHEELWRIGHT, Frederick, b18--, wElizabeth Alexander
Sarah, b1834, Heathsville, Nhld Co, hHenry C DeShields
Thomas S, b2/19/1866, Warr Co, fWilliam Henry, mMargaret Kerfoot, wSusan Carter, md1893
William Henry, b7/23/1824, West Co, fJoseph, mLavisa Dodge, wMargaret Kerfoot
WHETSEL, Alexander, b185-, Fred Co?, wCarrie Funkhouser
WHISMAN, Nancy, b18--, Lee Co?, hWilliam Younger Tucker
WHISSEN, Jennie, b18--, Fred Co, hThomas W Massie
WHITACRE, Addie, b185-, Fauq Co, fRobert, (1)mRebecca Jane (Elgin) Nixon, hS Lodge Cochran
Amos, b18--, nrHamilton, Loud Co, wLydia Craven
Amos B C, b1/1/1860, Fauq Co, fRobert, (1)mRebecca Jane (Elgin) Nixon, wLucy Harmison
Amos H, bc1850, Fauq Co, wGustavia Lee Whitacre
Ella P, b186-, Fauq Co, fRobert, (1)mRebecca Jane (Elgin) Nixon
Elma J, bc1870, Fauq Co, fRobert, (2)mFannie McCarty

WHITACRE (continued)
Gustavia Lee, b186-, Fauq Co, fRobert, (1)mRebecca Jane (Elgin) Nixon, hAmos H Whitacre
Hester A, bc1870, Fauq Co, fRobert, (2)mFannie McCarty, hMilton Rogers
Robert, b18--, nrHamilton, Loud Co, d1901, fAmos, mLydia Craven, 1wRebecca Jane (Elgin) Nixon, 2wFannie McCarty
WHITAKER, Mariah Elizabeth, b9/1/1836, Rich Neck, Warw Co, d1919, hHumphrey Howard Curtis
WHITE, --, bc1840, Rkhm Co, wBelle Thuma
--, bc1860, KiGe Co?, wSallie Billingsley
--, b18--, Madi Co, fJohn, hWilliam K Bowie
--, b185-, Augu Co, fWilliam, mFrances E Sproul, hHarry D Irwin
Agnes, b17--, Pitt Co, fJohn, hWilliam Easley
Annie, b184-, nrTimberville, Rkhm Co, mCatherine Adams, h-- Shelton
Archibald S, bc1850, Augu Co, fWilliam, mFrances E Sproul, wLulu Johnston
Bettie W, b18--, Abingdon, Wash Co, fW Y C, hThomas Preston Trigg
Buena, bc1870, Wash Co, hJohn C Pruner
Catherine, b18--, Wash Co, hFrank Clark
Charlotte F, bc1838, Math Co, hJohn H MIles
Christian A, b1844, nrTimberville, Rkhm Co, mCatherine Adams, wAlice V Hoover
D Frank White, Sr, b5/8/1841, Acco Co, d1899, fDavid, wDora Melson
Elijah B, b4/6/1864, nrLuray, Page Co, fElijah V, mElizabeth Gott, 1wRosalie Pancast, md 1886, 2wLalla B Harrison, md1/21/1900
Elizabeth, b17--, Hano Co?, hEdward Garland Sydnor
Elizabeth, b1821, Bedf Co, d1865, 1w of Joshua Laughon
Elizabeth, b18--, Albe Co?,

WHITE (continued)
1h-- Kent, 2hEgbert Read Watson (his 3w), md1860
Elizabeth Susan, b9/7/1831, Math Co, d1922, fJames, mLucy --, hFrederick Richardson
Emeline Josephine, bc1838, Caro Co, hJoseph Alsop Chandler
Emma C, b186-, nrStephens City, Fred Co, fSamuel, mSarah Gardner, h-- Willis
Emma Tell, b18--, Nels Co?, fPeter, mFannie Ruffner, hJohn W Dillard, md1880
Fannie, b18--, Oran Co, hLewis Graves
Fannie B, b18--, Spot Co?, hJohn T Goolrick, Sr
Frances, bc1830, Albe Co, fJohn S, hAlfred Carpenter
Frank, bc1840, Lune Co?, d1913, wNannie E Smith
Garrett, b17--, Albe Co?, wBettsey E Piper
Gertrude, bc1860, nrStephens City, Fred Co, fSamuel, mSarah Gardner, h-- Ebersole
H D, b18--, Bedf Co?, wMary --
H M, b18--, Roan Co?, wMaria Blanche McClanahan
Hamden Murray, b11/13/1861, Fauq Co, fJohn L, mCamilla A Brown, wKate E Stone, md12/21/1884
Hilah, b18--, Portsmouth, Norf Co?, 2w of John M White
Holcomb, b18--, Bedf Co, wMary Jennings
Hugh A, b18--, wJane Graham McIlwaine
Ichabod P, bc1850, Pitt Co?, wEmily Johnson
Isaac, b184-, nrTimberville, Rkhm Co, mCatherine Adams
James, bc1800, Math Co?, wLucy
James Garrett, b2/24/1864, nr Charlottesville, Albe Co, fJohn S, mMartha O Moon, wMary Carpenter, md11/30/1887
James M, bc1850, Bedf Co?, wLavinia E Laughon
John, b18--, Albe Co, fGarrett, mBettsey E Piper, wCaroline Moore
John, b18--, Norf Co?, wLouise Hodges

WHITE (continued)
John, b184-, Augu Co, fWilliam, mFrances E Sproul
John, b186-, nrCharlottesville, Albe Co, fJohn S, mMartha Moon
John G, b18--, Wash Co?, wMary Preston
John H, b5/30/1859, Richmond, fWilliam F, mMargaret S Greanor, wEmma Lee Stewart
John L, b18--, nrWarrenton, Fauq Co, wCamilla A Brown
John M, b11/16/1846, Deep Creek, Norf Co, fJohn, mLouise Hodges, 1wGay Pendleton Leake, md1868, 2wHilah White
John S, b18--, nrCharlottesville, Albe Co, wMartha O Moon
John T, b18--, Acco Co
Joseph K, b184-, Augu Co, fWilliam, mFrances Sproul
Josie, b1854, Fran Co, hHenry T Adams
Louisa, b1813, Saltville, Smyt Co, d1887, hJames Sanders
Louise, bc1870, Albe Co?, fJohn M, (1)mGay Pendleton Leake, hHunter Pendleton
Lucy M, b18--, Spot Co, fWilliam, m-- Cropp, hEdloe James Sudduth
M Carrie, b10/1863, nrCharlottesville, Albe Co, fJohn S, mMartha O Moon, hRichard D Adnerson, Sr
Martha, bc1822, Lexington, Rkbr Co, fMatthew, hJacob D Williamson
Mary S, b186-, nrStephens City, Fred Co, fSamuel, mSarah Gardner, h-- Gruver
Matilda Scott, b184-, Augu Co, fWilliam, mFrances E Sproul
Rachel, b18--, Taze Co, fJames W M Witten
Rawley, b17--, Pitt Co, wAnn --
Rebekah Martha, b18--, Pitt Co, d1887, fRawley, mAnn --, hChesley Martin
Reid, b3/28/1868, Lexington, Rkbr Co, fJ J, mMary Louisa Reid, wLucy W Preston, md1895
Rosa B, b2/22/1870, nrStephens City, Fred Co, fSamuel, mSarah Gardner, hClarence E Cougill, md5/30/1892

WHITE (continued)
Samuel, b18--, Fred Co, wSarah Gardner
Sarah, b18--, Fred Co?, hWilliam McIlwee
Virginia Jones, b1826, Meck Co, d1909, hJohn R Yancey
W S, b184-, Fred Co?, wCatherine Baker
William, b18--, Cripple Creek, Wyth Co, w-- Boy
William, b18--, Spot Co? w-- Cropp
William, bc1813, Augu Co?, d1897, wFrances E Sproul
William, b18--, Bedf Co, wLucy Wheat
William, b18--, Berk Co, wAlicia Bell
William C, b3/31/1854, Scottsville, Albe Co, wEugenia Haynes
William F, b18--, fP K, wMargret S Greanor
William M, b186-, nrStephens City, Fred Co, fSamuel, mSarah Gardner
William S, bc1850, Augu Co, fWilliam, mFrances E Sproul
Willie A, b18--, Wheats Valley, Bedf Co, fWilliam, mLucy Wheat, hHubert Watson
WHITEHEAD, --, b18--, Rkhm Co?, hJacob Swartz
Alexander Robert, b1831, Nels Co, wLucy William Stratton
Burcher, b1764, NewK Co?, wNancy Camden, md1788
David Garland, b186-, Amherst Court House, Amhe Co, fThomas, (2)mMartha Henry Garland
Edgar, b182-, Amhe Co?, fJohn, mAnna Mahoney
Floyd Kincaid, b1/7/1870, Nels Co, fAlexander Robert, mLucy Williams Stratton, wLaura Nelson, md11/30/1898
Irving Powell, bc1870, Amherst Court House, Amhe Co, fThomas, (2)mMartha Henry Garland
John, b1735, NewK Co, d1787, wSarah Burcher
John, b1789, Amhe Co, fBurcher, mNancy Camden, wAnna Mahoney, md2/24/1812
John, b185-, Amherst Court

WHITEHEAD (continued)
House, Amhe Co, fThomas, (2)m Martha Henry Garland
John D, b186-, Nels Co, fAlexander Robert, mLucy William Stratton
John Early, bc1846, Back Bay District, PrAn Co, wSarah Frances Whitehurst
Marcellus, b181-, Amherst, Amhe Co, fJohn, mAnna Mahoney
Martha Garland, bc1870, Amherst Court House, Amhe Co, fThomas, (2)mMartha Henry Garland, hStuart Michaux
Mary B, b186-, Nels Co, fRobert, (2)mMargaret Daniel Baldwin
Mary Irving, b186-, Amherst Court House, Amhe Co, fThomas, (2)m Martha Henry Garland, hEdward Schneider
Mildred Powell, b185-, Amherst Court House, Amhe Co, fThomas, (2)mMartha Henry Garland, hJohn D Murrell
Paul, b182-, Amhe Co?, fJohn, mAnna Mahoney
Richard H, bc1820, Amherst, Amhe Co, fJohn, mAnna Mahoney
Robert, b1815, Amherst, Amhe Co, fJohn, mAnna Mahoney, 2wMargaret Daniel Baldwin
Robert Frederick, b186-, Nels Co, fRobert, (2)mMargaret Daniel Baldwin
S B, Sr, b10/3/1859, Nels Co, fRobert, (2)mMargaret Daniel Baldwin, wSusan M Massie, md6/21/1893
Sarah A, b186-, Nels Co, fRobert, (2)mMargaret Daniel Baldwin
Sarah Ann Brown, bc1870, Amherst Court House, Amhe Co, fThomas, (2)mMartha Henry Garland, hHenry D Perkins
Thomas, b18--, Ches Co?, wElizabeth Erwin
Thomas, b12/27/1825, nrLovingston, Nels Co, d1901, fJohn, mAnna Mahoney, 1wMary Kincade Irving, 2wMartha Henry Garland
Thomas, bc1860, Amherst Court House, Amhe Co, fThomas, (2)m Martha Henry Garland

WHITEHEAD (continued)
Virginia C, bc1833, Amhe Co, hAlsen Thomas
WHITED, Jerome Bonaparte, b18--, Russ Co, fRobert M, mAnna Meadows, wLucy Plaster
Robert M, b1818, Russ Co, d1914, wAnna Meadows
Thomas C, b18--, Russ Co, fRobert M, mAnna Meadows
WHITEHURST, Alice V, b18--, Norfolk?, hC T Gordon
Anne Elizabeth, b18--, PrAn Co?, hJonathan Whitehead Old
Edward H, bc1860, Midd Co?, wSusan Pierce Lawson
George Leonard, b18--, Norfolk?, wSarah Anne Taylor
Sarah Frances, bc1852, Back Bay District, PrAn Co, hJohn Early Whitehead
Virginia E, b18--, PrAn Co, hJohn Thomas Woodhouse
WHITESEL, Alice, hC Luther Rogers
WHITING, --, b18--, ElCi Co?, hSamuel Read Chisman
John, b17--, Glou Co?, wLettice Lee
Lettice Lee, bc1800, Midd Co?, fJohn, mLettice Lee, 2w of Richard Woodward, md6/22/1820
Mary, b18--, ElCi Co, hJames A Watkins
WHITLEY, Reece, bc1860, Taze Co?, wRachel W Witten
WHITLOCK, --, bc1870, Capon Bridge, Hamp Co, fDarias M, hFrank Getridge
Albert, b186-, Capon Bridge, Hamp Co, fDarias M, mLucy Alverson
Darias M, b1844, Hamp Co, m-- Parrish, wLucy Alverson
Emma, b186-, Capon Bridge, Hamp Co, fDarias M, mLucy Alverson
James Reeves, bc184-, Hamp Co, m-- Parrish
Jane, bc1850, Hamp Co, m-- Parrish
Joanna, bc1850, Loui Co, hJohn Richard Payne, Sr
Minnie, b186-, Capon Bridge, Hamp Co, fDarias M, mLucy Alverson
Nannie, b184-, Hamp Co, m--

WHITLOCK (continued)
Parrish
Robert, bc1840, Hamp Co, m-- Parrish
Stanley, bc1870, Capon Bridge, Hamp Co, fDarias M, mLucy Alverson
Susie, bc1850, Hamp Co, m- Parrish
William Joseph, b3/29/1849, Hamp Co, m-- Parrish, 1wSophia Michael, 2wAnnie W (Alexander) Ritter, md10/19/1893
WHITLOW, May E, b18--, Fran Co, hJohn G Hurt
WHITMAN, Andrew, b3/15/1844, Cripple Creek Valley, Wyth Co, d1901, fDavid Whitman, (2)m Elizabeth Hale, wCaroline Kegley, md1/8/1868
David, b8/7/1796, Bunger's Mill, Grbr Co, fAndreas, mElizabeth Stevens, 1wElizabeth Horne, 2wElizabeth Hale, 3w Elizabeth Cassell
John Alexander, b4/29/1869, Cripple Creek Valley, Wyth Co, fAndrew Clay, mCaroline Kegley, wCaroline F Heuser, md4/12/1889
W O, bc1860, Loud Co?, w-- Robey
WHITMIRE, Jacob, b18--, Shen Co?, wSallie Zirkle
John, bc1800, Shen Co, wRebecca Harpine
WHITMORE, Annie Bowman, b5/22/1870, nrMt Clinton, Rkhm Co, fW C, mRachel Thompson, hCharles Hopkins Ralston, md5/22/1890
Franklin, b182-, Parnassus, Augu Co, fMartin
Sarah Elizabeth, b18--, Ashby District, Rkhm Co, fEmanuel, hGeorge Miller
Susan B, b1/12/1828, Parnassus, Augu Co, d1919, fMartin, hDavid Coiner, md1850
W C, b18--, Rkhm Co, wRachel Thompson
WHITNEY, Martha Ann, b12/8/1828, Sout Co, d1891, hJames Madison Corbett, md4/30/1861
WHITT, Alice, b1867, Russ Co, d1922, hJohn F Griffith

WHITTAKER, Lydia, b1830, Hyters Gap, Wash Co, hJohn W Littton
Nannie, b1856, Taze Co, hAlexander Altizer
Virginia, b18--, Smyt Co, 2w of Robert B Witten
WHITTLE, Elizabeth Beverley, b18--, fWilliam Conway, m--Sinclair, hJohn Coles Terry
Lucy T, bc1850, Richmond?, fFrancis M, 1w of John Nottingham Upshur, md11/19/1873
WIATT, Sarah Elizabeth, b18--, Camp Co?, hWalter Hayes Otey
WICKENS, Georgia A, b12/23/1837, PrAn Co, fJ Edward, mAlice White, hGeorge Alexander Martin, Sr
Elizabeth Hill Carter, b18-- Richmond?, fJohn, mElizabeth Hill Carter, hHenry V Strayer, md12/4/1883
WICKHAM, John, bc1800, Richmond?, wElizabeth Hill Carter
WICKS, John J, b18--, wFrances Ford
WIERMAN, Benjamin D, bc1810, Shen Co?, wCatherine Moore
WIGGINSON, Mary, bAlexandria?, hCave English
WIGGLESWORTH, John, b17--, fJohn, mMary Lindsay, wPhiladelphia Claibourne Fox
Lucy J, b18--, Mont Co?, hCephas Shelburne
Maria Claibourne, bc1800, Spot Co, fThomas, mMatilda Foster, hBenjamin Spindle
Thomas, b17--, fJohn, mPhiladelphia Claibourne Fox, wMatilda Foster
WIGHT, Annie L, b1837, Richmond, 2w of Edmund Waddill II
Edward Cunningham, b10/21/1867, Gooc Co, fWilliam Washington, mAriana Peyton Cunningham
Elizabeth Berkeley, b9/1/1870, Gooc Co, fWilliam Washington, mAriana Peyton Cunningham, hWilliam Henry Venable
Henry Theodore, b180-, Tuckahoe, Gooc Co, fWilliam Leeds, mGrace Hughes
William Leeds, b1802, Tuckahoe, Gooc Co, wGrace Hughes
William Leeds, b7/6/1869, Gooc

WIGHT (continued)
Co, fWilliam Washington, mAriana Peyton Cunningham
William Washington, b3/7/1837, Tuckahoe, Gooc Co, fWilliam Leeds, mGrace Hughes, wAriana Peyton Cunningham
WILBORN, Stephen M, b12/20/1852, South Boston, Hali Co, fWilliam H, mElizabeth Childress, wMary S Tuck
William H, b18--, nrSouth Boston, Hali Co, wElizabeth Childress
WILBURN, Elizabeth, b18--, Suss Co, hWilliam Nicholas Jarratt
WILCOXEN, Hattie, bc1860, PrWi Co, hMars Lewis
WILEY, --, bc1800, KiWi Co?, hLarkin Garrett
C P, b186-, Sinking Creek, Crai Co, fOscar, mMelvina Price
Ephraim E, b18--, Wash Co?, wElizabeth Reeves
Frances Elizabeth, b9/6/1841, Emory, Wash Co, fEphraim E, Jr, mElizabeth Hackett Hammond, hJohn Lee Buchanan
George E, b10/19/1851, Emory, Wash Co, fEphraim E, Jr, mElizabeth Hackett Hammond, wSarah E Scarff
Henrietta, b18--, Clar Co?, hJoseph W Lloyd
Margaret Ann, b1840, Emory, Wash Co, fEphraim E, Jr, mElizabeth Hackett Hammond, hJohn C Storey
Mary Helen, b18--, Wash Co, fEphraim E, mElizabeth Reeves, hJoseph Leonard Jarman, md12/22/1891
Olin Fisk, b12/28/1849, Emory, Wash Co, fEphraim E, Jr, mElizabeth Hackett Hammond, wMary Richmond
Oscar, b1830, Fincastle, Bote Co, d1904, wMelvina Price
Robert, bc1830, Fincastle, Bote Co
Robert Minor, b1/8/1870, Sinking Creek, Crai Co, fOscar, mMelvina Price, wEllen Blair, md11/14/1900
Virginia Watson, b10/7/847, Emory, Wash Co, fEphraim E,

WILEY (continued)
Jr, mElizabeth Hackett Hammond, hFrank A Parker
William Harlow, b5/19/1845, Emory, Wash Co, fEphraim E, Jr, mElizabeth Hackett Hammond, wHelen Palmiter
WILKINS, Albert Jefferson, bc1853, nrSassafras, Glou Co, wMartha Susan Hurst
George, b184-, Shen Co, fIsaac, m-- Hockman
Giedon, b1851, Shen Co, d1920, fIsaac, m-- Hockman, wJosephine Dyer Bowman
Isaac, b1813, Strasburg, Shen Co, d1893, w-- Hockman
Jacob, b184-, Shen Co, fIsaac, m-- Hockman
Lydia, b184-, Shen Co, fIsaac, m-- Hockman, hJ O Wakeman
Magnus Taliaferro, b4/4/1868, Alexandria, fJohn Quincy Adams, mLucy Frances Peyton, wCora Laws
WILKINSON, Eveline, b185-, nr Hillsville, Carr Co, d1900, fJohn, mElizabeth Anderson, hCharles L Jennings
Isabella W, b18--, Richmond?, hJohn G Robertson
Laura, b186-, nrHillsville, Carr Co, fJohn, mElizabeth Anderson
Lavinia, b186-, nrHillsville, Carr Co, fJohn, mElizabeth Anderson, hNicholas P Oglesby
Mildred Minerva, b18--, 2w of Daniel Hobson Browne, md6/30/1858
Robert G, b6/20/1860, nrHillsville, Carr Co, fJohn, mElizabeth Anderson, wLaura J Carter, md9/14/1880
Stephen Ellis, b4/3/1865, nr Hillsville, Carr Co, fJohn, mElizabeth Anderson, wFlora L Hanks, md3/4/1896
WilliamJ, b185-, nrHillsville, Carr Co, d1887, fJohn, mElizabeth Anderson
WILL, Barbara, bc1850, Shen Co, fWilliam, mMadaline Dellinger, hWilliam Jones
Caroline, b184-, Shen Co, fWilliam, mMadaline Dellinger,

WILL (continued)
hWilliam Sauerwine
Jacob, b184-, Shen Co, fWilliam, mMadaline Dellinger
Jeff, b185-, Shen Co, d1922, fWilliam, mMadaline Dellinger
John, b5/27/1847, Shen Co, d1922, fWilliam, mMadaline Dellingr, wAnnie Jones
John F, bc1870, nrTimberville, Rkhm Co, fWilliam Anderson, mCatherine Garber
Joseph, b185-, Shen Co, fWilliam, mMadaline Dellinger
Joseph M, bc1870, nrTimberville, Rkhm Co, fWilliam Anderson, mCatherine Garber
Lizzie, b186-, nrTimberville, Rkhm Co, fWilliam Anderson, mCatherine Garber, hC C Lindamood
Sallie, b9/22/1868, nrTimberville, Rkhm Co, fWilliam Anderson, mCatherine Garber, hGeorge F Bull
Sarah, bc1870, Rkhm Co, fJohn, mAnnie Jones, hHugh Armentrout
William, b18--, Rkhm Co, wMadaline Dellinger
William II, b185-, Shen Co, fWilliam, mMadaline Dellinger
William Anderson, bc1842, nr Timberville, Rkhm Co, d1903, wCatherine Garber
WILLARD, Emma, b18--, Wise Co?, hRobert W James
WILLCOX, Thomas, b18--, Norf Co
WILLIAMS, --, b18--, Oran Co, hGeorge Morton
--, b18--, Crai Co?, 1w of William J Layman
Albert, bc1850, Clar Co?, wBettie Glaize
Albert Henry, b8/20/1839, Lune Co, wMatilda Anne Berkeley
Alfred Brockenbrough, b1/10/1856, Richmond, fRobert Afred, mElizabeth Marshall Colston, wMamie Young Bryce, md1882
Annie M, b186-, Charlotte Court House, Char Co, fAlbert Henry, mMatilda Anne Berkeley, hCabell Morton
Archie H, b5/12/1863, Pitt Co, fRobert, mElizabeth Martin, wNannie Lee Grayson

WILLIAMS (continued)
Benjamin, b1796, Fred Co, d1889
Benjamin, bc1820, Oran Co, fJoseph, m-- Catterton
Benjamin F, bc1850, nrWinchester, Fred Co, fPhilip Benjamin, mMary Vance
Bettie, bc1860, Rkhm Co?, 2w of James Van Meter
Charles A, bnrWinchester, Fred Co, fPhilip Benjamin, mMary Vance
Christina, b18--, hWilliam Robertson
Cyrus, b183-, Taze Co, fWilliam, mMargaret Gillespie
David A, bc1840, Nott Co?, wObedience Beville
Dicey, b18--, Scot Co?, hJoseph Salling
Edward, bc1820, Avon, Nels Co, fWilliam, m-- Fulton
Eliza, b18--, Roan Co, hArmistead Neal
Elizabeth, b18--, Bote Co, hBenjamin F Brock
Ellen, bc1870, Buck Co, fWilliam, mEmily Guthrie, hJ E Tapscott
Ennion G, b18--, fJohn Langbourne, mMaria Ward Skelton, wLila LeFebyre Isaacs, md1895
Ernest, b10/21/1862, Lynchburg, Camp Co, fFayette, mMary Malvina Snead, wMary L Thomas, md1888
Eula, bc1870, Charlotte Court House, Char Co, fAlbert Henry, mMatilda Anne Wardell
Fayette, b1829, Camp Co, d1901, fLewis E, wMary Malvina Snead
Fayette C, b18--, Nott Co, wAnnie Harrison
Florence L, bc1870, Taze Co, fJulius C, mMary Davis, hJohn Henry Stinson, md8/31/1893
Forest Ashton, bc1870, Greenfield, Nels Co, fWilliam Lewis, mSusan H Patrick
G J, b18--, Taze Co, fJulius C, mMary Davis
George, b184-, nrWoodstock, Shen Co, d186-, fSamuel, mSarah Ott
George D, bc1840, Powh Co?, wVirginia Baugh

WILLIAMS (continued)
Harriet, b182-, Fred Co, fBenjamin, hJacob W Richard
Helen, b186-, Buck Co, fWilliam, mEmily Guthrie, hB L Snoddy
Henrietta V, b1/1852, d1901, hJames H Porterfield, Sr
Herbert F, b3/1867, The Plains, Fauq Co, fFranklin, mKatrina Ferguson, wAnnie M Taylor, md11/2/1892
Ida L,bc1870, Charlotte Court House, Char Co, fAlbert Henry, mMatilda Anne Berkeley
Isaac, b9/12/1846, Clinchpot, Scot Co, fNeri, 1wSarah Scott, 2wOllie Bryant, 3wLina Speers, 4wLora Worf
J Hunter, b9/25/1858, nrWinchester, Fred Co, fPhilip Benjamin, mMary Vance, wMargaret A Barrett, md10/27/1886
James, b18--, Waverley, Clar Co, w-- Williams
James L, b18--, Russ Co?, wEliza Meade
James W W, b182-, Fred Co, fBenjamin
James W, b11/4/1840, Washington, Rapp Co, d1917, wMary Agnes Easley
John, Jr, bc1800, PrWi Co, fJohn, Sr
John, b182-, Oran Co, fJoseph, m-- Catterton
John C, b18--, Richmond?, wAlberta Wortham
John C, bc1870, nrPounding Mill Station, Taze Co, fWilliam Cyrus
John Edward, b9/17/1867, nr Charlotte Court House, Char Co, fAlbert Henry, mMatilda Anne Berkeley, wSallie Taylor Patton, md8/28/1905
John G, b1/19/1843, Oran Co, fLewis Burwell, wCatherine Murat Willis
John Langbourne, b7/13/1831, Richmond, fJohn, mSianna Dandridge, wMaria Ward Skelton, md10/13/ 1864
John S, b18--, Camp Co?, wLina
John Skelton, b7/6/1865, Richmond, fJohn Langbourne, mMaria

WILLIAMS (continued)
Ward Skelton
John W, bc1870, Flint Hill, Rapp Co, fWilliam J, mAdeline Chappelear
John William, b3/23/1869, Pearisburg, Gile Co, fJames W, mMary Agnes Easley, wAnnie Johnston Snidow
John William, b186-, Greenfield, Nels Co, fWilliam Lewis, mSusan H Patrick
Joseph, b17--, Oran Co?, w-- Catterton
Joseph Benjamin, b5/5/1870, Flint Hill, Rapp Co, fWilliam J, mAdeline Chappelear, wGrace Hart
Julius C, b2/22/1829, Taze Co, d1910, fWilliam, mMargaret Gillespie, wMary Davis
Kate H, bc1870, Marysville, Camp Co, d1917, fJohn S, mLina --, hRobley M Perrow, md1892
L E, b18--, KiWi Co?, wMary Alice Skidmore
Lena, bc1845, nrWaverley, Clar Co, fJames, m-- Williams, hClaude Baxley, md1866
Lewis, b2/1/1868, Buck Co, fWilliam, mEmily Guthrie, wJennie C Forbes, md5/25/1904
Lewis Burwell, b1802, Fredericksburg, Spot Co, fWilliam C
Louisa B, b183-, Taze Co, fWilliam, mMargaret Gillespie
Marcus, b183-, Taze Co, fWilliam, mMargaret Gillespie
Margaret, bc1830, Fred Co, fBenjamin, hWilliam E Reed
Margaret, bc1840, Taze Co, fWilliam
Margaret Mary, b18-- Taze Co, fJulius C, mMary Davis
Martin, b186-, Pitt Co, fRobert, mElizabeth Martin
Mary, b182-, Fred Co, fBenjamin, hWilliam N Eddy
Mary A, b18--, Taze Co, fWilliam, mMargaret Gillespie
Mary Carson, b5/26/1793, nrFront Royal, Warr Co, fJared, mMartha Carson, hSamuel Simpson, md1820
Mary Jane, b18--, Rapp Co, hEdward Thomas Keyser

WILLIAMS (continued)
Mary Jane, b18--, Sout Co?, hJohn Henry Rawlings
Mary Virginia, b185-, nrWinchester, Fred Co, fPhilip Benjamin, mMary Vance, hTheodore Eddy
Nellie, b18--, Norf Co?, hJohn Chapman Little
Neri, b1813, d1903
Newton A, bc1860, nrWinchester, Fred Co, fPhilip Benjamin, mMary Vance
Octavia, b18--, Taze Co, fJulius C, mMary Davis, hW B Harris
Patrick, b183-, Taze Co, fWilliam, mMargaret Gillespie
Philip Benjamin, b11/5/1824, Fred Co, d1896, fBenjamin, wMary Vance
R Lancaster, bc1860, Richmond, fJohn Langbourne, mMaria Ward Skelton
Robert, b18--, d1863, wElizabeth Martin
Robert Alfred, b1822, Richmond, fJohn, mCyane Armistead Dandridge, wElizabeth Marshall Colston
Robert S, bc1870, nrPounding Mill Station, Taze Co, fWilliam Cyrus, mOctavia Dais
Robert Wesley, b186-, Charlotte Court House, Char Co, fAlbert Henry, mMatilda Anne Berkeley
S M, bc1850, Fred Co, wSarah E Larrick
Sallie Greene, bc1800, Rapp Co?, fJames, hJames French Strother, Sr
Samuel, b18--, Shen Co, d186-, fPhilip, wSarah Ott
Samuel W, b186-, Pitt Co, fRobert, mElizabeth Martin
Sara, b17--, Henrico Co, fJonathan, 1h-- Roberts, 2hJames Throckmorton
Sarah F, bc1836, PrWi Co, fJohn, Jr, hThomas W Lion
Sarah India, b18--, Nott Co?, fFayette C, mAnnie Harrison, 1w of Henry Stokes, Jr, md4/10/1884
Susan E, b1844, nrKilmarnock, Lanc Co, d1920, 2w of William

WILLIAMS (continued)
M Sanders
Thomas B, b18--, fThomas W, mHarriet E Jones, wBelle Horner
Thomas J, b185-, nrWinchester, Fred Co, fPhilip Benjamin, mMary Vance
Thomas W, b18--, Albe Co, wHarriet E Jones
Titus V, b183-, Taze Co, fWilliam, mMargaret Gillespie
Walter Gregory, b11/17/1865, Charlotte Court House, Char Co, fAlbert Henry, mMatilda Anne Berkeley, wMartha Friend Rice
William, b1833, Buck Co, wEmily Guthrie
William Clayton, b2/8/1859, Orange, Oran Co, fWilliam G, mRoberta Banks Hansbrough, wEveline Johnson
William Cyrus, b1839, Taze Co, d1905, m-- Gillespie, wOctavia Davis
William J, b1/1824, Oran Co, Joseph, m-- Catterton, wAdaline Chappelear
William Lewis, b4/18/1818, Avon, Nels Co, d1902, fWilliam, m-- Fulton, wSusan H Patrick
William Twyman, b3/31/1849, nrWoodstock, Shen Co, fSamuel, mSarah Ott, wSallie Madison Bird, md1882
WILLIAMSON, --, b18--, Shen Co, wFannie A Ripley
Belle O, b18--, Wise Co?, hHarry L Rollins
Birtea, b186-, Char Co, fE M, mMary Virginia Spencer, hWillis J Dance
Catherine, b184-, nrNew Market, Rkhm Co, fJacob D, mMartha White, hA A Waldon
E M, b8/28/1835, Char Co, fWilliam B, mPermelia Jackson, wMary Virginia Spencer, md1859
Gilbert M, b184-, nrNew Market, Rkhm Co, fJacob D, mMartha White
Henry, Jr, b18--, Bedf Co, fHenry, Sr, mLucy Bowles, wRebecca Mason

WILLIAMSON (continued)
J G, b185-, nrNew Market, Rkhm Co, fJacob D, mMartha White
Jacob D, b1819, Jeff Co, fThomas Lemen, mMary Williamson, wMartha White (Jacob's original surname was Lemen)
Jacob D, bc1850, nrNew Market, Rkhm Co, fJacob D, mMartha White
James Pinkney, b186-, Char Co?, fE M, mMary Virginia Spencer
Joseph A, b18--,wMary Mann Page
M White, b184-, nrNew Market, Rkhm Co, fJacob D, mMartha White
Mary, b17--, hThomas Lemen
Roberta Page, b18--, fJoseph A, mMary Mann Page, hJohn Brockenbrough Newton
Thomas Lemen, b10/7/1847, nrNew Market, Rkhm Co, d1875, fJacob D, mMartha White, wBettie B Burnley, md6/7/1876
Thomas S, b186-, Char Co, fE M, mMary Viginia Spencer
William B, bc1800, Char Co, wPermelia Jackson
William Littleberry, b1837, Bedf Co, fHenry, Jr, mRebecca Mason, wNancy Campbell, md1872
William W, b186-, Char Co?, fE M, mMary Virginia Spencer
WILLIS, --, bc1860, Fred Co, wEmma C White
A G, b18--, Culp Co
Claudia Marshall, b185-, Oran Co, fJohn, mLucy Madison, hWilliam Wallace Scott, md9/29/1869
Evelyn Byrd, b1856, Ches Co, fRich A, mVirginia Martin Drewry, hDavid L Pulliam
James, b184-, shen Co?, wLone Cordelia
John, b18--, Oran Co?, wLucy Madison
Joseph W, bc1860, Hano Co?, wLula Lee Mann
Malinda, b1840, Walnut Hill, Lee Co, hThomas S Ely
Mary Lewis, b18--, hJohn Armistead Browning, Sr
Rich A, b18--, wVirginia Martin Drewry
Virginia, b4/18/1853, Oran Co,

WILLIS (continued)
hCharles Edward Cary
William Byrd, b18--, Oran Co?,
wNellie Conway
WILLS, Bessie Haskins, b1857,
Loui Co, hJohn W Flannagan, Sr
Elowise, b18--, Nels Co, hJames
W C Meeks
James L, b1/29/1818, Nels Co,
wMargaret C Reid
James Reid, b7/22/1852, Augu
Co, fJames L, mMargaret C
Reid, wVirginia Carper, md1/
21/1880
Sarah Frances, b18--, Bedf Co,
hNathaniel Angle
WILLSON, Estelline Montgomery,
b1830, nrBrownsburg, Rkbr Co,
d1876, 1w of Andrew A McClung,
md1856
J Frank, b185-, Augu Co?,
wPhoebe W McClung
James, bc1830, nrBrownsburg,
Rkbr Co, d1865
Mary, b1831, Rkbr Co, d1886,
fThomas, hJohn Alexander
McClung
WILSHIRE, Susan, b18--, Amhe Co,
hW Dillard tucker
WILSON, --, b17--, Russ Co?,
fAbner, hGeorge Finney
A J, b18--, Lee Co
Abner, b17--, Russ Co?, fJoab
Adam, b18--, Russ Co, d1861,
wRebecca Fields
Alice, b18--, Wayn Co, hCharles
N Crouch
Annie, bc1870, Pitt Co, hRorer
A James, md10/12/1892
Annie G, b18--, Augu Co, fS C,
hCharles S McClung
Benjamin, b12/6/1733, PrAn Co?,
fWillis, m-- Goodrich, wAnn
Seay
Calla Hill, b182-, Bedf Co, 1h
of Martha Lydia Bond
Calvin, b18--, wAnnie Randolph
Charlotte, b18--, High Co?,
hAdam Stephenson
Daniel A, bc1800, Cumb Co,
fRichard
Darius A, bc1840, Nott Co, wAnn
Jane Beville
Elizabeth A, b18--, Shen Co?,
d1893, fJohn, hJoseph Bausrman
Ella Edward, b8/11/1845, PrEd

WILSON (continued)
Co, 2w of William Taylor
Barret
George M, b1/1843, Amel Co,
fWilliam H, mHenningham Elam,
wMary Eppes Thweatt
Goodrich, b17--, Cumb Co, fBenjamin, mAnn Seay, wElizabeth
Venable
Grace A, b18--, fDaniel A,
hWilliam V Wilson, Sr
Jennie D, b185-, Bedf Co,
fCalla Hill, mMartha Lydia
Bond, hH W Nichols
John, b18--, Norfolk, wPenelope
Campbell
John, b185-, d1899, wSusan Colston Minor
Martha J, b4/4/1846, Monterey,
High Co, fJohn E, mMary J
Hills, hCharles Pinckney Jones
Mary, b18--, Amel Co, fGeorge
M, mMary Eppes Thweatt, hJohn
G Robert
Mary, b1675, ElCi Co, fWilliam,
mJane --, hMiles Cary II
Mary Elizabeth, b18--, Fauq Co,
d1892, hThomas H Alexander
Melissa E, b10/3/1837, Swords
Creek, Russ Co, hLilburn
Finney
Minerva, bc1850, Lee Co, fA J,
hRobert W Orr
Nimrod, bc1860, Hamp Co?,
wMinerva Orndorff
Norvill, bc1860, Richmond?,
wSarah Frances Betts
Paul, b1813, Lune Co, d1901,
w-- Wrigglesworth
Richard T, b8/17/1869, Briarfield, Amel Co, fGeorge M,
mMary Eppes Thweatt, wEllen
Beirne Blair
Robert H, b18--, wMaria Osborne
S C, b18--, Augu Co
Sallie Ann, b18--, Rkbr Co,
hNapoleon B McCluer
Samuel, b16--, Poplar Grove,
PrAn Co, fJames, w-- Mason
Sarah, b18--, Lee Co, hJoseph
Jones
Susan, b1856, Oak Grove, West
Co, hWilliam Catesby Latane
Thornton, b184-, Hali Co?,
wFannie Owen
William, b1838, nrFinney, Russ

WILSON (continued)
Co, d1923, fAdam, mRebecca Fields, wViola Honaker
William A, b3/1844, Lune Co, fPaul, m-- Wrigglesworth, wPauline Cheatham
William H, b18--, Amel Co, wHenningham Elam
William V, Sr, b18--, fGoodrich, mElizabeth Venable, wGrace A Wilson
William V, Jr, b4/22/1854, Petersburg, Dinw Co, fWilliam V, Sr, mGrace A Wilson
Willis, bc1700, PrAn Co?, fSamuel, m-- Mason, w-- Goodrich
Woodrow, b12/28/1855, Staunton, Augu Co, fJoseph R, mJessie Woodrow, 1wEllen Louise Axsen, md6/24/1885, 2wEdith Bolling Galt, md12/18/1915
WILTSHIRE, Elizabeth, b18--, Rkbr Co?, hHarry McGown
WIMBISH, Eppay, bc1800, Peytonsburg, Pitt Co
Fanny Clopton, b1827, Pitt Co, fEppay, hRandolph V Barksdale
Judith, bc1800, hJohn Bonaparte Carrington
Sarah Ann, b18--, Hali Co, 1w of Thomas Leigh
WINCH, Edith, bc1870, Richmond?, fGeorge, mMary Winch, hJames Scott Parrish, Sr, md12/6/1893
Enoch, b18--, Richmond?, wMary Fuller
George, b18--, Richmond?, fEnoch, mMary Fuller, wMary Winch
Mary, b18--, Richmond?, fRussell, mMary Carver, hGeorge Winch
Russell, b18--, Richmond?, wMary Carver
WINDLE, Jemimah, bc1848, Shen Co, d1880, fSamuel, hGeorge W Hillyard, md186-
Samuel, b18--, Shen Co
Samuel, bc1861, nrEdinburg, Shen Co, d1892, fGeorge, 1h of Laura Artz
WINE, --, b18--, Rkhm Co, hSamuel Miller
Anna, b18--, Rkhm Co?, hJames A Fry
Anna, b1/21/1844, Forrestville,

WINE (continued)
Shen Co, fJacob, mSusanna Neff, hJonathan Harpine
Barbara, b17--, Shen Co, hSamuel Myers
Catherine, b184-, Forrestville, fJacob, mSusanna Neff, hJohn Humbert
Daniel P, b1856, Shen Co, fJacob, mSusanna Neff, wRebecca Good
Elizabeth, b18--, Rkhm Co, hMartin Garber
Jacob, b18--, Quicksburg, Shen Co, fMichael, mMary Hoover
Jacob, b18--, Shen Co, wSusanna Neff
John, b18--, Quicksburg, Shen Co, fMichael, mMary Hoover
Katie, b18--, Quicksburg, Shen Co, fMichael, mMary Hoover, hBenjamin Wine
Mary, b18--, Quicksburg, Shen Co, fMichael, mMary Hoover, hReuben Golliday
Newton, bc1850, Rkhm Co, wMattie C Driver
Rebecca, bc1840, Forrestville, Shen Co, fJacob, mSusanna Neff, hJacob Miller
Samuel A, b5/14/1838, Quicksburg, Shen Co, fMichael, mMary Hoover, wSarah Jane Coffman
Susanna, b184-, Forrestville, Shen Co, fJacob, mSusanna Neff, hChristian Holler
William, bc1850, Augu Co?, wMary V Plecker
WINEGOARD, Isaac, b18--, Rkhm Co?, wAnnie Grove
WINESETT, Julia Ann, b1860, Woodlawn, Carr Co, d1920, hJames W Edwards
Will, bc1860, Wyth Co, wLaura Poole
WINFIELD, Katherine, b18--, Rkhm Co, 2w of Samuel M Yost, md186-
WINFREE, Catherine Virginia, b1824, Lynchburg, Camp Co, fChristopher, mCornelia Meyer Tilden
Christopher, b10/23/1785, Ches Co, fValentine, Jr, mLucy Cheatham, 1wPolly Warwick, 2w Cornelia Meyer Tilden, md11/

WINFREE (continued)
19/1817
Christopher Valentine, b11/14/1826, Lynchburg, Camp Co, fChristopher, mCornelia Meyer Tilden, 1wVirginia A Brown, md11/14/1860, 2wSarah C Doniphan
Edwin, bc1800, Ches Co
Elizabeth Owen, b1/27/1803, Ches Co, fValentine, Jr, mLucy Cheatham, hJohn Dance, md1/1824
George, b1838, Ches Co, fEdwin, 1wAdelhide Snellings, 2wElton Cole
Henry Lee, b1/16/1864, Lynchburg, Camp Co, fChristopher Valentine, (1)mVirginia A Brown, wElsie Cleaveland, md7/9/1912
James, b176-, Ches Co, fValentine, Sr, mMartha Johnson
Jane Margaret, b7/18/1821, Lynchburg, Camp Co, fChristopher (2)mCornelia Meyer Tilden, hEdward S Brown, md5/1845
John Bell Tilden, b5/8/1829, Lynchburg, Camp Co, fChristopher, (2)mCornelia Meyer Tilden, wAnn E Pennington, md12/16/ 1857
Lizzie Kent, b11/23/1866, Lynchburg, Camp Co, fChristopher Valentine, (1)mVirginia A Brown, hWalter B Ryan, md11/16/1893
Louisa Ann, b18--, Lynchburg, Camp Co, fChristopher, (1)m Polly Warwick
Lucy Adeline, b18--, Lynhburg, Camp Co, fChristopher, (1)m Polly Warwick
Lucy, b1837, Ches Co?, hWilliam Tilghman Cogvill
Lucy Hobson, b11/18/1791, Ches Co, fValentine, Jr, mLucy Cheatham
Major, b176-, Ches Co, fValentine, Sr, mMartha Johnson
Margaret, b3/7/1798, Ches Co, fValentine, Jr, mLucy Cheatham
Martha Caroline, b18--, Lynchburg, Camp Co, fChristopher, (1)mPolly Warwick
Martha Johnson, b2/11/1790,

WINFREE (continued)
Ches Co, fValentine, Jr, mLucy Cheatham
Mary Cornelia, b1/30/1819, Lynchburg, Camp Co, fChristopher, (2)mCornelia Meyer Tilden, hThaddeus H Ivey, md7/1842
Nelson, b10/24/1783, Ches Co, fValentine, Jr, mLucy Cheatham, w-- Vairden
Peyton Brown, b9/10/1868, Lynchburg, Camp Co, fChristopher Valentine, (1)mVirginia A Brown, wMabel Louise Wilbur, md11/25/ 1896
Polly Cheatham, b1/7/1794, Ches Co, fValentine, Jr, mLucy Cheatham
Robert Burton, b3/2/1800, Ches Co, fValentine, Jr, mLucy Chatham
Reuben, b176-, Ches Co, fValentine, Sr, mMartha Johnson
Thomas, b11/23/1796, Ches Co, fValentine, Jr, mLucy Cheatham
Valentine, Sr, b17--, Ches Co?, wMartha Johnson
Valentine, jr, b7/15/1762, Ches Co, fValentine, Sr, mMartha Johnson, wLucy Cheatham, md1/3/ 1783
Valentine III, b10/27/1787, Ches Co, fValentine, Jr, mLucy Cheatham, w-- Lafon
Virginia Elizabeth, b11/19/1831, Lynchburg, Camp Co, fChristopher, (2)mCornelia Meyer Tilden
William Washington, b10/15/1806, Ches Co, fValentine, Jr, mLucy Cheatham
WINFREY, Elisha William, b18--, fGeorge Hill, wRoberta Jones Layne
George Hill, b1838, Buck Co, w-- Layne
WINGETER, Sarah, bc1860, Fred Co?, fJohn W, hGeorge H Clark
WINGFIELD, Cornelia, b18--, Albe Co, hJames M Garnett
Douglas, b18--, Fauq Co?, wDora L Parr
Edward Campbell, b10/20/1820, Albe Co, fJohn M, mAnn Buster, wEliza Mildred Simms

WINGFIELD (continued)
Indiana, b18--, Hano Co, hWilliam H Carpenter
J R, bc1840, Albe Co, fEdward C, mEliza M Sims, wIda R Vest, md1876
John, b1700, Hano Co, wMary Hudson
John M, b5/6/1765, Albe Co, fJohn, mMary Hudson, wAnn Buster
Lucy Sledd, b18--, Albe Co, fEdward Campbell, mEliza Mildred Sims, hJames Benjamin Morris
Mary, b18--, Hano Co, hCallom B Jones
Molly, b18--, Richmond?, hJohn L Grubbs
Richard W, b18--, Albe Co, fJohn M, mAnn Buster
WINN, Ann, bc1800, Caro Co, hJames Goodloe
Bertie, b1856, Hano Co, hWalter M Shelton
Helen, b18--, Fluv Co, hCornelius P Snead
Julia Butler, b1867, Charlottesville, Albe Co, hEmmett St Clair Watson
WINSTON, Barrett C, b186-, Albe Co, fNathaniel W, Sr, mNannie Barrett
Charles, b18--, wNannie Steger
Charlotte Bryce, bc1850, Loui Co, d1923, hAlexander West
Chiswell Barrett, b18--, Loui Co, wLucy Nelson
Josephine, 18--, Ches Co, hWilliam S Bland
Josie, bc1870, PrEd Co, fPeter, mMollie Rice, hThomas A Woodson, md1/6/1892
Lucy M, bc1870, Albe Co, fNathaniel W, S, mNannie Barrett
Mary Mead, b18--, fCharles H, mNannie Steger, hHill Montague, md6/26/1894
Minerva, b18--, hWilliam Winter Payne
Myrtle, b186-, Albe Co, fNathaniel W, Sr, mNannie Barrett
Nannie M, b186-, Albe Co, fNathaniel W, Sr, mNannie Bar-

WINSTON (continued)
rett
Nathaniel W, Sr, b11/22/1842, nrMonticello, Albe Co, d1923, fChiswell Barrett, mLucy Nelson, wNannie Barrett, md11/1865
Octavus Madison, b18--, KiWi Co?, wNannie Nelson
Peter, Sr, b18--, Richmond?, wEliza Ann Woodward
Peter, Jr, b6/5/1836, Richmond, d1920, fPeter, mEliza Ann Woodward, wMollie Rice
Virginia Henry, b18--, Richmond, hMicajah Quincy Holt
William A, b18--, Loui Co?, wLucy Payne
WINTER, Lula, b18--, hThomas Griffith
WISE, --, b17--, Fred Co?, wElizabeth Canter
Elizabeth, bc1800, Norfolk, hWilliam Deans II
Elizabeth, bc1800, Rkhm Co, m-- Haigler, hJacob Plecker/Blaecher
Frank, bc1840, Richmnd?, wEllen Tompkins
James B, bc1860, Hano Co?, wRosa Alice Mann
James I, bc1860, Fred Co?, wClara Kline
John, b184-, Bath Co, d186-, fMichael
Julia, b18--, Acco Co?, hGustave Teagle Westcott
Lucy, bc1700, Nels Co?, hJames Stephen Dillard, Jr, md1724
Mary, b5/10/1843, Bath Co, fMichael, hAndrew Bird McClintic, md7/25/1865
Michael, b18--, Augu Co
Newton B, bc1855, Rkhm Co, fWilliam, wNettie V Reeves
William, b18--, Rkhm Co
WISELY, Ella Florence, b18--, Gate City, Scot Co, d1910, fIsaac, 1w of John Edward Lane, Sr
WISMAN, Annie C, b9/17/1850, nrWoodstock, Shen Co, fW F, mSarah Orwick, hGeorge W Dellinger, md12/30/1869
Bettie, b18--, Shen Co?, fPhilip, hSamuel Hollar

WISEMAN (continued)
John H, b18--, Shen Co, wJennie Maphis
Josiah,, bc1860, Shen Co?, fJames William, mMargaret Stickley, wAnnie Smoot
Mary,, bc1870, Shen Co, d189-, fJohn H, mJennie Maphis, 1w of James Henry Smoot
Mary Catherine, b18--, Shen Co?, d1907, fPhilip, hLewis J Funkhouser
Rebecca, b18--, Shen Co, fPhilip, hJoseph Burner
Samuel, b18--, Shen Co?, fPhilip, wMargaret Elizabeth Bowman
W F, b18--, Shen Co?, wSarah Orwick
WITCHER, John Glass, Sr, b18--, Pitt Co?, wExcie Clay Wright
WITHERS, Sarah, b18--, Fauq Co?, fHoward, hAlbert Fletcher, Sr
Zuleika Lemmon, b18--, Camp Co, fE B, hAbram Irvin Clark, md1854
WITT, Alfred, b184-, nrKeokee, Lee Co, fEdmond, mAnnie Thompson
Anthony, b1771, Russ Co, w-- Mace
Archibald, b184-, nrKeokee, Lee Co, fEdmond, mAnnie Thompson
Bettie, b183-, nrKeokee, Lee Co, fEdmond, mAnnie Thompson
Edmond, b5/4/1808, Russ Co, d1870, fAnthony, m-- Mace, wAnnie Thompson, d12/22/1831
Jasper Franklin, b1/25/1857, nrKeokee, Lee Co, fEdmond, mAnnie Thompson, wDora Hurst
John, bc1840, nrKeokee, Lee Co, fEdmond, mAnnie Thompson
John B F, b2/9/1862, Lee Co, fWilliam, mElizabeth Clark, wEllen DeBusk
Martha, bc1850, nrKeokee, Lee Co, fEdmond, mAnnie Thompson, hMarion Morris
Mary Ann, b184-, nrKeokee, Lee Co, fEdmond, mAnnie Thompson, hHenry H Clarkston
Rebecca, b183-, nrKeokee, Lee Co, d186-, fEdmond, mAnnie Thompson, hJames Clarkston
William, b6/5/1837, nrKeokee,

WITT (continued)
Lee Co, d1922, fEdmond, mAnnie Thompson, wElizabeth Clark
WITTEN, Ancil Davidson, b4/4/1862, Wittens Mills, Taze Co, fJames R, mMatilda Davidson, wBetty Montague Stephens, md2/1895
E H, bc1860, Taze Co, fJames R, mMatilda Davidson
Elizabeth, b18--, Abbs Valley, Taze Co, 1w of Robert Craig Graham
James W M, b18--, Taze Co, wRachel White
James R, bc1831, Taze Co, wMatilda Davidson
Pauline, bc1870, Taze Co, fRobert B, (1)mVirginia Custer, hJohn Graham
Rachel W, bc1870, Taze Co, fRobert, (1)mVirginia Custer, hReece Whitley
Robert B, b1843, Taze C, fJames W M, mRachel White, 1wVirginia "Kate" Custer, 2wVirginia Whittaker
William, bc1860, Taze Co, fJames R, mMatilda Davidson
WITTIG, George W, bc1870, Brock's Gap, Rkhm Co, fHenry, mMary Moyers
John, b186-, Brock's Gap, Rkhm Co, fHenry, mMary Moyers
WOHLFORD, James, bc1850, Wyth Co?, wKate S Johnson
WOLF, --, b17--, Fred Co?, wAnna Maria Miller
Kate, b18--, Rkhm Co?, hCharles B Harnsberger
William, b18--, Richmond?, wAnnie Watson
WOLFE, Clinton M, b186-, Dungannon, Scot Co, fJasper Marion, mMary Anne Davis
Elbert F, b1/18/1861, Dungannon, Scot Co, fJasper Marion, mMary Anne Davis, wLula E Smith
Jacob, b17--, nrDungannon, Scot Co, wFrankie Stallard
Jaley A, bc1860, Dungannon, Scot Co, fJasper Marion, mMary Anne Davis, hJohn H Reynolds
Jasper Marion, b1818, Dungannon, Scot Co, fJacob, mFrankie

WOLFE (continued)
Stallad, wMary Anne Davis
Joseph B, Sr, b2/18/1832, Charlottesville, Albe Co, fEzra M, mLucy Bishop
Maggie, b185-, Dungannon, Scot Co, fJasper Marion, mMary Anne Davis, hJohn H Osborne
Melissa J, bc1870, Dungannon, Scot Co, fJasper Marion, mMary Anne Davis, hPhillip S Banner
Preston, bc1860, Wash Co?, wMatilda Jane Edmondson
William R, b186-, Dungannon, Scot Co, fJasper Marion, mMary Anne Davis
WOLFORD, Mary M, bc1840, Wyth Co, 2w of John G Kegley
Sarah, b1866, Grant Co, hBazzle Hess
WOLVERTON, Mary, b18--, Shen Co?, hJohn Kibler
WOLWINE, Bettie, b18--, KiWi Co?, hAlfred F Hargrave
WOMACK, Mary Ann, b18--, Meck Co, hCharles B Watkins
Polk Dallas, b1845, Pitt Co, fCharles, m-- Glasscock, wMary L Tucker
WOMBLE, Susan Ann, b1842, Isle Co, hAbner B Cofer
WOOD, --, b18--, Rkhm Co?, 1h of Matilda Riddel
A J, bc1840, Loui Co?, wLouisa M Vest
A J, b186-, Patr Co?, wNancy S Via
Alice, b18--, Culpeper, Culp Co, fPollard, mJemima Spillman, hW E Hackley
Annie Ashford, b186-, Rkbr Co, fGeorge Godfey, mMartha Ann Grimsley
Archibald, b182-, Newcastle, Crai Co, fJohn M, mRachel Mason
B J, b18--, Rapp Co?, wNellie D Roberts
Beryl, b18--, Rapp Co
Cabell S, b10/2/1870, Charlotte Court House, Char Co, fHenry, Jr, mMary J Wood, wLouise Neilson, md2/21/1900
Catherine, bc1800, Winchester, Fred Co, fRobert, hThomas Glass

WOOD (continued)
Charles B, b18--, Rapp Co, fBeryl, wMary Catherine Miller
D M, b18--, wSarah Eleanor Reynolds
Daniel Pollard, b6/11/1852, Culpeper, Culp Co, fPollard, mJemima Spillman, wSallie Parkinson, md4/17/1777
David, b17--, wMargaret Lewis
Elisha G, b182-, Newcastle, Crai Co, fJohn M, mRachel Moon
Eliza, b17--, Fran Co, hJohn Spotswood Burwell
Eliza, b182-, Newcastle, Crai Co, fJohn M, mRachel Mason
Elizabeth, b18--, Charlottesville, Albe Co, fJohn, Jr, 2w of Clement D Fishburne, md1867
Elizabeth, bc1830, Newcastle, Crai Co, fJohn M, mRachel Mason
Emma V, b18--, Nhtn Co?, hJohn Wesley Richardson
Fannie C, bc1870, Madi Co?, fJames Madison, mAnne E Bragg, hWilliam Jackson Smith, md2/7/1894
Florilla, b18--, Pitt Co?, hWhitefield West
Frank, b18--, Rapp Co, fCharles B, mMary Catherine Miller
George Godfrey, b18--, Rapp Co, wMartha Ann Grimsley, mdc1857
Georgie, b186-, Rapp Co, fGeorge Godfrey, mMartha Ann Grimsley, hCarey Stout
Henry Virginia, bc1823, Albe Co?, d1900, fHenry, hThomas H Campbell
Henry, Sr, b1810, Amel Co
Henry, Jr, b5/13/1843, Clarksville, Meck Co, d1921, fHenry, Sr, 1wMary J Wood, 2wSallie Morton
Henry Ashford, b18--, Rapp Co, fJohn, wLucy Ann Smith
Hugh, b182-, Newcastle, Crai Co, fJohn M, mRachel Mason
J J, bc1850, Camp Co, wMary B Robertson
Jacquelin, b18--, fJames
James, b18--, fJames
James Barnett, b186-, Rapp Co, fGeorge Godfrey, mMartha Ann Grimsley

WOOD (continued)
James Madison, b18--, Madi Co, fJohn Hay, mLucy Miller, wAnna E Bragg
James W, b1853, Albe Co, wMildred S Craig
Jane, b18--, fJames, hJohn Borden
John F, b182-, Newcastle, Crai Co, fJohn M, mRachel Mason
John H, b186-, Rkbr C, fGeorge Godfrey, mMartha Ann Grimsley
John M, b17--, Monr Co, wRachel Mason
John R, b6/4/1842, Batesville, Albe Co, wAbbie Rogers
John W, b18--, Rapp Co, fCharles D, wFannie Taylor Dudley
Lelia D, b18--, fD M, mSarah Eleanor Reynolds, 1hA W Ruff, 2w of Samuel Hutchings Price, md5/24/1899
Lewis, b182-, fJames
Lucy Jane, b18--, Albe Co, 1w of William Taylor Barret
Lula, b18--, Rapp Co, fCharles B, mMary Catherine Miller, hHubert Forest Keyser, md12/10/1890
Martha, b18--, fJames, h-- Lippincott
Martha, b1837, Lee Co, d1916, 2w of John N Cridlin
Mary, b17--, PrEd Co, fValentine, mLucy Henry, 1w of Peter Johnston II
Mary Ewing, b4/17/1860, Big Moccasin, Scot Co, d1886, 1w of Charles M Carter
Mary J, b18--, Gooc Co, d1873, w1 of Henry Wood, Jr
Mary Ruth, b186-, Rkbr Co, fGeorge Godfrey, mMartha Ann Grimsley, hJ P Millan
Pollard, b1825, fJames, 1wJemima Spillman, 2wColumbia Doors
Robert, b17--, Winchester, Fred Co, fJames
Robert Warner, bc1800, Albe Co?, fDavid, mMargaret Lewis, 1h of Mary Miller
Susan, b17--, Lune Co, hJohn F Adams
Susan Moore, b186-, Rapp Co, fGeorge Godfrey, mMartha Ann

WOOD (continued)
Grimsley, hC E Johnson
Thomas A, bc1870, Rapp Co, fGeorge Godfrey, mMartha Ann Grimsley
Valentine, b17--, wLucy Henry
W F, bc1850, Camp Co, wMittie Robertson
Warner, b9/1825, Albe Co, d1902, fRobert, mMary Willer, wMargaret Lynn Woods, md1/5/1888
Wesley, b182-, fJames
William Grimsley, b3/1/1861, Rkbr Co, fGeorge Godfrey, mMartha Ann Grimsley, wAnnie Washington (Jones) Clopton
William M, b1825, Newcastle, Crai Co, fJohn M, mRachel Mason, wMary Early Wright
William Woodford, b18--, Culpeper, Culp Co, fPollard, mJemima Spillman
Woodford, bc1820, fJames
WOODALL, Sarah, b18--, Camp Co, hWilliam E Nichols
WOODARD, J J, b18--, nrBoykins, Sout Co, fAnthony, wSally Dudly
WOODHOUSE, John Thomas, bc1839, PrAn Co, d1917, wVirginia E Whitehurst
Robert Woodside, Sr, b18--, PrAn Co, wBettie James
WOODING, Harry, Sr, b4/27/1844, fWilliam H, mJane W Grasly, wMary Ella Coleman, md1873
William H, b18--, Pitt Co, fThomas, wJane W Grasly
WOODROOF, Ella, bc1858, Amhe Co, hJames Spotswood Dillard, Jr
WOODRUM, Josephine Elizabeth, b18-- Pearisburg, Gile Co, hCharles Carroll Woolwine, Sr
Robert H, bc1857, Roan Co?, wAnna T Musgrove
WOODS, Amine, bc1860, Roan Co, fWilliam, (2)mSarah Jane Edington
Annie L, b186-, Roan Co, fWilliam, (2)mSarah Jane Edington
Archibald, b173-, Albe Co, fMichael
Hudson James, b11/13/1866, nrPearisburg, Gile Co, fJames Hudson, mLucretia Jordan,

WOODS (continued)
wStella Kinzie
James Hudson, b1826, Gile Co, d1908, wLucretia Jordan
James P, Sr, b2/4/1868, Roan Co, fWilliam, (2)mSarah Jane Edington, wSusie K Moon
John, b1770, Catawba, Roan Co, fArchibald, wElizabeth Smith
John Rodes, b18--, Albe Co, fMicajah, wSabina Lewis Stuart Creigh
John W, bc1860, Roan Co, d1912, fWilliam, (2)mSarah Jane Edington
Joseph R, b186-, Roan Co, fWilliam, (2)mSarah Jane Edington
Margaret Lynn, bc1860, "Holkham", Albe Co, fJohn Rodes, mSabina Lewis Stuart Creigh, hWarner Wood, md1/5/1888
Mary Jane, b17--, Scot Co, hGeorge Morison
Micajah, b17--, Albe Co, fWilliam
Micajah, b5/17/1844, "Holkham", Albe Co, d1911, fJohn Rodes, mSabina Lewis Stuart Creigh, wMatilda Minor Morris, md6/9/1874
Oscar W, bc1870, Roan Co, d1908, fWilliam, (2)mSarah Jane Edington
Susan, bc1800, Albe Co?, hNathaniel Massie
William, b17--, Albe Co
William, b1817, Roan Co, fJohn, mElizabeth Smith, 2wSarah Jane Edington
William P, b18--, Albe Co?, wEllen Willie Benton, bc1850, Albe Co, fWilliam P, mEllen -- hJames Monroe Ellison
WOODSON, Agnes, b18--, fRichard, mNannie Micheaux, hFrancis Watkins
Amanda, bc1830, Appo Co, fDrury, mLouise Hendrick
Charles A, bc1842, New Amsterdam, Bote Co, d1922, wGeorgie Callen
Drury A, b1836, Appo Co, fDrury W, mLouisa Hendrick, 1wElla S Bruce, md9/30/1866, 2wEmma W Bruce, md2/1/1877
Drury W, bc1804, PrEd Co,

WOODSON (continued)
d1895, fObediah, mMary Watson, wLouise Hendrick
Elizabeth Eleanor, bc1870, PrEd Co, fDrury A, (1)mElla S Bruce, hW B Gates
Ella, bc1830, Appo Co, fDrury W, mLouise Hendrick
Emaline Marcella, b18--, Lexington, Rkbr Co, 1w of Albert Lawrence West
Henry Palmer, bc1860, Appo Co, fJohn William, mMary Elizabeth Christian
Jacob, b1748, PrEd Co, d1839, fObediah, mConstant Watkins, wElizabeth Morton
Jacob, b1753, Gooc Co, wMary Gray
Jacob, bc1830, Appo Co, fDrury W, mLouise Hendrick
James, bc1830, Appo Co, fDrury W, mLouise Hendrick
Jane, b1798, Gooc Co, fJacob, mMary Gray, hIsrael Nuckols
Jane Randolph, b17--, fJohn, mDorothea Randolph, hArchibald Pleasants
John, b1632, nrJamestown, (now) PrGe Co, fJohn, mSarah --
John, bc1660, PrGe Co, fRobert, mElizabeth Ferris
John, b17--, wDorothea Randolph
John William, b1823, Appo Co, d1864, fDrury W, mLouise Hendrick, wMary Elizabeth Christian, md185-
Jonathan Christian, b1/30/1853, Appo Co, fJohn William, mMary Elizabeth Christian, 1wFannie Christian Binford, md1885, 2w Bennie Gipson, md1890, 3wLily Cabell Scott, md1913
Keith, b1850, Richmond, hCharles O Saville
Martha, b18--, Augu Co, hAbram Wayland
Martha, bc1830, Appo Co, fDrury W, mLouise Hendrick
Mary, bc1700, Fluv Co?, hGeorge Payne
Mary Elizabeth, b185-, Appo Co, fJohn William, mMary Elizabeth Christian, hLewis D Isbell
Molly, bc1830, Appo Co, fDrury W, mLouise Hendrick

WOODSON (continued)
Obediah, b1712, Henrico Co?, fRichard, mAnn Smith, wConstant Watkins, md1734
Obediah, b17--, PrEd Co, fJacob, mElizabeth Morton, wMary Watson
Richard, bc1660, PrEd Co, fRobert, mElizabeth Ferris, wAnn Smith
Robert, b1634, nrJamestown, (now) PrGe Co, fJohn, mSarah --, wElizabeth Ferris
Robert, b1660, PrGe Co, fRobert, mElizabeth Ferris, 1wSarah Lewis, 2wRachel Watkins
S B, bc180, Bote Co?, wNellie Huff
Sarah, b16--, hHenry Terrell
Sarah Louisa, b185-, Appo Co, fJohn William, mMary Elizabeth Christian, hJohn H Nowlin
Thomas A, b8/14/1869, PrEd Co, fDrury A, (1)mElla S Bruce, wJosie Winston, md1/6/1892
William McGuffy, b185-, Appo Co, d1917, fJohn William, mMary Elizabeth Christian, wMaude Thornhill
WOODWARD, --, b18--, KiQu Co?, 3w of Thomas Beverly Evans
Alberta Frances, b18--, Page Co?, m-- Holland, hRichard Grubbs Morrison
Anna, bc1850, Augu Co, fPeter H, mEliza Doak, hL D Young
Anne, b181-, Midd Co, fRichard, (1)m-- Thresley, hJohn D McGill
Annie, b184-, Rectortown, Fauq Co, fLuke Edward, Sr, (1)m-- Jolley, hStephen D Boyd
Ashby W, bc1850, Augu Co, fPeter H, mEliza Doak
Betty H, bc1850, Augu Co, fPeter H, mEliza Doak
Catherine, b18--, Augu Co, fSamuel, mMary C Hanger, hWilliam E Burnett
Eliza Ann, b18--, Richmond?, hPeter Winston, Sr
Eveline, b18--, Augu Co, fSamuel M, mMary C Hanger, hCaleb Crone
George, b17--, NewK Co?,

WOODWARD (continued)
fGeorge/Lancelott, wSusanna --
Hannah, b18--, Augu Co, fSamuel M, mMary C Hanger, hWilliam J Hunter
Harry Duke, b9/3/1758, NewK Co, fSamuel mMary --
Henley, bc1760, NewK Co, fGeorge, mSusanna --
Isabella, b181-, Midd Co, fRichard, (1)m-- Thresley, hWilliam Shepherd
James, b18--, Lee Co
James H, bc1850, Augu Co, fPeter H, mEliza Doak
Jesse L, bc1870, nrJonesville, Lee Co, fWilliam, mJane Sorber
John Douglas, bc1850, Midd Co?, fJohn Pitt Lee, mMary Mildred Minor, wMaria Louise Simmons, md2/1875
John H, b18--, Augu Co, fSamuel M, mMary C Hanger
John H, bc1850, Augu Co, fPeter H, mEliza Doak
John Pitt Lee, b5/7/1821, Midd Co, fRichard, (2)mLettice Lee Whiting, wMary Mildred Minor, md10/26/1843
John W, bc1850, Lee Co?, wMargaret Jane Wynn
Joseph B, b5/6/1850, Staunton, Augu Co, fPeter H, mEliza Doak
Joseph N, b18--, Augu Co, fSamuel M, mMary C Hanger
Luke Edward, b1812, Fred Co, 1w-- Jolley, 2wEliza Fred
Luke Edward, Jr, b36/1845, Rectortown, Fauq Co, fLuke Edward, Sr, (1)m-- Jolley, wEugenia Lambert
Martha, b186-, nrJonesville, Lee Co, fWilliam, mJane Serber, hJames McCauley
Mary E, b18--, Augu Co, fSamuel M, mMary C Hanger, hWilliam McNiel
Peter H, b1/6/1823, Augu Co, fSamuel M, mMary C Hanger, wEliza Doak
Philemon, b8/24/1758, NewK Co, fGeorge, mSusanna --
Porter M, bc1850, Augu Co, fPeter H, mEliza Doak
Richard, bc1760, NewK Co, fGeorge, mSusanna --, 1w--

WOODWARD (continued)
Thresley, 2wLettice Lee Whiting, md6/22/ 1820
Richard, bc1840, Rectortown, Fauq Co, fLuke Edward, Sr, (1)m-- Jolley
Sallie E, bc1840, Rectortown, Fauq Co, fLuke Edward, Sr, (1)m-- Jolley, hJames R Dorrell
Samuel M, b1791, Augu Co, fJoseph, mJane Morris, wMary C Hanger
Samuel N, bc1850, Augu Co, fPeter H, mEliza Doak
Thomas E, bc1850, Augu Co, fPeter H, mEliza Doak
Wallace W, b18--, York Co?, wKate
Warner Minor, b10/14/1844, Midd Co, fJohn Pitt Lee, mMary Mildred Minor, wMary E Stewart, md10/28/1869
William, b1839, Lee Co, d1906, fJames, wJane Serber
William E, b18--, Augu Co, fSamuel M, mMary C Hanger
William G, bc1850, Augu Co, fPeter H, mEliza Doak
WOODY, Archer Lester, b18--, Appo Co?, wEdna MHamlet
Mary, b1812, 2w of John E Green
WOODYARD, Virginia, b18--, Fair Co?, hJohn Broders
WOOLDRIDGE, Albert Burton, b184- Ches Co, fDaniel Spencer, mMinerva Archer Cox
Caroline, b18--, Powh Co, hEdward C Archer
Daniel, b17--, Cumb Co, d1824, fThomas, wAnne Grant Spencer
Daniel Spencer, b1809, Ches Co, fSpencer, mMartha Hannah Walke, wMinerva Archer Cox, md1835
Edwin Spencer, b184-, Ches Co, d1875, fDaniel Spencer, mMinerva Archer Cox
Martha H, b5/14/1839, Ches Co, d1871, fDaniel Spencer, mMinerva Archer Cox, hHenry Winston Cox, md11/8/1859
Spencer, b178-, Ches Co, fDaniel, mAnne Grant Spencer, wMartha Hannah Walke, md1808
Thomas, b17--, Ches Co?, d1760

WOOLDRIDGE (continued)
Thomas James, b184-, Ches Co, fDaniel Spencer, mMinerva Archer Cox
WOOLF, Adam, b181-, nrRectortown, Fauq Co, fAndrew, mSophie Michael
Agnes Sophia, b185-, Scott District, Fauq Co, fHenry, mCatherine E Dowell, hMatthew Woolf
Andrew, bc1775, Scott District, Fauq Co, wSophie Michael
Andrew, b181-, nrRectortown, Fauq Co, fAndrew, mSophie Michael, wAnn Dowell
Ann Maria, b181-, Rectortown, Fauq Co, fAndrew, mSophie Michael
Annie Mary, b185-, Scott District, Fauq Co, Henry M, mCatherine E Dowell, hHenry Saunders
Bessie, bc1860, Scott District, Fauq Co, fHenry M, mCatherine E Dowell, 1hWilliam Waters, 2hHurrah Reed
Charles Marion, b185-, Scott District, Fauq Co, fHenry M, mCatherine E Dowell
Daniel, b181-, nrRectortown, Fauq Co, fAndew, mSophie Michael
Ernest Lee, bc1860, Scott District, Fauq Co, fHenry M, mCatherine E Dowell
Gertrude T, bc1860, Fauq Co, fAndrew, mAnn Dowell, hFenton M Love, Jr, md6/1/1881
Hardwick E, b185-, Scott District, Fauq Co, fHenry M, mCatherine E Dowell
Henry M, b1816, nrRectortown, Fauq Co, fAndrew, mSophie Michael, wCatherine E Dowell
James Edgar, b185-, Scott District, Fauq Co, fHenry M, mCatherine E Dowell
John, b181-, nrRectortown, Fauq Co, fAndrew, mSophie Michael
John Andrew, b10/5/1848, Scott District, Fauq Co, fHenry M, mCatherine E Dowell, wJosephine L Burgess, md1/7/1881
Mary Magdalene, b181-, nrRectortown, Fauq Co, fAndrew,

WOOLF (continued)
mSophie Michael
Matthew, bc1850, Fauq Co?, wAgnes Sophia Woolf
Phoebe, b 181-, nrRectortown, Fauq Co, fAndrew, mSophie Michael
Robert D, bc1850, Scott District, Fauq Co, fHenry M, mCatherine E Dowell
Simon, b181-, nrRectortown, Fauq Co, fAndrew, mSophie Michael
Sophia, b181-, nrRectortown, Fauq Co, fAndrew, mSophie Michael
Thurston, bc1840, Fauq Co?, wJennie Ashby
William H, b185-, Scott District, Fauq Co, fHenry M, mSophie Michael
WOOLWINE, Charles Carroll, Sr, b18--, Christiansburg, Mont Co, wJosephine Elizabeth Woodrum
Emma L, b18--, Camp Co?, fRobert L, mElizabeth Charlton, 1w of John Martin Oakey
Luemma, b1/19/1851, Patr Co, hJohn Merritt
Robert L, b18--, Camp Co?, wElizabeth Charlton
WOOTEN, Mattie A, b18--, Green Bay, PrEd Co, fFrank Taylor, hJames L Stone, md1863
WOOTTON, Fannie, b18--, PrEd Co, hAlexander Storton Clark
WORD, John, b181-, Hali Co
Martha, bc1825, Hali Co, dc1896, hWilliam H Peak
WORRELL, Cordelia, b186-, Carr Co, fJonathan, mMatilda Branscome
Jane, b18--, Carr Co? hPeter Early
Jonathan, b18--, Carr Co, wMatilda Branscome
Lawson, bc1870, Carr Co, fJonathan, mMatilda Branscome, wAnnye L Hall, md6/25/1902
Wiley, b186-, Carr Co, fJonathan, mMatilda Branscome
WORSHAM, John Henry, b18--, fRichard, mClarke Roxanna Goddin, wMary Bell Pilcher
Maria, b18--, Amel Co, hDabney

WORSHAM (continued)
Hardy
Richard, b18--, wClarke Roxanna Goddin
WORTHAM, Alberta, b18--, Richmond?, hJohn C Williams
WREN, Albert, bc1850, Fair Co?, wHannah Harrison
Bell, b18--, Amhe Co, hJohn Wesley Joyner
Lucy Jane, b1858, Buck Co, hRobert Henry Hudgins, Jr
WRIGGLESWORTH, --, b18--, Spot Co, hPaul Wilson
WRIGHT, Ann, b181-, Middletown, Fred Co, fGeorge, mCatherine Sensenny
Annie B, b18--, Sout Co, hThomas L Lea
Anthony W, b1844, KiWi Co, fDavid, wIsabella Granger
Benjamin T, b18--, Buck Co?, fThomas Smith, mElizabeth Patterson
Dora A, bc1870, nrVinton, Roan Co, fStephen, mMargaret Jane Muse
Eliza A, b18--, Bote Co?, hJohn B Lemon
Elizabeth, b18--, Wise Co?, fVincent, mMelinda Baldwin, 1h-- Lewis, 2w of William W G Dotson
Elizabeth, b18--, Russ Co?, 2w of William Gilmer
Ellis L, bc1870, nrVinton, Roan Co, fStephen, mMargaret Jane Muse
Estelle A, b18--, Camp Co?, fJohn M, hOscar Bayne Barker
Excie Clay, b18--, Pitt Co?, hJohn Glass Witcher, Sr
Frances Catherine, b186-, Camp Co, fThomas Smith, mElizabeth Patterson
Franklin P, b18--, Bedf Co, fThomas Smith, mElizabeth Patterson
George, b17--, Rich Co?, wCatherine Pope Sanford
George, b17--, Esse Co?
George Butler, b3/22/1858, nr Middletown, Fred Co, fJohn William, mJacquelin Hite, wEttie Canter, md10/6/1880
George W, bc1860, Bedf Co?,

WRIGHT (continued)
fThomas Smith, mElizabeth Patterson
Hannah, bc1800, West Co, hBenedict Walker
Howard F, bc1850, wVirginia Parrish
Ida F, b18--, nrVinton, Roan Co, fStephen, mMargaret Jane Muse, hJohn Thomas Graves, md10/11/ 1883
James B, bc1850, Amhe Co?, wBettis McGinnis
James D, b18--, Russ Co? wLucy Cox
John, b18--, Esse Co?, fGeorge, wEliza John Noel
John James, b18--, Buck Co, fThomas Smith, mElizabeth Patterson
John R, bc1850, wMary Lucy Parrish
John William, b7/26/1822, Middletown, Fred Co, d1899, fGeorge, (1)mCatherine Sensenney, wJacquelin Hite
Kate, b18--, Pitt Co?, hRobert Temple Johnson
Kate, b18--, Culp Co, hConaway Compton
Luther, b18--, Caro Co?, wSusan Withers Coleman
Maria Louise, b185-, nrMiddletown, Fred Co, fJohn William, mJacquelin Hite, hS W Cooley
Mary, bc1800, Richmond, fGeorge, mCatherine Pope Sanford, 2w of Christopher DeAtley Ficklin
Mary, b1855, Elk Creek, Gray Co, hKenley C Cornett
Mary Ann, b186-, Caro Co, fLuther, mSusan Wither Coleman, hCharles Woodson Throckmorton
Mary Elizabeth, b186-, Camp Co, fThomas Smith, mElizabeth Patterson
Mary H, b182-, Middletown, Fred Co, fGeorge, (1)mCatherine Sensenny, hArthur Bragg
Matthew, b17--, Bedf Co, wNancy Holland
Matthew, b17--, Bedf Co, fJoseph
Maude, bc1830, Fred Co, hSen-

WRIGHT (continued)
senny Wright
Nancy, bc1800, Bedf Co?, fMatthew, mNancy Holland, hFrancis Johnson
Nancy, b18--, Bedf Co?, hC H McManaway
Peter M, bc1802, Bedf Co, fMatthew, wSusan James
Polly, b17--, Roan Co? hDavid Gish
Rachel, bc1820, Middletown, Fred Co, fGeorge, (1)mCatherine Sensenny
Richard H, b18--, Gooc Co, wLillie M Hobson
Robert H, bc1860, Bedf Co?, fThomas Smith, mElizabeth Patterson
Sarah, b17--, PrAn Co, hWilliam Consalvo II
Sarah, b1811, Nels Co, hNelson Bryant, Sr
Sensenny, b182-, Middletown, Fred Co, fGeorge, (1)mCatherine Sensenny, wMaude Wright
Stephen, b5/21/1836, nrStuartsville, Bedf Co, fPeter M, mSusan James, wMargaret Jane Muse
Stephen, b186-, Carr Co, wLula L Hylton
Susan Jones, b18--, "Springfield Farm", nrRexburg, Esse Co, d1886, fJohn, mEliza Jones Noel, 1hJohn Milton Gouldin, Sr, md187-, 2hJohn Rosler
T S, bc1860, Bedf Co?, w-- Mc Manaway
Themer Turner, b18--, Bedf Co, fThomas Smith, mElizabeth Patterson
Thomas, b18--, Buck Co?, fThomas, mElizabeth Patterson
Thomas Smith, b1809, Buck Co, wElizabeth Patterson
Vincent, b18--, Wise Co?, wMelinda Baldwin
Wesley D, b186-, Camp Co, fThomas Smith, mElizabeth Patterson, wMollie Elizabeth Poindexter
William H, bc1840, Rkbr Co?, wMary Clinedinst
William Patterson, b18--, Buck Co, fThomas Smith, mElizabeth

WRIGHT (continued)
Patterson
WUNDER, Charles S, Jr, b185-, Moore's Store, Shen Co, fCharles S, Sr, mElizabeth Mary Moore
Henry S, b185-, Moore's Store, Shen Co, fCharles S, mElizabeth Mary Moore
Mark Bird, b5/23/1857, Moore's Store, Shen Co, fCharles S, mElizabeth Mary Moore, wCaroline Mary Newman, md10/18/1883
Mary Hagey, b185-, Moore's Store, Shen Co, d1922, fCharles S, mElizabeth Mary Moore, hWilliam A Pence
Milton M, b185-, Moore's Store, Shen Co, fCharles S, mElizabeth Mary Moore
Reuben M, b185-, Moore's Store, Shen Co, fCharles S, mElizabeth Mary Moore
WYANT, Alexander, b18--, nrElkton, Rkhm Co, d186-, fJohn, wJulia Long
Alexander E, b2/16/1861, nrElkton, Rkhm Co, fAlexander, mJulia Long, wSallie A Wyant
Annie, bc1860, nrElkton, Rkhm Co, fAlexander, mJulia Long, hD C Davis
Cordelia, b185-, nrElkton, Rkhm Co, fAlexander, mJulia Long, h-- Powell
Jesse, b18--, Rkhm Co, wMartha Garrison
John, b17--, nrElkton, Rkhm Co, fPeter
Sallie A, b186-, Rkhm Co, fJesse, mMartha Garrison, hAlexander E Wyant
Victoria, b185-, nrElkton, Rkhm Co, fAlexander, mJulia Long, hSamuel Hall
WYATT, Anne Harrison, bc1800, Gooc Co, hSamuel Atwell Guy
George M, b5/17/1854, Richmond, fWest
WYCLIFFE, Dorcas, b17--, Fair Co, fRobert, hCornelius Kincheloe
WYGAL, Mary, b18--, Pula Co, hJohn Trolinger
Newton, bc1850, Lee Co?, wNancy Alice Wynn

WYGAL (continued)
Rhoda, b1824, nrNewburn, Pula Co, d1873, 2w of James W Early Sebastian, bc1850, Lee Co?, wMary Malindan Wynn
WYNDHAM, Jane Norris, b18--, nrBerryville, Clar Co, fThomas, hJohn W Martin
Thomas, b18--, nrBerryville, Clar Co
WYNN, Alexander, b1824, nrJonesville, Lee Co, fWilliam, mAlice Sims, wSusan Marshall
Anne, b18--, PrGe Co?, hJames Nathaniel Nichols
Charles W, b186-, nrJoneville, Lee Co, fAlexander, mSusan Marshall
Elkanah, b17--, Taze Co, w-- Muncy
Elkanah, Jr, b1829, Lee Co, d1899, fElkanah, Sr, 2h of Fannie Robbins
Frank J, b186-, nrJoneville, Lee Co, fAlexander, mSusan Marshall
John C Breckenridge, b185-, nrJonesville, Lee Co, fAlexander, mSusan Marshall
Margaret Jane, b185-, nrJonesville, Lee Co, fAlexander, mSusan Marshall, hJohn W Woodward
Mary Malindan, b185-, nrJonesville, Lee Co, fAlexander, mSusan Marshall, hSebastian Wygal
Nancy Alice, b185-, nrJonesville, Lee Co, fAlexander, mSusan Marshall, hNewton Wygal
Ursula Belle, bc860, nJonesville, Lee Co, fAlexander, mSusan Marshall, hStephen S Surganer
William, b17--, nrJonesville, Lee Co, fElkanah, m-- Muncy, wAlice Sims
William Elkanah, b1/27/1850, nrJonesville, Lee Co, fAlexander, mSusan Marshall, wDocia Jane Thomas, md10/18/1874
WYNNE, Martha, b1846, JaCi Co, d1882, hThomas Newman
YAGER, Martha C, b18--, Page Co, hHenry J Smoot
Mollie, b18--, Madi Co?, hWil-

YAGER (continued)
liam L Payne
YANCEY, Albert S, b18--, Rkhm Co, fWilliam B II, mVictoria Winsborough, wBertie Shipp, md1895
Carrie, b18--, Camp Co?, fWilliam Tudor, hWaller Massie Boyd, Sr
Charles, bc1720, Rapp Co?, fLewis Davis, mWinifred Cavanaugh
Ed S, bc1840, Rkh Co?, wFannie V Mauzy
Ella W, bc1870, nrClarksville, Meck Co, fJohn R, mVirginia Jones White
John, b18--, wElizabeth Field
John Gibbons, b1852, Stonewall District, Rkhm Co, d1913, wFannie Bennett Bradley
John J, b1859, nrClarksville, Meck Co, d1905, fJohn R, mVirginia Jones White
John R, b1820, nrBuffalo Springs, Meck Co, d1907, fRichard, wVirginia Jones White
John William, bc1804, Rapp Co?, d1894, fThomas, wJane Elizabeth Terrell
Laura V, b1864, nrClarksville, Meck Co, d1906, fJohn R, mVirginia Jones White
Lewis Davis, b16--, Rapp Co?, wWinifred Cavanaugh, md1710
Mary Columbia, b18--, Rkhm Co?, hFountain Taliaferro
Robert Edward, b10/4/1862, nrClarksville, Meck Co, fJohn R, mVirginia Jones White, wOtelia V Harris, md1/6/1891
Thomas, b17--, Rapp Co?, fCharles
William B II, b18--, Rkhm Co, fWilliam B, m-- Smith, wVictoria Winsborough
William Terrell, b5/3/1857, Oak Forest, Rapp Co, fJohn William, mJane Elizabeth Terrell, 1wNannie Stevenson, md4/25/1883, 2w Annie Belle Mason, md7/27/1917
William Tudor, b18--, Camp Co
YATES, Addie Moore, b186-, Yatesville, Lune Co, fBenjamin

YATES (continued)
L, Sr, mSophia M Ralls, hPaul H Dodson
Anna M, bc1860, Yatesville, Lune Co, d1922, fBenjamin L, Sr, mSophia M Ralls, 1hWilliam E Jeter, 2hGeorge F Moore
Benjamin L, Sr, b1830, Mill Grove, Meck Co, d1913, fJohn Murray, mAnne (Bailey) Moring, wSophia M Ralls
Benjamin L, Jr, b185-, Yatesville, Lune Co, fBenjamin L, Sr, mSophia M Ralls
Catherine, b17--, "Nottingham", Spot Co, hRobert Wellford
Charles, b18--, Rapp Co
Charles Lewis, b18--, Rapp Co, fCharles, wSusan Mary Bragg
Charles N, b185-, Yatesville, Lune Co, d1905, fBenjamin L, Sr, mSophia M Ralls
Cynthia, b18--, Russ Co, hJoseph H Perkins
Elijah, b184-, Dick Co? wMary Keel
Elizabeth Jury, b18--, hE Lawrence Brown
Garrett, b18--, Rapp Co
George M, b186-, Yatesville, Lune Co, fBenjamin L, Sr, mSophia M Ralls
Henry Tucker, bc1870, Yatesville, Lune Co, fBenjamin L, Sr, mSophia Ralls
James, b18--, Rapp Co?, wMary Moore
James Massillon, b11/23/1869, Rosewood Farm, Rapp Co, fCharles Lewis, mSusan Mary Bragg, wDaisy Elizabeth Menefee, md10/18/1899
John Leroy, b9/21/1854, Yatesville, Lune Co, fBenjamin L, Sr, mSophia M Ralls, wMary Frances Cooksey, md4/7/1881
John Murray, bc1800, nrPetersburg, Dinw Co, d1856, 2h of Anne (Bailey) Moring
Joseph M, b186-, Yatesville, Lune Co, d1901, fBenjamin L, Sr, mSophia M Ralls
Lucy, b11/8/1856, Wilton, West Co, d1919, hEdward Colston Newton
Luther Edward, b186-, Yates-

YATES (continued)
ville, Lune Co, fBenjamin L, Sr, mSophia M Ralls W B, bc1860, PrEd Co, wElizabeth Eleanor Woodson
William A, b185-, Yatesville, Lune Co, fBenjamin L, Sr, mSophia M Ralls
YEAGER, Jane, b18--, hThomas Alexander Gordon
YEATMAN, Charity Evelyn, b18--, West Co, fCharles, mEmily Arnest, hFrederick Griffith, md9/14/1897
Charles, b18--, West Co, wEmily Arnest
YEATTS, Thomas Alfred, b1850, Pitt Co, wFannie P Cook
YOST, Isaac, bc1800, Augu Co
Jacob, b18--, Strasburg, Shen Co
Jacob, b4/1/1853, Staunton, Augu Co, fSamuel M, (1)mHenrietta Cushing, wMary S Young, md1/13/ 1881
Kate, b18--, Strasburg, Shen Co, fJacob, hJohn Eaton Rogers, Sr
Mary E, b18--, Pula Co?, hJohn B Darst
Samuel M, b11/13/1828, Augu Co, fIsaac, 1wHenrietta Cushing, 2wKatherine Winfield
YOUELL, William, b18--, Rkbr Co, w-- Davidson
William A, bc1860, Rkbr Co, fWilliam, m-- Davidson, wSusie McNutt
YOUNG, Andrew Jackson, b2/7/ 1864, Elkton, Rkhm Co, fJames Absalom, mDelilah Frances Maiden, wMollie Rebecca Boutz, md1887
Betty Wethered Young, b2/10/1848, Lovington, Nels Co, fPereguin Wethered, mEleanor Perrow, hTuley Joseph Mitchell, md11/4/ 1869
David S, b18--, Augu Co?, wElizabeth Kemper
Elizabeth, bc1810, Rkhm Co, hSamuel Flory
Emeline, b18--, Fair Co?, 2w of George West Gunnell
Frank M, b18--, Augu Co
James Absalom, bc1839, Page Co,

YOUNG (continued)
d1907, fJames, wDelilah Frances Maiden
John, b17--, wMary Wethered
John Wesley, b18--, Meck Co, wAlice Neblett Love
Lee, bc1860, Shen Co?, wFannie Smoot
Lucy, b1820, Gray Co, hJohn H Perkins
Loudema, b1840, Gray Co, d1902, hEli Washington Greear
Mary Elizabeth, b1858, Berryville, Clar Co, hCyrus D Baughman
Mary S, b18--, Staunton, Augu Co, fFrank M, hJacob Yost, md1/31/ 1881
May Jeanette, b8/29/1862, Portsmouth, Norf Co, hR Finley Gayle, Sr
Nancy, b18--, Lee Co, d1856, hElkanah Flanary
Pereguin Wethered, b18--, Grbr Co, fJohn, mMary Wethered, wEleanor Perrow
Rosa, b18--, Math Co?, hLewis Montague
Sallie S, bc1860, Staunton, Augu Co, fDavid S, mElizabeth Kemper, hWilliam Carter Camp, md10/1882
Sarah, b18--, Lee Co, hRufus Boyd Fugate
T L H, bc1840, Dinw Co?, wEmma Davis
W Ormond, bc1860, Richmond?, wClaudia Palmer
William H, b18--, wMary Frances Kemper
William J, b18--, Richmond?, wCaroline V Mercer
YOWELL, Joel, b18--, Rapp Co?, wMargaret Thornhill
Joseph Lewis, b18--, Rapp Co?, fJoel, mMargaret Thornhill, wMary Francis Lillard
ZERING, Mary, b18--, Shen Co, 1w of Andrew Funkhouser
Sallie, bc1850, nrWoodstock, Shen Co, hPhilip A Funkhouser, Jr
ZETTY, Mamie, bc1870, Rkhm Co?, 1w of William Thomas Moore
ZIGLER, David H, b12/26/1857, nrBroadway, Rkhm Co, fSamuel,

ZIGLER (continued)
mAnna Miller, wSarah E Shank, md2/14/1885
Samuel, b10/11/1816, fJohn, Jr, mElizabeth Kline, wAnna Miller
ZIMMERMAN, Elizabeth, b18--, West Co, hWalter Randolph Crabbe
ZIRKLE, Gideon, b18--, Forrestville, Shen Co, wRebecca Pence
Hannah, b184-, Forrestville, Shen Co, fGideon, mRebecca Pence, hJohn Admas
John W, b1846, Forrestville, Shen Co, fGideon, mRebecca Pence, wEmma O'Roark
Jonathan, b17--, Shen Co
Julius, b185-, Forrestville, Shen Co, fGideon, mRebecca Pence
Kate, b184-, Forrestville, Shen Co, fGideon, mRebecca Pence, hWilliam Burkett

ZIRKLE (continued)
Lydia, b18--, Shen Co?, hJohn Balser Dingledine
Lydia, b185-, Forrestville, Shen Co, fGideon, mRebecca Pence, hL L Shadwell
Sallie, b5/3/1824, Shen Co, d1898, fJonathan, hJonas Pence
Sallie, bc1850, Forrestville, Shen Co, fGideon, mRebecca Pence, hJacob Whitmire
Silone, b184-, Forrestville, Shen Co, fGideon, mRebecca Pence
Susanna, bc1800, Shen Co, hAbraham Harpine
William, bc1830, Winchester, Fred Co, wMartha Miller
ZOLMAN, Charles, bc1850, Nels Co?, wJulia Meeks
ZUVERS, Christana, bc1800, hDavid Brown

FAMILY NAME INDEX BY VOLUME

This partial index to the three biographical volumes of the History of Virginia has been prepared for the benefit of researchers wishing to locate the original articles from which the data in this volume has been abstracted. The citations have the obvious meanings, e.g., AARON: V4-91 549 means that there are article on the AARON family on pages 91 and 549 of volume 4.

AARON: V4-91 549
ABBOTT: V6-37 493
ABDELL: V5-515
ABELL: V4-324
ABY: V5-71
ACKER: V4-235
ADAIR: V6-391
ADAMS: V4-98 453 487; V5-161
  240 284 296 351 364 526 545
  564; V6-100 268 271 468
ADAMSON: V4-115; V6-349 393
ADDINGTON: V4-440; V6-432
ADDISON: V4-143; V6-91
ADKERSON: V4-323
AGNOR: V5-412
AICHELMAN: V5-269
AIKEN: V4-504
ALBERT: V5-475; V6-326
ALBIN: V5-68 182 192
ALBY: V6-86
ALDERMAN: V5-7
ALESHIRE: V5-370 396
ALEXANDER: V4-81 377 409 525;
  V5-317 411 450; V6-83 268 587
ALFRED: V5-111
ALLEN: V4-54; V5-153 164 202
  204 269 428; V6-226
ALLEY: V5-461
ALLPORT: V4-15
ALMOND: V5-199
ALPHIN: V6-227
ALSTON: V5-265
ALTIZER: V4-76; V5-459
ALVERSON: V4-408
AMBLER: V6-205
AMBROSE: V5-80
AMES: V6-318 520
AMISS: V4-400; V5-92 217
AMMEN: V6-405
AMOS: V5-355
ANDERSON: V4-27 33 357 388; V5-
  125 144 189 296 334 409 411
  487 540; V6-63 116 142 238
  278 290 322 518 634
ANDREWS: V4-213; V5-58 75; V6-
  418 495

ANGELL: V5-413; V6-549
ANGLE: V6-369 397
ANSLEY: V4-546
APPERSON: V6-282
APPICH: V6-146
APPLEWHITE: V4-553
ARBOGAST: V6-80
ARCHER: V4-135; V5-543; V6-634
ARESON: V5-61
ARGENBRIGHT: V5-548; V6-108
ARISS: V4-451
ARMES: V5-504
ARMISTEAD: V4-460;   V5-61 308
  336; V6-435
ARMSTRONG: V5-242; V6-265 376
ARNOLD: V5-176; V6-325
ARPS: V5-258
ARTHUR: V5-8 474
ASH: V5-335; V6-70
ASHBROOK: V6-325 353
ASHBY: V4-452 574; V5-71 312 323
  341 363; V6-164 224 364 394
ASHWORTH: V5-451
AST: V6-51
ATKINSON: V4-16; V6-171
ATWOOD: V5-281
AVENT: V5-438
AVERILL: V6-527
AVERY: V5-531
AYERS: V6-477
AYLOR: V4-49; V6-350
AYRE: V5-346
BABCOCK: V5-332
BACKER: V4-450
BAGBY: V5-54 366
BAGLEY: V5-148 153 272
BAILEY: V4-344 355; V6-50 430
BAKER: V4-356 401 407 411 555;
  V5-12 188 192 267 308 382 283;
  V6-203 272
BALDWIN: V4-434; V5-56; V6-173
  482
BALL: V4-223; V5-313 433 436;
  V6-110 157 473
BALLARD: V4-567; V5-152; V6-253
BANDY: V6-303

417

BANE: B6-502
BANISTER: V5-125
BANKS: V5-209 213
BANNER: V5-514
BARBEE: V4-461; V6-15 537
BARBOUR: V5-358; V6-554 640
BARCLAY: V6-418
BARGAMIN: V4-327
BARKER: V5-142
BARKSDALE: V4-198; V5-143 216; V6-562 581
BARLOW: V5-86 413
BARNES: V4-22; V5-386 452
BARNETT: V4-212
BARNHAM: V4-499
BARNHART: V5-315
BARNITZ: V4-464; V6-242
BARR: V4-498; V5-27 28 310
BARRET: V4-121
BARRETT: V5-226; V6-130
BARRIE: V5-403
BARRINGER: V4-34
BARRON: V4-516; V6-406
BARROW: V5-498
BARRY: V5-118
BARTH: V6-88
BASKERVILLE: V5-288
BASSETT: V5-336 515; V6-576
BATTLE: V5-53
BAUGH: V5-123
BAUMGARDNER: V4-561; V5-111
BAUSERMAN: V4-271 327; V5-224
BAYLOR: V5-394; V6-599
BAYNE: V4-476 531; V5-34 323
BEALE: V4-477; V5-112 253 255
BEAMER: V6-467
BEAR: V6-490
BEARD: V5-528
BEATIE: V6-177
BEAVER: V4-323
BEAZLEY: V5-255; V6-609
BECKHAM: V5-497; V6-389
BECKLEY: V5-557
BEDINGER: V5-63
BERRY: V4-219; V6-203
BEIRNE: V5-393
BELCHER: V5-524
BELL: V4-452; V5-138 207 215 322 504; V6-62 81 148 347 348 418
BELT: V4-485; V6-91
BELVIN: V6-247
BEMISS: V4-69
BENCHOFF: V4-291
BENNETT: V5-430; V6-52 547
BENT: V6-11
BENTLEY: V6-295

BERGER: V5-209 235
BERKELEY: V4-560; V5-103; V6-638
BERLIN: V5-316
BERRY: V5-293 421 464; V6-413
BERTRAM: V4-300
BEST: V4-426
BEVERLEY: V4-228; V5-249; V6-57 232 247 264
BEVILLE: V5-179
BEVINS: V6-636
BIBB: V5-356 361
BICKFORD: V4-544
BICKWELL: V6-326
BIDGOOD: V5-173
BIEDLER: V5-392
BILISOLY: V6-18 516
BILLHEIMER: V5-411
BILLINGSLEY: V4-580
BINNS: V4-364
BIRCKHEAD: V6-618
BIRD: B5-199 341 556; V6-444
BIRDSON: V6-557
BISHOP: V4-66
BLACK: V6-282
BLACKARD: V5-495
BLACKBURN: V4-284; V5-176; V6-62 385
BLACKFORD: V5-8
BLACKWELL: V4-84 276; V5-88 94 491; V6-12 162 328
BLAIR: V4-184 441; V5-412; V6-574
BLAKE: V4-151
BLAKEMORE: V6-39
BLAKESLEE: V5-416
BLAND: V6-333 437
BLANKENBECKER: V5-218
BLANTON: V4-149; V5-63 107 146
BLEDSOE: V4-470
BLOOMER: V4-470; V6-344
BLOSSER: V4-225
BLOXOM: V5-531
BOARD: V6-324
BOATWRIGHT: V5-501
BOAZ: V4-46 328; V5-151
BOCK: V6-452
BOCOCK: V4-202
BOGGAN: V5-419
BOISSEAU: V5-443
BOLEN: V4-316; V5-150; V6-461
BOLLING: V5-274; V6-461
BOND: V4-414; V5-244; V6-529
BONDURANT: V5-257
BONIFANT: V5-377 378
BONNER: V6-152 222
BOOKER: V5-137 160 264; V6-497

BOONE: V6-455
BOOTHE: V6-279 280
BOOTON: V5-388
BORCHERS: V5-373
BORDEN: V4-333
BOSCHEN: V4-176
BOSHER: V4-435
BOSWELL: V6-310
BOTTOM: V4-136
BOTTS: V6-485
BOUGHTON: V5-81
BOULDIN: V5-106; V6-120 612
BOUTON: V4-451
BOUTWELL: V4-447
BOWE: V4-23
BOWEN: V5-342 534; V6-210 647
BOWERING: V5-19
BOWERS: V4-289; V6-583
BOWERSITT: V6-445
BOWIE: V6-151 350
BOWLES: V5-372 527; V6-317
BOWMAN: V4-250 261 288 325 346 357; V5-24 312 381 403; V6-86 147 284
BOWYER: V6-311
BOXLEY: V5-220; V6-189 236
BOYD: V4-479; V5-426; V6-14
BOYER: V4-257 353
BOYKIN: V4-244
BOYLE: V4-376
BRADBURY: V6-590
BRADLEY: V5-220; V6-433
BRADSHAW: V5-207 486; V6-107 138 154
BRAGG: V4-424
BRANCH: V5-17 125 164; V6-184
BRATTON: V5-405
BREADY: V6-260
BRECKENRIDGE: V6-226
BRELSFORD: V6-277
BRENAMAN: V5-48
BRENNAN: V5-511
BRENT: V5-3 240; V6-89 521
BREVINGTON: V5-235
BREWER: V4-262; V5-313 467 491
BRIDGEFORTH: V5-154
BRIDGES: V5-348
BRIGGS: V6-493
BRIGHT: V5-44
BRILL: V4-352; V5-376
BRINKLEY: V5-494; V6-220
BRISTOW: V5-277 373
BRITTAIN: V6-362
BRITTINGHAM: V4-548; V5-40
BRITTLE: V6-210
BRITTS: V6-342

BRIZZOLARA: V6-452
BROADNAX: V4-108
BROADWATER: V6-482
BROCK: V5-149; V6-350
BROCKENBROUGH: V5-260 433; V6-274 388
BRODERS: V6-584
BRODNAX: V5-232
BROMLEY: V4-412; V5-27
BROOKE: V4-460 560; V6-49
BROOKS: V6-72
BROWER: V5-228
BROWN: See BROWNE
BROWNE: V4-56 222 238 413 464 540 569; V5-13 28 29 32 33 40 56 124 257 324 356 377 398 409 442 562; V6-55 117 204 419 489 508 593 644 649
BROWNING: V5-463; V6-195 219 266 408 484 590 598 618
BROWNLOW: V4-18
BROYLES: V5-219
BRUBAKER: V5-396
BRUBECK: V6-149
BRUCE: V4-74 167; V5-51
BRUGH: V4-497
BRULLE: V5-72
BRUMBACH: V5-115 208 223 392; V6-129 358
BRUNK: V4-110
BRYAN: V6-58 59
BRYANT: V4-353; V6-283
BRYDON: V4-76
BUCHANAN: V4-154 529; V5-184; V6-647
BUCHER: V4-298 338
BUCK: V6-11 144 535
BUCKNER: V4-165 451
BUDD: V4-82
BUGG: V5-134 146
BUHRMAN: V5-454
BULL: V4-290
BULLITT: V5-465
BULLY: V6-487
BUMGARDNER: V6-88
BUNN: V6-291
BUNTING: V6-557
BUNTS: V6-621
BURAKER: V6-550
BURCH: V5-470
BURGES: V6-539
BURGESS: V6-209 235
BURKE: V4-213 477; V5-263
BURNER: V5-25
BURNETT: V4-226: V6-615
BURNHAM: V6-30

BURROUGHS: V5-422
BURRUSS: V6-449
BURTON: V5-351 397 555; V6-25 291 413
BURWELL: V4-560; V5-15 183 472; V6-234 390 473
BUSHONG: V4-37
BUSTER: V4-281
BUSTON: V6-154
BUTCHER: V4-205
BUTLER: V4-480
BUTTON: V4-116
BYERS: V4-286
BYRD: V5-248 481 494; V6-75 646
BYRNE: V4-427
CABELL: V4-372 379 431; V5-51 158
CADWALLADER: V5-191
CAGE: V5-217; V6-495
CALDWELL: V4-490 539; V5-365; V6-648
CALL: V4-125; V5-559
CALLAHAM: V5-139
CALLAWAY: V4-372 423
CALLIHAN: V6-618
CALLIS: V5-211
CALLISON: V5-379
CALLOWAY: V5-474 522; V5-186
CALROW: V4-439
CALVERT: V5-310
CAMBLOS: V4-456
CAMDEN: V4-380; V5-117; V6-60 563
CAMERON: V5-287
CAMP: V4-62 195; V6-24 93 433
CAMPBELL: V5-135 159 197 200; V6-208 285 371 374 500 521 647
CANDLER: V6-354
CANNON: V4-167; V6-47
CANTER: V5-74
CAPLES: V4-442
CAPPER: V4-411
CAPPS: V4-440 444
CARBAUGH: V5-195
CARDER: V5-276; V6-417
CARDWELL: V4-191; V5-332 490
CARLIN: V6-125
CARNE: V6-146
CARNEGY: V4-186
CARNER: V5-66
CARPENTER: V4-323; V5-277 544; V6-65
CARR: V4-469 483; V5-43 184 247 328; V6-183 197
CARRIER: V6-168 369
CARRINGTON: V4-12 27 113 114

CARRINGTON (continued) 390; V5-525; V6-271 360 494
CARROLL: V4-363 396; V5-525 566
CARSON: V5-157; V6-334
CARTER: V4-42 245 254 347 416 421 472 473 560; V5-6 184 383; V6-57 58 97 111 183 211 216 220 230 232 240 265 329 423 466 468 483 561
CARTWRIGHT: V6-144
CARVER: V4-237; V5-363
CARY: V4-63; V5-345 508; V6-415
CASEY: V5-123
CASKIE: V4-394; V5-130; V6-576
CASSELL: V5-398
CATHER: V4-393; V5-40 178 179
CAUDLE: V4-441
CAUDILL: V6-551
CAVANAUGH: V4-448
CAVE: V4-451
CAWSEY: V4-426
CECIL: V5-566
CHALKLEY: V6-179 497
CHAMBERLAIN: V6-213
CHAMBERLAYNE: V5-327
CHANBERLIN: V5-270
CHANCELLOR: V5-23
CHANDLER: V4-304; V6-455 625 629 640
CHAPIN: V4-558; V6-28
CHAPPELEAR: V5-464; V6-263
CHAPPELL: V4-242; V5-101
CHARLES: V5-394
CHASE: V6-353
CHERNAULT: V5-281
CHERRY: V4-545
CHESNEY: V6-128
CHICHESTER: V6-506
CHILDS: V6-375
CHILES: V5-372
CHILTON: V5-170; V6-162
CHINN: V5-287; V6-90 275
CHISOLM: V4-45
CHISMAN: V4-549
CHITWOOD: V4-466; V6-197 373 612
CHOWNING: V5-340
CHRISTIAN: V4-85; V5-58 278 351
CHUMBLEY: V6-436
CHURCH: V6-198
CHURCHILL: V6-99 180
CHURCHMAN: V4-206
CLAGETT: V5-188
CLAIBORNE: V6-44 212
CLARDY: V5-179
CLARK: V4-103 401 456 515; V5-20 21 30 103 107 168; V6-254 265

CLARK (continued)
  435 640
CLARKSON: V4-380
CLAUD: V6-257
CLAYBROOK: V5-168
CLAYTON: V5-60
CLEVELAND: V5-32
CLEEK: V6-67 221
CLEGG: V6-343
CLEM: V4-346; V6-73
CLEMENT: V6-561
CLEMENTS: V4-369
CLEMER: V5-418
CLEMMER: V5-427
CLENDENEN: V4-481
CLEVINGER: V6-503
CLINE: V5-192 194 283 437; V6-476
CLINEDINST: V4-245 360; V5-209
CLOWSER: V5-30
COATS: V5-305
COBB: V6-93 320 367
COCHRAN: V5-272 378 514 558; V6-229 327 555
COCKE: V4-381; V5-444 507; V6-39
COCKERILL: V6-274
COFER: V4-75
COFFELT: V5-27
COFFEY: V6-205
COFFMAN: V4-351; V6-123
COGBILL: V4-78 206; V5-407
COGGIN: V6-509
COHOON: V5-507
COLAW: V6-190
COLBERT: V4-382; V5-70
COLE: V5-528
COLEMAN: V4-77 550; V5-119 151 221 222 493; V6-511 576
COLLEY: V5-524
COLLIE: V6-535
COLLIR: V4-538; V6-478
COLLINS: V6-278 580
COLOGNE: V6-179
COLONNA: V5-10 511
COLSTON: V5-10
COLVIN: V4-241; V6-420
COMBS: V5-241 294; V6-354 455
COMPHER: V6-98 200
COMPTON: V5-150 526; V6-421
COMYN: V6-553
CONN: V4-555
CONNALLY: V5-358
CONNELLEE: V5-260
CONNER: V5-497
CONNOR: V5-335 411
CONRAD: V5-95 341; V6-52

CONSALVO: V4-465
CONTESSE: V5-61
COOK: V6-504 543
COOKE: V4-573; V5-338; V6-110 187 284 567
COOKSEY: V5-109
COOLEY: V5-85
COONTZ: V4-579
COOPER: V4-164; V5-298 457; V6-241 420
COPENHAVER: V4-579; V6-277
COPP: V4-312; V5-208
COPPRIDGE: V4-420
CORBIN: V5-449
CORBITT: V4-537 545
CORDER: V6-343
CORNETT: V6-614
CORNS: V6-337 379
CORNWELL: V6-319 538
CORR: V5-350; V6-14
COSBY: V5-43; V6-385
COTTRELL: V5-98 136; V6-492 581
COUCH: V5-408; V6-154
COUGILL: V5-77
COUK: V6-247
COULBORN: V4-93; V5-499
COUNTS: V5-482 519
COURTNEY: V6-370
COVER: V4-312; V5-223 540; V6-50
COWLES: V4-542; V6-564
COX: V4-114 329 442; V5-101 159 366; V6-23 164 251 288 297 307 568
COYNER: V6-356
CRABB: V5-260
CRADDOCK: V4-464; V5-401; V6-582
CRAIG: V6-121 168
CRAIGHEAD: V5-493
CRALLE: V4-223; V5-49 237 429; V6-300
CRANK: V5-53
CRASS: V5-425
CRAWFORD: V4-153; V6-13 586
CRAWLEY: V5-168
CREASY: V5-150; V6-467
CRENSHAW: V6-376 402
CRESAP: V6-91
CREVELING: V6-565
CREWS: V6-438
CRIDLIN: V6-478
CRIGLER: V6-375
CRIM: V5-209
CRISMOND: V5-68 431
CRIST: V4-193
CRITCHER: V6-20
CRITTENDEN: V5-544; V6-422

CROCKETT: V6-312 474 545
CROOK: V6-481
CROSBY: V6-425
CROSS: V4-176; V6-524
CROSWELL: V5-156
CROUCH: V6-600
CROUNSE: V5-287
CROW: V5-316
CROWDER: V4-388 400
CROWELL: V5-553
CROWN: V5-460
CRUMP: V4-39; V5-349
CRUMPLER: V6-440
CRUMPTON: V5-361
CRUSER: V6-36
CRUTE: V5-143
CRYMBLE: V6-258
CUMMOCK: V5-274; V6-571
CUNNINGHAM: V5-360
CURTIS: V6-483 566
CUTCHINS: V4-84
CUTLER: V6-338
DABBS: V5-107
DABNEY: V4-146; V5-216 247; V6-625
DAILY: V5-152
DAINGERFIELD: V5-250
DAMERON: V5-374
DANCE: V5-102
DANDRIDGE: V5-142
DANIEL: V4-32; V5-54 106
DARDEN: V5-489
DARNALL: V5-521
DARST: V6-569
DAUGHTON: V5-616
DAVES: V4-569
DAVIDSON: V4-567; V5-135 245 475; V6-486 620
DAVIES: V5-422; V6-26 391 444
DAVIS: V4-143 217 359 364 516 539 551; V5-21 45 121 243 310 368 369 379 470 524 530 534; V6-104 238 267 418 534 543 559 573 592
DAWSON: V5-404
DAY: V6-59 365
DEAL: V6-503
DEAN: V5-212
DEANS: V4-123
DEARBORN: V5-116
DEARING: V4-570; V5-351; V6-69
DEARMONT: V5-430
DeATLEY: V5-242
DEATON: V4-437; V6-330
DeBUTTS: V5-441; V6-241 245 394
DECHERT: V4-502

DeCORMIS: V5-463
DEEBLE: V5-313
DeFRIECE: V6-254
DeHART: V5-496
DeHAVEN: V5-11
DeJARNETTE: V6-472
DELANEY: V4-491
DELAPLANE: V6-25 233
DeLASHMUTT: V5-303
DELKE: V6-313
DELLENGER: V5-327
DELLINGER: V6-440
DELP: V6-598
DEMPSEY: V5-512
DENBY: V5-50
DENNETT: V4-461
DENNIS: V6-533
DERRICK: V6-535
DeSAUSSURE: V4-35
DeSHIELDS: V5-300
DETTOR: V5-448
DETTRA: V5-11
DEVANY: V4-455
DEVIER: V4-239
DEVINE: V6-54
DEW: V6-189 643
DEWITT: V5-131
DEY: V6-631
DEYERLE: V4-211
DIBRELL: V6-97
DICKEN: V5-79
DICKENSON: V5-16 65 68 455 503; V6-293 336
DICKERSON: V4-60 446; V5-103 166 262; V6-595
DICKEY: V5-131; V6-206 287
DICKIE: V4-355
DIDLAKE: V6-343
DIGGES: V6-520
DIGGS: V4-140 178; V5-336
DILL: V6-61
DILLARD: V4-47 286 467; V5-129 157 281 311; V6-291
DILLON: V5-456 457
DINGES: V5-190 193 201
DINGLEDINE: V4-197
DINWIDDLE: V5-301
DIVERS: V5-445; V6-197
DIVINE: V5-411
DIX: V6-532
DOBLER: V4-384
DODD: V5-114
DODGE: V4-123
DODSON: V4-218 477; V5-112
DOHERTY: V4-359
DONALD: V6-314

DONNAN: V4-17; V5-141
DONOHOE: V6-465
DOOLEY: V5-272
DOOSING: V5-567
DORNIN: V5-159; V6-249
DOTSON: V4-471
DOUBLES: V4-126
DOUGHERTY: V6-432
DOUGLAS: V5-243 246; V6-140 275
DOUGLASS: V5-221
DOVE: V6-252
DOVEL: V5-384
DOVELL: V6-525
DOWDELL: V6-243
DOWELL: V4-475 562
DOWNES: V5-472; V6-514
DOWNING: V4-427; V5-83 169
DOYLE: V4-431; V6-122
DRAKE: V4-325; V5-271
DRAPER: V4-455; V6-479
DREWRY: V4-20 131
DRISCOLL: V4-214
DRIVER: V4-295
DRUMMOND: V5-529
DUDLEY: V4-140 430 468; V5-410 502; V6-259 459
DUFF: V5-481
DUFFEL: V6-66
DUFFY: V6-235
DUGUID: V5-135
DUKE: V4-50; V5-6 7
DULANEY: V6-233 245
DUNCAN: V5-419 489; V6-304 318 559 648
DUNFORD: V4-178
DUNLAP: V5-188 388; V6-480
DUNLOP: V4-379; V5-381
DUNN: V6-509
DUNNINGTON: V5-141 269 321
DUNSCOMBE: V5-351
DUPUY: V5-166; V6-8
DURRETT: V4-402; V5-21
DUVALL: V5-133 526
DWYER: V5-34
DYER: V4-438
EDS: V6-140
EAGLE: V5-567
EARLY: V4-373; V6-72 175 229 454 461 569
EARNEST: V4-157; V5-455
EASLEY: V4-485; V6-561
EAST: V5-563
EASTWOOD: V5-64
EATON: V4-430
EBERT: V5-186
ECHOLS: V6-499

EDDS: V6-254
EDENS: V4-172; V5-384
EDMONDS: V5-365; V6-407
EDMONDSON: V5-150; V6-476 631
EDMUNDS: V5-114; V6-497
EDWARDS: V6-459
EGE: V5-91
EGGLESTON: V5-108; V6-6
EICHBERG: V4-278
ELAM: V4-221; V5-169
ELEY: V5-493
ELLETT: V5-310 314
ELLIOTT: V4-24; V5-467
ELLIS: V4-258 483
ELLISON: V5-46; V6-110
ELLZEY: V5-322; V6-181
ELMORE: V5-528
ELSEA: V5-320
ELY: V5-523; V6-253
EMBREY: V4-381; V5-17
EMERICK: V6-200
EMMETT: V5-538
ENGELDOVE: V4-400
ENGELMAN: V5-411
ENGLISH: V5-458 555
EPPARD: V5-81
EPPES: V5-47 148 388
ERWIN: V5-110
ESKRIDGE: V6-308 475
ESSER: V6-231
ESSEX: V5-202
ESTES: V5-503
ETHERIDGE: V5-257
ETTER: V6-536
EUBANK: V4-360; V5-432; V6-12
EUKER: V5-373
EUTSLER: V5-454
EVANS: V4-243; V5-331; V6-340 539
EVERETT: V5-53 222
EVERSOLE: V6-296
EWELL: V4-425
EWING: V6-210
EYSTER: V5-555
FADELEY: V5-325
FAGAN: V5-12
FAGGE: V6-551
FAIRCLOTH: V5-462
FAIRFAX: V6-398
FAISON: V5-449
FALLIN: V5-337
FARINHOLT: V4-127
FARISH: V4-42
FARLEY: V6-425 601
FARRAR: V5-110
FARRIER: V6-596

FARROW: V4-97
FASS: V5-483
FATHERLY: V6-512
FAULCONER: V5-298 308
FAULKNER: V5-85 160 278
FAUST: V6-313
FENTRESS: V6-463
FEREBEE: V6-504
FERGUSON: V4-420; V5-273 435 557; V6-26 415 460
FERNALD: V4-486
FERRELL: V4-490; V5-174; V6-385 386
FICKLEN: V6-389
FICKLIN: V5-241 409
FIFER: V5-23
FILLSMOYER: V4-357
FINDLAY: V6-645 646
FINE: V4-499
FINLEY: V5-439
FINNEGAN: V4-120
FINNELL: V6-416
FINNEY: V6-325
FIREBAUGH: V5-419
FISHBACK: V4-500; V6-248
FISHBURN: V4-55; V6-119 178 455
FISHER: V4-195 444 515; V6-512
FITCHETT: V5-336
FITERY: V5-472
FITTS: V6-433
FITZGERALD: V4-88 253; V5-40; V6-281 448
FITZHUGH: V4-29; V5-59 465; V6-407
FITZPATRICK: V4-352; V5-146 221
FLANARY: V6-636
FLANNAGAN: V4-128 318; V6-351
FLANNERY: V4-439
FLEENOR: V6-356
FLEET: V5-86 366
FLEETWOOD: V4-33
FLEISHER: V6-193
FLEMING: V5-73; V6-231 299 322
FLETCHER: V4-149 420; V5-464; V6-103 203 215 384 534
FLINT: V5-395
FLIPPIN: V6-445
FLIPPO: V5-236 405
FLOOD: V5-248; V6-313 628
FLORA: V5-500
FLORY: V4-270 331; V5-94
FLOYD: V5-467; V6-647
FLYNN: V5-140; V6-569
FOGG: V5-301
FOGLEMAN: V6-15
FOLKES: V5-348

FOLTZ: V5-381; V6-583
FORBES: V4-141; V5-127
FORD: V4-139 343 489; V5-204 523; V6-380
FOREMAN: V6-157
FORMAN: V5-96
FORTUNE: V4-363
FOSTER: V5-279 380; V6-215 570
FOWLER: V4-556; V6-32
FOX: V4-12; V5-507; V6-194 276 315 472
FOXCROFT: V6-218
FRALEY: V6-85
FRANCE: V4-28; V6-578
FRANCIS: V4-495; V5-185; V6-24 304 446 487
FRANKLIN: V5-359
FRAVEL: V4-112; V5-24
FRAY: V4-498; V6-199 375
FRED: V6-244
FREE: V6-392
FREEMAN: V5-103 211; V6-359
FRENCH: V4-63; V5-487 488; V6-519
FRIEND: V6-460
FRIES: V5-185
FRITES: V5-327
FRY: V4-251
FUDGE: V5-243; V6-537
FUGATE: V4-470; V6-345
FULLER: V5-31; V6-288 383
FULTON: V6-147 217 294
FULWIDER: V5-310
FUNK: V4-179; V5-75
FUNKHAUSER: V4-293 333 426; V5-76 326 441 443; V6-6 477
FUQUA: V6-186
GALE: V5-516
GAMBILL: V5-476
GAMMON: V6-602
GAMON: V5-272
GANNAWAY: V4-396
GARBER: V4-189 272 292 294 381; V6-75 447
GARDNER: V4-392; V5-29 61 204 235 502 568; V6-145 515 570
GARGES: V5-35
GARLAND: V6-131 174 564
GARNER: V6-218
GARNETT: V5-105 501 534; V6-643
GARRETT: V5-180 346 355; V6-96 557
GARRISON: V4-290; V5-152 153
GARST: V6-548
GARTEN: V6-326
GARTH: V4-52

GARVIN: V5-188 190
GARY: V4-387; V5-108
GATEWOOD: V5-440; V6-213 406 585
GAULDING: V5-98
GAYLE: V4-160; V5-547
GEE: V5-108 153 449
GENTRY: V4-46
GEORGE: V6-133
GIBBON: V6-329
GIBSON: V4-444 570; V5-44 157 293 406 517; V6-82 423 574
GIDEON: V5-295
GIFFIN: V5-190
GILBERT: V6-610
GILES: V5-89; V6-535 602
GILKESON: V4-560; V6-462
GILL: V4-20
GILLESPIE: V6-164 336 363
GILLIAM: V4-16 83 375 574; V5-243; V6-286
GILMER: V4-38; V6-279
GILMORE: V4-446; V6-229 305 447 537
GILPIN: V5-307; V6-81
GINN: V4-411
GISH: V4-518; V6-469
GIVENS: V4-474; V6-625
GLAIZE: V5-88 185
GLASCOCK: V6-209 327 384 403
GLASGOW: V4-425; V6-54
GLASS: V4-410
GLEASON: V4-301
GLEBE: V5-33
GLOTH: V5-423
GLOVER: V5-316
GOAD: V6-573
GOBLE: V6-303 304
GOCHENOUR: V6-250
GODDIN: V6-324
GODSEY: V4-416; V5-176
GODWIN: V5-198 556
GOFF: V5-516
GOGGIN: V5-162 500
GOLDMAN: V4-216
GOLDSMITH: V5-314
GOLLADAY: V4-352
GOODALL: V5-554
GOODBAR: V5-554
GOOD: V4-249 305 326 403; V5-329
GOODE: V4-194; V5-33 175; V6-153 556
GOODLOE: V5-14 434
GOODRIDGE: V5-292
GOODWIN: V4-327; V5-25
GOODWYN: V4-80
GOOLRICK: V5-237

GORDON: V4-3 43 159 381 442; V5-85
GORE: V6-263 416
GORMAN: V5-353
GORRELL: V6-127
GORSLINE: V4-217
GOSE: V5-561; V6-335
GOULDIN: V5-376
GRAHAM: V4-457 492; V5-408 421; V6-297 471 545 597
GRANBERG: V5-320
GRANDSTAFF: V4-279 335
GRANDY: V6-47
GRASTY: V4-355
GRAVATT: V4-576; V5-387
GRAVELEY: V5-520; V6-323 549
GRAVES: V4-274 276; V6-323 392 403 581
GRAY: V4-101 196 417; V5-239; V6-227 294
GRAYBEAL: V6-643
GRAYBILL: V5-41
GRAYSON: V5-392
GREEAR: V6-300 327 552 613
GREEN: V4-473; V5-76 105 289 486; V6-120 234 323 462 621
GREENE: see GREEN
GREENWOOD: V4-502
GREGG: V5-434; V6-98
GREGORY: V4-563; V6-634
GREIDER: V5-551
GRESHAM: V4-57 423; V5-332; V6-572
GRICE: V6-16
GRIFFIN: V6-63
GRIFFITH: V4-478 505; V5-382 544; V6-431
GRIMSLEY: V6-414
GRINNAN: V4-188
GRIZZARD: V4-72 363
GRONIGER: V5-195
GROOME: V6-266
GROVE: V4-335; V5-223 309; V6-170
GRUBB: V4-540
GRUBBS: V4-479
GRUVER: V5-267
GRYMES: V5-15 259
GUDE: V4-560
GUERRANT: V5-120; V6-417
GUGGENHEIMER: V5-137 291
GUIGON: V4-237
GUINN: V6-420
GUNNELL: V5-293
GUTHRIE: V4-369 370; V5-360
GUY: V4-200; V6-234

GUYER: V5-71
GWYNN: V5-441 562
HADDON: V4-152
HADDOX: V6-238
HADEN: V4-52 53; V5-330; V6-101
HAEGER: V6-248
HAINES: V5-12; V6-186
HAIRSTON: V5-521
HALDEMAN: V5-40
HALE: V6-106 473
HALEY: V6-189 503
HALLEY: V5-467
HALLIGAN: V4-362; V6-49
HALSEY: V4-367; V6-290
HAMILTON: V4-502; V5-271; V6-212 360 404 617
HAMLIN: V6-466
HAMMER: V5-219
HAMMETT: V6-464
HAMMOCK: V5-236
HAMMOND: V6-358
HAMNER: V5-161 279
HAMPTON: V5-357; V6-526
HAMSBERGER: V4-417
HANCE: V6-588
HANCKEL: V4-58
HANCOCK: V4-64; V5-103 130; V6-279 379 439
HAND: V5-338
HANGER: V6-86
HANKINS: V4-61; V5-473
HANKLA: V4-528; V5-280
HANKS: V6-572
HANNA: V5-450
HANNAH: V5-558
HANNAN: V5-286
HANSBROUGH: V5-202; V6-439
HARAHAN: V4-436
HARBISON: 6-456
HARDAWAY: V5-165 551
HARDESTY: V5-322
HARDIN: V4-384; V5-158
HARDWICK: V5-418
HARDY: V4-55 407; V5-35 162 165 547; V6-78
HARDYMAN: V4-254
HARGRAVE: V5-353
HARLOW: V5-285 545
HARMAN: V5-326 381 418; V6-159 165
HARMANSON: V4-475
HARMISON: V5-338 564
HARNESBARGER: V5-228; V6-442
HARPER: V5-437; V6-330 448
HARPINE: V4-273
HARRELL: V5-446; V6-558

HARRIS: V4-71 380 488; V5-55 67 81 118 275 347 356 361 505 513; V6-211 330 441
HARRISON: V4-12 432 460; V5-5 151 183 210 345 567; V6-183 267 360 412
HART: V5-513; V6-323 392
HARTLEY: V6-637
HARTMAN: V5-522
HARVEY: V4-372 493; V5-101 126 359
HARWOOD: V4-490; V5-342
HASKINS: V5-17; V6-445
HASLUP: V5-198
HATCH: V5-88
HATCHER: V4-73; V5-205; V6-141
HATFIELD: V6-532
HATHAWAY: V5-295 563; V6-465
HATTON: V5-264; V6-17
HAWES: V5-222; V6-142
HAWKINS: V4-37; V6-241 492
HAWSE: V4-280
HAY: V5-277
HAYDEN: V6-500
HAYES: V6-511
HAYNES: V4-399 426; V5-335 400; V6-537
HEADLEY: V5-201 431
HEALE: V5-354
HEARON: V5-559
HEATER: V5-195
HEATH: V4-378
HEATWOLE: V5-22
HERB: V5-428
HECHLER: V5-77
HEDGECOCK: V6-590
HEDGMAN: V6-106
HEFLIN: V6-268
HELMINTOLLER: V6-178 402
HELMS: V4-496
HENDRICKSON: V5-80
HENING: V5-306
HENKEL: V4-347 349 383 389; V5-196; V6-84 220
HENLEY: V4-543; V6-241
HENNINGER: V4-536
HENRITZE: V4-419
HENRY: V4-574; V6-223 435
HENSLEY: V5-250
HENSON: V4-99; V6-332
HEPLER: V5-452; V6-324
HERBERT: V4-153 328
HERMAN: V6-301
HERMANCE: V5-529
HERNDON: V4-453; V5-12 428; V6-345

HERRING: V4-181 287
HESS: V5-22; V6-278
HEUSER: V6-29 474
HEVENER: V6-85 192
HEWITT: V5-216
HICKMAN: V5-543; V6-9 45
HICKS: V5-451
HICKSON: V5-86
HIETT: V5-87 309 435
HIGGINBOTHAM: V4-435 477; V6-339
HIGGS: V6-347
HILL: V4-14; V5-126; V6-538 555
HILLIDGE: V5-266
HILLMAN: V4-471; V5-38
HILLYARD: V4-579; V5-182
HINCHMAN: V4-358
HINEGARDNER: V6-351
HINER: V6-79
HINKINS: V5-76
HINKLE: V5-79
HINTON: V5-155; V6-145
HIRSCHBERG: V4-177
HISEY: V5-382
HITE: V4-352; V5-116 187; V6-481
HIX: V5-473; V6-293
HOBBS: V6-310
HOBGOOD: V5-58
HOBSON: V4-158; V6-611
HOCKADAY: V6-310
HOCKMAN: V4-344
HODGSON: V4-579; V6-29
HOFFMAN: V4-385
HOGGAN: V4-111
HOGSHEAD: V5-428; V6-95
HOGUE: V5-244 522; V6-74 183 464
HOLDEN: V5-357
HOLLAND: V5-478 490; V6-69 279 524 550
HOLLAR: V6-259
HOLLINGSWORTH: V4-347
HOLMAN: V5-20
HOLMES: V4-432; V5-95 403 538
HOLT: V4-548; V5-36; V6-226 599
HOLTON: V6-243 540
HONEYSTOFFLE: V4-395
HOOE: V6-165
HOOK: V5-189 225
HOOKER: V6-491
HOOPER: V5-540
HOOVER: V4-287 371 491
HOPE: V6-432 522
HOPKINS: V4-418 554; V5-436; V6-185 187 484
HOPWOOD: V5-447
HORN: V5-453
HORNBAKER: V6-47 270

HORNBARGER: V6-396
HORNE: V6-344
HORNER: V5-27
HORSLEY: V4-373; V5-47; V6-398
HORTENSTINE: V5-382
HORTON: V6-201
HOSKINS: V5-340
HOTCHKISS: V5-276
HOTTEL: V4-263 332; V5-65
HOUSTON: V4-546; V5-114 398
HOVEY: V4-556
HOWARD: V5-490 513; V6-378 569
HOWELL: V4-95
HOWLE: V4-219; V5-160
HOWSON: V6-164 165
HOYE: V5-50
HUBARD: V4-256 285; V5-470
HUBBARD: V4-370; V5-163 530
HUDDLE: V6-533 636
HUDDLESTON: V5-349; V6-9
HUDGINS: V4-570; V5-177 451 523; V6-18
HUDSON: V5-110 225 330 383; V6-397
HUFF: V4-575; V5-560; V6-202 487
HUFFARD: V6-335
HUFFMAN: V4-341; V5-116 326; V6-436 499
HUFFORD: V6-401
HUGER: V6-63
HUGHES: V4-408 515 563; V5-391 504 505; V6-269 640
HUGHSON: V5-448
HULINGS: V5-321
HULL: V6-191 296
HULTS: V6-169
HULVEY: V5-430
HUMBERT: V5-395
HUME: V4-432
HUMPHREY: V5-464; V6-528
HUMSTON: V5-375
HUNDLEY: V5-105 257; V6-372 547 549 577
HUNKLE: V5-402
HUNT: V4-531; V6-64 225 234
HUNTER: V5-4 377
HUNTON: V6-215
HUPP: V5-555
HURFF: V6-525
HURLEY: V5-461; V6-638
HURST: V6-16 426 616
HURT: V5 21; V6-376 399 561 581
HUTCHESON: V4-169 253; V5-88 109; V6-280 359 628
HUTT: V5-262 291
HUTTER: V4-517; V5-136

427

HUTTON: V5-466; V6-633
HYATT: V6-147
HYLTON: V5-500 615
HYSLOP: V6-518
INGE: V5-174 312
INGLE: V4-454; V6-479
INGRAM: V5-231
INSKEEP: V6-420
IRION: V5-206
IRVIN: V5-20
IRVING: V4-259; V5-149 542; V6-239
IRWIN: V4-277 519 525
ISETT: V5-213
ISHAM: V6-360
IVEY: V5-128
JACKSON: V4-409; V5-130 257 358 468; V6-225 226 248 457 632
JACOBS: V5-153
JAMES: V4-16; V5-295 505; V6-457
JAMISON: V6-161 579
JANES: V6-378
JANNEY: V5-517
JARMAN: V4-203; V5-223 385
JARRATT: V4-70
JARRETT: V5-61
JARVIS: V5-469
JAVINS: V6-328
JEFFERSON: V5-154
JEFFREYS: V6-153
JEFFRIES: V5-251 537; V6-392
JELLIS: V5-364
JENKINS: V5-122; V6-320
JENNEY: V5-447
JENNINGS: V6-53 573
JESSE: V6-114
JESSEE: V6-400
JETER: V4-135 388; V6-41
JETT: V5-260 321 391; V6-317
JOACHIM: V4-325
JOHNS: V4-224
JOHNSON: V4-88 170 378 467; V5-214 322 367 371 474 501 508 566; V6-7 55 90 105 174 285 326 357 416 435 469 581
JOHNSTON: V4-9 73 564; V5-135 375; V6-32 341 505 547 647
JONES: V4-108 146 208 403 483 485 540 552 558; V5-70 80 130 154 245 254 286 299 303 315 333 351 367 376 501 546; V6-19 23 33 68 364 376 389 390 415 594 637 639
JORDAN: V5-527 536; V6-85 224 237 348 531 588
JOYNER: V4-579

JOYNES: V6-521
JUDY: V6-190
JUNKIN: V4-114
JUREY: V4-455
KABLE: V5-431
KABLER: V5-216
KAGEY: V4-191
KARNES: V6-26
KAST: V5-420
KAVANAUGH: V6-52
KEANE: V5-239
KEAR: V5-530
KECKLEY: V6-444
KEEL: V5-483
KEEN: V4-239
KEESEE: V4-495
KEEZELL: V5-226
KEFFER: V6-203
KEISTER: V4-233 297 532; V5-229
KEITH: V5-155; V6-162
KELLAM: V4-429; V5-399; V6-517
KELLEY: V4-23; V5-478 484; V6-520
KELLOGG: V6-517
KELLS: V6-448
KELLY: V4-12 429; V5-79; V6-641
KELSEY: V4-324
KEMP: V5-417; V6-611
KEMPER: V4-229
KENDRICK: V4-474; V5-94
KENNER: V6-242
KENNERLY: V4-186
KENNEY: V5-304
KENT: V6-290
KER: V5-517; V6-24
KERBY: V6-587
KERFOOT: V4-558
KERN: V4-397; V5-83; V6-49
KERR: V4-577
KESSLR: V6-404
KEYS: V6-354 477
KEYSER: V4-361 426; V5-383; V6-472
KIBLER: V5-345 357
KIDD: V4-90; V5-234 345
KIEFFER: V4-179; V6-419
KILGORE: V6-519
KIME: V6-39
KINCHELOE: V5-343; V6-621
KING: V5-123 403 444; V6-286 294 595 639 645
KINNEY: V6-80
KINNIER: V5-427
KINSEY: V5-499
KINZLEY: V6-71
KIRK: V5-311; V6-392

KIRKPATRICK: V5-364
KIRTNER: V6-175
KISER: V6-354
KITE: V5-390
KITTS: V6-509
KIZER: V4-93; V6-408
KLINE: V4-273
KNIGHT: V4-393; V5-359; V6-69
KNIGHTON: V5-199
KNOTT: V5-22
KNOWLES: V6-71
KOINER: V4-383; V5-324
KOONTZ: V4-279; V5-147 230 468; V6-487
KREBS: V5-85
KRIGG: V6-645
KURTZ: V4-383; V5-59
KYLE: V6-168 468
LACKEY: V4-547
LACY: V6-452 496 501
LaFOLLETTE: V5-225
LAFON: V4-341; V6-531
LAGRANDE: V5-104
LAIRD: V5-35
LAKE: V4-494; V5-191; V6-203
LAM: V6-362
LAMAR: V6-91
LAMB: V4-236; V6-516
LAMBERT: V6-174 240
LAMBETH: V5-273
LAMP: V6-70
LANCASTER: V6-546
LAND: V5-253
LANDACRE: V6-476
LANDES: V6-90
LANE: V4-525; V5-215 329; V6-101 397 526
LANG: V5-428; V6-76
LANGFORD: V4-323
LANGHORNE: V4-317 570; V5-142 215 449; V6-43
LANGLEY: V4-435
LANHAM: V6-123
LARKIN: V5-147
LARMER: V6-253
LARRICK: V5-65 198
LARUE: V6-152 220
LATANE: V5-297 334; V6-106 126
LAUCK: V5-388
LAUFLAND: V6-173
LAVENDER: V6-641
LAVINDER: V5-282
LAW: V5-101; V6-168
LAWLESS: V6-387
LAWRENCE: V5-151 266
LAWS: V6-139

LAWSON: V5-159 235 396; V6-372
LAYMAN: V4-433 463 497; V5-526 560; V6-404
LEA: V4-171 380 382; V6-498
LEACHMAN: V5-458
LEADBEATER: V6-567
LEAKE: V4-193 488
LEATHERS: V5-154
LECKEY: V5-405
LEDENHAM: V4-268
LEE: V4-29 116; V5-39 42 43 46 81 356 381 518; V6-226 393 524
LEEDY: V5-227; V6-125
LEFTWICH: V6-185
LeHEW: V5-159
LEIGH: V5-263; V6-562 641
LEMON: V5-454; V6-401
LENZ: V4-559
LEONARD: V6-152
LESLIE: V6-333
LESNER: V4-451
LESTER: V4-565; V5-33; V6-488
LETCHER: V5-13
LEVI: V5-318
LEVY: V4-65
LEWIS: V4-97 158 367 494 565; V5-43 120 205 237 242 296 322 352 458 463 507; V6-26 183 196 262 346 371 500
LICHLITER: V4-364
LIGHTFOOT: V6-389
LIGHTNER: V6-67
LIGON: V5-360; V6-205
LILLARD: V4-425 500; V6-195 442 648
LILLY: V4-514
LIMING: V6-477
LINCOLN: V4-227; V5-82; V6-182 286 299
LINDAMOOD: V4-334
LINDSAY: V4-339; V5-329 385; V6-323 463 482 591
LINEWEAVER: V4-207
LINTHICUM: V5-64 181
LINTZ: V5-528
LION: V6-348 456
LIPFORD: V6-146
LIPSCOMB: V5-461; V6-281
LIPSCOMBE: V4-419
LITTLE: V6-568
LITTLEPAGE: V5-233
LITTLETON: V6-141
LITTON: V6-134 230 304
LITZ: V5-561; V6-335
LIVESAY: V6-333

LIVESEY: V4-555
LLEWELLYN: V5-521
LLOYD: V4-536; V5-179; V6-24
LOCHER: V6-317
LOCKE: V4-559
LOCKETT: V6-194
LOCKHART: V4-475; V5-68
LOCKWOOD: V6-109
LODGE: V5-558
LOMAX: V5-377
LONG: V4-223 296 302 415 427 517; V5-78 390 401 478; V6-118 148
LONGLEY: V6-588
LOONEY: V5-462
LOTTIER: V4-568
LOTTS: V5-309
LOUGHEED: V5-157
LOVE: V5-295
LOVELACE: V4-426; V6-493
LOVING: V4-567; V5-358
LOWRY: V4-171; V5-278
LOYD: V5-360
LUCAS: V6-37 44 624
LUCK: V5-487; V6-213 255 264
LUCKE: V5-139
LUDWIG: V4-346
LUMPKIN: V5-260
LUPTON: V4-304 384; V5-67 182 241; V6-152
LUTTON: V5-112
LUTTRELL: V6-270
LUTZ: V6-269
LUXFORD: V6-343
LUZIER: V5-214
LYDICK: V4-400
LYLE: V5-409 513
LYNCH: V5-351; V6-70
LYNN: V6-47 217 480
LYON: V6-123 133 205 301
LYONS: V6-589
McADAMS: V4-142
McALLISTER: V5-283 456 541; V6-62
McALPINE: V6-528
McBRYDE: V4-567
McCALL: V6-139 322
McCAM: V6-53
McCANDLISH: V6-145
MacCARTNEY: V5-154; V6-417
McCARTY: V4-439
McCAULEY: V5-74
McCAW: V5-543
MACE: V6-566
McCHESNEY: V6-304
McCLELLAN: V5-111

McCLINTIC: V6-623
McCLINTOCK: V5-115
McCLUNG: V5-418 420 453; V6-77
McCLURE: V5-380 416; V6-82
McCOMAS: V6-312
MACON: V4-56; V6-166
McCONNELL: V5-459; V6-623
McCORKLE: V6-289
McCORMICK: V4-458; V5-317 321 322 329; V6-181 271
McCOY: V5-485; V6-243 431 457
McCRACKEN: V6-477
McCRARY: V6-257
McCUE: V6-87
McCUNE: V6-78
McCUTCHEON: V5-563
MacDONALD: V6-25 179
McDONALD: V6-268 453
McDONOUGH: V5-290
McDOWELL: V5-557; V6-301
McELHONE: V6-629
McELROY: V6-339
McELWEE: V5-249
McENERY: V5-347
McFADDEN: V6-601
McFALL: V5-483 517
McFARLAND: V6-72 543
McFARRAN: V5-559
McGAVOCK: V4-7
McGHEE: V5-307
McGINNIS: V5-84
McGOWN: V5-304
McGRADY: V5-479
McGUFFIN: V6-222
McGUIRE: V4-7 165 221; V6-180
McHENRY: V5-124
McHUGH: V4-108; V5-211
McILWAINE: V4-132; V5-371; V6-200
McILWEE: V5-28
McINTIRE: V6-64
McINTOSH: V6-100 197
McINTYRE: V5-553
McKAY: V5-156; V6-165 173 364
McKINNEY: V6-454
McLANAHAN: V6-376
McLAUGHLIN: V5-562
McLEAN: V4-502
McLEMORE: V4-89; V6-408 557
McMANAMAY: V6-74
McMANAWAY: V5-399
McMATH: V6-608
McMILLEN: V6-319
McMULLAN: V5-59
McMURRAN: V6-504
McNAIR: V5-529; V6-193

MacNAMARA: V5-154
McNEER: V6-429 600
McNEIL: V4-486
McNEILL: V4-354; V5-157
McNULTY: V6-141
McNUTT: V4-28
McQUILKIN: V5-471
McRAE: V5-307
McSHEA: V6-356
McVEA: V5-301
McVEIGH: V6-421
McVITTY: V5-470
MADDOX: V5-154; V6-279
MADISON: V4-565; V6-226
MAGINNIS: V4-518
MAGRI: V5-479
MAGRUDER: V4-148 315; V6-183
MAHER: V6-105
MAHONEY: V6-563
MAHOOD: V4-367
MAJOR: V4-366; V5-457; V6-11 112
MALBON: V6-631
MALLON: V5-124
MALLORY: V5-250
MANN: V5-37 389; V6-3 568
MANNING: V4-436 437; V5-537
MANSFIELD: V5-511
MAPHIS: V4-317 342; V5-26
MAPP: V6-30
MARCHANT: V6-62
MARPLE: V6-169
MARSH: V5-261
MARSHALL: V5-125 153 154 164 219 344; V6-164 388
MARSTELLER: V6-151
MARTIN: V4-10 18 535 558; V5-129 222 478; V6-129 157 166 214 304 381 523 551 644
MARTZ: V4-282
MASON: V4-417; V5-212 259; V6-19 45
MASSENBURG: V6-487
MASSEY: V6-640
MASSIE: V4-329 356 361 374; V5-30 183 206 238 247 286 427; V6-215
MASTIN: V4-89
MATHENY: V5-555
MATHEWS: V6-513
MATHIS: V6-364
MATTHEWS: V5-38 492; V6-170
MAUCK: V5-228
MAUZY: V4-270
MAXEY: V5-174 461
MAXWELL: V4-569; V5-400
MAY: V4-489; V5-108 306; V6-641

MAYER: V5-507
MAYHEW: V5-472
MAYO: V4-496; V5-258
MAYS: V6-548
MEADE: V4-444 482; V6-352
MEADOR: V6-162
MEARS: V5-477 515; V6-554 607
MEBANE: V6-637
MEEKS: V4-382
MEEM: V5-98 142
MEETZ: V6-269
MEGGINSON: V5-306
MELTON: V5-93
MENEFEE: V4-302 400 423 473; V5-323 394; V6-550
MERCER: V4-182
MERCEREAU: V5-381; V6-81
MERCHANT: V6-393
MEREDITH: V4-51 568; V5-97
MERIWETHER: V4-56
MERRIFIELD: V4-50
MERRILL: V6-618
MERRITT: V4-519
MERRYMAN: V5-383
METZ: V5-41; V6-346
MEYER: V5-32
MEYERHOEFFER: V4-296
MEZICK: V5-48
MICHAELS: V5-81
MICHAUX: V6-435
MICHIE: V4-19 30 333
MICKS: V5-62
MIDDLETON: V5-47 112; V6-164
MIDYETT: V5-181
MIKESELL: V4-332
MILEY: V6-14
MILES: V5-453; V6-309 575
MILLAR: V5-156 212
MILLER: V4-152 173 192 246 267 335 383 424; V5-22 52 74 120 138 202 208 218 276 384 395 417 435 492 528 539; V6-140 150 200 209 266 310 390 406 412 442 510 519 648
MILLIGAN: V6-24
MILTON: V4-155
MINER: V4-530
MINGE: V6-460
MINNICK: V4-175; V6-62 358
MINOR: V4-5 307 309 310 375; V5-8 43
MINTER: V5-336; V6-162
MITCHELL: V4-441 448; V5-51 245 274 433 560; V6-308 316 433
MODESITT: V5-396
MOFFETT: V4-330 472; V5-409 433;

MOFFETT (continued)
V6-209 390
MOHERMAN: V6-457
MOLER: V4-388
MONCURE: V5-302 387; V6-109 506 585
MONEYHUN: V6-274
MONROE: V5-331 409; V6-8
MONTAGUE: V4-118 349
MONTGOMERY: V4-398; V5-458 563; V6-312
MOOERS: V5-37
MOOMAW: V4-433; V6-376 614
MOON: V5-247; V6-158 418
MOORE: V4-14 199 249 470; V5-311 313 322 323 324 350 444 544; V6-43 163 266 334 339 348 362 366 395 406 465 504 508 575 595
MOORMAN: V5-384 422 550
MORAN: V5-468
MOREHEAD: V6-440
MORGAN: V5-156 400 422 494; V6-531
MORISON: V6-306 438
MORLOK: V4-107
MORRIS: V4-337 459 462; V5-169 178 295 320 493; V6-462 493
MORRISON: V4-288; V5-434; V6-171 550 555
MORRISSETT: V4-96
MORRISSETTE: V6-305
MORTON: V5-301 457; V6-368 621
MOSBY: V5-280
MOSES: V6-535
MOSS: V4-202; V5-304 318; V6-339 400
MOTLEY: V5-244 264 445; V6-309 600
MOTTROM: V5-405
MOULTON: V5-424
MOUNTS: V5-148
MOYERS: V5-384
MULLEN: V4-223; V5-246
MULLINS: V4-568; V6-542
MUMFORD: V5-565
MUNCE: V4-337
MURPHY: V6-341
MURRAY: V6-90 245 248 258
MURRELL: V4-573
MUSE: V5-197; V6-187
MUSSAEUS: V5-269
MUSTOE: V6-143
MYERS: V4-209 259 306 433; V5-28 219; V6-486
NANCE: V4-370

NASH: V4-467; V5-17
NAUMAN: V6-118
NAYLOR: V6-180
NEALE: V4-566; V5-3 496; V6-388
NEEB: V4-255
NEEL: V6-593
NEIGHBORS: V6-469
NEILSON: V5-206
NELMS: V5-287
NELSON: V4-58 449 560; V5-15 16 162 299 449 550; V6-270 390
NETTLETON: V5-415
NEVE: V5-191
NEVES: V4-557
NEW: V5-507
NEWBILL: V5-230 429
NEWCOMB: V5-379; V6-642
NEWCOMER: V5-307
NEWELL: V5-21
NEWHOUSE: V6-529
NEWMAN: V4-354 358 551; V5-170 536; V6-9 330
NEWTON: V5-265; V6-308 388
NICHOLS: V4-281 413 431; V6-555 610
NICHOLSON: V4-438; V5-80
NICKELS: V6-399
NICKLES: V4-417 472 489
NOBLETT: V5-239
NOBLIN: V6-640
NOEL: V4-376 413 436 439
NOELL: V5-143 538; V6-57
NOFFSINGER: V6-348
NOLLEY: V4-131 324
NOLTING: V6-240
NORRIS: V5-167; V6-96
NORTHAM: V6-521
NORTHROP: V5-244
NORTHRUP: V6-199
NORTON: V4-405
NORVELL: V5-139
NOTTINGHAM: V5-475; V6-23
NOWELL: V5-120 446
NOWLIN: V4-404
NUCKOLS: V4-220; V6-457
NUNLEY: V5-438
NUNNALLY: V6-179
NUTT: V6-90
NYE: V6-432
OAKES: V5-217
OAKEY: V5-469
O'BANNON: V6-442
O'BYRNE: V4-519
O'FERRALL: V5-146
OGILVIE: V5-549
OGLE: V6-43

OGLESBY: V6-596
OLD: V4-437; V6-564
OLDFIELD: V5-506
OLDHAM: V5-294
OLIVER: V4-173 453; V5-446; V6-128 585
OLSSON: V5-319
OMOHUNDRO: V5-262 304
O'NEALE: V4-428
O'NEILL: V4-323
OPIE: V4-577
OREBAUGH: V4-330
ORGAIN: V5-88
ORNDORFF: V5-282
ORR: V4-515; V6-338
ORRICK: V6-317
OSBORNE: V4-98; V5-17; V6-36
OSBOURN: V6-345
OSBURN: V5-224 373
OTEY: V4-571 572; V5-119 138; V6-186 532
OVERBY: V5-537
OVERSTREET: V5-276
OWEN: V4-133
OWENS: V4-428
OWSLEY: V5-398
OZLIN: V5-57
PACE: V4-473; V6-151
PAGE: V4-4 204 277 321 449 560; V5-15 185 315
PAGGETT: V5-360
PAINTER: V4-385; V5-431; V6-40 140 286 336 590
PALEN: V6-579
PALMATARY: V5-361
PALMER: V4-79 111; V5-91 547; V6-584
PANCAKE: V5-545
PANNETT: V5-10
PARHAM: V6-133
PARISH: V4-320 461
PARKER: V5-91 273 305 465 540; V6-368
PARKINS: V6-86
PARKS: V6-22 554
PARR: V6-264 266
PARRISH: V4-71 146 419; V5-13 29 363 364 497; V6-194
PARROTT: V6-407
PARSONS: V6-24
PATRICK: V5-405
PATTERSON: V5-114; V6-30
PATTESON: V4-47
PATTON: V4-54; V5-451; V6-498
PATTY: V6-370
PAUL: V5-444
PAULETT: V5-144
PAXTON: V5-201 406 529
PAYNE: V4-446 448 534 574; V5-4 18 19 20 142 273 429 487 528 548 553; V6-52 74 264
PEAK: V6-365 617
PEARCE: V6-249
PEARSON: V4-501; V5-352
PEATROSS: V6-549
PEDDICORD: V6-198 374
PEDIGO: V5-519; V6-587
PEERMAN: V6-551
PEERY: V6-157 158 163 281 355 363 427
PEIRCE: V4-430 574; V5-240
PENCE: V4-267 338; V5-48; V6-422
PENDLETON: V5-275 528; V6-11
PENICK: V4-242; V6-155 551
PENN: V4-373; V6-225
PENNINGTON: V5-435
PENNYBACKER: V6-9
PENROSE: V5-394
PEOPLES: V5-450
PERDUE: V4-78; V5-408; V6-69
PERKINS: V4-311; V5-26 53 512 564; V6-284 543 624
PERROWS: V4-392; V5-18 20 133
PERRY: V6-257
PETERS: V6-60 161 233 363 423
PETTIT: V4-351; V6-38
PETTUS: V6-185
PETTY: V6-422
PETTYJOHN: V4-391
PEYTON: V4=224 473; V5-57 122 378
PHELPS: V5-424
PHILLIPPI: V6-537
PHILLIPS: V4-171 307 535; V5-66 325 378; V6-119 238
PHIPPS: V5-487; V6-507
PHLEGAR: V4-532; V6-553
PHOEBUS: V4-544
PIERPONT: V6-502
PIERSON: V6-156
PIFER: V5-268
PIGG: V5-102 537
PIKE: V5-201
PILSON: V6-276
PIRKEY: V6-598
PITMAN: V5-386
PITT: V4-172
PITZER: V4-565; V6-105
PLASTER: V6-283
PLEASANTS: V5-507 508; V6-37
PLECKE: V4-294; V5-397 398
PLUMMER: V6-372

POE: V4-556
POINDEXTER: V4-551 552; V5-447; V6-552
POLE: V6-178 223 623
POLHAMUS: V6-70
POLK: V5-456
POLLARD: V4-231; V6-438 472
POLLOCK: V5-518
POOLE: V4-122; V5-384; V6-329
POORE: V5-119
POPE: V5-323; V6-446 649
POPKINS: V4-451
PORTER: V5-18; V6-535
PORTERFIELD: V6-508
POTTER: V5-403
POTTS: V6-125
POWELL: V5-39 496; V6-554 591 595
POWERS: V5-71 141; V6-359
PRATT: V6-94 638
PREDERGRAF: V5-220
PRESCOTT: V5-129
PRESLEY: V5-433; V6-595
PRESTON: V4-174 489; V6-51 632 647
PRETLOW: V6-557
PRICE: V4-361; V5-274 423 454 500; V6-117 391
PRIDDY: V5-97 100
PRIDEMORE: V6-443
PRILLAMAN: V6-490 505
PRINCE: V6-439
PRITCHETT: V4-268 495; V5-565
PROFFITT: V6-550
PROW: V5-409
PRDEN: V6-626
PRUITT: V5-459
PRUNER: V6-352
PUCKETT: V5-219
PUGH: V5-354; V6-217
PULLEN: V4-67
PULLER: V4-61
PULLIAM: V4-106; V5-445
PURCELL: V4-289; V5-84 211 294
PUTNEY: V4-384
QUACKENBUSH: V6-357
QUAINTANCE: V6-183
QUARLES: V5-279; V6-627
QUESENBERRY: V4-539
QUILLEN: V6-337 352
QUINN: V4-443
QUISENBERRY: V5-495; V6-515 615
RAGER: V5-204
RALSTON: V4-260
RAMEY: V5-464; V6-230 322
RAMSAUR: V5-77

RAMSAY: V4-441
RAMSEY: V5-525; V6-448
RANDOLPH: V4-216 314; V5-15 184 212 535; V6-4 162 360 415
RANGLEY: V6-596
RANKIN: V4-457
RANSOM: V4-578
RANSON: V6-22
RAPER: V6-523 545
RASNICK: V5-484 495
RATCLIFFE: V4-475 561; V6-142
RATLIFF: V6-542
RAUHOF: V5-542
RAWLINGS: V5-23; V6-242 417
RAWLS: V4-435 489; V6-525 526
RAYBURN: V6-225
REA: V4-283
READ: V5-105; V6-120
REAGUER: V6-420
REAMER: V6-78
REAMY: V5-457
RECTOR: V6-214 242
REDD: V4-164
REED: V4-454; V5-116; V6-248 273
REEKES: V5-63
REEVES: V6-458 499
REID: V5-333 443 556; V6-48 98
REILLY: V6-376
REINHART: V5-171
REITER: V4-292
RENFORD: V4-549
RENICK: V5-530
REPASS: V6-508
REVERCOMB: V6-222
REYNER: V6-18
REYNOLDS: V4-464; V5-308 495; V6-456 600
RHEA: V6-297
RHODES: V4-265; V5-71 200; V6-418
RICE: V5-166 170 274 318; V6-228 431
RICHARDS: V4-395; V-39 230 322
RICHARDSON: V4-200; V5-147 527 565; V6-144 178 228 421 546 553 585 645
RICHMOND: V4-415; V6-227 323
RIDDEL: V4-329
RIDDICK: V5-451
RIDGEWAY: V5-187
RIEDEL: V5-213
RIELY: V4-112 433
RIFE: V5-421
RIGGIN: V5-485
RILEE: V5-184
RILEY: V5-404

RINEHART: V5-172 267 325
RINKER: V5-69 442; V6-216
RIPLEY: V6-475
RISON: V6-548
RISQUE: V4-517; V5-136
RITTENOUR: V5-343
RITTER: V4-406; V5-40
RITZ: V6-128
RIVES: V4-428; V6-489
RIXEY: V4-414
ROANE: V5-240 362; V6-71
ROBERTS: V5-115 399; V6-20 21 202 381 408 515 619
ROBERTSON: V5-97 132 163 363 379 522; V6-71 256 309 397 647
ROBEY: V5-402 404; V6-260
ROBINETT: V6-482
ROBINS: V6-637
ROBINSON: V4-117 210 319 468 544 548; V5-202 371 376 408; V6-148 545
ROCK: V5-234 247
RODES: V4-357; V5-443; V6-117 131
RODGERS: V5-178
RODIER: V5-254
ROGERS: V4-366; V5-254; V6-42 203 538 591
ROGERSON: V5-497
ROHR: V5-290
ROLLER: V5-389 550
ROLLINS: V4-541 542
ROOP: V4-534
ROOTES: V5-508
ROPER: V4-275; V6-526 608 609
RORER: V5-330
ROSE: V4-438; V5-485; V6-435
ROSEN: V5-563
ROSS: V5-477
ROSSER: V5-162; V6-131
ROSZEL: V6-245
ROTH: V5-75
ROUNTREE: V5-96
ROUSE: V6-256
ROWAN: V6-55
ROWE: V5-165 290; V6-542
ROWLETT: V6-320
ROYALL: V5-498; V6-155
RUCKER: V4-180; V5-200 304
RUDASILL: V4-425
RUDD: V4-76; V5-123
RUEBUSH: V4-179 248; V6-5 419
RUFFIN: V4-412
RUFFNER: V5-36
RUMBLE: V6-462
RUSH: V4-354; V5-265

RUSSELL: V5-99 431 537; V6-264 267 336 519
RUST: V6-164 364
RUTHERFOORD: V4-545; V5-551
RUTTER: V6-215
RYAN: V4-150; V5-32
SAGER: V5-531 536
ST GEORGE: V5-4
ST JOHN: V6-174
SALE: V4-11; V6-555
SALLE: V5-253
SALLING: V4-528
SAMBELL: V5-152
SAMPLE: V4-490
SAMS: V5-425
SAMUEL: V6-550
SANDERLIN: V4-428
SANDERS: V4-503; V5-164 236
SANFORD: V5-126 173 392 513; V6-323
SANGER: V4-104
SANTMIERS: V4-372; V5-25
SAUL: V6-401 448
SAUM: V4-255
SAUNDERS: V4-121 144 236; V5-152 533; V6-189
SAVAGE: V6-608
SCAISBROOK: V5-216
SCARBOROUGH: V6-556
SCARFF: V6-136
SCHERER: V4-87; V5-374
SCHMUCKER: V5-224
SCHNEIDER: V5-424
SCHOFIELD: V6-577 578
SCHOTTLAND: V6-517
SCHRADER: V6-293
SCHULTZ: V4-383
SCHWANK: V5-520
SCHWARTZ: V4-424
SCOLLAY: V5-16
SCOTT: V4-141 308 322; V5-17 39 58 138 239 365 385; V6-35 153 212 445 465 572
SCRUGGS: V5-427
SEARS: V5-264
SEAWELL: V6-53
SEAY: V5-45 46; V6-204
SEBRELL: V6-439
SEDDON: V5-51
SEESE: V6-350
SEGAR: V5-340; V6-406
SEHORN: V6-29
SELDON: V6-611
SELECMAN: V6-480
SELMAN: V5-317
SENSENEY: V5-200

SENTER: V6-274
SERGENT: V6-442
SERPELL: V4-562
SETTLE: V4-475; V6-413 494
SEWARD: V5-121 278
SEXTON: V6-182 381
SHACKELFORD: V4-39 278; V5-158; V6-21
SHADRACH: V4-316
SHAFFER: V4-303
SHANER: V4-552
SHANK: V6-151
SHANKS: V4-532; V5-448
SHANNON: V5-72; V6-56
SHAUT: V5-523
SHAVER: V4-299 320 497
SHEAIN: V4-119
SHEETZ: V4-353
SHEFFEY: V4-530; V6-60
SHEILD: V4-550
SHELBURNE: V4-334; V6-315
SHELOR: V4-495; V6-615
SHELTON: V4-95; V5-34 47 444; V6-291 513
SHENK: V5-388
SHEPHERD: V4-49; V5-276
SHEPPARD: V4-397; V5-152; V6-490
SHEPPERD: V6-541
SHERARD: V5-207
SHERERTZ: V6-44
SHERMAN: V4-402
SHEWMAKE: V6-611
SHICKEL: V6-361
SHIELDS: V5-140 251
SHIPP: V6-63
SHIRLEY: V4-247
SHOEMAKER: V4-79
SHORT: V4-466
SHOWALTER: V4-226; V6-451 578
SHREVE: V5-297 313
SHRUM: V4-183 294
SHRYOCK: V4-397; V5-190
SHUE: V4-301; V6-156
SHUFF: V6-73
SHULER: V5-229 380; V6-332
SHUMATE: V4-53; V6-267
SIBERT: V4-406; V6-79 143 550
SIFERS: V5-483 525
SIGMON: V5-446
SILLING: V4-476
SIMMERMAN: V6-39 617
SIMMONS: V5-449 494
SIMPSON: V5-66 132
SIMS: V4-438
SINCLAIR: V6-485 585
SINE: V4-363

SINGER: V6-81
SINGLETON: V6-271 434 495
SINK: V5-498
SISK: V4-501
SISSON: V5-463
SIZER: V6-532
SKAGGS: V5-198; V6-426
SKEEN: V5-326 374
SKINKER: V6-228
SKINNER: V4-463 557 559; V6-230 460
SKIPWITH: V5-4
SLADE: V6-498
SLAGLE: V4-67
SLATE: V6-453
SLATER: V6-136 383
SLAUGHTER: V5-180 436; V6-257 266 389 502
SLEMP: V6-536
SLOAN: V6-265
SMALLWOOD: V5-320
SMITH: V4-37 41 48 187 233 319 325 445 464 516 535 564 569; V5-25 29 104 164 175 176 189 271 279 286 306 354 362 367 392 460 466 508 513 525 527 533 536 545 553; V6-7 53 186 209 213 239 299 312 335 363 405 414 421 423 441 479 481 645
SMITHSON: V5-531
SMOOT: V4-342; V5-225 397
SMYTH: V4-134; V5-280
SMYTHE: V4-432
SNAPP: V5-201 442; V6-441
SNARR: V4-281; V5-40
SNEAD: V4-26; V5-116 163; V6-493
SNEED: V5-29; V6-234
SNIDOW: V6-501
SNODDY: V4-255
SNYDER: V5-147 522; V6-85 291 402
SOMMERVILLE: V6-642
SORG: V5-119
SOURS: V5-380
SOUTH: V5-482
SOUTHGATE: V6-530
SOWARD: V5-484
SOWDER: V4-533
SOWERS: V5-71; V6-244
SPAID: V4-311; V5-333
SPANGLER: V6-419
SPARKS: V4-432; V5-480
SPARROW: V5-360
SPEAKMAN: V6-152
SPEARMAN: V5-33

SPECHT: V6-424
SPEED: V6-193
SPEERS: V5-174
SPEIDEN: V6-567
SPENCER: V4-542; V5-25 102 148 525; V6-194 341
SPENGLR: V4-552
SPESSARD: V4-232 564
SPIGGLE: V6-126
SPILLER: V6-312
SPILMAN: V6-59 206
SPINDLE: V6-315
SPITZER: V4-280
SPIVEY: V6-509
SPOTSWOOD: V4-560; V5-142 472; V6-234 489
SPRATLEY: V4-421
SPRINT: V4-374
SPROULE: V6-184
SPURRIER: V5-375
STABLES: V5-90
STACY: V4-564; V5-125 365
STAFFORD: V6-511 586
STAIR: V5-492
STALEY: V4-529; V6-296
STALLARD: V5-460
STALLING: V5-125
STANFORD: V4-87
STANT: V6-249
STAPLES: V6-225 252
STARK: V4-22; V6-482
STARKE: V5-405
STARKEY: V4-415
STARNES: V4-413
STAUBER: V5-561
STAUFFER: V6-495
STEDMAN: V5-496; V6-251
STEEL: V6-66
STEGER: V5-551
STEPHENS: V5-214; V6-262
STEPHENSON: V6-87 239 371 444
STEPTOE: V5-216
STEVENS: V4-230 575; V5-52
STEVENSON: V4-448
STEWART: V4-528; V5-42 43; V6-310
STICKLEY: V5-69 76 83 193 195
STIFF: V5-391 396
STIMSON: V5-548
STINE: V4-499
STINSON: V6-221 618
STIPES: V5-222
STIREWALT: V4-347
STITH: V5-263
STOKES: V5-49 267
STONE: V4-483; V5-361 514 554;

STONE (continued) V6-132
STONEMAN: V4-92
STONER: V4-346
STOUT: V4-147
STOVALL: V6-640
STOVER: V4-546; V5-83 445; V6-193
STRATTON: V4-553; V5-284
STRAYER: V5-392
STREIT: V5-185
STRICKLAND: V4-516; V6-43 210
STRICKLER: V5-431
STRINGFELLOW: V5-473
STROLE: V5-469; V6-119
STRONG: V5-463
STROSNIDER: V4-408
STROTHER: V5-323 459; V6-20 412
STRYKER: V4-551
STUART: V5-5 44 57 256; V6-72 592
STUBBLEFIELD: V6-81
STUBBS: V5-352
STULL: V4-504; V5-400
STUMP: V6-51
STURGIS: V5-47
STURTZ: V4-406
SUDDUTH: V6-204
SUHLING: V5-122
SULLIVAN: V6-147
SUMMERS: V4-541; V5-30; V6-27 192 302
SUMNER: V5-54
SURBER: V4-381
SURFACE: V4-430; V6-335
SUTER: V4-298; V5-442
SUTHERLAND: V4-26 481; V5-481 495 517 518
SUTPHIN: V4-426
SWANGER: V5-468
SWANK: V4-262 283
SWANSON: V5-5; V6-187
SWART: V6-244 591
SWARTZ: V5-22
SWEM: V6-438
SWINDLER: V4-424
SYCLE: V4-212
SYDNOR: V4-21 156; V5-170 437
SYKES: V4-466; V5-486 511
TABB: V4-545; V5-348
TABOR: V4-431
TAGGERT: V5-516
TALBOT: V4-473
TALIAFERRO: V4-562; V5-160; V6-350 589
TALLEY: V4-75; V6-68

TANNEHILL: V5-145
TANNER: V5-17 427
TANSILL: V6-128
TAPSCOTT: V4-574; V5-161
TATE: V6-239 331 647
TAUSCHER: V6-272
TAYLOE: V5-259 377; V6-42
TAYLOR: V4-79 148 163 205   373
  413   528; V5-52 81 120 130 164
  233 473 476; V6-71 79 80 137
  142   144 272 273 330 332 393
  459 475 513 556 573
TEARNEY: V5-127
TEAS: V6-316
TEEL: V4-40
TEETER: V6-84
TEMPLE: V4-32; V6-237
TEMPLETON: V4-528
TERRELL: V4-365 448; V5-21 547
TERRILL: V6-340
TERRY: V5-206 209 502; V6-446
  579 585
TEVALT: V5-282
THACKER: V5-89
THARP: V5-187
THAXTON: V6-29
THEOBOLD: V4-553
THOMAS: V4-26 41 52 438; V5-78
  210 261: V6-233 452 616 634
THOMASON: V5-89
THOMPSON: V4-504; V5-17 145 179
  283 320; V6-96 137 511 541
THORNHILL: V4-87 449; V5-443
THORNTON: V5-323 433 465; V6-132
  183 391 444
THORPE: V6-520
THRESHER: V6-469
THROCKMORTON: V4-190
THUMA: V4-247
THURMAN: V4-129; V6-182
THWAITE: V4-399
TIDD: V4-43
TILDEN: V5-32
TILGHMAN: V4-59; V6-22
TILLAR: V5-254
TILLER: V4-203
TILLEY: V4-482
TILMAN: V4-378
TILTON: V4-31
TIMBERLAKE: V5-43; V6-85 95 220
  491
TIPTON: V6-613
TISDALE: V5-113 270
TITUS: V6-101
TOD: V5-245
TODD: V6-79 300

TOLBERT: V5-453
TOMKINS: V4-168; V6-391 646
TORRENCE: V6-222
TOTTY: V6-523
TOWLES: V4-15; V5-288
TOWNES: V6-548
TOWNSEND: V5-471
TRAINR: V6-65
TRAUB: V6-194
TRAVERS: V5-433
TRAYLOR: V5-101
TREADWAY: V5-440
TREDWAY: V4-566; V6-66
TRENARY: V5-36
TRIBLE: V5-299
TRIGG: V6-186
TRINKLE: V4-6; V6-470 575
TRIPLETT: V4-494 519
TRIVETT: V6-518
TROLINGER: V5-435
TROUP: V5-96
TROUT: V6-579
TROWER: V5-475
TUCKER: V4-243 528; V5-4 35 62
  219 357 465; V6-183
TUNE: V5-220
TUNSTALL: V4-382 459; V6-548
TURMAN: V5-200
TURNBULL: V6-405
TURNER: V5-543; V5-34 49 133 134
  211 495 557; V6-18 27 185 211
  246 262 409 418
TURPIN: V4-378
TUTTLE: V6-219
TWYFORD: V4-425
TWYMAN: V4-215 260 350
TYLER: V4-10 505; V5-61 180 258
  283 428 441; V6-464 512
TYNES: V5-439
TYREE: V5-200
TYSON: V5-307 441
UNDERWOOD: V5-362
UPSHUR: V4-161; V5-469
URBACH: V4-105
URQUHART: V6-539
UTLEY: V5-438
VAIDEN: V6-189
VAN ALLEN: V4-545
VANDERHOOF: V4-113
VANDERSLICE: V4-544
VANMETER: V6-374
VAN NORT: V5-188
VANOVER: V5-485
VAN WAGENEN: V4-335
VAUGHN: V4-387 458; V5-14 111
  177 407; V6-210 492

VEITCH: V6-114
VELLINES: V5-491
VENABLE: V5-145 150 525; V6-73
VERSER: V5-77
VEST: V6-586
VIA: V5-447 457
VICARS: V6-287 382
VICTOR: V5-140
VINCENT: V5-131
VIRDEN: V5-86
VON HERBULES: V5-299
WADDEY: V6-494
WADDILL: V4-31
WADE: V4-549; V5-417 453; V6-243
WAGENER: V6-344 545
WAGGONER: V6-593
WAGINGTON: V4-494
WAGNER: V4-266 496; V6-510
WAID: V6-380
WAKEMAN: V5-214
WALDEN: V5-443; V6-556
WALDRON: V5-476
WALFORD: V4-128
WALKE: V5-102
WALKER: V4-68 264 358; V5-6 105 130 157 263 279 354 390 405; V6-48 394 500 592
WALL: V5-28 173
WALLACE: V5-540; V6-366 506
WALLER: V5-203 233; V6-493
WALLNER: V4-533
WALTHALL: V5-217
WALTON: V4-13 269; V5-33 77 214; V6-10 434
WAMPLER: V4-313 331; V6-429
WARD: V4-318 404 570; V5-488; V6-622
WARDEN: V5-187
WARING: V5-298
WARREN: V5-221 436; V6-133 225 462 484
WARWICK: V6-88
WASHINGTON: V4-560; V5-263; V6-220
WASSOM: V6-532
WATERS: V5-512; V6-29
WATKINS: V4-547; V5-102 107 127 167 168 301; V6-194 434
WATSON: V4-30 49 186 310 566; V5-445; V6-7 177 307 315 373 600
WATTS: V4-402; V5-21 315; V6-226
WATTSON: V4-321
WAYLAND: V4-169 328
WAYT: V6-76
WEATHERLY: V6-552

WEAVER: V5-218 339
WEBB: V4-468; V5-182; V6-52 289 453 492
WEBER: V6-174
WEBSTER: V6-161
WEDDING: V6-631
WEEDON: V5-549; V6-538
WEEMS: V4-101
WEINDEL: V6-292
WEIR: V5-3
WEISZ: V5-397
WEITZEL: V4-20
WELCH: V5-70 246; V6-90 248
WELFORD: V5-449
WELLBURN: V5-447; V6-263
WELLER: V5-548
WELLES: V5-301
WELLS: V5-14 407 440; V6-541 620
WELSH: V4-53
WENGER: V4-374
WEST: V4-59 103 105 557; V5-294 430 506; V6-313 522 553
WESTRAY: V5-54
WETHERED: V6-316
WETZEL: V6-358
WHALING: V6-550
WHARTON: V5-328; V6-252
WHEAT: V4-194
WHEELER: V4-231; V6-361
WHEELWRIGHT: V4-240; V6-430
WHITACRE: V5-337
WHITE: V4-46 94 181 221 330 388 466 558 561; V5-73 78 134 454 472; V6-50 54 257 307 400 409 411 503 526 645 647
WHITED: V4-478
WHITEHEAD: V4-177; V5-38; V6-238 329 563 564
WHITING: V5-42
WHITLOCK: V4-376 408; V5-492
WHITMAN: V6-473
WHITMORE: V5-325
WHITTLE: V6-585
WHYTE: V5-221
WICKENS: V6-157
WICKHAM: V5-392
WIGHT: V4-226
WIGGLESWORTH: V6-315
WILDER: V5-440
WILEY: V5-385; V6-135 167 574
WILKINS: V4-251 556; V6-514
WILKINSON: V6-142 465 571
WILL: V4-275
WILLARD: V4-437
WILLCOX: V5-526
WILLIAMS: V4-11 74 124 137 340

WILLIAMS (continued)
  345 501 537; V5-49 106 152
  163 177 180 226 319 320 330
  533; V6-36 56 122 137 222 262
  348 352 377 392 413 478 497
WILLIAMSON: V4-310; V5-421 433;
  V6-38 308 498
WILLIS: V4-139; V5-356; V6-220
  644
WILLITS: V6-382
WILLS: V5-17
WILLSON: V6-81
WILSON: V4-86 252 357 422 565
  576; V5-46 90 165 207 418 504;
  V6-53 142 191
WIMBISH: V6-562
WIMER: V6-193
WINCH: V5-364
WINCHESTER: V4-478
WINDLE: V5-432
WINDSOR: V6-128
WINE: V4-274 343; V5-23; V6-123
WINFREE: V4-210; V5-31 132
WINFREY: V4-81
WINGETER: V5-30
WINGFIELD: V4-48
WINNE: V4-130
WINMILL: V6-208
WINSTON: V5-193 568
WISE: V5-373; V6-359 623
WISELY: V6-397
WISMAN: V5-328
WITCHER: V4-491
WITHERS: V4-401; V5-500
WITT: V6-355 425
WITTEN: V4-493; V6-261 337
WITTIG: V4-272
WOLCOTT: V5-148; V6-446
WOLFE: V4-468; V6-31 454
WOLFORD: V5-516
WOMACK: V4-578
WOOD: V4-331 410 424 426; V5-13
  126 161 197 206 457; V6-46 195

WOOD (continued)
  206 213 390 414 448 545 647
WOODARD: V4-70
WOODHOUSE: V6-539 570
WOODING: V6-45
WOODRUM: V6-471
WOODS: V4-505; V5-46 251; V6-29
  507
WOODSON: V4-220 386 396 404; V5-
  21 162
WOODWARD: V5-41 382; V6-14 82
  240 625
WOODY: V5-107 194
WOODYARD: V6-345
WOOLF: V5-296; V6-235
WOOLRIDGE: V5-102
WOOLWINE: V4-567; V6-112 506
WOOTEN: V6-132
WORRELL: V6-583
WORSHAM: V4-83
WORTHINGTON: V6-84 95
WRIGHT: V4-147 471; V5-73 143
  242 377; V6-124 544 552 581
WUNDER: V4-340; V5-195
WYANT: V4-201
WYATT: V4-120
WYCLIFFE: V5-343
WYNDHAM: V6-214
WYNN: V5-414; V6-245 525
WYNNE: V6-475
YANCEY: V4-25 284 448; V5-118
YATES: V4-473; V5-94 95 109
YEATMAN: V4-505
YEATTS: V6-616
YELLMAN: V6-383
YERGER: V6-495
YODER: V4-398
YOST: V6-149 607
YOUELL: V4-234
YOWELL: V4-500
YOUNG: V5-110 549; V6-316 607
ZIGLER: V6-150
ZIRKLE: V5-23; V6-123

Other Heritage Books by Patrick G. Wardell:

Adventures in Genealogy

Alexandria City and County, Virginia Deed Books Extracts, 1801-1818

Alexandria City and County, Virginia Wills, Administrations, and Guardian Bonds, 1800-1870

CD: Virginia/West Virginia Revolutionary War Records, Volumes 1-6

Genealogical Data from United States Military Academy Application Papers, 1805-1866 Volumes 1 and 2

Timesaving Aid to Virginia-West Virginia Ancestors (A Genealogical Index of Surnames from Published Sources)

Virginia and West Virginia Genealogical Data from Revolutionary War Pension and Bounty Land Warrant Records: Volume 1

Virginia and West Virginia Genealogical Data from Revolutionary War Pension and Bounty Land Warrant Records, Volume 2: Dabbs - Hyslop

Virginia and West Virginia Genealogical Data from Revolutionary War Pension and Bounty Land Warrant Records, Volume 3: Iams - Myres

Virginia and West Virginia Genealogical Data from Revolutionary War Pension and Bounty Land Warrant Records, Volume 4: Nabors - Rymer

Virginia and West Virginia Genealogical Data from Revolutionary War Pension and Bounty Land Warrant Records, Volume 5: Sacrey - Tyree

Virginia and West Virginia Genealogical Data from Revolutionary War Pension and Bounty Land Warrant Records, Volume 6: Ullum - Zumwalt

Virginia/West Virginia Husbands and Wives Volumes 1 and 2

Virginians and West Virginians, 1607-1870 Volumes 1-3

War of 1812: Virginia Bounty Land and Pension Applicants

www.ingramcontent.com/pod-product-compliance
Lightning Source LLC
Chambersburg PA
CBHW050830230426
43667CB00012B/1937